Collins

Pocket Dictionary

Collins
An Imprint of HarperCollins*Publishers*

fourth edition 2000

latest reprint 2002

HarperCollins Publishers
Westerhill Road, Bishopbriggs, Glasgow G64 2QT
Great Britain

www.collinsdictionaries.com

ISBN 0-00-472387-2 Vinyl Cover
ISBN 0-00-472386-4 Hardback

Acknowledgements
We would like to thank those authors and publishers who kindly gave permission for copyright material to be used in the Bank of English. We would also like to thank Times Newspapers Ltd for providing valuable data.

Note
Entered words that we have reason to believe constitute trademarks have been designated as such. However, neither the presence nor absence of such designation should be regarded as affecting the legal status of any trademark.

A catalogue record for this book is available from the British Library

Typeset by John Podbielski

Printed and bound in Italy by Amadeus S.p.A.

This dictionary has been compiled by referring to the Bank of English, a unique database of the English language with examples of over 323 million words enabling Collins lexicographers to analyse how English is actually used today and how it is changing. This is the evidence on which the changes in this dictionary are based.

The Bank of English was set up as a joint initiative by HarperCollins Publishers and Birmingham University to be a resource for language research and lexicography. It contains a very wide range of material from books, newspapers, radio, TV, magazines, letters and talks reflecting the whole spectrum of English today. Its size and range make it an unequalled resource and the purpose-built software for its analysis is unique to Collins Dictionaries.

This ensures that Collins Dictionaries accurately reflect English as it is used today in a way that is most helpful to the dictionary user as well as including the full range of rarer and historical words and meanings.

FEATURES OF THE DICTIONARY

Usage Note

Entry Word

Alternative Form

Pronunciation

Part of Speech

Cross Reference

chill

childbirth *n* giving birth to a child. **child's play** very easy task.

> Note that *childish* has overtones of *foolish* while *childlike* suggests an *innocent* quality.

chill *n* **1** a feverish cold. **2** moderate coldness. ♦ *v* **3** make (something) cool or cold. **4** cause (someone) to feel cold or frightened. ♦ *adj* **5** unpleasantly cold. **chilly** *adj* **chillier, chilliest 1** moderately cold. **2** unfriendly. **chilliness** *n*

chilli, chili *n* **1** small red or green hot-tasting capsicum pod, used in cooking. **2** (also **chilli con carne**) hot-tasting Mexican dish of meat, onions, beans, and chilli powder.

chime *n* **1** musical ringing sound of a bell or clock. ♦ *v* **2** make a musical ringing sound. **3** indicate (the time) by chiming. **4** (foll. by *with*) be consistent with.

chimera [kime-**meer**-a] *n* **1** unrealistic hope or idea. **2** fabled monster with a lion's head, goat's body, and serpent's tail. **chimerical** *adj*

chimney *n* hollow vertical structure for carrying away smoke from a fire. **chimney breast** walls surrounding the base of a chimney or fireplace. **chimneypot** *n* short pipe on the top of a chimney. **chimney sweep** person who cleans soot from chimneys.

chimp *n Informal* short for CHIMPANZEE.

chimpanzee *n* intelligent black African ape.

chin *n* part of the face below the mouth. **chinwag** *n Informal* chat.

china *n* **1** fine earthenware or porcelain. **2** dishes or ornaments made of this. **china clay** same as KAOLIN.

chinchilla *n* **1** S American rodent bred for its soft grey fur. **2** its fur.

chine *n* **1** cut of meat including part of the backbone. ♦ *v* **2** cut (meat) along the backbone.

Chinese *adj* **1** of China. ♦ *n* **2** *pl* **-nese** person from China. **3** any of the languages of China. **Chinese chequers**

FEATURES OF THE DICTIONARY

game played with marbles or pegs on a star-shaped board. **Chinese lantern** collapsible lantern made of thin paper.

chink[1] *n* small narrow opening, e.g. *a chink of light.* — Example

chink[2] *v, n* (make) a light ringing sound.

chintz *n* printed cotton fabric with a glazed finish.

chip *n* **1** strip of potato, fried in deep fat. **2** tiny wafer of semiconductor material forming an integrated circuit. **3** counter used to represent money in gambling games. — Sense Number **4** small piece removed by chopping, breaking, etc. **5** mark left where a small piece has been broken off something. ♦ *v* **chipping, chipped 6** break small pieces from. **have a chip on one's shoulder** *Informal* bear a grudge. **chip in** *v Informal* **1** contribute (money). — Phrasal Verb **2** interrupt with a remark.

chipboard *n* thin board made of compressed wood particles.

chipmunk *n* small squirrel-like N American rodent with a striped back.

chipolata *n* small sausage.

chiropodist [kir-**rop**-pod-ist] *n* person who treats minor foot complaints. **chiropody** *n*

chiropractic [kire-oh-**prak**-tik] *n* system of treating bodily disorders by manipulation of the spine. **chiropractor** *n* — Related Word

chirp, chirrup *v* **1** (of a bird or insect) make a short high-pitched sound. **2** speak in a lively fashion. ♦ *n* **3** chirping sound. **chirpy** *adj* **chirpier, chirpiest** *Informal* lively and cheerful. — Spelling Help

chisel *n* **1** metal tool with a sharp end for shaping wood or stone. ♦ *v* **-elling, -elled 2** carve or form with a chisel.

chit[1] *n* short official note, such as a receipt.

chit[2] *n Old-fashioned* pert or impudent girl. — Usage Label

chitchat *n* chat, gossip.

chitterlings *pl n* pig's intestines cooked as food.

chivalry *n* **1** courteous behaviour, esp. by men towards women. **2** medieval system and principles of knighthood. **chivalrous** *adj*

EDITORIAL STAFF

Editorial Director
Diana Treffry

Managing Editor
Sheila Ferguson

Senior Lexicographer
Elspeth Summers

Lexicographers
Andrew Holmes
Ian Brookes   Lorna Gilmour
Mary O'Neill

Computing Staff
John Podbielski

ABBREVIATIONS USED IN THE DICTIONARY

AD	anno Domini
adj	adjective
adv	adverb
Anat	Anatomy
Archit	Architecture
Astrol	Astrology
Aust	Australia(n)
BC	before Christ
Biol	Biology
Brit	British
Chem	Chemistry
C of E	Church of England
conj	conjunction
E	East
e.g.	for example
esp.	especially
etc.	et cetera
fem	feminine
foll.	followed
Geom	Geometry
Hist	History
interj	interjection
Lit	Literary
masc	masculine
Med	Medicine
Meteorol	Meteorology
Mil	Military
n	noun
N	North
Naut	Nautical
NZ	New Zealand
Obs	Obsolete
Offens	Offensive
orig.	originally
Photog	Photography
pl	plural
prep	preposition
pron	pronoun
Psychol	Psychology
®	Trademark
RC	Roman Catholic
S	South
S Afr	South Africa(n)
Scot	Scottish
sing	singular
US	United States
usu.	usually
v	verb
W	West
Zool	Zoology

A a

a *adj* indefinite article, used before a noun being mentioned for the first time.
A *n, pl* **A's, As** highest grade in an examination. **from A to Z** from start to finish.
Å angstrom unit.
a- *prefix* not or without, e.g. *apolitical; amoral.*
A1 *adj Informal* first-class, excellent.
AA **1** Alcoholics Anonymous. **2** Automobile Association.
aardvark *n* S African anteater with long ears and snout.
AB **1** able-bodied seaman. **2** Alberta.
aback *adv* **taken aback** startled or disconcerted.
abacus [**ab**-a-cuss] *n* beads on a wire frame, used for doing calculations.
abaft *adj, adv Naut* closer to the rear of (a ship).
abalone [ab-a-**lone**-ee] *n* edible sea creature with a shell lined with mother of pearl.
abandon *v* **1** desert or leave (one's wife, children, etc.). **2** give up (hope etc.) altogether. ♦ *n* **3** lack of inhibition. **abandoned** *adj* **1** deserted. **2** uninhibited. **abandonment** *n*
abase *v* humiliate or degrade (oneself). **abasement** *n*
abashed *adj* embarrassed and ashamed.
abate *v* make or become less strong. **abatement** *n*
abattoir [**ab**-a-twahr] *n* slaughterhouse.
abbess *n* nun in charge of a convent.
abbey *n* dwelling place of, or a church belonging to, a community of monks or nuns.
abbot *n* head of an abbey of monks.
abbreviate *v* shorten (a word) by leaving out some letters. **abbreviation** *n* shortened form of a word or words.
ABC *n* **1** alphabet. **2** basics of a subject.
abdicate *v* give up (the throne or a responsibility). **abdication** *n*
abdomen *n* part of the body containing the stomach and intestines. **abdominal** *adj*
abduct *v* carry off, kidnap. **abduction** *n* **abductor** *n*
aberration *n* **1** sudden change from what is normal, accurate, or correct. **2** brief lapse in control of one's thoughts or feelings. **aberrant** *adj* showing aberration.
abet *v* **abetting, abetted** help or encourage in wrongdoing. **abettor** *n*
abeyance *n* **in abeyance** not in use.
abhor *v* **-horring, -horred** detest utterly. **abhorrent** *adj* hateful, loathsome. **abhorrence** *n*
abide *v* **1** endure, put up with. **2** *Obs* stay or dwell, e.g. *abide with me.* **abide by** *v* obey (the law, rules, etc.). **abiding** *adj* lasting.
ability *n, pl* **-ties** **1** competence, power. **2** talent.
abject *adj* **1** utterly miserable. **2** lacking all self-respect. **abjectly** *adv*
abjure *v* deny or renounce on oath.
ablative [**ab**-lat-iv] *n* case of nouns in Latin and other languages, indicating source, agent, or instrument of action.
ablaze *adj* **1** burning fiercely. **2** emotionally aroused, e.g. *ablaze with desire.*
able *adj* capable, competent. **ably** *adv* **able-bodied** *adj* strong and healthy. **able-bodied seaman** seaman who is trained in certain skills.
-able *adj suffix* able to be acted on as specified, e.g. *washable.* **-ably** *adv suffix* **-ability** *n suffix*
ablutions *pl n* act of washing.
ABM antiballistic missile.
abnormal *adj* not normal or usual. **abnormally** *adv* **abnormality** *n*
aboard *adv, prep* on, in, onto, or into (a ship, train, or plane).
abode *n* home, dwelling.
abolish *v* do away with. **abolition** *n* **abolitionist** *n* person who wishes to do

away with something, esp. slavery.

A-bomb *n* short for ATOMIC BOMB.

abominable *adj* detestable, very bad. **abominable snowman** large apelike creature said to live in the Himalayas. **abominably** *adv*

abomination *n* **1** someone or something that is detestable. **2** strong dislike.

aborigine [ab-or-**rij**-in-ee], **aboriginal** *n* original inhabitant of a country or region, esp. (**A-**) Australia. **aboriginal** *adj*

abort *v* **1** have an abortion or perform an abortion on. **2** have a miscarriage. **3** end a plan or process before completion. **abortion** *n* **1** operation to end a pregnancy. **2** *Informal* something grotesque. **abortionist** *n* **1** person in favour of legal abortion. **2** person who performs abortions, esp. illegally. **abortive** *adj* unsuccessful.

abound *v* be plentiful. **abounding** *adj*

about *prep* **1** concerning, on the subject of. **2** in or near (a place). ♦ *adv* **3** nearly, approximately. **4** nearby. **about to** shortly going to, e.g. *about to leave.* **not about to** determined not to, e.g. *I'm not about to give up now.* **about-turn** *n* **1** turn to the opposite direction. **2** complete change of attitude.

above *adv, prep* **1** over or higher (than). **2** greater (than). **3** superior (to). **above board** in the open, without dishonesty.

abracadabra *n* supposedly magic word.

abrasion *n* scraped area on the skin.

abrasive *adj* **1** harsh and unpleasant in manner. **2** tending to rub or scrape. ♦ *n* **3** substance for cleaning or polishing by rubbing.

abreast *adv, adj* side by side. **abreast of** up to date with.

abridge *v* shorten by using fewer words. **abridgment, abridgement** *n*

abroad *adv* **1** to or in a foreign country. **2** at large.

abrogate *v* cancel (a law or agreement) formally. **abrogation** *n*

abrupt *adj* **1** sudden, unexpected. **2** blunt and rude. **abruptly** *adv* **abruptness** *n*

abscess [**ab**-sess] *n* inflamed swelling containing pus.

abscond *v* leave secretly.

abseil [**ab**-sale] *v* go down a steep drop by a rope fastened at the top and tied around one's body.

absent *adj* **1** not present. **2** lacking. **3** inattentive. ♦ *v* **4** stay away. **absently** *adv* **absence** *n* **1** being away. **2** lack. **absentee** *n* person who should be present but is not. **absenteeism** *n* persistent absence from work or school. **absent-minded** *adj* inattentive or forgetful. **absent-mindedly** *adv*

absinthe *n* strong green aniseed-flavoured liqueur.

absolute *adj* **1** complete, perfect. **2** not limited, unconditional. **3** pure, e.g. *absolute alcohol.* **absolute zero** *Physics* lowest possible temperature, -273.15°C. **absolutely** *adv* **1** completely. ♦ *interj* **2** certainly, yes. **absolutism** *n* government by a ruler with unrestricted power.

absolve *v* declare to be free from blame or sin. **absolution** *n*

absorb *v* **1** soak up (a liquid). **2** take in. **3** engage the interest of (someone). **absorption** *n* **absorbent** *adj* able to absorb liquid. **absorbency** *n*

abstain *v* **1** choose not to do something. **2** choose not to vote. **abstainer** *n* **abstention** *n* abstaining, esp. from voting. **abstinence** *n* abstaining, esp. from drinking alcohol. **abstinent** *adj*

abstemious [ab-**steem**-ee-uss] *adj* taking very little alcohol or food. **abstemiousness** *n*

abstract *adj* **1** existing as a quality or idea rather than a material object. **2** theoretical. **3** (of art) using patterns of shapes and colours rather than realistic likenesses. ♦ *n* **4** summary. **5** abstract work of art. **6** abstract word or idea. ♦ *v* **7** summarize. **8** remove. **abstracted** *adj* lost in thought. **abstractedly** *adv* **abstraction** *n*

abstruse *adj* not easy to understand.

absurd *adj* incongruous or ridiculous. **absurdly** *adv* **absurdity** *n*

abundant *adj* plentiful. **abundantly** *adv* very, e.g. *it is abundantly clear.* **abun-**

dance *n*

abuse *v* **1** use wrongly. **2** ill-treat violently. **3** speak harshly and rudely to. ♦ *n* **4** prolonged ill-treatment. **5** harsh and vulgar comments. **6** wrong use. **abuser** *n* **abusive** *adj* **abusively** *adv* **abusiveness** *n*

abut *v* **abutting, abutted** be next to or touching.

abuzz *adj* noisy, busy with activity etc.

abysmal *adj Informal* extremely bad, awful. **abysmally** *adv*

abyss *n* very deep hole or chasm.

Ac *Chem* actinium.

AC alternating current.

a/c account.

acacia [a-**kay**-sha] *n* tree or shrub with yellow or white flowers.

academy *n, pl* **-mies** **1** society to advance arts or sciences. **2** institution for training in a particular skill. **3** *Scot* secondary school. **academic** *adj* **1** of an academy or university. **2** of theoretical interest only. ♦ *n* **3** lecturer or researcher at a university. **academically** *adv* **academician** *n* member of an academy.

acanthus *n* **1** prickly plant. **2** ornamental carving in the shape of an acanthus leaf.

ACAS Advisory Conciliation and Arbitration Service.

acc. account.

accede *v* **1** consent or agree (to). **2** take up (an office or position).

accelerate *v* (cause to) move faster. **acceleration** *n* **accelerator** *n* pedal in a motor vehicle to increase speed.

accent *n* **1** distinctive style of pronunciation of a local, national, or social group. **2** mark over a letter to show how it is pronounced. **3** stress on a syllable or musical note. ♦ *v* **4** place emphasis on.

accentuate *v* stress, emphasize. **accentuation** *n*

accept *v* **1** receive willingly. **2** agree to. **3** consider to be true. **accepted** *adj* generally approved. **acceptance** *n* **acceptable** *adj* **1** tolerable. **2** satisfactory. **acceptably** *adv* **acceptability** *n*

access *n* **1** means of or right to approach or enter. ♦ *v* **2** obtain (data) from a computer. **accessible** *adj* **1** easy to reach. **2** easy to understand. **accessibility** *n*

accession *n* taking up of an office or position.

accessory *n, pl* **-ries** **1** supplementary part or object. **2** person involved in a crime although not present when it is committed.

accident *n* **1** mishap, usu. one causing injury or death. **2** event happening by chance. **accidental** *adj* **1** happening by chance or unintentionally. ♦ *n* **2** *Music* symbol indicating that a sharp, flat, or natural note is not a part of the key signature. **accidentally** *adv* **accident-prone** *adj* often having accidents.

acclaim *v* **1** applaud, praise. ♦ *n* **2** enthusiastic approval. **acclamation** *n*

acclimatize *v* adapt to a new climate or environment. **acclimatization** *n*

accolade *n* **1** award, honour, or praise. **2** award of knighthood.

accommodate *v* **1** provide with lodgings. **2** have room for. **3** oblige, do a favour for. **4** adapt or adjust (to something). **accommodation** *n* house or room for living in. **accommodating** *adj* obliging.

> Note the double 'c' and double 'm'. This word is very commonly misspelled.

accompany *v* **-nying, -nied** **1** go along with. **2** occur with. **3** provide a musical accompaniment for. **accompaniment** *n* **1** something that accompanies. **2** *Music* supporting part that goes with a solo. **accompanist** *n*

accomplice *n* person who helps another to commit a crime.

accomplish *v* **1** manage to do. **2** finish. **accomplishment** *n* **1** completion. **2** personal ability or skill. **accomplished** *adj* expert, proficient.

> The usual pronunciation of the sylla-

ble 'com' in British English sounds like 'kum', but the sound 'kom' is increasingly used.

accord *n* **1** agreement, harmony. ♦ *v* **2** fit in with. **3** grant or give. **of one's own accord** voluntarily.

Do not confuse *of one's own accord* with *on one's own account* 'for one's own benefit'.

accordance *n* **in accordance with** conforming to or according to.
according *adv* **according to 1** as stated by. **2** in conformity with. **accordingly** *adv* **1** in an appropriate manner. **2** consequently.
accordion *n* portable musical instrument played by moving the two sides apart and together, and pressing a keyboard or buttons to produce the notes. **accordionist** *n*
accost *v* approach and speak to.
account *n* **1** report, description. **2** business arrangement making credit available. **3** record of money received and paid out with the resulting balance. **4** person's money held in a bank. **5** importance, value. ♦ *v* **6** judge to be. **on account of** because of. **accountable** *adj* responsible to someone or for something. **accountability** *n* **account for** *v* **1** explain. **2** make up, constitute.
accounting *n* skill or practice of maintaining and auditing business accounts. **accountant** *n* person who maintains and audits business accounts. **accountancy** *n*
accoutrements [ak-**koo**-tra-ments] *pl n* clothing and equipment for a particular activity.
accredited *adj* authorized, officially recognized.
accretion [ak-**kree**-shun] *n* **1** gradual growth. **2** something added.
accrue *v* **-cruing, -crued** increase gradually. **accrual** *n*
accumulate *v* gather together in increasing quantity. **accumulation** *n* **accumulative** *adj* **accumulator** *n* rechargeable electric battery.
accurate *adj* exact, correct. **accurately** *adv* **accuracy** *n*
accursed [a-**curse**-id] *adj* **1** under a curse. **2** detestable.
accusative *n* grammatical case indicating the direct object.
accuse *v* charge with wrongdoing. **accused** *n* *Law* person or people accused of a crime in a court. **accuser** *n* **accusing** *adj* **accusation** *n* **accusatory** *adj*
accustom *v* make used to. **accustomed** *adj* **1** usual. **2** used (to). **3** in the habit (of).
ace *n* **1** playing card with one symbol on it. **2** *Informal* expert. **3** *Tennis* unreturnable serve. ♦ *adj* **4** *Informal* excellent.
acerbic [ass-**sir**-bik] *adj* harsh or bitter. **acerbity** *n*
acetate [**ass**-it-tate] *n* **1** *Chem* salt or ester of acetic acid. **2** (also **acetate rayon**) synthetic textile fibre.
acetic [ass-**see**-tik] *adj* of or involving vinegar. **acetic acid** colourless liquid used to make vinegar.
acetone [**ass**-it-tone] *n* colourless liquid used as a solvent.
acetylene [ass-**set**-ill-een] *n* colourless flammable gas used in welding metals.
ache *n* **1** dull continuous pain. ♦ *v* **2** be in or cause continuous dull pain. **aching** *adj, n* **achingly** *adv*
achieve *v* gain by hard work or ability. **achievement** *n* something accomplished. **achiever** *n*

Note the 'ie'. This word is very commonly misspelled.

Achilles heel [ak-**kill**-eez] *n* small but fatal weakness.
Achilles tendon *n* cord connecting the calf to the heel bone.
achromatic *adj* **1** colourless. **2** *Music* with no sharps or flats.
acid *n* **1** *Chem* one of a class of compounds, corrosive and sour when dis-

solved in water, that combine with a base to form a salt. **2** *Slang* LSD. ♦ *adj* **3** containing acid. **4** sour-tasting. **5** sharp or sour in manner. **acidly** *adv* **acidic** *adj* **acidify** *v* **-fying, -fied** **acidity** *n* **Acid (House)** *n* type of funk-based electronically edited disco music with hypnotic sound effects. **acid rain** rain containing acid from atmospheric pollution. **acid test** conclusive test of value.

acknowledge *v* **1** admit, recognize. **2** indicate recognition of (a person). **3** say one has received. **acknowledgment, acknowledgement** *n*

> The alternative spellings with or without an 'e' between 'g' and 'm' are equally acceptable.

acme [**ak**-mee] *n* highest point of achievement or excellence.

acne [**ak**-nee] *n* pimply skin disease.

acolyte *n* **1** follower or attendant. **2** *Christianity* person who assists a priest.

aconite *n* **1** poisonous plant with hoodlike flowers. **2** poison obtained from this plant.

acorn *n* nut of the oak tree.

acoustic *adj* **1** of sound and hearing. **2** (of a musical instrument) not electronically amplified. **acoustics** *n* **1** science of sounds. ♦ *pl* **2** features of a room or building determining how sound is heard within it. **acoustically** *adv*

acquaint *v* make familiar, inform. **acquainted** *adj* **acquaintance** *n* **1** person known. **2** personal knowledge.

> The idiom is *acquaint* someone *with* something.

acquiesce [ak-wee-**ess**] *v* agree to what someone wants. **acquiescence** *n* **acquiescent** *adj*

> The use of *to* after *acquiesce* was formerly regarded as incorrect, but is now acceptable.

acquire *v* gain, get. **acquisition** *n* **1** thing acquired. **2** act of getting. **acquired taste** **1** liking for something at first considered unpleasant. **2** the thing liked.

acquisitive *adj* eager to gain material possessions. **acquisitiveness** *n*

acquit *v* **-quitting, -quitted** **1** pronounce (someone) innocent. **2** behave in a particular way. **acquittal** *n*

acre *n* measure of land, 4840 square yards. **acreage** [**ake**-er-rij] *n* land area in acres.

acrid [**ak**-rid] *adj* pungent, bitter. **acridity** *n*

acrimonious *adj* bitter in speech or manner. **acrimony** *n*

acrobat *n* person skilled in gymnastic feats requiring agility and balance. **acrobatic** *adj* **acrobatics** *pl n* acrobatic feats.

acronym *n* word formed from the initial letters of other words, such as NASA.

acrophobia *n* fear of heights.

acropolis [a-**crop**-pol-liss] *n* citadel of an ancient Greek city.

across *adv, prep* **1** from side to side (of). **2** on or to the other side (of). **across the board** applying equally to all.

acrostic *n* lines of writing in which the first or last letters of each line spell a word or saying.

acrylic *n, adj* (synthetic fibre, paint, etc.) made from acrylic acid. **acrylic acid** strong-smelling corrosive liquid.

act *n* **1** thing done. **2** law or decree. **3** section of a play or opera. **4** one of several short performances in a show. **5** pretended attitude. ♦ *v* **6** do something. **7** behave in a particular way. **8** perform in a play, film, etc. **act of God** unpredictable natural event. **acting** *n* **1** art of an actor. ♦ *adj* **2** temporarily performing the duties of. **actor, actress** *n* person who acts in a play, film, etc.

ACT Australian Capital Territory.

actinide series *n* series of 15 radioactive elements with increasing atomic numbers from actinium to lawrencium.

actinium *n Chem* radioactive chemical element.

action *n* **1** process of doing something. **2** thing done. **3** lawsuit. **4** operating mechanism. **5** events forming the plot of a story or play. **6** *Slang* main activity in a place. **7** minor battle. **actionable** *adj* giving grounds for a lawsuit. **action replay** rerun of an event on a television tape.

active *adj* **1** moving, working, e.g. *he remained active in public affairs.* **2** busy, energetic. **3** *Grammar* (of a verb) in a form indicating that the subject is performing the action, e.g. *threw* in *Kim threw the ball.* **actively** *adv* **activity** *n* **1** state of being active. **2** (*pl* **-ties**) leisure pursuit. **activate** *v* make active. **activation** *n* **activator** *n* **activist** *n* person who works energetically to achieve political or social goals. **activism** *n*

actual *adj* existing in reality. **actually** *adv* really, indeed. **actuality** *n*

> Avoid using *actual* or *actually* when it adds nothing to the sense of the sentence. Compare: *It's an actual fact: It's a fact.*

actuary *n, pl* **-aries** statistician who calculates insurance risks. **actuarial** *adj*

actuate *v* **1** start up (a device). **2** motivate (someone).

acuity [ak-**kew**-it-ee] *n* keenness of vision or thought.

acumen [**ak**-yew-men] *n* ability to make good judgments.

acupuncture *n* medical treatment involving the insertion of needles at various points on the body. **acupuncturist** *n*

acute *adj* **1** severe. **2** keen, shrewd. **3** sharp, sensitive. **4** (of an angle) less than 90 . ♦ *n* **5** accent (´) over a letter to indicate the quality or length of its sound, as in cafØ. **acutely** *adv* **acuteness** *n*

ad *n Informal* advertisement.

AD anno Domini.

adage [**ad**-ij] *n* wise saying, proverb.

adagio [ad-**dahj**-yo] *n, pl* **-gios,** *adv Music* (piece to be played) slowly and gracefully.

adamant *adj* unshakable in determination or purpose. **adamantly** *adv*

Adam's apple *n* projecting lump of thyroid cartilage at the front of the throat.

adapt *v* alter for new use or new conditions. **adaptable** *adj* **adaptability** *n* **adaptation** *n* **1** thing produced by adapting something. **2** adapting. **adaptor, adapter** *n* device for connecting several electrical appliances to a single socket.

ADC aide-de-camp.

add *v* **1** combine (numbers or quantities). **2** join (to something). **3** say or write further. **add up** *v* **1** calculate the sum of (two or more numbers). **2** *Informal* make sense. **add up to** *v* amount to.

addendum *n, pl* **-da** **1** an addition. **2** appendix to a book etc.

adder *n* small poisonous snake.

addict *n* **1** person who is unable to stop taking drugs. **2** *Informal* person devoted to something. **addicted** *adj* **addiction** *n* **addictive** *adj* causing addiction.

addition *n* **1** adding. **2** thing added. **in addition** besides, as well. **additional** *adj* **additionally** *adv* **additive** *n* something added, esp. to a foodstuff, to improve it or prevent deterioration.

addled *adj* confused or unable to think clearly.

address *n* **1** place where a person lives. **2** direction on a letter. **3** location. **4** formal public speech. ♦ *v* **5** mark the destination, as on an envelope. **6** speak to. **7** give attention to (a problem, task, etc.). **addressee** *n* person addressed.

adduce *v* mention something as evidence or proof.

adenoids [**ad**-in-oidz] *pl n* mass of tissue at the back of the throat. **adenoidal** *adj* having a nasal voice caused by swollen adenoids.

adept *adj, n* very skilful (person).

adequate *adj* **1** sufficient, enough. **2** not outstanding. **adequately** *adv* **adequacy** *n*

à deux [ah **der**] *adv French* of or for two

people.

adhere *v* **1** stick (to). **2** be devoted (to). **adherence** *n* **adherent** *n* devotee, fol›lower. **adhesion** *n* **1** sticking (to). **2** joining together of parts of the body that are normally separate, as after sur›gery.

adhesive *n* **1** substance used to stick things together. ♦ *adj* **2** able to stick to things.

ad hoc *adj, adv Latin* for a particular pur›pose only.

adieu [a›**dew**] *interj* farewell, goodbye.

ad infinitum *adv Latin* endlessly.

adipose *adj* of or containing fat.

adj. adjective.

adjacent *adj* **1** near or next (to). **2** hav›ing a common boundary. **3** *Geom* (of a side in a right›angled triangle) lying be›tween a specified angle and the right angle.

adjective *n* word that adds information about a noun or pronoun. **adjectival** *adj*

adjoin *v* be next to. **adjoining** *adj*

adjourn *v* **1** close (a court) at the end of a session. **2** postpone temporarily. **3** *In›formal* go elsewhere. **adjournment** *n*

adjudge *v* declare (to be).

adjudicate *v* **1** give a formal decision on (a dispute). **2** judge (a competition). **adjudication** *n* **adjudicator** *n*

adjunct *n* subordinate or additional per›son or thing.

adjure *v* **1** command (to do). **2** appeal earnestly. **adjuration** *n*

adjust *v* **1** adapt to new conditions. **2** al›ter slightly so as to be suitable. **adjust›able** *adj* **adjuster** *n* **adjustment** *n*

adjutant [**aj**›oo›tant] *n* army officer in charge of routine administration.

ad-lib *v* **-libbing, -libbed** **1** improvise a speech etc. without preparation. ♦ *n* **2** improvised remark.

Adm. Admiral(ty).

admin *n Informal* administration.

administer *v* **1** manage (business af›fairs). **2** organize and put into practice. **3** give (medicine or treatment).

administrate *v* manage (an organiza›tion). **administration** *n* **administra›tive** *adj* **administrator** *n*

admiral *n* highest naval rank. **Admiral›ty** *n* former government department in charge of the Royal Navy.

admire *v* regard with esteem and ap›proval. **admirable** [**ad**›mer›a›bl] *adj* **admirably** *adv* **admiration** *n* **admirer** *n* **admiring** *adj* **admiringly** *adv*

admissible *adj* allowed to be brought in as evidence in court. **admissibility** *n*

admission *n* **1** permission to enter. **2** permission to join (an organization). **3** entrance fee. **4** confession.

admit *v* **-mitting, -mitted** **1** confess, ac›knowledge. **2** concede the truth of. **3** al›low in. **admittance** *n* permission to en›ter. **admittedly** *adv* it must be agreed.

admixture *n* **1** mixture. **2** ingredient.

admonish *v* reprove sternly. **admoni›tion** *n*

ad nauseam [**ad naw**›zee›am] *adv Latin* to a boring or sickening extent.

ado *n* fuss, trouble.

adobe [ad›**oh**›bee] *n* sun›dried brick.

adolescence *n* period between puberty and adulthood. **adolescent** *n, adj* (per›son) between puberty and adulthood.

Adonis *n* handsome young man.

adopt *v* **1** take (someone else's child) as one's own. **2** take up (a plan or princi›ple). **adoption** *n* **adoptive** *adj* related by adoption.

adore *v* **1** love intensely. **2** worship. **3** *In›formal* like very much, e.g. *I adore being in the country.* **adorable** *adj* **adoration** *n* **adoring** *adj* **adoringly** *adv*

adorn *v* decorate, embellish. **adorn›ment** *n*

ADP automatic data processing.

adrenal [ad›**reen**›al] *adj* near the kid›neys. **adrenal glands** glands covering the top of the kidneys.

adrenalin, adrenaline *n* hormone se›creted by the adrenal glands in re›sponse to stress.

adrift *adj, adv* **1** drifting. **2** without a clear purpose.

adroit *adj* quick and skilful. **adroitly** *adv* **adroitness** *n*

adsorb *v* (of a gas or vapour) condense and form a thin film on a surface. **adsorbent** *adj* **adsorption** *n*

adulation *n* uncritical admiration.

adult *adj* **1** fully grown, mature. ♦ *n* **2** adult person or animal. **adulthood** *n*

adulterate *v* spoil something by adding inferior material. **adulteration** *n*

adultery *n, pl* **-teries** sexual unfaithfulness of a husband or wife. **adulterer, adulteress** *n* **adulterous** *adj*

adv. adverb.

advance *v* **1** go or bring forward. **2** further (a cause). **3** propose (an idea). **4** lend (a sum of money). ♦ *n* **5** forward movement. **6** improvement. **7** loan. ♦ *pl* **8** approaches to a person with the hope of starting a romantic or sexual relationship. ♦ *adj* **9** done or happening before an event. **in advance** ahead. **advanced** *adj* **1** at a late stage in development. **2** not elementary. **advancement** *n* promotion.

advantage *n* **1** more favourable position or state. **2** benefit or profit. **3** *Tennis* point scored after deuce. **take advantage of 1** use (a person) unfairly. **2** use (an opportunity). **advantageous** *adj* **advantageously** *adv* **advantaged** *adj* in a superior social or financial position.

advent *n* **1** arrival. **2** (**A-**) season of four weeks before Christmas. **Adventist** *n* member of a Christian sect that believes in the imminent return of Christ.

adventitious *adj* added or appearing accidentally.

adventure *n* exciting and risky undertaking or exploit. **adventurer, adventuress** *n* **1** person who unscrupulously seeks money or power. **2** person who seeks adventures. **adventurous** *adj* **adventurously** *adv*

adverb *n* word that adds information about a verb, adjective, or other adverb. **adverbial** *adj*

adversary [**ad**-verse-er-ree] *n, pl* **-saries** opponent or enemy.

adverse *adj* **1** unfavourable. **2** antagonistic or hostile. **adversely** *adv* **adversity** *n* very difficult or hard circumstances.

advert *n Informal* advertisement.

advertise *v* **1** present or praise (goods or services) to the public in order to encourage sales. **2** make (a vacancy, event, etc.) known publicly. **advertisement** *n* public announcement to sell goods or publicize an event. **advertiser** *n* **advertising** *adj, n*

> Note that the standard pronunciation of *advertisement* differs from *advertise*. The main stress is on 'ver', while 'tise' is pronounced 'tiz'.

advice *n* recommendation as to what to do. **advise** *v* **1** offer advice to. **2** notify (someone). **adviser, advisor** *n* **advisable** *adj* prudent, sensible. **advisability** *n* **advisory** *adj* giving advice. **advised** *adj* considered, thought-out, e.g. *ill-advised.* **advisedly** [ad-**vize**-id-lee] *adv* deliberately.

advocaat *n* liqueur with a raw egg base.

advocate *v* **1** propose or recommend. ♦ *n* **2** person who publicly supports a cause. **3** *Scot* barrister. **advocacy** *n*

adze *n* tool with an arched blade at right angles to the handle.

aegis [**ee**-jiss] *n* sponsorship, protection.

aeolian harp [ee-**oh**-lee-an] *n* musical instrument that produces sounds when the wind passes over its strings.

aeon [**ee**-on] *n* immeasurably long period of time.

aerate *v* put gas into (a liquid), as when making a fizzy drink. **aeration** *n*

aerial *adj* **1** in, from, or operating in the air. **2** relating to aircraft. ♦ *n* **3** metal pole, wire, etc., for receiving or transmitting radio or TV signals.

aero- *combining form* air or aircraft, e.g. *aeronautics.*

aerobatics *pl n* stunt flying. **aerobatic** *adj*

aerobics *n* exercises designed to increase the amount of oxygen in the blood. **aerobic** *adj* **aerobically** *adv*

aerodrome *n* small airport.

aerodynamics *n* study of how air flows around moving solid objects. **aerodynamic** *adj*
aerofoil *n* part of an aircraft, such as the wing, designed to give lift.
aerogram *n* airmail letter on a single sheet of paper that seals to form an envelope.
aeronautics *n* study or practice of aircraft flight. **aeronautical** *adj*
aeroplane *n* powered flying vehicle with fixed wings.
aerosol *n* pressurized can from which a substance can be dispensed as a fine spray.

> Be careful not to confuse the spelling 'aer-' with 'air-'.

aerospace *n* **1** earth's atmosphere and space beyond. ♦ *adj* **2** of rockets or space vehicles, e.g. *the aerospace industry.*
aesthetic [iss-**thet**-ik] *adj* relating to the appreciation of art and beauty. **aesthetics** *n* study of art, beauty, and good taste. **aesthetically** *adv* **aesthete** [**eess**-theet] *n* person who has or affects an extravagant love of art. **aestheticism** *n*
aether *n* same as ETHER.
aetiology [ee-tee-**ol**-a-jee] *n* same as ETIOLOGY.
afar *adv* **from afar** from or at a great distance.
affable *adj* friendly and easy to talk to. **affably** *adv* **affability** *n*
affair *n* **1** event or happening. **2** sexual relationship outside marriage. **3** thing to be done or attended to. ♦ *pl* **4** personal or business interests. **5** matters of public interest.
affect[1] *v* **1** act on, influence. **2** move (someone) emotionally.

> Note the difference between the verbs *affect* meaning 'influence' and *effect* meaning 'accomplish'.

affect[2] *v* **1** put on a show of. **2** wear or use by preference. **affectation** *n* attitude or manner put on to impress. **affected** *adj* **1** displaying affectation. **2** pretended.
affection *n* fondness or love. **affectionate** *adj* loving. **affectionately** *adv*
affianced [af-**fie**-anst] *adj Old-fashioned* engaged to be married.
affidavit [af-fid-**dave**-it] *n* written statement made on oath.
affiliate *v* (of a group) link up with a larger group. **affiliation** *n*
affinity *n, pl* **-ties** **1** close connection or liking. **2** close resemblance. **3** chemical attraction.
affirm *v* **1** declare to be true. **2** uphold or confirm (an idea or belief). **affirmation** *n* **affirmative** *n, adj* (word or phrase) indicating agreement.
affix *v* **1** attach or fasten. ♦ *n* **2** word or syllable added to a word to change its meaning.
afflict *v* give pain or grief to. **affliction** *n*
affluent *adj* having plenty of money. **affluence** *n* wealth.
afford *v* **1** have enough money to buy. **2** be able to spare (the time etc.). **3** give or supply. **affordable** *adj*
afforest *v* plant trees on. **afforestation** *n*
affray *n* noisy fight, brawl.
affront *v, n* insult.

> *Affront* is often followed by 'to': *An affront to my feelings.*

Afghan *n* **1** language of Afghanistan. **2** person from Afghanistan. ♦ *adj* **3** of Afghanistan or its language. **Afghan hound** large slim dog with long silky hair.
aficionado [af-fish-yo-**nah**-do] *n, pl* **-dos** enthusiastic fan of something or someone.
afield *adv* **far afield** far away.
aflame *adj* burning.
afloat *adv, adj* **1** floating. **2** at sea.
afoot *adv, adj* happening, in operation.
aforesaid, aforementioned *adj* referred to previously.

aforethought *adj* premeditated, e.g. *with malice aforethought.*

a fortiori [**eh** for›tee›**or**›rye] *adv* for a stronger reason.

Afr. Africa(n).

afraid *adj* **1** frightened. **2** regretful.

afresh *adv* again, anew.

African *adj* **1** of Africa. ♦ *n* **2** person from Africa. **African-American** *n* **1** American of African descent. ♦ *adj* **2** of African› Americans. **African violet** house plant with pink or purple flowers and hairy leaves.

Afrikaans *n* language used in S Africa, related to Dutch.

Afrikaner *n* White S African whose moth› er tongue is Afrikaans.

Afro- *combining form* African, e.g. *Afro-Caribbean.*

aft *adv* at or towards the rear of a ship or aircraft.

after *prep* **1** following in time or place. **2** in pursuit of. **3** in imitation of. ♦ *conj* **4** at a later time than. ♦ *adv* **5** at a later time. **afters** *pl n Informal* dessert.

afterbirth *n* material expelled from the womb after childbirth.

aftercare *n* **1** support given to a person discharged from a hospital or prison. **2** regular care required to keep some› thing in good condition.

aftereffect *n* result occurring some time after its cause.

afterglow *n* **1** glow left after a source of light has gone. **2** pleasant feeling left af› ter an enjoyable experience.

afterlife *n* life after death.

aftermath *n* results of an event consid› ered together.

afternoon *n* time between noon and evening.

afterpains *pl n* pains caused by the con› traction of the womb after childbirth.

aftershave *n* lotion applied to the face after shaving.

afterthought *n* **1** idea occurring later. **2** something added later.

afterwards, afterward *adv* later.

Ag *Chem* silver.

again *adv* **1** once more. **2** in addition.

against *prep* **1** in opposition or contrast to. **2** in contact with. **3** as a protection from.

agape *adj* **1** (of the mouth) wide open. **2** (of a person) very surprised.

agaric *n* fungus with gills on the under› side of the cap, such as a mushroom.

agate [**ag**›git] *n* semiprecious form of quartz with striped colouring.

agave [a›**gave**›vee] *n* tropical American plant with tall flower stalks and thick leaves.

age *n* **1** length of time a person or thing has existed. **2** time of life. **3** latter part of human life. **4** period of history. **5** long time. ♦ *v* **ageing** *or* **aging, aged 6** make or grow old. **aged** *adj* **1** [**ay**›jid] old. **2** [rhymes with **raged**] being at the age of. **ageing, aging** *n, adj* **ageless** *adj* **1** apparently never growing old. **2** seeming to have existed for ever. **age-old** *adj* very old.

> Both spellings of *ageing,* with or without an 'e', are equally acceptable.

agency *n, pl* **-cies 1** organization provid› ing a service. **2** business or function of an agent. **3** *Old-fashioned* power or ac› tion by which something happens.

agenda *n* list of things to be dealt with, esp. at a meeting.

agent *n* **1** person acting on behalf of an› other. **2** person or thing producing an effect.

agent provocateur [**azh**›on prov›vok› at›**tur**] *n, pl* **agents provocateurs** [**azh**›on prov›vok›at›**tur**] person em› ployed by the authorities to tempt peo› ple to commit illegal acts and so be dis› credited or punished.

agglomeration *n* confused mass or clus› ter.

aggrandize *v* make greater in size, pow› er, or rank. **aggrandizement** *n*

aggravate *v* **1** make worse. **2** *Informal* annoy. **aggravating** *adj* **aggravation** *n*

aggregate *n* **1** total. **2** rock consisting of a mixture of minerals. **3** sand or gravel used to make concrete. ♦ *adj* **4** gathered into a mass. **5** total or final. ♦ *v* **6** combine into a whole. **aggregation** *n*

aggression *n* **1** hostile behaviour. **2** unprovoked attack. **aggressive** *adj* **1** showing aggression. **2** forceful. **aggressively** *adv* **aggressiveness** *n* **aggressor** *n*

aggrieved *adj* upset and angry.

aggro *n Slang* aggressive behaviour.

aghast *adj* overcome with amazement or horror.

agile *adj* **1** nimble, quick-moving. **2** mentally quick. **agilely** *adv* **agility** *n*

agin *prep Dialect* against, opposed to.

agitate *v* **1** disturb or excite. **2** stir or shake (a liquid). **3** stir up public opinion for or against something. **agitated** *adj* anxious or worried. **agitatedly** *adv* **agitation** *n* **agitator** *n*

agitprop *n* political agitation and propaganda.

aglitter *adj* sparkling, glittering.

aglow *adj* glowing.

AGM annual general meeting.

agnostic *n* **1** person who believes that it is impossible to know whether God exists. ♦ *adj* **2** of agnostics. **agnosticism** *n*

ago *adv* in the past.

agog *adj* eager or curious.

agony *n, pl* **-nies** extreme physical or mental pain. **agonize** *v* **1** worry greatly. **2** (cause to) suffer agony. **agonizing** *adj* **agonizingly** *adv* **agony aunt** journalist who gives advice in an agony column. **agony column** newspaper or magazine feature offering advice on personal problems.

agoraphobia *n* fear of open spaces. **agoraphobic** *n, adj*

agrarian *adj* of land or agriculture.

agree *v* **agreeing, agreed** **1** be of the same opinion. **2** consent. **3** reach a joint decision. **4** be consistent. **5** (foll. by *with*) be suitable to (one's health or digestion). **agreeable** *adj* **1** pleasant and enjoyable. **2** prepared to consent. **agreeably** *adv* **agreement** *n* **1** agreeing. **2** contract.

> *Agree* is usually followed by a preposition. Use agree *on* something; agree *with* someone; agree *to* do something.

agriculture *n* raising of crops and livestock. **agricultural** *adj* **agriculturalist** *n*

agrimony *n* yellow-flowered plant with bitter-tasting fruits.

agronomy [ag-**ron**-om-mee] *n* science of soil management and crop production. **agronomist** *n*

aground *adv* onto the bottom of shallow water.

ague [**aig**-yew] *n* periodic fever with shivering.

ah *interj* exclamation of pleasure, pain, etc.

aha *interj* exclamation of triumph, surprise, etc.

ahead *adv* **1** in front. **2** forwards.

ahem *interj* clearing of the throat to attract attention etc.

ahoy *interj* shout used at sea to attract attention.

AI **1** artificial insemination. **2** artificial intelligence.

aid *v, n* (give) assistance or support.

AID formerly, artificial insemination by donor: see DI.

aide *n* assistant.

aide-de-camp [**aid**-de-**kom**] *n, pl* **aides-de-camp** [**aid**-de-**kom**] military officer serving as personal assistant to a senior.

AIDS acquired immunodeficiency syndrome, a viral disease that destroys the body's ability to fight infection.

AIH artificial insemination by husband.

ail *v* **1** trouble, afflict. **2** be ill. **ailing** *adj* **1** sickly. **2** unsuccessful over a long time. **ailment** *n* illness.

aileron [**ale**-er-on] *n* movable flap on an aircraft wing which controls rolling.

aim *v* **1** point (a weapon or missile) or direct (a blow or remark) at a target. **2** propose or intend. ♦ *n* **3** aiming. **4** intention, purpose. **aimless** *adj* having no purpose. **aimlessly** *adv*

> The idiom is *aim at* something or

aim to do something.

ain't *Not standard* **1** am not. **2** is not. **3** are not. **4** has not. **5** have not.

air *n* **1** mixture of gases forming the earth's atmosphere. **2** space above the ground, sky. **3** breeze. **4** quality or manner. **5** tune. ♦ *pl* **6** affected manners. ♦ *v* **7** make known publicly. **8** expose to air to dry or ventilate. **on the air** in the act of broadcasting on radio or television. **airless** *adj* stuffy. **air base** centre from which military aircraft operate. **airborne** *adj* **1** carried by air. **2** (of aircraft) flying. **airbrush** *n* atomizer spraying paint by compressed air. **airfield** *n* place where aircraft can land and take off. **air force** branch of the armed forces responsible for air warfare. **air gun** gun fired by compressed air. **air hostess** stewardess on an aircraft. **airlift** *n* **1** transport of troops or cargo by aircraft when other routes are blocked. ♦ *v* **2** transport by airlift. **airlock** *n* **1** air bubble blocking the flow of liquid in a pipe. **2** airtight chamber. **airmail** *n* **1** system of sending mail by aircraft. **2** mail sent in this way. **airman** *n* member of the air force. **air miles** miles of free air travel that can be earned by buying airline tickets and various other products. **airplane** *n US* aeroplane. **airplay** *n* broadcast performances of a record on radio. **airport** *n* airfield for civilian aircraft, with facilities for aircraft maintenance and passengers. **air raid** attack by aircraft. **airship** *n* lighter-than-air self-propelled aircraft. **airsick** *adj* nauseated from travelling in an aircraft. **airspace** *n* atmosphere above a country, regarded as its territory. **airstrip** *n* cleared area where aircraft can take off and land. **airtight** *adj* sealed so that air cannot enter.

air conditioning *n* system that controls the temperature and humidity of the air in a building. **air-conditioned** *adj* **air conditioner**

aircraft *n* any machine that flies, such as an aeroplane. **aircraft carrier** warship for the launching and landing of aircraft.

Airedale *n* large rough-coated terrier.

airing *n* **1** exposure to air for drying or ventilation. **2** exposure to public debate.

airline *n* company providing scheduled flights for passengers and cargo. **airliner** *n* large passenger aircraft.

airworthy *adj* (of aircraft) fit to fly. **airworthiness** *n*

airy *adj* **airier, airiest 1** well-ventilated. **2** light-hearted and casual. **airily** *adv*

aisle [rhymes with **mile**] *n* passageway separating seating areas in a church, theatre, etc., or row of shelves in a supermarket.

ajar *adj, adv* (of a door) partly open.

AK Alaska.

akimbo *adv* **with arms akimbo** with hands on hips and elbows outwards.

akin *adj* **akin to** similar, related.

Al *Chem* aluminium.

AL Alabama.

à la *prep* in the manner of.

alabaster *n* soft white translucent stone.

à la carte *adj, adv* (of a menu) having dishes individually priced.

alacrity *n* speed, eagerness.

à la mode *adj* fashionable.

alarm *n* **1** sudden fear caused by awareness of danger. **2** warning sound. **3** device that gives this. **4** alarm clock. ♦ *v* **5** fill with fear. **alarming** *adj* **alarmingly** *adv* **alarmist** *n* person who alarms others needlessly. **alarm clock** clock which sounds at a set time to wake someone up.

alas *adv* unfortunately, regrettably.

alb *n* long white robe worn by a Christian priest.

albacore *n* tuna found in warm seas, eaten for food.

albatross *n* large sea bird with very long wings.

albeit *conj* even though.

albino *n, pl* **-nos** person or animal with white skin and hair and pink eyes. **albinism** *n*

Albion *n Poetic* **1** Britain. **2** England.

album *n* **1** book with blank pages for

keeping photographs or stamps in. **2** long-playing record.

albumen *n* egg white.

albumin, albumen *n* protein found in blood plasma, egg white, milk, and muscle.

alchemy *n* medieval form of chemistry concerned with trying to turn base metals into gold and to find the elixir of life. **alchemist** *n*

alcohol *n* **1** colourless flammable liquid present in intoxicating drinks. **2** intoxicating drinks generally. **alcoholic** *adj* **1** of alcohol. ♦ *n* **2** person addicted to alcohol. **alcoholism** *n* addiction to alcohol.

alcopop *n Informal* alcoholic drink that tastes like a soft drink.

alcove *n* recess in the wall of a room.

aldehyde *n* one of a group of chemical compounds derived from alcohol by oxidation.

alder *n* tree related to the birch.

alderman *n* formerly, senior member of a local council.

ale *n* kind of beer.

alembic *n* anything that distils or purifies, esp. an obsolete vessel used for distillation.

alert *adj* **1** watchful, attentive. ♦ *n* **2** warning of danger. ♦ *v* **3** warn of danger. **4** make (someone) aware of (a fact). **on the alert** watchful. **alertness** *n*

A level *n* (pass in a subject at) the advanced level of the GCE.

alfalfa *n* kind of plant used to feed livestock.

alfresco *adv, adj* in the open air.

algae [**al**-jee] *pl n* plants which live in or near water and have no true stems, leaves, or roots.

algebra *n* branch of mathematics using symbols to represent numbers. **algebraic** *adj*

ALGOL *n Computers* computer programming language designed for mathematical and scientific purposes.

algorithm *n* logical arithmetical or computational procedure for solving a problem.

alias *adv* **1** also known as, e.g. *William Bonney, alias Billy the Kid.* ♦ *n* **2** false name.

alibi *n* **1** plea of being somewhere else when a crime was committed. **2** *Informal* excuse.

Alice band *n* band worn across the head to hold the hair back from the face.

alien *adj* **1** foreign. **2** repugnant (to). **3** from another world. ♦ *n* **4** foreigner. **5** being from another world. **alienable** *adj Law* able to be transferred to another owner. **alienate** *v* cause to become hostile. **alienation** *n*

alight[1] *v* **1** step out of (a vehicle). **2** land.

alight[2] *adj* **1** on fire. **2** lit up.

align [a-**line**] *v* **1** bring (a person or group) into agreement with the policy of another. **2** place in a line. **alignment** *n*

alike *adj* **1** like, similar. ♦ *adv* **2** in the same way.

alimentary *adj* of nutrition. **alimentary canal** food passage in the body.

alimony *n* allowance paid under a court order to a separated or divorced spouse.

A-line *adj* (of a skirt) slightly flared.

aliped [**al**-lee-ped] *n* animal, like the bat, whose toes are joined by membrane that serves as wing.

aliphatic *adj* (of an organic compound) having an open chain structure.

aliquot *Maths* ♦ *adj* **1** of or denoting an exact divisor of a number. ♦ *n* **2** exact divisor.

alive *adj* **1** living, in existence. **2** lively. **alive to** aware of. **alive with** swarming with.

alkali [**alk**-a-lie] *n* substance which combines with acid and neutralizes it to form a salt. **alkaline** *adj* **alkalinity** *n* **alkaloid** *n* any of a group of organic compounds containing nitrogen.

all *adj* **1** whole quantity or number (of). ♦ *adv* **2** wholly, entirely. **3** (in the score of games) each. **give one's all** make the greatest possible effort. **all in** *adj* **1**

exhausted. **2** (of wrestling) with no style forbidden. ♦ *adv* **3** with all expenses included. **all-clear** *n* signal indicating that danger is over. **all right** *adj* **1** adequate, satisfactory. **2** unharmed. ♦ *interj* **3** expression of approval or agreement. **all-rounder** *n* person with ability in many fields.

Allah *n* name of God in Islam.

allay *v* reduce (fear or anger).

allege *v* state without proof. **alleged** *adj* **allegedly** [al-**lej**-id-lee] *adv* **allegation** *n* unproved accusation.

allegiance *n* loyalty to a person, country, or cause.

allegory *n, pl* **-ries** story with an underlying meaning as well as the literal one. **allegorical** *adj*

allegretto *n, pl* **-tos,** *adv Music* (piece to be played) fairly quickly or briskly.

allegro *n, pl* **-gros,** *adv Music* (piece to be played) in a brisk lively manner.

alleluia *interj* same as HALLELUJAH.

allergy *n, pl* **-gies** extreme sensitivity to a substance, which causes the body to react to it. **allergic** *adj* having or caused by an allergy. **allergic to** having a strong dislike of, e.g. *allergic to work.* **allergen** [**al**-ler-jen] *n* substance capable of causing an allergic reaction.

alleviate *v* lessen (pain or suffering). **alleviation** *n*

alley *n* **1** narrow street or path. **2** long narrow enclosure in which tenpin bowling or skittles is played.

alliance *n* **1** state of being allied. **2** formal relationship between countries or groups for a shared purpose.

alligator *n* reptile of the crocodile family, found in the southern US and China.

alliteration *n* use of the same sound at the start of words occurring together. **alliterative** *adj*

allocate *v* assign to someone or for a particular purpose. **allocation** *n*

allopathy [al-**lop**-ath-ee] *n* orthodox method of treating disease, by using drugs that produce an effect opposite to the effect of the disease being treated, as contrasted with homeopathy. **allopathic** *adj*

allot *v* **-lotting, -lotted** assign as a share or for a particular purpose. **allotment** *n* **1** distribution. **2** portion allotted. **3** small piece of public land rented to grow vegetables on.

allotrope *n* any of two or more physical forms in which an element can exist. **allotropic** *adj* **allotropy** *n*

allow *v* **1** permit. **2** set aside. **3** acknowledge (a point or claim). **allow for** *v* take into account. **allowable** *adj* **allowance** *n* **1** amount of money given at regular intervals. **2** amount permitted. **make allowances for 1** treat or judge (someone) less severely because he or she has special problems. **2** take into account.

alloy *n* **1** mixture of two or more metals. ♦ *v* **2** mix (metals).

allspice *n* spice made from the berries of a tropical American tree.

allude *v* (foll. by *to*) refer indirectly to. **allusion** *n* indirect reference. **allusive** *adj*

> *Allude* is followed by *to*. Be careful not to confuse this word with *elude* meaning 'escape'. Also be careful not to confuse *allusion* with *illusion* meaning 'fallacy' or 'fantasy'.

allure *n* **1** attractiveness. ♦ *v* **2** entice or attract. **alluring** *adj*

alluvium *n* fertile soil deposited by flowing water. **alluvial** *adj*

ally *n, pl* **-lies 1** country, person, or group with an agreement to support another. ♦ *v* **-lying, -lied 2 ally oneself with** join as an ally. **allied** *adj*

alma mater *n* school, university, or college that one attended.

almanac *n* yearly calendar with detailed information on anniversaries, phases of the moon, etc.

almighty *adj* **1** having absolute power. **2** *Informal* very great. ♦ *n* **3 the Almighty** God.

almond *n* edible oval-shaped nut which grows on a small tree.

almoner *n* formerly, a hospital social worker.
almost *adv* very nearly.
alms [**ahmz**] *pl n Old-fashioned* gifts to the poor.
aloe *n* **1** plant with fleshy spiny leaves. ♦ *pl* **2** bitter drug made from aloe leaves. **aloe vera** plant producing a juice used for skin and hair care.
aloft *adv* **1** in the air. **2** in a ship's rigging.
alone *adj, adv* without anyone or anything else.
along *prep* **1** over part or all the length of. ♦ *adv* **2** forward. **3** in company with others, e.g. *come along for the ride*. **alongside** *prep, adv* beside (something).

> Avoid following *alongside* with *of*. Its use is unnecessary.

aloof *adj* distant or haughty in manner. **aloofness** *n*
alopecia [al-loh-**pee**-sha] *n* loss of hair.
aloud *adv* in an audible voice.
alp *n* high mountain. **the Alps** high mountain range in S central Europe.
alpaca *n* **1** Peruvian llama. **2** wool or cloth made from its hair.
alpenstock *n* iron-tipped stick used by climbers.
alpha *n* **1** first letter in the Greek alphabet. **2** highest grade in an examination. **alpha and omega** the first and last. **alpha particle** positively charged particle emitted during some radioactive transformations. **alpha ray** stream of alpha particles.
alphabet *n* set of letters used in writing a language. **alphabetical** *adj* in the conventional order of the letters of an alphabet. **alphabetically** *adv* **alphabetize** *v* put in alphabetical order. **alphabetization** *n*
alphanumeric *adj* consisting of alphabetical and numerical symbols.
alpine *adj* **1** of high mountains. **2** (**A-**) of the Alps. ♦ *n* **3** mountain plant.
already *adv* **1** before the present time. **2** sooner than expected.
alright *adj, interj* all right.

> While this compact form is commonly acceptable, many people still regard it as an error and prefer *all right*.

Alsatian *n* large wolflike dog.
also *adv* in addition, too. **also-ran** *n* loser in a race, competition, or election.
altar *n* **1** table used for Communion in Christian churches. **2** raised structure on which sacrifices are offered and religious rites are performed. **altarpiece** *n* work of art above and behind the altar in some Christian churches.
alter *v* make or become different. **alteration** *n*
altercation *n* heated argument.
alter ego *n* **1** second self. **2** very close friend.
alternate *v* **1** (cause to) occur by turns. ♦ *adj* **2** occurring by turns. **3** every second (one) of a series, e.g. *alternate Fridays*. **alternately** *adv* **alternation** *n* **alternator** *n* electric generator for producing alternating current. **alternating current** electric current that reverses direction at frequent regular intervals.
alternative *n* **1** one of two choices. ♦ *adj* **2** able to be done or used instead of something else. **3** (of medicine, lifestyle, etc.) not conventional. **alternatively** *adv*

> Although the strict meaning of *alternative*, 'a choice between two things', is not usually observed nowadays, it is preferable to say *there are three choices* rather than *there are three alternatives*.

although *conj* despite the fact that.
altimeter [al-**tim**-it-er] *n* instrument that measures altitude.
altitude *n* height above sea level.
alto *n, pl* **-tos** *Music* **1** short for CONTRALTO. **2** (singer with) the highest adult male voice. **3** instrument with the second-highest pitch in its group.

altogether *adv* **1** entirely. **2** on the whole. **3** in total.

altruism *n* unselfish concern for the welfare of others. **altruist** *n* **altruistic** *adj* **altruistically** *adv*

alum *n* double sulphate of aluminium and potassium.

aluminium *n Chem* light silvery-white metal that does not rust.

alumnus [al-**lumm**-nuss] *n, pl* **-ni** [-nie] *Chiefly US* graduate of a college. **alumna** [al-**lumm**-na] *n fem, pl* **-nae** [-nee]

always *adv* **1** at all times. **2** for ever. **3** in any case, e.g. *you could always work abroad.*

alyssum *n* garden plant with small yellow or white flowers.

am *v* see BE.

Am *Chem* americium.

AM amplitude modulation.

Am. America(n).

a.m. ante meridiem: before noon.

amalgam *n* **1** blend or combination. **2** alloy of mercury and another metal.

amalgamate *v* combine or unite. **amalgamation** *n*

amanuensis [am-man-yew-**en**-siss] *n, pl* **-ses** [-seez] person who writes from dictation.

amaranth *n* **1** imaginary flower that never fades. **2** lily-like plant with red, green, or purple flowers.

amaryllis *n* lily-like plant with large red, pink, or white flowers.

amass *v* collect or accumulate.

amateur *n* **1** person who engages in a sport or activity as a pastime rather than as a profession. **2** person unskilled in something. ♦ *adj* **3** not professional. **amateurish** *adj* lacking skill. **amateurishly** *adv* **amateurism** *n*

amatory *adj* relating to romantic or sexual love.

amaze *v* surprise greatly, astound. **amazing** *adj* **amazingly** *adv* **amazement** *n*

Amazon *n* **1** strong and powerful woman. **2** legendary female warrior. **Amazonian** *adj*

ambassador *n* senior diplomat who represents his or her country in another country. **ambassadorial** *adj*

amber *n* **1** clear yellowish fossil resin. ♦ *adj* **2** brownish-yellow.

ambergris [**am**-ber-greece] *n* waxy substance secreted by the sperm whale, used in making perfumes.

ambidextrous *adj* able to use both hands with equal ease.

ambience, ambiance *n* atmosphere of a place.

ambient *adj* surrounding.

ambiguous *adj* having more than one possible meaning. **ambiguously** *adv* **ambiguity** *n, pl* **-ties**

ambit *n* limits or boundary.

ambition *n* **1** desire for success. **2** something so desired, goal. **ambitious** *adj* **ambitiously** *adv*

ambivalence [am-**biv**-a-lenss] *n* state of feeling two conflicting emotions at the same time. **ambivalent** *adj* **ambivalently** *adv*

amble *v* **1** walk at a leisurely pace. ♦ *n* **2** leisurely walk or pace.

ambrosia *n* **1** anything delightful to taste or smell. **2** *Myth* food of the gods. **ambrosial** *adj*

ambulance *n* motor vehicle designed to carry sick or injured people.

ambulatory *adj* **1** of or relating to walking. **2** able to walk. ♦ *n, pl* **-ries** **3** place for walking in, such as a cloister.

ambush *n* **1** act of waiting in a concealed position to make a surprise attack. **2** attack from a concealed position. ♦ *v* **3** attack from a concealed position.

ameliorate [am-**meal**-yor-rate] *v* make (something) better. **amelioration** *n*

amen *interj* so be it: used at the end of a prayer.

amenable [a-**mean**-a-bl] *adj* likely or willing to cooperate.

amend *v* make small changes to correct or improve (something). **amendment** *n*

amends *pl n* **make amends for** compensate for.

amenity *n, pl* **-ties** useful or enjoyable feature.

American *adj* **1** of the United States of America or the American continent. ♦ *n* **2** person from America or the American continent. **Americanism** *n* expression or custom characteristic of Americans. **Americanize** *v* make American in outlook, form, etc.

americium *n Chem* white metallic element artificially produced from plutonium.

amethyst [**am**-myth-ist] *n* bluish-violet variety of quartz used as a gemstone.

Amharic *n* official language of Ethiopia.

amiable *adj* friendly, pleasant-natured. **amiably** *adv* **amiability** *n*

amicable *adj* friendly. **amicably** *adv* **amicability** *n*

amid, amidst *prep* in the middle of, among. **amidships** *adv* at or towards the middle of a ship.

> The meaning of *amid* overlaps with that of *among*, but the form *amidst* is old-fashioned. Nowadays use *amid* or *among*.

amino acid [am-**mean**-oh] *n* organic compound found in protein.

amiss *adv* **1** wrongly, badly. ♦ *adj* **2** wrong, faulty. **take something amiss** be offended by something.

amity *n* friendship.

ammeter *n* instrument for measuring electric current.

ammo *n Informal* ammunition.

ammonia *n* **1** strong-smelling alkaline gas containing hydrogen and nitrogen. **2** solution of this in water.

ammonite *n* fossilized spiral shell of an extinct sea creature.

ammunition *n* **1** bullets, bombs, and shells that can be fired from or as a weapon. **2** facts that can be used in an argument.

amnesia *n* loss of memory. **amnesiac** *adj, n*

amnesty *n, pl* **-ties** general pardon for offences against a government.

amniocentesis *n, pl* **-ses** removal of some amniotic fluid to test for possible abnormalities in a fetus.

amniotic fluid *n* fluid surrounding a fetus in the womb.

amoeba [am-**mee**-ba] *n, pl* **-bae** [-bee], **-bas** microscopic single-celled animal able to change its shape.

amok *adv* **run amok** run about in a violent frenzy.

among, amongst *prep* **1** in the midst of. **2** in the group or number of. **3** to each of, e.g. *divide it among yourselves.*

> *Among* is generally used when more than two things are mentioned: *It's hard to choose among friends.* The form *amongst* is rather old-fashioned.

amoral [aim-**mor**-ral] *adj* without moral standards. **amorality** *n*

> *Amoral* should not be confused with *immoral*, 'acting contrary to moral standards'.

amorous *adj* feeling, showing, or relating to sexual love. **amorously** *adv*

amorphous *adj* without distinct shape.

amortize *v* pay off (a debt) gradually by periodic transfers to a sinking fund.

amount *n* **1** extent or quantity. ♦ *v* **2** (foll. by *to*) be equal or add up to.

amour *n* (secret) love affair.

amour-propre [am-**moor-prop**-ra] *n French* self-respect.

amp *n* **1** ampere. **2** *Informal* amplifier.

ampere [**am**-pair] *n* basic unit of electric current.

ampersand *n* the character (&), meaning *and.*

> It is best to avoid using an *ampersand* (&) to replace the word *and* in formal writing.

amphetamine [am-**fet**-am-mean] *n* drug used as a stimulant.

amphibian *n* **1** animal that lives on land but breeds in water. **2** vehicle that can travel on both land and water. **amphibious** *adj* living or operating both on land and in water.

amphitheatre *n* open oval or circular building with tiers of seats rising round an arena.

amphora [**am**-for-ra] *n, pl* **-phorae** [-for-ree] two-handled ancient Greek or Roman jar.

ample *adj* **1** more than sufficient. **2** large. **amply** *adv*

amplify *v* **-fying, -fied 1** increase the strength of (a current or sound signal). **2** explain in more detail. **3** increase the size or effect of. **amplification** *n* **amplifier** *n* device used to amplify a current or sound signal.

amplitude *n* greatness of extent.

ampoule *n* small sealed glass vessel containing liquid for injection.

amputate *v* cut off (a limb or part of a limb) for medical reasons. **amputation** *n* **amputee** *n* person who has had a limb amputated.

amuck *adv* same as AMOK.

amulet *n* something carried or worn as a protection against evil.

amuse *v* **1** cause to laugh or smile. **2** entertain or divert. **amusing** *adj* **amusingly** *adv* **amusement** *n* **1** state of being amused. **2** something that amuses.

amylase *n* enzyme, present in saliva, that helps to change starch into sugar.

an *adj* form of A: used before vowels, and sometimes before *h*, e.g. *an hour.*

> This form of the indefinite article is also used with abbreviations which have a vowel sound when read aloud: *an MA*. It is old-fashioned to use *an* before words like *hotel* or *historic.*

anabolic steroid *n* synthetic steroid hormone used to stimulate muscle and bone growth.

anabolism *n Biol* metabolic process in which body tissues are synthesized from food.

anachronism [an-**nak**-kron-iz-zum] *n* person or thing placed in the wrong historical period or seeming to belong to another time. **anachronistic** *adj*

anaconda *n* large S American snake which kills by constriction.

anaemia [an-**neem**-ee-a] *n* deficiency in the number of red blood cells. **anaemic** *adj* **1** having anaemia. **2** pale and sickly. **3** lacking vitality.

anaerobic *adj Biol* not requiring oxygen.

anaesthetic [an-niss-**thet**-ik] *n, adj* (substance) causing loss of bodily feeling. **anaesthesia** [an-niss-**theez**-ee-a] *n* loss of bodily feeling. **anaesthetist** [an-**neess**-thet-ist] *n* doctor trained to administer anaesthetics. **anaesthetize** *v*

Anaglypta *n* ® thick embossed wallpaper, designed to be painted.

anagram *n* word or phrase made by rearranging the letters of another word or phrase.

anal [**ain**-al] *adj* of the anus.

analgesic [an-nal-**jeez**-ik] *n, adj* (drug) relieving pain. **analgesia** *n* absence of pain.

analogous *adj* similar in some respects.

analogue *n* **1** something that is similar in some respects to something else. ♦ *adj* **2** displaying information by means of a dial, e.g. *analogue speedometers.*

analogy *n, pl* **-gies 1** similarity in some respects. **2** comparison made to show such a similarity. **analogical** *adj* **analogize** *v* **1** use analogy. **2** show analogy between.

analysis [an-**nal**-liss-iss] *n, pl* **-ses** [-seez] **1** separation of a whole into its parts for study and interpretation. **2** psychoanalysis. **analyse** [**an**-nal-lize] *v* **1** make an analysis of (something). **2** psychoanalyse. **analyst** *n* **1** person skilled in analysis. **2** psychoanalyst. **analytical, analytic** *adj* **analytically** *adv*

anarchism *n* doctrine advocating the abolition of government. **anarchist** *n* **anarchistic** *adj*

anarchy [**an**-ark-ee] *n* **1** lawlessness and disorder. **2** lack of government in a state. **anarchic** *adj*

anastigmat *n* lens corrected for astigmatism. **anastigmatic** *adj* (of lens) not astigmatic.

anathema [an-**nath**-im-a] *n* detested person or thing. **anathematize** *v* curse (a person or thing).

anatomy *n, pl* **-mies 1** science of the structure of the body. **2** physical structure. **3** person's body, e.g. *a delicate part of his anatomy.* **4** detailed analysis. **anatomical** *adj* **anatomically** *adv* **anatomist** *n* expert in anatomy.

ancestor *n* **1** person from whom one is descended. **2** forerunner. **ancestral** *adj* **ancestry** *n* lineage or descent.

anchor *n* **1** heavy hooked device attached to a boat by a cable and dropped overboard to fasten the ship to the sea bottom. **2** source of stability or security. ♦ *v* **3** fasten with or as if with an anchor. **anchorage** *n* place where boats can be anchored. **anchorman, anchorwoman** *n* **1** broadcaster in a central studio who links up and presents items from outside camera units and other studios. **2** last person to compete in a relay team.

anchorite *n* religious recluse.

anchovy [**an**-chov-ee] *n, pl* **-vies** small strong-tasting fish.

ancien régime [**on**-syan ray-**zheem**] *n French* a former system, esp. the political and social system in France before the 1789 Revolution.

ancient *adj* **1** dating from very long ago. **2** very old. **ancients** *pl n* people who lived very long ago.

ancillary *adj* **1** supporting the main work of an organization. **2** used as an extra or supplement.

and *conj* **1** in addition to. **2** as a consequence. **3** then, afterwards. **and/or** *conj* either or both.

> Avoid using *and/or* where *or* alone will do. Its use generally suggests commercial and official correspondence.

andante [an-**dan**-tay] *n, adv Music* (piece to be played) moderately slowly.

andantino [an-dan-**tee**-no] *n, pl* **-nos,** *adv Music* (piece to be played) slightly faster or slower than andante.

andiron *n* iron stand for supporting logs in a fireplace.

androgynous *adj* having both male and female characteristics.

android *n* robot resembling a human.

anecdote *n* short amusing account of an incident. **anecdotal** *adj*

anemometer *n* instrument for recording wind speed.

anemone [an-**nem**-on-ee] *n* plant with white, purple, or red flowers.

aneroid barometer *n* device for measuring air pressure, consisting of a partially evacuated chamber in which variations in pressure cause a pointer on the lid to move.

aneurysm, aneurism [**an**-new-riz-zum] *n* permanent swelling of a blood vessel.

anew *adv* **1** once more. **2** in a different way.

angel *n* **1** spiritual being believed to be an attendant or messenger of God. **2** person who is kind, pure, or beautiful. **angelic** *adj* **angelically** *adv*

angelica [an-**jell**-ik-a] *n* **1** aromatic plant. **2** its candied stalks, used in cookery.

Angelus [**an**-jell-uss] *n* **1** (in the Roman Catholic Church) prayers recited in the morning, at midday, and in the evening. **2** bell signalling the times of these prayers.

anger *n* **1** fierce displeasure or extreme annoyance. ♦ *v* **2** make (someone) angry.

angina [an-**jine**-a] *n* heart disorder causing sudden severe chest pains (also **angina pectoris**).

angle[1] *n* **1** space between or shape formed by two lines or surfaces that meet. **2** divergence between these, measured in degrees. **3** corner. **4** point of view. ♦ *v* **5** bend or place (something) at an angle.

angle[2] *v* **1** fish with a hook and line. **2**

(foll. by *for*) try to get by hinting. **angler** *n* **angling** *n*

Anglican *n, adj* (member) of the Church of England. **Anglicanism** *n*

anglicize *v* make or become English in outlook, form, etc. **Anglicism** *n* expression or custom characteristic of the English.

Anglo *n, pl* **-glos** *Canadian* English-speaking Canadian.

Anglo- *combining form* **1** English, e.g. *Anglo-Scottish.* **2** British, e.g. *Anglo-American.*

Anglophile *n* person who admires England or the English. **Anglophilia** *n*

Anglophobe *n* person who dislikes England or the English. **Anglophobia** *n*

Anglo-Saxon *n* **1** member of any of the W Germanic tribes that settled in England from the fifth century AD. **2** language of the Anglo-Saxons. ♦ *adj* **3** of the Anglo-Saxons or their language.

angora *n* **1** variety of goat, cat, or rabbit with long silky hair. **2** hair of the angora goat or rabbit. **3** cloth made from this hair.

Angostura Bitters *pl n* ® bitter tonic, used as a flavouring in alcoholic drinks.

angry *adj* **-grier, -griest 1** full of anger. **2** inflamed, e.g. *an angry wound.* **angrily** *adv*

angst *n* feeling of anxiety.

angstrom *n* unit of length used to measure wavelengths.

anguish *n* great mental pain. **anguished** *adj*

angular *adj* **1** (of a person) lean and bony. **2** having angles. **3** measured by an angle. **angularity** *n*

anhydrous *adj Chem* containing no water.

anil *n* West Indian shrub, from which indigo is obtained.

aniline *n* colourless oily liquid obtained from coal tar and used for making dyes, plastics, and explosives.

animal *n* **1** living creature with specialized sense organs and capable of voluntary motion, esp. one other than a human being. **2** quadruped. ♦ *adj* **3** of animals. **4** sensual, physical. **animality** *n* animal instincts of human beings. **animalcule** *n* microscopic animal.

animate *v* **1** give life to. **2** make lively. **3** make a cartoon film of. ♦ *adj* **4** having life. **animated** *adj* **animatedly** *adv* **animation** *n* **1** technique of making cartoon films. **2** liveliness and enthusiasm. **animator** *n*

animism *n* belief that natural objects possess souls. **animist** *n, adj* **animistic** *adj*

animosity *n, pl* **-ties** hostility, hatred.

animus *n* hatred, animosity.

anion [**an**-eye-on] *n* ion with negative charge.

anise [**an**-niss] *n* plant with liquorice-flavoured seeds.

aniseed *n* liquorice-flavoured seeds of the anise plant.

ankle *n* joint between the foot and leg. **anklet** *n* ornamental chain worn round the ankle.

ankylosis [ang-kill-**loh**-siss] *n* abnormal immobility of a joint, caused by a fibrous growth.

anna *n* former Indian coin worth one sixteenth of rupee.

annals *pl n* yearly records of events. **annalist** *n*

anneal *v* toughen (metal or glass) by heating and slow cooling.

annelid *n* worm with a segmented body, such as an earthworm.

annex *v* **1** seize (territory). **2** take (something) without permission. **3** join or add (something) to something larger. **annexation** *n*

annexe *n* **1** extension to a building. **2** nearby building used as an extension.

annihilate *v* destroy utterly. **annihilation** *n*

anniversary *n, pl* **-ries 1** date on which something occurred in a previous year. **2** celebration of this.

anno Domini *adv Latin* (indicating years numbered from the supposed year of the birth of Christ) in the year of our Lord.

annotate *v* add notes to (a written work). **annotation** *n*

announce *v* **1** make known publicly. **2** proclaim. **announcement** *n* **announcer** *n* person who introduces radio or television programmes.

annoy *v* irritate or displease. **annoyance** *n* **annoying** *adj* **annoyingly** *adv*

annual *adj* **1** happening once a year. **2** lasting for a year. ♦ *n* **3** plant that completes its life cycle in a year. **4** book published once every year. **annually** *adv*

annuity *n, pl* **-ties** fixed sum paid every year.

annul *v* **-nulling, -nulled** declare (something, esp. a marriage) invalid. **annulment** *n*

annular [**an**-new-lar] *adj* ring-shaped.

Annunciation *n Christianity* angel Gabriel's announcement to the Virgin Mary of her conception of Christ.

anode *n Electricity* positive electrode in a battery, valve, etc. **anodize** *v* coat (metal) with a protective oxide film by electrolysis.

anodyne *n* **1** something that relieves pain or distress. ♦ *adj* **2** relieving pain or distress.

anoint *v* smear with oil as a sign of consecration.

anomaly [an-**nom**-a-lee] *n, pl* **-lies** something that deviates from the normal, irregularity. **anomalous** *adj*

anomie [**an**-oh-mee] *n Sociology* lack of social or moral standards. **anomic** [an-**nom**-mik] *adj*

anon *adv Obs* in a short time, soon.

anon. anonymous.

anonymous *adj* **1** by someone whose name is unknown or withheld. **2** having no known name. **anonymously** *adv* **anonymity** *n*

anorak *n* waterproof hooded jacket.

anorexia *n* psychological disorder characterized by fear of becoming fat and refusal to eat (also **anorexia nervosa**). **anorexic** *adj, n*

another *adj, pron* **1** one more. **2** a different (one).

answer *n* **1** reply to a question, request, letter, etc. **2** solution to a problem. **3** reaction or response. ♦ *v* **4** give an answer (to). **5** be responsible to (a person). **6** respond or react. **answerable** *adj* (foll. by *for* or *to*) responsible for or accountable to. **answering machine** device for answering a telephone automatically and recording messages.

ant *n* small insect living in highly organized colonies. **anteater** *n* mammal which feeds on ants by means of a long snout. **ant hill** mound built by ants around their nest.

antacid *n* substance that counteracts acidity, esp. in the stomach.

antagonist *n* opponent or adversary. **antagonism** *n* open opposition or hostility. **antagonistic** *adj* **antagonize** *v* arouse hostility in, annoy.

antalkali [ant-**alk**-a-lie] *n* substance that neutralizes alkalis.

Antarctic *n* **1 the Antarctic** area around the South Pole. ♦ *adj* **2** of this region.

ante *n* **1** player's stake in poker. ♦ *v* **-teing, -ted** or **-teed 2** place (one's stake) in poker.

ante- *prefix* before in time or position, e.g. *antedate; antechamber.*

antecedent *n* **1** event or circumstance happening or existing before another. ♦ *adj* **2** preceding, prior.

antechamber *n* same as ANTEROOM.

antedate *v* precede in time.

antediluvian *adj* **1** of the time before the biblical Flood. **2** old-fashioned.

antelope *n* deerlike mammal with long legs and horns.

antenatal *adj* during pregnancy, before birth.

antenna *n* **1** (*pl* **-nae**) insect's feeler. **2** (*pl* **-nas**) aerial.

antepenultimate *adj* third last.

ante-post *adj* (of a bet) placed before the runners in a race are confirmed.

anterior *adj* **1** to the front. **2** earlier.

anteroom *n* small room leading into a larger one, often used as a waiting room.

anthem *n* **1** song of loyalty, esp. to a country. **2** piece of music for a choir, usu. set to words from the Bible.

anther *n* part of a flower's stamen con›taining pollen.

anthology *n, pl* **-gies** collection of poems or other literary pieces by vari›ous authors. **anthologist** *n*

anthracite *n* hard coal burning slowly with little smoke or flame but intense heat.

anthrax *n* dangerous disease of cattle and sheep, communicable to humans.

anthropocentric *adj* regarding human beings as the most important factor in the universe.

anthropoid *adj* **1** like a human. ♦ *n* **2** ape, such as a chimpanzee, that resem›bles a human.

anthropology *n* study of human ori›gins, institutions, and beliefs. **anthropo-logical** *adj* **anthropologist** *n*

anthropomorphic *adj* attributing hu›man form or personality to a god, ani›mal, or object. **anthropomorphism** *n*

anti *adj, prep Informal* opposed (to).

anti- *prefix* **1** against, opposed to, e.g. *anti-war*. **2** opposite to, e.g. *anticlimax*. **3** counteracting, e.g. *antifreeze*.

anti-aircraft *adj* for defence against air›craft attack.

antiballistic missile *n* missile designed to destroy a ballistic missile in flight.

antibiotic *n* **1** chemical substance ca›pable of destroying bacteria. ♦ *adj* **2** of antibiotics.

antibody *n, pl* **-bodies** protein produced in the blood, which destroys bacteria.

Antichrist *n* **1** *New Testament* the an›tagonist of Christ. **2** any enemy of Christ or Christianity.

anticipate *v* **1** foresee and act in ad›vance of. **2** look forward to. **3** make use of (something) before receiving it. **an-ticipation** *n* **anticipatory** *adj*

anticlimax *n* disappointing conclusion to a series of events. **anticlimactic** *adj*

anticlockwise *adv, adj* in the opposite direction to the rotation of the hands of a clock.

antics *pl n* absurd acts or postures.

anticyclone *n* area of moving air of high pressure in which the winds rotate outwards.

antidote *n* **1** substance that counteracts a poison. **2** anything that counteracts a harmful condition.

antifreeze *n* liquid added to water to lower its freezing point, used in car ra›diators.

antigen [**an**›tee›jen] *n* substance, usu. a toxin, causing the blood to produce antibodies.

antihero *n, pl* **-roes** central character in a book, film, etc., who lacks the tradi›tional heroic virtues.

antihistamine *n* drug used to treat aller›gies.

antimacassar *n* cloth put over a chair› back to prevent soiling.

antimony [**an**›tim›mon›ee] *n Chem* brit›tle silvery›white metallic element.

antinuclear *adj* opposed to nuclear weapons or nuclear power.

antipasto *n, pl* **-tos** appetizer in an Ital›ian meal.

antipathy [an›**tip**›a›thee] *n* dislike, hostil›ity. **antipathetic** *adj*

antiperspirant *n* substance used to re›duce or prevent sweating.

antiphon *n* hymn sung in alternate parts by two groups of singers. **antiphonal** *adj*

antipodes [an›**tip**›pod›deez] *pl n* any two places diametrically opposite one another on the earth's surface. **the Antipodes** Australia and New Zealand. **antipodean** *adj*

antipyretic *adj* **1** reducing fever. ♦ *n* **2** drug that reduces fever.

antiquary *n, pl* **-quaries** student or col›lector of antiques or ancient works of art. **antiquarian** *adj* **1** of or relating to antiquities or rare books. ♦ *n* **2** anti›quary.

antiquated *adj* out›of›date.

antique *n* **1** object of an earlier period,

valued for its beauty, workmanship, or age. ♦ *adj* **2** made in an earlier period. **3** old›fashioned.

antiquity *n* **1** great age. **2** ancient times. **antiquities** *pl n* objects dating from an›cient times.

antiracism *n* policy of challenging rac›ism and promoting racial tolerance. **antiracist** *n, adj*

antirrhinum *n* two›lipped flower of vari›ous colours.

antiscorbutic *adj* preventing or curing scurvy.

anti-Semitism *n* discrimination against Jews. **anti-Semite** *n* person who per›secutes or discriminates against Jews. **anti-Semitic** *adj*

antiseptic *adj* **1** preventing infection by killing germs. ♦ *n* **2** antiseptic substance.

antisocial *adj* **1** avoiding the company of other people. **2** (of behaviour) harm›ful to society.

antistatic *adj* reducing the effects of stat›ic electricity.

antithesis [an›**tith**›iss›iss] *n, pl* **-ses** [›seez] **1** exact opposite. **2** placing to›gether of contrasting ideas or words to produce an effect of balance. **antitheti-cal** *adj*

antitoxin *n* (serum containing) an anti›body that acts against a toxin.

antitrades *pl n* winds blowing in the op›posite direction from and above the trade winds.

antler *n* branched horn of male deer.

antonym *n* word that means the oppo›site of another.

anus [**ain**›uss] *n* opening at the end of the alimentary canal, through which fae›ces are discharged.

anvil *n* heavy iron block on which metals are hammered into particular shapes.

anxiety *n, pl* **-ties** state of being anxious.

anxious *adj* **1** worried and tense. **2** in›tensely desiring. **anxiously** *adv*

any *adj, pron* **1** one or some, no matter which. ♦ *adv* **2** at all, e.g. *it isn't any worse.* **anybody** *pron* anyone. **anyhow** *adv* anyway. **anyone** *pron* **1** any per›son. **2** person of any importance. **any-thing** *pron* any object, event, or action whatever. **anyway** *adv* **1** at any rate, nevertheless. **2** in any manner. **any-where** *adv* in, at, or to any place.

> It is acceptable to use *anyone* with a following plural form as in *Has any-one lost their purse?*.

Anzac *n* (in World War 1) a soldier serv›ing with the Australian and New Zea›land Army Corps.

AOB (on the agenda for a meeting) any other business.

aorta [eh›**or**›ta] *n* main artery of the body, carrying oxygen›rich blood from the heart.

apace *adv Lit* swiftly.

Apache *n, pl* **Apaches, Apache** Native American of the SW US and N Mexico.

apart *adv* **1** to or in pieces. **2** to or at a distance. **3** individual, distinct. **apart from** other than.

apartheid *n* former official government policy of racial segregation in S Africa.

apartment *n* **1** room in a building. **2** flat.

apathy *n* lack of interest or enthusiasm. **apathetic** *adj* **apathetically** *adv*

ape *n* **1** tailless monkey such as the chim›panzee or gorilla. **2** stupid, clumsy, or ugly man. ♦ *v* **3** imitate. **apeman** *n* ex›tinct primate thought to have been the forerunner of true humans.

aperient [ap›**peer**›ee›ent] *adj* **1** having a mild laxative effect. ♦ *n* **2** mild laxative.

aperitif [ap›per›rit›**teef**] *n* alcoholic drink taken before a meal.

aperture *n* opening or hole.

apex *n* highest point.

APEX Advance Purchase Excursion: re›duced fare for journeys booked a speci›fied period in advance.

aphasia *n* disorder of the central nerv›ous system that affects the ability to speak and understand words.

aphelion [ap›**heel**›lee›on] *n, pl* **-lia** [›lee›a] point of a planet's orbit that is far›thest from the sun.

aphid [**eh**-fid], **aphis** [**eh**-fiss] *n* small insect which sucks the sap from plants.

aphorism *n* short clever saying expressing a general truth.

aphrodisiac [af-roh-**diz**-zee-ak] *n* **1** substance that arouses sexual desire. ♦ *adj* **2** arousing sexual desire.

apiary [**ape**-yar-ee] *n, pl* **-ries** place where bees are kept. **apiarist** *n* beekeeper.

apiculture *n* breeding and care of bees.

apiece *adv* each, e.g. *they were given two apples apiece.*

aplomb [ap-**plom**] *n* calm self-possession.

apocalypse *n* **1** end of the world. **2** event of great destruction. **the Apocalypse** book of Revelation, the last book of the New Testament. **apocalyptic** *adj*

Apocrypha [ap-**pok**-rif-fa] *pl n* **the Apocrypha** collective name for the 14 books of the Old Testament which are not accepted as part of the Hebrew scriptures. **apocryphal** *adj* (of a story) of questionable authenticity.

apogee [**ap**-oh-jee] *n* **1** point of the moon's or a satellite's orbit that is farthest from the earth. **2** highest point.

apolitical *adj* not concerned with political matters.

apologia *n* formal written defence of a cause.

apology *n, pl* **-gies** **1** expression of regret for wrongdoing. **2** (foll. by *for*) poor example (of). **3** same as APOLOGIA. **apologetic** *adj* showing or expressing regret. **apologetically** *adv* **apologetics** *n* branch of theology concerned with the reasoned defence of Christianity. **apologist** *n* person who formally defends a cause. **apologize** *v* make an apology.

apoplexy *n Med* stroke. **apoplectic** *adj* **1** of apoplexy. **2** *Informal* furious.

apostasy [ap-**poss**-stass-ee] *n, pl* **-sies** abandonment of one's religious faith or other belief. **apostate** *n, adj*

a posteriori [**eh** poss-steer-ee-**or**-rye] *adj* involving reasoning from effect to cause.

Apostle *n* **1** one of the twelve disciples chosen by Christ to preach his gospel. **2** (**a-**) ardent supporter of a cause or movement. **apostolic** [ap-poss-**stoll**-ik] *adj*

apostrophe [ap-**poss**-trof-fee] *n* **1** punctuation mark (') showing the omission of a letter or letters in a word, e.g. *don't*, or forming the possessive, e.g. *Jill's car.* **2** digression from a speech to address an imaginary or absent person or thing. **apostrophize** *v* address an apostrophe to.

apothecary *n, pl* **-caries** *Obs* chemist.

apotheosis [ap-poth-ee-**oh**-siss] *n, pl* **-ses** [-seez] **1** perfect example. **2** elevation to the rank of a god.

appal *v* **-palling, -palled** dismay, terrify. **appalling** *adj* dreadful, terrible. **appallingly** *adv*

apparatus *n* equipment for a particular purpose.

apparel [ap-**par**-rel] *n Old-fashioned* clothing.

apparent *adj* **1** readily seen, obvious. **2** seeming as opposed to real. **apparently** *adv*

apparition *n* ghost or ghostlike figure.

appeal *v* **1** make an earnest request. **2** attract, please, or interest. **3** request a review of a lower court's decision by a higher court. ♦ *n* **4** earnest request. **5** attractiveness. **6** request for a review of a lower court's decision by a higher court. **appealing** *adj* **appealingly** *adv*

appear *v* **1** become visible or present. **2** seem. **3** be seen in public. **appearance** *n* **1** sudden or unexpected arrival of someone or something at a place. **2** an appearing. **3** outward aspect.

appease *v* **1** pacify (a person) by yielding to his or her demands. **2** satisfy or relieve (a feeling). **appeasement** *n*

appellant *n* person who makes an appeal to a higher court.

appellation *n* name, title.

append *v* join on, add. **appendage** *n* thing joined on or added.

appendicitis *n* inflammation of the appendix.

appendix *n, pl* **-dices, -dixes** **1** separate additional material at the end of a book. **2** *Anat* short closed tube attached to the large intestine.

> Extra sections at the end of a book are *appendices*. The plural *appendixes* is used in medicine.

appertain *v* (foll. by *to*) **1** belong to. **2** be connected with.

appetite *n* **1** desire for food or drink. **2** liking or willingness. **appetizer** *n* thing eaten or drunk to stimulate the appetite. **appetizing** *adj* stimulating the appetite.

applaud *v* **1** show approval of by clapping one's hands. **2** approve strongly. **applause** *n* approval shown by clapping one's hands.

apple *n* round firm fleshy fruit that grows on trees. **in apple-pie order** *Informal* very tidy.

appliance *n* device with a specific function.

applicable *adj* relevant, appropriate. **applicability** *n*

applicant *n* person who applies for something.

application *n* **1** formal request. **2** act of applying something to a particular use. **3** diligent effort. **4** act of putting something onto a surface.

applicator *n* simple device for applying cosmetics, medication, etc.

appliqué [ap-**plee**-kay] *n* kind of decoration in which one material is cut out and attached to another.

apply *v* **-plying, -plied** **1** make a formal request. **2** put to practical use. **3** put onto a surface. **4** be relevant or appropriate. **apply oneself** concentrate one's efforts. **applied** *adj* (of a skill, science, etc.) put to practical use.

appoint *v* **1** assign to a job or position. **2** fix or decide, e.g. *appoint a time.* **3** equip or furnish. **appointee** *n* **appointment** *n* **1** arrangement to meet a person. **2** act of placing someone in a job. **3** the job itself. ♦ *pl* **4** fixtures or fittings.

apportion *v* divide out in shares.

apposite *adj* suitable, apt. **apposition** *n* grammatical construction in which two nouns or phrases referring to the same thing are placed one after another without a conjunction, e.g. *my son the doctor.*

appraise *v* estimate the value or quality of. **appraisal** *n* **appraising** *adj* **appraisingly** *adv*

appreciate *v* **1** value highly. **2** be aware of and understand. **3** be grateful for. **4** rise in value. **appreciable** *adj* enough to be noticed. **appreciably** *adv* **appreciation** *n* **appreciative** *adj* feeling or showing appreciation. **appreciatively** *adv*

apprehend *v* **1** arrest and take into custody. **2** grasp (something) mentally. **apprehension** *n* **1** dread, anxiety. **2** arrest. **3** understanding. **apprehensive** *adj* fearful or anxious. **apprehensively** *adv*

apprentice *n* **1** someone working for a skilled person for a fixed period in order to learn his or her trade. ♦ *v* **2** take or place (someone) as an apprentice. **apprenticeship** *n*

apprise *v* make aware (of).

appro *n* **on appro** *Informal* on approval.

approach *v* **1** come near or nearer (to). **2** make a proposal or suggestion to. **3** begin to deal with (a matter). ♦ *n* **4** approaching or means of approaching. **5** proposal or suggestion made to someone. **6** approximation. **approachable** *adj* **1** friendly. **2** accessible.

approbation *n* approval.

appropriate *adj* **1** suitable, fitting. ♦ *v* **2** take for oneself. **3** put aside for a particular purpose. **appropriately** *adv* **appropriateness** *n* suitability. **appropriation** *n* act of putting (something) aside for a particular purpose.

approve *v* **1** consider good or right. **2** authorize, agree to. **approval** *n* **1** consent. **2** favourable opinion. **on approval** (of goods) with an option to be returned without payment if unsatisfactory. **approving** *adj* **approvingly** *adv*

approx. approximate(ly).

approximate *adj* **1** almost but not quite exact. ♦ *v* (foll. by *to*) **2** come close to. **3** be almost the same as. **approximately** *adv* **approximation** *n*

appurtenances *pl n* minor or additional features.

Apr. April.

après-ski [ap›ray›**skee**] *n* social activities after a day's skiing.

apricot *n* **1** yellowish›orange juicy fruit like a small peach. ♦ *adj* **2** yellowish›orange.

April *n* fourth month of the year. **April fool** victim of a practical joke played on April 1 (**April Fools' Day**).

a priori [**eh** pry›**or**›rye] *adj* involving rea›soning from cause to effect.

apron *n* **1** garment worn over the front of the body to protect the clothes. **2** area at an airport or hangar for manoeu›vring and loading aircraft. **3** part of a stage in front of the curtain.

apropos [ap›prop›**poh**] *adj, adv* appro›priate(ly). **apropos of** with regard to.

apse *n* arched or domed recess, esp. in a church.

apt *adj* **1** having a specified tendency. **2** suitable. **3** quick to learn. **aptly** *adv* **aptness** *n* **aptitude** *n* natural ability.

APT Advanced Passenger Train.

aqua *adj* short for AQUAMARINE (sense 2).

aqualung *n* mouthpiece attached to air cylinders, worn for underwater swim›ming.

aquamarine *n* **1** greenish›blue gem›stone. ♦ *adj* **2** greenish›blue.

aquaplane *n* **1** board on which a person stands to be towed by a motorboat. ♦ *v* **2** ride on an aquaplane. **3** (of a motor vehicle) skim uncontrollably on a thin film of water.

aquarium *n, pl* **aquariums, aquaria 1** tank in which fish and other underwater creatures are kept. **2** building contain›ing such tanks.

Aquarius *n* (the water bearer) eleventh sign of the zodiac.

aquatic *adj* **1** living in or near water. **2** done in or on water. **aquatics** *pl n* wa›ter sports.

aquatint *n* print like a watercolour, pro›duced by etching copper.

aqua vitae [**ak**›wa **vee**›tie] *n Obs* bran›dy.

aqueduct *n* structure carrying water across a valley or river.

aqueous *adj* of, like, or containing water.

aquiline *adj* **1** (of a nose) curved like an eagle's beak. **2** of or like an eagle.

Ar *Chem* argon.

AR Arkansas.

Arab *n* **1** member of a Semitic people originally from Arabia. ♦ *adj* **2** of the Arabs. **Arabian** *adj* of Arabia or the Arabs. **Arabic** *n* **1** language of the Arabs. ♦ *adj* **2** of Arabic, Arabs, or Ara›bia. **Arabic numerals** the symbols 1, 2, 3, 4, 5, 6, 7, 8, 9, 0, used to represent numbers.

arabesque [ar›ab›**besk**] *n* **1** ballet posi›tion in which one leg is raised behind and the arms are extended. **2** elaborate ornamental design.

arable *adj* suitable for growing crops on.

arachnid [ar›**rak**›nid] *n* eight›legged in›vertebrate, such as a spider, scorpion, tick, or mite.

arak *n* same as ARRACK.

Aramaic *n* an ancient Semitic language of the Middle East.

Aran *adj* (of sweaters etc.) knitted in a complicated pattern traditional to the Aran Islands, usu. with natural un›bleached wool.

arbiter *n* **1** person empowered to judge in a dispute. **2** person with influential opinions about something.

arbitrary *adj* based on personal choice or chance, rather than reason. **arbitrari-ly** *adv* **arbitrariness** *n*

arbitration *n* hearing and settling of a dispute by an impartial referee chosen by both sides. **arbitrate** *v* **arbitrator** *n*

arboreal [ahr›**bore**›ee›al] *adj* of or living in trees.

arboretum [ahr›bore›**ee**›tum] *n, pl* **-ta** [›ta] place where rare trees or shrubs are cultivated.

arboriculture *n* cultivation of trees or shrubs. **arboriculturist** *n*

arbour *n* glade sheltered by trees.

arbutus [ar›**byew**›tuss] *n, pl* **-tuses** ever›green shrub with strawberry›like berries.

arc *n* **1** part of a circle or other curve. **2** luminous discharge of electricity across a small gap between two electrodes. ♦ *v* **3** form an arc.

arcade *n* **1** covered passageway lined with shops. **2** set of arches and their supporting columns.

Arcadian *adj* rustic in an idealized way.

arcane *adj* mysterious and secret.

arch[1] *n* **1** curved structure supporting a bridge or roof. **2** something curved. **3** curved lower part of the foot. ♦ *v* **4** (cause to) form an arch. **archway** *n* passageway under an arch.

arch[2] *adj* **1** superior, knowing. **2** coyly playful. **archly** *adv* **archness** *n*

arch- *combining form* chief, principal, e.g. *archenemy.*

archaeology *n* study of ancient cultures from their physical remains. **archaeological** *adj* **archaeologist** *n*

archaeopteryx *n* extinct bird with teeth, a long tail, and well›developed wings.

archaic [ark›**kay**›ik] *adj* **1** ancient. **2** out›of›date. **archaism** [**ark**›kay›iz›zum] *n* ar›chaic word or phrase.

archangel [**ark**›ain›jell] *n* chief angel.

archbishop *n* chief bishop.

archdeacon *n* priest ranking just below a bishop.

archdiocese *n* diocese of an archbishop.

archduke *n* duke of specially high rank. **archduchess** *n fem* **archduchy** *n* terri›tory of an archduke or archduchess.

archer *n* person who shoots with a bow and arrow. **archery** *n*

archetype [**ark**›ee›type] *n* **1** perfect specimen. **2** original model. **archetypal** *adj*

archipelago [ark›ee›**pel**›a›go] *n, pl* **-gos** **1** group of islands. **2** sea full of small is›lands.

architect *n* person qualified to design and supervise the construction of build›ings. **architecture** *n* **1** style in which a building is designed and built. **2** design›ing and construction of buildings. **architectural** *adj* **architecturally** *adv*

architrave *n Archit* **1** beam that rests on columns. **2** moulding round a doorway or window.

archive [**ark**›ive] *n* **1** (often pl) collection of records or documents. **2** place where these are kept. **archival** *adj* **archivist** [**ark**›iv›ist] *n* person in charge of ar›chives.

Arctic *n* **1** **the Arctic** area around the North Pole. ♦ *adj* **2** of this region. **3** (**a-**) *Informal* very cold.

ardent *adj* **1** passionate. **2** eager, zeal›ous. **ardently** *adv* **ardour** *n* **1** passion. **2** enthusiasm, zeal.

arduous *adj* hard to accomplish, strenu›ous. **arduously** *adv*

are[1] *v* see BE.

are[2] *n* unit of measure, 100 square me›tres.

area *n* **1** part or region. **2** size of a two›dimensional surface. **3** subject field. **4** small sunken yard giving access to a basement.

arena *n* **1** seated enclosure for sports events. **2** area of a Roman amphitheatre where gladiators fought. **3** sphere of in›tense activity.

aren't are not.

areola *n, pl* **-lae, -las** small circular area, such as the coloured ring around the human nipple.

arête *n* sharp ridge separating valleys.

argon *n Chem* inert gas found in the air.

argosy *n, pl* **-sies** *Poetic* large merchant ship.

argot [**ahr**›go] *n* slang or jargon.

argue *v* **-guing, -gued** **1** try to prove by giving reasons. **2** debate. **3** quarrel, dis›pute. **arguable** *adj* **arguably** *adv* **argument** *n* **1** quarrel. **2** discussion. **3** point presented for or against some›thing. **argumentation** *n* process of rea›soning methodically. **argumentative** *adj* given to arguing.

argy-bargy *n, pl* **-bargies** *Informal*

squabbling argument.

aria [**ah**-ree-a] *n* elaborate song for solo voice, esp. one from an opera.

arid *adj* **1** parched, dry. **2** uninteresting. **aridity** *n*

Aries *n* (the ram) first sign of the zodiac.

aright *adv* rightly.

arise *v* **arising, arose, arisen 1** come about. **2** come into notice. **3** get up.

aristocracy *n, pl* **-cies 1** highest social class. **2** government by this class. **aristocrat** *n* member of the aristocracy. **aristocratic** *adj* **aristocratically** *adv*

arithmetic *n* **1** calculation by or of numbers. ♦ *adj* **2** of arithmetic. **arithmetical** *adj* **arithmetically** *adv* **arithmetician** *n*

ark *n* **1** *Old Testament* boat built by Noah, which survived the Flood. **2** (**A-**) *Judaism* chest containing the writings of Jewish Law.

arm[1] *n* **1** upper limb from the shoulder to the wrist. **2** sleeve of a garment. **3** side of a chair. **armful** *n* as much as can be held in the arms. **armlet** *n* band worn round the arm. **armchair** *n* upholstered chair with side supports for the arms. **armhole** *n* opening in a garment through which the arm passes. **armpit** *n* hollow under the arm at the shoulder.

arm[2] *v* **1** supply with weapons. **2** prepare (a bomb etc.) for use. **arms** *pl n* **1** weapons. **2** military exploits. **3** heraldic emblem.

armada *n* large number of warships.

armadillo *n, pl* **-los** small S American mammal covered in strong bony plates.

Armageddon *n* **1** *New Testament* final battle between good and evil at the end of the world. **2** catastrophic conflict.

armament *n* **1** military weapons. **2** preparation for war.

armature *n* revolving structure in an electric motor or generator, wound with coils carrying the current.

armistice [**arm**-miss-stiss] *n* agreed suspension of fighting.

armour *n* **1** metal clothing formerly worn to protect the body in battle. **2** metal plating of tanks, warships, etc. **armoured** *adj* **1** having a protective covering. **2** consisting of armoured vehicles. **armourer** *n* maker, repairer, or keeper of arms or armour. **armoury** *n* place where weapons are stored.

army *n, pl* **armies 1** military land forces of a nation. **2** great number.

aroma *n* pleasant smell. **aromatic** *adj* **aromatherapy** *n* massage with fragrant oils to relieve tension.

arose *v* past tense of ARISE.

around *prep, adv* **1** on all sides (of). **2** from place to place (in). **3** somewhere in or near. **4** approximately.

arouse *v* **1** stimulate, make active. **2** awaken. **arousal** *n*

arpeggio [arp-**pej**-ee-oh] *n, pl* **-gios** *Music* notes of a chord played or sung in quick succession.

arr. **1** arranged (by). **2** arrival. **3** arrive(d).

arrack *n* alcoholic drink distilled from grain or rice.

arraign [ar-**rain**] *v* **1** bring (a prisoner) before a court to answer a charge. **2** accuse. **arraignment** *n*

arrange *v* **1** plan. **2** agree. **3** put in order. **4** adapt (music) for performance in a certain way. **arrangement** *n*

arrant *adj* utter, downright.

arras *n* tapestry wall-hanging.

array *n* **1** impressive display or collection. **2** orderly arrangement, esp. of troops. **3** *Poetic* rich clothing. ♦ *v* **4** arrange in order. **5** dress in rich clothing.

arrears *pl n* money owed. **in arrears** late in paying a debt.

arrest *v* **1** take (a person) into custody. **2** stop the movement or development of. **3** catch and hold (the attention). ♦ *n* **4** act of taking a person into custody. **5** slowing or stopping. **arresting** *adj* attracting attention, striking.

arrive *v* **1** reach a place or destination. **2** happen, come. **3** *Informal* be born. **4** *Informal* attain success. **arrival** *n* **1** arriving. **2** person or thing that has just arrived.

arrivederci [ar-reeve-a-**der**-chee] *interj Italian* goodbye.

arrogant *adj* proud and overbearing. **arrogantly** *adv* **arrogance** *n*

arrogate *v* claim or seize without justification.

arrow *n* **1** pointed shaft shot from a bow. **2** arrow-shaped sign or symbol used to show direction. **arrowhead** *n* pointed tip of an arrow.

arrowroot *n* nutritious starch obtained from the root of a W Indian plant.

arse *n Taboo* buttocks or anus. **arsehole** *n Taboo* **1** anus. **2** stupid or annoying person.

arsenal *n* place where arms and ammunition are made or stored.

arsenic *n* **1** toxic grey element. **2** highly poisonous compound of this. **arsenical** *adj*

arson *n* crime of intentionally setting property on fire. **arsonist** *n*

art *n* **1** creation of works of beauty, esp. paintings or sculpture. **2** works of art collectively. **3** skill. ♦ *pl* **4** nonscientific branches of knowledge. **artist** *n* **1** person who produces works of art, esp. paintings or sculpture. **2** person skilled at something. **3** artiste. **artiste** *n* professional entertainer such as a singer or dancer. **artistic** *adj* **artistically** *adv* **artistry** *n* artistic skill. **arty** *adj* **artier, artiest** *Informal* having an affected interest in art.

artefact *n* something made by human beings.

arteriosclerosis [art-ear-ee-oh-skler-**oh**-siss] *n* hardening of the arteries.

artery *n, pl* **-teries 1** one of the tubes carrying blood from the heart. **2** major road or means of communication. **arterial** *adj* **1** of an artery. **2** (of a route) major.

artesian well [art-**teez**-yan] *n* well bored vertically so that the water is forced to the surface by natural pressure.

Artex *n* ® textured plaster-like covering for ceilings and walls.

artful *adj* cunning, wily. **artfully** *adv* **artfulness** *n*

arthritis *n* painful inflammation of a joint or joints. **arthritic** *adj, n*

arthropod *n* animal, such as a spider or insect, with jointed limbs and a segmented body.

artic *n Informal* articulated lorry.

artichoke *n* flower head of a thistle-like plant, cooked as a vegetable.

article *n* **1** written piece in a magazine or newspaper. **2** item or object. **3** clause in a document. **4** *Grammar* any of the words *the, a,* or *an.*

articled *adj* bound (as an apprentice) by a written contract.

articulate *adj* **1** able to express oneself clearly and coherently. **2** (of speech) clear, distinct. **3** *Zool* having joints. ♦ *v* **4** speak or say clearly and coherently. **articulately** *adv* **articulated** *adj* jointed. **articulated lorry** large lorry in two separate sections joined by a pivoted bar. **articulation** *n*

artifact *n* same as ARTEFACT.

artifice *n* **1** clever trick. **2** cleverness, skill. **artificer** [art-**tiff**-iss-er] *n* craftsman.

artificial *adj* **1** man-made, not occurring naturally. **2** made in imitation of something natural. **3** not sincere. **artificial insemination** introduction of semen into the womb by means other than sexual intercourse. **artificial intelligence** branch of computer science aiming to produce machines which can imitate intelligent human behaviour. **artificial respiration** method of restarting a person's breathing after it has stopped. **artificially** *adv* **artificiality** *n*

artillery *n* **1** large-calibre guns. **2** branch of the army who use these.

artisan *n* skilled worker, craftsman.

artless *adj* **1** free from deceit or cunning. **2** natural, unpretentious. **artlessly** *adv*

arum lily [**air**-rum] *n* plant with a white funnel-shaped leaf surrounding a spike of flowers.

Aryan [**air**-ree-an] *n* **1** (in Nazi Germany) non-Jewish person of the Nordic type. **2** person supposedly of Indo-European descent. ♦ *adj* **3** of Aryans.

as *conj* **1** while, when. **2** in the way that.

3 that which, e.g. *do as you are told.* **4** since, seeing that. **5** for instance. ♦ *adv, conj* **6** used to indicate amount or extent in comparisons, e.g. *he is as tall as you.* ♦ *prep* **7** in the role of, being, e.g. *as a mother, I am concerned.*

As *Chem* arsenic.

ASA Advertising Standards Authority.

asafoetida *n* strong-smelling plant resin used as a spice in Eastern cookery.

a.s.a.p. as soon as possible.

asbestos *n* fibrous mineral which does not burn. **asbestosis** *n* lung disease caused by inhalation of asbestos fibre.

ascend *v* go or move up. **ascent** *n* **1** ascending. **2** upward slope. **ascendant** *adj* **1** dominant or influential. ♦ *n* **2** **in the ascendant** increasing in power or influence. **ascendancy** *n* condition of being dominant. **the Ascension** *Christianity* passing of Jesus Christ from earth into heaven.

ascertain *v* find out definitely. **ascertainable** *adj* **ascertainment** *n*

ascetic [ass-**set**-tik] *n, adj* (person) abstaining from worldly pleasures and comforts. **asceticism** *n*

ascorbic acid [ass-**core**-bik] *n* vitamin C.

ascribe *v* attribute, as to a particular origin. **ascription** *n*

aseptic [eh-**sep**-tik] *adj* free from harmful bacteria. **asepsis** [eh-**sep**-siss] *n* aseptic condition.

asexual [eh-**sex**-yew-al] *adj* without sex. **asexually** *adv*

ash[1] *n* **1** powdery substance left when something is burnt. ♦ *pl* **2** remains after burning, esp. of a human body after cremation. **the Ashes** cricket trophy competed for in test matches by England and Australia. **ashen** *adj* pale with shock. **ashtray** *n* receptacle for tobacco ash and cigarette butts. **Ash Wednesday** first day of Lent.

ash[2] *n* tree with grey bark.

ashamed *adj* feeling shame.

ashlar *n* square block of hewn stone used in building.

ashore *adv* towards or on land.

ashram *n* religious retreat where a Hindu holy man lives.

Asian *adj* **1** (also **Asiatic**) of the continent of Asia or any of its peoples or languages. **2** of the Indian subcontinent. ♦ *n* **3** person from Asia or a descendant of one. **4** person from the Indian subcontinent or a descendant of one. **Asian pear** apple-shaped pear with crisp juicy flesh.

> Use *Asian* for 'someone who comes from Asia'. *Asiatic* in this context can be offensive.

aside *adv* **1** to one side. **2** out of other people's hearing, e.g. *he took me aside to tell me his plans.* ♦ *n* **3** remark not meant to be heard by everyone present.

asinine [**ass**-in-nine] *adj* stupid, idiotic.

ask *v* **1** say or write (something) in a form that requires an answer. **2** make a request or demand. **3** invite.

askance [ass-**kanss**] *adv* **look askance at** **1** look at with an oblique glance. **2** regard with suspicion.

askew *adv, adj* to one side, crooked.

aslant *adv, prep* at a slant (to), slanting (across).

asleep *adj* **1** sleeping. **2** (of limbs) numb.

asp *n* small poisonous snake.

asparagus *n* plant whose shoots are cooked as a vegetable.

aspect *n* **1** feature or element. **2** position facing a particular direction. **3** appearance or look.

aspen *n* kind of poplar tree.

asperity [ass-**per**-rit-ee] *n* roughness of temper.

aspersion *n* **cast aspersions on** make derogatory remarks about.

asphalt *n* **1** black hard tarlike substance used for road surfaces etc. ♦ *v* **2** cover with asphalt.

asphodel *n* plant with clusters of yellow or white flowers.

asphyxia [ass-**fix**-ee-a] *n* suffocation. **asphyxiate** *v* suffocate. **asphyxiation** *n*

aspic *n* savoury jelly used to coat meat,

eggs, fish, etc.

aspidistra *n* plant with long tapered leaves.

aspirate *Phonetics* ♦ *v* **1** pronounce with an *h* sound. ♦ *n* **2** an *h* sound.

aspire *v* (foll. by *to*) yearn (for), hope (to do or be). **aspirant** *n* person who aspires. **aspiration** *n* strong desire or aim. **aspiring** *adj*

aspirin *n* **1** drug used to relieve pain and fever. **2** tablet of this.

ass *n* **1** donkey. **2** stupid person.

assagai *n* same as ASSEGAI.

assail *v* attack violently. **assailant** *n*

assassin *n* person who murders a prominent person. **assassinate** *v* murder (a prominent person). **assassination** *n*

assault *n* **1** violent attack. ♦ *v* **2** attack violently. **assault course** series of obstacles used in military training.

assay *n* **1** analysis of a substance, esp. a metal, to ascertain its purity. ♦ *v* **2** make such an analysis.

assegai *n* slender spear used in S Africa.

assemble *v* **1** collect or congregate. **2** put together the parts of (a machine). **assemblage** *n* **1** collection or group. **2** assembling. **assembly** *n* **1** (*pl* **-blies**) assembled group. **2** assembling. **assembly line** sequence of machines and workers in a factory assembling a product.

assent *n* **1** agreement or consent. ♦ *v* **2** agree or consent.

assert *v* **1** declare forcefully. **2** insist upon (one's rights etc.). **assert oneself** put oneself forward forcefully. **assertion** *n* **1** positive statement, usu. made without evidence. **2** act of asserting. **assertive** *adj* **assertively** *adv* **assertiveness** *n*

assess *v* **1** judge the worth or importance of. **2** estimate the value of (income or property) for taxation purposes. **assessment** *n* **assessor** *n*

asset *n* **1** valuable or useful person or thing. ♦ *pl* **2** property that a person or firm can sell, esp. to pay debts.

asseverate *v* declare solemnly. **asseveration** *n*

assiduous *adj* **1** hard-working. **2** done with care. **assiduously** *adv* **assiduity** *n*

assign *v* **1** appoint (someone) to a job or task. **2** allot (a task). **3** attribute. **assignation** [ass-sig-**nay**-shun] *n* **1** assigning. **2** secret arrangement to meet. **assignment** *n* **1** task assigned. **2** assigning.

assimilate *v* **1** learn and understand (information). **2** absorb or be absorbed or incorporated. **assimilable** *adj* **assimilation** *n*

assist *v* give help or support. **assistance** *n* **assistant** *n* **1** helper. ♦ *adj* **2** junior or deputy.

assizes *pl n* court sessions formerly held in each county of England and Wales.

assoc. association.

associate *v* **1** connect in the mind. **2** mix socially. ♦ *n* **3** partner in business. **4** friend or companion. ♦ *adj* **5** having partial rights or subordinate status, e.g. *associate member*. **association** *n* **1** society or club. **2** associating.

assonance *n* rhyming of vowel sounds but not consonants, as in *time* and *light*. **assonant** *adj*

assorted *adj* consisting of various types mixed together. **assortment** *n* assorted mixture.

asst assistant.

assuage [ass-**wage**] *v* relieve (pain, grief, thirst, etc.).

assume *v* **1** take to be true without proof. **2** take upon oneself, e.g. *he assumed command*. **3** pretend, e.g. *I assumed indifference*. **assumption** *n* **1** thing assumed. **2** assuming.

assure *v* **1** promise or guarantee. **2** convince. **3** make (something) certain. **4** insure against loss of life. **assured** *adj* **1** confident. **2** certain to happen. **assuredly** [a-**sure**-id-lee] *adv* definitely. **assurance** *n* assuring or being assured.

> When used in the context of business, *assurance* and *insurance* have the same meaning.

astatine *n* *Chem* radioactive nonmetallic element.

aster *n* plant with daisy-like flowers.
asterisk *n* **1** star-shaped symbol (*) used in printing or writing to indicate a footnote etc. ♦ *v* **2** mark with an asterisk.
astern *adv* **1** at or towards the stern of a ship. **2** backwards.
asteroid *n* any of the small planets that orbit the sun between Mars and Jupiter.
asthma [**ass**-ma] *n* illness causing difficulty in breathing. **asthmatic** *adj, n*
astigmatism [eh-**stig**-mat-tiz-zum] *n* inability of a lens, esp. of the eye, to focus properly. **astigmatic** *adj*
astir *adj* **1** out of bed. **2** in motion.
astonish *v* surprise greatly. **astonishment** *n* **astonishing** *adj* **astonishingly** *adv*
astound *v* overwhelm with amazement. **astounding** *adj* **astoundingly** *adv*
astrakhan *n* **1** dark curly fleece of lambs from Astrakhan in Russia. **2** fabric resembling this.
astral *adj* **1** of stars. **2** of the spirit world.
astray *adv* off the right path.
astride *adv, prep* with a leg on either side (of).
astringent *adj* **1** causing contraction of body tissue. **2** checking the flow of blood from a cut. **3** severe or harsh. ♦ *n* **4** astringent substance. **astringency** *n*
astro- *combining form* star.
astrolabe *n* instrument formerly used to measure the altitude of stars and planets.
astrology *n* study of the alleged influence of the stars, planets, and moon on human affairs. **astrologer** *n* **astrological** *adj*
astronaut *n* person trained for travelling in space.
astronautics *n* science and technology of space flight. **astronautical** *adj*
astronomy *n* scientific study of heavenly bodies. **astronomer** *n* **astronomical** *adj* **1** very large. **2** of astronomy. **astronomically** *adv*
astrophysics *n* science of the physical and chemical properties of stars, planets, etc. **astrophysical** *adj* **astrophysicist** *n*
astute *adj* perceptive or shrewd. **astutely** *adv* **astuteness** *n*
asunder *adv* into parts or pieces.
asylum *n* **1** refuge or sanctuary. **2** old name for a mental hospital.
asymmetry *n* lack of symmetry. **asymmetrical, asymmetric** *adj*
asymptote [**ass**-im-tote] *n* straight line closely approached but never met by a curve.
at *prep* indicating position in space or time, movement towards an object, etc., e.g. *at midnight; throwing stones at windows.*
At *Chem* astatine.
atavism [**at**-a-viz-zum] *n* recurrence of a trait present in distant ancestors. **atavistic** *adj*
ate *v* past tense of EAT.
atelier [**at**-tell-yay] *n* workshop, artist's studio.
atheism [**aith**-ee-iz-zum] *n* belief that there is no God. **atheist** *n* **atheistic** *adj*
atherosclerosis *n, pl* **-ses** disease in which deposits of fat cause the walls of the arteries to thicken.
athlete *n* person trained in or good at athletics. **athletic** *adj* **1** physically fit or strong. **2** of an athlete or athletics. **athletics** *pl n* track-and-field sports such as running, jumping, throwing, etc. **athletically** *adv* **athleticism** *n*
at-home *n* social gathering in a person's home.
athwart *prep* **1** across. ♦ *adv* **2** transversely.
atlas *n* book of maps.
atmosphere *n* **1** mass of gases surrounding a heavenly body, esp. the earth. **2** prevailing tone or mood (of a place etc.). **3** unit of pressure. **atmospheric** *adj* **atmospherics** *pl n* radio interference due to electrical disturbance in the atmosphere.
atoll *n* ring-shaped coral reef enclosing a lagoon.
atom *n* **1** smallest unit of matter which can take part in a chemical reaction. **2**

very small amount. **atom bomb** same as ATOMIC BOMB.

atomic *adj* **1** of or using atomic bombs or atomic energy. **2** of atoms. **atomic bomb** bomb in which the energy is provided by nuclear fission. **atomic energy** nuclear energy. **atomic number** number of protons in the nucleus of an atom. **atomic weight** ratio of the mass per atom of an element to one twelfth of the mass of a carbon atom.

atomize *v* reduce to atoms or small particles. **atomizer** *n* device for discharging a liquid in a fine spray.

atonal [eh-**tone**-al] *adj* (of music) not written in an established key. **atonality** *n*

atone *v* make amends (for sin or wrongdoing). **atonement** *n*

atop *prep* on top of.

atrium *n, pl* **atria** **1** upper chamber of either half of the heart. **2** central hall extending through several storeys of a modern building. **3** main courtyard of an ancient Roman house.

atrocious *adj* **1** extremely cruel or wicked. **2** horrifying or shocking. **3** *Informal* very bad. **atrociously** *adv* **atrocity** *n* **1** wickedness. **2** (*pl* **-ties**) act of cruelty.

atrophy [**at**-trof-fee] *n, pl* **-phies** **1** wasting away of an organ or part. **2** failure to grow. ♦ *v* **-phying, -phied** **3** (cause to) waste away.

atropine *n* poisonous alkaloid obtained from deadly nightshade.

attach *v* **1** join, fasten, or connect. **2** attribute or ascribe, e.g. *he attaches great importance to his looks.* **attached** *adj* (foll. by *to*) fond of. **attachment** *n*

attaché [at-**tash**-shay] *n* specialist attached to a diplomatic mission. **attaché case** flat rectangular briefcase for papers.

attack *v* **1** launch a physical assault (against). **2** criticize. **3** set about (a job or problem) with vigour. **4** affect adversely. ♦ *n* **5** act of attacking. **6** sudden bout of illness. **attacker** *n*

attain *v* **1** achieve or accomplish (a task or aim). **2** reach. **attainable** *adj* **attainment** *n* accomplishment.

attar *n* fragrant oil made from roses.

attempt *v* **1** try, make an effort. ♦ *n* **2** effort or endeavour.

attend *v* **1** be present at. **2** go regularly to a school, college, etc. **3** look after. **4** pay attention. **5** apply oneself (to). **attendance** *n* **1** attending. **2** number attending. **attendant** *n* **1** person who assists, guides, or provides a service. ♦ *adj* **2** accompanying. **attention** *n* **1** concentrated direction of the mind. **2** consideration. **3** care. **4** alert position in military drill. **attentive** *adj* **1** giving attention. **2** considerately helpful. **attentively** *adv* **attentiveness** *n*

attenuated *adj* **1** weakened. **2** thin and extended. **attenuation** *n*

attest *v* affirm the truth of, be proof of. **attestation** *n*

attic *n* space or room within the roof of a house.

attire *n* fine or formal clothes.

attired *adj* dressed in a specified way.

attitude *n* **1** way of thinking and behaving. **2** posture of the body. **3** *Informal* hostile manner.

attorney *n* **1** person legally appointed to act for another. **2** *US* lawyer.

attract *v* **1** arouse the interest or admiration of. **2** draw (something) closer by exerting a force on it. **attraction** *n* **1** power to attract. **2** something that attracts. **attractive** *adj* **attractively** *adv* **attractiveness** *n*

attribute *v* **1** (usu. foll. by *to*) regard as belonging to or produced by. ♦ *n* **2** quality or feature representative of a person or thing. **attributable** *adj* **attribution** *n* **attributive** *adj Grammar* (of an adjective) preceding the noun modified.

attrition *n* constant wearing down to weaken or destroy, e.g. *war of attrition.*

attune *v* adjust or accustom (a person or thing).

atypical [eh-**tip**-ik-al] *adj* not typical.

Au *Chem* gold.

aubergine [**oh**-bur-zheen] *n* dark purple tropical fruit, cooked and eaten as a vegetable.

aubrietia [aw-**bree**-sha] *n* trailing plant with purple flowers.
auburn *adj* (of hair) reddish-brown.
auction *n* **1** public sale in which articles are sold to the highest bidder. ♦ *v* **2** sell by auction. **auctioneer** *n* person who conducts an auction.
audacious *adj* **1** recklessly bold or daring. **2** impudent. **audaciously** *adv* **audacity** *n*
audible *adj* loud enough to be heard. **audibly** *adv* **audibility** *n*
audience *n* **1** group of spectators or listeners. **2** formal interview.
audio *adj* **1** of sound or hearing. **2** of or for the transmission or reproduction of sound. **audiotypist** *n* typist trained to type from a dictating machine. **audiovisual** *adj* (esp. of teaching aids) involving both sight and hearing.
audit *n* **1** official examination of business accounts. ♦ *v* **auditing, audited 2** examine (business accounts) officially. **auditor** *n*
audition *n* **1** test of a performer's ability for a particular role or job. ♦ *v* **2** test or be tested in an audition.
auditorium *n, pl* **-toriums, -toria** area of a concert hall or theatre where the audience sits.
auditory *adj* of or relating to hearing.
au fait [oh **fay**] *adj French* **1** fully informed. **2** expert.
auf Wiedersehen [owf **vee**-der-zay-en] *interj German* goodbye.
Aug. August.
auger *n* carpenter's tool for boring holes.
aught *pron Old-fashioned* anything whatever.
augment *v* increase or enlarge. **augmentation** *n*
au gratin [oh **grat**-tan] *adj* covered and cooked with breadcrumbs and sometimes cheese.
augur *v* be a sign of (future events). **augury** *n* **1** foretelling of the future. **2** (*pl* **-ries**) omen.
august *adj* dignified and imposing.
August *n* eighth month of the year.
auk *n* northern sea bird with short wings and black-and-white plumage.
auld lang syne *n* times past.
aunt *n* **1** father's or mother's sister. **2** uncle's wife. **auntie, aunty** *n, pl* **aunties** *Informal* aunt. **Aunt Sally 1** figure used in fairgrounds as a target. **2** target of abuse or criticism.
au pair *n* young foreign woman who does housework in return for board and lodging.
aura *n* distinctive air or quality of a person or thing.
aural *adj* of or using the ears or hearing.
aureate *adj* **1** covered with gold, gilded. **2** (of style of writing or speaking) excessively elaborate.
aureole, aureola *n* halo.
au revoir [**oh** riv-**vwahr**] *interj French* goodbye.
auricle *n* **1** upper chamber of the heart. **2** outer part of the ear. **auricular** *adj*
auriferous *adj* containing gold.
aurochs *n, pl* **aurochs** recently extinct European wild ox.
aurora *n, pl* **-ras, -rae** bands of light sometimes seen in the sky in polar regions. **aurora australis** aurora seen near the South Pole. **aurora borealis** aurora seen near the North Pole.
auscultation *n* listening to the internal sounds of the body, usu. with a stethoscope, to help with diagnosis.
auspices [**aw**-spiss-siz] *pl n* **under the auspices of** with the support and approval of.
auspicious *adj* showing signs of future success, favourable. **auspiciously** *adv*
Aussie *n, adj Informal* Australian.
austere *adj* **1** stern or severe. **2** ascetic or self-disciplined. **3** severely simple or plain. **austerely** *adv* **austerity** *n*
austral *adj* southern.
Australasian *n, adj* (person) from Australia, New Zealand, and neighbouring islands.
Australian *n, adj* (person) from Australia.
Austrian *n, adj* (person) from Austria.
autarchy [**aw**-tar-kee] *n* absolute power

or autocracy.

autarky [**aw**-tar-kee] *n* policy of economic self-sufficiency.

authentic *adj* known to be real, genuine. **authentically** *adv* **authenticity** *n* **authenticate** *v* establish as genuine. **authentication** *n*

author *n* **1** writer of a book etc. **2** originator or creator. **authorship** *n*

authority *n, pl* **-ties 1** power to command or control others. **2** (often pl) person or group having this power. **3** expert in a particular field. **authoritarian** *n, adj* (person) insisting on strict obedience to authority. **authoritative** *adj* **1** recognized as being reliable, e.g. *the authoritative book on Shakespeare.* **2** possessing authority. **authoritatively** *adv* **authorize** *v* **1** give authority to. **2** give permission for. **authorization** *n*

autism *n Psychiatry* disorder, usu. of children, characterized by lack of response to people and limited ability to communicate. **autistic** *adj*

auto- *combining form* self-, e.g. *autobiography.*

autobahn *n* German motorway.

autobiography *n, pl* **-phies** account of a person's life written by that person. **autobiographical** *adj* **autobiographically** *adv*

autocrat *n* **1** ruler with absolute authority. **2** dictatorial person. **autocratic** *adj* **autocratically** *adv* **autocracy** *n* government by an autocrat.

autocross *n* motor-racing over a rough course.

Autocue *n* ® electronic television prompting device displaying a speaker's script, unseen by the audience.

autogiro, autogyro *n, pl* **-ros** self-propelled aircraft resembling a helicopter but with an unpowered rotor.

autograph *n* **1** handwritten signature of a (famous) person. ♦ *v* **2** write one's signature on or in.

automat *n US* vending machine.

automate *v* make (a manufacturing process) automatic. **automation** *n*

automatic *adj* **1** (of a device) operating mechanically by itself. **2** (of a process) performed by automatic equipment. **3** done without conscious thought. **4** (of a firearm) self-loading. ♦ *n* **5** self-loading firearm. **6** vehicle with automatic transmission. **automatically** *adv* **automatic transmission** transmission system in a motor vehicle in which the gears change automatically.

automaton *n* **1** robot. **2** person who acts mechanically.

automobile *n US* motor car.

automotive *adj* relating to motor vehicles.

autonomy *n* self-government. **autonomous** *adj*

autopsy *n, pl* **-sies** examination of a corpse to determine the cause of death.

autoroute *n* French motorway.

autostrada *n* Italian motorway.

autosuggestion *n* process in which a person unconsciously influences his or her own behaviour or beliefs.

autumn *n* season between summer and winter. **autumnal** *adj*

auxiliary *adj* **1** secondary or supplementary. **2** supporting. ♦ *n, pl* **-ries 3** person or thing that supplements or supports. **auxiliary verb** verb used to form the tense, voice, or mood of another, such as *will* in *I will go.*

avail *v* **1** be of use or advantage (to). ♦ *n* **2** use or advantage, esp. in *to no avail.* **avail oneself of** make use of.

available *adj* obtainable or accessible. **availability** *n*

avalanche *n* **1** mass of snow or ice falling down a mountain. **2** sudden overwhelming quantity of anything.

avant-garde [av-ong-**gard**] *n* **1** group of innovators, esp. in the arts. ♦ *adj* **2** innovative and progressive.

avarice [**av**-a-riss] *n* greed for wealth. **avaricious** *adj*

avast *interj Naut* stop.

avatar *n Hinduism* appearance of a god in animal or human form.

Ave. Avenue.

Ave Maria [**ah**-vay ma-**ree**-a] *n* same as

HAIL MARY.

avenge *v* take revenge in retaliation for (harm done) or on behalf of (a person harmed). **avenger** *n*

avenue *n* **1** wide street. **2** road between two rows of trees. **3** way of approach.

aver [av-**vur**] *v* **averring, averred** state to be true.

average *n* **1** typical or normal amount or quality. **2** result obtained by adding quantities together and dividing the total by the number of quantities. ♦ *adj* **3** usual or typical. **4** calculated as an average. ♦ *v* **5** calculate the average of. **6** amount to as an average.

averse *adj* (usu. foll. by *to*) disinclined or unwilling. **aversion** *n* **1** strong dislike. **2** person or thing disliked.

avert *v* **1** turn away. **2** ward off.

aviary *n, pl* **aviaries** large cage or enclosure for birds.

aviation *n* art of flying aircraft. **aviator** *n*

avid *adj* **1** keen or enthusiastic. **2** greedy (for). **avidly** *adv* **avidity** *n*

avocado *n, pl* **-dos** pear-shaped tropical fruit with a leathery green skin and yellowish-green flesh.

avocation *n Old-fashioned* **1** occupation. **2** hobby.

avocet *n* long-legged wading bird with a long slender upward-curving bill.

avoid *v* **1** prevent from happening. **2** refrain from. **3** keep away from. **avoidable** *adj* **avoidance** *n*

avoirdupois [av-er-de-**poise**] *n* system of weights based on pounds and ounces.

avow *v* **1** state or affirm. **2** admit openly. **avowal** *n* **avowed** *adj* **avowedly** [a-**vow**-id-lee] *adv*

avuncular *adj* (of a man) friendly, helpful, and caring towards someone younger.

await *v* **1** wait for. **2** be in store for.

awake *v* **awaking, awoke, awoken 1** emerge or rouse from sleep. **2** (cause to) become alert. ♦ *adj* **3** not sleeping. **4** alert.

awaken *v* awake. **awakening** *n*

award *v* **1** give (something, such as a prize) formally. ♦ *n* **2** something awarded, such as a prize.

aware *adj* having knowledge, informed. **awareness** *n*

awash *adv* washed over by water.

away *adv* **1** from a place, e.g. *go away.* **2** to another place, e.g. *put that gun away.* **3** out of existence, e.g. *fade away.* **4** continuously, e.g. *laughing away.* ♦ *adj* **5** not present. **6** distant, e.g. *two miles away.* **7** *Sport* played on an opponent's ground.

awe *n* **1** wonder and respect mixed with dread. ♦ *v* **2** fill with awe. **awesome** *adj* **1** inspiring awe. **2** *Slang* excellent or outstanding. **awestruck** *adj* filled with awe.

aweigh *adj Naut* (of an anchor) no longer hooked into the bottom.

awful *adj* **1** very bad or unpleasant. **2** *Informal* very great. **3** *Obs* inspiring awe. **awfully** *adv* **1** in an unpleasant way. **2** *Informal* very. **awfulness** *n*

awhile *adv* for a brief time.

awkward *adj* **1** clumsy or ungainly. **2** embarrassed. **3** difficult to use or handle. **4** inconvenient. **awkwardly** *adv* **awkwardness** *n*

awl *n* pointed tool for piercing wood, leather, etc.

awning *n* canvas roof supported by a frame to give protection against the weather.

awoke *v* past tense of AWAKE. **awoken** *v* past participle of AWAKE.

AWOL [**eh**-woll] *adj Mil* absent without leave.

awry [a-**rye**] *adv, adj* **1** with a twist to one side, askew. **2** amiss.

axe *n* **1** tool with a sharp blade for felling trees or chopping wood. **2** *Informal* dismissal from employment etc. ♦ *v* **3** *Informal* dismiss (employees), restrict (expenditure), or terminate (a project).

axil *n* angle where the stalk of a leaf joins a stem.

axiom *n* **1** generally accepted principle. **2** self-evident statement. **axiomatic** *adj* **1** containing axioms. **2** self-evident.

axis *n, pl* **axes** **1** (imaginary) line round which a body can rotate or about which an object or geometrical figure is symmetrical. **2** one of two fixed lines on a graph, against which quantities or positions are measured. **axial** *adj*

axle *n* shaft on which a wheel or pair of wheels turns.

axolotl *n* aquatic salamander of central America.

ayah *n* (in parts of the former British Empire) native maidservant or nursemaid.

ayatollah *n* Islamic religious leader in Iran.

aye, ay *interj* **1** yes. ♦ *n* **2** affirmative vote or voter.

AZ Arizona.

azalea [az-**zale**-ya] *n* garden shrub grown for its showy flowers.

azimuth *n* **1** arc of the sky between the zenith and the horizon. **2** horizontal angle of a bearing measured clockwise from the north.

Aztec *n, adj* (person) of the race ruling Mexico before the Spanish conquest in the 16th century.

azure *adj, n* (of) the colour of a clear blue sky.

B b

B *Chem* boron.

Ba *Chem* barium.

BA Bachelor of Arts.

baa *v* **baaing, baaed 1** make the characteristic bleating sound of a sheep. ♦ *n* **2** cry made by a sheep.

baas *n S Afr* boss.

babble *v* **1** talk excitedly or foolishly. **2** (of streams) make a low murmuring sound. ♦ *n* **3** muddled or foolish speech.

babe *n* **1** baby. **2** *Slang* an attractive girl.

babel [**babe**-el] *n* confused mixture of noises or voices.

baboon *n* large monkey with a pointed face and a long tail.

baby *n, pl* **-bies 1** very young child or animal. **2** *Slang* sweetheart. ♦ *adj* **3** comparatively small of its type, e.g. *baby carrots.* **babyish** *adj* **baby-sit** *v* take care of a child while the parents are out. **baby-sitter** *n*

baccarat [**back**-a-rah] *n* card game involving gambling.

bacchanalia *n* wild drunken party or orgy. **bacchanalian** *adj*

bachelor *n* **1** unmarried man. **2** person who holds the lowest university or college degree, e.g. *a Bachelor of Science.*

bacillus [bass-**ill**-luss] *n, pl* **-li** [-lie] rod-shaped bacterium. **bacillary** *adj*

back *n* **1** rear part of the human body, from the neck to the pelvis. **2** spinal column. **3** part or side of an object opposite the front. **4** part of anything less often seen or used. **5** *Ball games* defensive player or position. ♦ *v* **6** (cause to) move backwards. **7** provide money for (a person or enterprise). **8** bet on the success of. **9** (foll. by *onto*) have the back facing towards. ♦ *adj* **10** situated behind, e.g. *back garden.* **11** owing from an earlier date, e.g. *back pay.* ♦ *adv* **12** at, to, or towards the rear. **13** to or towards the original starting point or condition. **backer** *n* person who gives financial support. **backing** *n* **1** support. **2** musical accompaniment for a pop singer. **backward** *adj* **1** directed towards the rear. **2** retarded in physical, material, or intellectual development. **backwardness** *n* **backwards** *adv* **1** towards the rear. **2** with the back foremost. **3** in the reverse of the usual direction. **back door** secret or underhand means of entry to a job etc. **back down** *v* withdraw an earlier claim. **back number** old issue of a newspaper or magazine. **back out** *v* withdraw (from an agreement). **back room** place where secret research or planning is done. **back up** *v* support. **backup** *n* **1** support or reinforcement. **2** reserve or substitute.

backbencher *n* Member of Parliament who does not hold office in the government or opposition.

backbiting *n* spiteful talk about an absent person.

backbone *n* **1** spinal column. **2** strength of character.

backbreaking *adj* (of work or effort) exhausting.

backchat *n Informal* impudent replies.

backcloth, backdrop *n* painted curtain at the back of a stage set.

backdate *v* make (a document) effective from a date earlier than its completion.

backfire *v* **1** (of a plan) fail to have the desired effect. **2** (of an engine) make a loud noise like an explosion.

backgammon *n* game played with counters and dice.

background *n* **1** events or circumstances that help to explain something. **2** person's social class, education, or experience. **3** part of a scene or picture furthest from the viewer.

backhand *n Tennis etc.* stroke played with the back of the hand facing the direction of the stroke. **backhanded** *adj* ambiguous or implying criticism, e.g. *a backhanded compliment.* **backhander** *n*

Slang bribe.

backlash *n* sudden and adverse reaction.

backlog *n* accumulation of things to be dealt with.

backpack *n* **1** rucksack. ♦ *v* **2** go hiking with a backpack. **backpacker** *n*

back-pedal *v* retract or modify a previous statement.

back-seat driver *n Informal* person who offers unwanted advice.

backside *n Informal* buttocks.

backslide *v* relapse into former bad habits. **backslider** *n*

backstage *adv, adj* behind the stage in a theatre.

backstairs *adj* underhand, e.g. *backstairs deals.*

backstreet *n* **1** street far from any main road. ♦ *adj* **2** secret or illegal, e.g. *a backstreet abortion.*

backstroke *n* swimming stroke performed on the back.

backtrack *v* **1** return by the same route by which one has come. **2** retract or reverse one's opinion or policy.

backwash *n* **1** water washed backwards by the motion of a boat. **2** repercussion.

backwater *n* isolated or backward place or condition.

backwoods *pl n* remote sparsely populated area.

bacon *n* salted or smoked pig meat.

bacteria *pl n, sing* **-rium** large group of microorganisms, many of which cause disease. **bacterial** *adj* **bacteriology** *n* study of bacteria. **bacteriologist** *n*

> Note that the word *bacteria* is already plural and does not need an '-s'.

bad *adj* **worse, worst 1** of poor quality. **2** lacking skill or talent. **3** harmful. **4** immoral or evil. **5** naughty or mischievous. **6** rotten or decayed. **7** unpleasant. **badly** *adv* **badness** *n* **bad blood** feeling of intense hatred.

bade *v* a past tense of BID.

badge *n* emblem worn to show membership, rank, etc.

badger *n* **1** nocturnal burrowing mammal with a black and white head. ♦ *v* **2** pester or harass.

badinage [**bad**-in-nahzh] *n* playful and witty conversation.

badminton *n* game played with rackets and a shuttlecock, which is hit back and forth over a high net.

baffle *v* **1** perplex or puzzle. ♦ *n* **2** device to limit or regulate the flow of fluid, light, or sound. **bafflement** *n*

bag *n* **1** flexible container with an opening at one end. **2** handbag or piece of luggage. **3** loose fold of skin under the eyes. **4** *Offens* ugly or bad-tempered woman. **5** amount of game killed by a hunter. ♦ *v* **bagging, bagged 6** put into a bag. **7** succeed in capturing, killing or scoring, e.g. *he has bagged over 40 goals this season.* **bags of** *Informal* lots (of). **baggy** *adj* **-gier, -giest** (of clothes) hanging loosely.

bagatelle *n* **1** something of little value. **2** board game in which balls are struck into holes.

bagel *n* hard ring-shaped bread roll.

baggage *n* **1** suitcases packed for a journey. **2** *Informal* previous knowledge or experience that affects contemporary behaviour, e.g. *ideological baggage.*

bagpipes *pl n* musical wind instrument with reed pipes and an inflatable bag.

bah *interj* expression of contempt or disgust.

bail[1] *n* **1** *Law* money deposited with a court as security for a person's reappearance in court. **2** person giving such security. ♦ *v* **3** pay bail for (a person).

bail[2], **bale** *v* (foll. by *out*) **1** remove (water) from (a boat). **2** *Informal* help (a person or organization) out of a predicament. **3** make an emergency parachute jump from an aircraft.

bail[3] *n Cricket* either of two wooden bars across the tops of the stumps.

bailey *n* outermost wall or court of a castle.

bailiff *n* **1** sheriff's officer who serves writs and summonses. **2** landlord's agent.

bailiwick *n* area a person is interested in or operates in.

bairn *n Scot* child.

bait *n* **1** piece of food on a hook or in a trap to attract fish or animals. **2** enticement or temptation. ♦ *v* **3** put a piece of food on or in (a hook or trap). **4** persecute or tease.

> The phrase *with bated breath* is sometimes wrongly spelled *with baited breath.*

baize *n* woollen fabric used to cover billiard and card tables.

bake *v* **1** cook by dry heat as in an oven. **2** make or become hardened by heat. **3** *Informal* be extremely hot. **baker** *n* person whose business is to make or sell bread, cakes, etc. **baker's dozen** thirteen. **bakery** *n, pl* **-eries** place where bread, cakes, etc. are baked or sold. **baking powder** powdered mixture containing sodium bicarbonate, used as a raising agent in baking.

baksheesh *n* (in some Eastern countries) money given as a tip.

Balaclava, Balaclava helmet *n* close-fitting woollen hood that covers the ears and neck.

balalaika *n* guitar-like musical instrument with a triangular body.

balance *n* **1** stability of mind or body. **2** state in which a weight or amount is evenly distributed. **3** amount that remains, e.g. *the balance of what you owe.* **4** weighing device. **5** difference between the credits and debits of an account. ♦ *v* **6** weigh in a balance. **7** make or remain steady. **8** consider or compare. **9** compare or equalize the money going into or coming out of an account. **balance of payments** difference between the payments for the imports and exports of a country. **balance of power** equal distribution of military and economic power among countries. **balance of trade** difference in value between a country's imports and exports. **balance sheet** statement showing the financial position of a business.

balcony *n, pl* **-nies** **1** platform on the outside of a building with a rail along the outer edge. **2** upper tier of seats in a theatre or cinema.

bald *adj* **1** having little or no hair on the scalp. **2** plain or blunt, e.g. *the bald facts.* **3** (of a tyre) having a worn tread. **balding** *adj* becoming bald. **baldly** *adv* **baldness** *n*

balderdash *n* stupid talk.

bale[1] *n* **1** large bundle of hay or goods tightly bound together. ♦ *v* **2** make or put into bales.

bale[2] *v* same as BAIL[2].

baleen *n* whalebone.

baleful *adj* vindictive or menacing. **balefully** *adv*

balk, baulk *v* **1** be reluctant to (do something). **2** thwart or hinder.

Balkan *adj* of any of the countries of the Balkan Peninsula: Romania, Bulgaria, Albania, Greece, the former Yugoslavia, and the European part of Turkey.

ball[1] *n* **1** round or nearly round object, esp. one used in games. **2** single delivery of the ball in a game. **3** bullet. **4** more or less rounded part of the body, e.g. *the ball of the foot.* ♦ *pl Taboo slang* **5** testicles. **6** nonsense. ♦ *v* **7** form into a ball, e.g. *he balled his fist.* **ball bearings** steel balls between moving parts of a machine to reduce friction. **ball cock** device with a floating ball and a valve for regulating the flow of water. **ballpoint, ballpoint pen** *n* pen with a tiny ball bearing as a writing point.

ball[2] *n* formal social function for dancing. **ballroom** *n*

ballad *n* **1** narrative poem or song. **2** slow sentimental song.

ballast *n* **1** substance, such as sand, used to stabilize a ship when it is not carrying cargo. **2** crushed rock used for road or railway foundation. ♦ *v* **3** give stability or weight to.

ballet *n* **1** classical style of expressive dancing based on conventional steps. **2** theatrical performance of this. **balleri-**

na *n* female ballet dancer.
ballistics *n* study of the flight of projectiles, such as bullets. **ballistic** *adj* **ballistic missile** missile guided automatically in flight but which falls freely at its target.
balloon *n* **1** inflatable rubber bag used as a plaything or decoration. **2** large bag inflated with air or gas, designed to float in the atmosphere with passengers in a basket underneath. ♦ *v* **3** fly in a balloon. **4** swell or increase rapidly in size, e.g. *his weight ballooned.* **balloonist** *n*
ballot *n* **1** method of voting secretly. **2** actual vote or paper indicating a person's choice. ♦ *v* **-loting, -loted 3** vote or ask for a vote from.
ballyhoo *n* exaggerated fuss.
balm *n* **1** aromatic substance used for healing and soothing. **2** anything that comforts or soothes.
balmy *adj* **balmier, balmiest** (of weather) mild and pleasant.
baloney *n Informal* nonsense.
balsa [**bawl**-sa] *n* very light wood from a tropical American tree.
balsam *n* **1** aromatic resin obtained from various trees and shrubs. **2** soothing ointment. **3** flowering plant.
Baltic *adj* of the Baltic Sea in N Europe or the states bordering it.
baluster *n* set of posts supporting a rail. **balustrade** *n* ornamental rail supported by balusters.
bamboo *n* tall treelike tropical grass with hollow stems.
bamboozle *v* **1** *Informal* cheat or mislead. **2** confuse, puzzle.
ban *v* **banning, banned 1** prohibit or forbid officially. ♦ *n* **2** official prohibition.
banal [ban-**nahl**] *adj* ordinary and unoriginal. **banality** *n*
banana *n* yellow crescent-shaped fruit. **banana republic** small politically unstable country whose economy is dominated by foreign interests.
band[1] *n* **1** group of musicians playing together. **2** group of people having a common purpose. **bandmaster** *n* conductor of a band. **bandsman** *n* **bandstand** *n* roofed outdoor platform for a band. **band together** *v* unite.
band[2] *n* **1** strip of some material, used to hold objects. **2** strip of contrasting colour or texture. **3** *Physics* range of frequencies or wavelengths between two limits.
bandage *n* **1** piece of material used to cover a wound or wrap an injured limb. ♦ *v* **2** cover with a bandage.
bandanna, bandana *n* large brightly coloured handkerchief or neckerchief.
B & B bed and breakfast.
bandicoot *n* ratlike Australian marsupial.
bandit *n* robber, esp. a member of an armed gang. **banditry** *n*
bandolier *n* shoulder belt for holding cartridges.
bandwagon *n* **jump, climb on the bandwagon** join a party or movement that seems assured of success.
bandy *adj* **-dier, -diest 1** (also **bandy-legged**) having legs curved outwards at the knees. ♦ *v* **-dying, -died 2** exchange (words) in a heated manner. **3** use (a name, term, etc.) frequently.
bane *n* person or thing that causes misery or distress. **baneful** *adj*
bang *n* **1** short loud explosive noise. **2** hard blow or loud knock. ♦ *v* **3** hit or knock, esp. with a loud noise. **4** close (a door) noisily. ♦ *adv* **5** precisely, e.g. *bang in the middle.* **6** with a sudden impact.
banger *n* **1** *Informal* old decrepit car. **2** *Slang* sausage. **3** firework that explodes loudly.
bangle *n* bracelet worn round the arm or the ankle.
banish *v* **1** send (someone) into exile. **2** drive away, e.g. *she has banished all thoughts of retirement.* **banishment** *n*
banisters *pl n* railing supported by posts on a staircase.
banjo *n, pl* **-jos, -joes** guitar-like musical instrument with a circular body.
bank[1] *n* **1** institution offering services such as the safekeeping and lending of money. **2** any supply, store, or reserve. ♦ *v* **3** deposit (cash or cheques) in a

bank. **4** transact business with a bank. **banking** *n* **bank holiday** public holiday when banks are closed by law. **banknote** *n* piece of paper money. **bank on** *v* rely on.

bank^{2} *n* **1** raised mass, esp. of earth. **2** slope, as of a hill. **3** sloping ground at the side of a river. ♦ *v* **4** form into a bank. **5** cover (a fire) with ashes and fuel so that it will burn slowly. **6** cause (an aircraft) or (of an aircraft) to tip to one side on turning.

bank^{3} *n* arrangement of switches, keys, oars, etc. in a row or in tiers.

banker *n* **1** manager or owner of a bank. **2** keeper of the bank in gambling games.

bankrupt *n* **1** person declared by a court to be unable to pay his or her debts. ♦ *adj* **2** financially ruined. **3** completely lacking a particular quality, e.g. *morally bankrupt.* ♦ *v* **4** make bankrupt. **bankruptcy** *n*

banner *n* **1** long strip of cloth displaying a slogan, advertisement, etc. **2** placard carried in a demonstration or procession.

bannisters *pl n* same as BANISTERS.

banns *pl n* public declaration, esp. in a church, of an intended marriage.

banquet *n* **1** elaborate formal dinner. ♦ *v* **-queting, -queted 2** hold or take part in a banquet.

banshee *n* (in Irish folklore) female spirit whose wailing warns of a coming death.

bantam *n* small breed of chicken. **bantamweight** *n* boxer weighing up to 118lb (professional) or 54kg (amateur).

banter *v* **1** tease jokingly. ♦ *n* **2** teasing or joking conversation.

Bantu *n* **1** group of languages of Africa. **2** *Offens* Black speaker of a Bantu language.

banyan *n* Indian tree whose branches grow down into the soil forming additional trunks.

baobab [**bay**›oh›bab] *n* African tree with a thick trunk and angular branches.

bap *n Brit* large soft bread roll.

baptism *n* Christian religious ceremony in which a person is immersed in or sprinkled with water as a sign of being cleansed from sin and accepted into the Church. **baptismal** *adj* **baptize** *v* **1** perform baptism on. **2** give a name to.

Baptist *n* member of a Protestant denomination that believes in adult baptism by immersion.

bar^{1} *n* **1** rigid length of metal, wood, etc. **2** solid, usu. rectangular block, of any material. **3** anything that obstructs or prevents. **4** counter or room where drinks are served. **5** heating element in an electric fire. **6** place in court where the accused stands during trial. **7** *Music* group of beats repeated throughout a piece of music. ♦ *v* **barring, barred 8** secure with a bar. **9** obstruct. **10** ban or forbid. ♦ *prep* **11** (also **barring**) except for. **the Bar** barristers collectively. **barman, barmaid, bartender** *n*

bar^{2} *n* unit of atmospheric pressure.

barb *n* **1** cutting remark. **2** point facing in the opposite direction to the main point of a fish›hook etc. **barbed** *adj* **barbed wire** strong wire with protruding sharp points.

barbarian *n* member of a primitive or uncivilized people. **barbaric** *adj* cruel or brutal. **barbarism** *n* condition of being backward or ignorant. **barbarity** *n* **1** state of being barbaric or barbarous. **2** (*pl* **-ties**) vicious act. **barbarous** *adj* **1** uncivilized. **2** brutal or cruel.

barbecue *n* **1** grill on which food is cooked over hot charcoal, usu. outdoors. **2** outdoor party at which barbecued food is served. ♦ *v* **3** cook (food) on a barbecue.

barber *n* person who cuts men's hair and shaves beards.

barbican *n* walled defence to protect a gate or drawbridge of a fortification.

barbiturate *n* drug used as a sedative.

bard *n Lit* poet. **the Bard** William Shakespeare.

bare *adj* **1** unclothed, naked. **2** without the natural or usual covering. **3** unembellished, simple. **4** just sufficient, e.g. *the bare minimum.* ♦ *v* **5** uncover. **bare-**

ly *adv* only just. **bareness** *n*

> As *barely* already has a negative meaning, it should never be used with *not* or other negatives.

bareback *adj, adv* (of horse-riding) without a saddle.
barefaced *adj* shameless or obvious.
barefoot, barefooted *adj, adv* with the feet uncovered.
bareheaded *adj, adv* with the head uncovered.
bargain *n* **1** agreement establishing what each party will give, receive, or perform in a transaction. **2** something bought or offered at a low price. ♦ *v* **3** negotiate the terms of an agreement. **into the bargain** besides, in addition. **bargain for** *v* anticipate or take into account.
barge *n* **1** flat-bottomed boat used to transport freight. ♦ *v* **2** *Informal* push violently. **bargee** *n* person in charge of a barge. **barge in, into** *v* interrupt rudely.
baritone *n* (singer with) the second lowest adult male voice.
barium [**bare**-ee-um] *n Chem* soft white metallic element. **barium meal** preparation of barium sulphate swallowed by a patient before an x-ray of the alimentary canal.
bark[1] *n* **1** loud harsh cry of a dog. ♦ *v* **2** (of a dog) make its typical cry. **3** shout in an angry tone. **barker** *n* person at a fairground who calls loudly to passers-by in order to attract customers.
bark[2] *n* **1** tough outer layer of a tree. ♦ *v* **2** scrape or rub off skin.
barking *adj Slang* mad
barley *n* **1** tall grasslike plant cultivated for grain. **2** grain of this plant used in making malt and whisky and in soups. **barley sugar** brittle clear amber-coloured sweet. **barley water** drink made from an infusion of barley.
bar mitzvah *n Judaism* ceremony marking the 13th birthday of a boy, who then assumes full religious obligations.
barmy *adj* **-mier, -miest** *Slang* insane.
barn *n* large building on a farm used for storing grain. **barn dance** informal party with country dancing. **barn owl** owl with pale brown and white plumage. **barnstorm** *v US* tour rural districts putting on shows or making speeches in a political campaign.
barnacle *n* shellfish that lives attached to rocks, ship bottoms, etc. **barnacle goose** goose with a black-and-white head and body.
barney *n Informal* noisy fight or argument.
barometer *n* instrument for measuring atmospheric pressure. **barometric** *adj*
baron *n* **1** member of the lowest rank of nobility. **2** powerful businessman, e.g. *a press baron*. **baroness** *n* **baronial** *adj*
baronet *n* commoner who holds the lowest hereditary British title.
baroque [bar-**rock**] *n* **1** highly ornate style of art, architecture, or music from the late 16th to the early 18th century. ♦ *adj* **2** ornate in style.
barque [**bark**] *n* sailing ship, esp. one with three masts.
barrack *v* criticize loudly or shout against (a team or speaker).
barracks *pl n* building used to accommodate military personnel.
barracuda [bar-rack-**kew**-da] *n* fierce tropical sea fish.
barrage [**bar**-rahzh] *n* **1** continuous delivery of questions, complaints, etc. **2** continuous artillery fire. **3** artificial barrier across a river to control the water level.
barrel *n* **1** cylindrical container with rounded sides and flat ends. **2** amount that a barrel can hold. **3** tube in a firearm through which the bullet is fired. **barrel organ** musical instrument played by turning a handle.
barren *adj* **1** (of a woman or female animal) incapable of producing offspring. **2** (of land) unable to support the growth of crops, fruit, etc. **3** unprofitable, e.g. *a barren period*. **barrenness** *n*
barricade *n* **1** barrier, esp. one erected hastily for defence. ♦ *v* **2** erect a barri-

cade across (an entrance).

barrier *n* anything that prevents access, progress, or union. **barrier cream** cream that protects the skin. **barrier reef** long narrow coral reef lying close to the shore.

barrister *n* lawyer qualified to plead in a higher court.

barrow[1] *n* **1** wheelbarrow. **2** movable stall used by street traders.

barrow[2] *n* mound of earth over a prehistoric tomb.

barter *v* **1** trade (goods) in exchange for other goods. ♦ *n* **2** trade by the exchange of goods.

basal *adj* **1** of, at, or constituting a base. **2** fundamental.

basalt [**bass**-awlt] *n* dark volcanic rock. **basaltic** *adj*

bascule *n* drawbridge that operates by a counterbalanced weight.

base[1] *n* **1** bottom or supporting part of anything. **2** fundamental part. **3** centre of operations, organization, or supply. **4** starting point. **5** chemical compound that combines with an acid to form a salt. **6** *Maths* the number of units in a counting system that is equivalent to one in the next higher counting place. ♦ *v* **7** (foll. by *on* or *upon*) use as a basis (for). **8** (foll. by *at* or *in*) to station or place. **baseless** *adj* **base rate** rate of interest as a basis for bank lending rates.

base[2] *adj* **1** dishonourable or immoral. **2** of inferior quality or value. **3** debased or counterfeit. **basely** *adv* **baseness** *n*

baseball *n* **1** team game in which runs are scored by hitting a ball with a bat then running round four bases. **2** ball used for this.

basement *n* partly or wholly underground storey of a building.

bases *n* plural of BASIS.

bash *Informal* ♦ *v* **1** hit violently or forcefully. ♦ *n* **2** heavy blow. **have a bash** *Informal* make an attempt.

bashful *adj* shy or modest. **bashfully** *adv* **bashfulness** *n*

basic *adj* **1** of or forming a base or basis. **2** elementary or simple. **3** *Chem* of or containing a base. **basics** *pl n* fundamental principles, facts, etc. **basically** *adv*

BASIC *n* computer programming language that uses common English words.

basil *n* aromatic herb used in cooking.

basilica *n* rectangular church with a rounded end and two aisles.

basilisk *n* legendary serpent said to kill by its breath or glance.

basin *n* **1** round open container. **2** sink for washing the hands and face. **3** sheltered area of water where boats may be moored. **4** catchment area of a particular river.

basis *n, pl* **-ses** fundamental principles etc. from which something is started or developed.

bask *v* **1** lie in or be exposed to something, esp. pleasant warmth. **2** enjoy (approval or favourable conditions).

basket *n* container made of interwoven strips of wood or cane. **basketwork** *n*

basketball *n* **1** team game in which points are scored by throwing the ball through a high horizontal hoop. **2** ball used for this.

basque *n* tight-fitting bodice for women.

Basque *n, adj* (member or language) of a people living in the W Pyrenees in France and Spain.

bas-relief *n* sculpture in which the figures project slightly from the background.

bass[1] [**base**] *n* **1** (singer with) the lowest adult male voice. **2** *Informal* same as BASS GUITAR *or* DOUBLE BASS. ♦ *adj* **3** of the lowest range of musical notes. **bass guitar** electric guitar with same pitch and tuning as a double bass.

bass[2] *n* edible sea fish.

basset hound *n* smooth-haired dog with short legs and long ears.

bassoon *n* low-pitched woodwind instrument.

bastard *n* **1** *Offens* obnoxious or despicable person. **2** person born of parents not married to each other. **bastardize** *v* debase or corrupt.

baste[1] *v* moisten (meat) during cooking with hot fat.

baste[2] *v* sew with loose temporary stitches.

bastion *n* **1** projecting part of a fortification. **2** thing or person regarded as defending a principle.

bat[1] *n* **1** any of various types of club used to hit the ball in certain sports. ♦ *v* **batting, batted 2** strike with or as if with a bat. **3** *Cricket* take a turn at batting. **batsman** *n Cricket* person who bats or specializes in batting.

bat[2] *n* nocturnal mouselike flying animal.

bat[3] *v* **not bat an eyelid** *Informal* show no surprise.

batch *n* group of people or things dealt with at the same time.

bated *adj* **with bated breath** in suspense or fear.

bath *n* **1** large container in which to wash the body. **2** act of washing in such a container. ♦ *pl* **3** public swimming pool. ♦ *v* **4** wash in a bath. **bathroom** *n* room with a bath, sink, and usu. a toilet.

Bath chair *n* wheelchair for an invalid.

bathe *v* **1** swim in open water for pleasure. **2** apply liquid to (the skin or a wound) in order to cleanse or soothe. **3** (foll. by *in*) fill (with), e.g. *bathed in sunlight.* ♦ *n* **4** *Brit* instance of bathing. **bather** *n*

bathos [**bay**-thoss] *n* sudden ludicrous change in speech or writing from a serious subject to a trivial one.

bathyscaph, bathyscaphe, bathysphere *n* deep-sea diving vessel for observation.

batik [bat-**teek**] *n* **1** process of printing fabric using wax to cover areas not to be dyed. **2** fabric printed in this way.

batman *n* officer's servant in the armed forces.

baton *n* **1** thin stick used by the conductor of an orchestra. **2** short bar transferred in a relay race. **3** police officer's truncheon.

batrachian [bat-**tray**-kee-an] *n* **1** amphibian, esp. a frog or toad. ♦ *adj* **2** of or relating to frogs and toads.

battalion *n* army unit consisting of three or more companies.

batten[1] *n* strip of wood fixed to something, esp. to hold it in place. **batten down** *v* secure with battens.

batten[2] *v* **batten on** thrive at the expense of (someone else).

batter[1] *v* **1** hit repeatedly. **2** damage or injure, as by blows, heavy wear, etc., e.g. *battered by gales.* **battering ram** large beam used to break down fortifications.

batter[2] *n* mixture of flour, eggs, and milk, used in cooking.

battery *n, pl* **-teries 1** device that produces electricity in a torch, radio, etc. **2** number of similar things occurring together. **3** *Law* assault by beating. **4** group of heavy guns operating as a single unit. ♦ *adj* **5** kept in series of cages for intensive rearing, e.g. *battery hens.*

battle *n* **1** fight between large armed forces. **2** conflict or struggle. ♦ *v* **3** struggle.

battle-axe *n* **1** *Informal* domineering woman. **2** (formerly) large heavy axe.

battledress *n* ordinary uniform of a soldier.

battlefield, battleground *n* place where a battle is fought.

battlement *n* wall with gaps along the top for firing through.

battleship *n* large heavily armoured warship.

batty *adj* **-tier, -tiest** *Slang* eccentric or crazy.

bauble *n* trinket of little value.

baulk *v* same as BALK.

bauxite *n* claylike substance that is the chief source of aluminium.

bawdy *adj* **bawdier, bawdiest** (of writing etc.) containing humorous references to sex. **bawdiness** *n*

bawl *v* **1** shout or weep noisily. ♦ *n* **2** loud shout or cry.

bay[1] *n* stretch of coastline that curves inwards.

bay[2] *n* **1** recess in a wall. **2** area set aside

for a particular purpose, e.g. *loading bay.* **3** compartment in an aircraft, e.g. *bomb bay.* **bay window** window projecting from a wall.

bay[3] *n* **1** deep howl of a hound or wolf. ♦ *v* **2** howl in deep prolonged tones. **at bay 1** forced to turn and face attackers. **2** at a safe distance.

bay[4] *n* Mediterranean laurel tree. **bay leaf** its dried leaf, used in cooking.

bay[5] *adj, n* reddish-brown (horse).

bayonet *n* **1** sharp blade that can be fixed to the end of a rifle. ♦ *v* **-neting, -neted 2** stab with a bayonet.

bazaar *n* **1** sale in aid of charity. **2** market area, esp. in Eastern countries.

bazooka *n* portable rocket launcher that fires an armour-piercing projectile.

BB Boys' Brigade.

BBC British Broadcasting Corporation.

BC 1 before Christ. **2** British Columbia.

BCG antituberculosis vaccine.

BD Bachelor of Divinity.

BDS Bachelor of Dental Surgery.

be *v, present sing 1st person* **am.** *2nd person* **are.** *3rd person* **is.** *present pl* **are.** *past sing 1st person* **was.** *2nd person* **were.** *3rd person* **was.** *past pl* **were.** *present participle* **being.** *past participle* **been 1** exist or live. **2** pay a visit, e.g. *have you been to Spain?* **3** take place, e.g. *my birthday was last Monday.* **4** used as a linking between the subject of a sentence and its complement, e.g. *John is a musician.* **5** forms the progressive present tense, e.g. *the man is running.* **6** forms the passive voice of all transitive verbs, e.g. *a good film is being shown on television tonight.*

Be *Chem* beryllium.

BE Bachelor of Engineering.

be- *prefix* **1** surround or cover, e.g. *befog.* **2** affect completely, e.g. *bedazzle.* **3** consider as or cause to be, e.g. *befriend.* **4** provide or cover with, e.g. *bejewelled.* **5** at, for, against, on, or over, e.g. *bewail.*

beach *n* **1** area of sand or pebbles on a shore. ♦ *v* **2** run or haul (a boat) onto a beach. **beachcomber** *n* person who searches shore debris for anything of worth. **beachhead** *n* beach captured by an attacking army on which troops can be landed.

beacon *n* **1** fire or light on a hill or tower, used as a warning. **2** lighthouse. **3** radio or other signal used in air navigation.

bead *n* **1** small piece of plastic, wood, etc., pierced for threading on a string to form a necklace etc. **2** small drop of moisture. **3** small metal knob acting as the sight of a firearm. **beaded** *adj* **beading** *n* strip of moulding used for edging furniture. **beady** *adj* **beadier, beadiest** small, round, and glittering, e.g. *beady eyes.*

beagle *n* small hound with short legs and drooping ears.

beak[1] *n* **1** projecting horny jaws of a bird. **2** *Slang* nose. **beaky** *adj* **beakier, beakiest**

beak[2] *n Slang* judge, magistrate, or headmaster.

beaker *n* **1** large drinking cup. **2** lipped glass container used in laboratories.

beam *n* **1** broad smile. **2** ray of light. **3** narrow flow of electromagnetic radiation or particles. **4** long thick piece of wood, metal, etc., used in building. **5** breadth of a ship at its widest part. ♦ *v* **6** smile broadly. **7** divert or aim (a radio signal, light, etc.) in a certain direction.

bean *n* seed or pod of various plants, eaten as a vegetable or used to make coffee etc. **full of beans** *Informal* full of energy and vitality. **beansprout** *n* small edible shoot grown from a bean seed.

beano *n, pl* **beanos** *Brit slang* celebration or party.

bear[1] *v* **bearing, bore, borne 1** support or hold up. **2** bring, e.g. *to bear gifts.* **3** (*passive* **born**) give birth to. **4** produce as by natural growth. **5** tolerate or endure. **6** stand up to, e.g. *his story does not bear scrutiny.* **7** hold in the mind, e.g. *to bear a grudge.* **8** show or be marked with, e.g. *he still bears the scars.* **9** have or be in (relation or comparison), e.g. *her account bears no relation to the facts.* **10** move in a specified direction, e.g. *bring to bear.* **bearable** *adj* **bear down on** *v* **1** press down on. **2** approach (someone) in a determined manner. **bear out** *v* show to be truthful.

bear[2] *n* large heavy mammal with a shaggy coat. **bear hug** rough tight embrace. **bearskin** *n* tall fur helmet worn by some British soldiers.

beard *n* **1** hair growing on the lower parts of a man's face. ♦ *v* **2** oppose boldly. **bearded** *adj*

bearer *n* person who carries, presents, or upholds something.

bearing *n* **1** relevance (to). **2** person's general social conduct. **3** part of a machine that supports another part, esp. one that reduces friction. ♦ *pl* **4** sense of one's own relative position, e.g. *I lost my bearings in the fog.*

beast *n* **1** large wild animal. **2** brutal or uncivilized person. **beastly** *adj* unpleasant or disagreeable.

beat *v* **beating, beat, beaten** *or* **beat 1** hit hard and repeatedly. **2** move (wings) up and down. **3** throb rhythmically. **4** stir or mix vigorously. **5** *Music* indicate (time) by one's hand or a baton. **6** overcome or defeat. **7** (foll. by *back* or *off*) drive, push, or thrust. **8** *Slang* puzzle or baffle. ♦ *n* **9** (sound made by) a stroke or blow. **10** regular throb. **11** assigned route, as of a policeman. **12** basic rhythmic unit in a piece of music. **beat up** *v* injure (someone) by repeated blows or kicks.

beatify [bee-**at**-if-fie] *v* **-fying, -fied** *RC Church* declare (a dead person) to be among the blessed in heaven: the first step towards canonization. **beatific** *adj* displaying great happiness. **beatification** *n* **beatitude** *n Christianity* any of the blessings on the poor, meek, etc., in the Sermon on the Mount.

beatnik *n* young person in the late 1950s who rebelled against conventional attitudes etc.

beau [**boh**] *n, pl* **beaux, beaus 1** boyfriend or admirer. **2** man greatly concerned with his appearance.

Beaufort scale *n* scale for measuring wind speeds.

Beaujolais *n* wine, usu. red, from southern Burgundy in France.

beauteous *adj Lit* beautiful.

beautician *n* person who gives beauty treatments professionally.

beautiful *adj* **1** very attractive to look at. **2** very pleasant. **beautifully** *adv*

beautify *v* **-fying, -fied** make beautiful. **beautification** *n*

beauty *n, pl* **-ties 1** combination of all the qualities of a person or thing that delight the senses and mind. **2** very attractive woman. **3** *Informal* something outstanding of its kind. **beauty queen** woman who has been judged the most beautiful in a contest. **beauty spot 1** place of outstanding beauty. **2** small black spot formerly worn on a lady's face as decoration.

beaver *n* **1** amphibious rodent with a big flat tail. **2** (hat made of) its fur. **beaver away** *v* work industriously.

becalmed *adj* (of a sailing ship) motionless through lack of wind.

became *v* past tense of BECOME.

because *conj* on account of the fact that. **because of** on account of.

> It is unnecessary to follow *Because* with *the reason is/was: He was cold because the window was open* or *The reason he was cold was that the window was open.*

beck[1] *n* **at someone's beck and call** having to be constantly available to do as someone asks.

beck[2] *n N English* stream.

beckon *v* summon with a gesture.

become *v* **-coming, -came, -come 1** come to be. **2** (foll. by *of*) happen to, e.g. *what became of him?* **3** suit, e.g. *that dress really becomes you.* **becoming** *adj* **1** attractive or pleasing. **2** appropriate or proper.

bed *n* **1** piece of furniture on which to sleep. **2** garden plot. **3** bottom of a river, lake, or sea. **4** layer of rock. ♦ *v* **bedding, bedded 5** plant in a bed. **go to**

bed with have sexual intercourse with. **bed and breakfast** overnight accommodation plus breakfast. **bedclothes** *pl n* coverings for a bed. **bed down** *v* go to or put into a place to sleep or rest. **bedpan** *n* shallow bowl used as a toilet by bedridden people. **bedridden** *adj* confined to bed because of illness or old age. **bedrock** *n* **1** solid rock beneath the surface soil. **2** basic facts or principles. **bedroom** *n* **bedsit, bedsitter** *n* furnished sitting room with a bed. **bedspread** *n* top cover on a bed. **bedstead** *n* framework of a bed.

BEd Bachelor of Education.

bedaub *v* smear with something sticky or dirty.

bedding *n* **1** sheets and covers that are used on a bed. **2** litter, such as straw, for animals.

bedeck *v* cover with decorations.

bedevil [bid-**dev**-ill] *v* **-illing, -illed** harass, confuse, or torment.

bedlam *n* noisy confused situation.

Bedouin *n, pl* **-in, -ins** member of a nomadic Arab race.

bedraggled *adj* untidy, wet, or dirty.

bee[1] *n* insect that makes wax and honey. **have a bee in one's bonnet** be obsessed with an idea. **beehive** *n* structure in which bees live. **beeswax** *n* wax secreted by bees, used in polishes etc.

bee[2] *n US* social gathering to carry out a communal task, e.g. *quilting bee.*

Beeb *n Informal* the BBC.

beech *n* European tree with a smooth greyish bark.

beef *n* **1** flesh of a cow, bull, or ox. **2** *Informal* complaint. ♦ *v* **3** *Informal* complain. **beefy** *adj* **beefier, beefiest 1** like beef. **2** *Informal* strong and muscular. **beefburger** *n* flat grilled or fried cake of minced beef. **beefeater** *n* yeoman warder at the Tower of London. **beef tomato, beefsteak tomato** large fleshy tomato. **beef up** *v* make stronger or more effective.

been *v* past participle of BE.

beep *n* **1** high-pitched sound, like that of a car horn. ♦ *v* **2** (cause to) make this noise.

beer *n* alcoholic drink brewed from malt and hops. **beery** *adj*

beet *n* plant with an edible root and leaves. **beetroot** *n* type of beet plant with a dark red root.

beetle[1] *n* insect with a hard wing cover on its back.

beetle[2] *adj* overhang or jut. **beetling** *adj* **beetle-browed** *adj* having bushy or overhanging eyebrows.

befall *v Old-fashioned* happen to (someone).

befit *v* be appropriate or suitable for. **befitting** *adj*

before *conj, prep, adv* indicating something earlier in time, in front of, or preferred to, e.g. *before the war; brought before a judge; death before dishonour.* **beforehand** *adv* in advance.

befriend *v* become friends with.

befuddled *adj* stupefied or confused, as through alcoholic drink.

beg *v* **begging, begged 1** solicit (for money or food), esp. in the street. **2** ask formally or humbly. **beg the question** assume the thing under examination as proved. **go begging** be unwanted or unused.

began *v* past tense of BEGIN.

beget *v* **-getting, -got** *or* **-gat, -gotten** *or* **-got** *Old-fashioned* **1** cause or create. **2** father.

beggar *n* **1** person who lives by begging. **2** *Brit* fellow. ♦ *v* **3 beggar description** be impossible to describe. **beggarly** *adj*

begin *v* **-ginning, -gan, -gun 1** start. **2** bring or come into being. **beginner** *n* person who has just started learning to do something. **beginning** *n*

begone *interj* go away!

begonia *n* tropical plant with waxy flowers.

begot *v* a past of BEGET. **begotten** *v* a past participle of BEGET.

begrudge *v* **1** envy (someone) the possession of something, e.g. *I don't be-*

grudge him his success. **2** give or allow unwillingly, e.g. *he begrudged her an apology.*

beguile [big-**gile**] *v* **1** cheat or mislead. **2** charm or amuse. **beguiling** *adj*

beguine [big-**geen**] *n* **1** S American dance. **2** music for this.

begum [**bay**-gum] *n* Muslim woman of high rank.

begun *v* past participle of BEGIN.

behalf *n* **on behalf of** in the interest of or for the benefit of.

behave *v* **1** act or function in a particular way. **2** conduct (oneself) properly.

behaviour *n* manner of behaving.

behead *v* remove the head from.

beheld *v* past of BEHOLD.

behemoth [bee-**hee**-moth] *n* huge person or thing.

behest *n* order or earnest request, e.g. *I came at her behest.*

behind *prep, adv* **1** indicating position to the rear, lateness, responsibility, etc., e.g. *behind the wall; behind schedule; the reasons behind her departure.* ♦ *n* **2** *Informal* buttocks.

behold *v* **-holding, -held** *Old-fashioned* look (at). **beholder** *n*

beholden *adj* indebted or obliged.

behove *v Old-fashioned* be necessary or fitting for.

beige *adj* pale brown.

being *n* **1** state or fact of existing. **2** something that exists or is thought to exist. **3** human being. ♦ *v* **4** present participle of BE.

belabour *v* attack verbally or physically.

belated *adj* late or too late. **belatedly** *adv*

belch *v* **1** expel wind from the stomach noisily through the mouth. **2** expel or be expelled forcefully, e.g. *smoke belched from the factory.* ♦ *n* **3** act of belching.

beleaguered *adj* **1** struggling against difficulties or criticism. **2** besieged by an enemy.

belfry *n, pl* **-fries** part of a tower where bells are hung.

belie *v* **1** show to be untrue. **2** misrepresent.

belief *n* **1** faith or confidence. **2** opinion. **3** principle accepted as true, often without proof. **believe** *v* **1** accept as true or real. **2** think, assume, or suppose **3** accept (someone's) statement or opinion as true, e.g. *I don't believe you!* **believe in** be convinced of the truth or existence of. **believable** *adj* **believer** *n*

Belisha beacon [bill-**lee**-sha] *n* flashing orange globe mounted on a post, marking a pedestrian crossing.

belittle *v* treat as having little value or importance.

bell *n* **1** hollow, usu. metal, cup-shaped instrument that emits a ringing sound when struck. **2** device that rings or buzzes as a signal. **ring a bell** bring to mind something previously known or experienced. **bell-bottoms** *pl n* trousers that flare from the knee.

belladonna *n* (drug obtained from) deadly nightshade.

belle *n* beautiful woman, esp. the most attractive woman at a function.

belles-lettres [bell-**let**-tra] *n* literary works, esp. essays and poetry.

bellicose *adj* warlike and aggressive.

belligerent *adj* **1** hostile and aggressive. **2** engaged in war. ♦ *n* **3** person or country engaged in war. **belligerence** *n*

bellow *v* **1** make a low deep cry like that of a bull. **2** shout in anger. ♦ *n* **3** loud deep roar.

bellows *pl n* instrument for pumping a stream of air into something.

belly *n, pl* **-lies** **1** part of the body of a vertebrate which contains the intestines. **2** stomach. **3** front, lower, or inner part of something. ♦ *v* **-lying, -lied** **4** (cause to) swell out. **bellyful** *n Slang* more than one can tolerate. **belly laugh** loud deep laugh.

belong *v* **1** (foll. by *to*) be the property of. **2** (foll. by *to*) be a part or member of. **3** (foll. by *to* or *with*) be classified with. **belongings** *pl n* personal possessions.

beloved *adj* **1** dearly loved. ♦ *n* **2** person

dearly loved.

below *prep, adv* at or to a position lower than, under.

belt *n* **1** band of cloth, leather, etc., worn usu. around the waist. **2** long narrow area, e.g. *a belt of trees.* **3** circular strip of rubber that drives moving parts in a machine. ♦ *v* **4** fasten with a belt. **5** *Slang* hit very hard. **6** *Slang* move very fast. **belt out** *v* sing (a song) loudly.

bemoan *v* express sorrow or dissatisfaction about.

bemused *adj* puzzled or confused.

ben *n Scot & Irish* mountain peak.

bench *n* **1** long seat. **2** long narrow work table. **the bench 1** judge or magistrate sitting in court, or judges and magistrates collectively. **2** place where substitutes sit during a sports match. **benchmark** *n* criterion by which to measure something.

bend *v* **bending, bent 1** (cause to) form a curve. **2** (often foll. by *down*) etc. incline the body. **3** (cause to) submit. ♦ *n* **4** curved part. ♦ *pl* **5** *Informal* decompression sickness. **bend the rules** *Informal* ignore or change rules to suit oneself. **bendy** *adj* **bendier, bendiest**

beneath *adv, prep* **1** below. **2** not worthy of.

Benedictine *adj* **1** of an order of Christian monks and nuns founded by Saint Benedict. ♦ *n* **2** liqueur first made by Benedictine monks.

benediction *n* prayer for divine blessing. **benedictory** *adj*

benefactor, benefactress *n* someone who supports a person or institution by giving money. **benefaction** *n* **1** act of doing good. **2** gift to charity.

benefice *n Christianity* church office providing its holder with an income.

beneficent [bin-**eff**-iss-ent] *adj* charitable or generous. **beneficence** *n*

beneficial *adj* helpful or advantageous.

beneficiary *n, pl* **-ciaries** person who gains or benefits.

benefit *n* **1** something that improves or promotes. **2** advantage or sake, e.g. *I'm doing this for your benefit.* **3** payment made by a government to a poor, ill, or unemployed person. **4** theatrical performance or sports event to raise money for charity. ♦ *v* **-fiting, -fited 5** do or receive good.

benevolence *n* **1** inclination to do good. **2** act of kindness. **benevolent** *adj* **benevolently** *adv*

Bengali *n, adj* (member or language) of a people living chiefly in Bangladesh and W Bengal.

benighted *adj* ignorant or uncultured.

benign [bin-**nine**] *adj* **1** showing kindliness. **2** favourable or propitious. **3** (of a tumour) not threatening to life. **benignly** *adv*

bent *v* **1** past of BEND. ♦ *adj* **2** curved. **3** *Slang* dishonest or corrupt, e.g. *a bent cop.* **4** *Offens slang* homosexual. ♦ *n* **5** personal inclination or aptitude. **bent on** determined to pursue (a course of action).

benumb *v* **1** make numb or powerless. **2** stupefy (the mind etc.).

benzene *n* flammable poisonous liquid used as a solvent, insecticide, etc.

benzine *n* volatile liquid used as a solvent.

bequeath *v* **1** dispose of (property) as in a will. **2** hand down. **bequest** *n* legal gift of money or property by someone who has died.

berate *v* scold harshly.

berberis *n* shrub with red berries.

bereaved *adj* having recently lost a close friend or relative through death. **bereavement** *n*

bereft *adj* (foll. by *of*) deprived.

beret [**ber**-ray] *n* round flat close-fitting brimless cap.

berg *n* iceberg.

bergamot *n* small Asian tree, the fruit of which yields an oil used in perfumery.

beri-beri *n* disease caused by vitamin B deficiency.

berk *n Brit, Aust & NZ slang* stupid person.

berkelium *n Chem* radioactive element.

Bermuda shorts *pl n* shorts that come

down to the knees.

berry *n, pl* **-ries** small soft stoneless fruit.

berserk *adj* **go berserk** become violent or destructive.

berth *n* **1** bunk in a ship or train. **2** place assigned to a ship at a mooring. ♦ *v* **3** dock (a ship). **give a wide berth to** keep clear of.

beryl *n* hard transparent mineral.

beryllium *n Chem* toxic silvery-white metallic element.

beseech *v* **-seeching, -sought** *or* **-seeched** ask earnestly; beg.

beset *v* **1** trouble or harass constantly. **2** attack from all sides.

beside *prep* **1** at, by, or to the side of. **2** as compared with. **3** away from, e.g. *beside the point.* **beside oneself** overwhelmed or overwrought. **besides** *adv, prep* in addition.

besiege *v* **1** surround with military forces. **2** hem in. **3** overwhelm, as with requests.

besmirch *v* tarnish (someone's name or reputation).

besom *n* broom made of twigs.

besotted *adj* infatuated.

besought *v* a past of BESEECH.

bespatter *v* splash, e.g. with dirty water.

bespeak *v* indicate or suggest. **bespoke** *adj* **1** (esp. of a suit) made to the customer's specifications. **2** making or selling such suits, e.g. *a bespoke tailor.*

best *adj* **1** most excellent of a particular group etc. ♦ *adv* **2** in a manner surpassing all others. ♦ *n* **3** the utmost effort, e.g. *I did my best.* **4** most outstanding or excellent person, thing, or group in a category. ♦ *v* **5** defeat. **best man** groom's attendant at a wedding. **bestseller** *n* book or other product that has sold in great numbers. **bestselling** *adj*

bestial *adj* **1** brutal or savage. **2** of or like a beast. **bestiality** *n*

bestir *v* cause (oneself) to become active.

bestow *v* present (a gift) or confer (an honour). **bestowal** *n*

bestride *v* have or put a leg on either side of.

bet *n* **1** the act of staking a sum of money or other stake on the outcome of an event. **2** stake risked. **3** course of action, e.g. *your best bet is to go by train.* ♦ *v* **betting, bet** *or* **betted 4** make or place (a bet). **5** *Informal* predict.

beta *n* second letter in the Greek alphabet. **beta-blocker** *n* drug used to treat high blood pressure and angina. **beta particle** electron or positron emitted by a nucleus during radioactive decay or nuclear fission.

betake *v* **betake oneself** *Formal* go or move.

betel [**bee**-tl] *n* Asian climbing plant, the leaves and nuts of which can be chewed.

bête noire [**bet nwahr**] *n, pl* **bêtes noires** person or thing that one particularly dislikes.

betide *v* happen (to).

betoken *v* indicate or signify.

betray *v* **1** hand over or expose (one's nation, friend, etc.) treacherously to an enemy. **2** disclose (a secret or confidence) treacherously. **3** reveal unintentionally. **betrayal** *n* **betrayer** *n*

betrothed *adj* engaged to be married. **betrothal** *n*

better *adj* **1** more excellent than others. **2** improved or fully recovered in health. ♦ *adv* **3** in a more excellent manner. **4** in or to a greater degree. ♦ *pl n* **5** one's superiors. ♦ *v* **6** improve upon. **get the better of** defeat or outwit. **betterment** *n* improvement. **better off** in more favourable circumstances, esp. financially. **better-off** *adj* reasonably wealthy.

between *prep, adv* indicating position in the middle, alternatives, etc.

> *Between* is used when two people or things are mentioned: *the trade war between Europe and America.* Otherwise use *among.*

betwixt *prep, adv Old-fashioned* between.

bevel *n* **1** slanting edge. ♦ *v* **-elling, -elled 2** slope. **3** cut a bevel on (a piece of timber etc.).

beverage *n* drink.
bevy *n, pl* **bevies** flock or group.
bewail *v* express great sorrow over.
beware *v* be on one's guard (against).
bewilder *v* confuse utterly. **bewildering** *adj* **bewilderment** *n*
bewitch *v* **1** attract and fascinate. **2** cast a spell over. **bewitching** *adj*
beyond *prep* **1** at or to a point on the other side of. **2** outside the limits or scope of. ♦ *adv* **3** at or to the far side of something. ♦ *n* **4** the unknown, esp. life after death.
bezique *n* card game for two or more players.
bhaji *n, pl* **bhaji, bhajis** Indian deep-fried savoury of chopped vegetables in spiced batter.
bhp brake horsepower.
Bi *Chem* bismuth.
bi- *combining form* two or twice, e.g. *bifocal; biweekly.*
biannual *adj* occurring twice a year. **biannually** *adv*
bias *n* **1** mental tendency, esp. prejudice. **2** diagonal cut across the weave of a fabric. **3** *Bowls* bulge or weight on one side of a bowl that causes it to roll in a curve. ♦ *v* **-asing, -ased** *or* **-assing, -assed 4** cause to have a bias. **biased, biassed** *adj* **bias binding** strip of material used for binding hems.
bib *n* **1** piece of cloth or plastic worn to protect a young child's clothes when eating. **2** upper front part of dungarees etc.
Bible *n* **1** sacred writings of the Christian religion. **2** (**b-**) book regarded as authoritative. **biblical** *adj*
bibliography *n, pl* **-phies 1** list of books on a subject. **2** list of sources used in a book etc. **bibliographer** *n*
bibliophile *n* person who collects or is fond of books.
bibulous *adj* addicted to alcohol.
bicameral *adj* (of a legislature) consisting of two chambers.
bicarbonate *n* salt of carbonic acid. **bicarbonate of soda** powder used in baking or as medicine.
bicentenary, *US* **bicentennial** ♦ *adj* **1** marking a 200th anniversary. ♦ *n, pl* **-naries 2** 200th anniversary.
biceps *n* muscle with two origins, esp. the muscle that flexes the forearm.
bicker *v* argue over petty matters.
bicycle *n* **1** vehicle with two wheels, one behind the other, pedalled by the rider. ♦ *v* **2** ride a bicycle.
bid *v* **bidding, bade, bidden 1** say (a greeting), e.g. *to bid farewell.* **2** command. **3** (*past* **bid**) offer (an amount) in an attempt to buy something. ♦ *n* **4** offer of a specified amount. **5** attempt. **bidder** *n* **biddable** *adj* obedient. **bidding** *n* **1** command. **2** invitation.
bide *v* **bide one's time** wait patiently for an opportunity.
bidet [**bee**-day] *n* low basin for washing the genital area.
biennial *adj* **1** occurring every two years. ♦ *n* **2** plant that completes its life cycle in two years.
bier *n* stand on which a corpse or coffin rests before burial.
biff *Slang* ♦ *n* **1** blow with the fist. ♦ *v* **2** give (someone) such a blow.
bifocals *pl n* spectacles with lenses permitting near and distant vision. **bifocal** *adj* having two different focuses.
bifurcate *v* fork into two branches.
big *adj* **bigger, biggest 1** of considerable size, height, number, or capacity. **2** important through having power, wealth, etc. **3** elder. **4** generous. ♦ *adv* **5** on a grand scale, e.g. *think big.* **bighead** *n Informal* conceited person. **big-headed** *adj* **big shot, bigwig** *n Informal* important person. **big top** *Informal* main tent of a circus.
bigamy *n* crime of marrying a person while still legally married to someone else. **bigamist** *n* **bigamous** *adj*
bight *n* **1** long curved shoreline. **2** curve or loop in a rope.
bigot *n* person who is intolerant, esp. regarding religion or race. **bigoted** *adj* **bigotry** *n*
bijou [**bee**-zhoo] *adj* (of a house) small

but elegant.

bike *n Informal* bicycle or motorcycle.

bikini *n* woman's brief two-piece swimming costume.

bilateral *adj* affecting or undertaken by two parties.

bilberry *n* bluish-black edible berry.

bile *n* **1** bitter yellow fluid secreted by the liver. **2** irritability or peevishness.

bilge *n* **1** *Informal* nonsense. **2** ship's bottom. **3** dirty water that collects in a ship's bilge.

bilingual *adj* involving or using two languages.

bilious *adj* **1** sick, nauseous. **2** *Informal* bad-tempered or irritable.

bilk *v* cheat, esp. by not paying.

bill[1] *n* **1** statement of money owed for goods or services supplied. **2** draft of a proposed new law. **3** poster. **4** *Chiefly US & Canadian* piece of paper money. **5** list of events, such as a theatre programme. ♦ *v* **6** send or present a bill to. **7** advertise by posters. **bill of fare** menu. **clean bill of health** favourable account of a person or thing's physical or financial condition. **fit, fill the bill** *Informal* be suitable or adequate.

bill[2] *n* bird's beak. **bill and coo** (of lovers) kiss and whisper amorously.

billabong *n Aust* stagnant pool in an intermittent stream.

billboard *n Chiefly US & Canadian* hoarding.

billet *v* **-leting, -leted 1** assign a lodging to (a soldier). ♦ *n* **2** accommodation for a soldier in civil lodgings.

billet-doux [bill-ee-**doo**] *n, pl* **billets-doux** love letter.

billhook *n* tool with a hooked blade, used for chopping etc.

billiards *n* game played on a table with balls and a cue.

billion *n* **1** one thousand million. **2** formerly, one million million. **billionth** *adj* **billionaire** *n* person who owns at least a billion pounds, dollars, etc.

billow *n* **1** large sea wave. **2** swelling or surging mass, as of smoke or sound. ♦ *v* **3** rise up or swell out. **billowy, billowing** *adj*

billy, billycan *n, pl* **-lies, -lycans** metal can or pot for cooking on a camp fire.

billy goat *n* male goat.

bimbo *n Slang* attractive but empty-headed young person, esp. a woman.

bimonthly *adv, adj* **1** every two months. **2** twice a month.

bin *n* **1** container for rubbish or for storing grain, coal, etc. **2** a large container for bulk storage. ♦ *v* **3** put in a rubbish bin.

binary [**bine**-a-ree] *adj* **1** composed of two parts. **2** *Maths, computers* of or in a counting system with only two digits, 0 and 1.

bind *v* **binding, bound 1** make secure with or as if with a rope. **2** place (someone) under obligation. **3** place under certain constraints, e.g. *bound by the rules*. **4** stick together or cause to stick, e.g. *egg binds fat and flour*. **5** enclose and fasten (the pages of a book) between covers. ♦ *n* **6** *Informal* annoying situation. **binder** *n* **1** firm cover for holding loose sheets of paper together. **2** something used to fasten or hold together. **3** *Obs* machine for cutting and binding sheaves. **binding** *n* **1** anything that binds or fastens. **2** book cover. ♦ *adj* **3** imposing an obligation or duty.

bindweed *n* plant that twines around a support.

binge *n Informal* bout of excessive indulgence, esp. in drink.

bingo *n* gambling game in which numbers are called out and covered by the players on their individual cards.

binnacle *n* box holding a ship's compass.

binoculars *pl n* optical instrument consisting of two small telescopes joined together. **binocular** *adj* involving both eyes.

binomial *n, adj* (mathematical expression) consisting of two terms.

bio- *combining form* life or living organisms, e.g. *biology*.

biochemistry *n* study of the chemistry of living things. **biochemist** *n*

biodegradable *adj* capable of being de›composed by natural means.
biodiversity *n* existence of a wide vari›ety of species in their natural environ›ment.
biography *n, pl* **-phies** account of a per›son's life by another person. **biographi-cal** *adj* **biographer** *n*
biological *adj* **1** of or relating to biology. **2** (of a detergent) containing enzymes that remove natural stains. **biological warfare** use of living organisms or their toxic products to kill or disable.
biology *n* study of living organisms. **bi-ologist** *n*
bionic *adj* having a part of the body that is operated electronically.
biopsy *n, pl* **-sies** examination of tissue from a living body.
biosphere *n* part of the earth's surface and atmosphere inhabited by living things.
biotechnology *n* use of microorgan›isms, such as cells or bacteria, in indus›try and technology.
bipartite *adj* **1** consisting of two parts. **2** affecting or made by two parties.
biped [**bye**›ped] *n* animal with two feet.
biplane *n* aeroplane with two sets of wings, one above the other.
bipolar *adj* **1** having two poles. **2** having two extremes.
birch *n* **1** tree with thin peeling bark. **2** birch rod or twigs used, esp. formerly, for flogging offenders. ♦ *v* **3** flog with a birch.
bird *n* **1** creature with feathers and wings, most types of which can fly. **2** *Slang* young woman. **bird's-eye view** **1** view seen from above. **2** general or overall impression.
birdie *n Golf* score of one stroke under par for a hole.
biretta *n* stiff square cap worn by the Catholic clergy.
Biro *n* ﬁ ballpoint pen.
birth *n* **1** process of bearing young; child›birth. **2** act of being born. **3** origin or beginning. **4** ancestry. **give birth to** bear (offspring). **birth control** any method of contraception. **birthday** *n* anniversary of the day of one's birth. **birthmark** *n* blemish on the skin formed before birth. **birth rate** ratio of live births to population. **birthright** *n* privileges or possessions that someone is entitled to as soon as he or she is born.
biscuit *n* **1** small flat dry sweet or plain cake. **2** porcelain that has been fired but not glazed. ♦ *adj* **3** pale brown.
bisect *v* divide into two equal parts.
bisexual *adj* **1** sexually attracted to both men and women. **2** showing characteris›tics of both sexes. ♦ *n* **3** bisexual per›son. **bisexuality** *n*
bishop *n* **1** clergyman who governs a diocese. **2** chessman which is moved di›agonally. **bishopric** *n* diocese or office of a bishop.
bismuth *n Chem* pinkish›white metallic element.
bison *n, pl* **-son** large hairy animal of the cattle family.
bisque[1] *n* thick rich soup made from shellfish.
bisque[2] *adj* pinkish›tan.
bistro *n, pl* **-tros** small restaurant.
bit[1] *n* **1** small piece, portion, or quantity. **2** short time or distance. **a bit** rather, somewhat. **bit by bit** gradually.
bit[2] *n* **1** metal mouthpiece on a bridle. **2** cutting or drilling part of a tool.
bit[3] *v* past tense of BITE.
bit[4] *n Maths, computers* **1** single digit of binary notation, either 0 or 1. **2** smallest unit of information.
bitch *n* **1** female dog, fox, or wolf. **2** *Offens* spiteful woman. ♦ *v* **3** *Informal* complain or grumble. **bitchy** *adj* **bitchi-er, bitchiest** **bitchiness** *n*
bite *v* **biting, bit, bitten** **1** grip, tear, or puncture the skin, as with the teeth or jaws. **2** take firm hold of or act effective›ly upon. **3** (of corrosive material) eat away or into. ♦ *n* **4** act of biting. **5** wound or sting inflicted by biting. **6** snack. **biter** *n* **biting** *adj* **1** piercing or keen. **2** sarcastic.

bitter *adj* **1** having a sharp unpleasant taste. **2** showing or caused by hostility or resentment. **3** extremely cold. ♦ *n* **4** beer with a slightly bitter taste. ♦ *pl* **5** bitter-tasting alcoholic drink. **bitterly** *adv* **bitterness** *n* **bittersweet** *adj* **1** tasting of bitterness and sweetness. **2** pleasant but tinged with sadness.

bittern *n* wading marsh bird with a booming call.

bitty *adj* **-tier, -tiest** lacking unity, disjointed. **bittiness** *n*

bitumen *n* black sticky substance obtained from tar or petrol.

bivalve *n, adj* (marine mollusc) with two hinged segments to its shell.

bivouac *n* **1** temporary camp in the open air. ♦ *v* **-acking, -acked 2** camp in a bivouac.

bizarre *adj* odd or unusual.

Bk *Chem* berkelium.

blab *v* **blabbing, blabbed** reveal (secrets) indiscreetly.

blabber *v* talk without thinking.

black *adj* **1** of the darkest colour, like coal. **2** without light. **3** (**B-**) dark-skinned. **4** without hope. **5** angry or resentful, e.g. *black looks.* **6** unpleasant in a macabre manner, e.g. *black comedy.* **7** (of coffee or tea) without milk or cream. ♦ *n* **8** darkest colour. **9** (**B-**) member of a dark-skinned race. **10** complete darkness. ♦ *v* **11** make black. **12** (of trade unionists) boycott (goods or people). **blackness** *n* **blacken** *v* **1** make or become black. **2** defame or slander. **blacking** *n* preparation for giving a black finish to shoes, metals, etc. **black-and-blue** *adj* bruised, as from a beating. **black-and-white** *adj* **1** not in colour. ♦ *n* **in black and white 2** in print or writing. **black box** *Informal* flight recorder. **black eye** bruising round the eye. **black hole** *Astronomy* hypothetical region of space from which neither matter nor radiation can escape. **black ice** thin transparent layer of new ice on a road. **black magic** magic used for evil purposes. **Black Maria** police van for transporting prisoners. **black market** illegal trade in goods or currencies. **black pudding** sausage made from blood, suet, etc. **black sheep** person who is regarded as a disgrace by his or her family. **black spot** place on a road where accidents frequently occur. **black widow** American spider, the female of which eats its mate.

> When *black* is used as a political or racial term it has a capital letter.

blackball *v* exclude from a group.

blackberry *n* small blackish edible fruit.

blackbird *n* common European thrush.

blackboard *n* hard black surface used for writing on with chalk.

blackcurrant *n* very small blackish edible fruit that grows in bunches.

blackguard [**blag**-gard] *n* unprincipled person.

blackhead *n* small black spot on the skin.

blackleg *n* person who continues to work during a strike.

blacklist *n* **1** list of people or organizations considered untrustworthy etc. ♦ *v* **2** put on a blacklist.

blackmail *n* **1** act of attempting to extort money by threats. ♦ *v* **2** (attempt to) obtain money by blackmail.

blackout *n* **1** extinguishing of all light as a precaution against an air attack. **2** momentary loss of consciousness or memory. **black out** *v* **1** extinguish (lights). **2** lose consciousness or memory temporarily.

blacksmith *n* person who works iron with a furnace, anvil, etc.

blackthorn *n* thorny shrub with white flowers and small sour plumlike fruits.

black-tie *adj* denoting an occasion when a dinner jacket should be worn.

bladder *n* **1** sac in the body where urine is held. **2** hollow bag which may be filled with air or liquid.

blade *n* **1** cutting edge of a weapon or tool. **2** thin flattish part of a propeller, oar, etc. **3** leaf of grass.

blame *v* **1** consider (someone) responsible for, e.g. *I blame her for the failure.* **2** (foll. by *on*) put responsibility for (something) on (someone), e.g. *she blames the failure on me.* ♦ *n* **3** responsibility for something that is wrong. **4** expression of condemnation. **blameless** *adj* **blameworthy** *adj* deserving blame.

blanch *v* **1** become white or pale. **2** prepare (vegetables etc.) by plunging them in boiling water.

blancmange [blam-**monzh**] *n* jelly-like dessert made with milk.

bland *adj* **1** dull and uninteresting. **2** smooth in manner. **blandly** *adv*

blandishments *pl n* flattery intended to coax or persuade.

blank *adj* **1** not written on. **2** with spaces left for details to be filled in. **3** without decoration. **4** showing no interest or expression, e.g. *a blank stare.* **5** lacking ideas or inspiration, e.g. *his mind went blank.* ♦ *n* **6** empty space. **7** condition of not understanding. **8** cartridge containing no bullet. **blankly** *adv* **blank cheque 1** signed cheque without the amount payable specified. **2** complete freedom of action. **blank verse** unrhymed verse.

blanket *n* **1** large thick cloth used as covering for a bed. **2** concealing cover, as of snow. ♦ *adj* **3** applying to a wide group of people, situations, conditions, etc. ♦ *v* **4** cover as with a blanket.

blare *v* **1** sound loudly and harshly. ♦ *n* **2** loud harsh noise.

blarney *n* flattering talk.

blasé [**blah**-zay] *adj* indifferent or bored through familiarity.

blaspheme *v* **1** speak disrespectfully of (God or sacred things). **2** utter curses. **blasphemy** *n* **blasphemous** *adj* **blasphemer** *n*

blast *n* **1** explosion. **2** sudden strong gust of air or wind. **3** sudden loud sound, as of a trumpet. **4** *US slang* very enjoyable or thrilling experience. ♦ *v* **5** blow up (a rock etc.) with explosives. **6** make a loud harsh noise. **7** criticize severely. ♦ *interj* **8** *Slang* expression of annoyance. **blasted** *adj, adv Slang* extreme or extremely. **blast furnace** furnace for smelting, using a preheated blast of air. **blastoff** *n* launching of a rocket.

blatant [**blay**-tant] *adj* glaringly obvious. **blatantly** *adv*

blather *v, n* same as BLETHER.

blaze[1] *n* **1** strong fire or flame. **2** very bright light. **3** outburst of passion. ♦ *v* **4** burn or shine brightly. **5** become stirred with anger or excitement.

blaze[2] *n* **1** mark made on a tree to indicate a route. **2** light-coloured marking on the face of an animal. ♦ *v* **3** mark (a tree etc.) with a blaze.

blaze[3] *v* **blaze something abroad** make something widely known.

blazer *n* lightweight jacket, often in the colours of a school etc.

blazon *v* proclaim publicly.

bleach *v* **1** make or become white or colourless. ♦ *n* **2** bleaching agent.

bleak *adj* **1** exposed and barren. **2** offering little hope.

bleary *adj* **-rier, -riest** with eyes dimmed, as by tears or tiredness. **blearily** *adv*

bleat *v* **1** (of a sheep, goat, or calf) utter its plaintive cry. **2** whine. ♦ *n* **3** cry of sheep, goats, and calves.

bleed *v* **bleeding, bled 1** lose or emit blood. **2** draw blood from (a person or animal). **3** *Informal* obtain money by extortion. **4** draw off or emit liquid or gas.

bleep *n* **1** short high-pitched sound made by an electrical device. ♦ *v* **2** make a bleeping sound. **bleeper** *n* small portable radio receiver that makes a bleeping signal.

blemish *n* **1** defect or stain. ♦ *v* **2** spoil or tarnish.

blench *v* shy away, as in fear.

blend *v* **1** mix or mingle (components or ingredients). **2** look good together. ♦ *n* **3** mixture. **blender** *n* electrical appliance for puréeing vegetables etc.

blende *n* mineral consisting mainly of zinc sulphide.

blenny *n, pl* **-nies** small fish with a tapering scaleless body.

bless *v* **1** make holy by means of a religious rite. **2** call upon God to protect. **3** give thanks to. **4** endow with health, talent, etc. **blessed** *adj* **1** holy. **2** *RC Church* beatified by the Pope. **3** *Euphemistic* damned. **blessing** *n* **1** invoking of divine aid. **2** approval. **3** happy event.

blether *Scot* ♦ *v* **1** talk, esp. foolishly or at length. ♦ *n* **2** conversation. **3** talkative person.

blew *v* past tense of BLOW[1].

blight *n* **1** person or thing that spoils or prevents growth. **2** withering plant disease. ♦ *v* **3** cause to suffer a blight. **4** frustrate or disappoint.

blighter *n Informal* irritating person.

blimey *interj Slang* exclamation of surprise or annoyance.

blimp *n* small airship.

blind *adj* **1** unable to see. **2** unable or unwilling to understand. **3** not determined by reason, e.g. *blind hatred.* ♦ *v* **4** deprive of sight. **5** deprive of good sense, reason, or judgment. ♦ *n* **6** covering for a window. **7** something that serves to conceal the truth. **blindly** *adv* **blindness** *n* **blind alley** alley open at one end only. **blind date** *Informal* prearranged social meeting between two people who have not met. **blind man's buff** game in which a blindfolded person tries to catch and identify other players. **blind spot 1** area of the retina where vision is not experienced. **2** place where vision is obscured. **3** subject about which a person is ignorant.

> The use of *the blind, the disabled,* etc. can be offensive and should be avoided. Instead you should talk about *blind people, disabled people,* etc.

blindfold *v* **1** prevent (a person) from seeing by covering the eyes. ♦ *n* **2** piece of cloth used to cover the eyes. ♦ *adj, adv* **3** with the eyes covered by a cloth.

blink *v* **1** close and immediately reopen (the eyes). **2** shine intermittently. ♦ *n* **3** act of blinking. **on the blink** *Slang* not working properly.

blinkers *pl n* leather flaps on a horse's bridle to prevent sideways vision. **blinkered** *adj* considering only a narrow point of view.

blip *n* **1** spot of light on a radar screen indicating the position of an object. **2** temporary irregularity in performance.

bliss *n* perfect happiness. **blissful** *adj* **blissfully** *adv*

blister *n* **1** small bubble on the skin. **2** swelling, as on a painted surface. ♦ *v* **3** (cause to) have blisters. **blistering** *adj* **1** (of weather) very hot. **2** (of criticism) extremely harsh.

blithe *adj* **1** casual and indifferent. **2** very happy. **blithely** *adv*

blithering *adj Informal* stupid.

blitz *n* **1** violent and sustained attack by aircraft. **2** intensive attack or concerted effort. ♦ *v* **3** attack suddenly and intensively.

blizzard *n* blinding storm of wind and snow.

bloat *v* cause to swell, as with liquid or air.

bloater *n* salted smoked herring.

blob *n* **1** soft mass or drop. **2** indistinct or shapeless form.

bloc *n* people or countries combined by a common interest.

block *n* **1** large solid piece of wood, stone, etc. **2** large building of offices, flats, etc. **3** group of buildings enclosed by intersecting streets. **4** obstruction or hindrance. **5** piece of wood or metal engraved for printing. **6** one of a set of wooden or plastic cubes used as a toy. **7** *Slang* person's head. ♦ *v* **8** obstruct or impede by introducing an obstacle. **blockage** *n* **blockbuster** *n* highly successful film, novel, etc. **blockhead** *n* stupid person. **block letter** plain capital letter.

blockade *n* **1** sealing off of a place to prevent the passage of goods. ♦ *v* **2** impose a blockade on.

bloke *n Informal* man.

blonde, (*masc*) **blond** *adj, n* fair-haired (person).

blood *n* **1** red fluid that flows around the body. **2** bloodshed. **3** race or kinship. ♦ *v* **4** initiate (a person) to war or hunting. **in cold blood** done deliberately. **bloodless** *adj* **1** without blood or bloodshed. **2** pale. **3** lacking vitality. **blood bath** massacre. **bloodcurdling** *adj* terrifying. **bloodhound** *n* large dog formerly used for tracking. **blood poisoning** same as SEPTICAEMIA. **blood pressure** pressure exerted by the blood on the inner walls of the blood vessels. **bloodshed** *n* slaughter or killing. **bloodshot** *adj* (of an eye) inflamed. **blood sport** sport involving the killing of animals. **bloodstream** *n* flow of blood round the body. **bloodsucker** *n* **1** animal that sucks blood. **2** *Informal* person who extorts money from other people. **bloodthirsty** *adj* taking pleasure in violence. **blood vessel** tube that carries the blood in the body.

bloody *adj* **1** covered with blood. **2** marked by much killing. ♦ *adj, adv* **3** *Slang* extreme or extremely. ♦ *v* **4** stain with blood. **bloody-minded** *adj* deliberately unhelpful.

bloom *n* **1** blossom on a flowering plant. **2** period when flowers open. **3** flourishing condition. **4** youthful or healthy glow. **5** whitish coating on fruit, leaves, etc. ♦ *v* **6** (of flowers) open. **7** bear flowers. **8** be in a healthy, glowing condition.

bloomer *n Informal* stupid mistake.

bloomers *pl n* woman's baggy knickers.

blossom *n* **1** flowers of a plant. ♦ *v* **2** (of plants) flower. **3** come to a promising stage.

blot *n* **1** spot or stain. **2** something that spoils. ♦ *v* **blotting, blotted 3** cause a blemish in or on. **4** soak up (ink) by using blotting paper. **blotter** *n* **blot out** *v* darken or hide completely. **blotting paper** soft absorbent paper for soaking up ink.

blotch *n* discoloured area or stain. **blotchy** *adj* **blotchier, blotchiest**

blotto *adj Slang* extremely drunk.

blouse *n* woman's shirtlike garment.

blouson *n* short loose jacket with a tight waist.

blow[1] *v* **blowing, blew, blown 1** (of air, the wind, etc.) move. **2** move or be carried as if by the wind. **3** expel (air etc.) through the mouth or nose. **4** cause (a musical instrument) to sound by forcing air into it. **5** burn out (a fuse etc.). **6** *Slang* spend (money) freely. **7** *Slang* use (an opportunity) ineffectively. **blower** *n* **blowy** *adj* windy. **blow-dry** *v* style (the hair) with a hand-held dryer. **blowfly** *n* fly that lays its eggs in meat. **blowtorch** *n* small burner producing a very hot flame. **blowout** *n* **1** sudden loss of air in a tyre. **2** escape of oil or gas from a well. **3** *Slang* filling meal. **blowpipe** *n* long tube from which darts etc. are shot by blowing. **blow up** *v* **1** explode. **2** fill with air. **3** *Informal* lose one's temper. **4** exaggerate the importance of. **5** *Informal* enlarge (a photograph).

blow[2] *n* **1** hard hit. **2** sudden setback. **3** attacking action, e.g. *a blow for freedom.*

blown *v* past participle of BLOW[1].

blowsy *adj* fat, untidy, and red-faced.

blubber *n* **1** fat of whales, seals, etc. ♦ *v* **2** sob without restraint.

bludgeon *n* **1** short thick club. ♦ *v* **2** hit with a bludgeon. **3** force or bully.

blue *n* **1** colour of a clear unclouded sky. **2** sportsman representing Oxford or Cambridge University. ♦ *pl* **3** feeling of depression. **4** type of folk music of Black American origin. ♦ *adj* **bluer, bluest 5** of the colour blue. **6** depressed. **7** pornographic. **out of the blue** unexpectedly. **bluish** *adj* **bluebell** *n* flower with blue bell-shaped flowers. **bluebottle** *n* large fly with a dark-blue body. **blue cheese** cheese containing a blue mould. **blue-collar** *adj* denoting manual industrial workers. **blueprint** *n* **1** photographic print of a plan. **2** description of how a plan is expected to work. **blue ribbon** first prize in a competition. **bluestocking** *n* intellectual woman.

bluff[1] *v* **1** pretend to be confident in order to influence (someone). ♦ *n* **2** act of bluffing.

bluff[2] *n* **1** steep cliff or bank. ♦ *adj* **2** good-naturedly frank and hearty.

blunder *n* **1** clumsy mistake. ♦ *v* **2** make a blunder. **3** act clumsily.

blunderbuss *n* obsolete gun with a wide flared muzzle.

blunt *adj* **1** not having a sharp edge or point. **2** (of people, speech, etc.) straightforward or uncomplicated. ♦ *v* **3** make less sharp. **bluntly** *adv*

blur *v* **blurring, blurred 1** make or become vague or less distinct. **2** smear or smudge. ♦ *n* **3** something vague, hazy, or indistinct. **blurry** *adj* **-rier, -riest**

blurb *n* promotional description, as on the jacket of a book.

blurt *v* (foll. by *out*) utter suddenly and involuntarily.

blush *v* **1** become red in the face, esp. from embarrassment or shame. ♦ *n* **2** reddening of the face. **blusher** *n* cosmetic for giving the cheeks a rosy colour.

bluster *v* **1** speak loudly or in a bullying way. ♦ *n* **2** empty threats or protests. **blustery** *adj* (of weather) rough and windy.

BMA British Medical Association.

B-movie *n* film originally made as a supporting film, now considered a genre in its own right.

BO *Informal* body odour.

boa *n* **1** large nonvenomous snake. **2** long scarf of fur or feathers. **boa constrictor** large snake that kills its prey by crushing.

boar *n* **1** uncastrated male pig. **2** wild pig.

board *n* **1** long flat piece of sawn timber. **2** smaller flat piece of rigid material for a specific purpose, e.g. *ironing board; chess board.* **3** group of people who administer a company, trust, etc. **4** meals provided for money. ♦ *pl* **5** the stage. ♦ *v* **6** go aboard (a train, aeroplane, etc.). **7** cover with boards. **8** receive meals and lodgings in return for money. **on board** on or in a ship, aeroplane, etc. **boarder** *n* pupil who lives at school during the school term. **boarding house** private house that provides meals and accommodation for paying guests. **boarding school** school providing living accommodation for pupils. **boardroom** *n* room where the board of a company meets.

boast *v* **1** speak too proudly about one's talents etc. **2** possess (something to be proud of). ♦ *n* **3** bragging statement. **4** something that is bragged about. **boastful** *adj*

boat *n* **1** small vehicle for travelling across water. **2** *Informal* ship. **3** boat-shaped dish, e.g. *gravy boat.* ♦ *v* **4** travel in a boat. **boater** *n* flat straw hat. **boating** *n* **boat train** train scheduled to take passengers to or from a ship.

boatswain *n* same as BOSUN.

bob[1] *v* **bobbing, bobbed 1** move up and down repeatedly. ♦ *n* **2** short abrupt movement.

bob[2] *n* **1** hairstyle in which the hair is cut short evenly all round the head. **2** weight on a pendulum or plumb line. ♦ *v* **bobbing, bobbed 3** cut (the hair) in a bob.

bob[3] *n, pl* **bob** *Brit informal* (formerly) shilling.

bobbin *n* reel on which thread is wound.

bobble *n* small ball of material, usu. for decoration.

bobby *n, pl* **-bies** *Informal* policeman.

bobsleigh *n* **1** sledge for racing down an icy track. ♦ *v* **2** ride on a bobsleigh.

bod *n Informal* person.

bode *v* be an omen of (good or ill).

bodega *n* shop in a Spanish-speaking country that sells wine.

bodge *v Informal* make a mess of.

bodice *n* upper part of a dress.

bodkin *n* blunt large-eyed needle.

body *n, pl* **bodies 1** entire physical structure of an animal or human. **2** trunk or torso. **3** corpse. **4** group regarded as a single entity. **5** main part of anything. **6** separate mass of water or land. **7** person. **8** woman's one-piece undergarment. **bodily** *adj* **1** relating to the body. ♦ *adv* **2** by taking hold of the body. **bodyguard** *n* person or group of people employed to protect someone. **body shop** place where vehicle bodywork is repaired. **body stocking** woman's one-piece undergarment, covering the torso. **bodywork** *n* outer shell of a motor vehicle.

Boer *n* descendant of the Dutch settlers in S Africa.

boffin *n Informal* scientist.

bog *n* **1** wet spongy ground. **2** *Slang* toilet. **boggy** *adj* **-gier, -giest** **bog down** *v* **bogging, bogged** impede physically or mentally.

bogey, bogy *n* **1** evil or mischievous spirit. **2** something that worries or annoys. **3** *Golf* score of one stroke over par on a hole.

boggle *v* **1** be surprised, confused, or alarmed. **2** hesitate when confronted with a problem.

bogie, bogy *n* set of wheels, as on a railway carriage.

bog-standard *adj Slang* completely ordinary.

bogus [**boh**-guss] *adj* not genuine.

bogy *n, pl* **-gies** same as BOGEY *or* BOGIE.

bohemian *n, adj* (person) leading an unconventional life.

boil[1] *v* **1** (cause to) change from a liquid to a vapour so quickly that bubbles are formed. **2** reach or cause to reach boiling point. **3** cook by the process of boiling. **4** bubble like something boiling. **5** be extremely angry. ♦ *n* **6** state or action of boiling. **boiler** *n* piece of equipment which provides hot water. **boiler suit** one-piece overall. **boiling point** temperature at which a liquid boils.

boil[2] *n* red pus-filled swelling on the skin.

boisterous *adj* **1** noisy and lively. **2** turbulent or stormy. **boisterously** *adv*

bold *adj* **1** confident and fearless. **2** immodest or impudent. **3** standing out distinctly. **boldly** *adv* **boldness** *n*

bole *n* tree trunk.

bolero *n, pl* **-ros** **1** (music for) traditional Spanish dance. **2** short open jacket.

boll *n* rounded seed capsule of cotton, flax, etc.

bollard *n* **1** short thick post used to prevent the passage of motor vehicles. **2** post on a quay etc. for securing mooring lines.

boloney *n* same as BALONEY.

Bolshevik *n* (formerly) Russian Communist. **bolshie, bolshy** *adj Informal* difficult or rebellious.

bolster *v* **1** support or strengthen. ♦ *n* **2** long narrow pillow.

bolt *n* **1** sliding metal bar for fastening a door etc. **2** metal pin which screws into a nut. **3** flash (of lightning). **4** sudden movement, esp. in order to escape. **5** arrow for a crossbow. ♦ *v* **6** run away suddenly. **7** fasten with a bolt. **8** eat hurriedly. **bolt upright** stiff and rigid. **bolt hole** place of escape.

bomb *n* **1** container fitted with explosive material. **2** *Slang* large amount of money. ♦ *v* **3** attack with bombs. **4** move very quickly. **the bomb** nuclear bomb. **bomber** *n* **1** aircraft that drops bombs. **2** person who throws or puts a bomb in a particular place. **bombshell** *n* shocking or unwelcome surprise.

bombard *v* **1** attack with heavy gunfire or bombs. **2** attack verbally, esp. with questions. **bombardier** *n* noncommissioned rank in the Royal Artillery. **bombardment** *n*

bombast *n* pompous language. **bombastic** *adj*

bona fide [**bone**-a **fide**-ee] *adj* genuine.

bonanza *n* sudden good luck or wealth.

bonbon *n* sweet.

bond *n* **1** something that binds, fastens or holds together. **2** something that unites people, e.g. *a bond of friendship*. **3** written or spoken agreement. **4** *Finance* certificate of debt issued to raise funds. ♦ *pl* **5** something that restrains or imprisons. ♦ *v* **6** bind. **bonded** *adj*

bondage *n* **1** slavery. **2** subjection to some influence or duty. **3** sexual practice in which one partner is tied or chained up.

bone *n* **1** any of the hard parts in the

body that form the skeleton. ♦ *pl* **2** human skeleton. ♦ *v* **3** remove the bones from (meat for cooking etc.). **boneless** *adj* **bony** *adj* **bonier, boniest 1** having many bones. **2** thin or emaciated. **bone china** porcelain containing powdered bone. **bone-dry** *adj* completely dry. **bone-idle** *adj* extremely lazy. **bone meal** ground bones used as a fertilizer.

bonfire *n* large outdoor fire.

bongo *n, pl* **-gos, -goes** small drum played with the fingers.

bonhomie [**bon**-om-ee] *n* cheerful friendliness.

bonk *v Informal* **1** have sex with. **2** hit. **bonking** *n*

bonkers *adj Slang* crazy.

bon mot [bon **moh**] *n, pl* **bons mots** clever and fitting remark.

bonnet *n* **1** metal cover over a vehicle's engine. **2** hat which ties under the chin. **3** *Scot* soft cloth cap.

bonny *adj* **-nier, -niest** *Scot* **1** beautiful. **2** good or fine.

bonsai *n, pl* **-sai** ornamental miniature tree or shrub.

bonus *n* something given, paid, or received above what is due or expected.

bon voyage *interj* phrase used to wish a traveller a pleasant journey.

boo *interj* **1** shout of disapproval. **2** shout to startle someone. ♦ *v* **booing, booed 3** shout 'boo' to show disapproval.

boob *Slang* ♦ *n* **1** foolish mistake. **2** female breast. ♦ *v* **3** make a foolish mistake.

booby *n, pl* **-bies** foolish person. **booby prize** prize given for the lowest score in a competition. **booby trap 1** hidden bomb primed to be set off by an unsuspecting victim. **2** trap for an unsuspecting person, intended as a joke.

boogie *v Informal* dance to fast pop music.

book *n* **1** number of pages bound together between covers. **2** long written work. **3** number of tickets, stamps, etc. fastened together. **4** libretto of a musical etc. **5** record of betting transactions. ♦ *pl* **6** record of transactions of a business or society. ♦ *v* **7** reserve (a place, passage, etc.) in advance. **8** record the name of (a person) who has committed an offence. **bookcase** *n* piece of furniture containing shelves for books. **bookish** *adj* **1** fond of reading. **2** forming opinions through reading rather than experience. **booklet** *n* thin book with paper covers.

bookie *n Informal* short for BOOKMAKER.

book-keeping *n* systematic recording of business transactions. **book-keeper** *n*

bookmaker *n* person whose occupation is taking bets.

bookworm *n* **1** person devoted to reading. **2** small insect that feeds on books.

boom[1] *v* **1** make a loud deep echoing sound. **2** prosper vigorously and rapidly. ♦ *n* **3** loud deep echoing sound. **4** period of high economic growth.

boom[2] *n* **1** pole to which the foot of a sail is attached. **2** pole carrying an overhead microphone. **3** barrier across a waterway.

boomerang *n* **1** curved wooden missile which can be made to return to the thrower. ♦ *v* **2** (of a plan) recoil unexpectedly.

boon[1] *n* something helpful or beneficial.

boon[2] *adj* close or intimate.

boor *n* rude or insensitive person. **boorish** *adj*

boost *n* **1** encouragement or help. **2** upward thrust or push. **3** increase. ♦ *v* **4** improve. **5** increase. **booster** *n* **1** small additional injection of a vaccine. **2** radio-frequency amplifier to strengthen signals. **3** first stage of a multistage rocket.

boot[1] *n* **1** outer covering for the foot that extends above the ankle. **2** space in a car for luggage. **3** *Informal* kick. **4** *Slang* dismissal from employment. ♦ *v* **5** *Informal* kick. **6** start up (a computer). **bootee** *n* baby's soft shoe. **boot camp** centre for young offenders, with strict discipline and hard physical exercise.

boot[2] *n* **to boot** in addition.

booth *n* **1** small partly enclosed cubicle. **2** stall at a fair or market.

bootleg *adj* **1** produced, distributed, or sold illicitly. ♦ *v* **-legging, -legged 2** make, carry, or sell (illicit goods). **bootlegger** *n*

booty *n, pl* **-ties** valuable articles obtained as plunder.

booze *v, n Informal* (consume) alcoholic drink. **boozy** *adj* **boozer** *n Informal* **1** person who is fond of drinking. **2** pub. **booze-up** *n Informal* drinking spree.

bop *v* **bopping, bopped** *Informal* dance to pop music.

borage *n* Mediterranean plant with star-shaped blue flowers.

borax *n* white mineral used in making glass. **boracic** *adj*

Bordeaux *n* red or white wine from SW France.

border *n* **1** dividing line between political or geographical regions. **2** band around or along the edge of something. ♦ *v* **3** provide with a border. **4** be adjacent to. **5** be nearly the same as, e.g. *resentment that borders on hatred.*

bore[1] *v* **1** make (a hole) with a drill etc. ♦ *n* **2** hole or tunnel drilled in search of oil, minerals, etc. **3** (diameter of) the hollow of a gun barrel.

bore[2] *v* **1** make weary by being dull or repetitious. ♦ *n* **2** dull or repetitious person or thing. **bored** *adj* **boredom** *n*

> *Bored* is followed by *with* or *by*: *...bored by his conversation; ...bored with reading*. The usage *bored of* is not fully accepted.

bore[3] *n* high wave in a narrow estuary, caused by the tide.

bore[4] *v* past tense of BEAR[1].

boric *adj* of or containing boron. **boric acid** white soluble solid used as a mild antiseptic.

born *v* **1** a past participle of BEAR[1]. ♦ *adj* **2** possessing certain qualities from birth, e.g. *a born musician.*

born-again *adj* **1** having experienced conversion, esp. to evangelical Christianity. **2** showing the enthusiasm of someone newly converted to a cause, e.g. *a born-again romantic.*

borne *v* a past participle of BEAR[1].

boron *n Chem* element used in hardening steel.

borough *n* town or district with its own council.

borrow *v* **1** obtain (something) temporarily. **2** adopt (ideas etc.) from another source. **borrower** *n*

> *Borrow* is followed by *from*: *Borrow a pound from Frank*. The use of *borrow* followed by *off of* is nonstandard. Avoid confusing the meanings of *borrow* and *lend*.

borscht, borsch *n* Russian soup based on beetroot.

borstal *n* (formerly) prison for young criminals.

borzoi *n* tall dog with a long silky coat.

bosh *n Informal* empty talk, nonsense.

Bosnian *n, adj* (person) from Bosnia.

bosom *n* **1** chest of a person, esp. the female breasts. ♦ *adj* **2** very dear, e.g. *a bosom friend.*

boss[1] *n* **1** person in charge of or employing others. ♦ *v* **2 boss around, about** be domineering towards. **bossy** *adj* **bossier, bossiest**

boss[2] *n* raised knob or stud.

bosun *n* officer responsible for the maintenance of a ship.

bot. 1 botanical. **2** botany.

botany *n* study of plants. **botanical, botanic** *adj* **botanist** *n*

botch *v* **1** spoil through clumsiness. **2** repair badly. ♦ *n* **3** (also **botch-up**) badly done piece of work or repair.

both *adj, pron* two considered together.

> After *both* the use of *of* is optional: *both of the boys* or *both (the) boys.*

bother *v* **1** take the time or trouble. **2** give annoyance or trouble to. **3** pester. ♦ *n* **4** trouble, fuss, or difficulty. ♦ *interj* **5** *Chiefly Brit* exclamation of slight annoyance. **bothersome** *adj*

bothy *n, pl* **-ies** *Chiefly Scot* hut used for temporary shelter.

bottle *n* **1** container for holding liquids. **2** *Slang* courage. ♦ *v* **3** put in a bottle. **bottle bank** container into which people can throw glass bottles for recycling. **bottle-green** *adj* dark green. **bottleneck** *n* narrow stretch of road where traffic is held up. **bottle up** *v* restrain (powerful emotion).

bottom *n* **1** lowest, deepest, or farthest removed part of a thing. **2** least important or successful position. **3** ground underneath a sea, lake, or river. **4** buttocks. ♦ *adj* **5** lowest or last. **bottomless** *adj* **bottom out** *v* reach the lowest point and level out.

botulism *n* severe food poisoning.

bouclé *n* looped yarn giving a knobbly effect.

boudoir [**boo**-dwahr] *n* woman's bedroom or private sitting room.

bouffant [**boof**-fong] *adj* (of a hairstyle) having extra height through backcombing.

bougainvillea *n* climbing plant with red or purple flowers.

bough *n* large branch of a tree.

bought *v* past of BUY.

> Be careful not to confuse the past forms *bought* (from *buy*) with *brought* (from *bring*).

bouillon [**boo**-yon] *n* thin clear broth or stock.

boulder *n* large rounded rock.

boulevard *n* wide, usu. tree-lined, street.

bounce *v* **1** (of a ball etc.) rebound from an impact. **2** *Slang* (of a cheque) be returned uncashed owing to a lack of funds in the account. ♦ *n* **3** act of rebounding. **4** springiness. **5** *Informal* vitality or vigour. **bouncer** *n* person employed at a disco etc. to remove unwanted people. **bouncing** *adj* vigorous and robust. **bouncy** *adj* **bouncier, bounciest**

bound[1] *v* **1** past of BIND. ♦ *adj* **2** destined or certain. **3** compelled or obliged.

bound[2] *v* **1** move forwards by jumps. ♦ *n* **2** jump upwards or forwards.

bound[3] *v* **1** limit or place restrictions on. **2** form a boundary of. ♦ *pl n* **3** limit, e.g. *his ignorance knows no bounds* **boundary** *n, pl* **-aries** dividing line that indicates the farthest limit.

bound[4] *adj* going or intending to go towards, e.g. *homeward bound.*

bounder *n Old-fashioned Brit slang* morally reprehensible person.

bounty *n, pl* **-ties 1** generosity. **2** generous gift or reward. **bountiful, bounteous** *adj*

bouquet *n* **1** bunch of flowers. **2** aroma of wine. **bouquet garni** bunch of herbs tied together and used for flavouring soups etc.

bourbon [**bur**-bn] *n* whiskey made from maize.

bourgeois [**boor**-zhwah] *adj, n Offens* middle-class (person). **bourgeoisie** *n* middle classes.

bourn *n* (in S Britain) stream.

Bourse [**boorss**] *n* stock exchange, esp. of Paris.

bout *n* **1** period of activity or illness. **2** boxing or wrestling match.

boutique *n* small clothes shop.

bouzouki *n* Greek stringed musical instrument.

bovine *adj* **1** relating to cattle. **2** rather slow and stupid.

bow[1] [rhymes with **now**] *v* **1** lower (one's head) or bend (one's knee or body) as a sign of respect or shame. **2** comply or accept. ♦ *n* **3** movement made when bowing.

bow[2] [rhymes with **go**] *n* **1** knot with two loops and loose ends. **2** weapon for shooting arrows. **3** something curved, bent, or arched. **4** long stick stretched with horsehair for playing stringed instruments. **bow-legged** *adj* having legs that curve outwards at the knees. **bow window** curved bay window.

bow[3] [rhymes with **now**] *n* front end of a ship.

bowdlerize *v* remove words regarded as indecent from (a play, novel, etc.).

bowdlerization *n*
bowel *n* **1** intestine, esp. the large intestine. ♦ *pl* **2** innermost part.
bower *n* shady leafy shelter.
bowie knife *n* stout hunting knife.
bowl[1] *n* **1** round container with an open top. **2** hollow part of an object.
bowl[2] *n* **1** large heavy ball. ♦ *pl* **2** game played on smooth grass with wooden bowls. ♦ *v* **3** roll smoothly along the ground. **4** *Cricket* send (a ball) towards the batsman. **5** *Cricket* dismiss (a batsman) by delivering a ball that breaks his wicket. **6** play bowls. **bowler** *n* **bowling** *n* game in which bowls are rolled at a group of pins.
bowler *n* stiff felt hat with a rounded crown.
box[1] *n* **1** container with a firm flat base and sides. **2** separate compartment in a theatre, stable, etc. **3** place to which mail is sent and from which it is collected or redistributed, e.g. *a post-office box.* ♦ *v* **4** put into a box. **the box** *Informal* television. **boxy** *adj* **boxier, boxiest** squarish or chunky. **box in** *v* prevent from moving freely. **box junction** road junction marked with yellow lines which may only be entered if the exit is clear. **box lacrosse** *Canadian* lacrosse played indoors. **box office** place where theatre or cinema tickets are sold. **box pleat** flat double pleat.
box[2] *v* **1** fight (an opponent) in a boxing match. **2** hit (a person's ears) with the fist. **boxer** *n* **1** person who participates in the sport of boxing. **2** medium-sized dog with smooth hair and a short nose. **boxer shorts, boxers** *pl n* men's underpants shaped like shorts but with a front opening. **boxing** *n* sport of fighting with the fists.
box[3] *n* evergreen tree with shiny leaves.
Boxing Day *n* first weekday after Christmas.
boy *n* male child. **boyish** *adj* **boyhood** *n* **boyfriend** *n* male friend with whom a person is romantically or sexually involved.
boycott *v* **1** refuse to deal with (an organization or country). ♦ *n* **2** instance of boycotting.
BP blood pressure.
Br *Chem* bromine.
bra *n* woman's undergarment for supporting the breasts.
brace *n* **1** object fastened to something to straighten or support it. **2** pair, esp. of game birds. ♦ *pl* **3** straps worn over the shoulders to hold up trousers. ♦ *v* **4** steady or prepare (oneself) for something unpleasant. **5** strengthen or fit with a brace. **bracing** *adj* refreshing and invigorating.
bracelet *n* ornamental chain or band for the wrist.
bracken *n* large fern.
bracket *n* **1** pair of characters used to enclose a section of writing. **2** group falling within certain defined limits. **3** support fixed to a wall. ♦ *v* **-eting, -eted 4** put in brackets. **5** class together.
brackish *adj* (of water) slightly salty.
bract *n* leaf at the base of a flower.
bradawl *n* small boring tool.
brae *n Scot* hill or slope.
brag *v* **bragging, bragged 1** speak arrogantly and boastfully. ♦ *n* **2** boastful talk or behaviour. **3** card game similar to poker. **braggart** *n* person who boasts loudly.
Brahma *n* Hindu god, the Creator. **Brahman, Brahmin** *n* member of the highest Hindu caste.
braid *v* **1** interweave (hair, thread, etc.). ♦ *n* **2** length of hair etc. that has been braided. **3** narrow ornamental tape of woven silk etc.
Braille *n* system of writing for the blind, consisting of raised dots interpreted by touch.
brain *n* **1** soft mass of nervous tissue in the head. **2** intellectual ability. ♦ *v* **3** hit (someone) hard on the head. **brainless** *adj* stupid. **brainy** *adj* **brainier, brainiest** *Informal* clever. **brainchild** *n* idea produced by creative thought. **brain-dead** *adj* **1** having suffered irreversible stoppage of breathing due to brain damage. **2** *Informal* not using or show-

ing intelligence. **brainstorm** *n* sudden mental aberration. **brainwash** *v* cause (a person) to alter his or her beliefs, esp. by methods based on isolation, sleeplessness, etc. **brainwave** *n* sudden idea.

braise *v* cook slowly in a covered pan with a little liquid.

brake[1] *n* **1** device for slowing or stopping a vehicle. ♦ *v* **2** slow down or stop by using a brake. **brake horsepower** rate at which an engine does work. **brake light** red light at the rear of a motor vehicle that comes on when the brakes are applied.

brake[2] *n* area of dense undergrowth.

bramble *n* **1** prickly shrub that produces blackberries. **2** *Scot* blackberry.

bran *n* husks of cereal grain.

branch *n* **1** secondary stem of a tree. **2** offshoot or subsidiary part of something larger or more complex. ♦ *v* **3** (of stems, roots, etc.) divide, then develop in different directions. **branch out** *v* expand one's interests.

brand *n* **1** particular product. **2** particular kind or variety. **3** identifying mark burnt onto the skin of an animal. **4** *Lit* burning piece of wood. ♦ *v* **5** mark with a brand. **6** denounce as being, e.g. *he was branded a fascist.* **brand-new** *adj* absolutely new.

brandish *v* wave (a weapon etc.) in a threatening way.

brandy *n, pl* **-dies** alcoholic spirit distilled from wine. **brandy snap** tube-shaped crisp sweet biscuit.

brash *adj* offensively loud, showy, or self-confident. **brashness** *n*

brass *n* **1** alloy of copper and zinc. **2** family of wind instruments made of brass. **3** engraved brass memorial tablet in a church. **4** *N English dialect* money. **5** *Informal* bold self-confidence. **brassy** *adj* **brassier, brassiest 1** brazen or flashy. **2** like brass, esp. in colour. **brass hat** *Informal* top-ranking military officer.

brasserie *n* restaurant serving drinks and cheap meals.

brassica *n* any plant of the cabbage and turnip family.

brassiere *n* bra.

brat *n* unruly child.

bravado *n* showy display of self-confidence.

brave *adj* **1** having or showing courage, resolution, and daring. **2** splendid. ♦ *n* **3** Native American warrior. ♦ *v* **4** confront with resolution or courage. **bravery** *n*

bravo *interj* well done!

bravura *n* **1** display of boldness or daring. **2** *Music* brilliance of execution.

brawl *n* **1** noisy fight. ♦ *v* **2** fight noisily.

brawn *n* **1** physical strength. **2** pressed meat from the head of a pig or calf. **brawny** *adj*

bray *v* **1** (of a donkey) utter its loud harsh sound. ♦ *n* **2** donkey's loud harsh sound.

braze *v* join (two metal surfaces) with brass.

brazen *adj* **1** shameless and bold. ♦ *v* **2 brazen it out** overcome a difficult situation boldly or shamelessly. **brazenly** *adv*

brazier [**bray**-zee-er] *n* portable container for burning charcoal or coal.

brazil nut *n* large three-sided nut of a tropical American tree.

breach *n* **1** breaking of a promise, obligation, etc. **2** serious quarrel or separation. **3** gap or break. ♦ *v* **4** break (a promise, law, etc.). **5** make a gap in.

bread *n* **1** food made by baking a mixture of flour and water or milk. **2** *Slang* money. **breadwinner** *n* person whose earnings support a family.

breadline *n* **on the breadline** living at subsistence level.

breadth *n* **1** extent of something from side to side. **2** lack of restriction, esp. of viewpoint or interest.

break *v* **breaking, broke, broken 1** separate or become separated into two or more pieces. **2** damage or become damaged so as to be inoperative. **3** fail to observe (an agreement etc.). **4** disclose or be disclosed, e.g. *he broke the news.* **5** bring or come to an end, e.g. *the good weather broke at last.* **6** weaken or be weakened, as in spirit. **7** cut through or penetrate, e.g. *silence broken by shouts.* **8** improve on or surpass, e.g. *break a record.* **9** accustom (a horse) to being ridden. **10** (of the male voice) become permanently deeper at puberty. ♦ *n* **11** act or result of breaking. **12** gap or interruption in continuity. **13** sudden rush, esp. to escape. **14** *Informal* fortunate opportunity. **15** *Billiards, snooker* series of successful shots during one turn. **break even** make neither a profit nor a loss. **breakable** *adj* **breakage** *n* **breaker** *n* large wave. **breakaway** *adj, n* (consisting of) a dissenting group who have left a larger unit. **break down** *v* **1** cease to function. **2** yield to strong emotion. **3** decompose or separate into component parts. **breakdown** *n* **1** act or instance of breaking down. **2** nervous breakdown. **3** separation of something into its component parts. **break-in** *n* illegal entering of a building, esp. by thieves. **break into** *v* start doing, esp. suddenly, e.g. *she broke into song.* **breakneck** *adj* fast and dangerous. **break off** *v* **1** sever or detach. **2** end (a relationship etc.). **break out** *v* begin or arise suddenly. **breakthrough** *n* important development or discovery. **break up** *v* **1** (cause to) separate. **2** come to an end. **3** (of a school) close for the holidays. **breakwater** *n* wall that extends into the sea to protect a harbour or beach from the force of waves.

breakfast *v, n* (eat) the first meal of the day.

bream *n* freshwater silvery fish.

breast *n* **1** either of the two soft fleshy milk-secreting glands on a woman's chest. **2** chest. **3** source of human emotions. ♦ *v* **4** *Lit* reach the summit of. **breastbone** *n* long flat bone in the front of the body, to which most of the ribs are attached. **breast-feed** *v* feed (a baby) with milk from the breast. **breaststroke** *n* swimming stroke in which the arms are extended in front of the head and swept back on either side.

breath *n* **1** taking in and letting out of air during breathing. **2** air taken in and let out during breathing. **3** slight gust of air. **breathless** *adj* **breathtaking** *adj* causing awe or excitement. **breathe** *v* **1** take in oxygen and give out carbon dioxide. **2** be alive. **3** whisper. **4** impart or instil, e.g. *the move breathed new life into his career.* **breather** *n Informal* short rest. **breathing** *n*

Breathalyser *n* ® device for estimating the amount of alcohol in the breath. **breathalyse** *v*

bred *v* past of BREED.

breech *n* **1** buttocks. **2** part of a firearm behind the barrel. **breech birth, breech delivery** birth of a baby with the feet or buttocks appearing first.

breeches *pl n* trousers extending to just below the knee.

breed *v* **breeding, bred 1** produce new or improved strains of (domestic animals or plants). **2** bear (offspring). **3** bring up, e.g. *he was born and bred in Hull.* **4** produce or be produced, e.g. *breed trouble.* ♦ *n* **5** group of animals etc. within a species that have certain clearly defined characteristics. **6** kind or sort. **breeder** *n* **breeder reactor** nuclear reactor that produces more fissionable material than it uses. **breeding** *n* result of good upbringing or training.

breeze *n* **1** gentle wind. ♦ *v* **2** move quickly or casually. **breezy** *adj* **breezier, breeziest 1** windy. **2** casual or carefree.

breeze block *n* light building brick made of ashes bonded by cement.

Bren gun *n* gas-operated light machine gun.

brent *n* small goose with a dark grey plumage.

brethren *pl n Old-fashioned* (used in religious contexts) brothers.

Breton *adj* **1** of Brittany. ♦ *n* **2** person from Brittany. **3** language of Brittany.

breviary *n, pl* **-aries** book of prayers to be recited daily by a Roman Catholic priest.

brevity *n* shortness.

brew *v* **1** make (beer etc.) by steeping,

boiling, and fermentation. **2** prepare (a drink) by infusing. **3** be about to happen or forming, e.g. *trouble was brewing.* ♦ *n* **4** beverage produced by brewing. **brewer** *n* **brewery** *n, pl* **-ries** place where beer etc. is brewed.

briar[1], **brier** *n* **1** European shrub with a hard woody root. **2** tobacco pipe made from this root.

briar[2] *n* same as BRIER[1].

bribe *v* **1** offer or give something to someone to gain favour, influence, etc. ♦ *n* **2** something given or offered as a bribe. **bribery** *n*

bric-a-brac *n* miscellaneous small ornamental objects.

brick *n* **1** (rectangular block of) baked clay used in building. ♦ *v* **2** (foll. by *up* or *over*) build, enclose, or fill with bricks. **brickbat** *n* blunt criticism. **bricklayer** *n* person who builds with bricks.

bride *n* woman who has just been or is about to be married. **bridal** *adj* **bridegroom** *n* man who has just been or is about to be married. **bridesmaid** *n* girl who attends a bride at her wedding.

bridge[1] *n* **1** structure for crossing a river etc. **2** platform from which a ship is steered or controlled. **3** upper part of the nose. **4** dental plate with artificial teeth that is secured to natural teeth. **5** piece of wood supporting the strings of a violin etc. ♦ *v* **6** build a bridge over (something). **7** connect or reduce the distance between. **bridgehead** *n* fortified position at the end of a bridge nearest the enemy. **bridging loan** loan made to cover the period between two transactions.

bridge[2] *n* card game based on whist, played between two pairs.

bridle *n* **1** headgear for controlling a horse. **2** something that curbs or restrains. ♦ *v* **3** show anger or indignation. **4** put a bridle on (a horse). **bridle path** path suitable for riding horses.

Brie [**bree**] *n* soft creamy white cheese.

brief *adj* **1** short in duration. **2** concise. ♦ *n* **3** condensed statement or written synopsis. **4** (also **briefing**) set of instructions. ♦ *pl* **5** men's or women's underpants. ♦ *v* **6** give information and instructions to (a person). **briefly** *adv* **briefcase** *n* small flat case for carrying papers, books, etc.

brier[1], **briar** *n* wild rose with long thorny stems.

brier[2] *n* same as BRIAR[1].

brig *n* two-masted square-rigged ship.

Brig. Brigadier.

brigade *n* **1** army unit smaller than a division. **2** group of people organized for a certain task. **brigadier** *n* high-ranking army officer.

brigand *n* bandit.

brigantine *n* two-masted sailing ship.

bright *adj* **1** emitting or reflecting much light. **2** (of colours) intense. **3** full of promise. **4** lively or cheerful. **5** clever. **brightly** *adv* **brightness** *n* **brighten** *v*

brill *n* edible European flatfish.

brilliant *adj* **1** shining with light. **2** (of a colour) vivid. **3** splendid. **4** extremely clever. ♦ *n* **5** diamond cut so as to increase its sparkle. **brilliance, brilliancy** *n*

brilliantine *n* perfumed hair oil.

brim *n* **1** upper rim of a cup etc. **2** projecting edge of a hat. ♦ *v* **brimming, brimmed 3** be full to the brim.

brimstone *n Obs* sulphur.

brindled *adj* brown or grey streaked with a darker colour.

brine *n* salt water. **briny** *adj* very salty. **the briny** *Informal* the sea.

bring *v* **bringing, brought 1** carry, convey, or take to a designated place or person. **2** cause to happen. **3** *Law* put forward (charges) officially. **bring about** *v* cause to happen. **bring off** *v* succeed in achieving. **bring out** *v* **1** publish or have (a book) published. **2** reveal or cause to be seen. **bring up** *v* **1** rear (a child). **2** mention. **3** vomit (food).

brink *n* edge of a steep place. **on the brink of** very near. **brinkmanship** *n* pressing of a dangerous situation to the limit of safety in order to win an advantage.

briquette *n* block of compressed coal dust.

brisk *adj* **1** lively and quick. **2** invigorating or sharp, e.g. *a brisk breeze.* **3** practical and businesslike. **briskly** *adv*

brisket *n* beef from the breast of a cow.

bristle *n* **1** short stiff hair. ♦ *v* **2** (cause to) stand up like bristles. **3** show anger. **bristly** *adj* **bristlier, bristliest**

Brit *n Informal* British person.

Brit. **1** Britain. **2** British.

Britannia *n* female warrior personifying Great Britain.

Britannic *adj* of Britain, esp. in *Her Britannic Majesty.*

British *adj* **1** of Great Britain or the British Commonwealth. ♦ *pl n* **2** people of Great Britain.

Briton *n* native or inhabitant of Britain.

brittle *adj* hard but easily broken. **brittleness** *n*

broach *v* **1** introduce (a topic) for discussion. **2** open (a bottle or barrel).

broad *adj* **1** having great breadth or width. **2** not detailed. **3** extensive, e.g. *broad support.* **4** obvious, e.g. *broad hints.* **5** strongly marked, e.g. *a broad Bristol accent.* ♦ *n* **6** *Slang chiefly US* woman. **broadly** *adv* **broaden** *v* **broad bean** thick flat edible bean. **broad-leaved** *adj* (of trees) having broad rather than needle-shaped leaves. **broad-minded** *adj* tolerant. **broadsheet** *n* newspaper in a large format. **broadside** *n* **1** strong verbal or written attack. **2** *Naval* firing of all the guns on one side of a ship at once.

B-road *n* secondary road in Britain.

broadcast *n* **1** programme or announcement on radio or television. ♦ *v* **2** transmit (a programme or announcement) on radio or television. **3** make widely known. **4** scatter (seed etc.). **broadcaster** *n* **broadcasting** *n*

brocade *n* rich fabric woven with a raised design.

broccoli *n* type of cabbage with greenish flower heads.

brochure *n* booklet that contains information about a product or service.

broderie anglaise *n* open embroidery on white cotton etc.

brogue[1] *n* sturdy walking shoe.

brogue[2] *n* strong accent, esp. Irish.

broil *v Aust, NZ, US & Canadian* same as GRILL. **broiler** *n* young tender chicken for roasting.

broke *v* **1** past tense of BREAK. ♦ *adj* **2** *Informal* having no money.

broken *v* **1** past participle of BREAK. ♦ *adj* **2** fractured or smashed. **3** (of the speech of a foreigner) noticeably imperfect, e.g. *broken English.* **broken-hearted** *adj* overwhelmed by grief. **broken home** family where the parents are separated or divorced.

broker *n* agent who buys or sells goods, securities, etc. **brokerage** *n* commission charged by a broker.

brolly *n, pl* **-lies** *Informal* umbrella.

bromide *n* **1** chemical compound used in medicine and photography. **2** boring or meaningless remark.

bromine *n Chem* dark red liquid element that gives off a pungent vapour.

bronchus [**bronk**-uss] *n, pl* **bronchi** [**bronk**-eye] either of the two branches of the windpipe. **bronchial** *adj* **bronchitis** *n* inflammation of the bronchi.

bronco *n, pl* **-cos** (in the US) wild or partially tamed pony.

brontosaurus *n* very large plant-eating four-footed dinosaur.

bronze *n* **1** alloy of copper and tin. **2** statue, medal, etc. made of bronze. ♦ *adj* **3** made of, or coloured like, bronze. ♦ *v* **4** (esp. of the skin) make or become brown. **Bronze Age** era when bronze tools and weapons were used. **bronze medal** medal awarded as third prize.

brooch *n* ornament with a pin, worn fastened to clothes.

brood *n* **1** number of birds produced at one hatching. **2** all the children of a family. ♦ *v* **3** (of a bird) sit on or hatch eggs. **4** think long and unhappily. **broody** *adj* **1** moody and sullen. **2** (of a hen) wishing to hatch eggs. **3** *Informal* (of a woman) wishing to have a baby.

brook[1] *n* small stream.
brook[2] *v* bear or tolerate.
broom *n* **1** long-handled sweeping brush. **2** yellow-flowered shrub. **broomstick** *n* handle of a broom.
bros., Bros. brothers.
broth *n* soup, usu. containing vegetables.
brothel *n* house where men pay to have sex with prostitutes.
brother *n* **1** boy or man with the same parents as another person. **2** close friend or comrade. **3** member of a male religious order. **brotherly** *adj* **brotherhood** *n* **1** fellowship. **2** association, such as a trade union. **brother-in-law** *n, pl* **brothers-in-law 1** brother of one's husband or wife. **2** husband of one's sister.
brought *v* past of BRING.
brouhaha *n* loud confused noise.
brow *n* **1** part of the face from the eyes to the hairline. **2** eyebrow. **3** top of a hill.
browbeat *v* frighten (someone) with threats.
brown *n* **1** colour of earth or wood. ♦ *adj* **2** (of bread) made from wheatmeal or wholemeal flour. **3** of the colour brown. ♦ *v* **4** make or become brown. **brownish** *adj* **browned-off** *adj Informal* bored and depressed.
brownie *n* **1** elf said to do household chores at night. **2** small square nutty chocolate cake.
Brownie Guide, Brownie *n* junior Guide. **Brownie point** credit for being seen to do the right thing.
browse *v* **1** look through (a book or articles for sale) in a casual manner. **2** nibble on young shoots or leaves. ♦ *n* **3** instance of browsing.
brucellosis *n* infectious disease of animals which can be transmitted to humans.
bruise *n* **1** discoloured area on the skin caused by an injury. ♦ *v* **2** cause a bruise on. **bruiser** *n* strong tough person.
brunch *n Informal* breakfast and lunch combined.
brunette *n* girl or woman with dark brown hair.
brunt *n* main force or shock of a blow, attack, etc.
brush[1] *n* **1** device made of bristles, wires, etc. used for cleaning, painting, etc. **2** brief unpleasant encounter. **3** fox's tail. ♦ *v* **4** clean, scrub, or paint with a brush. **5** touch lightly and briefly. **brush off** *v Slang* dismiss or ignore (someone). **brush up** *v* refresh one's knowledge of (a subject).
brush[2] *n* thick growth of shrubs. **brushwood** *n* cut or broken-off tree branches and twigs.
brusque *adj* blunt or curt in manner or speech. **brusquely** *adv* **brusqueness** *n*
Brussels sprout *n* vegetable like a tiny cabbage.
brute *n* **1** brutal person. **2** animal other than man. ♦ *adj* **3** wholly instinctive or physical, like an animal. **4** without reason. **brutish** *adj* of or like an animal. **brutal** *adj* **1** cruel and vicious. **2** extremely honest in speech or manner. **brutally** *adv* **brutality** *n* **brutalize** *v*
bryony *n* wild climbing hedge plant.
BSc Bachelor of Science.
BSE bovine spongiform encephalopathy: fatal virus disease of cattle.
BSI British Standards Institution.
BST British Summer Time.
Bt Baronet.
bubble *n* **1** ball of air in a liquid or solid. **2** thin film of liquid forming a ball around air or a gas. **3** transparent dome. **4** something initially very pleasing or successful which suddenly disappears or goes wrong. ♦ *v* **5** form bubbles. **6** move or flow with a gurgling sound. **bubbly** *adj* **-blier, -bliest 1** excited and lively. **2** full of bubbles. ♦ *n* **3** *Informal* champagne. **bubble over** *v* express an emotion freely.
bubonic plague [bew-**bonn**-ik] *n* acute infectious disease characterized by swellings.
buccaneer *n* pirate.
buck[1] *n* **1** male of the goat, hare, kangaroo, rabbit, and reindeer. ♦ *v* **2** (of a horse etc.) jump with legs stiff and back

arched. **3** *Informal* resist or oppose obstinately, e.g. *to buck a trend.* **buckshot** *n* large lead pellets used for shooting game. **buck up** *v* make or become more cheerful.

buck[2] *n US, Canadian & Aust slang* dollar.

buck[3] *n* **pass the buck** *Informal* shift blame or responsibility onto someone else.

bucket *n* **1** open-topped round container with a handle. ♦ *v* **-eting, -eted 2** (also **bucket down**) rain heavily. **kick the bucket** *Slang* die. **bucketful** *n*

buckle *n* **1** clasp for fastening a belt or strap. ♦ *v* **2** fasten or be fastened with a buckle. **3** (cause to) bend out of shape through pressure or heat. **buckle down** *v Informal* apply oneself with determination.

buckshee *adj Slang* free.

buckteeth *pl n* projecting upper front teeth. **buck-toothed** *adj*

buckwheat *n* small black grain used for making flour.

bucolic [bew-**koll**-ik] *adj* of the countryside or country life.

bud *n* **1** swelling on a tree or plant that develops into a leaf or flower. **2** partially opened flower. ♦ *v* **budding, budded 3** produce buds. **budding** *adj* beginning to develop or grow, e.g. *a budding actor.*

Buddhism *n* eastern religion founded by Buddha. **Buddhist** *n, adj*

buddleia *n* shrub with long spikes of purple flowers.

buddy *n, pl* **-dies** *Informal* friend.

budge *v* **1** move slightly. **2** change (an opinion).

budgerigar *n* small cage bird bred in many different-coloured varieties.

budget *n* **1** financial plan for a period of time. **2** money allocated for a specific purpose. ♦ *v* **-eting, -eted 3** plan the expenditure of (money or time). ♦ *adj* **4** cheap. **the Budget** statement of government's financial plans for the coming year. **budgetary** *adj*

budgie *n Informal* short for BUDGERIGAR.

buff[1] *n* **1** soft flexible undyed leather. ♦ *adj* **2** dull yellowish-brown. ♦ *v* **3** clean or polish with soft material. **in the buff** *Informal* naked.

buff[2] *n Informal* expert on or devotee of a given subject.

buffalo *n* **1** type of cattle. **2** *US* bison.

buffer[1] *n* something that lessens shock or protects from damaging impact, circumstances, etc. **buffer state** small state between two rival powers.

buffer[2] *n Brit informal* stupid or bumbling man.

buffet[1] [**boof**-ay] *n* **1** counter where drinks and snacks are served. **2** meal at which guests serve themselves from a range of dishes.

buffet[2] [**buff**-it] *v* **-feting, -feted 1** knock against or about. **2** hit, esp. with the fist. ♦ *n* **3** blow, esp. with the hand.

buffoon *n* clown or fool. **buffoonery** *n*

bug *n* **1** small insect. **2** *Informal* minor illness. **3** small mistake in a computer program. **4** concealed microphone. ♦ *v* **bugging, bugged 5** *Informal* irritate (someone). **6** conceal a microphone in (a room or phone).

bugbear *n* thing that causes obsessive anxiety.

bugger *n* **1** *Taboo slang* unpleasant or difficult person or thing. **2** *Slang* any person, e.g. *poor old bugger.* **3** person who practises buggery. ♦ *v* **4** *Slang* tire. **5** practise buggery with. **bugger off** *v Taboo slang* go away. **buggery** *n* anal intercourse.

buggy *n, pl* **-gies 1** light horse-drawn carriage having two or four wheels. **2** lightweight folding pram.

bugle *n* instrument like a small trumpet. **bugler** *n*

build *v* **building, built 1** make, construct, or form by joining parts or materials. **2** establish and develop. ♦ *n* **3** shape of the body. **builder** *n* **building** *n* structure with walls and a roof. **building society** organization where money can be borrowed or invested. **build-up** *n* gradual increase. **build up** *v* construct or establish gradually.

built *v* past of BUILD. **built-in** *adj* incorporated as an integral part. **built-up** *adj* having many buildings.

bulb *n* **1** same as LIGHT BULB. **2** onion-shaped root which grows into a flower or plant. **bulbous** *adj* round and fat.

bulge *n* **1** swelling on a normally flat surface. **2** sudden increase in number. ♦ *v* **3** swell outwards. **bulging** *adj*

bulimia *n* disorder characterized by compulsive overeating followed by vomiting.

bulk *n* **1** size or volume, esp. when great. **2** main part. ♦ *v* **3 bulk large** be or seem important. **in bulk** in large quantities. **bulky** *adj*

bulkhead *n* partition in a ship or aeroplane.

bull[1] *n* male of some animals, such as cattle, elephants, and whales. **bullock** *n* castrated bull. **bulldog** *n* thickset dog with a broad head and a muscular body. **bulldozer** *n* powerful tractor for moving earth. **bulldoze** *v* **1** demolish or flatten with a bulldozer. **2** *Informal* achieve (something) or persuade (someone) by intimidation, e.g. *the new law was bulldozed through parliament.* **bullfight** *n* public show in which a matador kills a bull. **bullfinch** *n* common European songbird. **bullfrog** *n* large American frog with a deep croak. **bull's-eye** *n* central disc of a target. **bull terrier** terrier with a short smooth coat.

bull[2] *n Informal* complete nonsense.

bull[3] *n* papal decree.

bullet *n* small piece of metal fired from a gun.

bulletin *n* short official report or announcement.

bullion *n* gold or silver in the form of bars.

bully *n, pl* **-lies 1** person who hurts, persecutes, or intimidates a weaker person. ♦ *v* **-lying, -lied 2** hurt, intimidate, or persecute (a weaker person).

bully beef *n* canned corned beef.

bully-off *n Hockey* method of restarting play in which opposing players strike their sticks together before trying to hit the ball. **bully off** *v Hockey* restart play with a bully-off.

bulrush *n* tall stiff reed.

bulwark *n* **1** wall used as a fortification. **2** person or thing acting as a defence.

bum[1] *n Slang* buttocks or anus. **bumbag** *n* small bag attached to a belt and worn round the waist.

bum[2] *Informal* ♦ *n* **1** disreputable idler. **2** *US* tramp or hobo. ♦ *v* **bumming, bummed 3** get by begging. ♦ *adj* **4** of poor quality.

bumble *v* speak, do, or move in a clumsy way. **bumbling** *adj, n*

bumblebee *n* large hairy bee.

bumf, bumph *n Informal* official documents or forms.

bump *v* **1** knock or strike with a jolt. **2** travel in jerks and jolts. ♦ *n* **3** dull thud from an impact or collision. **4** lump on the body caused by a blow. **5** raised uneven part. **bumpy** *adj* **bumpier, bumpiest bump into** *v Informal* meet (someone) by chance. **bump off** *v Informal* murder.

bumper[1] *n* bar on the front and back of a vehicle to protect against damage.

bumper[2] *n* **1** glass filled to the brim. ♦ *adj* **2** unusually large or abundant.

bumph *n* same as BUMF.

bumpkin *n* awkward simple country person.

bumptious *adj* offensively self-assertive.

bun *n* **1** small sweet bread roll or cake. **2** hair gathered into a bun shape at the back of the head.

bunch *n* **1** number of things growing, fastened, or grouped together. **2** group, e.g. *a bunch of cowards.* ♦ *v* **3** group or be grouped together in a bunch.

bundle *n* **1** number of things gathered loosely together. ♦ *v* **2** cause to go roughly or unceremoniously. **bundle up** *v* make into a bundle.

bung *n* **1** stopper for a cask etc. ♦ *v* **2** (foll. by *up*) *Informal* close with a bung. **3** *Slang* throw (something) somewhere in a careless manner.

bungalow *n* one-storey house.

bungee jumping, bungy jumping *n* sport of leaping from a high bridge, tower, etc., to which one is connected by a rubber rope.

bungle *v* **1** spoil through incompetence. ♦ *n* **2** blunder or muddle. **bungler** *n* **bungling** *adj, n*

bunion *n* inflamed swelling on the big toe.

bunk[1] *n* narrow shelflike bed. **bunk bed** one of a pair of beds constructed one above the other.

bunk[2] *n* same as BUNKUM.

bunk[3] *n* **do a bunk** *Slang* make a hurried and secret departure.

bunker *n* **1** sand-filled hollow forming an obstacle on a golf course. **2** underground shelter. **3** large storage container for coal etc.

bunkum *n* nonsense.

bunny *n, pl* **-nies** child's word for a rabbit.

Bunsen burner *n* gas burner used in laboratories.

bunting[1] *n* decorative flags.

bunting[2] *n* songbird with a short stout bill.

buoy *n* **1** floating marker anchored in the sea. ♦ *v* **2** prevent from sinking. **3** encourage or hearten. **buoyant** *adj* **1** able to float. **2** cheerful or resilient. **buoyancy** *n*

bur *n* same as BURR[1].

burble *v* **1** make a bubbling sound. **2** talk quickly and excitedly.

burden[1] *n* **1** heavy load. **2** something difficult to cope with. ♦ *v* **3** put a burden on. **4** oppress. **burdensome** *adj*

burden[2] *n* **1** theme of a speech etc. **2** chorus of a song.

burdock *n* weed with prickly burrs.

bureau *n, pl* **-reaus, -reaux** **1** office that provides a service. **2** writing desk with shelves and drawers.

bureaucracy *n, pl* **-cies** **1** administrative system based on complex rules and procedures. **2** excessive adherence to complex procedures. **bureaucrat** *n* **bureaucratic** *adj*

burette *n* glass tube for dispensing known volumes of fluids.

burgeon *v* develop or grow rapidly.

burger *n Informal* hamburger.

burgess *n* citizen or freeman of a borough.

burgh *n* Scottish borough. **burgher** *n* citizen.

burglar *n* person who enters a building to commit a crime, esp. theft. **burglary** *n, pl* **-ries** **burgle** *v*

Burgundy *n* type of French wine. **burgundy** *adj* dark-purplish red.

burial *n* burying of a dead body.

burlesque *n* artistic work which satirizes a subject by caricature.

burly *adj* **-lier, -liest** (of a person) broad and strong.

burn[1] *v* **burning, burnt** *or* **burned** **1** be or set on fire. **2** destroy or be destroyed by fire. **3** damage, injure, or mark by heat. **4** feel strong emotion. ♦ *n* **5** injury or mark caused by fire or exposure to heat. **burner** *n* part of a stove or lamp that produces the flame. **burning** *adj* **1** intense. **2** urgent or crucial.

> Either *burnt* or *burned* may be used as a past form.

burn[2] *n Scot* small stream.

burnish *v* make smooth and shiny by rubbing.

burnous *n* long circular cloak with a hood, worn esp. by Arabs.

burnt *v* a past of BURN[1].

burp *v, n Informal* belch.

burr[1] *n* head of a plant with prickles or hooks.

burr[2] *n* **1** soft trilling sound given to the letter *r* in some dialects. **2** whirring sound. **3** rough edge left after cutting.

burrow *n* **1** hole dug in the ground by a rabbit etc. ♦ *v* **2** dig holes in the ground. **3** delve deeply, e.g. *he burrowed into his coat pocket.*

bursar *n* treasurer of a school, college, or university. **bursary** *n, pl* **-ries** scholarship.

burst *v* **bursting, burst** **1** (cause to) break open or apart noisily and suddenly. **2** come or go suddenly and forcibly. **3** be full to the point of breaking open.

♦ *n* **4** instance of breaking open suddenly. **5** sudden outbreak or occurrence. **burst into** *v* give vent to (an emotion) suddenly.

bury *v* **burying, buried 1** place in a grave. **2** place in the earth and cover with soil. **3** conceal or hide. **4** occupy (oneself) with deep concentration.

bus *n* **1** large motor vehicle for carrying passengers. ♦ *v* **bussing, bussed 2** travel or transport by bus.

busby *n, pl* **-bies** tall fur hat worn by some soldiers.

bush *n* **1** dense woody plant, smaller than a tree. **2** wild uncultivated part of a country. **bushy** *adj* **bushier, bushiest** (of hair) thick and shaggy. **bushbaby** *n* small African tree-living mammal with large eyes. **Bushman** *n* member of a hunting and gathering people of Southern Africa. **bush telegraph** means of spreading gossip.

bushel *n* obsolete unit of measure equal to 8 gallons.

business *n* **1** purchase and sale of goods and services. **2** commercial establishment. **3** trade or profession. **4** proper concern or responsibility. **5** affair, e.g. *it's a dreadful business.* **businesslike** *adj* efficient and methodical. **businessman, businesswoman** *n*

busker *n* street entertainer. **busk** *v* act as a busker.

bust[1] *n* **1** woman's bosom. **2** sculpture of the head and shoulders.

bust[2] *Informal* ♦ *v* **busting, bust** *or* **busted 1** burst or break. **2** (of the police) raid (a place) or arrest (someone). ♦ *adj* **3** broken. **go bust** become bankrupt. **bust-up** *n Informal* **1** serious quarrel. **2** brawl or disturbance.

bustle[1] *v* **1** hurry with a show of activity or energy. ♦ *n* **2** energetic and noisy activity. **bustling** *adj*

bustle[2] *n* cushion or framework formerly worn under the back of a woman's skirt to hold it out.

busy *adj* **busier, busiest 1** actively employed. **2** crowded or full of activity. ♦ *v* **busying, busied 3** keep (someone, esp. oneself) busy. **busily** *adv* **busybody** *n* meddlesome or nosy person.

but *conj* **1** contrary to expectation. **2** in contrast. **3** other than. **4** without it happening. ♦ *prep* **5** except. ♦ *adv* **6** only. **but for** were it not for.

butane [**bew**-tane] *n* gas used for fuel.

butch *adj Slang* markedly or aggressively masculine.

butcher *n* **1** person who slaughters animals or sells their meat. **2** brutal murderer. ♦ *v* **3** kill and prepare (animals) for meat. **4** kill (people) brutally or indiscriminately. **5** make a mess of. **butchery** *n*

butler *n* chief male servant.

butt[1] *n* **1** thicker end of something. **2** unused end of a cigar or cigarette. **3** *Chiefly US & Canadian slang* buttocks.

butt[2] *n* **1** person or thing that is the target of ridicule. **2** mound of earth behind a target. ♦ *pl* **3** target range.

butt[3] *v* **1** strike with the head or horns. ♦ *n* **2** blow with the head or horns. **butt in** *v* interrupt a conversation.

butt[4] *n* large cask.

butter *n* **1** edible fatty solid made by churning cream. ♦ *v* **2** put butter on. **buttery** *adj* **butter up** *v* flatter.

butter bean *n* large pale flat edible bean.

buttercup *n* small yellow flower.

butterfingers *n Informal* person who drops things by mistake.

butterfly *n* **1** insect with brightly coloured wings. **2** swimming stroke in which both arms move together in a forward circular action.

buttermilk *n* sourish milk that remains after the butter has been separated from milk.

butterscotch *n* kind of hard brittle toffee.

buttock *n* either of the two fleshy masses that form the human rump.

button *n* **1** small disc or knob sewn to clothing, which can be passed through a slit in another piece of fabric to fasten them. **2** knob that operates a piece of equipment when pressed. ♦ *v* **3** fasten with buttons. **buttonhole** *n* **1** slit in a garment through which a button is passed. **2** flower worn on a lapel. ♦ *v* **3** detain (someone) in conversation.

buttress *n* **1** structure to support a wall. ♦ *v* **2** support with, or as if with, a buttress.

buxom *adj* (of a woman) healthily plump and full-bosomed.

buy *v* **buying, bought 1** acquire by paying money for. **2** be capable of purchasing, e.g. *money can't buy love.* **3** acquire by any exchange or sacrifice. **4** *Slang* accept as true. **5** bribe. ♦ *n* **6** thing acquired through payment. **buyer** *n* **1** customer. **2** person employed to buy merchandise.

> Be careful not to confuse the past forms *bought* (from *buy*) with *brought* (from *bring*).

buzz *n* **1** rapidly vibrating humming sound. **2** *Informal* telephone call. **3** *Informal* sense of excitement. ♦ *v* **4** make a humming sound. **5** be filled with an air of excitement. **6** *Informal* fly an aircraft very low over. **buzzer** *n* **buzz around** *v* move around quickly and busily. **buzz word** jargon word which becomes fashionably popular.

buzzard *n* bird of prey of the hawk family.

by *prep* **1** indicating the doer of an action, nearness, movement past, time before or during which, etc., e.g. *bitten by a dog; down by the river; driving by the school; in bed by midnight.* ♦ *adv* **2** near. **3** past. **by and by** eventually. **by and large** in general.

bye[1] *n* **1** *Sport* situation where a player or team wins a round by having no opponent. **2** *Cricket* run scored off a ball not touched by the batsman.

bye[2], **bye-bye** *interj Informal* goodbye.

by-election *n* election held during parliament to fill a vacant seat.

bygone *adj* **1** past or former. ♦ *pl n* **2 let bygones be bygones** agree to forget past quarrels.

bylaw, bye-law *n* rule made by a local authority.

by-line *n* line under the title of a newspaper or magazine article giving the author's name.

bypass *n* **1** main road built to avoid a city. **2** operation to divert blood flow away from a damaged part of the heart. ♦ *v* **3** go round or avoid.

by-product *n* secondary or incidental product of a process.

byre *n* shelter for cows.

bystander *n* person present but not involved.

byte *n* *Computers* group of bits processed as one unit of data.

byway *n* minor road.

byword *n* person or thing regarded as a perfect example of something.

Byzantine *adj* **1** of Byzantium or the Byzantine Empire. **2** of the style of architecture developed in the Byzantine Empire. **3** complicated.

C c

C **1** *Chem* carbon. **2** Celsius. **3** centigrade. **4** century. **5** the Roman numeral for 100.

c. circa.

Ca *Chem* calcium.

CA **1** California. **2** Chartered Accountant.

ca. circa.

cab *n* **1** taxi. **2** enclosed driver's compartment on a train, lorry, etc. **cabbie, cabby** *n, pl* **-bies** *Informal* taxi driver.

cabal [kab-**bal**] *n* **1** small group of political plotters. **2** secret plot.

cabaret [**kab**-a-ray] *n* **1** dancing and singing show in a nightclub. **2** place providing a cabaret.

cabbage *n* **1** vegetable with a large head of green leaves. **2** *Informal* person with no mental faculties.

caber *n* tree trunk tossed in competition at Highland games.

cabin *n* **1** compartment in a ship or aircraft. **2** small hut. **cabin boy** boy who waits on the officers and passengers of a ship. **cabin cruiser** motorboat with a cabin.

cabinet *n* **1** piece of furniture with drawers or shelves. **2** (**C-**) committee of senior government ministers. **cabinetmaker** *n* person who makes fine furniture.

cable *n* **1** strong thick rope. **2** bundle of wires that carries electricity or electronic signals. **3** telegram sent abroad. ♦ *v* **4** send (someone) a message by cable. **cable car** vehicle pulled up a steep slope by a moving cable. **cable television** television service conveyed by cable to subscribers.

caboodle *n* **the whole caboodle** *Informal* the whole lot.

caboose *n US* guard's van on a train.

cabriolet [kab-ree-oh-**lay**] *n* small horse-drawn carriage with a folding hood.

cacao [kak-**kah**-oh] *n* tropical tree with seed pods from which chocolate and cocoa are made.

cachalot *n* sperm whale.

cache [**kash**] *n* hidden store of weapons or treasure.

cachet [**kash**-shay] *n* prestige, distinction.

cachou *n* lozenge eaten to sweeten the breath.

cack-handed *adj Informal* clumsy.

cackle *v* **1** laugh shrilly. **2** (of a hen) squawk with shrill broken notes. ♦ *n* **3** cackling noise.

cacophony [kak-**koff**-on-ee] *n* harsh discordant sound. **cacophonous** *adj*

cactus *n, pl* **-tuses, -ti** fleshy desert plant with spines but no leaves.

cad *n Old-fashioned* dishonourable man. **caddish** *adj*

cadaver [kad-**dav**-ver] *n* corpse. **cadaverous** *adj* pale, thin, and haggard.

caddie, caddy *n, pl* **-dies** **1** person who carries a golfer's clubs. ♦ *v* **-dying, -died** **2** act as a caddie.

caddis fly *n* insect whose larva (**caddis worm**) lives underwater in a protective case of sand and stones.

caddy *n, pl* **-dies** small container for tea.

cadence [**kade**-enss] *n* **1** rise and fall in the pitch of the voice. **2** close of a musical phrase.

cadenza *n* complex solo passage in a piece of music.

cadet *n* young person training for the armed forces or police.

cadge *v Informal* get (something) by taking advantage of someone's generosity. **cadger** *n*

cadi *n, pl* **-dis** judge in a Muslim community.

cadmium *n Chem* bluish-white metallic element used in alloys.

cadre [**kah**-der] *n* small group of people selected and trained to form the core of a political organization or military unit.

caecum [**seek**-um] *n, pl* **-ca** [-ka] pouch at the beginning of the large intestine.

Caerphilly *n* creamy white mild-flavoured cheese.

Caesarean section [see-**zair**-ee-an] *n* surgical incision into the womb to deliver a baby.

caesium *n Chem* silvery-white metallic element used in photocells.

caesura [siz-**your**-ra] *n, pl* **-ras, -rae** [-ree] pause in a line of verse.

café *n* small or inexpensive restaurant serving light refreshments. **cafeteria** *n* self-service restaurant.

caffeine *n* stimulant found in tea and coffee.

caftan *n* same as KAFTAN.

cage *n* **1** enclosure of bars or wires, for keeping animals or birds. **2** enclosed platform of a lift in a mine. **caged** *adj* kept in a cage.

cagey *adj* **cagier, cagiest** *Informal* reluctant to go into details. **cagily** *adv*

cagoule [kag-**gool**] *n* lightweight hooded waterproof jacket.

cahoots *pl n* **in cahoots** *Informal* conspiring together.

caiman *n* same as CAYMAN.

cairn *n* mound of stones erected as a memorial or marker.

cairngorm *n* yellow or brownish quartz gemstone.

caisson [**kay**-son] *n* watertight chamber used to carry out construction work under water.

cajole *v* persuade by flattery. **cajolery** *n*

cake *n* **1** sweet food baked from a mixture of flour, eggs, etc. **2** flat compact mass of something, such as soap. ♦ *v* **3** form into a hardened mass or crust.

calabash *n* **1** type of large round gourd. **2** bowl made from this.

calamine *n* pink powder consisting chiefly of zinc oxide, used in skin lotions and ointments.

calamity *n, pl* **-ties** disaster. **calamitous** *adj*

calciferol *n* substance found in fish oils and used to treat rickets.

calcify *v* **-fying, -fied** harden by the depositing of calcium salts. **calcification** *n*

calcium *n Chem* silvery-white metallic element found in bones, teeth, limestone, and chalk.

calculate *v* **1** solve or find out by a mathematical procedure or by reasoning. **2** aim to have a particular effect. **calculable** *adj* **calculated** *adj* deliberate, premeditated. **calculating** *adj* selfishly scheming. **calculation** *n* **calculator** *n* small electronic device for making calculations.

calculus *n, pl* **-luses** **1** branch of mathematics dealing with infinitesimal changes to a variable number or quantity. **2** *Pathology* hard deposit in kidney or bladder.

caldron *n* same as CAULDRON.

Caledonian *adj* Scottish.

calendar *n* **1** chart showing a year divided up into months, weeks, and days. **2** system for determining the beginning, length, and division of years. **3** schedule of events or appointments.

calender *n* machine in which paper or cloth is smoothed by passing it between rollers.

calends *pl n* first day of each month in the ancient Roman calendar.

calendula *n* marigold.

calf[1] *n, pl* **calves** **1** young cow, bull, elephant, whale, or seal. **2** leather made from calf skin. **calve** *v* give birth to a calf. **calf love** adolescent infatuation.

calf[2] *n, pl* **calves** back of the leg between the ankle and knee.

calibre [**kal**-lib-ber] *n* **1** person's ability or worth. **2** diameter of the bore of a gun or of a shell or bullet. **calibrate** *v* mark the scale or check the accuracy of (a measuring instrument). **calibration** *n*

calico *n, pl* **-coes, -cos** white cotton fabric.

californium *n Chem* radioactive element produced artificially.

caliph *n Hist* Muslim ruler.

call *v* **1** name. **2** shout to attract attention. **3** telephone. **4** summon. **5** (often foll. by *on*) visit. **6** arrange (a meeting, strike, etc.). ♦ *n* **7** cry, shout. **8** animal's or bird's cry. **9** telephone communication. **10** short visit. **11** summons, invitation. **12** need, demand. **caller** *n* **calling** *n* vocation, profession. **call box** kiosk for a public telephone. **call for** *v* require. **call girl** prostitute with whom appointments are made by telephone. **call off** *v* cancel. **call up** *v* **1** summon to serve in the armed forces. **2** cause one to remember.

calligraphy *n* (art of) beautiful handwriting. **calligrapher** *n*

calliper *n* **1** metal splint for supporting the leg. **2** instrument for measuring diameters.

callisthenics *pl n* light keep-fit exercises. **callisthenic** *adj*

callous *adj* showing no concern for other people's feelings. **calloused** *adj* (of skin) thickened and hardened. **callously** *adv* **callousness** *n*

callow *adj* young and inexperienced.

callus *n, pl* **-luses** area of thick hardened skin.

calm *adj* **1** not agitated or excited. **2** not ruffled by the wind. **3** windless. ♦ *n* **4** peaceful state. ♦ *v* **5** (often foll. by *down*) make or become calm. **calmly** *adv* **calmness** *n*

Calor Gas *n* ® butane gas liquefied under pressure in containers for domestic use.

calorie *n* **1** unit of measurement for the energy value of food. **2** unit of heat. **calorific** *adj* of calories or heat.

calumny *n, pl* **-nies** false or malicious statement. **calumniate** *v* make false or malicious statements about.

Calvary *n* place outside the walls of Jerusalem where Jesus was crucified.

calves *n* plural of CALF.

Calvinism *n* theological system of Calvin, stressing predestination and salvation solely by God's grace. **Calvinist** *n, adj* **Calvinistic** *adj*

calypso *n, pl* **-sos** West Indian song with improvised topical lyrics.

calyx *n, pl* **calyxes, calyces** outer leaves that protect a flower bud.

cam *n* device that converts a circular motion to a to-and-fro motion. **camshaft** *n* part of an engine consisting of a rod to which cams are fixed.

camaraderie *n* comradeship.

camber *n* slight upward curve to the centre of a surface.

cambric *n* fine white linen fabric.

camcorder *n* combined portable video camera and recorder.

came *v* past tense of COME.

camel *n* humped mammal that can survive long periods without food or water in desert regions.

camellia [kam-**meal**-ya] *n* evergreen ornamental shrub with white, pink, or red flowers.

Camembert [**kam**-mem-bare] *n* soft creamy French cheese.

cameo *n, pl* **cameos** **1** brooch or ring with a profile head carved in relief. **2** small part in a film or play performed by a well-known actor or actress.

camera *n* apparatus used for taking photographs or pictures for television or cinema. **in camera** in private session. **cameraman** *n* man who operates a camera for television or cinema.

camiknickers *pl n* woman's undergarment consisting of knickers attached to a camisole.

camisole *n* woman's bodice-like garment.

camomile *n* aromatic plant, used to make herbal tea.

camouflage [**kam**-moo-flahzh] *n* **1** use of natural surroundings or artificial aids to conceal or disguise something. ♦ *v* **2** conceal by camouflage.

camp[1] *n* **1** (place for) temporary lodgings consisting of tents, huts, or cabins. **2** group supporting a particular doctrine. ♦ *v* **3** stay in a camp. **camper** *n* **camp follower** person who supports a particular group without being a member of it.

camp[2] *adj Informal* **1** effeminate or homosexual. **2** consciously artificial or affected. **camp it up** *Informal* behave in a camp way.

campaign *n* **1** series of coordinated activities designed to achieve a goal. **2**

number of military operations aimed at achieving an objective. ♦ *v* **3** take part in a campaign.

campanile [camp-an-**neel**-lee] *n* bell tower, usu. one not attached to another building.

campanology *n* art of ringing bells. **campanologist** *n*

campanula *n* plant with blue or white bell-shaped flowers.

camphor *n* aromatic crystalline substance used medicinally and in mothballs. **camphorated** *adj*

campion *n* red, pink, or white wild flower.

campus *n, pl* **-puses** grounds of a university or college.

can[1] *v, past* **could** **1** be able to. **2** be allowed to.

can[2] *n* **1** metal container for food or liquids. ♦ *v* **canning, canned** **2** put (something) into a can. **canned** *adj* **1** preserved in a can. **2** (of music) prerecorded. **cannery** *n, pl* **-neries** factory where food is canned.

Canadian *n, adj* (person) from Canada.

canal *n* **1** artificial waterway. **2** passage in the body. **canalize** *v* **1** give direction to. **2** convert into a canal.

canapé [**kan**-nap-pay] *n* small piece of bread or toast with a savoury topping.

canard *n* false report.

canary *n, pl* **-ries** small yellow songbird often kept as a pet.

canasta *n* card game like rummy, played with two packs.

cancan *n* lively high-kicking dance performed by a female group.

cancel *v* **-celling, -celled** **1** stop (something that has been arranged) from taking place. **2** mark (a cheque or stamp) with an official stamp to prevent further use. **cancellation** *n* **cancel out** *v* counterbalance, neutralize.

cancer *n* **1** serious disease resulting from a malignant growth or tumour. **2** malignant growth or tumour. **3** evil influence that spreads dangerously. **cancerous** *adj*

Cancer *n* (the crab) fourth sign of the zodiac. **tropic of Cancer** see TROPIC.

candela [kan-**dee**-la] *n* unit of luminous intensity.

candelabrum *n, pl* **-bra** large branched candle holder.

candid *adj* honest and straightforward. **candidly** *adv*

candidate *n* **1** person seeking a job or position. **2** person taking an examination. **candidacy, candidature** *n*

candle *n* stick of wax enclosing a wick, which is burned to produce light. **candlestick** *n* holder for a candle. **candlewick** *n* cotton fabric with a tufted surface.

Candlemas *n Christianity* Feb. 2, Feast of the Purification of the Virgin Mary.

candour *n* honesty and straightforwardness.

candy *n, pl* **-dies** *US* a sweet or sweets. **candied** *adj* coated with sugar. **candyfloss** *n* light fluffy mass of spun sugar on a stick. **candy-striped** *adj* having coloured stripes on a white background.

candytuft *n* garden plant with clusters of white, pink, or purple flowers.

cane *n* **1** stem of the bamboo or similar plant. **2** flexible rod used to beat someone. **3** slender walking stick. ♦ *v* **4** beat with a cane.

canine [**kay**-nine] *adj* **1** of or like a dog. ♦ *n* **2** sharp pointed tooth between the incisors and the molars.

canister *n* metal container.

canker *n* **1** ulceration, ulcerous disease. **2** something evil that spreads and corrupts.

cannabis *n* drug obtained from the hemp plant.

cannelloni *pl n* tubular pieces of pasta filled with meat etc.

cannibal *n* **1** person who eats human flesh. **2** animal that eats others of its own kind. **cannibalism** *n* **cannibalize** *v* use parts from (one machine) to repair another.

cannon *n* **1** large gun on wheels. **2** billiard stroke in which the cue ball hits two balls successively. **cannonade** *n* continuous heavy gunfire. **cannonball** *n* heavy metal ball fired from a cannon. **cannon into** *v* collide with.

cannot can not.

canny *adj* **-nier, -niest** shrewd, cautious. **cannily** *adv*

canoe *n* light narrow open boat propelled by a paddle or paddles. **canoeing** *n* sport of rowing in a canoe. **canoeist** *n*

canon[1] *n* priest serving in a cathedral.

canon[2] *n* **1** Church decree regulating morals or religious practices. **2** general rule or standard. **3** list of the works of an author that are accepted as authentic. **4** piece of music in which the same melody is taken up in different parts. **canonical** *adj* **canonize** *v* declare (a person) officially to be a saint. **canonization** *n*

canoodle *v Slang* kiss and cuddle.

canopy *n, pl* **-pies 1** covering above a bed, door, etc. **2** any large or wide covering. **canopied** *adj* covered with a canopy.

cant[1] *n* **1** insincere talk. **2** specialized vocabulary of a particular group. ♦ *v* **3** use cant.

cant[2] *n* **1** tilted position. ♦ *v* **2** tilt, overturn.

can't can not.

cantaloupe, cantaloup *n* kind of melon with sweet orange flesh.

cantankerous *adj* quarrelsome, bad-tempered.

cantata [kan-**tah**-ta] *n* musical work consisting of arias, duets, and choruses.

canteen *n* **1** restaurant attached to a workplace or school. **2** box containing a set of cutlery.

canter *n* **1** horse's gait between a trot and a gallop. ♦ *v* **2** move at a canter.

canticle *n* short hymn with words from the Bible.

cantilever *n* beam or girder fixed at one end only. **cantilever bridge** bridge made of two cantilevers that meet in the middle.

canto [**kan**-toe] *n, pl* **-tos** main division of a long poem.

canton *n* political division of a country, esp. Switzerland.

cantonment [kan-**toon**-ment] *n* military camp.

cantor *n* man employed to lead services in a synagogue.

canvas *n* **1** heavy coarse cloth used for sails and tents, and for oil painting. **2** an oil painting on canvas. **under canvas** in a tent.

canvass *v* **1** try to get votes or support (from). **2** find out the opinions of (people) by conducting a survey. ♦ *n* **3** canvassing.

canyon *n* deep narrow valley.

caoutchouc [**cow**-chook] *n* raw rubber.

cap *n* **1** soft close-fitting covering for the head. **2** cap given to player selected for a national team. **3** small lid. **4** small explosive device used in a toy gun. **5** contraceptive device. ♦ *v* **capping, capped 6** cover or top with something. **7** select (a player) for a national team. **8** impose an upper limit on (a tax). **9** outdo, excel.

CAP (in the EU) Common Agricultural Policy.

cap. capital.

capable *adj* **1** (foll. by *of*) having the ability (for). **2** competent and efficient. **capably** *adv* **capability** *n, pl* **-ties**

capacity *n, pl* **-ties 1** ability to contain, absorb, or hold. **2** maximum amount that can be contained or produced. **3** physical or mental ability. **4** position, function. **capacious** *adj* roomy. **capacitance** *n* (measure of) the ability of a system to store electrical charge. **capacitor** *n* device for storing electrical charge.

caparisoned [kap-**par**-riss-sond] *adj* magnificently decorated.

cape[1] *n* short cloak.

cape[2] *n* large piece of land that juts out into the sea.

caper *n* **1** high-spirited prank. ♦ *v* **2** skip about.

capercaillie, capercailzie [kap-per-**kale**-yee] *n* large black European grouse.

capers *pl n* pickled flower buds of a Mediterranean shrub used in sauces.

capillary [kap-**pill**-a-ree] *n, pl* **-laries** **1** very fine blood vessel. ♦ *adj* **2** (of a tube) having a fine bore.

capital[1] *n* **1** chief city of a country. **2** accumulated wealth. **3** wealth used to produce more wealth. **4** large letter, as used at the beginning of a name or sentence. ♦ *adj* **5** involving or punishable by death. **6** *Old-fashioned* excellent. **capitalize** *v* **1** write or print (words) in capitals. **2** convert into or provide with capital. **capitalize on** *v* take advantage of (a situation). **capital gain** profit from the sale of an asset.

capital[2] *n* top part of a pillar.

capitalism *n* economic system based on the private ownership of industry. **capitalist** *adj* **1** of capitalists or capitalism. **2** supporting capitalism. ♦ *n* **3** supporter of capitalism. **4** person who owns a business.

capitation *n* tax of a fixed amount per person.

capitulate *v* surrender on agreed terms. **capitulation** *n*

capon [**kay**-pon] *n* castrated cock fowl fattened for eating.

cappuccino [kap-poo-**cheen**-oh] *n, pl* **-nos** coffee with steamed milk, sprinkled with powdered chocolate.

caprice [kap-**reess**] *n* sudden change of attitude. **capricious** *adj* tending to have sudden changes of attitude. **capriciously** *adv*

Capricorn *n* (the goat) tenth sign of the zodiac. **tropic of Capricorn** see TROPIC.

capsicum *n* kind of pepper used as a vegetable or as a spice.

capsize *v* overturn accidentally.

capstan *n* rotating cylinder round which a ship's rope is wound.

capsule *n* **1** soluble gelatine case containing a dose of medicine. **2** plant's seed case. **3** *Anat* membrane surrounding an organ. **4** detachable crew compartment of a spacecraft.

Capt. Captain.

captain *n* **1** commander of a ship or civil aircraft. **2** middle-ranking naval officer. **3** junior officer in the army. **4** leader of a team or group. ♦ *v* **5** be captain of. **captaincy** *n*

caption *n* **1** title or explanation accompanying an illustration. ♦ *v* **2** provide with a caption.

captious *adj* tending to make trivial criticisms.

captivate *v* attract and hold the attention of. **captivating** *adj*

captive *n* **1** person kept in confinement. ♦ *adj* **2** kept in confinement. **3** (of an audience) unable to leave. **captivity** *n*

captor *n* person who captures a person or animal.

capture *v* **1** take by force. **2** succeed in representing (something elusive) artistically. ♦ *n* **3** capturing.

capuchin [**kap**-yoo-chin] *n* S American monkey with thick hair on the top of its head.

capybara *n* very large S American rodent.

car *n* **1** motor vehicle designed to carry a small number of people. **2** passenger compartment of a cable car, lift, etc. **3** *US* railway carriage. **carjack** *v* attack (a car driver) to rob them or to steal the car. **car park** area or building reserved for parking cars.

carafe [kar-**raff**] *n* glass bottle for serving water or wine.

caramel *n* **1** chewy sweet made from sugar and milk. **2** burnt sugar, used for colouring and flavouring food. **caramelize** *v* turn into caramel.

carapace *n* hard upper shell of tortoises and crustaceans.

carat *n* **1** unit of weight of precious stones. **2** measure of the purity of gold in an alloy.

caravan *n* **1** large enclosed vehicle for living in, designed to be towed by a car or horse. **2** group travelling together in Eastern countries. **caravanserai** *n* large inn enclosing a courtyard, providing accommodation for caravans in Eastern countries.

caraway *n* plant whose seeds are used

as a spice.

carbide *n* compound of carbon with a metal.

carbine *n* light automatic rifle.

carbohydrate *n* any of a large group of energy-producing compounds in food, such as sugars and starches.

carbolic acid *n* disinfectant derived from coal tar.

carbon *n* nonmetallic element occurring as charcoal, graphite, and diamond, found in all organic matter. **carbonate** *n* salt or ester of carbonic acid. **carbonated** *adj* (of a drink) containing carbon dioxide. **carboniferous** *adj* producing coal or carbon. **carbonize** *v* **1** turn into carbon as a result of heating. **2** coat with carbon. **carbon copy 1** copy made with carbon paper. **2** very similar person or thing. **carbon dioxide** colourless gas exhaled by people and animals. **carbonic acid** weak acid formed from carbon dioxide and water. **carbon paper** paper coated on one side with a dark waxy pigment, used to make a copy of something as it is typed or written.

Carborundum *n* ® compound of silicon and carbon, used for grinding and polishing.

carboy *n* large bottle with a protective casing.

carbuncle *n* inflamed boil.

carburettor *n* device which mixes petrol and air in an internal-combustion engine.

carcass, carcase *n* **1** dead body of an animal. **2** *Informal* person's body.

carcinogen *n* substance that produces cancer. **carcinogenic** *adj* **carcinoma** *n* malignant tumour.

card[1] *n* **1** piece of thick stiff paper or cardboard used for identification, reference, or sending greetings or messages. **2** one of a set of cards with a printed pattern, used for playing games. **3** small rectangle of stiff plastic with identifying numbers for use as a credit card, cheque card, or charge card. **4** *Old-fashioned* witty or eccentric person. ♦ *pl* **5** any card game, or card games in general. **cardboard** *n* thin stiff board made from paper pulp. **cardsharp** *n* professional card player who cheats.

card[2] *n* **1** machine or tool for combing wool before spinning. ♦ *v* **2** process with such a machine or tool.

cardamom *n* spice obtained from the seeds of a tropical plant.

cardiac *adj* of the heart. **cardiogram** *n* electrocardiogram. **cardiograph** *n* electrocardiograph. **cardiology** *n* study of the heart and its diseases. **cardiologist** *n* **cardiovascular** *adj* of the heart and the blood vessels.

cardigan *n* knitted jacket.

cardinal *n* **1** any of the high-ranking clergymen of the RC Church who elect the Pope and act as his counsellors. ♦ *adj* **2** fundamentally important. **cardinal number** number denoting quantity but not order in a group, for example four as distinct from fourth. **cardinal points** the four main points of the compass.

care *v* **1** be concerned. **2** like (to do something). **3** (foll. by *for*) like, be fond of. **4** (foll. by *for*) look after. ♦ *n* **5** careful attention, caution. **6** protection, charge. **7** trouble, worry. **in, into care** made the legal responsibility of a local authority. **careful** *adj* **carefully** *adv* **carefulness** *n* **careless** *adj* **carelessly** *adv* **carelessness** *n* **caring** *adj*

careen *v* tilt over to one side.

> Be careful not to confuse *careen*, 'tilt', with *career*, 'rush headlong'.

career *n* **1** series of jobs in a profession or occupation that a person has through their life. **2** part of a person's life spent in a particular occupation. ♦ *v* **3** rush in an uncontrolled way. **careerist** *n* person who seeks advancement by any possible means.

> Do not confuse *career* 'rush' with *careen* 'tilt'.

carefree *adj* without worry or responsibility.

caress *n* **1** gentle affectionate touch or embrace. ♦ *v* **2** touch gently and affectionately.

caret [**kar**-rett] *n* symbol (‸) indicating a place in written or printed matter where something is to be inserted.

caretaker *n* person employed to look after a place.

careworn *adj* showing signs of worry.

cargo *n, pl* **-goes** goods carried by a ship, aircraft, etc.

caribou *n, pl* **-bou** *or* **-bous** large N American reindeer.

caricature *n* **1** drawing or description of a person that exaggerates features for comic effect. ♦ *v* **2** make a caricature of.

caries [**care**-reez] *n* tooth decay.

carillon [kar-**rill**-yon] *n* **1** set of bells played by keyboard or mechanically. **2** tune played on such bells.

Carmelite *n, adj* (friar or nun) of the Order of Our Lady of Carmel.

carminative *n, adj* (drug) able to relieve flatulence.

carmine *adj* vivid red.

carnage *n* extensive slaughter of people.

carnal *adj* of a sexual or sensual nature. **carnal knowledge** sexual intercourse.

carnation *n* cultivated plant with fragrant white, pink, or red flowers.

carnelian *n* reddish-yellow gemstone.

carnival *n* **1** festive period with processions, music, and dancing in the street. **2** travelling funfair.

carnivore *n* meat-eating animal. **carnivorous** *adj*

carob *n* pod of a Mediterranean tree, used as a chocolate substitute.

carol *n* **1** joyful Christmas hymn. ♦ *v* **-olling, -olled 2** sing carols. **3** sing joyfully.

carotid [kar-**rot**-id] *adj, n* (of) either of the two arteries supplying blood to the head.

carouse *v* have a merry drinking party. **carousal** *n* merry drinking party.

carousel [kar-roo-**sell**] *n* **1** revolving conveyor belt for luggage or photographic slides. **2** *US* merry-go-round.

carp[1] *n* large freshwater fish.

carp[2] *v* complain, find fault.

carpal *n* wrist bone.

carpel *n* female reproductive organ of a flowering plant.

carpenter *n* person who makes or repairs wooden structures. **carpentry** *n*

carpet *n* **1** heavy fabric for covering floors. **2** covering like a carpet. ♦ *v* **carpeting, carpeted 3** cover with a carpet. **on the carpet** *Informal* being reprimanded. **carpetbagger** *n* politician seeking office in a place where he or she has no connections.

carpus *n, pl* **-pi** set of eight bones of the wrist.

carriage *n* **1** one of the sections of a train for passengers. **2** way a person holds his or her head and body. **3** four-wheeled horse-drawn vehicle. **4** moving part of a machine that supports and shifts another part. **5** charge made for conveying goods. **carriageway** *n* part of a road along which traffic passes in one direction.

carrier *n* **1** person or thing that carries something. **2** person or animal that does not suffer from a disease but can transmit it to others. **carrier bag** large plastic or paper bag for shopping. **carrier pigeon** homing pigeon used for carrying messages.

carrion *n* dead and rotting flesh. **carrion crow** scavenging European crow.

carrot *n* **1** long tapering orange root vegetable. **2** something offered as an incentive. **carroty** *adj* (of hair) reddish-orange.

carry *v* **-rying, -ried 1** take from one place to another. **2** have with one habitually, in one's pocket etc. **3** transmit (a disease). **4** have as a factor or result. **5** hold (one's head or body) in a specified manner. **6** secure the adoption of (a bill or motion). **7** (of sound) travel a certain distance. **carrycot** *n* light portable bed for a baby, with handles and a hood. **carry on** *v* **1** continue. **2** do, run, or take part in. **3** *Informal* cause a fuss. **carry out** *v* follow, accomplish. **carry through** *v* bring to completion.

cart *n* **1** open two-wheeled horse-drawn vehicle for carrying goods or passengers. **2** small vehicle pulled or pushed by hand. ♦ *v* **3** carry, usu. with some effort. **carthorse** *n* large heavily built horse. **cartwheel** *n* **1** sideways somersault supported by the hands with legs outstretched. **2** large spoked wheel of a cart.

carte blanche *n French* complete authority.

cartel *n* association of competing firms formed to fix prices.

Carthusian *n, adj* (monk or nun) of a strict monastic order founded in 1084.

cartilage [**kar**-till-ij] *n* strong flexible tissue forming part of the skeleton. **cartilaginous** *adj*

cartography *n* map making. **cartographer** *n* **cartographic** *adj*

carton *n* container made of cardboard or waxed paper.

cartoon *n* **1** humorous or satirical drawing. **2** sequence of these telling a story. **3** film made by photographing a series of drawings which give the illusion of movement when projected. **cartoonist** *n*

cartouche, cartouch *n* **1** ornamental tablet or panel in the form of a scroll. **2** oval figure containing royal or divine Egyptian names.

cartridge *n* **1** casing containing an explosive charge and bullet for a gun. **2** part of the pick-up of a record player that converts the movements of the stylus into electrical signals. **3** sealed container of film, tape, etc. **cartridge paper** strong thick drawing paper.

carve *v* **1** cut to form an object. **2** form (an object or design) by cutting. **3** slice (cooked meat). **carving** *n* **carve out** *v Informal* make or create (a career).

caryatid [kar-ree-**at**-id] *n* supporting column in the shape of a female figure.

Casanova *n* promiscuous man.

casbah *n* citadel of a N African city.

cascade *n* **1** waterfall. **2** something flowing or falling like a waterfall. ♦ *v* **3** flow or fall in a cascade.

cascara *n* bark of a N American shrub, used as a laxative.

case[1] *n* **1** instance, example. **2** matter for discussion. **3** condition, state of affairs. **4** set of arguments supporting an action or cause. **5** person or problem dealt with by a doctor, social worker, or solicitor. **6** action, lawsuit. **7** evidence offered in court to support a claim. **8** *Grammar* form of a noun, pronoun, or adjective showing its relation to other words in the sentence. **in case** so as to allow for the possibility that.

case[2] *n* **1** container, protective covering. **2** suitcase. ♦ *v* **3** *Slang* inspect (a building) with the intention of burgling it. **case-hardened** *adj* having been made callous by experience.

casein *n* protein found in milk and its products.

casement *n* window that is hinged on one side.

cash *n* **1** banknotes and coins. ♦ *adj* **2** of, for, or paid in cash. ♦ *v* **3** obtain cash for. **cash-and-carry** *adj* operating on a basis of cash payment for goods that are taken away by the buyer. **cash in on** *v Informal* gain profit or advantage from. **cash register** till that displays and adds the prices of the goods sold.

cashew *n* edible kidney-shaped nut.

cashier[1] *n* person responsible for handling cash in a bank, shop, etc.

cashier[2] *v* dismiss with dishonour from the armed forces.

cashmere *n* fine soft wool obtained from goats.

casing *n* protective case, covering.

casino *n, pl* **-nos** public building or room where gambling games are played.

cask *n* barrel used to hold alcoholic drink.

casket *n* **1** small box for valuables. **2** *US* coffin.

Cassandra *n* someone whose prophecies of doom are unheeded.

cassava *n* starch obtained from the

roots of a tropical American plant, used to make tapioca.

casserole *n* **1** covered dish in which food is cooked slowly, usu. in an oven. **2** dish cooked in this way. ♦ *v* **3** cook in a casserole.

cassette *n* plastic case containing a reel of film or magnetic tape.

cassia *n* tropical plant whose pods yield a mild laxative. **cassia bark** cinnamon-like bark used as a spice.

cassock *n* long tunic, usu. black, worn by priests.

cassowary *n, pl* **-waries** large flightless bird of Australia and New Guinea.

cast *n* **1** actors in a play or film collectively. **2** object shaped by a mould while molten. **3** mould used to shape such an object. **4** rigid plaster-of-Paris casing for immobilizing broken bones while they heal. **5** sort, kind. **6** slight squint in the eye. ♦ *v* **casting, cast 7** select (an actor) to play a part in a play or film. **8** give (a vote). **9** let fall, shed. **10** shape (molten material) in a mould. **11** throw with force. **12** direct (a glance). **castaway** *n* shipwrecked person. **casting vote** deciding vote used by the chairman of a meeting when the votes on each side are equal. **cast-iron** *adj* **1** made of a hard but brittle type of iron. **2** definite, unchallengeable. **cast-off** *adj, n* discarded (person or thing). **cast off** *v* **1** discard (something no longer wanted). **2** untie a ship from a dock. **3** knot and remove (stitches) from the needle in knitting. **cast on** *v* make (stitches) on the needle in knitting.

castanets *pl n* musical instrument, used by Spanish dancers, consisting of curved pieces of hollow wood clicked together in the hand.

caste *n* **1** any of the hereditary classes into which Hindu society is divided. **2** social rank.

castellated *adj* having battlements.

caster *n* same as CASTOR.

caster sugar finely ground white sugar.

castigate *v* reprimand severely. **castigation** *n*

castle *n* **1** large fortified building, often built as a ruler's residence. **2** rook in chess. **castle in the air** daydream.

castor *n* small swivelling wheel fixed to the bottom of a piece of furniture for easy moving.

castor oil *n* oil obtained from an Indian plant, used as a lubricant and purgative.

castrate *v* **1** remove the testicles of. **2** deprive of vigour or masculinity. **castration** *n*

casual *adj* **1** careless, nonchalant. **2** (of work or workers) occasional. **3** shallow, superficial. **4** for informal wear. **5** happening by chance. ♦ *n* **6** occasional worker. **casually** *adv*

casualty *n, pl* **-ties 1** person killed or injured in an accident or war. **2** hospital department treating victims of accidents. **3** person or thing that has suffered as the result of something.

casuistry *n* reasoning that is misleading or oversubtle. **casuist** *n*

cat *n* **1** small domesticated furry mammal. **2** related wild mammal, such as the lion or tiger. **catty** *adj* **-tier, -tiest** *Informal* spiteful. **catkin** *n* drooping flower spike of certain trees. **catcall** *n* derisive whistle or cry. **catgut** *n* strong cord used to string musical instruments and sports rackets. **catnap** *n, v* doze. **cat-o'-nine-tails** *n* whip with nine knotted thongs. **Catseyes** *pl n* ® glass reflectors set in the road to indicate traffic lanes. **cat's paw** person used by another to do unpleasant things for him or her. **catwalk** *n* **1** narrow pathway or platform. **2** narrow platform where models display clothes in a fashion show.

catabolism *n* breaking down of complex molecules into simple ones.

cataclysm [**kat**-a-kliz-zum] *n* **1** violent upheaval. **2** disaster, such as an earthquake. **cataclysmic** *adj*

catacombs [**kat**-a-koomz] *pl n* underground burial place consisting of tunnels with recesses for tombs.

catafalque [**kat**-a-falk] *n* raised platform on which a body lies in state before or during a funeral.

catalepsy *n* trancelike state in which the body is rigid. **cataleptic** *adj*

catalogue *n* **1** book containing details of items for sale. **2** systematic list of items. ♦ *v* **3** enter (an item) in a catalogue. **4** make a systematic list of.

catalyst *n* **1** substance that speeds up a chemical reaction without itself changing. **2** person or thing that causes a change. **catalyse** *v* speed up (a chemical reaction) by a catalyst. **catalysis** *n* **catalytic** *adj*

catamaran *n* boat with twin parallel hulls.

catapult *n* **1** Y-shaped device with a loop of elastic, used by children for firing stones. ♦ *v* **2** shoot forwards or upwards violently. **3** cause (someone) suddenly to be in a particular situation.

cataract *n* **1** eye disease in which the lens becomes opaque. **2** opaque area of an eye. **3** large waterfall.

catarrh [kat-**tar**] *n* excessive mucus in the nose and throat, during or following a cold. **catarrhal** *adj*

catastrophe [kat-**ass**-trof-fee] *n* great and sudden disaster. **catastrophic** *adj*

catatonia *n* form of schizophrenia characterized by stupor, with outbreaks of excitement. **catatonic** *adj*

catch *v* **catching, caught 1** seize, capture. **2** surprise in an act, e.g. *two boys were caught stealing.* **3** hit unexpectedly. **4** be in time for (a bus, train, etc.). **5** see or hear. **6** be infected with (an illness). **7** entangle. **8** understand, make out. **9** start burning. ♦ *n* **10** device for fastening a door, window, etc. **11** total number of fish caught. **12** *Informal* concealed or unforeseen drawback. **13** *Informal* person considered worth having as a husband or wife. **catch it** *Informal* be punished. **catching** *adj* infectious. **catchy** *adj* **catchier, catchiest** (of a tune) pleasant and easily remembered. **catchment area** area served by a particular school or hospital. **catch on** *v Informal* **1** become popular. **2** understand. **catch out** *v Informal* trap (someone) in an error or lie. **catchpenny** *adj* designed to have instant appeal without regard for quality. **catch phrase** well-known phrase associated with a particular entertainer. **catch 22** inescapable dilemma. **catch up with** *v* reach or pass. **catchword** *n* well-known and frequently used phrase.

catechism [**kat**-ti-kiz-zum] *n* instruction on the doctrine of a Christian Church in a series of questions and answers. **catechize** *v* **1** instruct by using a catechism. **2** question (someone) thoroughly.

category *n, pl* **-ries** class, group. **categorical** *adj* absolutely clear and certain. **categorically** *adv* **categorize** *v* put in a category. **categorization** *n*

cater *v* provide what is needed or wanted, esp. food or services. **caterer** *n*

caterpillar *n* **1** wormlike larva of a moth or butterfly. **2** ® endless track, driven by cogged wheels, used to propel a heavy vehicle.

caterwaul *v, n* wail, yowl.

catharsis [kath-**thar**-siss] *n, pl* **-ses 1** relief of strong suppressed emotions. **2** evacuation of the bowels, esp. with a laxative. **cathartic** *adj* **1** causing catharsis. ♦ *n* **2** drug that causes catharsis.

cathedral *n* principal church of a diocese.

Catherine wheel *n* rotating firework.

catheter [**kath**-it-er] *n* tube inserted into a body cavity to drain fluid.

cathode *n* negative electrode, by which electrons leave a circuit. **cathode rays** stream of electrons from a cathode in a vacuum tube. **cathode-ray tube** vacuum tube in which a beam of electrons produces a visible image, used in television receivers etc.

catholic *adj* **1** (of tastes or interests) covering a wide range. ♦ *n, adj* **2** (**C-**) (member) of the Roman Catholic Church. **Catholicism** *n*

> Note that the meaning of *catholic* can change depending on whether it begins with a capital letter or not.

cation [**kat**-eye-on] *n* positively charged ion.

cattle *pl n* domesticated cows and bulls. **cattle-grid** *n* grid over a ditch in the road to prevent livestock crossing.

Caucasian, Caucasoid *n, adj* (member) of the light-skinned racial group of humankind.

caucus *n, pl* **-cuses** **1** local committee or faction of a political party. **2** political meeting to decide future plans.

caudal *adj* at or near an animal's tail.

caught *v* past of CATCH.

caul *n Anat* membrane sometimes covering a child's head at birth.

cauldron, caldron *n* large pot used for boiling.

cauliflower *n* vegetable with a large head of white flower buds surrounded by green leaves.

caulk *v* fill in (cracks) with paste etc.

causal *adj* of or being a cause. **causally** *adv* **causation, causality** *n* relationship of cause and effect.

cause *n* **1** something that produces a particular effect. **2** (foll. by *for*) reason, motive. **3** aim or principle supported by a person or group. ♦ *v* **4** be the cause of.

cause célèbre [**kawz** sill-**leb**-ra] *n, pl* **causes célèbres** [**kawz** sill-**leb**-ra] controversial legal case or issue.

causeway *n* raised path or road across water or marshland.

caustic *adj* **1** capable of burning by chemical action. **2** bitter and sarcastic. ♦ *n* **3** caustic substance. **caustically** *adv* **caustic soda** same as SODIUM HYDROXIDE.

cauterize *v* burn (a wound) with heat or a caustic agent to prevent infection. **cauterization** *n*

caution *n* **1** care, esp. in the face of danger. **2** warning. ♦ *v* **3** warn, advise. **cautionary** *adj* warning. **cautious** *adj* showing caution. **cautiously** *adv*

cavalcade *n* procession of people on horseback or in cars.

cavalier *adj* **1** showing haughty disregard. ♦ *n* **2** *Old-fashioned* gallant gentleman. **3** (**C-**) supporter of Charles I in the English Civil War.

cavalry *n, pl* **-ries** part of the army orig. on horseback, but now often using fast armoured vehicles.

cave *n* hollow in the side of a hill or cliff. **caving** *n* sport of exploring caves. **cave in** *v* **1** collapse inwards. **2** *Informal* yield under pressure. **caveman** *n* **1** prehistoric cave dweller. **2** *Informal* man who is primitive in his behaviour.

caveat [**kav**-vee-at] *n* warning.

cavern *n* large cave. **cavernous** *adj*

caviar, caviare *n* salted sturgeon roe, regarded as a delicacy.

cavil *v* **-illing, -illed** **1** make petty objections. ♦ *n* **2** petty objection.

cavity *n, pl* **-ties** **1** hollow space. **2** decayed area on a tooth.

cavort *v* skip about.

caw *n* **1** cry of a crow, rook, or raven. ♦ *v* **2** make this cry.

cay *n* low island or bank composed of sand and coral fragments.

cayenne pepper, cayenne *n* hot red spice made from capsicum seeds.

cayman *n, pl* **-mans** S American reptile similar to an alligator.

CB Citizens' Band.

CBE Commander of the Order of the British Empire.

CBI Confederation of British Industry.

cc cubic centimetre.

Cd *Chem* cadmium.

CD compact disc.

CD-ROM compact disc read-only memory.

Ce *Chem* cerium.

cease *v* bring or come to an end. **ceaseless** *adj* **ceaselessly** *adv* **ceasefire** *n* temporary truce.

cedar *n* **1** evergreen coniferous tree. **2** its wood.

cede *v* surrender (territory or legal rights).

cedilla *n* character (¸) placed under a *c* in some languages, to show that it is pronounced *s*, not *k*.

Ceefax *n* ® BBC teletext service.

ceilidh [**kay**-lee] *n* informal social gathering for singing and dancing, esp. in Scotland.

ceiling *n* **1** inner upper surface of a room. **2** upper limit set on something. **3** upper altitude to which an aircraft can climb.

celandine *n* wild plant with yellow flowers.

celebrate *v* **1** hold festivities to mark (a happy event, anniversary, etc.). **2** perform (a religious ceremony). **3** praise publicly. **celebrated** *adj* well known. **celebration** *n* **celebrant** *n* person who performs a religious ceremony. **celebrity** *n, pl* **-rities** **1** famous person. **2** state of being famous.

celeriac [sill-**ler**-ee-ak] *n* variety of celery with a large turnip-like root.

celerity [sill-**ler**-rit-tee] *n* swiftness.

celery *n* vegetable with long green crisp edible stalks.

celestial *adj* **1** heavenly, divine. **2** of the sky.

celibate *adj* **1** unmarried or abstaining from sex, esp. because of a religious vow of chastity. ♦ *n* **2** celibate person. **celibacy** *n*

cell *n* **1** smallest unit of an organism that is able to function independently. **2** small room for a prisoner, monk, or nun. **3** small compartment of a honeycomb etc. **4** small group operating as the core of a larger organization. **5** device that produces electrical energy by chemical reaction. **cellular** *adj* **1** of or consisting of cells. **2** woven with an open texture. **3** designed for or using cellular radio. **cellular radio** radio communication, used esp. in car phones, based on a network of transmitters each serving a small area.

cellar *n* **1** underground room for storage. **2** stock of wine.

cello [**chell**-oh] *n, pl* **-los** large low-pitched instrument of the violin family. **cellist** *n*

Cellophane *n* ® thin transparent cellulose sheeting used as wrapping.

cellulite *n* fat deposits under the skin alleged to resist dieting.

celluloid *n* kind of plastic used to make toys and, formerly, photographic film.

cellulose *n* main constituent of plant cell walls, used in making paper, plastics, etc.

Celsius *adj* of the temperature scale in which water freezes at 0° and boils at 100°.

Celt [**kelt**] *n* person from Scotland, Ireland, Wales, Cornwall, or Brittany. **Celtic** [**kel**-tik, **sel**-tik] *n* **1** group of languages including Gaelic and Welsh. ♦ *adj* **2** of the Celts or the Celtic languages.

cement *n* **1** fine grey powder mixed with water and sand to make mortar or concrete. **2** something that unites, binds, or joins. **3** material used to fill teeth. ♦ *v* **4** join, bind, or cover with cement. **5** make (a relationship) stronger.

cemetery *n, pl* **-teries** place where dead people are buried.

cenotaph *n* monument honouring soldiers who died in a war.

censer *n* container for burning incense.

censor *n* **1** person authorized to examine films, books, etc., to ban or cut anything considered obscene or objectionable. ♦ *v* **2** ban or cut parts of (a film, book, etc.). **censorship** *n* **censorious** *adj* harshly critical.

censure *n* **1** severe disapproval. ♦ *v* **2** criticize severely.

census *n, pl* **-suses** official count of a population.

cent *n* hundredth part of a monetary unit such as the dollar or euro.

centaur *n* mythical creature with the head, arms, and torso of a man, and the lower body and legs of a horse.

centenary [sen-**teen**-a-ree] *n, pl* **-naries** 100th anniversary or its celebration. **centenarian** *n* person at least 100 years old. **centennial** *n US* centenary.

centi- *prefix* **1** one hundredth, e.g. *centimetre*. **2** a hundred, e.g. *centipede*.

centigrade *adj* same as CELSIUS.

> Scientists now use *Celsius* in preference to *centigrade*.

centigram, centigramme *n* one hundredth of a gram.
centilitre *n* one hundredth of a litre.
centime [**son**-teem] *n* monetary unit worth one hundredth of a franc.
centimetre *n* one hundredth of a metre.
centipede *n* small wormlike creature with many legs.
central *adj* **1** of, at, or forming the centre. **2** main, principal. **centrally** *adv* **centrality** *n* **centralism** *n* principle of central control of a country or organization. **centralize** *v* bring under central control. **centralization** *n* **central heating** system for heating a building from one central source of heat. **central processing unit** part of a computer that performs logical and arithmetical operations on the data.
centre *n* **1** middle point or part. **2** place for a specified activity. **3** person or thing that is a focus of interest. **4** political party or group favouring moderation. **5** *Sport* player who plays in the middle of the field. ♦ *v* **6** put in the centre of something. **centrist** *n* person favouring political moderation. **centre on** *v* have as a centre or main theme.
centrifugal *adj* moving away from a centre. **centrifuge** *n* machine that separates substances by centrifugal force. **centrifugal force** force that acts outwards on any body that rotates or moves along a curved path.
centripetal *adj* moving towards a centre.
centurion *n* (in ancient Rome) officer commanding 100 men.
century *n, pl* **-ries** **1** period of 100 years. **2** cricket score of 100 runs.
cephalopod [**seff**-a-loh-pod] *n* sea mollusc with a head and tentacles, such as the octopus.
ceramic *n* **1** hard brittle material made by heating clay to a very high temperature. **2** object made of this. ♦ *pl* **3** art of producing ceramic objects. ♦ *adj* **4** made of ceramic.
cereal *n* **1** grass plant with edible grain, such as oat or wheat. **2** this grain. **3** breakfast food made from this grain, eaten mixed with milk.
cerebellum [serr-rib-**bell**-lum] *n, pl* **-lums, -la** [-la] back part of the brain.
cerebral [**ser**-rib-ral] *adj* **1** of the brain. **2** intellectual.
cerebrum [**serr**-rib-rum] *n, pl* **-brums, -bra** [-bra] main part of the brain. **cerebrospinal** *adj* of the brain and spinal cord.
ceremony *n, pl* **-nies** **1** formal act or ritual. **2** formally polite behaviour. **ceremonial** *adj, n* **ceremonially** *adv* **ceremonious** *adj* excessively polite or formal. **ceremoniously** *adv*
cerise [ser-**reess**] *adj* cherry-red.
cerium *n Chem* steel-grey metallic element.
cert *n Informal* certainty, e.g. *a dead cert.*
certain *adj* **1** positive and confident. **2** definite. **3** some but not much. **4** named but not known, e.g. *a certain Miss Watson taught me English.* **certainly** *adv* **certainty** *n* **1** state of being sure. **2** (*pl* **-ties**) something that is inevitable.
certificate *n* official document stating the details of a birth, academic course, etc.
certify *v* **-fying, -fied** **1** confirm, attest to. **2** guarantee. **3** declare legally insane. **certifiable** *adj* considered legally insane. **certification** *n*
certitude *n* confidence, certainty.
cervix *n, pl* **cervixes, cervices** **1** narrow entrance of the womb. **2** neck. **cervical** *adj*
cessation *n* ceasing.
cession *n* ceding.
cesspit, cesspool *n* covered tank or pit for sewage.
cetacean [sit-**tay**-shun] *n* fish-shaped sea mammal such as a whale or dolphin.
cetane [**see**-tane] *n* colourless liquid hydrocarbon, used as a solvent.
cf compare.
Cf *Chem* californium.
CFC chlorofluorocarbon.
cg centigram.
ch. **1** chapter. **2** church.

cha-cha, cha-cha-cha *n* (music for) a modern ballroom dance from Latin America.

chafe *v* **1** make sore or worn by rubbing. **2** be annoyed or impatient.

chafer *n* large beetle.

chaff[1] *n* **1** grain husks. **2** something of little worth.

chaff[2] *v* tease good-naturedly.

chaffinch *n* small European songbird.

chagrin [**shag**-grin] *n* annoyance and disappointment. **chagrined** *adj* annoyed and disappointed.

chain *n* **1** flexible length of connected metal links. **2** (usu. pl) anything that restricts or restrains. **3** series of connected facts or events. **4** group of shops, hotels, etc. owned by one firm. ♦ *v* **5** restrict or fasten with or as if with a chain. **chain gang** *US* group of prisoners chained together. **chain mail** same as MAIL[2]. **chain reaction** series of events, each of which causes the next. **chain-smoke** *v* smoke (cigarettes) continuously. **chain smoker**

chair *n* **1** seat with a back, for one person. **2** official position of authority. **3** person holding this. **4** professorship. ♦ *v* **5** preside over (a meeting). **chairlift** series of chairs suspended from a moving cable for carrying people up a slope. **chairman, chairwoman** *n* person in charge of a company's board of directors or a meeting (also **chairperson**).

> *Chairman* can seem inappropriate when applied to a woman, while *chairwoman* can be offensive. *Chair* and *chairperson* can be applied to either a man or a woman; *chair* is generally preferred to *chairperson*.

chaise [**shaze**] *n* light horse-drawn carriage.

chaise longue [**long**] *n* couch with a back and a single armrest.

chalcedony [kal-**sed**-don-ee] *n, pl* **-nies** variety of quartz.

chalet *n* **1** kind of Swiss wooden house with a steeply sloping roof. **2** similar house, used as a holiday home.

chalice [**chal**-liss] *n* **1** large goblet. **2** goblet containing the wine at Communion.

chalk *n* **1** soft white rock consisting of calcium carbonate. **2** piece of chalk, often coloured, used for drawing and writing on blackboards. ♦ *v* **3** draw or mark with chalk. **chalky** *adj*

challenge *n* **1** demanding or stimulating situation. **2** call to take part in a contest or fight. **3** questioning of a statement of fact. **4** demand by a sentry for identification or a password. ♦ *v* **5** issue a challenge to. **challenger** *n*

chamber *n* **1** hall used for formal meetings. **2** legislative or judicial assembly. **3** *Old-fashioned* bedroom. **4** compartment, cavity. **5** compartment for a cartridge in a gun. ♦ *pl* **6** set of rooms used as offices by a barrister. **chambermaid** *n* woman employed to clean bedrooms in a hotel. **chamber music** classical music to be performed by a small group of musicians. **chamber pot** bowl for urine, formerly used in bedrooms.

chamberlain *n Hist* officer who managed the household of a king or nobleman.

chameleon [kam-**meal**-yon] *n* small lizard that changes colour to blend in with its surroundings.

chamfer [**cham**-fer] *v* bevel the edge of.

chamois [**sham**-wah] *n, pl* **-ois 1** small mountain antelope. **2** [**sham**-ee] soft suede leather. **3** piece of this, used for cleaning or polishing.

chamomile [**kam**-mo-mile] *n* same as CAMOMILE.

champ[1] *v* chew noisily. **champ at the bit** *Informal* be impatient to do something.

champ[2] *n* short for CHAMPION.

champagne *n* sparkling white French wine.

champion *n* **1** overall winner of a competition. **2** (foll. by *of*) someone who defends a person or cause. ♦ *v* **3** support. ♦ *adj* **4** *Dialect* excellent. **championship** *n*

chance *n* **1** likelihood, probability. **2** opportunity to do something. **3** risk, gamble. **4** unpredictable element that causes things to happen one way rather than another. ♦ *v* **5** risk, hazard. **6** (foll. by *to*) do something without planning to. **chancy** *adj* **chancier, chanciest** uncertain, risky. **by chance** without planning.

chancel *n* part of a church containing the altar and choir.

chancellery *n, pl* **-leries 1** residence or office of a chancellor. **2** office of an embassy or consulate.

chancellor *n* **1** head of government in some European countries. **2** honorary head of a university. **chancellorship** *n* **Chancellor of the Exchequer** cabinet minister responsible for finance.

Chancery *n* division of the British High Court of Justice.

chancre [**shang**-ker] *n* small hard growth which is the first sign of syphilis.

chandelier [shan-dill-**eer**] *n* ornamental light with branches and holders for several candles or bulbs.

chandler *n* dealer, esp. in ships' supplies.

change *n* **1** becoming different. **2** variety or novelty. **3** different set, esp. of clothes. **4** balance received when the amount paid is more than the cost of a purchase. **5** coins of low value. ♦ *v* **6** make or become different. **7** give and receive (something) in return. **8** exchange (money) for its equivalent in a smaller denomination or different currency. **9** put on other clothes. **10** leave one vehicle and board another. **changeable** *adj* changing often. **changeling** *n* child believed to have been exchanged by fairies for another.

channel *n* **1** band of broadcasting frequencies. **2** means of access or communication. **3** broad strait connecting two areas of sea. **4** bed or course of a river, stream, or canal. **5** groove. ♦ *v* **-nelling, -nelled 6** direct or convey through a channel.

chant *v* **1** utter or sing (a slogan or psalm). ♦ *n* **2** rhythmic or repetitious slogan. **3** psalm that has a short simple melody with several words sung on one note.

chanter *n* (on bagpipes) pipe on which the melody is played.

chanty *n, pl* **-ties** same as SHANTY[2].

chaos *n* complete disorder or confusion. **chaotic** *adj* **chaotically** *adv*

chap *n Informal* man or boy.

chapati, chapatti *n* (in Indian cookery) flat thin unleavened bread.

chapel *n* **1** place of worship with its own altar, within a church. **2** similar place of worship in a large house or institution. **3** Nonconformist place of worship. **4** section of a trade union in the print industry.

chaperone [**shap**-per-rone] *n* **1** older person who accompanies and supervises a young person or young people on a social occasion. ♦ *v* **2** act as a chaperone to.

chaplain *n* clergyman attached to a chapel, military body, or institution. **chaplaincy** *n, pl* **-cies**

chaplet *n* garland for the head.

chapped *adj* (of the skin) raw and cracked, through exposure to cold.

chaps *pl n* leather leggings without a seat, worn by cowboys.

chapter *n* **1** division of a book. **2** period in a life or history. **3** sequence of events, e.g. *chapter of accidents.* **4** branch of a society or club.

char[1] *v* **charring, charred** blacken by partial burning.

char[2] *Informal* ♦ *n* **1** charwoman. ♦ *v* **charring, charred 2** clean other people's houses as a job.

char[3] *n Old-fashioned slang* tea.

char[4] *n* small troutlike fish.

charabanc [**shar**-rab-bang] *n Old-fashioned* coach for sightseeing.

character *n* **1** combination of qualities distinguishing a person, group, or place. **2** reputation, esp. good reputation. **3** person represented in a play, film, or story. **4** unusual or amusing person. **5** letter, numeral, or symbol used in writing or printing. **characteristic** *n*

1 distinguishing feature or quality. ♦ *adj* 2 typical. **characteristically** *adv* **characterize** *v* 1 be a characteristic of. 2 (foll. by *as*) describe. **characterization** *n*

charade [shar-**rahd**] *n* 1 absurd pretence. ♦ *pl* 2 game in which one team acts out a word or phrase, which the other team has to guess.

charcoal *n* black substance formed by partially burning wood.

charge *v* 1 ask as a price. 2 enter a debit against a person's account for (a purchase). 3 accuse formally. 4 make a rush at or sudden attack upon. 5 fill (a glass). 6 fill (a battery) with electricity. 7 command, assign. ♦ *n* 8 price charged. 9 formal accusation. 10 attack. 11 command, exhortation. 12 custody, guardianship. 13 person or thing entrusted to someone's care. 14 cartridge, shell. 15 amount of electricity stored in a battery. **in charge of** in control of. **chargeable** *adj* **charger** *n* 1 device for charging an accumulator. 2 (in the Middle Ages) warhorse.

chargé d'affaires [**shar**-zhay daf-**fair**] *n, pl* **chargés d'affaires** head of a diplomatic mission in the absence of an ambassador or in a small mission.

chariot *n* two-wheeled horse-drawn vehicle used in ancient times in wars and races. **charioteer** *n* chariot driver.

charisma [kar-**rizz**-ma] *n* person's power to attract or influence people. **charismatic** [kar-rizz-**mat**-ik] *adj*

charity *n, pl* **-ties** 1 organization that gives help, such as money or food, to those in need. 2 giving of help to those in need. 3 help given to those in need. 4 kindly attitude towards people. **charitable** *adj* **charitably** *adv*

charlady *n* same as CHARWOMAN.

charlatan [**shar**-lat-tan] *n* person who claims expertise that he or she does not have.

charleston *n* lively dance of the 1920s.

charlock *n* weed with hairy leaves and yellow flowers.

charlotte *n* dessert made with fruit and bread or cake crumbs.

charm *n* 1 attractive quality. 2 trinket worn on a bracelet. 3 small object with supposed magical powers. 4 magic spell. ♦ *v* 5 attract, delight. 6 influence by personal charm. 7 protect or influence as if by magic. **charmer** *n* **charming** *adj* attractive. **charmingly** *adv*

charnel house *n* building or vault for the bones of the dead.

chart *n* 1 graph, table, or diagram showing information. 2 map of the sea or stars. ♦ *v* 3 plot the course of. 4 make a chart of. **the charts** *Informal* weekly lists of the bestselling pop records.

charter *n* 1 document granting or demanding certain rights. 2 fundamental principles of an organization. 3 hire of transport for private use. ♦ *v* 4 hire by charter. 5 grant a charter to. **chartered** *adj* officially qualified to practise a profession, e.g. *chartered accountant.*

chartreuse [shar-**trerz**] *n* sweet-smelling green or yellow liqueur.

charwoman *n* woman whose job is to clean other people's homes.

chary [**chair**-ee] *adj* **-rier, -riest** wary, careful. **charily** *adv*

chase[1] *v* 1 run after quickly in order to catch or drive away. 2 *Informal* rush, run. 3 *Informal* try energetically to obtain. ♦ *n* 4 chasing, pursuit. **chaser** *n* milder drink drunk after another stronger one.

chase[2] *v* engrave or emboss (metal).

chasm [**kaz**-zum] *n* 1 deep crack in the earth. 2 wide difference.

chassis [**shass**-ee] *n, pl* **-sis** frame, wheels, and mechanical parts of a vehicle.

chaste *adj* 1 abstaining from sex outside marriage or altogether. 2 (of style) simple. **chastely** *adv* **chastity** *n*

chasten [**chase**-en] *v* subdue by criticism.

chastise *v* 1 scold severely. 2 punish by beating. **chastisement** *n*

chasuble [**chazz**-yew-bl] *n* long sleeveless robe worn by a priest when celebrating Mass.

chat *n* **1** informal conversation. ♦ *v* **chatting, chatted 2** have an informal conversation. **chatty** *adj* **-tier, -tiest**

chateau [**shat**-toe] *n, pl* **-teaux, -teaus** French castle.

chatelaine [**shat**-tell-lane] *n* (formerly) mistress of a large house or castle.

chattels *pl n* possessions.

chatter *v* **1** speak quickly and continuously about unimportant things. **2** (of a bird or monkey) make rapid repetitive high-pitched noises. **3** (of the teeth) rattle with cold or fear. ♦ *n* **4** idle talk. **chatterbox** *n* person who chatters a lot.

chauffeur *n* person employed to drive a car for someone. **chauffeuse** *n fem*

chauvinism [**show**-vin-iz-zum] *n* irrational belief that one's own country, race, group, or sex is superior. **chauvinist** *n, adj* **chauvinistic** *adj*

cheap *adj* **1** costing relatively little. **2** of poor quality. **3** not valued highly. **4** mean, despicable. **cheaply** *adv* **cheapen** *v* **1** lower the reputation of. **2** reduce the price of. **cheap-jack** *n Informal* person who sells cheap and shoddy goods. **cheapskate** *n Informal* miserly person.

cheat *v* **1** act dishonestly to gain profit or advantage. **2** (usu. foll. by *on*) be unfaithful (to). ♦ *n* **3** person who cheats. **4** fraud, deception.

check *v* **1** examine, investigate. **2** slow the growth or progress of. **3** correspond, agree. ♦ *n* **4** test to ensure accuracy or progress. **5** break in progress. **6** *US* cheque. **7** pattern of squares or crossed lines. **8** *Chess* position of a king under attack. **checked** *adj* having a pattern of squares. **check in** *v* register one's arrival. **checkmate** *n* **1** *Chess* winning position in which an opponent's king is under attack and unable to escape. **2** utter defeat. ♦ *v* **3** *Chess* place the king of (one's opponent) in checkmate. **4** thwart, defeat. **check out** *v* **1** pay the bill and leave a hotel. **2** examine, investigate. **3** *Informal* have a look at. **checkout** *n* counter in a supermarket, where customers pay. **checkup** *n* thorough medical examination.

checkers *n US* same as DRAUGHTS.

Cheddar *n* firm orange or yellowy-white cheese.

cheek *n* **1** either side of the face below the eye. **2** *Informal* impudence, boldness. ♦ *v* **3** *Informal* speak impudently to. **cheeky** *adj* **cheekier, cheekiest** impudent, disrespectful. **cheekily** *adv* **cheekiness** *n*

cheep *n* **1** young bird's high-pitched cry. ♦ *v* **2** utter a cheep.

cheer *v* **1** applaud or encourage with shouts. **2** make or become happy. ♦ *n* **3** shout of applause or encouragement. **4** feeling of happiness. **cheerful** *adj* **cheerfully** *adv* **cheerfulness** *n* **cheerless** *adj* dreary, gloomy. **cheery** *adj* **cheerily** *adv*

cheerio *interj Informal* goodbye.

cheese *n* **1** food made from coagulated milk curd. **2** block of this. **cheesy** *adj* **cheeseburger** *n* hamburger topped with melted cheese. **cheesecake** *n* **1** dessert with a biscuit-crumb base covered with a sweet cream-cheese mixture. **2** *Slang* photographs of naked or near-naked women. **cheesecloth** *n* light cotton cloth. **cheesed off** bored, annoyed. **cheeseparing** *adj* mean, miserly.

cheetah *n* large fast-running spotted African wild cat.

chef *n* cook in a restaurant.

chef-d'oeuvre [shay-**durv**] *n, pl* **chefs-d'oeuvre** masterpiece.

chemical *n* **1** substance used in or resulting from a reaction involving changes to atoms or molecules. ♦ *adj* **2** of chemistry or chemicals. **chemically** *adv*

chemise [shem-**meez**] *n Old-fashioned* woman's loose-fitting slip.

chemistry *n* science of the composition, properties, and reactions of substances. **chemist** *n* **1** shop selling medicines and cosmetics. **2** qualified dispenser of prescribed medicines. **3** specialist in chemistry.

chemotherapy *n* treatment of disease, often cancer, using chemicals.

chenille [shen-**neel**] *n* (fabric of) thick

tufty yarn.

cheque *n* written order to one's bank to pay money from one's account. **cheque book** book of detachable blank cheques issued by a bank. **cheque card** plastic card issued by a bank guaranteeing payment of a customer's cheques.

chequer *n* **1** piece used in Chinese chequers. ♦ *pl* **2** game of draughts. **chequered** *adj* **1** marked by varied fortunes, e.g. *a chequered career.* **2** having a pattern of squares.

cherish *v* **1** cling to (an idea or feeling). **2** care for.

cheroot [sher-**root**] *n* cigar with both ends cut flat.

cherry *n, pl* **-ries** **1** small red or black fruit with a stone. **2** tree on which it grows. ♦ *adj* **3** deep red. **cherry tomato** miniature tomato.

cherub *n, pl* **-ubs, -ubim** **1** angel, often represented as a winged child. **2** sweet child. **cherubic** [cher-**rew**-bik] *adj*

chervil *n* aniseed-flavoured herb.

chess *n* game for two players with 16 pieces each, played on a chequered board of 64 squares. **chessman** *n* piece used in chess.

chest *n* **1** front of the body, from neck to waist. **2** large strong box. **chest of drawers** piece of furniture consisting of drawers in a frame.

chesterfield *n* couch with high padded sides and back.

chestnut *n* **1** reddish-brown edible nut. **2** tree on which it grows. **3** reddish-brown horse. **4** *Informal* old joke. ♦ *adj* **5** (of hair or a horse) reddish-brown.

chesty *adj* **chestier, chestiest** *Informal* symptomatic of chest disease.

cheval glass [shev-**val**] *n* full-length mirror mounted to swivel within a frame.

Cheviot *n* large British sheep reared for its wool.

chevron [**shev**-ron] *n* V-shaped pattern, esp. on the sleeve of a military uniform to indicate rank.

chew *v* grind (food) between the teeth. **chewy** *adj* **chewier, chewiest** requiring a lot of chewing. **chewing gum** flavoured gum to be chewed but not swallowed. **chew over** *v* consider carefully.

chianti [kee-**ant**-ee] *n* dry red Italian wine.

chiaroscuro [kee-ah-roh-**skew**-roh] *n, pl* **-ros** distribution of light and shade in a picture.

chic [**sheek**] *adj* **1** stylish, elegant. ♦ *n* **2** stylishness, elegance.

chicane [shik-**kane**] *n* obstacle in a motor-racing circuit.

chicanery *n* trickery, deception.

chick *n* **1** baby bird. **2** *Slang* young woman. **chickpea** *n* edible yellow pealike seed. **chickweed** *n* weed with small white flowers.

chicken *n* **1** domestic fowl. **2** its flesh, used as food. **3** *Slang* coward. ♦ *adj* **4** *Slang* cowardly. **chicken feed** *Slang* trifling amount of money. **chicken out** *v* *Informal* fail to do something through cowardice. **chickenpox** *n* infectious disease with an itchy rash.

chicory *n, pl* **-ries** **1** plant whose leaves are used in salads. **2** root of this plant, used as a coffee substitute.

chide *v* **chiding, chided** *or* **chid, chid** *or* **chidden** rebuke, scold.

chief *n* **1** head of a group of people. ♦ *adj* **2** most important. **chiefly** *adv* **1** especially. **2** mainly. **chieftain** *n* leader of a tribe.

chiffchaff *n* common European warbler.

chiffon [**shif**-fon] *n* fine see-through fabric.

chignon [**sheen**-yon] *n* knot of hair pinned up at the back of the head.

chigoe [**chig**-go] *n* tropical flea that burrows into the skin.

chihuahua [chee-**wah**-wah] *n* tiny short-haired dog.

chilblain *n* inflammation of the fingers or toes, caused by exposure to cold.

child *n, pl* **children** **1** young human being, boy or girl. **2** son or daughter. **3** product of an influence or environment, e.g. *a child of the Sixties.* **childhood** *n* **childish** *adj* **1** immature, silly. **2** of or like a child. **childishly** *adv* **childless** *adj* **childlike** *adj* innocent, trustful.

childbirth *n* giving birth to a child. **child's play** very easy task.

> Note that *childish* has overtones of *foolish* while *childlike* suggests an *innocent* quality.

chill *n* **1** a feverish cold. **2** moderate coldness. ♦ *v* **3** make (something) cool or cold. **4** cause (someone) to feel cold or frightened. ♦ *adj* **5** unpleasantly cold. **chilly** *adj* **chillier, chilliest 1** moderately cold. **2** unfriendly. **chilliness** *n*

chilli, chili *n* **1** small red or green hot-tasting capsicum pod, used in cooking. **2** (also **chilli con carne**) hot-tasting Mexican dish of meat, onions, beans, and chilli powder.

chime *n* **1** musical ringing sound of a bell or clock. ♦ *v* **2** make a musical ringing sound. **3** indicate (the time) by chiming. **4** (foll. by *with*) be consistent with.

chimera [kime-**meer**-a] *n* **1** unrealistic hope or idea. **2** fabled monster with a lion's head, goat's body, and serpent's tail. **chimerical** *adj*

chimney *n* hollow vertical structure for carrying away smoke from a fire. **chimney breast** walls surrounding the base of a chimney or fireplace. **chimneypot** *n* short pipe on the top of a chimney. **chimney sweep** person who cleans soot from chimneys.

chimp *n Informal* short for CHIMPANZEE.

chimpanzee *n* intelligent black African ape.

chin *n* part of the face below the mouth. **chinwag** *n Informal* chat.

china *n* **1** fine earthenware or porcelain. **2** dishes or ornaments made of this. **china clay** same as KAOLIN.

chinchilla *n* **1** S American rodent bred for its soft grey fur. **2** its fur.

chine *n* **1** cut of meat including part of the backbone. ♦ *v* **2** cut (meat) along the backbone.

Chinese *adj* **1** of China. ♦ *n* **2** (*pl* **-nese**) person from China. **3** any of the languages of China. **Chinese chequers** game played with marbles or pegs on a star-shaped board. **Chinese lantern** collapsible lantern made of thin paper.

chink[1] *n* small narrow opening, e.g. *a chink of light.*

chink[2] *v, n* (make) a light ringing sound.

chintz *n* printed cotton fabric with a glazed finish.

chip *n* **1** strip of potato, fried in deep fat. **2** tiny wafer of semiconductor material forming an integrated circuit. **3** counter used to represent money in gambling games. **4** small piece removed by chopping, breaking, etc. **5** mark left where a small piece has been broken off something. ♦ *v* **chipping, chipped 6** break small pieces from. **have a chip on one's shoulder** *Informal* bear a grudge. **chip in** *v Informal* **1** contribute (money). **2** interrupt with a remark.

chipboard *n* thin board made of compressed wood particles.

chipmunk *n* small squirrel-like N American rodent with a striped back.

chipolata *n* small sausage.

chiropodist [kir-**rop**-pod-ist] *n* person who treats minor foot complaints. **chiropody** *n*

chiropractic [kire-oh-**prak**-tik] *n* system of treating bodily disorders by manipulation of the spine. **chiropractor** *n*

chirp, chirrup *v* **1** (of a bird or insect) make a short high-pitched sound. **2** speak in a lively fashion. ♦ *n* **3** chirping sound. **chirpy** *adj* **chirpier, chirpiest** *Informal* lively and cheerful.

chisel *n* **1** metal tool with a sharp end for shaping wood or stone. ♦ *v* **-elling, -elled 2** carve or form with a chisel.

chit[1] *n* short official note, such as a receipt.

chit[2] *n Old-fashioned* pert or impudent girl.

chitchat *n* chat, gossip.

chitterlings *pl n* pig's intestines cooked as food.

chivalry *n* **1** courteous behaviour, esp. by men towards women. **2** medieval system and principles of knighthood. **chivalrous** *adj*

chives *pl n* herb with a mild onion flavour.

chivvy *v* **-vying, -vied** *Informal* harass, nag.

chlorine *n* strong-smelling greenish-yellow gaseous element, used to disinfect water. **chlorinate** *v* disinfect (water) with chlorine. **chlorination** *n* **chloride** *n* compound of chlorine and another substance.

chlorofluorocarbon *n* any of various gaseous compounds of carbon, hydrogen, chlorine, and fluorine, used in refrigerators and aerosol propellants, some of which break down the ozone in the atmosphere.

chloroform *n* strong-smelling liquid formerly used as an anaesthetic.

chlorophyll *n* green colouring matter of plants, which enables them to convert sunlight into energy.

chock *n* **1** block or wedge used to prevent a heavy object from moving. ♦ *v* **2** secure by a chock. **chock-full, chock-a-block** *adj* completely full.

chocolate *n* **1** sweet food made from cacao seeds. **2** sweet or drink made from this. ♦ *adj* **3** dark brown.

choice *n* **1** choosing. **2** opportunity or power of choosing. **3** person or thing chosen or that may be chosen. **4** alternative action or possibility. ♦ *adj* **5** of high quality.

choir *n* **1** organized group of singers, esp. in church. **2** part of a church occupied by the choir.

choke *v* **1** hinder or stop the breathing of (a person) by strangling or smothering. **2** have trouble in breathing. **3** block, clog up. ♦ *n* **4** device controlling the amount of air that is mixed with the fuel in a petrol engine. **choker** *n* tight-fitting necklace. **choke back** *v* suppress (tears or anger).

cholera [**kol**-ler-a] *n* serious infectious disease causing severe vomiting and diarrhoea.

choleric [**kol**-ler-ik] *adj* bad-tempered. **choler** *n Old-fashioned* bad temper.

cholesterol [kol-**lest**-er-oll] *n* fatty substance found in animal tissue, an excess of which can cause heart disease.

chomp *v* chew noisily.

choose *v* **choosing, chose, chosen 1** select from a number of alternatives. **2** decide (to do something) because one wants to. **choosy** *adj* **choosier, choosiest** *Informal* fussy, hard to please.

chop[1] *v* **chopping, chopped 1** cut with a blow from an axe or knife. **2** cut into pieces. **3** *Boxing, karate* hit (an opponent) with a short sharp blow. ♦ *n* **4** cutting or sharp blow. **5** slice of lamb or pork, usu. with a rib. **chopper** *n* **1** *Informal* helicopter. **2** small axe. **3** butcher's cleaver. **4** cycle with very high handlebars. **choppy** *adj* **-pier, -piest** (of the sea) fairly rough.

chop[2] *v* **chopping, chopped. chop and change** change one's mind repeatedly.

chops *pl n Informal* jaws, cheeks.

chopsticks *pl n* pair of thin sticks used to eat Chinese food.

chop suey *n* Chinese dish of chopped meat and vegetables in a sauce.

choral *adj* of a choir.

chorale [kor-**rahl**] *n* slow stately hymn tune.

chord[1] *n Maths* straight line joining two points on a curve.

chord[2] *n* simultaneous sounding of three or more musical notes.

chore *n* **1** routine task. **2** unpleasant task.

chorea [kor-**ree**-a] *n* disorder of the nervous system characterized by uncontrollable brief jerky movements.

choreography *n* composition of steps and movements for dancing. **choreographer** *n* **choreographic** *adj*

chorister *n* singer in a choir.

chortle *v* **1** chuckle in amusement. ♦ *n* **2** amused chuckle.

chorus *n, pl* **-ruses 1** large choir. **2** part of a song repeated after each verse. **3** something expressed by many people at once. **4** group of singers or dancers who perform together in a show. ♦ *v* **chorusing, chorused 5** sing or say together. **in chorus** in unison.

chose *v* past tense of CHOOSE. **chosen** *v* past participle of CHOOSE.

chough [**chuff**] *n* large black bird of the crow family.

choux pastry [**shoo**] *n* very light pastry made with eggs.

chow *n* **1** thick-coated dog with a curled tail, orig. from China. **2** *Informal* food.

chowder *n* thick soup containing clams or fish.

chow mein *n* Chinese-American dish of chopped meat or vegetables fried with noodles.

chrism *n* consecrated oil used for anointing in some churches.

Christ *n* **1** Jesus of Nazareth, regarded by Christians as the Messiah. ♦ *interj* **2** *Taboo slang* oath of annoyance or surprise.

christen *v* **1** baptize. **2** give a name to. **3** *Informal* use for the first time. **christening** *n*

Christendom *n* all Christian people or countries.

Christian *n* **1** person who believes in and follows Christ. ♦ *adj* **2** of Christ or Christianity. **3** kind, good. **Christianity** *n* religion based on the life and teachings of Christ. **Christian name** person's first name. **Christian Science** religious system which emphasizes spiritual healing.

Christmas *n* **1** annual festival on Dec. 25 commemorating the birth of Christ. **2** period around this time. **Christmassy** *adj* **Christmas box** tip given at Christmas to postmen or tradesmen. **Christmas Day** Dec. 25. **Christmas Eve** Dec. 24. **Christmas tree** evergreen tree or imitation of one, decorated as part of Christmas celebrations.

chromatic *adj* **1** of colour or colours. **2** *Music* (of a scale) proceeding by semitones. **chromatically** *adv*

chromatography *n* separation and analysis of the components of a substance by slowly passing it through an adsorbing material.

chromium, chrome *n Chem* grey metallic element used in steel alloys and for electroplating.

chromosome *n* microscopic gene-carrying body in the nucleus of a cell.

chronic *adj* **1** (of an illness) lasting a long time. **2** habitual, e.g. *chronic drinking*. **3** *Informal* of poor quality. **chronically** *adv*

chronicle *n* **1** record of events in order of occurrence. ♦ *v* **2** record in or as if in a chronicle. **chronicler** *n*

chronology *n, pl* **-gies** arrangement or list of events in order of occurrence. **chronological** *adj* **chronologically** *adv*

chronometer *n* timepiece designed to be accurate in all conditions.

chrysalis [**kriss**-a-liss] *n* insect in the stage between larva and adult, when it is in a cocoon.

chrysanthemum *n* garden flower with a large head made up of thin petals.

chub *n* freshwater fish of the carp family.

chubby *adj* **-bier, -biest** plump and round. **chubbiness** *n*

chuck[1] *v* **1** *Informal* throw. **2** *Informal* give up, reject. **3** touch (someone) affectionately under the chin.

chuck[2] *n* **1** cut of beef from the neck to the shoulder. **2** device that holds a workpiece in a lathe or a tool in a drill.

chuckle *v* **1** laugh softly. ♦ *n* **2** soft laugh.

chuff *v* (of a steam engine) move while making a puffing sound.

chuffed *adj Informal* very pleased.

chug *n* **1** short dull sound like the noise of an engine. ♦ *v* **chugging, chugged 2** operate or move with this sound.

chukka, chukker *n* period of play in polo.

chum *Informal* ♦ *n* **1** close friend. ♦ *v* **chumming, chummed 2 chum up with** form a close friendship with. **chummy** *adj* **-mier, -miest**

chump *n* **1** *Informal* stupid person. **2** thick piece of meat. **3** thick block of wood.

chunk *n* **1** thick solid piece. **2** considerable amount. **chunky** *adj* **chunkier, chunkiest 1** (of a person) broad and heavy. **2** (of an object) large and thick.

church *n* **1** building for public Christian worship. **2** particular Christian denomination. **3** (**C-**) Christians collectively. **4** clergy. **churchgoer** *n* person who attends church regularly. **churchwarden** *n* member of a congregation who assists the vicar. **churchyard** *n* grounds round a church, used as a graveyard.

churlish *adj* surly and rude.

churn *n* **1** machine in which cream is shaken to make butter. **2** large container for milk. ♦ *v* **3** stir (cream) vigorously to make butter. **4** move about violently. **churn out** *v Informal* produce (things) rapidly in large numbers.

chute[1] [**shoot**] *n* steep slope down which things may be slid.

chute[2] *n Informal* short for PARACHUTE.

chutney *n* pickle made from fruit, vinegar, spices, and sugar.

chyle *n* milky fluid formed in the small intestine during digestion.

chyme *n* thick fluid mass of partially digested food that leaves the stomach.

CIA (in the US) Central Intelligence Agency.

cicada [sik-**kah**-da] *n* large insect that makes a high-pitched drone.

cicatrix [**sik**-a-trix] *n, pl* **-trices** scar.

CID Criminal Investigation Department.

cider *n* alcoholic drink made from fermented apple juice.

cigar *n* roll of cured tobacco leaves for smoking.

cigarette *n* thin roll of shredded tobacco in thin paper, for smoking.

cilium *n, pl* **cilia** *Biol* **1** short thread projecting from a cell, whose rhythmic beating causes movement. **2** eyelash.

cinch [**sinch**] *n Informal* easy task.

cinchona [sing-**kone**-a] *n* **1** S American tree with medicinal bark. **2** (drug made from) the dried bark of this tree, which yields quinine.

cinder *n* piece of material that will not burn, left after burning coal.

Cinderella *n* poor, neglected, or unsuccessful person.

cine camera *n* camera for taking moving pictures.

cinema *n* **1** place for showing films. **2** films collectively. **cinematic** *adj* **cinematograph** *n* combined camera, printer, and projector. **cinematography** *n* technique of making films. **cinematographer** *n*

cineraria *n* garden plant with daisy-like flowers.

cinerarium *n, pl* **-raria** place for keeping the ashes of the dead after cremation.

cinnabar *n* heavy red mineral containing mercury.

cinnamon *n* spice obtained from the bark of an Asian tree.

cinquefoil *n* plant with five-lobed leaves.

cipher [**sife**-er] *n* **1** system of secret writing. **2** unimportant person. **3** *Obs* numeral zero.

circa [**sir**-ka] *prep Latin* approximately, about.

circle *n* **1** perfectly round geometric figure, line, or shape. **2** group of people sharing an interest or activity. **3** *Theatre* section of seats above the main level of the auditorium. ♦ *v* **4** move in a circle (round). **5** enclose in a circle.

circlet *n* circular ornament worn on the head.

circuit *n* **1** complete route or course, esp. a circular one. **2** complete path through which an electric current can flow. **3** periodical journey round a district, as made by judges. **4** motor-racing track. **5** series of sports tournaments. **circuitous** [sir-**kew**-it-uss] *adj* indirect and lengthy. **circuitry** [**sir**-kit-tree] *n* electrical circuit(s).

circular *adj* **1** in the shape of a circle. **2** moving in a circle. ♦ *n* **3** letter for general distribution. **circularity** *n*

circulate *v* **1** send, go, or pass from place to place or person to person. **2** move about a party, talking to different people. **circulation** *n* **1** flow of blood around the body. **2** number of copies of a newspaper or magazine sold. **3** sending or moving round. **circulatory** *adj*

circum- *prefix* around, on all sides, e.g. *circumlocution*.

circumcise *v* **1** remove the foreskin of. **2** cut or remove the clitoris of. **circumcision** *n*

circumference *n* **1** boundary of a specified area or shape, esp. of a circle. **2** distance round this.

circumflex *n* mark (ˆ) over a vowel to show that it is pronounced in a particular way.

circumlocution *n* indirect way of saying something. **circumlocutory** *adj*

circumnavigate *v* sail right round. **circumnavigation** *n*

circumscribe *v* **1** limit, restrict. **2** draw a line round. **circumscription** *n*

circumspect *adj* cautious and careful not to take risks. **circumspectly** *adv* **circumspection** *n*

circumstance *n* (usu. pl) occurrence or condition that accompanies or influences a person or event. **pomp and circumstance** formal display or ceremony. **circumstantial** *adj* **1** (of evidence) strongly suggesting something but not proving it. **2** very detailed. **circumstantiate** *v* prove by giving details.

circumvent *v* **1** avoid or get round (a rule etc.). **2** outwit. **circumvention** *n*

circus *n, pl* **-cuses** (performance given by) a travelling company of acrobats, clowns, performing animals, etc.

cirque *n* steep-sided semicircular hollow found in mountainous areas.

cirrhosis [sir-**roh**-siss] *n* serious liver disease, often caused by drinking too much alcohol.

cirrus *n, pl* **-ri** high wispy cloud.

CIS Commonwealth of Independent States.

Cistercian *n, adj* (monk or nun) of a strict Benedictine order.

cistern *n* water tank, esp. one that holds water for flushing a toilet.

citadel *n* fortress in a city.

cite *v* **1** quote, refer to. **2** bring forward as proof. **3** summon to appear before a court of law. **citation** *n* **1** commendation for bravery. **2** summons to appear before a court of law. **3** quotation.

citizen *n* **1** native or naturalized member of a state or nation. **2** inhabitant of a city or town. **citizenship** *n* **Citizens' Band** range of radio frequencies for private communication by the public.

citric acid *n* weak acid found in citrus fruits.

citron *n* lemon-like fruit of a small Asian tree.

citrus fruit *n* juicy sharp-tasting fruit such as an orange or lemon.

city *n, pl* **-ties** **1** large or important town. **2** town that has received this title from the Crown. **the City** area of London as a financial centre.

civet [**siv**-vit] *n* **1** spotted catlike African mammal. **2** musky fluid from its glands used in perfume.

civic *adj* of a city or citizens. **civics** *n* study of the rights and responsibilities of citizenship.

civil *adj* **1** relating to the citizens of a state as opposed to the armed forces or the Church. **2** polite, courteous. **civilly** *adv* **civility** *n* polite or courteous behaviour. **civilian** *n, adj* (person) not belonging to the armed forces. **civil law** law relating to private and civilian affairs. **civil service** service responsible for the administration of the government. **civil servant** member of the civil service. **civil war** war between people of the same country.

civilize *v* **1** refine or educate (a person). **2** make (a place) more pleasant or more acceptable. **civilization** *n* **1** high level of human cultural and social development. **2** particular society which has reached this level.

civvies *pl n Slang* ordinary clothes that are not part of a uniform.

cl centilitre.

Cl *Chem* chlorine.

clack *n* **1** sound made by two hard objects striking each other. ♦ *v* **2** make this sound.

clad *v* a past of CLOTHE.

cladding *n* material used to cover the outside of a building.

claim *v* **1** assert as a fact. **2** demand as a

right. **3** need, require. ♦ *n* **4** assertion that something is true. **5** assertion of a right. **6** something claimed as a right. **7** demand for payment in connection with an insurance policy. **claimant** *n*

clairvoyance *n* power of perceiving things beyond the natural range of the senses. **clairvoyant** *n, adj*

clam *n* **1** edible shellfish with a hinged shell. ♦ *v* **clamming, clammed 2 clam up** *Informal* stop talking, esp. through nervousness.

clamber *v* climb awkwardly.

clammy *adj* **-mier, -miest** unpleasantly moist and sticky. **clamminess** *n*

clamour *n* **1** loud protest. **2** loud persistent noise or outcry. ♦ *v* **3** make a loud noise or outcry. **clamorous** *adj* **clamour for** *v* demand noisily.

clamp *n* **1** tool with movable jaws for holding things together tightly. **2** short for WHEEL CLAMP. ♦ *v* **3** fasten with a clamp. **4** immobilize (a car) with a wheel clamp. **clamp down on** *v* **1** become stricter about. **2** suppress.

clan *n* **1** group of families with a common ancestor, esp. among Scottish Highlanders. **2** close group. **clannish** *adj* (of a group) tending to exclude outsiders.

clandestine *adj* secret and concealed.

clang *v* **1** make a loud ringing metallic sound. ♦ *n* **2** ringing metallic sound. **clanger** *n Informal* obvious mistake.

clangour *n* loud continuous clanging sound. **clangorous** *adj*

clank *n* **1** harsh metallic sound. ♦ *v* **2** make such a sound.

clap[1] *v* **clapping, clapped 1** applaud by hitting the palms of one's hands sharply together. **2** put quickly or forcibly. **3** strike (someone) lightly with an open hand, for example in greeting. ♦ *n* **4** act or sound of clapping. **5** sudden loud noise, e.g. *a clap of thunder.* **clapped out** *Slang* worn out, dilapidated.

clap[2] *n Slang* gonorrhoea.

clapper *n* piece of metal inside a bell, which causes it to sound when struck against the side. **clapperboard** *n* pair of hinged boards clapped together during filming to help in synchronizing sound and picture.

claptrap *n Informal* foolish or pretentious talk.

claque *n* group of people hired to applaud.

claret [**klar**-rit] *n* dry red wine from Bordeaux.

clarify *v* **-fying, -fied 1** make (a matter) clear and unambiguous. **2** remove the water from (butter) by heating it. **clarification** *n*

clarinet *n* keyed woodwind instrument with a single reed. **clarinettist** *n*

clarion *n* **1** obsolete high-pitched trumpet. **2** its sound. **clarion call** strong encouragement to do something.

clarity *n* clearness.

clash *v* **1** come into conflict. **2** (of events) happen at the same time. **3** (of colours) look unattractive together. **4** (of objects) make a loud harsh sound by being hit together. ♦ *n* **5** fight, argument. **6** fact of two events happening at the same time. **7** loud harsh noise, esp. of things striking together.

clasp *n* **1** device for fastening things. **2** firm grasp or embrace. ♦ *v* **3** grasp or embrace firmly. **4** fasten with a clasp. **clasp knife** large knife with blades that fold into the handle.

class *n* **1** group of people sharing a similar social position. **2** system of dividing society into such groups. **3** group of people or things sharing a common characteristic. **4** group of pupils or students taught together. **5** standard of quality. **6** *Informal* elegance or excellence, e.g. *a touch of class.* ♦ *v* **7** place in a class.

classic *adj* **1** being a typical example of something. **2** of lasting interest because of excellence. **3** attractive because of simplicity of form. ♦ *n* **4** author, artist, or work of art of recognized excellence. ♦ *pl* **5** study of ancient Greek and Roman literature and culture. **classical** *adj* **1** of or in a restrained conservative style. **2** denoting serious art music. **3** of or influenced by ancient Greek and Roman culture. **classically** *adv* **classicism** *n* artistic style showing emotional restraint and regularity of form. **classicist** *n*

> *Classic* and *classical* are synonyms except in the context of Greek and Roman culture, which is called *classical*, or highly rated art and literature, which is called *classic*.

classify *v* **-fying, -fied 1** divide into groups with similar characteristics. **2** declare (information) to be officially secret. **classifiable** *adj* **classification** *n*

classy *adj* **classier, classiest** *Informal* stylish and elegant.

clatter *v, n* (make) a rattling noise.

clause *n* **1** section of a legal document. **2** part of a sentence, containing a verb.

claustrophobia *n* abnormal fear of confined spaces. **claustrophobic** *adj*

clavichord *n* early keyboard instrument.

clavicle *n* same as COLLARBONE.

claw *n* **1** sharp hooked nail of a bird or beast. **2** similar part, such as a crab's pincer. ♦ *v* **3** tear with claws or nails.

clay *n* fine-grained earth, soft when moist and hardening when baked, used to make bricks and pottery. **clayey** *adj* **clay pigeon** baked clay disc hurled into the air as a target for shooting.

claymore *n* large two-edged sword formerly used by Scottish Highlanders.

clean *adj* **1** free from dirt or impurities. **2** not yet used. **3** morally acceptable, inoffensive. **4** (of a reputation or record) free from dishonesty or corruption. **5** complete, e.g. *a clean break.* **6** smooth and regular. ♦ *v* **7** make (something) free from dirt. ♦ *adv* **8** *Not standard* completely, e.g. *I clean forgot.* **come clean** *Informal* reveal or admit something. **cleaner** *n* **cleanly** *adv* **cleanliness** *n* **clean-cut** *adj* **1** clearly outlined. **2** wholesome in appearance.

cleanse *v* make clean. **cleanser** *n*

clear *adj* **1** free from doubt or confusion. **2** easy to see or hear. **3** able to be seen through. **4** free from darkness or obscurity. **5** free of obstruction. **6** (of weather) free from clouds. **7** (of skin) without blemish. **8** (of money) without deduction. ♦ *adv* **9** in a clear or distinct manner. **10** out of the way, e.g. *he lifted him clear of the deck.* ♦ *v* **11** make or become clear. **12** pass by or over (something) without contact. **13** prove (someone) innocent of a crime or mistake. **14** make as profit. **clearly** *adv* **clearance** *n* **1** clearing. **2** official permission. **3** space between two parts in motion. **clear-cut** *adj* easy to understand, not vague. **clearing** *n* treeless area in a wood. **clear off** *v Informal* go away. **clear out** *v* **1** remove and sort the contents of. **2** *Informal* go away. **clear-sighted** *adj* having good judgment. **clearway** *n* stretch of road on which motorists may stop in an emergency.

cleat *n* **1** wedge. **2** piece of wood or iron with two projecting ends round which ropes are fastened.

cleave[1] *v* **cleaving, cleft, cleaved** *or* **clove, cleft, cleaved** *or* **cloven** split apart. **cleavage** *n* **1** space between a woman's breasts, as revealed by a low-cut dress. **2** division, split. **cleaver** *n* butcher's heavy knife with a square blade.

cleave[2] *v* cling or stick.

clef *n Music* symbol at the beginning of a stave to show the pitch.

cleft *n* **1** narrow opening or crack. ♦ *v* **2** a past of CLEAVE[1]. **in a cleft stick** in a very difficult position.

clematis *n* climbing plant with large colourful flowers.

clement *adj* (of weather) mild. **clemency** *n* kind or lenient treatment.

clementine *n* small orange citrus fruit.

clench *v* **1** close or squeeze (one's teeth or fist) tightly. **2** grasp firmly.

clerestory [**clear**-store-ee] *n, pl* **-ries** row of windows at the top of a wall above an adjoining roof.

clergy *n* priests and ministers as a group. **clergyman** *n*

cleric *n* member of the clergy.

clerical *adj* **1** of clerks or office work. **2** of the clergy.

clerk *n* employee in an office, bank, or court who keeps records, files, and accounts.

clever *adj* **1** intelligent, quick at learning. **2** showing skill. **cleverly** *adv* **cleverness** *n*

cliché [**klee**-shay] *n* expression or idea that is no longer effective because of overuse. **clichéd** *adj*

click *n* **1** short sharp sound. ♦ *v* **2** make this sound. **3** *Informal* (of two people) get on well together. **4** *Informal* become suddenly clear. **5** *Computers* press and release (a button on a mouse). **6** *Slang* be a success.

client *n* person who uses the services of a professional person or company. **clientele** [klee-on-**tell**] *n* clients collectively.

cliff *n* steep rock face, esp. along the sea shore. **cliffhanger** *n* film, game, etc., that is tense and exciting because its outcome is uncertain.

climacteric *n* **1** same as MENOPAUSE. **2** diminishing sex drive and fertility experienced by men in middle age.

climate *n* **1** typical weather conditions of an area. **2** prevailing trend. **climatic** *adj* **climatically** *adv*

> *Climatic* is sometimes wrongly used where *climactic* is meant. *Climatic* should be used to talk about things relating to climate; *climactic* is used to describe something which forms a climax.

climax *n* **1** most intense point of an experience, series of events, or story. **2** same as ORGASM. ♦ *v* **3** *Not universally accepted* reach a climax. **climactic** *adj*

climb *v* **1** go up, ascend. **2** rise to a higher point or intensity. ♦ *n* **3** climbing. **4** place to be climbed. **climber** *n* **climb down** *v* retreat from an opinion or position.

clime *n Poetic* place or its climate.

clinch *v* **1** settle (an argument or agreement) decisively. ♦ *n* **2** *Boxing, wrestling* movement in which one competitor holds on to the other to avoid punches. **3** *Informal* lover's embrace. **clincher** *n Informal* something decisive.

cling *v* **clinging, clung** hold tightly or stick closely. **clingfilm** *n* thin polythene material for wrapping food.

clinic *n* **1** building where outpatients receive medical treatment or advice. **2** private or specialized hospital. **clinical** *adj* **1** of a clinic. **2** logical and unemotional. **clinically** *adv*

clink[1] *v, n* (make) a light sharp metallic sound.

clink[2] *n Slang* prison.

clinker *n* fused coal left over in a fire or furnace.

clinker-built *adj* (of a boat) made of overlapping planks.

clip[1] *v* **clipping, clipped 1** cut with shears or scissors. **2** *Informal* hit sharply. ♦ *n* **3** short extract of a film. **4** *Informal* sharp blow. **clipped** *adj* (of speech) abrupt and disjointed. **clippers** *pl n* tool for clipping. **clipping** *n* something cut out, esp. an article from a newspaper.

clip[2] *n* **1** device for attaching or holding things together. ♦ *v* **clipping, clipped 2** attach or hold together with a clip.

clipper *n* fast commercial sailing ship.

clique [**kleek**] *n* small exclusive group. **cliquey** *adj*

clitoris [**klit**-or-iss] *n* small sexually sensitive organ at the front of the vulva. **clitoral** *adj*

cloak *n* **1** loose sleeveless outer garment. **2** something that covers or conceals. ♦ *v* **3** cover or conceal. **cloakroom** *n* room where coats may be left temporarily.

clobber[1] *v Informal* **1** hit. **2** defeat utterly.

clobber[2] *n Informal* belongings, esp. clothes.

cloche [**klosh**] *n* **1** cover to protect young plants. **2** woman's close-fitting hat.

clock *n* **1** instrument for showing the time. **2** device with a dial for recording or measuring. ♦ *v* **3** record (time) with a stopwatch. **clockwise** *adv, adj* in the direction in which the hands of a clock rotate. **clock in** *or* **on, out** *or* **off** *v* register arrival at *or* departure from work on an automatic time recorder. **clock up** *v* reach (a total). **clockwork** *n* mechanism similar to the kind in a clock, used in wind-up toys. **like clockwork** with complete regularity and precision.

clod *n* **1** lump of earth. **2** stupid person. **cloddish** *adj* **clodhopper** *n Informal* clumsy person.

clog *v* **clogging, clogged 1** obstruct. ♦ *n* **2** wooden or wooden-soled shoe.

cloisonné [klwah-**zon**-nay] *n* design made by filling in a wire outline with coloured enamel.

cloister *n* **1** covered pillared arcade, usu. in a monastery. **2** place of religious seclusion. **cloistered** *adj* sheltered.

clone *n* **1** animal or plant produced artificially from the cells of another animal or plant, and identical to the original. **2** *Informal* person who closely resembles another. ♦ *v* **3** produce as a clone.

close[1] *v* [rhymes with **nose**] **1** shut. **2** prevent access to. **3** end, terminate. **4** bring or come nearer together. ♦ *n* **5** end, conclusion. **6** [rhymes with **dose**] street closed at one end. **7** [rhymes with **dose**] courtyard, quadrangle. **closed-circuit television** television system used within a limited area such as a building. **closed shop** place of work in which all workers must belong to a particular trade union.

close[2] *adj* [rhymes with **dose**] **1** near. **2** intimate. **3** careful, thorough. **4** compact, dense. **5** oppressive, stifling. **6** secretive. ♦ *adv* **7** closely, tightly. **closely** *adv* **closeness** *n* **close season** period when it is illegal to kill certain game or fish. **close shave** *Informal* narrow escape. **close-up** *n* photograph or film taken at close range.

closet *n* **1** *US* cupboard. **2** small private room. ♦ *adj* **3** private, secret. ♦ *v* **closeting, closeted 4** shut (oneself) away in private.

closure *n* **1** closing. **2** ending of a debate by immediate vote.

clot *n* **1** soft thick lump formed from liquid. **2** *Informal* stupid person. ♦ *v* **clotting, clotted 3** form soft thick lumps.

cloth *n* **1** (piece of) woven fabric. **2** (preceded by *the*) the clergy.

clothe *v* **clothing, clothed** *or* **clad 1** put clothes on. **2** provide with clothes. **clothes** *pl n* **1** articles of dress. **2** bed coverings. **clothier** *n Old-fashioned* maker or seller of clothes or cloth. **clothing** *n* clothes collectively.

cloud *n* **1** mass of condensed water vapour floating in the sky. **2** floating mass of smoke, dust, etc. **3** large number of insects etc. in flight. **4** something that threatens or causes gloom. ♦ *v* **5** (foll. by *over*) become cloudy. **6** confuse. **7** make gloomy or depressed. **cloudless** *adj* **cloudy** *adj* **1** having a lot of clouds. **2** (of liquid) not clear. **cloudburst** *n* heavy fall of rain.

clout *Informal* ♦ *n* **1** hard blow. **2** power, influence. ♦ *v* **3** hit hard.

clove[1] *n* dried flower bud of a tropical tree, used as a spice.

clove[2] *n* segment of a bulb of garlic.

clove[3] *v* a past tense of CLEAVE[1]. **clove hitch** knot used to fasten a rope to a spar.

cloven *v* a past participle of CLEAVE[1]. **cloven hoof** divided hoof of a cow, goat, etc.

clover *n* plant with three-lobed leaves. **in clover** in luxury.

clown *n* **1** comic entertainer in a circus. **2** amusing person. **3** stupid person. ♦ *v* **4** behave foolishly. **5** perform as a clown. **clownish** *adj*

cloying *adj* sickeningly sweet.

club *n* **1** association of people with common interests. **2** building used by such a group. **3** thick stick used as a weapon. **4** stick with a curved end used to hit the ball in golf. **5** playing card with black three-leaved symbols. ♦ *v* **clubbing, clubbed 6** hit with a club. **club together** *v* combine resources for a common purpose.

club foot *n* deformity of the foot causing inability to put the foot flat on the ground.

cluck *n* **1** low clicking noise made by a hen. ♦ *v* **2** make this noise.

clue *n* something that helps to solve a mystery or puzzle. **not have a clue** be completely baffled. **clueless** *adj* stupid. **clued-up** *adj* shrewd and well-informed.

clump *n* **1** small group of things or people. **2** dull heavy tread. ♦ *v* **3** walk heavily. **4** form into clumps.

clumsy *adj* **-sier, -siest 1** lacking skill or physical coordination. **2** badly made or done. **clumsily** *adv* **clumsiness** *n*

clung *v* past of CLING.

clunk *n* **1** dull metallic sound. ♦ *v* **2** make such a sound.

cluster *n* **1** small close group. ♦ *v* **2** gather in clusters.

clutch[1] *v* **1** grasp tightly. **2** (foll. by *at*) try to get hold of. ♦ *n* **3** device enabling two revolving shafts to be connected and disconnected, esp. in a motor vehicle. **4** tight grasp.

clutch[2] *n* **1** set of eggs laid at the same time. **2** small group of things.

clutter *v* **1** scatter objects about (a place) untidily. ♦ *n* **2** untidy mess.

Clydesdale *n* heavy powerful carthorse.

cm centimetre.

Cm *Chem* curium.

CND Campaign for Nuclear Disarmament.

Co *Chem* cobalt.

CO 1 Colorado. **2** Commanding Officer.

Co. 1 Company. **2** County.

co- *prefix* together, joint, or jointly, e.g. *coproduction.*

c/o 1 care of. **2** *Book-keeping* carried over.

coach *n* **1** long-distance bus. **2** railway carriage. **3** large four-wheeled horse-drawn carriage. **4** trainer, instructor. ♦ *v* **5** train, teach. **coachman** *n* driver of a horse-drawn coach or carriage.

coagulate [koh-**ag**-yew-late] *v* change from a liquid to a semisolid mass. **coagulation** *n* **coagulant** *n* substance causing coagulation.

coal *n* black rock consisting mainly of carbon, used as fuel. **coalface** *n* exposed seam of coal in a mine. **coalfield** *n* area with coal under the ground. **coal gas** mixture of gases produced from coal, used for heating and lighting. **coal tar** black tar made from coal, used for making drugs and chemical products.

coalesce [koh-a-**less**] *v* come together, merge. **coalescence** *n*

coalition [koh-a-**lish**-un] *n* temporary alliance, esp. between political parties.

coaming *n* raised frame round a ship's hatchway for keeping out water.

coarse *adj* **1** rough in texture. **2** unrefined, indecent. **3** of inferior quality. **coarsely** *adv* **coarseness** *n* **coarsen** *v* **coarse fish** any freshwater fish not of the salmon family.

coast *n* **1** place where the land meets the sea. ♦ *v* **2** move by momentum, without the use of power. **3** proceed without great effort. **coastal** *adj* **coaster** *n* **1** small mat placed under a glass. **2** small ship. **coastguard** *n* **1** organization that aids ships and swimmers in trouble and prevents smuggling. **2** member of this. **coastline** *n* outline of a coast.

coat *n* **1** outer garment with long sleeves. **2** animal's fur or hair. **3** covering layer, e.g. *a coat of paint.* ♦ *v* **4** cover with a layer. **coating** *n* covering layer. **coat of arms** heraldic emblem of a family or institution.

coax *v* **1** persuade gently. **2** obtain by persistent coaxing.

coaxial [koh-**ax**-ee-al] *adj* (of a cable) transmitting by means of two concentric conductors separated by an insulator.

cob *n* **1** stalk of an ear of maize. **2** thickset type of horse. **3** round loaf of bread. **4** male swan.

cobalt *n Chem* brittle silvery-white metallic element.

cobble *n* cobblestone. **cobbler** *n* shoe mender. **cobblestone** *n* rounded stone used for paving. **cobble together** *v* put together clumsily.

cobblers *pl n Taboo slang* nonsense.

COBOL *n* high-level computer programming language for general commercial use.

cobra *n* venomous hooded snake of Asia and Africa.

cobweb *n* spider's web.

coca *n* dried leaves of a S American shrub which contain cocaine.

Coca-Cola *n* ® dark brown fizzy soft drink.

cocaine *n* addictive drug used as a narcotic and as an anaesthetic.

coccyx [**kok**-six] *n, pl* **coccyges** [kok-**sije**-eez] bone at the base of the spinal column.

cochineal *n* red dye obtained from a Mexican insect, used for food colouring.

cochlea [**kok**-lee-a] *n, pl* **-leae** [-li-**ee**] spiral tube in the internal ear, which converts sound vibrations into nerve impulses.

cock *n* **1** male bird, esp. of domestic fowl. **2** *Taboo slang* penis. **3** stopcock. ♦ *v* **4** draw back (the hammer of a gun) to firing position. **5** lift and turn (part of the body). **cockerel** *n* young domestic cock. **cock-a-hoop** *adj* in high spirits. **cock-and-bull story** improbable story.

cockade *n* feather or rosette worn on a hat as a badge.

cockatoo *n* crested parrot of Australia or the East Indies.

cocker spaniel *n* small spaniel.

cockeyed *adj* **1** *Informal* crooked, askew. **2** foolish, absurd.

cockle *n* edible shellfish. **cockleshell** *n* **1** shell of the cockle. **2** small light boat.

Cockney *n* **1** native of the East End of London. **2** London dialect.

cockpit *n* **1** pilot's compartment in an aircraft. **2** driver's compartment in a racing car. **3** site of many battles or contests.

cockroach *n* beetle-like insect which is a household pest.

cockscomb *n* same as COXCOMB.

cocksure *adj* overconfident, arrogant.

cocktail *n* **1** mixed alcoholic drink. **2** appetizer of seafood or mixed fruits.

cocky *adj* **cockier, cockiest** conceited and overconfident. **cockily** *adv* **cockiness** *n*

coco *n* coconut palm.

cocoa *n* **1** powder made from the seed of the cacao tree. **2** drink made from this powder.

coconut *n* **1** large hard fruit of a type of palm tree. **2** edible flesh of this fruit.

cocoon *n* **1** silky protective covering of a silkworm. **2** protective covering. ♦ *v* **3** wrap up tightly for protection.

cocotte *n* small fireproof dish in which individual portions of food are cooked.

cod *n* large food fish of the North Atlantic. **cod-liver oil** oil extracted from fish, rich in vitamins A and D.

COD cash on delivery.

coda [**kode**-a] *n* final part of a musical composition.

coddle *v* **1** pamper, overprotect. **2** cook (eggs) in water just below boiling point.

code *n* **1** system of letters, symbols, or prearranged signals by which messages can be communicated secretly or briefly. **2** set of principles or rules. ♦ *v* **3** put into code. **codify** [**kode**-if-fie] *v* **-fying, -fied** organize (rules or procedures) systematically. **codification** *n*

codeine [**kode**-een] *n* drug used as a painkiller.

codex *n, pl* **codices** volume of manuscripts of an ancient text.

codger *n Informal* old man.

codicil [**kode**-iss-ill] *n* addition to a will.

codpiece *n Hist* bag covering the male genitals, attached to the breeches.

codswallop *n Slang* nonsense.

coeducation *n* education of boys and girls together. **coeducational** *adj*

coefficient *n* **1** *Maths* number or constant placed before and multiplying a quantity. **2** *Physics* number or constant used to calculate the behaviour of a substance under specified conditions.

coelacanth [**seel**-a-kanth] *n* primitive marine fish.

coeliac disease [**seel**-ee-ak] *n* disease which hampers digestion of food.

coequal *adj, n* equal.
coerce [koh-**urss**] *v* compel, force. **coercion** *n* **coercive** *adj*
coeval [koh-**eev**-al] *adj, n* contemporary.
coexist *v* exist together, esp. peacefully despite differences. **coexistence** *n*
coextensive *adj* covering the same area.
C of E Church of England.
coffee *n* **1** drink made from the roasted and ground seeds of a tropical shrub. **2** beanlike seeds of this shrub. ♦ *adj* **3** medium-brown. **coffee bar** café, snack bar. **coffee table** small low table. **coffee-table book** large expensive illustrated book.
coffer *n* **1** chest for valuables. ♦ *pl* **2** store of money.
cofferdam *n* watertight enclosure pumped dry to enable construction work to be done.
coffin *n* box in which a corpse is buried or cremated.
cog *n* **1** one of the teeth on the rim of a gearwheel. **2** unimportant person in a big organization.
cogent [**koh**-jent] *adj* forcefully convincing. **cogency** *n* **cogently** *adv*
cogitate [**koj**-it-tate] *v* think deeply about. **cogitation** *n*
cognac [**kon**-yak] *n* French brandy.
cognate *adj* derived from a common original form.
cognition *n* act or experience of knowing or acquiring knowledge. **cognitive** *adj*
cognizance *n* knowledge, understanding. **cognizant** *adj*
cognomen [kog-**noh**-men] *n, pl* **-nomens, -nomina** [-**nom**-min-a] **1** nickname. **2** surname.
cognoscenti [kon-yo-**shen**-tee] *pl n* connoisseurs.
cohabit *v* live together as husband and wife without being married. **cohabitation** *n*
cohere *v* **1** hold or stick together. **2** be logically connected or consistent. **coherence** *n* **coherent** *adj* **1** logical and consistent. **2** capable of intelligible speech. **3** sticking together. **coherently** *adv* **cohesion** *n* sticking together. **cohesive** *adj*
cohort *n* **1** band of associates. **2** tenth part of an ancient Roman legion.
coif *v* **coiffing, coiffed 1** arrange the hair of. ♦ *n* **2** close-fitting cap worn in the Middle Ages.
coiffure *n* hairstyle. **coiffeur, coiffeuse** *n* hairdresser.
coil *v* **1** wind in loops. **2** move in a winding course. ♦ *n* **3** something coiled. **4** single loop of this. **5** coil-shaped contraceptive device inserted in the womb. **6** electrical conductor wound into a spiral.
coin *n* **1** piece of metal money. **2** metal currency collectively. ♦ *v* **3** invent (a word or phrase). **4** make or stamp (coins). **coin it in** *Informal* earn money quickly. **coinage** *n* **1** coins collectively. **2** word or phrase coined. **3** coining.
coincide *v* **1** happen at the same time. **2** agree or correspond exactly. **coincidence** *n* **1** occurrence of simultaneous or apparently connected events. **2** coinciding. **coincident** *adj* in agreement. **coincidental** *adj* resulting from coincidence. **coincidentally** *adv*
coir *n* coconut fibre, used for matting.
coitus [**koh**-it-uss], **coition** [koh-**ish**-un] *n* sexual intercourse. **coital** *adj*
coke[1] *n* solid fuel left after gas has been distilled from coal.
coke[2] *n Slang* cocaine.
Coke *n* ® short for COCA-COLA.
col *n* high mountain pass.
Col. Colonel.
cola *n* dark brown fizzy soft drink.
colander *n* perforated bowl for straining or rinsing foods.
cold *adj* **1** lacking heat. **2** lacking affection or enthusiasm. **3** (of a colour) giving an impression of coldness. **4** (of a scent in hunting) faint. **5** *Slang* unconscious, e.g. *out cold.* ♦ *n* **6** lack of heat. **7** mild illness causing a runny nose, sneezing, and coughing. **coldly** *adv* **coldness** *n* **cold-blooded** *adj* **1** cruel, unfeeling. **2** having a body temperature that varies according to the surround-

ing temperature. **cold cream** creamy preparation for softening and cleansing the skin. **cold feet** *Slang* nervousness, fear. **cold-shoulder** *v* treat with indifference. **cold sore** cluster of blisters near the lips, caused by a virus. **cold war** political hostility between countries without actual warfare.

coleslaw *n* salad dish of shredded raw cabbage in a dressing.

coley *n* codlike food fish of the N Atlantic.

colic *n* severe pains in the stomach and bowels. **colicky** *adj*

colitis [koh-**lie**-tiss] *n* inflammation of the colon.

collaborate *v* **1** work with another on a project. **2** cooperate with an enemy invader. **collaboration** *n* **collaborative** *adj* **collaborator** *n*

collage [kol-**lahzh**] *n* **1** art form in which various materials or objects are glued onto a surface. **2** picture made in this way.

collapse *v* **1** fall down suddenly. **2** fail completely. **3** fold compactly. ♦ *n* **4** collapsing. **5** sudden failure or breakdown. **collapsible** *adj*

collar *n* **1** part of a garment round the neck. **2** band put round an animal's neck. **3** cut of meat from an animal's neck. ♦ *v* **4** *Informal* seize, arrest. **5** catch in order to speak to. **collarbone** *n* bone joining the shoulder blade to the breastbone.

collate *v* gather together, examine, and put in order. **collation** *n* **1** collating. **2** light meal. **collator** *n*

collateral *n* **1** security pledged for the repayment of a loan. ♦ *adj* **2** descended from a common ancestor but through different lines. **3** additional but subordinate.

colleague *n* fellow worker, esp. in a profession.

collect[1] *v* **1** gather together. **2** accumulate (stamps etc.) as a hobby. **3** fetch. **4** receive payments of (taxes etc.). **5** regain control of (oneself). **collected** *adj* calm and controlled. **collection** *n* **1** things collected. **2** collecting. **3** sum of money collected. **collector** *n*

collect[2] *n* short prayer.

collective *adj* **1** of or done by a group. ♦ *n* **2** group of people working together on an enterprise and sharing the benefits from it. **collective bargaining** negotiation between a trade union and an employer on the wages etc. of the employees. **collectively** *adv* **collectivism** *n* theory that the state should own all means of production. **collectivize** *v* organize according to the theory of collectivism.

colleen *n Irish* girl.

college *n* **1** place of higher education. **2** *Brit* name given to some secondary schools. **3** group of people of the same profession or with special duties. **collegian** *n* member of a college. **collegiate** *adj*

collide *v* **1** crash together violently. **2** have an argument. **collision** *n*

collie *n* silky-haired sheepdog.

colliery *n, pl* **-lieries** coal mine. **collier** *n* **1** coal miner. **2** coal ship.

collocate *v* (of words) occur together regularly. **collocation** *n*

colloid *n* suspension of particles in a solution. **colloidal** *adj*

colloquial *adj* suitable for informal speech or writing. **colloquialism** *n* colloquial word or phrase.

colloquium *n, pl* **-quiums, -quia** academic seminar.

colloquy *n, pl* **-quies** conversation or conference.

collusion *n* secret or illegal cooperation. **collude** *v* act in collusion.

collywobbles *pl n Slang* nervousness.

cologne *n* mild perfume.

colon[1] *n* punctuation mark (:).

colon[2] *n* part of the large intestine connected to the rectum. **colonic** *adj*

colonel *n* senior commissioned army or air-force officer.

colonnade *n* row of columns.

colony *n, pl* **-nies** **1** group of people who settle in a new country but remain under the rule of their homeland. **2** territory occupied by a colony. **3** group of people or animals of the same kind living together. **colonial** *adj, n* (inhabitant) of a colony. **colonialism** *n* policy of acquiring and maintaining colonies. **colonist** *n* settler in a colony. **colonize** *v* make into a colony. **colonization** *n*

Colorado beetle *n* black-and-yellow beetle that is a serious pest of potatoes.

coloration, colouration *n* arrangement of colours.

coloratura *n Music* **1** complicated vocal passage. **2** soprano who specializes in such music.

colossal *adj* very large.

colossus *n, pl* **-si, -suses** **1** huge statue. **2** huge or important person or thing.

colostomy *n, pl* **-mies** operation to form an opening from the colon onto the surface of the body, for emptying the bowel.

colour *n* **1** appearance of things as a result of reflecting light. **2** substance that gives colour. **3** complexion. **4** vividness, authenticity. ♦ *pl* **5** flag of a country or regiment. **6** *Sport* badge or symbol denoting membership of a team. ♦ *v* **7** apply colour to. **8** influence (someone's judgment). **9** blush. **coloured** *adj* **1** having colour. **2** (**C-**) (in S Africa) of mixed White and non-White parentage. **colourful** *adj* **1** with bright or varied colours. **2** vivid, distinctive. **colourfully** *adv* **colouring** *n* **1** application of colour. **2** something added to give colour. **3** complexion. **colourless** *adj* **1** dull and uninteresting. **2** without colour. **colour-blind** *adj* unable to distinguish between certain colours.

colt *n* young male horse.

columbine *n* garden flower with five petals.

column *n* **1** pillar. **2** vertical division of a newspaper page. **3** regular feature in a newspaper. **4** vertical arrangement of numbers. **5** narrow formation of troops. **columnist** *n* journalist who writes a regular feature in a newspaper.

com-, con- *prefix* together, jointly, e.g. *commingle.*

coma *n* state of deep unconsciousness. **comatose** *adj* **1** in a coma. **2** sound asleep.

comb *n* **1** toothed implement for arranging the hair. **2** cock's crest. **3** honeycomb. ♦ *v* **4** use a comb on. **5** search with great care.

combat *n, v* **-bating, -bated** fight, struggle. **combatant** *n* **1** fighter. ♦ *adj* **2** fighting. **combative** *adj*

combe *n* same as COOMB.

combine *v* **1** join together. **2** form a chemical compound. ♦ *n* **3** association of people or firms for a common purpose. **combination** *n* **1** combining. **2** people or things combined. **3** set of numbers that opens a special lock. ♦ *pl* **4** old-fashioned undergarment with long sleeves and long legs. **combine harvester** machine that reaps and threshes grain in one process.

combo *n, pl* **-bos** small group of jazz musicians.

combustion *n* process of burning. **combustible** *adj* burning easily.

come *v* **coming, came, come** **1** move towards a place, arrive. **2** occur. **3** reach a specified point or condition. **4** be produced. **5** (foll. by *from*) be born in. **6** become, e.g. *a dream come true.* **come across** *v* **1** meet or find by accident. **2** (often foll. by *as*) give an impression of (being). **comeback** *n Informal* **1** return to a former position. **2** retort. **come by** *v* find, obtain. **comedown** *n* **1** decline in status. **2** disappointment. **come into** *v* **1** enter. **2** inherit. **come of** *v* result from. **come to** *v* **1** regain consciousness. **2** amount to (a total figure). **come up** *v* be mentioned, arise. **comeuppance** *n Informal* deserved punishment.

comedy *n, pl* **-dies** **1** humorous play, film, or programme. **2** humorous aspect of events. **comedian, comedienne** *n* **1** entertainer who tells jokes. **2** person who performs in comedy.

comely *adj* **-lier, -liest** *Old-fashioned* nice-looking.

comestibles *pl n Formal* food.

comet *n* heavenly body with a long luminous tail.

comfit *n* sugar-coated sweet.

comfort *n* **1** physical ease or wellbeing. **2** consolation. **3** means of consolation. ♦ *v* **4** soothe, console. **comfortable** *adj* **1** giving comfort. **2** free from pain. **3** *Informal* well-off financially. **comfortably** *adv* **comforter** *n* **1** person or thing that comforts. **2** baby's dummy. **3** *Brit* woollen scarf.

comfrey *n* tall plant with bell-shaped flowers.

comfy *adj* **-fier, -fiest** *Informal* comfortable.

comic *adj* **1** humorous, funny. **2** of comedy. ♦ *n* **3** comedian. **4** magazine containing strip cartoons. **comical** *adj* amusing. **comically** *adv*

comma *n* punctuation mark (,).

command *v* **1** order. **2** have authority over. **3** deserve and get. **4** look down over. ♦ *n* **5** authoritative instruction that something must be done. **6** authority to command. **7** knowledge. **8** military or naval unit with a specific function. **9** instruction given to a computer. **commandant** *n* officer commanding a military group. **commandeer** *v* **1** seize for military use. **2** take (something to which one is not entitled). **commander** *n* **1** military officer in command of a group or operation. **2** middle-ranking naval officer. **commander-in-chief** *n, pl* **commanders-in-chief** supreme commander of a nation's armed forces. **commandment** *n* command from God.

commando *n, pl* **-dos, -does** (member of) a military unit trained for swift raids in enemy territory.

commemorate *v* honour the memory of. **commemoration** *n* **commemorative** *adj*

commence *v* begin. **commencement** *n*

commend *v* **1** praise. **2** recommend. **commendable** *adj* **commendably** *adv* **commendation** *n*

commensurable *adj* measurable by the same standards.

commensurate *adj* corresponding in degree, size, or value.

comment *n* **1** remark. **2** talk, gossip. **3** explanatory note. ♦ *v* **4** make a comment. **commentary** *n, pl* **-taries** **1** spoken accompaniment to a broadcast or film. **2** explanatory notes. **commentate** *v* provide a commentary. **commentator** *n*

commerce *n* **1** buying and selling, trade. **2** *Lit* social relations. **commercial** *adj* **1** of commerce. **2** (of television or radio) paid for by advertisers. **3** having profit as the main aim. ♦ *n* **4** television or radio advertisement. **commercialize** *v* make commercial. **commercialization** *n* **commercial traveller** sales representative.

commie *n, adj Informal offens* communist.

commingle *v* mix or be mixed.

commis *n, pl* **-mis** apprentice waiter or chef.

commiserate *v* (foll. by *with*) express sympathy (for). **commiseration** *n*

commissar *n* (formerly) official responsible for political education in Communist countries.

commissariat *n* military department in charge of food supplies.

commissary *n, pl* **-saries** *US* shop supplying food or equipment, esp. in a military camp.

commission *n* **1** piece of work that an artist is asked to do. **2** duty, task. **3** percentage paid to a salesperson for each sale made. **4** group of people appointed to perform certain duties. **5** committing of a crime. **6** *Mil* rank or authority officially given to an officer. ♦ *v* **7** place an order for. **8** *Mil* give a commission to. **9** grant authority to. **out of commission** not in working order. **commissioner** *n* **1** appointed official in a government department. **2** member of a commission.

commissionaire *n* uniformed doorman at a hotel, theatre, etc.

commit *v* **-mitting, -mitted** **1** perform (a crime or error). **2** hand over, allocate. **3** pledge (oneself) to a course of action.

4 send (someone) to prison or hospital. **committal** *n* sending someone to prison or hospital. **commitment** *n* **1** dedication to a cause. **2** responsibility that restricts freedom of action.

committee *n* group of people appointed to perform a specified service or function.

commode *n* **1** seat with a hinged flap concealing a chamber pot. **2** chest of drawers.

commodious *adj* roomy.

commodity *n, pl* **-ities** article of trade.

commodore *n* senior commissioned officer in the navy.

common *adj* **1** occurring often. **2** belonging to two or more people. **3** public, general. **4** lacking in taste or manners. ♦ *n* **5** area of grassy land belonging to a community. ♦ *pl* **6** shared food. **House of Commons, the Commons** lower chamber of the British parliament. **in common** shared. **commonly** *adv* **commoner** *n* person who does not belong to the nobility. **common-law** *adj* (of a relationship) regarded as a marriage through being long-standing. **Common Market** European Union. **commonplace** *adj* **1** ordinary, everyday. ♦ *n* **2** trite remark. **common room** sitting room for students or staff in a school or college. **common sense** good practical understanding.

commonwealth *n* **1** state or nation viewed politically. **2** (**C-**) association of independent states that used to be ruled by Britain.

commotion *n* noisy disturbance.

commune[1] *n* **1** group of people who live together and share everything. **2** smallest district of local government in some countries. **communal** *adj* shared. **communally** *adv*

commune[2] *v* (foll. by *with*) feel very close (to), e.g. *communing with nature.* **communion** *n* **1** sharing of thoughts or feelings. **2** (**C-**) Christian ritual of sharing consecrated bread and wine. **3** religious group with shared beliefs and practices.

communicate *v* **1** make known or share (information, thoughts, or feelings). **2** receive Communion. **communicable** *adj* (of a disease) able to be passed on. **communicant** *n* person who receives Communion. **communicating** *adj* (of a door) joining two rooms. **communication** *n* **1** communicating. **2** thing communicated. ♦ *pl* **3** means of travelling or sending messages. **communicative** *adj* talking freely.

communiqué [kom-**mune**-ik-kay] *n* official announcement.

communism *n* **1** belief that all property and means of production should be shared by the community. **2** (**C-**) system of state control of the economy and society in some countries. **communist** *n, adj* **communistic** *adj*

community *n, pl* **-ties** **1** all the people living in one district. **2** group with shared origins or interests. **3** the public, society. **community centre** building used by a community for activities.

commute *v* **1** travel daily to and from work. **2** reduce (a sentence) to a less severe one. **commuter** *n* person who commutes to and from work. **commutator** *n* device used to change alternating electric current into direct current.

compact[1] *adj* **1** closely packed. **2** neatly arranged. **3** concise, brief. ♦ *n* **4** small flat case containing a mirror and face powder. ♦ *v* **5** pack closely together. **compactly** *adv* **compactness** *n* **compact disc** small digital audio disc on which the sound is read by an optical laser system.

compact[2] *n* contract, agreement.

companion *n* **1** person who associates with or accompanies someone. **2** woman paid to live with another woman. **companionable** *adj* friendly. **companionship** *n*

companionway *n* ladder linking the decks of a ship.

company *n, pl* **-nies** **1** business organization. **2** group of actors. **3** small unit of troops. **4** crew of a ship. **5** fact of being with someone. **6** gathering of people. **7**

guest or guests. **8** person's associates.

compare *v* **1** examine (things) and point out the resemblances or differences. **2** (foll. by *to*) declare to be (like). **3** (foll. by *with*) be worthy of comparison. **comparable** *adj* **1** worthy of comparison. **2** able to be compared. **comparability** *n* **comparative** *adj* **1** relative. **2** involving comparison. **3** *Grammar* denoting the form of an adjective or adverb indicating *more*. ♦ *n* **4** *Grammar* comparative form of a word. **comparatively** *adv* **comparison** *n* **1** comparing. **2** similarity or equivalence.

compartment *n* **1** section of a railway carriage. **2** separate section.

compass *n* **1** instrument for showing direction, with a needle that points north. **2** limits, range. ♦ *pl* **3** hinged instrument for drawing circles.

> The drawing instrument is technically *a pair of compasses* and some people insist on this usage.

compassion *n* pity, sympathy. **compassionate** *adj*

compatible *adj* able to exist, work, or be used together. **compatibility** *n*

compatriot *n* fellow countryman or countrywoman.

compel *v* **-pelling, -pelled** force (to be or do). **compelling** *adj* **1** convincing. **2** arousing strong interest.

compendium *n, pl* **-diums, -dia** selection of board games in one box. **compendious** *adj* brief but comprehensive.

compensate *v* **1** make amends to (someone), esp. for injury or loss. **2** (foll. by *for*) cancel out (a bad effect). **compensation** *n* payment to make up for loss or injury. **compensatory** *adj*

compere *n* **1** person who presents a stage, radio, or television show. ♦ *v* **2** be the compere of.

compete *v* try to win or achieve (a prize, profit, etc.). **competition** *n* **1** competing. **2** event in which people compete. **3** people against whom one competes. **competitive** *adj* **1** involving rivalry. **2** eager to be more successful than other people. **3** offering good value compared with commercial rivals. **competitor** *n*

competent *adj* having the skill or knowledge to do something well. **competently** *adv* **competence** *n*

compile *v* collect and arrange (information), esp. to make a book. **compilation** *n* **compiler** *n*

complacent *adj* self-satisfied. **complacently** *adv* **complacency** *n*

complain *v* **1** express resentment or displeasure. **2** (foll. by *of*) say that one is suffering from (an illness). **complaint** *n* **1** complaining. **2** mild illness. **complainant** *n Law* plaintiff.

complaisant [kom-**play**-zant] *adj* willing to please. **complaisance** *n*

complement *n* **1** thing that completes something. **2** complete amount or number. **3** *Grammar* word or words added to a verb to complete the meaning. **4** *Maths* angle added to a specified angle to produce a right angle. ♦ *v* **5** make complete. **complementary** *adj*

> Avoid confusion with *compliment.*

complete *adj* **1** thorough, absolute. **2** finished. **3** having all the necessary parts. ♦ *v* **4** finish. **5** make whole or perfect. **completely** *adv* **completeness** *n* **completion** *n* finishing.

complex *adj* **1** made up of parts. **2** complicated. ♦ *n* **3** whole made up of parts. **4** group of unconscious feelings that influences behaviour. **complexity** *n*

complexion *n* **1** skin of the face. **2** character, nature.

compliance *n* **1** complying. **2** tendency to do what others want. **compliant** *adj*

complicate *v* make or become complex or difficult to deal with. **complication** *n* **1** complicating factor. **2** medical condition arising as a result of another.

complicity *n* fact of being an accomplice in a crime.

compliment *n* **1** expression of praise. ♦ *pl* **2** formal greetings. ♦ *v* **3** praise.

complimentary *adj* **1** expressing praise. **2** free of charge.

> Avoid confusion with *complement*.

compline *n* last service of the day in the Roman Catholic Church.

comply *v* **-plying, -plied** (foll. by *with*) act in accordance (with).

component *n, adj* (being) part of a whole.

comport *v* behave (oneself) in a specified way.

compose *v* **1** put together. **2** be the component parts of. **3** create (a piece of music or writing). **4** calm (oneself). **5** arrange artistically. **composed** *adj* calm. **composer** *n*

> For sense 2 the usual idiom is: *it is/was composed of.*

composite *n, adj* (something) made up of separate parts.

composition *n* **1** way that something is put together or arranged. **2** work of art, esp. a musical one. **3** essay. **4** composing.

compositor *n* person who arranges type for printing.

compos mentis *adj Latin* sane.

compost *n* decayed plants used as a fertilizer.

composure *n* calmness.

compote *n* fruit stewed with sugar.

compound[1] *n, adj* **1** (thing, esp. chemical) made up of two or more combined parts or elements. ♦ *v* **2** combine or make by combining. **3** intensify, make worse. **compound fracture** fracture in which the broken bone pierces the skin. **compound interest** interest paid on a sum and its accumulated interest.

compound[2] *n* fenced enclosure containing buildings.

comprehend *v* understand. **comprehensible** *adj* **comprehension** *n* **comprehensive** *adj* **1** of broad scope, fully inclusive. ♦ *n* **2** comprehensive school. **comprehensive school** secondary school for children of all abilities.

compress *v* [kum-**press**] **1** squeeze together. **2** make shorter. ♦ *n* [**kom**-press] **3** pad applied to stop bleeding or cool inflammation. **compression** *n* **compressor** *n* machine that compresses gas or air.

comprise *v* be made up of or make up.

> *Comprise* is not followed by *of* but directly by its object.

compromise [**kom**-prom-mize] *n* **1** settlement reached by concessions on each side. ♦ *v* **2** settle a dispute by making concessions. **3** put in a dishonourable position.

comptroller *n* (in titles) financial controller.

compulsion *n* **1** irresistible urge. **2** forcing by threats or violence. **compulsive** *adj* **compulsively** *adv* **compulsory** *adj* required by rules or laws.

compunction *n* feeling of guilt or shame.

compute *v* calculate, esp. using a computer. **computation** *n* **computer** *n* electronic machine that stores and processes data. **computerize** *v* **1** adapt (a system) to be handled by computer. **2** store or process in a computer. **computerization** *n*

comrade *n* **1** fellow member of a union or socialist political party. **2** companion. **comradeship** *n*

con[1] *Informal* ♦ *n* **1** short for CONFIDENCE TRICK. ♦ *v* **conning, conned 2** deceive, swindle.

con[2] *n* **pros and cons** see PRO[1].

con[3] *n Slang* convict.

concatenation *n* series of linked events.

concave *adj* curving inwards. **concavity** *n*

conceal *v* **1** cover and hide. **2** keep secret. **concealment** *n*

concede *v* **1** admit to be true. **2** acknowledge defeat in (a contest or argument). **3** grant as a right.

conceit *n* **1** too high an opinion of oneself. **2** far-fetched or clever comparison. **conceited** *adj*

conceive *v* **1** imagine, think. **2** form in the mind. **3** become pregnant. **conceivable** *adj* imaginable, possible. **conceivably** *adv*

concentrate *v* **1** fix one's attention or efforts on something. **2** bring or come together in large numbers in one place. **3** make (a liquid) stronger by removing water from it. ♦ *n* **4** concentrated liquid. **concentration** *n* **1** concentrating. **2** proportion of a substance in a mixture or solution. **concentration camp** prison camp for civilian prisoners, esp. in Nazi Germany.

concentric *adj* having the same centre.

concept *n* abstract or general idea. **conceptual** *adj* of or based on concepts. **conceptualize** *v* form a concept of.

conception *n* **1** general idea. **2** becoming pregnant.

concern *n* **1** anxiety, worry. **2** something that is of importance to someone. **3** business, firm. ♦ *v* **4** worry (someone). **5** involve (oneself). **6** be relevant or important to. **concerned** *adj* **1** interested, involved. **2** anxious, worried. **concerning** *prep* about, regarding.

concert *n* musical entertainment. **in concert 1** working together. **2** (of musicians) performing live. **concerted** *adj* done together.

concertina *n* **1** small musical instrument similar to an accordion. ♦ *v* **-naing, -naed 2** collapse or fold up like a concertina.

concerto [kon-**chair**-toe] *n, pl* **-tos, -ti** large-scale composition for a solo instrument and orchestra.

concession *n* **1** grant of rights, land, or property. **2** reduction in price for a specified category of people. **3** conceding. **4** thing conceded. **concessionary** *adj*

conch *n* **1** shellfish with a large spiral shell. **2** its shell.

concierge [kon-see-**airzh**] *n* (in France) caretaker in a block of flats.

conciliate *v* try to end a disagreement (with). **conciliation** *n* **conciliator** *n* **conciliatory** *adj*

concise *adj* brief and to the point. **concisely** *adv* **concision, conciseness** *n*

conclave *n* **1** secret meeting. **2** private meeting of cardinals to elect a new pope.

conclude *v* **1** decide by reasoning. **2** end, finish. **3** arrange or settle finally. **conclusion** *n* **1** decision based on reasoning. **2** ending. **3** final arrangement or settlement. **conclusive** *adj* ending doubt, convincing. **conclusively** *adv*

concoct *v* **1** make up (a story or plan). **2** make by combining ingredients. **concoction** *n*

concomitant *adj* existing along with something else.

concord *n* state of peaceful agreement, harmony. **concordance** *n* **1** similarity or consistency. **2** index of words in a book. **concordant** *adj* agreeing.

concordat *n* pact or treaty.

concourse *n* **1** large open public place where people can gather. **2** large crowd.

concrete *n* **1** mixture of cement, sand, stone, and water, used in building. ♦ *v* **2** cover with concrete. ♦ *adj* **3** made of concrete. **4** particular, specific. **5** real or solid, not abstract.

concubine [**kon**-kew-bine] *n* woman living with a man as his wife, but not married to him.

concupiscence [kon-**kew**-piss-enss] *n* *Formal* lust. **concupiscent** *adj*

concur *v* **-curring, -curred** agree. **concurrence** *n* **concurrent** *adj* happening at the same time or place. **concurrently** *adv* at the same time.

concussion *n* period of unconsciousness caused by a blow to the head. **concussed** *adj* having concussion.

condemn *v* **1** express disapproval of. **2** sentence, e.g. *he was condemned to death.* **3** force into an unpleasant situation. **4** declare unfit for use. **condemnation** *n* **condemnatory** *adj*

condense *v* **1** make shorter. **2** turn from gas into liquid. **condensation** *n* **condenser** *n* *Electricity* capacitor.

condescend *v* **1** behave patronizingly towards someone. **2** agree to do something, but as if doing someone a favour. **condescension** *n*

condiment *n* seasoning for food, such as salt or pepper.

condition *n* **1** particular state of being. **2** necessary requirement for something else to happen. **3** restriction, qualification. **4** state of health, physical fitness. **5** medical problem, e.g. *a heart condition.* ♦ *pl* **6** circumstances. ♦ *v* **7** train or influence to behave in a particular way. **8** treat with conditioner. **9** control. **on condition that** only if. **conditional** *adj* depending on circumstances. **conditioner** *n* thick liquid used when washing to make hair or clothes feel softer.

condolence *n* **1** sympathy, e.g. *a message of condolence.* ♦ *pl* **2** expression of sympathy.

condom *n* rubber sheath worn on the penis or in the vagina during sexual intercourse to prevent conception or infection.

condominium *n Aust, US & Canadian* block of flats in which each flat is owned by the occupant.

condone *v* overlook or forgive (wrongdoing).

condor *n* large vulture of S America.

conducive *adj* (foll. by *to*) likely to lead (to).

conduct *n* **1** management of an activity. **2** behaviour. ♦ *v* **3** carry out (a task). **4** behave (oneself). **5** direct (musicians) by moving the hands or a baton. **6** lead, guide. **7** transmit (heat or electricity). **conduction** *n* transmission of heat or electricity. **conductivity** *n* ability to transmit heat or electricity. **conductive** *adj* **conductor** *n* **1** person who conducts musicians. **2** (*fem* **conductress**) official on a bus who collects fares. **3** something that conducts heat or electricity.

conduit [**kon**-dew-it] *n* channel or tube for fluid or cables.

cone *n* **1** object with a circular base, tapering to a point. **2** cone-shaped ice-cream wafer. **3** plastic cone used as a traffic marker on the roads. **4** scaly fruit of a conifer tree.

coney *n* same as CONY.

confab *n Informal* conversation (also **confabulation**).

confection *n* **1** any sweet food. **2** elaborate article of clothing. **confectioner** *n* maker or seller of confectionery. **confectionery** *n* sweets.

confederate *n* **1** member of a confederacy. **2** accomplice. ♦ *adj* **3** united, allied. ♦ *v* **4** unite in a confederacy. **confederacy** *n, pl* **-cies** union of states or people for a common purpose. **confederation** *n* alliance of political units.

confer *v* **-ferring, -ferred 1** discuss together. **2** grant, give. **conference** *n* meeting for discussion. **conferment** *n* granting, giving.

confess *v* **1** admit (a fault or crime). **2** admit to be true. **3** declare (one's sins) to God or a priest, in hope of forgiveness. **confession** *n* **1** something confessed. **2** confessing. **3** declaring one's sins to God or a priest, in hope of forgiveness. **confessional** *n* small stall in which a priest hears confessions. **confessor** *n* priest who hears confessions.

confetti *n* small pieces of coloured paper thrown at weddings.

confidant *n* person confided in. **confidante** *n fem*

confide *v* **1** tell someone (a secret). **2** entrust. **confidence** *n* **1** trust. **2** self-assurance. **3** something confided. **in confidence** as a secret. **confidence trick** swindle involving gaining a person's trust in order to cheat him or her. **confident** *adj* sure, esp. of oneself. **confidently** *adv* **confidential** *adj* **1** private, secret. **2** entrusted with someone's secret affairs. **confidentially** *adv* **confidentiality** *n*

configuration *n* arrangement of parts.

confine *v* **1** keep within bounds. **2** restrict the free movement of. **confines** *pl n* boundaries, limits. **confinement** *n* **1** being confined. **2** period of childbirth.

confirm *v* **1** prove to be true. **2** reaffirm,

strengthen. **3** administer the rite of confirmation to. **confirmation** *n* **1** confirming. **2** something that confirms. **3** *Christianity* rite that admits a baptized person to full church membership. **confirmed** *adj* firmly established in a habit or condition, e.g. *a confirmed bachelor.*

confiscate *v* seize (property) by authority. **confiscation** *n*

conflagration *n* large destructive fire.

conflate *v* combine or blend into a whole. **conflation** *n*

conflict *n* **1** disagreement. **2** struggle or fight. ♦ *v* **3** be incompatible.

confluence *n* **1** place where two rivers join. **2** gathering.

conform *v* **1** comply with accepted standards or customs. **2** (foll. by *to* or *with*) be like or in accordance with. **conformist** *n, adj* (person) complying with accepted standards or customs. **conformity** *n* compliance with accepted standards or customs.

confound *v* **1** astound, bewilder. **2** confuse. **confounded** *adj Informal* damned, e.g. *what a confounded nuisance!*

confront *v* come face to face with. **confrontation** *n* serious argument.

confuse *v* **1** mix up. **2** perplex, disconcert. **3** make unclear. **confusion** *n*

confute *v* prove wrong. **confutation** *n*

conga *n* **1** dance performed by a number of people in single file. **2** large single-headed drum played with the hands.

congeal *v* (of a liquid) become thick and sticky.

congenial *adj* **1** pleasant, agreeable. **2** having similar interests and attitudes. **congeniality** *n*

congenital *adj* (of a condition) existing from birth. **congenitally** *adv*

conger *n* large sea eel.

congested *adj* crowded to excess. **congestion** *n*

conglomerate *n* **1** large corporation made up of many companies. **2** thing made up of several different elements. ♦ *v* **3** form into a mass. ♦ *adj* **4** made up of several different elements. **conglomeration** *n*

congratulate *v* express one's pleasure to (someone) at his or her good fortune or success. **congratulations** *pl n, interj* **congratulatory** *adj*

congregate *v* gather together in a crowd. **congregation** *n* people who attend a church. **congregational** *adj* **Congregationalism** *n* Protestant denomination in which each church is self-governing. **Congregationalist** *adj, n*

congress *n* **1** formal meeting for discussion. **2** (**C-**) federal parliament of the US. **congressional** *adj* **Congressman, Congresswoman** *n* member of Congress.

congruent *adj* **1** similar, corresponding. **2** *Geom* identical in shape and size. **congruence** *n*

conical *adj* cone-shaped.

conic section *n Geom* figure formed by the intersection of a plane and a cone.

conifer *n* cone-bearing tree, such as the fir or pine. **coniferous** *adj*

conjecture *n, v* guess. **conjectural** *adj*

conjugal [**kon**-jew-gal] *adj* of marriage.

conjugate *v* give the inflections of (a verb). **conjugation** *n* complete set of inflections of a verb.

conjunction *n* **1** combination. **2** simultaneous occurrence of events. **3** part of speech joining words, phrases, or clauses.

conjunctivitis *n* inflammation of the membrane covering the eyeball and inner eyelid. **conjunctiva** *n* this membrane.

conjuncture *n* combination of events.

conjure *v* **1** perform tricks that appear to be magic. **2** summon (a spirit) by magic. **conjuror, conjurer** *n* **conjure up** *v* produce as if by magic.

conk *n Slang* nose.

conker *n Informal* nut of the horse chestnut. **conkers** *n* game played with conkers tied on strings.

conk out *v Informal* **1** (of a machine) break down. **2** fall asleep suddenly.

connect *v* **1** join together. **2** put into telephone communication with. **3** associate in the mind. **connection, connexion** *n* **1** relationship, association. **2** link or bond. **3** opportunity to transfer from one public vehicle to another. **4** Influential acquaintance. **connective** *adj*

conning tower *n* raised observation tower containing the periscope on a submarine.

connive *v* **1** (foll. by *at*) allow (wrongdoing) by ignoring it. **2** conspire. **connivance** *n*

connoisseur [kon-noss-**sir**] *n* person with special knowledge of the arts, food, or drink.

connotation *n* associated idea conveyed by a word. **connote** *v*

connubial [kon-**new**-bee-al] *adj* of marriage.

conquer *v* **1** defeat. **2** overcome (a difficulty). **3** take (a place) by force. **conqueror** *n* **conquest** *n* **1** conquering. **2** person or thing conquered. **3** person whose affections have been won.

consanguinity *n Formal* relationship by blood.

conscience *n* sense of right or wrong as regards thoughts and actions. **conscience-stricken** *adj* feeling anxious or guilty.

conscientious *adj* **1** painstaking. **2** governed by conscience. **conscientiously** *adv* **conscientious objector** person who refuses to serve in the armed forces on moral or religious grounds.

conscious *adj* **1** alert and awake. **2** aware. **3** deliberate, intentional. **4** of the part of the mind that determines the choices of action. **consciously** *adv* **consciousness** *n*

conscript *n* **1** person enrolled for compulsory military service. ♦ *v* **2** enrol (someone) for compulsory military service. **conscription** *n*

consecrate *v* **1** make sacred. **2** dedicate to a specific purpose. **consecration** *n*

consecutive *adj* in unbroken succession. **consecutively** *adv*

consensus *n* general agreement.

> Note the spelling of this word, often confused with that of *census*. In view of its meaning, it is redundant to say 'a consensus of opinion'.

consent *n* **1** agreement, permission. ♦ *v* **2** (foll. by *to*) permit, agree to.

consequence *n* **1** result, effect. **2** importance. **consequent** *adj* resulting. **consequently** *adv* as a result, therefore. **consequential** *adj* **1** important. **2** following as a result.

conservative *adj* **1** opposing change. **2** moderate, cautious. **3** conventional in style. **4** (**C-**) of the Conservative Party, the British right-wing political party which believes in private enterprise and capitalism. ♦ *n* **5** conservative person. **6** (**C-**) supporter or member of the Conservative Party. **conservatism** *n*

conservatoire [kon-**serv**-a-twahr] *n* school of music.

conservatory *n, pl* **-ries** **1** room with glass walls and a glass roof, attached to a house. **2** conservatoire.

conserve *v* **1** protect from harm, decay, or loss. **2** preserve (fruit) with sugar. ♦ *n* **3** jam containing large pieces of fruit. **conservancy** *n* environmental conservation. **conservation** *n* **1** protection of natural resources and the environment. **2** conserving. **conservationist** *n*

consider *v* **1** regard as. **2** think about. **3** be considerate of. **4** discuss. **5** look at. **considerable** *adj* large in amount or degree. **considerably** *adv* **considerate** *adj* thoughtful towards others. **considerately** *adv* **consideration** *n* **1** careful thought. **2** fact that should be considered. **3** thoughtfulness. **4** payment for a service. **considered** *adj* thought out with care. **considering** *prep* taking (a specified fact) into account.

consign *v* **1** put somewhere. **2** send (goods). **consignee** *n* **consignor** *n* **consignment** *n* shipment of goods.

consist *v* **1 consist of** be made up of. **2 consist in** have as its main or only feature.

consistent *adj* **1** unchanging, constant.

2 (foll. by *with*) in agreement. **consistently** *adv* **consistency** *n, pl* **-cies** **1** being consistent. **2** degree of thickness or smoothness.

console[1] *v* comfort in distress. **consolation** *n* **1** consoling. **2** person or thing that consoles.

console[2] *n* **1** panel of controls for electronic equipment. **2** cabinet for a television or audio equipment. **3** ornamental wall bracket. **4** part of an organ containing the pedals, stops, and keys.

consolidate *v* **1** make or become stronger or more stable. **2** combine into a whole. **consolidation** *n*

consommé [kon-**som**-may] *n* thin clear meat soup.

consonant *n* **1** speech sound made by partially or completely blocking the breath stream, such as *b* or *f*. **2** letter representing this. ♦ *adj* **3** (foll. by *with*) agreeing (with). **consonance** *n* agreement, harmony.

consort *v* **1** (foll. by *with*) keep company (with). ♦ *n* **2** husband or wife of a monarch.

consortium *n, pl* **-tia** association of business firms.

conspectus *n Formal* survey or summary.

conspicuous *adj* **1** clearly visible. **2** noteworthy, striking. **conspicuously** *adv*

conspire *v* **1** plan a crime together in secret. **2** act together as if by design. **conspiracy** *n* **1** conspiring. **2** (*pl* **-cies**) plan made by conspiring. **conspirator** *n* **conspiratorial** *adj*

constable *n* police officer of the lowest rank. **constabulary** *n, pl* **-laries** police force of an area.

constant *adj* **1** continuous. **2** unchanging. **3** faithful. ♦ *n* **4** unvarying quantity. **5** something that stays the same. **constantly** *adv* **constancy** *n*

constellation *n* group of stars.

consternation *n* anxiety or dismay.

constipation *n* difficulty in defecating. **constipated** *adj* having constipation.

constituent *n* **1** member of a constituency. **2** component part. ♦ *adj* **3** forming part of a whole. **constituency** *n, pl* **-cies** **1** area represented by a Member of Parliament. **2** voters in such an area.

constitute *v* **1** be, amount to. **2** form, make up. **constitution** *n* **1** principles on which a state is governed. **2** physical condition. **3** structure. **constitutional** *adj* **1** of a constitution. **2** in accordance with a political constitution. **3** being inherent to a person or thing. ♦ *n* **4** walk taken for exercise. **constitutionally** *adv*

constrain *v* **1** compel, force. **2** limit, restrict. **constrained** *adj* embarrassed or unnatural. **constraint** *n* something that limits or controls a person's actions.

constrict *v* **1** make narrower by squeezing. **2** limit, restrict. **constriction** *n* **constrictive** *adj* **constrictor** *n* **1** large snake that squeezes its prey to death. **2** muscle that compresses an organ.

construct *v* **1** build or put together. **2** *Geom* draw (a figure). **construction** *n* **1** constructing. **2** thing constructed. **3** interpretation. **4** *Grammar* way in which words are arranged in a sentence, clause, or phrase. **constructive** *adj* (of advice, criticism, etc.) useful and helpful. **constructively** *adv*

construe *v* **-struing, -strued** interpret.

consul *n* **1** official representing a state in a foreign country. **2** one of the two chief magistrates in ancient Rome. **consular** *adj* **consulate** *n* workplace or position of a consul. **consulship** *n*

consult *v* go to for advice or information. **consultant** *n* **1** specialist doctor with a senior position in a hospital. **2** specialist who gives professional advice. **consultancy** *n, pl* **-cies** work or position of a consultant. **consultation** *n* (meeting for) consulting. **consultative** *adj* giving advice.

consume *v* **1** eat or drink. **2** use up. **3** destroy. **4** obsess. **consumer** *n* person who buys goods or uses services. **consumerism** *n* protection of the rights of consumers. **consumption** *n* **1** amount consumed. **2** consuming. **3** purchase of goods and services. **4** *Old-fashioned* tuberculosis. **consumptive** *n, adj Old-fashioned* (person) having tuberculosis.

consummate [**kon**-sum-mate] *v* **1** make (a marriage) legal by sexual intercourse. **2** complete or fulfil. ♦ *adj* [kon-**sum**-mit] **3** supremely skilled. **4** complete, extreme. **consummation** *n*

cont. continued.

contact *n* **1** communicating. **2** touching. **3** useful acquaintance. **4** connection between two electrical conductors in a circuit. ♦ *v* **5** get in touch with. **contact lens** lens placed on the eyeball to correct defective vision.

contagion *n* **1** passing on of disease by contact. **2** disease spread by contact. **3** spreading of a harmful influence. **contagious** *adj* spreading by contact, catching.

contain *v* **1** hold or be capable of holding. **2** consist of. **3** control, restrain. **container** *n* **1** object used to hold or store things in. **2** large standard-sized box for transporting cargo by lorry or ship. **containerize** *v* pack (cargo) into containers. **containment** *n* prevention of the spread of something harmful.

contaminate *v* **1** make impure, pollute. **2** make radioactive. **contaminant** *n* contaminating substance. **contamination** *n*

contemn *v Formal* regard with contempt.

contemplate *v* **1** think deeply. **2** consider as a possibility. **3** gaze at. **contemplation** *n* **contemplative** *adj* deeply thoughtful.

contemporary *adj* **1** present-day, modern. **2** living or occurring at the same time. **3** of roughly the same age. ♦ *n, pl* **-raries 4** person or thing living or occurring at the same time as another. **contemporaneous** *adj* happening at the same time.

contempt *n* **1** dislike and disregard. **2** open disrespect for the authority of a court. **contemptible** *adj* deserving contempt. **contemptuous** *adj* showing contempt. **contemptuously** *adv*

contend *v* **1** (foll. by *with*) deal with. **2** state, assert. **3** compete. **contender** *n*

content[1] *n* **1** meaning or substance of a piece of writing. **2** amount of a substance in a mixture. ♦ *pl* **3** what something contains. **4** list of chapters at the front of a book.

content[2] *adj* **1** satisfied with things as they are. **2** willing to accept a proposed course of action. ♦ *v* **3** make (someone) content. ♦ *n* **4** happiness and satisfaction. **contented** *adj* **contentment** *n*

contention *n* **1** disagreement or dispute. **2** point asserted in argument. **contentious** *adj* **1** causing disagreement. **2** quarrelsome.

contest *n* **1** competition or struggle. ♦ *v* **2** dispute, object to. **3** fight or compete for. **contestant** *n*

context *n* **1** circumstances of an event or fact. **2** words before and after a word or sentence that help make its meaning clear. **contextual** *adj*

contiguous *adj* very near or touching.

continent[1] *n* one of the earth's large masses of land. **the Continent** mainland of Europe. **continental** *adj* **continental breakfast** light breakfast of coffee and rolls. **continental quilt** same as DUVET.

continent[2] *adj* **1** able to control one's bladder and bowels. **2** sexually restrained. **continence** *n*

contingent *n* **1** group of people that represents or is part of a larger group. ♦ *adj* **2** (foll. by *on*) dependent on (something uncertain). **contingency** *n, pl* **-cies** something that may happen.

continue *v* **-tinuing, -tinued 1** (cause to) remain in a condition or place. **2** carry on (doing something). **3** resume. **4** go on beyond a place. **continual** *adj* **1** constant. **2** recurring frequently. **continually** *adv* **continuance** *n* continuing. **continuation** *n* **1** continuing. **2** part added. **continuity** *n, pl* **-ties 1** smooth development or sequence. **2** arrangement of scenes in a film so that they follow each other logically and without breaks. **continuous** *adj* continuing uninterrupted. **continuously** *adv*

continuo *n, pl* **-tinuos** *Music* continuous bass part, usu. played on a keyboard instrument.

continuum *n, pl* **-tinua, -tinuums** continuous series.

contort *v* twist out of shape. **contortion** *n* **contortionist** *n* performer who contorts his or her body to entertain.

contour *n* **1** outline. **2** (also **contour line**) line on a map joining places of the same height.

contra- *prefix* against or contrasting, e.g. *contraflow.*

contraband *n, adj* smuggled (goods).

contraception *n* prevention of pregnancy by artificial means. **contraceptive** *n* **1** device used or pill taken to prevent pregnancy. ♦ *adj* **2** preventing pregnancy.

contract *n* **1** (document setting out) a formal agreement. ♦ *v* **2** make a formal agreement (to do something). **3** make or become smaller or shorter. **4** catch (an illness). **5** tighten (muscles) or (of muscles) be tightened. **contraction** *n* **1** contracting. **2** shortened word. **contractor** *n* firm that supplies materials or labour, esp. for building. **contractual** *adj*

contradict *v* **1** declare the opposite of (a statement) to be true. **2** be at variance with. **contradiction** *n* **contradictory** *adj*

contradistinction *n* distinction made by contrasting different qualities.

contraflow *n* flow of traffic going alongside but in an opposite direction to the usual flow.

contralto *n, pl* **-tos** (singer with) the lowest female voice.

contraption *n* strange-looking device.

contrapuntal *adj Music* of or in counterpoint.

contrary *n* **1** complete opposite. ♦ *adj* **2** opposed, completely different. **3** perverse, obstinate. ♦ *adv* **4** in opposition. **contrarily** *adv* **contrariness** *n* **contrariwise** *adv*

contrast *n* **1** obvious difference. **2** person or thing very different from another. **3** degree of difference between colours in a photograph or television picture. ♦ *v* **4** compare in order to show differences. **5** (foll. by *with*) be very different (from).

contravene *v* break (a rule or law). **contravention** *n*

contretemps [**kon**-tra-tahn] *n, pl* **-temps** embarrassing minor disagreement.

contribute *v* **1** give for a common purpose or fund. **2** (foll. by *to*) be partly responsible (for). **3** write articles for a publication. **contribution** *n* **contributor** *n* **contributory** *adj*

contrite *adj* sorry and apologetic. **contritely** *adv* **contrition** *n*

contrive *v* **1** make happen. **2** devise or construct. **contrivance** *n* **1** device. **2** plan. **3** contriving. **contrived** *adj* planned or artificial.

control *n* **1** power to direct something. **2** curb or check. **3** standard of comparison in an experiment. ♦ *pl* **4** instruments used to operate a machine. ♦ *v* **-trolling, -trolled 5** have power over. **6** limit, restrain. **7** regulate, operate. **controllable** *adj* **controller** *n*

controversy *n, pl* **-sies** fierce argument or debate. **controversial** *adj* causing controversy.

> Note that the stress used always to be on the first syllable, 'kon', but is now more often on the second syllable, 'trov'.

contumely [**kon**-tume-mill-ee] *n Lit* scornful or insulting treatment.

contusion *n Formal* bruise.

conundrum *n* riddle.

conurbation *n* large urban area formed by the growth and merging of towns.

convalesce *v* recover after an illness or operation. **convalescence** *n* **convalescent** *n, adj*

convection *n* transmission of heat in liquids or gases by the circulation of currents. **convector** *n* heater that gives out hot air.

convene *v* gather or summon for a formal meeting. **convener, convenor** *n* person who calls a meeting.

convenient *adj* **1** suitable or opportune. **2** easy to use. **3** nearby. **conveniently** *adv* **convenience** *n* **1** quality of being convenient. **2** useful object. **3** *Euphemistic* public toilet.

convent *n* **1** building where nuns live. **2** school run by nuns.

conventicle *n* secret or unauthorized religious meeting.

convention *n* **1** widely accepted view of proper behaviour. **2** assembly or meeting. **3** formal agreement. **conventional** *adj* **1** (unthinkingly) following the accepted customs. **2** customary. **3** (of weapons or warfare) not nuclear. **conventionally** *adv* **conventionality** *n*

converge *v* meet or join. **convergence** *n* **convergent** *adj*

conversant *adj* **conversant with** having knowledge or experience of.

converse[1] *v* have a conversation. **conversation** *n* informal talk. **conversational** *adj* **conversationalist** *n* person with a specified ability at conversation.

converse[2] *adj, n* opposite or contrary. **conversely** *adv*

convert *v* **1** change in form, character, or function. **2** cause to change in opinion or belief. **3** change (money) into a different currency. **4** *Rugby* make a conversion after (a try). ♦ *n* **5** person who has converted to a different belief or religion. **conversion** *n* **1** (thing resulting from) converting. **2** *Rugby* score made after a try by kicking the ball over the crossbar. **convertible** *adj* **1** capable of being converted. ♦ *n* **2** car with a folding or removable roof.

convex *adj* curving outwards. **convexity** *n*

convey *v* **1** communicate (information). **2** carry, transport. **3** transfer (the title to property). **conveyance** *n* **1** *Old-fashioned* vehicle. **2** transfer of the legal title to property. **conveyancing** *n* branch of law dealing with the transfer of ownership of property. **conveyor belt** continuous moving belt for transporting things, esp. in a factory.

convict *v* **1** declare guilty. ♦ *n* **2** person serving a prison sentence. **conviction** *n* **1** firm belief. **2** instance of being convicted.

convince *v* persuade by argument or evidence. **convincing** *adj* **convincingly** *adv*

convivial *adj* sociable, lively. **conviviality** *n*

convocation *n* **1** calling together. **2** large formal meeting. **convoke** *v* call together.

convoluted *adj* **1** coiled, twisted. **2** (of an argument or sentence) complex and hard to understand. **convolution** *n*

convolvulus *n* twining plant with funnel-shaped flowers.

convoy *n* group of vehicles or ships travelling together.

convulse *v* **1** (of part of the body) undergo violent spasms. **2** (of a person) shake violently. **3** *Informal* (be) overcome with laughter. **convulsion** *n* **1** violent muscular spasm. ♦ *pl* **2** uncontrollable laughter. **convulsive** *adj*

cony *n, pl* **conies 1** rabbit. **2** rabbit fur.

coo *v* **cooing, cooed** (of a dove or pigeon) make a soft murmuring sound.

cooee *interj* call to attract attention.

cook *v* **1** prepare (food) by heating. **2** (of food) be cooked. ♦ *n* **3** person who cooks food. **cook the books** falsify accounts. **cooker** *n* **1** apparatus for cooking heated by gas or electricity. **2** apple suitable for cooking. **cookery** *n* art of cooking. **cookie** *n US* biscuit. **cook up** *v Informal* devise (a story or scheme).

cool *adj* **1** moderately cold. **2** calm and unemotional. **3** indifferent or unfriendly. **4** *Informal* sophisticated or excellent. **5** *Informal* (of a large sum of money) without exaggeration, e.g. *a cool million.* ♦ *v* **6** make or become cool. ♦ *n* **7** coolness. **8** *Slang* calmness, composure. **coolly** *adv* **coolness** *n* **coolant** *n* fluid used to cool machinery while it is working. **cooler** *n* container for making or keeping things cool.

coolie *n Old-fashioned offens* unskilled Oriental labourer.

coomb, coombe *n* valley.

coop[1] *n* cage or pen for poultry. **coop up** *v* confine in a restricted place.

coop[2] [**koh**-op] *n* (shop run by) a co-operative society.

cooper *n* person who makes or repairs barrels.

cooperate *v* work or act together. **cooperation** *n* **cooperative** *adj* **1** willing to cooperate. **2** (of an enterprise) owned and managed collectively. ♦ *n* **3** cooperative organization.

coopt [koh-**opt**] *v* add (someone) to a group by the agreement of the existing members.

coordinate *v* **1** bring together and cause to work together efficiently. ♦ *n* **2** *Maths* any of a set of numbers defining the location of a point. ♦ *pl* **3** clothes designed to be worn together. **coordination** *n* **coordinator** *n*

coot *n* **1** small black water bird. **2** foolish person.

cop *Slang* ♦ *n* **1** policeman. ♦ *v* **copping, copped 2** take or seize. **cop it** get into trouble or be punished. **cop out** *v* avoid taking responsibility or committing oneself. **cop-out** *n*

copal *n* resin used in varnishes.

cope[1] *v* (often foll. by *with*) **1** deal successfully (with). **2** tolerate, endure.

cope[2] *n* large ceremonial cloak worn by some Christian priests.

cope[3] *v* provide with a coping.

copier *n* see COPY.

copilot *n* second pilot of an aircraft.

coping *n* sloping top row of a wall.

copious [**kope**-ee-uss] *adj* abundant, plentiful. **copiously** *adv*

copper[1] *n* **1** soft reddish-brown metal. **2** copper or bronze coin. **3** large metal container used to boil water. ♦ *adj* **4** reddish-brown. **copper-bottomed** *adj* financially reliable. **copperplate** *n* **1** fine handwriting style. **2** (print taken from) an engraved copper plate.

copper[2] *n Slang* policeman.

coppice, copse *n* small group of trees growing close together.

copra *n* dried oil-yielding kernel of the coconut.

copula *n, pl* **-las, -lae** verb used to link the subject and complement of a sentence, e.g. *become* in *they become chums*.

copulate *v* have sexual intercourse. **copulation** *n*

copy *n, pl* **copies 1** thing made to look exactly like another. **2** single specimen of a book etc. **3** material for printing. **4** suitable material for a newspaper article. ♦ *v* **copying, copied 5** make a copy of. **6** act or try to be like. **copier** *n* machine that copies. **copybook** *n* **blot one's copybook** *Informal* spoil one's reputation. **copyright** *n* **1** exclusive legal right to reproduce and control a book, work of art, etc. ♦ *v* **2** take out a copyright on. ♦ *adj* **3** protected by copyright. **copywriter** *n* person who writes advertising copy.

coquette *n* woman who flirts. **coquettish** *adj*

coracle *n* small round boat of wicker covered with skins.

coral *n* **1** hard substance formed from the skeletons of very small sea animals. ♦ *adj* **2** orange-pink.

cor anglais *n, pl* **cors anglais** woodwind instrument similar to the oboe.

corbel *n* stone or timber support sticking out of a wall.

cord *n* **1** thin rope or thick string. **2** cordlike structure in the body. **3** corduroy. **4** *US* electrical flex. ♦ *pl* **5** corduroy trousers. ♦ *adj* **6** (also **corded**) (of fabric) ribbed.

cordate *adj* heart-shaped.

cordial *adj* **1** warm and friendly. ♦ *n* **2** drink with a fruit base. **cordially** *adv* **cordiality** *n*

cordite *n* explosive used in guns and bombs.

cordon *n* chain of police, soldiers, etc., guarding an area. **cordon off** *v* form a cordon round.

cordon bleu [**bluh**] *adj* (of cookery or cooks) of the highest standard.

corduroy *n* cotton fabric with a velvety

ribbed surface.

core *n* **1** central part of certain fruits, containing the seeds. **2** central or essential part. **3** region of a nuclear reactor that contains fissionable material. ♦ *v* **4** remove the core from.

co-respondent *n* person with whom someone being sued for divorce is claimed to have committed adultery.

corgi *n* short-legged sturdy dog.

coriander *n* **1** plant grown for its aromatic seeds and leaves. **2** its dried seeds, used as a flavouring.

cork *n* **1** thick light bark of a Mediterranean oak. **2** piece of this used as a stopper. ♦ *v* **3** seal with a cork. **corked** *adj* (of wine) spoiled through having a decayed cork. **corkage** *n* restaurant's charge for serving wine bought elsewhere. **corkscrew** *n* **1** spiral metal tool for pulling corks from bottles. ♦ *adj* **2** like a corkscrew in shape.

corm *n* bulblike underground stem of certain plants.

cormorant *n* large dark-coloured long-necked sea bird.

corn[1] *n* **1** cereal plant such as wheat or oats. **2** grain of such plants. **3** *US* maize. **4** *Slang* something unoriginal or oversentimental. **corny** *adj* **cornier, corniest** *Slang* unoriginal or oversentimental. **cornflakes** *pl n* breakfast cereal made from toasted maize. **cornflour** *n* fine maize flour. **cornflower** *n* plant with blue flowers.

corn[2] *n* painful hard skin on the toe.

corncrake *n* brown bird with a harsh cry.

cornea [**korn**-ee-a] *n, pl* **-neas, -neae** transparent membrane covering the eyeball. **corneal** *adj*

corned beef *n* beef preserved in salt.

cornelian *n* same as CARNELIAN.

corner *n* **1** area or angle where two converging lines or surfaces meet. **2** place where two streets meet. **3** sharp bend in a road. **4** remote place. **5** *Sport* free kick or shot from the corner of the field. ♦ *v* **6** force into a difficult or inescapable position. **7** (of a vehicle) turn a corner. **8** obtain a monopoly of. **cornerstone** *n* **1** indispensable part or basis. **2** stone at the corner of a wall.

cornet *n* **1** brass instrument similar to the trumpet. **2** cone-shaped ice-cream wafer.

cornice [**korn**-iss] *n* decorative moulding round the top of a wall.

Cornish *pl n, adj* (people) of Cornwall. **Cornish pasty** pastry case with a filling of meat and vegetables.

cornucopia [korn-yew-**kope**-ee-a] *n* **1** great abundance. **2** symbol of plenty, consisting of a horn overflowing with fruit and flowers.

corolla *n* petals of a flower collectively.

corollary [kor-**oll**-a-ree] *n, pl* **-laries** idea, fact, or proposition which is the natural result of something else.

corona [kor-**rone**-a] *n, pl* **-nas, -nae** **1** ring of light round the moon or sun. **2** long cigar with blunt ends.

coronary [**kor**-ron-a-ree] *adj* **1** of the arteries surrounding the heart. ♦ *n, pl* **-naries** **2** coronary thrombosis. **coronary thrombosis** condition in which the flow of blood to the heart is blocked by a blood clot.

coronation *n* ceremony of crowning a monarch.

coroner *n* official responsible for the investigation of violent, sudden, or suspicious deaths.

coronet *n* small crown.

corpora *n* plural of CORPUS.

corporal[1] *n* noncommissioned officer in an army.

corporal[2] *adj* of the body. **corporal punishment** physical punishment, such as caning.

corporation *n* **1** large business or company. **2** city or town council. **3** *Informal* large paunch. **corporate** *adj* **1** of business corporations. **2** shared by a group.

corporeal [kore-**pore**-ee-al] *adj* physical or tangible.

corps [**kore**] *n, pl* **corps** **1** military unit with a specific function. **2** organized body of people.

corpse *n* dead body.

corpulent *adj* fat or plump. **corpulence** *n*

corpus *n, pl* **corpora** collection of writings, esp. by a single author.

corpuscle *n* red or white blood cell.

corral *US* ♦ *n* **1** enclosure for cattle or horses. ♦ *v* **-ralling, -ralled 2** put in a corral.

correct *adj* **1** free from error, true. **2** in accordance with accepted standards. ♦ *v* **3** put right. **4** indicate the errors in. **5** rebuke or punish. **6** make conform to a standard. **correctly** *adv* **correctness** *n* **correction** *n* **1** correcting. **2** alteration correcting something. **3** punishment. **corrective** *adj* intended to put right something wrong.

correlate *v* place or be placed in a mutual relationship. **correlation** *n*

correspond *v* **1** be consistent or compatible (with). **2** be the same or similar. **3** communicate by letter. **corresponding** *adj* **correspondingly** *adv* **correspondence** *n* **1** communication by letters. **2** letters so exchanged. **3** relationship or similarity. **correspondence course** study conducted by post. **correspondent** *n* **1** person employed by a newspaper etc. to report on a special subject or from a foreign country. **2** letter writer.

corridor *n* **1** passage in a building or train. **2** strip of land or airspace providing access through foreign territory.

corrie *n Scot* circular hollow on a hillside.

corrigendum [kor-rij-**end**-um] *n, pl* **-da** error to be corrected.

corroborate *v* support (a fact or opinion) by giving proof. **corroboration** *n* **corroborative** *adj*

corrode *v* **1** eat or be eaten away by chemical action or rust. **2** destroy gradually. **corrosion** *n* **corrosive** *adj*

corrugate *v* fold into alternate grooves and ridges. **corrugated** *adj*

corrupt *adj* **1** open to or involving bribery. **2** morally depraved. **3** (of a text or data) unreliable through errors or alterations. ♦ *v* **4** make corrupt. **corruptly** *adv* **corruption** *n* **corruptible** *adj*

corsage [kor-**sahzh**] *n* small bouquet worn on the bodice of a dress.

corsair *n* **1** pirate. **2** pirate ship.

corselet *n* **1** one-piece undergarment combining a corset and bra. **2** piece of armour to cover the trunk.

corset *n* women's close-fitting undergarment worn to shape the torso.

cortege [kor-**tayzh**] *n* funeral procession.

cortex *n, pl* **-tices** *Anat* outer layer of the brain or other internal organ. **cortical** *adj*

cortisone *n* steroid hormone used to treat various diseases.

corundum *n* hard mineral used as an abrasive.

coruscate *v Formal* sparkle. **coruscation** *n*

corvette *n* lightly armed escort warship.

cos[1], **cos lettuce** *n* long crisp-leaved lettuce.

cos[2] *Maths* cosine.

cosh *n* **1** heavy blunt weapon. ♦ *v* **2** hit with a cosh.

cosine [**koh**-sine] *n* (in trigonometry) ratio of the length of the adjacent side to that of the hypotenuse in a right-angled triangle.

cosmetic *n* **1** preparation used to improve the appearance of a person's skin. ♦ *adj* **2** improving the appearance only.

cosmic *adj* of the whole universe. **cosmic rays** electromagnetic radiation from outer space.

cosmonaut *n* Russian name for an astronaut.

cosmopolitan *adj* **1** composed of people or elements from many countries. **2** having lived and travelled in many countries. ♦ *n* **3** cosmopolitan person. **cosmopolitanism** *n*

cosmos *n* the universe. **cosmogony** *n* study of the origin of the universe. **cosmology** *n* study of the origin and nature of the universe. **cosmological** *adj*

Cossack *n* member of a S Russian people famous as horsemen and dancers.

cosset *v* **cosseting, cosseted** pamper.

cost *n* **1** amount of money, time, labour,

etc., required for something. ♦ *pl* **2** expenses of a lawsuit. ♦ *v* **costing, cost 3** have as its cost. **4** involve the loss or sacrifice of. **5** (*past* **costed**) estimate the cost of. **costly** *adj* **-lier, -liest 1** expensive. **2** involving great loss or sacrifice. **costliness** *n* **cost of living** average cost of the basic necessities of life.

costal *adj* of the ribs.

costermonger *n* person who sells fruit and vegetables from a street barrow.

costive *adj Old-fashioned* having or causing constipation.

costume *n* **1** style of dress of a particular place or time, or for a particular activity. **2** clothes worn by an actor or performer. **costumier** *n* maker or seller of costumes. **costume jewellery** inexpensive artificial jewellery.

cosy *adj* **-sier, -siest 1** warm and snug. **2** intimate, friendly. ♦ *n* **3** cover for keeping things warm, e.g. *a tea cosy.* **cosily** *adv* **cosiness** *n*

cot[1] *n* **1** baby's bed with high sides. **2** small portable bed. **cot death** unexplained death of a baby while asleep.

cot[2] *n* **1** *Lit* small cottage. **2** cote.

cote *n* shelter for birds or animals.

coterie [**kote**-er-ee] *n* exclusive group, clique.

cotoneaster [kot-tone-ee-**ass**-ter] *n* garden shrub with red berries.

cottage *n* small house in the country. **cottager** *n* **cottage cheese** soft mild white cheese. **cottage industry** craft industry in which employees work at home. **cottage pie** dish of minced meat topped with mashed potato.

cotter *n* pin or wedge used to secure machine parts.

cotton *n* **1** white downy fibre covering the seeds of a tropical plant. **2** cloth or thread made from this. **cottony** *adj* **cotton on (to)** *v Informal* understand. **cotton wool** fluffy cotton used for surgical dressings etc.

cotyledon [kot-ill-**ee**-don] *n* first leaf of a plant embryo.

couch *n* **1** piece of upholstered furniture for seating more than one person. ♦ *v* **2** express in a particular way. **couch potato** *Slang* lazy person whose only hobby is watching television.

couchette [koo-**shett**] *n* bed converted from seats on a train or ship.

couch grass *n* quickly spreading grassy weed.

cougar [**koo**-gar] *n* puma.

cough *v* **1** expel air from the lungs abruptly and noisily. ♦ *n* **2** act or sound of coughing. **3** illness which causes coughing. **cough up** *v Informal* hand over or pay (money).

could *v* past tense of CAN[1].

couldn't could not.

coulomb [**koo**-lom] *n* SI unit of electric charge.

coulter [**kole**-ter] *n* blade at the front of a ploughshare.

council *n* **1** group meeting for discussion or consultation. **2** local governing body of a town or region. ♦ *adj* **3** of or by a council. **councillor** *n* member of a council. **council tax** tax based on the value of property, to fund local services.

counsel *n* **1** advice or guidance. **2** discussion or consultation. **3** barrister or barristers. ♦ *v* **-selling, -selled 4** give guidance to. **5** urge, recommend. **counsellor** *n*

count[1] *v* **1** say numbers in order. **2** find the total of. **3** be important. **4** regard as. **5** take into account. ♦ *n* **6** counting. **7** number reached by counting. **8** *Law* one of a number of charges. **countless** *adj* too many to count. **count on** *v* rely or depend on. **count out** *v* **1** exclude. **2** declare (a boxer) defeated when he has not risen from the floor within ten seconds.

count[2] *n* European nobleman.

countdown *n* counting backwards to zero of the seconds before an event.

countenance *n* **1** (expression of) the face. ♦ *v* **2** allow or tolerate.

counter[1] *n* **1** long flat surface in a bank or shop, on which business is transacted. **2** small flat disc used in board games.

counter[2] *v* **1** oppose, retaliate against.

♦ *adv* **2** in the opposite direction. **3** in direct contrast. ♦ *n* **4** opposing or retaliatory action.

counter[3] *n* apparatus for counting things.

counter- *prefix* **1** opposite, against, e.g. *counterattack.* **2** complementary, corresponding, e.g. *counterpart.*

counteract *v* act against or neutralize. **counteraction** *n*

counterattack *n, v* attack in response to an attack.

counterbalance *n* **1** weight or force balancing or neutralizing another. ♦ *v* **2** act as a counterbalance to.

counterblast *n* aggressive response to a verbal attack.

counterclockwise *adv, adj US* anticlockwise.

counterespionage *n* activities to counteract enemy espionage.

counterfeit *adj* **1** fake, forged. ♦ *n* **2** fake, forgery. ♦ *v* **3** fake, forge.

counterfoil *n* part of a cheque or receipt kept as a record.

counterintelligence *n* activities designed to frustrate enemy espionage.

countermand *v* cancel (a previous order).

counterpane *n* bed covering.

counterpart *n* person or thing complementary to or corresponding to another.

counterpoint *n Music* **1** technique of combining melodies. **2** part or melody so combined.

counterpoise *n, v* counterbalance.

counterproductive *adj* having an effect opposite to the one intended.

countersign *v* sign (a document already signed by someone) as confirmation.

countersink *v* drive (a screw) into a shaped hole so that its head is below the surface.

countertenor *n* male alto.

countess *n* **1** woman holding the rank of count or earl. **2** wife or widow of a count or earl.

country *n, pl* **-tries** **1** nation. **2** nation's territory. **3** nation's people. **4** part of the land away from cities. **5** person's native land. **countrified** *adj* rustic in manner or appearance. **country and western, country music** popular music based on American White folk music. **country dancing** British folk dancing in rows or circles. **countryman, countrywoman** *n* **1** person from one's native land. **2** person who lives in the country. **countryside** *n* land away from cities.

county *n, pl* **-ties** **1** division of a country. ♦ *adj* **2** *Informal* upper-class.

coup [**koo**] *n* **1** successful action. **2** coup d'état.

coup de grâce [**koo** de **grahss**] *n* final or decisive action.

coup d'état [**koo** day-**tah**] *n* sudden violent overthrow of a government.

coupé [**koo**-pay] *n* sports car with two doors and a sloping fixed roof.

couple *n* **1** two people who are married or romantically involved. **2** two partners in a dance or game. ♦ *v* **3** connect, associate. **4** *Lit* have sexual intercourse. **a couple** **1** a pair. **2** *Informal* a few. **couplet** *n* two consecutive lines of verse, usu. rhyming and of the same metre. **coupling** *n* device for connecting things, such as railway carriages.

coupon *n* **1** piece of paper entitling the holder to a discount or gift. **2** detachable order form. **3** football pools entry form.

courage *n* ability to face danger or pain without fear. **courageous** *adj* **courageously** *adv*

courgette *n* type of small vegetable marrow.

courier *n* **1** person employed to look after holiday-makers. **2** person employed to deliver urgent messages.

course *n* **1** series of lessons or medical treatment. **2** onward movement in space or time. **3** route or direction taken. **4** area where golf is played or a race is run. **5** any of the successive parts of a meal. **6** continuous layer of masonry at one level in a building. **7** mode of conduct or action. **8** natural development of events. ♦ *v* **9** (of liquid) run swiftly. **10** hunt with hounds that follow the quarry by sight and not scent. **of course** as expected, naturally. **courser** *n Lit* swift horse

court *n* **1** body which decides legal cases. **2** place where it meets. **3** marked area for playing a racket game. **4** courtyard. **5** residence, household, or retinue of a sovereign. ♦ *v* **6** *Old-fashioned* try to gain the love of. **7** try to win the favour of. **8** invite, e.g. *to court disaster.* **courtier** *n* attendant at a royal court. **courtly** *adj* **-lier, -liest** ceremoniously polite. **courtliness** *n* **courtship** *n* courting of an intended spouse or mate. **court martial** *n, pl* **courts martial** court for trying naval or military offences. **court shoe** woman's low-cut shoe without straps or laces. **courtyard** *n* paved space enclosed by buildings or walls.

courtesan [kor-tiz-**zan**] *n Hist* mistress or high-class prostitute.

courtesy *n* **1** politeness, good manners. **2** (*pl* **-sies**) courteous act. **(by) courtesy of** by permission of. **courteous** *adj* polite. **courteously** *adv*

cousin *n* child of one's uncle or aunt.

couture [koo-**toor**] *n* high-fashion designing and dressmaking. **couturier** *n* person who designs women's fashion clothes.

cove *n* small bay or inlet.

coven [**kuv**-ven] *n* meeting of witches.

covenant [**kuv**-ven-ant] *n* **1** formal agreement to make an annual (charitable) payment. ♦ *v* **2** agree by a covenant.

Coventry *n* **send someone to Coventry** punish someone by refusing to speak to them.

cover *v* **1** place something over, to protect or conceal. **2** extend over or lie on the surface of. **3** travel over. **4** keep a gun aimed at. **5** insure against loss or risk. **6** include. **7** report (an event) for a newspaper. **8** be enough to pay for. ♦ *n* **9** anything that covers. **10** outside of a book or magazine. **11** pretext or disguise. **12** individual table setting. **13** insurance. **14** shelter or protection. **coverage** *n* amount or extent covered. **coverlet** *n* bed cover. **cover charge** fixed service charge in a restaurant.

covert *adj* **1** concealed, secret. ♦ *n* **2** thicket giving shelter to game birds or animals. **covertly** *adv*

covet *v* **coveting, coveted** long to possess (what belongs to someone else). **covetous** *adj* **covetousness** *n*

covey [**kuv**-vee] *n* small flock of grouse or partridge.

cow[1] *n* **1** mature female of cattle and of certain other mammals, such as the elephant or seal. **2** *Informal, offens* a disagreeable woman. **cowboy** *n* **1** (in the US) ranch worker who herds and tends cattle, usu. on horseback. **2** *Informal* irresponsible or unscrupulous worker. **cowpat** *n* pool of cow dung. **cowpox** *n* disease of cows, the virus of which is used in the smallpox vaccine.

cow[2] *v* intimidate, subdue.

coward *n* person who lacks courage. **cowardly** *adj* **cowardice** *n* lack of courage.

cower *v* cringe in fear.

cowl *n* **1** loose hood. **2** monk's hooded robe. **3** cover on a chimney to increase ventilation.

cowling *n* cover on an engine.

cowrie *n* brightly-marked sea shell.

cowslip *n* small yellow wild flower.

cox *n* **1** coxswain. ♦ *v* **2** act as cox of (a boat).

coxcomb *n* **1** comb of a domestic cock. **2** *Informal* conceited dandy.

coxswain [**kok**-sn] *n* person who steers a rowing boat.

coy *adj* affectedly shy or modest. **coyly** *adv* **coyness** *n*

coyote [koy-**ote**-ee] *n* prairie wolf of N America.

coypu *n* beaver-like aquatic rodent, bred for its fur.

cozen *v Lit* cheat, trick.

CPU *Computers* central processing unit.

Cr *Chem* chromium.

crab *n* **1** edible shellfish with ten legs, the first pair modified into pincers. **2** crab louse. **crab louse** parasitic louse living in the pubic area of humans.

crab apple *n* small sour apple.

crabbed *adj* **1** (of handwriting) hard to read. **2** (also **crabby**) bad-tempered.

crack *v* **1** break or split partially. **2** break with a sharp noise. **3** (cause to) make a sharp noise. **4** (of the voice) become harsh or change pitch suddenly. **5** break down or yield under strain. **6** hit suddenly. **7** force (a safe) open. **8** solve (a code or problem). **9** tell (a joke). ♦ *n* **10** sudden sharp noise. **11** narrow gap. **12** sharp blow. **13** *Informal* gibe, joke. **14** *Slang* highly addictive form of cocaine. ♦ *adj* **15** *Informal* first-rate, excellent, e.g. *a crack shot.* **cracking** *adj* **1** very fast, e.g. *a cracking pace.* **2** very good. **crackdown** *n* severe disciplinary measures. **crack down on** *v* take severe measures against. **crack up** *v Informal* have a physical or mental breakdown.

cracker *n* **1** thin dry biscuit. **2** decorated cardboard tube, pulled apart with a bang, containing a paper hat and a joke or toy. **3** small explosive firework. **4** *Slang* an outstanding thing or person.

crackers *adj Slang* insane.

crackle *v* **1** make small sharp popping noises. ♦ *n* **2** crackling sound. **crackling** *n* **1** crackle. **2** crisp skin of roast pork.

crackpot *n, adj Informal* eccentric (person).

cradle *n* **1** baby's bed on rockers. **2** place where something originates. **3** supporting structure. ♦ *v* **4** hold gently as if in a cradle.

craft *n* **1** occupation requiring skill with the hands. **2** skill or ability. **3** (*pl* **craft**) boat, ship, aircraft, or spaceship. ♦ *v* **4** make skilfully. **crafty** *adj* **craftier, craftiest** skilled in deception. **craftily** *adv* **craftiness** *n* **craftsman, craftswoman** *n* skilled worker. **craftsmanship** *n*

crag *n* steep rugged rock. **craggy** *adj*

cram *v* **cramming, crammed 1** force into too small a space. **2** fill too full. **3** study hard just before an examination.

cramp[1] *n* **1** painful muscular contraction. **2** clamp for holding masonry or timber together. ♦ *v* **3** affect with a cramp.

cramp[2] *v* confine, restrict. **cramped** *adj* **1** closed in. **2** (of handwriting) small and irregular.

crampon *n* spiked plate strapped to a boot for climbing on ice.

cranberry *n* sour edible red berry.

crane *n* **1** machine for lifting and moving heavy weights. **2** large wading bird with a long neck and legs. ♦ *v* **3** stretch (one's neck) to see something.

crane fly *n* long-legged insect with slender wings.

cranesbill *n* plant with pink or purple flowers.

cranium *n, pl* **-niums, -nia 1** skull. **2** part of the skull enclosing the brain. **cranial** *adj*

crank *n* **1** arm projecting at right angles from a shaft, for transmitting or converting motion. **2** *Informal* eccentric person. ♦ *v* **3** turn with a crank. **4** start (an engine) with a crank. **cranky** *adj* **crankier, crankiest** *Informal* **1** eccentric. **2** bad-tempered. **crankshaft** *n* shaft driven by a crank.

cranny *n, pl* **-nies** narrow opening.

crap *Slang* ♦ *n* **1** rubbish, nonsense. **2** *Taboo* faeces. ♦ *v* **crapping, crapped 3** *Taboo* defecate. **crappy** *adj*

crape *n* same as CREPE.

craps *n* gambling game played with two dice.

crash *n* **1** collision involving a vehicle or vehicles. **2** sudden loud smashing noise. **3** financial collapse. ♦ *v* **4** (cause to) collide violently with a vehicle, a stationary object, or the ground. **5** (cause to) make a loud smashing noise. **6** (cause to) fall with a crash. **7** collapse or fail financially. **8** *Informal* gate-crash. **crash barrier** safety barrier along a road or racetrack. **crash course** short, very intensive course in a particular subject. **crash helmet** protective helmet worn by a motorcyclist. **crash-land** *v* (of an aircraft) land in an emergency, causing damage. **crash-landing** *n*

crass *adj* stupid and insensitive. **crassly** *adv* **crassness** *n*

crate *n* **1** large wooden container for packing goods. ♦ *v* **2** put in a crate.
crater *n* **1** very large hole in the ground or in the surface of the moon. **2** mouth of a volcano.
cravat *n* man's scarf worn like a tie.
crave *v* **1** desire intensely. **2** beg or plead for. **craving** *n*
craven *adj* cowardly.
craw *n* **stick in one's craw** *Informal* be difficult for one to accept.
crawfish *n* same as CRAYFISH.
crawl *v* **1** move on one's hands and knees. **2** move very slowly. **3** (foll. by *to*) flatter in order to gain some advantage. **4** feel as if covered with crawling creatures. ♦ *n* **5** crawling motion or pace. **6** overarm swimming stroke. **crawler** *n*
crayfish *n* edible freshwater shellfish like a lobster.
crayon *v, n* (draw or colour with) a stick or pencil of coloured wax or clay.
craze *n* short-lived fashion or enthusiasm. **crazed** *adj* **1** wild and uncontrolled. **2** (of porcelain) having fine cracks. **crazy** *adj* **crazier, craziest 1** ridiculous. **2** (foll. by *about*) very fond (of). **3** insane. **craziness** *n* **crazy paving** paving made of irregularly shaped slabs of stone.
creak *v, n* (make) a harsh squeaking sound. **creaky** *adj* **creakier, creakiest**
cream *n* **1** fatty part of milk. **2** food or cosmetic resembling cream in consistency. **3** best part (of something). ♦ *adj* **4** yellowish-white. ♦ *v* **5** beat to a creamy consistency. **6** remove the cream from. **creamer** *n* powdered milk substitute for use in coffee. **creamery** *n, pl* **-eries** place where dairy products are made or sold. **creamy** *adj* **creamier, creamiest cream cheese** rich soft white cheese. **cream off** *v* take the best part from. **cream of tartar** purified tartar used in baking powder.
crease *n* **1** line made by folding or pressing. **2** wrinkle or furrow. **3** *Cricket* line marking the bowler's and batsman's positions. ♦ *v* **4** crush or line.
create *v* **1** make, cause to exist. **2** appoint to a new rank or position. **3** *Slang* make an angry fuss. **creation** *n* **creative** *adj* imaginative or inventive. ♦ *n* person who is creative professionally. **creativity** *n* **creator** *n* **1** person who creates. **2** (**C-**) God.
creature *n* **1** animal, person, or other being. **2** person controlled by another.
crèche *n* place where small children are looked after while their parents are working, shopping, etc.
credence [**kreed**-enss] *n* belief in the truth or accuracy of a statement.
credentials *pl n* document giving evidence of a person's identity or qualifications.
credible *adj* **1** believable. **2** trustworthy. **credibly** *adv* **credibility** *n*
credit *n* **1** system of allowing customers to receive goods and pay later. **2** reputation for trustworthiness in paying debts. **3** money at one's disposal in a bank account. **4** side of an account book on which such sums are entered. **5** (source or cause of) praise or approval. **6** influence or reputation based on the good opinion of others. **7** belief or trust. ♦ *pl* **8** list of people responsible for the production of a film, programme, or record. ♦ *v* **crediting, credited 9** enter as a credit in an account. **10** (foll. by *with*) attribute (to). **11** believe. **creditable** *adj* praiseworthy. **creditably** *adv* **creditor** *n* person to whom money is owed. **credit card** card allowing a person to buy on credit.
credo *n, pl* **-dos** creed.
credulous *adj* too willing to believe. **credulity** *n*
creed *n* statement or system of (Christian) beliefs or principles.
creek *n* **1** narrow inlet or bay. **2** *Aust, NZ, US & Canadian* small stream.
creel *n* wicker basket used by anglers.
creep *v* **creeping, crept 1** move quietly and cautiously. **2** crawl with the body near to the ground. **3** have a crawling sensation on the skin, from fear or disgust. **4** (of a plant) grow along the ground or over rocks. ♦ *n* **5** creeping

movement. **6** *Slang* obnoxious or servile person. **give one the creeps** *Informal* make one feel fear or disgust. **creeper** *n* creeping plant. **creepy** *adj* **creepier, creepiest** *Informal* causing a feeling of fear or disgust. **creepy-crawly** *n, pl* **-crawlies** *Informal* insect, viewed with fear or disgust.

cremate *v* burn (a corpse) to ash. **cremation** *n* **crematorium** *n* building where corpses are cremated.

crème de menthe *n* peppermint-flavoured liqueur.

crenellated *adj* having battlements.

creole *n* **1** language developed from a mixture of languages. **2** (**C-**) native-born W Indian or Latin American of mixed European and African descent.

creosote *n* **1** dark oily liquid made from coal tar and used for preserving wood. ♦ *v* **2** treat with creosote.

crepe [**krayp**] *n* **1** fabric or rubber with a crinkled texture. **2** very thin pancake. **crepe paper** paper with a crinkled texture.

crept *v* past of CREEP.

crepuscular *adj Lit* of or like twilight.

Cres. Crescent.

crescendo [krish-**end**-oh] *n, pl* **-dos 1** gradual increase in loudness, esp. in music. ♦ *adv* **2** gradually getting louder.

crescent *n* **1** (curved shape of) the moon as seen in its first or last quarter. **2** crescent-shaped street. ♦ *adj* **3** crescent-shaped.

cress *n* plant with strong-tasting leaves, used in salads.

crest *n* **1** top of a mountain, hill, or wave. **2** tuft or growth on a bird's or animal's head. **3** heraldic design used on a coat of arms and elsewhere. ♦ *v* **4** come to or be at the top of. **crested** *adj* **crestfallen** *adj* disheartened.

cretin *n* **1** *Informal* stupid person. **2** *Obs* person afflicted with physical and mental retardation caused by a thyroid deficiency. **cretinism** *n* **cretinous** *adj*

cretonne *n* heavy printed cotton fabric used in furnishings.

crevasse *n* deep open crack in a glacier.

crevice *n* narrow crack or gap in rock.

crew[1] *n* **1** people who work on a ship or aircraft. **2** group of people working together. **3** *Informal* any group of people. ♦ *v* **4** serve as a crew member (on). **crew cut** man's closely cropped haircut.

crew[2] *v Old-fashioned* past tense of CROW[2].

crewel *n* fine worsted yarn used in embroidery.

crib *n* **1** piece of writing stolen from elsewhere. **2** translation or list of answers used by students, often illicitly. **3** baby's cradle. **4** rack for fodder. **5** short for CRIBBAGE. ♦ *v* **cribbing, cribbed 6** copy (someone's work) dishonestly.

cribbage *n* card game for two to four players.

crick *n* **1** muscle spasm or cramp in the back or neck. ♦ *v* **2** cause a crick in.

cricket[1] *n* outdoor game played with bats, a ball, and wickets by two teams of eleven. **cricketer** *n*

cricket[2] *n* chirping insect like a grasshopper.

cried *v* past of CRY.

crier *n* (formerly) official who made public announcements (also **town crier**).

crime *n* **1** unlawful act. **2** unlawful acts collectively. **3** *Informal* disgraceful act. **criminal** *n* **1** person guilty of a crime. ♦ *adj* **2** of crime. **3** *Informal* deplorable. **criminally** *adv* **criminality** *n* **criminology** *n* study of crime. **criminologist** *n*

crimp *v* **1** fold or press into ridges. **2** curl (hair) tightly.

crimson *adj* deep purplish-red.

cringe *v* **1** flinch in fear. **2** behave in a submissive or timid way.

crinkle *v, n* wrinkle, crease, or fold. **crinkly** *adj*

crinoline *n* hooped petticoat.

cripple *n* **1** person who is lame or disabled. **2** person with a mental or social problem, e.g. *an emotional cripple.* ♦ *v* **3** make lame or disabled. **4** damage (something).

crisis *n, pl* **-ses 1** crucial stage, turning point. **2** time of extreme trouble.

crisp *adj* **1** fresh and firm. **2** dry and brittle. **3** clean and neat. **4** (of weather) cold but invigorating. **5** clear and sharp. **6** lively or brisk. ♦ *n* **7** very thin slice of potato fried till crunchy. ♦ *v* **8** make or become crisp. **crisply** *adv* **crispness** *n* **crispy** *adj* **crispier, crispiest** hard and crunchy. **crispbread** *n* thin dry biscuit.

crisscross *v* **1** move in or mark with a crosswise pattern. ♦ *adj* **2** (of lines) crossing in different directions.

criterion *n, pl* **-ria** standard of judgment.

> It is incorrect to use *criteria* as a singular, though this use is often found.

critic *n* **1** professional judge of any of the arts. **2** person who finds fault. **critical** *adj* **1** very important or dangerous. **2** very seriously ill or injured. **3** fault-finding. **4** able to examine and judge carefully. **5** of a critic or criticism. **critically** *adv* **criticism** *n* **1** fault-finding. **2** analysis of a work of art. **criticize** *v* **1** find fault with. **2** analyse. **critique** *n* critical essay.

croak *v* **1** (of a frog or crow) give a low hoarse cry. **2** utter or speak with a croak. **3** *Slang* die. ♦ *n* **4** low hoarse sound. **croaky** *adj* hoarse.

Croatian [kroh-**ay**-shun], **Croat** *adj* **1** of Croatia. ♦ *n* **2** person from Croatia. **3** dialect of Serbo-Croat spoken in Croatia.

crochet [**kroh**-shay] *v* **-cheting, -cheted** **1** make by looping and intertwining yarn with a hooked needle. ♦ *n* **2** work made in this way.

crock[1] *n* earthenware pot or jar. **crockery** *n* dishes.

crock[2] *n Informal* old or decrepit person or thing.

crocodile *n* **1** large amphibious tropical reptile. **2** a line of people, esp. schoolchildren, walking two by two. **crocodile tears** insincere show of grief.

crocus *n, pl* **-cuses** small plant with yellow, white, or purple flowers in spring.

croft *n* small farm worked by one family in Scotland. **crofter** *n*

croissant [**krwah**-son] *n* rich flaky crescent-shaped roll.

cromlech *n* circle of prehistoric standing stones.

crone *n* witchlike old woman.

crony *n, pl* **-nies** close friend.

crook *n* **1** *Informal* criminal. **2** bent or curved part. **3** hooked pole. ♦ *v* **4** bend or curve. **crooked** *adj* **1** bent or twisted. **2** set at an angle. **3** *Informal* dishonest.

croon *v* sing, hum, or speak in a soft low tone. **crooner** *n* male singer of sentimental ballads.

crop *n* **1** cultivated plant. **2** season's total yield of produce. **3** group of things appearing at one time. **4** (handle of) a whip. **5** pouch in a bird's gullet. **6** very short haircut. ♦ *v* **cropping, cropped** **7** cut very short. **8** produce or harvest as a crop. **9** (of animals) feed on (grass). **cropper** *n* **come a cropper** *Informal* have a disastrous failure or heavy fall. **crop up** *v Informal* happen unexpectedly.

croquet [**kroh**-kay] *n* game played on a lawn in which balls are hit through hoops.

croquette [kroh-**kett**] *n* fried cake of potato, meat, or fish.

crosier *n* same as CROZIER.

cross *v* **1** move or go across (something). **2** meet and pass. **3** draw two lines across (a cheque) to make it payable only into a bank account. **4** mark with a cross. **5** (with *out*) delete with a cross or lines. **6** place (one's arms or legs) crosswise. **7** make the sign of the cross on (oneself). **8** challenge or oppose. **9** cross-fertilize. ♦ *n* **10** structure, symbol, or mark of two intersecting lines. **11** such a structure of wood as a means of execution. **12** representation of the Cross as an emblem of Christianity. **13** crossbred animal or plant. **14** mixture of two things. **15** hindrance or misfortune, e.g. *that's my cross to bear.* ♦ *adj* **16** angry, annoyed. **17** lying or placed across. **the Cross** *Christianity* the cross on which Christ was crucified. **crossing** *n* **1** place where a street may be crossed safely. **2** place where one thing crosses another. **3** journey across water. **crossly** *adv* **crossness** *n* **crossbar** *n* horizontal bar across goalposts or on a bicycle. **cross-bench** *n* seat in Parliament for a member belonging to neither the government nor the opposition. **crossbow** *n* weapon consisting of a bow fixed across a wooden stock. **crossbred** *adj* bred from two different types of animal or plant. **crossbreed** *n* crossbred animal or plant. **crosscheck** *v* check using a different method. **cross-country** *adj, adv* **1** by way of open country or fields. ♦ *n* **2** race across open ground. **cross-examine** *v Law* question (a witness for the opposing side) to check his or her testimony. **cross-examination** *n* **cross-eyed** *adj* with eyes looking towards each other. **cross-fertilize** *v* fertilize (an animal or plant) from one of a different kind. **cross-fertilization** *n* **crossfire** *n* gunfire crossing another line of fire. **cross-ply** *adj* (of a tyre) having the fabric cords in the outer casing running diagonally. **cross-purposes** *pl n* **at cross-purposes** misunderstanding each other. **cross-reference** *n* reference within a text to another part. **crossroads** *n* place where roads intersect. **cross section** **1** (diagram of) a surface made by cutting across something. **2** representative sample. **crosswise** *adj, adv* **1** across. **2** in the shape of a cross. **crossword puzzle, crossword** *n* puzzle in which words suggested by clues are written into a grid of squares.

crotch *n* part of the body between the tops of the legs.

crotchet *n* musical note half the length of a minim.

crotchety *adj Informal* bad-tempered.

crouch *v* **1** bend low with the legs and body close. ♦ *n* **2** this position.

croup[1] [**kroop**] *n* throat disease of children, with a cough.

croup[2] [**kroop**] *n* hind quarters of a horse.

croupier [**kroop**-ee-ay] *n* person who collects bets and pays out winnings at a gambling table in a casino.

crouton *n* small piece of fried or toasted bread served in soup.

crow[1] *n* large black bird with a harsh call. **as the crow flies** in a straight line. **crow's feet** wrinkles at the corners of the eyes. **crow's nest** lookout platform at the top of a ship's mast.

crow[2] *v* **1** (of a cock) make a shrill squawking sound. **2** boast or gloat. **3** (of a baby) utter cries of pleasure.

crowbar *n* iron bar used as a lever.

crowd *n* **1** large group of people or things. **2** particular group of people. ♦ *v* **3** gather together in large numbers. **4** press together in a confined space. **5** fill or occupy fully.

crown *n* **1** monarch's headdress of gold and jewels. **2** wreath for the head, given as an honour. **3** top of the head or of a hill. **4** artificial cover for a broken or decayed tooth. **5** former British coin worth 25 pence. ♦ *v* **6** put a crown on the head of (someone) to proclaim him or her monarch. **7** put on or form the top of. **8** put the finishing touch to (a series of events). **9** attach a crown to (a tooth). **10** *Informal* hit on the head. **the Crown** power of the monarchy. **crown court** local criminal court in England and Wales. **crown jewels** jewellery used by a sovereign on state occasions. **crown prince, crown princess** heir to a throne.

crozier *n* bishop's hooked staff.

crucial *adj* **1** very important. **2** *Slang* excellent. **crucially** *adv*

crucible *n* pot in which metals are melted.

crucify *v* **-fying, -fied** **1** put to death by fastening to a cross. **2** *Informal* punish severely. **crucifix** *n* model of Christ on the Cross. **crucifixion** *n* crucifying. **the Crucifixion** *Christianity* crucifying of Christ. **cruciform** *adj* cross-shaped.

crude *adj* **1** rough and simple. **2** tasteless, vulgar. **3** in a natural or unrefined state. **crude oil** unrefined petroleum. **crudely** *adv* **crudity, crudeness** *n*

cruel *adj* **1** delighting in others' pain. **2**

causing pain or suffering. **cruelly** *adv* **cruelty** *n*

cruet *n* small container for salt, pepper, etc., at table.

cruise *n* **1** sail for pleasure. ♦ *v* **2** sail from place to place for pleasure. **3** (of a vehicle) travel at a moderate and economical speed. **cruiser** *n* **1** fast warship. **2** motorboat with a cabin. **cruiserweight** *n* same as LIGHT HEAVYWEIGHT. **cruise missile** low-flying guided missile.

crumb *n* **1** small fragment of bread or other dry food. **2** small amount. **crumby** *adj* **crumbier, crumbiest**

crumble *v* **1** break into fragments. **2** fall apart or decay. ♦ *n* **3** pudding of stewed fruit with a crumbly topping. **crumbly** *adj* **-blier, -bliest**

crummy *adj* **-mier, -miest** *Slang* of poor quality.

crumpet *n* **1** round soft yeast cake, eaten buttered. **2** *Slang* sexually attractive women collectively.

crumple *v* **1** crush, crease. **2** collapse, esp. from shock. **crumpled** *adj*

crunch *v* **1** bite or chew with a noisy crushing sound. **2** make a crisp or brittle sound. ♦ *n* **3** crunching sound. **4** *Informal* critical moment. **crunchy** *adj*

crupper *n* strap that passes from the back of a saddle under a horse's tail.

crusade *n* **1** medieval Christian war to recover the Holy Land from the Muslims. **2** vigorous campaign in favour of a cause. ♦ *v* **3** take part in a crusade. **crusader** *n*

cruse *n* small earthenware jug or pot.

crush *v* **1** compress so as to injure, break, or crumple. **2** break into small pieces. **3** defeat or humiliate utterly. ♦ *n* **4** dense crowd. **5** *Informal* infatuation. **6** drink made by crushing fruit.

crust *n* **1** hard outer part of something, esp. bread. **2** solid outer shell of the earth. ♦ *v* **3** cover with or form a crust. **crusty** *adj* **crustier, crustiest** **1** having a crust. **2** irritable.

crustacean *n* hard-shelled, usu. aquatic animal with several pairs of legs, such as the crab or lobster.

crutch *n* **1** long sticklike support with a rest for the armpit, used by a lame person. **2** person or thing that gives support. **3** crotch.

crux *n, pl* **cruxes** crucial or decisive point.

cry *v* **crying, cried** **1** shed tears. **2** call or utter loudly. ♦ *n, pl* **cries** **3** fit of weeping. **4** loud utterance. **5** urgent appeal, e.g. *a cry for help.* **crying** *adj* **a crying shame** something demanding immediate attention. **crybaby** *n* person, esp. a child, who cries too readily. **cry off** *v* *Informal* withdraw from an arrangement. **cry out for** *v* need urgently.

cryogenics *n* branch of physics concerned with very low temperatures. **cryogenic** *adj*

crypt *n* vault under a church, esp. one used as a burial place.

cryptic *adj* obscure in meaning, secret. **cryptically** *adv* **cryptography** *n* art of writing in and deciphering codes.

crystal *n* **1** (single grain of) a symmetrically shaped solid formed naturally by some substances. **2** very clear and brilliant glass, usu. with the surface cut in many planes. **3** tumblers, vases, etc., made of crystal. ♦ *adj* **4** bright and clear. **crystalline** *adj* **1** of or like crystal or crystals. **2** clear. **crystallize** *v* **1** make or become definite. **2** form into crystals. **crystallization** *n*

Cs *Chem* caesium.

CS gas *n* gas causing tears and painful breathing, used to control civil disturbances.

CT Connecticut.

Cu *Chem* copper.

cu. cubic.

cub *n* **1** young wild animal such as a bear or fox. **2** (**C-**) Cub Scout. ♦ *adj* **3** young or inexperienced, e.g. *a cub reporter.* ♦ *v* **cubbing, cubbed** **4** give birth to cubs. **Cub Scout** member of a junior branch of the Scout Association.

cubbyhole *n* small enclosed space or room.

cube *n* **1** object with six equal square sides. **2** number resulting from multiplying a number by itself twice. ♦ *v* **3** cut into cubes. **4** find the cube of (a number). **cubic** *adj* **1** having three dimensions. **2** cube-shaped. **3** involving the cubes of numbers. **cubism** *n* style of art in which objects are represented by geometrical shapes. **cubist** *adj, n* **cube root** number whose cube is a given number.

cubicle *n* enclosed part of a large room, screened for privacy.

cubit *n* old measure of length based on the length of the forearm.

cuckold *n* **1** man whose wife has been unfaithful. ♦ *v* **2** be unfaithful to (one's husband).

cuckoo *n* **1** migratory bird with a characteristic two-note call, which lays its eggs in the nests of other birds. ♦ *adj* **2** *Informal* insane or foolish. **cuckoo spit** white frothy mass produced on plants by larvae.

cucumber *n* long green-skinned fleshy fruit used in salads.

cud *n* partially digested food which a ruminant brings back into its mouth to chew again. **chew the cud** think deeply.

cuddle *v, n* hug. **cuddle up** *v* lie close to and hug someone. **cuddly** *adj*

cudgel *n* short thick stick used as a weapon.

cue[1] *n* **1** signal to an actor or musician to begin speaking or playing. **2** signal or reminder. ♦ *v* **cueing, cued 3** give a cue to.

cue[2] *n* **1** long tapering stick used in billiards, snooker, or pool. ♦ *v* **cueing, cued 2** hit (a ball) with a cue.

cuff[1] *n* end of a sleeve. **off the cuff** *Informal* without preparation. **cuff link** one of a pair of decorative fastenings for shirt cuffs.

cuff[2] *v* **1** hit with an open hand. ♦ *n* **2** blow with an open hand.

cuisine [quiz-**zeen**] *n* style of cooking.

cul-de-sac *n* road with one end blocked off.

culinary *adj* of kitchens or cookery.

cull *v* **1** choose, gather. **2** remove or kill (inferior or surplus animals) from a herd. ♦ *n* **3** culling.

culminate *v* reach the highest point or climax. **culmination** *n*

culottes *pl n* women's knee-length trousers cut to look like a skirt.

culpable *adj* deserving blame. **culpability** *n*

culprit *n* person guilty of an offence or misdeed.

cult *n* **1** specific system of worship. **2** sect devoted to the beliefs of a cult. **3** devotion to a person, idea, or activity. **4** popular fashion.

cultivate *v* **1** prepare (land) to grow crops. **2** grow (plants). **3** develop or improve (something). **4** try to develop a friendship with (someone). **cultivated** *adj* well-educated. **cultivation** *n* **cultivator** *n* farm implement for breaking up soil.

culture *n* **1** ideas, customs, and art of a particular society. **2** particular society. **3** developed understanding of the arts. **4** development by special training. **5** cultivation of plants or rearing of animals. **6** growth of bacteria for study. ♦ *v* **7** grow (bacteria) for study. **cultural** *adj* **cultured** *adj* showing good taste or manners. **cultured pearl** pearl artificially grown in an oyster shell.

culvert *n* drain under a road or railway.

cum *prep* with, e.g. *a kitchen-cum-dining room.*

cumbersome, cumbrous *adj* **1** awkward because of size or shape. **2** difficult because of complexity.

cumin, cummin *n* sweet-smelling seeds of a Mediterranean plant, used in cooking.

cummerbund *n* wide sash worn round the waist.

cumquat *n* same as KUMQUAT.

cumulative [**kew**-myew-la-tiv] *adj* increasing steadily.

cumulus [**kew**-myew-luss] *n, pl* **-li** thick white or dark grey cloud.

cuneiform [**kew**-nif-form] *n, adj* (written in) an ancient system of writing using wedge-shaped characters.

cunning *adj* **1** clever at deceiving. **2** ingenious. ♦ *n* **3** cleverness at deceiving. **4** ingenuity. **cunningly** *adv*

cup *n* **1** small bowl-shaped drinking container with a handle. **2** contents of a cup. **3** (competition with) a cup-shaped trophy given as a prize. **4** hollow rounded shape. ♦ *v* **cupping, cupped 5** form (one's hands) into the shape of a cup. **6** hold in cupped hands. **cupful** *n* **cup tie** eliminating match between two teams in a cup competition.

cupboard *n* piece of furniture or alcove with a door, for storage.

Cupid *n* Roman god of love, represented as a winged boy with a bow and arrow.

cupidity [kew-**pid**-it-ee] *n* greed for money or possessions.

cupola [**kew**-pol-la] *n* domed roof or ceiling.

cupreous *adj* of copper.

cur *n Lit* **1** mongrel dog. **2** contemptible person.

curaçao [**kew**-rah-so] *n* orange-flavoured liqueur.

curare [kew-**rah**-ree] *n* poisonous resin of a S American tree, used as a muscle relaxant in medicine.

curate *n* clergyman who assists a parish priest. **curacy** [**kew**-rah-see] *n, pl* **-cies** work or position of a curate.

curative *adj, n* (something) able to cure.

curator *n* person in charge of a museum or art gallery. **curatorship** *n*

curb *n* **1** something that restrains. **2** strap under a horse's jaw, used to check it. ♦ *v* **3** control, restrain.

curd *n* coagulated milk, used to make cheese. **curdle** *v* turn into curd, coagulate.

cure *v* **1** get rid of (an illness or problem). **2** make (someone) well again. **3** preserve by salting, smoking, or drying. ♦ *n* **4** (treatment causing) curing of an illness or person. **5** remedy or solution. **curable** *adj*

curette *n* **1** surgical instrument for scraping tissue from body cavities. ♦ *v* **2** scrape with a curette. **curettage** *n*

curfew *n* **1** law ordering people to stay inside their homes after a specific time at night. **2** time set as a deadline by such a law.

Curia *n, pl* **-riae** court and government of the Roman Catholic Church.

curie *n* standard unit of radioactivity.

curio [**kew**-ree-oh] *n, pl* **-rios** rare or unusual object valued as a collector's item.

curious *adj* **1** eager to learn or know. **2** eager to find out private details. **3** unusual or peculiar. **curiously** *adv* **curiosity** *n* **1** eagerness to know or find out. **2** (*pl* **-ties**) rare or unusual object.

curium [**kew**-ree-um] *n Chem* radioactive element artificially produced from plutonium.

curl *n* **1** curved piece of hair. **2** curved spiral shape. ♦ *v* **3** make (hair) into curls or (of hair) grow in curls. **4** make into a curved spiral shape. **curly** *adj* **curler** *n* pin or small tube for curling hair. **curling** *n* game like bowls, played with heavy stones on ice.

curlew *n* long-billed wading bird.

curlicue *n* ornamental curl or twist.

curmudgeon *n* bad-tempered person.

currant *n* **1** small dried grape. **2** small round berry, such as a redcurrant.

current *adj* **1** of the immediate present. **2** most recent, up-to-date. **3** commonly accepted. ♦ *n* **4** flow of water or air in one direction. **5** flow of electricity. **6** general trend. **currently** *adv* **currency** *n, pl* **-cies 1** money in use in a particular country. **2** general acceptance or use. **current account** bank account from which money may be drawn at any time by cheque or computerized card.

curriculum *n, pl* **-la, -lums** all the courses of study offered by a school or college. **curriculum vitae** [**vee**-tie] outline of someone's educational and professional history, prepared for job applications.

curry[1] *n, pl* **-ries 1** Indian dish of meat or vegetables in a hot spicy sauce. ♦ *v* **-rying, -ried 2** prepare (food) with curry powder. **curry powder** mixture of spices for making curry.

curry[2] *v* **-rying, -ried 1** groom (a horse). **2** dress (leather). **curry favour** ingratiate oneself with an important person. **currycomb** *n* ridged comb for grooming a horse.

curse *v* **1** swear (at). **2** ask a supernatural power to cause harm to. ♦ *n* **3** swearword. **4** (result of) a call to a supernatural power to cause harm to someone. **5** something causing trouble or harm. **cursed** *adj* **1** under a curse. **2** (foll. by *with*) having (something unfortunate).

cursive *adj, n* (handwriting) done with joined letters.

cursor *n* movable point of light that shows a specific position on a visual display unit.

cursory *adj* quick and superficial. **cursorily** *adv*

curt *adj* brief and rather rude. **curtly** *adv* **curtness** *n*

curtail *v* **1** cut short. **2** restrict. **curtailment** *n*

curtain *n* **1** piece of cloth hung at a window or opening as a screen. **2** hanging cloth separating the audience and the stage in a theatre. **3** fall or closing of the curtain at the end, or the rise or opening of the curtain at the start of a theatrical performance. **4** something forming a barrier or screen. ♦ *pl* **5** *Informal* death, the end. ♦ *v* **6** provide with curtains. **7** (foll. by *off*) separate by a curtain. **curtain call** return to the stage by performers to receive applause.

curtsy, curtsey *n, pl* **-sies, -seys** **1** woman's gesture of respect made by bending the knees and bowing the head. ♦ *v* **-sying, -sied** *or* **-seying, -seyed** **2** make a curtsy.

curve *n* **1** continuously bending line with no straight parts. **2** something that curves or is curved. ♦ *v* **3** form or move in a curve. **curvy** *adj* **curvier, curviest** **curvaceous** *adj Informal* (of a woman) having a shapely body. **curvature** *n* curved shape. **curvilinear** *adj* consisting of or bounded by a curve.

cushion *n* **1** bag filled with soft material, to make a seat more comfortable. **2** something that provides comfort or absorbs shock. **3** padded edge of a billiard, snooker, or pool table. ♦ *v* **4** lessen the effects of. **5** protect from injury or shock.

cushy *adj* **cushier, cushiest** *Informal* easy, e.g. *a cushy job.*

cusp *n* **1** pointed end, esp. on a tooth. **2** *Astrol* division between houses or signs of the zodiac.

cuss *Informal* ♦ *n* **1** curse, oath. **2** annoying person. ♦ *v* **3** swear (at). **cussed** [**kuss**-id] *adj Informal* obstinate.

custard *n* sweet yellow sauce made from milk and eggs.

custody *n* **1** keeping safe. **2** imprisonment prior to being tried. **custodial** *adj* **custodian** *n* person in charge of a public building.

custom *n* **1** long-established activity or action. **2** usual habit. **3** regular use of a shop or business. ♦ *pl* **4** duty charged on imports or exports. **5** government department which collects these. **6** area at a port, airport, or border where baggage and freight are examined for dutiable goods. **customary** *adj* **1** usual. **2** established by custom. **customarily** *adv* **customer** *n* **1** person who buys goods or services. **2** *Informal* person who behaves in a specified way, e.g. *a cool customer.* **custom-built, custom-made** *adj* made to the specifications of an individual customer.

cut *v* **cutting, cut** **1** open up, penetrate, wound, or divide with a sharp instrument. **2** divide. **3** trim or shape by cutting. **4** abridge, shorten. **5** reduce, restrict. **6** *Informal* hurt the feelings of. **7** pretend not to recognize. **8** *Informal* not attend (classes). **9** grow (teeth) through the gums. **10** call a halt to a shooting sequence in a film. **11** move quickly to another scene in a film. **12** divide (a pack of cards) at random. ♦ *n* **13** act of cutting. **14** stroke or incision made by cutting. **15** piece cut off. **16** reduction. **17** deletion in a text, film, or play. **18** *Informal* share, esp. of profits. **19** style in which hair or a garment is cut. **cut and dried** *Informal* settled in advance. **cutback** *n* decrease or reduction. **cut back**

(on) *v* decrease or reduce. **cut in** *v* **1** interrupt. **2** obstruct another vehicle in overtaking it. **cut off** *v* **1** separate. **2** stop the supply of. **cut out** *v* **1** shape by cutting. **2** delete, remove. **3** *Informal* stop doing (something). **4** (of an engine) cease to operate suddenly. **5** **be cut out for** be suited for or to. **cut-price** *adj* at a reduced price. **cut up** *v* **1** cut into pieces. **2** **be cut up** *Informal* be very upset.

cutaneous [kew-**tane**-ee-uss] *adj* of the skin.

cute *adj* **1** appealing or attractive. **2** *Informal* clever or shrewd. **cutely** *adv* **cuteness** *n*

cuticle [**kew**-tik-kl] *n* skin at the base of a fingernail or toenail.

cutlass *n* curved one-edged sword formerly used by sailors.

cutlery *n* knives, forks, and spoons. **cutler** *n* maker of cutlery.

cutlet *n* **1** small piece of meat like a chop. **2** flat croquette of chopped meat or fish.

cutter *n* **1** person or tool that cuts. **2** any of various small fast boats.

cut-throat *adj* **1** fierce or relentless. ♦ *n* **2** murderer. **3** razor with a long folding blade.

cutting *n* **1** article cut from a newspaper or magazine. **2** piece cut from a plant from which to grow a new plant. **3** passage cut through high ground for a road or railway. ♦ *adj* **4** (of a remark) hurtful.

cuttlefish *n* squidlike sea mollusc.

CV curriculum vitae.

cwm [**koom**] *n* (in Wales) valley.

cwt hundredweight.

cyanide *n* extremely poisonous chemical compound.

cyanosis *n* blueness of the skin, caused by a deficiency of oxygen in the blood.

cybernetics *n* branch of science in which electronic and mechanical systems are studied and compared to biological systems.

cyberspace *n* place said to contain all the data stored in computers.

cyclamen [**sik**-la-men] *n* plant with red, pink, or white flowers.

cycle *v* **1** ride a bicycle. ♦ *n* **2** bicycle. **3** *US* motorcycle. **4** complete series of recurring events. **5** time taken for one such series. **6** single complete movement in an electrical, electronic, or mechanical process. **7** set of plays, songs, or poems about a figure or event. **cyclical, cyclic** *adj* occurring in cycles. **cyclist** *n* person who rides a bicycle.

cyclone *n* violent wind moving clockwise round a central area.

cyclotron *n* apparatus that accelerates charged particles by means of a strong vertical magnetic field.

cygnet *n* young swan.

cylinder *n* **1** solid or hollow body with straight sides and circular ends. **2** container with this shape. **3** chamber within which the piston moves in an internal-combustion engine. **cylindrical** *adj*

cymbal *n* percussion instrument consisting of a brass plate which is struck against another or hit with a stick.

Cymric [**kim**-rik] *adj* Welsh.

cynic [**sin**-ik] *n* person who believes that people always act selfishly. **cynical** *adj* **cynically** *adv* **cynicism** *n*

cynosure [**sin**-oh-zyure] *n* centre of attention.

cypher *n* same as CIPHER.

cypress *n* evergreen tree with dark green leaves.

Cypriot *n, adj* (person) from Cyprus.

cyst [**sist**] *n* (abnormal) sac in the body containing fluid or soft matter. **cystic** *adj* **cystitis** [siss-**tite**-iss] *n* inflammation of the bladder.

cytology [site-**ol**-a-jee] *n* study of plant and animal cells. **cytological** *adj* **cytologist** *n*

cytoplasm *n* protoplasm of a cell excluding the nucleus.

czar [**zahr**] *n* same as TSAR.

Czech *n, adj* **1** (person) from the Czech Republic. ♦ *n* **2** language of the Czech Republic.

D d

d *Physics* density.

D **1** *Chem* deuterium. **2** the Roman numeral for 500.

d. **1** *Brit* (before decimalization) penny. **2** died.

dab[1] *v* **dabbing, dabbed** **1** pat lightly. **2** apply with short tapping strokes. ♦ *n* **3** small amount of something soft or moist. **4** light stroke or tap. **dab hand** *Informal* person who is particularly good at something.

dab[2] *n* small flatfish with rough scales.

dabble *v* **1** be involved in something superficially. **2** splash about. **dabbler** *n*

dace *n* small freshwater fish.

dacha *n* country cottage in Russia.

dachshund *n* dog with a long body and short legs.

dad *n Informal* father.

Dada, Dadaism *n* early 20th-century artistic movement that systematically used arbitrary and absurd concepts. **Dadaist** *n, adj*

daddy *n, pl* **-dies** *Informal* father.

daddy-longlegs *n Informal* crane fly.

dado [**day**-doe] *n, pl* **-does, -dos** lower part of an interior wall, below a rail, decorated differently from the upper part.

daffodil *n* yellow trumpet-shaped flower that blooms in spring.

daft *adj Informal* foolish or crazy.

dagger *n* short knifelike weapon with a pointed blade.

daguerreotype [dag-**gair**-oh-type] *n* type of early photograph produced on chemically treated silver.

dahlia [**day**-lya] *n* brightly coloured garden flower.

Dáil Éireann [**doil air**-in], **Dáil** *n* lower chamber of parliament in the Irish Republic.

daily *adj* **1** occurring every day or every weekday. ♦ *adv* **2** every day. ♦ *n, pl* **-lies** **3** daily newspaper. **4** *Brit informal* person who cleans other people's houses.

dainty *adj* **-tier, -tiest** **1** delicate or elegant. ♦ *n, pl* **-ties** **2** small cake or sweet. **daintily** *adv*

daiquiri [**dak**-eer-ee] *n* iced drink containing rum, lime juice, and sugar.

dairy *n, pl* **dairies** **1** place for the processing or sale of milk and its products. ♦ *adj* **2** of milk or its products. **dairy cattle** cows kept mainly for their milk. **dairy farm** farm where cows are kept mainly for their milk. **dairymaid** *n* (formerly) woman employed to milk cows. **dairyman** *n* man employed to look after cows.

dais [**day**-iss] *n* raised platform in a hall, used by a speaker.

daisy *n, pl* **-sies** small wild flower with a yellow centre and white petals. **daisy chain** string of daisies joined together by their stems to make a necklace. **daisywheel** *n* flat disc in a word processor with radiating spokes for printing letters.

Dalai Lama *n* chief lama and (until 1959) ruler of Tibet.

dale *n* (esp. in N England) valley.

dally *v* **-lying, -lied** **1** waste time. **2** (foll. by *with*) deal frivolously (with). **dalliance** *n* flirtation.

Dalmatian *n* large dog with a white coat and black spots.

dam[1] *n* **1** barrier built across a river to create a lake. **2** lake created by this. ♦ *v* **damming, dammed** **3** build a dam across (a river).

dam[2] *n* mother of an animal such as a sheep or horse.

damage *v* **1** harm, spoil. ♦ *n* **2** harm to a person or thing. **3** *Informal* cost, e.g. *what's the damage?* ♦ *pl* **4** money awarded as compensation for injury or loss.

damask *n* fabric with a pattern woven into it, used for tablecloths etc.

dame *n* **1** *Slang* woman. **2** (**D-**) title of a woman who has been awarded the OBE or another order of chivalry.

damn *interj* **1** *Slang* exclamation of annoyance. ♦ *adv, adj* **2** (also **damned**) *Slang* extreme(ly). ♦ *v* **3** condemn as bad or worthless. **4** (of God) condemn to hell. **damnable** *adj* annoying. **damnably** *adv* **damnation** *interj, n* **damning** *adj* proving or suggesting guilt, e.g. *a damning report.*

damp *adj* **1** slightly wet. ♦ *n* **2** slight wetness, moisture. ♦ *v* (also **dampen**) **3** make damp. **4** (foll. by *down*) reduce the intensity of (feelings or actions). **damply** *adv* **dampness** *n* **damper** *n* **1** movable plate to regulate the draught in a fire. **2** pad in a piano that deadens the vibration of each string. **put a damper on** have a depressing or inhibiting effect on. **damp course, damp-proof course** layer of water-resistant material built into the foot of a wall to stop moisture rising.

damsel *n Old-fashioned* young woman.

damson *n* small blue-black plumlike fruit.

dan *n Martial arts* **1** any of the 10 black-belt grades of proficiency. **2** competitor entitled to a dan grading.

dance *v* **1** move the feet and body rhythmically in time to music. **2** perform (a particular dance). **3** skip or leap. **4** move rhythmically. ♦ *n* **5** series of steps and movements in time to music. **6** social meeting arranged for dancing. **dancer** *n*

D and C *n Med* dilatation and curettage: a minor operation in which the neck of the womb is stretched and the lining of the womb scraped, to clear the womb or remove tissue for diagnosis.

dandelion *n* yellow-flowered wild plant.

dander *n* **get one's dander up** *Slang* become angry.

dandle *v* move (a child) up and down on one's knee.

dandruff *n* loose scales of dry dead skin shed from the scalp.

dandy *n, pl* **-dies** **1** man who is overconcerned with the elegance of his appearance. ♦ *adj* **-dier, -diest** **2** *Informal* very good. **dandified** *adj*

Dane *n* person from Denmark. **Danish** *n, adj* (language) of Denmark. **Danish blue** strong white cheese with blue veins. **Danish pastry** iced puff pastry filled with fruit, almond paste, etc.

danger *n* **1** possibility of being injured or killed. **2** person or thing that may cause injury or harm. **3** likelihood that something unpleasant will happen. **danger money** extra money paid for doing dangerous work. **dangerous** *adj* **dangerously** *adv*

dangle *v* **1** hang loosely. **2** display as an enticement.

dank *adj* unpleasantly damp and chilly.

dapper *adj* (of a man) neat in appearance and slight in build.

dappled *adj* **1** marked with spots of a different colour. **2** covered in patches of light and shadow. **dapple-grey** *n* horse with a grey coat and darker coloured spots.

Darby and Joan *n* happily married elderly couple. **Darby and Joan Club** club for elderly people.

dare *v* **1** be courageous enough to try (to do something). **2** challenge to do something risky. ♦ *n* **3** challenge to do something risky. **I dare say** probably. **daring** *adj* **1** willing to take risks. ♦ *n* **2** courage to do dangerous things. **daringly** *adv* **daredevil** *adj, n* recklessly bold (person).

> When *dare* is used in a question or as a negative, it does not take an *-s: He dare not come.*

dark *adj* **1** having little or no light. **2** (of a colour) reflecting little light. **3** (of hair or skin) brown or black. **4** gloomy, sad. **5** sinister, evil. **6** secret, e.g. *keep it dark.* ♦ *n* **7** absence of light. **8** night. **in the dark** not knowing, uninformed. **darkly** *adv* **darkness** *n* **darken** *v* **dark age** period of ignorance or barbarism. **Dark Ages** period of European history between 500 and 1000 AD. **dark horse** person about whom little is known. **darkroom** *n* darkened room for processing photographic film.

darling *n* **1** much-loved person. **2** favourite, e.g. *the darling of the financial press.* ♦ *adj* **3** much-loved.

darn[1] *v* **1** mend (a garment) with a series of interwoven stitches. ♦ *n* **2** patch of darned work.

darn[2] *interj, adv, adj, v Euphemistic* damn.

dart *n* **1** small narrow pointed missile that is thrown or shot, esp. in the game of darts. **2** sudden quick movement. **3** tapered tuck made in dressmaking. ♦ *pl* **4** game in which darts are thrown at a circular numbered board. ♦ *v* **5** move or direct quickly and suddenly.

Darwinism *n* theory of the origin of animal and plant species by evolution. **Darwinian, Darwinist** *adj, n*

dash *v* **1** move quickly. **2** hurl or crash. **3** frustrate (someone's hopes). ♦ *n* **4** sudden quick movement. **5** small amount. **6** mixture of style and courage. **7** punctuation mark (–) indicating a change of subject. **8** longer symbol used in Morse code. **dashing** *adj* stylish and attractive. **dashboard** *n* instrument panel in a vehicle. **dash off** *v* write or produce quickly.

dastardly *adj* wicked and cowardly.

data *n* **1** information consisting of observations, measurements, or facts. **2** numbers, digits, etc., stored by a computer. **data base** store of information that can be easily handled by a computer. **data capture** process for converting information into a form that can be handled by a computer. **data processing** series of operations performed on data, esp. by a computer, to extract or interpret information.

> *Data* is a Latin plural word but it is generally used as a singular word in English.

date[1] *n* **1** specified day of the month. **2** particular day or year when an event happened. **3** *Informal* appointment, esp. with a person of the opposite sex. **4** *Informal* person with whom one has a date. ♦ *v* **5** mark with the date. **6** assign a date of occurrence to. **7** become old-fashioned. **8** (foll. by *from*) originate from, e.g. *the church dates from Norman times.* **dated** *adj* old-fashioned. **dateline** *n Journalism* information about the place and time a story was written, placed at the top of the article. **Date Line** line, approx. equal to 180°, on the east side of which the date is one day earlier than on the west.

date[2] *n* dark-brown sweet-tasting fruit of the date palm. **date palm** tall palm grown in tropical regions for its fruit.

dative *n* (in certain languages) the form of the noun that expresses the indirect object.

datum *n, pl* **data** single piece of information in the form of a fact or statistic.

daub *v* smear or spread quickly or clumsily.

daughter *n* **1** female child. **2** woman who comes from a certain place or is connected with a certain thing, e.g. *daughter of the Catholic church.* **daughterly** *adj* **daughter-in-law** *n, pl* **daughters-in-law** son's wife.

daunting *adj* intimidating or worrying. **dauntless** *adj* fearless.

dauphin [**doe**-fan] *n* (formerly) eldest son of the king of France.

davenport *n* **1** small writing table with drawers. **2** *Aust, US & Canadian* large couch.

davit [**dav**-vit] *n* crane, usu. one of a pair, at a ship's side, for lowering and hoisting a lifeboat.

Davy Jones's locker *n* the sea, considered as a grave for sailors.

Davy lamp *n* miner's lamp designed to prevent it from igniting gas.

dawdle *v* walk slowly, lag behind. **dawdler** *n*

dawn *n* **1** daybreak. **2** beginning (of something). ♦ *v* **3** begin to grow light. **4** begin to develop or appear. **5** (foll. by *on*) become apparent (to).

day *n* **1** period of 24 hours. **2** period of light between sunrise and sunset. **3** part of a day occupied with regular activity, esp. work. **4** period or point in time. **5** time of success. **daybreak** *n* time in the morning when light first appears. **day centre** place providing meals etc., where elderly or handicapped people can spend the day. **daydream** *n* **1** pleasant fantasy indulged in while awake. ♦ *v* **2** indulge in idle fantasy. **daydreamer** *n* **daylight** *n* light from the sun. **daylight robbery** *Informal* blatant overcharging. **daylight-saving time** time set one hour ahead of the local standard time, to provide an extra hour of light in the evening in summer. **day release** system in which workers go to college one day a week. **day return** reduced fare for a journey to a place and back again on the same day. **day room** communal living-room in a hospital or similar institution. **day-to-day** *adj* routine.

daze *v* **1** stun, by a blow or shock. ♦ *n* **2** state of confusion or shock. **dazed** *adj*

dazzle *v* **1** impress greatly. **2** blind temporarily by sudden excessive light. ♦ *n* **3** bright light that dazzles. **dazzling** *adj* **dazzlingly** *adv*

dB, db decibel(s).

DC **1** direct current. **2** District of Columbia.

DD Doctor of Divinity.

D-day *n* day selected for the start of some operation, orig. the Allied invasion of Europe in 1944.

DDT *n* kind of insecticide.

DE Delaware.

de- *prefix* indicating: **1** removal, e.g. *dethrone.* **2** reversal, e.g. *declassify.* **3** departure, e.g. *decamp.*

deacon *n Christianity* **1** ordained minister ranking immediately below a priest. **2** (in some Protestant churches) lay official who assists the minister.

deactivate *v* make (a bomb etc.) harmless or inoperative.

dead *adj* **1** no longer alive. **2** no longer in use. **3** numb, e.g. *my leg has gone dead.* **4** complete, absolute, e.g. *dead silence.* **5** *Informal* very tired. **6** (of a place) lacking activity. ♦ *n* **7** period during which coldness or darkness is most intense, e.g. *in the dead of night.* ♦ *adv* **8** extremely. **9** suddenly, e.g. *I stopped dead.* **the dead** dead people. **dead set** firmly decided, e.g. *he really was dead set against it.* **deadbeat** *n Informal* lazy useless person. **dead beat** *Informal* exhausted. **dead end** **1** road with one end blocked off. **2** situation in which further progress is impossible. **dead heat** tie for first place between two participants in a contest. **deadline** *n* time limit. **deadlock** *n* point in a dispute at which no agreement can be reached. **deadlocked** *adj* **dead loss** *Informal* useless person or thing. **deadpan** *adj, adv* showing no emotion or expression. **dead reckoning** method of establishing one's position using the distance and direction travelled. **dead weight** heavy weight. **dead wood** *Informal* useless people or things.

deaden *v* make less intense.

deadly *adj* **-lier, -liest** **1** likely to cause death. **2** *Informal* extremely boring. ♦ *adv* **3** extremely. **deadly nightshade** plant with poisonous black berries.

deaf *adj* unable to hear. **deaf to** refusing to listen to or take notice of. **deafen** *v* make deaf, esp. temporarily. **deafness** *n* **deaf-mute** *n* person unable to hear or speak.

> The use of *the deaf, the disabled,* etc. can be offensive and should be avoided. Instead you should talk about *deaf people, disabled people,* etc.

deal[1] *n* **1** agreement or transaction. **2** kind of treatment, e.g. *a fair deal.* **3** large amount. ♦ *v* **dealing, dealt** [**delt**] **4** inflict (a blow) on. **5** *Cards* give out (cards) to the players. **dealer** *n* **1** person whose business involves buying and selling. **2** *Slang* person who sells illegal drugs. **3** *Cards* person who gives out the cards. **dealings** *pl n* transactions or business relations. **deal in** *v* buy or sell (goods). **deal out** *v* distribute. **deal with** *v* **1** take action on. **2** be concerned with.

deal[2] *n* plank of fir or pine wood.

dean *n* **1** chief administrative official of a college or university faculty. **2** chief administrator of a cathedral. **deanery** *n, pl* **-eries 1** office or residence of a dean. **2** parishes of a dean.

dear *n* **1** someone regarded with affection. ♦ *adj* **2** much-loved. **3** costly. **dearly** *adv* **dearness** *n*

dearth [**dirth**] *n* inadequate amount, scarcity.

death *n* **1** permanent end of life in a person or animal. **2** instance of this. **3** ending, destruction. **deathly** *adj, adv* like death, e.g. *a deathly silence; deathly pale.* **deathless** *adj* everlasting, because of fine qualities. **deathbed** *n* bed where a person is about to die or has just died. **death certificate** document signed by a doctor certifying the death of a person and giving the cause of death if known. **death duty** former name for INHERITANCE TAX. **death knell** something that heralds death or destruction. **death mask** cast taken from the face of a person who has recently died. **death row** *US* part of a prison where convicts awaiting execution are held. **death's-head** *n* human skull or a representation of one. **deathtrap** *n* place or vehicle considered very unsafe. **death warrant** official authorization for a death sentence. **deathwatch beetle** beetle that bores into wood and makes a tapping sound.

deb *n Informal* debutante.

debacle [day-**bah**-kl] *n* disastrous failure.

debar *v* prevent, bar.

debase *v* lower in value, quality, or character. **debasement** *n*

debate *n* **1** discussion. **2** formal discussion of a proposition, at the end of which people vote on whether to accept it. ♦ *v* **3** discuss formally. **4** consider (a course of action). **debatable** *adj* not absolutely certain.

debauch [dib-**bawch**] *v* make (someone) bad or corrupt, esp. sexually. **debauched** *adj* immoral, sexually corrupt. **debauchery** *n*

debenture *n* long-term bond bearing fixed interest, issued by a company or a government agency.

debilitate *v* weaken, make feeble. **debilitation** *n* **debility** *n* weakness, infirmity.

debit *n* **1** acknowledgment of a sum owing by entry on the left side of an account. ♦ *v* **debiting, debited 2** charge (an account) with a debt. **3** record as a debit.

debonair *adj* (of a man) charming and refined.

debouch *v* move out from a narrow place to a wider one.

debrief *v* receive a report from (a soldier, diplomat, etc.) after an event. **debriefing** *n*

debris [**deb**-ree] *n* fragments of something destroyed.

debt *n* something owed, esp. money. **bad debt** debt that is unlikely to be repaid. **debt of honour** debt that is morally but not legally binding. **in debt** owing money. **debtor** *n*

debug *v* **1** *Informal* find and remove defects in (a computer program). **2** remove concealed microphones from (a room or telephone).

debunk *v Informal* expose the falseness of.

debut [**day**-byoo] *n* first public appearance of a performer. **debutante** [**day**-byoo-tont] *n* young upper-class woman being formally presented to society.

Dec. December.

decade *n* period of ten years.

decadence [**dek**-a-denss] *n* deterioration in morality or culture. **decadent** *adj*

decaffeinated [dee-**kaf**-fin-ate-id] *adj* (of coffee, tea, or cola) with caffeine removed.

decagon *n* geometric figure with ten faces. **decagonal** *adj*

decahedron [deck-a-**heed**-ron] *n* solid figure with ten sides.

Decalogue *n* the Ten Commandments.

decamp *v* depart secretly or suddenly.

decant *v* **1** pour (a liquid) from one container to another. **2** rehouse (people) while their homes are being renovated. **decanter** *n* stoppered bottle for wine or spirits.

decapitate *v* behead. **decapitation** *n*

decathlon *n* athletic contest with ten events. **decathlete** *n*

decay *v* **1** become weaker or more corrupt. **2** rot. ♦ *n* **3** process of decaying. **4** state brought about by this process.

decease *n Formal* death. **deceased** *adj Formal* dead. **the deceased** dead person.

deceive *v* **1** mislead by lying. **2** be unfaithful to (one's sexual partner). **deceiver** *n* **deceit** *n* behaviour intended to deceive. **deceitful** *adj*

decelerate *v* slow down. **deceleration** *n*

December *n* twelfth month of the year.

decent *adj* **1** (of a person) polite and morally acceptable. **2** fitting or proper. **3** conforming to conventions of sexual behaviour. **4** *Informal* kind. **decently** *adv* **decency** *n, pl* **-cies**

decentralize *v* reorganize into smaller local units. **decentralization** *n*

deception *n* **1** deceiving. **2** something that deceives, trick. **deceptive** *adj* likely or designed to deceive. **deceptively** *adv* **deceptiveness** *n*

deci- *combining form* one tenth.

decibel *n* unit for measuring the intensity of sound.

decide *v* **1** (cause to) reach a decision. **2** settle (a contest or question). **decided** *adj* **1** unmistakable. **2** determined. **decidedly** *adv*

deciduous *adj* (of a tree) shedding its leaves annually.

decimal *n* **1** fraction written in the form of a dot followed by one or more numbers. ♦ *adj* **2** relating to or using powers of ten. **3** expressed as a decimal. **decimalize** *v* change (a system or number) to the decimal system. **decimalization** *n* **decimal currency** system of currency in which the units are parts or powers of ten. **decimal point** dot between the unit and the fraction of a number in the decimal system. **decimal system** number system with a base of ten, in which numbers are expressed by combinations of the digits 0 to 9.

decimate *v* destroy or kill a large proportion of. **decimation** *n*

decipher *v* work out the meaning of (something illegible or in code). **decipherable** *adj*

decision *n* **1** judgment, conclusion, or resolution. **2** act of making up one's mind. **3** firmness of purpose. **decisive** *adj* **1** having a definite influence, e.g. *the decisive factor.* **2** having the ability to make quick decisions. **decisively** *adv* **decisiveness** *n*

deck *n* **1** area of a ship that forms a floor. **2** similar area in a bus. **3** platform that supports the turntable and pick-up of a record player. **4** *US* pack (of cards). **deck chair** folding chair made of canvas over a wooden frame. **deck hand** sailor assigned duties on the deck of a ship. **deck out** *v* decorate.

declaim *v* **1** speak loudly and dramatically. **2** protest loudly. **declamation** *n* **declamatory** *adj*

declare *v* **1** state firmly and forcefully. **2** announce officially. **3** acknowledge for tax purposes. **declaration** *n* **declaratory** *adj*

declassify *v* state officially that (information or a document) is no longer secret. **declassification** *n*

declension *n Grammar* changes in the form of nouns, pronouns, or adjectives to show case, number, and gender.

decline *v* **1** become smaller, weaker, or less important. **2** refuse politely to accept or do. **3** *Grammar* list the inflections of (a noun, pronoun, or adjective). ♦ *n* **4** gradual weakening or loss.

declivity *n, pl* **-ties** downward slope.

declutch *v* disengage the clutch of a motor vehicle.

decoct *v* extract the essence from (a substance) by boiling. **decoction** *n*

decode *v* convert from code into ordinary language. **decoder** *n*

décolleté [day-**kol**-tay] *adj* (of a woman's garment) low-cut. **décolletage** [day-**kol**-tazh] *n* low-cut dress or neckline.

decommission *v* dismantle (a nuclear reactor, weapon, etc.) which is no longer needed.

decompose *v* be broken down through chemical or bacterial action. **decomposition** *n*

decompress *v* **1** free from pressure. **2** return (a diver) to normal atmospheric pressure. **decompression** *n* **decompression sickness** severe pain and difficulty in breathing, caused by a sudden change in atmospheric pressure.

decongestant *n* medicine that relieves nasal congestion.

decontaminate *v* make safe by removing poisons, radioactivity, etc. **decontamination** *n*

decor [**day**-core] *n* style in which a room or house is decorated.

decorate *v* **1** make more attractive by adding something ornamental. **2** paint or wallpaper. **3** award a (military) medal to. **decoration** *n* **decorative** *adj* **decorator** *n*

decorous [**dek**-a-russ] *adj* polite, calm, and sensible in behaviour. **decorously** *adv*

decorum [dik-**core**-um] *n* polite and socially correct behaviour.

decoy *n* **1** person or thing used to lure someone into danger. **2** dummy bird or animal, used to lure game within shooting range. ♦ *v* **3** lure away by means of a trick.

decrease *v* **1** make or become less. ♦ *n* **2** lessening, reduction. **3** amount by which something has decreased.

decree *n* **1** law made by someone in authority. **2** court judgment. ♦ *v* **3** order by decree. **decree absolute** final court order in a divorce case, which leaves the parties free to remarry. **decree nisi** court order in a divorce case, which will become absolute unless valid reasons are produced to oppose it.

decrepit *adj* weakened or worn out by age or long use. **decrepitude** *n*

decretal *n* *RC Church* papal decree.

decriminalize *v* make (an illegal act) no longer a crime. **decriminalization** *n*

decry *v* **-crying, -cried** express disapproval of.

dedicate *v* **1** commit (oneself or one's time) wholly to a special purpose or cause. **2** inscribe or address (a book etc.) to someone as a tribute. **dedicated** *adj* devoted to a particular purpose or cause. **dedication** *n*

deduce *v* reach (a conclusion) by reasoning from evidence. **deducible** *adj*

deduct *v* subtract. **deductible** *adj*

deduction *n* **1** deducting. **2** something that is deducted. **3** deducing. **4** conclusion reached by deducing. **deductive** *adj*

deed *n* **1** something that is done. **2** legal document. **deed box** strong box in which legal documents are stored. **deed poll** *Law* deed made by one party only, esp. to change one's name.

deejay *n* *Informal* disc jockey.

deem *v* consider, judge.

deep *adj* **1** extending or situated far down, inwards, backwards, or sideways. **2** of a specified dimension downwards, inwards, or backwards, e.g. *three inches deep.* **3** difficult to understand. **4** of great intensity. **5** (foll. by *in*) absorbed in (an activity). **6** (of a colour) strong or dark. **7** low in pitch. **the deep** *Poetic* the sea. **deeply** *adv* profoundly or intensely (also **deep down**). **deepen** *v* **deep-freeze** *n* same as FREEZER. **deep-fry** *v* cook in hot oil deep enough to cover the food completely. **deep-rooted** *adj* (of an idea or belief) firmly fixed or held. **deep-seated** *adj* (of a problem, fear, etc.) affecting one strongly.

deer *n, pl* **deer** large wild animal, the male of which has antlers. **deerstalker** *n* cloth hat with peaks at the back and front and earflaps.

deface *v* deliberately spoil the appearance of. **defacement** *n*

de facto *adv* **1** in fact. ♦ *adj* **2** existing in fact, whether legally recognized or not.

defame *v* attack the good reputation of. **defamation** *n* **defamatory** [dif-**fam**-a-tree] *adj*

default *n* **1** failure to do something. **2** *Computers* instruction to a computer to select a particular option unless the user specifies otherwise. ♦ *v* **3** fail to fulfil an obligation. **by default** (happening) only because something else has not happened. **in default of** in the absence of. **defaulter** *n*

defeat *v* **1** win a victory over. **2** thwart, frustrate. ♦ *n* **3** defeating. **defeatism** *n* ready acceptance or expectation of defeat. **defeatist** *adj, n*

defecate *v* discharge waste from the body through the anus. **defecation** *n*

defect *n* **1** imperfection, blemish. ♦ *v* **2** desert one's cause or country to join the opposing forces. **defective** *adj* imperfect, faulty. **defection** *n* **defector** *n*

defence *n* **1** resistance against attack. **2** argument in support of something. **3** a country's military resources. **4** defendant's case in a court of law. **5** *Sport* players whose chief task is to stop the opposition scoring. **defenceless** *adj*

defend *v* **1** protect from harm or danger. **2** support in the face of criticism. **3** represent (a defendant) in court. **4** *Sport* protect (a title) against a challenge. **defendant** *n* person accused of a crime. **defender** *n* **defensible** *adj* capable of being defended because believed to be right. **defensibility** *n* **defensive** *adj* **1** intended for defence. **2** overanxious to protect oneself against (threatened) criticism. **on the defensive** protecting oneself, esp. against (threatened) criticism. **defensively** *adv*

defer[1] *v* **-ferring, -ferred** delay (something) until a future time. **deferment, deferral** *n*

defer[2] *v* **-ferring, -ferred** (foll. by *to*) comply with the wishes (of). **deference** *n* polite and respectful behaviour. **deferential** *adj* **deferentially** *adv*

defiance *n* see DEFY.

deficient *adj* **1** lacking some essential thing or quality. **2** inadequate in quality or quantity. **deficiency** *n, pl* **-cies 1** state of being deficient. **2** lack, shortage. **deficiency disease** condition, such as scurvy, caused by a lack of vitamins or other nutrients. **deficit** *n* amount by which a sum of money is too small.

defile[1] *v* treat (something sacred or important) without respect. **defilement** *n*

defile[2] *n* narrow valley or pass.

define *v* **1** state precisely the meaning of. **2** show clearly the outline of. **definable** *adj* **definite** *adj* **1** firm, clear, and precise. **2** having precise limits. **3** known for certain. **definite article** the word *the*. **definitely** *adv* **definition** *n* **1** statement of the meaning of a word or phrase. **2** quality of being clear and distinct. **definitive** *adj* **1** providing an unquestionable conclusion. **2** being the best example of something. **definitively** *adv*

deflate *v* **1** (cause to) collapse through the release of air. **2** take away the self-esteem or conceit from. **3** *Economics* cause deflation of (an economy). **deflation** *n* **1** *Economics* reduction in economic activity resulting in lower output and investment. **2** feeling of sadness following excitement. **deflationary** *adj*

deflect *v* (cause to) turn aside from a course. **deflection** *n* **deflector** *n*

deflower *v Lit* deprive (a woman) of her virginity.

defoliate *v* deprive (a plant) of its leaves. **defoliant** *n* **defoliation** *n*

deforestation *n* destruction of all the trees in an area.

deform *v* put out of shape or spoil the appearance of. **deformation** *n* **deformed** *adj* **deformity** *n, pl* **-ties 1** *Pathology* distortion of a body part. **2** state of being deformed.

defraud *v* cheat out of money, property, etc.

defray *v* provide money for (costs or expenses).

defrock *v* deprive (a priest) of priestly

status.

defrost *v* **1** make or become free of ice. **2** thaw (frozen food) by removing it from a freezer.

deft *adj* quick and skilful in movement. **deftly** *adv* **deftness** *n*

defunct *adj* no longer existing or operative.

defuse *v* **1** remove the fuse of (an explosive device). **2** remove the tension from (a situation).

defy *v* **-fying, -fied 1** resist openly and boldly. **2** make impossible, e.g. *the condition of the refugees defied description.* **defiance** *n* open resistance or disobedience. **defiant** *adj*

degenerate *adj* **1** having deteriorated to a lower mental, moral, or physical level. ♦ *n* **2** degenerate person. ♦ *v* **3** become degenerate. **degeneracy** *n* degenerate behaviour. **degeneration** *n* **degenerative** *adj* (of a disease or condition) getting steadily worse.

degrade *v* **1** reduce to dishonour or disgrace. **2** reduce in status or quality. **3** *Chem* decompose into smaller molecules. **degrading** *adj* **degradation** *n*

degree *n* **1** stage in a scale of relative amount or intensity. **2** academic award given by a university or college on successful completion of a course. **3** unit of measurement for temperature, angles, or latitude and longitude.

dehumanize *v* **1** deprive of human qualities. **2** make (an activity) mechanical or routine. **dehumanization** *n*

dehumidifier *n* device for removing moisture from the air.

dehydrate *v* remove water from (food) to preserve it. **be dehydrated** become weak through losing too much water from the body. **dehydration** *n*

de-ice *v* free of ice. **de-icer** *n*

deify [**day**-if-fie] *v* **-fying, -fied** treat or worship as a god. **deification** *n*

deign [**dane**] *v* agree (to do something), but as if doing someone a favour.

deism [**dee**-iz-zum] *n* belief in god but not in divine revelation. **deist** *n*

deity [**dee**-it-ee] *n, pl* **-ties 1** god or goddess. **2** state of being divine.

déjà vu [**day**-zhah **voo**] *n* feeling of having experienced before something that is actually happening now.

dejected *adj* unhappy. **dejectedly** *adv* **dejection** *n*

de jure *adv, adj* according to law.

dekko *n Brit & Aust slang* **have a dekko** have a look.

delay *v* **1** put off to a later time. **2** slow up or cause to be late. ♦ *n* **3** act of delaying. **4** interval of time between events.

delectable *adj* delightful, very attractive. **delectation** *n Formal* great pleasure.

delegate *n* **1** person chosen to represent others, esp. at a meeting. ♦ *v* **2** entrust (duties or powers) to someone. **3** appoint as a delegate. **delegation** *n* **1** group chosen to represent others. **2** delegating.

delete *v* remove (something written or printed). **deletion** *n*

deleterious [del-lit-**eer**-ee-uss] *adj* harmful, injurious.

Delft *n* type of earthenware, orig. from Delft in the Netherlands, usu. with blue decoration on a white background (also **delftware**).

deli *n Informal* delicatessen.

deliberate *adj* **1** planned in advance, intentional. **2** careful and unhurried. ♦ *v* **3** think something over. **deliberately** *adv* **deliberation** *n* **deliberative** *adj*

delicate *adj* **1** fine or subtle in quality or workmanship. **2** having a fragile beauty. **3** (of a taste etc.) pleasantly subtle. **4** easily damaged. **5** requiring tact. **delicately** *adv* **delicacy** *n* **1** being delicate. **2** (*pl* **-cies**) something particularly good to eat.

delicatessen *n* shop selling imported or unusual foods, often already cooked or prepared.

delicious *adj* very appealing to taste or smell. **deliciously** *adv*

delight *n* **1** (source of) great pleasure. ♦ *v* **2** please greatly. **3** (foll. by *in*) take great pleasure (in). **delightful** *adj* **delightfully** *adv*

delimit *v* mark or lay down the limits of. **delimitation** *n*

delineate [dill-**lin**-ee-ate] *v* **1** show by drawing. **2** describe in words. **delineation** *n*

delinquent *n* **1** someone, esp. a young person, who repeatedly breaks the law. ♦ *adj* **2** repeatedly breaking the law. **delinquency** *n, pl* **-cies**

delirium *n* **1** state of excitement and mental confusion, often with hallucinations. **2** great excitement. **delirium tremens** [**treh**-menz] trembling and hallucinations caused by chronic alcoholism. **delirious** *adj* **deliriously** *adv*

deliver *v* **1** carry (goods etc.) to a destination. **2** hand over. **3** aid in the birth of. **4** present (a lecture or speech). **5** release or rescue. **6** strike (a blow). **deliverance** *n* rescue from captivity or evil. **delivery** *n, pl* **-eries 1** delivering. **2** something that is delivered. **3** act of giving birth to a baby. **4** style in public speaking.

dell *n* small wooded hollow.

Delphic *adj* ambiguous, like the ancient Greek oracle at Delphi.

delphinium *n* large garden plant with blue flowers.

delta *n* **1** fourth letter in the Greek alphabet. **2** flat area at the mouth of some rivers where the main stream splits up into several branches.

delude *v* deceive.

deluge [**del**-lyooj] *n* **1** great flood. **2** torrential rain. **3** overwhelming number. ♦ *v* **4** flood. **5** overwhelm.

delusion *n* **1** mistaken idea or belief. **2** state of being deluded. **delusive** *adj*

de luxe *adj* rich or sumptuous, superior in quality.

delve *v* **1** research deeply (for information). **2** *Old-fashioned* dig.

demagnetize *v* remove magnetic properties from.

demagogue *n* political agitator who appeals to the prejudice and passions of the mob. **demagogic** *adj* **demagogy** *n*

demand *v* **1** request forcefully. **2** require as just, urgent, etc. **3** claim as a right. ♦ *n* **4** forceful request. **5** *Economics* willingness and ability to purchase goods and services. **6** something that requires special effort or sacrifice. **demanding** *adj* requiring a lot of time or effort.

> The verb *demand* is followed by either *of* or *from: demand too much of them; demand an explanation from you.*

demarcation *n Formal* establishing limits or boundaries, esp. between the work performed by different trade unions.

demean *v* **demean oneself** do something unworthy of one's status or character.

demeanour *n* way a person behaves.

demented *adj* mad. **dementedly** *adv* **dementia** [dim-**men**-sha] *n* state of serious mental deterioration.

demerara sugar *n* brown crystallized cane sugar.

demerger *n* separation of two or more companies which have previously been merged.

demerit *n* fault, disadvantage.

demesne [dim-**mane**] *n* **1** land surrounding a house. **2** *Law* possession of one's own property or land.

demi- *combining form* half.

demigod *n* **1** being who is part mortal, part god. **2** godlike person.

demijohn *n* large bottle with a short neck, often encased in wicker.

demilitarize *v* remove the military forces from. **demilitarization** *n*

demimonde *n* **1** (esp. in the 19th century) class of women considered to be outside respectable society because of promiscuity. **2** group considered not wholly respectable.

demise *n* **1** eventual failure (of something successful). **2** *Formal* death.

demist *v* remove condensation from (a windscreen). **demister** *n*

demo *n, pl* **demos** *Informal* **1** demonstration, organized expression of public opinion. **2** demonstration record or tape.

demob *v Informal* demobilize.

demobilize *v* release from the armed forces. **demobilization** *n*

democracy *n, pl* **-cies 1** government by the people or their elected representatives. **2** state governed in this way. **democrat** *n* **1** advocate of democracy. **2** (**D-**) member or supporter of the Democratic Party in the US. **democratic** *adj* **1** of democracy. **2** upholding democracy. **3** (**D-**) of the Democratic Party, the more liberal of the two main political parties in the US. **democratically** *adv*

demography *n* study of population statistics, such as births and deaths. **demographer** *n* **demographic** *adj*

demolish *v* **1** knock down or destroy (a building). **2** disprove (an argument). **demolisher** *n* **demolition** *n*

demon *n* **1** evil spirit. **2** person who does something with great energy or skill, e.g. *I worked like a demon.* **demonic** *adj* evil. **demoniac, demoniacal** *adj* **1** appearing to be possessed by a devil. **2** frenzied. **demoniacally** *adv* **demonology** *n* study of demons.

demonetize *v* withdraw from use as currency. **demonetization** *n*

demonstrate *v* **1** show or prove by reasoning or evidence. **2** display and explain the workings of. **3** reveal the existence of. **4** show support or opposition by public parades or rallies. **demonstrable** *adj* able to be proved. **demonstrably** *adv* **demonstration** *n* **1** organized expression of public opinion. **2** explanation or display of how something works. **3** proof. **demonstrative** *adj* tending to show one's feelings unreservedly. **demonstratively** *adv* **demonstrator** *n* **1** person who demonstrates how a device or machine works. **2** person who takes part in a public demonstration.

demoralize *v* undermine the morale of. **demoralization** *n*

demote *v* reduce in status or rank. **demotion** *n*

demotic *adj* of the common people.

demur *v* **-murring, -murred 1** show reluctance. ♦ *n* **2 without demur** without objecting.

demure *adj* quiet, reserved, and rather shy. **demurely** *adv* **demureness** *n*

demystify *v* remove the mystery from. **demystification** *n*

den *n* **1** home of a wild animal. **2** small secluded room in a home. **3** place where people indulge in criminal or immoral activities, e.g. *a den of thieves.*

denarius *n, pl* **-narii** ancient Roman silver coin, often called a penny in translation.

denationalize *v* transfer (an industry) from public to private ownership. **denationalization** *n*

denature *v* **1** change the nature of. **2** make (alcohol) unfit to drink.

dengue fever, dengue [**deng**-gee] *n* infectious tropical fever.

denial *n* see DENY.

denier [**den**-yer] *n* unit of weight used to measure the fineness of nylon or silk.

denigrate *v* criticize unfairly. **denigration** *n* **denigrator** *n*

denim *n* **1** hard-wearing cotton fabric, usu. blue. ♦ *pl* **2** jeans made of denim.

denizen *n* inhabitant.

denominate *v* give a specific name to. **denomination** *n* **1** group having a distinctive interpretation of a religious faith. **2** unit in a system of weights, values, or measures. **denominational** *adj* **denominator** *n* number below the line in a fraction.

denote *v* **1** be a sign of. **2** have as a literal meaning. **denotation** *n*

denouement [day-**noo**-mon] *n* final outcome or solution in a play or book.

denounce *v* **1** speak vehemently against. **2** give information against. **denunciation** *n* open condemnation.

dense *adj* **1** closely packed. **2** difficult to see through. **3** stupid. **densely** *adv* **density** *n, pl* **-ties 1** degree to which something is filled or occupied. **2** measure of the compactness of a substance, expressed as its mass per unit volume.

dent *n* **1** hollow in the surface of something, made by hitting it. ♦ *v* **2** make a dent in.

dental *adj* of teeth or dentistry. **dental floss** waxed thread used to remove food particles from between the teeth. **dental surgeon** dentist. **dentate** *adj* having teeth or teethlike notches. **dentifrice** [**den**-tif-riss] *n* paste or powder for cleaning the teeth. **dentine** [**den**-teen] *n* hard dense tissue forming the bulk of a tooth. **dentition** *n* typical arrangement of teeth in a species. **denture** *n* false tooth.

dentist *n* person qualified to practise dentistry. **dentistry** *n* branch of medicine concerned with the teeth and gums.

denude *v* remove the covering or protection from. **denudation** *n*

denunciation *n* see DENOUNCE.

deny *v* **-nying, -nied 1** declare to be untrue. **2** refuse to give or allow. **3** refuse to acknowledge. **deniable** *adj* **denial** *n* **1** statement that something is not true. **2** rejection of a request.

deodorize *v* remove or disguise the smell of. **deodorization** *n* **deodorant** *n* substance applied to the body to mask the smell of perspiration.

deoxyribonucleic acid *n* same as DNA.

depart *v* **1** leave. **2** differ, deviate. **departed** *adj Euphemistic* dead. **the departed** *Euphemistic* a dead person. **departure** *n*

department *n* **1** specialized division of a large organization. **2** major subdivision of the administration of a government. **3** administrative division of France and some other countries. **4** *Informal* task for which someone is responsible, e.g. *gardening is my department*. **departmental** *adj* **department store** large shop selling many kinds of goods.

depend *v* (foll. by *on*) **1** put trust (in). **2** be influenced or determined (by). **3** rely (on) for income or support. **dependable** *adj* **dependably** *adv* **dependability** *n* **dependant** *n* person who depends on another for financial support. **dependence** *n* state of being dependent. **dependency** *n, pl* **-cies 1** country controlled by another country. **2** overreliance on another person or on a drug. **dependent** *adj* depending on someone or something.

depict *v* **1** produce a picture of. **2** describe in words. **depiction** *n*

depilatory [dip-**pill**-a-tree] *n, pl* **-tories,** *adj* (substance) designed to remove unwanted hair.

deplete *v* **1** use up. **2** reduce in number. **depletion** *n*

deplore *v* condemn strongly. **deplorable** *adj* very bad or unpleasant.

deploy *v* organize (troops or resources) into a position ready for immediate action. **deployment** *n*

deponent *n Law* person who makes a statement on oath.

depopulate *v* reduce the population of. **depopulation** *n*

deport *v* remove forcibly from a country. **deport oneself** behave in a specified way. **deportation** *n* **deportee** *n*

deportment *n* way in which a person moves or stands.

depose *v* **1** remove from an office or position of power. **2** *Law* testify on oath.

deposit *v* **1** put down. **2** entrust for safekeeping, esp. to a bank. **3** lay down naturally. ♦ *n* **4** sum of money paid into a bank account. **5** money given in part payment for goods or services. **6** accumulation of sediments, minerals, etc. **deposit account** bank account that earns interest. **depositary** *n, pl* **-taries** person to whom something is entrusted for safety. **depositor** *n* **depository** *n, pl* **-tories** store for furniture etc.

deposition *n* **1** *Law* sworn statement of a witness used in court in his or her absence. **2** deposing. **3** depositing. **4** something deposited.

depot [**dep**-oh] *n* **1** building where goods or vehicles are kept when not in use. **2** *Chiefly US* bus or railway station.

depraved *adj* morally bad. **depravity** *n*

deprecate *v* express disapproval of. **deprecation** *n* **deprecatory** *adj*

depreciate *v* **1** decline in value or price. **2** criticize. **depreciation** *n*

depredation *n* plundering.

depress *v* **1** make sad. **2** lower (prices or wages). **3** push down. **depressing** *adj* **depressingly** *adv* **depressant** *n, adj* (drug) able to reduce nervous activity. **depression** *n* **1** mental state in which a person has feelings of gloom and inadequacy. **2** economic condition in which there is high unemployment and low output and investment. **3** area of low air pressure. **4** sunken place. **the Depression** the worldwide economic depression of the early 1930s. **depressive** *adj* **1** tending to cause depression. ♦ *n* **2** person who suffers from depression.

deprive *v* (foll. by *of*) prevent from (having or enjoying). **deprivation** *n* **deprived** *adj* lacking adequate living conditions, education, etc.

dept department.

depth *n* **1** distance downwards, backwards, or inwards. **2** intensity of emotion. **3** profundity of character or thought. **4** intensity of colour. ♦ *pl* **5** remote inaccessible place, e.g. *the depths of the Universe.* **6** most severe point, e.g. *in the depths of the Depression; the depths of their anguish.* **depth charge** bomb used to attack submarines by exploding at a preset depth of water.

depute *v* appoint (someone) to act on one's behalf. **deputation** *n* body of people appointed to represent others. **deputize** *v* act as deputy. **deputy** *n, pl* **-ties** person appointed to act on behalf of another.

derail *v* cause (a train) to go off the rails. **derailment** *n*

derailleur [dee-**rail**-yer] *n* type of gear-change mechanism for bicycles.

deranged *adj* **1** insane or uncontrolled. **2** in a state of disorder. **derangement** *n*

derby[1] [**der**-bee] *n, pl* **-bies** *US* bowler hat.

derby[2] [**dah**-bee] *n, pl* **-bies** sporting event between teams from the same area. **the Derby** annual horse race run at Epsom Downs.

deregulate *v* remove regulations or controls from. **deregulation** *n*

derelict *adj* **1** unused and falling into ruins. ♦ *n* **2** social outcast, vagrant. **dereliction** *n* state of being abandoned. **dereliction of duty** failure to do one's duty.

derestrict *v* make (a road) free from speed limits.

deride *v* treat with contempt or ridicule. **derision** *n* **derisive** *adj* mocking, scornful. **derisory** *adj* too small or inadequate to be considered seriously.

de rigueur [de rig-**gur**] *adj* required by fashion.

derive *v* (foll. by *from*) take or develop (from). **derivation** *n* **derivative** *adj* **1** based on other sources, not original. ♦ *n* **2** word, idea, etc., derived from another. **3** *Maths* rate of change of one quantity in relation to another.

dermatitis *n* inflammation of the skin.

dermatology *n* branch of medicine concerned with the skin. **dermatologist** *n*

derogate *v* (foll. by *from*) detract from. **derogation** *n*

derogatory [dir-**rog**-a-tree] *adj* intentionally offensive.

derrick *n* **1** simple crane. **2** framework erected over an oil well.

derring-do *n Old-fashioned or lit* spirited bravery, boldness.

derringer *n* small large-bored pistol.

derv *n* diesel oil, when used for road transport.

dervish *n* member of a Muslim religious order noted for a frenzied whirling dance.

desalination *n* process of removing salt, esp. from sea water.

descale *v* remove a hard coating from inside (a kettle or pipe).

descant *n Music* **1** tune played or sung above a basic melody. ♦ *adj* **2** denoting the highest member in a family of musical instruments, e.g. *descant clarinets.*

descend *v* **1** move down (a slope etc.). **2** move to a lower level, pitch, etc. **3** (foll. by *to*) stoop to (unworthy behaviour). **4** (foll. by *on*) visit unexpectedly. **be descended from** be connected by a blood relationship to. **descendant** *n* person or animal descended from an individual, race, or species. **descendant** *adj* descending. **descent** *n* **1** descending. **2** downward slope. **3** derivation from an ancestor.

describe *v* **1** give an account of (something or someone) in words. **2** trace the outline of (a circle etc.). **description** *n* **1** statement that describes something or someone. **2** sort, e.g. *flowers of every description.* **descriptive** *adj* **descriptively** *adv*

descry *v* **-scrying, -scried 1** catch sight of. **2** discover by looking carefully.

desecrate *v* damage or insult (something sacred). **desecration** *n*

desegregate *v* end racial segregation in. **desegregation** *n*

deselect *v Brit politics* refuse to select (an MP) for re-election. **deselection** *n*

desensitize *v* make insensitive or less sensitive.

desert[1] *n* region with little or no vegetation because of low rainfall. **desert island** small uninhabited island in the tropics.

desert[2] *v* **1** abandon (a person or place) without intending to return. **2** *Mil* leave (a post or duty) with no intention of returning. **deserter** *n* **desertion** *n*

deserts *pl n* **get one's just deserts** get the punishment one deserves.

deserve *v* be entitled to or worthy of. **deserved** *adj* rightfully earned. **deservedly** [dee-**zerv**-id-lee] *adv* **deserving** *adj* worthy of help, praise, or reward.

deshabille [day-zab-**beel**] *n* state of being partly dressed.

desiccate *v* remove most of the water from. **desiccation** *n*

design *v* **1** work out the structure or form of (something), by making a sketch or plans. **2** plan and make artistically. **3** intend for a specific purpose. ♦ *n* **4** preliminary drawing. **5** arrangement or features of an artistic or decorative work. **6** art of designing. **7** intention, e.g. *by design.* **designedly** [dee-**zine**-id-lee] *adv* intentionally. **designer** *n* **1** person who draws up original sketches or plans from which things are made. ♦ *adj* **2** designed by a well-known designer. **designing** *adj* cunning and scheming.

designate [**dez**-zig-nate] *v* **1** give a name to. **2** select (someone) for an office or duty. ♦ *adj* **3** appointed but not yet in office, e.g. *the Prime Minister designate.* **designation** *n* name.

desire *v* **1** want very much. ♦ *n* **2** wish, longing. **3** sexual appetite. **4** person or thing desired. **desirable** *adj* **1** worth having. **2** arousing sexual desire. **desirability** *n* **desirous of** having a desire for.

desist *v* (foll. by *from*) stop (doing something).

desk *n* **1** piece of furniture with a writing surface and drawers. **2** service counter in a public building. **3** section of a newspaper covering a specific subject, e.g. *the sports desk.* **desktop** *adj* (of a computer) small enough to use at a desk. **desktop publishing** means of publishing reports etc. using a desktop computer and a laser printer.

desolate *adj* **1** uninhabited and bleak. **2** very sad. ♦ *v* **3** deprive of inhabitants. **4** make (someone) very sad. **desolation** *n*

despair *n* **1** total loss of hope. ♦ *v* **2** lose hope.

despatch *v, n* same as DISPATCH.

desperado *n, pl* **-does, -dos** reckless person ready to commit any violent illegal act.

desperate *adj* **1** in despair and reckless. **2** (of an action) undertaken as a last resort. **3** having a strong need or desire, e.g. *desperate to get away.* **desperately** *adv* **desperation** *n*

despise *v* regard with contempt. **despicable** *adj* deserving contempt. **despicably** *adv*

despite *prep* in spite of.

despoil *v Formal* plunder. **despoliation** *n*

despondent *adj* unhappy. **despondent-**

ly *adv* **despondency** *n*

despot *n* person in power who acts unfairly or cruelly. **despotic** *adj* **despotically** *adv* **despotism** *n* unfair or cruel government or behaviour.

dessert *n* sweet course served at the end of a meal. **dessertspoon** *n* spoon between a tablespoon and a teaspoon in size.

destabilize *v* make (a country or government) politically or economically unstable. **destabilization** *n*

destination *n* place to which someone or something is going.

destined [**dess**-tind] *adj* certain to be or to do something, e.g. *destined to fail.*

destiny *n, pl* **-nies** **1** future marked out for a person or thing. **2** the power that predetermines the course of events.

destitute *adj* having no money or possessions. **destitution** *n*

destroy *v* **1** ruin, demolish. **2** put an end to. **3** kill (an animal). **destroyer** *n* **1** small heavily armed warship. **2** person or thing that destroys.

destruction *n* **1** destroying. **2** cause of ruin. **destructible** *adj* able to be destroyed. **destructive** *adj* (capable of) causing destruction. **destructively** *adv* **destructiveness** *n*

desuetude [diss-**syoo**-it-tude] *n* condition of not being in use.

desultory [**dez**-zl-tree] *adj* **1** jumping from one thing to another, disconnected. **2** random. **desultorily** *adv*

detach *v* disengage and separate. **detachable** *adj* **detached** *adj* **1** (of a house) not joined to another house. **2** showing no emotional involvement. **detachment** *n* **1** lack of emotional involvement. **2** small group of soldiers.

detail *n* **1** individual piece of information. **2** unimportant item. **3** small individual features of something, considered collectively. **4** *Chiefly mil* (personnel assigned) a specific duty. ♦ *v* **5** list fully. **6** *Chiefly mil* assign to a specific duty.

detain *v* **1** delay (someone). **2** hold (someone) in custody. **detainee** *n* **detainment** *n*

detect *v* **1** notice. **2** discover, find. **detectable** *adj* **detection** *n* **detective** *n* policeman or private agent who investigates crime. **detector** *n* instrument used to find something, e.g. *a metal detector.*

detente [day-**tont**] *n* easing of tension between nations.

detention *n* **1** imprisonment. **2** form of punishment in which a pupil is detained after school.

deter *v* **-terring, -terred** discourage (someone) from doing something by instilling fear or doubt. **deterrent** *n* **1** something that deters. **2** weapon, esp. nuclear, intended to deter attack. ♦ *adj* **3** tending to deter. **deterrence** *n*

detergent *n* chemical substance for washing clothes or dishes.

deteriorate *v* become worse. **deterioration** *n*

determine *v* **1** settle (an argument or a question) conclusively. **2** find out the facts about. **3** make a firm decision (to do something). **determinant** *n* factor that determines. **determinate** *adj* definitely limited or fixed. **determination** *n* **1** being determined or resolute. **2** determining. **determined** *adj* firmly decided, unable to be dissuaded. **determinedly** *adv* **determiner** *n Grammar* word that determines the object to which a noun phrase refers, e.g. *all.* **determinism** *n* theory that human choice is not free, but decided by past events. **determinist** *n, adj* **deterministic** *adj*

detest *v* dislike intensely. **detestable** *adj* **detestation** *n*

dethrone *v* remove from a throne or position of power.

detonate *v* explode. **detonation** *n* **detonator** *n* small amount of explosive, or a device, used to set off an explosion.

detour *n* route that is not the most direct one.

detox *v, n Informal* (undergo) treatment to rid the body of poisonous substances.

detoxify *v* **-fying, -fied** remove poison from. **detoxification** *n*

detract *v* (foll. by *from*) make (something) seem less good. **detractor** *n* **detraction** *n*

detriment *n* disadvantage or damage. **detrimental** *adj* **detrimentally** *adv*

detritus [dit-**trite**-uss] *n* **1** loose mass of stones and silt worn away from rocks. **2** debris.

de trop [de **troh**] *adj French* unwanted, unwelcome.

detumescence *n* subsidence of swelling. **detumescent** *adj*

deuce [**dyewss**] *n* **1** *Tennis* score of forty all. **2** playing card with two symbols or dice with two spots.

deuterium *n* isotope of hydrogen twice as heavy as the normal atom.

Deutschmark [**doytch**-mark], **Deutsche Mark** [**doytch**-a] *n* monetary unit of Germany.

devalue *v* **-valuing, -valued 1** reduce the exchange value of (a currency). **2** reduce the value of (something or someone). **devaluation** *n*

devastate *v* destroy. **devastated** *adj* shocked and extremely upset. **devastation** *n*

develop *v* **1** grow or bring to a later, more elaborate, or more advanced stage. **2** come or bring into existence. **3** build houses or factories on (an area of land). **4** produce (photographs) by making negatives or prints from a film. **developer** *n* **1** person who develops property. **2** chemical used to develop photographs or films. **development** *n* **1** developing. **2** product of developing. **3** event or incident that changes a situation. **4** area of land that has been developed. **developmental** *adj* **developing country** poor or nonindustrial country that is trying to develop its resources by industrialization.

deviate *v* **1** differ from others in belief or thought. **2** depart from one's previous behaviour. **deviation** *n* **deviant** *n, adj* (person) deviating from what is considered acceptable behaviour. **deviance** *n*

device *n* **1** machine or tool used for a specific task. **2** scheme or plan. **leave someone to his, her own devices** let someone do as he *or* she wishes.

devil *n* **1** evil spirit. **2** evil person. **3** person, e.g. *poor devil.* **4** daring person, e.g. *be a devil!* **5** *Informal* something difficult or annoying, e.g. *a devil of a long time.* ♦ *v* **-illing, -illed 6** prepare (food) with a highly flavoured spiced mixture. **the Devil** *Theology* chief spirit of evil and enemy of God. **devilish** *adj* **1** cruel or unpleasant. ♦ *adv* **2** (also **devilishly**) *Informal* extremely. **devilment** *n* mischievous conduct. **devilry** *n* mischievousness. **devil-may-care** *adj* carefree and cheerful. **devil's advocate** person who takes an opposing or unpopular point of view for the sake of argument.

devious *adj* **1** insincere and dishonest. **2** indirect. **deviously** *adv* **deviousness** *n*

devise *v* work out (something) in one's mind.

devoid *adj* (foll. by *of*) completely lacking (in).

devolve *v* (foll. by *on* or *to*) pass (power or duties) or (of power or duties) be passed to a successor or substitute. **devolution** *n* transfer of authority from a central government to regional governments.

devote *v* apply or dedicate to a particular purpose. **devoted** *adj* showing loyalty or devotion. **devotedly** *adv* **devotee** [dev-vote-**tee**] *n* **1** person who is very enthusiastic about something. **2** zealous follower of a religion. **devotion** *n* **1** strong affection for or loyalty to someone or something. **2** religious zeal. ♦ *pl* **3** prayers. **devotional** *adj*

devour *v* **1** eat greedily. **2** (of an emotion) engulf and destroy. **3** read eagerly.

devout *adj* deeply religious. **devoutly** *adv*

dew *n* drops of water that form on the ground at night from vapour in the air. **dewy** *adj* **dewier, dewiest** **dewy-eyed** *adj* innocent and inexperienced.

dewlap *n* loose fold of skin hanging under the throat in dogs, cattle, etc.

dexterity *n* **1** skill in using one's hands. **2** mental quickness. **dexterous** *adj*

dexterously *adv*
dextrin, dextrine *n* sticky substance obtained from starch, used as a thickening agent in food.
dextrose *n* glucose occurring in fruit, honey, and the blood of animals.
dg decigram.
DH Department of Health.
dhal, dal *n* curry made from lentils or beans.
dharma *n* **1** *Hinduism* moral law or behaviour. **2** *Buddhism* ideal truth.
dhoti *n, pl* **-tis** long loincloth worn by men in India.
dhow *n* Arab sailing ship.
DI donor insemination: method of making a woman pregnant by transferring sperm from a man other than her regular partner using artificial means.
di- *prefix* **1** twice, two, or double, e.g. *dicotyledon.* **2** containing two specified atoms or groups of atoms, e.g. *carbon dioxide.*
diabetes [die-a-**beet**-eez] *n* disorder in which an abnormal amount of urine containing an excess of sugar is excreted. **diabetic** *n* **1** person who has diabetes. ♦ *adj* **2** of or having diabetes. **3** suitable for people with diabetes.
diabolic *adj* of the Devil. **diabolical** *adj Informal* extremely bad, e.g. *the conditions were diabolical.* **diabolically** *adv* **diabolism** *n* witchcraft, devil worship.
diaconate *n* position or period of office of a deacon.
diacritic *n* sign above or below a character to indicate phonetic value or stress.
diadem *n Old-fashioned* crown.
diaeresis *n, pl* **-ses** mark (¨) placed over a vowel to show that it is pronounced separately from the preceding one, for example in *Noël.*
diagnosis [die-ag-**no**-siss] *n, pl* **-ses** [-seez] discovery and identification of diseases from the examination of symptoms. **diagnose** *v* **diagnostic** *adj*
diagonal *adj* **1** from corner to corner. **2** slanting. ♦ *n* **3** diagonal line. **diagonally** *adv*
diagram *n* sketch showing the form or workings of something. **diagrammatic** *adj*
dial *n* **1** face of a clock or watch. **2** graduated disc on a measuring instrument. **3** control on a radio or television set used to change the station. **4** numbered disc on the front of some telephones. ♦ *v* **dialling, dialled 5** operate the dial or buttons on a telephone in order to contact (a number). **dialling tone** continuous sound heard on picking up a telephone, indicating that a number can be dialled.
dialect *n* form of a language spoken in a particular area. **dialectal** *adj*
dialectic *n* logical debate by question and answer to resolve differences between two views. **dialectical** *adj*
dialogue *n* **1** conversation between two people, esp. in a book, film, or play. **2** discussion between representatives of two nations or groups.
dialysis [die-**al**-iss-iss] *n Med* filtering of blood through a membrane to remove waste products.
diamagnetism *n* phenomenon exhibited by substances that are repelled by both poles of a magnet.
diamanté [die-a-**man**-tee] *adj* decorated with artificial jewels or sequins.
diameter *n* (length of) a straight line through the centre of a circle or sphere. **diametric, diametrical** *adj* **1** of a diameter. **2** completely opposed, e.g. *the diametric opposite.* **diametrically** *adv*
diamond *n* **1** exceptionally hard, usu. colourless, precious stone. **2** *Geom* figure with four sides of equal length forming two acute and two obtuse angles. **3** playing card marked with red diamond-shaped symbols. **4** *Baseball* the playing field. **diamond jubilee** sixtieth anniversary of an event. **diamond wedding** sixtieth anniversary of a wedding.
diapason [die-a-**pay**-zon] *n* **1** either of two stops found throughout the range of a pipe organ. **2** range of an instrument or voice.
diaper *n US* nappy.

diaphanous [die-**af**-fan-ous] *adj* fine and almost transparent.

diaphoretic *n, adj* (drug) causing sweating.

diaphragm [**die**-a-fram] *n* **1** muscular partition that separates the abdominal cavity and chest cavity. **2** contraceptive device placed over the neck of the womb.

diarrhoea [die-a-**ree**-a] *n* frequent discharge of abnormally liquid faeces.

diary *n, pl* **-ries** (book for) a record of daily events, appointments, or observations. **diarist** *n* person who writes a diary.

Diaspora [die-**ass**-spore-a] *n* **1** dispersion of the Jews after the Babylonian conquest of Palestine. **2** (**d-**) dispersion of people originally of one nation.

diastole [die-**ass**-stoh-lee] *n* dilation of the chambers of the heart. **diastolic** *adj*

diatomic *adj* containing two atoms.

diatonic *adj Music* of a regular major or minor scale.

diatribe *n* bitter critical attack.

dibble *n* small hand tool used to make holes in the ground for seeds or plants.

dice *n, pl* **dice 1** small cube each of whose sides has a different number of spots (1 to 6), used in games of chance. **2** game played with dice. ♦ *v* **3** cut (food) into small cubes. **dice with death** take a risk. **dicey** *adj* **dicier, diciest** *Informal* dangerous or risky.

dichotomy [die-**kot**-a-mee] *n, pl* **-mies** division into two opposed groups or parts.

dick *n Taboo slang* penis. **clever dick** person who likes to show how clever he or she is.

Dickensian *adj* denoting poverty, distress, and exploitation as depicted in Dickens's novels.

dicky[1] *n, pl* **dickies** false shirt front. **dicky-bird** *n* child's word for a bird.

dicky[2] *adj* **dickier, dickiest** *Informal* shaky or weak, e.g. *a dicky heart.*

Dictaphone *n* ® tape recorder for recording dictation for subsequent typing.

dictate *v* **1** say aloud for someone else to write down. **2** (foll. by *to*) seek to impose one's will on (other people). ♦ *n* **3** authoritative command. **4** guiding principle. **dictation** *n* **dictator** *n* **1** ruler who has complete power. **2** person in power who acts unfairly or cruelly. **dictatorship** *n* **dictatorial** *adj* like a dictator.

diction *n* manner of pronouncing words and sounds.

dictionary *n, pl* **-aries 1** book consisting of an alphabetical list of words with their meanings. **2** similar book giving equivalent words in two languages. **3** alphabetically ordered reference book of terms relating to a particular subject.

dictum *n, pl* **-tums, -ta 1** formal statement. **2** popular saying.

did *v* past tense of DO[1].

didactic *adj* **1** intended to instruct. **2** overeager to instruct. **didactically** *adv*

diddle *v Informal* swindle.

didgeridoo *n Music* Australian Aboriginal deep-toned wind instrument.

didn't did not.

die[1] *v* **dying, died 1** (of a person, animal, or plant) cease all biological activity permanently. **2** (of something inanimate) cease to exist or function. **be dying for, to do something** *Informal* be eager for *or* to do something. **die down** *v* lose strength or power by degrees. **die-hard** *n* person who resists change.

die[2] *n* **1** shaped block used to cut or form metal. **2** same as DICE (sense 1).

dieldrin *n* highly toxic insecticide.

dielectric *n* **1** substance which does not conduct electricity well, insulator. ♦ *adj* **2** not conducting electricity well.

dieresis [die-**air**-iss-iss] *n, pl* **-ses** [-seez] same as DIAERESIS.

diesel *n* **1** diesel engine. **2** vehicle driven by a diesel engine. **3** diesel oil. **diesel engine** internal-combustion engine in which oil is ignited by compression. **diesel oil** fuel obtained from petroleum distillation.

diet[1] *n* **1** food that a person or animal regularly eats. **2** specific range of foods, to control weight or for health reasons. ♦ *v* **3** follow a special diet so as to lose weight. ♦ *adj* **4** (of food) suitable for a weight-reduction diet. **dietary** *adj* **dietary fibre** fibrous substances in fruit and vegetables that aid digestion. **dieter** *n* **dietetic** *adj* prepared for special dietary requirements. **dietetics** *n* study of diet and nutrition. **dietician** *n* person who specializes in dietetics.

diet[2] *n* parliament of some countries.

differ *v* **1** be unlike. **2** disagree. **difference** *n* **1** state of being unlike. **2** disagreement. **3** remainder left after subtraction. **different** *adj* **1** unlike. **2** unusual. **differently** *adv*

> The accepted idiom is *different from* but *different to* is also used. *Different than* is an Americanism.

differential *adj* **1** of or using a difference. **2** *Maths* involving differentials. ♦ *n* **3** factor that differentiates between two comparable things. **4** *Maths* tiny difference between values in a scale. **5** difference between rates of pay for different types of work. **differential calculus** branch of calculus concerned with derivatives and differentials. **differential gear** mechanism in a road vehicle that allows one driving wheel to rotate faster than the other when cornering. **differentiate** *v* **1** perceive or show the difference (between). **2** make (one thing) distinct from other such things. **differentiation** *n*

difficult *adj* **1** requiring effort or skill to do or understand. **2** not easily pleased. **difficulty** *n, pl* **-ties**

diffident *adj* lacking self-confidence. **diffidence** *n* **diffidently** *adv*

diffract *v* cause to undergo diffraction. **diffraction** *n Physics* **1** deviation in the direction of a wave at the edge of an obstacle in its path. **2** formation of light and dark fringes by the passage of light through a small aperture.

diffuse *v* **1** spread over a wide area. ♦ *adj* **2** widely spread. **3** lacking concision. **diffusely** *adv* **diffusion** *n*

dig *v* **digging, dug 1** cut into, break up, and turn over or remove (earth), esp. with a spade. **2** excavate (a hole or tunnel) by digging. **3** (foll. by *out* or *up*) find by effort or searching. **4** (foll. by *in* or *into*) thrust or jab. ♦ *n* **5** digging. **6** archaeological excavation. **7** thrust or poke. **8** spiteful remark. ♦ *pl* **9** *Informal* lodgings. **digger** *n* machine used for digging.

digest *v* **1** subject to a process of digestion. **2** absorb mentally. ♦ *n* **3** shortened version of a book, report, or article. **digestible** *adj* **digestion** *n* (body's system for) breaking down food into easily absorbed substances. **digestive** *adj* **digestive biscuit** biscuit made from wholemeal flour.

digit [**dij**-it] *n* **1** finger or toe. **2** numeral from 0 to 9. **digital** *adj* **1** displaying information as numbers rather than with hands and a dial, e.g. *a digital clock.* **2** representing data as a series of numerical values. **digital recording** sound-recording process that converts audio or analogue signals into a series of pulses. **digitally** *adv*

digitalis *n* drug made from foxglove leaves, used as a heart stimulant.

dignity *n, pl* **-ties 1** serious, calm, and controlled behaviour or manner. **2** quality of being worthy of respect. **3** sense of self-importance. **dignify** *v* **-fying, -fied** add distinction to. **dignitary** *n, pl* **-taries** person of high official position.

digress *v* depart from the main subject in speech or writing. **digression** *n*

dihedral *adj* having or formed by two intersecting planes.

dike *n* same as DYKE.

diktat *n* dictatorial decree.

dilapidated *adj* (of a building) having fallen into ruin. **dilapidation** *n*

dilate *v* make or become wider or larger. **dilation, dilatation** *n*

dilatory [**dill**-a-tree] *adj* tending or intended to waste time. **dilatoriness** *n*

dildo *n, pl* **-dos** object used as a substitute for an erect penis.

dilemma *n* situation offering a choice between two equally undesirable alternatives.

> If a difficult choice involves more than two courses of action, it is preferable to speak of a *problem* or *difficulty*.

dilettante [dill-it-**tan**-tee] *n, pl* **-tantes, -tanti** person whose interest in a subject is superficial rather than serious. **dilettantism** *n*

diligent *adj* **1** careful and persevering in carrying out duties. **2** carried out with care and perseverance. **diligently** *adv* **diligence** *n*

dill *n* sweet-smelling herb.

dilly-dally *v* **-lying, -lied** *Informal* dawdle, waste time.

dilute *v* **1** make (a liquid) less concentrated, esp. by adding water. **2** make (a quality etc.) weaker in force. ♦ *adj* **3** (of a liquid) thin and watery. **dilution** *n*

diluvial, diluvian *adj* of a flood, esp. the great Flood described in the Old Testament.

dim *adj* **dimmer, dimmest 1** badly lit. **2** not clearly seen. **3** unintelligent. ♦ *v* **dimming, dimmed 4** make or become dim. **take a dim view of** disapprove of. **dimly** *adv* **dimness** *n* **dimmer** *n* device for dimming an electric light.

dime *n* coin of the US and Canada, worth ten cents.

dimension *n* **1** measurement of the size of something in a particular direction. **2** aspect, factor.

diminish *v* make or become smaller, fewer, or less. **diminished responsibility** *Law* mental derangement which makes a person unaware that he or she is committing a crime. **diminution** *n* **diminutive** *adj* **1** very small. ♦ *n* **2** word or affix which implies smallness or unimportance. **diminutiveness** *n*

diminuendo *n Music* gradual decrease in loudness.

dimple *n* **1** small natural dent, esp. in the cheeks or chin. ♦ *v* **2** produce dimples by smiling. **dimpled** *adj*

dimwit *n Informal* stupid person. **dimwitted** *adj*

din *n* **1** loud unpleasant confused noise. ♦ *v* **dinning, dinned 2** (foll. by *into*) instil (something) into someone by constant repetition.

dinar [**dee**-nahr] *n* monetary unit of various Balkan, Middle Eastern, and North African countries.

dine *v* eat dinner. **diner** *n* **1** person eating a meal. **2** *Chiefly US* small cheap restaurant. **dining car** railway coach where meals are served. **dining room** room where meals are eaten.

ding-dong *n* **1** sound of a bell. **2** *Informal* lively quarrel or fight.

dinghy [**ding**-ee] *n, pl* **-ghies** small boat, powered by sails, oars, or a motor.

dingo *n, pl* **-goes** Australian wild dog.

dingy [**din**-jee] *adj* **-gier, -giest** dull and drab. **dinginess** *n*

dinkum *adj Aust & NZ informal* genuine or right.

dinky *adj* **-kier, -kiest** *Brit & Aust informal* small and neat.

dinner *n* main meal of the day, eaten either in the evening or at midday. **dinner jacket** man's semiformal black evening jacket.

dinosaur *n* extinct gigantic prehistoric reptile.

dint *n* **by dint of** by means of.

diocese [**die**-a-siss] *n* district over which a bishop has control. **diocesan** *adj*

diode *n* semiconductor device for converting alternating current to direct current.

Dionysian [die-on-**niz**-zee-an] *adj* wild or unrestrained.

dioptre [die-**op**-ter] *n* unit for measuring the refractive power of a lens.

diorama *n* miniature three-dimensional scene, in which models of figures are seen against a three-dimensional background.

dioxide *n* oxide containing two oxygen atoms per molecule.

dip *v* **dipping, dipped 1** plunge quickly

or briefly into a liquid. **2** slope downwards. **3** switch (car headlights) from the main to the lower beam. **4** lower briefly. ♦ *n* **5** dipping. **6** brief swim. **7** liquid chemical in which farm animals are dipped to rid them of insects. **8** depression in a landscape. **9** creamy mixture into which pieces of food are dipped before being eaten. **dip into** *v* read passages at random from (a book or journal).

Dip Ed Diploma in Education.

diphtheria [dif-**theer**-ya] *n* contagious disease producing fever and difficulty in breathing and swallowing.

diphthong *n* union of two vowel sounds in a single compound sound.

diploma *n* qualification awarded by a college on successful completion of a course.

diplomacy *n* **1** conduct of the relations between nations by peaceful means. **2** tact or skill in dealing with people. **diplomat** *n* official engaged in diplomacy. **diplomatic** *adj* **1** of diplomacy. **2** tactful in dealing with people. **diplomatic immunity** freedom from legal action and taxation which diplomats have in the country where they are working. **diplomatically** *adv*

dipper *n* **1** ladle used for dipping. **2** (also **ousel, ouzel**) songbird that lives by a river.

dipsomania *n* compulsive craving for alcohol. **dipsomaniac** *n, adj*

dipstick *n* notched rod dipped into a container to measure the level of a liquid.

diptych [**dip**-tik] *n* painting on two hinged panels.

dire *adj* disastrous, urgent, or terrible.

direct *adj* **1** (of a route) shortest, straight. **2** without anyone or anything intervening. **3** likely to have an immediate effect. **4** honest, frank. ♦ *adv* **5** in a direct manner. ♦ *v* **6** lead and organize. **7** tell (someone) to do something. **8** tell (someone) the way to a place. **9** address (a letter, package, remark, etc.). **10** provide guidance to (actors, cameramen, etc.) in (a play or film). **directly** *adv* **1** in a direct manner. **2** at once. ♦ *conj* **3** as soon as. **directness** *n* **direct current** electric current that flows in one direction only. **direct debit** order given to a bank by an account-holder to pay an amount of money directly from the account to a specified person or company. **direct object** noun or pronoun receiving the direct action of the verb, e.g. *a book* in *I bought you a book*. **direct speech** reporting of what someone has said by quoting his or her exact words. **direct tax** tax paid by the person or organization on which it is levied.

direction *n* **1** course or line along which a person or thing moves, points, or lies. **2** management or guidance. ♦ *pl* **3** instructions for doing something or for reaching a place. **directional** *adj*

directive *n* instruction, order.

director *n* **1** person or thing that directs or controls. **2** member of the governing board of a business etc. **3** person responsible for the artistic and technical aspects of the making of a film etc. **directorial** *adj* **directorship** *n* **directorate** *n* **1** board of directors. **2** position of director. **director-general** *n, pl* **directors-general** person in overall charge of a large organization.

directory *n, pl* **-tories** **1** book listing names, addresses, and telephone numbers. **2** *Computers* area of a disk containing the names and locations of the files it currently holds.

dirge *n* slow sad song of mourning.

dirigible [**dir**-rij-jib-bl] *adj* **1** able to be steered. ♦ *n* **2** airship.

dirk *n* dagger, formerly worn by Scottish Highlanders.

dirndl *n* full gathered skirt.

dirt *n* **1** unclean substance, filth. **2** earth, soil. **3** obscene speech or writing. **4** *Informal* harmful gossip. **dirt-cheap** *adj, adv* at a very low price. **dirt track** racetrack made of packed earth or cinders.

dirty *adj* **dirtier, dirtiest** **1** covered or marked with dirt. **2** unfair or dishonest.

3 obscene. 4 displaying dislike or anger, e.g. *a dirty look.* ♦ *v* **dirtying, dirtied** 5 make dirty. **dirtiness** *n*

dis- *prefix* indicating: 1 reversal, e.g. *disconnect.* 2 negation or lack, e.g. *dissimilar; disgrace.* 3 removal or release, e.g. *disembowel.*

disable *v* make ineffective, unfit, or incapable. **disabled** *adj* lacking a physical power, such as the ability to walk. **disablement** *n* **disability** *n, pl* **-ties** 1 condition of being disabled. 2 something that disables someone.

> The use of *the disabled, the blind* etc. can be offensive and should be avoided. Instead you should talk about *disabled people, blind people,* etc.

disabuse *v* (foll. by *of*) rid (someone) of a mistaken idea.

disadvantage *n* unfavourable or harmful circumstance. **disadvantageous** *adj* **disadvantaged** *adj* socially or economically deprived.

disaffected *adj* having lost loyalty to or affection for someone or something. **disaffection** *n*

disagree *v* **-greeing, -greed** 1 argue or have different opinions. 2 be different, conflict. 3 (foll. by *with*) cause physical discomfort (to), e.g. *curry disagrees with me.* **disagreement** *n* **disagreeable** *adj* 1 unpleasant. 2 (of a person) unfriendly or unhelpful. **disagreeably** *adv*

disallow *v* reject as untrue or invalid.

disappear *v* 1 cease to be visible. 2 cease to exist. **disappearance** *n*

disappoint *v* fail to meet the expectations or hopes of. **disappointment** *n* 1 feeling of being disappointed. 2 person or thing that disappoints.

disapprobation *n* disapproval.

disapprove *v* (foll. by *of*) consider wrong or bad. **disapproval** *n*

disarm *v* 1 deprive of weapons. 2 win the confidence or affection of. 3 (of a country) decrease the size of one's armed forces. **disarmament** *n* **disarming** *adj* removing hostility or suspicion. **disarmingly** *adv*

disarrange *v* throw into disorder.

disarray *n* 1 confusion and lack of discipline. 2 extreme untidiness.

disassociate *v* same as DISSOCIATE.

disaster *n* 1 occurrence that causes great distress or destruction. 2 project etc. that fails. **disastrous** *adj* **disastrously** *adv*

disavow *v* deny connection with or responsibility for. **disavowal** *n*

disband *v* (cause to) cease to function as a group.

disbelieve *v* 1 reject as false. 2 (foll. by *in*) have no faith (in). **disbelief** *n*

disburse *v* pay out. **disbursement** *n*

disc *n* 1 flat circular object. 2 gramophone record. 3 *Anat* circular flat structure in the body, esp. between the vertebrae. 4 *Computers* same as DISK. **disc brake** brake in which two plates rub against a flat disc. **disc jockey** person who introduces and plays pop records on a radio programme or at a disco.

discard *v* get rid of (something or someone) as useless or undesirable.

discern *v* see or be aware of (something) clearly. **discernible** *adj* **discernibly** *adv* **discerning** *adj* having good judgment. **discernment** *n*

discharge *v* 1 release, allow to go. 2 dismiss (someone) from duty or employment. 3 fire (a gun). 4 pour forth, send out. 5 meet the demands of (a duty or responsibility). 6 relieve oneself of (a debt). ♦ *n* 7 substance that comes out from a place. 8 discharging.

disciple [diss-**sipe**-pl] *n* follower of the doctrines of a teacher, esp. Jesus Christ.

discipline *n* 1 practice of imposing strict rules of behaviour. 2 area of academic study. ♦ *v* 3 attempt to improve the behaviour of (oneself or another) by training or rules. 4 punish. **disciplined** *adj* able to behave and work in a controlled way. **disciplinarian** *n* person who practises strict discipline. **disciplinary** *adj*

disclaim *v* deny (responsibility for or knowledge of something). **disclaimer** *n* statement denying responsibility.

disclose *v* **1** make known. **2** allow to be seen. **disclosure** *n*

disco *n, pl* **-cos** **1** nightclub where people dance to amplified pop records. **2** occasion at which people dance to amplified pop records. **3** mobile equipment for providing music for a disco.

discography *n, pl* **-phies** classified list of gramophone records.

discolour *v* change in colour, fade. **discoloration** *n*

discomfit *v* make uneasy or confused. **discomfiture** *n*

discomfort *n* inconvenience, distress, or mild pain.

discommode *v* cause inconvenience to.

discompose *v* disturb, upset. **discomposure** *n*

disconcert *v* embarrass or upset.

disconnect *v* **1** undo or break the connection between (two things). **2** stop the supply of electricity or gas of. **disconnected** *adj* (of speech or ideas) not logically connected. **disconnection** *n*

disconsolate *adj* sad beyond comfort. **disconsolately** *adv*

discontent *n* lack of contentment. **discontented** *adj* **discontentedly** *adv*

discontinue *v* come or bring to an end. **discontinuous** *adj* characterized by interruptions. **discontinuity** *n*

discord *n* **1** lack of agreement or harmony between people. **2** harsh confused sounds. **discordant** *adj* **discordance** *n*

discotheque *n* same as DISCO.

discount *v* **1** take no account of (something) because it is considered to be unreliable, prejudiced, or irrelevant. **2** deduct (an amount) from the price of something. ♦ *n* **3** deduction from the full price of something.

discountenance *v* make (someone) ashamed or confused.

discourage *v* **1** deprive of the will to persist in something. **2** oppose by expressing disapproval. **discouraging** *adj* **discouragement** *n*

discourse *n* **1** conversation. **2** formal treatment of a subject in speech or writing. ♦ *v* **3** (foll. by *on*) speak or write (about) at length.

discourteous *adj* showing bad manners. **discourteously** *adv* **discourtesy** *n*

discover *v* **1** be the first to find or to find out about. **2** learn about for the first time. **3** find after study or search. **discoverer** *n* **discovery** *n, pl* **-eries** **1** discovering. **2** person, place, or thing that has been discovered.

discredit *v* **1** damage the reputation of. **2** cause (an idea) to be disbelieved or distrusted. ♦ *n* **3** damage to someone's reputation. **discreditable** *adj* bringing shame.

discreet *adj* **1** careful to avoid embarrassment, esp. by keeping confidences secret. **2** unobtrusive. **discreetly** *adv*

discrepancy *n, pl* **-cies** conflict or variation between facts, figures, or claims.

discrete *adj* separate, distinct.

discretion [diss-**kresh**-on] *n* **1** quality of behaving in a discreet way. **2** freedom or authority to make judgments and decide what to do. **discretionary** *adj*

discriminate *v* **1** (foll. by *against* or *in favour of*) single out (a particular person or group) for worse or better treatment than others. **2** (foll. by *between*) recognize or understand the difference (between). **discriminating** *adj* showing good taste and judgment. **discrimination** *n* **discriminatory** *adj* based on prejudice.

discursive *adj* passing from one topic to another.

discus *n* heavy disc-shaped object thrown in sports competitions.

discuss *v* **1** consider (something) by talking it over. **2** treat (a subject) in speech or writing. **discussion** *n*

disdain *n* **1** feeling of superiority and dislike. ♦ *v* **2** refuse with disdain. **disdainful** *adj* **disdainfully** *adv*

disease *n* illness, sickness. **diseased** *adj*

disembark *v* get off a ship, aircraft, or bus. **disembarkation** *n*

disembodied *adj* **1** lacking a body. **2** seeming not to be attached to or coming from anyone.

disembowel *v* **-elling, -elled** remove the entrails of.

disenchanted *adj* disappointed and disillusioned. **disenchantment** *n*

disenfranchise *v* deprive (someone) of the right to vote or of other rights of citizenship.

disengage *v* release from a connection. **disengagement** *n*

disentangle *v* release from entanglement or confusion. **disentanglement** *n*

disequilibrium *n* loss or absence of stability or balance.

disestablish *v* remove state support from (a church etc.). **disestablishment** *n*

disfavour *n* disapproval or dislike.

disfigure *v* spoil the appearance of. **disfigurement** *n*

disfranchise *v* same as DISENFRANCHISE.

disgorge *v* empty out, discharge.

disgrace *n* **1** condition of shame, loss of reputation, or dishonour. **2** shameful person or thing. ♦ *v* **3** bring shame upon (oneself or others). **disgraceful** *adj* **disgracefully** *adv*

disgruntled *adj* sulky or discontented. **disgruntlement** *n*

disguise *v* **1** change the appearance or manner in order to conceal the identity of (someone or something). **2** misrepresent (something) in order to obscure its actual nature or meaning. ♦ *n* **3** mask, costume, or manner that disguises. **4** state of being disguised.

disgust *n* **1** great loathing or distaste. ♦ *v* **2** sicken, fill with loathing. **disgusted** *adj* **disgusting** *adj* **disgustingly** *adv*

dish *n* **1** shallow container used for holding or serving food. **2** particular kind of food. **3** short for DISH AERIAL. **4** *Informal* attractive person. **dish aerial** aerial consisting of a concave disc-shaped reflector, used esp. for satellite television. **dishcloth** *n* cloth for washing dishes. **dish out** *v Informal* distribute. **dish up** *v Informal* serve (food).

dishabille [diss-a-**beel**] *n* same as DESHABILLE.

disharmony *n* lack of agreement, discord.

dishearten *v* weaken or destroy the hope, courage, or enthusiasm of.

dishevelled *adj* (of a person's hair, clothes, or general appearance) disordered and untidy.

dishonest *adj* not honest or fair. **dishonestly** *adv* **dishonesty** *n*

dishonour *v* **1** treat with disrespect. **2** refuse to cash (a cheque). ♦ *n* **3** lack of respect. **4** state of shame or disgrace. **5** something that causes a loss of honour. **dishonourable** *adj* **dishonourably** *adv*

disillusion *v* **1** destroy the illusions or false ideas of. ♦ *n* **2** (also **disillusionment**) state of being disillusioned.

disincentive *n* something that acts as a deterrent.

disinclined *adj* unwilling, reluctant. **disinclination** *n*

disinfect *v* rid of harmful germs, chemically. **disinfectant** *n* substance that destroys harmful germs. **disinfection** *n*

disinformation *n* false information intended to mislead.

disingenuous *adj* not sincere. **disingenuously** *adv*

disinherit *v Law* deprive (an heir) of inheritance. **disinheritance** *n*

disintegrate *v* break up. **disintegration** *n*

disinter *v* **-terring, -terred 1** dig up. **2** reveal, make known. **disinterment** *n*

disinterested *adj* free from bias or involvement. **disinterest** *n*

> Distinguish *disinterested* from *uninterested*, meaning 'apathetic, not caring': *We asked him to decide because he was a disinterested observer.*

disjointed *adj* having no coherence, disconnected.

disjunction *n* disconnection, separation. **disjunctive** *adj*

disk *n Computers* storage device, consisting of a stack of plates coated with a magnetic layer, which rotates rapidly as a single unit.

dislike *v* **1** consider unpleasant or disagreeable. ♦ *n* **2** feeling of not liking something or someone.

dislocate *v* **1** displace (a bone or joint) from its normal position. **2** disrupt or shift out of place. **dislocation** *n*

dislodge *v* remove (something) from a previously fixed position.

disloyal *adj* not loyal, deserting one's allegiance. **disloyalty** *n*

dismal *adj* **1** gloomy and depressing. **2** *Informal* of poor quality. **dismally** *adv*

dismantle *v* take apart piece by piece.

dismay *v* **1** fill with alarm or depression. ♦ *n* **2** alarm mixed with sadness.

dismember *v* **1** remove the limbs of. **2** cut to pieces. **dismemberment** *n*

dismiss *v* **1** remove (an employee) from a job. **2** allow (someone) to leave. **3** put out of one's mind. **4** (of a judge) state that (a case) will not be brought to trial. **dismissal** *n* **dismissive** *adj* scornful, contemptuous.

dismount *v* get off a horse or bicycle.

disobey *v* neglect or refuse to obey. **disobedient** *adj* **disobedience** *n*

disobliging *adj* unwilling to help.

disorder *n* **1** state of untidiness and disorganization. **2** public violence or rioting. **3** an illness. **disordered** *adj* untidy. **disorderly** *adj* **1** untidy and disorganized. **2** uncontrolled, unruly.

disorganize *v* disrupt the arrangement or system of. **disorganization** *n*

disorientate, disorient *v* cause (someone) to lose his or her bearings. **disorientation** *n*

disown *v* deny any connection with (someone).

disparage *v* speak contemptuously of. **disparagement** *n*

disparate *adj* completely different. **disparity** *n, pl* **-ties** inequality or difference.

dispassionate *adj* not influenced by emotion. **dispassionately** *adv*

dispatch *v* **1** send off to a destination or to perform a task. **2** carry out (a duty or a task) with speed. **3** *Old-fashioned* kill. ♦ *n* **4** official communication or report, sent in haste. **5** report sent to a newspaper by a correspondent. **dispatch rider** motorcyclist who carries dispatches.

dispel *v* **-pelling, -pelled** destroy or remove.

dispense *v* **1** distribute in portions. **2** prepare and distribute (medicine). **3** administer (the law etc.). **dispensable** *adj* not essential. **dispensation** *n* **1** dispensing. **2** exemption from an obligation. **dispenser** *n* **dispensary** *n, pl* **-saries** place where medicine is dispensed. **dispense with** *v* do away with, manage without.

disperse *v* **1** scatter over a wide area. **2** (cause to) leave a gathering. **3** separate (light) into its different wavelengths. **dispersal, dispersion** *n*

dispirit *v* make downhearted. **dispirited** *adj* **dispiriting** *adj*

displace *v* **1** move from the usual location. **2** remove from office. **displacement** *n* **displaced person** person forced from his or her home or country, esp. by war.

display *v* **1** make visible or noticeable. ♦ *n* **2** displaying. **3** something displayed. **4** exhibition. **5** electronic device for representing information visually. **6** *Zool* pattern of behaviour an animal uses to draw attention to itself when courting, defending its territory, etc.

displease *v* annoy or upset. **displeasure** *n*

disport *v* **disport oneself** indulge oneself in pleasure.

dispose *v* place in a certain order. **disposed** *adj* **1** willing or eager. **2** having an attitude as specified, e.g. *he felt well disposed towards her.* **disposable** *adj* **1** designed to be thrown away after use. **2** available for use, e.g. *disposable income.* **disposal** *n* getting rid of something. **at one's disposal** available for use. **disposition** *n* **1** person's usual temperament. **2** desire or tendency to do something. **3** arrangement. **dispose of** *v* **1** throw away, get rid of. **2** deal with (a problem etc.). **3** kill.

dispossess *v* (foll. by *of*) deprive (someone) of (a possession). **dispossessed** *adj* **dispossession** *n*

disproportion *n* lack of proportion or equality. **disproportionate** *adj* **disproportionately** *adv*

disprove *v* show (an assertion or claim) to be incorrect.

dispute *n* **1** disagreement, argument. ♦ *v* **2** argue about (something). **3** doubt the validity of. **4** fight over possession of.

disqualify *v* stop (someone) officially from taking part in something for wrongdoing. **disqualification** *n*

disquiet *n* **1** feeling of anxiety. ♦ *v* **2** make (someone) anxious. **disquietude** *n*

disquisition *n* detailed explanation of a subject.

disregard *v* **1** give little or no attention to. ♦ *n* **2** lack of attention or respect.

disrepair *n* condition of being worn out or in poor working order.

disrepute *n* loss or lack of good reputation. **disreputable** *adj* having or causing a bad reputation.

disrespect *n* lack of respect. **disrespectful** *adj* **disrespectfully** *adv*

disrobe *v* undress.

disrupt *v* interrupt the progress of. **disruption** *n* **disruptive** *adj*

dissatisfied *adj* not pleased or contented. **dissatisfaction** *n*

dissect *v* **1** cut open (a corpse) to examine it. **2** examine critically and minutely. **dissection** *n*

dissemble *v* conceal one's real motives or emotions by pretence.

disseminate *v* spread (information). **dissemination** *n*

dissent *v* **1** disagree. **2** *Christianity* reject the doctrines of an established church. ♦ *n* **3** disagreement. **4** *Christianity* separation from an established church. **dissension** *n* **dissenter** *n* **dissentient** *adj* dissenting.

dissertation *n* **1** written thesis, usu. required for a higher university degree. **2** long formal speech.

disservice *n* harmful action.

dissident *n* **1** person who disagrees with and criticizes the government. ♦ *adj* **2** disagreeing with the government. **dissidence** *n*

dissimilar *adj* not alike, different. **dissimilarity** *n*

dissimulate *v* conceal one's real feelings by pretence. **dissimulation** *n*

dissipate *v* **1** waste or squander. **2** scatter, disappear. **dissipated** *adj* showing signs of overindulgence in alcohol and other physical pleasures. **dissipation** *n*

dissociate *v* regard or treat as separate. **dissociate oneself from** deny or break an association with. **dissociation** *n*

dissolute *adj* leading an immoral life.

dissolution *n* **1** official breaking up of an organization or institution, such as Parliament. **2** official ending of a formal agreement, such as a marriage.

dissolve *v* **1** (cause to) become liquid. **2** break up or end officially. **3** break down emotionally, e.g. *she dissolved into tears.*

dissonance *n* lack of agreement or harmony. **dissonant** *adj*

dissuade *v* deter (someone) by persuasion from doing something. **dissuasion** *n*

distaff *n* rod on which wool etc. is wound for spinning. **distaff side** female side of a family.

distance *n* **1** space between two points. **2** state of being apart. **3** remoteness in manner. **the distance** most distant part of the visible scene. **distance oneself from** separate oneself mentally from. **distant** *adj* **1** far apart. **2** separated by a specified distance. **3** remote in manner. **distantly** *adv*

distaste *n* dislike, disgust. **distasteful** *adj* unpleasant, offensive. **distastefully** *adv*

distemper[1] *n* highly contagious viral disease of dogs.

distemper[2] *n* paint mixed with water, glue, etc., used for painting walls.

distend *v* (of part of the body) swell. **distension** *n*

distil *v* **-tilling, -tilled 1** subject to or obtain by distillation. **2** give off (a substance) in drops. **3** extract the essence of. **distillation** *n* **1** process of evaporating a liquid and condensing its vapour. **2** (also **distillate**) concentrated essence. **distiller** *n* person or company that makes strong alcoholic drink, esp. whisky. **distillery** *n, pl* **-leries** place where a strong alcoholic drink, esp. whisky, is made.

distinct *adj* **1** not the same. **2** easily sensed or understood. **3** clear and definite. **distinctly** *adv* **distinction** *n* **1** act of distinguishing. **2** distinguishing feature. **3** state of being different. **4** special honour, recognition, or fame. **distinctive** *adj* easily recognizable. **distinctively** *adv* **distinctiveness** *n*

distinguish *v* **1** (usu. foll. by *between*) make, show, or recognize a difference (between). **2** be a distinctive feature of. **3** make out by hearing, seeing, etc. **distinguishable** *adj* **distinguished** *adj* **1** dignified in appearance. **2** highly respected.

distort *v* **1** misrepresent (the truth or facts). **2** twist out of shape. **3** *Electronics* reproduce or amplify (a signal) inaccurately. **distortion** *n*

distract *v* **1** draw the attention of (a person) away from something. **2** entertain. **distracted** *adj* unable to concentrate, preoccupied. **distraction** *n*

distrait [diss-**tray**] *adj* absent-minded or preoccupied.

distraught [diss-**trawt**] *adj* extremely anxious or agitated.

distress *n* **1** extreme unhappiness. **2** great physical pain. **3** poverty. ♦ *v* **4** upset badly. **distressed** *adj* **1** extremely upset. **2** in financial difficulties. **3** (of furniture or fabric) made to look old. **distressing** *adj* **distressingly** *adv*

distribute *v* **1** hand out or deliver. **2** share out. **distribution** *n* **1** distributing. **2** arrangement or spread. **distributor** *n* **1** wholesaler who distributes goods to retailers in a specific area. **2** device in a petrol engine that sends the electric current to the spark plugs. **distributive** *adj*

district *n* area of land regarded as an administrative or geographical unit. **district nurse** nurse who attends to patients in their homes.

distrust *v* **1** regard as untrustworthy. ♦ *n* **2** feeling of suspicion or doubt. **distrustful** *adj*

disturb *v* **1** intrude on. **2** worry, make anxious. **3** change the position or shape of. **disturbance** *n* **disturbing** *adj* **disturbingly** *adv* **disturbed** *adj Psychiatry* emotionally upset or maladjusted.

disunite *v* cause disagreement among. **disunity** *n*

disuse *n* state of being no longer used. **disused** *adj*

ditch *n* **1** narrow channel dug in the earth for drainage or irrigation. ♦ *v* **2** *Slang* abandon.

dither *v* **1** be uncertain or indecisive. ♦ *n* **2** state of indecision or agitation. **ditherer** *n* **dithery** *adj*

ditto *n, pl* **-tos 1** the same. ♦ *adv* **2** in the same way.

ditty *n, pl* **-ties** short simple poem or song.

diuretic [die-yoor-**et**-ik] *n* drug that increases the flow of urine.

diurnal [die-**urn**-al] *adj* happening during the day or daily.

diva *n* distinguished female singer.

divan *n* **1** low backless bed. **2** backless sofa or couch.

dive *v* **diving, dived 1** plunge headfirst into water. **2** (of a submarine or diver) submerge under water. **3** fly in a steep nose-down descending path. **4** move quickly in a specified direction. **5** (foll. by *in* or *into*) start doing (something) enthusiastically. ♦ *n* **6** diving. **7** steep nose-down descent. **8** *Slang* disreputable bar or club. **diver** *n* **1** person who works or explores underwater. **2** person who dives for sport. **3** water bird that swims and dives. **dive bomber** military aircraft designed to release bombs during a dive. **diving bell** diving apparatus with an open bottom, supplied with compressed air from above. **diving**

board platform from which swimmers may dive. **diving suit** diver's waterproof suit, with a helmet and air supply.

diverge *v* **1** separate and go in different directions. **2** deviate (from a prescribed course). **divergence** *n* **divergent** *adj*

divers *adj Old-fashioned* various.

diverse *adj* **1** having variety, assorted. **2** different in kind. **diversity** *n, pl* **-ties 1** quality of being different or varied. **2** range of difference. **diversify** *v* **-fying, -fied diversification** *n*

divert *v* **1** change the direction of. **2** entertain, distract the attention of. **diversion** *n* **1** official detour used by traffic when a main route is closed. **2** something that distracts someone's attention. **3** diverting. **4** amusing pastime. **diversionary** *adj*

divest *v* **1** strip (of clothes). **2** deprive (of a role or function).

divide *v* **1** separate into parts. **2** share or be shared out in parts. **3** (cause to) disagree. **4** keep apart, be a boundary between. **5** calculate how many times (one number) can be contained in (another). ♦ *n* **6** division, split. **dividend** *n* **1** sum of money representing part of the profit made, paid by a company to its shareholders. **2** extra benefit. **3** number to be divided by another number. **divider** *n* **1** screen used to divide a room into separate areas. ♦ *pl* **2** compasses with two pointed arms, used for measuring or dividing lines.

divine *adj* **1** of God or a god. **2** godlike. **3** *Informal* splendid. ♦ *v* **4** discover (something) by intuition or guessing. **divinely** *adv* **divination** *n* art of discovering future events, as though by supernatural powers. **divinity** *n* **1** study of religion. **2** (*pl* **-ties**) god. **3** state of being divine. **divining rod** forked twig said to move when held over ground in which water or metal is to be found.

division *n* **1** dividing, sharing out. **2** one of the parts into which something is divided. **3** mathematical operation of dividing. **4** difference of opinion. **5** several departments in an organization that are grouped together. **divisional** *adj* of a division in an organization. **divisible** *adj* **divisibility** *n* **divisive** [div-**vice**-iv] *adj* tending to cause disagreement. **divisor** *n* number to be divided into another number.

divorce *n* **1** legal ending of a marriage. **2** any separation, esp. a permanent one. ♦ *v* **3** legally end one's marriage (to). **4** separate, consider separately. **divorcée,** (*masc*) **divorcé** *n* person who is divorced.

divot *n* small piece of turf.

divulge *v* make known, disclose. **divulgence** *n*

divvy *v* **-vying, -vied** (foll. by *up*) *Informal* divide and share.

Diwali *n* annual Hindu festival honouring Lakshmi, the goddess of wealth.

Dixie *n* southern states of the US (also **Dixieland**).

DIY *Brit, Aust & NZ* do-it-yourself.

dizzy *adj* **-zier, -ziest 1** having or causing a whirling sensation. **2** mentally confused. ♦ *v* **-zying, -zied 3** make dizzy. **dizzily** *adv* **dizziness** *n*

DJ 1 disc jockey. **2** dinner jacket.

djinni *n, pl* **djinn** same as JINNI.

dl decilitre.

dm decimetre.

DM Deutschmark.

DNA *n* deoxyribonucleic acid, the main constituent of the chromosomes of all living things.

D-notice *n Brit* official notice sent to newspapers etc., prohibiting publication of certain security information.

do[1] *v* **does, doing, did, done 1** perform or complete (a deed or action). **2** be adequate, e.g. *that one will do.* **3** provide, serve. **4** make (hair) neat or attractive. **5** suit or improve, e.g. *that style does nothing for you.* **6** find the answer to (a problem or puzzle). **7** cause, produce, e.g. *it does no harm to think ahead.* **8** give, grant, e.g. *do me a favour.* **9** work at, as a course of study or a job. **10** mimic. **11** *Informal* cheat or rob. **12** *Slang* use (illegal drugs). **13** used to form questions, e.g. *how do you know?* **14** used to intensify positive statements and commands, e.g. *I do like port; do go on.* **15** used to form negative statements and commands, e.g. *I do not know her well; do not get up.* **16** used to replace an earlier verb, e.g. *he gets paid more than I do.* ♦ *n, pl* **dos, do's 17** *Informal* party, celebration. **do away with** *v* get rid of. **do down** *v* belittle, criticize. **do for** *v* *Informal* cause the death or ruin of. **do-gooder** *n* *Informal* well-intentioned but naive or impractical person. **do in** *v* *Slang* **1** kill. **2** exhaust. **do-it-yourself** *n* constructing and repairing things oneself. **do up** *v* **1** fasten. **2** decorate and repair. **do with** *v* find useful or benefit from, e.g. *I could do with a rest.* **do without** *v* manage without.

do[2] *n, pl* **dos** same as DOH.

Doberman pinscher, Doberman *n* large dog with a black-and-tan coat.

docile *adj* (of a person or animal) easily controlled. **docilely** *adv* **docility** *n*

dock[1] *n* **1** enclosed area of water where ships are loaded, unloaded, or repaired. ♦ *v* **2** bring or be brought into dock. **3** link (two spacecraft) or (of two spacecraft) be linked together in space. **docker** *n* person employed to load and unload ships. **dockyard** *n* place where ships are built or repaired.

dock[2] *v* **1** deduct money from (a person's wages). **2** remove part of (an animal's tail) by cutting through the bone.

dock[3] *n* enclosed space in a court of law where the accused person sits or stands.

dock[4] *n* weed with broad leaves.

docket *n* label on a package or other delivery, stating contents, delivery instructions, etc.

doctor *n* **1** person licensed to practise medicine. **2** person who has been awarded a doctorate. ♦ *v* **3** alter in order to deceive. **4** poison or drug (food or drink). **5** *Informal* castrate (an animal). **doctoral** *adj* **doctorate** *n* highest academic degree in any field of knowledge.

doctrine [**dock**-trin] *n* **1** body of teachings of a religious, political, or philosophical group. **2** principle or body of principles that is taught or advocated. **doctrinal** *adj* of doctrines. **doctrinaire** *adj* stubbornly insistent on the application of a theory without regard to practicality.

document *n* **1** piece of paper providing an official record of something. ♦ *v* **2** record or report (something) in detail. **3** support (a claim) with evidence. **documentation** *n*

documentary *n, pl* **-ries 1** film or television programme presenting the facts about a particular subject. ♦ *adj* **2** (of evidence) based on documents.

docu-soap *n* television documentary series presenting the lives of the people filmed as entertainment.

dodder *v* move unsteadily. **doddery** *adj*

doddle *n* *Informal* something easily accomplished.

dodecagon [doe-**deck**-a-gon] *n* geometric figure with twelve sides.

dodecahedron [doe-deck-a-**heed**-ron] *n* solid figure with twelve faces.

dodge *v* **1** avoid (a blow, being seen, etc.) by moving suddenly. **2** evade by cleverness or trickery. ♦ *n* **3** cunning or deceitful trick. **dodger** *n* **dodgy** *adj* **dodgier, dodgiest** *Informal* **1** dangerous, risky. **2** untrustworthy.

Dodgem *n* ® small electric car driven and bumped against similar cars in a rink at a funfair.

dodo *n, pl* **dodos, dodoes** large flightless extinct bird.

doe *n* female deer, hare, or rabbit.

does *v* third person singular of the present tense of DO[1].

doesn't does not.

doff *v* take off or lift (one's hat) in polite greeting.

dog *n* **1** domesticated four-legged mammal of many different breeds. **2** related wild mammal, such as the dingo or coyote. **3** male animal of the dog family. **4** *Informal* person, e.g. *you lucky dog!* ♦ *v* **dogging, dogged 5** follow (someone) closely. **6** trouble, plague. **the dogs** *Brit informal* greyhound racing. **go to the**

dogs *Informal* go to ruin physically or morally. **let sleeping dogs lie** leave things undisturbed. **doggy, doggie** *n, pl* **-gies** child's word for a dog. **doggy bag** bag in which leftovers from a meal may be taken away. **dogcart** *n* light horse-drawn two-wheeled cart. **dog collar 1** collar for a dog. **2** *Informal* white collar fastened at the back, worn by members of the clergy. **dog days** hottest part of the summer. **dog-eared** *adj* **1** (of a book) having pages folded down at the corner. **2** shabby, worn. **dog-end** *n Informal* cigarette end. **dog-fight** *n* close-quarters combat between fighter aircraft. **dogfish** *n* small shark. **doghouse** *n US* kennel. **in the dog-house** *Informal* in disgrace. **dogleg** *n* sharp bend. **dog paddle** swimming stroke in which the hands are paddled in imitation of a swimming dog. **dog rose** wild rose with pink or white flowers. **dog-tired** *adj Informal* exhausted.

doge [**doje**] *n* (formerly) chief magistrate of Venice or Genoa.

dogged [**dog**-gid] *adj* obstinately determined. **doggedly** *adv* **doggedness** *n*

doggerel *n* poorly written poetry, usu comic.

doggo *adv* **lie doggo** *Informal* hide and keep quiet.

dogma *n* doctrine or system of doctrines proclaimed by authority as true. **dogmatic** *adj* habitually stating one's opinions forcefully or arrogantly. **dogmatically** *adv* **dogmatism** *n*

dogsbody *n, pl* **-bodies** *Informal* person who carries out boring tasks for others.

doh *n Music* in tonic sol-fa, first degree of any major scale.

doily *n, pl* **-lies** decorative lacy paper mat, laid on a plate.

Dolby *n* ® system used in tape recorders that reduces noise level on recorded or broadcast sound.

doldrums *pl n* **1** depressed state of mind. **2** state of inactivity. **3** area of sea round the equator where there is hardly any wind.

dole *n* **1** *Informal* money received from the state while unemployed. ♦ *v* **2** (foll. by *out*) distribute in small quantities. **on the dole** *Brit informal* receiving unemployment benefit.

doleful *adj* dreary, unhappy. **dolefully** *adv* **dolefulness** *n*

doll *n* **1** small model of a human being, used as a toy. **2** *Slang* pretty girl or young woman. **doll up** *v Slang* dress up smartly or showily.

dollar *n* standard monetary unit of the US, Canada, and various other countries.

dollop *n Informal* lump (of food).

dolly *n, pl* **-lies 1** child's word for a doll. **2** wheeled support on which a camera may be moved.

dolman sleeve *n* sleeve that is very wide at the armhole, tapering to a tight wrist.

dolmen *n* prehistoric monument consisting of a horizontal stone supported by vertical stones.

dolomite *n* mineral consisting of calcium magnesium carbonate.

dolorous *adj* sad, mournful.

dolphin *n* sea mammal of the whale family, with a beaklike snout. **dolphinarium** *n* aquarium for dolphins.

dolt *n* stupid person. **doltish** *adj*

domain *n* **1** field of knowledge or activity. **2** land under one ruler or government.

dome *n* **1** rounded roof built on a circular base. **2** something shaped like this. **domed** *adj*

domestic *adj* **1** of one's own country or a specific country, e.g. *domestic and foreign policy.* **2** of the home or family. **3** enjoying running a home. **4** (of an animal) kept as a pet or to produce food. ♦ *n* **5** person whose job is to do housework in someone else's house. **domestically** *adv* **domesticity** *n* **domesticate** *v* **1** bring or keep (a wild animal or plant) under control or cultivation. **2** accustom (someone) to home life. **domestication** *n* **domestic science** study of household skills.

domicile [**dom**-miss-ile] *n* place where one lives. **domiciliary** *adj*

dominant *adj* **1** having authority or influence. **2** main, chief. **dominance** *n*

dominate *v* **1** control or govern. **2** tower above (surroundings). **3** be very significant in. **domination** *n*

domineering *adj* forceful and arrogant.

Dominican *n, adj* (friar or nun) of an order founded by Saint Dominic.

dominion *n* **1** control or authority. **2** land governed by one ruler or government. **3** (formerly) self-governing division of the British Empire.

domino *n, pl* **-noes** **1** small rectangular block marked with dots, used in dominoes. ♦ *pl* **2** game in which dominoes with matching halves are laid together.

don[1] *v* **donning, donned** put on (clothing).

don[2] *n* **1** *Brit* member of the teaching staff at a university or college. **2** Spanish gentleman or nobleman. **3** head of a Mafia family. **donnish** *adj* serious and academic.

donate *v* give, esp. to a charity or organization. **donation** *n* **1** donating. **2** thing donated. **donor** *n* **1** *Med* person who gives blood or organs for use in the treatment of another person. **2** person who makes a donation.

done *v* **1** past participle of DO[1]. ♦ *adj* **2** completed. **3** used up. **4** socially acceptable. **5** *Informal* cheated, tricked.

doner kebab *n* see KEBAB.

Don Juan *n* man who has seduced many women.

donkey *n* long-eared member of the horse family. **donkey jacket** man's long thick jacket with a waterproof panel across the shoulders. **donkey's years** *Informal* a long time. **donkey-work** *n* tedious hard work.

Don Quixote [**don** kee-**hoe**-tee] *n* impractical idealist.

don't do not.

doodle *v* **1** scribble or draw aimlessly. ♦ *n* **2** shape or picture drawn aimlessly.

doom *n* **1** death or a terrible fate. ♦ *v* **2** destine or condemn to death or a terrible fate. **doomsday** *n* **1** *Christianity* day on which the Last Judgment will occur. **2** any dreaded day.

door *n* **1** hinged or sliding panel for closing the entrance to a building, room, etc. **2** entrance. **doorjamb, doorpost** *n* vertical post forming one side of a door frame. **doorman** *n* man employed to be on duty at the entrance to a large public building. **doormat** *n* **1** mat for wiping dirt from shoes before going indoors. **2** *Informal* person who offers little resistance to ill-treatment. **door-to-door** *adj* **1** (of selling) from one house to the next. **2** (of a journey) direct. **doorway** *n* opening into a building or room.

dope *n* **1** *Slang* illegal drug, usu. cannabis. **2** medicine, drug. **3** *Informal* stupid person. ♦ *v* **4** give a drug to, esp. in order to improve performance in a race. **dopey, dopy** *adj* **1** half-asleep, drowsy. **2** *Slang* silly.

doppelgänger *n Legend* ghostly double of a living person.

Doppler effect *n* change in the apparent frequency of a sound or light wave as a result of relative motion between the observer and the source.

Doric *adj* **1** of a style of ancient Greek architecture. ♦ *n* **2** country dialect, esp. a Scots one.

dormant *adj* temporarily quiet, inactive, or not being used. **dormancy** *n*

dormer, dormer window *n* window that sticks out from a sloping roof.

dormitory *n, pl* **-ries** **1** large room, esp. at a school, containing several beds. ♦ *adj* **2** (of a town or suburb) having many inhabitants who travel to work in a nearby city.

dormouse *n, pl* **-mice** small mouselike rodent with a furry tail.

dorsal *adj* of or on the back.

dory, John Dory *n, pl* **-ries** spiny-finned edible sea fish.

dose *n* **1** specific quantity of a medicine taken at one time. **2** *Informal* something unpleasant to experience, e.g. *a dose of the jitters.* ♦ *v* **3** give a dose to. **dosage** *n* size of a dose.

dosh *n Slang* money.

doss *v* **doss down** *Brit & Aust slang* sleep in an uncomfortable place. **dosshouse** *n Brit slang* cheap lodging house for homeless people.

dossier [**doss**-ee-ay] *n* collection of documents about a subject or person.

dot *n* **1** small round mark. **2** shorter symbol used in Morse code. ♦ *v* **dotting, dotted 3** mark with a dot. **4** scatter, spread around. **on the dot** at exactly the arranged time. **dotty** *adj* **-tier, -tiest** *Slang* rather eccentric.

dote *v* **dote on** love to an excessive degree. **dotage** *n* weakness as a result of old age. **doting** *adj*

dotterel *n* rare kind of plover.

dottle *n* tobacco left in a pipe after smoking.

double *adj* **1** as much again in number, amount, size, etc. **2** composed of two equal or similar parts. **3** designed for two users, e.g. *double room.* **4** folded in two. ♦ *adv* **5** twice over. ♦ *n* **6** twice the number, amount, size, etc. **7** person who looks almost exactly like another. ♦ *pl* **8** game between two pairs of players. ♦ *v* **9** make or become twice as much or as many. **10** bend or fold (material etc.). **11** play two parts. **12** turn sharply. **at, on the double** quickly or immediately. **doubly** *adv* **double agent** spy employed by two enemy countries at the same time. **double-barrelled** *adj* **1** (of a gun) having two barrels. **2** (of a surname) having two hyphenated parts. **double bass** stringed instrument, largest and lowest member of the violin family. **double-breasted** *adj* (of a jacket or coat) having overlapping fronts. **double-check** *v* make certain by checking again. **double chin** fold of fat under the chin. **double cream** thick cream with a high fat content. **double-cross** *v* **1** cheat or betray. ♦ *n* **2** double-crossing. **double-dealing** *n* treacherous or deceitful behaviour. **double-decker** *n* **1** bus with two passenger decks one on top of the other. ♦ *adj* **2** *Informal* (of a sandwich) made from three slices of bread with two fillings. **double Dutch** *Informal* incomprehensible talk, gibberish. **double-edged** *adj* **1** (of a remark) malicious in intent though apparently complimentary. **2** (of a knife) having a cutting edge on each side of the blade. **double glazing** two panes of glass in a window, fitted to reduce heat loss. **double-jointed** *adj* (of a person) having unusually flexible joints. **double-park** *v* park (a vehicle) alongside another, causing an obstruction. **double standard** set of principles that allows greater freedom to one person or group than to another. **double take** esp. in comedy, delayed reaction by a person to a remark or situation. **double talk** deceptive or ambiguous talk. **double whammy** *Informal* devastating setback made up of two elements.

double entendre [**doob**-bl on-**tond**-ra] *n* word or phrase that can be interpreted in two ways, one of which is rude.

doublet [**dub**-lit] *n Hist* man's close-fitting jacket, with or without sleeves.

doubloon *n* former Spanish gold coin.

doubt *n* **1** uncertainty about the truth, facts, or existence of something. **2** unresolved difficulty or point. ♦ *v* **3** question the truth of. **4** distrust or be suspicious of (someone). **doubter** *n* **doubtful** *adj* **1** unlikely. **2** feeling doubt. **doubtfully** *adv* **doubtless** *adv* probably or certainly.

> If *doubt* is followed by a clause it is connected by *whether: I doubt whether she means it.* If it is used with a negative it is followed by *that: I don't doubt that he is sincere.*

douche [**doosh**] *n* **1** (instrument for applying) a stream of water directed onto or into the body for cleansing or medical purposes. ♦ *v* **2** cleanse or treat by means of a douche.

dough *n* **1** thick mixture of flour and water or milk, used for making bread etc. **2** *Slang* money. **doughy** *adj* **doughier, doughiest** **doughnut** *n* small cake of sweetened dough fried in deep fat.

doughty [**dowt**-ee] *adj* **-tier, -tiest** *Old-fashioned* brave and determined.

dour [**doo**-er] *adj* sullen and unfriendly. **dourness** *n*

douse [rhymes with **mouse**] *v* **1** drench with water or other liquid. **2** put out (a light).

dove *n* **1** bird with a heavy body, small head, and short legs. **2** *Politics* person opposed to war. **dovecote, dovecot** *n* structure for housing pigeons. **dovetail** *n* **1** joint containing wedge-shaped tenons. ♦ *v* **2** fit together neatly.

dowager *n* widow possessing property or a title obtained from her husband.

dowdy *adj* **-dier, -diest** dull and old-fashioned. **dowdily** *adv* **dowdiness** *n*

dowel *n* wooden or metal peg that fits into two corresponding holes to join two adjacent parts.

dower *n* life interest in a part of her husband's estate allotted to a widow by law.

down[1] *prep, adv* **1** indicating movement to or position in a lower place. ♦ *adv* **2** indicating completion of an action, lessening of intensity, etc., e.g. *calm down.* ♦ *adj* **3** depressed, unhappy. ♦ *v* **4** *Informal* drink quickly. **have a down on** *Informal* feel hostile towards. **down under** *Informal* (in or to) Australia or New Zealand. **downward** *adj, adv* (descending) from a higher to a lower level, condition, or position. **downwards** *adv* from a higher to a lower level, condition, or position. **down-and-out** *n* **1** person who is homeless and destitute. ♦ *adj* **2** without any means of support. **down-to-earth** *adj* sensible or practical.

down[2] *n* soft fine feathers. **downy** *adj*

downbeat *adj* **1** *Informal* gloomy. **2** relaxed.

downcast *adj* **1** sad, dejected. **2** (of the eyes) directed downwards.

downfall *n* (cause of) a sudden loss of position or reputation.

downgrade *v* reduce in importance or value.

downhearted *adj* sad and discouraged.

downhill *adj* **1** going or sloping down. ♦ *adv* **2** towards the bottom of a hill. **go downhill** *Informal* deteriorate.

Downing Street *n Informal* British prime minister or government.

downpour *n* heavy fall of rain.

downright *adj, adv* extreme(ly).

downs *pl n* low grassy hills, esp. in S England.

Down's syndrome *n* genetic disorder characterized by a flat face, slanting eyes, and mental retardation.

downstage *adv, adj* to or at the front part of the stage.

downstairs *adv* **1** to or on a lower floor. ♦ *n* **2** lower or ground floor.

downtrodden *adj* oppressed and lacking the will to resist.

dowry *n, pl* **-ries** property brought by a woman to her husband at marriage.

dowse [rhymes with **cows**] *v* search for underground water or minerals using a divining rod. **dowser** *n*

doxology *n, pl* **-gies** short hymn of praise to God.

doyen [**doy**-en] *n* senior member of a group, profession, or society. **doyenne** [doy-**en**] *n fem*

doyley *n* same as DOILY.

doze *v* **1** sleep lightly or briefly. ♦ *n* **2** short sleep. **dozy** *adj* **dozier, doziest 1** feeling sleepy. **2** *Informal* stupid. **doze off** *v* fall into a light sleep.

dozen *adj, n* twelve. **dozenth** *adj*

DPP Director of Public Prosecutions.

Dr 1 Doctor. **2** Drive.

drab *adj* **drabber, drabbest 1** dull and dreary. **2** dull brown. **drabness** *n*

drachm [**dram**] *n Brit* one eighth of a fluid ounce.

drachma *n, pl* **-mas, -mae** standard monetary unit of Greece.

draconian *adj* severe, harsh.

draft *n* **1** plan, sketch, or drawing of something. **2** preliminary outline of a book, speech, etc. **3** written order for payment of money by a bank. **4** *US & Aust* selection for compulsory military service. ♦ *v* **5** draw up an outline or plan of. **6** send (people) from one place to another to do a specific job. **7** *US & Aust* select for compulsory military service.

drag *v* **dragging, dragged 1** pull with force, esp. along the ground. **2** trail on the ground. **3** persuade or force (oneself or someone else) to go somewhere. **4** (foll. by *on* or *out*) last or be prolonged tediously. **5** search (a river) with a dragnet or hook. **6** *Computers* move (an image) on the screen by use of the mouse. ♦ *n* **7** person or thing that slows up progress. **8** *Informal* tedious thing or person. **9** *Slang* women's clothes worn by a man. **10** resistance to the motion of a body passing through air or a liquid. **dragnet** *n* net used to scour the bottom of a pond or river to search for something. **drag race** race in which specially built cars or motorcycles are timed over a measured course.

dragoman *n, pl* **-mans, -men** (in some Middle Eastern countries) professional interpreter or guide.

dragon *n* **1** mythical fire-breathing monster like a huge lizard. **2** *Informal* fierce woman. **dragonfly** *n* brightly coloured insect with a long slender body and two pairs of wings.

dragoon *n* **1** heavily armed cavalryman. ♦ *v* **2** coerce, force.

drain *n* **1** pipe or channel that carries off water or sewage. **2** cause of a continuous reduction in energy or resources. ♦ *v* **3** draw off or remove liquid from. **4** flow away or filter off. **5** drink the entire contents of (a glass or cup). **6** make constant demands on (energy or resources), exhaust. **drainage** *n* **1** system of drains. **2** process or method of draining. **draining board** sloping grooved surface at the side of a sink, used for draining washed dishes. **drainpipe** *n* **1** pipe for carrying off rainwater or sewage. ♦ *pl* **2** trousers with very narrow legs.

drake *n* male duck.

dram *n* **1** small amount of a strong alcoholic drink, esp. whisky. **2** one sixteenth of an ounce.

drama *n* **1** serious play for theatre, television, or radio. **2** plays collectively. **3** writing, producing, or acting in plays. **4** situation that is exciting or highly emotional. **dramatic** *adj* **1** of or like drama. **2** behaving flamboyantly. **dramatically** *adv* **dramatist** *n* person who writes plays. **dramatize** *v* **1** rewrite (a book) in the form of a play. **2** express (something) in a dramatic or exaggerated way. **dramatization** *n*

dramatis personae [**drah**-mat-tiss per-**soh**-nigh] *pl n* characters in a play.

dramaturgy *n* art and technique of the theatre. **dramaturge** *n* **1** playwright. **2** literary adviser to a theatre, film company, etc. **dramaturgical, dramaturgic** *adj*

drank *v* past tense of DRINK.

drape *v* **1** cover with material, usu. in folds. **2** place casually. ♦ *n* **3** *Aust, US & Canadian* curtain. **draper** *n Brit, Aust & NZ* person who sells fabrics and sewing materials. **drapery** *n, pl* **-peries 1** fabric or clothing arranged and draped. **2** fabrics and cloth collectively.

drastic *adj* strong and severe. **drastically** *adv*

draught *n* **1** current of cold air, esp. in an enclosed space. **2** portion of liquid to be drunk, esp. medicine. **3** gulp or swallow. **4** one of the flat discs used in the game of draughts. ♦ *pl* **5** game for two players using a chessboard and twelve draughts each. ♦ *adj* **6** (of an animal) used for pulling heavy loads. **draughty** *adj* **draughtier, draughtiest** exposed to draughts of air. **draughtsman** *n* **1** person employed to prepare detailed scale drawings of machinery, buildings, etc. **2** person skilled in drawing. **draughtsmanship** *n* **draught beer** beer stored in a cask.

draw *v* **drawing, drew, drawn 1** sketch (a figure, picture, etc.) with a pencil or pen. **2** pull (a person or thing) closer to or further away from a place. **3** move in a specified direction, e.g. *the car drew near.* **4** take from a source, e.g. *draw* *money from bank accounts.* **5** attract, interest. **6** formulate or decide, e.g. *to draw conclusions.* **7** (of two teams or contestants) finish a game with an equal number of points. ♦ *n* **8** raffle or lottery. **9** contest or game ending in a tie. **10** event, act, etc., that attracts a large audience. **drawing** *n* **1** picture or plan made by means of lines on a surface. **2** art of making drawings. **drawing pin** short tack with a broad smooth head. **drawing room** *Old-fashioned* room where visitors are received and entertained. **drawback** *n* disadvantage. **drawbridge** *n* bridge that may be raised to prevent access or to enable vessels to pass. **draw out** *v* **1** encourage (someone) to talk freely. **2** make longer. **drawstring** *n* cord run through a hem around an opening, so that when it is pulled tighter, the opening closes. **draw up** *v* **1** prepare and write out (a contract). **2** (of a vehicle) come to a stop.

drawer *n* **1** sliding box-shaped part of a piece of furniture, used for storage. ♦ *pl* **2** *Old-fashioned* undergarment worn on the lower part of the body.

drawl *v* **1** speak slowly, with long vowel sounds. ♦ *n* **2** drawling manner of speech.

drawn *v* **1** past participle of DRAW. ♦ *adj* **2** haggard, tired, or tense in appearance.

dray *n* low cart used for carrying heavy loads.

dread *v* **1** anticipate with apprehension or fear. ♦ *n* **2** great fear. **dreadful** *adj* **1** very disagreeable or shocking. **2** extreme, e.g. *a dreadful anticlimax.* **dreadfully** *adv*

dreadlocks *pl n* hair worn in the Rastafarian style of tightly twisted strands.

dream *n* **1** imagined series of events experienced in the mind while asleep. **2** daydream. **3** cherished hope. **4** *Informal* wonderful person or thing. ♦ *v* **dreaming, dreamed** *or* **dreamt** **5** see imaginary pictures in the mind while asleep. **6** (often foll. by *of* or *about*) have an image (of) or fantasy (about). **7** (foll. by *of*) consider the possibility (of). ♦ *adj* **8** ideal, e.g. *a dream house.* **dreamer** *n* **dreamy** *adj* **dreamier, dreamiest** **1** vague or impractical. **2** *Informal* wonderful. **dreamily** *adv* **dream up** *v* invent by imagination and ingenuity.

dreary *adj* **drearier, dreariest** dull, boring. **drearily** *adv* **dreariness** *n*

dredge[1] *v* clear or search (a river bed or harbour) by removing silt or mud. **dredger** *n* boat fitted with machinery for dredging. **dredge up** *v* *Informal* remember (something) obscure or half-forgotten.

dredge[2] *v* sprinkle (food) with flour etc.

dregs *pl n* **1** solid particles that settle at the bottom of some liquids. **2** most despised elements, e.g. *the dregs of society.*

drench *v* make completely wet.

Dresden china, Dresden *n* delicate decorative porcelain made near Dresden in Germany.

dress *n* **1** one-piece garment for a woman or girl, consisting of a skirt and bodice and sometimes sleeves. **2** complete style of clothing. ♦ *v* **3** put clothes on. **4** put on formal clothes. **5** apply a protective covering to (a wound). **6** arrange or prepare. **dressing** *n* **1** sauce for salad. **2** covering for a wound. **dressing-down** *n* *Informal* severe scolding. **dressing gown** coat-shaped garment worn over pyjamas or nightdress. **dressing room** room used for changing clothes, esp. backstage in a theatre. **dressing table** piece of bedroom furniture with a mirror and drawers. **dressy** *adj* **dressier, dressiest** (of clothes) elegant. **dress circle** first gallery in a theatre. **dressmaker** *n* person who makes women's clothes. **dressmaking** *n* **dress rehearsal** last rehearsal of a play or show, using costumes, lighting, etc. **dress up** *v* **1** put on glamorous or stylish clothes. **2** put on fancy dress. **3** make (something) seem better than it really is, e.g. *to dress up profits.*

dressage [**dress**-ahzh] *n* training of a horse to perform manoeuvres in response to the rider's body signals.

dresser[1] *n* piece of furniture with shelves and with cupboards, for storing or displaying dishes.

dresser[2] *n Theatre* person employed to assist actors with their costumes.

drew *v* past tense of DRAW.

drey *n* squirrel's nest.

dribble *v* **1** (allow to) flow in drops. **2** allow saliva to trickle from the mouth. **3** *Sport* propel (a ball) by repeatedly tapping it with the foot, hand, or a stick. ♦ *n* **4** small quantity of liquid falling in drops. **5** dribbling. **dribbler** *n*

driblet *n* small amount.

dribs and drabs *pl n Informal* small occasional amounts.

dried *v* past of DRY.

drier[1] *adj* a comparative of DRY.

drier[2] *n* same as DRYER.

driest *adj* a superlative of DRY.

drift *v* **1** be carried along by currents of air or water. **2** move aimlessly from one place or activity to another. **3** (of snow) pile up in heaps. ♦ *n* **4** something piled up by the wind or current, such as a snowdrift. **5** general movement or development. **6** point, meaning, e.g. *catch my drift?* **drifter** *n* **1** person who moves aimlessly from place to place or job to job. **2** fishing boat equipped with drift nets. **drift net** fishing net that is allowed to drift with the tide. **driftwood** *n* wood floating on or washed ashore by the sea.

drill[1] *n* **1** tool or machine for boring holes. **2** strict and often repetitious training. **3** *Informal* correct procedure. ♦ *v* **4** bore a hole in (something) with or as if with a drill. **5** teach by rigorous exercises or training.

drill[2] *n* **1** machine for sowing seed in rows. **2** small furrow for seed. ♦ *v* **3** sow (seed) in drills or furrows.

drill[3] *n* hard-wearing cotton cloth.

drily *adv* same as DRYLY.

drink *v* **drinking, drank, drunk 1** swallow (a liquid). **2** consume alcohol, esp. to excess. ♦ *n* **3** (portion of) a liquid suitable for drinking. **4** alcohol, or its habitual or excessive consumption. **drinkable** *adj* **drinker** *n* **drink-driving** *adj, n* (of) driving a car after drinking alcohol. **drink in** *v* pay close attention to. **drink to** *v* drink a toast to.

drip *v* **dripping, dripped 1** (let) fall in drops. ♦ *n* **2** falling of drops of liquid. **3** sound made by falling drops. **4** *Informal* weak dull person. **5** *Med* device by which a solution is passed in small drops through a tube into a vein. **drip-dry** *adj* denoting clothing that will dry free of creases if hung up when wet. **drip-feed** *v* feed (someone) a liquid drop by drop, usu. through a vein.

dripping *n* fat that comes from meat while it is being roasted or fried.

drive *v* **driving, drove, driven 1** guide the movement of (a vehicle). **2** transport in a vehicle. **3** goad into a specified state. **4** push or propel. **5** *Sport* hit (a ball) very hard and straight. **6** make (people or animals) go to or from a place. ♦ *n* **7** journey by car, van, etc. **8** (also **driveway**) path for vehicles connecting a building to a public road. **9** united effort towards a common goal, e.g. *a recruitment drive.* **10** energy and ambition. **11** *Psychol* motive or interest, e.g. *sex drive.* **12** means by which power is transmitted in a mechanism. **driver** *n* **drive at** *v Informal* intend or mean, e.g. *what was he driving at?* **drive-in** *adj, n* (denoting) a cinema, restaurant, etc., used by people in their cars. **driving licence** official document authorizing a person to drive a motor vehicle.

drivel *n* **1** foolish talk. ♦ *v* **-elling, -elled 2** speak foolishly.

drizzle *n* **1** very light rain. ♦ *v* **2** rain lightly. **drizzly** *adj* **-zlier, -zliest**

droll *adj* quaintly amusing. **drolly** *adv* **drollery** *n*

dromedary [**drom**-mid-er-ee] *n, pl* **-daries** camel with a single hump.

drone[1] *n* male bee.

drone[2] *v, n* (make) a monotonous low dull sound. **drone on** *v* talk for a long time in a monotonous tone.

drool *v* **1** (foll. by *over*) show excessive

enthusiasm (for). **2** allow saliva to flow from the mouth.

droop *v* hang downwards loosely. **droopy** *adj* **droopier, droopiest**

drop *v* **dropping, dropped 1** (allow to) fall vertically. **2** decrease in amount, strength, or value. **3** (of ground) go down to a lower level. **4** mention (a hint or name) casually. **5** drive (someone or something) to a place. **6** discontinue. ♦ *n* **7** small quantity of liquid forming a round shape. **8** any small quantity of liquid. **9** decrease in amount, strength, or value. **10** vertical distance that something may fall. ♦ *pl* **11** liquid medication applied in small drops. **droplet** *n* **droppings** *pl n* faeces of certain animals, such as rabbits or birds. **drop in, by** *v* pay someone a casual visit. **drop kick** (in rugby etc.) kick in which the ball is dropped from the hands and kicked as it hits the ground. **drop off** *v* **1** *Informal* fall asleep. **2** same as DROP (sense 5). **3** grow smaller or less. **dropout** *n* **1** person who rejects conventional society. **2** person who does not complete a course of study. **drop out (of)** *v* abandon or withdraw from (a school, job, etc.).

dropsy *n* illness in which watery fluid collects in the body.

dross *n* **1** scum formed on the surfaces of molten metals. **2** anything worthless.

drought *n* prolonged shortage of rainfall.

drove[1] *v* past tense of DRIVE.

drove[2] *n* very large group, esp. of people. **drover** *n* person who drives sheep or cattle.

drown *v* **1** die or kill by immersion in liquid. **2** forget (one's sorrows) temporarily by drinking alcohol. **3** drench thoroughly. **4** make (a sound) inaudible by being louder.

drowse *v* be sleepy, dull, or sluggish. **drowsy** *adj* **drowsily** *adv* **drowsiness** *n*

drubbing *n* utter defeat in a contest etc.

drudge *n* **1** person who works hard at uninteresting tasks. ♦ *v* **2** work at such tasks. **drudgery** *n*

drug *n* **1** substance used in the treatment or prevention of disease. **2** chemical substance, esp. a narcotic, taken for the effects it produces. ♦ *v* **drugging, drugged 3** give a drug to (a person or animal) to cause sleepiness or unconsciousness. **4** mix a drug with (food or drink). **drugstore** *n US* pharmacy where a wide range of goods are available.

Druid *n* member of an ancient order of Celtic priests. **Druidic, Druidical** *adj*

drum *n* **1** percussion instrument sounded by striking a membrane stretched across the opening of a hollow cylinder. **2** cylindrical object or container. ♦ *v* **drumming, drummed 3** play (music) on a drum. **4** tap rhythmically or regularly. **drummer** *n* **drum into** *v* instil into (someone) by constant repetition. **drum machine** synthesizer programmed to reproduce the sound of percussion instruments. **drum major** person in charge of a marching band. **drum out (of)** *v* force to leave (an organization). **drumstick** *n* **1** stick used for playing a drum. **2** lower joint of the leg of a cooked chicken etc. **drum up** *v* obtain (support or business) by making requests or canvassing.

drunk *v* **1** past participle of DRINK. ♦ *adj* **2** intoxicated with alcohol to the extent of losing control over normal functions. **3** overwhelmed by a strong influence or emotion, e.g. *drunk with success.* ♦ *n* **4** person who is drunk or who frequently gets drunk. **drunkard** *n* person who frequently gets drunk. **drunken** *adj* **1** drunk or frequently drunk. **2** caused by or relating to alcoholic intoxication. **drunkenly** *adv* **drunkenness** *n*

dry *adj* **drier, driest** *or* **dryer, dryest 1** lacking moisture. **2** having little or no rainfall. **3** *Informal* thirsty. **4** (of wine) not sweet. **5** uninteresting, e.g. *a dry book.* **6** (of humour) subtle and sarcastic. **7** prohibiting the sale of alcohol, e.g. *a dry town.* ♦ *v* **drying, dried 8** make or become dry. **9** preserve (food) by removing the moisture. **drily, dryly**

adv **dryness** *n* **dryer** *n* apparatus for removing moisture. **dry-clean** *v* clean (clothes etc.) with chemicals rather than water. **dry-cleaner** *n* **dry-cleaning** *n* **dry dock** dock that can be pumped dry to permit work on a ship's bottom. **dry ice** solid carbon dioxide. **dry out** *v* **1** make or become dry. **2** (cause to) undergo treatment for alcoholism. **dry rot** crumbling and drying of timber, caused by certain fungi. **dry run** *Informal* rehearsal. **dry-stone** *adj* (of a wall) made without mortar. **dry up** *v* **1** dry (washed dishes) with a tea towel. **2** stop being productive. **3** *Informal* stop speaking.

dryad *n* wood nymph.

DSc Doctor of Science.

DSS Department of Social Security.

DT's *Informal* delirium tremens.

dual *adj* having two parts, functions, or aspects. **duality** *n* **dualism** *n* state of having or being believed to have two distinct parts or aspects. **dual carriageway** *Brit, Aust & NZ* road on which traffic travelling in opposite directions is separated by a central strip of grass or concrete.

dub[1] *v* **dubbing, dubbed** give (a person or place) a name or nickname.

dub[2] *v* **dubbing, dubbed 1** provide (a film) with a new soundtrack, esp. in a different language. **2** provide (a film or tape) with a soundtrack. ♦ *n* **3** style of reggae record production involving exaggeration of instrumental parts, echo, etc.

dubbin *n* thick grease applied to leather to soften and waterproof it.

dubious [**dew**-bee-uss] *adj* feeling or causing doubt. **dubiously** *adv* **dubiety** [dew-**by**-it-ee] *n*

ducal [**duke**-al] *adj* of a duke.

ducat [**duck**-it] *n* former European gold or silver coin.

duchess *n* **1** woman who holds the rank of duke. **2** wife or widow of a duke.

duchy *n, pl* **duchies** territory of a duke or duchess.

duck[1] *n* **1** water bird with short legs, webbed feet, and a broad blunt bill. **2** its flesh, used as food. **3** female of this bird. **4** *Cricket* score of nothing. **duckling** *n* baby duck. **duck-billed platypus** see PLATYPUS.

duck[2] *v* **1** move (the head or body) quickly downwards, to avoid being seen or to dodge a blow. **2** plunge suddenly under water. **3** *Informal* dodge (a duty or responsibility).

duct *n* **1** tube, pipe, or channel through which liquid or gas is conveyed. **2** bodily passage conveying secretions or excretions.

ductile *adj* (of a metal) able to be shaped into sheets or wires.

dud *Informal* ♦ *n* **1** ineffectual person or thing. ♦ *adj* **2** bad or useless, e.g. *dud cheques.*

dude *n US informal* **1** man. **2** *Old-fashioned* dandy. **3** any person.

dudgeon *n* **in high dudgeon** angry, resentful.

due *adj* **1** expected or scheduled to be present or arrive. **2** owed as a debt. **3** fitting, proper. ♦ *n* **4** something that is owed or required. ♦ *pl* **5** charges for membership of a club or organization. ♦ *adv* **6** directly or exactly, e.g. *due south.* **due to** attributable to or caused by.

> The use of *due to* as a compound preposition as in *the performance has been cancelled due to bad weather* was formerly considered incorrect, but is now acceptable.

duel *n* **1** formal fight with deadly weapons between two people, to settle a quarrel. ♦ *v* **duelling, duelled 2** fight in a duel. **duellist** *n*

duenna *n* (esp. in Spain) elderly woman acting as chaperone to a young woman.

duet *n* piece of music for two performers.

duff *adj Chiefly Brit* broken or useless. **duff up** *v Brit informal* beat (someone) severely.

duffel, duffle *n* short for DUFFEL COAT. **duffel bag** cylindrical canvas bag fastened with a drawstring. **duffel coat** wool coat with toggle fastenings, usu. with a hood.

duffer *n Informal* dull or incompetent person.

dug[1] *v* past of DIG.

dug[2] *n* teat or udder.

dugong *n* whalelike mammal of tropical waters.

dugout *n* **1** (at a sports ground) covered bench where managers and substitutes sit. **2** canoe made by hollowing out a log. **3** *Mil* covered excavation to provide shelter.

duke *n* **1** nobleman of the highest rank. **2** prince or ruler of a small principality or duchy. **dukedom** *n*

dulcet [**dull**-sit] *adj* (of a sound) soothing or pleasant.

dulcimer *n* tuned percussion instrument consisting of a set of strings stretched over a sounding board and struck with hammers.

dull *adj* **1** not interesting. **2** (of an ache) not acute. **3** (of weather) not bright or clear. **4** lacking in spirit. **5** not very intelligent. **6** (of a blade) not sharp. ♦ *v* **7** make or become dull. **dullness** *n* **dully** *adv* **dullard** *n* dull or stupid person.

dulse *n* seaweed with large red edible fronds.

duly *adv* **1** in a proper manner. **2** at the proper time.

dumb *adj* **1** lacking the power to speak. **2** silent. **3** *Informal* stupid. **dumbly** *adv* **dumbness** *n* **dumbbell** *n* short bar with a heavy ball or disc at each end, used for physical exercise. **dumbfounded** *adj* speechless with astonishment. **dumb show** meaningful gestures without speech. **dumbwaiter** *n* **1** lift for carrying food etc. between floors. **2** stand for holding food at a dining table.

dumdum *n* soft-nosed bullet that expands on impact and causes serious wounds.

dummy *n, pl* **-mies** **1** figure representing the human form, used for displaying clothes etc. **2** copy of an object, often lacking some essential feature of the original. **3** rubber teat for a baby to suck. **4** *Slang* stupid person. ♦ *adj* **5** imitation, substitute. **dummy run** rehearsal.

dump *v* **1** drop or let fall in a careless manner. **2** *Informal* get rid of (someone or something no longer wanted). **3** dispose of (nuclear waste). **4** market (goods) in bulk and at low prices, esp. abroad. ♦ *n* **5** place where waste materials are left. **6** *Informal* dirty unattractive place. **7** *Mil* place where weapons or supplies are stored. **down in the dumps** *Informal* depressed and miserable.

dumpling *n* **1** small ball of dough cooked and served with stew. **2** round pastry case filled with fruit.

dumpy *adj* **dumpier, dumpiest** short and plump.

dun[1] *adj* brownish-grey.

dun[2] *v* **dunning, dunned** **1** demand payment from (a debtor). ♦ *n* **2** demand for payment.

dunce *n* person who is stupid or slow to learn.

dunderhead *n* slow-witted person.

dune *n* mound or ridge of drifted sand.

dung *n* faeces from animals such as cattle.

dungarees *pl n* trousers with a bib attached.

dungeon *n* underground prison cell.

dunk *v* **1** dip (a biscuit or bread) in a drink or soup before eating it. **2** put (something) in liquid.

dunlin *n* small sandpiper with a brown back.

duo *n, pl* **duos** **1** pair of performers. **2** *Informal* pair of closely connected people.

duodenum [dew-oh-**deen**-um] *n, pl* **-na, -nums** first part of the small intestine, just below the stomach. **duodenal** *adj*

duologue *n* (in drama) conversation between only two speakers.

dupe *v* **1** deceive or cheat. ♦ *n* **2** person who is easily deceived.

duple *adj Music* having two beats in a

bar.

duplex *n* **1** *Chiefly US & Aust* apartment on two floors. **2** *US* semidetached house.

duplicate *adj* **1** copied exactly from an original. ♦ *n* **2** exact copy. ♦ *v* **3** make an exact copy of. **4** do again (something that has already been done). **duplication** *n* **duplicator** *n*

duplicity *n* deceitful behaviour.

durable *adj* long-lasting. **durability** *n* **durable goods, durables** *pl n* goods that require infrequent replacement.

duration *n* length of time that something lasts.

duress *n* compulsion by use of force or threats.

during *prep* throughout or within the limit of (a period of time).

dusk *n* time just before nightfall, when it is almost dark. **dusky** *adj* **duskier, duskiest** **1** dark in colour. **2** shadowy. **duskiness** *n*

dust *n* **1** small dry particles of earth, sand, or dirt. ♦ *v* **2** remove dust from (furniture) by wiping. **3** sprinkle (something) with a powdery substance. **duster** *n* cloth used for dusting. **dusty** *adj* **dustier, dustiest** covered with dust. **dustbin** *n* large container for household rubbish. **dust bowl** dry area in which the surface soil is exposed to wind erosion. **dustcart** *n* lorry for collecting household rubbish. **dust jacket** removable paper cover used to protect a book. **dustman** *n Brit* man whose job is to collect household rubbish. **dustpan** *n* short-handled shovel into which dust is swept from floors. **dustsheet** *n Brit* large cloth cover to protect furniture from dust. **dust-up** *n Informal* fight or argument.

Dutch *adj* **1** of the Netherlands. ♦ *n* **2** language of the Netherlands. **go Dutch** *Informal* share the expenses on an outing. **Dutch auction** auction in which the price is gradually lowered until a buyer is found. **Dutch barn** farm building with a steel frame and a curved roof. **Dutch courage** false courage gained from drinking alcohol. **Dutch elm disease** fungal disease of elm trees.

duty *n, pl* **-ties** **1** work or a task performed as part of one's job. **2** task that a person feels morally bound to do. **3** government tax on imports. **on duty** at work. **dutiable** *adj* (of goods) requiring payment of duty. **dutiful** *adj* doing what is expected. **dutifully** *adv* **duty-bound** *adj* morally obliged. **duty-free** *adj, adv* with exemption from customs or excise duties.

duvet [**doo**-vay] *n* kind of quilt used in bed instead of a top sheet and blankets.

DVD Digital Versatile (or Video) Disk.

dwarf *n, pl* **dwarfs, dwarves** **1** person who is smaller than average. **2** (in folklore) small ugly manlike creature, often possessing magical powers. ♦ *adj* **3** (of an animal or plant) much smaller than the usual size for the species. ♦ *v* **4** cause (someone or something) to seem small by being much larger.

dwell *v* **dwelling, dwelt** *or* **dwelled** live, reside. **dweller** *n* **dwelling** *n* place of residence. **dwell on, upon** *v* think, speak, or write at length about.

dwindle *v* grow less in size, strength, or number.

Dy *Chem* dysprosium.

dye *n* **1** colouring substance. **2** colour produced by dyeing. ♦ *v* **dyeing, dyed** **3** colour (hair or fabric) by applying a dye. **dyer** *n* **dyed-in-the-wool** *adj* uncompromising or unchanging in opinion.

dying *v* present participle of DIE[1].

dyke[1] *n* wall built to prevent flooding.

dyke[2] *n Slang* lesbian.

dynamic *adj* **1** full of energy, ambition, and new ideas. **2** *Physics* of energy or forces that produce motion. **dynamically** *adv* **dynamism** *n* great energy and enthusiasm.

dynamics *n* **1** branch of mechanics concerned with the forces that change or produce the motions of bodies. ♦ *pl* **2** forces that produce change in a system.

dynamite *n* **1** explosive made of nitroglycerine. **2** *Informal* dangerous or exciting person or thing. ♦ *v* **3** blow (something) up with dynamite.

dynamo *n, pl* **-mos** device for converting mechanical energy into electrical energy.

dynasty *n, pl* **-ties** sequence of hereditary rulers. **dynastic** *adj* **dynast** *n* hereditary ruler.

dysentery *n* infection of the intestine causing severe diarrhoea.

dysfunction *n* **1** *Med* disturbance or abnormality in the function of an organ or part. **2** (of a family) failure to show the characteristics accepted as normal. **dysfunctional** *adj*

dyslexia *n* disorder causing impaired ability to read. **dyslexic** *adj*

dysmenorrhoea *n* painful menstruation.

dyspepsia *n* indigestion. **dyspeptic** *adj, n*

dysprosium *n Chem* metallic element of the lanthanide series.

dystopia *n* imaginary place where everything is as bad as it can be.

dystrophy [**diss**-trof-fee] *n* see MUSCULAR DYSTROPHY.

E e

E 1 East(ern). 2 *Slang* ecstasy (the drug).

each *adj, pron* every (one) taken separately.

> The expressions *each other* and *one another* are interchangeable.

eager *adj* showing or feeling great desire, keen. **eagerly** *adv* **eagerness** *n*

eagle *n* 1 large bird of prey with keen eyesight. 2 *Golf* score of two strokes under par for a hole. **eaglet** *n* young eagle.

ear[1] *n* 1 organ of hearing, esp. the external part of it. 2 sensitivity to musical or other sounds. **earache** *n* pain in the ear. **eardrum** *n* thin piece of skin inside the ear which enables one to hear sounds. **earmark** *v* 1 set (something) aside for a specific purpose. ♦ *n* 2 distinguishing mark. **earphone** *n* receiver for a radio etc., held to or put in the ear. **ear-piercing** *adj* deafening. **earplug** *n* piece of soft material placed in the ear to keep out water or noise. **earring** *n* ornament for the lobe of the ear. **earshot** *n* hearing range.

ear[2] *n* head of corn.

earl *n* British nobleman ranking next below a marquess. **earldom** *n*

early *adj, adv* **-lier, -liest** 1 before the expected or usual time. 2 in the first part of a period. 3 in a period far back in time.

earn *v* 1 obtain by work or merit. 2 (of investments etc.) gain (interest). **earnings** *pl n* money earned.

earnest[1] *adj* serious and sincere. **in earnest** seriously. **earnestly** *adv*

earnest[2] *n* part payment given in advance, esp. to confirm a contract.

earth *n* 1 planet that we live on. 2 land, the ground. 3 soil. 4 fox's hole. 5 wire connecting an electrical apparatus with the earth. ♦ *v* 6 connect (a circuit) to earth. **come down to earth** return to reality from a daydream. **earthen** *adj* made of baked clay or earth. **earthenware** *n* pottery made of baked clay. **earthly** *adj* conceivable or possible, e.g. *no earthly reason*. **earthy** *adj* 1 coarse or crude. 2 of or like earth. **earthquake** *n* violent vibration of the earth's surface. **earthwork** *n* fortification made of earth. **earthworm** *n* worm which burrows in the soil.

earwig *n* small insect with a pincer-like tail.

ease *n* 1 freedom from difficulty, discomfort, or worry. 2 rest or leisure, e.g. *at one's ease*. ♦ *v* 3 give bodily or mental ease to. 4 lessen (severity, tension, pain, etc.). 5 move carefully or gradually. **ease off** *v* become less severe.

easel *n* frame to support an artist's canvas or a blackboard.

east *n* 1 (direction towards) the part of the horizon where the sun rises. 2 region lying in this direction. ♦ *adj* 3 to or in the east. 4 (of a wind) from the east. ♦ *adv* 5 in, to, or towards the east. **easterly** *adj* **eastern** *adj* **easterner** *n* person from the east of a country or area. **eastward** *adj, adv* **eastwards** *adv*

Easter *n* Christian spring festival commemorating the Resurrection of Jesus Christ. **Easter egg** chocolate egg given at Easter.

easy *adj* **easier, easiest** 1 not needing much work or effort. 2 free from pain, care, or anxiety. 3 easy-going. **easily** *adv* **easiness** *n* **easy chair** comfortable armchair. **easy-going** *adj* relaxed in attitude, tolerant.

> *Easy* may be used as an adverb in set phrases like *take it easy*.

eat *v* **eating, ate, eaten** 1 take (food) into the mouth and swallow it. 2 have a meal. 3 (foll. by *away* or *up*) destroy. **eatable** *adj* fit or suitable for eating.

eau de Cologne [**oh** de kol-**lone**] *n French* light perfume.

eaves *pl n* overhanging edges of a roof.

eavesdrop *v* **-dropping, -dropped** listen secretly to a private conversation. **eavesdropper** *n* **eavesdropping** *n*

ebb *v* **1** (of tide water) flow back. **2** fall away or decline, e.g. *her anger ebbed away.* ♦ *n* **3** flowing back of the tide. **at a low ebb** in a state of weakness.

ebony *n, pl* **-onies 1** hard black wood. ♦ *adj* **2** deep black.

ebullient *adj* full of enthusiasm or excitement. **ebullience** *n*

EC 1 European Commission. **2** European Community: a former name for the European Union.

eccentric *adj* **1** odd or unconventional. **2** (of circles) not having the same centre. ♦ *n* **3** eccentric person. **eccentrically** *adv* **eccentricity** *n*

ecclesiastic *n* **1** clergyman. ♦ *adj* **2** (also **ecclesiastical**) of the Christian Church or clergy.

ECG electrocardiogram.

echelon [**esh**-a-lon] *n* **1** level of power or responsibility. **2** *Mil* formation in which units follow one another but are spaced out sideways to allow each a line of fire ahead.

echidna [ik-**kid**-na] *n, pl* **-s, -nae** [-nee] mammal with a protective layer of spines, found in Australia and New Guinea (also **spiny anteater**).

echo *n, pl* **-oes 1** repetition of sounds by reflection of sound waves off a surface. **2** close imitation. ♦ *v* **-oing, -oed 3** repeat or be repeated as an echo. **4** imitate (what someone else has said). **echo sounder** sonar.

éclair *n* finger-shaped pastry filled with cream and covered with chocolate.

éclat [ake-**lah**] *n* **1** brilliant success. **2** splendour.

eclectic *adj* selecting from various styles, ideas, or sources. **eclecticism** *n*

eclipse *n* **1** temporary obscuring of one star or planet by another. ♦ *v* **2** surpass or outclass. **ecliptic** *n* apparent path of the sun.

eco- *combining form* ecology or ecological, e.g. *ecotourism.*

ecological *adj* **1** of ecology. **2** intended to protect the environment, e.g. *an ecological approach to agriculture.* **ecologically** *adv* **ecology** *n* study of the relationships between living things and their environment. **ecologist** *n*

economy *n, pl* **-mies 1** system of interrelationship of money, industry, and employment in a country. **2** careful use of money or resources to avoid waste. **economic** *adj* **1** of economics. **2** profitable. **3** *Informal* inexpensive or cheap. **economics** *n* **1** social science concerned with the production and consumption of goods and services. ♦ *pl* **2** financial aspects. **economical** *adj* not wasteful, thrifty. **economically** *adv* **economist** *n* specialist in economics. **economize** *v* reduce expense or waste.

ecosystem *n* system involving interactions between a community and its environment.

ecru *adj* pale creamy-brown.

ecstasy *n* **1** state of intense delight. **2** *Slang* powerful drug that can produce hallucinations. **ecstatic** *adj* **ecstatically** *adv*

ECT electroconvulsive therapy.

ectoplasm *n Spiritualism* substance that supposedly is emitted from the body of a medium during a trance.

ECU European Currency Unit.

ecumenical *adj* of the Christian Church throughout the world, esp. with regard to its unity.

eczema [**ek**-sim-a] *n* skin disease causing intense itching.

ed. 1 edition. **2** editor.

Edam *n* round Dutch cheese with a red waxy cover.

eddy *n, pl* **eddies 1** circular movement of air, water, etc. ♦ *v* **eddying, eddied 2** move with a circular motion.

edelweiss [**ade**-el-vice] *n* alpine plant with white flowers.

Eden *n* **1** *Bible* garden in which Adam and Eve were placed at the Creation. **2** place of delight or contentment.

edge *n* **1** border or line where something ends or begins. **2** cutting side of a blade. **3** sharpness of tone. ♦ *v* **4** provide an edge or border for. **5** push (one's way) gradually. **have the edge on** have an advantage over. **on edge** nervous or irritable. **edgeways** *adv* with the edge forwards or uppermost. **edging** *n* anything placed along an edge to finish it. **edgy** *adj* nervous or irritable.

edible *adj* fit to be eaten. **edibility** *n*

edict [**ee**-dikt] *n* order issued by an authority.

edifice [**ed**-if-iss] *n* large building.

edify [**ed**-if-fie] *v* **-fying, -fied** improve morally by instruction. **edification** *n*

edit *v* prepare (a book, film, etc.) for publication or broadcast. **edition** *n* **1** number of copies of a new publication printed at one time. **2** single television or radio programme which forms part of a series. **editor** *n* **1** person who edits. **2** person in charge of one section of a newspaper or magazine. **editorial** *n* **1** newspaper article stating the opinion of the editor. ♦ *adj* **2** of editing or editors.

educate *v* **1** teach. **2** provide schooling for. **education** *n* **educational** *adj* **educationally** *adv* **educationalist** *n* expert in the theory of education. **educative** *adj* educating.

Edwardian *adj* of the reign of King Edward VII of Great Britain and Ireland (1901–10).

EEG electroencephalogram.

eel *n* snakelike fish.

eerie *adj* **eerier, eeriest** uncannily frightening or disturbing. **eerily** *adv*

efface *v* **1** remove by rubbing. **2** make (oneself) inconspicuous. **effacement** *n*

effect *n* **1** change or result caused by someone or something. **2** condition of being operative, e.g. *the law comes into effect next month.* **3** overall impression. ♦ *pl* **4** personal belongings. **5** lighting, sounds, etc. to accompany a film or a broadcast. ♦ *v* **6** cause to happen, accomplish. **effective** *adj* **1** producing a desired result. **2** operative. **3** impressive. **effectively** *adv* **effectual** *adj* producing the intended result. **effectually** *adv*

> Note the difference between *effect* meaning 'accomplish' and *affect* meaning 'influence'.

effeminate *adj* (of a man) displaying characteristics thought to be typical of a woman. **effeminacy** *n*

effervescent *adj* **1** (of a liquid) giving off bubbles of gas. **2** (of a person) lively and enthusiastic. **effervescence** *n*

effete [if-**feet**] *adj* powerless, feeble.

efficacious *adj* producing the intended result. **efficacy** *n*

efficient *adj* functioning effectively with little waste of effort. **efficiently** *adv* **efficiency** *n*

effigy [**ef**-fij-ee] *n, pl* **-gies** image or likeness of a person.

efflorescence *n* flowering.

effluent *n* liquid discharged as waste.

effluvium *n, pl* **-via** unpleasant smell, as of decaying matter or gaseous waste.

effort *n* **1** physical or mental exertion. **2** attempt. **effortless** *adj* **effortlessly** *adv*

effrontery *n* brazen impudence.

effusion *n* **1** unrestrained outburst. **2** sudden pouring out of light or liquid. **effusive** *adj* openly emotional, demonstrative. **effusively** *adv* **effusiveness** *n*

EFTA European Free Trade Association.

EFTPOS electronic funds transfer at point of sale.

e.g. for example.

egalitarian *adj* **1** upholding the equality of all people. ♦ *n* **2** person who holds egalitarian beliefs. **egalitarianism** *n*

egg[1] *n* **1** oval or round object laid by the females of birds and other creatures, containing a developing embryo. **2** hen's egg used as food. **3** (also **egg cell**) ovum. **egghead** *n Informal* intellectual person. **eggplant** *n US, Canadian, & Aust* aubergine. **eggshell** *n* hard covering round the egg of a bird or animal. **egg timer** *n* device used for measuring the time needed to boil an egg.

egg[2] *v* **egg on** encourage or incite, esp. to do wrong.

ego *n, pl* **egos** **1** the conscious mind of an individual. **2** self-esteem. **egoism, egotism** *n* **1** excessive concern for one's own interests. **2** excessively high opinion of oneself. **egotist, egoist** *n* **egotistic, egoistic** *adj* **egocentric** *adj* self-centred.

egregious [ig-**greej**-uss] *adj* outstandingly bad.

egress [**ee**-gress] *n* **1** departure. **2** way out.

egret [**ee**-grit] *n* lesser white heron.

Egyptian *adj* **1** relating to Egypt. ♦ *n* **2** person from Egypt.

Egyptology *n* study of the culture of ancient Egypt.

eh *interj* exclamation of surprise or inquiry, or to seek confirmation of a statement or question.

eider *n* Arctic duck. **eiderdown** *n* quilt (orig. stuffed with eider feathers).

eight *adj, n* **1** one more than seven. ♦ *n* **2** eight-oared boat. **3** its crew. **eighth** *adj, n* (of) number eight in a series. **eighteen** *adj, n* eight and ten. **eighteenth** *adj, n* **eighty** *adj, n* eight times ten. **eightieth** *adj, n*

einsteinium *n Chem* radioactive element artificially produced from plutonium.

Eire *n* Ireland or the Republic of Ireland.

eisteddfod [ice-**sted**-fod] *n* Welsh festival with competitions in music and other performing arts.

either *adj, pron* **1** one or the other (of two). **2** each of two. ♦ *conj* **3** used preceding two or more possibilities joined by *or*. ♦ *adv* **4** likewise, e.g. *I don't eat meat and he doesn't either.*

> When *either* is followed by a plural noun, it is acceptable to make the verb plural too: *Either of these books are useful.*

ejaculate *v* **1** eject (semen). **2** utter abruptly. **ejaculation** *n*

eject *v* force out, expel. **ejection** *n* **ejector** *n* **ejector seat** *n* seat in an aircraft that ejects the occupant in an emergency.

eke out *v* **1** make (a supply) last by frugal use. **2** make (a living) with difficulty.

elaborate *adj* **1** with a lot of fine detail. ♦ *v* **2** expand upon. **elaborately** *adv* **elaboration** *n*

élan [ale-**an**] *n* style and vigour.

eland [**eel**-and] *n* large antelope of southern Africa.

elapse *v* (of time) pass by.

elastic *adj* **1** resuming normal shape after distortion. **2** adapting easily to change. ♦ *n* **3** tape or fabric containing interwoven strands of flexible rubber. **elasticity** *n*

elated *v* extremely happy and excited. **elatedly** *adv* **elation** *n*

elbow *n* **1** joint between the upper arm and the forearm. **2** part of a garment that covers this. ♦ *v* **3** shove or strike with the elbow. **elbow grease** vigorous physical labour. **elbow room** sufficient room to move freely.

elder[1] *adj* **1** older. ♦ *n* **2** older person. **3** (in certain Protestant Churches) lay officer. **elderly** *adj* (fairly) old. **eldest** *adj* oldest.

> *Elder* (*eldest*) is used for age comparison in families, *older* for other age comparisons.

elder[2] *n* small tree with white flowers and black berries.

El Dorado [el dor-**rah**-doe] *n* fictitious country rich in gold.

eldritch *adj Scot* weird, uncanny.

elect *v* **1** choose by voting. **2** decide (to do something). ♦ *adj* **3** appointed but not yet in office, e.g. *president elect.* **election** *n* **1** choosing of representatives by voting. **2** act of choosing. **electioneering** *n* active participation in a political campaign. **elective** *adj* **1** chosen by election. **2** optional. **elector** *n* someone who has the right to vote in an election. **electoral** *adj* **electorate** *n* people who have the right to vote.

electricity *n* **1** form of energy associated with stationary or moving electrons or other charged particles. **2** electric current or charge. **electric** *adj* **1** produced by, transmitting, or powered by electricity. **2** exciting or tense. **electrical** *adj* using or concerning electricity. **electrician** *n* person trained to install and repair electrical equipment. **electrics** *pl n* electric appliances. **electric chair** *US* chair in which criminals who have been sentenced to death are electrocuted. **electric shock** effect of an electric current passing through the body.

> Note that *electric* is an adjective. Avoid its use as a noun: *The electricity* (not *the electric) has failed.*

electrify *v* **-fying, -fied 1** adapt for operation by electric power. **2** charge with electricity. **3** startle or excite intensely. **electrification** *n*

electro- *combining form* operated by or caused by electricity.

electrocardiograph *n* instrument for recording the electrical activity of the heart. **electrocardiogram** *n* tracing produced by this.

electroconvulsive therapy *n* treatment of severe mental disorders by passing an electric current through the brain.

electrocute *v* kill or injure by electricity. **electrocution** *n*

electrode *n* conductor through which an electric current enters or leaves a battery, vacuum tube, etc.

electrodynamics *n* branch of physics concerned with the interactions between electrical and mechanical forces.

electroencephalograph [ill-lek-tro-en-**sef**-a-loh-graf] *n* instrument for recording the electrical activity of the brain. **electroencephalogram** *n* tracing produced by this.

electrolysis [ill-lek-**troll**-iss-iss] *n* **1** conduction of electricity by an electrolyte, esp. to induce chemical change. **2** destruction of living tissue such as hair roots by an electric current.

electrolyte *n* solution or molten substance that conducts electricity. **electrolytic** *adj*

electromagnet *n* magnet containing a coil of wire through which an electric current is passed. **electromagnetic** *adj* **electromagnetism** *n*

electron *n* elementary particle in all atoms that has a negative electrical charge. **electron microscope** microscope that uses electrons, rather than light, to produce a magnified image. **electronvolt** *n* unit of energy used in nuclear physics.

electronic *adj* **1** (of a device) dependent on the action of electrons. **2** (of a process) using electronic devices. **electronic mail** see E-MAIL. **electronic publishing** publication of information on discs etc., so that it can be accessed by computer. **electronics** *n* technology concerned with the development of electronic devices and circuits.

electroplate *v* coat with silver etc. by electrolysis.

elegant *adj* **1** pleasing or graceful in dress, style, or design. **2** cleverly simple and clear, e.g. *an elegant summary.* **elegance** *n* **elegantly** *adv*

elegy [**el**-lij-ee] *n, pl* **-egies** mournful poem, esp. a lament for the dead. **elegiac** *adj* mournful or plaintive.

element *n* **1** component part. **2** substance which cannot be separated into other substances by ordinary chemical techniques. **3** section of people within a larger group, e.g. *the rowdy element.* **4** heating wire in an electric kettle, stove, etc. ♦ *pl* **5** basic principles of something. **6** weather conditions, esp. wind, rain, and cold. **in one's element** in a situation where one is happiest. **elemental** *adj* of primitive natural forces or passions. **elementary** *adj* simple and straightforward. **elementary particle** entity that is less complex than an atom.

elephant *n* huge four-footed thick-skinned animal with ivory tusks and a long trunk. **elephantine** *adj* unwieldy, clumsy. **elephantiasis** [el-lee-fan-**tie**-a-siss] *n* disease with hardening of the skin and enlargement of the legs etc.

elevate *v* **1** raise in rank or status. **2** lift up. **elevated** *adj* **1** higher than normal, e.g. *elevated cholesterol levels.* **2** (of ideas or pursuits) dignified or of a high rank. **elevation** *n* **1** raising. **2** height above sea level. **3** scale drawing of one side of a building. **elevator** *n Aust, US & Canadian* lift for carrying people.

eleven *adj, n* **1** one more than ten. ♦ *n* **2** *Sport* team of eleven people. **eleventh** *adj, n* (of) number eleven in a series. **elevenses** *n Informal* mid-morning snack. **eleventh hour** the last moment.

elf *n, pl* **elves** (in folklore) small mischievous fairy. **elfin** *adj* small and delicate.

elicit *v* **1** bring about (a response or reaction), e.g. *her remarks elicited a sharp retort.* **2** find out (information) by careful questioning.

elide *v* omit (a vowel or syllable) from a spoken word. **elision** *n*

eligible *adj* **1** meeting the requirements or qualifications needed. **2** desirable as a spouse. **eligibility** *n*

eliminate *v* **1** get rid of. **2** remove (a team or competitor) from a contest, esp. following a defeat. **elimination** *n*

elision *n* see ELIDE.

elite [ill-**eet**] *n* most powerful, rich, or gifted members of a group. **elitism** *n* belief that society should be governed by a small group of superior people. **elitist** *n, adj*

elixir [ill-**ix**-er] *n* imaginary liquid that can prolong life or turn base metals into gold.

Elizabethan *adj* of the reign of Elizabeth I of England (1558–1603).

elk *n* large deer of N Europe and Asia.

ellipse *n* oval shape. **elliptical** *adj* **1** oval-shaped. **2** (of speech or writing) obscure or ambiguous.

ellipsis [ill-**lip**-siss] *n, pl* **-ses** omission of letters or words in a sentence.

elm *n* tree with serrated leaves.

elocution *n* art of speaking clearly in public. **elocutionist** *n*

elongate [**eel**-long-gate] *v* make or become longer. **elongation** *n*

elope *v* (of two people) run away secretly to get married. **elopement** *n*

eloquence *n* fluent powerful use of language. **eloquent** *adj* **eloquently** *adv*

else *adv* **1** in addition or more, e.g. *what else can I do?* **2** other or different, e.g. *it was unlike anything else that had happened.* **elsewhere** *adv* in or to another place.

elucidate *v* make (something difficult) clear. **elucidation** *n*

elude *v* **1** escape from by cleverness or quickness. **2** baffle. **elusive** *adj* difficult to catch or remember.

elver *n* young eel.

elves *n* plural of ELF.

Elysium [ill-**liz**-zee-um] *n* **1** *Greek myth* (also **Elysian fields**) dwelling place of the blessed after death. **2** state or place of perfect bliss.

emaciated [im-**mace**-ee-ate-id] *adj* abnormally thin. **emaciation** *n*

e-mail *n* **1** (also **electronic mail**) sending of messages between computer terminals. ♦ *v* **2** communicate in this way.

emanate [**em**-a-nate] *v* issue, proceed from a source. **emanation** *n*

emancipate *v* free from social, political, or legal restraints. **emancipation** *n*

emasculate *v* deprive of power. **emasculation** *n*

embalm *v* preserve (a corpse) from decay by the use of chemicals etc.

embankment *n* man-made ridge that carries a road or railway or holds back water.

embargo *n, pl* **-goes 1** order by a government prohibiting trade with a country. ♦ *v* **-going, -goed 2** put an embargo on.

embark *v* **1** board a ship or aircraft. **2** (foll. by *on*) begin (a new project). **embarkation** *n*

embarrass *v* cause to feel self-conscious or ashamed. **embarrassed** *adj* **embarrassing** *adj* **embarrassment** *n*

embassy *n, pl* **-sies** **1** offices or official residence of an ambassador. **2** ambassador and his staff.

embattled *adj* having a lot of difficulties.

embed *v* **-bedding, -bedded** fix firmly in something solid.

embellish *v* **1** decorate. **2** embroider (a story). **embellishment** *n*

ember *n* glowing piece of wood or coal in a dying fire.

embezzle *v* steal money that has been entrusted to one. **embezzlement** *n* **embezzler** *n*

embittered *adj* feeling anger as a result of misfortune. **embitterment** *n*

emblazon [im-**blaze**-on] *v* **1** decorate with bright colours. **2** proclaim or publicize.

emblem *n* object or design that symbolizes a quality, type, or group. **emblematic** *adj*

embody *v* **-bodying, -bodied** **1** be an example or expression of. **2** comprise, include. **embodiment** *n*

embolden *v* encourage (someone).

embolism *n* blocking of a blood vessel by a blood clot or air bubble. **embolus** *n, pl* **-li** material, such as a blood clot, that blocks a blood vessel.

embossed *adj* (of a design or pattern) standing out from a surface.

embrace *v* **1** clasp in the arms, hug. **2** accept (an idea) eagerly. **3** comprise. ♦ *n* **4** act of embracing.

embrasure *n* **1** door or window having splayed sides so that the opening is larger on the inside. **2** opening like this in a fortified wall, for shooting through.

embrocation *n* lotion for rubbing into the skin to relieve pain.

embroider *v* **1** decorate with needlework. **2** make (a story) more interesting with fictitious detail. **embroidery** *n*

embroil *v* involve (a person) in problems. **embroilment** *n*

embryo [**em**-bree-oh] *n, pl* **-bryos** **1** unborn creature in the early stages of development. **2** something at an undeveloped stage. **embryonic** *adj* at an early stage. **embryology** *n* scientific study of embryos.

emend *v* remove errors from. **emendation** *n*

emerald *n* **1** bright green precious stone. ♦ *adj* **2** bright green.

emerge *v* **1** come into view. **2** (foll. by *from*) come out of. **3** become known. **emergence** *n* **emergent** *adj*

emergency *n, pl* **-cies** sudden unforeseen occurrence needing immediate action.

emeritus [im-**mer**-rit-uss] *adj* retired, but retaining an honorary title, e.g. *emeritus professor.*

emery *n* hard mineral used for smoothing and polishing. **emery board** cardboard strip coated with crushed emery, for filing the nails.

emetic [im-**met**-ik] *n* **1** substance that causes vomiting. ♦ *adj* **2** causing vomiting.

EMF electromotive force.

emigrate *v* go and settle in another country. **emigrant** *n* **emigration** *n*

émigré [**em**-mig-gray] *n* someone who has left his native country for political reasons.

eminent *adj* distinguished, well-known. **eminently** *adv* **eminence** *n* **1** position of superiority or fame. **2** (**E-**) title of a cardinal.

emir [em-**meer**] *n* Muslim ruler. **emirate** *n* his country.

emissary *n, pl* **-saries** agent sent on a mission by a government.

emit *v* **emitting, emitted** **1** give out (heat, light, or a smell). **2** utter. **emission** *n*

emollient *adj* **1** softening, soothing. ♦ *n* **2** substance which softens or soothes the skin.

emolument *n Formal* fees or wages from employment.

emotion *n* strong feeling. **emotional** *adj* readily affected by or appealing to the emotions. **emotionally** *adv* **emotive** *adj* tending to arouse emotion.

empathy *n* ability to understand someone else's feelings as if they were one's own. **empathize** *v*

emperor *n* ruler of an empire. **empress** *n fem*

emphasis *n, pl* **-ses** **1** special importance or significance. **2** stress on a word or phrase in speech. **emphasize** *v* **emphatic** *adj* showing emphasis. **emphatically** *adv*

emphysema [em-fiss-**see**-ma] *n* condition in which the air sacs of the lungs are grossly enlarged, causing breathlessness.

empire *n* **1** group of territories under the rule of one state or person. **2** large organization that is directed by one person or group.

empirical *adj* relying on experiment or experience, not on theory. **empirically** *adv* **empiricism** *n* doctrine that all knowledge derives from experience. **empiricist** *n*

emplacement *n* prepared position for a gun.

employ *v* **1** hire (a person). **2** provide work or occupation for. **3** use. ♦ *n* **4** **in the employ of** doing regular paid work for. **employee** *n* **employer** *n* **employment** *n* **1** state of being employed. **2** work done by a person to earn money.

emporium *n, pl* **-riums, -ria** *Old-fashioned* large general shop.

empower *v* enable, authorize.

empress *n* see EMPEROR.

empty *adj* **-tier, -tiest** **1** containing nothing. **2** unoccupied. **3** without purpose or value. **4** (of words) insincere. ♦ *v* **-tying, -tied** **5** make or become empty. **empties** *pl n* empty boxes, bottles, etc. **emptiness** *n*

empyrean [em-pie-**ree**-an] *n Poetic* heavens or sky.

EMS European Monetary System.

emu *n* large Australian flightless bird with long legs.

EMU European Monetary Union.

emulate *v* attempt to equal or surpass by imitating. **emulation** *n*

emulsion *n* **1** light-sensitive coating on photographic film. **2** type of water-based paint. ♦ *v* **3** paint with emulsion paint. **emulsify** *v* **-fying, -fied** (of two liquids) join together or join (two liquids) together. **emulsifier** *n*

enable *v* provide (a person) with the means, opportunity, or authority (to do something). **enabling act** legislative act giving certain powers to a person or organization.

enact *v* **1** establish by law. **2** perform (a story or play) by acting. **enactment** *n*

enamel *n* **1** glasslike coating applied to metal etc. to preserve the surface. **2** hard white coating on a tooth. ♦ *v* **-elling, -elled** **3** cover with enamel.

enamoured *adj* inspired with love.

en bloc *adv French* as a whole, all together.

encamp *v* set up in a camp. **encampment** *n*

encapsulate *v* **1** summarize. **2** enclose as in a capsule.

encase *v* enclose or cover completely. **encased** *adj*

encephalitis [en-sef-a-**lite**-iss] *n* inflammation of the brain.

encephalogram *n* short for ELECTROENCEPHALOGRAM.

enchant *v* delight and fascinate. **enchanting** *adj* **enchantment** *n* **enchanter** *n* **enchantress** *n fem*

enchilada *n* Mexican dish of a tortilla filled with meat, served with chilli sauce.

encircle *v* form a circle around. **encirclement** *n*

enclave *n* part of a country entirely surrounded by foreign territory.

enclose *v* **1** surround completely. **2** include along with something else. **enclosure** *n* **enclosed order** Christian religious order whose members do not go into the outside world.

encomium *n, pl* **-miums, -mia** formal expression of praise.

encompass *v* **1** surround. **2** include comprehensively.

encore *interj* **1** again, once more. ♦ *n* **2** extra performance due to enthusiastic demand.

encounter *v* **1** meet unexpectedly. **2** be faced with. ♦ *n* **3** unexpected meeting. **4** game or battle.

encourage *v* **1** inspire with confidence. **2** spur on. **encouraging** *adj* **encouragement** *n*

encroach *v* intrude gradually on a person's rights or land. **encroachment** *n*

encrust *v* cover with a layer of something.

encumber *v* hinder or impede. **encumbrance** *n* something that impedes or is burdensome.

encyclical [en-**sik**-lik-kl] *n* letter sent by the Pope to all bishops.

encyclopedia, encyclopaedia *n* book or set of books containing facts about many subjects, usu. in alphabetical order. **encyclopedic, encyclopaedic** *adj* comprehensive.

end *n* **1** furthest point or part. **2** limit. **3** last part of something. **4** fragment. **5** death or destruction. **6** purpose. **7** *Sport* either of the two defended areas of a playing field. ♦ *v* **8** bring or come to a finish. **make ends meet** have just enough money for one's needs. **ending** *n* **endless** *adj* **endways** *adv* having the end forwards or upwards. **end product** final result of a process, esp. in manufacturing.

endanger *v* put in danger.

endear *v* cause to be liked. **endearing** *adj* **endearment** *n* affectionate word or phrase.

endeavour *v* **1** try. ♦ *n* **2** effort.

endemic *adj* present within a localized area or peculiar to a particular group of people.

endive *n* curly-leaved plant used in salads.

endocardium *n* lining membrane of the heart.

endocrine *adj* relating to the glands which secrete hormones directly into the bloodstream.

endogenous [en-**dodge**-in-uss] *adj* originating from within.

endorphin *n* chemical occurring in the brain, which has a similar effect to morphine.

endorse *v* **1** give approval to. **2** sign the back of (a cheque). **3** record a conviction on (a driving licence). **endorsement** *n*

endow *v* provide permanent income for. **endowed with** provided with. **endowment** *n*

endure *v* **1** bear (hardship) patiently. **2** last for a long time. **endurable** *adj* **endurance** *n* act or power of enduring. **enduring** *adj* long-lasting.

enema [**en**-im-a] *n* medicine injected into the rectum to empty the bowels.

enemy *n, pl* **-mies** hostile person or nation, opponent.

energy *n, pl* **-gies** **1** capacity for intense activity. **2** capacity to do work and overcome resistance. **3** source of power, such as electricity. **energetic** *adj* **energetically** *adv* **energize** *v* give vigour to.

enervate *v* deprive of strength or vitality. **enervated** *adj* **enervation** *n*

enfant terrible [**on**-fon ter-**reeb**-la] *n, pl* **enfants terribles** *French* clever but unconventional or indiscreet person.

enfeeble *v* weaken. **enfeebled** *adj* **enfeeblement** *n*

enfold *v* **1** cover by wrapping something around. **2** embrace.

enforce *v* **1** impose obedience (to a law etc.). **2** impose (a condition). **enforceable** *adj* **enforcement** *n*

enfranchise *v* grant (a person) the right to vote. **enfranchised** *adj* **enfranchisement** *n*

engage *v* **1** take part, participate. **2** involve (a person or his or her attention) intensely. **3** employ (a person). **4** begin a battle with. **5** bring (a mechanism) into operation. **engaged** *adj* **1** pledged to be married. **2** in use. **engagement** *n* **engaging** *adj* charming.

engender *v* produce, cause to occur.

engine *n* **1** any machine which converts energy into mechanical work. **2** railway locomotive.

engineer *n* **1** person trained in any branch of engineering. ♦ *v* **2** plan in a clever manner. **3** design or construct as

an engineer.
engineering *n* profession of applying scientific principles to the design and construction of engines, cars, buildings, or machines.
English *n* **1** official language of Britain, the US, most of the Commonwealth, and certain other countries. ♦ *adj* **2** relating to England. **the English** the people of England.
engorge *v Pathology* clog with blood. **engorgement** *n*
engrave *v* **1** carve (a design) onto a hard surface. **2** fix deeply in the mind. **engraver** *n* **engraving** *n* print made from an engraved plate.
engross [en-**groce**] *v* occupy the attention of (a person) completely. **engrossing** *adj*
engulf *v* cover or surround completely.
enhance *v* increase in quality, value, or attractiveness. **enhancement** *n*
enigma *n* puzzling thing or person. **enigmatic** *adj* **enigmatically** *adv*
enjoin *v* order (someone) to do something.
enjoy *v* **1** take joy in. **2** have the benefit of. **3** experience. **enjoyable** *adj* **enjoyment** *n*
enlarge *v* **1** make or grow larger. **2** (foll. by *on*) speak or write about in greater detail. **enlargement** *n*
enlighten *v* give information to. **enlightened** *adj* **1** guided by rational thought. **2** tolerant and unprejudiced. **enlightenment** *n*
enlist *v* **1** enter the armed forces. **2** obtain the support of. **enlistment** *n*
enliven *v* make lively or cheerful.
en masse *adv French* in a group, all together.
enmeshed *adj* deeply involved, e.g. *enmeshed in turmoil.*
enmity *n, pl* **-ties** ill will, hatred.
ennoble *v* make noble, elevate.
ennui [on-**nwee**] *n* boredom, dissatisfaction.
enormous *adj* very big, vast. **enormously** *adv* **enormity** *n, pl* **-ties** **1** great wickedness. **2** gross offence. **3** *Informal* great size.
enough *adj* **1** as much or as many as necessary. ♦ *n* **2** sufficient quantity. ♦ *adv* **3** sufficiently. **4** fairly or quite, e.g. *that's a common enough experience.*
en passant [**on pass**-on] *adv French* in passing, by the way.
enquire *v* same as INQUIRE. **enquiry** *n*
enraptured *adj* filled with delight and fascination.
enrich *v* **1** improve in quality. **2** make wealthy or wealthier. **enriched** *adj* **enrichment** *n*
enrol *v* **-rolling, -rolled** (cause to) become a member. **enrolment** *n*
en route *adv French* on the way.
ensconce *v* settle firmly or comfortably.
ensemble [on-**som**-bl] *n* **1** all the parts of something taken together. **2** complete outfit of clothes. **3** company of actors or musicians. **4** *Music* group of musicians playing together.
enshrine *v* cherish or treasure.
enshroud *v* cover or hide as with a shroud.
ensign *n* **1** naval flag. **2** banner. **3** *US* naval officer.
enslave *v* make a slave of (someone). **enslavement** *n*
ensnare *v* catch in or as if in a snare.
ensue *v* come next, result. **ensuing** *adj*
en suite *adv French* connected to a bedroom and entered directly from it.
ensure *v* **1** make certain or sure. **2** make safe or protect.
ENT *Med* ear, nose, and throat.
entablature *n Archit* part of a classical temple above the columns, with an architrave, frieze, and cornice.
entail *v* **1** bring about or impose inevitably. **2** *Law* restrict (ownership of property) to designated heirs.
entangle *v* catch or involve in or as if in a tangle. **entanglement** *n*
entente [on-**tont**] *n* friendly understanding between nations.
enter *v* **1** come or go in. **2** join. **3** become involved in, take part in. **4** record

(an item) in a journal etc. **5** begin. **entrance** *n* **1** way into a place. **2** act of entering. **3** right of entering. **entrant** *n* person who enters a university, contest, etc. **entry** *n, pl* **-tries 1** entrance. **2** entering. **3** item entered in a journal etc.

enteric [en-**ter**-ik] *adj* intestinal. **enteritis** [en-ter-**rite**-iss] *n* inflammation of the intestine, causing diarrhoea.

enterprise *n* **1** company or firm. **2** bold or difficult undertaking. **3** boldness and energy. **enterprising** *adj* full of boldness and initiative.

entertain *v* **1** amuse. **2** receive as a guest. **3** consider (an idea). **entertainer** *n* **entertaining** *adj* **entertainment** *n*

enthral [en-**thrawl**] *v* **-thralling, -thralled** hold the attention of. **enthralling** *adj*

enthrone *v* **1** place (someone) on a throne. **2** praise or honour (something). **enthronement** *n*

enthusiasm *n* ardent interest, eagerness. **enthuse** *v* (cause to) show enthusiasm. **enthusiast** *n* ardent supporter of something. **enthusiastic** *adj* **enthusiastically** *adv*

entice *v* attract by exciting hope or desire, tempt. **enticing** *adj* **enticement** *n*

entire *adj* including every detail, part, or aspect of something. **entirely** *adv* **entirety** *n*

entitle *v* **1** give a right to. **2** give a title to. **entitlement** *n*

entity *n, pl* **-ties** separate distinct thing.

entomb *v* **1** place (a corpse) in a tomb. **2** serve as a tomb for. **entombment** *n*

entomology *n* study of insects. **entomological** *adj* **entomologist** *n*

entourage [**on**-toor-ahzh] *n* group of people who assist an important person.

entozoon [en-toe-**zoe**-on] *n, pl* **-zoa** [-**zoe**-a] internal parasite. **entozoic** *adj*

entr'acte [on-**tract**] *n* interval between acts of a play etc.

entrails *pl n* **1** intestines. **2** innermost parts of something.

entrance[1] *n* see ENTER.

entrance[2] *v* **1** delight. **2** put into a trance. **entrancing** *adj*

entrap *v* **1** trick into difficulty etc. **2** catch in a trap, or catch as if in a trap. **entrapment** *n*

entreat *v* ask earnestly. **entreaty** *n, pl* **-ties** earnest request.

entrecôte [**on**-tra-coat] *n* beefsteak cut from between the ribs.

entrée [**on**-tray] *n* **1** dish served before a main course. **2** main course. **3** right of admission.

entrench *v* **1** establish firmly. **2** establish in a fortified position with trenches. **entrenched** *adj* **entrenchment** *n*

entrepreneur *n* business person who attempts to make a profit by risk and initiative.

entropy [**en**-trop-ee] *n* **1** lack of organization. **2** *Physics* unavailability of the heat energy of a system for mechanical work.

entrust *v* put into the care or protection of.

entwine *v* twist together or around.

E number *n* any of a series of numbers with the prefix E indicating a specific food additive recognized by the EU.

enumerate *v* name one by one. **enumeration** *n*

enunciate *v* **1** pronounce clearly. **2** state precisely or formally. **enunciation** *n*

enuresis [en-yoo-**reece**-iss] *n* involuntary discharge of urine, esp. during sleep. **enuretic** *adj*

envelop *v* **enveloping, enveloped** wrap up, enclose. **envelopment** *n*

envelope *n* folded gummed paper cover for a letter.

environment [en-**vire**-on-ment] *n* **1** external conditions and surroundings in which people, animals, or plants live. **2** natural world of land, sea, air, plants, and animals. **environmental** *adj* **environmentalist** *n* person concerned with the protection of the natural environment.

> Note the 'n' before the 'm' in the spelling of *environment*.

environs *pl n* surrounding area, esp. of a town.

envisage *v* conceive of as a possibility.

envoy *n* **1** messenger. **2** diplomat ranking below an ambassador.

envy *n* **1** feeling of discontent aroused by another's good fortune. ♦ *v* **-vying, -vied 2** grudge (another's good fortune, success, or qualities). **enviable** *adj* arousing envy, fortunate. **envious** *adj* full of envy.

enzyme *n* any of a group of complex proteins that act as catalysts in specific biochemical reactions.

Eolithic *adj* of the early part of the Stone Age.

epaulette *n* shoulder ornament on a uniform.

ephedrine [**eff**-fid-dreen] *n* alkaloid used for treatment of asthma and hay fever.

ephemeral *adj* short-lived.

epic *n* **1** long poem, book, or film about heroic events or actions. ♦ *adj* **2** very impressive or ambitious.

epicene *adj* **1** common to both sexes. **2** effeminate.

epicentre *n* point on the earth's surface immediately above the origin of an earthquake.

epicure *n* person who enjoys good food and drink. **epicurism** *n* **epicurean** *adj* **1** devoted to sensual pleasures, esp. food and drink. ♦ *n* **2** epicure. **epicureanism** *n*

epidemic *n* **1** widespread occurrence of a disease. **2** rapid spread of something.

epidermis *n* outer layer of the skin.

epidural [ep-pid-**dure**-al] *adj, n* (of) spinal anaesthetic injected to relieve pain during childbirth.

epiglottis *n* thin flap that covers the opening of the larynx during swallowing.

epigram *n* short witty remark or poem. **epigrammatic** *adj*

epigraph *n* **1** quotation at the start of a book. **2** inscription.

epilepsy *n* disorder of the nervous system causing loss of consciousness and sometimes convulsions. **epileptic** *adj* **1** of or having epilepsy. ♦ *n* **2** person who has epilepsy.

epilogue *n* short speech or poem at the end of a literary work, esp. a play.

Epiphany *n* Christian festival held on January 6 commemorating the manifestation of Christ to the Magi.

episcopal [ip-**piss**-kop-al] *adj* of or governed by bishops. **episcopalian** *adj* **1** advocating Church government by bishops. ♦ *n* **2** advocate of such Church government.

episode *n* **1** incident in a series of incidents. **2** section of a serialized book, television programme, etc. **episodic** *adj* occurring at irregular intervals.

epistemology [ip-iss-stem-**ol**-a-jee] *n* study of the source, nature, and limitations of knowledge. **epistemological** *adj* **epistemologist** *n*

epistle *n* letter, esp. of an apostle. **epistolary** *adj*

epitaph *n* **1** commemorative inscription on a tomb. **2** commemorative speech or passage.

epithet *n* descriptive word or name.

epitome [ip-**pit**-a-mee] *n* typical example. **epitomize** *v* be the epitome of.

> Avoid the use of *epitome* to mean 'the peak' of something.

epoch [**ee**-pok] *n* period of notable events. **epoch-making** *adj* extremely important.

eponymous [ip-**pon**-im-uss] *adj* after whom a book, play, etc. is named. **eponymously** *adv*

EPOS electronic point of sale.

Epsom salts *pl n* medicinal preparation of magnesium sulphate and water, used to empty the bowels.

equable [**ek**-wab-bl] *adj* even-tempered. **equably** *adv*

equal *adj* **1** identical in size, quantity, degree, etc. **2** having identical rights or status. **3** evenly balanced. **4** (foll. by *to*) having the necessary ability (for). ♦ *n* **5** person or thing equal to another. ♦ *v*

equalling, equalled 6 be equal to. **equally** *adv* **equality** *n* state of being equal. **equalize** *v* 1 make or become equal. 2 reach the same score as one's opponent. **equalization** *n* **equal opportunity** nondiscrimination as to sex, race, etc. in employment.

equanimity *n* calmness of mind.

equate *v* make or regard as equivalent. **equation** *n* 1 mathematical statement that two expressions are equal. 2 act of equating. 3 representation of a chemical reaction using symbols of the elements.

equator *n* imaginary circle round the earth, equidistant from the poles. **equatorial** *adj*

equerry [**ek**-kwer-ee] *n, pl* **-ries** officer who acts as an attendant to a member of a royal family.

equestrian *adj* of horses and riding.

equidistant *adj* equally distant.

equilateral *adj* having equal sides.

equilibrium *n, pl* **-ria** steadiness or stability.

equine *adj* of or like a horse.

equinox *n* time of year when day and night are of equal length. **equinoctial** *adj*

equip *v* **equipping, equipped** provide with supplies, components, etc. **equipment** *n* 1 set of tools or devices used for a particular purpose. 2 act of equipping.

equipoise *n* perfect balance.

equitation *n* riding and horsemanship.

equity *n, pl* **-ties** 1 fairness. 2 legal system, founded on the principles of natural justice, that supplements common law. ♦ *pl* 3 interest of ordinary shareholders in a company. **equitable** *adj* fair and reasonable. **equitably** *adv*

equivalent *adj* 1 equal in value. 2 having the same meaning or result. ♦ *n* 3 something that is equivalent. **equivalence** *n*

equivocal *adj* 1 ambiguous. 2 deliberately misleading. 3 of doubtful character or sincerity. **equivocally** *adv* **equivocate** *v* use vague or ambiguous language to mislead people. **equivocation** *n*

er *interj* sound made when hesitating in speech.

Er *Chem* erbium.

ER Queen Elizabeth.

era *n* period of time considered as distinctive.

eradicate *v* destroy completely. **eradication** *n*

erase *v* 1 destroy all traces of, e.g. *he could not erase the memory of his earlier defeat.* 2 rub out. 3 remove sound or information from (a magnetic tape or disk). **eraser** *n* object for erasing something written. **erasure** *n* 1 erasing. 2 place or mark where something has been erased.

erbium *n Chem* metallic element of the lanthanide series.

ere *prep, conj Poetic* before.

erect *v* 1 build. 2 found or form. ♦ *adj* 3 upright. 4 (of the penis, clitoris, or nipples) rigid as a result of sexual excitement. **erectile** *adj* capable of becoming erect from sexual excitement. **erection** *n*

erg *n* unit of work or energy.

ergo *adv* therefore.

ergonomics *n* study of the relationship between workers and their environment. **ergonomic** *adj* 1 designed to minimize effort. 2 of ergonomics.

ergot *n* 1 fungal disease of cereal. 2 dried fungus used in medicine.

erica *n* genus of plants including heathers.

ermine *n* 1 stoat in northern regions. 2 its white winter fur.

erne, ern *n* fish-eating sea eagle.

Ernie *n Brit* machine that randomly selects winning numbers of Premium Bonds.

erode *v* wear away. **erosion** *n*

erogenous [ir-**roj**-in-uss] *adj* sensitive to sexual stimulation.

erotic *adj* relating to sexual pleasure or desire. **eroticism** *n* **erotica** *n* sexual literature or art.

err *v* 1 make a mistake. 2 sin. **erratum** *n,*

pl **-ta** error in writing or printing. **erroneous** *adj* incorrect, mistaken. **erroneously** *adv*

errand *n* short trip to do something for someone.

errant *adj* behaving in a manner considered to be unacceptable.

erratic *adj* irregular or unpredictable. **erratically** *adv*

error *n* mistake, inaccuracy, or misjudgment.

ersatz [**air**-zats] *adj* made in imitation, e.g. *ersatz coffee.*

Erse *n* **1** Gaelic. ♦ *adj* **2** of or relating to the Gaelic language.

erstwhile *adj* former.

erudite [**air**-rude-ite] *adj* having great academic knowledge. **erudition** *n*

erupt *v* **1** eject (steam, water, or volcanic material) violently. **2** burst forth suddenly and violently. **3** (of a blemish) appear on the skin. **eruption** *n*

erysipelas [err-riss-**sip**-pel-ass] *n* acute skin infection causing purplish patches.

erythema [err-rith-**theme**-a] *n* patchy inflammation of the skin.

erythrocyte [ir-**rith**-roe-site] *n* red blood cell of vertebrates that transports oxygen and carbon dioxide.

Es *Chem* einsteinium.

escalate *v* increase in extent or intensity. **escalation** *n*

escalator *n* moving staircase.

escalope [**ess**-kal-lop] *n* thin slice of meat, esp. veal.

escapade *n* mischievous adventure.

escape *v* **1** get free (of). **2** avoid, e.g. *escape attention.* **3** (of a gas, liquid, etc.) leak gradually. **4** be forgotten by, e.g. *the figure escapes me.* ♦ *n* **5** act of escaping. **6** means of relaxation. **escapee** *n* person who has escaped. **escapism** *n* taking refuge in fantasy to avoid unpleasant reality. **escapologist** *n* entertainer who specializes in freeing himself from confinement. **escapology** *n*

escarpment *n* steep face of a ridge or mountain.

eschatology [ess-cat-**tol**-loh-jee] *n* branch of theology concerned with the end of the world. **eschatological** *adj*

escheat [iss-**cheat**] *Law* ♦ *n* **1** private possessions that become state property in the absence of an heir. ♦ *v* **2** attain such property.

eschew [iss-**chew**] *v* abstain from, avoid.

escort *n* **1** people or vehicles accompanying another person for protection or as an honour. **2** person who accompanies a person of the opposite sex to a social event. ♦ *v* **3** act as an escort to.

escritoire [ess-kree-**twahr**] *n* type of writing desk.

escudo [ess-**kyoo**-doe] *n, pl* **-dos** monetary unit of Portugal.

escutcheon *n* shield with a coat of arms. **blot on one's escutcheon** stain on one's honour.

Eskimo *n* **1** member of the aboriginal race inhabiting N Canada, Greenland, Alaska, and E Siberia. **2** their language.

> *Eskimo* is considered by many people to be offensive, and in North America the term *Inuit* is often used.

ESN *Obs* educationally subnormal.

esoteric [ee-so-**ter**-rik] *adj* understood by only a small number of people with special knowledge.

ESP extrasensory perception.

esp. especially.

espadrille [**ess**-pad-drill] *n* light canvas shoe with a braided cord sole.

espalier [ess-**pal**-yer] *n* **1** shrub or fruit tree trained to grow flat. **2** trellis for this.

esparto *n, pl* **-tos** grass used for making rope etc.

especial *adj Formal* special. **especially** *adv* particularly.

> *Special(ly)* is more common than *especial(ly)* and is always used in preference to *especial* when the sense is 'out of the ordinary'.

Esperanto *n* universal artificial language.

espionage [**ess**-pyon-ahzh] *n* spying.

esplanade *n* wide open road used as a public promenade.

espouse *v* adopt or give support to (a cause etc.). **espousal** *n*

espresso *n, pl* **-sos** strong coffee made by forcing steam or boiling water through ground coffee beans.

> Note that the second letter is 's' not 'x'.

esprit [ess-**pree**] *n* spirit, liveliness, or wit. **esprit de corps** [de **core**] pride in and loyalty to a group.

espy *v* **espying, espied** catch sight of.

Esq. esquire.

esquire *n* courtesy title placed after a man's name.

essay *n* **1** short literary composition. **2** short piece of writing on a subject done as an exercise by a student. ♦ *v* **3** attempt. **essayist** *n*

essence *n* **1** most important feature of a thing which determines its identity. **2** concentrated liquid used to flavour food. **essential** *adj* **1** vitally important. **2** basic or fundamental. ♦ *n* **3** something fundamental or indispensable. **essentially** *adv*

est. **1** established. **2** estimate(d).

establish *v* **1** set up on a permanent basis. **2** make secure or permanent in a certain place, job, etc. **3** prove. **4** cause to be accepted. **establishment** *n* **1** act of establishing. **2** commercial or other institution. **the Establishment** group of people having authority within a society.

estate *n* **1** landed property. **2** large area of property development, esp. of new houses or factories. **3** property of a deceased person. **estate agent** agent concerned with the valuation, lease, and sale of property. **estate car** car with a rear door and luggage space behind the rear seats.

esteem *n* **1** high regard. ♦ *v* **2** think highly of. **3** judge or consider.

ester *n Chem* compound produced by the reaction between an acid and an alcohol.

estimate *v* **1** calculate roughly. **2** form an opinion about. ♦ *n* **3** approximate calculation. **4** statement from a workman etc. of the likely charge for a job. **5** opinion. **estimable** *adj* worthy of respect. **estimation** *n* considered opinion.

estranged *adj* no longer living with one's spouse. **estrangement** *n*

estuary *n, pl* **-aries** mouth of a river.

ETA estimated time of arrival.

et al. **1** and elsewhere. **2** and others.

etc. et cetera.

> *Etc.* means 'and the rest' so it is redundant to write *and etc.* Note the spelling; it comes from the Latin *et cetera*.

et cetera [et **set**-ra] *Latin* **1** and the rest, and others. **2** or the like. **etceteras** *pl n* miscellaneous extra things or people.

etch *v* **1** wear away or cut the surface of (metal, glass, etc.) with acid. **2** imprint vividly (on someone's mind). **etching** *n* picture printed from an etched metal plate.

eternal *adj* **1** without beginning or end. **2** unchanging. **eternally** *adv* **eternity** *n* **1** infinite time. **2** seemingly endless period of time. **3** timeless existence after death. **eternity ring** ring given as a token of lasting affection.

ethane *n* odourless flammable gas obtained from natural gas and petroleum.

ether *n* **1** colourless sweet-smelling liquid used as an anaesthetic. **2** region above the clouds. **ethereal** [eth-**eer**-ee-al] *adj* extremely delicate.

ethic *n* moral principle. **ethical** *adj* **ethically** *adv* **ethics** *n* **1** code of behaviour. **2** study of morals.

Ethiopian *adj* **1** of Ethiopia, its people, or their languages. ♦ *n* **2** person from Ethiopia.

ethnic *adj* **1** relating to a people or group that shares a culture, religion, or language. **2** belonging or relating to such a group, esp. one that is a minority group in a particular place. **ethnology** *n* study of human races. **ethnological** *adj* **ethnologist** *n*

ethos [**eeth**-oss] *n* distinctive spirit and attitudes of a people, culture, etc.

ethyl [**eeth**-ile] *adj* of, consisting of, or containing the hydrocarbon group C_2H_5. **ethylene** *n* poisonous gas used as an anaesthetic and as fuel.

etiolate [**ee**-tee-oh-late] *v* **1** become pale and weak. **2** *Botany* whiten through lack of sunlight.

etiology *n* study of the causes of diseases.

etiquette *n* conventional code of conduct.

étude [**ay**-tewd] *n* short musical composition for a solo instrument, esp. intended as a technical exercise.

etymology *n, pl* **-gies** study of the sources and development of words. **etymological** *adj* **etymologist** *n*

Eu *Chem* europium.

EU European Union.

eucalyptus, eucalypt *n* tree, mainly grown in Australia, that provides timber, gum, and medicinal oil from the leaves.

Eucharist [**yew**-kar-ist] *n* **1** Christian sacrament commemorating Christ's Last Supper. **2** consecrated elements of bread and wine. **Eucharistic** *adj*

eugenics [yew-**jen**-iks] *n* study of methods of improving the human race.

eulogy *n, pl* **-gies** speech or writing in praise of a person. **eulogize** *v* praise (a person or thing) highly in speech or writing. **eulogist** *n* **eulogistic** *adj*

eunuch *n* castrated man, esp. (formerly) a guard in a harem.

euphemism *n* inoffensive word or phrase substituted for one considered offensive or upsetting. **euphemistic** *adj* **euphemistically** *adv*

euphony *n, pl* **-nies** pleasing sound. **euphonious** *adj* pleasing to the ear. **euphonium** *n* brass musical instrument, tenor tuba.

euphoria *n* sense of elation. **euphoric** *adj*

Eurasian *adj* **1** of Europe and Asia. **2** of mixed European and Asian parentage. ♦ *n* **3** person of Eurasian parentage.

eureka [yew-**reek**-a] *interj* exclamation of triumph at finding something.

euro *n, pl* **euros** unit of the single currency of the European Union.

Eurodollar *n* US dollar as part of a European holding.

Euroland *n* the countries within the European Union that have adopted the euro.

European *n, adj* (person) from Europe. **European Union** association of a number of European nations with some shared monetary and political goals.

europium *n Chem* silvery-white element of the lanthanide series.

Eurozone same as EUROLAND.

Eustachian tube *n* passage leading from the ear to the throat.

euthanasia *n* act of killing someone painlessly, esp. to relieve his or her suffering.

eV electronvolt.

evacuate *v* **1** send (someone) away from a place of danger. **2** empty. **evacuation** *n* **evacuee** *n*

evade *v* **1** get away from or avoid. **2** elude. **evasion** *n* **evasive** *adj* not straightforward, e.g. *an evasive answer.* **evasively** *adv*

evaluate *v* find or judge the value of. **evaluation** *n*

evanescent *adj* quickly fading away. **evanescence** *n*

evangelical *adj* **1** of or according to gospel teaching. **2** of certain Protestant sects which maintain the doctrine of salvation by faith. ♦ *n* **3** member of an evangelical sect. **evangelicalism** *n*

evangelist *n* **1** writer of one of the four gospels. **2** travelling preacher. **evangelism** *n* teaching and spreading of the Christian gospel. **evangelize** *v* preach the gospel. **evangelization** *n*

evaporate *v* **1** change from a liquid or solid to a vapour. **2** disappear. **evaporation** *n* **evaporated milk** thick unsweetened tinned milk.

eve *n* **1** evening or day before some special event. **2** period immediately before an event. **evensong** *n* evening prayer.

even *adj* **1** flat or smooth. **2** (foll. by *with*) on the same level (as). **3** constant. **4** calm. **5** equally balanced. **6** divisible by two. ♦ *adv* **7** equally. **8** simply. **9** nevertheless. ♦ *v* **10** make even.

evening *n* **1** end of the day or early part of the night. ♦ *adj* **2** of or in the evening. **evening class** educational class for adults, held during the evening. **evening dress** attire for a formal occasion during the evening.

event *n* **1** anything that takes place. **2** planned and organized occasion. **3** contest in a sporting programme. **eventful** *adj* full of exciting incidents.

eventing *n* riding competitions, usu. involving cross-country, jumping, and dressage.

eventual *adj* ultimate. **eventually** *adv* **eventuality** *n* possible event.

ever *adv* **1** at any time. **2** always. **evergreen** *n, adj* (tree or shrub) having leaves throughout the year. **everlasting** *adj* **1** eternal. **2** lasting for an indefinitely long period. **evermore** *adv* for all time to come.

every *adj* **1** each without exception. **2** all possible. **everybody** *pron* every person. **everyday** *adj* usual or ordinary. **everyone** *pron* every person. **everything** *pron* **everywhere** *adv* in all places.

> *Everybody* and *everyone* are interchangeable. Although strict usage treats these pronouns as singular, modern practice is to use a plural after them: *Everyone nodded their head.*

evict *v* legally expel (someone) from his or her home. **eviction** *n*

evidence *n* **1** ground for belief. **2** matter produced before a lawcourt to prove or disprove a point. **3** sign, indication. ♦ *v* **4** demonstrate, prove. **in evidence** conspicuous. **evident** *adj* easily seen or understood. **evidently** *adv* **evidential** *adj* of, serving as, or based on evidence. **evidentially** *adv*

evil *n* **1** wickedness. **2** wicked deed. ♦ *adj* **3** harmful. **4** morally bad. **5** very unpleasant. **evilly** *adv* **evildoer** *n* wicked person. **evil eye** look superstitiously supposed to have the power of inflicting harm.

evince *v* make evident.

eviscerate *v* disembowel. **evisceration** *n*

evoke *v* call or summon up (a memory, feeling, etc.). **evocation** *n* **evocative** *adj*

evolve *v* **1** develop gradually. **2** (of an animal or plant species) undergo evolution. **evolution** *n* **1** gradual change in the characteristics of living things over successive generations, esp. to a more complex form. **2** gradual development. **evolutionary** *adj*

ewe *n* female sheep.

ewer *n* large jug with a wide mouth.

ex *n Informal* former wife or husband.

ex- *prefix* **1** out of, outside, from, e.g. *exodus.* **2** former, e.g. *ex-wife.*

exacerbate [ig-**zass**-er-bate] *v* make (pain, emotion, or a situation) worse. **exacerbation** *n*

exact *adj* **1** correct and complete in every detail. **2** precise, as opposed to approximate. ♦ *v* **3** demand (payment or obedience). **exactly** *adv* precisely, in every respect. **exactness, exactitude** *n* **exacting** *adj* making rigorous or excessive demands.

exaggerate *v* **1** regard or represent as greater than is true. **2** make greater or more noticeable. **exaggeratedly** *adv* **exaggeration** *n*

exalt *v* **1** praise highly. **2** raise to a higher rank. **exalted** *adj* **exaltation** *n*

exam *n* short for EXAMINATION.

examine *v* **1** look at closely. **2** test the knowledge of. **3** ask questions of. **examination** *n* **1** examining. **2** test of a candidate's knowledge or skill. **examinee** *n* person who sits an exam. **examiner** *n* person who sets or marks an exam.

example *n* **1** specimen typical of its

group. **2** instance that illustrates a fact or opinion. **3** person or thing worthy of imitation. **4** punishment regarded as a warning to others.

exasperate *v* cause great irritation to. **exasperation** *n*

excavate *v* **1** unearth buried objects from (a piece of land) methodically to learn about the past. **2** make (a hole) in solid matter by digging. **excavation** *n* **excavator** *n* large machine used for digging.

exceed *v* **1** be greater than. **2** go beyond (a limit). **exceedingly** *adv* very.

excel *v* **-celling, -celled 1** be superior to. **2** be outstandingly good at something. **excellent** *adj* exceptionally good. **excellence** *n*

Excellency *n* title used to address a high-ranking official, such as an ambassador.

except *prep* **1** (sometimes foll. by *for*) other than, not including. ♦ *v* **2** not include. **except that** but for the fact that. **excepting** *prep* except. **exception** *n* **1** excepting. **2** thing that is excluded from or does not conform to the general rule. **exceptionable** *adj* causing offence. **exceptional** *adj* **1** not ordinary. **2** much above the average. **exceptionally** *adv*

excerpt *n* passage taken from a book, speech, etc.

excess *n* **1** state or act of exceeding the permitted limits. **2** immoderate amount. **3** amount by which a thing exceeds the permitted limits. **excessive** *adj* **excessively** *adv*

exchange *v* **1** give or receive (something) in return for something else. ♦ *n* **2** act of exchanging. **3** thing given or received in place of another. **4** centre in which telephone lines are interconnected. **5** *Finance* place where securities or commodities are traded. **6** transfer of sums of money of equal value between different currencies. **exchangeable** *adj* **exchange rate** rate at which the currency unit of one country may be exchanged for that of another.

Exchequer *n Brit* government department in charge of state money.

excise[1] *n* tax on goods produced for the home market.

excise[2] *v* cut out or away. **excision** *n*

excite *v* **1** arouse to strong emotion. **2** arouse or evoke (an emotion). **3** arouse sexually. **excitement** *n* **excitable** *adj* easily excited. **excitability** *n* **exciting** *adj*

exclaim *v* speak suddenly, cry out. **exclamation** *n* **exclamation mark** punctuation mark (!) used after exclamations. **exclamatory** *adj*

exclude *v* **1** keep out, leave out. **2** leave out of consideration. **exclusion** *n* **exclusive** *adj* **1** excluding everything else. **2** not shared. **3** catering for a privileged minority. ♦ *n* **4** story reported in only one newspaper. **exclusively** *adv* **exclusivity, exclusiveness** *n*

excommunicate *v* exclude from membership and the sacraments of the Church. **excommunication** *n*

excoriate *v* **1** censure severely. **2** strip skin from. **excoriation** *n*

excrement *n* waste matter discharged from the body.

excrescence *n* lump or growth on the surface of an animal or plant. **excrescent** *adj*

excrete *v* discharge (waste matter) from the body. **excretion** *n* **excreta** [ik-**skree**-ta] *n* excrement. **excretory** *adj*

excruciating *adj* **1** agonizing. **2** hard to bear, e.g. *he spoke at excruciating length.* **excruciatingly** *adv*

exculpate *v* free from blame or guilt.

excursion *n* short journey, esp. for pleasure.

excuse *n* **1** explanation offered to justify (a fault etc.). ♦ *v* **2** put forward a reason or justification for (a fault etc.). **3** forgive (a person) or overlook (a fault etc.). **4** make allowances for. **5** exempt. **6** allow to leave. **excusable** *adj*

ex-directory *adj* not listed in a telephone directory by request.

execrable [**eks**-sik-rab-bl] *adj* of very poor quality.

execute *v* **1** put (a condemned person)

to death. **2** carry out or accomplish. **3** produce (a work of art). **4** render (a legal document) effective, as by signing. **execution** *n* **executioner** *n*

executive *n* **1** person or group in an administrative position. **2** branch of government responsible for carrying out laws etc. ♦ *adj* **3** having the function of carrying out plans, orders, laws, etc.

executor, executrix *n* person appointed to perform the instructions of a will.

exegesis [eks-sij-**jee**-siss] *n, pl* **-ses** [-seez] explanation of a text, esp. of the Bible.

exemplar *n* **1** person or thing to be copied, model. **2** example. **exemplary** *adj* **1** being a good example. **2** serving as a warning.

exemplify *v* **-fying, -fied 1** show an example of. **2** be an example of. **exemplification** *n*

exempt *adj* **1** not subject to an obligation etc. ♦ *v* **2** release from an obligation etc. **exemption** *n*

exequies [**eks**-sik-wiz] *pl n* funeral rites.

exercise *n* **1** activity to train the body or mind. **2** set of movements or tasks designed to improve or test a person's ability. **3** performance of a function. ♦ *v* **4** make use of, e.g. *to exercise one's rights*. **5** take exercise or perform exercises.

exert *v* use (influence, authority, etc.) forcefully or effectively. **exert oneself** make a special effort. **exertion** *n*

exeunt [**eks**-see-unt] *Latin* they go out: used as a stage direction.

exfoliate *v* peel in scales or layers.

ex gratia [**eks gray**-sha] *adj* given as a favour where no legal obligation exists.

exhale *v* breathe out. **exhalation** *n*

exhaust *v* **1** tire out. **2** use up. **3** discuss (a subject) thoroughly. ♦ *n* **4** gases ejected from an engine as waste products. **5** pipe through which an engine's exhaust fumes pass. **exhaustible** *adj* **exhaustion** *n* **1** extreme tiredness. **2** exhausting. **exhaustive** *adj* comprehensive. **exhaustively** *adv*

exhibit *v* **1** display to the public. **2** show (a quality or feeling). ♦ *n* **3** object exhibited to the public. **4** *Law* document or object produced in court as evidence. **exhibitor** *n* **exhibition** *n* **1** public display of art, skills, etc. **2** exhibiting. **exhibitionism** *n* **1** compulsive desire to draw attention to oneself. **2** compulsive desire to display one's genitals in public. **exhibitionist** *n*

exhilarate *v* make lively and cheerful. **exhilaration** *n*

exhort *v* urge earnestly. **exhortation** *n*

exhume [ig-**zyume**] *v* dig up (something buried, esp. a corpse). **exhumation** *n*

exigency *n, pl* **-cies** urgent demand or need. **exigent** *adj*

exiguous *adj* scanty or meagre.

exile *n* **1** prolonged, usu. enforced, absence from one's country. **2** person banished or living away from his or her country. ♦ *v* **3** expel from one's country.

exist *v* **1** have being or reality. **2** eke out a living. **3** live. **existence** *n* **existent** *adj*

existential *adj* of or relating to existence, esp. human existence. **existentialism** *n* philosophical movement stressing the personal experience and responsibility of the individual, who is seen as a free agent. **existentialist** *adj, n*

exit *n* **1** way out. **2** going out. **3** actor's going off stage. ♦ *v* **4** go out. **5** go offstage: used as a stage direction.

exocrine *adj* relating to a gland, such as the sweat gland, that secretes externally through a duct.

exodus [**eks**-so-duss] *n* departure of a large number of people.

ex officio [**eks** off-**fish**-ee-oh] *adv, adj Latin* by right of position or office.

exonerate *v* free from blame or a criminal charge. **exoneration** *n*

exorbitant *adj* (of prices, demands, etc.) excessive, immoderate. **exorbitantly** *adv*

exorcize *v* expel (evil spirits) by prayers and religious rites. **exorcism** *n* **exorcist** *n*

exotic *adj* **1** having a strange allure or

beauty. **2** originating in a foreign country. ♦ *n* **3** non-native plant. **exotically** *adv* **exotica** *pl n* (collection of) exotic objects.

expand *v* **1** make or become larger. **2** spread out. **3** (foll. by *on*) enlarge (on). **4** become more relaxed, friendly, and talkative. **expansion** *n* **expansionism** *n* policy of expanding the economy or territory of a country. **expansionist** *adj* **expanse** *n* uninterrupted wide area. **expansive** *adj* **1** wide or extensive. **2** friendly and talkative.

expatiate [iks-**pay**-shee-ate] *v* (foll. by *on*) speak or write at great length (on). **expatiation** *n*

expatriate [eks-**pat**-ree-it] *adj* **1** living outside one's native country. ♦ *n* **2** person living outside his or her native country. **expatriation** *n*

expect *v* **1** regard as probable. **2** look forward to, await. **3** require as an obligation. **expectancy** *n* **1** something expected on the basis of an average, e.g. *life expectancy*. **2** feeling of anticipation. **expectant** *adj* **1** expecting or hopeful. **2** pregnant. **expectantly** *adv* **expectation** *n* **1** act or state of expecting. **2** something looked forward to. **3** attitude of anticipation or hope.

expectorate *v* spit out (phlegm etc.). **expectoration** *n* **expectorant** *n* medicine that helps to bring up phlegm from the respiratory passages.

expedient [iks-**pee**-dee-ent] *n* **1** something that achieves a particular purpose. ♦ *adj* **2** suitable to the circumstances, appropriate. **expediency** *n*

expedite *v* hasten the progress of. **expedition** *n* **1** organized journey, esp. for exploration. **2** people and equipment comprising an expedition. **3** pleasure trip or excursion. **expeditionary** *adj* relating to an expedition, esp. a military one. **expeditious** *adj* done quickly and efficiently.

expel *v* **-pelling, -pelled 1** drive out with force. **2** dismiss from a school etc. permanently. **expulsion** *n*

expend *v* spend, use up. **expendable** *adj* able to be sacrificed to achieve an objective. **expenditure** *n* **1** something expended, esp. money. **2** amount expended. **expense** *n* **1** cost. **2** (cause of) spending. ♦ *pl* **3** charges, outlay incurred. **expense account** arrangement by which an employee's expenses are refunded by the employer. **expensive** *adj* high-priced.

experience *n* **1** direct personal participation. **2** particular incident, feeling, etc. that a person has undergone. **3** accumulated knowledge. ♦ *v* **4** participate in. **5** be affected by (an emotion). **experienced** *adj* skilful from extensive participation.

experiment *n* **1** test to provide evidence to prove or disprove a theory. **2** attempt at something new. ♦ *v* **3** carry out an experiment. **experimental** *adj* **experimentally** *adv* **experimentation** *n*

expert *n* **1** person with extensive skill or knowledge in a particular field. ♦ *adj* **2** skilful or knowledgeable. **expertise** [eks-per-**teez**] *n* special skill or knowledge. **expertly** *adv*

expiate *v* make amends for. **expiation** *n*

expire *v* **1** finish or run out. **2** breathe out. **3** *Lit* die. **expiration** *n* **expiry** *n* end, esp. of a contract period.

explain *v* **1** make clear and intelligible. **2** account for. **explanation** *n* **explanatory** *adj*

expletive [iks-**plee**-tiv] *n* swearword.

explicable *adj* able to be explained. **explicate** *v Formal* explain. **explication** *n*

explicit *adj* **1** precisely and clearly expressed. **2** shown in realistic detail. **explicitly** *adv*

explode *v* **1** burst with great violence, blow up. **2** react suddenly with emotion. **3** increase rapidly. **4** show (a theory etc.) to be baseless. **explosion** *n* **explosive** *adj* **1** tending to explode. ♦ *n* **2** substance that causes explosions.

exploit *v* **1** take advantage of for one's own purposes. **2** make the best use of. ♦ *n* **3** notable feat or deed. **exploitation** *n* **exploiter** *n*

explore *v* **1** investigate. **2** travel into (unfamiliar regions), esp. for scientific purposes. **exploration** *n* **exploratory** *adj* **explorer** *n*

expo *n, pl* **expos** *Informal* exposition, large public exhibition.

exponent *n* **1** person who advocates an idea, cause, etc. **2** skilful performer, esp. a musician.

exponential *adj Informal* very rapid. **exponentially** *adv*

export *n* **1** selling or shipping of goods to a foreign country. **2** product shipped or sold to a foreign country. ♦ *v* **3** sell or ship (goods) to a foreign country. **exporter** *n*

expose *v* **1** uncover or reveal. **2** make vulnerable, leave unprotected. **3** subject (a photographic film) to light. **expose oneself** display one's sexual organs in public. **exposure** *n* **1** exposing. **2** lack of shelter from the weather, esp. the cold. **3** appearance before the public, as on television. **4** *Photog* act of exposing film or plates to light. **5** *Photog* intensity of light falling on a film or plate multiplied by the time of the exposure.

exposé [iks-**pose**-ay] *n* bringing of a crime, scandal, etc. to public notice.

exposition *n* see EXPOUND.

expostulate *v* (foll. by *with*) reason (with), esp. to dissuade. **expostulation** *n*

expound *v* explain in detail. **exposition** *n* **1** explanation. **2** large public exhibition.

express *v* **1** put into words. **2** show (an emotion). **3** indicate by a symbol or formula. **4** squeeze out (juice etc.). ♦ *adj* **5** explicitly stated. **6** (of a purpose) particular. **7** of or for rapid transportation of people, mail, etc. ♦ *n* **8** fast train or bus stopping at only a few stations. ♦ *adv* **9** by express delivery. **expression** *n* **1** expressing. **2** word or phrase. **3** showing or communication of emotion. **4** look on the face that indicates mood. **5** *Maths* variable, function, or some combination of these. **expressionless** *adj* **expressive** *adj* **expressiveness** *n*

expressionism *n* early 20th-century artistic movement which sought to express emotions rather than represent the physical world. **expressionist** *n, adj*

expropriate *v* deprive an owner of (property). **expropriation** *n*

expulsion *n* see EXPEL.

expunge [iks-**sponge**] *v* delete, erase, blot out.

expurgate [**eks**-per-gate] *v* remove objectionable parts from (a book etc.).

exquisite *adj* **1** of extreme beauty or delicacy. **2** sensitive or discriminating, e.g. *exquisite manners*. **3** intense in feeling. **exquisitely** *adv*

ex-serviceman *n* man who has served in the armed forces.

extant *adj* still existing.

> *Extant* suggests that something still exists because it has survived: *The only example of this fossil extant.*

extemporize *v* speak, perform, or compose without preparation.

extend *v* **1** draw out or be drawn out, stretch. **2** last for a certain time. **3** (foll. by *to*) include. **4** increase in size or scope. **5** offer, e.g. *extend one's sympathy*. **extendable** *adj* **extension** *n* **1** room or rooms added to an existing building. **2** additional telephone connected to the same line as another. **3** extending. **extensive** *adj* having a large extent, widespread. **extensor** *n* muscle that extends a part of the body. **extent** *n* range over which something extends, area.

extenuate *v* make (an offence or fault) less blameworthy. **extenuating** *adj* **extenuation** *n*

exterior *n* **1** part or surface on the outside. **2** outward appearance. ♦ *adj* **3** of, on, or coming from the outside.

exterminate *v* destroy (animals or people) completely. **extermination** *n* **exterminator** *n*

external *adj* of, situated on, or coming from the outside. **externally** *adv* **externalize** *v* express (feelings) in words or actions.

extinct *adj* **1** having died out. **2** (of a volcano) no longer liable to erupt. **extinction** *n*

extinguish *v* **1** put out (a fire or light). **2** remove or destroy entirely. **extinguisher** *n*

extirpate [**eks**-ter-pate] *v* destroy utterly.

extol *v* **-tolling, -tolled** praise highly.

extort *v* get (something) by force or threats. **extortion** *n* **extortionate** *adj* (of prices) excessive.

extra *adj* **1** more than is usual, expected or needed. ♦ *n* **2** additional person or thing. **3** something for which an additional charge is made. **4** *Films* actor hired for crowd scenes. **5** *Cricket* run not scored off the bat. ♦ *adv* **6** unusually or exceptionally.

extra- *prefix* outside or beyond an area or scope, e.g. *extrasensory; extraterritorial.*

extract *v* **1** pull out by force. **2** remove. **3** derive. **4** copy out (an article, passage, etc.) from a publication. ♦ *n* **5** something extracted, such as a passage from a book etc. **6** preparation containing the concentrated essence of a substance, e.g. *beef extract.* **extraction** *n* **extractor** *n* **extractor fan** device for removing stale air or fumes from a room.

extracurricular *adj* taking place outside the normal school timetable.

extradite *v* send (an accused person) back to his or her own country for trial. **extradition** *n*

extramural *adj* connected with but outside the normal courses of a university or college.

extraneous [iks-**train**-ee-uss] *adj* irrelevant.

extraordinary *adj* **1** very unusual. **2** (of a meeting) specially arranged to deal with a particular subject. **extraordinarily** *adv*

extrapolate [iks-**trap**-a-late] *v* **1** infer (something not known) from the known facts. **2** *Maths* estimate (a value of a function or measurement) beyond the known values by the extension of a curve. **extrapolation** *n*

extrasensory *adj* **extrasensory perception** supposed ability to obtain information other than through the normal senses.

extraterrestrial *adj* of or from outside the earth's atmosphere.

extravagant *adj* **1** spending money excessively. **2** going beyond reasonable limits. **extravagance** *n* **extravaganza** *n* elaborate and lavish entertainment, display, etc.

extreme *adj* **1** of a high or the highest degree or intensity. **2** severe. **3** immoderate. **4** farthest or outermost. ♦ *n* **5** either of the two limits of a scale or range. **extremely** *adv* **extremism** *n* behaviour or beliefs that are immoderate. **extremist** *n* **1** person who favours immoderate methods. ♦ *adj* **2** holding extreme opinions. **extremity** *n, pl* **-ties** **1** farthest point. **2** extreme condition, as of misfortune. ♦ *pl* **3** hands and feet.

extricate *v* free from complication or difficulty. **extrication** *n*

extrinsic *adj* not contained or included within. **extrinsically** *adv*

extrovert *adj* **1** lively and outgoing. **2** concerned more with external reality than inner feelings. ♦ *n* **3** extrovert person. **extroversion** *n*

extrude *v* squeeze or force out. **extrusion** *n*

exuberant *adj* **1** high-spirited. **2** growing luxuriantly. **exuberance** *n* **exuberantly** *adv*

exude *v* **1** (of a liquid or smell) seep or flow out slowly and steadily. **2** make apparent by mood or behaviour, e.g. *exude confidence.*

exult *v* be joyful or jubilant. **exultation** *n* **exultant** *adj*

eye *n* **1** organ of sight. **2** external part of an eye. **3** (often pl) ability to see. **4** attention, e.g. *his new shirt caught my eye.* **5** ability to judge or appreciate, e.g. *a good eye for detail.* **6** one end of a sewing needle. **7** small area of calm at the centre of a hurricane. **8** dark spot on a potato from which a stem grows. ♦ *v*

eyeing *or* **eying, eyed 9** look at carefully or warily. **eyeless** *adj* **eyelet** *n* **1** small hole for a lace or cord to be passed through. **2** ring that strengthens this. **eyeball** *n* ball-shaped part of the eye. **eyebrow** *n* line of hair on the bony ridge above the eye. **eye-catching** *adj* attracting attention. **eyeful** *n Informal* **1** view. **2** attractive sight, esp. a woman. **eyeglass** *n* lens for aiding defective vision. **eyelash** *n* short hair that grows out from the eyelid. **eyelid** *n* fold of skin that covers the eye when it is closed. **eyeliner** *n* cosmetic used to outline the eyes. **eye-opener** *n Informal* something startling or revealing. **eye shadow** coloured cosmetic worn on the upper eyelids. **eyesight** *n* ability to see. **eyesore** *n* ugly object. **eyetooth** *n* canine tooth. **eyewash** *n Informal* nonsense. **eyewitness** *n* person who was present at an event and can describe what happened.

eyrie *n* **1** nest of an eagle or other bird of prey, built in a high inaccessible place. **2** high isolated position or place.

F f

f *Music* forte.

F **1** Fahrenheit. **2** farad. **3** *Chem* fluorine. **4** franc(s).

f. and the following (page).

fa *n* same as FAH.

FA Football Association.

fable *n* **1** story with a moral. **2** false or fictitious account. **3** legend. **fabled** *adj* made famous in legend.

fabric *n* **1** knitted or woven cloth. **2** framework or structure.

fabricate *v* **1** make up (a story or lie). **2** make or build. **fabrication** *n*

fabulous *adj* **1** *Informal* excellent. **2** astounding. **3** told of in fables. **fabulously** *adv*

facade [fas-**sahd**] *n* **1** front of a building. **2** (false) outward appearance.

face *n* **1** front of the head. **2** facial expression. **3** distorted expression. **4** outward appearance. **5** front or main side. **6** dial of a clock. **7** exposed area of coal or ore in a mine. **8** dignity, self-respect. ♦ *v* **9** look or turn towards. **10** be opposite. **11** be confronted by. **12** provide with a surface. **set one's face against** oppose determinedly. **faceless** *adj* impersonal, anonymous. **face-lift** *n* operation to tighten facial skin, to remove wrinkles. **face-saving** *adj* maintaining dignity or self-respect. **face up to** *v* accept (an unpleasant fact or reality). **face value** apparent worth or meaning.

facet *n* **1** aspect. **2** surface of a cut gem.

facetious [fas-**see**-shuss] *adj* funny or trying to be funny, esp. at inappropriate times. **facetiously** *adv*

facia *n, pl* **-ciae** same as FASCIA.

facial *adj* **1** of the face. ♦ *n* **2** beauty treatment for the face.

facile [**fas**-sile] *adj* **1** (of a remark, argument, etc.) superficial and showing lack of real thought. **2** easily performed or achieved.

facilitate *v* make easy. **facilitation** *n*

facility *n, pl* **-ties** **1** skill. **2** easiness. ♦ *pl* **3** means or equipment for an activity.

facing *n* **1** lining or covering for decoration or reinforcement. ♦ *pl* **2** contrasting collar and cuffs on a jacket.

facsimile [fak-**sim**-ill-ee] *n* exact copy. **facsimile transmission** same as FAX (sense 1).

fact *n* **1** event or thing known to have happened or existed. **2** provable truth. **fact of life** inescapable, often unpleasant, truth. **facts of life** details of sex and reproduction. **factual** *adj*

faction[1] *n* **1** (dissenting) minority group within a larger body. **2** dissension. **factious** *adj* of or producing factions.

faction[2] *n* dramatized presentation of a factual event.

factitious *adj* artificial.

factor *n* **1** element contributing to a result. **2** *Maths* one of the integers multiplied together to give a given number. **3** level on a scale of measurement, e.g. *suntan oil with a factor of 5*. **4** *Scot* property manager. **factorial** *n* product of all the integers from one to a given number. **factorize** *v* calculate the factors of (a number).

factory *n, pl* **-ries** building where goods are manufactured. **factory farm** farm on which animals are reared using modern industrial methods. **factory ship** ship that processes fish caught by a fleet.

factotum *n* person employed to do all sorts of work.

faculty *n, pl* **-ties** **1** physical or mental ability. **2** department in a university or college.

fad *n* **1** short-lived fashion. **2** whim. **faddy, faddish** *adj*

fade *v* **1** (cause to) lose brightness, colour, or strength. **2** vanish slowly. **fade-in, -out** *n* gradual increase or decrease, as of vision or sound in a film or broadcast.

faeces [**fee**-seez] *pl n* waste matter discharged from the anus. **faecal** [**fee**-kl] *adj*

faff *v* (often foll. by *about*) *Brit informal* dither or fuss.

fag[1] *n* **1** *Informal* boring task. **2** young public schoolboy who does menial chores for a senior boy. ♦ *v* **3** do menial chores in a public school.

fag[2] *n Slang* cigarette. **fag end 1** last and worst part. **2** *Slang* cigarette stub.

fag[3] *n US offens* male homosexual.

faggot[1] *n* **1** ball of chopped liver, herbs, and bread. **2** bundle of sticks for fuel.

faggot[2] *n US & Aust offens* male homosexual.

fah *n Music* (in tonic sol-fa) fourth degree of any major scale.

Fahrenheit [**far**-ren-hite] *adj* of a temperature scale with the freezing point of water at 32° and the boiling point at 212°.

faïence [**fie**-ence] *n* tin-glazed earthenware.

fail *v* **1** be unsuccessful. **2** stop operating. **3** be or judge to be below the required standard in a test. **4** disappoint or be useless to (someone). **5** neglect or be unable to do (something). **6** go bankrupt. ♦ *n* **7** instance of not passing an exam or test. **without fail 1** regularly. **2** definitely. **failing** *n* **1** weak point. ♦ *prep* **2** in the absence of. **failure** *n* **1** act or instance of failing. **2** unsuccessful person or thing. **fail-safe** *adj* designed to return to a safe condition if something goes wrong.

fain *adv Obs* gladly.

faint *adj* **1** lacking clarity, brightness, or volume. **2** feeling dizzy or weak. **3** lacking conviction or force. ♦ *v* **4** lose consciousness temporarily. ♦ *n* **5** temporary loss of consciousness. **faint-hearted** *adj* lacking courage and confidence.

fair[1] *adj* **1** unbiased and reasonable. **2** in agreement with rules. **3** light in colour. **4** beautiful. **5** quite good, e.g. *a fair attempt*. **6** quite large, e.g. *a fair amount of money*. **7** (of weather) fine. ♦ *adv* **8** fairly. **9** absolutely. **fairly** *adv* **1** moderately. **2** to a great degree or extent. **3** as deserved, reasonably. **fairness** *n* **fair copy** neat copy, without mistakes or alterations, of a piece of writing. **fair game** person regarded as a justifiable target for criticism or ridicule. **fair play** conventional standard of honourable behaviour. **fairway** *n Golf* smooth area between the tee and the green. **fair-weather** *adj* unreliable in difficult situations, e.g. *a fair-weather friend*.

fair[2] *n* **1** travelling entertainment with sideshows, rides, and amusements. **2** exhibition of commercial or industrial products. **fairground** *n* open space used for a fair.

fairing *n* curved metal structure fitted round part of a car, aircraft, etc. to reduce drag.

Fair Isle *n* intricate multicoloured knitted pattern.

fairy *n, pl* **fairies 1** imaginary small creature with magic powers. **2** *Offens* male homosexual. **fairy godmother** person who helps in time of trouble. **fairyland** *n* **fairy lights** small coloured electric bulbs used as decoration. **fairy ring** ring of dark grass caused by fungi. **fairy tale, story 1** story about fairies or magic. **2** unbelievable story or explanation.

fait accompli [**fate** ak-**kom**-plee] *n French* something already done that cannot be altered.

faith *n* **1** strong belief, esp. without proof. **2** religion. **3** complete confidence or trust. **4** allegiance to a person or cause. **faithful** *adj* **1** loyal. **2** maintaining sexual loyalty to one's lover or spouse. **3** consistently reliable. **4** accurate in detail. **faithfully** *adv* **faithless** *adj* disloyal or dishonest. **faith-healing** *n* healing of bodily ailments by religious rather than medical means. **faith-healer** *n*

fake *v* **1** cause something not genuine to appear real or more valuable by fraud. **2** pretend to have (an illness, emotion, etc.). ♦ *n* **3** person, thing, or act that is not genuine. ♦ *adj* **4** not genuine.

fakir [**fay**-keer] *n* **1** member of any Islamic religious order. **2** Hindu holy man.

falcon *n* small bird of prey. **falconry** *n* **1** art of training falcons. **2** sport of hunting with falcons. **falconer** *n*

fall *v* **falling, fell, fallen 1** drop from a higher to a lower place through the force of gravity. **2** collapse to the ground. **3** decrease in number or quality. **4** slope downwards. **5** die in battle. **6** be captured. **7** pass into a specified condition. **8** (of the face) take on a sad expression. **9** occur. **10** yield to temptation. ♦ *n* **11** falling. **12** thing or amount that falls. **13** decrease in value or number. **14** decline in power or influence. **15** capture or overthrow. **16** *US* autumn. ♦ *pl* **17** waterfall. **fall flat** fail utterly. **fall behind** *v* **1** fail to keep up. **2** be in arrears with a payment etc. **fall for** *v* **1** *Informal* fall in love with. **2** be deceived by (a lie or trick). **fall guy 1** *Informal* victim of a confidence trick. **2** scapegoat. **fall in** *v* **1** collapse. **2** (of a soldier etc.) take his or her place in a formation. **fall in with** *v* **1** meet with and join. **2** agree with or support a person or idea. **fallout** *n* radioactive particles spread as a result of a nuclear explosion. **fall out** *v* **1** *Informal* stop being friendly, disagree. **2** (of a soldier etc.) leave his or her place in a formation. **fall through** *v* fail. **fall to** *v* **1** (of a task or duty) become (someone's) responsibility. **2** begin some activity.

fallacy *n, pl* **-cies 1** false belief. **2** unsound reasoning. **fallacious** *adj*

fallen *v* past participle of FALL.

fallible *adj* (of a person) liable to make mistakes. **fallibility** *n*

Fallopian tube *n* either of a pair of tubes through which egg cells pass from the ovary to the womb.

fallow[1] *adj* (of land) ploughed but left unseeded to regain fertility.

fallow[2] *adj* light yellowish-brown. **fallow deer** reddish-brown deer with white spots in summer.

false *adj* **1** not true or correct. **2** artificial, fake. **3** deceptive, e.g. *false promises.* **4** forced or insincere, e.g. *false cheer.* **falsely** *adv* **falseness** *n* **falsity** *n, pl* **-ties 1** state of being false. **2** lie. **falsehood** *n* **1** quality of being untrue. **2** lie.

falsetto *n, pl* **-tos** voice pitched higher than one's natural range.

falsify *v* **-fying, -fied** alter fraudulently. **falsification** *n*

falter *v* **1** be hesitant, weak, or unsure. **2** lose power momentarily. **3** utter hesitantly. **4** move unsteadily. **faltering** *adj*

fame *n* state of being widely known or recognized. **famed** *adj* famous.

familiar *adj* **1** well-known. **2** frequent or common. **3** intimate, friendly. **4** too friendly. ♦ *n* **5** demon supposed to attend a witch. **6** friend. **familiarly** *adv* **familiarity** *n, pl* **-ties familiarize** *v* acquaint fully with a particular subject. **familiarization** *n*

family *n, pl* **-lies 1** group of parents and their children. **2** one's spouse and children. **3** one's children. **4** group descended from a common ancestor. **5** group of related objects or beings. ♦ *adj* **6** suitable for parents and children together. **familial** *adj* **family doctor** *Informal* same as GENERAL PRACTITIONER. **family name** surname, esp. when seen as representing a family's good reputation. **family planning** control of the number of children in a family by the use of contraception. **family tree** chart showing the relationships between individuals in a family over many generations.

famine *n* severe shortage of food.

famished *adj* very hungry.

famous *adj* very well-known. **famously** *adv Informal* excellently.

fan[1] *n* **1** hand-held or mechanical object used to create a current of air for ventilation or cooling. ♦ *v* **fanning, fanned 2** blow or cool with a fan. **3** spread out like a fan. **fan belt** belt that drives a cooling fan in a car engine. **fan heater** heater which uses a fan to spread warmed air through a room. **fanlight** *n* semicircular window over a door or window.

fan[2] *n Informal* devotee of a pop star, sport, or hobby.

fanatic *n* person who is excessively enthusiastic about something. **fanatical** *adj* **fanatically** *adv* **fanaticism** *n*

fancy *adj* **-cier, -ciest 1** elaborate, not plain. **2** (of prices) higher than usual. ♦ *n, pl* **-cies 3** sudden irrational liking or desire. **4** uncontrolled imagination. ♦ *v* **-cying, -cied 5** *Informal* be sexually attracted to. **6** *Informal* have a wish for. **7** picture in the imagination. **8** suppose. **fancy oneself** *Informal* have a high opinion of oneself. **fancier** *n* person who is interested in and often breeds plants or animals, e.g. *a pigeon fancier.* **fanciful** *adj* **1** not based on fact. **2** excessively elaborate. **fancifully** *adv* **fancy dress** party costume representing a historical figure, animal, etc. **fancy-free** *adj* not in love. **fancy goods** small decorative gifts.

fandango *n, pl* **-gos** lively Spanish dance.

fanfare *n* short loud tune played on brass instruments.

fang *n* **1** snake's tooth which injects poison. **2** long pointed tooth.

fanny *n, pl* **-nies** *Slang* **1** *Brit taboo* female genitals. **2** *US* buttocks.

fantasia *n* musical composition of an improvised nature.

fantastic *adj* **1** *Informal* very good. **2** unrealistic or absurd. **3** strange or difficult to believe. **fantastically** *adv*

fantasy *n, pl* **-sies 1** far-fetched notion. **2** imagination unrestricted by reality. **3** daydream. **4** fiction with a large fantasy content. **fantasize** *v* indulge in daydreams.

fanzine [**fan**-zeen] *n* magazine produced by fans of a specific interest, football club, etc., for fellow fans.

far *adv* **farther** *or* **further, farthest** *or* **furthest 1** at, to, or from a great distance. **2** at or to a remote time. **3** very much. ♦ *adj* **4** remote in space or time. **faraway** *adj* **1** very distant. **2** absent-minded. **Far East** East Asia. **far-fetched** *adj* hard to believe. **far-flung** *adj* **1** distributed over a wide area. **2** very distant. **far-reaching** *adj* extensive in influence, effect, or range. **far-sighted** *adj* having or showing foresight and wisdom.

> *Farther* is often used, rather than *further,* when distance, not time or effort, is involved.

farad *n* unit of electrical capacitance.

farce *n* **1** boisterous comedy. **2** ludicrous situation. **farcical** *adj* ludicrous. **farcically** *adv*

fare *n* **1** charge for a passenger's journey. **2** passenger. **3** food provided. ♦ *v* **4** get on (as specified), e.g. *we fared badly.* **fare stage 1** section of a bus journey for which a set charge is made. **2** bus stop marking the end of such a section.

farewell *interj* **1** goodbye. ♦ *n* **2** act of saying goodbye and leaving.

farinaceous *adj* containing starch or having a starchy texture.

farm *n* **1** area of land for growing crops or rearing livestock. **2** area of land or water for growing or rearing a specified animal or plant, e.g. *fish farm.* ♦ *v* **3** cultivate (land). **4** rear (stock). **farmer** *n* **farm hand** person employed to work on a farm. **farmhouse** *n* **farm out** *v* send (work) to be done by others. **farmstead** *n* farm and its buildings. **farmyard** *n*

farrago [far-**rah**-go] *n, pl* **-gos, -goes** jumbled mixture of things.

farrier *n* person who shoes horses.

farrow *n* **1** litter of piglets. ♦ *v* **2** (of a sow) give birth.

fart *Taboo* ♦ *n* **1** emission of gas from the anus. ♦ *v* **2** emit gas from the anus.

farther, farthest *adv, adj* see FAR.

farthing *n* former British coin equivalent to a quarter of a penny.

farthingale *n Obs* hoop worn under skirts in the Elizabethan period.

fascia [**fay**-shya] *n, pl* **-ciae, -cias 1** outer surface of a dashboard. **2** flat surface above a shop window.

fascinate *v* **1** attract and interest strongly. **2** make motionless from fear or awe. **fascinating** *adj* **fascination** *n*

fascism [**fash**-iz-zum] *n* right-wing totalitarian political system characterized by state control and extreme nationalism. **fascist** *adj, n*

fashion *n* **1** style in clothes, hairstyle, etc., popular at a particular time. **2** way something happens or is done. ♦ *v* **3** form or make into a particular shape. **fashionable** *adj* currently popular. **fashionably** *adv*

fast[1] *adj* **1** (capable of) acting or moving quickly. **2** done in or lasting a short time. **3** adapted to or allowing rapid movement. **4** (of a clock or watch) showing a time later than the correct time. **5** dissipated. **6** firmly fixed, fastened, or shut. **7** (of colours and dyes) not likely to fade. ♦ *adv* **8** quickly. **9** soundly, deeply, e.g. *fast asleep.* **10** tightly and firmly. **pull a fast one** *Informal* trick or deceive someone. **fast food** food, such as hamburgers, prepared and served very quickly. **fast lane 1** outside lane on a motorway. **2** quickest but most competitive route to success. **fast-track** *adj* taking the quickest but most competitive route to success, e.g. *fast-track executives.*

fast[2] *v* **1** go without food, esp. for religious reasons. ♦ *n* **2** period of fasting.

fasten *v* **1** make or become firmly fixed or joined. **2** close by fixing in place or locking. **3** (foll. by *on*) direct (one's attention) towards. **fastener, fastening** *n* device that fastens.

fastidious *adj* **1** very fussy about details. **2** excessively concerned with cleanliness. **fastidiously** *adv* **fastidiousness** *n*

fastness *n* fortress, safe place.

fat *adj* **fatter, fattest 1** having excess flesh on the body. **2** (of meat) containing a lot of fat. **3** thick. **4** profitable. ♦ *n* **5** extra flesh on the body. **6** oily substance obtained from animals or plants. **fatness** *n* **fatten** *v* (cause to) become fat. **fatty** *adj* **fattier, fattiest** containing fat. **fathead** *n Informal* stupid person. **fat-headed** *adj* **fat stock** livestock fattened and ready for market.

fatal *adj* causing death or ruin. **fatally** *adv* **fatality** *n, pl* **-ties** death caused by an accident or disaster.

fatalism *n* belief that all events are predetermined and people are powerless to change their destinies. **fatalist** *n* **fatalistic** *adj*

fate *n* **1** power supposed to predetermine events. **2** inevitable fortune that befalls a person or thing. **fated** *adj* **1** destined. **2** doomed to death or destruction. **fateful** *adj* having important, usu. disastrous, consequences.

father *n* **1** male parent. **2** person who founds a line or family. **3** man who starts, creates, or invents something. **4** (**F-**) God. **5** (**F-**) title of some priests. ♦ *v* **6** be the father of (offspring). **fatherhood** *n* **fatherless** *adj* **fatherly** *adj* **father-in-law** *n, pl* **fathers-in-law** father of one's husband or wife. **fatherland** *n* one's native country.

fathom *n* **1** unit of measurement of the depth of water, equal to six feet. ♦ *v* **2** understand. **fathomable** *adj* **fathomless** *adj* too deep or difficult to fathom.

fatigue [fat-**eeg**] *n* **1** extreme physical or mental tiredness. **2** weakening of a material due to stress. **3** soldier's nonmilitary duty. ♦ *pl* **4** soldier's clothing for nonmilitary duty. ♦ *v* **5** tire out.

fatuous *adj* foolish. **fatuously** *adv* **fatuity** *n, pl* **-ties 1** foolish thoughtlessness. **2** fatuous remark.

faucet [**faw**-set] *n US* tap.

fault *n* **1** responsibility for something wrong. **2** defect or flaw. **3** mistake or error. **4** *Geology* break in layers of rock. **5** *Tennis, squash, etc.* invalid serve. ♦ *v* **6** criticize or blame. **at fault** guilty of error. **find fault with** seek out minor imperfections in. **to a fault** excessively. **faulty** *adj* **faultless** *adj* **faultlessly** *adv*

faun *n* (in Roman legend) creature with a human face and torso and a goat's horns and legs.

fauna *n, pl* **-nas, -nae** animals of a given place or time.

faux pas [**foe pah**] *n, pl* **faux pas** social blunder.

favour *n* **1** approving attitude. **2** act of

goodwill or generosity. **3** partiality. ♦ *v* **4** prefer. **5** regard or treat with especial kindness. **6** support or advocate.

favourable *adj* **1** encouraging or advantageous. **2** giving consent. **3** useful or beneficial. **favourably** *adv*

favourite *adj* **1** most liked. ♦ *n* **2** preferred person or thing. **3** *Sport* competitor expected to win. **favouritism** *n* practice of giving special treatment to a person or group.

fawn[1] *n* **1** young deer. ♦ *adj* **2** light yellowish-brown.

fawn[2] *v* **1** (foll. by *on*) seek attention from (someone) by insincere flattery. **2** (of a dog) try to please by a show of extreme affection.

fax *n* **1** electronic system for sending facsimiles of documents by telephone. **2** document sent by this system. ♦ *v* **3** send (a document) by this system.

faze *v Informal* disconcert or fluster.

FBI *US* Federal Bureau of Investigation.

FC Football Club.

Fe *Chem* iron.

fealty *n* (in feudal society) subordinate's loyalty to his ruler or lord.

fear *n* **1** distress or alarm caused by impending danger or pain. **2** something that causes distress. ♦ *v* **3** be afraid of (something or someone). **fear for** feel anxiety about something. **fearful** *adj* **1** feeling fear. **2** causing fear. **3** *Informal* very unpleasant. **fearfully** *adv* **fearless** *adj* **fearlessly** *adv* **fearsome** *adj* terrifying.

feasible *adj* able to be done, possible. **feasibly** *adv* **feasibility** *n*

feast *n* **1** lavish meal. **2** something extremely pleasing. **3** annual religious celebration. ♦ *v* **4** eat a feast. **5** give a feast to. **6** (foll. by *on*) eat a large amount of. **feast one's eyes on** look at (someone or something) with a great deal of pleasure.

feat *n* remarkable, skilful, or daring action.

feather *n* **1** one of the barbed shafts forming the plumage of birds. ♦ *v* **2** fit or cover with feathers. **3** turn (an oar) edgeways. **feather in one's cap** achievement one can be pleased with. **feather one's nest** make one's life comfortable. **feathered** *adj* **feathery** *adj* **featherbedding** *n* practice of working deliberately slowly so that more workers are employed than are necessary. **featherweight** *n* **1** boxer weighing up to 126lb (professional) or 57kg (amateur). **2** insignificant person or thing.

feature *n* **1** part of the face, such as the eyes. **2** prominent or distinctive part. **3** special article in a newspaper or magazine. **4** main film in a cinema programme. ♦ *v* **5** have as a feature or be a feature in. **6** give prominence to. **featureless** *adj*

Feb. February.

febrile [**fee**-brile] *adj* **1** very active and nervous, e.g. *increasingly febrile activity at the Stock Exchange.* **2** feverish.

February *n* second month of the year.

feckless *adj* ineffectual or irresponsible.

fecund *adj* fertile. **fecundity** *n*

fed *v* past of FEED. **fed up** *Informal* bored, dissatisfied.

federal *adj* **1** of a system in which power is divided between one central government and several regional governments. **2** of the central government of a federation. **federalism** *n* **federalist** *n* **federate** *v* unite in a federation. **federation** *n* **1** union of several states, provinces, etc. **2** association.

fedora [fid-**or**-a] *n* man's soft hat with a brim.

fee *n* **1** charge paid to be allowed to do something. **2** payment for professional services.

feeble *adj* **1** lacking physical or mental power. **2** unconvincing. **feebleness** *n* **feebly** *adv* **feeble-minded** *adj* unable to think or understand effectively.

feed *v* **feeding, fed 1** give food to. **2** give (something) as food. **3** eat. **4** supply or prepare food for. **5** supply (what is needed). ♦ *n* **6** act of feeding. **7** food, esp. for babies or animals. **8** *Informal* meal. **feeder** *n* **1** baby's bib. **2** device used to feed an animal, child, or sick person. **3** road or railway line linking outlying areas to the main traffic network. **feedback** *n* **1** information received in response to something done. **2** return of part of the output of an electrical circuit or loudspeaker to its source.

feel *v* **feeling, felt 1** have a physical or emotional sensation of. **2** become aware of or examine by touch. **3** sense by intuition. **4** believe. ♦ *n* **5** act of feeling. **6** impression. **7** way something feels. **8** sense of touch. **9** instinctive aptitude. **feeler** *n* **1** organ of touch in some animals. **2** remark made to test others' opinion. **feeling** *n* **1** emotional reaction. **2** intuitive understanding. **3** opinion. **4** sympathy, understanding. **5** ability to experience physical sensations. **6** sensation experienced. ♦ *pl* **7** emotional sensitivities. **feel like** wish for, want. **feel for** *v* **1** attempt to find by touch alone. **2** have sympathy or compassion for someone in trouble. **feel up to** *v* be fit or energetic enough to.

> *Feel* is followed by an adjective when it refers back to the subject: *I feel sick.* Otherwise it is followed by an adverb: *She feels strongly about it.*

feet *n* plural of FOOT.

feign [**fane**] *v* pretend. **feigned** *adj*

feint[1] [**faint**] *n* **1** sham attack or blow meant to distract an opponent. ♦ *v* **2** make a feint.

feint[2] [**faint**] *n* narrow lines on ruled paper.

feldspar *n* hard mineral that is the main constituent of igneous rocks.

felicity *n* **1** happiness. **2** (*pl* **-ties**) appropriate expression or style. **felicitations** *pl n* congratulations. **felicitous** *adj*

feline *adj* **1** of cats. **2** catlike. ♦ *n* **3** member of the cat family.

fell[1] *v* past tense of FALL.

fell[2] *v* **1** cut down (a tree). **2** knock down.

fell[3] *adj* **in one fell swoop** in a single action or occurrence.

fell[4] *n Scot & N English* a mountain, hill, or moor.

fell[5] *n* animal's skin or hide with its hair.

felloe *n* (segment of) the rim of a wheel.

fellow *n* **1** *Old-fashioned* man or boy. **2** comrade or associate. **3** person in the same group or condition. **4** member of a learned society or the governing body of a college. ♦ *adj* **5** in the same group or condition. **fellowship** *n* **1** sharing of aims or interests. **2** group with shared aims or interests. **3** feeling of friendliness. **4** paid research post in a college or university. **fellow feeling** sympathy between people who have undergone the same experience. **fellow traveller** Communist sympathizer who is not a Communist Party member.

felon *n Criminal law* (formerly) person guilty of a felony. **felony** *n, pl* **-nies** serious crime. **felonious** *adj*

felspar *n* same as FELDSPAR.

felt[1] *v* past of FEEL.

felt[2] *n* matted fabric made by bonding fibres by pressure. **felt-tip pen** pen with a writing point made from pressed fibres.

fem. feminine.

female *adj* **1** of the sex which bears offspring. **2** (of plants) producing fruits. ♦ *n* **3** female person or animal.

feminine *adj* **1** having qualities traditionally regarded as suitable for, or typical of, women. **2** of women. **3** belonging to a particular class of grammatical inflection in some languages. **femininity** *n* **feminism** *n* advocacy of equal rights for women. **feminist** *n, adj*

femme fatale [**fam** fat-**tahl**] *n, pl* **femmes fatales** alluring woman who leads men into dangerous situations by her charm.

femur [**fee**-mer] *n* thighbone. **femoral** *adj* of the thigh.

fen *n* low-lying flat marshy land. **fenland** *n*

fence *n* **1** barrier of posts linked by wire or wood, enclosing an area. **2** obstacle for a horse to jump in steeplechasing or showjumping. **3** *Slang* dealer in stolen property. ♦ *v* **4** enclose with or as if with a fence. **5** fight with swords as a sport. **6** avoid a question. **fencing** *n* **1** sport of fighting with swords. **2** material for making fences. **fencer** *n*

fend *v* **fend for oneself** provide for oneself. **fend off** *v* defend oneself against (verbal or physical attack).

fender *n* **1** low metal frame in front of a fireplace. **2** soft but solid object hung over a ship's side to prevent damage when docking. **3** *Chiefly US* wing of a car.

Fenian [**feen**-yan] *n* member of a 19th-century Irish revolutionary organization founded to fight for an independent Ireland.

fennel *n* fragrant plant whose seeds, leaves, and root are used in cookery.

fenugreek *n* Mediterranean plant grown for its heavily scented seeds.

feoff [**feef**] *n Hist* same as FIEF.

feral *adj* wild.

ferment *n* **1** commotion, unrest. ♦ *v* **2** undergo or cause to undergo fermentation. **fermentation** *n* reaction in which an organic molecule splits into simpler substances, esp. the conversion of sugar to alcohol.

fermium *n Chem* element artificially produced by neutron bombardment of plutonium.

fern *n* flowerless plant with fine fronds.

ferocious *adj* savagely fierce or cruel. **ferocity** *n*

ferret *n* **1** tamed polecat used to catch rabbits or rats. ♦ *v* **ferreting, ferreted 2** hunt with ferrets. **3** search around. **ferret out** *v* find by searching.

ferric, ferrous *adj* of or containing iron.

Ferris wheel *n* large vertical fairground wheel with hanging seats for riding in.

ferrule *n* metal cap to strengthen the end of a stick.

ferry *n, pl* **-ries 1** boat for transporting people and vehicles. **2** route or service operated by such a boat. ♦ *v* **-rying, -ried 3** carry by ferry. **4** convey (goods or people). **ferryboat** *n* **ferryman** *n*

fertile *adj* **1** capable of producing young, crops, or vegetation. **2** highly productive, e.g. *a fertile mind.* **fertility** *n* **fertilize** *v* **1** provide (an animal or plant) with sperm or pollen to bring about fertilization. **2** supply (soil) with nutrients. **fertilization** *n* **fertilizer** *n* substance added to the soil to increase its productivity.

fervent, fervid *adj* intensely passionate and sincere. **fervently** *adv* **fervour** *n* intensity of feeling.

fescue *n* pasture and lawn grass with stiff narrow leaves.

fester *v* **1** grow worse and increasingly hostile, e.g. *the bitterness which had been festering beneath the surface.* **2** (of a wound) form pus. **3** rot and decay, e.g. *rubbish festered in the heat.*

festival *n* **1** organized series of special events or performances. **2** day or period of celebration. **festive** *adj* of or like a celebration. **festivity** *n, pl* **-ties 1** happy celebration. ♦ *pl* **2** celebrations.

festoon *v* hang decorations in loops.

feta *n* white salty Greek cheese.

fetal *adj* see FETUS.

fetch *v* **1** go after and bring back. **2** be sold for. **3** *Informal* deal (a blow). **fetching** *adj* attractive. **fetch up** *v Informal* arrive or end up.

fete [**fate**] *n* **1** gala, bazaar, etc., usu. held outdoors. ♦ *v* **2** honour or entertain regally.

fetid *adj* stinking.

fetish *n* **1** form of behaviour in which sexual pleasure is derived from looking at or handling an inanimate object. **2** thing with which one is excessively concerned. **3** object believed to have magical powers. **fetishism** *n* **fetishist** *n*

fetlock *n* projection behind and above a horse's hoof.

fetter *n* **1** chain or shackle for the foot. ♦ *pl* **2** restrictions. ♦ *v* **3** restrict. **4** bind in fetters.

fettle *n* state of health or spirits.

fetus, foetus [**fee**-tuss] *n, pl* **-tuses** embryo of a mammal in the later stages of development. **fetal, foetal** *adj*

feu *n* (in Scotland) right of use of land in return for a fixed annual payment.

feud *n* **1** long bitter hostility between two people or groups. ♦ *v* **2** carry on a feud.

feudalism *n* medieval system in which people held land from a lord, and in return worked and fought for him. **feudal** *adj* of or like feudalism.

fever *n* **1** (illness causing) high body temperature. **2** nervous excitement. **fevered** *adj* **feverish** *adj* **1** suffering from fever. **2** in a state of nervous excitement. **feverishly** *adv* **fever pitch** state of great excitement.

few *adj* not many. **a few** a small number. **quite a few, a good few** several.

> *Few(er)* is used of things that can be counted: *Fewer than five visits.* Compare *less,* which is used for quantity: *It uses less sugar.*

fey *adj* **1** whimsically strange. **2** having the ability to look into the future.

fez *n, pl* **fezzes** brimless tasselled cap, orig. from Turkey.

ff *Music* fortissimo.

ff. and the following (pages).

fiancé [fee-**on**-say] *n* man engaged to be married. **fiancée** *n fem*

fiasco *n, pl* **-cos, -coes** ridiculous or humiliating failure.

fiat [**fee**-at] *n* **1** arbitrary order. **2** official permission.

fib *n* **1** trivial lie. ♦ *v* **fibbing, fibbed 2** tell a lie. **fibber** *n*

fibre *n* **1** thread that can be spun into yarn. **2** threadlike animal or plant tissue. **3** fibrous material in food. **4** strength of character. **5** essential substance or nature. **fibrous** *adj* **fibreboard** *n* building material made of compressed wood. **fibreglass** *n* material made of fine glass fibres, used as insulation. **fibre optics** transmission of information by light along very thin flexible fibres of glass.

fibrillation *n* uncontrollable twitching of muscles, esp. those in the heart.

fibroid [**fibe**-royd] *adj* **1** *Anat* (of structures or tissues) containing or resembling fibres. ♦ *n* **2** benign tumour composed of fibrous connective tissue. **fibrositis** [fibe-roh-**site**-iss] *n* inflammation of the tissues of muscle sheaths.

fibula [**fib**-yew-la] *n, pl* **-lae, -las** slender outer bone of the lower leg. **fibular** *adj*

fiche [**feesh**] *n* sheet of film for storing publications in miniaturized form.

fickle *adj* changeable, inconstant. **fickleness** *n*

fiction *n* **1** literary works of the imagination, such as novels. **2** invented story. **fictional** *adj* **fictionalize** *v* turn into fiction. **fictitious** *adj* **1** not genuine. **2** of or in fiction.

fiddle *n* **1** violin. **2** *Informal* dishonest action or scheme. ♦ *v* **3** play the violin. **4** falsify (accounts). **5** move or touch something restlessly. **fiddling** *adj* trivial. **fiddly** *adj* **-lier, -liest** awkward to do or use. **fiddlesticks** *interj* expression of annoyance or disagreement.

fidelity *n* **1** faithfulness. **2** accuracy in detail. **3** quality of sound reproduction.

fidget *v* **1** move about restlessly. ♦ *n* **2** person who fidgets. ♦ *pl* **3** restlessness. **fidgety** *adj*

fiduciary [fid-**yew**-she-er-ee] *Law* ♦ *n, pl* **-aries 1** person bound to act for someone else's benefit, as a trustee. ♦ *adj* **2** of a trust or trustee.

fie *interj Obs or facetious* exclamation of disapproval.

fief [**feef**] *n Hist* land granted by a lord in return for war service.

field *n* **1** enclosed piece of agricultural land. **2** marked off area for sports. **3** area rich in a specified natural resource. **4** all the competitors in a competition. **5** all the competitors except the favourite. **6** battlefield. **7** sphere of knowledge or activity. **8** place away from the laboratory or classroom where practical work is done. **9** background, as of a flag. **10** area over which electric, gravitational, or magnetic force is exerted. ♦ *v* **11** *Sport* catch and return (a ball). **12** send (a player or team) on to the field. **13** play as a fielder. **14** deal with (a question) successfully. **fielder** *n Sport* player whose task is to field the ball. **field day**

day or time of exciting activity. **field events** throwing and jumping events in athletics. **fieldfare** *n* type of large thrush. **field glasses** binoculars. **field hockey** *US* hockey played on grass, as distinguished from ice hockey. **field marshal** army officer of the highest rank. **fieldmouse** *n, pl* **-mice** nocturnal mouse that lives in fields and woods. **field sports** hunting, shooting, and fishing. **fieldwork** *n* investigation made in the field as opposed to the classroom or the laboratory.

fiend [**feend**] *n* **1** evil spirit. **2** cruel or wicked person. **3** *Informal* person devoted to something, e.g. *fitness fiend.* **fiendish** *adj* **fiendishly** *adv*

fierce *adj* **1** wild or aggressive. **2** intense or strong. **fiercely** *adv* **fierceness** *n*

fiery [**fire**-ee] *adj* **fierier, fieriest 1** consisting of or like fire. **2** easily angered. **3** (of food) very spicy.

fiesta *n* religious festival, carnival.

FIFA [**fee**-fa] Fédération Internationale de Football Association (International Association Football Federation).

fife *n* small high-pitched flute.

fifteen *adj, n* **1** five and ten. ♦ *n* **2** Rugby Union team. **fifteenth** *adj, n*

fifth *adj, n* **1** (of) number five in a series. ♦ *n* **2** one of five equal parts of something. **fifth column** group secretly helping the enemy.

fifty *adj, n, pl* **-ties** five times ten. **fifty-fifty** *Informal* ♦ *adv* **1** equally divided, e.g. *they split the profits fifty-fifty.* ♦ *adj* **2** having an equal chance of happening or not happening, e.g. *a fifty-fifty chance of success.* **fiftieth** *adj, n*

fig *n* **1** soft pear-shaped fruit. **2** tree bearing it. **fig leaf 1** representation of the leaf of a fig tree, used to cover the genitals of a nude statue or painting. **2** anything used to conceal something thought to be shameful.

fig. 1 figurative(ly). **2** figure.

fight *v* **fighting, fought 1** struggle (against) in battle or physical combat. **2** struggle to overcome someone or obtain something. **3** carry on (a battle or contest). **4** make (one's way) somewhere with difficulty. ♦ *n* **5** aggressive conflict between two (groups of) people. **6** quarrel or contest. **7** resistance. **8** boxing match. **fighter** *n* **1** boxer. **2** determined person. **3** aircraft designed to destroy other aircraft. **fight off** *v* **1** drive away (an attacker). **2** struggle to avoid.

figment *n* **figment of one's imagination** imaginary thing.

figure *n* **1** numerical symbol. **2** amount expressed in numbers. **3** bodily shape. **4** well-known person. **5** representation in painting or sculpture of a human form. **6** diagram or illustration. **7** set of movements in dancing or skating. **8** *Maths* any combination of lines, planes, points, or curves. ♦ *pl* **9** calculations with numbers. ♦ *v* **10** calculate (sums or amounts). **11** *US & Aust* consider, conclude. **12** (usu. foll. by *in*) be included (in). **figure of speech** expression in which words do not have their literal meaning. **figurative** *adj* (of language) abstract, imaginative, or symbolic. **figuratively** *adv* **figurine** *n* statuette. **figurehead** *n* **1** nominal leader. **2** carved bust at the bow of a ship. **figure out** *v* solve or understand.

filament *n* **1** fine wire in a light bulb that gives out light. **2** fine thread.

filbert *n* hazelnut.

filch *v* steal (small amounts).

file[1] *n* **1** box or folder used to keep documents in order. **2** documents in a file. **3** information about a person or subject. **4** line of people one behind the other. **5** *Computers* organized collection of related material. ♦ *v* **6** place (a document) in a file. **7** place (a legal document) on official record. **8** bring a lawsuit, esp. for divorce. **9** walk or march in a line. **filing cabinet** piece of office furniture with deep drawers used for storing documents.

file[2] *n* **1** tool with a roughened blade for smoothing or shaping. ♦ *v* **2** shape or smooth with a file. **filings** *pl n* shavings removed by a file.

filial *adj* of or befitting a son or daughter.

filibuster *n* **1** obstruction of legislation by making long speeches. **2** person who filibusters. ♦ *v* **3** obstruct (legislation) with such delaying tactics.

filigree *n* **1** delicate ornamental work of gold or silver wire. ♦ *adj* **2** made of filigree.

Filipino [fill-lip-**pee**-no] *adj* **1** of the Philippines. ♦ *n* **2** (*fem* **Filipina**) person from the Philippines.

fill *v* **1** make or become full. **2** occupy completely. **3** plug (a gap). **4** satisfy (a need). **5** hold and perform the duties of (a position). **6** appoint to (a job or position). **one's fill** sufficient for one's needs or wants. **filler** *n* substance that fills a gap or increases bulk. **fill in** *v* **1** complete (a form or drawing). **2** act as a substitute. **3** *Informal* give (a person) fuller details. **filling** *n* **1** substance that fills a gap or cavity, esp. in a tooth. ♦ *adj* **2** (of food) substantial and satisfying. **filling station** garage selling petrol, oil, etc.

fillet *n* **1** boneless piece of meat or fish. ♦ *v* **filleting, filleted 2** remove the bones from.

fillip *n* something that adds stimulation or enjoyment.

filly *n, pl* **-lies** young female horse.

film *n* **1** sequence of images projected on a screen, creating the illusion of movement. **2** story told in such a sequence of images. **3** thin strip of light-sensitive cellulose used to make photographic negatives and transparencies. **4** thin sheet or layer. ♦ *v* **5** photograph with a movie or video camera. **6** make a film of (a scene, story, etc.). **7** cover or become covered with a thin layer. ♦ *adj* **8** connected with films or the cinema. **filmy** *adj* **filmier, filmiest** very thin, delicate. **film strip** set of pictures on a strip of film, projected separately as slides.

filter *n* **1** material or device permitting fluid to pass but retaining solid particles. **2** device that blocks certain frequencies of sound or light. **3** traffic signal that allows vehicles to turn either left or right while the main signals are at red. ♦ *v* **4** remove impurities from (a substance) with a filter. **5** pass slowly or faintly. **filter tip** (cigarette with) a built-in filter to reduce the amount of nicotine etc. inhaled by a smoker.

filth *n* **1** disgusting dirt. **2** offensive material or language. **filthy** *adj* **filthier, filthiest filthily** *adv* **filthiness** *n*

filtrate *n* **1** filtered gas or liquid. ♦ *v* **2** remove impurities with a filter. **filtration** *n*

fin *n* **1** projection from a fish's body enabling it to balance and swim. **2** vertical tailplane of an aircraft.

finagle [fin-**nay**-gl] *v* get or achieve by craftiness or trickery.

final *adj* **1** at the end. **2** having no possibility of further change, action, or discussion. ♦ *n* **3** deciding contest between winners of previous rounds in a competition. ♦ *pl* **4** last examinations in an educational course. **finally** *adv* **finality** *n* **finalist** *n* competitor in a final. **finalize** *v* put into final form. **finale** [fin-**nah**-lee] *n* concluding part of a dramatic performance or musical work.

finance *v* **1** provide or obtain funds for. ♦ *n* **2** system of money, credit, and investment. **3** management of money, loans, or credits. **4** (provision of) funds. ♦ *pl* **5** money resources. **financial** *adj* **financially** *adv* **financier** *n* person involved in large-scale financial business. **financial year** twelve-month period used for financial calculations.

finch *n, pl* **finches** small songbird with a short strong beak.

find *v* **finding, found 1** discover by chance. **2** discover by search or effort. **3** become aware of. **4** consider to have a particular quality. **5** experience (a particular feeling). **6** *Law* pronounce (the defendant) guilty or not guilty. **7** provide, esp. with difficulty. ♦ *n* **8** person or thing found, esp. when valuable. **finder** *n* **finding** *n* conclusion from an investigation. **find out** *v* **1** gain knowledge of. **2** detect (a crime, deception, etc.).

fine[1] *adj* **1** very good. **2** (of weather) clear and dry. **3** in good health. **4** satisfactory. **5** of delicate workmanship. **6** thin or slender. **7** in small particles. **8** very small, e.g. *fine print.* **9** subtle or abstruse, e.g. *a fine distinction.* **finely** *adv* **fineness** *n* **finery** *n* showy clothing. **fine art** art produced to appeal to the sense of beauty. **fine-tune** *v* make small adjustments to (something) so that it works really well.

fine[2] *n* **1** payment imposed as a penalty. ♦ *v* **2** impose a fine on.

finesse [fin-**ness**] *n* **1** delicate skill. **2** subtlety and tact.

finger *n* **1** one of the four long jointed parts of the hand. **2** part of a glove that covers a finger. **3** something that resembles a finger in shape or function. **4** quantity of liquid in a glass as deep as a finger is wide. ♦ *v* **5** touch or handle with the fingers. **fingering** *n* technique of using the fingers in playing a musical instrument. **fingerboard** *n* part of a stringed instrument against which the strings are pressed. **finger bowl** small bowl of water for diners to rinse their hands in at the table. **fingerprint** *n* **1** impression of the ridges on the tip of the finger. ♦ *v* **2** take the fingerprints of (someone). **fingerstall** *n* cover to protect an injured finger.

finial *n Archit* ornament at the apex of a gable or spire.

finicky *adj* **1** excessively particular, fussy. **2** overelaborate.

finis *n Latin* end: used at the end of a book.

finish *v* **1** bring to an end, stop. **2** use up. **3** bring to a desired or completed condition. **4** put a surface texture on (wood, cloth, or metal). **5** defeat or destroy. ♦ *n* **6** end, last part. **7** death or defeat. **8** surface texture. **finishing school** private school for girls that teaches social graces.

finite [**fine**-ite] *adj* having limits in space, time, or size.

Finn *n* native of Finland. **Finnish** *adj* **1** of Finland. ♦ *n* **2** official language of Finland.

finnan haddock, haddie *n* smoked haddock.

fiord *n* same as FJORD.

fipple flute *n* end-blown flute with a plug (**fipple**) at the mouthpiece, such as a recorder.

fir *n* pyramid-shaped tree with needle-like leaves and erect cones.

fire *n* **1** state of combustion producing heat, flames, and smoke. **2** burning coal or wood, or a gas or electric device, used to heat a room. **3** uncontrolled destructive burning. **4** shooting of guns. **5** intense passion, ardour. ♦ *v* **6** operate (a weapon) so that a bullet or missile is released. **7** *Informal* dismiss from employment. **8** bake (ceramics etc.) in a kiln. **9** (of an internal-combustion engine) start. **10** excite. **firearm** *n* rifle, pistol, or shotgun. **fireball** *n* **1** ball of fire at the centre of an explosion. **2** large bright meteor. **3** *Slang* energetic person. **firebrand** *n* person who causes unrest. **firebreak** *n* strip of cleared land to stop the advance of a fire. **firebrick** *n* heat-resistant brick used for lining furnaces, fireplaces, etc. **fire brigade** organized body of people whose job is to put out fires. **firecracker** *n* firework which produces a loud bang. **firedamp** *n* explosive gas, composed mainly of methane, formed in mines. **fire drill** rehearsal of procedures for escape from a fire. **fire engine** vehicle with apparatus for extinguishing fires. **fire escape** metal staircase or ladder down the outside of a building for escape in the event of fire. **firefighter** *n* member of a fire brigade. **firefly** *n, pl* **-flies** beetle that glows in the dark. **fireguard** *n* protective grating in front of a fire. **fire irons** tongs, poker, and shovel for tending a domestic fire. **fireplace** *n* recess in a room for a fire. **fire power** *Mil* amount a weapon or unit can fire. **fire raiser** person who deliberately starts fires. **fire station** building where firefighters are stationed. **fire trap** building which could easily catch fire or which would be difficult to escape from if it did. **firework** *n* **1** device containing chemicals that is ignited to produce spectacular explosions and coloured sparks. ♦ *pl* **2** show of fireworks. **3** *Informal* outburst of temper. **firing line** leading or most vulnerable position. **firing squad** group of soldiers ordered to execute an offender by shooting.

firm[1] *adj* **1** not soft or yielding. **2** securely in position. **3** definite. **4** having determination or strength. ♦ *adv* **5** in an unyielding manner, e.g. *hold firm.* ♦ *v* **6** make or become firm. **firmly** *adv* **firmness** *n*

firm[2] *n* business company.

firmament *n Lit* sky or the heavens.

first *adj* **1** earliest in time or order. **2** graded or ranked above all others. ♦ *n* **3** person or thing coming before all others. **4** outset or beginning. **5** first-class honours degree at university. **6** lowest forward gear in a motor vehicle. ♦ *adv* **7** before anything else. **8** for the first time. **firstly** *adv* **first aid** immediate medical assistance given in an emergency. **first-class** *adj* **1** of the highest class or grade. **2** excellent. **first-foot** *Scot* ♦ *n, pl* **first-foots** **1** first person to enter a house in the New Year. ♦ *v* **2** visit (someone) as a first-foot. **first-footing** *n* **first-hand** *adj, adv* (obtained) directly from the original source. **first mate** officer of a merchant ship second in command to the captain. **first person** *Grammar* category of verbs and pronouns used by a speaker to refer to himself or herself. **first-rate** *adj* excellent. **first refusal** right to buy something before it is offered to others. **first-strike** *adj* (of a nuclear missile) for use in an opening attack to destroy enemy weapons.

firth *n* narrow inlet of the sea.

fiscal *adj* **1** of government finances, esp. taxes. ♦ *n* **2** short for PROCURATOR FISCAL.

fish *n, pl* **fish, fishes** **1** cold-blooded vertebrate with gills, that lives in water. **2** its flesh as food. ♦ *v* **3** try to catch fish. **4** fish in (a particular area of water). **5** (foll. by *for*) grope for and find with difficulty. **6** (foll. by *for*) seek indirectly. **fisherman** *n* person who catches fish for a living or for pleasure. **fishery** *n, pl* **-eries** area of the sea used for fishing. **fishing** *n* job or pastime of catching fish. **fishy** *adj* **fishier, fishiest** **1** of or like fish. **2** *Informal* suspicious or questionable. **fishfinger** *n* oblong piece of fish covered in breadcrumbs. **fishmeal** dried ground fish used as animal feed or fertilizer. **fishmonger** *n* seller of fish. **fishnet** *n* open mesh fabric resembling netting. **fishwife** *n, pl* **-wives** coarse scolding woman.

fishplate *n* metal plate holding rails together.

fission *n* **1** splitting. **2** *Biol* asexual reproduction involving a division into two or more equal parts. **3** splitting of an atomic nucleus with the release of a large amount of energy. **fissionable** *adj* **fissile** *adj* **1** capable of undergoing nuclear fission. **2** tending to split.

fissure [**fish**-er] *n* long narrow cleft or crack.

fist *n* clenched hand. **fisticuffs** *pl n* fighting with the fists.

fistula [**fist**-yew-la] *n* long narrow ulcer.

fit[1] *v* **fitting, fitted** **1** be appropriate or suitable for. **2** be of the correct size or shape (for). **3** adjust so as to make appropriate. **4** try (clothes) on and note any adjustments needed. **5** make competent or ready. **6** correspond with the facts or circumstances. ♦ *adj* **7** appropriate. **8** in good health. **9** worthy or deserving. ♦ *n* **10** way in which something fits. **fitness** *n* **fitted** *adj* **1** designed for excellent fit, e.g. *a fitted suit.* **2** (of a kitchen, bathroom, etc.) having equipment and furniture built or selected to suit the measurements of the room. **3** (of a carpet) covering a floor completely. **fitter** *n* **1** person skilled in the installation and adjustment of machinery. **2** person who fits garments. **fitting** *adj* **1** appropriate, suitable. ♦ *n* **2** accessory or part. **3** trying on of clothes for size. ♦ *pl* **4** furnishings and accessories in a building. **fitment** *n* **1** accessory attached to a machine. **2** detachable part of the furnishings of a room. **fit in** *v* **1** give a place or time to. **2** belong or conform. **fit out** *v* provide with the necessary equipment.

fit[2] *n* **1** sudden attack or convulsion, such as an epileptic seizure. **2** sudden short burst or spell.

fitful *adj* occurring in irregular spells. **fitfully** *adv*

five *adj, n* one more than four. **fiver** *n* *Informal* five-pound note. **fives** *n* ball game resembling squash but played with bats or the hands.

fix *v* **1** make or become firm, stable, or secure. **2** repair. **3** place permanently. **4** settle definitely. **5** direct (the eyes etc.) steadily. **6** *Informal* unfairly influence the outcome of. ♦ *n* **7** *Informal* difficult situation. **8** ascertaining of the position of a ship by radar etc. **9** *Slang* injection of a narcotic drug. **fixed** *adj* **fixedly** [**fix**-id-lee] *adv* steadily. **fixer** *n* **1** solution used to make a photographic image permanent. **2** *Slang* person who arranges things. **fix up** *v* **1** arrange. **2** provide (with).

fixation *n* obsessive interest in something. **fixated** *adj* obsessed.

fixative *n* liquid used to preserve or hold things in place.

fixture *n* **1** permanently fitted piece of household equipment. **2** person whose presence seems permanent. **3** sports match or the date fixed for it.

fizz *v* **1** make a hissing or bubbling noise. **2** give off small bubbles. ♦ *n* **3** hissing or bubbling noise. **4** releasing of small bubbles of gas by a liquid. **5** effervescent drink. **fizzy** *adj* **fizzier, fizziest** **fizziness** *n*

fizzle *v* make a weak hissing or bubbling sound. **fizzle out** *v* *Informal* come to nothing, fail.

fjord [fee-**ord**] *n* long narrow inlet of the sea between cliffs, esp. in Norway.

FL Florida.

flab *n* *Informal* unsightly body fat.

flabbergasted *adj* completely astonished.

flabby *adj* **-bier, -biest** **1** having flabby flesh. **2** loose or limp. **flabbiness** *n*

flaccid [**flas**-sid] *adj* soft and limp. **flaccidity** *n*

flag[1] *n* **1** piece of cloth attached to a pole as an emblem or signal. ♦ *v* **flagging, flagged** **2** mark with a flag or sticker. **3** (often foll. by *down*) signal (a vehicle) to stop by waving the arm. **flag day** day on which small stickers are sold in the streets for charity. **flagpole, flagstaff** *n* pole for a flag. **flagship** *n* **1** admiral's ship. **2** most important product of an organization.

flag[2] *v* **flagging, flagged** lose enthusiasm or vigour.

flag[3], **flagstone** *n* flat paving-stone. **flagged** *adj* paved with flagstones.

flag[4] *n* any of various plants with sword-shaped leaves, esp. the iris.

flagellate [**flaj**-a-late] *v* whip, esp. in religious penance or for sexual pleasure. **flagellation** *n* **flagellant** *n* person who whips himself or herself.

flagellum [flaj-**jell**-lum] *n, pl* **-la** [-la], **-lums** **1** *Biol* whiplike outgrowth from a cell that acts as an organ of movement. **2** *Botany* long thin shoot.

flageolet [flaj-a-**let**] *n* small instrument like a recorder.

flagon *n* **1** wide bottle for wine or cider. **2** narrow-necked jug for liquid.

flagrant [**flayg**-rant] *adj* openly outrageous. **flagrantly** *adv* **flagrancy** *n*

flail *v* **1** wave about wildly. **2** beat or thrash. ♦ *n* **3** tool formerly used for threshing grain by hand.

flair *n* **1** natural ability. **2** stylishness.

flak *n* **1** anti-aircraft fire. **2** *Informal* severe criticism.

flake *n* **1** small thin piece, esp. chipped off something. ♦ *v* **2** peel off in flakes. **flaky** *adj* **flakier, flakiest** **flake out** *v* *Informal* collapse or fall asleep from exhaustion.

flambé [**flahm**-bay] *v* **flambéing, flambéed** cook or serve (food) in flaming brandy.

flamboyant *adj* **1** behaving in a very noticeable, extravagant way. **2** very bright and showy. **flamboyance** *n*

flame *n* **1** luminous burning gas coming from burning material. ♦ *v* **2** burn brightly. **3** become bright red. **old flame** *Informal* former sweetheart.

flamenco *n, pl* **-cos** **1** rhythmical Spanish dance accompanied by a guitar and vocalist. **2** music for this dance.

flamingo *n, pl* **-gos, -goes** large pink wading bird with a long neck and legs.

flammable *adj* easily set on fire. **flammability** *n*

> This now replaces *inflammable* in labelling and packaging because *inflammable* was often mistaken to mean 'not flammable'.

flan *n* open sweet or savoury tart.

flange *n* projecting rim or collar.

flank *n* **1** part of the side between the hips and ribs. **2** side of a body of troops. ♦ *v* **3** be at or move along the side of.

flannel *n* **1** small piece of cloth for washing the face. **2** soft woollen fabric for clothing. **3** *Informal* evasive talk. ♦ *pl* **4** trousers made of flannel. ♦ *v* **-nelling, -nelled** **5** *Informal* talk evasively. **flannelette** *n* cotton imitation of flannel.

flap *v* **flapping, flapped** **1** move back and forwards or up and down. ♦ *n* **2** action or sound of flapping. **3** piece of something attached by one edge only. **4** hinged section of an aircraft's wing that is raised and lowered to control the speed. **5** *Informal* state of excitement or panic.

flapjack *n* chewy biscuit made with oats.

flare *v* **1** blaze with a sudden unsteady flame. **2** *Informal* (of temper, violence, or trouble) break out suddenly. **3** (of a skirt or trousers) become wider towards the hem. ♦ *n* **4** sudden unsteady flame. **5** signal light. ♦ *pl* **6** flared trousers. **flared** *adj* (of a skirt or trousers) becoming wider towards the hem.

flash *n* **1** sudden burst of light or flame. **2** sudden occurrence (of intuition or emotion). **3** very short time. **4** brief unscheduled news announcement. **5** *Photog* small bulb that produces an intense flash of light. ♦ *adj* **6** (also **flashy**) vulgarly showy. ♦ *v* **7** (cause to) burst into flame. **8** (cause to) emit light suddenly or intermittently. **9** move very fast. **10** come rapidly (to mind or view). **11** *Informal* display ostentatiously. **12** *Slang* expose oneself indecently. **flasher** *n Slang* man who exposes himself indecently. **flashback** *n* scene in a book, play, or film, that shows earlier events. **flash flood** sudden short-lived flood. **flashlight** *n US* torch. **flash point** **1** critical point beyond which a situation will inevitably erupt into violence. **2** lowest temperature at which vapour given off by a liquid can ignite.

flashing *n* watertight material used to cover joins in a roof.

flask *n* **1** same as VACUUM FLASK. **2** flat bottle for carrying alcoholic drink in the pocket. **3** narrow-necked bottle.

flat[1] *adj* **flatter, flattest** **1** level and horizontal. **2** even and smooth. **3** (of a tyre) deflated. **4** outright. **5** fixed. **6** without variation or emotion. **7** (of a drink) no longer fizzy. **8** (of a battery) with no electrical charge. **9** *Music* below the true pitch. ♦ *adv* **10** in or into a flat position. **11** completely or absolutely. **12** exactly. **13** *Music* too low in pitch. ♦ *n* **14** flat surface. **15** *Music* symbol lowering the pitch of a note by a semitone. **16** punctured car tyre. **17** level ground. **18** mudbank exposed at low tide. **flat out** with maximum speed or effort. **flatly** *adv* **flatness** *n* **flatten** *v* **flatfish** *n* sea fish, such as the sole, which has a flat body. **flat-footed** *adj* **1** having a less than usually arched instep. **2** clumsy or insensitive. **flat racing** horse racing over level ground with no jumps.

flat[2] *n* set of rooms for living in which are part of a larger building. **flatlet** *n* small flat. **flatmate** *n* person with whom one shares a flat.

flatter *v* **1** praise insincerely. **2** show to advantage. **3** make (a person) appear more attractive in a picture than in reality. **flatterer** *n* **flattery** *n*

flatulent *adj* suffering from or caused by too much gas in the intestines. **flatulence** *n*

flaunt *v* display (oneself or one's possessions) arrogantly.

> Be careful not to confuse this with *flout* meaning 'disobey'.

flautist [**flaw**-tist] *n* flute player.

flavour *n* **1** distinctive taste. **2** distinctive characteristic or quality. ♦ *v* **3** give flavour to. **flavouring** *n* substance used to flavour food. **flavourless** *adj*

flaw *n* **1** imperfection or blemish. **2** mistake that makes a plan or argument invalid. **flawed** *adj* **flawless** *adj*

flax *n* **1** plant grown for its stem fibres and seeds. **2** its fibres, spun into linen thread. **flaxen** *adj* (of hair) pale yellow.

flay *v* **1** strip the skin off. **2** criticize severely.

flea *n* small wingless jumping bloodsucking insect. **flea market** market for cheap goods. **fleapit** *n Informal* shabby cinema or theatre.

fleck *n* **1** small mark, streak, or speck. ♦ *v* **2** speckle.

fled *v* past of FLEE.

fledged *adj* **1** (of young birds) able to fly. **2** (of people) fully trained. **fledgling, fledgeling** *n* **1** young bird. ♦ *adj* **2** new or inexperienced.

flee *v* **fleeing, fled** run away (from).

fleece *n* **1** sheep's coat of wool. **2** sheepskin used as a lining for coats etc. ♦ *v* **3** defraud or overcharge. **fleecy** *adj* made of or like fleece.

fleet[1] *n* **1** number of warships organized as a unit. **2** number of vehicles under the same ownership.

fleet[2] *adj* swift in movement. **fleeting** *adj* rapid and soon passing. **fleetingly** *adv*

Fleet Street *n* **1** street in London where many newspaper offices were formerly situated. **2** British national newspapers collectively.

Flemish *n* **1** one of two official languages of Belgium. ♦ *adj* **2** of Flanders, in Belgium.

flesh *n* **1** soft part of a human or animal body. **2** *Informal* excess fat. **3** meat of animals as opposed to fish or fowl. **4** thick soft part of a fruit or vegetable. **5** human body as opposed to the soul. **in the flesh** in person, actually present. **one's own flesh and blood** one's family. **flesh-coloured** *adj* yellowish-pink. **fleshly** *adj* **1** carnal. **2** worldly. **fleshy** *adj* **fleshier, fleshiest** **1** plump. **2** like flesh. **flesh wound** wound affecting only superficial tissue.

fleur-de-lys, fleur-de-lis [flur-de-**lee**] *n, pl* **fleurs-de-lys, fleurs-de-lis** heraldic lily with three petals.

flew *v* past tense of FLY[1].

flex *n* **1** flexible insulated electric cable. ♦ *v* **2** bend. **flexible** *adj* **1** easily bent. **2** adaptable. **flexibly** *adv* **flexibility** *n* **flexitime** *n* system permitting variation in starting and finishing times of work.

flick *v* **1** touch or move with the finger or hand in a quick movement. **2** move with a short sudden movement, often repeatedly, e.g. *the windscreen wipers flicked back and forth.* ♦ *n* **3** tap or quick stroke. ♦ *pl* **4** *Slang* the cinema. **flick knife** knife with a spring-loaded blade which shoots out when a button is pressed. **flick through** *v* look at (a book or magazine) quickly or idly.

flicker *v* **1** shine unsteadily or intermittently. **2** move quickly to and fro. ♦ *n* **3** unsteady brief light. **4** brief faint indication.

flier *n* see FLY[1].

flight[1] *n* **1** journey by air. **2** act or manner of flying through the air. **3** group of birds or aircraft flying together. **4** aircraft flying on a scheduled journey. **5** set of stairs between two landings. **6** stabilizing feathers or plastic fins on an arrow or dart. **flightless** *adj* (of certain birds or insects) unable to fly. **flight deck** **1** crew compartment in an airliner. **2** runway deck on an aircraft carrier. **flight lieutenant** junior commissioned officer in an air force. **flight of fancy** imaginative but impractical idea. **flight recorder** electronic device in an aircraft storing information about its flight.

flight[2] *n* act of running away.

flighty *adj* **flightier, flightiest** frivolous and fickle.

flimsy *adj* **-sier, -siest 1** not strong or substantial. **2** thin. **3** not very convincing. **flimsily** *adv* **flimsiness** *n*

flinch *v* draw back or wince, as from pain. **flinch from** *v* shrink from or avoid.

fling *v* **flinging, flung 1** throw, send, or move forcefully or hurriedly. ♦ *n* **2** spell of self-indulgent enjoyment. **3** brief romantic or sexual relationship. **fling oneself into** (start to) do with great vigour.

flint *n* **1** hard grey stone. **2** piece of this. **3** small piece of an iron alloy, used in cigarette lighters. **flinty** *adj* **1** cruel. **2** of or like flint. **flintlock** *n* obsolete gun in which the powder was lit by a spark from a flint.

flip *v* **flipping, flipped 1** throw (something small or light) carelessly. **2** turn (something) over. **3** throw (a coin) so that it turns over in the air. **4** (also **flip one's lid**) *Slang* fly into an emotional state. ♦ *n* **5** snap or tap. ♦ *adj* **6** *Informal* flippant. **flipper** *n* **1** limb of a sea animal adapted for swimming. **2** one of a pair of paddle-like rubber devices worn on the feet to help in swimming. **flipchart** *n* large pad of paper mounted on a stand, used in giving lectures etc. **flip-flop** *n* rubber-soled sandal held on by a thong between the big toe and the next toe. **flip through** *v* look at (a book or magazine) quickly or idly.

flippant *adj* treating serious things lightly. **flippancy** *n*

flirt *v* **1** behave as if sexually attracted to someone. **2** consider lightly, toy (with). ♦ *n* **3** person who flirts. **flirtation** *n* **flirtatious** *adj*

flit *v* **flitting, flitted 1** move lightly and rapidly. **2** *Scot* move house. **3** *Informal* depart hurriedly and secretly. ♦ *n* **4** act of flitting.

float *v* **1** rest on the surface of a liquid. **2** move lightly and freely. **3** move about aimlessly. **4** launch (a company). **5** offer for sale on the stock market. **6** allow (a currency) to fluctuate against other currencies. ♦ *n* **7** light object used to help someone or something float. **8** indicator on a fishing line that moves when a fish bites. **9** decorated lorry in a procession. **10** small delivery vehicle. **11** sum of money used for minor expenses or to provide change. **floating** *adj* **1** moving about, changing, e.g. *floating population.* **2** (of a voter) not committed to one party.

flock[1] *n* **1** number of animals of one kind together. **2** large group of people. **3** *Christianity* congregation. ♦ *v* **4** gather in a crowd.

flock[2] *n* **1** wool or cotton waste used as stuffing. ♦ *adj* **2** (of wallpaper) with a velvety raised pattern.

floe *n* sheet of floating ice.

flog *v* **flogging, flogged 1** beat with a whip or stick. **2** *Slang* sell. **flogging** *n*

flood *n* **1** overflow of water onto a normally dry area. **2** large amount of water. **3** rising of the tide. ♦ *v* **4** cover or become covered with water. **5** fill to overflowing. **6** come in large numbers or quantities. **7** supply excess petrol to (an engine) so that it does not work properly. **floodgate** *n* gate used to control the flow of water. **floodlight** *n* **1** lamp that casts a broad intense beam of light. ♦ *v* **-lighting, -lit 2** illuminate by floodlight.

floor *n* **1** lower surface of a room. **2** level of a building. **3** flat bottom surface. **4** (right to speak in) a legislative hall. ♦ *v* **5** knock down. **6** *Informal* disconcert or defeat. **floored** *adj* covered with a floor. **flooring** *n* material for floors. **floorboard** *n* long plank used for making floors. **floor show** entertainment in a nightclub.

floozy *n, pl* **-zies** *Old-fashioned slang* disreputable woman.

flop *v* **flopping, flopped 1** bend, fall, or collapse loosely or carelessly. **2** *Informal* fail. ♦ *n* **3** *Informal* failure. **4** flopping movement. **floppy** *adj* **floppier, floppiest** hanging downwards, loose. **floppy disk** *Computers* flexible magnetic disk that stores information.

flora *n* plants of a given place or time.

floral *adj* consisting of or decorated with flowers.

floret [**flaw**-ret] *n* small flower forming part of a composite flower head.

floribunda *n* type of rose whose flowers grow in large clusters.

florid *adj* **1** with a red or flushed complexion. **2** ornate.

florin *n* former British coin equivalent to ten pence.

florist *n* seller of flowers.

floss *n* **1** fine silky fibres. **2** see DENTAL FLOSS.

flotation *n* launching or financing of a business enterprise.

flotilla *n* small fleet or fleet of small ships.

flotsam *n* floating wreckage. **flotsam and jetsam 1** odds and ends. **2** homeless or vagrant people.

flounce[1] *v* **1** go with emphatic movements. ♦ *n* **2** flouncing movement.

flounce[2] *n* ornamental frill on a garment.

flounder[1] *v* **1** move with difficulty, as in mud. **2** behave or speak in a bungling or hesitating manner.

flounder[2] *n* edible flatfish.

flour *n* **1** powder made by grinding grain, esp. wheat. ♦ *v* **2** sprinkle with flour. **floury** *adj*

flourish *v* **1** be active, successful, or widespread. **2** be at the peak of development. **3** wave (something) dramatically. ♦ *n* **4** dramatic waving motion. **5** ornamental curly line in writing. **flourishing** *adj*

flout [rhymes with **out**] *v* deliberately disobey (a rule, law, etc.).

> Be careful not to confuse this with *flaunt* meaning 'display'.

flow *v* **1** (of liquid) move in a stream. **2** (of blood or electricity) circulate. **3** proceed smoothly. **4** hang loosely. **5** be abundant. ♦ *n* **6** act, rate, or manner of flowing. **7** continuous stream or discharge. **flow chart** diagram showing a sequence of operations in a process.

flower *n* **1** part of a plant that produces seeds. **2** plant grown for its colourful flowers. **3** best or finest part. ♦ *v* **4** produce flowers, bloom. **5** reach full growth or maturity. **in flower** with flowers open. **flowered** *adj* decorated with a floral design. **flowery** *adj* **1** decorated with a floral design. **2** (of language or style) elaborate. **flowerbed** *n* piece of ground for growing flowers.

flown *v* past participle of FLY[1].

fl. oz. fluid ounce(s).

flu *n* short for INFLUENZA.

fluctuate *v* change frequently and erratically. **fluctuation** *n*

flue *n* passage or pipe for smoke or hot air.

fluent *adj* **1** able to speak or write with ease. **2** spoken or written with ease. **fluently** *adv* **fluency** *n*

fluff *n* **1** soft fibres. **2** *Informal* mistake. ♦ *v* **3** make or become soft and puffy. **4** *Informal* make a mistake. **fluffy** *adj* **fluffier, fluffiest**

fluid *n* **1** substance able to flow and change its shape; a liquid or a gas. ♦ *adj* **2** able to flow or change shape easily. **fluidity** *n* **fluid ounce** one twentieth of a pint.

fluke[1] *n* accidental stroke of luck. **fluky** *adj*

fluke[2] *n* **1** flat triangular point of an anchor. **2** lobe of a whale's tail.

fluke[3] *n* parasitic worm.

flume *n* **1** narrow sloping channel for water. **2** enclosed water slide at a swimming pool.

flummox *v* puzzle or confuse.

flung *v* past of FLING.

flunk *v* *US, Aust & NZ Informal* fail.

flunky, flunkey *n, pl* **flunkies, flunkeys** **1** servile person. **2** manservant who wears a livery.

fluorescence *n* emission of light from a

substance bombarded by particles, such as electrons, or by radiation. **fluorescent** *adj* **fluorescent lamp** lamp in which ultraviolet radiation causes the chemical lining of a glass tube to glow. **fluoresce** *v* exhibit fluorescence.

fluoride *n* compound containing fluorine. **fluoridate** *v* add fluoride to (water) as protection against tooth decay. **fluoridation** *n*

fluorine *n Chem* toxic yellow gas, most reactive of all the elements.

flurry *n, pl* **-ries** **1** sudden commotion. **2** gust of rain or wind or fall of snow. ♦ *v* **-rying, -ried** **3** confuse.

flush[1] *v* **1** blush or cause to blush. **2** send water through (a toilet or pipe) so as to clean it. **3** elate. ♦ *n* **4** blush. **5** rush of water. **6** excitement or elation. **flushed** *adj*

flush[2] *adj* **1** level with the surrounding surface. **2** *Informal* having plenty of money.

flush[3] *v* drive out of a hiding place.

flush[4] *n* (in card games) hand all of one suit.

fluster *v* **1** make nervous or upset. ♦ *n* **2** nervous or upset state.

flute *n* **1** wind instrument consisting of a tube with sound holes and a mouth hole in the side. **2** tall narrow wineglass. **fluted** *adj* having decorative grooves. **fluting** *n* design of decorative grooves.

flutter *v* **1** wave rapidly. **2** flap the wings. **3** move quickly and irregularly. **4** (of the heart) beat abnormally quickly. ♦ *n* **5** flapping movement. **6** nervous agitation. **7** *Informal* small bet. **8** abnormally fast heartbeat.

fluvial [**flew**-vee-al] *adj* of rivers.

flux *n* **1** constant change or instability. **2** flow or discharge. **3** substance mixed with metal to assist in fusion. **4** *Physics* strength of a field in a given area.

fly[1] *v* **flying, flew, flown** **1** move through the air on wings or in an aircraft. **2** control the flight of. **3** float, flutter, display, or be displayed in the air. **4** transport or be transported by air. **5** move quickly or suddenly. **6** (of time) pass rapidly. **7** flee. ♦ *n, pl* **flies** **8** (often pl) fastening at the front of trousers. **9** flap forming the entrance to a tent. ♦ *pl* **10** space above a stage, used for storage. **flyer, flier** *n* **1** small advertising leaflet. **2** aviator. **fly-by-night** *adj Informal* unreliable or untrustworthy. **flyleaf** *n* blank leaf at the beginning or end of a book. **flyover** *n* road passing over another by a bridge. **fly-past** *n* ceremonial flight of aircraft. **flywheel** *n* heavy wheel regulating the speed of a machine.

fly[2] *n, pl* **flies** two-winged insect. **flycatcher** *n* small insect-eating songbird. **fly-fishing** *n* fishing with an artificial fly as a lure. **flypaper** *n* paper with a sticky poisonous coating, used to kill flies. **flyweight** *n* boxer weighing up to 112lb (professional) or 51kg (amateur).

fly[3] *adj Slang* sharp and cunning.

flying *adj* hurried and brief. **flying boat** aircraft fitted with floats instead of landing wheels. **flying colours** conspicuous success, e.g. *pass with flying colours.* **flying fish** fish with winglike fins used for gliding above the water. **flying fox** large fruit-eating bat. **flying officer** junior officer in an air force. **flying saucer** unidentified disc-shaped flying object, supposedly from outer space. **flying squad** small group of police, soldiers, etc., ready to act quickly. **flying start** very good start.

Fm *Chem* fermium.

FM frequency modulation.

foal *n* **1** young of a horse or related animal. ♦ *v* **2** give birth to a foal.

foam *n* **1** mass of small bubbles on a liquid. **2** frothy saliva. **3** light spongelike solid used for insulation, packing, etc. ♦ *v* **4** produce foam. **5** be very angry, e.g. *he makes me foam at the mouth.* **foamy** *adj* **foamier, foamiest**

fob *n* **1** short watch chain. **2** small pocket in a waistcoat.

fob off *v* **fobbing, fobbed** **1** pretend to satisfy (a person) with lies or excuses. **2** sell or pass off (inferior goods) as valuable.

fo'c's'le *n* same as FORECASTLE.

focus *n, pl* **-cuses, -ci** [-sye] **1** point at which light or sound waves converge. **2** state of an optical image when it is clearly defined. **3** state of an instrument producing such an image. **4** centre of interest or activity. ♦ *v* **-cusing, -cused** *or* **-cussing, -cussed 5** bring or come into focus. **6** concentrate (on). **focal** *adj* of or at a focus. **focal length** distance from a lens or a mirror to its focal point. **focal point 1** point where the object seen in a lens or a mirror is in perfect focus. **2** centre of interest or attention.

fodder *n* feed for livestock.

foe *n* enemy, opponent.

foetid *adj* same as FETID.

foetus *n, pl* **-tuses** same as FETUS.

fog *n* **1** mass of condensed water vapour in the lower air, often greatly reducing visibility. **2** blurred area on a developed photograph. ♦ *v* **fogging, fogged 3** cover with steam. **foggy** *adj* **foggier, foggiest fogbound** *adj* prevented from operating by fog. **foghorn** *n* large horn sounded to warn ships in fog.

fogey, fogy *n, pl* **-geys, -gies** old-fashioned person.

foible *n* minor weakness or slight peculiarity.

foil[1] *v* ruin (someone's plan).

foil[2] *n* **1** metal in a thin sheet. **2** anything which sets off another thing to advantage.

foil[3] *n* light slender flexible sword tipped with a button.

foist *v* (foll. by *on* or *upon*) force or impose on.

fold[1] *v* **1** bend so that one part covers another. **2** interlace (the arms). **3** clasp (in the arms). **4** *Cooking* mix gently. **5** *Informal* fail or go bankrupt. ♦ *n* **6** folded piece or part. **7** mark, crease, or hollow made by folding. **folder** *n* piece of folded cardboard for holding loose papers.

fold[2] *n* **1** enclosure for sheep. **2** church or its members.

foliage *n* leaves. **foliaceous** *adj* of or like leaves. **foliation** *n* process of producing leaves.

folio *n, pl* **-lios 1** sheet of paper folded in half to make two leaves of a book. **2** book made up of such sheets. **3** page number.

folk *n* **1** people in general. **2** race of people. **3** *Informal* folk music. ♦ *pl* **4** relatives. **folksy** *adj* simple and unpretentious. **folk dance** traditional country dance. **folklore** *n* traditional beliefs and stories of a people. **folk music 1** music handed down from generation to generation. **2** piece written in the style of such music. **folk song 1** song handed down among the common people. **2** modern song like this. **folk singer**

follicle *n* small cavity in the body, esp. one from which a hair grows.

follow *v* **1** go or come after. **2** accompany. **3** be a logical or natural consequence of. **4** keep to the course or track of. **5** act in accordance with. **6** accept the ideas or beliefs of. **7** understand. **8** have a keen interest in. **follower** *n* disciple or supporter. **following** *adj* **1** about to be mentioned. **2** next in time. ♦ *n* **3** group of supporters. ♦ *prep* **4** as a result of. **follow-on** *n Cricket* immediate second innings forced on a team scoring a set number of runs fewer than its opponents in the first innings. **follow through** *v* **1** continue an action or series of actions until finished. **2** *Sport* continue a stroke, kick, etc. after striking the ball. **follow up** *v* **1** investigate. **2** do a second, often similar, thing after (a first). **follow-up** *n* something done to reinforce an initial action.

folly *n, pl* **-lies 1** foolishness. **2** foolish action or idea. **3** useless extravagant building.

foment [foam-**ent**] *v* encourage or stir up (trouble).

fond *adj* **1** tender, loving. **2** unlikely to be realized, e.g. *a fond hope.* **fond of** having a liking for. **fondly** *adv* **fondness** *n*

fondant *n* (sweet made from) flavoured paste of sugar and water.

fondle *v* caress.

fondue *n* Swiss dish of a hot melted cheese sauce into which pieces of bread are dipped.

font *n* bowl in a church for baptismal water.

fontanelle *n* soft membranous gap between the bones of a baby's skull.

food *n* what one eats, solid nourishment. **foodie** *n Informal* gourmet. **food chain** *Ecology* series of living organisms each member of which feeds on another in the chain and is in turn eaten. **food poisoning** illness caused by eating contaminated food. **food processor** machine for chopping, liquidizing, or mixing food. **foodstuff** *n* substance used as food.

fool[1] *n* **1** person lacking sense or judgment. **2** person made to appear ridiculous. **3** *Hist* jester, clown. ♦ *v* **4** deceive (someone). **foolish** *adj* unwise, silly, or absurd. **foolishly** *adv* **foolishness** *n* **foolery** *n* foolish behaviour. **fool around** *v* act or play irresponsibly or aimlessly. **foolproof** *adj* unable to fail. **fool's paradise** state of happiness based on false hopes or beliefs.

fool[2] *n* dessert of puréed fruit mixed with cream.

foolhardy *adj* recklessly adventurous. **foolhardiness** *n*

foolscap *n* size of paper, 34.3 × 43.2 centimetres.

foot *n, pl* **feet** **1** part of the leg below the ankle. **2** unit of length of twelve inches (0.3048 metre). **3** lowest part of anything. **4** unit of poetic rhythm. **foot it** *Informal* walk. **foot the bill** pay the entire cost. **footage** *n* amount of film used. **foot-and-mouth disease** infectious viral disease of sheep, cattle, etc. **footbridge** *n* bridge for pedestrians. **footfall** *n* sound of a footstep. **foothills** *pl n* hills at the foot of a mountain. **foothold** *n* **1** secure position from which progress may be made. **2** small place giving a secure grip for the foot. **footlights** *pl n* lights across the front of a stage. **footloose** *adj* free from ties. **footman** *n* male servant in uniform. **footnote** *n* note printed at the foot of a page. **footpath** *n* narrow path for walkers only. **footplate** *n* platform in the cab of a locomotive for the driver. **footprint** *n* mark left by a foot. **footstep** *n* **1** step in walking. **2** sound made by walking. **footstool** *n* low stool used to rest the feet on while sitting. **footwear** *n* anything worn to cover the feet. **footwork** *n* skilful use of the feet, as in sport or dancing.

football *n* **1** game played by two teams of eleven players kicking a ball in an attempt to score goals, soccer. **2** any of various similar games, such as rugby. **3** ball used for this. **footballer** *n* **football pools** form of gambling on the results of football matches.

footing *n* **1** basis or foundation. **2** relationship between people. **3** secure grip by or for the feet.

footle *v Informal* loiter aimlessly. **footling** *adj* trivial.

footsie *n Informal* flirtation involving the touching together of feet.

fop *n* man excessively concerned with fashion. **foppery** *n* **foppish** *adj*

for *prep* **1** indicating a person intended to benefit from or receive something, span of time or distance, person or thing represented by someone, etc., e.g. *a gift for you; for five miles; playing for his country.* ♦ *conj* **2** because. **for it** *Informal* liable for punishment or blame.

forage [**for**-ridge] *v* **1** search about (for). ♦ *n* **2** food for cattle or horses.

foray *n* **1** brief raid or attack. **2** first attempt or new undertaking.

forbear[1] *v* cease or refrain (from doing something). **forbearance** *n* tolerance, patience.

forbear[2] *n* same as FOREBEAR.

forbid *v* prohibit, refuse to allow. **forbidden** *adj* **forbidden fruit** anything attractive because prohibited. **forbidding** *adj* severe, threatening.

force *n* **1** strength or power. **2** compulsion. **3** *Physics* influence tending to produce a change in a physical system. **4** mental or moral strength. **5** person or thing with strength or influence. **6** vehemence or intensity. **7** group of people organized for a particular task or duty. ♦ *v* **8** compel, make (someone) do something **9** acquire or produce through effort, strength, etc. **10** propel or drive. **11** break open. **12** impose or inflict. **13** cause to grow at an increased rate. **in force 1** having legal validity. **2** in great numbers. **forced** *adj* **1** compulsory. **2** false or unnatural. **3** due to an emergency. **force-feed** *v* **-feeding, -fed** compel (a person or animal) to swallow food. **forceful** *adj* **1** emphatic and confident. **2** effective. **forcefully** *adv* **forcible** *adj* **1** involving physical force or violence. **2** strong and emphatic. **forcibly** *adv*

forcemeat *n* mixture of chopped ingredients used for stuffing.

forceps *pl n* surgical pincers.

ford *n* **1** shallow place where a river may be crossed. ♦ *v* **2** cross (a river) at a ford. **fordable** *adj*

fore *adj* **1** in, at, or towards the front. ♦ *n* **2** front part. ♦ *interj* **3** golfer's shouted warning to a person in the path of a ball. **to the fore** in a conspicuous position.

fore- *prefix* **1** before in time or rank, e.g. *forefather*. **2** at the front, e.g. *forecourt*.

fore-and-aft *adj* located at both ends of a ship.

forearm[1] *n* arm from the wrist to the elbow.

forearm[2] *v* prepare beforehand.

forebear *n* ancestor.

foreboding *n* feeling that something bad is about to happen.

forecast *v* **-casting, -cast** *or* **-casted 1** predict (weather, events, etc.). ♦ *n* **2** prediction.

forecastle [**foke**-sl] *n* raised front part of a ship.

foreclose *v* take possession of (property bought with borrowed money which has not been repaid). **foreclosure** *n*

forecourt *n* courtyard or open space in front of a building.

forefather *n* ancestor.

forefinger *n* finger next to the thumb.

forefoot *n* either of the front feet of an animal.

forefront *n* **1** most active or prominent position. **2** very front.

foregather *v* meet together or assemble.

forego *v* same as FORGO.

foregoing *adj* going before, preceding. **foregone conclusion** inevitable result.

foreground *n* part of a view, esp. in a picture, nearest the observer.

forehand *n Tennis etc.* stroke played with the palm of the hand facing forward.

forehead *n* part of the face above the eyebrows.

foreign *adj* **1** not of, or in, one's own country. **2** relating to or connected with other countries. **3** unfamiliar, strange. **4** in an abnormal place or position, e.g. *foreign matter*. **foreigner** *n* **foreign minister, secretary** government minister who deals with other countries. **foreign office** ministry that deals with other countries.

foreknowledge *n* knowledge of something before it actually happens.

foreleg *n* either of the front legs of an animal.

forelock *n* lock of hair over the forehead. **tug the forelock** behave servilely or obsequiously.

foreman *n* **1** person in charge of a group of workers. **2** leader of a jury.

foremast *n* mast nearest the bow of a ship.

foremost *adj, adv* first in time, place, or importance.

forename *n* first name.

forenoon *n* morning.

forensic [for-**ren**-sik] *adj* used in or connected with courts of law. **forensic medicine** use of medical knowledge for the purposes of the law.

foreordain *v* determine events in the future.

forepaw *n* either of the front feet of a land mammal that does not have hooves.

foreplay *n* sexual stimulation before intercourse.

forerunner *n* person or thing that goes before, precursor.

foresail *n* main sail on the foremast of a ship.

foresee *v* see or know beforehand. **foreseeable** *adj*

foreshadow *v* show or indicate beforehand.

foreshore *n* part of the shore between high- and low-tide marks.

foreshorten *v* represent (an object) in a picture as shorter than it really is, in accordance with perspective.

foresight *n* ability to anticipate and provide for future needs.

foreskin *n* fold of skin covering the tip of the penis.

forest *n* large area with a thick growth of trees. **forested** *adj* **forestry** *n* **1** science of planting and caring for trees. **2** management of forests. **forester** *n* person skilled in forestry.

forestall *v* prevent or guard against in advance.

foretaste *n* early limited experience of something to come.

foretell *v* tell or indicate beforehand.

forethought *n* thoughtful planning for future events.

forever, for ever *adv* **1** without end. **2** at all times. **3** *Informal* for a long time.

forewarn *v* warn beforehand.

foreword *n* introduction to a book.

forfeit [**for**-fit] *n* **1** thing lost or given up as a penalty for a fault or mistake. ♦ *v* **2** lose as a forfeit. ♦ *adj* **3** lost as a forfeit. **forfeiture** *n*

forgather *v* same as FOREGATHER.

forgave *v* past tense of FORGIVE.

forge[1] *n* **1** place where metal is worked, smithy. **2** furnace for melting metal. ♦ *v* **3** make a fraudulent imitation of (something). **4** shape (metal) by heating and hammering it. **5** create (an alliance etc.).

forge[2] *v* advance steadily. **forge ahead** increase speed or take the lead.

forgery *n, pl* **-ries** **1** illegal copy of something. **2** crime of making an illegal copy. **forger** *n*

forget *v* **-getting, -got, -gotten** **1** fail to remember. **2** neglect. **3** leave behind by mistake. **forgetful** *adj* tending to forget. **forgetfulness** *n* **forget-me-not** *n* plant with clusters of small blue flowers.

forgive *v* **-giving, -gave, -given** cease to blame or hold resentment against, pardon. **forgiveness** *n* **forgivable** *adj* able to be forgiven. **forgiving** *adj* willing to forgive.

forgo *v* do without or give up.

forgot *v* past tense of FORGET. **forgotten** *v* past participle of FORGET.

fork *n* **1** tool for eating food, with prongs and a handle. **2** large similarly-shaped tool for digging or lifting. **3** point where a road, river, etc. divides into branches. **4** one of the branches. ♦ *v* **5** pick up, dig, etc. with a fork. **6** branch. **7** take one or other branch at a fork in the road. **forked** *adj* **fork-lift truck** vehicle with a forklike device at the front which can be raised or lowered to move loads. **fork out** *v Informal* pay.

forlorn *adj* lonely and unhappy. **forlorn hope** hopeless enterprise. **forlornly** *adv*

form *n* **1** shape or appearance. **2** mode in which something appears. **3** type or kind. **4** printed document with spaces for details. **5** physical or mental condition. **6** previous record of an athlete, racehorse, etc. **7** class in school. **8** procedure or etiquette. **9** bench. **10** hare's nest. ♦ *v* **11** give a (particular) shape to or take a (particular) shape. **12** come or bring into existence. **13** make or be made. **14** train. **15** acquire or develop. **16** be an element of. **formless** *adj*

formal *adj* **1** of or characterized by established conventions of ceremony and behaviour. **2** of or for formal occasions. **3** stiff in manner. **4** organized. **5** symmetrical. **formally** *adv* **formalism** *n* concern with outward appearances and structure at the expense of content. **formalist** *n, adj* **formality** *n, pl* **-ties** **1** requirement of custom or etiquette. **2** necessary procedure without real importance. **formalize** *v* make official or formal.

formaldehyde [for-**mal**-de-hide] *n* colourless pungent gas used to make formalin. **formalin** *n* solution of formaldehyde in water, used as a disinfectant or a preservative for biological specimens.

format *n* **1** size and shape of a publication. **2** style in which something is arranged. ♦ *v* **-matting, -matted 3** arrange in a format.

formation *n* **1** forming. **2** thing formed. **3** structure or shape. **4** arrangement of people or things acting as a unit.

formative *adj* **1** of or relating to development. **2** shaping.

former *adj* of an earlier time, previous. **the former** first mentioned of two. **formerly** *adv*

Formica *n* ® kind of laminated sheet used to make heat-resistant surfaces.

formic acid *n* acid derived from ants.

formidable *adj* **1** frightening because difficult to overcome or manage. **2** extremely impressive. **formidably** *adv*

formula *n, pl* **-las, -lae 1** group of numbers, letters, or symbols expressing a scientific or mathematical rule. **2** method or rule for doing or producing something. **3** set form of words used in religion, law, etc. **4** specific category of car in motor racing. **5** *US* powder used to produce a milky drink for babies. **formulaic** *adj* **formulate** *v* plan or describe precisely and clearly. **formulation** *n*

fornicate *v* have sexual intercourse without being married. **fornication** *n* **fornicator** *n*

forsake *v* **-saking, -sook, -saken 1** withdraw support or friendship from. **2** give up, renounce.

forsooth *adv Obs* indeed.

forswear *v* **-swearing, -swore, -sworn** renounce or reject.

forsythia [for-**syth**-ee-a] *n* shrub with yellow flowers in spring.

fort *n* fortified building or place. **hold the fort** *Informal* keep things going during someone's absence.

forte[1] [**for**-tay] *n* thing at which a person excels.

forte[2] [**for**-tay] *adv Music* loudly.

forth *adv* forwards, out, or away. **and so forth** and so on.

forthcoming *adj* **1** about to appear or happen. **2** available. **3** (of a person) communicative.

forthright *adj* direct and outspoken.

forthwith *adv* at once.

fortieth *adj, n* see FORTY.

fortify *v* **-fying, -fied 1** make (a place) defensible, as by building walls. **2** strengthen. **3** add vitamins etc. to (food). **4** add alcohol to (wine) to make sherry or port. **fortification** *n*

fortissimo *adv Music* very loudly.

fortitude *n* courage in adversity or pain.

fortnight *n* two weeks. **fortnightly** *adv, adj*

FORTRAN *n Computers* programming language for mathematical and scientific purposes.

fortress *n* large fort or fortified town.

fortuitous [for-**tyew**-it-uss] *adj* happening by (lucky) chance. **fortuitously** *adv*

fortunate *adj* **1** having good luck. **2** occurring by good luck. **fortunately** *adv*

fortune *n* **1** luck, esp. when favourable. **2** power regarded as influencing human destiny. **3** wealth, large sum of money. ♦ *pl* **4** person's destiny. **fortune-teller** *n* person who claims to predict the future of others.

forty *adj, n, pl* **-ties** four times ten. **fortieth** *adj, n* **forty winks** short light sleep.

forum *n* meeting or medium for open discussion or debate.

forward *adj* **1** directed or moving ahead. **2** in, at, or near the front. **3** presumptuous. **4** well developed or advanced. **5** relating to the future. ♦ *n* **6** attacking player in various team games, such as football or hockey. ♦ *adv* **7** forwards. ♦ *v* **8** send (a letter etc.) on to an ultimate destination. **9** advance or promote. **forwards** *adv* **1** towards or at a place further ahead in space or time. **2** towards the front.

forwent *v* past tense of FORGO.

fossil *n* **1** hardened remains of a prehistoric animal or plant preserved in rock. ♦ *adj* **2** of, like, or being a fossil. **fossil fuel** fuel such as coal or oil that is formed from the decayed remains of prehistoric animals or plants. **fossilize** *v* **1** turn into a fossil. **2** become out-of-date or inflexible.

foster *v* **1** promote the growth or development of. **2** bring up (a child not one's own). ♦ *adj* **3** of or involved in fostering a child, e.g. *foster parents.* **fostering** *n*

fought *v* past of FIGHT.

foul *adj* **1** loathsome or offensive. **2** stinking or dirty. **3** (of language) obscene or vulgar. **4** unfair. **5** very bad-tempered. ♦ *n* **6** *Sport* violation of the rules. ♦ *v* **7** make dirty or polluted. **8** make or become entangled or clogged. **9** *Sport* commit a foul against (an opponent). **fall foul of** come into conflict with. **foul-mouthed** *adj* habitually using foul language. **foul play** unfair conduct, esp. involving violence.

found[1] *v* past of FIND.

found[2] *v* **1** establish or bring into being. **2** lay the foundation of. **3** (foll. by *on* or *upon*) have a basis (in). **founder** *n* **founder member** one of the original members of a club or organization, often someone involved in setting it up.

found[3] *v* **1** cast (metal or glass) by melting and setting in a mould. **2** make (articles) by this method.

foundation *n* **1** basis or base. **2** part of a building or wall below the ground. **3** act of founding. **4** institution supported by an endowment. **5** cosmetic used as a base for make-up.

founder *v* **1** break down or fail. **2** (of a ship) sink. **3** stumble or fall.

foundling *n* abandoned baby.

foundry *n, pl* **-ries** place where metal is melted and cast.

fount[1] *n* **1** *Lit* fountain. **2** source.

fount[2] *n* set of printing type of one style and size.

fountain *n* **1** jet of water. **2** structure from which such a jet spurts. **3** source. **fountainhead** *n* original source. **fountain pen** pen supplied with ink from a container inside it.

four *adj, n* **1** one more than three. ♦ *n* **2** (crew of) four-oared rowing boat. **on all fours** on hands and knees. **four-letter word** short obscene word referring to sex or excrement. **four-poster** *n* bed with four posts supporting a canopy. **foursome** *n* group of four people. **foursquare** *adv* **1** squarely or firmly. ♦ *adj* **2** solid and strong. **3** forthright.

fourteen *adj, n* four and ten. **fourteenth** *adj, n*

fourth *adj, n* **1** (of) number four in a series. ♦ *n* **2** quarter. **fourthly** *adv* **fourth dimension** time. **fourth estate** the press.

fowl *n* **1** domestic cock or hen. **2** any bird used for food or hunted as game.

fox *n* **1** reddish-brown bushy-tailed animal of the dog family. **2** its fur. **3** cunning person. ♦ *v* **4** *Informal* perplex or deceive. **foxy** *adj* **foxier, foxiest** of or like a fox, esp. in craftiness. **foxglove** *n* tall plant with purple or white flowers. **foxhole** *n Mil* small pit dug for protection. **foxhound** *n* dog bred for hunting foxes. **fox terrier** small short-haired terrier. **foxtrot** *n* **1** ballroom dance with slow and quick steps. **2** music for this.

foyer [**foy**-ay] *n* entrance hall in a theatre, cinema, or hotel.

Fr **1** *Chem* francium. **2** Father.

Fr. Franc.

fracas [**frak**-ah] *n, pl* **-cas** noisy quarrel.

fraction *n* **1** numerical quantity that is not a whole number. **2** fragment, piece. **3** *Chem* substance separated by distillation. **fractional** *adj* **fractionally** *adv*

fractious *adj* easily upset and angered.

fracture *n* **1** breaking, esp. of a bone. ♦ *v* **2** break.

fragile *adj* **1** easily broken or damaged. **2** in a weakened physical state. **fragility** *n*

fragment *n* **1** piece broken off. **2** incomplete piece. ♦ *v* **3** break into pieces. **fragmentary** *adj* **fragmentation** *n*

fragrant *adj* sweet-smelling. **fragrance** *n* **1** pleasant smell. **2** perfume, scent.

frail *adj* **1** physically weak. **2** easily damaged. **frailty** *n, pl* **-ties** physical or moral weakness.

frame *n* **1** structure giving shape or support. **2** enclosing case or border, as round a picture. **3** person's build. **4** individual exposure on a strip of film. **5** individual game of snooker in a match. ♦ *v* **6** put together, construct. **7** put into words. **8** put into a frame. **9** *Slang* incriminate (a person) on a false charge. **frame of mind** mood or attitude. **frame-up** *n Slang* false incrimination. **framework** *n* supporting structure.

franc *n* monetary unit of France, Switzerland, Belgium, and various African countries.

franchise *n* **1** right to vote. **2** authorization to sell a company's goods.

Franciscan *n, adj* (friar or nun) of the order founded by St. Francis of Assisi.

francium *n Chem* radioactive metallic element.

Franco- *combining form* of France or the French.

frank *adj* **1** honest and straightforward in speech or attitude. ♦ *n* **2** official mark on a letter permitting delivery. ♦ *v* **3** put such a mark on (a letter). **frankly** *adv* **frankness** *n*

frankfurter *n* smoked sausage.

frankincense *n* aromatic gum resin burned as incense.

frantic *adj* **1** distracted with rage, grief, joy, etc. **2** hurried and disorganized. **frantically** *adv*

frappé *adj* (of drinks) chilled.

fraternal *adj* of a brother, brotherly. **fraternally** *adv* **fraternity** *n, pl* **-ties 1** group of people with shared interests, aims, etc. **2** brotherhood. **3** *US* male social club at college. **fraternize** *v* associate on friendly terms. **fraternization** *n* **fratricide** *n* **1** crime of killing one's brother. **2** person who does this.

Frau [rhymes with **how**] *n, pl* **Fraus, Frauen** German title, equivalent to *Mrs.* **Fräulein** [**froy**-line] *n, pl* **-leins, -lein** German title, equivalent to *Miss.*

fraud *n* **1** (criminal) deception, swindle. **2** person who acts in a deceitful way. **fraudulent** *adj* **fraudulence** *n*

fraught [**frawt**] *adj* tense or anxious. **fraught with** involving, filled with.

fray[1] *n* noisy quarrel or conflict.

fray[2] *v* **1** make or become ragged at the edge. **2** become strained.

frazzle *n Informal* exhausted state. **frazzled** *adj Informal* exhausted and irritable.

freak *n* **1** abnormal person or thing. **2** person who is excessively enthusiastic about something. ♦ *adj* **3** abnormal. **freakish** *adj* **freak out** *v Informal* (cause to) be in a heightened emotional state. **freaky** *adj* **freakier, freakiest** *Informal* weird, peculiar.

freckle *n* small brown spot on the skin. **freckled** *adj* marked with freckles.

free *adj* **freer, freest 1** able to act at will, not compelled or restrained. **2** not subject (to). **3** independent. **4** provided without charge. **5** generous, lavish. **6** not in use. **7** (of a person) not busy. **8** not fixed or joined. **9** (of a translation) not exact or literal. ♦ *v* **freeing, freed 10** release, liberate. **11** remove (obstacles, pain, etc.) from. **12** make available or usable. **a free hand** unrestricted freedom to act. **freely** *adv* **free-and-easy** *adj* casual and tolerant. **freebooter** *n* pirate. **free enterprise** economic system in which businesses compete for profit with little state control. **free fall** part of a parachute descent before the parachute opens. **free-for-all** *n Informal* brawl. **freehand** *adj* drawn without guiding instruments. **freehold** *n* tenure of land for life without restrictions. **freeholder** *n* **free house** public house not bound to sell only one brewer's products. **freelance** *adj, n* (of) a self-employed person doing specific pieces of work for various employers. **freeloader** *n Slang* habitual scrounger. **freeman** *n* person who has been given the freedom of a city. **free-market** *adj* denoting an economic system in which supply and demand regulate prices, wages, etc. **free-range** *adj* kept or produced in natural conditions. **freestanding** *adj* not attached to or supported by another object. **free-style** *n* competition, esp. in swimming, in which each participant uses the style of his or her choice. **freethinker** *n* person who forms his or her ideas independently of authority, esp. on religious matters. **free verse** unrhymed verse without a fixed rhythm. **freeway** *n Chiefly US* motorway. **freewheel** *v* travel downhill on a bicycle without pedalling. **free will 1** ability to make choices that are not externally determined. **2** ability to make a decision without outside coercion, e.g. *she left of her own free will.*

> *Free of* means 'not subject to': *free of charge. Free from* suggests a change of circumstances: *They were free from danger.*

-free *combining form* without, e.g. *a trouble-free journey.*

freedom *n* **1** being free. **2** exemption or immunity, e.g. *freedom from hunger.* **3** right or privilege of unlimited access, e.g. *the freedom of the city.*

Freemason *n* member of a secret fraternity pledged to help each other. **Freemasonry** *n*

freesia *n* plant with fragrant tubular flowers.

freeze *v* **freezing, froze, frozen 1** change from a liquid to a solid by the reduction of temperature, as water to ice. **2** preserve (food etc.) by extreme cold. **3** (cause to) be very cold. **4** become motionless with fear, shock, etc. **5** fix (prices or wages) at a particular level. **6** ban the exchange or collection of (loans, assets, etc.). ♦ *n* **7** period of very cold weather. **8** freezing of prices or wages. **freezer** *n* insulated cabinet for cold-storage of perishable foods. **freeze-dry** *v* preserve (food) by rapid freezing and drying in a vacuum. **freeze-frame** *n* single frame from a film or video recording shown as a still photograph. **freezing** *adj Informal* very cold. **freezing point** temperature below which a liquid turns into a solid.

freight [**frate**] *n* **1** commercial transport of goods. **2** cargo transported. **3** cost of this. ♦ *v* **4** send by freight. **freighter** *n* ship or aircraft for transporting goods.

French *n* **1** language of France, also spoken in parts of Belgium, Canada, and Switzerland. ♦ *adj* **2** of France, its people, or their language. **French bean** green bean whose pods are eaten. **French bread** white bread in a long thin crusty loaf. **French-Canadian** *adj* of or from the part of Canada where French is spoken. **French dressing** salad dressing of oil and vinegar. **French fries** potato chips. **French horn** brass wind instrument with a coiled tube. **French letter** *Slang* condom. **French polish** shellac varnish for wood. **French window** window extending to floor level, used as a door.

frenetic [frin-**net**-ik] *adj* uncontrolled, excited. **frenetically** *adv*

frenzy *n, pl* **-zies 1** violent mental derangement. **2** wild excitement. **frenzied** *adj* **frenziedly** *adv*

frequent *adj* **1** happening often. **2** habitual. ♦ *v* **3** visit habitually. **frequently** *adv* **frequency** *n, pl* **-cies 1** rate of occurrence. **2** *Physics* number of times a wave repeats itself in a given time.

fresco *n, pl* **-coes, -cos** watercolour painting done on wet plaster on a wall.

fresh *adj* **1** newly made, acquired, etc. **2** novel, original. **3** most recent. **4** further, additional. **5** (of food) not preserved. **6** (of water) not salty. **7** (of weather) brisk or invigorating. **8** not tired. **9** *Informal* impudent. **freshly** *adv* **freshness** *n* **freshen** *v* **1** make or become fresh or fresher. **2** (foll. by *up*) refresh oneself, esp. by washing. **3** (of the wind) increase. **fresher, freshman** *n* first-year student. **freshwater** *adj* of or living in fresh water.

fret[1] *v* **fretting, fretted 1** be worried. **2** rub or wear away. ♦ *n* **3** worried state. **fretful** *adj* irritable.

fret[2] *n* small bar on the fingerboard of a guitar etc.

fretwork *n* decorative carving in wood.

fret saw fine saw with a narrow blade, used for fretwork.

Freudian [**froy**-dee-an] *adj* of or relating to the psychoanalyst Sigmund Freud or his theories. **Freudian slip** action or error which may reveal an unconscious wish.

Fri. Friday.

friable [**fry**-a-bl] *adj* easily crumbled. **friability** *n*

friar *n* member of a male Roman Catholic religious order. **friary** *n, pl* **-ries** house of friars.

fricassee *n* stewed meat served in a thick white sauce.

fricative *n* **1** consonant produced by friction of the breath through a partially open mouth, such as (f) or (z). ♦ *adj* **2** relating to or being a fricative.

friction *n* **1** resistance met with by a body moving over another. **2** rubbing. **3** clash of wills or personalities. **frictional** *adj*

Friday *n* sixth day of the week. **Good Friday** Friday before Easter.

fridge *n* apparatus in which food and drinks are kept cool.

fried *v* past of FRY[1].

friend *n* **1** person whom one knows well and likes. **2** supporter or ally. **3** (**F-**) Quaker. **friendly** *adj* **-lier, -liest 1** showing or expressing liking. **2** not hostile, on the same side. ♦ *n, pl* **-lies 3** *Sport* match played for its own sake and not as part of a competition. **-friendly** *combining form* good or easy for the person or thing specified, e.g. *user-friendly*. **friendly society** association of people who pay regular dues in return for pensions, sickness benefits, etc. **friendliness** *n* **friendless** *adj* **friendship** *n*

fries *pl n* see FRY[1] (sense 3).

Friesian [**free**-zhan] *n* breed of black-and-white dairy cattle.

frieze [**freeze**] *n* ornamental band on a wall.

frigate [**frig**-it] *n* medium-sized fast warship.

fright *n* **1** sudden fear or alarm. **2** sudden alarming shock. **3** *Informal* grotesque person. **frighten** *v* **1** scare or terrify. **2** force (someone) to do something from fear. **frightening** *adj* **frighteningly** *adv* **frightful** *adj* **1** horrifying. **2** *Informal* very great. **frightfully** *adv*

frigid [**frij**-id] *adj* **1** (of a woman) sexually unresponsive. **2** very cold. **3** excessively formal. **frigidity** *n*

frill *n* **1** gathered strip of fabric attached at one edge. ♦ *pl* **2** superfluous decorations or details. **frilled** *adj* **frilly** *adj*

fringe *n* **1** hair cut short and hanging over the forehead. **2** ornamental edge of hanging threads, tassels, etc. **3** outer edge. **4** less important parts of an activity or group. ♦ *v* **5** decorate with a fringe. ♦ *adj* **6** (of theatre) unofficial or unconventional. **fringed** *adj* **fringe benefit** benefit given in addition to a regular salary.

frippery *n, pl* **-peries 1** useless ornamentation. **2** trivia.

Frisian *n* **1** language spoken in the NW Netherlands and adjacent islands. **2** speaker of this language. ♦ *adj* **3** of this language or its speakers.

frisk *v* **1** move or leap playfully. **2** *Informal* search (a person) for concealed weapons etc. ♦ *n* **3** playful movement. **4** *Informal* instance of searching a person. **frisky** *adj* **friskier, friskiest** lively or high-spirited. **friskily** *adv*

frisson [**frees**-sonn] *n* shiver of fear or excitement.

fritter *n* piece of food fried in batter.

fritter away *v* waste.

frivolous *adj* **1** not serious or sensible. **2** enjoyable but trivial. **frivolity** *n, pl* **-ties**

frizz *v* form (hair) into stiff wiry curls. **frizzy** *adj* **frizzier, frizziest**

frizzle *v* cook or heat until crisp and shrivelled.

fro *adv* away, only in *to and fro*.

frock *n* dress. **frock coat** man's skirted coat as worn in the 19th century.

frog *n* smooth-skinned tailless amphibian with long back legs used for jumping. **frog in one's throat** phlegm on the vocal cords, hindering speech. **frogman** *n* swimmer with a rubber suit and breathing equipment for working underwater. **frogmarch** *v* force (a resisting person) to move by holding his arms. **frogspawn** *n* jelly-like substance containing frog's eggs.

frolic *v* **-icking, -icked 1** run and play in a lively way. ♦ *n* **2** lively and merry behaviour. **frolicsome** *adj* playful.

from *prep* indicating the point of departure, source, distance, cause, change of state, etc.

> The use of *off* to mean *from* is very informal: *They bought milk from* (rather than *off*) *a farmer.*

frond *n* long leaf or leaflike part of a fern, palm, or seaweed.

front *n* **1** fore part. **2** position directly before or ahead. **3** seaside promenade. **4** battle line or area. **5** *Meteorol* dividing line between two different air masses. **6** outward appearance. **7** *Informal* cover for another, usu. criminal, activity. **8** group with a common goal. **9** particular field of activity, e.g. *on the economic front.* ♦ *adj* **10** of or at the front. ♦ *v* **11** face (onto). **12** be a front of or for. **13** be the presenter of (a television show). **frontal** *adj* **frontage** *n* facade of a building. **front bench** parliamentary leaders of the government or opposition. **front-bencher** *n* **frontrunner** *n* *Informal* person regarded as most likely to win a race, election, etc.

frontier *n* **1** area of a country bordering on another. **2** edge of the settled area of a country. ♦ *pl* **3** limit of knowledge in a particular field.

frontispiece *n* illustration facing the title page of a book.

frost *n* **1** white frozen dew or mist. **2** atmospheric temperature below freezing point. ♦ *v* **3** become covered with frost. **frosted** *adj* (of glass) having a rough surface to make it opaque. **frosting** *n* *Chiefly US* sugar icing. **frosty** *adj* **frostier, frostiest 1** characterized or covered by frost. **2** unfriendly. **frostily** *adv* **frostiness** *n* **frostbite** *n* destruction of tissue, esp. of the fingers or ears, by cold. **frostbitten** *adj*

froth *n* **1** mass of small bubbles. **2** trivial but superficially attractive ideas or entertainment. ♦ *v* **3** foam. **frothy** *adj* **frothier, frothiest**

frown *v* **1** wrinkle one's brows in worry, anger, or thought. **2** look disapprovingly (on). ♦ *n* **3** frowning expression.

frowsty *adj* stale or musty.

frowzy, frowsy *adj* **-zier, -ziest** *or* **-sier, -siest** dirty or unkempt.

froze *v* past tense of FREEZE. **frozen** *v* past participle of FREEZE.

FRS Fellow of the Royal Society.

fructify *v* **-fying, -fied** (cause to) bear fruit. **fructification** *n*

fructose *n* crystalline sugar occurring in many fruits.

frugal [**froo**-gl] *adj* **1** thrifty, sparing. **2** meagre and inexpensive. **frugally** *adv* **frugality** *n*

fruit *n* **1** part of a plant containing seeds, esp. if edible. **2** any plant product useful to man. **3** (often pl) result of an action or effort. ♦ *v* **4** bear fruit. **fruiterer** *n* person who sells fruit. **fruitful** *adj* useful or productive. **fruitfully** *adv* **fruitless** *adj* useless or unproductive. **fruitlessly** *adv* **fruity** *adj* **fruitier, fruitiest 1** of or like fruit. **2** (of a voice) mellow. **3** *Informal* mildly bawdy. **fruitcake** *n* cake containing dried fruit. **fruit machine** coin-operated gambling machine. **fruit salad, cocktail** dish consisting of pieces of different kinds of fruit.

fruition [froo-**ish**-on] *n* fulfilment of something worked for or desired.

frump *n* dowdy woman. **frumpy** *adj* **frumpier, frumpiest**

frustrate *v* **1** upset or anger. **2** hinder or prevent. **frustrated** *adj* **frustrating** *adj* **frustration** *n*

frustum *n, pl* **-tums, -ta** *Geom* part of a cone or pyramid contained between the base and a plane parallel to the base that intersects the solid.

fry[1] *v* **frying, fried 1** cook or be cooked in fat or oil. ♦ *n, pl* **fries 2** (also **fry-up**) dish of fried food. ♦ *pl* **3** potato chips.

frying pan shallow pan used for frying food. **out of the frying pan into the fire** from a bad situation into a worse one.

fry[2] *pl n* young fishes. **small fry** young or insignificant people.

ft. **1** foot. **2** feet.

fuchsia [**fyew**-sha] *n* ornamental shrub with hanging flowers.

fuck *Taboo* ♦ *v* **1** have sexual intercourse (with). ♦ *n* **2** act of sexual intercourse. ♦ *interj* **3** expression of strong disgust or anger. **fuck off** *v Taboo slang* go away. **fuck up** *v Taboo slang* make a mess of (something).

fuddle *v* **1** cause to be intoxicated or confused. ♦ *n* **2** confused state. **fuddled** *adj*

fuddy-duddy *adj, n, pl* **-dies** *Informal* old-fashioned (person).

fudge[1] *n* soft caramel-like sweet.

fudge[2] *v* **1** make (an issue) less clear deliberately. **2** avoid making a firm statement or decision.

fuel *n* **1** substance burned or treated to produce heat or power. **2** something that intensifies (a feeling etc.). ♦ *v* **fuelling, fuelled 3** provide with fuel.

fug *n* hot stale atmosphere. **fuggy** *adj* **fuggier, fuggiest**

fugitive [**fyew**-jit-iv] *n* **1** person who flees, esp. from arrest or pursuit. ♦ *adj* **2** fleeing. **3** transient.

fugue [**fyewg**] *n* musical composition in which a theme is repeated in different parts.

Führer *n German* leader: title used by Hitler as Nazi dictator.

-ful *adj suffix* **1** full of or characterized by, e.g. *painful; restful.* **2** able or tending to, e.g. *useful.* ♦ *n suffix* **3** as much as will fill the thing specified, e.g. *mouthful.*

fulcrum *n, pl* **-crums, -cra** pivot about which a lever turns.

fulfil *v* **-filling, -filled 1** bring about the achievement of (a desire or promise). **2** carry out (a request or order). **3** do what is required. **fulfilment** *n* **fulfil oneself** *v* achieve one's potential.

full[1] *adj* **1** containing as much or as many as possible. **2** abundant in supply. **3** having had enough to eat. **4** plump. **5** complete, whole. **6** (of a garment) of ample cut. **7** (of a sound or flavour) rich and strong. ♦ *adv* **8** completely. **9** directly. **10** very. **fully** *adv* **fullness** *n* **in full** without shortening. **full back** defensive player in various sports. **full-blooded** *adj* vigorous or enthusiastic. **full-blown** *adj* fully developed. **full board** provision by a hotel of a bed and all meals. **full-bodied** *adj* having a full rich flavour or quality. **full house 1** theatre filled to capacity. **2** (in bingo) set of numbers needed to win. **full-length** *adj* **1** (of a mirror, portrait, etc.) showing the whole human body. **2** not abridged. **full moon** phase of the moon when it is visible as a fully illuminated disc. **full-scale** *adj* **1** (of a plan) of actual size. **2** using all resources. **full stop** punctuation mark (.) at the end of a sentence and after abbreviations. **full time** (in football, rugby, etc.) end of the game. **full-time** *adj* for all of the normal working week. **full up** filled to capacity.

full[2] *v* clean, shrink, and press cloth. **fuller** *n* **fuller's earth** absorbent clay used for clarifying oils and fats, fulling cloth, etc.

fulmar *n* Arctic sea bird.

fulminate *v* (foll. by *against*) criticize or denounce angrily. **fulmination** *n*

fulsome *adj* distastefully excessive or insincere.

fumble *v* **1** handle awkwardly. **2** say awkwardly. ♦ *n* **3** act of fumbling.

fume *v* **1** be very angry. **2** give out smoke or vapour. **3** treat with fumes. ♦ *n* **4** pungent smoke or vapour.

fumigate [**fyew**-mig-gate] *v* disinfect with fumes. **fumigation** *n*

fun *n* enjoyment or amusement. **make fun of** mock or tease. **funny** *adj* **funnier, funniest 1** comical, humorous. **2** odd. **funny bone** part of the elbow where the nerve is near the surface. **funnily** *adv*

function *n* **1** purpose something exists for. **2** way something works. **3** large or formal social event. **4** *Maths* quantity whose value depends on the varying value of another. **5** sequence of operations performed by a computer at a key stroke. ♦ *v* **6** operate or work. **7** (foll. by *as*) fill the role of. **functional** *adj* **1** of or as a function. **2** practical rather than decorative. **3** in working order. **functionally** *adv* **functionary** *n, pl* **-aries** official.

fund *n* **1** stock of money for a special purpose. **2** supply or store. ♦ *pl* **3** money resources. ♦ *v* **4** provide money to. **funding** *n*

fundamental *adj* **1** essential or primary. **2** basic. ♦ *n* **3** basic rule or fact. **fundamentally** *adv* **fundamentalism** *n* literal or strict interpretation of a religion. **fundamentalist** *n, adj*

funeral *n* ceremony of burying or cremating a dead person. **funeral director** undertaker. **funeral parlour** place where the dead are prepared for burial or cremation.

funerary *adj* of or for a funeral.

funereal [fyew-**neer**-ee-al] *adj* gloomy or sombre.

funfair *n* entertainment with machines to ride on and stalls.

fungus *n, pl* **-gi, -guses** plant without leaves, flowers, or roots, such as a mushroom or mould. **fungal, fungous** *adj* **fungicide** *n* substance that destroys fungi.

funicular [fyew-**nik**-yew-lar] *n* cable railway on a mountainside or cliff.

funk[1] *n* style of dance music with a strong beat. **funky** *adj* **funkier, funkiest** (of music) having a strong beat.

funk[2] *Informal* ♦ *n* **1** nervous or fearful state. ♦ *v* **2** avoid (doing something) through fear.

funnel *n* **1** cone-shaped tube for pouring liquids into a narrow opening. **2** chimney of a ship or locomotive. ♦ *v* **-nelling, -nelled 3** (cause to) move through or as if through a funnel.

funny *adj* see FUN.

fur *n* **1** soft hair of a mammal. **2** animal skin with the fur left on. **3** garment made of this. **4** whitish coating on the tongue or inside a kettle. ♦ *v* **5** cover or become covered with fur. **furry** *adj* **furrier, furriest** **furrier** *n* dealer in furs.

furbish *v* smarten up.

furcate *v* **1** divide into two parts. ♦ *adj* **2** forked, branching.

furious *adj* **1** very angry. **2** violent or unrestrained. **furiously** *adv*

furl *v* roll up and fasten (a sail, umbrella, or flag). **furled** *adj*

furlong *n* eighth of a mile.

furlough [**fur**-loh] *n* leave of absence from military duty.

furnace *n* **1** enclosed chamber containing a very hot fire. **2** *Informal* very hot place.

furnish *v* **1** provide (a house or room) with furniture. **2** supply, provide. **furnishings** *pl n* furniture, carpets, and fittings. **furniture** *n* large movable articles such as chairs and wardrobes.

furore [fyew-**ror**-ee] *n* very excited or angry reaction.

furrow *n* **1** trench made by a plough. **2** groove, esp. a wrinkle on the forehead. ♦ *v* **3** make or become wrinkled. **4** make furrows in.

further *adv* **1** in addition. **2** to a greater distance or extent. ♦ *adj* **3** additional. **4** more distant. ♦ *v* **5** assist the progress of. **further education** education beyond school other than at a university. **furthest** *adv* **1** to the greatest distance or extent. ♦ *adj* **2** most distant. **furtherance** *n* **furthermore** *adv* besides. **furthermost** *adj* most distant.

furtive *adj* sly and secretive. **furtively** *adv*

fury *n, pl* **-ries 1** wild anger. **2** uncontrolled violence. **3** person with a violent temper.

furze *n* gorse.

fuse[1] *n* cord containing an explosive for detonating a bomb.

fuse[2] *n* **1** safety device for electric circuits, containing a wire that melts and breaks the connection when the circuit is overloaded. ♦ *v* **2** (cause to) fail as a result of a blown fuse. **3** equip (a plug) with a fuse. **4** join or combine. **5** unite by melting. **6** melt with heat.

fuselage [**fyew**-zill-lahzh] *n* body of an aircraft.

fusible *adj* capable of being melted.

fusilier [fyew-zill-**leer**] *n* soldier of certain regiments.

fusillade [fyew-zill-**lade**] *n* **1** continuous discharge of firearms. **2** outburst of criticism, questions, etc.

fusion *n* **1** melting. **2** product of fusing. **3** (also **nuclear fusion**) combination of the nucleus of two atoms with the release of energy. **4** something new created by a mixture of qualities, ideas, or things. **5** popular music blending styles, esp. jazz and funk.

fuss *n* **1** needless activity or worry. **2** complaint or objection. **3** great display of attention. ♦ *v* **4** make a fuss. **fussy** *adj* **fussier, fussiest 1** inclined to fuss. **2** overparticular. **3** overelaborate. **fussily** *adv* **fussiness** *n*

fusty *adj* **-tier, -tiest 1** stale-smelling. **2** behind the times. **fustiness** *n*

futile [**fyew**-tile] *adj* unsuccessful or useless. **futility** *n*

futon [**foo**-tonn] *n* Japanese padded quilt, laid on the floor as a bed.

future *n* **1** time to come. **2** what will happen. **3** prospects. ♦ *adj* **4** yet to come or be. **5** of or relating to time to come. **6** (of a verb tense) indicating that the action specified has not yet taken place. **futuristic** *adj* of a design appearing to belong to some future time.

fuzz[1] *n* mass of fine or curly hairs or fibres. **fuzzy** *adj* **fuzzier, fuzziest 1** of, like, or covered with fuzz. **2** blurred or indistinct. **3** (of hair) tightly curled. **fuzzily** *adv* **fuzziness** *n*

fuzz[2] *n Slang* police.

fwd forward.

G g

g **1** gram(s). **2** (acceleration due to) gravity.

Ga *Chem* gallium.

GA Georgia.

gab *n, v* **gabbing, gabbed** *Informal* talk or chatter. **gift of the gab** eloquence. **gabby** *adj* **-bier, -biest** *Informal* talkative.

gabardine, gaberdine *n* strong twill cloth used esp. for raincoats.

gabble *v* **1** speak rapidly and indistinctly. ♦ *n* **2** rapid indistinct speech.

gable *n* triangular upper part of a wall between sloping roofs. **gabled** *adj*

gad *v* **gadding, gadded. gad about, around** go around in search of pleasure. **gadabout** *n* pleasure-seeker.

gadfly *n* **1** fly that bites cattle. **2** constantly annoying person.

gadget *n* small mechanical device or appliance. **gadgetry** *n* gadgets.

gadoid [**gay**-doid] *adj* **1** of the cod family of marine fishes. ♦ *n* **2** gadoid fish.

gadolinium *n Chem* silvery-white metallic element.

Gael [**gayl**] *n* speaker of Gaelic. **Gaelic** [**gal**-lik, **gay**-lik] *n* **1** any of the Celtic languages of Ireland and the Scottish Highlands. ♦ *adj* **2** of the Gaels or their language.

gaff[1] *n* stick with an iron hook for landing large fish.

gaff[2] *n* **blow the gaff** *Slang* divulge a secret.

gaffe *n* social blunder.

gaffer *n* **1** *Informal* foreman or boss. **2** old man.

gag[1] *v* **gagging, gagged** **1** choke or retch. **2** stop up the mouth of (a person) with cloth etc. **3** deprive of free speech. ♦ *n* **4** cloth etc. put into or tied across the mouth.

gag[2] *n Informal* joke.

gaga [**gah**-gah] *adj Slang* **1** senile. **2** foolishly doting.

gage *n, v US* gauge.

gaggle *n* **1** *Informal* disorderly crowd. **2** flock of geese.

gaiety *n* **1** cheerfulness. **2** merrymaking. **gaily** *adv* **1** merrily. **2** colourfully.

gain *v* **1** acquire or obtain. **2** increase or improve. **3** reach. **4** (of a watch or clock) be or become too fast. ♦ *n* **5** profit or advantage. **6** increase or improvement. **gainful** *adj* useful or profitable. **gainfully** *adv* **gain on, upon** *v* get nearer to or catch up with.

gainsay *v* **-saying, -said** deny or contradict.

gait *n* manner of walking.

gaiter *n* cloth or leather covering for the lower leg.

gal *n Slang* girl.

gal. gallon.

gala [**gah**-la] *n* **1** festival. **2** competitive sporting event.

galaxy *n, pl* **-axies** **1** system of stars. **2** gathering of famous people. **3** (**G-**) Milky Way. **galactic** *adj*

gale *n* **1** strong wind. **2** *Informal* loud outburst.

gall[1] [**gawl**] *n* **1** *Informal* impudence. **2** bitter feeling. **3** bile. **gall bladder** sac attached to the liver, storing bile. **gallstone** *n* hard mass formed in the gall bladder or its ducts.

gall[2] [**gawl**] *v* **1** annoy. **2** make sore by rubbing. ♦ *n* **3** sore caused by rubbing. **galling** *adj* annoying or bitterly humiliating.

gall[3] [**gawl**] *n* abnormal outgrowth on a tree or plant.

gallant *adj* **1** brave and noble. **2** (of a man) attentive to women. **gallantly** *adv* **gallantry** *n* **1** showy, attentive treatment of women. **2** bravery.

galleon *n* large three-masted sailing ship of the 15th–17th centuries.

gallery *n, pl* **-ries** **1** room or building for displaying works of art. **2** balcony in a church, theatre, etc. **3** passage in a mine. **4** covered walk with side openings. **5** long narrow room for a specific purpose, e.g. *shooting gallery.*

galley *n* **1** kitchen of a ship or aircraft. **2** *Hist* ship propelled by oars, usu. rowed by slaves. **galley slave 1** slave forced to row in a galley. **2** *Informal* drudge.

Gallic *adj* **1** French. **2** of ancient Gaul. **Gallicism** *n* French word or idiom.

gallinaceous *adj* of an order of birds including poultry, pheasants, and grouse.

gallium *n Chem* soft grey metallic element used in semiconductors.

gallivant *v* go about in search of pleasure.

gallon *n* liquid measure of eight pints, equal to 4.55 litres.

gallop *n* **1** horse's fastest pace. **2** galloping. ♦ *v* **galloping, galloped 3** go or ride at a gallop. **4** move or progress rapidly.

gallows *n* wooden structure used for hanging criminals.

Gallup poll *n* public opinion poll carried out by questioning a cross section of the population.

galore *adv* in abundance, e.g. *presents galore.*

galoshes *pl n* waterproof overshoes.

galumph *v Informal* leap or move about clumsily.

galvanic *adj* **1** of or producing an electric current generated by chemical means. **2** *Informal* stimulating or startling. **galvanize** *v* **1** stimulate into action. **2** coat (metal) with zinc. **galvanometer** *n* instrument for measuring small electric currents.

gambit *n* **1** opening line or move intended to secure an advantage. **2** *Chess* opening move involving the sacrifice of a pawn.

gamble *v* **1** play games of chance to win money. **2** act on the expectation of something. ♦ *n* **3** risky undertaking. **4** bet or wager. **gambler** *n* **gambling** *n*

gamboge [gam-**boje**] *n* gum resin used as a yellow pigment and purgative.

gambol *v* **-bolling, -bolled 1** jump about playfully, frolic. ♦ *n* **2** frolic.

game[1] *n* **1** amusement or pastime. **2** contest for amusement. **3** single period of play in a contest. **4** score needed to win a contest. **5** animals or birds hunted for sport or food. **6** their flesh. **7** scheme or trick. ♦ *pl* **8** athletic contests. ♦ *v* **9** gamble. ♦ *adj* **10** brave. **11** willing. **gamely** *adv* **gaming** *n* gambling. **gamey, gamy** *adj* **gamier, gamiest** having the smell or flavour of game. **gamekeeper** *n* person employed to breed game and prevent poaching. **gamesmanship** *n* art of winning by cunning practices without actually cheating.

game[2] *adj* lame, crippled.

gamete [**gam**-eet] *n Biol* reproductive cell.

gamin *n* street urchin.

gamine [**gam**-een] *n* slim boyish young woman.

gamma *n* third letter of the Greek alphabet. **gamma ray** electromagnetic ray of shorter wavelength and higher energy than an x-ray.

gammon *n* **1** cured or smoked ham. **2** hindquarter of a side of bacon.

gammy *adj* **-mier, -miest** same as GAME[2].

gamp *n Informal* umbrella.

gamut *n* whole range or scale (of music, emotions, etc.).

gander *n* **1** male goose. **2** *Informal* quick look.

gang *n* **1** (criminal) group. **2** organized group of workmen. **gangland** *n* criminal underworld. **gang up** *v* form an alliance (against).

gangling *adj* lanky and awkward.

ganglion *n* **1** group of nerve cells. **2** small harmless tumour.

gangplank *n* portable bridge for boarding or leaving a ship.

gangrene *n* decay of body tissue as a result of disease or injury. **gangrenous** *adj*

gangsta rap *n* style of music portraying life in Black ghettos in the US.

gangster *n* member of a criminal gang.

gangue *n* valueless material in an ore.

gangway *n* **1** passage between rows of

seats. **2** gangplank. **3** opening in a ship's side for a gangplank.

gannet *n* **1** large sea bird. **2** *Slang* greedy person.

gantry *n, pl* **-tries** structure supporting something such as a crane or rocket.

gaol [**jayl**] *n* same as JAIL.

gap *n* **1** break or opening. **2** interruption or interval. **3** divergence or difference. **gappy** *adj*

gape *v* **1** stare in wonder. **2** open the mouth wide. **3** be or become wide open. **gaping** *adj*

garage *n* **1** building used to house cars. **2** place for the refuelling, sale, and repair of cars. ♦ *v* **3** put or keep a car in a garage.

garb *n* **1** clothes. ♦ *v* **2** clothe.

garbage *n* rubbish.

garbled *adj* (of a story etc.) jumbled and confused.

garden *n* **1** piece of land for growing flowers, fruit, or vegetables. ♦ *pl* **2** ornamental park. ♦ *v* **3** cultivate a garden. **gardener** *n* **gardening** *n* **garden centre** place selling plants and gardening equipment.

gardenia [gar-**deen**-ya] *n* **1** large fragrant white waxy flower. **2** shrub bearing this.

gargantuan *adj* huge.

gargle *v* **1** wash the throat with (a liquid) by breathing out slowly through the liquid. ♦ *n* **2** liquid used for gargling. **3** act or sound of gargling.

gargoyle *n* waterspout carved in the form of a grotesque face, esp. on a church.

garish *adj* crudely bright or colourful. **garishly** *adv* **garishness** *n*

garland *n* **1** wreath of flowers worn or hung as a decoration. ♦ *v* **2** decorate with garlands.

garlic *n* pungent bulb of a plant of the onion family, used in cooking.

garment *n* **1** article of clothing. ♦ *pl* **2** clothes.

garner *v* collect or store.

garnet *n* red semiprecious stone.

garnish *v* **1** decorate (food). ♦ *n* **2** decoration for food.

garret *n* attic in a house.

garrison *n* **1** troops stationed in a town or fort. **2** fortified place. ♦ *v* **3** station troops in.

garrotte, garotte *n* **1** Spanish method of execution by strangling. **2** cord or wire used for this. ♦ *v* **3** kill by this method. **4** strangle.

garrulous *adj* talkative. **garrulously** *adv*

garter *n* band worn round the leg to hold up a sock or stocking. **the Garter** highest order of British knighthood.

gas *n, pl* **gases, gasses** **1** airlike substance that is not liquid or solid. **2** fossil fuel in the form of a gas, used for heating. **3** gaseous anaesthetic. **4** *Chiefly US* petrol. **5** poisonous gas used in warfare. ♦ *v* **gassing, gassed** **6** poison or render unconscious with gas. **7** *Informal* talk idly or boastfully. **gassy** *adj* **-sier, -siest** filled with gas. **gaseous** *adj* of or like gas. **gasbag** *n Informal* person who talks too much. **gas chamber** airtight room which is filled with poison gas to kill people or animals. **gasholder, gasometer** [gas-**som**-it-er] *n* large tank for storing gas. **gasify** *v* **-fying, -fied** change into a gas. **gasification** *n* **gas mask** mask with a chemical filter to protect the wearer against poison gas. **gasworks** *n* plant where coal gas is made.

gash *v* **1** make a long deep cut in. ♦ *n* **2** long deep cut.

gasket *n* piece of rubber etc. placed between the faces of a metal joint to act as a seal.

gasoline *n US* petrol.

gasp *v* **1** draw in breath sharply or with difficulty. **2** utter breathlessly. **3** (foll. by *for*) crave. ♦ *n* **4** convulsive intake of breath.

gastric *adj* of the stomach. **gastritis** *n* inflammation of the stomach lining.

gastroenteritis *n* inflammation of the stomach and intestines.

gastronomy *n* art of good eating. **gastronomic** *adj*

gastropod *n* mollusc, such as a snail,

with a single flattened muscular foot.

gate *n* **1** movable barrier, usu. hinged, in a wall or fence. **2** opening with a gate. **3** any entrance or way in. **4** (entrance money paid by) those attending a sporting event. **5** exit at an airport by which passengers get to an aircraft. **gatecrash** *v* enter (a party) uninvited. **gatehouse** *n* building at or above a gateway. **gateway** *n* **1** entrance with a gate. **2** means of access, e.g. *Bombay, gateway to India.*

gâteau [**gat**-toe] *n, pl* **-teaux** [-toes] rich elaborate cake.

gather *v* **1** assemble. **2** collect gradually. **3** increase gradually. **4** learn from information given. **5** pick or harvest. **6** draw (material) into small tucks or folds. **gathers** *pl n* gathered folds in material. **gathering** *n* assembly.

GATT General Agreement on Tariffs and Trade.

gauche [**gohsh**] *adj* socially awkward. **gaucheness** *n*

gaucho [**gow**-choh] *n, pl* **-chos** S American cowboy.

gaudy *adj* **gaudier, gaudiest** vulgarly bright or colourful. **gaudily** *adv* **gaudiness** *n*

gauge [**gayj**] *v* **1** estimate or judge. **2** measure the amount or condition of. ♦ *n* **3** measuring instrument. **4** scale or standard of measurement. **5** distance between the rails of a railway track. **6** capacity or extent.

Gaul *n* **1** native of ancient Gaul. **2** Frenchman.

gaunt *adj* **1** lean and haggard. **2** (of a place) desolate or bleak. **gauntness** *n*

gauntlet[1] *n* **1** heavy glove with a long cuff. **2** medieval armoured glove. **throw down the gauntlet** offer a challenge.

gauntlet[2] *n* **run the gauntlet** be exposed to criticism or unpleasant treatment.

gauze *n* transparent loosely-woven fabric, often used for surgical dressings. **gauzy** *adj*

gave *v* past tense of GIVE.

gavel [**gav**-el] *n* small hammer banged on a table by a judge, auctioneer, or chairman to call for attention.

gavotte *n* **1** old formal dance. **2** music for this.

gawk *v* **1** stare stupidly. ♦ *n* **2** clumsy awkward person. **gawky** *adj* **gawkier, gawkiest** clumsy or awkward. **gawkiness** *n*

gawp *v Slang* stare stupidly.

gay *adj* **1** homosexual. **2** carefree and merry. **3** colourful. ♦ *n* **4** homosexual. **gayness** *n* homosexuality.

> The meaning 'homosexual' is now the most frequent use of *gay,* which retains the meaning 'happy' only in older books.

gaze *v* **1** look fixedly. ♦ *n* **2** fixed look.

gazebo [gaz-**zee**-boh] *n, pl* **-bos, -boes** summerhouse with a good view.

gazelle *n* small graceful antelope.

gazette *n* official publication containing announcements. **gazetteer** *n* (part of) a book that lists and describes places.

gazump *v Brit & Aust* raise the price of a property after verbally agreeing it with (a prospective buyer).

gazunder *v Brit* reduce an offer on a property immediately before exchanging contracts having earlier agreed a higher price with the seller.

GB Great Britain.

GBH grievous bodily harm.

GC George Cross.

GCE **1** General Certificate of Education. **2** pass in a GCE examination.

GCSE **1** General Certificate of Secondary Education. **2** pass in a GCSE examination.

Gd *Chem* gadolinium.

Ge *Chem* germanium.

gear *n* **1** set of toothed wheels connecting with another or with a rack to change the direction or speed of transmitted motion. **2** mechanism for transmitting motion by gears. **3** setting of a gear to suit engine speed, e.g. *first gear.*

4 clothing or belongings. **5** equipment. ♦ *v* **6** prepare or organize for something. **in, out of gear** with the gear mechanism engaged *or* disengaged. **gearbox** *n* case enclosing a set of gears in a motor vehicle. **gear lever** lever for changing gears in a motor vehicle. **gear up** *v* prepare for an activity.

gecko *n, pl* **geckos, geckoes** small tropical lizard.

gee *interj US informal* mild exclamation of surprise, admiration, etc.

geek *n Informal* boring, unattractive person.

geese *n* plural of GOOSE.

geezer *n Informal* man.

Geiger counter [**guy**-ger] *n* instrument for detecting and measuring radiation.

geisha [**gay**-sha] *n, pl* **-sha, -shas** (in Japan) professional female companion for men.

gel [**jell**] *n* **1** jelly-like substance, esp. one used to secure a hairstyle. ♦ *v* **gelling, gelled 2** form a gel. **3** *Informal* take on a definite form.

gelatine [**jel**-at-teen], **gelatin** *n* **1** substance made by boiling animal bones. **2** edible jelly made of this. **gelatinous** [jel-**at**-in-uss] *adj* of or like jelly.

geld *v* castrate. **gelding** *n* castrated horse.

gelignite *n* type of dynamite used for blasting.

gem *n* **1** precious stone or jewel. **2** highly valued person or thing.

Gemini *n* (the twins) third sign of the zodiac.

gen *n Informal* information. **gen up on** *v* **genning, genned** *Informal* make or become fully informed about.

gendarme [**zhohn**-darm] *n* member of the French police force.

gender *n* **1** state of being male or female. **2** *Grammar* classification of nouns in certain languages as masculine, feminine, or neuter.

gene [**jean**] *n* part of a cell which determines inherited characteristics.

genealogy [jean-ee-**al**-a-gee] *n, pl* **-gies** (study of) the history and descent of a family or families. **genealogical** *adj* **genealogist** *n*

genera [**jen**-er-a] *n* plural of GENUS.

general *adj* **1** common or widespread. **2** of or affecting all or most. **3** not specific. **4** including or dealing with various or miscellaneous items. **5** highest in authority or rank, e.g. *general manager.* ♦ *n* **6** very senior army officer. **in general** mostly or usually. **generally** *adv* **generality** *n, pl* **-ties 1** general principle. **2** state of being general. **generalize** *v* **1** draw general conclusions. **2** speak in generalities. **3** make widely known or used. **generalization** *n* **general election** election in which representatives are chosen for every constituency. **general practitioner** nonspecialist doctor serving a local area.

generalissimo *n, pl* **-mos** supreme commander of combined armed forces.

generate *v* produce or bring into being. **generative** *adj* capable of producing. **generator** *n* machine for converting mechanical energy into electrical energy.

generation *n* **1** all the people born about the same time. **2** successive stage in descent of people or animals. **3** average time between two generations (about 30 years). **4** generating.

generic [jin-**ner**-ik] *adj* of a class, group, or genus. **generically** *adv*

generous *adj* **1** free in giving. **2** free from pettiness. **3** plentiful. **generously** *adv* **generosity** *n*

genesis [**jen**-iss-iss] *n, pl* **-eses** [-iss-eez] beginning or origin.

genetic [jin-**net**-tik] *adj* of genes or genetics. **genetics** *n* study of heredity and variation in organisms. **geneticist** *n* **genetic engineering** alteration of the genetic structure of an organism for a particular purpose. **genetic fingerprinting** use of a person's unique DNA pattern for identification.

Geneva Convention *n* international agreement establishing a code for wartime treatment of the sick, wounded, and prisoners of war.

genial [**jean**-ee-al] *adj* cheerful and friendly. **genially** *adv* **geniality** *n*
genie [**jean**-ee] *n* (in fairy tales) servant who appears by magic and grants wishes.
genital *adj* of the sexual organs or reproduction. **genitals, genitalia** [jen-it-**ail**-ya] *pl n* external sexual organs.
genitive *n* grammatical case indicating possession or association.
genius [**jean**-yuss] *n* **1** (person with) exceptional ability in a particular field. **2** person considered as exerting influence of a certain sort.
genocide [**jen**-no-side] *n* murder of a race of people.
genre [**zhohn**-ra] *n* style of literary, musical, or artistic work.
gent *n Informal* gentleman. **gents** *n* men's public toilet.
genteel *adj* affectedly proper and polite. **genteelly** *adv* **gentility** *n* **1** noble birth or ancestry. **2** polite and well-mannered behaviour.
gentian [**jen**-shun] *n* mountain plant with deep blue flowers. **gentian violet** violet dye used as an antiseptic.
gentile *adj, n* non-Jewish (person).
gentle *adj* **1** mild or kindly. **2** not rough or severe. **3** gradual. **4** easily controlled, tame. **gentleness** *n* **gently** *adv* **gentlefolk, gentlefolks** *pl n* people of good breeding. **gentleman** *n* **1** polite well-bred man. **2** man of high social position. **3** polite name for a man. **gentlemanly** *adj* **gentlewoman** *n fem*
gentry *n* people just below the nobility in social rank. **gentrification** *n* taking-over of a traditionally working-class area by middle-class incomers. **gentrify** *v* **-fying, -fied**
genuflect *v* bend the knee as a sign of reverence or deference. **genuflection, genuflexion** *n*
genuine *adj* **1** not fake, authentic. **2** sincere. **genuinely** *adv* **genuineness** *n*
genus [**jean**-uss] *n, pl* **genera** **1** group into which a family of animals or plants is divided. **2** kind, type.
geocentric *adj* **1** having the earth as a centre. **2** measured as from the earth's centre.
geodesic *adj* **1** of the geometry of curved surfaces. ♦ *n* **2** shortest line between two points on a curve.
geodesy *n* study of the shape and size of the earth.
geography *n* **1** study of the earth's physical features, climate, population, etc. **2** physical features of a region. **geographer** *n* **geographical, geographic** *adj* **geographically** *adv*
geology *n* **1** study of the earth's origin, structure, and composition. **2** geological features of an area. **geological** *adj* **geologically** *adv* **geologist** *n*
geometry *n* branch of mathematics dealing with points, lines, curves, and surfaces. **geometric, geometrical** *adj* **geometrically** *adv* **geometrician** *n*
Geordie *n* **1** person from, or dialect of, Tyneside. ♦ *adj* **2** of Tyneside or its dialect.
George Cross *n* British award for bravery.
georgette [jor-**jet**] *n* fine silky fabric.
Georgian *adj* of the time of any of the kings of Britain called George, esp. 1714–1830.
geostationary *adj* (of a satellite) orbiting so as to remain over the same point of the earth's surface.
geothermal *adj* of or using the heat in the earth's interior.
geranium *n* cultivated plant with red, pink, or white flowers.
gerbil [**jer**-bill] *n* burrowing desert rodent of Asia and Africa.
geriatrics *n* branch of medicine dealing with old age and its diseases. **geriatric** *adj, n* old (person). **geriatrician** *n*
germ *n* **1** microbe, esp. one causing disease. **2** beginning from which something may develop. **3** simple structure that can develop into a complete organism. **germicide** *n* substance that kills germs.
German *n* **1** language of Germany, Austria, and part of Switzerland. **2** person from Germany. ♦ *adj* **3** of Germany or

its language. **Germanic** *adj* **German measles** contagious disease accompanied by a cough, sore throat, and red spots. **German shepherd dog** Alsatian.

germane *adj* **germane to** relevant to.

germanium *n Chem* brittle grey element that is a semiconductor.

germinate *v* (cause to) sprout or begin to grow. **germination** *n* **germinal** *adj* **1** of or in the earliest stage of development. **2** of germs.

gerontology *n* study of ageing and the problems of elderly people. **gerontologist** *n*

gerrymandering *n* division of voting constituencies in order to give an unfair advantage to one party.

gerund [**jer**-rund] *n* noun formed from a verb, such as *living.*

Gestapo *n* secret state police of Nazi Germany.

gestation *n* **1** (period of) carrying of young in the womb between conception and birth. **2** developing of a plan or idea in the mind.

gesticulate *v* make expressive movements with the hands and arms. **gesticulation** *n*

gesture *n* **1** movement to convey meaning. **2** thing said or done to show one's feelings. ♦ *v* **3** gesticulate.

get *v* **getting, got 1** obtain or receive. **2** bring or fetch. **3** contract (an illness). **4** capture or seize. **5** (cause to) become as specified, e.g. *get wet.* **6** understand. **7** (often foll. by *to*) come (to) or arrive (at). **8** go on board (a plane, bus, etc.). **9** persuade. **10** receive a broadcast signal. **11** *Informal* annoy. **12** *Informal* have the better of. **13** be revenged on. **get across** *v* (cause to) be understood. **get at** *v* **1** gain access to. **2** imply or mean. **3** criticize. **getaway** *adj, n* (used in) escape. **get by** *v* manage in spite of difficulties. **get off** *v* **1** leave (a bus, train, etc.). **2** (cause to) avoid the consequences of, or punishment for, an action. **get off with** *v Informal* start a romantic or sexual relationship with. **get on** *v* **1** board (a bus, train, etc.). **2** be friends with. **3** (foll. by *with*) continue to do. **4** grow old. **get over** *v* recover from. **get through** *v* **1** (cause to) succeed. **2** use up (money or supplies). **get through to** *v* **1** make (a person) understand. **2** contact by telephone. **get-up** *n Informal* costume. **get up to** *v* be involved in.

geyser [**geez**-er] *n* **1** spring that discharges steam and hot water. **2** domestic gas water heater.

ghastly *adj* **-lier, -liest 1** *Informal* unpleasant. **2** deathly pale. **3** *Informal* unwell. **4** *Informal* horrible. **ghastliness** *n*

ghat *n* **1** (in India) steps leading down to a river. **2** (in India) place of cremation. **3** mountain pass.

ghee [**gee**] *n* (in Indian cookery) clarified butter.

gherkin *n* small pickled cucumber.

ghetto *n, pl* **-tos, -toes** slum area inhabited by a deprived minority. **ghetto-blaster** *n Informal* large portable cassette recorder or CD player.

ghillie *n* same as GILLIE.

ghost *n* **1** disembodied spirit of a dead person. **2** faint trace. **3** faint secondary image on a television screen. ♦ *v* **4** ghostwrite. **ghostly** *adj* **ghost town** deserted town. **ghostwrite** *v* write (a book or article) on behalf of another person who is credited as the author. **ghostwriter** *n*

ghoul [**gool**] *n* **1** person with morbid interests. **2** demon that eats corpses. **ghoulish** *adj*

GHQ *Mil* General Headquarters.

GI *n Informal* US soldier.

giant *n* **1** mythical being of superhuman size. **2** very large person or thing. **3** person of exceptional ability or importance. ♦ *adj* **4** huge. **giantess** *n fem*

gibber [**jib**-ber] *v* speak or utter rapidly and unintelligibly. **gibberish** *n* rapid unintelligible talk.

gibbet [**jib**-bit] *n* gallows for displaying executed criminals.

gibbon [**gib**-bon] *n* agile tree-dwelling ape of S Asia.

gibbous *adj* (of the moon) more than

half but less than fully illuminated.

gibe [**jibe**] *v, n* same as JIBE[1].

giblets [**jib**-lets] *pl n* gizzard, liver, heart, and neck of a fowl.

giddy *adj* **-dier, -diest 1** having or causing a feeling of dizziness. **2** happy and excited. **giddily** *adv* **giddiness** *n*

gift *n* **1** present. **2** natural talent. ♦ *v* **3** make a present of. **gifted** *adj* talented.

gig[1] *n* **1** single performance by pop or jazz musicians. ♦ *v* **gigging, gigged 2** play a gig or gigs.

gig[2] *n* **1** light two-wheeled horse-drawn carriage. **2** long light rowing boat.

giga- *prefix* **1** denoting 10^9, e.g. *gigavolt.* **2** *Computers* denoting 2^{30}, e.g. *gigabyte.*

gigantic *adj* enormous.

giggle *v* **1** laugh nervously or foolishly. ♦ *n* **2** such a laugh. **3** *Informal* amusing person or thing. **giggly** *adj*

gigolo [**jig**-a-lo] *n, pl* **-los** man paid by an older woman to be her escort or lover.

gigot *n* leg of lamb or mutton.

gild *v* **gilding, gilded** *or* **gilt 1** put a thin layer of gold on. **2** make falsely attractive.

gill[1] [**gill**] *n* radiating structure beneath the cap of a mushroom.

gill[2] [**jill**] *n* liquid measure of quarter of a pint, equal to 0.142 litres.

gillie *n* (in Scotland) attendant for hunting or fishing.

gills [**gillz**] *pl n* breathing organs in fish and other water creatures.

gillyflower *n* fragrant flower.

gilt[1] *v* **1** past of GILD. ♦ *adj* **2** covered with a thin layer of gold. ♦ *n* **3** thin layer of gold used as decoration. **gilt-edged** *adj* denoting government stocks on which interest payments and final repayments are guaranteed.

gilt[2] *n* young female pig.

gimbals *pl n* set of pivoted rings which allow nautical instruments to remain horizontal at sea.

gimcrack [**jim**-krak] *adj* **1** showy but cheap. **2** shoddy.

gimlet [**gim**-let] *n* small tool with a screwlike tip for boring holes in wood. **gimlet-eyed** *adj* having a piercing glance.

gimmick *n* something designed to attract attention or publicity. **gimmickry** *n* **gimmicky** *adj*

gin[1] *n* alcoholic drink flavoured with juniper berries.

gin[2] *n* **1** wire noose used to trap small animals. **2** machine for separating seeds from raw cotton.

ginger *n* **1** root of a tropical plant, used as a spice. **2** light orange-brown colour. **gingery** *adj* **ginger ale, beer** fizzy ginger-flavoured soft drink. **gingerbread** *n* moist cake flavoured with ginger. **ginger group** group within a larger group that agitates for a more active policy. **ginger nut, snap** crisp ginger-flavoured biscuit.

gingerly *adv* **1** cautiously. ♦ *adj* **2** cautious.

gingham *n* cotton cloth, usu. checked or striped.

gingivitis [jin-jiv-**vite**-iss] *n* inflammation of the gums.

ginkgo [**gink**-go] *n, pl* **-goes** ornamental Chinese tree.

ginseng [**jin**-seng] *n* (root of) a plant believed to have tonic and energy-giving properties.

Gipsy *n, pl* **-sies** same as GYPSY.

giraffe *n* African ruminant mammal with a spotted yellow skin and long neck and legs.

gird *v* **girding, girded** *or* **girt 1** put a belt round. **2** secure with or as if with a belt. **3** surround. **gird (up) one's loins** prepare for action.

girder *n* large metal beam.

girdle[1] *n* **1** woman's elastic corset. **2** belt. **3** *Anat* encircling structure or part. ♦ *v* **4** surround or encircle.

girdle[2] *n Scot* griddle.

girl *n* **1** female child. **2** young woman. **3** girlfriend. **4** *Informal* any woman. **girlhood** *n* **girlish** *adj* **girlie** *adj Informal* featuring photographs of naked or scantily clad women. **girlfriend** *n* **1** girl or woman with whom a person is romantically or sexually involved. **2** female friend. **Girl Guide** same as GUIDE.

giro [**jire**-oh] *n, pl* **-ros** **1** system of transferring money within a post office or bank directly from one account to another. **2** *Informal* social security payment by giro cheque.

girt *v* a past of GIRD.

girth *n* **1** measurement round something. **2** band round a horse to hold the saddle in position.

gist [**jist**] *n* substance or main point of a matter.

give *v* **giving, gave, given** **1** present (something) to another person. **2** transfer in exchange or payment. **3** impart. **4** attribute. **5** administer. **6** be a source of. **7** utter or emit. **8** sacrifice or devote. **9** organize or host. **10** concede. **11** yield or break under pressure. ♦ *n* **12** resilience or elasticity. **give away** *v* **1** donate as a gift. **2** reveal. **3** hand over (a bride) formally to her husband in a marriage ceremony. **giveaway** *n* **1** something that reveals hidden feelings or intentions. ♦ *adj* **2** very cheap or free. **give in** *v* admit defeat. **give off** *v* emit. **give out** *v* **1** distribute. **2** emit. **3** come to an end or fail. **give over** *v* **1** set aside for a specific purpose. **2** *Informal* cease. **give up** *v* **1** abandon. **2** acknowledge defeat.

gizzard *n* part of a bird's stomach.

glacé [**glass**-say] *adj* preserved in a thick sugary syrup.

glacier *n* slow-moving mass of ice formed by accumulated snow. **glacial** *adj* **1** of ice or glaciers. **2** very cold. **3** unfriendly. **glaciated** *adj* covered with or affected by glaciers. **glaciation** *n*

glad *adj* **gladder, gladdest** **1** pleased and happy. **2** causing happiness. **glad to** very willing to (do something). **the glad eye** *Informal* inviting or seductive glance. **gladly** *adv* **gladness** *n* **gladden** *v* make glad. **gladsome** *adj Old-fashioned* joyous or cheerful. **glad rags** *Informal* best clothes.

glade *n* open space in a forest.

gladiator *n* (in ancient Rome) man trained to fight in arenas to provide entertainment.

gladiolus *n, pl* **-lus, -li, -luses** garden plant with sword-shaped leaves.

glamour *n* alluring charm or fascination. **glamorous** *adj* alluring. **glamorize** *v*

glance *v* **1** look rapidly or briefly. **2** glint or gleam. ♦ *n* **3** brief look. **glancing** *adj* hitting at an oblique angle. **glance off** *v* strike and be deflected off (an object) at an oblique angle.

gland *n* **1** organ that produces and secretes substances in the body. **2** similar organ in a plant. **glandular** *adj* **glandular fever** infectious viral disease characterized by fever and swollen lymph nodes.

glare *v* **1** stare angrily. **2** be unpleasantly bright. ♦ *n* **3** angry stare. **4** unpleasant brightness. **glaring** *adj* **1** conspicuous. **2** unpleasantly bright. **glaringly** *adv*

glasnost *n* policy of openness and accountability, esp., formerly, in the USSR.

glass *n* **1** hard brittle, usu. transparent substance consisting of metal silicates or similar compounds. **2** tumbler. **3** its contents. **4** objects made of glass. **5** mirror. **6** barometer. ♦ *pl* **7** spectacles. **glassy** *adj* **1** like glass. **2** expressionless. **glassiness** *n* **glasshouse** *n* **1** greenhouse. **2** *Informal* army prison.

glaucoma *n* eye disease.

glaze *v* **1** fit or cover with glass. **2** cover with a protective shiny coating. **3** cover (food) with beaten egg or milk before cooking. **4** become glassy. ♦ *n* **5** transparent coating. **6** substance used for this. **glazier** *n* person who fits windows with glass.

gleam *n* **1** small beam or glow of light. **2** brief or faint indication. ♦ *v* **3** emit a gleam. **gleaming** *adj*

glean *v* **1** gather (facts etc.) bit by bit. **2** gather (the useful remnants of a crop) after harvesting. **gleaner** *n*

glee *n* triumph and delight. **gleeful** *adj* **gleefully** *adv*

glen *n* deep narrow valley.

glengarry *n, pl* **-ries** brimless Scottish cap with a crease down the crown.

glib *adj* **glibber, glibbest** fluent but insincere or superficial. **glibly** *adv* **glibness** *n*

glide *v* **1** move easily and smoothly. **2** (of an aircraft) move without the use of engines. **3** pass gradually and imperceptibly. ♦ *n* **4** smooth easy movement. **glider** *n* aircraft without an engine which floats on air currents. **gliding** *n* sport of flying gliders.

glimmer *v* **1** shine faintly, flicker. ♦ *n* **2** faint gleam. **3** faint indication.

glimpse *n* **1** brief or incomplete view. **2** vague indication. ♦ *v* **3** catch a glimpse of.

glint *v* **1** gleam brightly. ♦ *n* **2** bright gleam.

glissade *n* **1** gliding step in ballet. **2** controlled slide down a snow slope. ♦ *v* **3** perform a glissade.

glissando *n Music* slide between two notes in which all intermediate notes are played.

glisten *v* gleam by reflecting light.

glitch *n* small problem that stops something from working properly.

glitter *v* **1** shine with bright flashes. **2** be showy. ♦ *n* **3** sparkle or brilliance. **4** superficial glamour. **5** tiny pieces of shiny decorative material.

glitzy *adj* **glitzier, glitziest** *Slang* showily attractive.

gloaming *n* twilight.

gloat *v* (often foll. by *over*) regard one's own good fortune or the misfortune of others with smug or malicious pleasure.

glob *n* rounded mass of thick fluid.

globe *n* **1** sphere with a map of the earth on it. **2** spherical object. **the globe** the earth. **global** *adj* **1** worldwide. **2** total or comprehensive. **global warming** increase in the overall temperature worldwide believed to be caused by the greenhouse effect. **globally** *adv* **globetrotter** *n* habitual worldwide traveller. **globetrotting** *n, adj*

globule *n* small round drop. **globular** *adj*

globulin *n* simple protein found in living tissue.

glockenspiel *n* percussion instrument consisting of small metal bars played with hammers.

gloom *n* **1** melancholy or depression. **2** darkness. **gloomy** *adj* **gloomier, gloomiest** **gloomily** *adv*

glory *n, pl* **-ries** **1** praise or honour. **2** splendour. **3** praiseworthy thing. **4** adoration or worship. ♦ *v* **-rying, -ried** **5** (foll. by *in*) triumph or exalt. **glorify** *v* **-fying, -fied** **1** make (something) seem more worthy than it is. **2** praise. **3** worship. **glorification** *n* **glorious** *adj* **1** brilliantly beautiful. **2** delightful. **3** full of or conferring glory. **gloriously** *adv* **glory hole** *Informal* untidy cupboard or storeroom.

gloss[1] *n* **1** surface shine or lustre. **2** superficially attractive appearance. **3** paint or cosmetic giving a shiny finish. ♦ *v* **4** make glossy. **glossy** *adj* **-sier, -siest** **1** smooth and shiny. **2** (of a magazine) printed on shiny paper. **3** superficially attractive or sophisticated. **glossily** *adv* **glossiness** *n* **gloss over** *v* (try to) cover up or pass over (a fault or error).

gloss[2] *n* **1** explanatory comment added to the text of a book. ♦ *v* **2** add glosses to.

glossary *n, pl* **-ries** list of special or technical words with definitions.

glottis *n, pl* **-tises, -tides** vocal cords and the space between them. **glottal** *adj* **glottal stop** speech sound made by closing and then opening the glottis.

glove *n* covering for the hand with individual sheaths for each finger and the thumb. **gloved** *adj* covered by a glove or gloves. **glove compartment** small storage area in the dashboard of a car.

glow *v* **1** emit light and heat without flames. **2** shine. **3** have a feeling of wellbeing or satisfaction. **4** (of a colour) look warm. **5** be hot. ♦ *n* **6** glowing light. **7** warmth of colour. **8** feeling of wellbeing. **glow-worm** *n* insect giving out a green light.

glower [rhymes with **power**] *v, n* scowl.

gloxinia *n* tropical plant with large bell-shaped flowers.

glucose *n* kind of sugar found in fruit.

glue *n* **1** natural or synthetic sticky substance used as an adhesive. ♦ *v* **gluing** *or* **glueing, glued 2** fasten with glue. **3** (foll. by *to*) pay full attention to, e.g. *her eyes were glued to the TV.* **gluey** *adj* **glue-sniffing** *n* inhaling of glue fumes for intoxicating or hallucinatory effects.

glum *adj* **glummer, glummest** sullen or gloomy. **glumly** *adv*

glut *n* **1** excessive supply. ♦ *v* **glutting, glutted 2** oversupply. **3** feed or fill to excess.

gluten [**gloo**-ten] *n* protein found in cereal grain.

glutinous [**gloo**-tin-uss] *adj* sticky or gluey.

glutton *n* **1** greedy person. **2** person with a great capacity for something. **gluttonous** *adj* **gluttony** *n*

glycerine, glycerin [**gliss**-ser-in] *n* colourless sweet liquid used widely in chemistry and industry.

glycerol [**gliss**-ser-ol] *n* technical name for GLYCERIN.

gm gram.

GM 1 grant-maintained. **2** genetically modified.

G-man *n, pl* **G-men** *US slang* FBI agent.

GMO genetically modified organism.

GMT Greenwich Mean Time.

gnarled *adj* rough, twisted, and knobbly.

gnash *v* grind (the teeth) together in anger or pain.

gnat *n* small biting two-winged fly.

gnaw *v* **gnawing, gnawed, gnawed** *or* **gnawn 1** bite or chew steadily. **2** (foll. by *at*) cause constant distress (to). **gnawing** *adj*

gneiss *n* coarse-grained metamorphic rock.

gnome *n* **1** imaginary creature like a little old man. **2** *Facetious* international banker or financier.

gnomic [**no**-mik] *adj* of pithy sayings.

Gnosticism *n* religious movement believing in intuitive spiritual knowledge. **Gnostic** *n, adj*

GNP Gross National Product.

gnu [**noo**] *n* oxlike S African antelope.

go *v* **going, went, gone 1** move to or from a place. **2** be in regular attendance at. **3** depart. **4** function. **5** be, do, or become as specified. **6** contribute to a result, e.g. *it just goes to show.* **7** be allotted to a specific purpose or recipient. **8** be sold. **9** blend or harmonize. **10** fail or break down. **11** elapse. **12** be got rid of. **13** attend. **14** reach or exceed certain limits, e.g. *she's gone too far this time.* **15** be acceptable. **16** carry authority. ♦ *n* **17** attempt. **18** verbal attack. **19** turn. **20** *Informal* energy or vigour. **make a go of** be successful at. **on the go** active and energetic. **go-ahead** *adj* enterprising or ambitious. **go back on** *v* break (a promise etc.). **go-between** *n* intermediary. **go for** *v* **1** *Informal* choose. **2** attack. **3** apply to equally. **go-getter** *n* energetically ambitious person. **go-go dancer** scantily dressed erotic dancer. **go off** *v* **1** stop functioning. **2** explode. **3** ring or sound. **4** occur as specified. **5** *Informal* become stale or rotten. **6** *Informal* stop liking. **go out** *v* **1** go to entertainments or social functions. **2** be romantically involved (with). **3** be extinguished. **4** (of a broadcast) be transmitted. **go over** *v* examine or check. **go-slow** *n* deliberate slowing of work-rate as an industrial protest. **go through** *v* **1** suffer or undergo. **2** examine or search.

goad *v* **1** provoke (someone) to take some kind of action, usu. in anger. ♦ *n* **2** spur or provocation. **3** spiked stick for driving cattle.

goal *n* **1** *Sport* posts through which the ball or puck has to be propelled to score. **2** score made in this way. **3** aim or purpose. **goalie** *n Informal* goalkeeper. **goalkeeper** *n* player whose task is to stop shots entering the goal. **goalpost** *n* one of the two posts supporting the crossbar of a goal. **move the goalposts** change the aims of an activity to ensure the desired result.

goat *n* **1** sure-footed ruminant animal with horns. **2** foolish person. **get some-**

one's goat *Slang* annoy someone. **goatee** *n* pointed tuftlike beard.

gob *n* **1** lump of a soft substance. **2** *Slang* mouth.

gobbet *n* lump, esp. of food.

gobble[1] *v* eat hastily and greedily.

gobble[2] *n* **1** rapid gurgling cry of the male turkey. ♦ *v* **2** make this noise.

gobbledegook, gobbledygook *n* unintelligible (official) language or jargon.

goblet *n* drinking cup without handles.

goblin *n* (in folklore) small malevolent creature.

goby *n, pl* **-by, -bies** small spiny-finned fish.

god *n* **1** spirit or being worshipped as having supernatural power. **2** object of worship, idol. **3** (**G-**) (in monotheistic religions) the Supreme Being, creator and ruler of the universe. **the gods** top balcony in a theatre. **goddess** *n fem* **godlike** *adj* **godly** *adj* devout or pious. **godliness** *n* **god-fearing** *adj* pious and devout. **godforsaken** *adj* desolate or dismal. **godsend** *n* something unexpected but welcome.

godetia *n* plant with showy flowers.

godparent *n* person who promises at a child's baptism to bring the child up as a Christian. **godchild** *n* child for whom a person stands as godparent. **goddaughter** *n* **godfather** *n* **1** male godparent. **2** head of a criminal, esp. Mafia, organization. **godmother** *n* **godson** *n*

godwit *n* shore bird with long legs and an upturned bill.

goer *n* person who attends something regularly, e.g. *filmgoer.*

goggle *v* **1** (of the eyes) bulge. **2** stare. **goggles** *pl n* protective spectacles. **gogglebox** *n Slang* television set.

Goidelic *adj, n* (of) the group of Celtic languages consisting of Scottish Gaelic, Irish Gaelic, and Manx.

going *n* **1** condition of the ground for walking or riding over. **2** speed or progress. **3** departure. ♦ *adj* **4** thriving. **5** current or accepted. **going-over** *n, pl* **goings-over 1** *Informal* investigation or examination. **2** scolding or thrashing. **goings-on** *pl n* mysterious or unacceptable events.

goitre [**goy**-ter] *n* swelling of the thyroid gland in the neck.

go kart *n* small low-powered racing car.

gold *n* **1** yellow precious metal. **2** coins or articles made of this. **3** colour of gold. **4** wealth. ♦ *adj* **5** made of gold. **6** gold-coloured. **goldcrest** *n* small bird with a yellow crown. **gold-digger** *n* **1** person who digs for gold. **2** *Informal* woman who uses her sexual attractions to get money from a man. **goldfinch** *n* kind of finch, the male of which has yellow-and-black wings. **goldfish** *n* orange fish kept in ponds or aquariums. **gold leaf** thin gold sheet used for gilding. **gold medal** medal given to the winner of a competition or race. **gold rush** migration of people to a territory where gold has been found. **goldsmith** *n* dealer in or maker of gold articles.

golden *adj* **1** made of gold. **2** gold-coloured. **3** very successful or promising. **golden eagle** large mountain eagle of the N hemisphere. **golden goal** *Soccer* first goal scored in extra time, which wins the match for the side scoring it. **golden handshake** *Informal* payment to a departing employee. **golden mean** middle course between extremes. **golden rule** important principle. **golden wedding** fiftieth wedding anniversary.

golf *n* **1** outdoor game in which a ball is struck with clubs into a series of holes. ♦ *v* **2** play golf. **golfer** *n*

golliwog *n* soft black-faced doll.

golly *interj* exclamation of mild surprise.

goloshes *pl n* same as GALOSHES.

gonad *n* organ producing reproductive cells, such as a testicle or ovary.

gondola *n* **1** long narrow boat used in Venice. **2** suspended cabin of a cable car, airship, etc. **gondolier** *n* person who propels a gondola.

gone *v* past participle of GO. **goner** *n Informal* person or thing beyond help or recovery.

gong *n* **1** rimmed metal disc that produces a note when struck. **2** *Slang* medal.

gonorrhoea [gon-or-**ree**-a] *n* venereal disease with a discharge from the genitals.

good *adj* **better, best 1** giving pleasure. **2** morally excellent. **3** beneficial. **4** kindly. **5** talented. **6** well-behaved. **7** valid. **8** reliable. **9** financially sound. **10** complete or full. ♦ *n* **11** benefit. **12** positive moral qualities. ♦ *pl* **13** merchandise. **14** property. **as good as** virtually. **for good** permanently. **goodness** *n* **goodly** *adj* considerable. **goody** *n, pl* **-dies 1** *Informal* hero in a book or film. **2** enjoyable thing. **goody-goody** *adj, n* smugly virtuous (person). **good-for-nothing** *adj, n* irresponsible or worthless (person). **Good Friday** Friday before Easter, observed by Christians as a commemoration of the Crucifixion. **good-natured** *adj* tolerant and kindly. **Good Samaritan** person who helps another in distress. **goodwill** *n* **1** kindly feeling. **2** value of a business in reputation etc. over and above its tangible assets.

> Note that *good* is an adjective. To modify a verb, use *well: She did well.*

goodbye *interj, n* expression used on parting.

gooey *adj* **gooier, gooiest** *Informal* **1** sticky and soft. **2** sentimental.

goof *Informal* ♦ *n* **1** mistake. **2** stupid person. ♦ *v* **3** make a mistake. **goofy** *adj* **goofier, goofiest**

googly *n, pl* **-lies** *Cricket* ball that spins unexpectedly from off to leg on the bounce.

goon *n* **1** *Informal* stupid person. **2** *Chiefly US* hired thug.

goosander *n* type of duck.

goose *n, pl* **geese 1** web-footed bird like a large duck. **2** female of this bird. **3** silly person. **goose flesh, pimples** bumpy condition of the skin and bristling of the hair due to cold or fright. **goose step** march step in which the leg is raised rigidly.

gooseberry *n* **1** edible yellowy-green berry. **2** *Informal* unwanted third person accompanying a couple.

gopher [**go**-fer] *n* American burrowing rodent.

gore[1] *n* blood from a wound.

gore[2] *v* pierce with horns.

gore[3] *n* tapering piece of material in a garment, sail, or umbrella.

gorge *n* **1** deep narrow valley. ♦ *v* **2** eat greedily. **make one's gorge rise** cause feelings of disgust or nausea.

gorgeous *adj* **1** strikingly beautiful or attractive. **2** *Informal* very pleasant. **gorgeously** *adv*

gorgon *n* terrifying or repulsive woman.

Gorgonzola *n* sharp-flavoured blue-veined Italian cheese.

gorilla *n* largest of the apes, found in Africa.

gormless *adj Informal* stupid.

gorse *n* prickly yellow-flowered shrub.

gory *adj* **gorier, goriest 1** horrific or bloodthirsty. **2** involving bloodshed.

gosh *interj* exclamation of mild surprise or wonder.

goshawk *n* large hawk.

gosling *n* young goose.

gospel *n* **1** (**G-**) any of the first four books of the New Testament. **2** doctrine held to be of great importance. **3** unquestionable truth. **4** Black religious music originating in the churches of the Southern US.

gossamer *n* **1** very fine fabric. **2** filmy cobweb.

gossip *n* **1** idle talk, esp. about other people. **2** person who engages in gossip. ♦ *v* **gossiping, gossiped 3** engage in gossip. **gossipy** *adj*

got *v* past of GET. **have got** possess. **have got to** need or be required to.

Goth *n* member of an East Germanic people who invaded the Roman Empire.

Gothic *adj* **1** (of architecture) of or in the style common in Europe from the 12th–16th centuries, with pointed arches. **2** of or in an 18th-century literary style characterized by gloom and the supernatural. **3** (of print) using a heavy ornate typeface. **4** barbarous.

gotten *v US* past participle of GET.

gouache *n* (painting using) watercolours mixed with glue.

Gouda *n* mild-flavoured Dutch cheese.

gouge [**gowj**] *v* **1** scoop or force out. **2** cut (a hole or groove) in (something). ♦ *n* **3** hole or groove. **4** chisel with a curved cutting edge.

goulash [**goo**-lash] *n* rich stew seasoned with paprika.

gourd [**goord**] *n* **1** fleshy fruit of a climbing plant. **2** its dried shell, used as a container.

gourmand [**goor**-mand] *n* person who is very keen on food and drink.

gourmet [**goor**-may] *n* connoisseur of food and drink.

gout [**gowt**] *n* disease causing inflammation of the joints. **gouty** *adj*

govern *v* **1** rule, direct, or control. **2** exercise restraint over (temper etc.). **3** decide or determine. **governable** *adj* **governance** *n* governing. **governess** *n* woman teacher in a private household. **government** *n* **1** executive policy-making body of a state. **2** exercise of political authority over a country or state. **3** system by which a country or state is ruled. **governmental** *adj* **governor** *n* **1** official governing a province or state. **2** senior administrator of a society, institution, or prison. **3** chief executive of a US state. **4** *Informal* person's father or employer. **governor general** representative of the Crown in a Commonwealth country.

gown *n* **1** woman's long formal dress. **2** surgeon's overall. **3** official robe worn by judges, clergymen, etc.

goy *n, pl* **goyim, goys** *Slang* Jewish word for a non-Jew.

GP general practitioner.

GPO General Post Office.

grab *v* **grabbing, grabbed 1** grasp suddenly, snatch. **2** take (food, drink, or rest) hurriedly. **3** seize illegally. ♦ *n* **4** sudden snatch. **5** mechanical device for gripping.

grace *n* **1** beauty and elegance. **2** polite, kind behaviour. **3** goodwill or favour. **4** courtesy or decency. **5** delay granted. **6** free favour of God shown towards man. **7** short prayer of thanks for a meal. **8** (**G-**) title of a duke, duchess, or archbishop. ♦ *pl* **9** (**G-**) (in Greek mythology) three sister goddesses, givers of charm and beauty. ♦ *v* **10** honour. **11** add grace to. **graceful** *adj* **gracefully** *adv* **graceless** *adj* **gracious** *adj* **1** kind and courteous. **2** condescendingly polite. **3** elegant. **graciously** *adv* **grace note** *Music* note ornamenting a melody.

grade *n* **1** place on a scale of quality, rank, or size. **2** mark or rating. **3** *US & Aust* class in school. ♦ *v* **4** arrange in grades. **5** assign a grade to. **make the grade** succeed. **gradation** *n* **1** (stage in) a series of degrees or steps. **2** arrangement in stages.

gradient *n* (degree of) slope.

gradual *adj* occurring, developing, or moving in small stages. **gradually** *adv*

graduate *v* **1** receive a degree or diploma. **2** (often foll. by *to*) change by degrees. **3** group by type or quality. **4** mark (a container etc.) with units of measurement. ♦ *n* **5** holder of a degree. **graduation** *n*

graffiti [graf-**fee**-tee] *pl n* words or drawings scribbled or sprayed on walls etc.

> English does not have a singular form for this word and tends to use *graffiti* for both singular and multiple examples.

graft[1] *n* **1** surgical transplant of skin or tissue. **2** shoot of a plant set in the stalk of another. ♦ *v* **3** transplant (living tissue) surgically. **4** insert (a plant shoot) in another stalk.

graft[2] *Informal* ♦ *n* **1** hard work. **2** obtaining of money by misusing one's position. ♦ *v* **3** work hard. **grafter** *n*

grail *n* same as HOLY GRAIL.

grain *n* **1** seedlike fruit of a cereal plant. **2** cereal plants in general. **3** small hard particle. **4** very small amount. **5** arrangement of fibres, as in wood. **6** texture or pattern resulting from this. ♦ *v* **7** paint in imitation of the grain of wood or leather. **go against the grain** be contrary to one's natural inclination. **grainy** *adj*

gram, gramme *n* metric unit of mass equal to one thousandth of a kilogram.

gramineous, graminaceous *adj* of or like grass.

graminivorous *adj* (of animals) feeding on grass.

grammar *n* **1** branch of linguistics dealing with the form, function, and order of words. **2** use of words. **3** book on the rules of grammar. **grammarian** *n* **grammatical** *adj* according to the rules of grammar. **grammatically** *adv* **grammar school** esp. formerly, a secondary school providing an education with a strong academic bias.

gramme *n* same as GRAM.

gramophone *n* old-fashioned type of record player.

grampus *n, pl* **-puses** dolphin-like mammal.

gran *n Informal* grandmother.

granary *n, pl* **-ries** **1** storehouse for grain. **2** region that produces a large amount of grain.

grand *adj* **1** large or impressive, imposing. **2** ambitious or important. **3** dignified or haughty. **4** *Informal* excellent. **5** (of a total) final. ♦ *n* **6** *Slang* thousand pounds or dollars. **7** grand piano. **grandchild** *n* child of one's child. **granddaughter** *n* female grandchild. **grandfather** *n* male grandparent. **grandfather clock** tall standing clock with a pendulum and wooden case. **grandmother** *n* female grandparent. **grandparent** *n* parent of one's parent. **grand piano** large harp-shaped piano with the strings set horizontally. **grand slam** winning of all the games or major tournaments in a sport in one season. **grandson** *n* male grandchild. **grandstand** *n* terraced block of seats giving the best view at a sports ground.

grandee *n* **1** Spanish nobleman of the highest rank. **2** person of high station.

grandeur *n* **1** magnificence. **2** nobility or dignity.

grandiloquent *adj* using pompous language. **grandiloquence** *n*

grandiose *adj* **1** imposing. **2** pretentiously grand. **grandiosity** *n*

Grand Prix [gron **pree**] *n* international formula motor race.

grange *n* country house with farm buildings.

granite [**gran**-nit] *n* very hard igneous rock often used in building.

granivorous *adj* feeding on grain or seeds.

granny, grannie *n, pl* **-nies** *Informal* grandmother. **granny flat** flat in or added to a house, suitable for an elderly parent.

grant *v* **1** consent to fulfil (a request). **2** give formally. **3** admit. ♦ *n* **4** sum of money provided by a government for a specific purpose, such as education. **take for granted** **1** accept as true without proof. **2** take advantage of without due appreciation.

Granth *n* sacred scripture of Sikhism.

granule *n* small grain. **granular** *adj* of or like grains. **granulated** *adj* (of sugar) in the form of coarse grains. **granulation** *n*

grape *n* small juicy green or purple berry, eaten raw or used to produce wine, raisins, currants, or sultanas. **grapeshot** *n* bullets which scatter when fired. **grapevine** *n* **1** grape-bearing vine. **2** *Informal* unofficial way of spreading news.

grapefruit *n* large round yellow citrus fruit.

graph *n* drawing showing the relation of different numbers or quantities plotted against a set of axes.

graphic *adj* **1** vividly descriptive. **2** of or using drawing, painting, etc. **graphics** *pl n* diagrams, graphs, etc., esp. as used on a television programme or computer screen. **graphically** *adv*

graphite *n* soft black form of carbon, used in pencil leads.

graphology *n* study of handwriting.

graphologist *n*

grapnel *n* device with several hooks, used to grasp or secure things.

grapple *v* **1** try to cope with (something difficult). **2** come to grips with (a person). ♦ *n* **3** grapnel. **grappling iron** grapnel.

grasp *v* **1** grip something firmly. **2** understand. **3** try to seize. ♦ *n* **4** grip or clasp. **5** understanding. **6** total rule or possession. **grasping** *adj* greedy or avaricious.

grass *n* **1** common type of plant with jointed stems and long narrow leaves, including cereals and bamboo. **2** lawn. **3** pasture land. **4** *Slang* marijuana. **5** *Slang* person who informs, esp. on criminals. ♦ *v* **6** cover with grass. **7** (often foll. by *on*) *Slang* inform on. **grassy** *adj* **-sier, -siest** **grasshopper** *n* jumping insect with long hind legs. **grass roots** **1** ordinary members of a group, as distinct from its leaders. **2** essentials. **grassroots** *adj* **grass snake** harmless European snake. **grass widow** wife whose husband is absent for a time.

grate[1] *v* **1** rub into small bits on a rough surface. **2** scrape with a harsh rasping noise. **3** annoy. **grater** *n* **grating** *adj* **1** harsh or rasping. **2** annoying.

grate[2] *n* framework of metal bars for holding fuel in a fireplace. **grating** *n* framework of metal bars covering an opening.

grateful *adj* feeling or showing gratitude. **gratefully** *adv* **gratefulness** *n*

gratify *v* **-fying, -fied** **1** satisfy or please. **2** indulge (a desire or whim). **gratification** *n*

gratis *adv, adj* free, for nothing.

gratitude *n* feeling of being thankful for a favour or gift.

gratuitous [grat-**tyoo**-it-uss] *adj* **1** unjustified, e.g. *gratuitous violence.* **2** given free. **gratuitously** *adv*

gratuity [grat-**tyoo**-it-ee] *n, pl* **-ties** money given for services rendered, tip.

grave[1] *n* hole for burying a corpse. **the grave** death. **gravestone** *n* stone marking a grave. **graveyard** *n* cemetery.

grave[2] *adj* **1** causing concern. **2** serious and solemn. **3** important. **gravely** *adv*

grave[3] [rhymes with **halve**] *n* accent (`) over a vowel to indicate a special pronunciation.

gravel *n* **1** mixture of small stones and coarse sand. **2** small rough stones in the kidneys or bladder. ♦ *v* **-elling, -elled** **3** cover with gravel. **gravelled** *adj* covered with gravel. **gravelly** *adj* **1** covered with gravel. **2** rough-sounding.

graven [**grave**-en] *adj* carved or engraved.

gravid [**grav**-id] *adj Med* pregnant.

gravitate *v* **1** be influenced or drawn towards. **2** *Physics* move by gravity. **gravitation** *n* **gravitational** *adj*

gravity *n, pl* **-ties** **1** force of attraction of one object for another, esp. of objects to the earth. **2** seriousness or importance. **3** solemnity.

gravy *n, pl* **-vies** **1** juices from meat in cooking. **2** sauce made from these.

gray *adj Chiefly US* grey.

grayling *n* fish of the salmon family.

graze[1] *v* feed on grass. **grazier** *n* person who feeds cattle for market. **grazing** *n* land on which grass for livestock is grown.

graze[2] *v* **1** scratch or scrape the skin. **2** touch lightly in passing. ♦ *n* **3** slight scratch or scrape.

grease *n* **1** soft melted animal fat. **2** any thick oily substance. ♦ *v* **3** apply grease to. **greasy** *adj* **greasier, greasiest** **1** covered with or containing grease. **2** unctuous in manner. **greasiness** *n* **grease gun** appliance for injecting oil or grease into machinery. **greasepaint** *n* theatrical make-up.

great *adj* **1** large in size or number. **2** extreme or more than usual. **3** important. **4** pre-eminent. **5** *Informal* excellent. **the greats** the most successful people in a particular field. **great-** *prefix* one generation older or younger than, e.g. *great-grandfather.* **greatly** *adv* **greatness** *n* **greatcoat** *n* heavy overcoat. **Great Dane** very large dog with short smooth hair.

greave *n* piece of armour for the shin.

grebe *n* diving water bird.

Grecian [**gree**-shan] *adj* of ancient Greece.

greed *n* excessive desire for food, wealth, etc. **greedy** *adj* **greedier, greediest** **greedily** *adv* **greediness** *n*

Greek *n* **1** language of Greece. **2** person from Greece. ♦ *adj* **3** of Greece, the Greeks, or the Greek language.

green *adj* **1** of a colour between blue and yellow. **2** characterized by green plants or foliage. **3** (**G-**) of or concerned with environmental issues. **4** unripe. **5** envious or jealous. **6** immature or gullible. ♦ *n* **7** colour between blue and yellow. **8** area of grass kept for a special purpose. **9** (**G-**) person concerned with environmental issues. ♦ *pl* **10** green vegetables. ♦ *v* **11** make or become green. **greenness** *n* **greenish, greeny** *adj* **greenery** *n* vegetation. **green belt** protected area of open country around a town. **greenfinch** *n* European finch with dull green plumage in the male. **green fingers** skill in gardening. **greenfly** *n* green aphid, a common garden pest. **greengage** *n* sweet green plum. **greengrocer** *n* shopkeeper selling vegetables and fruit. **greenhorn** *n* novice. **greenhouse** *n* glass building for rearing plants. **greenhouse effect** rise in the temperature of the earth caused by heat absorbed from the sun being unable to leave the atmosphere. **green light** **1** signal to go. **2** permission to proceed with something. **greenroom** *n* room for actors when offstage. **greenshank** *n* large European sandpiper.

Greenwich Mean Time *n* local time of the 0° meridian passing through Greenwich, England: the basis for calculating times throughout the world.

greet *v* **1** meet with expressions of welcome. **2** receive in a specified manner. **3** be immediately noticeable to. **greeting** *n*

gregarious *adj* **1** fond of company. **2** (of animals) living in flocks or herds.

Gregorian calendar *n* calendar introduced by Pope Gregory XIII and still widely used.

Gregorian chant *n* same as PLAINSONG.

gremlin *n* imaginary being blamed for mechanical malfunctions.

grenade *n* small bomb thrown by hand or fired from a rifle. **grenadier** *n* soldier of a regiment formerly trained to throw grenades.

grenadine [gren-a-**deen**] *n* syrup made from pomegranates.

grew *v* past tense of GROW.

grey *adj* **1** of a colour between black and white. **2** (of hair) partly turned white. **3** dismal or dark. **4** dull or boring. ♦ *n* **5** grey colour. **6** grey or white horse. **greying** *adj* (of hair) turning grey. **greyish** *adj* **greyness** *n* **grey matter** *Informal* brains.

greyhound *n* swift slender dog used in racing.

greylag *n* large grey goose.

grid *n* **1** network of horizontal and vertical lines, bars, etc. **2** national network of electricity supply cables.

griddle *n* flat iron plate for cooking.

gridiron *n* **1** frame of metal bars for grilling food. **2** American football pitch.

gridlock *n* situation where traffic is not moving. **gridlocked** *adj*

grief *n* deep sadness. **come to grief** end unsuccessfully. **grieve** *v* (cause to) feel grief. **grievance** *n* real or imaginary cause for complaint. **grievous** *adj* **1** very severe or painful. **2** very serious.

griffin *n* mythical monster with an eagle's head and wings and a lion's body.

grill *n* **1** device on a cooker that radiates heat downwards. **2** grilled food. **3** gridiron. **4** grillroom. ♦ *v* **5** cook under a grill. **6** question relentlessly. **grilling** *n* relentless questioning. **grillroom** *n* restaurant serving grilled foods.

grille, grill *n* grating over an opening.

grilse [**grillss**] *n* salmon on its first return from the sea to fresh water.

grim *adj* **grimmer, grimmest** **1** stern. **2** harsh or forbidding. **3** very unpleasant. **4** harshly ironic or sinister. **grimly** *adv*

grimness *n*

grimace *n* **1** ugly or distorted facial expression of pain, disgust, etc. ♦ *v* **2** make a grimace.

grimalkin *n* old female cat.

grime *n* **1** ingrained dirt. ♦ *v* **2** make very dirty. **grimy** *adj* **griminess** *n*

grin *v* **grinning, grinned 1** smile broadly, showing the teeth. ♦ *n* **2** broad smile.

grind *v* **grinding, ground 1** crush or rub to a powder. **2** smooth or sharpen by friction. **3** scrape together with a harsh noise. **4** oppress. **5** *Informal* work or study hard. ♦ *n* **6** *Informal* hard work. **7** act or sound of grinding. **grind out** *v* produce in a routine or uninspired manner. **grindstone** *n* stone used for grinding.

grip *n* **1** firm hold or grasp. **2** way in which something is grasped. **3** mastery or understanding. **4** *US* travelling bag. **5** handle. ♦ *v* **gripping, gripped 6** grasp or hold tightly. **7** affect strongly. **8** hold the interest or attention of. **gripping** *adj*

gripe *v* **1** *Informal* complain persistently. ♦ *n* **2** *Informal* complaint. **3** sudden intense bowel pain.

grisly *adj* **-lier, -liest** horrifying or ghastly.

grist *n* grain for grinding. **grist to one's mill** something which can be turned to advantage.

gristle *n* tough stringy animal tissue found in meat. **gristly** *adj*

grit *n* **1** rough particles of sand. **2** courage. **3** coarse sandstone. ♦ *pl* **4** coarsely ground grain. ♦ *v* **gritting, gritted 5** spread grit on (an icy road etc.). **6** clench or grind (the teeth). **gritty** *adj* **-tier, -tiest gritter** *n* **grittiness** *n*

grizzle *v Informal* whine or complain.

grizzled *adj* grey-haired.

grizzly *n, pl* **-zlies** large American bear (also **grizzly bear**).

groan *n* **1** deep sound of grief or pain. **2** *Informal* complaint. ♦ *v* **3** utter a groan. **4** *Informal* complain. **5** (usu. foll. by *beneath* or *under*) be weighed down (by).

groat *n Hist* fourpenny piece.

groats *pl n* hulled and crushed grain of various cereals.

grocer *n* shopkeeper selling foodstuffs. **grocery** *n, pl* **-ceries 1** business or premises of a grocer. ♦ *pl* **2** goods sold by a grocer.

grog *n* spirit, usu. rum, and water.

groggy *adj* **-gier, -giest** *Informal* faint, shaky, or dizzy.

groin *n* **1** place where the legs join the abdomen. **2** edge made by the intersection of two vaults.

grommet *n* **1** ring or eyelet. **2** *Med* tube inserted in the ear to drain fluid from the middle ear.

groom *n* **1** person who looks after horses. **2** bridegroom. **3** officer in a royal household. ♦ *v* **4** make or keep one's clothes and appearance neat and tidy. **5** brush or clean a horse. **6** train (someone) for a future role.

groove *n* **1** long narrow channel in a surface. **2** spiral channel in a gramophone record. **3** routine. **grooved** *adj* **groovy** *adj* **groovier, grooviest** *Dated slang* attractive or exciting.

grope *v* feel about or search uncertainly. **groping** *n*

grosbeak *n* finch with a large powerful bill.

grosgrain [**grow**-grain] *n* heavy ribbed silk or rayon fabric.

gross *adj* **1** flagrant. **2** vulgar. **3** *Slang* disgusting or repulsive. **4** repulsively fat. **5** total, without deductions. ♦ *n* **6** twelve dozen. ♦ *v* **7** make as total revenue before deductions. **grossly** *adv* **grossness** *n*

grotesque [grow-**tesk**] *adj* **1** strangely distorted. **2** absurd. ♦ *n* **3** grotesque person or thing. **4** artistic style mixing distorted human, animal, and plant forms. **grotesquely** *adv*

grotto *n, pl* **-toes, -tos 1** small picturesque cave. **2** construction imitating a cave.

grotty *adj* **-tier, -tiest** *Informal* nasty or in bad condition.

grouch *Informal* ♦ *v* **1** grumble or complain. ♦ *n* **2** person who is always complaining. **3** persistent complaint.

grouchy *adj*

ground[1] *n* **1** surface of the earth. **2** soil. **3** area used for a specific purpose, e.g. *rugby ground.* **4** position in an argument or controversy. **5** background colour of a painting. ♦ *pl* **6** enclosed land round a house. **7** reason or motive. **8** coffee dregs. ♦ *adj* **9** on or of the ground. ♦ *v* **10** base or establish. **11** instruct in the basics. **12** ban an aircraft or pilot from flying. **13** run (a ship) aground. **14** place on the ground. **groundless** *adj* without reason. **grounding** *n* basic knowledge of a subject. **ground-breaking** *adj* innovative. **ground floor** floor of a building level with the ground. **groundnut** *n* peanut. **groundsheet** *n* waterproof sheet put on the ground under a tent. **groundsman** *n* person employed to maintain a sports ground or park. **groundswell** *n* rapidly developing general feeling or opinion. **groundwork** *n* preliminary work.

ground[2] *v* past of GRIND. **ground beef** finely chopped beef used in beefburgers etc.

groundsel [**grounce**-el] *n* yellow-flowered weed.

group *n* **1** number of people or things regarded as a unit. **2** small band of musicians or singers. ♦ *v* **3** place or form into a group. **group captain** middle-ranking air force officer.

grouper *n* large edible sea fish.

grouse[1] *n* **1** stocky game bird. **2** its flesh.

grouse[2] *v* **1** grumble or complain. ♦ *n* **2** complaint.

grout *n* **1** thin mortar. ♦ *v* **2** fill up with grout.

grove *n* small group of trees.

grovel [**grov**-el] *v* **-elling, -elled 1** behave humbly in order to win a superior's favour. **2** crawl on the floor.

grow *v* **growing, grew, grown 1** develop physically. **2** (of a plant) exist. **3** cultivate (plants). **4** increase in size or degree. **5** originate. **6** become gradually, e.g. *it was growing dark.* **growth** *n* **1** growing. **2** increase. **3** something grown or growing. **4** tumour. **grown** *adj* developed or advanced. **grown-up** *adj, n* adult. **grow on** *v* become more acceptable to. **grow up** *v* mature.

growl *v* **1** make a low rumbling sound. **2** utter with a growl. ♦ *n* **3** growling sound.

groyne *n* wall built out from the shore to control erosion.

grub *n* **1** legless insect larva. **2** *Slang* food. ♦ *v* **grubbing, grubbed 3** search carefully for something by digging or by moving things about. **4** dig up the surface of (soil).

grubby *adj* **-bier, -biest** dirty. **grubbiness** *n*

grudge *v* **1** be unwilling to give or allow. ♦ *n* **2** resentment. **grudging** *adj* **grudgingly** *adv*

gruel *n* thin porridge.

gruelling *adj* exhausting or severe.

gruesome *adj* causing horror and disgust.

gruff *adj* rough or surly in manner or voice. **gruffly** *adv* **gruffness** *n*

grumble *v* **1** complain. **2** rumble. ♦ *n* **3** complaint. **4** rumble. **grumbler** *n* **grumbling** *adj, n*

grumpy *adj* **grumpier, grumpiest** bad-tempered. **grumpily** *adv* **grumpiness** *n*

grunge *n* **1** style of rock music with a fuzzy guitar sound. **2** deliberately untidy and uncoordinated fashion style.

grunt *v* **1** make a low short gruff sound, like a pig. ♦ *n* **2** pig's sound. **3** gruff noise.

Gruyère [**grew**-yair] *n* hard yellow Swiss cheese with holes.

gryphon *n* same as GRIFFIN.

G-string *n* small strip of cloth covering the genitals and attached to a waistband.

G-suit *n* close-fitting pressurized garment worn by the crew of high-speed aircraft.

GT gran turismo, used of a sports car.

guanaco [gwah-**nah**-koh] *n, pl* **-cos** S American animal related to the llama.

guano [**gwah**-no] *n* dried sea-bird manure, used as fertilizer.

guarantee *n* **1** formal assurance, esp. in writing, that a product will meet certain standards. **2** something that makes a specified condition or outcome certain. **3** guarantor. **4** guaranty. ♦ *v* **-teeing, -teed 5** give a guarantee. **6** secure against risk etc. **7** ensure. **guarantor** *n* person who gives or is bound by a guarantee. **guaranty** *n, pl* **-ties 1** pledge of responsibility for fulfilling another person's obligations in case of default. **2** thing given as security for a guaranty.

guard *v* **1** watch over to protect or to prevent escape. **2** protect (a right or privilege). ♦ *n* **3** person or group that guards. **4** official in charge of a train. **5** protection. **6** screen for enclosing anything dangerous. **7** posture of defence in sports such as boxing or fencing. ♦ *pl* **8** (**G-**) regiment with ceremonial duties. **guarded** *adj* cautious or noncommittal. **guardedly** *adv* **guard against** *v* take precautions against. **guardhouse, guardroom** *n* military police office for holding prisoners. **guardsman** *n* member of the Guards.

guardian *n* **1** keeper or protector. **2** person legally responsible for a child, mentally ill person, etc. **guardianship** *n*

guava [**gwah**-va] *n* yellow-skinned tropical American fruit.

gubernatorial *adj US* of or relating to a governor.

gudgeon[1] *n* small freshwater fish.

gudgeon[2] *n* socket for a hinge or rudder.

guelder-rose [**geld**-er-rose] *n* shrub with clusters of white flowers.

Guernsey [**gurn**-zee] *n* breed of dairy cattle.

guerrilla, guerilla *n* member of an unofficial armed force fighting regular forces.

guess *v* **1** estimate or draw a conclusion without proper knowledge. **2** estimate correctly by guessing. **3** *Chiefly US* suppose. ♦ *n* **4** estimate or conclusion reached by guessing. **guesswork** *n* process or results of guessing.

guest *n* **1** person entertained at another's house or at another's expense. **2** invited performer or speaker. **3** customer at a hotel or restaurant. ♦ *v* **4** appear as a visiting player or performer. **guesthouse** *n* boarding house.

guff *n Slang* nonsense.

guffaw *n* **1** crude noisy laugh. ♦ *v* **2** laugh in this way.

guide *n* **1** person who conducts tour expeditions. **2** person who shows the way. **3** book of instruction or information. **4** model for behaviour. **5** something used to gauge something or to help in planning one's actions. **6** (**G-**) member of an organization for girls equivalent to the Scouts. ♦ *v* **7** act as a guide for. **8** control, supervise, or influence. **guidance** *n* leadership, instruction, or advice. **guidebook** *n* handbook with information for visitors to a place. **guided missile** missile whose flight is controlled electronically. **guide dog** dog trained to lead a blind person. **guideline** *n* set principle for doing something.

guild *n* **1** organization or club. **2** *Hist* society of men in the same trade or craft.

guilder *n* monetary unit of the Netherlands.

guile [**gile**] *n* cunning or deceit. **guileful** *adj* **guileless** *adj*

guillemot [**gil**-lee-mot] *n* black-and-white diving sea bird.

guillotine *n* **1** machine for beheading people. **2** device for cutting paper or sheet metal. **3** method of preventing lengthy debate in parliament by fixing a time for taking the vote. ♦ *v* **4** behead by guillotine. **5** limit debate by the guillotine.

guilt *n* **1** fact or state of having done wrong. **2** remorse for wrongdoing. **guiltless** *adj* innocent. **guilty** *adj* **guiltier, guiltiest 1** responsible for an offence or misdeed. **2** feeling or showing guilt. **guiltily** *adv*

guinea *n* **1** former British monetary unit worth 21 shillings (1.05 pounds). **2** former gold coin of this value. **guinea fowl** bird related to the pheasant. **guinea pig 1** tailless S American rodent, commonly kept as a pet. **2** *Informal* person used for experimentation.

guise [rhymes with **size**] *n* **1** false appearance. **2** external appearance.

guitar *n* stringed instrument with a flat back and a long neck, played by plucking or strumming. **guitarist** *n*

Gulag *n* system or department that silences dissidents, esp. in the former Soviet Union.

gulch *n US* deep narrow valley.

gulf *n* **1** large deep bay. **2** chasm. **3** large difference in opinion or understanding. **Gulf Stream** warm ocean current flowing from the Gulf of Mexico towards NW Europe.

gull[1] *n* long-winged sea bird.

gull[2] *v* cheat or deceive.

gullet *n* muscular tube through which food passes from the mouth to the stomach.

gullible *adj* easily tricked. **gullibility** *n*

gully *n, pl* **-lies** channel cut by running water.

gulp *v* **1** swallow hastily. **2** gasp. ♦ *n* **3** gulping. **4** thing gulped.

gum[1] *n* firm flesh in which the teeth are set. **gummy** *adj* **-mier, -miest** toothless. **gumboil** *n* abscess on the gum.

gum[2] *n* **1** sticky substance obtained from certain trees. **2** adhesive. **3** chewing gum. **4** gumdrop. **5** gumtree. ♦ *v* **gumming, gummed 6** stick with gum. **gummy** *adj* **-mier, -miest gumboots** *pl n* Wellington boots. **gumdrop** *n* hard jelly-like sweet. **gumtree** *n* eucalypt tree.

gumption *n Informal* **1** resourcefulness. **2** courage.

gun *n* **1** weapon with a metal tube from which missiles are fired by explosion. **2** device from which a substance is ejected under pressure. **3** member of a shooting party. ♦ *v* **gunning, gunned 4** cause (an engine) to run at high speed. **jump the gun** act prematurely. **gunner** *n* artillery soldier. **gunnery** *n* use or science of large guns. **gunboat** *n* small warship. **guncotton** *n* form of cellulose nitrate used as an explosive. **gun dog** dog used to retrieve game. **gun down** *v* shoot (a person). **gun for** *v* seek or pursue vigorously. **gunman** *n* armed criminal. **gunmetal** *n* **1** alloy of copper, tin, and zinc. ♦ *adj* **2** dark grey. **gunpowder** *n* explosive mixture of potassium nitrate, sulphur, and charcoal. **gunrunning** *n* smuggling of guns and ammunition. **gunrunner** *n* **gunshot** *n* **1** shot or range of a gun. **2** sound of a gun being fired.

gunge *n Informal* sticky unpleasant substance. **gungy** *adj* **-gier, -giest**

gunk *n Informal* slimy or filthy substance.

gunny *n* strong coarse fabric used for sacks.

gunwale, gunnel [**gun**-nel] *n* top of a ship's side.

guppy *n, pl* **-pies** small colourful aquarium fish.

gurgle *v, n* (make) a bubbling noise.

Gurkha *n* person, esp. a soldier, belonging to a Hindu people of Nepal.

gurnard *n* spiny armour-headed sea fish.

guru *n* **1** Hindu or Sikh religious teacher or leader. **2** leader or adviser.

gush *v* **1** flow out suddenly and profusely. **2** express admiration effusively. ♦ *n* **3** sudden copious flow. **4** sudden surge of strong feeling. **gusher** *n* spurting oil well. **gushing** *adj*

gusset *n* piece of material sewn into a garment to strengthen it.

gust *n* **1** sudden blast of wind. **2** sudden burst of rain, anger, etc. ♦ *v* **3** blow in gusts. **gusty** *adj*

gustation *n* act of tasting or the faculty of taste. **gustatory** *adj*

gusto *n* enjoyment or zest.

gut *n* **1** intestine. **2** *Informal* fat stomach. **3** short for CATGUT. ♦ *pl* **4** internal organs. **5** *Informal* courage. **6** *Informal* essential part. ♦ *v* **gutting, gutted 7** remove the guts from. **8** (of a fire) destroy the inside of (a building). ♦ *adj* **9** basic or instinctive, e.g. *a gut reaction.* **gutless** *adj Informal* cowardly. **gutsy** *adj* **-sier, -siest** *Informal* **1** courageous. **2** vigorous or robust, e.g. *a gutsy performance.* **3** greedy. **gutted** *adj Informal* disappointed and upset.

bent metal hairpin. **hairline** *n* **1** edge of hair at the top of the forehead. ♦ *adj* **2** very fine or narrow. **hairpiece** *n* section of false hair added to a person's real hair. **hairpin** *n* U-shaped wire used to hold the hair in place. **hairpin bend** very sharp bend in a road. **hair-raising** *adj* frightening or exciting. **hair's-breadth** *n* extremely small margin or distance. **hair shirt** shirt made of horsehair cloth worn against the skin as a penance. **hairsplitting** *n, adj* making petty distinctions. **hairstyle** *n* cut and arrangement of a person's hair.

hajj *n* pilgrimage a Muslim makes to Mecca. **hajji** *n* Muslim who has made a pilgrimage to Mecca.

hake *n* edible fish of the cod family.

halal *n* meat from animals slaughtered according to Muslim law.

halberd *n* spear with an axe blade.

halcyon [**hal**-see-on] *adj* peaceful and happy. **halcyon days** time of peace and happiness.

hale *adj* healthy, robust, e.g. *hale and hearty.*

half *n, pl* **halves** **1** either of two equal parts. **2** *Informal* half-pint of beer etc. **3** half-price ticket. ♦ *adj* **4** denoting one of two equal parts. ♦ *adv* **5** to the extent of half. **6** partially. **half-and-half** *adj* half one thing and half another thing. **halfback** *n Sport* player positioned immediately behind the forwards. **half-baked** *adj Informal* not properly thought out. **half board** (in a hotel) bed, breakfast, and evening meal. **half-brother, half-sister** *n* brother *or* sister related through one parent only. **half-caste** *n Offens* person with parents of different races. **half-cocked** *adj* **go off half-cocked, (at) half-cock** fail because of inadequate preparation. **half-day** *n* day when a person works only in the morning or only in the afternoon. **half-hearted** *adj* unenthusiastic. **half-heartedly** *adv* **half-life** *n* time taken for half the atoms in radioactive material to decay. **half-mast** *n* halfway position of a flag on a mast as a sign of mourning. **half-moon** *n* moon when half its face is illuminated. **half-nelson** *n* wrestling hold in which one wrestler's arm is pinned behind his back by his opponent. **half-term** *n* holiday midway through a school term. **half-timbered** *adj* (of a house) having an exposed wooden frame filled in with plaster. **half-time** *n Sport* short rest period between two halves of a game. **halftone** *n* illustration showing lights and shadows by means of very small dots. **halfway** *adv, adj* at or to half the distance. **halfwit** *n* foolish or stupid person. **half-witted** *adj*

halfpenny [**hayp**-nee] *n* former British coin worth half an old penny.

halibut *n* large edible flatfish.

halitosis *n* unpleasant-smelling breath.

hall *n* **1** (also **hallway**) entrance passage. **2** large room or building for public meetings, dances, etc. **3** large country house.

hallelujah [hal-ee-**loo**-ya] *interj* exclamation of praise to God.

hallmark *n* **1** typical feature. **2** mark indicating the standard of tested gold and silver. ♦ *v* **3** stamp with a hallmark.

hallo *interj* same as HELLO.

halloo *interj* shout used to call hounds at a hunt.

hallowed *adj* regarded as holy.

Halloween, Hallowe'en *n* October 31, celebrated by children by dressing up as ghosts, witches, etc.

hallucinate *v* seem to see something that is not really there. **hallucination** *n* **hallucinatory** *adj* **hallucinogen** *n* drug that causes hallucinations. **hallucinogenic** *adj*

halo [**hay**-loh] *n, pl* **-loes, -los** **1** ring of light round the head of a sacred figure. **2** circle of refracted light round the sun or moon.

halogen [**hal**-oh-jen] *n Chem* any of a group of nonmetallic elements including chlorine and iodine.

halt *v* **1** come or bring to a stop. ♦ *n* **2** temporary stop. **3** minor railway station without a building. **halting** *adj* hesitant, uncertain, e.g. *in a halting voice.* **haltingly** *adv*

halter *n* strap round a horse's head with a rope to lead it with. **halterneck** *n* woman's top or dress with a strap fastened at the back of the neck.

halve *v* **1** divide in half. **2** reduce by half.

halves *n* plural of HALF.

halyard *n* rope for raising a ship's sail or flag.

ham[1] *n* smoked or salted meat from a pig's thigh. **ham-fisted** *adj* clumsy.

ham[2] *Informal* ♦ *n* **1** amateur radio operator. **2** actor who overacts. ♦ *v* **hamming, hammed 3 ham it up** overact.

hamburger *n* minced beef shaped into a flat disc, cooked and usu. served in a bread roll.

hamlet *n* small village.

hammer *n* **1** tool with a heavy metal head and a wooden handle, used to drive in nails etc. **2** part of a gun which causes the bullet to be fired. **3** heavy metal ball on a wire, thrown as a sport. **4** auctioneer's mallet. **5** striking mechanism in a piano. ♦ *v* **6** hit (as if) with a hammer. **7** *Informal* punish or defeat utterly. **go at it hammer and tongs** do something, esp. argue, very vigorously. **hammerhead** *n* shark with a wide flattened head. **hammer out** *v* settle (differences) with great effort. **hammertoe** *n* condition in which a toe is permanently bent at the joint.

hammock *n* hanging bed made of canvas or net.

hamper[1] *v* make it difficult for (someone or something) to move or progress.

hamper[2] *n* **1** large basket with a lid. **2** selection of food and drink packed as a gift.

hamster *n* small rodent with a short tail and cheek pouches.

> Note the spelling. There is no 'p'.

hamstring *n* **1** tendon at the back of the knee. ♦ *v* **2** make it difficult for (someone) to take any action. **hamstrung** *adj*

hand *n* **1** part of the body at the end of the arm, consisting of a palm, four fingers, and a thumb. **2** style of handwriting. **3** round of applause. **4** manual worker. **5** pointer on a dial, esp. on a clock. **6** cards dealt to a player in a card game. **7** unit of length of four inches used to measure horses. ♦ *v* **8** pass, give. **have a hand in** be involved in. **lend a hand** help. **out of hand 1** beyond control. **2** definitely and finally, e.g. *the idea was rejected out of hand.* **to hand, at hand, on hand** nearby. **win hands down** win easily. **handbag** *n* woman's small bag for carrying personal articles in. **handbill** *n* small printed notice. **handbook** *n* small reference or instruction book. **handcuff** *n* **1** one of a linked pair of metal rings designed to be locked round a prisoner's wrists by the police. ♦ *v* **2** put handcuffs on. **hand-me-downs** *pl n Informal* clothes that someone has finished with and passed on to someone else. **hand-out** *n* **1** clothing, food, or money given to a needy person. **2** written information given out at a talk etc. **hand-pick** *v* select carefully for a particular purpose. **handrail** *n* rail alongside a stairway, to provide support. **handset** *n* telephone mouthpiece and earpiece in a single unit. **hands-on** *adj* involving practical experience of equipment. **handstand** *n* act of supporting the body on the hands in an upside-down position. **hand-to-hand** *adj* (of combat) at close quarters. **hand-to-mouth** *adj* having barely enough food or money to live on. **handwriting** *n* (style of) writing by hand. **handwritten** *adj*

h & c hot and cold (water).

handful *n* **1** amount that can be held in the hand. **2** small number. **3** *Informal* person or animal that is difficult to control.

handicap *n* **1** physical or mental disability. **2** something that makes progress difficult. **3** contest in which the competitors are given advantages or disadvantages in an attempt to equalize their chances. **4** advantage or disadvantage given. ♦ *v* **5** make it difficult for (someone) to do something. **handicapped** *adj*

handicraft *n* objects made by hand.

handiwork *n* something that one has made or done oneself, e.g. *I looked up to admire my handiwork.*

handkerchief *n* small square of fabric used to wipe the nose.

handle *n* **1** part of an object that is held so that it can be used. ♦ *v* **2** hold, feel, or move with the hands. **3** control or deal with. **handler** *n* person who controls an animal. **handlebars** *pl n* curved metal bar used to steer a cycle.

handsome *adj* **1** (esp. of a man) good-looking. **2** large or generous, e.g. *a handsome profit.* **handsomely** *adv*

handy *adj* **handier, handiest 1** convenient, useful. **2** good at manual work. **handily** *adv* **handyman** *n* man who is good at making or repairing things.

hang *v* **hanging, hung 1** attach or be attached at the top with the lower part free. **2** (of cloth or clothing) fall or flow in a particular way. **3** (*past* **hanged**) suspend or be suspended by the neck until dead. **4** fasten to a wall. **get the hang of** *Informal* begin to understand. **hanger** *n* curved piece of wood, wire, or plastic, with a hook, for hanging up clothes (also **coat hanger**). **hanger-on** *n, pl* **hangers-on** unwanted follower. **hanging** *n* **1** execution by hanging. **2** decorative drapery hung on a wall. **hang about, around** *v* **1** stand about idly. **2** (foll. by *with*) spend a lot of time in the company (of). **hang back** *v* hesitate, be reluctant. **hangman** *n* man who executes people by hanging. **hangover** *n* headache and nausea as a result of drinking too much alcohol. **hang-up** *n* *Informal* emotional or psychological problem.

hangar *n* large shed for storing aircraft.

hangdog *adj* guilty, ashamed, e.g. *a hangdog look.*

hang-glider *n* glider with a light framework from which the pilot hangs in a harness. **hang-gliding** *n*

hank *n* coil, esp. of yarn.

hanker *v* (foll. by *after*) desire intensely. **hankering** *n*

hanky, hankie *n, pl* **hankies** *Informal* handkerchief.

hanky-panky *n* *Informal* illicit sexual relations.

hansom cab, hansom *n* (formerly) two-wheeled horse-drawn carriage for hire.

haphazard *adj* not organized or planned. **haphazardly** *adv*

hapless *adj* unlucky.

happen *v* **1** take place, occur. **2** chance (to be or do something). **happening** *n* event, occurrence.

happy *adj* **-pier, -piest 1** feeling or causing joy. **2** lucky, fortunate. **3** willing (to do something). **happily** *adv* **happiness** *n* **happy-go-lucky** *adj* carefree and cheerful.

hara-kiri *n* (formerly, in Japan) ritual suicide by disembowelling.

harangue *v* **1** address angrily or forcefully. ♦ *n* **2** angry or forceful speech.

harass *v* annoy or trouble constantly. **harassed** *adj* **harassment** *n*

harbinger [**har**-binj-a] *n* someone or something that announces the approach of something, e.g. *a harbinger of doom.*

harbour *n* **1** sheltered port. ♦ *v* **2** maintain secretly in the mind. **3** give shelter or protection to.

hard *adj* **1** firm, solid, or rigid. **2** difficult. **3** requiring a lot of effort. **4** unkind, unfeeling. **5** causing pain, sorrow, or hardship. **6** (of water) containing calcium salts which stop soap lathering freely. **7** (of a drug) strong and addictive. ♦ *adv* **8** with great energy or effort. **9** with great intensity. **hard of hearing** unable to hear properly. **hard up** *Informal* short of money. **harden** *v* **hardness** *n* **hardship** *n* **1** suffering. **2** difficult circumstances. **hard-and-fast** *adj* (of rules) fixed and not able to be changed. **hard-bitten** *adj* tough and determined. **hard-boiled** *adj* **1** (of an egg) boiled until solid. **2** *Informal* tough, unemotional. **hard cash** notes and coins, as opposed to cheques or credit cards. **hard copy** computer output printed on paper. **hard core** the members of a group who most resist change. **hard-core** *adj* **1** (of pornography) showing sexual acts in explicit detail. **2** extremely committed, fanatical. **hard disk** *Computers* inflexible disk in a sealed container. **hard-headed** *adj* shrewd, practical. **hard-hearted** *adj* unsympathetic, uncaring. **hard line** uncompromising policy. **hard-line** *adj* **hard-liner** *n* **hard sell** aggressive sales technique. **hard shoulder** surfaced verge at the edge of a motorway for emergency stops.

hardback *n* book with a stiff cover.

hardboard *n* thin stiff board made of compressed sawdust and wood chips.

hardly *adv* **1** scarcely or not at all. **2** with difficulty.

> *Hardly* already has a negative sense and is not used with *no* or *not*.

hardware *n* **1** metal tools or implements. **2** machinery used in a computer system. **3** heavy military equipment, such as tanks and missiles.

hardwood *n* wood of a deciduous tree such as oak or ash.

hardy *adj* **hardier, hardiest** able to stand difficult conditions. **hardiness** *n*

hare *n* **1** animal like a large rabbit, with longer ears and legs. ♦ *v* **2** (usu. foll. by *off*) run (away) quickly. **harebell** *n* blue bell-shaped flower. **harebrained** *adj* foolish or impractical. **harelip** *n* slight split in the upper lip.

harem *n* (apartments of) a Muslim man's wives and concubines.

haricot bean, haricot [**har**-rik-oh] *n* small pale edible bean, usu. sold dried.

hark *v Old-fashioned* listen. **hark back** *v* return (to an earlier subject).

harlequin *n* **1** stock comic character with a diamond-patterned costume and mask. ♦ *adj* **2** in many colours.

harlot *n Lit* prostitute.

harm *v* **1** injure physically, mentally, or morally. ♦ *n* **2** physical, mental, or moral injury. **harmful** *adj* **harmless** *adj*

harmonica *n* small wind instrument played by sucking and blowing.

harmonium *n* keyboard instrument like a small organ.

harmony *n, pl* **-nies** **1** peaceful agreement and cooperation. **2** pleasant combination of notes sounded at the same time. **harmonious** *adj* **1** consisting of parts that blend together well. **2** of harmony. **harmoniously** *adv* **harmonic** *adj* of harmony. **harmonics** *n* science of musical sounds. **harmonize** *v* **1** sing or play in harmony. **2** blend well together. **harmonization** *n*

harness *n* **1** arrangement of straps for attaching a horse to a cart or plough. **2** set of straps fastened round someone's body to attach something, e.g. *a safety harness.* ♦ *v* **3** put a harness on. **4** control (something) in order to make use of it.

harp *n* large triangular stringed instrument played with the fingers. **harpist** *n* **harp on about** *v* talk about continuously.

harpoon *n* **1** barbed spear attached to a rope used for hunting whales. ♦ *v* **2** spear with a harpoon.

harpsichord *n* stringed keyboard instrument.

harpy *n, pl* **-pies** nasty or bad-tempered woman.

harridan *n* nagging or vicious woman.

harrier *n* cross-country runner.

harrow *n* **1** implement used to break up lumps of soil. ♦ *v* **2** draw a harrow over.

harrowing *adj* very distressing.

harry *v* **-rying, -ried** keep asking (someone) to do something, pester.

harsh *adj* **1** severe and difficult to cope with. **2** unkind, unsympathetic. **3** extremely hard, bright, or rough. **harshly** *adv* **harshness** *n*

hart *n* adult male deer.

hartebeest *n* large African antelope.

harum-scarum *adj* reckless.

harvest *n* **1** (season for) the gathering of crops. **2** crops gathered. ♦ *v* **3** gather (a ripened crop). **harvester** *n*

has *v* third person singular of the present tense of HAVE. **has-been** *n Informal* person who is no longer popular or successful.

hash[1] *n* dish of diced cooked meat and vegetables reheated. **make a hash of** *Informal* spoil, do badly.

hash[2] *n Informal* hashish.

hashish [**hash**-eesh] *n* drug made from the hemp plant, smoked for its intoxicating effects.

hasp *n* clasp that fits over a staple and is secured by a bolt or padlock, used as a fastening.

hassle *Informal* ♦ *n* **1** trouble, bother. **2** long argument. ♦ *v* **3** bother or annoy.

hassock *n* cushion for kneeling on in church.

haste *n* (excessive) quickness. **make haste** hurry, rush. **hasten** *v* (cause to) hurry. **hasty** *adj* **hastier, hastiest** (too) quick. **hastily** *adv*

hat *n* covering for the head, often with a brim, usu. worn to give protection from the weather. **keep something under one's hat** keep something secret. **hat trick** any three successive achievements, esp. in sport.

hatch[1] *v* **1** (cause to) emerge from an egg. **2** devise (a plot).

hatch[2] *n* **1** hinged door covering an opening in a floor or wall. **2** opening in the wall between a kitchen and a dining area. **3** door in an aircraft or spacecraft. **hatchback** *n* car with a lifting door at the back. **hatchway** *n* opening in the deck of a ship.

hatchet *n* small axe. **bury the hatchet** become reconciled. **hatchet job** malicious verbal or written attack. **hatchet man** *Informal* person carrying out unpleasant tasks for an employer.

hate *v* **1** dislike intensely. **2** be unwilling (to do something). ♦ *n* **3** intense dislike. **4** person or thing hated. **hateful** *adj* causing or deserving hate. **hater** *n* **hatred** *n* intense dislike.

haughty *adj* **-tier, -tiest** proud, arrogant. **haughtily** *adv* **haughtiness** *n*

haul *v* **1** pull or drag with effort. ♦ *n* **2** hauling. **3** amount gained by effort or theft. **long haul** something that takes a lot of time and effort. **haulage** *n* (charge for) transporting goods. **haulier** *n* firm or person that transports goods by road.

haulm [**hawm**] *n* stalks of beans, peas, or potatoes collectively.

haunch *n* human hip or fleshy hindquarter of an animal.

haunt *v* **1** visit in the form of a ghost. **2** remain in the memory or thoughts of. ♦ *n* **3** place visited frequently. **haunted** *adj* **1** frequented by ghosts. **2** worried. **haunting** *adj* memorably beautiful or sad. **hauntingly** *adv*

haute couture [**oat** koo-**ture**] *n French* high fashion.

hauteur [oat-**ur**] *n* haughtiness.

Havana *n* fine-quality cigar made in Cuba.

have *v* **has, having, had 1** possess, hold. **2** receive, take, or obtain. **3** experience or be affected by. **4** (foll. by *to*) be obliged, must, e.g. *I had to go.* **5** cause to be done. **6** give birth to. **7** *Slang* cheat or outwit. **8** used to form past tenses (with a past participle), e.g. *we have looked; she had done enough.* **have it out** *Informal* settle a matter by argument. **haves and have-nots** *Informal* rich people and poor people. **have on** *v* **1** wear. **2** *Informal* tease or trick. **have up** *v* bring to trial.

haven *n* place of safety.

haver *v Dialect* talk nonsense. **havers** *pl n Scot* nonsense.

haversack *n* canvas bag carried on the back or shoulder.

havoc *n* disorder and confusion.

haw *n* hawthorn berry.

hawk[1] *n* **1** bird of prey with a short hooked bill and very good eyesight. **2** *Politics* supporter or advocate of warlike policies. **hawkish, hawklike** *adj* **hawk-eyed** *adj* having very good eyesight.

hawk[2] *v* offer (goods) for sale in the

street or door-to-door. **hawker** *n*

hawk[3] *v* cough noisily.

hawser *n* large rope used on a ship.

hawthorn *n* thorny shrub or tree.

hay *n* grass cut and dried as fodder. **hay fever** allergy to pollen, causing sneezing and watery eyes. **haystack** *n* large pile of stored hay. **haywire** *adj* **go haywire** *Informal* not function properly.

hazard *n* **1** something that could be dangerous. ♦ *v* **2** put in danger. **3** make (a guess). **hazardous** *adj*

haze *n* mist, often caused by heat. **hazy** *adj* **hazier, haziest 1** not clear, misty. **2** confused or vague.

hazel *n* **1** small tree producing edible nuts. ♦ *adj* **2** (of eyes) greenish-brown. **hazelnut** *n*

HB (on pencils) hard-black.

H-bomb *n* hydrogen bomb.

he *pron* refers to: **1** male person or animal. **2** person or animal of unspecified sex.

> Try to avoid the use of *he* as a pronoun of general reference. It can appear sexist if the reference is to both men and women.

He *Chem* helium.

HE His (or Her) Excellency.

head *n* **1** upper or front part of the body, containing the sense organs and the brain. **2** mind and mental abilities. **3** upper or most forward part of anything. **4** person in charge of a group, organization, or school. **5** pus-filled tip of a spot or boil. **6** white froth on beer. **7** (*pl* **head**) person or animal considered as a unit. **8** headline or heading. **9** *Informal* headache. ♦ *adj* **10** chief, principal. ♦ *v* **11** be at the top or front of. **12** be in charge of. **13** move (in a particular direction). **14** hit (a ball) with the head. **15** provide with a heading. **go to one's head** make one drunk or conceited. **head over heels (in love)** very much in love. **not make head nor tail of** not understand. **off one's head** *Slang* foolish or insane. **heads** *adv Informal* with the side of a coin which has a portrait of a head on it uppermost. **header** *n* **1** striking a ball with the head. **2** headlong fall. **heading** *n* title written or printed at the top of a page. **heady** *adj* **headier, headiest** intoxicating or exciting. **headache** *n* **1** continuous pain in the head. **2** cause of worry or annoyance. **headboard** *n* vertical board at the top end of a bed. **headdress** *n* decorative head covering. **head-hunt** *v* (of a company) approach and offer a job to (a person working for a rival company). **head-hunting** *n* **head-hunter** *n* **headland** *n* area of land jutting out into the sea. **headlight** *n* powerful light on the front of a vehicle. **headline** *n* **1** title at the top of a newspaper article, esp. on the front page. ♦ *pl* **2** main points of a news broadcast. **headlong** *adv, adj* **1** with the head first. **2** hastily. **head-on** *adv, adj* **1** front foremost. **2** direct(ly) and uncompromising(ly). **headphones** *pl n* two small loudspeakers held against the ears by a strap. **headquarters** *pl n* centre from which operations are directed. **head start** advantage in a competition. **headstone** *n* memorial stone on a grave. **headstrong** *adj* self-willed, obstinate. **head teacher** person in charge of a school. **headway** *n* progress. **headwind** *n* wind blowing against the course of an aircraft or ship.

heal *v* make or become well. **healer** *n* **healing** *n, adj*

health *n* normal (good) condition of someone's body. **health centre** surgery and offices of the doctors in a district. **health food** natural food, organically grown and free from additives. **health visitor** nurse who visits elderly people and mothers of newborn babies in their homes. **healthy** *adj* **healthier, healthiest 1** having good health. **2** of or producing good health. **3** functioning well, sound. **healthily** *adv*

heap *n* **1** pile of things one on top of another. **2** (also **heaps**) large number or quantity. ♦ *v* **3** gather into a pile. **4** (foll. by *on*) give liberally (to), e.g. *Keegan* *heaped praise on his team.*

hear *v* **hearing, heard 1** perceive (a sound) by ear. **2** listen to. **3** learn or be informed. **4** *Law* try (a case). **hear! hear!** exclamation of approval or agreement. **hearer** *n* **hearing** *n* **1** ability to hear. **2** trial of a case. **within hearing** close enough to be heard.

hearken *v Obs* listen.

hearsay *n* gossip, rumour.

hearse *n* funeral car used to carry a coffin.

heart *n* **1** organ that pumps blood round the body. **2** centre of emotions, esp. love. **3** courage, spirit. **4** central or most important part. **5** figure representing a heart. **6** playing card with red heart-shaped symbols. **break someone's heart** cause someone great grief. **by heart** from memory. **set one's heart on something** greatly desire something. **take something to heart** be upset about something. **hearten** *v* encourage, make cheerful. **heartening** *adj* **heartless** *adj* cruel, unkind. **heartlessly** *adv* **hearty** *adj* **heartier, heartiest 1** substantial, nourishing. **2** friendly, enthusiastic. **3** strongly felt. **heartily** *adv* **heart attack** sudden severe malfunction of the heart. **heart failure** sudden stopping of the heartbeat. **heart-rending** *adj* causing great sorrow. **heart-throb** *n Slang* very attractive man, esp. a film or pop star. **heart-to-heart** *adj, n* intimate (conversation).

heartache *n* intense anguish.

heartbeat *n* one complete pulsation of the heart.

heartbreak *n* intense grief. **heartbreaking** *adj* **heartbroken** *adj*

heartburn *n* burning sensation in the chest caused by indigestion.

heartfelt *adj* felt sincerely or strongly.

hearth *n* floor of a fireplace.

heat *v* **1** make or become hot. ♦ *n* **2** state of being hot. **3** energy transferred as a result of a difference in temperature. **4** hot weather. **5** intensity of feeling. **6** preliminary eliminating contest in a competition. **on, in heat** (of some female animals) ready for mating. **heated** *adj* angry and excited. **heatedly** *adv* **heater** *n* **heating** *n* **heatstroke** *n* same as SUNSTROKE. **heat wave** spell of unusually hot weather.

heath *n* area of open uncultivated land.

heathen *adj, n* (of) a person who does not believe in an established religion.

heather *n* low-growing plant with small purple, pinkish, or white flowers, growing on heaths and mountains.

heave *v* **1** lift with effort. **2** throw (something heavy). **3** utter (a sigh). **4** rise and fall. **5** vomit. **6** (*past* **hove**) *Naut* move in a specified direction. ♦ *n* **7** heaving. **heave to** *v* (of a ship) stop moving.

heaven *n* **1** place believed to be the home of God, where good people go when they die. **2** place or state of bliss. **the heavens** sky. **heavenly** *adj* **1** of or like heaven. **2** of or occurring in space. **3** wonderful or beautiful.

heavy *adj* **heavier, heaviest 1** of great weight. **2** having a high density. **3** great in degree or amount. **4** (of breathing) deep and loud. **5** (of food) solid and difficult to digest. **6** *Informal* (of a situation) serious. **heavily** *adv* **heaviness** *n* **heavy-duty** *adj* made to withstand hard wear. **heavy industry** large-scale production of raw material or machinery. **heavy metal** very loud rock music featuring guitar riffs. **heavy water** water formed of oxygen and deuterium. **heavyweight** *n* boxer weighing over 175lb (professional) or 81kg (amateur).

Hebrew *n* **1** member of an ancient Semitic people. **2** ancient language of the Hebrews. **3** its modern form, used in Israel. ♦ *adj* **4** of the Hebrews.

heckle *v* interrupt (a public speaker) with comments, questions, or taunts. **heckler** *n*

hectare *n* one hundred ares or 10 000 square metres (2.471 acres).

hectic *adj* rushed or busy.

hector *v* bully. **hectoring** *adj, n*

hedge *n* **1** row of bushes forming a barrier or boundary. ♦ *v* **2** be evasive or noncommittal. **3** (foll. by *against*) protect oneself (from). **hedgerow** *n* bushes forming a hedge. **hedge sparrow** small brownish songbird.

hedgehog *n* small mammal with a protective covering of spines.

hedonism *n* doctrine that pleasure is the most important thing in life. **hedonist** *n* **hedonistic** *adj*

heed *n* **1** careful attention. ♦ *v* **2** pay careful attention to. **heedless** *adj* **heedless of** taking no notice of.

heel[1] *n* **1** back part of the foot. **2** part of a shoe supporting the heel. **3** *Slang* contemptible person. ♦ *v* **4** repair the heel of (a shoe).

heel[2] *v* (foll. by *over*) lean to one side.

hefty *adj* **heftier, heftiest 1** large, heavy, or strong. **2** (of a fine or bill) involving a large sum of money.

hegemony [hig-**em**-on-ee] *n* political domination.

Hegira *n* Mohammed's flight from Mecca to Medina in 622 AD.

heifer [**hef**-fer] *n* young cow.

height *n* **1** distance from base to top. **2** distance above sea level. **3** highest degree or topmost point. **heighten** *v* make or become higher or more intense. **heightened** *adj*

heinous *adj* evil and shocking.

heir *n* person entitled to inherit property or rank. **heiress** *n fem* **heir apparent** person whose right to inherit cannot be defeated. **heirloom** *n* object that has belonged to a family for generations. **heir presumptive** heir whose right may be defeated by the birth of a closer relative.

held *v* past of HOLD[1].

helical *adj* spiral.

helices [**hell**-iss-seez] *n* plural of HELIX.

helicopter *n* aircraft lifted and propelled by rotating overhead blades. **heliport** *n* airport for helicopters.

heliograph *n* signalling apparatus that uses a mirror to reflect the sun's rays.

heliotrope *n* **1** plant with purple flowers. ♦ *adj* **2** light purple.

helium [**heel**-ee-um] *n* *Chem* very light colourless odourless gas.

helix [**heel**-iks] *n, pl* **helices, helixes** spiral.

hell *n* **1** place believed to be where wicked people go when they die. **2** place or state of wickedness, suffering, or punishment. **hell for leather** at great speed. **hellish** *adj* **hellbent** *adj* (foll. by *on*) intent.

hellebore *n* plant with white flowers that bloom in winter.

Hellenic *adj* of the (ancient) Greeks or their language.

hello *interj* expression of greeting or surprise.

helm *n* tiller or wheel for steering a ship. **at the helm** in a position of leadership or control.

helmet *n* hard hat worn for protection.

help *v* **1** make something easier, better, or quicker for (someone). **2** improve (a situation). **3** refrain from, e.g. *I can't help smiling.* ♦ *n* **4** assistance or support. **5** person who gives assistance. **help oneself 1** take something, esp. food or drink, without being served. **2** *Informal* steal something. **helper** *n* **helpful** *adj* **helpfully** *adv* **helpfulness** *n* **helping** *n* single portion of food. **helpless** *adj* weak or incapable. **helplessly** *adv* **helplessness** *n* **helpline** *n* telephone line set aside for callers to contact an organization for help with a problem. **helpmate** *n* companion and helper, esp. a husband or wife.

helter-skelter *adj* **1** haphazard and careless. ♦ *adv* **2** in a haphazard and careless manner. ♦ *n* **3** high spiral slide at a fairground.

hem *n* **1** bottom edge of a garment, folded under and stitched down. ♦ *v* **hemming, hemmed 2** provide with a hem. **hem in** *v* surround and prevent from moving. **hemline** *n* level to which the hem of a skirt hangs.

he-man *n* *Informal* strong virile man.

hemisphere *n* half of a sphere, esp. the earth. **hemispherical** *adj*

hemlock *n* poison made from a plant with spotted stems and small white flowers.

hemp *n* **1** Asian plant with tough fibres. **2** its fibre, used to make canvas and rope. **3** narcotic drug obtained from hemp.

hen *n* **1** female domestic fowl. **2** female of any bird. **hen night, party** party for women only. **henpecked** *adj* (of a man) dominated by his wife.

henbane *n* poisonous plant with sticky hairy leaves.

hence *conj* **1** for this reason. ♦ *adv* **2** from this time. **henceforth, henceforward** *adv* from now on.

henchman *n* attendant or follower.

henna *n* **1** reddish dye made from a shrub or tree. ♦ *v* **2** dye (the hair) with henna.

henry *n, pl* **-ry, -ries, -rys** unit of electrical inductance.

hepatitis *n* inflammation of the liver.

heptagon *n* geometric figure with seven sides. **heptagonal** *adj*

heptathlon *n* athletic contest for women, involving seven events.

her *pron* **1** refers to a female person or animal or anything personified as feminine when the object of a sentence or clause. ♦ *adj* **2** belonging to her.

herald *n* **1** person who announces important news. **2** forerunner. ♦ *v* **3** signal the approach of. **heraldry** *n* study of coats of arms and family trees. **heraldic** *adj*

herb *n* plant used for flavouring in cookery, and in medicine. **herbal** *adj* **herbalist** *n* person who grows or specializes in the use of medicinal herbs. **herbaceous** *adj* (of a plant) soft-stemmed. **herbaceous border** flowerbed containing perennials rather than annuals. **herbicide** *n* chemical used to destroy plants, esp. weeds. **herbivore** *n* animal that eats only plants. **herbivorous** [her-**biv**-or-uss] *adj*

herculean [her-kew-**lee**-an] *adj* requiring great strength or effort.

herd *n* **1** group of animals feeding and living together. **2** large crowd of people. ♦ *v* **3** collect into a herd. **herdsman** *n* man who looks after a herd of animals.

here *adv* in, at, or to this place or point. **hereabouts** *adv* near here. **hereafter** *adv* after this point or time. **the hereafter** life after death. **hereby** *adv* by means of or as a result of this. **herein** *adv* in this place, matter, or document. **hereinafter** *adv Law* from this point on in this document, matter, or case. **heretofore** *adv Law* until now. **herewith** *adv* with this.

heredity [hir-**red**-it-ee] *n* passing on of characteristics from one generation to another. **hereditary** *adj* **1** passed on genetically from one generation to another. **2** passed on by inheritance.

heresy [**herr**-iss-ee] *n, pl* **-sies** opinion contrary to accepted opinion or belief. **heretic** [**herr**-it-ik] *n* person who holds unorthodox opinions. **heretical** [hir-**ret**-ik-al] *adj*

heritage *n* **1** something inherited. **2** anything from the past, considered as the inheritance of present-day society.

hermaphrodite [her-**maf**-roe-dite] *n* animal, plant, or person with both male and female reproductive organs.

hermetic *adj* sealed so as to be airtight. **hermetically** *adv*

hermit *n* person living in solitude, esp. for religious reasons. **hermitage** *n* home of a hermit. **hermit crab** small crab that lives in the shells of other shellfish.

hernia *n* protrusion of an organ or part through the lining of the surrounding body cavity.

hero *n, pl* **heroes 1** principal character in a film, book, etc. **2** man greatly admired for his exceptional qualities or achievements. **heroine** *n fem* **heroic** *adj* **1** courageous. **2** of or like a hero. **heroics** *pl n* extravagant behaviour. **heroically** *adv* **heroism** [**herr**-oh-izz-um] *n*

heroin *n* highly addictive drug derived from morphine.

heron *n* long-legged wading bird.

herpes [**her**-peez] *n* any of several inflammatory skin diseases, including shingles and cold sores.

Herr [**hair**] *n, pl* **Herren** German term of address equivalent to *Mr.*

herring *n* important food fish of northern seas. **herringbone** *n* pattern of zigzag lines.

hers *pron* something belonging to her.

herself *pron* emphatic or reflexive form of SHE *or* HER.

hertz *n, pl* **hertz** *Physics* unit of frequency.

hesitate *v* **1** be slow or uncertain in doing something. **2** be reluctant (to do something). **hesitation** *n* **hesitant** *adj* undecided or wavering. **hesitantly** *adv* **hesitancy** *n*

hessian *n* coarse jute fabric.

hetero- *combining form* other, different, e.g. *heterosexual.*

heterodox *adj* differing from accepted doctrines or beliefs. **heterodoxy** *n*

heterogeneous [het-er-oh-**jean**-ee-uss] *adj* composed of diverse elements. **heterogeneity** *n*

heterosexual *n, adj* (person) sexually attracted to members of the opposite sex. **heterosexuality** *n*

het up *adj Informal* agitated or anxious.

heuristic [**hew**-rist-ik] *adj* involving learning by investigation.

hew *v* **hewing, hewed, hewed** *or* **hewn** **1** cut with an axe. **2** carve from a substance.

hexagon *n* geometrical figure with six sides. **hexagonal** *adj*

hexagram *n* star formed by extending the sides of a regular hexagon to meet at six points.

hey *interj* expression of surprise or for catching attention. **hey presto!** exclamation used by conjurors at the climax of a trick.

heyday *n* time of greatest success, prime.

Hf *Chem* hafnium.

Hg *Chem* mercury.

HGV (formerly) heavy goods vehicle.

hi *interj Informal* hello.

HI Hawaii.

hiatus [hie-**ay**-tuss] *n, pl* **-tuses, -tus** pause or interruption in continuity.

hibernate *v* (of an animal) pass the winter as if in a deep sleep. **hibernation** *n*

Hibernian *adj Poetic* Irish.

hibiscus *n, pl* **-cuses** tropical plant with large brightly coloured flowers.

hiccup, hiccough *n* **1** spasm of the breathing organs with a sharp coughlike sound. **2** *Informal* small problem, hitch. ♦ *v* **3** make a hiccup.

hick *n US & Aust informal* unsophisticated country person.

hickory *n, pl* **-ries** **1** N American nut-bearing tree. **2** its wood.

hide[1] *v* **hiding, hid, hidden** **1** put (oneself or an object) somewhere difficult to see or find. **2** keep secret. ♦ *n* **3** place of concealment, esp. for a bird-watcher. **hiding** *n* state of concealment, e.g. *in hiding.* **hidden agenda** motives or intentions concealed from others who might object to them. **hideaway** *n* private place. **hide-out** *n* place to hide in.

hide[2] *n* skin of an animal. **hiding** *n Slang* severe beating. **hidebound** *adj* unwilling to accept new ideas.

hideous [**hid**-ee-uss] *adj* ugly, revolting. **hideously** *adv*

hie *v* **hying** *or* **hieing, hied** *Obs* hurry.

hierarchy [**hire**-ark-ee] *n, pl* **-chies** system of people or things arranged in a graded order. **hierarchical** *adj*

hieroglyphic [hire-oh-**gliff**-ik] *adj* **1** of a form of writing using picture symbols, as used in ancient Egypt. ♦ *n* **2** symbol that is difficult to decipher. **3** (also **hieroglyph**) symbol representing an object, idea, or sound.

hi-fi *n* **1** set of high-quality sound-reproducing equipment. ♦ *adj* **2** high-fidelity.

higgledy-piggledy *adv, adj* in a muddle.

high *adj* **1** of a great height. **2** far above ground or sea level. **3** being at its peak. **4** greater than usual in intensity or amount. **5** (of a sound) acute in pitch. **6** (of food) slightly decomposed. **7** of great importance, quality, or rank. **8** *Informal* under the influence of alcohol or drugs. ♦ *adv* **9** at or to a high level. ♦ *n* **10 on a high** *Informal* very excited and happy, (as if) intoxicated by alcohol or drugs. **highly** *adv* **highly strung** nervous and easily upset. **Highness** *n* title used to address or refer to a royal person. **High-Church** *adj* belonging to a section within the Church of England stressing the importance of ceremony and ritual. **high commissioner** senior diplomatic representative sent by one Commonwealth country to another. **higher education** education at colleges and universities. **high explosive** extremely powerful chemical explosive, such as TNT. **high-fidelity** *adj* able to reproduce sound with little or no distortion. **high-flown** *adj* (of language) extravagant or pretentious. **high-handed** *adj* excessively forceful. **high jump** athletic event in which competitors attempt to jump over a high bar. **high-minded** *adj* having high moral principles. **high-powered** *adj* dynamic and energetic. **high priest** head of a cult. **high priestess** *n fem* **high-rise** *adj* (of a building) having many storeys. **high school** secondary school. **high-spirited** *adj* lively, fun-loving. **high tea** early evening meal consisting of a cooked dish, bread, cakes, and tea. **high technology** use of advanced electronic processes in industry. **high time** latest possible time.

highball *n US* tall drink of whiskey with soda water or ginger ale and ice.

highbrow *adj, n* intellectual and serious (person).

highchair *n* long-legged chair with a tray attached, used by a very young child at mealtimes.

highfalutin [hie-fa-**loot**-in] *adj Informal* pompous or pretentious.

Highland *adj* of the Highlands, a mountainous region of N Scotland. **Highlander** *n*

highlands *pl n* area of high ground.

highlight *n* **1** outstanding part or feature. **2** light-toned area in a painting or photograph. **3** lightened streak in the hair. ♦ *v* **4** give emphasis to.

highway *n US, Aust & NZ* main road. **Highway Code** regulations and recommendations applying to all road users. **highwayman** *n* (formerly) robber, usu. on horseback, who robbed travellers at gunpoint.

hijack *v* seize control of (an aircraft or other vehicle) while travelling. **hijacker** *n* **hijacking** *n*

hike *n* **1** long walk in the country, esp. for pleasure. **2** rise in price. ♦ *v* **3** go for a long walk. **4** (foll. by *up*) pull (up) or raise. **hiker** *n*

hilarious *adj* very funny. **hilariously** *adv* **hilarity** *n*

hill *n* raised part of the earth's surface, less high than a mountain. **hilly** *adj* **hillier, hilliest** **hillock** *n* small hill. **hillbilly** *n, pl* **-billies** *US* unsophisticated country person.

hilt *n* handle of a sword or knife. **to the hilt, up to the hilt** to the full.

him *pron* refers to a male person or animal when the object of a sentence or clause. **himself** *pron* emphatic or reflexive form of HE *or* HIM.

hind[1] *adj* **hinder, hindmost** situated at the back. **hindsight** *n* ability to understand, after something has happened, what should have been done.

hind[2] *n* female deer.

hinder *v* get in the way of. **hindrance** *n*

Hinduism *n* dominant religion of India, which involves the worship of many gods and a belief in reincarnation. **Hindu** *n* **1** person who practises Hinduism. ♦ *adj* **2** of Hinduism. **Hindi** *n* language of N central India. **Hindustani** *n* group of N Indian languages including Hindi and Urdu.

hinge *n* **1** device for holding together two parts so that one can swing freely. ♦ *v* **2** (foll. by *on*) depend (on). **3** fit a hinge to.

hint *n* **1** indirect suggestion. **2** piece of advice. **3** small amount. ♦ *v* **4** suggest indirectly.

hinterland *n* land lying behind a coast or near a city, esp. a port.

hip[1] *n* either side of the body between the waist and the thigh.

hip[2] *n* rosehip.

hip[3] *adj* **hipper, hippest** *Slang* aware of or following the latest trends.

hip-hop *n* pop-culture movement of the 1980s, comprising rap music, graffiti, and break dancing.

hippie *adj, n* same as HIPPY.

hippo *n, pl* **-pos** *Informal* hippopotamus.

Hippocratic oath *n* oath taken by doctors to observe a code of medical ethics.

hippodrome *n* music hall, variety theatre, or circus.

hippopotamus *n, pl* **-muses, -mi** large African mammal with thick wrinkled skin, living near rivers.

hippy *adj, n, pl* **-pies** (esp. in the 1960s) (of) a person whose behaviour and dress imply a rejection of conventional values.

hire *v* **1** pay to have temporary use of. **2** employ for wages. ♦ *n* **3** hiring. **for hire** available to be hired. **hireling** *n* person who works only for wages. **hire-purchase** *n* system of purchase by which the buyer pays for goods by instalments.

hirsute [**her**-suit] *adj* hairy.

his *pron, adj* (something) belonging to him.

Hispanic *adj* Spanish or Latin-American.

hiss *n* **1** sound like that of a long *s* (as an expression of contempt). ♦ *v* **2** utter a hiss. **3** show derision or anger towards.

histamine [**hiss**-ta-meen] *n* substance released by the body tissues in allergic reactions.

histogram *n* statistical graph in which the frequency of values is represented by vertical bars of varying heights and widths.

histology *n* study of the tissues of an animal or plant. **histological** *adj*

history *n, pl* **-ries** **1** (record or account of) past events and developments. **2** study of these. **3** record of someone's past. **historian** *n* writer of history. **historic** *adj* famous or significant in history. **historical** *adj* **1** occurring in the past. **2** based on history. **historically** *adv*

histrionic *adj* excessively dramatic. **histrionics** *pl n* excessively dramatic behaviour.

hit *v* **hitting, hit** **1** strike, touch forcefully. **2** come into violent contact with. **3** affect badly. **4** reach (a point or place). ♦ *n* **5** hitting. **6** successful record, film, etc. **hit it off** *Informal* get on well together. **hit the road** *Informal* start a journey. **hit-and-miss, hit-or-miss** *adj* sometimes successful and sometimes not. **hit-and-run** *adj* denoting a motor-vehicle accident in which a driver drives away without stopping. **hit man** hired assassin. **hit on** *v* think of (an idea).

hitch *n* **1** minor problem. ♦ *v* **2** *Informal* obtain (a lift) by hitchhiking. **3** fasten with a knot or tie. **4** (foll. by *up*) pull up with a jerk. **get hitched** *Slang* get married. **hitchhike** *v* travel by obtaining free lifts. **hitchhiker** *n*

hi-tech *adj* using sophisticated technology.

hither *adv Old-fashioned* to or towards this place. **hitherto** *adv* until this time.

HIV human immunodeficiency virus, the cause of AIDS.

hive *n* same as BEEHIVE. **hive of activity** place where people are very busy. **hive off** *v* separate from a larger group.

hives *n* allergic reaction in which itchy red or whitish patches appear on the skin.

HM Her (or His) Majesty.

HMI Her (or His) Majesty's Inspector (of schools).

HMS Her (or His) Majesty's Ship.

HMSO Her (or His) Majesty's Stationery Office.

HNC Higher National Certificate.

HND Higher National Diploma.

Ho *Chem* holmium.

hoard *n* **1** store hidden away for future use. ♦ *v* **2** save or store. **hoarder** *n*

> Do not confuse *hoard* with *horde,* which means 'a large group'.

hoarding *n* large board for displaying advertisements.

hoarfrost *n* white ground frost.

hoarse *adj* **1** (of a voice) rough and unclear. **2** having a rough and unclear voice. **hoarsely** *adv* **hoarseness** *n*

hoary *adj* **hoarier, hoariest 1** grey or white(-haired). **2** very old.

hoax *n* **1** deception or trick. ♦ *v* **2** deceive or play a trick upon. **hoaxer** *n*

hob *n* flat top part of a cooker, or a separate flat surface, containing gas or electric rings for cooking on.

hobble *v* **1** walk lamely. **2** tie the legs of (a horse) together.

hobby *n, pl* **-bies** activity pursued in one's spare time. **hobbyhorse** *n* **1** favourite topic. **2** toy horse.

hobgoblin *n* mischievous goblin.

hobnail boots *pl n* heavy boots with short nails in the soles.

hobnob *v* **-nobbing, -nobbed** (foll. by *with*) be on friendly terms (with).

hobo *n, pl* **-bos** *US & Aust* tramp or vagrant.

Hobson's choice *n* the choice of taking what is offered or nothing at all.

hock[1] *n* joint in the back leg of an animal such as a horse that corresponds to the human ankle.

hock[2] *n* white German wine.

hock[3] *v Informal* pawn. **in hock** *Informal* in debt.

hockey *n* **1** team game played on a field with a ball and curved sticks. **2** *US* ice hockey.

hocus-pocus *n* trickery.

hod *n* open wooden box attached to a pole, for carrying bricks or mortar.

hoe *n* **1** long-handled tool used for loosening soil or weeding. ♦ *v* **2** scrape or weed with a hoe.

hog *n* **1** castrated male pig. **2** *Informal* greedy person. ♦ *v* **hogging, hogged 3** *Informal* take more than one's share of. **go the whole hog** *Slang* do something thoroughly or unreservedly. **hogshead** *n* large cask. **hogwash** *n Informal* nonsense.

Hogmanay *n* (in Scotland) New Year's Eve.

ho-ho *interj* representation of the sound of laughter.

hoick *v* raise abruptly and sharply.

hoi polloi *n* the ordinary people.

hoist *v* **1** raise or lift up. ♦ *n* **2** device for lifting things.

hoity-toity *adj Informal* arrogant or haughty.

hokum *n US slang* **1** rubbish, nonsense. **2** stereotyped sentimentality in a film or play.

hold[1] *v* **holding, held 1** keep or support in or with the hands or arms. **2** arrange for (a meeting, party, etc.) to take place. **3** consider to be as specified, e.g. *who are you holding responsible?* **4** maintain in a specified position or state. **5** have the capacity for. **6** *Informal* wait, esp. on the telephone. **7** reserve (a room etc.). **8** restrain or keep back. **9** own, possess. **10** (cause to) remain committed to (a promise etc.). **11** believe. ♦ *n* **12** act or way of holding. **13** controlling influence. **14** something to hold onto for support. **holder** *n* **holding** *n* property, such as land or stocks and shares. **holdall** *n* large strong travelling bag. **hold forth** *v* speak for a long time. **hold-up** *n* **1** armed robbery. **2** delay. **hold up** *v* **hold with** *v* approve of, e.g. *I don't hold with this theory.*

hold[2] *n* cargo compartment in a ship or aircraft.

hole *n* **1** area hollowed out in a solid. **2** opening or hollow. **3** animal's burrow. **4** *Informal* unattractive place. **5** *Informal* difficult situation. ♦ *v* **6** make holes in. **7** hit (a golf ball) into the target hole. **holey** *adj* **hole up** *v Informal* go into hiding.

holiday *n* **1** time spent away from home for rest or recreation. **2** day or other period of rest from work or studies.

holiness *n* **1** state of being holy. **2** (**H-**) title used to address or refer to the Pope.

holistic *adj* considering the complete person, physically and mentally, in the treatment of an illness. **holism** *n*

holler *v, n Informal* shout, yell.

hollow *adj* **1** having a hole or space inside. **2** (of a sound) as if echoing in a hollow place. **3** without any real value or worth. ♦ *n* **4** cavity or space. **5** dip in the land. ♦ *v* **6** form a hollow in. **hollowly** *adv* **hollowness** *n*

holly *n* evergreen tree with prickly leaves and red berries.

hollyhock *n* tall garden plant with spikes of colourful flowers.

holmium *n Chem* silver-white metallic element, the compounds of which are highly magnetic.

holm oak *n* evergreen oak tree with prickly leaves.

holocaust *n* destruction or loss of life on a massive scale.

hologram *n* three-dimensional photographic image.

holograph *n* document handwritten by the author.

holography *n* science of using lasers to produce holograms. **holographic** *adj*

holster *n* leather case for a pistol, hung from a belt.

holt *n* otter's lair.

holy *adj* **-lier, -liest 1** of God or a god. **2** devout or virtuous. **holier-than-thou** *adj* self-righteous. **Holy Communion** *Christianity* service in which people take bread and wine in remembrance of the death and resurrection of Jesus Christ. **Holy Grail** (in medieval legend) the bowl used by Jesus Christ at the Last Supper. **holy orders** status of an ordained Christian minister. **Holy Spirit, Ghost** *Christianity* one of the three aspects of God. **Holy Week** *Christianity* week before Easter.

homage *n* show of respect or honour towards someone or something.

homburg *n* man's soft felt hat with a dented crown and a stiff upturned brim.

home *n* **1** place where one lives. **2** place where one was born or grew up. **3** institution for the care of the elderly, orphans, etc. ♦ *adj* **4** of one's home, birthplace, or native country. **5** *Sport* played on one's own ground. ♦ *adv* **6** to or at home. ♦ *v* **7** (foll. by *in* or *in on*) direct towards (a point or target). **at home** at ease. **bring home to** make clear to. **home and dry** *Informal* safe or successful. **homeless** *adj* **1** having nowhere to live. ♦ *pl n* **2** people who have nowhere to live. **homelessness** *n* **homely** *adj* **1** simple, ordinary, and comfortable. **2** *US* unattractive. **homeliness** *n* **homeward** *adj, adv* **homewards** *adv* **homebrew** *n* beer made at home. **home economics** study of subjects concerned with running a home. **home help** person employed by a local authority to do housework in an elderly or disabled person's home. **home-made** *adj* made at home or on the premises. **Home Office** government department responsible for law and order, immigration, and other domestic matters. **Home Secretary** head of the Home Office. **home truths** unpleasant facts told to a person about himself or herself.

homeland *n* country from which a person's ancestors came.

homeopathy [home-ee-**op**-ath-ee] *n* treatment of disease by small doses of a drug that produces symptoms of the disease in healthy people. **homeopath** *n* person who practises homeopathy. **homeopathic** [home-ee-oh-**path**-ik] *adj*

homesick *adj* sad because missing one's home and family. **homesickness** *n*

homestead *n* farmhouse plus the adjoining land.

homework *n* school work done at home.

homicide *n* **1** killing of a human being. **2** person who kills someone. **homicidal** *adj*

homily *n, pl* **-lies** speech telling people how they should behave.

homing pigeon *n* pigeon trained to return home after travelling great distances, kept for racing.

hominid *n* man or any extinct forerunner of man.

hominoid *adj, n* manlike (animal).

homo- *combining form* same, like, e.g. *homosexual.*

homogeneous [home-oh-**jean**-ee-uss] *adj* formed of similar parts. **homogeneity** *n* **homogenize** *v* **1** break up fat globules in (milk or cream) to distribute them evenly. **2** make homogeneous.

homograph *n* word spelt the same as another, but with a different meaning.

homologous [hom-**ol**-log-uss] *adj* having a related or similar position or structure.

homonym *n* word spelt or pronounced the same as another, but with a different meaning.

homophobia *n* hatred or fear of homosexuals. **homophobic** *adj*

homophone *n* word pronounced the same as another, but with a different meaning or spelling.

Homo sapiens [**hoe**-moh **sap**-ee-enz] *n* human beings as a species.

homosexual *n, adj* (person) sexually attracted to members of the same sex. **homosexuality** *n*

Hon. Honourable.

hone *v* sharpen.

honest *adj* **1** truthful and moral. **2** open and sincere. **honestly** *adv* **honesty** *n* **1** quality of being honest. **2** plant with silvery seed pods.

honey *n* **1** sweet edible sticky substance made by bees from nectar. **2** term of endearment. **honeyed** *adj Poetic* flattering or soothing, e.g. *honeyed words.* **honeycomb** *n* waxy structure of six-sided cells in which honey is stored by bees in a beehive. **honeydew melon** melon with a yellow skin and sweet pale flesh. **honeymoon** *n* holiday taken by a newly married couple. **honeysuckle** *n* climbing shrub with sweet-smelling flowers.

honk *n* **1** sound made by a car horn. **2** sound made by a goose. ♦ *v* **3** (cause to) make this sound.

honour *n* **1** sense of honesty and fairness. **2** (award given out of) respect. **3** pleasure or privilege. ♦ *pl* **4** university degree of a higher standard than an ordinary degree. ♦ *v* **5** give praise and attention to. **6** give an award to (someone) out of respect. **7** accept or pay (a cheque or bill). **8** keep (a promise). **do the honours** act as host or hostess by pouring drinks or giving out food. **honourable** *adj* **1** worthy of respect or esteem. **2** (**H-**) denoting a title of respect placed before the names of some members of the nobility, judges, etc. **honourably** *adv* **honorary** *adj* **1** held or given only as an honour. **2** unpaid. **honorific** *adj* showing respect.

hooch [rhymes with **smooch**] *n US slang* alcoholic drink, esp. illicitly distilled spirits.

hood[1] *n* **1** head covering, often attached to a coat or jacket. **2** folding roof of a convertible car or a pram. **3** *US & Aust* car bonnet. **hooded** *adj* **1** (of a garment) having a hood. **2** (of eyes) having heavy eyelids that appear to be half-closed.

hood[2] *n Slang* hoodlum.

hoodlum *n Slang* violent criminal, gangster.

hoodoo *n, pl* **-doos** (cause of) bad luck.

hoodwink *v* trick, deceive.

hooey *n Slang* nonsense.

hoof *n, pl* **hooves, hoofs** horny covering of the foot of a horse, deer, etc. **hoof it** *Slang* walk.

hoo-ha *n* fuss or commotion.

hook *n* **1** curved piece of metal, plastic, etc., used to hang, hold, or pull something. **2** short swinging punch. ♦ *v* **3** fasten or catch (as if) with a hook. **hooked** *adj* **1** bent like a hook. **2** (foll. by *on*) *Slang* addicted (to) or obsessed (with). **hooker** *n* **1** *Slang* prostitute. **2** *Rugby* player who uses his feet to get the ball in a scrum. **hook-up** *n* linking of radio or television stations. **hookworm** *n* blood-sucking worm with hooked mouthparts.

hookah *n* oriental pipe in which smoke is drawn through water and a long tube.

hooligan *n* rowdy young person. **hooliganism** *n*

hoop *n* rigid circular band, used esp. as a child's toy or for animals to jump through in the circus. **jump, be put**

through the hoops go through an ordeal or test.

hoopla *n* fairground game in which hoops are thrown over objects in an attempt to win them.

hoopoe [**hoop**-oo] *n* bird with a pinkish-brown plumage and a fanlike crest.

hooray *interj* same as HURRAH.

hoot *n* **1** sound of a car horn. **2** cry of an owl. **3** cry of derision. **4** *Informal* amusing person or thing. ♦ *v* **5** sound (a car horn). **6** jeer or yell contemptuously (at someone). **hooter** *n* **1** device that hoots. **2** *Slang* nose.

Hoover *n* **1** ® vacuum cleaner. ♦ *v* **2** (**h-**) clean with a vacuum cleaner.

hooves *n* a plural of HOOF.

hop[1] *v* **hopping, hopped 1** jump on one foot. **2** move in short jumps. **3** *Informal* move quickly. ♦ *n* **4** instance of hopping. **5** *Informal* dance. **6** short journey, esp. by air. **hop it** *Slang* go away. **catch someone on the hop** *Informal* catch someone unprepared.

hop[2] *n* (often pl) climbing plant, the dried flowers of which are used to make beer.

hope *v* **1** want (something) to happen or be true. ♦ *n* **2** expectation of something desired. **3** thing that gives cause for hope or is desired. **hopeful** *adj* **1** having, expressing, or inspiring hope. ♦ *n* **2** person considered to be on the brink of success. **hopefully** *adv* **1** in a hopeful manner. **2** it is hoped. **hopefulness** *n* **hopeless** *adj* **hopelessly** *adv* **hopelessness** *n*

> Although many people dislike the use of *hopefully* as in *I'll see you in June, hopefully,* it is now well established.

hopper *n* container for storing substances such as grain or sand.

hopscotch *n* children's game of hopping in a pattern drawn on the ground.

horde *n* large crowd.

> Do not confuse *horde* with *hoard,* which means 'to store hidden away for future use'.

horizon *n* **1** apparent line that divides the earth and the sky. ♦ *pl* **2** limits of scope, interest, or knowledge.

horizontal *adj* parallel to the horizon, level, flat. **horizontally** *adv*

hormone *n* **1** substance secreted by certain glands which stimulates certain organs of the body. **2** synthetic substance with the same effect. **hormonal** *adj*

horn *n* **1** one of a pair of bony growths sticking out of the heads of cattle, sheep, etc. **2** substance of which horns are made. **3** musical instrument with a tube or pipe of brass fitted with a mouthpiece. **4** device on a vehicle sounded as a warning. **horned** *adj* **horny** *adj* **hornier, horniest 1** of or like horn. **2** *Slang* (easily) sexually aroused. **hornbeam** *n* tree with smooth grey bark. **hornbill** *n* bird with a bony growth on its large beak. **hornpipe** *n* (music for) a solo dance, traditionally performed by sailors.

hornblende *n* mineral containing aluminium, calcium, sodium, magnesium, and iron.

hornet *n* large wasp with a severe sting.

horoscope *n* **1** prediction of a person's future based on the positions of the planets, sun, and moon at his or her birth. **2** diagram of the positions of the planets, sun, and moon at a particular time and place.

horrendous *adj* very unpleasant and shocking. **horrendously** *adv*

horrible *adj* **1** disagreeable, unpleasant. **2** causing horror. **horribly** *adv*

horrid *adj* **1** disagreeable, unpleasant. **2** *Informal* nasty.

horrify *v* **-fying, -fied** cause to feel horror or shock. **horrifying** *adj* **horrifyingly** *adv* **horrific** *adj* causing horror. **horrifically** *adv*

horror *n* (thing or person causing) terror or hatred.

hors d'oeuvre [**or durv**] *n* appetizer served before a main meal.

horse *n* **1** large animal with hooves, a mane, and a tail, used for riding and pulling carts etc. **2** piece of gymnastic equipment used for vaulting over. **(straight) from the horse's mouth** from the original source. **horsey, horsy** *adj* **horsier, horsiest 1** very keen on horses. **2** of or like a horse. **horse around** *v Informal* play roughly or boisterously. **horsebox** *n* trailer used for transporting horses. **horse chestnut 1** tree with broad leaves and inedible large brown shiny nuts in spiky cases. **2** the nut. **horsefly** *n* large bloodsucking fly. **horsehair** *n* hair from the tail or mane of a horse. **horse laugh** loud coarse laugh. **horseman, horsewoman** *n* **1** person skilled in riding. **2** person riding a horse. **horsemanship** *n* **horseplay** *n* rough or rowdy play. **horsepower** *n* unit of power (equivalent to 745.7 watts), used to measure the power of an engine. **horseradish** *n* strong-tasting root of a plant, usu. made into a sauce. **horse sense** common sense. **horseshoe** *n* protective U-shaped piece of iron nailed to a horse's hoof, regarded as a symbol of good luck.

horticulture *n* art or science of cultivating gardens. **horticultural** *adj* **horticulturalist, horticulturist** *n*

hosanna *interj* exclamation of praise to God.

hose[1] *n* **1** flexible pipe for conveying liquid. ♦ *v* **2** water with a hose.

hose[2] *n* stockings, socks, and tights. **hosiery** *n* stockings, socks, and tights collectively.

hospice [**hoss**-piss] *n* nursing home for the terminally ill.

hospital *n* place where people who are ill are looked after and treated. **hospitalize** *v* send or admit to hospital. **hospitalization** *n*

hospitality *n* kindness in welcoming strangers or guests. **hospitable** *adj* welcoming to strangers or guests.

host[1] *n* **1** (*fem* **hostess**) person who entertains guests, esp. in his own home. **2** place or country providing the facilities for an event. **3** compere of a show. **4** animal or plant on which a parasite lives. ♦ *v* **5** be the host of.

host[2] *n* large number.

Host *n Christianity* bread used in Holy Communion.

hostage *n* person who is illegally held prisoner until certain demands are met by other people.

hostel *n* building providing accommodation at a low cost for travellers, homeless people, etc.

hostelry *n, pl* **-ries** *Old-fashioned or facetious* inn, pub.

hostile *adj* **1** unfriendly. **2** (foll. by *to*) opposed (to). **3** of an enemy. **hostility** *n, pl* **-ties 1** unfriendly and aggressive feelings or behaviour. ♦ *pl* **2** acts of warfare.

hot *adj* **hotter, hottest 1** having a high temperature. **2** strong, spicy. **3** (of news) very recent. **4** (of a contest) fiercely fought. **5** (of a temper) quick to rouse. **6** liked very much, e.g. *a hot favourite.* **7** *Slang* stolen. **in hot water** *Informal* in trouble. **in the hot seat** *Informal* in a difficult and responsible position. **hotly** *adv* **hotting** *n Informal* practice of stealing fast cars and putting on a show of skilful but dangerous driving. **hotter** *n* **hot air** *Informal* empty talk. **hot-blooded** *adj* passionate or excitable. **hot dog** long roll split lengthways with a hot frankfurter inside. **hot-headed** *adj* rash, having a hot temper. **hotline** *n* direct telephone link for emergency use. **hot-water bottle** rubber container filled with hot water, used for warming a bed.

hotbed *n* any place encouraging a particular activity, e.g. *hotbeds of unrest.*

hotchpotch *n* jumbled mixture.

hotel *n* commercial establishment providing lodging and meals. **hotelier** *n* owner or manager of a hotel.

hotfoot *adv Informal* quickly and eagerly. **hotfoot it** *Informal* go quickly and eagerly.

hothouse *n* greenhouse.

hotplate *n* **1** heated metal surface on an

electric cooker. **2** portable device for keeping food warm.

hotpot *n* casserole of meat and vegetables, topped with potatoes.

Hottentot *n* (member of) a race of people of South Africa, now almost extinct.

hound *n* **1** hunting dog. ♦ *v* **2** pursue relentlessly.

hour *n* **1** twenty-fourth part of a day, sixty minutes. **2** time of day. ♦ *pl* **3** period regularly appointed for work or business. **hourly** *adj, adv* **1** (happening) every hour. **2** frequent(ly). **hourglass** *n* device with two glass compartments, containing a quantity of sand that takes an hour to trickle from the top section to the bottom one.

houri *n Islam* any of the nymphs of paradise.

house *n* **1** building used as a home. **2** building used for some specific purpose, e.g. *the opera house.* **3** business firm. **4** law-making body or the hall where it meets. **5** family or dynasty. **6** theatre or cinema audience. ♦ *v* **7** give accommodation to. **8** contain or cover. ♦ *adj* **9** (of wine) sold in a restaurant at a lower price than wines on the wine list. **get on like a house on fire** *Informal* get on very well together. **on the house** *Informal* provided free by the management. **housing** *n* **1** (providing of) houses. **2** protective case or covering of a machine. **house arrest** confinement to one's home rather than in prison. **houseboat** *n* stationary boat used as a home. **housebound** *adj* unable to leave one's house, usu. because of illness. **housebreaker** *n* burglar. **housebreaking** *n* **housecoat** *n* woman's long loose coat-shaped garment for wearing at home. **household** *n* all the people living in a house. **household name, word** very well-known person or thing. **householder** *n* person who owns or rents a house. **housekeeper** *n* person employed to run someone else's household. **housekeeping** *n* (money for) running a household. **housemaid** *n* female servant employed to do housework. **houseman** *n* junior hospital doctor. **house-proud** *adj* excessively concerned with the appearance of one's house. **house-train** *v* train (a pet) to urinate and defecate outside. **housewarming** *n* party to celebrate moving into a new home. **housewife** *n* woman who runs her own household and does not have a job. **housewifely** *adj* **housework** *n* work of running a home, such as cleaning, cooking, and shopping.

House music, House *n* funk-based disco music with fragments of other recordings edited in electronically.

hove *v Naut* a past of HEAVE.

hovel *n* small dirty house or hut.

hover *v* **1** (of a bird etc.) remain suspended in one place in the air. **2** loiter. **3** be in a state of indecision. **hovercraft** *n* vehicle which can travel over both land and sea on a cushion of air.

how *adv* **1** in what way, by what means. **2** to what degree, e.g. *I know how hard it is.* **however** *adv* **1** nevertheless. **2** by whatever means. **3** no matter how, e.g. *however much it hurt, he could do it.*

howdah *n* canopied seat on an elephant's back.

howitzer *n* large gun firing shells at a steep angle.

howl *n* **1** loud wailing cry. **2** loud burst of laughter. ♦ *v* **3** utter a howl. **howler** *n Informal* stupid mistake.

hoyden *n* wild or boisterous girl.

HP, h.p. **1** hire-purchase. **2** horsepower.

HQ headquarters.

hr hour.

HRH Her (or His) Royal Highness.

HRT hormone replacement therapy.

hub *n* **1** centre of a wheel, through which the axle passes. **2** central point of activity.

hubble-bubble *n* same as HOOKAH.

hubbub *n* confused noise of many voices.

hubby *n, pl* **-bies** *Informal* husband.

hubris [**hew**-briss] *n Formal* pride, arrogance.

huckster *n* person using aggressive

methods of selling.

huddle *v* **1** hunch (oneself) through cold or fear. **2** crowd closely together. ♦ *n* **3** small group. **4** *Informal* impromptu conference.

hue *n* colour, shade.

hue and cry *n* public outcry.

huff *n* **1** passing mood of anger or resentment. ♦ *v* **2** blow or puff heavily. **huffy** *adj* **huffier, huffiest** **huffily** *adv*

hug *v* **hugging, hugged** **1** clasp tightly in the arms, usu. with affection. **2** keep close to (the ground, kerb, etc.). ♦ *n* **3** tight or fond embrace.

huge *adj* very big. **hugely** *adv*

huh *interj* exclamation of derision, bewilderment, or inquiry.

hula *n* swaying Hawaiian dance. **Hula Hoop** ® plastic hoop twirled round the body by gyrating the hips.

hulk *n* **1** body of an abandoned ship. **2** *Offens* large heavy person or thing. **hulking** *adj* bulky, unwieldy.

hull *n* **1** main body of a boat. **2** leaves round the stem of a strawberry, raspberry, etc. ♦ *v* **3** remove the hulls from.

hullabaloo *n, pl* **-loos** loud confused noise or clamour.

hullo *interj* same as HELLO.

hum *v* **humming, hummed** **1** make a low continuous vibrating sound. **2** sing with the lips closed. **3** *Slang* (of a place) be very busy. ♦ *n* **4** humming sound. **hummingbird** *n* very small American bird whose powerful wings make a humming noise as they vibrate.

human *adj* **1** of or typical of people. ♦ *n* **2** human being. **humanly** *adv* by human powers or means. **human being** man, woman, or child. **human nature** ordinary human behaviour, esp. when less than perfect. **human race** all men, women, and children collectively. **human rights** basic rights of people to liberty, justice, etc.

humane *adj* kind or merciful. **humanely** *adv*

humanism *n* belief in human effort rather than religion. **humanist** *n* **humanistic** *adj*

humanitarian *n, adj* (person) having the interests of humankind at heart. **humanitarianism** *n*

humanity *n, pl* **-ties** **1** human race. **2** the quality of being human. **3** kindness or mercy. ♦ *pl* **4** study of literature, philosophy, and the arts.

humanize *v* make human or humane. **humanization** *n*

humankind *n* human race.

humanoid *n, adj* (robot or creature) resembling a human being in appearance.

humble *adj* **1** conscious of one's failings. **2** modest, unpretentious. **3** unimportant. ♦ *v* **4** cause to feel humble, humiliate. **humbly** *adv*

humbug *n* **1** hard striped peppermint sweet. **2** nonsense. **3** dishonest person.

humdinger *n* *Slang* excellent person or thing.

humdrum *adj* ordinary, dull.

humerus [**hew**-mer-uss] *n, pl* **-meri** [-mer-rye] bone from the shoulder to the elbow.

humid *adj* damp and hot. **humidity** *n* **humidify** *v* **-fying, -fied** **humidifier** *n* device for increasing the amount of water vapour in the air in a room.

humiliate *v* lower the dignity or hurt the pride of. **humiliating** *adj* **humiliation** *n*

humility *n* quality of being humble.

hummock *n* very small hill.

humour *n* **1** ability to say or perceive things that are amusing. **2** amusing quality in a situation, film, etc. **3** state of mind, mood. **4** *Old-fashioned* fluid in the body. ♦ *v* **5** be kind and indulgent to. **humorous** *adj* **humorously** *adv* **humorist** *n* writer or entertainer who uses humour in his or her work. **humourless** *adj*

hump *n* **1** raised piece of ground. **2** large lump on the back of an animal or person. ♦ *v* **3** *Slang* carry or heave. **get, take the hump** *Informal* be annoyed, sulk. **humpback** *n* *Offens* hunchback. **humpbacked** *adj* **hump-back, humpbacked bridge** road bridge with a sharp slope on each side.

humus [**hew**-muss] *n* decomposing vegetable and animal mould in the soil.

Hun *n* **1** member of the Asian people who invaded the Roman Empire in the 4th and 5th centuries AD. **2** *Informal offens* (in World War 1) German.

hunch *n* **1** feeling or suspicion not based on facts. ♦ *v* **2** draw (one's shoulders) up or together. **hunchback** *n Offens* person with an abnormal curvature of the spine. **hunchbacked** *adj*

hundred *adj, n* **1** ten times ten. ♦ *n* **2** (often pl) large but unspecified number. **hundredth** *adj, n* **hundredweight** *n Brit* unit of weight of 112 pounds (50.8 kilograms).

hung *v* **1** past of HANG. ♦ *adj* **2** (of a parliament or jury) with no side having a clear majority. **hung over** *Informal* suffering the effects of a hangover.

Hungarian *adj* **1** of Hungary. ♦ *n* **2** person from Hungary. **3** language of Hungary.

hunger *n* **1** discomfort or weakness from lack of food. **2** lack of food that causes suffering or death, e.g. *refugees dying of hunger.* **3** desire or craving. ♦ *v* **4** (foll. by *for*) want very much. **hunger strike** refusal of all food, as a means of protest.

hungry *adj* **hungrier, hungriest** **1** desiring food. **2** (foll. by *for*) having a desire or craving (for). **hungrily** *adv*

hunk *n* **1** large piece. **2** *Slang* sexually attractive man.

hunt *v* **1** seek out and kill (wild animals) for food or sport. **2** (foll. by *for*) search (for). ♦ *n* **3** hunting. **4** (party organized for) hunting wild animals for sport. **hunter** *n* person or animal that hunts wild animals for food or sport. **hunting** *n* **huntsman** *n* man who hunts wild animals, esp. foxes.

hurdle *n* **1** *Sport* light barrier for jumping over in some races. **2** problem or difficulty. ♦ *pl* **3** race involving hurdles. ♦ *v* **4** jump over (something). **hurdler** *n*

hurdy-gurdy *n, pl* **-dies** mechanical musical instrument, such as a barrel organ.

hurl *v* throw or utter forcefully.

hurling, hurley *n* Irish game like hockey.

hurly-burly *n* loud confusion.

hurrah, hurray *interj* exclamation of joy or applause.

hurricane *n* very strong, often destructive, wind or storm. **hurricane lamp** paraffin lamp with a glass covering.

hurry *v* **-rying, -ried** **1** (cause to) move or act very quickly. ♦ *n* **2** doing something quickly or the need to do something quickly. **hurried** *adj* **hurriedly** *adv*

hurt *v* **hurting, hurt** **1** cause physical or mental pain to. **2** be painful. **3** *Informal* feel pain. ♦ *n* **4** physical or mental pain. **hurtful** *adj* unkind.

hurtle *v* move quickly or violently.

husband *n* **1** woman's partner in marriage. ♦ *v* **2** use economically. **husbandry** *n* **1** farming. **2** management of resources.

hush *v* **1** make or be silent. ♦ *n* **2** stillness or silence. **hushed** *adj* **hush-hush** *adj Informal* secret. **hush money** *Slang* money given to someone to ensure that something is kept secret. **hush up** *v* suppress information about.

husk *n* **1** outer covering of certain seeds and fruits. ♦ *v* **2** remove the husk from.

husky[1] *adj* **huskier, huskiest** **1** slightly hoarse. **2** *Informal* big and strong. **huskily** *adv*

husky[2] *n, pl* **huskies** Arctic sledge dog with thick hair and a curled tail.

hussar [hoo-**zar**] *n Hist* lightly armed cavalry soldier.

hussy *n, pl* **-sies** immodest or promiscuous woman.

hustings *pl n* political campaigns and speeches before an election.

hustle *v* **1** push about, jostle. ♦ *n* **2** lively activity or bustle.

hut *n* small house, shelter, or shed.

hutch *n* cage for pet rabbits etc.

hyacinth *n* sweet-smelling spring flower that grows from a bulb.

hyaena *n* same as HYENA.

hybrid *n* **1** offspring of two plants or animals of different species. **2** anything of mixed origin. ♦ *adj* **3** of mixed origin.

hydra *n* mythical many-headed water

serpent.

hydrangea *n* ornamental shrub with clusters of pink, blue, or white flowers.

hydrant *n* outlet from a water main with a nozzle for a hose.

hydrate *n* **1** chemical compound of water with another substance. ♦ *v* **2** treat or impregnate with water.

hydraulic *adj* operated by pressure forced through a pipe by a liquid such as water or oil. **hydraulics** *n* study of the mechanical properties of fluids as they apply to practical engineering. **hydraulically** *adv*

hydro[1] *n, pl* **hydros** hotel offering facilities for hydropathy.

hydro[2] *adj* short for HYDROELECTRIC.

hydro- *combining form* **1** water, e.g. *hydroelectric.* **2** hydrogen, e.g. *hydrochloric acid.*

hydrocarbon *n* compound of hydrogen and carbon.

hydrocephalus *n* accumulation of fluid within the cavities of the brain, causing enlargement of the head in children.

hydrochloric acid *n* strong colourless acid used in many industrial and laboratory processes.

hydrodynamics *n* branch of science concerned with the mechanical properties of fluids.

hydroelectric *adj* of the generation of electricity by water pressure.

hydrofoil *n* fast light boat with its hull raised out of the water on one or more pairs of fins.

hydrogen *n Chem* light flammable colourless gas that combines with oxygen to form water. **hydrogen bomb** extremely powerful bomb in which energy is released by fusion of hydrogen nuclei to give helium nuclei. **hydrogen peroxide** colourless liquid used as a hair bleach and as an antiseptic.

hydrology *n* study of the distribution, conservation, and use of the water of the earth and its atmosphere.

hydrolysis [hie-**drol**-iss-iss] *n* decomposition of a chemical compound reacting with water.

hydrometer [hie-**drom**-it-er] *n* instrument for measuring the density of a liquid.

hydropathy *n* method of treating disease by the use of large quantities of water both internally and externally. **hydropathic** *adj*

hydrophobia *n* **1** rabies. **2** fear of water.

hydroplane *n* light motorboat that skims the water.

hydroponics *n* method of growing plants in water rather than soil.

hydrotherapy *n Med* treatment of certain diseases by exercise in water.

hyena *n* scavenging doglike mammal of Africa and S Asia.

hygiene *n* **1** principles and practice of health and cleanliness. **2** study of these principles. **hygienic** *adj* **hygienically** *adv*

hymen *n* membrane partly covering the opening of a girl's vagina, which breaks before puberty or at the first occurrence of sexual intercourse.

hymn *n* Christian song of praise sung to God or a saint. **hymnal** *n* book of hymns (also **hymn book**).

hype *n* **1** intensive or exaggerated publicity or sales promotion. ♦ *v* **2** promote (a product) using intensive or exaggerated publicity.

hyper *adj Informal* overactive or overexcited.

hyper- *prefix* over, above, excessively, e.g. *hyperactive.*

hyperbola [hie-**per**-bol-a] *n Geom* curve produced when a cone is cut by a plane at a steeper angle to its base than its side.

hyperbole [hie-**per**-bol-ee] *n* deliberate exaggeration for effect. **hyperbolic** *adj*

hypermarket *n* huge self-service store.

hypersensitive *adj* **1** extremely sensitive to certain drugs, extremes of temperature, etc. **2** very easily upset.

hypersonic *adj* having a speed of at least five times the speed of sound.

hypertension *n* very high blood pressure.

hyperventilation *n* increase in the rate of breathing, sometimes resulting in cramp and dizziness. **hyperventilate** *v*

hyphen *n* punctuation mark (-) indicating that two words or syllables are connected. **hyphenated** *adj* (of two words or syllables) having a hyphen between them. **hyphenation** *n*

hypnosis *n* artificially induced state of relaxation in which the mind is more than usually receptive to suggestion. **hypnotic** *adj* of or (as if) producing hypnosis. **hypnotically** *adv* **hypnotism** *n* inducing hypnosis in someone. **hypnotist** *n* **hypnotize** *v*

hypo- *prefix* beneath, less than, e.g. *hypothermia.*

hypoallergenic *adj* (of cosmetics) not likely to cause an allergic reaction.

hypochondria *n* undue preoccupation with one's health. **hypochondriac** *n*

hypocrisy [hip-**ok**-rass-ee] *n, pl* **-sies** (instance of) pretence of having standards or beliefs that are contrary to one's real character or actual behaviour. **hypocrite** [**hip**-oh-krit] *n* person who pretends to be what he or she is not. **hypocritical** *adj* **hypocritically** *adv*

hypodermic *adj, n* (denoting) a syringe or needle used to inject a drug beneath the skin.

hypotension *n* very low blood pressure.

hypotenuse [hie-**pot**-a-news] *n* side of a right-angled triangle opposite the right angle.

hypothermia *n* condition in which a person's body temperature is dangerously low as a result of prolonged exposure to severe cold.

hypothesis [hie-**poth**-iss-iss] *n, pl* **-ses** [-seez] suggested but unproved explanation of something. **hypothesize** *v* **hypothetical** *adj* based on assumption rather than fact or reality. **hypothetically** *adv*

hyssop *n* sweet-smelling herb used in folk medicine.

hysterectomy *n, pl* **-mies** surgical removal of the womb.

hysteria *n* state of uncontrolled excitement, anger, or panic. **hysteric** *n* **1** hysterical person. **hysterical** *adj* **1** in a state of hysteria. **2** *Informal* wildly funny. **hysterically** *adv* **hysterics** *pl n* **1** attack of hysteria. **2** *Informal* uncontrollable laughter.

Hz hertz.

I i

I[1] *pron* used by a speaker or writer to refer to himself or herself as the subject of a verb.

I[2] **1** *Chem* iodine. **2** the Roman numeral for one.

IA Iowa.

IBA Independent Broadcasting Authority.

Iberian *adj* of Iberia, the peninsula comprising Spain and Portugal.

ibex [**ibe**-eks] *n* wild goat with large backward-curving horns.

ibid. (referring to a book, page, or passage already mentioned) in the same place.

ibis [**ibe**-iss] *n* large wading bird with long legs.

ICBM intercontinental ballistic missile.

ice *n* **1** frozen water. **2** portion of ice cream. ♦ *v* **3** (foll. by *up* or *over*) become covered with ice. **4** cover with icing. **break the ice** create a relaxed atmosphere, esp. between people meeting for the first time. **iced** *adj* **1** covered with icing. **2** (of a drink) containing ice. **icy** *adj* **icier, iciest 1** very cold. **2** covered with ice. **3** aloof and unfriendly. **icily** *adv* **iciness** *n* **Ice Age** period when much of the earth's surface was covered in glaciers. **iceberg** *n* large floating mass of ice. **icebox** *n US* refrigerator. **icebreaker** *n* ship designed to break a channel through ice. **icecap** *n* mass of ice permanently covering an area. **ice cream** sweet creamy frozen food. **ice cube** small square block of ice added to a drink to cool it. **ice floe** sheet of ice floating in the sea. **ice hockey** team game like hockey played on ice with a puck. **ice lolly** flavoured ice on a stick. **ice pick** pointed tool for breaking ice. **ice skate** boot with a steel blade fixed to the sole, to enable the wearer to glide over ice. **ice-skate** *v* **ice-skater** *n*

Icelandic *adj* **1** of Iceland. ♦ *n* **2** language of Iceland. **Icelander** *n*

ichthyology [ik-thi-**ol**-a-jee] *n* scientific study of fish. **ichthyological** *adj* **ichthyologist** *n*

icicle *n* tapering spike of ice hanging where water has dripped.

icing *n* mixture of sugar and water etc., used to cover and decorate cakes. **icing sugar** finely ground sugar for making icing.

icon *n* **1** picture of Christ or another religious figure, regarded as holy in the Orthodox Church. **2** picture on a computer screen representing a function that can be activated by moving the cursor over it.

iconoclast *n* person who attacks established ideas or principles. **iconoclastic** *adj* **iconoclasm** *n*

id *n Psychoanalysis* the mind's instinctive unconscious energies.

ID 1 Idaho. **2** identification.

idea *n* **1** plan or thought formed in the mind. **2** thought of something, e.g. *the idea overwhelms me.* **3** belief or opinion.

ideal *adj* **1** most suitable. **2** perfect. ♦ *n* **3** conception of something that is perfect. **4** perfect person or thing. **ideally** *adv* **idealism** *n* tendency to seek perfection in everything. **idealist** *n* **idealistic** *adj* **idealize** *v* regard or portray as perfect or nearly perfect. **idealization** *n*

idem *pron, adj Latin* the same: used to refer to an article, chapter, or book already quoted.

identical *adj* exactly the same. **identically** *adv*

identify *v* **-fying, -fied 1** prove or recognize as being a certain person or thing. **2** (foll. by *with*) understand and sympathize with (a person or group that one regards as being similar or similarly situated). **3** treat as being the same. **identifiable** *adj* **identification** *n*

Identikit *n* ® composite picture, assembled from descriptions given, of a person wanted by the police.

identity *n, pl* **-ties 1** state of being a specified person or thing. **2** individuality or personality. **3** state of being the same.

ideology *n, pl* **-gies** body of ideas and beliefs of a group, nation, etc. **ideological** *adj* **ideologically** *adv* **ideologist** *n*

ides *n* (in the Ancient Roman calendar) the 15th of March, May, July, or October, or the 13th of other months.

idiocy *n* utter stupidity.

idiom *n* **1** group of words which when used together have a different meaning from the words individually, e.g. *raining cats and dogs.* **2** way of expression natural or peculiar to a language or group. **idiomatic** *adj* **idiomatically** *adv*

idiosyncrasy *n, pl* **-sies** personal peculiarity of mind, habit, or behaviour. **idiosyncratic** *adj*

idiot *n* **1** foolish or stupid person. **2** *Offens* mentally retarded person. **idiotic** *adj* **idiotically** *adv*

idle *adj* **1** not doing anything. **2** not willing to work, lazy. **3** not being used. **4** useless or meaningless, e.g. *an idle threat.* ♦ *v* **5** (usu. foll. by *away*) spend (time) doing very little. **6** (of an engine) run slowly with the gears disengaged. **idleness** *n* **idler** *n* **idly** *adv*

idol [**ide**-ol] *n* **1** object of excessive devotion. **2** image of a god as an object of worship. **idolatry** [ide-**ol**-a-tree] *n* worship of idols. **idolatrous** *adj* **idolize** *v* love or admire excessively. **idolization** *n*

idyll [**id**-ill] *n* scene or time of great peace and happiness. **idyllic** *adj* **idyllically** *adv*

i.e. that is to say.

if *conj* **1** on the condition or supposition that. **2** whether. **3** even though. ♦ *n* **4** uncertainty or doubt, e.g. *no ifs, ands, or buts.* **iffy** *adj Informal* doubtful, uncertain.

igloo *n, pl* **-loos** dome-shaped Inuit house made of snow and ice.

igneous [**ig**-nee-uss] *adj* (of rock) formed as molten rock cools and hardens.

ignite *v* catch fire or set fire to.

ignition *n* **1** system that ignites the fuel-and-air mixture to start an engine. **2** igniting.

ignoble *adj* dishonourable. **ignobly** *adv*

ignominy [**ig**-nom-in-ee] *n* humiliating disgrace. **ignominious** *adj* **ignominiously** *adv*

ignoramus *n, pl* **-muses** ignorant person.

ignorant *adj* **1** lacking knowledge. **2** rude through lack of knowledge of good manners. **ignorance** *n*

ignore *v* refuse to notice, disregard deliberately.

iguana *n* large tropical American lizard.

ikebana [eek-a-**bah**-na] *n* Japanese art of flower arrangement.

ikon *n* same as ICON.

IL Illinois.

ileum *n* lowest part of the small intestine.

ilex *n* any of a genus of trees or shrubs that includes holly.

ilium *n, pl* **-ia** uppermost and widest of the three sections of the hipbone. **iliac** *adj*

ilk *n* type, e.g. *others of his ilk.*

ill *adj* **1** not in good health. **2** harmful or unpleasant, e.g. *ill effects.* ♦ *n* **3** evil, harm. ♦ *adv* **4** badly. **5** hardly, with difficulty, e.g. *I can ill afford to lose him.* **ill at ease** uncomfortable, unable to relax. **illness** *n* **ill-advised** *adj* **1** badly thought out. **2** unwise. **ill-bred** *adj* lacking good manners, rude. **ill-disposed** *adj* (often foll. by *towards*) unfriendly, unsympathetic. **ill-fated** *adj* doomed to end unhappily. **ill-favoured** *adj* ugly, unattractive. **ill-gotten** *adj* obtained dishonestly, e.g. *ill-gotten gains.* **ill-health** *n* condition of being unwell. **ill-mannered** *adj* having bad manners. **ill-starred** *adj* ill-fated, unlucky. **ill-tempered** *adj* displaying bad temper. **ill-timed** *adj* done or happening at an unsuitable time. **ill-treat** *v* treat cruelly. **ill-treatment** *n* **ill will** unkind feeling, hostility.

illegal *adj* against the law. **illegally** *adv* **illegality** *n, pl* **-ties**

illegible *adj* unable to be read or deciphered. **illegibility** *n*

illegitimate *adj* **1** born of parents not married to each other. **2** not lawful. **illegitimacy** *n*

illiberal *adj* narrow-minded, intolerant.

illicit *adj* **1** illegal. **2** forbidden or disapproved of by society.

illiterate *n, adj* (person) unable to read or write. **illiteracy** *n*

illogical *adj* **1** unreasonable. **2** not logical. **illogicality** *n*

illuminate *v* **1** light up. **2** make clear, explain. **3** decorate with lights. **4** *Hist* decorate (a manuscript) with designs of gold and bright colours. **illumination** *n* **illuminating** *adj*

illusion *n* deceptive appearance or belief. **illusionist** *n* conjuror. **illusory** *adj* seeming to be true, but actually false.

illustrate *v* **1** explain by use of examples. **2** provide (a book or text) with pictures. **3** be an example of. **illustration** *n* **1** picture or diagram. **2** example. **3** art of illustrating. **illustrative** *adj* **illustrator** *n*

illustrious *adj* famous and distinguished.

image *n* **1** mental picture of someone or something. **2** impression people have of a person, organization, etc. **3** representation of a person or thing in a work of art. **4** optical reproduction of someone or something, for example in a mirror. **5** person or thing that looks almost exactly like another. **6** figure of speech, esp. a metaphor or simile. **imagery** *n* images collectively, esp. in the arts.

imagine *v* **1** form a mental image of. **2** think, believe, or guess. **imaginable** *adj* **imaginary** *adj* existing only in the imagination. **imagination** *n* **1** ability to make mental images of things that may not exist in real life. **2** creative mental ability. **imaginative** *adj* having or showing a lot of creative mental ability. **imaginatively** *adv*

imago [im-**may**-go] *n, pl* **imagoes, imagines** [im-**maj**-in-ees] sexually mature adult insect.

imam *n* **1** leader of prayers in a mosque. **2** title of some Islamic leaders.

imbalance *n* lack of balance or proportion.

imbecile [**imb**-ess-eel] *n* **1** stupid person. **2** *Offens* mentally retarded person. ♦ *adj* **3** (also **imbecilic**) stupid or senseless. **imbecility** *n*

imbed *v* same as EMBED.

imbibe *v* **1** drink (alcoholic drinks). **2** *Lit* absorb (ideas etc.).

imbroglio [imb-**role**-ee-oh] *n, pl* **-ios** confusing and complicated situation.

imbue *v* **-buing, -bued** (usu. foll. by *with*) fill or inspire with (ideals or principles).

IMF International Monetary Fund.

imitate *v* **1** take as a model. **2** copy the voice and mannerisms of, esp. for entertainment. **imitation** *n* **1** copy of an original. **2** imitating. ♦ *adj* **3** made to look like a material of superior quality, e.g. *imitation leather.* **imitative** *adj* **imitator** *n*

immaculate *adj* **1** completely clean or tidy. **2** completely flawless. **immaculately** *adv*

immanent *adj* present within and throughout something. **immanence** *n*

immaterial *adj* not important, not relevant.

immature *adj* **1** not fully developed. **2** lacking wisdom or stability because of youth. **immaturity** *n*

immeasurable *adj* too great to be measured. **immeasurably** *adv*

immediate *adj* **1** occurring at once. **2** next or nearest in time, space, or relationship. **immediately** *adv* **immediacy** *n*

immemorial *adj* **since, from time immemorial** longer than anyone can remember.

immense *adj* extremely large. **immensely** *adv* to a very great degree. **immensity** *n*

immerse *v* **1** involve deeply, engross, e.g. *immersed in his work.* **2** plunge (something or someone) into liquid. **immersion** *n* **immersion heater** electrical device in a domestic hot-water tank for heating water.

immigration *n* coming to a foreign

country in order to settle there. **immigrate** *v* **immigrant** *n* person who comes to a foreign country in order to settle there.

imminent *adj* about to happen. **imminently** *adv* **imminence** *n*

immobile *adj* **1** not moving. **2** unable to move. **immobility** *n* **immobilize** *v* make unable to move or work.

immoderate *adj* excessive or unreasonable.

immodest *adj* **1** behaving in an indecent or improper manner. **2** behaving in a boastful or conceited manner. **immodesty** *n*

immolate *v* kill as a sacrifice. **immolation** *n*

immoral *adj* **1** morally wrong, corrupt. **2** sexually depraved or promiscuous. **immorality** *n*

> Do not confuse *immoral* with *amoral*, which means 'having no moral standards'.

immortal *adj* **1** living forever. **2** famous for all time. ♦ *n* **3** person whose fame will last for all time. **4** immortal being. **immortality** *n* **immortalize** *v*

immovable, immoveable *adj* **1** unable to be moved. **2** unwilling to change one's opinions or beliefs. **3** not affected by feeling, emotionless. **immovability, immoveability** *n* **immovably, immoveably** *adv*

immune *adj* **1** protected against a specific disease. **2** (foll. by *to*) secure (against). **3** (foll. by *from*) exempt (from). **immunity** *n, pl* **-ties 1** ability to resist disease. **2** freedom from prosecution, tax, etc. **immunize** *v* make immune to a disease. **immunization** *n*

immunodeficiency *n* deficiency in or breakdown of a person's ability to fight diseases.

immunology *n* branch of medicine concerned with the study of immunity. **immunological** *adj* **immunologist** *n*

immure *v Lit* imprison.

immutable [im-**mute**-a-bl] *adj* unchangeable. **immutability** *n*

imp *n* **1** (in folklore) mischievous small creature with magical powers. **2** mischievous child.

impact *n* **1** strong effect. **2** (force of) a collision. ♦ *v* **3** have a strong effect on. **4** press firmly into something.

impair *v* weaken or damage. **impairment** *n*

impala [imp-**ah**-la] *n* southern African antelope.

impale *v* pierce with a sharp object.

impalpable *adj* difficult to define or understand.

impart *v* **1** communicate (information). **2** give, e.g. *butter imparts a full rich taste to a cake.*

impartial *adj* not favouring one side or the other. **impartially** *adv* **impartiality** *n*

impassable *adj* (of a road etc.) impossible to travel through or over.

impasse [**am**-pass] *n* situation in which progress is impossible.

impassible *adj* impassive or unmoved.

impassioned *adj* full of emotion.

impassive *adj* showing no emotion, calm. **impassively** *adv*

impasto 1 paint applied thickly, so that brush marks are evident. **2** technique of painting in this way.

impatient *adj* **1** irritable at any delay or difficulty. **2** restless (to have or do something). **impatiently** *adv* **impatience** *n*

impeach *v* charge with a serious crime against the state. **impeachment** *n*

impeccable *adj* without fault, excellent. **impeccably** *adv*

impecunious *adj* penniless, poor.

impedance [imp-**eed**-anss] *n Electricity* measure of the opposition to the flow of an alternating current.

impede *v* hinder in action or progress. **impediment** *n* something that makes action, speech, or progress difficult. **impedimenta** *pl n* objects impeding progress, esp. baggage or equipment.

impel *v* **-pelling, -pelled** push or force (someone) to do something.

impending *adj* (esp. of something bad) about to happen.

impenetrable *adj* **1** impossible to get through. **2** impossible to understand.

imperative *adj* **1** extremely urgent, vital. **2** *Grammar* denoting a mood of verbs used in commands. ♦ *n* **3** *Grammar* imperative mood.

imperceptible *adj* too slight or gradual to be noticed. **imperceptibly** *adv*

imperfect *adj* **1** having faults or mistakes. **2** not complete. **3** *Grammar* denoting a tense of verbs describing continuous, incomplete, or repeated past actions. ♦ *n* **4** *Grammar* imperfect tense. **imperfection** *n*

imperial *adj* **1** of or like an empire or emperor. **2** denoting a system of weights and measures formerly used in Britain. **imperialism** *n* rule by one country over many others. **imperialist** *adj, n*

imperil *v* **-illing, -illed** put in danger.

imperious *adj* proud and domineering.

impersonal *adj* **1** not relating to any particular person, objective. **2** lacking human warmth or sympathy. **3** *Grammar* (of a verb) without a personal subject, e.g. *it is snowing*. **impersonality** *n*

impersonate *v* **1** pretend to be (another person). **2** copy the voice and mannerisms of, esp. for entertainment. **impersonation** *n* **impersonator** *n*

impertinent *adj* disrespectful or rude. **impertinently** *adv* **impertinence** *n*

imperturbable *adj* calm, not excitable.

impervious *adj* (foll. by *to*) **1** not letting (water etc.) through. **2** not influenced by (a feeling, argument, etc.).

impetigo [imp-it-**tie**-go] *n* contagious skin disease.

impetuous *adj* done or acting without thought, rash. **impetuously** *adv* **impetuosity** *n*

impetus [**imp**-it-uss] *n, pl* **-tuses** **1** incentive, impulse. **2** force that starts a body moving.

impinge *v* (foll. by *on*) affect or restrict.

impious [**imp**-ee-uss] *adj* showing a lack of respect or reverence.

impish *adj* mischievous.

implacable *adj* not prepared to be appeased, unyielding. **implacably** *adv* **implacability** *n*

implant *n* **1** *Med* something put into someone's body, usu. by surgical operation, e.g. *silicone implants*. ♦ *v* **2** put (something) into someone's body, usu. by surgical operation. **3** fix firmly in someone's mind. **implantation** *n*

implement *v* **1** carry out (instructions etc.). ♦ *n* **2** tool, instrument. **implementation** *n*

implicate *v* show to be involved, esp. in a crime. **implication** *n* something implied.

implicit *adj* **1** expressed indirectly. **2** absolute and unquestioning, e.g. *implicit support*. **implicitly** *adv*

implode *v* collapse inwards.

implore *v* beg earnestly.

imply *v* **-plying, -plied** **1** indicate by hinting, suggest. **2** involve as a necessary consequence.

impolite *adj* showing bad manners.

impolitic *adj* unwise or inadvisable.

imponderable *n, adj* (something) impossible to assess.

import *v* **1** bring in (goods) from another country. ♦ *n* **2** something imported. **3** importance. **4** meaning. **importation** *n* **importer** *n*

important *adj* **1** of great significance or value. **2** having influence or power. **importance** *n*

importunate *adj* persistent or demanding. **importune** *v* harass with persistent requests. **importunity** *n, pl* **-ties**

impose *v* **1** force the acceptance of. **2** (foll. by *on*) take unfair advantage (of). **imposing** *adj* grand, impressive. **imposition** *n* **1** imposing. **2** unreasonable demand.

impossible *adj* **1** not able to be done or to happen. **2** absurd or unreasonable. **impossibly** *adv* **impossibility** *n, pl* **-ties**

imposter, impostor *n* person who cheats or swindles by pretending to be someone else.

imposture *n* deception, esp. by pretending to be someone else.

impotent [**imp**-a-tent] *adj* **1** powerless. **2** (of a man) incapable of sexual intercourse. **impotence** *n* **impotently** *adv*

impound *v* take legal possession of, confiscate.

impoverish *v* make poor or weak. **impoverishment** *n*

impracticable *adj* incapable of being put into practice.

impractical *adj* not sensible.

imprecation *n* curse.

impregnable *adj* impossible to break into. **impregnability** *n*

impregnate *v* **1** saturate, spread all through. **2** make pregnant. **impregnation** *n*

impresario *n, pl* **-ios** person who runs theatre performances, concerts, etc.

impress *v* **1** affect strongly, usu. favourably. **2** stress, emphasize. **3** imprint, stamp. **impression** *n* **1** effect, esp. a strong or favourable one. **2** vague idea. **3** impersonation for entertainment. **4** mark made by pressing. **impressionable** *adj* easily impressed or influenced. **impressionist** *n* person who impersonates other people for entertainment.

Impressionism *n* art style that gives a general effect or mood rather than form or structure. **Impressionist** *n* **Impressionistic** *adj*

impressive *adj* making a strong impression, esp. through size, importance, or quality.

imprimatur [imp-rim-**ah**-ter] *n* official approval to print a book.

imprint *n* **1** mark made by printing or stamping. **2** publisher's name and address on a book. ♦ *v* **3** produce (a mark) by printing or stamping. **4** fix firmly in someone's mind.

imprison *v* put in prison. **imprisonment** *n*

improbable *adj* not likely to be true or to happen. **improbability** *n, pl* **-ties**

improbity *n* dishonesty or wickedness.

impromptu *adj* without planning or preparation.

improper *adj* **1** indecent. **2** incorrect or irregular. **improper fraction** fraction in which the numerator is larger than the denominator, as in $\frac{5}{3}$.

impropriety [imp-roe-**pry**-a-tee] *n, pl* **-ties** unsuitable or slightly improper behaviour.

improve *v* make or become better. **improvement** *n*

improvident *adj* not planning for future needs. **improvidence** *n*

improvise *v* **1** make use of whatever materials are available. **2** make up (a piece of music, speech, etc.) as one goes along. **improvisation** *n*

imprudent *adj* not sensible or wise. **imprudence** *n*

impudent *adj* cheeky, disrespectful. **impudently** *adv* **impudence** *n*

impugn [imp-**yoon**] *v* challenge the truth or validity of.

impulse *n* **1** sudden urge to do something. **2** short electrical signal passing along a wire or nerve or through the air. **on impulse** suddenly and without planning. **impulsive** *adj* acting or done without careful consideration. **impulsively** *adv*

impunity [imp-**yoon**-it-ee] *n* **with impunity** without punishment.

impure *adj* **1** having dirty or unwanted substances mixed in. **2** immoral, obscene. **impurity** *n, pl* **-ties**

impute *v* attribute responsibility to. **imputation** *n*

in *prep* **1** indicating position inside, state or situation, etc., e.g. *in the net; in tears.* ♦ *adv* **2** indicating position inside, entry into, etc., e.g. *she stayed in; come in.* ♦ *adj* **3** fashionable. **inward** *adj* **1** directed towards the middle. **2** situated within. **3** spiritual or mental. ♦ *adv* **4** (also **inwards**) towards the inside or middle. **inwardly** *adv*

In *Chem* indium.

IN Indiana.

in. inch.

in-[1] *prefix* **1** not, non-, e.g. *incredible.* **2** lack of, e.g. *inexperience.*

in-[2] *prefix* in, into, towards, within, on, e.g. *infiltrate.*

inability *n* lack of means or skill to do something.

inaccessible *adj* **1** impossible or very difficult to reach. **2** difficult to understand or appreciate. **inaccessibility** *n*

inaccurate *adj* not correct. **inaccuracy** *n, pl* **-cies**

inaction *n* doing nothing. **inactive** *adj* **inactivity** *n*

inadequate *adj* **1** not enough. **2** not good enough. **inadequacy** *n, pl* **-cies**

inadmissible *adj* not allowable or acceptable.

inadvertent *adj* unintentional. **inadvertently** *adv*

inalienable *adj* not able to be taken away, e.g. *an inalienable right.*

inamorata, (*masc*) **inamorato** *n, pl* **-s** *Lit* lover.

inane *adj* senseless, silly. **inanity** *n, pl* **-ties**

inanimate *adj* not living.

inapplicable *adj* not suitable or relevant.

inappropriate *adj* not suitable.

inapt *adj* not apt or fitting.

inarticulate *adj* unable to express oneself clearly or well.

inasmuch as *conj* because or in so far as.

inattentive *adj* not paying attention. **inattention** *n*

inaudible *adj* not loud enough to be heard. **inaudibly** *adv*

inaugurate *v* **1** open or begin the use of, esp. with ceremony. **2** formally establish (a new leader) in office. **inaugural** *adj* **inauguration** *n*

inauspicious *adj* unlucky, likely to have an unfavourable outcome.

inboard *adj* (of a boat's engine) inside the hull.

inborn *adj* existing from birth, natural.

inbred *adj* **1** produced as a result of inbreeding. **2** inborn or ingrained.

inbreeding *n* breeding of animals or people that are closely related.

inbuilt *adj* present from the start.

Inc. *US & Aust* (of a company) incorporated.

incalculable *adj* too great to be estimated.

in camera *adv* see CAMERA.

incandescent *adj* glowing with heat. **incandescence** *n*

incantation *n* ritual chanting of magic words or sounds.

incapable *adj* **1** (foll. by *of*) unable (to do something). **2** incompetent.

incapacitate *v* deprive of strength or ability. **incapacity** *n*

incarcerate *v* imprison. **incarceration** *n*

incarnate *adj* in human form, e.g. *she is evil incarnate.* **incarnation** *n* **Incarnation** *n Christianity* God's coming to earth in human form as Jesus Christ.

incendiary [in-**send**-ya-ree] *adj* **1** (of a bomb, attack, etc.) designed to cause fires. ♦ *n, pl* **-aries** **2** bomb designed to cause fires.

incense[1] *v* make very angry.

incense[2] *n* substance that gives off a sweet perfume when burned.

incentive *n* something that encourages effort or action.

inception *n* beginning.

incessant *adj* never stopping. **incessantly** *adv*

incest *n* sexual intercourse between two people too closely related to marry. **incestuous** *adj*

inch *n* **1** unit of length equal to one twelfth of a foot or 2.54 centimetres. ♦ *v* **2** move slowly and gradually.

inchoate [in-**koe**-ate] *adj* just begun and not yet properly developed.

incidence *n* extent or frequency of occurrence.

incident *n* **1** something that happens. **2** event involving violence.

incidental *adj* occurring in connection with or resulting from something more important. **incidentally** *adv* **incidental music** background music for a film or play.

incinerate *v* burn to ashes. **incineration** *n* **incinerator** *n* furnace for burning rubbish.

incipient *adj* just starting to appear or happen.

incise *v* cut into with a sharp tool. **incision** *n* **incisive** *adj* direct and forceful. **incisor** *n* front tooth, used for biting into food.

incite *v* stir up, provoke. **incitement** *n*

incivility *n, pl* **-ties** rudeness or a rude remark.

inclement *adj* (of weather) stormy or severe. **inclemency** *n*

incline *v* **1** lean, slope. **2** (cause to) have a certain disposition or tendency. ♦ *n* **3** slope. **inclination** *n* **1** liking, tendency, or preference. **2** slope.

include *v* **1** have as part of the whole. **2** put in as part of a set or group. **inclusion** *n* **inclusive** *adj* including everything (specified). **inclusively** *adv*

incognito [in-kog-**nee**-toe] *adj, adv* **1** having adopted a false identity. ♦ *n, pl* **-tos 2** false identity.

incoherent *adj* unclear and impossible to understand. **incoherence** *n* **incoherently** *adv*

income *n* amount of money earned from work, investments, etc. **income support** (formerly, in Britain) allowance paid by the government to people with a very low income. **income tax** personal tax levied on annual income.

incoming *adj* **1** coming in. **2** about to come into office.

incommode *v* cause inconvenience to.

incommunicado *adj, adv* deprived of communication with other people.

incomparable *adj* beyond comparison, unequalled. **incomparably** *adv*

incompatible *adj* inconsistent or conflicting. **incompatibility** *n*

incompetent *adj* **1** not having the necessary ability or skill to do something. ♦ *n* **2** incompetent person. **incompetence** *n*

inconceivable *adj* extremely unlikely, unimaginable.

inconclusive *adj* not giving a final decision or result.

incongruous *adj* inappropriate or out of place. **incongruously** *adv* **incongruity** *n, pl* **-ties**

inconsequential *adj* unimportant, insignificant.

inconsiderable *adj* **not inconsiderable** fairly large.

inconsiderate *adj* not considering other people.

inconsistent *adj* **1** changeable in behaviour or mood. **2** containing contradictory elements, e.g. *witnesses told inconsistent stories.* **3** not in accordance, e.g. *the outburst was inconsistent with his image.* **inconsistency** *n, pl* **-cies**

inconsolable *adj* very distressed. **inconsolably** *adv*

inconspicuous *adj* not easily noticed or seen. **inconspicuously** *adv*

inconstant *adj* liable to change one's loyalties or opinions.

incontestable *adj* impossible to deny or argue with.

incontinent *adj* unable to control one's bladder or bowels. **incontinence** *n*

incontrovertible *adj* impossible to deny or disprove.

inconvenience *n* **1** trouble or difficulty. ♦ *v* **2** cause trouble or difficulty to. **inconvenient** *adj*

incorporate *v* include or be included as part of a larger unit. **incorporation** *n*

incorporeal *adj* without material form.

incorrigible *adj* beyond correction or reform. **incorrigibly** *adv*

incorruptible *adj* **1** too honest to be bribed or corrupted. **2** not subject to decay.

increase *v* **1** make or become greater in size, number, etc. ♦ *n* **2** rise in number, size, etc. **3** amount by which something increases. **on the increase** becoming more common. **increasingly** *adv*

incredible *adj* **1** hard to believe or imagine. **2** *Informal* marvellous, amazing. **incredibly** *adv*

incredulous *adj* not willing to believe something. **incredulity** *n*

increment *n* increase in money or value, esp. a regular salary increase. **incre-**

mental *adj*

incriminate *v* make (someone) seem guilty of a crime. **incriminating** *adj*

incubate [**in**-cube-ate] *v* **1** (of a bird) hatch (eggs) by sitting on them. **2** grow (bacteria). **3** (of bacteria) remain inactive in an animal or person before causing disease. **incubation** *n* **incubator** *n* **1** heated enclosed apparatus for rearing premature babies. **2** apparatus for artificially hatching birds' eggs.

incubus [**in**-cube-uss] *n, pl* **-bi, -buses 1** (in folklore) demon believed to have sex with sleeping women. **2** nightmarish burden or worry.

inculcate *v* fix in someone's mind by constant repetition. **inculcation** *n*

inculpate *v* cause (someone) to be blamed for a crime.

incumbent *n* **1** person holding a particular office or position. ♦ *adj* **2** holding a particular office or position, e.g. *the incumbent president.* **3 it is incumbent on** it is the duty of. **incumbency** *n, pl* **-cies**

incur *v* **-curring, -curred** cause (something unpleasant) to happen

incurable *adj* **1** not able to be cured. **2** not willing or able to change, e.g. *an incurable romantic.* **incurably** *adv*

incurious *adj* showing no curiosity or interest.

incursion *n* sudden brief invasion.

indebted *adj* **1** owing gratitude for help or favours. **2** owing money. **indebtedness** *n*

indecent *adj* **1** morally or sexually offensive. **2** unsuitable or unseemly, e.g. *indecent haste.* **indecently** *adv* **indecency** *n* **indecent assault** sexual attack which does not include rape. **indecent exposure** showing of one's genitals in public.

indecipherable *adj* impossible to read.

indecisive *adj* unable to make decisions. **indecision** *n*

indeed *adv* **1** really, certainly. ♦ *interj* **2** expression of indignation or surprise.

indefatigable *adj* never getting tired. **indefatigably** *adv*

indefensible *adj* **1** unable to be justified. **2** impossible to defend.

indefinable *adj* difficult to describe or explain.

indefinite *adj* **1** without exact limits, e.g. *for an indefinite period.* **2** vague, unclear. **indefinite article** *Grammar* the word *a* or *an.* **indefinitely** *adv*

indelible *adj* **1** impossible to erase or remove. **2** making indelible marks. **indelibly** *adv*

indelicate *adj* offensive or embarrassing.

indemnify *v* **-ifying, -ified 1** secure against loss, damage, or liability. **2** compensate for loss or damage.

indemnity *n, pl* **-ties 1** insurance against loss or damage. **2** compensation for loss or damage.

indent *v* **1** start (a line of writing) further from the margin than the other lines. **2** order (goods) using a special order form. **indented** *adj* having indentations along the edge. **indentation** *n* dent in a surface or edge.

indenture *n* **1** contract, esp. one binding an apprentice to his or her employer. ♦ *v* **2** bind (an apprentice) by indenture.

independent *adj* **1** free from the control or influence of others. **2** separate. **3** financially self-reliant. **4** capable of acting for oneself or on one's own. ♦ *n* **5** politician who does represent any political party. **independently** *adv* **independence** *n*

in-depth *adj* detailed, thorough.

indescribable *adj* too intense or extreme for words. **indescribably** *adv*

indestructible *adj* not able to be destroyed.

indeterminate *adj* uncertain in extent, amount, or nature. **indeterminacy** *n*

index *n, pl* **indices** [**in**-diss-eez] **1** alphabetical list of names or subjects dealt with in a book. **2** file or catalogue used to find things. **3** system by which changes in the value of something can be measured. ♦ *v* **4** provide (a book) with an index. **5** enter in an index. **6** make index-linked. **index finger** finger next to the thumb. **index-linked** *adj* (of pensions, wages, etc.) rising or falling in line with the cost of living.

Indian *n, adj* **1** (person) from India. **2** Native American. **Indian summer** period of warm sunny weather in autumn.

indicate *v* **1** be a sign or symptom of. **2** point out. **3** state briefly. **4** use the indicators in a car to show that it is going to turn left or right. **5** (of a measuring instrument) show a reading of. **indication** *n* **indicative** [in-**dik**-a-tiv] *adj* **1** (foll. by *of*) suggesting, e.g. *outer mess is indicative of inner confusion.* **2** *Grammar* denoting a mood of verbs used to make a statement. ♦ *n* **3** *Grammar* indicative mood. **indicator** *n* **1** something acting as a sign or indication. **2** flashing light on a vehicle showing the driver's intention to turn. **3** dial or gauge.

indices *n* plural of INDEX.

indict [in-**dite**] *v* formally charge with a crime. **indictable** *adj* **indictment** *n* **1** indication of how bad something is, e.g. *that's a pretty sad indictment of the UN.* **2** formal charge.

indie *adj Informal* (of rock music) released by an independent record company.

indifferent *adj* **1** showing no interest or concern. **2** of poor quality. **indifference** *n* **indifferently** *adv*

indigenous [in-**dij**-in-uss] *adj* born in or natural to a country.

indigent *adj* extremely poor. **indigence** *n*

indigestion *n* (discomfort or pain caused by) difficulty in digesting food. **indigestible** *adj*

indignation *n* anger at something unfair or wrong. **indignant** *adj* feeling or showing indignation. **indignantly** *adv*

indignity *n, pl* **-ties** embarrassing or humiliating treatment.

indigo *adj* **1** deep violet-blue. ♦ *n* **2** dye of this colour.

indirect *adj* **1** done or caused by someone or something else. **2** not by a straight route. **indirectly** *adv* **indirect object** *Grammar* person or thing indirectly affected by the action of a verb, e.g. *Amy* in *I bought Amy a bag.* **indirect speech** same as REPORTED SPEECH. **indirect tax** tax, such as VAT, added to the price of something.

indiscernible *adj* not able to be seen clearly.

indiscreet *adj* incautious or tactless in revealing secrets. **indiscreetly** *adv* **indiscretion** *n*

indiscriminate *adj* showing lack of careful thought.

indispensable *adj* absolutely essential.

indisposed *adj* unwell, ill. **indisposition** *n*

indisputable *adj* beyond doubt. **indisputably** *adv*

indissoluble *adj* permanent.

indistinct *adj* unable to be seen or heard clearly.

indium *n Chem* soft silvery-white metallic element.

individual *adj* **1** characteristic of or meant for a single person or thing. **2** separate, distinct. **3** distinctive, unusual. ♦ *n* **4** single person or thing. **individually** *adv* **individuality** *n* **individualism** *n* principle of living one's life in one's own way. **individualist** *n* **individualistic** *adj*

indoctrinate *v* teach (someone) to accept a doctrine or belief uncritically. **indoctrination** *n*

Indo-European *adj, n* (of) a family of languages spoken in most of Europe and much of Asia, including English, Russian, and Hindi.

indolent *adj* lazy. **indolence** *n*

indomitable *adj* too strong to be defeated or discouraged. **indomitably** *adv*

indoor *adj* inside a building. **indoors** *adv*

indubitable [in-**dew**-bit-a-bl] *adj* beyond doubt, certain. **indubitably** *adv*

induce *v* **1** persuade or influence. **2** cause. **3** *Med* cause (a woman) to go into labour or bring on (labour) by the use of drugs etc. **inducement** *n* something used to persuade someone to do something.

induct *v* formally install (someone, esp. a

clergyman) in office.

inductance *n* property of an electric circuit creating voltage by a change of current.

induction *n* **1** reasoning process by which general conclusions are drawn from particular instances. **2** *Med* process of inducing labour. **3** process by which electrical or magnetic properties are produced by the proximity of an electrified or magnetic object. **4** formal introduction into an office or position. **inductive** *adj* **induction coil** transformer for producing a high voltage from a low voltage. **induction course** training course to help familiarize someone with a new job.

indulge *v* **1** allow oneself pleasure, e.g. *indulging in rich foods.* **2** allow (someone) to have or do everything he or she wants. **indulgence** *n* **1** something allowed because it gives pleasure. **2** act of indulging oneself or someone else. **3** liberal or tolerant treatment. **indulgent** *adj* **indulgently** *adv*

industrial *adj* of, used in, or employed in industry. **industrialize** *v* develop large-scale industry in (a country or region). **industrialization** *n* **industrialism** *n* social organization based on large-scale manufacturing industry rather than trade or farming. **industrialist** *n* person who owns or controls large amounts of money or property in industry. **industrial action** ways in which workers can protest about their conditions, e.g. by striking or working to rule. **industrial estate** area of land set aside for factories and warehouses. **industrial relations** relations between management and workers.

industry *n, pl* **-tries 1** manufacture of goods. **2** branch of this, e.g. *the music industry.* **3** quality of working hard. **industrious** *adj* hard-working.

inebriate *n, adj* (person who is) habitually drunk. **inebriated** *adj* drunk. **inebriation** *n*

inedible *adj* not fit to be eaten.

ineducable [in-**ed**-yuke-a-bl] *adj* incapable of being educated, esp. through mental retardation.

ineffable *adj* too great for words. **ineffably** *adv*

ineffectual *adj* having very little effect.

inefficient *adj* unable to perform a task or function to the best advantage. **inefficiency** *n*

inelegant *adj* lacking elegance or refinement.

ineligible *adj* not qualified for or entitled to something.

ineluctable *adj* impossible to avoid.

inept *adj* clumsy, lacking skill. **ineptitude** *n*

inequality *n, pl* **-ties 1** state or quality of being unequal. **2** instance of this.

inequitable *adj* unfair. **inequity** *n, pl* **-ties**

ineradicable *adj* impossible to remove.

inert *adj* **1** without the power of motion or resistance. **2** chemically unreactive. **inertly** *adv* **inertness** *n*

inertia *n* **1** feeling of unwillingness to do anything. **2** *Physics* tendency of a body to remain still or continue moving unless a force is applied to it. **inertia reel seat belt** car seat belt in which the belt is free to unwind from a metal drum except when the drum locks because of sudden braking. **inertia selling** practice of sending householders unrequested goods followed by a bill if the goods are not returned.

inescapable *adj* unavoidable.

inestimable *adj* too great to be estimated. **inestimably** *adv*

inevitable *adj* unavoidable, sure to happen. **the inevitable** something that cannot be prevented. **inevitably** *adv* **inevitability** *n*

inexorable *adj* unable to be prevented from continuing or progressing. **inexorably** *adv*

inexperienced *adj* having no knowledge or experience of a particular situation, activity, etc. **inexperience** *n*

inexpert *adj* lacking skill.

inexplicable *adj* impossible to explain.

inexplicably *adv*
in extremis *adv Latin* **1** in great difficulty. **2** on the point of death.
inextricable *adj* **1** impossible to escape from. **2** impossible to disentangle or separate. **inextricably** *adv*
infallible *adj* never wrong. **infallibly** *adv* **infallibility** *n*
infamous [**in**-fam-uss] *adj* well-known for something bad. **infamously** *adv* **infamy** *n*
infant *n* very young child. **infancy** *n* **1** early childhood. **2** early stage of development. **infantile** *adj* childish.
infanta *n* **1** (formerly) daughter of a king of Spain or Portugal. **2** wife of an infante.
infante *n* (formerly) any son of a king of Spain or Portugal, except the heir to the throne.
infanticide *n* **1** murder of an infant. **2** person guilty of this.
infantry *n* soldiers who fight on foot.
infatuate *v* inspire with intense unreasoning passion. **infatuated** *adj* **infatuation** *n*
infect *v* **1** affect with a disease. **2** affect with a feeling. **infection** *n* **infectious** *adj* **1** (of a disease) spreading without actual contact. **2** spreading from person to person, e.g. *infectious enthusiasm.*
infer *v* **-ferring, -ferred** work out from evidence. **inference** *n*

> Someone *infers* something by 'reading between the lines' of a remark. Do not confuse with *imply*, which means 'to hint'.

inferior *adj* **1** lower in quality, position, or status. ♦ *n* **2** person of lower position or status. **inferiority** *n* **inferiority complex** *Psychiatry* disorder arising from a feeling of inferiority to others, characterized by aggressiveness or extreme shyness.
infernal *adj* **1** of hell. **2** *Informal* irritating. **infernally** *adv*
inferno *n, pl* **-nos** intense raging fire.
infertile *adj* **1** unable to produce offspring. **2** (of soil) barren, not productive. **infertility** *n*
infest *v* inhabit or overrun in unpleasantly large numbers. **infestation** *n*
infidel *n* **1** person with no religion. **2** person who rejects a particular religion, esp. Christianity or Islam.
infidelity *n, pl* **-ties** (act of) sexual unfaithfulness to one's husband, wife, or lover.
infield *n* **1** *Cricket* area of the field near the pitch. **2** *Baseball* area of the playing field enclosed by the base lines.
infighting *n* quarrelling within a group.
infiltrate *v* enter gradually and secretly. **infiltration** *n* **infiltrator** *n*
infinite [**in**-fin-it] *adj* without any limit or end. **infinitely** *adv*
infinitesimal *adj* extremely small.
infinitive [in-**fin**-it-iv] *n Grammar* form of a verb not showing tense, person, or number, e.g. *to sleep.*
infinity *n* endless space, time, or number.
infirm *adj* physically or mentally weak. **infirmity** *n, pl* **-ties**
infirmary *n, pl* **-ries** hospital.
in flagrante delicto [in flag-**grant**-ee dee-**lick**-toe] *adv* while committing the offence.
inflame *v* make angry or excited. **inflamed** *adj* (of part of the body) red, swollen, and painful because of infection. **inflammation** *n*
inflammable *adj* easily set on fire.

> *Inflammable* means the same as *flammable* but is falling out of general use as it was often mistaken to mean 'not flammable'.

inflammatory *adj* likely to provoke anger.
inflate *v* **1** expand by filling with air or gas. **2** cause economic inflation in. **inflatable** *adj* **1** able to be inflated. ♦ *n* **2** plastic or rubber object which can be inflated.
inflation *n* **1** inflating. **2** increase in prices and fall in the value of money.

inflationary *adj*

inflection, inflexion *n* **1** change in the pitch of the voice. **2** *Grammar* change in the form of a word to show grammatical use.

inflexible *adj* **1** unwilling to be persuaded, obstinate. **2** (of a policy etc.) firmly fixed, unalterable. **3** incapable of being bent. **inflexibly** *adv* **inflexibility** *n*

inflict *v* impose (something unpleasant) on. **infliction** *n*

inflorescence *n Botany* arrangement of flowers on a stem.

inflow *n* **1** something, such as liquid or gas, that flows in. **2** flowing in, influx.

influence *n* **1** effect of one person or thing on another. **2** (person with) the power to have such an effect. ♦ *v* **3** have an effect on. **influential** *adj*

influenza *n* contagious viral disease causing headaches, muscle pains, and fever.

influx *n* arrival or entry of many people or things.

info *n Informal* information.

inform *v* **1** tell. **2** give incriminating information to the police. **informant** *n* person who gives information. **information** *n* knowledge or facts. **informative** *adj* giving useful information. **information superhighway** worldwide network of computers transferring information at high speed. **information technology** use of computers and electronic technology to store and communicate information. **informer** *n* person who informs to the police.

informal *adj* **1** relaxed and friendly. **2** appropriate for everyday life or use. **informally** *adv* **informality** *n*

infra dig *adj Informal* beneath one's dignity.

infrared *adj* of or using rays below the red end of the visible spectrum.

infrastructure *n* basic facilities, services, and equipment needed for a country or organization to function properly.

infrequent *adj* not happening often. **infrequently** *adv*

infringe *v* **1** break (a law or agreement). **2** (foll. by *on*) interfere (with), encroach (on). **infringement** *n*

infuriate *v* make very angry.

infuse *v* **1** fill (with an emotion or quality). **2** soak to extract flavour. **infusion** *n* **1** infusing. **2** liquid obtained by infusing.

ingenious [in-**jean**-ee-uss] *adj* showing cleverness and originality. **ingeniously** *adv* **ingenuity** [in-jen-**new**-it-ee] *n*

ingénue [**an**-jay-new] *n* naive young woman, esp. as a role played by an actress.

ingenuous [in-**jen**-new-uss] *adj* unsophisticated and trusting. **ingenuously** *adv*

ingest *v* take (food or liquid) into the body. **ingestion** *n*

inglenook *n* corner by a fireplace.

inglorious *adj* dishonourable, shameful.

ingot *n* oblong block of cast metal.

ingrained *adj* firmly fixed.

ingratiate *v* try to make (oneself) popular with someone. **ingratiating** *adj* **ingratiatingly** *adv*

ingratitude *n* lack of gratitude or thanks.

ingredient *n* component of a mixture or compound.

ingress *n* act or right of entering.

ingrowing *adj* (of a toenail) growing abnormally into the flesh.

inhabit *v* **-habiting, -habited** live in. **inhabitable** *adj* **inhabitant** *n*

inhale *v* breathe in (air, smoke, etc.). **inhalation** *n* **inhalant** [in-**hale**-ant] *n* medical preparation inhaled to help breathing problems. **inhaler** *n* container for an inhalant.

inherent *adj* existing as an inseparable part. **inherently** *adv*

inherit *v* **-heriting, -herited 1** receive (money etc.) from someone who has died. **2** receive (a characteristic) from an earlier generation. **3** receive from a predecessor. **inheritance** *n* **inheritance tax** tax paid on property left at death. **inheritor** *n*

inhibit *v* **-hibiting, -hibited 1** restrain (an impulse or desire). **2** hinder or prevent (action). **inhibited** *adj* **inhibition** *n* feeling of fear or embarrassment that stops one from behaving naturally.

inhospitable *adj* **1** not welcoming, unfriendly. **2** difficult to live in, harsh.

inhuman *adj* **1** cruel or brutal. **2** not human.

inhumane *adj* cruel or brutal. **inhumanity** *n*

inimical *adj* unfavourable or hostile.

inimitable *adj* impossible to imitate, unique.

iniquity *n, pl* **-ties 1** injustice or wickedness. **2** wicked act. **iniquitous** *adj*

initial *adj* **1** first, at the beginning. ♦ *n* **2** first letter, esp. of a person's name. ♦ *v* **-tialling, -tialled 3** sign with one's initials. **initially** *adv*

initiate *v* **1** begin or set going. **2** admit (someone) into a closed group. **3** instruct in the basics of something. ♦ *n* **4** recently initiated person. **initiation** *n* **initiator** *n*

initiative *n* **1** first step, commencing move. **2** ability to act independently.

inject *v* **1** put (a fluid) into the body with a syringe. **2** introduce (a new element), e.g. *try to inject a bit of humour.* **injection** *n*

injudicious *adj* showing poor judgment, unwise.

injunction *n* court order not to do something.

injure *v* hurt physically or mentally. **injury** *n, pl* **-ries injury time** *Sport* playing time added at the end of a match to compensate for time spent treating injured players. **injurious** *adj*

injustice *n* **1** unfairness. **2** unfair action.

ink *n* **1** coloured liquid used for writing or printing. ♦ *v* **2** (foll. by *in*) mark in ink (something already marked in pencil). **inky** *adj* **inkier, inkiest 1** dark or black. **2** covered in ink.

inkling *n* slight idea or suspicion.

inlaid *adj* **1** set in another material so that the surface is smooth. **2** made like this, e.g. *an inlaid table.*

inland *adj, adv* in or towards the interior of a country, away from the sea. **Inland Revenue** government department that collects taxes.

in-laws *pl n* one's husband's or wife's family.

inlay *n* inlaid substance or pattern.

inlet *n* **1** narrow strip of water extending from the sea into the land. **2** valve etc. through which liquid or gas enters.

in loco parentis [par-**rent**-iss] *Latin* in place of a parent.

inmate *n* person living in an institution such as a prison.

inmost *adj* innermost.

inn *n* pub or small hotel, esp. in the country. **innkeeper** *n*

innards *pl n Informal* **1** internal organs. **2** working parts of a machine.

innate *adj* being part of someone's nature, inborn.

inner *adj* **1** happening or located inside. **2** relating to private feelings, e.g. *the inner self.* **3** of a group with most power within a larger organization, e.g. *the inner circle.* **innermost** *adj* furthest inside. **inner city** parts of a city near the centre, esp. having social and economic problems.

innings *n* **1** *Sport* player's or side's turn of batting. **2** period of opportunity.

innocent *adj* **1** not guilty of a crime. **2** without experience of evil. **3** without malicious intent. ♦ *n* **4** innocent person, esp. a child. **innocently** *adv* **innocence** *n*

innocuous *adj* not harmful. **innocuously** *adv*

innovation *n* **1** new idea or method. **2** introduction of new ideas or methods. **innovate** *v* **innovative** *adj* **innovator** *n*

innuendo *n, pl* **-does** (remark making) an indirect reference to something rude or unpleasant.

innumerable *adj* too many to be counted.

innumerate *adj* having no understanding of mathematics or science. **innumeracy** *n*

inoculate *v* protect against disease by injecting with a vaccine. **inoculation** *n*

inoffensive *adj* causing no harm.

inoperable *adj* (of a tumour or cancer) unable to be surgically removed.

inoperative *adj* not working or functioning.

inopportune *adj* badly timed, unsuitable.

inordinate *adj* excessive. **inordinately** *adv*

inorganic *adj* **1** not having the characteristics of living organisms. **2** of chemical substances that do not contain carbon.

inpatient *n* patient who stays in a hospital for treatment.

input *n* **1** resources put into a project etc. **2** data fed into a computer. ♦ *v* **-putting, -put 3** enter (data) in a computer.

inquest *n* official inquiry into a sudden death.

inquietude *n* restlessness or anxiety.

inquire *v* seek information or ask (about). **inquirer** *n* **inquiry** *n, pl* **-ries 1** question. **2** investigation.

inquisition *n* **1** thorough investigation. **2** (**I-**) *Hist* organization within the Catholic Church for suppressing heresy. **inquisitor** *n* **inquisitorial** *adj*

inquisitive *adj* **1** excessively curious about other people's affairs. **2** eager to learn. **inquisitively** *adv*

inquorate *adj* without enough people present to make a quorum.

inroads *pl n* **make inroads into** start affecting or reducing, e.g. *Italy could make inroads into its interest burden.*

ins. inches.

insalubrious *adj* unpleasant, unhealthy, or sordid.

insane *adj* **1** mentally ill. **2** stupidly irresponsible. **insanely** *adv* **insanity** *n*

insanitary *adj* dirty or unhealthy.

insatiable [in-**saysh**-a-bl] *adj* unable to be satisfied.

inscribe *v* write or carve words on. **inscription** *n* words inscribed.

inscrutable *adj* mysterious, enigmatic. **inscrutably** *adv* **inscrutability** *n*

insect *n* small animal with six legs and usu. wings, such as an ant or fly. **insecticide** *n* substance for killing insects. **insectivorous** *adj* insect-eating.

insecure *adj* **1** anxious, not confident. **2** not safe or well-protected.

insemination *n* putting semen into a woman's or female animal's body to try to make her pregnant. **inseminate** *v*

insensate *adj* **1** without sensation, unconscious. **2** unfeeling.

insensible *adj* **1** unconscious, without feeling. **2** (foll. by *to* or *of*) not aware (of) or affected (by). **insensibility** *n*

insensitive *adj* unaware of or ignoring other people's feelings. **insensitivity** *n*

inseparable *adj* **1** (of two people) spending most of the time together. **2** (of two things) impossible to separate.

insert *v* **1** put inside or include. ♦ *n* **2** something inserted. **insertion** *n*

inset *n* small picture inserted within a larger one.

inshore *adj* **1** close to the shore. ♦ *adj, adv* **2** towards the shore.

inside *prep* **1** in or to the interior of. ♦ *adj* **2** on or of the inside. **3** by or from someone within an organization, e.g. *inside information.* ♦ *adv* **4** on, in, or to the inside, indoors. **5** *Slang* in(to) prison. ♦ *n* **6** inner side, surface, or part. ♦ *pl* **7** *Informal* stomach and bowels. **inside out** with the inside facing outwards. **know inside out** know thoroughly. **insider** *n* member of a group who has privileged knowledge about it.

> Avoid using the expression *inside of,* as the second preposition *of* is superfluous.

insidious *adj* subtle or unseen but dangerous. **insidiously** *adv*

insight *n* deep understanding.

insignia [in-**sig**-nee-a] *n, pl* **-nias, -nia** badge or emblem of honour or office.

insignificant *adj* not important. **insignificance** *n*

insincere *adj* showing false feelings, not genuine. **insincerely** *adv* **insincerity** *n, pl* **-ties**

insinuate *v* **1** suggest indirectly. **2** work (oneself) into a position by gradual manoeuvres. **insinuation** *n*

insipid *adj* lacking interest, spirit, or flavour. **insipidity** *n*

insist *v* demand or state firmly. **insistent** *adj* **1** making persistent demands. **2** demanding attention. **insistently** *adv* **insistence** *n*

in situ *adv, adj Latin* in its original position.

in so far as, insofar as *prep* to the extent that.

insole *n* inner sole of a shoe or boot.

insolent *adj* rude and disrespectful. **insolence** *n* **insolently** *adv*

insoluble *adj* **1** incapable of being solved. **2** incapable of being dissolved.

insolvent *adj* unable to pay one's debts. **insolvency** *n*

insomnia *n* inability to sleep. **insomniac** *n*

insomuch *adv* (foll. by *as* or *that*) to such an extent.

insouciant *adj* carefree and unconcerned. **insouciance** *n*

inspect *v* check closely or officially. **inspection** *n* **inspector** *n* **1** person who inspects. **2** high-ranking police officer.

inspire *v* **1** fill with enthusiasm, stimulate. **2** arouse (an emotion). **inspiration** *n* **1** creative influence or stimulus. **2** brilliant idea. **inspirational** *adj*

inst. instant (this month).

instability *n* lack of steadiness or reliability.

install *v* **1** put in and prepare (equipment) for use. **2** place (a person) formally in a position or rank. **installation** *n* **1** installing. **2** equipment installed. **3** place containing equipment for a particular purpose, e.g. *oil installations.*

instalment *n* any of the portions of a thing presented or a debt paid in successive parts.

instance *n* **1** particular example. ♦ *v* **2** mention as an example. **for instance** as an example.

instant *n* **1** very brief time. **2** particular moment. ♦ *adj* **3** happening at once. **4** (of foods) requiring little preparation. **instantly** *adv*

instantaneous *adj* happening at once. **instantaneously** *adv*

instead *adv* as a replacement or substitute. **instead of** in place of, as an alternative to.

instep *n* **1** part of the foot forming the arch between the ankle and toes. **2** part of a shoe etc. covering this.

instigate *v* cause to happen. **instigation** *n* **instigator** *n*

instil *v* **-stilling, -stilled** introduce (an idea etc.) gradually into someone's mind.

instinct *n* inborn tendency to behave in a certain way. **instinctive** *adj* **instinctively** *adv*

institute *n* **1** organization set up for a specific purpose, esp. research or teaching. ♦ *v* **2** start or establish.

institution *n* **1** large important organization such as a university or bank. **2** hospital etc. for people with special needs. **3** long-established custom. **institutional** *adj* **institutionalize** *v*

instruct *v* **1** order to do something. **2** teach (someone) how to do something. **instruction** *n* **1** order to do something. **2** teaching. ♦ *pl* **3** information on how to do or use something. **instructive** *adj* informative or helpful. **instructor** *n*

instrument *n* **1** tool used for particular work. **2** object played to produce a musical sound. **3** measuring device to show height, speed, etc. **4** *Informal* someone or something used to achieve an aim. **instrumental** *adj* **1** (foll. by *in*) having an important function (in). **2** played by or composed for musical instruments. **instrumentalist** *n* player of a musical instrument. **instrumentation** *n* **1** set of instruments in a car etc. **2** arrangement of music for instruments.

insubordinate *adj* not submissive to authority. **insubordination** *n*

insubstantial *adj* flimsy, fine, or slight.

insufferable *adj* unbearable.

insular *adj* not open to new ideas,

narrow-minded. **insularity** *n*

insulate *v* **1** prevent or reduce the transfer of electricity, heat, or sound by surrounding or lining with a nonconducting material. **2** isolate or set apart. **insulation** *n* **insulator** *n*

insulin [**in**-syoo-lin] *n* hormone produced in the pancreas that controls the amount of sugar in the blood.

insult *v* **1** behave rudely to, offend. ♦ *n* **2** insulting remark or action. **insulting** *adj*

insuperable *adj* impossible to overcome.

insupportable *adj* **1** impossible to tolerate. **2** impossible to justify.

insurance *n* **1** agreement by which one makes regular payments to a company who pay an agreed sum if damage, loss, or death occurs. **2** money paid to or by an insurance company. **3** means of protection. **insure** *v* protect by insurance. **insurance policy** contract of insurance.

insurgent *n, adj* (person) in revolt against an established authority. **insurgency** *n*

insurmountable *adj* impossible to overcome, e.g. *an insurmountable problem.*

insurrection *n* rebellion.

intact *adj* not changed or damaged in any way.

intaglio [in-**tah**-lee-oh] *n, pl* **-lios** (gem carved with) an engraved design.

intake *n* amount or number taken in.

intangible *adj* not clear or definite enough to be seen or felt easily, e.g. *an intangible quality.*

integer *n* positive or negative whole number or zero.

integral *adj* **1** being an essential part of a whole. ♦ *n* **2** *Maths* sum of a large number of very small quantities.

integrate *v* **1** combine into a whole. **2** amalgamate (a religious or racial group) into a community. **integration** *n* **integrated circuit** tiny electronic circuit on a silicon chip.

integrity *n* **1** quality of having high moral principles. **2** quality of being united.

intellect *n* power of thinking and reasoning. **intellectual** *adj* **1** of or appealing to the intellect. **2** clever, intelligent. ♦ *n* **3** intellectual person. **intellectually** *adv* **intellectualism** *n*

intelligent *adj* **1** able to understand, learn, and think things out quickly. **2** (of a computerized device) able to initiate or modify action in the light of ongoing events. **intelligence** *n* **1** quality of being intelligent. **2** secret government or military information. **3** people or department collecting such information. **intelligently** *adv* **intelligence quotient** a measure of the intelligence of a person calculated by dividing the person's mental age by his or her actual age and multiplying the result by 100.

intelligentsia *n* intellectual or cultured people in a society.

intelligible *adj* able to be understood. **intelligibility** *n*

intemperate *adj* **1** unrestrained, uncontrolled, e.g. *intemperate language.* **2** drinking alcohol to excess. **intemperance** *n*

intend *v* **1** propose or plan (to do something). **2** have as one's purpose. **intended** *adj* **1** planned or future. ♦ *n* **2** *Informal* person whom one is to marry.

intense *adj* **1** of great strength or degree. **2** deeply emotional. **intensity** *n* **intensify** *v* **-fying, -fied** make or become more intense. **intensification** *n*

intensive *adj* using or needing concentrated effort or resources. **intensively** *adv* **intensive care** thorough supervised treatment of an acutely ill patient in a hospital.

intent *n* **1** intention. **2** intention to commit a crime. ♦ *adj* **3** paying close attention. **intently** *adv* **intentness** *n* **intent on doing something** determined to do something. **to all intents and purposes** in almost every respect.

intention *n* something intended. **intentional** *adj* planned in advance, deliberate. **intentionally** *adv*

inter [in-**ter**] *v* **-terring, -terred** bury (a corpse). **interment** *n*

inter- *prefix* between or among, e.g.

international.

interact *v* act on or in close relation with each other. **interaction** *n* **interactive** *adj*

interbreed *v* breed within a related group.

intercede *v* try to end a dispute between two people or groups. **intercession** *n*

intercept *v* seize or stop in transit. **interception** *n* **interceptor** *n*

interchange *v* **1** (cause to) exchange places. ♦ *n* **2** motorway junction. **interchangeable** *adj*

Intercity *adj* ® denoting a fast train (service) travelling between cities.

intercom *n* internal communication system with loudspeakers.

intercommunion *n* association between Churches, involving mutual reception of Holy Communion.

intercontinental *adj* travelling between or linking continents.

intercourse *n* **1** sexual intercourse. **2** communication or dealings between people or groups.

interdenominational *adj* among or involving more than one denomination of the Christian Church.

interdiction, interdict *n* formal order forbidding something.

interdisciplinary *adj* involving more than one branch of learning.

interest *n* **1** desire to know or hear more about something. **2** something in which one is interested. **3** (often pl) advantage, benefit, e.g. *acting in the interests of the oil company.* **4** sum paid for the use of borrowed money. **5** (often pl) right or share. ♦ *v* **6** arouse the interest of. **interested** *adj* **1** feeling or showing interest. **2** involved in or affected by something. **interesting** *adj* **interestingly** *adv*

interface *n* **1** area where two things interact or link. **2** circuit linking a computer and another device.

interfere *v* **1** try to influence other people's affairs where one is not involved or wanted. **2** (foll. by *with*) clash (with). **3** (foll. by *with*) *Euphemistic* abuse (a child) sexually. **interfering** *adj* **interference** *n* **1** interfering. **2** *Radio* interruption of reception by atmospherics or unwanted signals.

interferon *n* protein that stops the development of an invading virus.

interim *adj* **1** temporary or provisional. ♦ *n* **2 in the interim** in the intervening time.

interior *n* **1** inside. **2** inland region. ♦ *adj* **3** inside, inner. **4** mental or spiritual.

interject *v* make (a remark) suddenly or as an interruption. **interjection** *n*

interlace *v* join together as if by weaving.

interleave *v* insert between other leaves, for example blank leaves in a book.

interlink *v* connect together.

interlock *v* join firmly together.

interlocutor [in-ter-**lok**-yew-ter] *n* person who takes part in a conversation.

interloper [**in**-ter-lope-er] *n* person in a place or situation where he or she has no right to be.

interlude *n* short rest or break in an activity or event.

intermarry *v* (of families, races, or religions) become linked by marriage. **intermarriage** *n*

intermediary *n, pl* **-ries** person trying to create agreement between others.

intermediate *adj* coming between two points or extremes.

intermezzo [in-ter-**met**-so] *n, pl* **-zos** short piece of music, esp. one performed between the acts of an opera.

interminable *adj* seemingly endless because boring. **interminably** *adv*

intermingle *v* mix together.

intermission *n* interval between parts of a play, film, etc.

intermittent *adj* occurring at intervals. **intermittently** *adv*

intern *v* **1** imprison, esp. during a war. ♦ *n* **2** *Chiefly US* trainee doctor in a hospital. **internment** *n* **internee** *n* person who is interned.

internal *adj* **1** of or on the inside. **2** within a country or organization. **3** spiritual or mental. **internally** *adv* **internal-combustion engine** engine powered by the explosion of a fuel-and-air mixture within the cylinders.

international *adj* **1** of or involving two or more countries. ♦ *n* **2** game or match between teams of different countries. **3** player in such a match. **internationally** *adv*

internecine *adj* mutually destructive.

Internet *n* large international computer network.

interplanetary *adj* of or linking planets.

interplay *n* action and reaction of two things upon each other.

Interpol International Criminal Police Organization.

interpolate [in-**ter**-pole-ate] *v* insert (a comment or passage) into (a conversation or text). **interpolation** *n*

interpose *v* **1** insert between or among things. **2** say as an interruption.

interpret *v* **1** explain the meaning of. **2** translate orally from one language into another. **3** convey the meaning of (a poem, song, etc.) in performance. **interpretation** *n* **interpreter** *n*

interregnum *n, pl* **-nums, -na** interval between reigns.

interrelate *v* connect (two or more things) to each other. **interrelation** *n*

interrogate *v* question closely. **interrogation** *n* **interrogative** *adj* **1** questioning. ♦ *n* **2** word used in asking a question, such as *how* or *why*. **interrogator** *n*

interrupt *v* **1** break into (a conversation etc.). **2** stop (a process or activity) temporarily. **interruption** *n*

intersect *v* **1** (of roads) meet and cross. **2** divide by passing across or through. **intersection** *n*

interspersed *adj* scattered (among, between, or on).

interstellar *adj* between or among stars.

interstice [in-**ter**-stiss] *n* small crack or gap between things.

intertwine *v* twist together.

interval *n* **1** time between two particular moments or events. **2** break between parts of a play, concert, etc. **3** difference in pitch between musical notes. **at intervals** **1** repeatedly. **2** with spaces left between.

intervene *v* **1** involve oneself in a situation, esp. to prevent conflict. **2** happen so as to stop something. **intervention** *n*

interview *n* **1** formal discussion, esp. between a job-seeker and an employer. **2** questioning of a well-known person about his or her career, views, etc., by a reporter. ♦ *v* **3** conduct an interview with. **interviewee** *n* **interviewer** *n*

interweave *v* weave together.

intestate *adj* not having made a will. **intestacy** *n*

intestine *n* (often pl) lower part of the alimentary canal between the stomach and the anus. **intestinal** *adj*

intimate[1] *adj* **1** having a close personal relationship. **2** personal or private. **3** (of knowledge) extensive and detailed. **4** (foll. by *with*) *Euphemistic* having a sexual relationship (with). **5** having a friendly quiet atmosphere. ♦ *n* **6** close friend. **intimately** *adv* **intimacy** *n, pl* **-cies**

intimate[2] *v* **1** hint at or suggest. **2** announce. **intimation** *n*

intimidate *v* subdue or influence by fear. **intimidating** *adj* **intimidation** *n*

into *prep* **1** indicating motion towards the centre, result of a change, division, etc., e.g. *into the valley; turned into a madman; cut into pieces.* **2** *Informal* interested in.

intolerable *adj* more than can be endured. **intolerably** *adv*

intolerant *adj* refusing to accept practices and beliefs different from one's own. **intolerance** *n*

intonation *n* sound pattern produced by variations in the voice.

intone *v* speak or recite in an unvarying tone of voice.

in toto *adv Latin* totally, entirely.

intoxicate *v* **1** make drunk. **2** excite to excess. **intoxicant** *n* intoxicating drink. **intoxication** *n*

intractable *adj* **1** (of a person) difficult to control. **2** (of a problem or issue) difficult to deal with.

intransigent *adj* refusing to change one's attitude. **intransigence** *n*

intransitive *adj* (of a verb) not taking a direct object.

intrauterine *adj* within the womb.

intravenous [in-tra-**vee**-nuss] *adj* into a vein. **intravenously** *adv*

intrepid *adj* fearless, bold. **intrepidity** *n*

intricate *adj* **1** involved or complicated. **2** full of fine detail. **intricately** *adv* **intricacy** *n, pl* **-cies**

intrigue *v* **1** make interested or curious. **2** plot secretly. ♦ *n* **3** secret plotting. **4** secret love affair. **intriguing** *adj*

intrinsic *adj* essential to the basic nature of something. **intrinsically** *adv*

introduce *v* **1** present (someone) by name (to another person). **2** present (a radio or television programme). **3** bring forward for discussion. **4** bring into use. **5** insert. **introduction** *n* **1** presentation of one person to another. **2** preliminary part or treatment. **introductory** *adj*

introspection *n* examination of one's own thoughts and feelings. **introspective** *adj*

introvert *n* person concerned more with his or her thoughts and feelings than with the outside world. **introverted** *adj* **introversion** *n*

intrude *v* come in or join in without being invited. **intruder** *n* **intrusion** *n* **intrusive** *adj*

intuition *n* instinctive knowledge or insight without conscious reasoning. **intuitive** *adj* **intuitively** *adv*

Inuit *n* Eskimo of North America or Greenland.

inundate *v* **1** flood. **2** overwhelm. **inundation** *n*

inured *adj* accustomed, esp. to hardship or danger.

invade *v* **1** enter (a country) by military force. **2** enter in large numbers. **3** disturb (someone's privacy). **invader** *n*

invalid[1] *adj, n* **1** disabled or chronically ill (person). ♦ *v* **2** (often foll. by *out*) dismiss from active service because of illness or injury. **invalidity** *n*

invalid[2] *adj* **1** having no legal force. **2** (of an argument etc.) not valid because based on a mistake. **invalidate** *v* make or show to be invalid.

invaluable *adj* of very great value or worth.

invasion *n* **1** invading. **2** intrusion, e.g. *an invasion of privacy.*

invective *n* abusive speech or writing.

inveigh [in-**vay**] *v* (foll. by *against*) criticize strongly.

inveigle *v* coax by cunning or trickery.

invent *v* **1** think up or create (something new). **2** make up (a story, excuse, etc.). **invention** *n* **1** something invented. **2** ability to invent. **inventive** *adj* creative and resourceful. **inventiveness** *n* **inventor** *n*

inventory [**in**-ven-tree] *n, pl* **-tories** detailed list of goods or furnishings.

inverse *adj* **1** reversed in effect, sequence, direction, etc. **2** *Maths* linking two variables in such a way that one increases as the other decreases. **inversely** *adv*

invert *v* turn upside down or inside out. **inversion** *n* **inverted commas** quotation marks.

invertebrate *n* animal with no backbone.

invest *v* **1** spend (money, time, etc.) on something with the expectation of profit. **2** (foll. by *with*) give (power or rights) to, e.g. *invested with the powers of government.* **investment** *n* **1** money invested. **2** something invested in. **investor** *n* **invest in** *v* buy.

investigate *v* inquire into, examine. **investigation** *n* **investigative** *adj* **investigator** *n*

investiture *n* formal installation of a person in an office or rank.

inveterate *adj* firmly established in a habit or condition, e.g. *an inveterate gambler.*

invidious *adj* likely to cause resentment.

invigilate [in-**vij**-il-late] *v* supervise people sitting an examination. **invigilator** *n*

invigorate *v* give energy to, refresh.

invincible *adj* impossible to defeat. **invincibility** *n*

inviolable *adj* unable to be broken or violated.

inviolate *adj* unharmed, unaffected.

invisible *adj* not able to be seen. **invisibly** *adv* **invisibility** *n*

invite *v* **1** request the company of. **2** ask politely for. **3** encourage or provoke, e.g. *the two works inevitably invite comparison.* ♦ *n* **4** *Informal* invitation. **inviting** *adj* tempting, attractive. **invitation** *n*

in-vitro *adj* happening outside the body in an artificial environment, e.g. *in-vitro fertilization.*

invoice *v, n* (present with) a bill for goods or services supplied.

invoke *v* **1** put (a law or penalty) into operation. **2** prompt or cause (a certain feeling). **3** call on (a god or spirit) for help, inspiration, etc. **invocation** *n*

involuntary *adj* not done consciously, unintentional. **involuntarily** *adv*

involve *v* **1** include as a necessary part. **2** affect, concern. **3** implicate (a person). **involved** *adj* **1** complicated. **2** concerned, taking part. **involvement** *n*

invulnerable *adj* not able to be wounded or harmed.

inward *adj, adv* see IN.

iodine *n Chem* bluish-black element used in medicine and photography. **iodize** *v* treat with iodine.

ion *n* electrically charged atom. **ionic** *adj* **ionize** *v* change into ions. **ionization** *n* **ionosphere** *n* region of ionized air in the upper atmosphere that reflects radio waves.

iota [eye-**oh**-ta] *n* **1** ninth letter in the Greek alphabet. **2** very small amount.

IOU *n* signed paper acknowledging debt.

IPA International Phonetic Alphabet.

ipecacuanha [ip-pee-kak-yoo-**an**-na], **ipecac** [**ip**-pee-kak] *n* drug made from the dried roots of a S American plant, used to cause vomiting.

ipso facto *adv Latin* by that very fact.

IQ intelligence quotient.

Ir *Chem* iridium.

IRA Irish Republican Army.

Iranian *n, adj* (person) from Iran.

Iraqi *n, adj* (person) from Iraq.

irascible *adj* easily angered. **irascibility** *n*

irate *adj* very angry.

ire *n Lit* anger.

iridescent *adj* having shimmering changing colours like a rainbow. **iridescence** *n*

iridium *n Chem* very hard corrosion-resistant metal.

iris *n* **1** coloured circular membrane of the eye containing the pupil. **2** tall plant with purple, yellow, or white flowers.

Irish *adj* of Ireland. **Irish coffee** hot coffee mixed with whiskey and topped with cream.

irk *v* irritate, annoy. **irksome** *adj* irritating, annoying.

iron *n* **1** strong silvery-white metallic element, widely used for structural and engineering purposes. **2** appliance used, when heated, to press clothes. **3** metal-headed golf club. ♦ *pl* **4** chains, restraints. ♦ *adj* **5** made of iron. **6** strong, inflexible, e.g. *iron will.* ♦ *v* **7** smooth (clothes or fabric) with an iron. **ironing** *n* clothes to be ironed. **ironing board** long cloth-covered board with folding legs, for ironing clothes on. **Iron Age** era when iron tools were used. **iron out** *v* settle (a problem) through discussion.

ironic, ironical *adj* **1** using irony. **2** odd or amusing because the opposite of what one would expect. **ironically** *adv*

ironmonger *n* shopkeeper or shop dealing in hardware. **ironmongery** *n*

ironstone *n* rock consisting mainly of iron ore.

irony *n, pl* **-nies** **1** mildly sarcastic use of words to imply the opposite of what is said. **2** aspect of a situation that is odd or amusing because the opposite of what one would expect.

irradiate *v* subject to or treat with radiation. **irradiation** *n*
irrational *adj* not based on or not using logical reasoning. **irrational number** *Maths* any real number that cannot be expressed as the ratio of two integers, such as π.
irreconcilable *adj* not able to be resolved or settled, e.g. *irreconcilable differences.* **irreconcilability** *n*
irredeemable *adj* not able to be reformed or corrected.
irreducible *adj* impossible to put in a simpler form.
irrefutable *adj* impossible to deny or disprove.
irregular *adj* **1** not regular or even. **2** not conforming to accepted practice. **3** (of a word) not following the typical pattern of formation in a language. **irregularly** *adv* **irregularity** *n, pl* **-ties**
irrelevant *adj* not connected with the matter in hand. **irrelevantly** *adv* **irrelevance** *n*
irreparable *adj* not able to be repaired or put right. **irreparably** *adv*
irreplaceable *adj* impossible to replace.
irrepressible *adj* lively and jolly. **irrepressibly** *adv*
irreproachable *adj* blameless, faultless. **irreproachably** *adv*
irresistible *adj* too attractive or strong to resist. **irresistibly** *adv*
irresolute *adj* unable to make decisions. **irresolution** *n*
irrespective of *prep* without taking account of.
irresponsible *adj* **1** not showing or not done with due care for the consequences of one's actions or attitudes. **2** not capable of accepting responsibility. **irresponsibility** *n*
irretrievable *adj* impossible to put right or make good. **irretrievably** *adv*
irreverent *adj* not showing due respect. **irreverence** *n*
irreversible *adj* not able to be reversed or put right again, e.g. *irreversible change.* **irreversibly** *adv*
irrevocable *adj* not possible to change or undo. **irrevocably** *adv*
irrigate *v* supply (land) with water by artificial channels or pipes. **irrigation** *n*
irritate *v* **1** annoy, anger. **2** cause (a body part) to itch or become inflamed. **irritable** *adj* easily annoyed. **irritability** *n* **irritably** *adv* **irritant** *n, adj* (person or thing) causing irritation. **irritation** *n*
is *v* third person singular present tense of BE.
ISA Individual Savings Account.
isinglass [**ize**-ing-glass] *n* kind of gelatine obtained from some freshwater fish.
Islam *n* **1** Muslim religion teaching that there is one God and that Mohammed is his prophet. **2** Muslim countries and civilization. **Islamic** *adj*
island *n* piece of land surrounded by water. **islander** *n* person who lives on an island.
isle *n Poetic* island. **islet** *n* small island.
-ism *n suffix* indicating: **1** political or religious belief, e.g. *Communism; Buddhism.* **2** characteristic quality, e.g. *cynicism.* **3** an action, e.g. *criticism.* **4** prejudice on the basis specified, e.g. *racism.*
isobar [**ice**-oh-bar] *n* line on a map connecting places of equal atmospheric pressure.
isolate *v* **1** place apart or alone. **2** *Chem* obtain (a substance) in uncombined form. **isolation** *n* **isolationism** *n* policy of not participating in international affairs. **isolationist** *n, adj*
isomer [**ice**-oh-mer] *n* substance whose molecules contain the same atoms as another but in a different arrangement.
isometric *adj* relating to muscular contraction without shortening of the muscle. **isometrics** *pl n* isometric exercises.
isosceles triangle [ice-**soss**-ill-eez] *n* triangle with two sides of equal length.
isotherm [**ice**-oh-therm] *n* line on a map connecting points of equal temperature.
isotope [**ice**-oh-tope] *n* one of two or more atoms with the same number of protons in the nucleus but a different number of neutrons.

Israeli *n, pl* **-lis, -li,** *adj* (person) from Israel.

issue *n* **1** topic of interest or discussion. **2** reason for quarrelling. **3** particular edition of a magazine or newspaper. **4** outcome or result. **5** *Law* child or children. ♦ *v* **6** make (a statement etc.) publicly. **7** supply officially (with). **8** produce and make available. **9** (foll. by *from*) come out of. **take issue with** disagree with.

-ist *n suffix* indicating: **1** person who performs a particular action, e.g. *exorcist.* **2** person who does a particular type of work, e.g. *physicist.* ♦ *adj suffix, n suffix* indicating: **3** (of) a person who holds a particular political or religious belief, e.g. *Communist; Buddhist.* **4** (of) a person who is prejudiced on the basis specified, e.g. *racist.*

isthmus [**iss**-muss] *n, pl* **-muses** narrow strip of land connecting two areas of land.

it *pron* **1** refers to a nonhuman, animal, plant, or inanimate object. **2** refers to a thing mentioned or being discussed. **3** used as the subject of impersonal verbs, e.g. *it's windy.* **4** *Informal* crucial or ultimate point. **its** *adj, pron* belonging to it. **it's 1** it is. **2** it has. **itself** *pron* emphatic form of IT.

> Beware of mistaking the possessive *its* (no apostrophe) as in *The cat has hurt its paw,* for the abbreviation *it's* meaning *it is* or *it has: It's been a long time.*

IT information technology.

Italian *n* **1** language of Italy and one of the languages of Switzerland. **2** person from Italy. ♦ *adj* **3** of Italy.

italic *adj* (of printing type) sloping to the right. **italics** *pl n* this type, used for emphasis. **italicize** *v* put in italics.

itch *n* **1** skin irritation causing a desire to scratch. **2** restless desire. ♦ *v* **3** have an itch. **itchy** *adj* **itchier, itchiest**

item *n* **1** single thing in a list or collection. **2** piece of information. **itemize** *v* make a list of.

iterate *v* repeat. **iteration** *n*

itinerant *adj* travelling from place to place.

itinerary *n, pl* **-aries** detailed plan of a journey.

ITV Independent Television.

IUD intrauterine device: a coil-shaped contraceptive fitted into the womb.

IVF in-vitro fertilization.

ivory *n* **1** hard white bony substance forming the tusks of elephants. ♦ *adj* **2** yellowish-white. **ivory tower** remoteness from the realities of everyday life.

ivy *n, pl* **ivies** evergreen climbing plant.

J j

J joule(s).

jab *v* **jabbing, jabbed 1** poke sharply. ♦ *n* **2** quick punch or poke. **3** *Informal* injection.

jabber *v* **1** talk rapidly or incoherently. ♦ *n* **2** rapid or incoherent talk.

jabot [**zhab**-oh] *n* frill or ruffle on the front of a blouse or shirt.

jacaranda *n* tropical tree with sweet-smelling wood.

jack *n* **1** device for raising a motor vehicle or other heavy object. **2** playing card with a picture of a pageboy. **3** *Bowls* small white bowl aimed at by the players. **4** socket in electrical equipment into which a plug fits. **5** flag flown at the bow of a ship, showing nationality. **6** piece used in the game of jacks. ♦ *pl* **7** game in which pieces are thrown and picked up between bounces of a ball. **jack in** *v Slang* abandon. **jack-in-the-box** *n* toy consisting of a figure on a spring in a box. **jack of all trades** person who can do many kinds of work. **jack up** *v* raise with a jack.

jackal *n* doglike wild animal of Africa and Asia.

jackass *n* **1** fool. **2** male of the ass. **laughing jackass** same as KOOKABURRA.

jackboot *n* **1** high military boot. **2** oppressive military rule.

jackdaw *n* black-and-grey bird of the crow family.

jacket *n* **1** short coat. **2** skin of a baked potato. **3** outer paper cover on a hardback book. **jacket potato** potato baked in its skin.

jackknife *v* **1** (of an articulated lorry) go out of control so that the trailer swings round at a sharp angle to the cab. ♦ *n* **2** large clasp knife. **3** dive with a sharp bend at the waist in mid-air.

jackpot *n* largest prize that may be won in a game. **hit the jackpot** be very successful through luck.

jack rabbit *n* American hare with long hind legs and large ears.

Jacobean [jak-a-**bee**-an] *adj* of the reign of James I of England.

Jacobite *n* supporter of James II of England and his descendants.

Jacquard [**jak**-ard] *n* fabric in which the design is incorporated into the weave.

Jacuzzi [jak-**oo**-zee] *n* ® circular bath with a device that swirls the water.

jade *n* **1** ornamental semiprecious stone, usu. dark green. ♦ *adj* **2** bluish-green.

jaded *adj* tired and unenthusiastic.

Jaffa *n* large orange with a thick skin.

jagged [**jag**-gid] *adj* having an uneven edge with sharp points.

jaguar *n* large S American spotted cat.

jail *n* **1** prison. ♦ *v* **2** send to prison. **jailer** *n* **jailbird** *n Informal* person who has often been in prison.

jalopy [jal-**lop**-ee] *n, pl* **-lopies** *Informal* old car.

jam[1] *v* **jamming, jammed 1** pack tightly into a place. **2** crowd or congest. **3** make or become stuck. **4** *Radio* block (another station) with impulses of equal wavelength. **5** play a jam session. ♦ *n* **6** hold-up of traffic. **7** *Informal* awkward situation. **jam on the brakes** apply brakes fiercely. **jam-packed** *adj* filled to capacity. **jam session** informal rock or jazz performance.

jam[2] *n* food made from fruit boiled with sugar.

jamb *n* side post of a door or window frame.

jamboree *n* large gathering or celebration.

jammy *adj* **-mier, -miest** *Slang* lucky.

Jan. January.

jangle *v* **1** (cause to) make a harsh ringing noise. **2** (of nerves) be upset or irritated. ♦ *n* **3** harsh ringing noise.

janitor *n* caretaker of a school or other building.

January *n* first month of the year.

japan *n* **1** very hard varnish, usu. black. ♦ *v* **-panning, -panned** **2** cover with this varnish.

Japanese *n, adj* (native or language) of Japan.

jape *n Old-fashioned* joke or prank.

japonica *n* shrub with red flowers.

jar[1] *n* **1** wide-mouthed container, usu. round and made of glass. **2** *Informal* glass of beer.

jar[2] *v* **jarring, jarred** **1** have a disturbing or unpleasant effect. **2** be in conflict. **3** jolt or bump. ♦ *n* **4** jolt or shock.

jardiniere *n* ornamental plant pot.

jargon *n* **1** specialized technical language of a particular subject. **2** pretentious language.

jasmine *n* shrub with sweet-smelling yellow or white flowers.

jasper *n* red, yellow, dark green, or brown variety of quartz.

jaundice *n* disease marked by yellowness of the skin. **jaundiced** *adj* **1** (of an attitude or opinion) bitter or cynical. **2** having jaundice.

jaunt *n* **1** short journey for pleasure. ♦ *v* **2** make such a journey.

jaunty *adj* **-tier, -tiest** **1** sprightly and cheerful. **2** smart. **jauntily** *adv*

javelin *n* light spear thrown in sports competitions.

jaw *n* **1** one of the bones in which the teeth are set. **2** lower part of the face. ♦ *pl* **3** mouth. **4** gripping part of a tool. **5** narrow opening of a gorge or valley. ♦ *v* **6** *Slang* talk lengthily. **jawbone** *n* lower jaw of a person or animal.

jay *n* bird with a pinkish body and blue-and-black wings.

jaywalking *n* crossing the road in a careless or dangerous manner. **jaywalker** *n*

jazz *n* kind of music with an exciting rhythm, usu. involving improvisation. **and all that jazz** *Slang* and other related things. **jazzy** *adj* **-zier, -ziest** **1** flashy or showy. **2** of or like jazz. **jazz up** *v* make more lively.

JCB *n* ® construction machine with a shovel at the front and an excavator at the rear.

jealous *adj* **1** fearful of losing a partner or possession to a rival. **2** envious. **3** suspiciously watchful. **jealously** *adv* **jealousy** *n, pl* **-sies**

jeans *pl n* casual denim trousers.

Jeep *n* ® four-wheel-drive motor vehicle.

jeer *v* **1** scoff or deride. ♦ *n* **2** cry of derision.

Jehovah *n* God. **Jehovah's Witness** member of a Christian sect believing that the end of the world is near.

jejune *adj* **1** simple or naive. **2** dull or boring.

jell *v* **1** form into a jelly-like substance. **2** take on a definite form.

jelly *n, pl* **-lies** **1** soft food made of liquid set with gelatine. **2** jam made from fruit juice and sugar. **jellied** *adj* prepared in a jelly.

jellyfish *n* small jelly-like sea animal.

jemmy *n, pl* **-mies** short steel crowbar used by burglars.

jenny *n, pl* **-nies** female ass or wren.

jeopardy *n* danger. **jeopardize** *v* place in danger.

jerboa *n* small mouselike rodent with long hind legs.

jerk *v* **1** move or throw abruptly. ♦ *n* **2** sharp or abruptly stopped movement. **3** *Slang* contemptible person. **jerky** *adj* **jerkier, jerkiest** sudden or abrupt. **jerkily** *adv* **jerkiness** *n*

jerkin *n* sleeveless jacket.

Jerry *n Brit slang* German or Germans collectively.

jerry-built *adj* built badly using flimsy materials.

jerry can *n* flat-sided can for carrying petrol etc.

jersey *n* **1** knitted jumper. **2** machine-knitted fabric. **3** (**J-**) breed of cow.

Jerusalem artichoke *n* small yellowish-white root vegetable.

jest *n, v* joke. **jester** *n Hist* professional clown at court.

Jesuit [**jezz**-yoo-it] *n* member of the Society of Jesus, a Roman Catholic order.

Jesus *n* **1** (also **Jesus Christ, Jesus of**

Nazareth) ?4 BC–?29 AD, founder of Christianity, believed by Christians to be the Son of God. ♦ *interj* **2** *Taboo slang* oath used to express intense surprise, dismay, etc.

jet[1] *n* **1** aircraft driven by jet propulsion. **2** stream of liquid or gas, esp. one forced from a small hole. **3** nozzle from which gas or liquid is forced. ♦ *v* **jetting, jetted** **4** fly by jet aircraft. **jet lag** fatigue caused by crossing time zones in an aircraft. **jet propulsion** propulsion by thrust provided by a jet of gas or liquid. **jet-propelled** *adj* **jet set** rich and fashionable people who travel the world for pleasure.

jet[2] *n* hard black mineral. **jet-black** *adj* glossy black.

jetsam *n* goods thrown overboard to lighten a ship.

jettison *v* **-soning, -soned** **1** abandon. **2** throw overboard.

jetty *n, pl* **-ties** **1** small pier. **2** structure built from a shore to protect a harbour.

Jew *n* **1** person whose religion is Judaism. **2** descendant of the ancient Hebrews. **Jewess** *n fem now often offens* **Jewish** *adj* **Jewry** *n* Jews collectively. **jew's-harp** *n* musical instrument held between the teeth and played by plucking a metal strip with one's finger.

jewel *n* **1** precious stone. **2** special person or thing. **jeweller** *n* dealer in jewels. **jewellery** *n* objects decorated with precious stones.

Jezebel *n* shameless or scheming woman.

jib[1] *n* triangular sail set in front of a mast.

jib[2] *v* **jibbing, jibbed** (of a horse, person, etc.) stop and refuse to go on. **jib at** *v* object to (a proposal etc.).

jib[3] *n* projecting arm of a crane or derrick.

jibe[1] *n, v* taunt or jeer.

jibe[2] *v* same as GYBE.

jiffy *n, pl* **-fies** *Informal* very short period of time.

jig *n* **1** type of lively dance. **2** music for it. **3** device that holds a component in place for cutting etc. ♦ *v* **jigging, jigged** **4** dance a jig. **5** make jerky up-and-down movements.

jiggery-pokery *n Informal* trickery or mischief.

jiggle *v* move up and down with short jerky movements.

jigsaw *n* **1** (also **jigsaw puzzle**) picture cut into interlocking pieces, which the user tries to fit together again. **2** mechanical saw for cutting along curved lines.

jihad *n* Islamic holy war against unbelievers.

jilt *v* leave or reject (one's lover).

jingle *n* **1** catchy verse or song used in a radio or television advert. **2** gentle ringing noise. ♦ *v* **3** (cause to) make a gentle ringing sound.

jingoism *n* aggressive nationalism. **jingoistic** *adj*

jinks *pl n* **high jinks** boisterous merrymaking.

jinni *n, pl* **jinn** spirit in Muslim mythology.

jinx *n* **1** person or thing bringing bad luck. ♦ *v* **2** be or put a jinx on.

jitters *pl n* worried nervousness. **jittery** *adj* nervous.

jive *n* **1** lively dance of the 1940s and '50s. ♦ *v* **2** dance the jive.

job *n* **1** occupation or paid employment. **2** task to be done. **3** performance of a task. **4** *Informal* difficult task. **5** *Informal* crime, esp. robbery. **jobbing** *adj* doing individual jobs for payment. **jobless** *adj, pl n* unemployed (people). **Jobcentre, job centre** *n* government office displaying information about available jobs. **job lot** assortment sold together. **job sharing** splitting of one post between two people working part-time.

Job's comforter *n* person who adds to distress while pretending to give sympathy.

jockey *n* **1** (professional) rider of racehorses. ♦ *v* **2** **jockey for position** manoeuvre to obtain an advantage.

jockstrap *n* belt with a pouch to support the genitals, worn by male athletes.

jocose [joke-**kohss**] *adj* playful or humorous. **jocosely** *adv*

jocular *adj* **1** fond of joking. **2** meant as a joke. **jocularity** *n* **jocularly** *adv*

jocund [**jok**-kund] *adj Lit* merry or cheerful.

jodhpurs *pl n* riding trousers, loose-fitting above the knee but tight below.

jog *v* **jogging, jogged 1** run at a gentle pace, esp. for exercise. **2** nudge slightly. ♦ *n* **3** slow run. **jog someone's memory** remind someone of something. **jogger** *n* **jogging** *n*

joggle *v* shake or move jerkily.

john *n US slang* toilet.

joie de vivre [jwah de **veev**-ra] *n French* enjoyment of life.

join *v* **1** become a member (of). **2** become part of. **3** come into someone's company. **4** take part (in). **5** come or bring together. **6** connect (two points). ♦ *n* **7** place where two things are joined. **join in** *v* take part in. **join up** *v* enlist in the armed services.

joiner *n* maker of finished woodwork. **joinery** *n* joiner's work.

joint *adj* **1** shared by two or more. ♦ *n* **2** place where bones meet but can move. **3** junction of two or more parts or objects. **4** piece of meat for roasting. **5** *Slang* house or place, esp. a disreputable bar or nightclub. **6** *Slang* marijuana cigarette. ♦ *v* **7** divide meat into joints. **8** provide with a joint. **out of joint 1** disorganized. **2** dislocated. **jointed** *adj* **jointly** *adv* **joint-stock company** firm whose capital is jointly owned by shareholders.

joist *n* horizontal beam that helps support a floor or ceiling.

jojoba [hoe-**hoe**-ba] *n* shrub whose seeds yield oil used in cosmetics.

joke *n* **1** thing said or done to cause laughter. **2** amusing or ridiculous person or thing. ♦ *v* **3** make jokes. **jokey** *adj* **jokingly** *adv* **joker** *n* **1** person who jokes. **2** *Slang* fellow. **3** extra card in a pack, counted as any other in some games.

jolly *adj* **-lier, -liest 1** (of a person) happy and cheerful. **2** (of an occasion) merry and festive. ♦ *adv* **3** *Informal* extremely. ♦ *v* **-lying, -lied 4 jolly along** try to keep (someone) cheerful by flattery or coaxing. **jollity** *n* **jollification** *n* merry-making.

jolt *n* **1** unpleasant surprise or shock. **2** sudden jerk or bump. ♦ *v* **3** surprise or shock. **4** move or shake with a jerk.

Jonah *n* person believed to bring bad luck to those around him or her.

jonquil *n* fragrant narcissus.

josh *v Chiefly US slang* tease.

joss stick *n* stick of incense giving off a sweet smell when burnt.

jostle *v* **1** knock or push against. **2** compete with someone.

jot *v* **jotting, jotted 1** write briefly. ♦ *n* **2** very small amount. **jotter** *n* notebook. **jottings** *pl n* notes jotted down.

joule [**jool**] *n Physics* unit of work or energy.

journal *n* **1** daily newspaper or magazine. **2** daily record of events. **journalese** *n* superficial style of writing, found in some newspapers. **journalism** *n* writing in or editing of newspapers and magazines. **journalist** *n* **journalistic** *adj*

journey *n* **1** act or process of travelling from one place to another. **2** time taken or distance travelled in a journey. ♦ *v* **3** travel.

journeyman *n* qualified craftsman employed by another.

joust *Hist* ♦ *n* **1** combat with lances between two mounted knights. ♦ *v* **2** fight on horseback using lances.

jovial *adj* happy and cheerful. **jovially** *adv* **joviality** *n*

jowl[1] *n* **1** lower jaw. ♦ *pl* **2** cheeks.

jowl[2] *n* fatty flesh hanging from the lower jaw.

joy *n* **1** feeling of great delight or pleasure. **2** cause of this feeling. **joyful** *adj* **joyless** *adj* **joyous** *adj* extremely happy and enthusiastic. **joyriding** *n* driving for pleasure, esp. in a stolen car. **joyride** *n* **joyrider** *n* **joystick** *n* control device for an aircraft or computer.

JP Justice of the Peace.

Jr Junior.

JSA jobseeker's allowance: in Britain, a payment made to unemployed people.

jubilant *adj* feeling or expressing great joy. **jubilantly** *adv* **jubilation** *n*

jubilee *n* special anniversary, esp. 25th (**silver jubilee**) or 50th (**golden jubilee**).

Judaism *n* religion of the Jews, based on the Old Testament and the Talmud. **Judaic** *adj*

Judas *n* person who betrays a friend.

judder *v* **1** vibrate violently. ♦ *n* **2** violent vibration.

judge *n* **1** public official who tries cases and passes sentence in a court of law. **2** person who decides the outcome of a contest. **3** person of reliable opinion on a subject. ♦ *v* **4** act as a judge. **5** appraise critically. **6** consider something to be the case. **judgment, judgement** *n* **1** opinion reached after careful thought. **2** verdict of a judge. **3** ability to appraise critically. **Judgment Day** occasion of the Last Judgment by God at the end of the world. **judgmental, judgemental** *adj*

> The alternative spellings with or without an 'e' between 'g' and 'm' are equally acceptable.

judicial *adj* **1** of or by a court or judge. **2** showing or using judgment. **judicially** *adv*

judiciary *n* system of courts and judges.

judicious *adj* well-judged and sensible. **judiciously** *adv*

judo *n* sport in which two opponents try to throw each other to the ground.

jug *n* container for liquids, with a handle and small spout. **jugged hare** hare stewed in an earthenware pot.

juggernaut *n* **1** large heavy lorry. **2** any irresistible destructive force.

juggle *v* **1** throw and catch (several objects) so that most are in the air at the same time. **2** manipulate (figures, situations, etc.) to suit one's purposes. **juggler** *n*

jugular, jugular vein *n* one of three large veins of the neck that return blood from the head to the heart.

juice *n* **1** liquid part of vegetables, fruit, or meat. **2** *Informal* petrol. ♦ *pl* **3** fluids secreted by an organ of the body. **juicy** *adj* **juicier, juiciest 1** full of juice. **2** interesting.

jujitsu *n* Japanese art of wrestling and self-defence.

juju *n* W African magic charm or fetish.

jukebox *n* coin-operated machine on which records, CDs, or videos can be played.

Jul. July.

julep *n* sweet alcoholic drink.

Julian calendar *n* calendar introduced by Julius Caesar, in which leap years occurred every fourth year.

julienne *adj* **1** (of vegetables or meat) cut into thin shreds. ♦ *n* **2** clear soup containing thinly shredded vegetables.

July *n* seventh month of the year.

jumble *n* **1** confused heap or state. **2** articles for a jumble sale. ♦ *v* **3** mix in a disordered way. **jumble sale** sale of miscellaneous second-hand items.

jumbo *adj* **1** *Informal* very large. ♦ *n* **2** (also **jumbo jet**) large jet airliner.

jump *v* **1** leap or spring into the air using the leg muscles. **2** move quickly and suddenly. **3** jerk with surprise. **4** increase suddenly. **5** change the subject abruptly. **6** *Informal* attack without warning. **7** pass over or miss out (intervening material). ♦ *n* **8** act of jumping. **9** sudden rise. **10** break in continuity. **11** step or degree. **jump the gun** act prematurely. **jump the queue** not wait one's turn. **jumpy** *adj* **jumpier, jumpiest** nervous. **jump at** *v* accept (a chance etc.) gladly. **jumped-up** *adj* arrogant because of recent promotion. **jump jet** fixed-wing jet that can take off and land vertically. **jump leads** electric cables to connect a flat car battery to an external battery to aid starting an engine. **jump on** *v* attack suddenly and forcefully. **jump suit** one-piece garment of trousers and top.

jumper[1] *n* sweater or pullover.
jumper[2] *n* person or animal that jumps.
Jun. **1** June. **2** Junior.
junction *n* place where routes, railway lines, or roads meet.
juncture *n* point in time, esp. a critical one.
June *n* sixth month of the year.
jungle *n* **1** tropical forest of dense tangled vegetation. **2** confusion or mess. **3** place of intense struggle for survival.
junior *adj* **1** of lower standing. **2** younger. ♦ *n* **3** junior person. **junior school** school for children between seven and eleven.
juniper *n* evergreen shrub with purple berries.
junk[1] *n* **1** discarded or useless objects. **2** *Informal* rubbish. **3** *Slang* narcotic drug, esp. heroin. **junkie, junky** *n, pl* **junkies** *Slang* drug addict. **junk food** snack food of low nutritional value. **junk mail** unwanted mail advertising goods or services.
junk[2] *n* flat-bottomed Chinese sailing boat.
junket *n* **1** excursion by public officials paid for from public funds. **2** sweetened milk set with rennet. **3** feast. **junketing** *n*
junta *n* group of military officers holding power in a country, esp. after a coup.
Jupiter *n* **1** king of the Roman gods. **2** largest of the planets.
juridical *adj* of law or the administration of justice.
jurisdiction *n* **1** right or power to administer justice and apply laws. **2** extent of this right or power. **3** authority in general.
jurisprudence *n* science or philosophy of law.
jurist *n* expert in law.
jury *n, pl* **-ries** **1** group of people sworn to deliver a verdict in a court of law. **2** judges of a competition. **juror** *n* member of a jury.
just *adv* **1** very recently. **2** at this instant. **3** merely, only. **4** exactly. **5** barely. **6** really. ♦ *adj* **7** fair or impartial in action or judgment. **8** proper or right. **justly** *adv* **justness** *n*
justice *n* **1** quality of being just. **2** judicial proceedings. **3** judge or magistrate. **justice of the peace** person who is authorized to act as a judge in a local court of law.
justify *v* **-fying, -fied** **1** prove right or reasonable. **2** explain the reasons for an action. **3** align (text) so the margins are straight. **justifiable** *adj* **justifiably** *adv* **justification** *n*
jut *v* **jutting, jutted** project or stick out.
jute *n* plant fibre, used for rope, canvas, etc.
juvenile *adj* **1** young. **2** of or suitable for young people. **3** immature and rather silly. ♦ *n* **4** young person or child. **juvenilia** *pl n* works produced in an author's youth. **juvenile delinquent** young person guilty of a crime.
juxtapose *v* put side by side. **juxtaposition** *n*

K k

K 1 *Chem* potassium. 2 *Informal* thousand(s).

Kaffir [**kaf**-fer] *n S Afr offens obs* Black African.

kaftan *n* 1 long loose Eastern garment. 2 woman's dress resembling this.

kai *n NZ informal* food.

kaiser [**kize**-er] *n Hist* German or Austro-Hungarian emperor.

Kalashnikov *n* Russian-made automatic rifle.

kale *n* cabbage with crinkled leaves.

kaleidoscope *n* 1 tube-shaped toy containing loose coloured pieces reflected by mirrors so that intricate patterns form when the tube is twisted. 2 complicated or rapidly changing set of colours, circumstances, etc. **kaleidoscopic** *adj*

kalends *pl n* same as CALENDS.

kamikaze [kam-mee-**kah**-zee] *n* 1 (in World War II) Japanese pilot who performed a suicide mission. ♦ *adj* 2 (of an action) undertaken in the knowledge that it will kill or injure the person performing it.

kangaroo *n, pl* **-roos** Australian marsupial which moves by jumping with its powerful hind legs. **kangaroo court** unofficial court set up by a group to discipline its members.

kaolin *n* fine white clay used to make porcelain and in some medicines.

kapok *n* fluffy fibre from a tropical tree, used to stuff cushions etc.

kaput [kap-**poot**] *adj Informal* ruined or broken.

karaoke *n* form of entertainment in which people sing over a prerecorded backing tape.

karate *n* Japanese system of unarmed combat using blows with the feet, hands, elbows, and legs.

karma *n Buddhism, Hinduism* person's actions affecting his or her fate in the next reincarnation.

karoo *n S Afr* high arid plateau.

kart *n* same as GO-KART.

kasbah *n* same as CASBAH.

katydid *n* large green grasshopper of N America.

kauri *n* large NZ conifer that yields valuable timber and resin.

kayak *n* 1 Inuit canoe made of sealskins stretched over a frame. 2 fibreglass or canvas-covered canoe of this design.

kazoo *n, pl* **-zoos** cigar-shaped metal musical instrument that produces a buzzing sound when the player hums into it.

KBE Knight Commander of the Order of the British Empire.

kbyte *Computers* kilobyte.

kcal kilocalorie.

kea *n* large brownish-green parrot of NZ.

kebab *n* 1 dish of small pieces of meat grilled on skewers. 2 (also **doner kebab**) grilled minced lamb served in a split slice of unleavened bread.

kedgeree *n* dish of fish with rice and eggs.

keel *n* main lengthways timber or steel support along the base of a ship. **keel over** *v* 1 turn upside down. 2 *Informal* collapse suddenly. **on an even keel** working or progressing smoothly.

keen[1] *adj* 1 eager or enthusiastic. 2 intense or strong. 3 intellectually acute. 4 (of the senses) capable of recognizing small distinctions. 5 sharp. 6 cold and penetrating. 7 competitive. **keenly** *adv* **keenness** *n*

keen[2] *v* wail over the dead.

keep *v* **keeping, kept** 1 have or retain possession of. 2 take temporary charge of. 3 store. 4 stay or cause to stay (in, on, or at a place or position). 5 continue or persist. 6 support financially. 7 detain (someone). 8 look after or maintain. 9 (of food) remain good. ♦ *n* 10 cost of food and everyday expenses. 11 central tower of a castle. **keeper** *n* 1 person who looks after animals in a zoo.

2 person in charge of a museum or collection. **3** short for GOALKEEPER. **keeping** *n* care or charge. **in, out of keeping with** appropriate *or* inappropriate for. **keep fit** exercises designed to promote physical fitness. **keepsake** *n* gift treasured for the sake of the giver. **keep up** *v* maintain at the current level. **keep up with** *v* maintain a pace set by (someone). **keep up with the Joneses** *Informal* compete with friends or neighbours in material possessions.

keg *n* small metal beer barrel.

kelp *n* large brown seaweed.

kelvin *n* SI unit of temperature. **Kelvin scale** temperature scale starting at absolute zero (-273.15° Celsius).

ken *v* **kenning, kenned** *or* **kent** *Scot* know. **beyond one's ken** beyond one's range of knowledge.

kendo *n* Japanese sport of fencing using wooden staves.

kennel *n* **1** hutlike shelter for a dog. ♦ *pl* **2** place for breeding, boarding, or training dogs.

kept *v* past of KEEP.

keratin *n* fibrous protein found in the hair and nails.

kerb *n* stone edging to a footpath. **kerb crawling** act of driving slowly beside a pavement to pick up a prostitute.

kerchief *n* piece of cloth worn over the head or round the neck.

kerfuffle *n Informal* commotion or disorder.

kernel *n* **1** seed of a nut, cereal, or fruit stone. **2** central and essential part of something.

kerosene *n Chiefly US* paraffin.

kestrel *n* type of small falcon.

ketch *n* two-masted sailing ship.

ketchup *n* thick cold sauce, usu. made of tomatoes.

kettle *n* container with a spout and handle used for boiling water. **a different kettle of fish** something entirely different. **kettledrum** *n* large bowl-shaped metal drum.

key[1] *n* **1** device for operating a lock by moving a bolt. **2** device turned to wind a clock, operate a machine, etc. **3** any of a set of levers or buttons pressed to operate a typewriter, computer, or musical keyboard instrument. **4** *Music* set of related notes. **5** something crucial in providing an explanation or interpretation. **6** means of achieving a desired end. **7** list of explanations of codes, symbols, etc. ♦ *adj* **8** of great importance. ♦ *v* **9** (also **key in**) enter (text) using a keyboard. **keyed up** very excited or nervous.

key[2] *n* same as CAY.

keyboard *n* **1** set of keys on a piano, computer, etc. **2** musical instrument played using a keyboard. ♦ *v* **3** enter (text) using a keyboard.

keyhole *n* opening for inserting a key into a lock. **keyhole surgery** surgery performed through a narrow hole cut in the body.

keynote *adj* **1** central or dominating. ♦ *n* **2** dominant idea of a speech etc. **3** basic note of a musical key.

keyring *n* decorative metal ring for keeping keys on.

keystone *n* **1** most important part of a process, organization, etc. **2** central stone of an arch which locks the others in position.

kg kilogram(s).

KG Knight of the Order of the Garter.

KGB *n* (formerly) Soviet secret police.

khaki *adj* **1** dull yellowish-brown. ♦ *n* **2** hard-wearing fabric of this colour used for military uniforms.

khan *n* title of respect in Afghanistan and central Asia.

kHz kilohertz.

kibbutz *n, pl* **kibbutzim** communal farm or factory in Israel.

kibosh *n* **put the kibosh on** *Slang* put a stop to.

kick *v* **1** drive, push, or strike with the foot. **2** (of a gun) recoil when fired. **3** *Informal* object or resist. **4** *Informal* free oneself of (an addiction). **5** *Rugby* score with a kick. ♦ *n* **6** thrust or blow with the foot. **7** recoil of a gun. **8** *Informal* excitement or thrill. **kickback** *n* money paid illegally for favours done. **kick off** *v* **1** start a game of football. **2** *Informal* begin. **kickoff** *n* **kick out** *v* dismiss or expel forcibly. **kick-start** *v* **1** start (a motorcycle) by kicking a pedal. **2** do something bold or drastic in order to begin or improve the performance of something. ♦ *n* **3** (also **kick-starter**) pedal on a motorcycle that is kicked downwards to start the engine. **kick up** *v Informal* create (a fuss).

kid[1] *n* **1** (also **kiddie**) *Informal* child. **2** young goat. **3** leather made from the skin of a young goat. **treat, handle someone with kid gloves** treat someone with great tact in order not to upset them.

kid[2] *v* **kidding, kidded** *Informal* tease or deceive (someone).

kidnap *v* **-napping, -napped** seize and hold (a person) to ransom. **kidnapper** *n* **kidnapping** *n*

kidney *n* **1** either of the pair of organs that filter waste products from the blood to produce urine. **2** animal kidney used as food. **kidney bean** reddish-brown kidney-shaped bean, edible when cooked.

kill *v* **1** cause the death of. **2** *Informal* cause (someone) pain or discomfort. **3** put an end to. **4** pass (time). ♦ *n* **5** act of killing. **6** animals or birds killed in a hunt. **killer** *n* **killing** *Informal* ♦ *adj* **1** very tiring. **2** very funny. ♦ *n* **3** sudden financial success. **killjoy** *n* person who spoils others' pleasure.

kiln *n* oven for baking, drying, or processing pottery, bricks, etc.

kilo *n* short for KILOGRAM.

kilo- *combining form* one thousand, e.g. *kilometre.*

kilobyte *n Computers* 1024 units of information.

kilocalorie *n* one thousand calories.

kilogram, kilogramme *n* one thousand grams.

kilohertz *n* one thousand hertz.

kilojoule *n* one thousand joules.

kilometre *n* one thousand metres.

kilowatt *n Electricity* one thousand watts. **kilowatt-hour** *n* unit of energy equal to the work done by a power of one thousand watts in an hour.

kilt *n* knee-length pleated tartan skirt worn orig. by Scottish Highlanders. **kilted** *adj*

kimono [kim-**moan**-no] *n, pl* **-nos 1** loose wide-sleeved Japanese robe, fastened with a sash. **2** European dressing gown resembling this.

kin, kinsfolk *n* person's relatives collectively. **kinship** *n* **1** blood relationship. **2** state of having common characteristics. **kinsman, kinswoman** *n* relative.

kind[1] *adj* considerate, friendly, and helpful. **kindness** *n* **kindly** *adj* **-lier, -liest 1** having a warm-hearted nature. **2** pleasant or agreeable. ♦ *adv* **3** in a considerate way. **4** please, e.g. *will you kindly be quiet!* **kindliness** *n* **kind-hearted** *adj*

kind[2] *n* **1** class or group with common characteristics. **2** essential nature or character. **in kind 1** (of payment) in goods rather than money. **2** with something similar. **kind of** to a certain extent.

> Note the singular/plural usage: *this* (or *that*) *kind of dog; these* (or *those*) *kinds of dog*. In the second, plural example, you can also say *these kinds of dogs*.

kindergarten *n* class or school for children of about four to six years old.

kindle *v* **1** set (a fire) alight. **2** (of a fire) start to burn. **3** arouse or be aroused. **kindling** *n* dry wood or straw for starting fires.

kindred *adj* **1** having similar qualities. **2** related by blood or marriage. ♦ *n* **3** same as KIN.

kine *pl n Obs* cows or cattle.

kinetic [kin-**net**-ik] *adj* relating to or caused by motion.

king *n* **1** male ruler of a monarchy. **2** ruler or chief. **3** best or most important of its kind. **4** piece in chess that must be defended. **5** playing card with a picture of a king on it. **kingship** *n* **kingdom** *n* **1** state ruled by a king or queen. **2** division of the natural world. **king-size, king-sized** *adj* larger than standard size.

kingfisher *n* small bird with a bright greenish-blue and orange plumage, that dives for fish.

kingpin *n* most important person in an organization.

kink *n* **1** twist or bend in rope, wire, hair, etc. **2** *Informal* quirk in someone's personality. **kinky** *adj* **kinkier, kinkiest 1** *Slang* given to unusual sexual practices. **2** full of kinks.

kiosk *n* **1** small booth selling drinks, cigarettes, newspapers, etc. **2** public telephone box.

kip *n, v* **kipping, kipped** *Informal* sleep.

kipper *n* cleaned, salted, and smoked herring.

kirk *n* *Scot* church.

Kirsch *n* brandy made from cherries.

kismet *n* fate or destiny.

kiss *v* **1** touch with the lips in affection or greeting. **2** join lips with a person in love or desire. ♦ *n* **3** touch with the lips. **kisser** *n* *Slang* mouth or face. **kissagram** *n* greetings service in which a messenger kisses the person celebrating. **kiss of life** mouth-to-mouth resuscitation.

kit *n* **1** outfit or equipment for a specific purpose. **2** set of pieces of equipment sold ready to be assembled. **kitbag** *n* bag for a soldier's or traveller's belongings. **kit out** *v* **kitting, kitted** provide with clothes or equipment needed for a particular activity.

kitchen *n* room used for cooking. **kitchenette** *n* small kitchen. **kitchen garden** garden for growing vegetables, herbs, etc.

kite *n* **1** light frame covered with a thin material flown on a string in the wind. **2** large hawk with a forked tail. **Kite mark** official mark on articles approved by the British Standards Institution.

kith *n* **kith and kin** friends and relatives.

kitsch *n* art or literature with popular sentimental appeal.

kitten *n* young cat. **kittenish** *adj* lively and flirtatious.

kittiwake *n* type of seagull.

kitty *n, pl* **-ties 1** communal fund. **2** total amount wagered in certain gambling games.

kiwi *n* **1** NZ flightless bird with a long beak and no tail. **2** *Informal* New Zealander. **kiwi fruit** edible fruit with a fuzzy brownish skin and green flesh.

kJ kilojoule(s).

klaxon *n* loud horn used on emergency vehicles as a warning signal.

kleptomania *n* compulsive tendency to steal. **kleptomaniac** *n*

km kilometre(s).

knack *n* **1** skilful way of doing something. **2** innate ability.

knacker *n* buyer of old horses for killing.

knackered *adj* *Slang* **1** extremely tired. **2** no longer functioning.

knapsack *n* soldier's or traveller's bag worn strapped on the back.

knave *n* **1** jack at cards. **2** *Obs* dishonest man.

knead *v* **1** work (dough) into a smooth mixture with the hands. **2** squeeze or press with the hands.

knee *n* **1** joint between thigh and lower leg. **2** lap. **3** part of a garment covering the knee. ♦ *v* **kneeing, kneed 4** strike or push with the knee. **kneecap** *n* **1** bone in front of the knee. ♦ *v* **2** shoot in the kneecap. **kneejerk** *adj* (of a reply or reaction) automatic and predictable. **knees-up** *n* *Informal* party.

kneel *v* **kneeling, kneeled** *or* **knelt** fall or rest on one's knees.

knell *n* **1** sound of a bell, esp. at a funeral or death. **2** portent of doom.

knew *v* past tense of KNOW.

knickerbockers *pl n* loose-fitting short trousers gathered in at the knee.

knickers *pl n* woman's or girl's undergarment covering the lower trunk and having legs or legholes.

knick-knack *n* trifle or trinket.

knife *n, pl* **knives 1** cutting tool or weapon consisting of a sharp-edged blade with a handle. ♦ *v* **2** cut or stab with a knife. **knife edge** critical point in the development of a situation.

knight *n* **1** man who has been given a knighthood. **2** *Hist* man who served his lord as a mounted armoured soldier. **3** chess piece shaped like a horse's head. ♦ *v* **4** award a knighthood to. **knighthood** *n* honorary title given to a man by the British sovereign. **knightly** *adj*

knit *v* **knitting, knitted** *or* **knit 1** make (a garment) by interlocking a series of loops in wool or other yarn. **2** join closely together. **3** draw (one's eyebrows) together. **knitting** *n* **knitwear** *n* knitted clothes, such as sweaters.

knives *n* plural of KNIFE.

knob *n* **1** rounded projection, such as a switch on a radio. **2** rounded handle on a door or drawer. **3** small amount of butter. **knobbly** *adj* covered with small bumps.

knock *v* **1** give a blow or push to. **2** rap audibly with the knuckles. **3** make or drive by striking. **4** *Informal* criticize adversely. **5** (of an engine) make a regular banging noise as a result of a fault. ♦ *n* **6** blow or rap. **7** knocking sound. **8** misfortune, rejection, or setback. **knocker** *n* metal fitting for knocking on a door. **knock about, around** *v* **1** wander or spend time aimlessly. **2** hit or kick brutally. **knockabout** *adj* (of comedy) boisterous. **knock back** *v Informal* **1** drink quickly. **2** cost. **3** reject or refuse. **knock down** *v* **1** demolish. **2** reduce the price of. **knockdown** *adj* (of a price) very low. **knock-knees** *pl n* legs that curve in at the knees. **knock-kneed** *adj* **knock off** *v* **1** *Informal* cease work. **2** *Informal* make or do (something) hurriedly or easily. **3** take (a specified amount) off a price. **4** *Informal* steal. **knock-on effect** indirect result of an action or decision. **knock out** *v* **1** render (someone) unconscious. **2** *Informal* overwhelm or amaze. **3** defeat in a knockout competition. **knockout** *n* **1** blow that renders an opponent unconscious. **2** competition from which competitors are progressively eliminated. **3** *Informal* overwhelmingly attractive person or thing. **knock up** *v* **1** *Informal* assemble (something) quickly. **2** *Informal* waken. **3** *Slang* make pregnant. **knock-up** *n* practice session at tennis, squash, or badminton.

knoll *n* small rounded hill.

knot *n* **1** fastening made by looping and pulling tight strands of string, cord, or rope. **2** tangle (of hair). **3** small cluster or huddled group. **4** round lump or spot in timber. **5** feeling of tightness, caused by tension or nervousness. **6** unit of speed used by ships, equal to one nautical mile per hour. ♦ *v* **knotting, knotted 7** tie with or into a knot. **knotty** *adj* **-tier, -tiest 1** full of knots. **2** puzzling or difficult.

know *v* **knowing, knew, known 1** be or feel certain of the truth of (information etc.). **2** be acquainted with. **3** have a grasp of or understand (a skill or language). **4** be aware of. **in the know** *Informal* informed or aware. **knowable** *adj* **knowing** *adj* suggesting secret knowledge. **knowingly** *adv* **1** deliberately. **2** in a way that suggests secret knowledge. **know-all** *n Informal* person who acts as if knowing more than other people. **know-how** *n Informal* ingenuity, aptitude, or skill.

knowledge *n* **1** facts or experiences known by a person. **2** state of knowing. **3** specific information on a subject. **knowledgeable, knowledgable** *adj* intelligent or well-informed. **knowledgeably, knowledgably** *adv*

knuckle *n* **1** bone at the finger joint. **2** knee joint of a calf or pig. **near the knuckle** *Informal* rather rude or offensive. **knuckle-duster** *n* metal appliance worn on the knuckles to add force to a blow. **knuckle under** *v* yield or submit.

KO knockout.

koala *n* tree-dwelling Australian marsupial with dense grey fur.

kohl *n* cosmetic powder used to darken the edges of the eyelids.

kook *n US informal* eccentric person. **kooky** *adj* **kookier, kookiest**

kookaburra *n* large Australian kingfisher with a cackling cry.

kopeck *n* former Russian monetary unit, one hundredth of a rouble.

kopje, koppie *n S Afr* small hill.

Koran *n* sacred book of Islam.

Korean *adj* **1** of North or South Korea or their language. ♦ *n* **2** person from North or South Korea. **3** language of North and South Korea.

kosher [**koh**-sher] *adj* **1** conforming to Jewish religious law, esp. (of food) to Jewish dietary law. **2** *Informal* legitimate or authentic. ♦ *n* **3** kosher food.

kowtow *v* be servile (towards).

kph kilometres per hour.

Kr *Chem* krypton.

kraal *n* S African village surrounded by a strong fence.

Kremlin *n* central government of Russia and, formerly, the Soviet Union.

krill *n, pl* **krill** small shrimplike sea creature.

krona *n, pl* **kronor** standard monetary unit of Sweden.

krone [**kroh**-na] *n, pl* **-ner** [-ner] standard monetary unit of Norway and Denmark.

krypton *n Chem* colourless gas present in the atmosphere and used in fluorescent lights.

KS Kansas.

kudos [**kyoo**-doss] *n* fame or credit.

kudu *n* African antelope with spiral horns.

Ku Klux Klan *n* secret organization of White Protestant Americans who use violence against African-Americans and Jews.

kumquat [**kumm**-kwott] *n* citrus fruit resembling a tiny orange.

kung fu *n* Chinese martial art combining hand, foot, and weapon techniques.

kW kilowatt.

kWh kilowatt-hour.

KY Kentucky.

L l

l litre.

L **1** large. **2** learner (driver). **3** the Roman numeral for fifty.

L. lake.

la *n Music* same as LAH.

La *Chem* lanthanum.

LA Louisiana.

lab *n Informal* short for LABORATORY.

Lab. Labour.

label *n* **1** piece of card or other material fixed to an object to show its ownership, destination, etc. **2** brief descriptive term. ♦ *v* **-elling, -elled 3** give a label to. **4** describe in a phrase.

labia *pl n, sing* **labium** four liplike folds of skin forming part of the female genitals. **labial** [**lay**-bee-al] *adj* of the lips.

laboratory *n, pl* **-ries** building or room designed for scientific research or for the teaching of practical science.

laborious *adj* involving great prolonged effort. **laboriously** *adv*

labour *n* **1** physical work or exertion. **2** workers in industry. **3** final stage of pregnancy, leading to childbirth. ♦ *v* **4** work hard. **5** make one's way with difficulty. **6** stress to excess or too persistently. **7** be at a disadvantage because of a mistake or false belief. **laboured** *adj* uttered or done with difficulty. **labourer** *n* person who labours, esp. someone doing manual work for wages. **Labour Party** major British political party advocating social equality.

labrador *n* large retriever dog with a usu. gold or black coat.

laburnum *n* ornamental tree with yellow hanging flowers.

labyrinth [**lab**-er-inth] *n* **1** complicated network of passages. **2** any complex system. **3** interconnecting cavities in the internal ear. **labyrinthine** *adj*

lace *n* **1** delicate decorative fabric made from threads woven into an open weblike pattern. **2** cord drawn through eyelets and tied. ♦ *v* **3** fasten with laces. **4** thread a cord or string through holes in something. **5** add a small amount of alcohol, a drug, etc. to (food or drink). **lacy** *adj* fine, like lace. **lace-ups** *pl n* shoes which fasten with laces.

lacerate [**lass**-er-rate] *v* tear (flesh). **laceration** *n*

lachrymose *adj* **1** tearful. **2** sad.

lack *n* **1** shortage or absence of something needed or wanted. ♦ *v* **2** need or be short of (something).

lackadaisical *adj* **1** lacking vitality and purpose. **2** lazy and careless in a dreamy way.

lackey *n* **1** servile follower. **2** uniformed male servant.

lacklustre *adj* lacking brilliance or vitality.

laconic *adj* using only a few words, terse. **laconically** *adv*

lacquer *n* **1** hard varnish for wood or metal. **2** clear sticky substance sprayed onto the hair to hold it in place. **lacquered** *adj*

lacrimal [**lack**-rim-al] *adj* of tears or the glands which produce them.

lacrosse *n* sport in which teams catch and throw a ball using long sticks with a pouched net at the end, in an attempt to score goals.

lactation *n* secretion of milk by female mammals to feed young. **lactic** *adj* of or derived from milk. **lactose** *n* white crystalline sugar found in milk.

lacuna [lak-**kew**-na] *n, pl* **-nae** gap or missing part, esp. in a document or series.

lad *n* boy or young man.

ladder *n* **1** frame of two poles connected by horizontal steps used for climbing. **2** system with ascending stages, e.g. *the social ladder.* **3** line of stitches that have come undone in tights or stockings. ♦ *v* **4** have or cause to have such a line of undone stitches.

laden *adj* **1** loaded. **2** burdened.

la-di-da, lah-di-dah *adj Informal* affected or pretentious.

ladle *n* **1** spoon with a long handle and a large bowl, used for serving soup etc. ♦ *v* **2** serve out.

lady *n, pl* **-dies** **1** woman regarded as having characteristics of good breeding or high rank. **2** polite term of address for a woman. **3** (**L-**) title of some female members of the nobility. **Our Lady** the Virgin Mary. **Lady Day** Feast of the Annunciation, March 25. **ladies, ladies' room** *n* women's public toilet. **lady-in-waiting** *n, pl* **ladies-in-waiting** female servant of a queen or princess. **ladykiller** *n Informal* man who is or thinks he is irresistible to women. **ladylike** *adj* polite and dignified. **Ladyship** *n* title used to address a Lady.

ladybird *n* small red beetle with black spots.

lag[1] *v* **lagging, lagged** **1** go too slowly, fall behind. ♦ *n* **2** delay between events. **laggard** *n* person who lags behind.

lag[2] *v* **lagging, lagged** wrap (a boiler, pipes, etc.) with insulating material. **lagging** *n* insulating material.

lag[3] *n* **old lag** *Slang* convict.

lager *n* light-bodied beer.

lagoon *n* body of water cut off from the open sea by coral reefs or sand bars.

lah *n Music* (in tonic sol-fa) sixth degree of any major scale.

laid *v* past of LAY[1]. **laid-back** *adj Informal* relaxed.

lain *v* past participle of LIE[2].

lair *n* **1** resting place of an animal. **2** *Informal* hiding place.

laird *n* Scottish landowner.

laissez-faire [less-ay-**fair**] *n* principle of nonintervention, esp. by a government in commercial affairs.

laity [**lay**-it-ee] *n* people who are not members of the clergy.

lake[1] *n* expanse of water entirely surrounded by land. **lakeside** *n*

lake[2] *n* red pigment.

lama *n* Buddhist priest in Tibet or Mongolia.

lamb *n* **1** young sheep. **2** its meat. ♦ *v* **3** (of sheep) give birth to a lamb or lambs. **lambskin** *n* **lambswool** *n*

lambast, lambaste *v* **1** beat or thrash. **2** reprimand severely.

lambent *adj Lit* (of a flame) flickering softly.

lame *adj* **1** having an injured or disabled leg or foot. **2** (of an excuse) unconvincing. ♦ *v* **3** make lame. **lamely** *adv* **lameness** *n* **lame duck** person or thing unable to cope without help.

lamé [**lah**-may] *n, adj* (fabric) interwoven with gold or silver thread.

lament *v* **1** feel or express sorrow (for). ♦ *n* **2** passionate expression of grief. **3** song of grief. **lamentable** *adj* very disappointing. **lamentation** *n* **lamented** *adj* grieved for.

laminate *v* **1** make (a sheet of material) by sticking together thin sheets. **2** cover with a thin sheet of material. **3** split or beat into thin sheets. ♦ *n* **4** laminated sheet. **laminated** *adj*

Lammas *n* August 1, formerly a harvest festival.

lamp *n* device which produces light from electricity, oil, or gas. **lamppost** *n* post supporting a lamp in the street. **lampshade** *n*

lampoon *n* **1** humorous satire ridiculing someone. ♦ *v* **2** satirize or ridicule.

lamprey *n* eel-like fish with a round sucking mouth.

lance *n* **1** long spear used by a mounted soldier. ♦ *v* **2** pierce (a boil or abscess) with a lancet. **lancer** *n* formerly, cavalry soldier armed with a lance. **lance corporal** noncommissioned army officer of the lowest rank.

lanceolate *adj* narrow and tapering to a point at each end.

lancet *n* **1** pointed two-edged surgical knife. **2** narrow window in the shape of a pointed arch.

land *n* **1** solid part of the earth's surface. **2** ground, esp. with reference to its type or use. **3** rural or agricultural area. **4** property consisting of land. **5** country or region. ♦ *v* **6** come or bring to earth after a flight, jump, or fall. **7** go or take from a ship at the end of a voyage. **8** come to or touch shore. **9** come or bring to some point or condition. **10** *Informal* obtain. **11** take (a hooked fish) from the water. **12** *Informal* deliver (a punch). **landed** *adj* possessing or consisting of lands. **landless** *adj* **landward** *adj* **1** nearest to or facing the land. ♦ *adv* **2** (also **landwards**) towards land. **landfall** *n* ship's first landing after a voyage. **landfill** *n* disposing of rubbish by covering it with earth. **landlocked** *adj* completely surrounded by land. **land mine** explosive device laid in the ground. **land up** *v* arrive at a final point or condition.

landau [**lan**-daw] *n* four-wheeled carriage with two folding hoods.

landing *n* **1** floor area at the top of a flight of stairs. **2** bringing or coming to land. **3** (also **landing stage**) place where people or goods go onto or come off a boat. **landing gear** undercarriage of an aircraft.

landlord, landlady *n* **1** person who rents out land, houses, etc. **2** owner or manager of a pub or boarding house.

landlubber *n* person who is not experienced at sea.

landmark *n* **1** prominent object in or feature of a landscape. **2** event, decision, etc. considered as an important development.

landscape *n* **1** extensive piece of inland scenery seen from one place. **2** picture of it. ♦ *v* **3** improve natural features of (a piece of land). **landscape gardener** person who designs gardens or parks so that they look attractive.

landslide *n* **1** (also **landslip**) falling of soil, rock, etc. down the side of a mountain. **2** overwhelming electoral victory.

lane *n* **1** narrow road. **2** area of road for one stream of traffic. **3** specified route followed by ships or aircraft. **4** strip of a running track or swimming pool for use by one competitor.

language *n* **1** system of sounds, symbols, etc. for communicating thought. **2** particular system used by a nation or people. **3** style or method of expression. **4** specialized words used by a particular group. **5** (also **programming language**) system of words and symbols for computer programming.

languid *adj* lacking energy or enthusiasm. **languidly** *adv*

languish *v* **1** suffer neglect or hardship. **2** lose or diminish in strength or vigour. **3** pine (for). **languishing** *adj*

languor [**lang**-ger] *n* **1** state of dreamy relaxation. **2** laziness or weariness. **languorous** *adj*

lank *adj* **1** (of hair) straight and limp. **2** thin or gaunt. **lanky** *adj* ungracefully tall and thin. **lankiness** *n*

lanolin *n* grease from sheep's wool used in ointments etc.

lantern *n* **1** light in a transparent protective case. **2** structure on top of a dome which lets in light. **3** upper part of a lighthouse that houses the light. **lantern jaw** long thin jaw. **lantern-jawed** *adj*

lanthanum *n Chem* silvery-white metallic element. **lanthanide series** class of 15 elements chemically related to lanthanum.

lanyard *n* **1** cord worn round the neck to hold a knife or whistle. **2** *Naut* short rope.

lap[1] *n* part between the waist and knees of a person when sitting. **in the lap of luxury** in conditions of great comfort and wealth. **laptop** *adj* (of a computer) small enough to fit on a user's lap.

lap[2] *n* **1** single circuit of a racecourse or track. **2** stage of a journey. ♦ *v* **lapping, lapped 3** overtake an opponent so as to be one or more circuits ahead.

lap[3] *v* **lapping, lapped** (of waves) beat softly against (a shore etc.). **lap up** *v* **1** drink by scooping up with the tongue. **2** accept (information or attention) eagerly.

lapel [lap-**pel**] *n* part of the front of a coat or jacket folded back towards the shoulders.

lapidary *adj* of or relating to stones.

lapis lazuli [**lap**-iss **lazz**-yoo-lie] *n* bright blue gemstone.

Lapp *n, adj* (member or language) of a people living chiefly in N Scandinavia.

lapse *n* **1** temporary drop in a standard, esp. through forgetfulness or carelessness. **2** instance of bad behaviour by someone usually well-behaved. **3** break in occurrence or usage. ♦ *v* **4** drop in standard. **5** end or become invalid, esp. through disuse. **6** drift (into a condition or habit). **7** abandon religious faith. **8** (of time) slip away. **lapsed** *adj*

lapwing *n* plover with a tuft of feathers on the head.

larboard *adj, n Old-fashioned* port (side of a ship).

larceny *n, pl* **-nies** *Law* theft.

larch *n* deciduous coniferous tree.

lard *n* **1** soft white fat obtained from a pig. ♦ *v* **2** insert strips of bacon in (meat) before cooking. **3** decorate (speech or writing) with strange words unnecessarily.

larder *n* storeroom for food.

large *adj* **1** great in size, number, or extent. **2** comprehensive. **at large 1** in general. **2** free, not confined. **3** fully. **largely** *adv* **largish** *adj* **large-scale** *adj* wide-ranging or extensive.

largesse, largess [lar-**jess**] *n* generous giving, esp. of money.

largo *n, pl* **-gos,** *adv Music* (piece to be played) in a slow and dignified manner.

lariat *n* **1** lasso. **2** rope for tethering animals.

lark[1] *n* small brown songbird, skylark.

lark[2] *n Informal* **1** harmless piece of mischief or fun. **2** unnecessary activity or job. **lark about** *v* play pranks.

larkspur *n* plant with spikes of blue, pink, or white flowers with spurs.

larva *n, pl* **-vae** insect in an immature stage, often resembling a worm. **larval** *adj*

larynx *n, pl* **larynges** part of the throat containing the vocal cords. **laryngeal** *adj* **laryngitis** *n* inflammation of the larynx.

lasagne, lasagna [laz-**zan**-ya] *n* **1** pasta in wide flat sheets. **2** dish made from layers of lasagne, meat, and cheese.

lascivious [lass-**iv**-ee-uss] *adj* showing or producing sexual desire. **lasciviously** *adv*

laser [**lay**-zer] *n* device that produces a very narrow intense beam of light, used for cutting very hard materials and in surgery etc.

lash[1] *n* **1** eyelash. **2** sharp blow with a whip. **3** flexible end of a whip. ♦ *v* **4** hit with a whip. **5** (of rain or waves) beat forcefully against. **6** attack verbally, scold. **7** flick or wave sharply to and fro. **8** urge as with a whip. **lash out** *v* **1** make a sudden physical or verbal attack. **2** *Informal* spend (money) extravagantly.

lash[2] *v* fasten or bind tightly with cord etc.

lashings *pl n Old-fashioned* large amounts.

lass, lassie *n* girl.

Lassa fever *n* serious African disease with high fever and muscular pains.

lassitude *n* physical or mental weariness.

lasso [lass-**oo**] *n, pl* **-sos, -soes 1** rope with a noose for catching cattle and horses. ♦ *v* **-soing, -soed 2** catch with a lasso.

last[1] *adj, adv* **1** coming at the end or after all others. **2** most recent(ly). ♦ *adj* **3** only remaining. ♦ *n* **4** last person or thing. **lastly** *adv* **last-ditch** *adj* done as a final resort. **Last Judgment** God's verdict on the destinies of all humans at the end of the world. **last post** army bugle-call played at sunset or funerals. **last straw** small irritation or setback that, coming after others, is too much to bear. **last word 1** final comment in an argument. **2** most recent or best example of something.

last[2] *v* **1** continue. **2** be sufficient for (a specified amount of time). **3** remain fresh, uninjured, or unaltered. **lasting** *adj*

last[3] *n* model of a foot on which shoes and boots are made or repaired.

lat. latitude.

latch *n* **1** fastening for a door with a bar and lever. **2** lock which can only be opened from the outside with a key. ♦ *v* **3** fasten with a latch. **latch onto** *v* become attached to (a person or idea).

late *adj* **1** after the normal or expected time. **2** towards the end of a period. **3** being at an advanced time. **4** recently dead. **5** recent. **6** former. ♦ *adv* **7** after the normal or expected time. **8** at a relatively advanced age. **9** recently. **lately** *adv* in recent times. **lateness** *n* **latish** *adj, adv* **latecomer** *n*

latent *adj* hidden and not yet developed. **latency** *n*

lateral [**lat**-ter-al] *adj* of or relating to the side or sides. **laterally** *adv* **lateral thinking** way of solving problems by apparently illogical methods.

latex *n* milky fluid found in some plants, esp. the rubber tree, used in making rubber.

lath *n* thin strip of wood used to support plaster, tiles, etc.

lathe *n* machine for turning wood or metal while it is being shaped.

lather *n* **1** froth of soap and water. **2** frothy sweat. **3** *Informal* state of agitation. ♦ *v* **4** make frothy. **5** rub with soap until lather appears.

Latin *n* **1** language of the ancient Romans. ♦ *adj* **2** of or in Latin. **3** of a people whose language derives from Latin. **4** of the Roman Catholic Church. **Latin America** parts of South and Central America whose official language is Spanish or Portuguese. **Latin American** *n, adj*

latitude *n* **1** angular distance measured in degrees N or S of the equator. **2** scope for freedom of action or thought. ♦ *pl* **3** regions considered in relation to their distance from the equator. **latitudinal** *adj*

latrine *n* toilet in a barracks or camp.

latter *adj* **1** second of two. **2** later. **3** recent. **latterly** *adv* **latter-day** *adj* modern.

> *Latter* is used for the last mentioned of two items. When there are more, use *last-named.*

lattice [**lat**-iss] *n* **1** framework of intersecting strips of wood, metal, etc. **2** gate, screen, etc. formed of such a framework. **latticed** *adj*

laud *v* praise or glorify. **laudable** *adj* praiseworthy. **laudably** *adv* **laudatory** *adj* praising or glorifying.

laudanum [**lawd**-a-num] *n* opium-based sedative.

laugh *v* **1** make inarticulate sounds with the voice expressing amusement, merriment, or scorn. **2** utter or express with laughter. ♦ *n* **3** act or instance of laughing. **4** *Informal* person or thing causing amusement. **laughable** *adj* ridiculously inadequate. **laughter** *n* sound or action of laughing. **laughing gas** nitrous oxide as an anaesthetic. **laughing stock** object of general derision. **laugh off** *v* treat (something serious or difficult) lightly.

launch[1] *v* **1** put (a ship or boat) into the water, esp. for the first time. **2** begin (a campaign, project, etc.). **3** put a new product on the market. **4** send (a missile or spacecraft) into space or the air. ♦ *n* **5** launching. **launcher** *n* **launch into** *v* start doing something enthusiastically. **launch out** *v* start doing something new.

launch[2] *n* open motorboat.

launder *v* **1** wash and iron (clothes and linen). **2** make (illegally obtained money) seem legal by passing it through foreign banks or legitimate businesses. **laundry** *n, pl* **-dries 1** clothes etc. for washing or which have recently been washed. **2** place for washing clothes and linen. **Launderette** *n* ® shop with coin-operated washing and drying machines.

laureate [**lor**-ee-at] *adj* see POET LAUREATE.

laurel *n* **1** glossy-leaved shrub, bay tree. ♦ *pl* **2** wreath of laurel, an emblem of victory or merit.

lava *n* molten rock thrown out by volcanoes, which hardens as it cools.

lavatory *n, pl* **-ries** toilet.

lavender *n* **1** shrub with fragrant flowers. ♦ *adj* **2** bluish-purple. **lavender water** light perfume made from lavender.

lavish *adj* **1** great in quantity or richness. **2** giving or spending generously. **3** extravagant. ♦ *v* **4** give or spend generously. **lavishly** *adv*

law *n* **1** rule binding on a community. **2** system of such rules. **3** *Informal* police. **4** invariable sequence of events in nature. **5** general principle deduced from facts. **lawful** *adj* allowed by law. **lawfully** *adv* **lawless** *adj* breaking the law, esp. in a violent way. **lawlessness** *n* **law-abiding** *adj* obeying the laws. **lawbreaker** *n* **Law Lords** members of the House of Lords who sit as the highest court of appeal. **lawsuit** *n* court case brought by one person or group against another.

lawn[1] *n* area of tended and mown grass. **lawn mower** machine for cutting grass. **lawn tennis** tennis, esp. when played on a grass court.

lawn[2] *n* fine linen or cotton fabric.

lawrencium *n Chem* element artificially produced from californium.

lawyer *n* professionally qualified legal expert.

lax *adj* not strict. **laxity** *n*

laxative *n, adj* (medicine) inducing the emptying of the bowels.

lay[1] *v* **laying, laid** **1** cause to lie. **2** devise or prepare. **3** set in a particular place or position. **4** attribute (blame). **5** put forward (a plan, argument, etc.). **6** (of a bird or reptile) produce eggs. **7** place (a bet). **8** arrange (a table) for a meal. **lay waste** devastate. **lay-by** *n* stopping place for traffic beside a road. **lay down** *v* **1** set down. **2** sacrifice. **3** formulate (a rule). **4** store (wine). **lay in** *v* accumulate and store. **lay into** *v Informal* attack or scold severely. **lay off** *v* dismiss staff during a slack period. **lay-off** *n* **lay on** *v* provide or supply. **lay out** *v* **1** arrange or spread out. **2** prepare (a corpse) for burial. **3** *Informal* spend money, esp. lavishly. **4** *Informal* knock unconscious. **layout** *n* arrangement, esp. of matter for printing or of a building. **lay up** *v* **1** *Informal* confine through illness. **2** store for future use.

> *Lay* and *lie* are often confused. *Lay* takes an object: *He laid down his weapon; lie* does not take an object: *I'm going to lie down.*

lay[2] *v* past tense of LIE[2]. **layabout** *n* lazy person.

lay[3] *adj* **1** of or involving people who are not clergymen. **2** nonspecialist. **layman, laywoman** *n* **1** person who is not a member of the clergy. **2** person without specialist knowledge.

lay[4] *n* short narrative poem designed to be sung.

layer *n* **1** single thickness of some substance, as a cover or coating on a surface. **2** laying hen. **3** shoot of a plant pegged down or partly covered with earth to encourage root growth. ♦ *v* **4** form a layer. **5** propagate plants by layers. **layered** *adj*

layette *n* clothes for a newborn baby.

laze *v* **1** be idle or lazy. ♦ *n* **2** time spent lazing.

lazy *adj* **lazier, laziest** **1** not inclined to work or exert oneself. **2** done in a relaxed manner without much effort. **3** (of movement) slow and gentle. **lazily** *adv* **laziness** *n* **lazybones** *n Informal* lazy person.

lb pound (weight).

lbw *Cricket* leg before wicket.

lea *n Poetic* meadow.

leach *v* remove or be removed from a substance by a liquid passing through it.

lead[1] *v* **leading, led** **1** guide or conduct. **2** cause to feel, think, or behave in a certain way. **3** be the most important person or thing in. **4** be, go, or play first. **5** (of a road, path, etc.) go towards. **6** control or direct. **7** result in. **8** pass or spend (one's life). ♦ *n* **9** first or most prominent place. **10** example or leadership. **11** amount by which a person or group is ahead of another. **12** clue. **13** length of leather or chain attached to a dog's collar to control it. **14** principal role or actor in a film, play, etc. **15** most important news story in a newspaper. **16** cable bringing current to an electrical device. ♦ *adj* **17** acting as a leader or lead. **leading** *adj* **1** principal. **2** in the first position. **leading light** important person in an organization. **leading question** question worded to prompt the answer desired. **lead-in** *n* introduction to a subject. **lead on** *v* lure or entice, esp. into wrongdoing. **lead up to** *v* act as a preliminary to.

lead[2] *n* **1** soft heavy grey metal. **2** (in a pencil) graphite. **3** lead weight on a line, used for sounding depths of water. ♦ *pl* **4** strips of lead used as a roof covering. ♦ *v* **5** cover or secure with lead. **leaded** *adj* (of windows) made from many small panes of glass held together by lead strips. **leaden** *adj* **1** heavy or sluggish. **2** dull grey. **3** made from lead.

leader *n* **1** person who leads. **2** (also **leading article**) article in a newspaper expressing editorial views. **3** principal first violinist of an orchestra. **leadership** *n*

leaf *n, pl* **leaves** **1** flat usu. green blade attached to the stem of a plant. **2** single sheet of paper in a book. **3** very thin sheet of metal. **4** extending flap on a table. **leafy** *adj* **leafless** *adj* **leaf mould** rich soil composed of decayed leaves. **leaf through** *v* turn pages without reading them.

leaflet *n* **1** sheet of printed matter for distribution. **2** small leaf.

league[1] *n* **1** association promoting the interests of its members. **2** association of sports clubs organizing competitions between its members. **3** *Informal* class or level.

league[2] *n Obs* measure of distance, about three miles.

leak *n* **1** hole or defect that allows the escape or entrance of liquid, gas, radiation, etc. **2** liquid etc. that escapes or enters. **3** disclosure of secrets. ♦ *v* **4** let liquid etc. in or out. **5** (of liquid etc.) find its way through a leak. **6** disclose secret information. **leakage** *n* act or instance of leaking. **leaky** *adj*

lean[1] *v* **leaning, leaned** *or* **leant** **1** rest against. **2** bend or slope from an upright position. **3** tend (towards). **leaning** *n* tendency. **lean on** *v* **1** *Informal* threaten or intimidate. **2** depend on for help or advice. **lean-to** *n* shed built against an existing wall.

lean[2] *adj* **1** thin but healthy-looking. **2** (of meat) lacking fat. **3** unproductive. ♦ *n* **4** lean part of meat. **leanness** *n*

leap *v* **leaping, leapt** *or* **leaped** **1** make a sudden powerful jump. ♦ *n* **2** sudden powerful jump. **3** abrupt increase, as in costs or prices. **leapfrog** *n* game in which a player vaults over another bending down. **leap year** year with February 29th as an extra day.

learn *v* **learning, learned** *or* **learnt** **1** gain skill or knowledge by study, practice, or teaching. **2** memorize (something). **3** find out or discover. **learned** *adj* **1** erudite, deeply read. **2** showing much learning. **learner** *n* **learning** *n* knowledge got by study.

lease *n* **1** contract by which land or property is rented for a stated time by the owner to a tenant. ♦ *v* **2** let or rent by lease. **new lease of life** prospect of renewed energy, health, or happiness. **leasehold** *n, adj* (land or property) held on lease. **leaseholder** *n*

leash *n* lead for a dog.

least *adj* **1** superlative of LITTLE. **2** smallest. ♦ *n* **3** smallest one. ♦ *adv* **4** in the smallest degree.

leather *n* **1** material made from specially treated animal skins. ♦ *adj* **2** made of leather. ♦ *v* **3** beat or thrash. **leathery** *adj* like leather, tough.

leave[1] *v* **leaving, left** **1** go away from. **2** allow to remain, accidentally or deliberately. **3** cause to be or remain in a specified state. **4** discontinue membership of. **5** permit. **6** entrust. **7** bequeath. **leavings** *pl n* something remaining, such as refuse. **leave out** *v* exclude or omit.

leave[2] *n* **1** permission to be absent from work or duty. **2** period of such absence. **3** permission to do something. **4** formal parting.

leaven [**lev**-ven] *n* **1** substance that causes dough to rise. **2** influence that produces a gradual change. ♦ *v* **3** raise with leaven. **4** spread through and influence (something).

lecherous [**letch**-er-uss] *adj* (of a man) having or showing excessive sexual desire. **lecher** *n* **lechery** *n*

lectern *n* sloping reading desk, esp. in a church.

lecture *n* **1** informative talk to an audience on a subject. **2** lengthy rebuke or scolding. ♦ *v* **3** give a talk. **4** scold. **lecturer** *n* **lectureship** *n* appointment as a lecturer.

led *v* past of LEAD[1].

LED light-emitting diode.

ledge *n* **1** narrow shelf sticking out from a wall. **2** shelflike projection from a cliff etc.

ledger *n* book of debit and credit accounts of a firm. **ledger line** *Music* short line above or below the staff for notes outside the range of the staff.

lee *n* **1** sheltered part or side. ♦ *adj* **2** away from the wind. **leeward** *adj, n* **1** (on) the lee side. ♦ *adv* **2** towards this side. **leeway** *n* **1** room for free movement within limits. **2** sideways drift of a boat or plane.

leech *n* **1** species of bloodsucking worm. **2** person who lives off others.

leek *n* vegetable of the onion family with a long bulb and thick stem.

leer *v* **1** look or grin at in a sneering or suggestive manner. ♦ *n* **2** sneering or suggestive look or grin.

leery *adj Informal* suspicious or wary (of).

lees *pl n* sediment of wine.

left[1] *adj* **1** of the side that faces west when the front faces north. ♦ *adv* **2** on or towards the left. ♦ *n* **3** left hand or part. **4** *Politics* people supporting socialism rather than capitalism. **leftist** *n, adj* (person) of the political left. **left-handed** *adj* **1** more adept with the left hand than with the right. **2** done with the left hand. **3** designed for use by the left hand. **left-wing** *adj* **1** socialist. **2** belonging to the more radical part of a political party. **left-winger** *n*

left[2] *v* past of LEAVE[1].

leftover *n* unused portion of food or material.

leg *n* **1** one of the limbs on which a person or animal walks, runs, or stands. **2** part of a garment covering the leg. **3** structure that supports, such as one of the legs of a table. **4** stage of a journey. **5** *Sport* (part of) one game or race in a series. **6** *Cricket* part of the field to the left of a right-handed batsman. **pull someone's leg** tease someone. **leggy** *adj* having long legs. **legless** *adj* **1** without legs. **2** *Slang* very drunk. **leggings** *pl n* **1** covering of leather or other material for the legs. **2** close-fitting trousers for women or children.

legacy *n, pl* **-cies** **1** thing left in a will. **2** thing handed down to a successor.

legal *adj* **1** established or permitted by law. **2** relating to law or lawyers. **legally** *adv* **legalistic** *adj* showing strict adherence to the letter of the law. **legality** *n* **legalize** *v* make legal. **legalization** *n*

legate *n* messenger or representative, esp. from the Pope. **legation** *n* **1** diplomatic minister and his staff. **2** official residence of a diplomatic minister.

legatee *n* recipient of a legacy.

legato [leg-**ah**-toe] *n, pl* **-tos,** *adv Music* (piece to be played) smoothly.

legend *n* **1** traditional story or myth. **2** traditional literature. **3** famous person or event. **4** stories about such a person or event. **5** inscription. **6** explanation of symbols on a map etc. **legendary** *adj* **1** famous. **2** of or in legend.

legerdemain [lej-er-de-**main**] *n* **1** sleight of hand. **2** cunning deception.

legible *adj* easily read. **legibility** *n* **legibly** *adv*

legion *n* **1** large military force. **2** large number. **3** association of veterans. **4** infantry unit in the Roman army. **legionary** *adj, n* **legionnaire** *n* member of a legion. **legionnaire's disease** serious bacterial disease similar to pneumonia.

legislate *v* make laws. **legislation** *n* **1** legislating. **2** laws made. **legislative** *adj* **legislator** *n* maker of laws. **legislature** *n* body of people that makes, amends, or repeals laws.

legitimate *adj* **1** authorized by or in accordance with law. **2** fairly deduced. **3** born to parents married to each other. ♦ *v* **4** make legitimate. **legitimacy** *n* **legitimately** *adv* **legitimize** *v* make legitimate, legalize. **legitimization** *n*

Lego *n* ® construction toy of plastic bricks fitted together by studs.

leguaan *n* large S African lizard.

legume *n* **1** pod of a plant of the pea or bean family. ♦ *pl* **2** peas or beans. **leguminous** *adj* (of plants) pod-bearing.

lei *n* (in Hawaii) garland of flowers.

leisure *n* time for relaxation or hobbies. **at one's leisure** when one has time. **leisurely** *adj* **1** deliberate, unhurried. ♦ *adv* **2** slowly. **leisured** *adj* with plenty of spare time. **leisure centre** building with facilities such as a swimming pool, gymnasium, and café.

leitmotif [**lite**-mote-eef] *n Music* recurring theme associated with a person, situation, or thought.

lemming *n* rodent of arctic regions, reputed to run into the sea and drown during mass migrations.

lemon *n* **1** yellow oval fruit that grows on trees. **2** *Slang* useless or defective person or thing. ♦ *adj* **3** pale-yellow. **lemonade** *n* lemon-flavoured soft drink, often fizzy. **lemon curd** creamy spread made of lemons, butter, etc. **lemon sole** edible flatfish.

lemur *n* nocturnal animal like a small monkey, found in Madagascar.

lend *v* **lending, lent 1** give the temporary use of. **2** provide (money) temporarily, often for interest. **3** add (a quality or effect), e.g. *her presence lent beauty to the scene.* **lend itself to** be suitable for. **lender** *n*

length *n* **1** extent or measurement from end to end. **2** period of time for which something happens. **3** quality of being long. **4** piece of something narrow and long. **at length 1** at last. **2** in full detail. **lengthy** *adj* very long or tiresome. **lengthily** *adv* **lengthen** *v* make or become longer. **lengthways, lengthwise** *adj, adv*

lenient [**lee**-nee-ent] *adj* tolerant, not strict or severe. **leniency** *n* **leniently** *adv*

lens *n, pl* **lenses 1** piece of glass or similar material with one or both sides curved, used to bring together or spread light rays in cameras, spectacles, telescopes, etc. **2** transparent structure in the eye that focuses light.

lent *v* past of LEND.

Lent *n* period from Ash Wednesday to Easter Saturday. **Lenten** *adj* of, in, or suitable to Lent.

lentil *n* edible seed of a leguminous Asian plant.

lento *n, pl* **-tos,** *adv Music* (piece to be played) slowly.

Leo *n* (the lion) fifth sign of the zodiac.

leonine *adj* like a lion.

leopard *n* large spotted carnivorous animal of the cat family. **leopardess** *n fem*

leotard *n* tight-fitting garment covering most of the body, worn for dancing or exercise.

leper *n* **1** person suffering from leprosy. **2** ignored or despised person.

lepidoptera *pl n* order of insects with four wings covered with fine gossamer scales, as moths and butterflies. **lepidopterous** *adj* **lepidopterist** *n* person who studies or collects butterflies or moths.

leprechaun *n* mischievous elf of Irish folklore.

leprosy *n* disease attacking the nerves and skin, resulting in loss of feeling in the affected parts. **leprous** *adj*

lesbian *n* **1** homosexual woman. ♦ *adj* **2** of homosexual women. **lesbianism** *n*

lese-majesty [lezz-**maj**-est-ee] *n* **1** treason. **2** taking of liberties against people in authority.

lesion *n* **1** structural change in an organ of the body caused by illness or injury. **2** injury or wound.

less *adj* **1** smaller in extent, degree, or duration. **2** not so much. **3** comparative of LITTLE. ♦ *pron* **4** smaller part or quantity. ♦ *adv* **5** to a smaller extent or degree. ♦ *prep* **6** after deducting, minus. **lessen** *v* make or become smaller or not as much. **lesser** *adj* not as great in quantity, size, or worth.

> Avoid confusion with *few(er)*. *Less* is used with amounts that cannot be counted: *less time; less fuss*. *Few(er)* is used of things that can be counted.

lessee *n* person to whom a lease is granted.

lesson *n* **1** single period of instruction in a subject. **2** content of this. **3** experience that teaches. **4** portion of Scripture read in church.

lest *conj* **1** so as to prevent any possibility that. **2** for fear that.

let[1] *v* **letting, let 1** allow, enable, or cause. **2** used as an auxiliary to express a proposal, command, threat, or assumption. **3** grant use of for rent, lease. **4** allow to escape. ♦ *n* **5** act of letting property. **let alone** not to mention. **let down** *v* **1** disappoint. **2** lower. **3** deflate. **letdown** *n* disappointment. **let off** *v* **1** excuse from (a duty or punishment). **2** fire or explode (a weapon). **3** emit (gas, steam, etc.). **let on** *v Informal* reveal (a secret). **let out** *v* **1** emit. **2** release. **3** rent out. **let up** *v* diminish or stop. **let-up** *n* lessening.

let[2] *n* **1** *Tennis* minor infringement or obstruction of the ball requiring a replay of the point. **2** hindrance.

lethal *adj* deadly.

lethargy *n* **1** sluggishness or dullness. **2** abnormal lack of energy. **lethargic** *adj* **lethargically** *adv*

letter *n* **1** written message, usu. sent by post. **2** alphabetical symbol. **3** strict meaning (of a law etc.). ♦ *pl* **4** literary knowledge or ability. **lettered** *adj* learned. **lettering** *n* **letter bomb** explosive device in a parcel or letter that explodes on opening. **letter box 1** slot in a door through which letters are delivered. **2** box in a street or post office where letters are posted. **letterhead** *n* printed heading on stationery giving the sender's name and address.

lettuce *n* plant with large green leaves used in salads.

leucocyte [**loo**-koh-site] *n* white blood cell.

leukaemia [loo-**kee**-mee-a] *n* disease caused by uncontrolled overproduction of white blood cells.

levee *n US* natural or artificial river embankment.

level *adj* **1** horizontal. **2** having an even surface. **3** of the same height as something else. **4** equal to or even with (someone or something else). **5** not going above the top edge of (a spoon etc.). **6** not irregular. ♦ *v* **-elling, -elled 7** make even or horizontal. **8** make equal in position or status. **9** direct (a gun, accusation, etc.) at. **10** raze to the ground. ♦ *n* **11** horizontal line or surface. **12** device for showing or testing if something is horizontal. **13** position on a scale. **14** standard or grade. **15** flat area of land. **on the level** *Informal* honest or trustworthy. **level crossing** point where a railway line and road cross. **level-headed** *adj* not apt to be carried away by emotion.

lever *n* **1** handle used to operate machinery. **2** bar used to move a heavy object or to open something. **3** rigid bar pivoted about a fulcrum to transfer a force to a load. **4** means of exerting pressure to achieve an aim. ♦ *v* **5** prise or move with a lever. **leverage** *n* **1** action or power of a lever. **2** influence or strategic advantage.

leveret [**lev**-ver-it] *n* young hare.

leviathan [lev-**vie**-ath-an] *n* **1** sea monster. **2** anything huge or formidable.

Levis *pl n* ® denim jeans.

levitation *n* raising of a solid body into

the air supernaturally. **levitate** *v* rise or cause to rise into the air.

levity *n, pl* **-ties** inclination to make a joke of serious matters.

levy [**lev**-vee] *v* **levying, levied 1** impose and collect (a tax). **2** raise (troops). ♦ *n, pl* **levies 3** imposition or collection of taxes. **4** money levied. **5** troops conscripted for service.

lewd *adj* lustful or indecent. **lewdly** *adv* **lewdness** *n*

lexicon *n* **1** dictionary. **2** vocabulary of a language. **lexical** *adj* relating to the vocabulary of a language. **lexicographer** *n* writer of dictionaries. **lexicography** *n*

LGV large goods vehicle.

Li *Chem* lithium.

liable *adj* **1** legally obliged or responsible. **2** given to or at risk from a condition. **liability** *n* **1** hindrance or disadvantage. **2** state of being liable. **3** financial obligation.

> The use of *liable* to mean 'likely' is informal. It generally means 'responsible for': *He was liable for any damage.*

liaise *v* establish and maintain communication (with). **liaison** *n* **1** communication and contact between groups. **2** secret or adulterous relationship.

liana *n* climbing plant in tropical forests.

liar *n* person who tells lies.

lib *n Informal* short for LIBERATION.

Lib. Liberal.

libation [lie-**bay**-shun] *n* drink poured as an offering to the gods.

libel *n* **1** published statement falsely damaging a person's reputation. ♦ *v* **-belling, -belled 2** falsely damage the reputation of (someone). **libellous** *adj*

liberal *adj* **1** having social and political views that favour progress and reform. **2** generous in behaviour or temperament. **3** tolerant. **4** abundant. **5** not rigid. **6** (of education) designed to develop general cultural interests. ♦ *n* **7** person who has liberal ideas or opinions. **liberally** *adv* **liberalism** *n* belief in democratic reforms and individual freedom. **liberality** *n* **1** generosity. **2** quality of being broad-minded. **liberalize** *v* make (laws, a country, etc.) less restrictive. **liberalization** *n* **Liberal Democrat** member of the Liberal Democrats, a British political party favouring a regulated market or mixed economy.

liberate *v* set free. **liberation** *n* **liberator** *n*

libertarian *n* **1** believer in freedom of thought and action. ♦ *adj* **2** having such a belief.

libertine [**lib**-er-teen] *n* morally dissolute person.

liberty *n, pl* **-ties 1** freedom. **2** act or comment regarded as forward or socially unacceptable. **at liberty 1** free. **2** having the right. **take liberties** be presumptuous.

libido [lib-**ee**-doe] *n, pl* **-dos 1** psychic energy. **2** emotional drive, esp. of sexual origin. **libidinal** *adj* **libidinous** *adj* lustful.

Libra *n* (the scales) seventh sign of the zodiac.

library *n, pl* **-braries 1** room or building where books are kept. **2** collection of books, records, etc. for consultation or borrowing. **3** set of books published in a series. **librarian** *n* keeper of or worker in a library. **librarianship** *n*

libretto *n, pl* **-tos, -ti** words of an opera. **librettist** *n*

lice *n* a plural of LOUSE.

licence *n* **1** document giving official permission to do something. **2** formal permission. **3** disregard of conventions for effect, e.g. *poetic licence.* **4** excessive liberty. **license** *v* grant a licence to. **licensed** *adj* **licensee** *n* holder of a licence, esp. to sell alcohol.

> Note the *-ce* ending for the noun *licence,* with *-se* for the verb *license.*

licentiate *n* person licensed as competent to practise a profession.

licentious *adj* sexually unrestrained or promiscuous. **licentiousness** *n*

lichen *n* small flowerless plant forming a crust on rocks, trees, etc.

licit *adj* lawful, permitted.

lick *v* **1** pass the tongue over. **2** touch lightly or flicker round. **3** *Slang* defeat. **4** *Slang* thrash. ♦ *n* **5** licking. **6** small amount (of paint etc.). **7** *Informal* blow. **8** *Informal* fast pace.

licorice *n* same as LIQUORICE.

lid *n* **1** movable cover. **2** short for EYELID.

lido [**lee**-doe] *n, pl* **-dos** open-air centre for swimming and water sports.

lie[1] *v* **lying, lied 1** make a deliberately false statement. **2** give a false impression. ♦ *n* **3** deliberate falsehood. **white lie** see WHITE.

lie[2] *v* **lying, lay, lain 1** place oneself or be in a horizontal position. **2** be situated. **3** be or remain in a certain state or position. **4** exist or be found. ♦ *n* **5** way something lies. **lie-down** *n* rest. **lie in** *v* remain in bed late into the morning. **lie-in** *n* long stay in bed in the morning.

> Note that the past of *lie* is *lay: She lay on the beach all day.* Do not confuse with the main verb *lay* meaning 'put'.

lied [**leed**] *n, pl* **lieder** *Music* setting for voice and piano of a romantic poem.

liege [**leej**] *adj* **1** bound to give or receive feudal service. ♦ *n* **2** lord.

lien *n* right to hold another's property until a debt is paid.

lieu [**lyew**] *n* **in lieu of** instead of.

lieutenant [lef-**ten**-ant] *n* **1** junior officer in the army or navy. **2** main assistant.

life *n, pl* **lives 1** state of living beings, characterized by growth, reproduction, and response to stimuli. **2** period between birth and death or between birth and the present time. **3** living person. **4** way of living. **5** sentence of imprisonment for life. **6** amount of time something is active or functions. **7** biography. **8** liveliness or high spirits. **9** living beings collectively. **lifeless** *adj* **1** dead. **2** not lively or exciting. **3** unconscious. **lifelike** *adj* **lifelong** *adj* lasting all of a person's life. **lifer** *n Informal* prisoner sentenced to imprisonment for life. **life belt, jacket** buoyant device to keep afloat a person in danger of drowning. **lifeblood** *n* **1** blood vital to life. **2** vital thing for success or development. **lifeboat** *n* boat used for rescuing people at sea. **life cycle** series of changes undergone by each generation of an animal or plant. **lifeguard** *n* person who saves people from drowning. **lifeline** *n* **1** means of contact or support. **2** rope used in rescuing a person in danger. **life science** any science concerned with living organisms, such as biology, botany, or zoology. **life-size, life-sized** *adj* representing actual size. **lifestyle** *n* particular attitudes, habits, etc. **life-support** *adj* (of equipment or treatment) necessary to keep a person alive. **lifetime** *n* length of time a person is alive.

lift *v* **1** move upwards in position, status, volume, etc. **2** revoke or cancel. **3** take (plants) out of the ground for harvesting. **4** disappear. **5** make or become more cheerful. **6** *Informal* plagiarize (music or writing). ♦ *n* **7** cage raised and lowered in a vertical shaft to transport people or goods. **8** ride in a car etc. as a passenger. **9** *Informal* feeling of cheerfulness. **10** lifting. **liftoff** *n* moment a rocket leaves the ground.

ligament *n* band of tissue joining bones.

ligature *n* **1** link, bond, or tie. **2** *Printing* two or more joined letters.

light[1] *n* **1** electromagnetic radiation by which things are visible. **2** source of this, lamp. **3** anything that lets in light, such as a window. **4** aspect or view. **5** mental vision. **6** brightness of countenance. **7** means of setting fire to. ♦ *pl* **8** traffic lights. ♦ *adj* **9** bright. **10** (of a colour) pale. ♦ *v* **lighting, lighted** *or* **lit 11** ignite. **12** illuminate or cause to illuminate. **13** guide by a light. **lighten** *v* make less dark. **lighting** *n* apparatus for and use of artificial light in theatres, films, etc. **light bulb** glass part of an electric lamp. **lighthouse** *n* tower with a light to guide ships. **lightship** *n* moored ship used as a lighthouse. **light up** *v* **1** illuminate. **2** make or become cheerful. **3** light a cigarette or pipe. **light year** *Astronomy* distance light travels in one year, about six million million miles.

light[2] *adj* **1** not heavy, weighing relatively little. **2** relatively low in strength, amount, density, etc. **3** lacking sufficient weight. **4** not clumsy. **5** not serious or profound. **6** easily digested. **7** free from care, cheerful. ♦ *adv* **8** with little equipment or luggage. ♦ *v* **lighting, lighted, lit 9** (esp. of birds) settle after flight. **10** come (upon) by chance. **lightly** *adv* **lightness** *n* **lighten** *v* **1** make less heavy or burdensome. **2** make more cheerful or lively. **light-fingered** *adj* skilful at stealing. **light-headed** *adj* feeling faint, dizzy. **light-hearted** *adj* carefree. **light heavyweight** boxer weighing up to 175lb (professional) or 81kg (amateur). **lightweight** *n, adj* **1** (person) of little importance. ♦ *n* **2** boxer weighing up to 135lb (professional) or 60kg (amateur).

lighter[1] *n* device for lighting cigarettes etc.

lighter[2] *n* flat-bottomed boat for unloading ships.

lightning *n* **1** visible discharge of electricity in the atmosphere. ♦ *adj* **2** fast and sudden. **lightning conductor** metal rod attached to the top of a building to divert lightning safely to earth.

lights *pl n* lungs of animals as animal food.

ligneous *adj* of or like wood.

lignite [**lig**-nite] *n* woody textured rock used as fuel.

like[1] *prep, conj, adj, pron* indicating similarity, comparison, etc. **liken** *v* compare. **likeness** *n* **1** resemblance. **2** portrait. **likewise** *adv* similarly.

like[2] *v* **1** find enjoyable. **2** be fond of. **3** prefer, choose, or wish. **likeable, likable** *adj* **liking** *n* **1** fondness. **2** preference.

likely *adj* **1** tending or inclined. **2** probable. **3** hopeful, promising. ♦ *adv* **4** probably. **not likely** *Informal* definitely not. **likelihood** *n* probability.

lilac *n* **1** shrub with pale mauve or white flowers. ♦ *adj* **2** light-purple.

Lilliputian [lil-lip-**pew**-shun] *adj* tiny.

Lilo *n, pl* **-los** ® inflatable rubber mattress.

lilt *n* **1** pleasing musical quality in speaking. **2** jaunty rhythm. **3** graceful rhythmic motion. ♦ *v* **4** speak with a lilt. **lilting** *adj*

lily *n, pl* **lilies** plant which grows from a bulb and has large, often white, flowers. **lily of the valley** small plant with fragrant white flowers.

limb *n* **1** arm, leg, or wing. **2** main branch of a tree. **out on a limb** in a dangerous or isolated position.

limber *adj* pliant or supple. **limber up** *v* loosen stiff muscles by exercising.

limbo[1] *n, pl* **-bos** supposed region intermediate between Heaven and Hell for the unbaptized. **in limbo** not knowing the result or next stage of something and powerless to influence it.

limbo[2] *n, pl* **-bos** West Indian dance in which dancers lean backwards to pass under a bar.

lime[1] *n* calcium compound used as a fertilizer or in making cement. **limelight** *n* glare of publicity. **limestone** *n* sedimentary rock used in building.

lime[2] *n* small green citrus fruit. **lime-green** *adj* greenish-yellow.

lime[3] *n* deciduous tree with heart-shaped leaves and fragrant flowers.

limerick [**lim**-mer-ik] *n* humorous verse of five lines.

limey *n US slang* British person.

limit *n* **1** ultimate extent, degree, or amount of something. **2** boundary or edge. ♦ *v* **-iting, -ited 3** restrict or confine. **limitation** *n* **limitless** *adj* **limited company** company whose shareholders' liability for debts is restricted. **limited edition** edition of a book, record, etc. which has been restricted to a particular number of copies.

limn *v* represent in drawing or painting.

limousine *n* large luxurious car.

limp[1] *v* **1** walk with an uneven step. **2** proceed with difficulty. ♦ *n* **3** limping walk.

limp[2] *adj* **1** without firmness or stiffness. **2** lacking strength or energy. **limply** *adv*

limpet *n* shellfish which sticks tightly to rocks.

limpid *adj* **1** clear or transparent. **2** easy to understand. **limpidity** *n*

linchpin, lynchpin *n* **1** pin to hold a wheel on its axle. **2** essential person or thing.

linctus *n, pl* **-tuses** syrupy cough medicine.

linden *n* same as LIME[3].

line[1] *n* **1** long narrow mark. **2** indented mark or wrinkle. **3** continuous length without breadth. **4** boundary or limit. **5** mark on a sports ground showing divisions of a pitch or track. **6** edge or contour of a shape. **7** string or wire for a particular use. **8** telephone connection. **9** wire or cable for transmitting electricity. **10** shipping company. **11** railway track. **12** course or direction of movement. **13** course or method of action. **14** prescribed way of thinking. **15** field of interest or activity. **16** row or queue of people. **17** class of goods. **18** row of words. **19** unit of verse. **20** military formation. ♦ *pl* **21** words of a theatrical part. **22** school punishment of writing out a sentence a specified number of times. ♦ *v* **23** mark with lines. **24** be or form a border or edge. **in line for** likely to receive. **in line with** in accordance with. **line-up** *n* people or things assembled for a particular purpose. **line up** *v* form or organize a line-up.

line[2] *v* **1** give a lining to. **2** cover the inside of.

lineage [**lin**-ee-ij] *n* descent from an ancestor. **lineal** *adj* in direct line of descent.

lineament *n* facial feature.

linear [**lin**-ee-er] *adj* of or in lines.

linen *n* **1** cloth or thread made from flax. **2** sheets, tablecloths, etc.

liner[1] *n* large passenger ship or aircraft.

liner[2] *n* something used as a lining.

linesman *n* **1** (in some sports) an official who helps the referee or umpire. **2** person who maintains railway, electricity, or telephone lines.

ling[1] *n* slender food fish.

ling[2] *n* heather.

linger *v* **1** delay or prolong departure. **2** continue in a weakened state for a long time before dying or disappearing. **3** spend a long time doing something. **lingering** *adj*

lingerie [**lan**-zher-ee] *n* women's underwear or nightwear.

lingo *n, pl* **-goes** *Informal* foreign or unfamiliar language or jargon.

lingua franca *n, pl* **lingua francas, linguae francae** language used for communication between people of different mother tongues.

lingual *adj* **1** of the tongue. **2** (of a sound) made by the tongue.

linguist *n* **1** person skilled in foreign languages. **2** person who studies linguistics. **linguistic** *adj* of languages. **linguistics** *n* scientific study of language.

liniment *n* medicated liquid rubbed on the skin to relieve pain or stiffness.

lining *n* **1** layer of cloth attached to the inside of a garment etc. **2** inner covering of anything.

link *n* **1** any of the rings forming a chain. **2** person or thing forming a connection. ♦ *v* **3** connect with or as if with links. **4** connect by association. **linkage** *n* **link-up** *n* joining together of two systems or groups.

links *pl n* golf course, esp. one by the sea.

linnet *n* songbird of the finch family.

lino *n* short for LINOLEUM.

linoleum *n* floor covering of hessian or jute with a smooth decorative coating of powdered cork.

Linotype *n* ® typesetting machine which casts lines of words in one piece.

linseed *n* seed of the flax plant.

lint *n* soft material for dressing a wound.

lintel *n* horizontal beam at the top of a door or window.

lion *n* **1** large animal of the cat family, the male of which has a shaggy mane. **2** courageous person. **lioness** *n fem* **the lion's share** the biggest part. **lionize** *v* treat as a celebrity. **lion-hearted** *adj* brave.

lip *n* **1** either of the fleshy edges of the mouth. **2** rim of a jug etc. **3** *Slang* impudence. **lip-reading** *n* method of understanding speech by interpreting lip movements. **lip-read** *v* **lip service** insincere tribute or respect. **lipstick** *n* cosmetic in stick form, for colouring the lips.

liquefy *v* **-fying, -fied** make or become liquid. **liquefaction** *n*

liqueur [lik-**cure**] *n* flavoured and sweetened alcoholic spirit.

liquid *n* **1** substance in a physical state which can change shape but not size. ♦ *adj* **2** of or being a liquid. **3** transparent and shining. **4** flowing smoothly. **5** (of assets) in the form of money or easily converted into money. **liquidize** *v* make or become liquid. **liquidizer** *n* kitchen appliance that liquidizes food. **liquidity** *n* state of being able to meet financial obligations.

liquidate *v* **1** pay (a debt). **2** dissolve a company and share its assets among creditors. **3** wipe out or kill. **liquidation** *n* **liquidator** *n* official appointed to liquidate a business.

liquor *n* **1** alcoholic drink, esp. spirits. **2** liquid in which food has been cooked.

liquorice [**lik**-ker-iss] *n* black substance used in medicine and as a sweet.

lira *n, pl* **-re, -ras** monetary unit of Italy and Turkey.

lisle [rhymes with **mile**] *n* strong fine cotton thread or fabric.

lisp *n* **1** speech defect in which *s* and *z* are pronounced *th*. ♦ *v* **2** speak or utter with a lisp.

lissom, lissome *adj* supple, agile.

list[1] *n* **1** item-by-item record of names or things, usu. written one below another. ♦ *v* **2** make a list of. **3** include in a list. **listed building** building protected from demolition or alteration because of its historical or architectural interest.

list[2] *v* **1** (of a ship) lean to one side. ♦ *n* **2** leaning to one side.

listen *v* **1** concentrate on hearing something. **2** heed or pay attention to. **listener** *n* **listen in** *v* listen secretly, eavesdrop.

listeriosis *n* dangerous form of food poisoning.

listing *n* **1** list or an entry in a list. ♦ *pl* **2** lists of films, concerts, etc. printed in newspapers and magazines.

listless *adj* lacking interest or energy. **listlessly** *adv*

lists *pl n* field of combat in a tournament. **enter the lists** engage in a conflict.

lit *v* past of LIGHT[1] *or* LIGHT[2].

litany *n, pl* **-nies** **1** prayer with responses from the congregation. **2** any tedious recital.

literacy *n* ability to read and write.

literal *adj* **1** according to the explicit meaning of a word or text, not figurative. **2** (of a translation) word for word. **3** dull or unimaginative. **4** actual, true. **literally** *adv*

> Note that *literally* means much the same as 'actually'. It is very loosely used to mean 'just about' but this can be ambiguous.

literary *adj* **1** of or knowledgeable about literature. **2** (of a word) formal, not colloquial. **literariness** *n*

literate *adj* **1** able to read and write. **2** educated. **literati** *pl n* literary people.

literature *n* **1** written works such as novels, plays, and poetry. **2** books and writings of a country, period, or subject. **3** printed matter on a subject.

lithe *adj* flexible or supple, pliant.

lithium *n Chem* chemical element, the lightest known metal.

litho *n, pl* **-thos** **1** short for LITHOGRAPH. ♦ *adj* **2** short for LITHOGRAPHIC.

lithography [lith-**og**-ra-fee] *n* method of printing from a metal or stone surface in which the printing areas are made receptive to ink. **lithograph** *n* **1** print made by lithography. ♦ *v* **2** reproduce by lithography. **lithographer** *n* **lithographic** *adj*

litigate *v* **1** bring or contest a law suit. **2** engage in legal action. **litigant** *n* person involved in a lawsuit. **litigation** *n* legal action. **litigious** [lit-**ij**-uss] *adj* frequently going to law.

litmus *n* blue dye turned red by acids and restored to blue by alkalis. **litmus paper** paper impregnated with litmus. **litmus test** something which is regarded as a simple and accurate test of a particular thing.

litotes [lie-**toe**-teez] *n* ironical understatement used for effect.

litre *n* unit of liquid measure equal to 1.76 pints.

litter *n* **1** untidy rubbish dropped in public places. **2** group of young animals produced at one birth. **3** straw etc. as bedding for an animal. **4** dry material to absorb a cat's excrement. **5** bed or seat on parallel sticks for carrying people. ♦ *v* **6** strew with litter. **7** scatter or be scattered about untidily. **8** give birth to young.

little *adj* **1** small or smaller than average. **2** young. ♦ *adv* **3** not a lot. **4** hardly. **5** not much or often. ♦ *n* **6** small amount, extent, or duration. **little by little** by small degrees.

littoral *adj* **1** of or by the seashore. ♦ *n* **2** coastal district.

liturgy *n, pl* **-gies** prescribed form of public worship. **liturgical** *adj*

live[1] *v* **1** be alive. **2** remain in life or existence. **3** exist in a specified way, e.g. *we live well.* **4** reside. **5** continue or last. **6** subsist. **7** enjoy life to the full. **liver** *n* person who lives in a specified way. **live down** *v* wait till people forget a past mistake or misdeed. **live-in** *adj* resident. **live together** *v* (of an unmarried couple) share a house and have a sexual relationship. **live up to** *v* meet (expectations). **live with** *v* tolerate.

live[2] *adj* **1** living, alive. **2** (of a broadcast) transmitted during the actual performance. **3** (of a performance) done in front of an audience. **4** (of a wire, circuit, etc.) carrying an electric current. **5** causing interest or controversy. **6** capable of exploding. **7** glowing or burning. ♦ *adv* **8** in the form of a live performance. **lively** *adj* **1** full of life or vigour. **2** animated. **3** vivid. **liveliness** *n* **liven up** *v* make (more) lively. **live wire 1** *Informal* energetic person. **2** wire carrying an electric current.

livelihood *n* occupation or employment.

liver *n* **1** organ secreting bile. **2** animal liver as food. **liverish** *adj* **1** having a disorder of the liver. **2** touchy or irritable.

liverwort *n* plant resembling seaweed or leafy moss.

livery *n, pl* **-eries 1** distinctive dress, esp. of a servant or servants. **2** distinctive design or colours of a company. **liveried** *adj* **livery stable** stable where horses are kept at a charge or hired out.

lives *n* plural of LIFE.

livestock *n* farm animals.

livid *adj* **1** *Informal* angry or furious. **2** bluish-grey.

living *adj* **1** possessing life, not dead or inanimate. **2** currently in use or existing. **3** of everyday life, e.g. *living conditions.* ♦ *n* **4** condition of being alive. **5** manner of life. **6** financial means. **7** church office yielding annual income. **living room** room in a house used for relaxation and entertainment. **living wage** wage adequate for a worker to live on in reasonable comfort.

lizard *n* four-footed reptile with a long body and tail.

llama *n* woolly animal of the camel family used as a beast of burden in S America.

LLB Bachelor of Laws.

lo *interj Old-fashioned* look!

loach *n* carplike freshwater fish.

load *n* **1** burden or weight. **2** amount carried. **3** source of worry. **4** amount of electrical energy drawn from a source. ♦ *pl* **5** *Informal* lots. ♦ *v* **6** put a load on or into. **7** burden or oppress. **8** supply in abundance. **9** cause to be biased. **10** put ammunition into (a weapon). **11** put film into (a camera). **12** transfer (a program) into computer memory. **a load of** *Informal* a quantity of. **loaded** *adj* **1** (of a question) containing a hidden trap or implication. **2** (of dice) dishonestly weighted. **3** *Slang* wealthy. **4** *Slang* drunk.

loaf[1] *n, pl* **loaves 1** shaped mass of baked bread. **2** shaped mass of food. **3** *Slang* head, esp. as the source of common sense, e.g. *use your loaf.*

loaf[2] *v* idle, loiter. **loafer** *n*

loam *n* fertile soil.

loan *n* **1** money lent at interest. **2** lending. **3** thing lent. ♦ *v* **4** lend. **loan shark** person who lends money at an extremely high interest rate.

loath, loth [rhymes with **both**] *adj* unwilling or reluctant (to).

> Distinguish between *loath* 'reluctant' and *loathe* 'be disgusted by'.

loathe *v* hate, be disgusted by. **loathing** *n* **loathsome** *adj*

loaves *n* plural of LOAF[1].

lob *Sport* ♦ *n* **1** ball struck or thrown in a high arc. ♦ *v* **lobbing, lobbed 2** strike or throw (a ball) in a high arc.

lobby *n, pl* **-bies 1** corridor into which rooms open. **2** group which tries to influence legislators. **3** hall in a legislative building to which the public has access. ♦ *v* **-bying, -bied 4** try to influence (legislators) in the formulation of policy. **lobbyist** *n*

lobe *n* **1** rounded projection. **2** soft hanging part of the ear. **3** subdivision of a body organ. **lobed** *adj*

lobelia *n* garden plant with blue, red, or white flowers.

lobotomy *n, pl* **-mies** surgical incision into a lobe of the brain to treat mental disorders.

lobster *n* shellfish with a long tail and claws, which turns red when boiled. **lobster pot** basket-like trap for catching lobsters.

local *adj* **1** of or existing in a particular place. **2** confined to a particular place. ♦ *n* **3** person belonging to a particular district. **4** *Informal* pub close to one's home. **locally** *adv* **locality** *n* **1** neighbourhood or area. **2** site. **localize** *v* restrict to a particular place. **locale** [loh-**kahl**] *n* scene of an event. **local anaesthetic** anaesthetic which produces loss of feeling in one part of the body. **local authority** governing body of a county or district. **local government** government of towns, counties, and districts by locally elected political bodies.

locate *v* **1** discover the whereabouts of. **2** situate or place. **location** *n* **1** site or position. **2** act of discovering where something is. **3** site of a film production away from the studio. **4** *S Afr* Black African or coloured township.

loch *n Scot* **1** lake. **2** long narrow bay.

loci *n* plural of LOCUS.

lock[1] *n* **1** appliance for fastening a door, case, etc. **2** section of a canal shut off by gates between which the water level can be altered to aid boats moving from one level to another. **3** extent to which a vehicle's front wheels will turn. **4** interlocking of parts. **5** mechanism for firing a gun. **6** wrestling hold. ♦ *v* **7** fasten or become fastened securely. **8** become or cause to become fixed or united. **9** become or cause to become immovable. **10** embrace closely. **lockout** *n* closing of a workplace by an employer to force workers to accept terms. **locksmith** *n* person who makes and mends locks. **lockup** *n* **1** prison. **2** garage or storage place away from the main premises. **lock up** *v* **1** imprison. **2** secure (a building) by locking.

lock[2] *n* strand of hair.

locker *n* small cupboard with a lock.

locket *n* small hinged pendant for a portrait etc.

lockjaw *n* tetanus.

locomotive *n* **1** self-propelled engine for pulling trains. ♦ *adj* **2** of locomotion. **locomotion** *n* action or power of moving.

locum *n* temporary stand-in for a doctor

or clergyman.

locus [**loh**-kuss] *n, pl* **loci** [**loh**-sigh] **1** area or place where something happens. **2** *Maths* set of points or lines satisfying one or more specified conditions.

locust *n* **1** destructive African insect that flies in swarms and eats crops. **2** N American tree with prickly branches.

lode *n* vein of ore. **lodestar** *n* star used in navigation or astronomy as a point of reference. **lodestone** *n* magnetic iron ore.

lodge *n* **1** gatekeeper's house. **2** house or cabin used occasionally by hunters, skiers, etc. **3** porters' room in a university or college. **4** local branch of some societies. **5** beaver's home. ♦ *v* **6** live in another's house at a fixed charge. **7** stick or become stuck (in a place). **8** leave for safety or storage. **9** make (a complaint etc.) formally. **lodger** *n* **lodging** *n* **1** temporary residence. ♦ *pl* **2** rented room or rooms in another person's house.

loft *n* **1** space between the top storey and roof of a building. **2** gallery in a church etc. **3** room over a stable used to store hay. ♦ *v* **4** *Sport* strike, throw, or kick (a ball) high into the air.

lofty *adj* **loftier, loftiest** **1** of great height. **2** exalted or noble. **3** haughty. **loftily** *adv* haughtily. **loftiness** *n*

log[1] *n* **1** portion of a felled tree stripped of branches. **2** detailed record of a journey of a ship, aircraft, etc. ♦ *v* **logging, logged** **3** saw logs from a tree. **4** record in a log. **logging** *n* work of cutting and transporting logs. **logbook** *n* book recording the details about a car or a ship's journeys. **log in, out** *v* gain entrance to *or* leave a computer system by keying in a special command.

log[2] *n* short for LOGARITHM.

loganberry *n* purplish-red fruit, similar to a raspberry.

logarithm *n* one of a series of arithmetical functions used to make certain calculations easier. **logarithmic** *adj*

loggerheads *pl n* **at loggerheads** quarrelling, disputing.

loggia [**loj**-ya] *n* covered gallery at the side of a building.

logic *n* **1** philosophy of reasoning. **2** particular system of reasoning. **3** reasoned thought or argument. **logical** *adj* **1** of logic. **2** capable of or using clear valid reasoning. **3** reasonable. **logically** *adv* **logician** *n*

logistics *n* detailed planning and organization of a large, esp. military, operation. **logistical, logistic** *adj* **logistically** *adv*

logo [**loh**-go] *n, pl* **-os** company emblem or similar device.

loin *n* **1** part of the body between the ribs and the hips. **2** cut of meat from this part of an animal. ♦ *pl* **3** hips and inner thighs. **4** *Euphemistic* genitals. **loincloth** *n* piece of cloth covering the loins only.

loiter *v* stand or wait aimlessly or idly.

loll *v* **1** lounge lazily. **2** hang loosely.

lollipop *n* **1** boiled sweet on a small wooden stick. **2** ice lolly. **lollipop man, lady** *Informal* person holding a circular sign on a pole, who controls traffic so that children may cross the road safely.

lollop *v* move clumsily.

lolly *n, pl* **-lies** **1** *Informal* lollipop or ice lolly. **2** *Slang* money.

lone *adj* **1** solitary. **2** isolated. **lonely** *adj* **1** sad because alone. **2** resulting from being alone. **3** unfrequented. **loneliness** *n* **loner** *n Informal* person who prefers to be alone. **lonesome** *adj* lonely.

long[1] *adj* **1** having length, esp. great length, in space or time. ♦ *adv* **2** for a certain time. **3** for an extensive period. **4** a considerable amount of time, e.g. *long ago.* **longways, longwise** *adv* lengthways. **longboat** *n* largest boat carried on a ship. **longbow** *n* large powerful bow. **long-distance** *adj* going between places far apart. **long face** glum expression. **longhand** *n* ordinary writing, not shorthand or typing. **long johns** *Informal* long underpants. **long jump** contest of jumping the farthest distance from a fixed mark. **long-life**

adj (of milk, batteries, etc.) lasting longer than the regular kind. **long-lived** *adj* living or lasting for a long time. **long-range** *adj* **1** extending into the future. **2** (of vehicles, weapons, etc.) designed to cover great distances. **long shot** competitor, undertaking, or bet with little chance of success. **long-sighted** *adj* able to see distant objects in focus but not nearby ones. **long-standing** *adj* existing for a long time. **long-suffering** *adj* enduring trouble or unhappiness without complaint. **long-term** *adj* lasting or effective for a long time. **long wave** radio wave with a wavelength of over 1000 metres. **long-winded** *adj* speaking or writing at tedious length.

long[2] *v* have a strong desire (for). **longing** *n* yearning. **longingly** *adv*

long. longitude.

longevity [lon-**jev**-it-ee] *n* long life.

longitude *n* distance east or west from a standard meridian. **longitudinal** *adj* **1** of length or longitude. **2** lengthways.

longshoreman *n US* docker.

loo *n Informal* toilet.

loofah *n* sponge made from the dried pod of a gourd.

look *v* **1** direct the eyes or attention (towards). **2** have the appearance of being. **3** face in a particular direction. **4** search (for). **5** hope (for). ♦ *n* **6** instance of looking. **7** view or sight. **8** (often pl) appearance. **look after** *v* take care of. **lookalike** *n* person who is the double of another. **look down on** *v* treat as inferior or unimportant. **look forward to** *v* anticipate with pleasure. **look-in** *n Informal* chance to participate. **look in** *v Informal* pay a short visit. **looking glass** mirror. **look on** *v* **1** be a spectator. **2** consider or regard. **lookout** *n* **1** act of watching for danger or for an opportunity. **2** guard. **3** place for watching. **4** *Informal* worry or concern. **5** chances or prospect. **look out** *v* be careful. **look up** *v* **1** discover or confirm by checking in a book. **2** improve. **3** visit. **look up to** *v* respect.

loom[1] *n* machine for weaving cloth.

loom[2] *v* **1** appear dimly. **2** seem ominously close.

loon *n* diving bird.

loony *Slang* ♦ *adj* **loonier, looniest 1** foolish or insane. ♦ *n, pl* **loonies 2** foolish or insane person.

loop *n* **1** rounded shape made by a curved line or rope crossing itself. **2** closed circuit through which an electronic signal can circulate. **3** continuous strip of film or tape. **4** set of instructions to be repeatedly performed in a computer program. ♦ *v* **5** form or fasten with a loop. **loop the loop** fly or be flown in a complete vertical circle. **loophole** *n* means of evading a rule without breaking it.

loose *adj* **1** not tight, fastened, fixed, or tense. **2** vague. **3** dissolute or promiscuous. ♦ *adv* **4** in a loose manner. ♦ *v* **5** free. **6** unfasten. **7** slacken. **8** let fly (an arrow, bullet, etc.). **at a loose end** bored, with nothing to do. **on the loose** free from confinement. **loosely** *adv* **looseness** *n* **loosen** *v* make loose. **loosen up** *v* relax, stop worrying. **loose-leaf** *adj* allowing the addition or removal of pages.

> Note the difference in spelling between the adjective *loose* and the verb *lose*.

loot *n, v* **1** plunder. ♦ *n* **2** *Informal* money. **looter** *n* **looting** *n*

lop *v* **lopping, lopped 1** cut away twigs and branches. **2** chop off.

lope *v* **1** run with long easy strides. ♦ *n* **2** loping stride.

lop-eared *adj* having drooping ears.

lopsided *adj* greater in height, weight, or size on one side.

loquacious *adj* talkative. **loquacity** *n*

lord *n* **1** person with power over others, such as a monarch or master. **2** male member of the nobility. **3** *Hist* feudal superior. **4** (**L-**) God or Jesus. **5** (**L-**) title given to certain male officials and peers. **House of Lords** unelected upper chamber of the British parliament. **lord it**

over act in a superior manner towards. **the Lord's Prayer** prayer taught by Christ to his disciples. **lordly** *adj* imperious, proud. **Lordship** *n* title of some male officials and peers.

lore *n* body of traditions on a subject.

lorgnette [lor-**nyet**] *n* pair of spectacles mounted on a long handle.

lorry *n, pl* **-ries** large vehicle for transporting loads by road.

lose *v* **losing, lost 1** come to be without, esp. by accident or carelessness. **2** fail to keep or maintain. **3** be deprived of. **4** get rid of. **5** fail to get or make use of. **6** be defeated in a competition etc. **7** fail to perceive or understand. **8** go astray or allow to go astray. **9** be or become engrossed, e.g. *lost in thought.* **10** die or be destroyed. **11** (of a clock etc.) run slow (by a specified amount). **loser** *n* **1** person or thing that loses. **2** *Informal* person who seems destined to fail.

> Note the difference in spelling between the verb *lose* and the adjective *loose.*

loss *n* **1** losing. **2** that which is lost. **3** damage resulting from losing. **at a loss 1** confused or bewildered. **2** not earning enough to cover costs. **loss leader** item sold at a loss to attract customers.

lost *v* **1** past of LOSE. ♦ *adj* **2** unable to find one's way. **3** unable to be found. **4** bewildered or confused. **5** (foll. by *on*) not used, noticed, or understood by. **6** no longer possessed or existing.

lot *pron* **1** great number. ♦ *n* **2** collection of people or things. **3** fate or destiny. **4** one of a set of objects drawn at random to make a selection or choice. **5** item at auction. **6** *US* area of land. ♦ *pl* **7** *Informal* great numbers or quantities. **a lot** *Informal* a great deal. **bad lot** disreputable person. **the lot** entire amount or number.

loth *adj* same as LOATH.

lotion *n* medical or cosmetic liquid for use on the skin.

lottery *n, pl* **-teries 1** method of raising money by selling tickets that win prizes by chance. **2** gamble.

lotto *n* game of chance like bingo.

lotus *n* **1** legendary plant whose fruit induces forgetfulness. **2** Egyptian water lily.

loud *adj* **1** relatively great in volume. **2** capable of making much noise. **3** insistent and emphatic. **4** unpleasantly patterned or colourful. **loudly** *adv* **loudness** *n* **loudspeaker** *n* instrument for converting electrical signals into sound.

lough *n Irish* loch.

lounge *n* **1** living room in a private house. **2** (also **lounge bar**) more expensive bar in a pub. **3** area for waiting in an airport. ♦ *v* **4** sit, lie, or stand in a relaxed manner. **lounge suit** man's suit for daytime wear.

lour *v* same as LOWER[2].

louse *n* **1** (*pl* **lice**) wingless parasitic insect. **2** (*pl* **louses**) unpleasant person. **lousy** *adj* **lousier, lousiest 1** *Slang* mean or unpleasant. **2** bad, inferior. **3** unwell. **4** infested with lice.

lout *n* crude, oafish, or aggressive person. **loutish** *adj*

louvre [**loo**-ver] *n* one of a set of parallel slats slanted to admit air but not rain. **louvred** *adj*

lovage *n* European plant used for flavouring food.

love *v* **1** have a great affection for. **2** feel sexual passion for. **3** enjoy (something) very much. ♦ *n* **4** great affection. **5** sexual passion. **6** wholehearted liking for something. **7** beloved person. **8** *Tennis, squash, etc.* score of nothing. **fall in love** become in love. **in love (with)** feeling a strong emotional (and sexual) attraction (for). **make love (to)** have sexual intercourse (with). **lovable, loveable** *adj* **loveless** *adj* **lovely** *adj* **-lier, -liest 1** very attractive. **2** highly enjoyable. **lover** *n* **1** person having a sexual relationship outside marriage. **2** person in love. **3** someone who loves a specified person or thing. **loving** *adj* affectionate, tender. **lovingly** *adv* **love affair** romantic or sexual relationship between two people who are not married to each other. **lovebird** *n* small parrot. **love child** *Euphemistic* child of an unmarried couple. **love life** person's romantic or sexual relationships. **lovelorn** *adj* miserable because of unhappiness in love. **lovemaking** *n*

low[1] *adj* **1** not tall, high, or elevated. **2** of little or less than the usual amount, degree, quality, or cost. **3** coarse or vulgar. **4** dejected. **5** ill. **6** not loud. **7** deep in pitch. **8** (of a gear) providing a relatively low speed. ♦ *adv* **9** in or to a low position, level, or degree. ♦ *n* **10** low position, level, or degree. **11** area of low atmospheric pressure, depression. **lowly** *adj* modest, humble. **lowliness** *n* **lowbrow** *n, adj* (person) with nonintellectual tastes and interests. **Low Church** section of the Anglican Church stressing evangelical beliefs and practices. **lowdown** *n Informal* inside information. **low-down** *adj Informal* mean, underhand, or dishonest. **low-key** *adj* subdued, restrained, not intense. **lowland** *n* **1** low-lying country. ♦ *pl* **2** (**L-**) less mountainous parts of Scotland. **low profile** position or attitude avoiding prominence or publicity. **low-spirited** *adj* depressed.

low[2] *n* **1** cry of cattle, moo. ♦ *v* **2** moo.

lower[1] *adj* **1** below one or more other things. **2** smaller or reduced in amount or value. ♦ *v* **3** cause or allow to move down. **4** behave in a way that damages one's respect. **5** lessen. **lower case** small, as distinct from capital, letters.

lower[2], **lour** *v* (of the sky or weather) look gloomy or threatening. **lowering** *adj*

loyal *adj* faithful to one's friends, country, or government. **loyally** *adv* **loyalty** *n* **loyalist** *n*

lozenge *n* **1** medicated tablet held in the mouth until it dissolves. **2** four-sided diamond-shaped figure.

LP *n* record playing approximately 20–25 minutes each side.

L-plate *n* sign on a car being driven by a learner driver.

Lr *Chem* lawrencium.

LSD lysergic acid diethylamide, a hallucinogenic drug.

Lt Lieutenant.

Ltd Limited (Liability).

Lu *Chem* lutetium.

lubricate [**loo**-brik-ate] *v* oil or grease to lessen friction. **lubricant** *n* lubricating substance, such as oil. **lubrication** *n*

lubricious [loo-**brish**-uss] *adj Lit* lewd.

lucerne *n* fodder plant like clover, alfalfa.

lucid *adj* **1** clear and easily understood. **2** able to think clearly. **3** bright and clear. **lucidly** *adv* **lucidity** *n*

Lucifer *n* Satan.

luck *n* **1** fortune, good or bad. **2** good fortune. **lucky** *adj* having or bringing good luck. **lucky dip** game in which prizes are picked from a tub at random. **luckily** *adv* fortunately. **luckless** *adj* having bad luck.

lucrative *adj* very profitable.

lucre [**loo**-ker] *n* **filthy lucre** *Facetious* money.

Luddite *n* person opposed to change in industrial methods.

ludicrous *adj* absurd or ridiculous. **ludicrously** *adv*

ludo *n* game played with dice and counters on a board.

luff *v* sail (a ship) towards the wind.

lug[1] *v* **lugging, lugged** carry or drag with great effort.

lug[2] *n* **1** projection serving as a handle. **2** *Informal* ear.

luggage *n* traveller's cases, bags, etc.

lugubrious [loo-**goo**-bree-uss] *adj* mournful, gloomy. **lugubriously** *adv*

lugworm *n* large worm used as bait.

lukewarm *adj* **1** moderately warm, tepid. **2** indifferent or half-hearted.

lull *v* **1** soothe (someone) by soft sounds or motions. **2** calm (fears or suspicions) by deception. ♦ *n* **3** brief time of quiet in a storm etc.

lullaby *n, pl* **-bies** quiet song to send a child to sleep.

lumbago [lum-**bay**-go] *n* pain in the lower back. **lumbar** *adj* relating to the lower back.

lumber[1] *n* **1** unwanted disused household articles. **2** *Chiefly US* sawn timber. ♦ *v* **3** *Informal* burden with something unpleasant. **lumberjack** *n US* man who fells trees and prepares logs for transport.

lumber[2] *v* move heavily and awkwardly. **lumbering** *adj*

luminous *adj* reflecting or giving off light. **luminosity** *n* **luminary** *n* **1** famous person. **2** *Lit* heavenly body giving off light. **luminescence** *n* emission of light at low temperatures by any process other than burning. **luminescent** *adj*

lump[1] *n* **1** shapeless piece or mass. **2** swelling. **3** *Informal* awkward or stupid person. ♦ *v* **4** consider as a single group. **lump in one's throat** tight dry feeling in one's throat, usu. caused by great emotion. **lumpish** *adj* stupid or clumsy. **lumpy** *adj* **lump sum** relatively large sum of money paid at one time.

lump[2] *v* **lump it** *Informal* tolerate or put up with it.

lunar *adj* relating to the moon.

lunatic *adj* **1** foolish and irresponsible. ♦ *n* **2** foolish or annoying person. **3** *Old-fashioned* insane person. **lunacy** *n*

lunch *n* **1** meal taken in the middle of the day. ♦ *v* **2** eat lunch. **luncheon** *n* formal lunch. **luncheon meat** tinned ground mixture of meat and cereal. **luncheon voucher** voucher for a certain amount, given to an employee and accepted by some restaurants as payment for a meal.

lung *n* organ that allows an animal or bird to breathe air: humans have two lungs in the chest.

lunge *n* **1** sudden forward motion. **2** thrust with a sword. ♦ *v* **3** move with or make a lunge.

lupin *n* garden plant with tall spikes of flowers.

lupine *adj* like a wolf.

lupus *n* ulcerous skin disease.

lurch[1] *v* **1** tilt or lean suddenly to one side. **2** stagger. ♦ *n* **3** lurching movement.

lurch[2] *n* **leave someone in the lurch** abandon someone in difficulties.

lurcher *n* crossbred dog trained to hunt silently.

lure *v* **1** tempt or attract by the promise of reward. ♦ *n* **2** person or thing that lures. **3** brightly-coloured artificial angling bait. **4** feathered decoy for attracting a falcon.

lurid *adj* **1** vivid in shocking detail, sensational. **2** glaring in colour. **luridly** *adv*

lurk *v* **1** lie hidden or move stealthily, esp. for sinister purposes. **2** be latent.

luscious [**lush**-uss] *adj* **1** extremely pleasurable to taste or smell. **2** very attractive.

lush[1] *adj* **1** (of grass etc.) growing thickly and healthily. **2** opulent.

lush[2] *n Slang* alcoholic.

lust *n* **1** strong sexual desire. **2** any strong desire. ♦ *v* **3** have passionate desire (for). **lustful** *adj* **lusty** *adj* vigorous, healthy. **lustily** *adv*

lustre *n* **1** gloss, sheen. **2** splendour or glory. **3** metallic pottery glaze. **lustrous** *adj* shining, luminous.

lute *n* ancient guitar-like musical instrument with a body shaped like a half pear.

lutetium [loo-**tee**-shee-um] *n Chem* silvery-white metallic element.

Lutheran *adj* of Martin Luther (1483–1546), German Reformation leader, his doctrines, or a Church following these doctrines.

lux *n, pl* **lux** unit of illumination.

luxuriant *adj* **1** rich and abundant. **2** very elaborate. **luxuriance** *n* **luxuriantly** *adv*

luxuriate *v* **1** take self-indulgent pleasure (in). **2** flourish.

luxury *n, pl* **-ries** **1** enjoyment of rich, very comfortable living. **2** enjoyable but not essential thing. ♦ *adj* **3** of or providing luxury. **luxurious** *adj* full of luxury, sumptuous. **luxuriously** *adv*

LV luncheon voucher.

lychee [lie-**chee**] *n* Chinese fruit with a whitish juicy pulp.

lych gate *n* roofed gate to a churchyard.

Lycra *n* ® elastic fabric used for tight-fitting garments, such as swimsuits.

lye *n* caustic solution made from wood ash.

lying *v* present participle of LIE[1] *or* LIE[2]. **lying-in** *n Old-fashioned* period of confinement during childbirth.

lymph *n* colourless bodily fluid consisting mainly of white blood cells. **lymphatic** *adj* **lymph node** mass of tissue that helps to fight infection in the body.

lymphocyte *n* type of white blood cell.

lynch *v* put to death without a trial.

lynx *n* animal of the cat family with tufted ears and a short tail.

lyre *n* ancient musical instrument like a U-shaped harp. **lyrebird** *n* Australian bird, the male of which spreads its tail into the shape of a lyre.

lyric *adj* **1** (of poetry) expressing personal emotion in songlike style. **2** like a song. ♦ *n* **3** short poem in a songlike style. ♦ *pl* **4** words of a popular song. **lyrical** *adj* **1** lyric. **2** enthusiastic. **lyricism** *n* **lyricist** *n* person who writes the words of songs or musicals.

M m

m 1 metre(s). 2 mile(s). 3 minute(s).

M 1 Motorway. 2 (*pl* **MM**) Monsieur. 3 mega-. 4 the Roman numeral for 1000.

m. 1 male. 2 married. 3 masculine. 4 meridian. 5 month.

ma *n Informal* mother.

MA 1 Master of Arts. 2 Massachusetts.

ma'am *n* madam.

mac *n Informal* mackintosh.

macabre [mak-**kahb**-ra] *adj* strange and horrible, gruesome.

macadam *n* road surface of pressed layers of small broken stones. **macadamize** *v* pave (a road) with macadam.

macaque [mac-**kahk**] *n* monkey of Asia and Africa with cheek pouches and either a short tail or no tail.

macaroni *n* pasta in short tube shapes.

macaroon *n* small biscuit or cake made with ground almonds.

macaw *n* large tropical American parrot.

mace[1] *n* 1 ceremonial staff of office. 2 medieval weapon with a spiked metal head.

mace[2] *n* spice made from the dried husk of the nutmeg.

macerate [**mass**-er-ate] *v* soften by soaking. **maceration** *n*

Mach [**mak**] *n* short for MACH NUMBER.

machete [mash-**ett**-ee] *n* broad heavy knife used for cutting or as a weapon.

Machiavellian [mak-ee-a-**vel**-yan] *adj* unprincipled, crafty, and opportunist.

machinations [mak-in-**nay**-shunz] *pl n* cunning plots and ploys.

machine *n* 1 apparatus, usu. powered by electricity, designed to perform a particular task. 2 vehicle, such as a car or aircraft. 3 controlling system of an organization. ♦ *v* 4 make or produce by machine. **machinery** *n* 1 machines or machine parts collectively. 2 standard procedures of an organization. **machinist** *n* person who operates a machine. **machine gun** automatic gun that fires rapidly and continuously. **machine-gun** *v* fire at with such a gun. **machine language** instructions for a computer in binary code that require no conversion or translation by the computer. **machine-readable** *adj* (of data) in a form suitable for processing by a computer.

machismo [mak-**izz**-moh] *n* exaggerated or strong masculinity.

Mach number [**mak**] *n* ratio of the speed of a body in a particular medium to the speed of sound in that medium.

macho [**match**-oh] *adj* strongly or exaggeratedly masculine.

mack *n Informal* mackintosh.

mackerel *n* edible sea fish with blue and silver stripes.

mackintosh, macintosh *n* 1 waterproof raincoat of rubberized cloth. 2 any raincoat.

macramé [mak-**rah**-mee] *n* ornamental work of knotted cord.

macro- *combining form* large, long, or great, e.g. *macroscopic.*

macrobiotics *n* dietary system advocating whole grains and vegetables grown without chemical additives. **macrobiotic** *adj*

macrocosm *n* 1 the universe. 2 any large complete system.

mad *adj* **madder, maddest** 1 mentally deranged, insane. 2 very foolish. 3 *Informal* angry. 4 frantic. 5 (foll. by *about* or *on*) very enthusiastic (about). **like mad** *Informal* with great energy, enthusiasm, or haste. **madly** *adv* 1 with great speed and energy. 2 *Informal* extremely or excessively. **madness** *n* **madden** *v* infuriate or irritate. **maddening** *adj* **maddeningly** *adv* **madman, madwoman** *n*

madam *n* 1 polite form of address to a woman. 2 *Informal* precocious or conceited girl.

madame [mad-**dam**] *n, pl* **mesdames** [may-**dam**] French title equivalent to

Mrs.

madcap *adj* foolish or reckless.

madder *n* **1** climbing plant. **2** red dye made from its root.

made *v* past of MAKE. **have (got) it made** *Informal* be assured of success.

Madeira [mad-**deer**-a] *n* fortified white wine. **Madeira cake** rich sponge cake.

mademoiselle [mad-mwah-**zel**] *n, pl* **mesdemoiselles** [maid-mwah-**zel**] French title equivalent to *Miss*.

madhouse *n* **1** *Informal* place filled with uproar or confusion. **2** *Old-fashioned* mental hospital.

Madonna *n* **1** the Virgin Mary. **2** picture or statue of her.

madrigal *n* 16th–17th-century part song for unaccompanied voices.

maelstrom [**male**-strom] *n* **1** great whirlpool. **2** turmoil.

maestro [**my**-stroh] *n, pl* **-tri, -tros** **1** outstanding musician or conductor. **2** any master of an art.

mae west *n* inflatable life jacket.

Mafia *n* international secret criminal organization founded in Sicily. **mafioso** *n, pl* **-sos, -si** member of the Mafia.

magazine *n* **1** periodical publication with articles by different writers. **2** television or radio programme made up of short nonfictional items. **3** appliance for automatically supplying cartridges to a gun or slides to a projector. **4** storehouse for explosives or arms.

magenta [maj-**jen**-ta] *adj* deep purplish-red.

maggot *n* larva of an insect. **maggoty** *adj*

Magi [**maje**-eye] *pl n* wise men from the East who came to worship the infant Jesus.

magic *n* **1** supposed art of invoking supernatural powers to influence events. **2** conjuring tricks done to entertain. **3** mysterious quality or power. ♦ *adj* **4** (also **magical**) of, using, or like magic. **5** *Informal* wonderful, marvellous. **magically** *adv* **magician** *n* **1** conjuror. **2** person with magic powers.

magistrate *n* **1** public officer administering the law. **2** justice of the peace. **magisterial** *adj* **1** commanding or authoritative. **2** of a magistrate.

magma *n* molten rock inside the earth's crust.

magnanimous *adj* noble and generous. **magnanimously** *adv* **magnanimity** *n*

magnate *n* influential or wealthy person, esp. in industry.

magnesia *n* white tasteless substance used as an antacid and a laxative; magnesium oxide.

magnesium *n Chem* silvery-white metallic element.

magnet *n* **1** piece of iron or steel capable of attracting iron and pointing north when suspended. **2** person or thing that exerts a great attraction. **magnetic** *adj* **1** having the properties of a magnet. **2** powerfully attractive. **magnetically** *adv* **magnetism** *n* **1** magnetic property. **2** powerful personal charm. **3** science of magnetic properties. **magnetize** *v* **1** make into a magnet. **2** attract strongly. **magnetic field** area around a magnet in which its power of attraction is felt. **magnetic north** direction in which a compass needle points. **magnetic tape** plastic strip coated with a magnetic substance for recording sound or video signals.

magneto [mag-**nee**-toe] *n, pl* **-tos** apparatus for ignition in an internal-combustion engine.

magnificent *adj* **1** splendid or impressive. **2** excellent. **magnificently** *adv* **magnificence** *n*

magnify *v* **-fying, -fied** **1** increase in apparent size, as with a lens. **2** exaggerate. **magnification** *n* **magnifying glass** convex lens used to produce an enlarged image of an object.

magnitude *n* relative importance or size.

magnolia *n* shrub or tree with showy white or pink flowers.

magnum *n* large wine bottle holding about 1.5 litres.

magnum opus *n* greatest single work of art or literature of a particular artist.

magpie *n* black-and-white bird.

Magyar *n* **1** member of the main ethnic group in Hungary. **2** Hungarian language. ♦ *adj* **3** of the Magyars.

maharajah *n* former title of some Indian princes. **maharani, maharanee** *n fem*

maharishi *n* Hindu religious teacher or mystic.

mahatma *n Hinduism* person revered for holiness and wisdom.

mah jong, mah-jongg *n* Chinese table game for four, played with tiles bearing different designs.

mahogany *n* hard reddish-brown wood of several tropical trees.

mahout [ma-**howt**] *n* (in India and the East Indies) elephant driver or keeper.

maid *n* **1** (also **maidservant**) female servant. **2** *Lit* young unmarried woman.

maiden *n* **1** *Lit* young unmarried woman. ♦ *adj* **2** unmarried. **3** first, e.g. *maiden voyage.* **maidenly** *adj* modest. **maidenhair** *n* fern with delicate fronds. **maidenhead** *n* virginity. **maiden name** woman's surname before marriage. **maiden over** *Cricket* over in which no runs are scored.

mail[1] *n* **1** letters and packages transported and delivered by the post office. **2** postal system. **3** single collection or delivery of mail. **4** train, ship, or aircraft carrying mail. **5** same as E-MAIL. ♦ *v* **6** send by mail. **mailing list** register of names and addresses to which information and advertising material is sent by post or electronic mail. **mail order** system of buying goods by post. **mailshot** *n* posting of advertising material to many selected people at once.

mail[2] *n* flexible armour of interlaced rings or links.

maim *v* cripple or mutilate.

main *adj* **1** chief or principal. ♦ *n* **2** principal pipe or line carrying water, gas, or electricity. ♦ *pl* **3** main distribution network for water, gas, or electricity. **in the main** on the whole. **mainly** *adv* for the most part, chiefly. **mainframe** *n, adj Computers* (denoting) a high-speed general-purpose computer. **mainland** *n* stretch of land which forms the main part of a country. **mainmast** *n* chief mast of a ship. **mainsail** *n* largest sail on a mainmast. **mainspring** *n* **1** chief cause or motive. **2** chief spring of a watch or clock. **mainstay** *n* **1** chief support. **2** rope securing a mainmast. **mainstream** *n* prevailing cultural trend.

maintain *v* **1** continue or keep in existence. **2** keep up or preserve. **3** support financially. **4** assert. **maintenance** *n* **1** maintaining. **2** upkeep of a building, car, etc. **3** provision of money for a separated or divorced spouse.

maisonette *n* flat with more than one floor.

maître d'hôtel [**met**-ra dote-**tell**] *n French* head waiter.

maize *n* type of corn with spikes of yellow grains.

Maj. Major.

majesty *n, pl* **-ties** **1** stateliness or grandeur. **2** supreme power. **majestic** *adj* **majestically** *adv*

majolica *n* type of ornamented Italian pottery.

major *adj* **1** greater in number, quality, or extent. **2** significant or serious. ♦ *n* **3** middle-ranking army officer. **4** scale in music. **5** *US & Aust* principal field of study at a university etc. ♦ *v* **6** (foll. by *in*) *US, Canadian, Aust & NZ* do one's principal study in (a particular subject). **majorette** *n* one of a group of girls who practise formation marching and baton twirling. **major-domo** *n, pl* **-domos** chief steward of a great household. **major-general** *n* senior military officer.

> *Major* strictly involves the comparison of one part with another: *He found the major part of the evidence.* Its use as a rough equivalent to 'large' is very informal.

majority *n, pl* **-ties** **1** greater number. **2** number by which the votes on one side exceed those on the other. **3** largest party voting together. **4** state of being legally an adult.

make *v* **making, made** **1** create, construct, or establish. **2** cause to do or be. **3** bring about or produce. **4** perform (an action). **5** appoint. **6** serve as or become. **7** amount to. **8** earn. ♦*n* **9** brand, type, or style. **make do** manage with an inferior alternative. **make it** *Informal* be successful. **on the make** *Informal* out for profit or conquest. **maker** *n* **1** person or company that makes something. **2** (**M-**) title given to God. **making** *n* **1** creation or production. ♦*pl* **2** necessary requirements or qualities. **make-believe** *n* fantasy or pretence. **make for** *v* head towards. **make off with** *v* steal or abduct. **make out** *v* **1** manage to see or hear (something), perceive. **2** understand. **3** write out (a cheque). **4** pretend. **5** attempt to establish or prove. **6** *Informal* manage or fare, e.g. *how did you make out in the competition?* **makeshift** *adj* serving as a temporary substitute. **make up** *v* **1** form or constitute. **2** prepare. **3** invent. **4** supply what is lacking, complete. **5** (foll. by *for*) compensate (for). **6** settle a quarrel. **7** apply cosmetics. **make-up** *n* **1** cosmetics. **2** way something is made. **3** mental or physical constitution. **makeweight** *n* something unimportant added to make up a lack.

mako *n, pl* **makos** powerful shark of the Atlantic and Pacific Oceans.

mal- *combining form* bad or badly, e.g. *malformation.*

malachite [**mal**-a-kite] *n* green mineral.

maladjusted *adj Psychol* unable to meet the demands of society. **maladjustment** *n*

maladministration *n* inefficient or dishonest administration.

maladroit [mal-a-**droyt**] *adj* clumsy or awkward.

malady [**mal**-a-dee] *n, pl* **-dies** disease or illness.

malaise [mal-**laze**] *n* **1** something wrong which affects a section of society or area of activity. **2** vague feeling of unease, illness, or depression.

malapropism *n* comical misuse of a word by confusion with one which sounds similar.

malaria *n* infectious disease caused by the bite of some mosquitoes. **malarial** *adj*

Malay *n* **1** member of a people of Malaysia or Indonesia. **2** language of this people. ♦*adj* **3** of the Malays or their language. **Malayan** *adj, n*

malcontent *n* discontented person.

male *adj* **1** of the sex which can fertilize female reproductive cells. ♦*n* **2** male person or animal. **maleness** *n* **male chauvinism** belief, held by some men, that men are superior to women. **male chauvinist** (characteristic of) a man who believes that men are superior to women.

malediction [mal-lid-**dik**-shun] *n* curse.

malefactor [**mal**-if-act-or] *n* criminal or wrongdoer.

malevolent [mal-**lev**-a-lent] *adj* wishing evil to others. **malevolently** *adv* **malevolence** *n*

malfeasance [mal-**fee**-zanss] *n* misconduct, esp. by a public official.

malformed *adj* misshapen or deformed. **malformation** *n*

malfunction *v* **1** function imperfectly or fail to function. ♦*n* **2** defective functioning or failure to function.

malice [**mal**-iss] *n* desire to cause harm to others. **malice aforethought** *Law* deliberate intention to do something unlawful. **malicious** *adj* **maliciously** *adv*

malign [mal-**line**] *v* **1** slander or defame. ♦*adj* **2** evil in influence or effect. **malignity** [mal-**lig**-nit-tee] *n* evil disposition.

malignant [mal-**lig**-nant] *adj* **1** seeking to harm others. **2** (of a tumour) harmful and uncontrollable. **malignancy** *n*

malinger [mal-**ling**-ger] *v* feign illness to avoid work. **malingerer** *n*

mall [**mawl**] *n* street or shopping area closed to vehicles.

mallard *n* wild duck.

malleable [**mal**-lee-a-bl] *adj* **1** capable of being hammered or pressed into shape. **2** easily influenced. **malleability**

n

mallet *n* **1** (wooden) hammer. **2** stick with a head like a hammer, used in croquet or polo.

mallow *n* plant with pink or purple flowers.

malnutrition *n* inadequate nutrition.

malodorous [mal-**lode**-or-uss] *adj* bad-smelling.

malpractice *n* immoral, illegal, or unethical professional conduct.

malt *n* **1** grain, such as barley, prepared for use in making beer or whisky. **2** malt whisky. ♦ *v* **3** make into or make with malt. **malty** *adj* **malted milk** drink made from powdered milk with malted cereals. **malt whisky** whisky made from malted barley.

Maltese *adj* **1** of Malta or its language. ♦ *n* **2** (*pl* **-tese**) person from Malta. **3** language of Malta. **Maltese cross** cross with triangular arms that taper towards the centre.

maltreat *v* treat badly. **maltreatment** *n*

mama [mam-**ma**] *n Old-fashioned* mother.

mamba *n* deadly S African snake.

mamma *n* same as MAMA.

mammal *n* animal of the type that suckles its young. **mammalian** *adj*

mammary *adj* of the breasts or milk-producing glands.

mammon *n* wealth regarded as a source of evil.

mammoth *n* **1** extinct elephant-like mammal. ♦ *adj* **2** colossal.

man *n, pl* **men** **1** adult male. **2** human being or person. **3** mankind. **4** manservant. **5** (usu. pl) member of the armed forces who is not an officer. **6** piece used in chess etc. ♦ *v* **manning, manned** **7** supply with sufficient people for operation or defence. **man in the street** average person. **manhood** *n* **mankind** *n* human beings collectively. **manly** *adj* **-lier, -liest** (possessing qualities) appropriate to a man. **manliness** *n* **manned** *adj* having a human personnel or crew. **mannish** *adj* like a man. **man-hour** *n* work done by one person in one hour. **man-made** *adj* made artificially.

> The use of words ending in *-man* is avoided as implying a male in job advertisements, where sexual discrimination is illegal, and in many other contexts where a term that is not gender-specific is available, such as *salesperson, barperson, camera operator.*

> Some people object to the use of *mankind* to refer to all human beings and prefer the term *humankind.*

manacle [**man**-a-kl] *n, v* handcuff or fetter.

manage *v* **1** succeed in doing. **2** be in charge of, administer. **3** handle or control. **4** cope with (financial) difficulties. **manageable** *adj* **management** *n* **1** managers collectively. **2** administration or organization. **manager, manageress** *n* person in charge of a business, institution, actor, sports team, etc. **managerial** *adj*

> In professional life the title *manager* is used for either men or women. Elsewhere the term *manageress* is still in use.

mañana [man-**yah**-na] *adv, n Spanish* **1** tomorrow. **2** some later (unspecified) time.

manatee *n* large tropical plant-eating aquatic mammal.

mandarin *n* **1** high-ranking government official. **2** kind of small orange.

Mandarin Chinese, Mandarin *n* official language of China.

mandate *n* **1** official or authoritative command. **2** authorization or instruction from an electorate to its representative or government. ♦ *v* **3** give authority to. **mandatory** *adj* compulsory.

mandible *n* lower jawbone or jawlike part.

mandolin *n* musical instrument with

four pairs of strings.

mandrake *n* plant with a forked root, formerly used as a narcotic.

mandrel *n* shaft on which work is held in a lathe.

mandrill *n* large blue-faced baboon.

mane *n* **1** long hair on the neck of a horse, lion, etc. **2** long thick human hair.

manful *adj* determined and brave. **manfully** *adv*

manganese *n Chem* brittle greyish-white metallic element.

mange *n* skin disease of domestic animals.

mangelwurzel *n* variety of beet used as cattle food.

manger *n* eating trough in a stable or barn.

mangetout [**mawnzh**-too] *n* variety of pea with an edible pod.

mangle[1] *v* **1** destroy by crushing and twisting. **2** spoil.

mangle[2] *n* **1** machine with rollers for squeezing water from washed clothes. ♦ *v* **2** put through a mangle.

mango *n, pl* **-goes, -gos** tropical fruit with sweet juicy yellow flesh.

mangrove *n* tropical tree with exposed roots, which grows beside water.

mangy *adj* **mangier, mangiest 1** having mange. **2** scruffy or shabby.

manhandle *v* treat roughly.

manhole *n* hole with a cover, through which a person can enter a drain or sewer.

manhunt *n* organized search, usu. by police, for a wanted man or a fugitive.

mania *n* **1** extreme enthusiasm. **2** madness. **maniac** *n* **1** mad person. **2** *Informal* person who has an extreme enthusiasm for something. **maniacal** [man-**eye**-a-kl] *adj*

manic *adj* **1** extremely excited or energetic. **2** affected by mania. **manic-depressive** *adj, n Psychiatry* (person afflicted with) a mental disorder that causes mood swings from extreme euphoria to deep depression.

manicure *n* **1** cosmetic care of the fingernails and hands. ♦ *v* **2** care for (the fingernails and hands) in this way. **manicurist** *n*

manifest *adj* **1** easily noticed, obvious. ♦ *v* **2** show plainly. **3** be evidence of. ♦ *n* **4** list of cargo or passengers for customs. **manifestly** *adv* **manifestation** *n*

manifesto *n, pl* **-tos, -toes** declaration of policy as issued by a political party.

manifold *adj* **1** numerous and varied. ♦ *n* **2** pipe with several outlets, esp. in an internal-combustion engine.

manikin *n* **1** little man or dwarf. **2** model of the human body.

manila, manilla *n* strong brown paper used for envelopes.

manipulate *v* **1** handle skilfully. **2** control cleverly or deviously. **manipulation** *n* **manipulative** *adj* **manipulator** *n*

manna *n* **1** *Bible* miraculous food which sustained the Israelites in the wilderness. **2** windfall.

mannequin *n* **1** woman who models clothes at a fashion show. **2** life-size dummy of the human body used to fit or display clothes.

manner *n* **1** way a thing happens or is done. **2** person's bearing or behaviour. **3** type or kind. **4** custom or style. ♦ *pl* **5** (polite) social behaviour. **mannered** *adj* affected. **mannerism** *n* person's distinctive habit or trait. **mannerly** *adj* having good manners, polite.

mannikin *n* same as MANIKIN.

manoeuvre [man-**noo**-ver] *n* **1** skilful movement. **2** contrived, complicated, and possibly deceptive plan or action. ♦ *pl* **3** military or naval exercises. ♦ *v* **4** manipulate or contrive skilfully or cunningly. **5** perform manoeuvres. **manoeuvrable** *adj*

manor *n* large country house and its lands. **manorial** *adj*

manpower *n* available number of workers.

manqué [**mong**-kay] *adj* would-be, e.g. *an actor manqué.*

mansard roof *n* roof with a break in its slope, the lower part being steeper than the upper.

manse *n* house provided for a minister in some religious denominations.

manservant *n, pl* **menservants** male servant, esp. a valet

mansion *n* large house.

manslaughter *n* unlawful but unintentional killing of a person.

mantel *n* structure round a fireplace. **mantelpiece, mantel shelf** *n* shelf above a fireplace.

mantilla *n* (in Spain) a lace scarf covering a woman's head and shoulders.

mantis *n, pl* **-tises, -tes** carnivorous insect like a grasshopper.

mantle *n* **1** loose cloak. **2** covering. **3** responsibilities and duties which go with a particular job or position. **4** incandescent gauze round a gas jet.

mantra *n Hinduism, Buddhism* any sacred word or syllable used as an object of concentration.

manual *adj* **1** of or done with the hands. **2** by human labour rather than automatic means. ♦ *n* **3** handbook. **4** organ keyboard. **manually** *adv*

manufacture *v* **1** process or make (goods) on a large scale using machinery. **2** invent or concoct (an excuse etc.). ♦ *n* **3** process of manufacturing goods. **manufacturer** *n*

manure *n* **1** animal excrement used as a fertilizer. ♦ *v* **2** fertilize (land) with this.

manuscript *n* **1** book or document, orig. one written by hand. **2** copy for printing.

Manx *adj* **1** of the Isle of Man or its inhabitants. ♦ *n* **2** almost extinct language of the Isle of Man. **Manx cat** tailless breed of cat.

many *adj* **more, most 1** numerous. ♦ *n* **2** large number.

Maoism *n* form of Marxism advanced by Mao Tse-tung in China. **Maoist** *n, adj*

Maori *n* **1** member of the indigenous race of New Zealand. **2** language of the Maoris. ♦ *adj* **3** of the Maoris or their language.

map *n* **1** representation of the earth's surface or some part of it, showing geographical features. **2** *Maths* (also **mapping**) same as FUNCTION (sense 4) *v* **mapping, mapped 3** make a map of. **4** *Maths* represent or transform (a function, figure, or set). **map out** *v* plan.

maple *n* tree with broad leaves, a variety of which (**sugar maple**) yields sugar. **maple syrup** very sweet syrup made from the sap of the sugar maple.

mar *v* **marring, marred** spoil or impair.

Mar. March.

marabou *n* **1** large black-and-white African stork. **2** its soft white down, used to trim hats etc.

maraca [mar-**rak**-a] *n* shaken percussion instrument made from a gourd containing dried seeds etc.

maraschino cherry [mar-rass-**kee**-no] *n* cherry preserved in a cherry liqueur with a taste like bitter almonds.

marathon *n* **1** long-distance race of 26 miles 385 yards (42.195 kilometres). **2** long or arduous task.

marauding *adj* wandering or raiding in search of plunder. **marauder** *n*

marble *n* **1** kind of limestone with a mottled appearance, which can be highly polished. **2** slab of or sculpture in this. **3** small glass ball used in playing marbles. ♦ *pl* **4** game of rolling these at one another. **marbled** *adj* having a mottled appearance like marble. **marbling** *n*

marcasite *n* crystals of iron pyrites, used in jewellery.

march[1] *v* **1** walk with a military step. **2** make (a person or group) proceed. **3** progress steadily. ♦ *n* **4** action of marching. **5** steady progress. **6** distance covered by marching. **7** piece of music, as for a march. **marcher** *n*

march[2] *n* border or frontier.

March *n* third month of the year.

marchioness [marsh-on-**ness**] *n* **1** woman holding the rank of marquis. **2** wife or widow of a marquis.

Mardi Gras [**mar**-dee **grah**] *n* festival of Shrove Tuesday, celebrated in some cities with great revelry.

mare *n* female horse or zebra. **mare's**

nest discovery which proves worthless.
margarine *n* butter substitute made from animal or vegetable fats.
marge *n Informal* margarine.
margin *n* **1** edge or border. **2** blank space round a printed page. **3** additional amount or one greater than necessary. **4** limit. **marginal** *adj* **1** insignificant, unimportant. **2** near a limit. **3** *Politics* (of a constituency) won by only a small margin. ♦ *n* **4** *Politics* marginal constituency. **marginally** *adv*
marguerite *n* large daisy.
marigold *n* plant with yellow or orange flowers.
marijuana [mar-ree-**wah**-na] *n* dried flowers and leaves of the hemp plant, used as a drug, esp. in cigarettes.
marimba *n* Latin American percussion instrument resembling a xylophone.
marina *n* harbour for yachts and other pleasure boats.
marinade *n* **1** seasoned liquid in which fish or meat is soaked before cooking. ♦ *v* **2** same as MARINATE. **marinate** *v* soak in marinade.
marine *adj* **1** of the sea or shipping. **2** used at or found in the sea. ♦ *n* **3** soldier trained for land and sea combat. **4** country's shipping or fleet. **mariner** [**mar**-in-er] *n* sailor.
marionette *n* puppet worked with strings.
marital *adj* relating to marriage.
maritime *adj* **1** relating to shipping. **2** of, near, or living in the sea.
marjoram *n* aromatic herb used for seasoning food and in salads.
mark[1] *n* **1** line, dot, scar, etc. visible on a surface. **2** distinguishing sign or symbol. **3** written or printed symbol. **4** letter or number used to grade academic work. **5** indication of position. **6** indication of some quality. **7** target or goal. ♦ *v* **8** make a mark on. **9** characterize or distinguish. **10** indicate. **11** pay attention to. **12** notice or watch. **13** grade (academic work). **14** stay close to (a sporting opponent) to hamper his or her play. **mark time 1** move the feet up and down as if marching, without moving forward. **2** wait for something more interesting to happen. **marked** *adj* noticeable. **markedly** [**mark**-id-lee] *adv* **marker** *n* **1** object used to show the position of something. **2** (also **marker pen**) thick felt-tipped pen for drawing and colouring. **marking** *n*
mark[2] *n* same as DEUTSCHMARK.
market *n* **1** assembly or place for buying and selling. **2** demand for goods. ♦ *v* **-keting, -keted 3** offer or produce for sale. **on the market** for sale. **marketable** *adj* **marketing** *n* part of a business that controls the way that goods or services are sold. **market garden** place where fruit and vegetables are grown for sale. **market maker** *Stock Exchange* person who uses a firm's money to create a market for a stock. **marketplace** *n* **1** market. **2** commercial world. **market research** research into consumers' needs and purchases.
marksman *n* person skilled at shooting. **marksmanship** *n*
marl *n* soil formed of clay and lime, used as fertilizer.
marlinespike, marlinspike [**mar**-lin-spike] *n* pointed hook used to separate strands of rope.
marmalade *n* jam made from citrus fruits.
marmoreal [mar-**more**-ee-al] *adj* of or like marble.
marmoset *n* small bushy-tailed monkey.
marmot *n* burrowing rodent.
maroon[1] *adj* reddish-purple.
maroon[2] *v* **1** abandon ashore, esp. on an island. **2** isolate without resources.
marquee *n* large tent used for a party or exhibition.
marquess [**mar**-kwiss] *n Brit* nobleman of the rank below a duke.
marquetry *n* ornamental inlaid work of wood.
marquis *n* (in various countries) nobleman of the rank above a count.
marquise [mar-**keez**] *n* same as MARCHIONESS.
marram grass *n* grass that grows on

sandy shores.

marrow *n* **1** fatty substance inside bones. **2** long thick striped green vegetable with whitish flesh

marry *v* **-rying, -ried 1** take as a husband or wife. **2** join or give in marriage. **3** unite closely. **marriage** *n* **1** state of being married. **2** wedding. **3** close union or relationship. **marriageable** *adj*

Mars *n* **1** Roman god of war. **2** fourth planet from the sun.

Marsala [mar-**sah**-la] *n* dark sweet wine.

Marseillaise [mar-say-**yaze**] *n* French national anthem.

marsh *n* low-lying wet land. **marshy** *adj* **marshier, marshiest**

marshal *n* **1** officer of the highest rank. **2** official who organizes ceremonies or events. **3** *US* law officer. ♦ *v* **-shalling, -shalled 4** arrange in order. **5** assemble. **6** conduct with ceremony. **marshalling yard** railway depot for goods trains.

marshmallow *n* spongy pink or white sweet.

marsupial [mar-**soop**-ee-al] *n* animal that carries its young in a pouch, such as a kangaroo.

mart *n* market.

Martello tower *n* round tower for coastal defence.

marten *n* **1** weasel-like animal. **2** its fur.

martial *adj* of war, warlike. **martial art** any of various philosophies and techniques of self-defence, orig. Eastern, such as karate. **martial law** law enforced by military authorities in times of danger or emergency.

Martian [**marsh**-an] *adj* **1** of Mars. ♦ *n* **2** supposed inhabitant of Mars.

martin *n* bird with a slightly forked tail.

martinet *n* person who maintains strict discipline.

martingale *n* strap from the reins to the girth of a horse, preventing it from throwing up its head.

martini *n* cocktail of vermouth and gin.

martyr *n* **1** person who dies or suffers for his or her beliefs. ♦ *v* **2** make a martyr of. **be a martyr to** be constantly suffering from. **martyrdom** *n*

marvel *v* **-velling, -velled 1** be filled with wonder. ♦ *n* **2** wonderful thing. **marvellous** *adj* **1** amazing. **2** wonderful. **marvellously** *adv*

Marxism *n* political philosophy of Karl Marx. **Marxist** *n, adj*

marzipan *n* paste of ground almonds, sugar, and egg whites.

masc. masculine.

mascara *n* cosmetic for darkening the eyelashes.

mascot *n* person, animal, or thing supposed to bring good luck.

masculine *adj* **1** relating to males. **2** manly. **3** *Grammar* of the gender of nouns that includes some male animate things. **masculinity** *n*

maser *n* device for amplifying microwaves.

mash *n* **1** a soft pulpy mass. **2** *Informal* mashed potatoes. **3** bran or meal mixed with warm water as food for horses etc. ♦ *v* **4** crush into a soft mass.

mask *n* **1** covering for the face, as a disguise or protection. **2** behaviour that hides one's true feelings. ♦ *v* **3** cover with a mask. **4** hide or disguise. **masking tape** adhesive tape used to protect surfaces surrounding an area to be painted.

masochism [**mass**-oh-kiz-zum] *n* condition in which (sexual) pleasure is obtained from feeling pain or from being humiliated. **masochist** *n* **masochistic** *adj* **masochistically** *adv*

mason *n* **1** person who works with stone. **2** (**M-**) Freemason. **Masonic** *adj* of Freemasonry. **masonry** *n* **1** stonework. **2** (**M-**) Freemasonry.

masque [**mask**] *n* *Hist* 16th–17th-century form of dramatic entertainment.

masquerade [mask-er-**aid**] *n* **1** deceptive show or pretence. **2** party at which masks and costumes are worn. ♦ *v* **3** pretend to be someone or something else.

mass *n* **1** coherent body of matter. **2** large quantity or number. **3** *Physics* amount of matter in a body. ♦ *adj* **4** large-scale. **5** involving many people.

♦ *v* **6** form into a mass. **massed** *adj* **the masses** ordinary people. **massive** *adj* large and heavy. **massively** *adv* **mass-market** *adj* for or appealing to a large number of people. **mass media** means of communication to many people, such as television and newspapers. **mass-produce** *v* manufacture (standardized goods) in large quantities. **mass production** manufacturing of standardized goods in large quantities.

Mass *n* service of the Eucharist, esp. in the RC Church.

massacre [**mass**-a-ker] *n* **1** indiscriminate killing of large numbers of people. ♦ *v* **2** kill in large numbers.

massage [**mass**-ahzh] *n* **1** rubbing and kneading of parts of the body to reduce pain or stiffness. ♦ *v* **2** give a massage to. **masseur** [mass-**ur**], (*fem*) **masseuse** [mass-**urz**] *n* person who gives massages.

massif [**mass**-seef] *n* connected group of mountains.

mast[1] *n* tall pole for supporting something, esp. a ship's sails. **masthead** *n* **1** *Naut* head of a mast. **2** name of a newspaper printed at the top of the front page.

mast[2] *n* fruit of the beech, oak, etc., used as pig fodder.

mastectomy [mass-**tek**-tom-ee] *n, pl* **-mies** surgical removal of a breast.

master *n* **1** person in control, such as an employer or an owner of slaves or animals. **2** expert. **3** great artist. **4** original thing from which copies are made. **5** male teacher. **6** (**M-**) title of a boy. ♦ *adj* **7** overall or controlling. **8** main or principal. ♦ *v* **9** acquire knowledge of or skill in. **10** overcome. **masterful** *adj* **1** domineering. **2** showing great skill. **masterly** *adj* showing great skill. **mastery** *n* **1** expertise. **2** control or command. **master key** key that opens all the locks of a set. **mastermind** *v* **1** plan and direct (a complex task). ♦ *n* **2** person who plans and directs a complex task. **master of ceremonies** person who presides over a public ceremony, formal dinner, or entertainment, introducing the events and performers. **masterpiece** *n* outstanding work of art. **masterstroke** *n* outstanding piece of strategy, skill, or talent.

mastic *n* **1** gum obtained from certain trees. **2** putty-like substance used as a filler, adhesive, or seal.

masticate *v* chew. **mastication** *n*

mastiff *n* large dog.

mastitis *n* inflammation of a breast or udder.

mastodon *n* extinct elephant-like mammal.

mastoid *n* projection of the bone behind the ear. **mastoiditis** *n* inflammation of this area.

masturbate *v* fondle the genitals (of). **masturbation** *n*

mat[1] *n* **1** piece of fabric used as a floor covering or to protect a surface. **2** thick tangled mass. ♦ *v* **matting, matted 3** tangle or become tangled into a dense mass. **on the mat** *Informal* summoned for a reprimand. **matted** *adj*

mat[2] *adj* same as MATT.

matador *n* man who kills the bull in bullfights.

match[1] *n* **1** contest in a game or sport. **2** person or thing exactly like, equal to, or in harmony with another. **3** marriage. ♦ *v* **4** be exactly like, equal to, or in harmony with. **5** put in competition (with). **6** find a match for. **7** join (in marriage). **matchless** *adj* unequalled. **matchmaker** *n* person who schemes to bring about a marriage. **matchmaking** *n, adj*

match[2] *n* small stick with a tip which ignites when scraped on a rough surface. **matchbox** *n* **matchstick** *n* **1** wooden part of a match. ♦ *adj* **2** (of drawn figures) thin and straight. **matchwood** *n* small splinters.

mate[1] *n* **1** *Informal* friend. **2** *Informal* common British and Australian term of address between males. **3** associate or colleague, e.g. *running mate; team-mate.* **4** sexual partner of an animal. **5** officer in a merchant ship. **6** tradesman's assistant. ♦ *v* **7** pair (animals) or (of animals) be paired for reproduction.

mate[2] *n, v Chess* checkmate.

material *n* **1** substance of which a thing is made. **2** cloth. **3** information on which a piece of work may be based. ♦ *pl* **4** things needed for an activity. ♦ *adj* **5** of matter or substance. **6** not spiritual. **7** affecting physical wellbeing. **8** relevant. **materially** *adv* considerably. **materialism** *n* **1** excessive interest in or desire for money and possessions. **2** belief that only the material world exists. **materialist** *adj, n* **materialistic** *adj* **materialize** *v* **1** actually happen. **2** come into existence or view. **materialization** *n*

maternal *adj* **1** of a mother. **2** related through one's mother. **maternity** *n* **1** motherhood. ♦ *adj* **2** of or for pregnant women, e.g. *maternity leave.*

matey *adj Informal* friendly or intimate.

mathematics *n* science of number, quantity, shape, and space. **mathematical** *adj* **mathematically** *adv* **mathematician** *n*

maths *n Informal* mathematics.

matinée [**mat**-in-nay] *n* afternoon performance in a theatre or cinema.

matins *pl n* early morning service in various Christian Churches.

matriarch [**mate**-ree-ark] *n* female head of a tribe or family. **matriarchal** *adj* **matriarchy** *n, pl* **-archies** society governed by a female, in which descent is traced through the female line.

matrices [**may**-triss-eez] *n* plural of MATRIX.

matricide *n* **1** crime of killing one's mother. **2** person who does this.

matriculate *v* enrol or be enrolled in a college or university. **matriculation** *n*

matrimony *n* marriage. **matrimonial** *adj*

matrix [**may**-trix] *n, pl* **matrices 1** substance or situation in which something originates, takes form, or is enclosed. **2** mould for casting. **3** *Maths* rectangular array of numbers or elements.

matron *n* **1** staid or dignified married woman. **2** woman who supervises the domestic or medical arrangements of an institution. **3** former name for NURSING OFFICER. **matronly** *adj* (of a woman) middle-aged and plump.

matt *adj* dull, not shiny.

matter *n* **1** substance of which something is made. **2** physical substance. **3** event, situation, or subject. **4** written material in general. **5** pus. ♦ *v* **6** be of importance. **what's the matter?** what is wrong? **matter-of-fact** *adj* unimaginative or emotionless. **matter-of-factly** *adv* **matter-of-factness** *n*

matting *n* coarsely woven fabric used as a floor-covering and packing material.

mattock *n* large pick with one of its blade ends flattened for loosening soil.

mattress *n* large stuffed flat case, often with springs, used on or as a bed.

mature *adj* **1** fully developed or grown-up. **2** ripe. ♦ *v* **3** make or become mature. **4** (of a bill or bond) become due for payment. **maturity** *n* state of being mature. **maturation** *n* process of becoming mature.

maudlin *adj* foolishly or tearfully sentimental.

maul *v* **1** handle roughly. **2** beat or tear.

maunder *v* talk or act aimlessly or idly.

Maundy money *n* special silver coins given to the poor in a symbolic ceremony on the Thursday before Easter.

mausoleum [maw-so-**lee**-um] *n* stately tomb.

mauve *adj* pale purple.

maverick *n, adj* independent and unorthodox (person).

maw *n* animal's mouth, throat, or stomach.

mawkish *adj* foolishly sentimental. **mawkishness** *n*

max. maximum.

maxim *n* general truth or principle.

maximum *adj, n, pl* **-mums, -ma** greatest possible (amount or number). **maximal** *adj* maximum. **maximize** *v* increase to a maximum. **maximization** *n*

may *v, past tense* **might** used as an auxiliary to express possibility, permission, opportunity, etc.

In very careful usage *may* is used in preference to *can* for asking permission. *Might* is used to express a more tentative request: *May/might I ask a favour?*.

May *n* **1** fifth month of the year. **2** (**m-**) same as HAWTHORN. **mayfly** *n* short-lived aquatic insect. **maypole** *n* pole set up for dancing round on the first day of May to celebrate spring.

maybe *adv* perhaps, possibly.

Mayday *n* international radio distress signal.

mayhem *n* violent destruction or confusion.

mayonnaise *n* creamy sauce of egg yolks, oil, and vinegar.

mayor *n* head of a municipality. **mayoress** *n* **1** mayor's wife. **2** female mayor. **mayoralty** *n, pl* **-ties** (term of) office of a mayor.

maze *n* **1** complex network of paths or lines designed to puzzle. **2** any confusing network or system.

mazurka *n* **1** lively Polish dance. **2** music for this.

MB **1** Bachelor of Medicine. **2** Manitoba.

MBE Member of the Order of the British Empire.

MC Master of Ceremonies.

MCC Marylebone Cricket Club.

Md *Chem* mendelevium.

MD **1** Doctor of Medicine. **2** Managing Director. **3** Maryland.

MDMA *n* same as ECSTASY (sense 2).

me[1] *pron* objective form of I[1].

The use of *it's me* in preference to *it's I* is accepted as quite standard.

me[2] *n Music* (in tonic sol-fa) third degree of any major scale.

ME **1** myalgic encephalomyelitis: painful muscles and general weakness sometimes persisting long after a viral illness. **2** Maine.

mead *n* alcoholic drink made from honey.

meadow *n* piece of grassland. **meadowsweet** *n* plant with dense heads of small fragrant flowers.

meagre *adj* scanty or insufficient.

meal[1] *n* **1** occasion when food is served and eaten. **2** the food itself. **make a meal of** *Informal* perform (a task) with an unnecessary amount of effort. **meals-on-wheels** *n* service taking hot meals to elderly or infirm people in their own homes. **meal ticket** *Slang* person or situation providing a source of livelihood or income.

meal[2] *n* grain ground to powder. **mealy** *adj* **mealier, mealiest** **mealy-mouthed** *adj* not outspoken enough.

mealie *n S Afr* maize.

mean[1] *v* **meaning, meant** **1** intend to convey or express. **2** signify, denote, or portend. **3** intend. **4** have importance as specified. **meaning** *n* sense, significance. **meaningful** *adj* important or significant. **meaningfully** *adv* **meaningfulness** *n* **meaningless** *adj* **meaninglessly** *adv* **meaninglessness** *n*

mean[2] *adj* **1** miserly, ungenerous, or petty. **2** despicable or callous. **3** *Chiefly US informal* bad-tempered. **meanly** *adv* **meanness** *n* **meanie** *n Informal* unkind or miserly person.

mean[3] *n* **1** middle point between two extremes. **2** average. ♦ *pl* **3** method by which something is done. **4** money. ♦ *adj* **5** intermediate in size or quantity. **6** average. **by all means** certainly. **by no means** in no way. **means test** inquiry into a person's means to decide on eligibility for financial aid.

meander [mee-**and**-er] *v* **1** follow a winding course. **2** wander aimlessly. ♦ *n* **3** winding course.

meant *v* past of MEAN[1].

meantime *n* **1** intervening period. ♦ *adv* **2** meanwhile.

meanwhile *adv* **1** during the intervening period. **2** at the same time.

measles *n* infectious disease producing red spots. **measly** *adj* **-lier, -liest** *Infor-*

mal meagre.

measure *n* **1** size or quantity. **2** graduated scale etc. for measuring size or quantity. **3** unit of size or quantity. **4** extent. **5** action taken. **6** law. **7** poetical rhythm. ♦ *v* **8** determine the size or quantity of. **9** be (a specified amount) in size or quantity. **measurable** *adj* **measured** *adj* **1** slow and steady. **2** carefully considered. **measurement** *n* **1** measuring. **2** size. **measure up to** *v* fulfil (expectations or requirements).

meat *n* animal flesh as food. **meaty** *adj* **meatier, meatiest 1** (tasting) of or like meat. **2** brawny. **3** full of significance or interest.

Mecca *n* **1** holy city of Islam. **2** place that attracts visitors.

> Most Muslims prefer the Arabic form *Makkah.*

mechanic *n* person skilled in repairing or operating machinery. **mechanics** *n* scientific study of motion and force. **mechanical** *adj* **1** of or done by machines. **2** (of an action) without thought or feeling. **mechanically** *adv*

mechanism *n* **1** way a machine works. **2** piece of machinery. **3** process or technique, e.g. *defence mechanism.* **mechanistic** *adj* **mechanize** *v* **1** equip with machinery. **2** make mechanical or automatic. **3** *Mil* equip (an army) with armoured vehicles. **mechanization** *n*

med. 1 medical. **2** medicine. **3** medieval. **4** medium.

medal *n* piece of metal with an inscription etc., given as a reward or memento. **medallion** *n* **1** disc-shaped ornament worn on a chain round the neck. **2** large medal. **3** circular decorative device in architecture. **medallist** *n* winner of a medal.

meddle *v* interfere annoyingly. **meddler** *n* **meddlesome** *adj*

media *n* **1** a plural of MEDIUM. **2** the mass media collectively. **media event** event that is staged for or exploited by the mass media.

> *Media* is a plural noun. There is an increasing tendency to use it also as a singular noun because of the ambiguous senses of *medium.*

mediaeval [med-ee-**eve**-al] *adj* same as MEDIEVAL.

medial [**mee**-dee-al] *adj* of or in the middle.

median *adj, n* middle (point or line).

mediate [**mee**-dee-ate] *v* intervene in a dispute to bring about agreement. **mediation** *n* **mediator** *n*

medic *n Informal* doctor or medical student.

medical *adj* **1** of the science of medicine. ♦ *n* **2** *Informal* medical examination. **medically** *adv* **medicament** [mid-**dik**-a-ment] *n* a medicine. **medicate** *v* treat with a medicinal substance. **medication** *n* (treatment with) a medicinal substance.

medicine *n* **1** substance used to treat disease. **2** science of preventing, diagnosing, or curing disease. **medicinal** [med-**diss**-in-al] *adj* having therapeutic properties. **medicinally** *adv* **medicine man** witch doctor.

medieval [med-ee-**eve**-al] *adj* of the Middle Ages.

mediocre [mee-dee-**oak**-er] *adj* **1** average in quality. **2** second-rate. **mediocrity** [mee-dee-**ok**-rit-ee] *n* **1** state of being mediocre. **2** (*pl* **-rities**) mediocre person.

meditate *v* **1** reflect deeply, esp. on spiritual matters. **2** think about or plan. **meditation** *n* **meditative** *adj* **meditatively** *adv* **meditator** *n*

Mediterranean *adj* of (the area around) the Mediterranean Sea, between S Europe, N Africa, and SW Asia.

medium *adj* **1** midway between extremes, average. ♦ *n, pl* **-dia, -diums 2** middle state, degree, or condition. **3** intervening substance producing an effect. **4** means of communicating news or information to the public, such as radio or newspapers. **5** person who can supposedly communicate with the dead. **6** surroundings or environment. **7** category of art according to the material used. **medium wave** radio wave with a wavelength between 100 and 1000 metres.

medlar *n* apple-like fruit of a small tree, eaten when it begins to decay.

medley *n* **1** miscellaneous mixture. **2** musical sequence of different tunes.

medulla [mid-**dull**-la] *n, pl* **-las, -lae** marrow, pith, or inner tissue.

meek *adj* submissive or humble. **meekly** *adv* **meekness** *n*

meerkat *n* S African mongoose.

meerschaum [**meer**-shum] *n* **1** white substance like clay. **2** tobacco pipe with a bowl made of this.

meet[1] *v* **meeting, met 1** come together (with). **2** come into contact (with). **3** be at the place of arrival of. **4** make the acquaintance of. **5** satisfy (a need etc.). **6** experience. ♦ *n* **7** sports meeting. **8** assembly of a hunt. **meeting** *n* **1** coming together. **2** assembly.

> *Meet* is only followed by *with* in the context of misfortune: *I met his son; I met with an accident.*

meet[2] *adj Obs* fit or suitable.

mega *adj Slang* extremely good, great, or successful.

mega- *combining form* **1** denoting one million, e.g. *megawatt.* **2** very great, e.g. *megastar.*

megabyte *n Computers* 2^{20} or 1 048 576 bytes.

megahertz *n, pl* **-hertz** one million hertz.

megalith *n* great stone, esp. as part of a prehistoric monument. **megalithic** *adj*

megalomania *n* craving for or mental delusions of power. **megalomaniac** *adj, n*

megaphone *n* cone-shaped instrument used to amplify the voice.

megaton *n* explosive power equal to that of one million tons of TNT.

meiosis [my-**oh**-siss] *n* type of cell division in which reproductive cells are produced, each containing half the chromosome number of the parent nucleus.

melamine *n* colourless crystalline compound used in making synthetic resins.

melancholy [**mel**-an-kol-lee] *n* **1** sadness or gloom. ♦ *adj* **2** sad or gloomy. **melancholia** [mel-an-**kole**-lee-a] *n* state of depression. **melancholic** *adj, n*

melange [may-**lahnzh**] *n* mixture.

melanin *n* dark pigment found in the hair, skin, and eyes of humans and animals.

Melba toast *n* very thin crisp toast.

mêlée [**mel**-lay] *n* noisy confused fight or crowd.

mellifluous [mel-**lif**-flew-uss] *adj* (of sound) smooth and sweet.

mellow *adj* **1** soft, not harsh. **2** kind-hearted, esp. through maturity. **3** (of fruit) ripe. ♦ *v* **4** make or become mellow.

melodrama *n* **1** play full of extravagant action and emotion. **2** overdramatic behaviour or emotion. **melodramatic** *adj*

melody *n, pl* **-dies 1** series of musical notes which make a tune. **2** sweet sound. **melodic** [mel-**lod**-ik] *adj* **1** of melody. **2** melodious. **melodious** [mel-**lode**-ee-uss] *adj* **1** pleasing to the ear. **2** tuneful.

melon *n* large round juicy fruit with a hard rind.

melt *v* **1** (cause to) become liquid by heat. **2** dissolve. **3** disappear. **4** blend (into). **5** soften through emotion. **meltdown** *n* (in a nuclear reactor) melting of the fuel rods, with the possible release of radiation. **melting pot** place or situation in which many races, ideas, etc., are mixed.

member *n* **1** individual making up a body or society. **2** limb. **membership** *n* **Member of Parliament** person elected to parliament.

membrane *n* thin flexible tissue in a plant or animal body. **membranous** *adj*

memento *n, pl* **-tos, -toes** thing serving to remind, souvenir.

memo *n, pl* **memos** short for MEMORANDUM.

memoir [**mem**-wahr] *n* **1** biography or historical account based on personal knowledge. ♦ *pl* **2** collection of these. **3** autobiography.

memorable *adj* worth remembering, noteworthy. **memorably** *adv* **memorabilia** *pl n* objects connected with famous people or events.

memorandum *n, pl* **-dums, -da 1** written record or communication within a business. **2** note of things to be remembered.

memory *n, pl* **-ries 1** ability to remember. **2** sum of things remembered. **3** particular recollection. **4** length of time one can remember. **5** commemoration. **6** part of a computer which stores information. **memorize** *v* commit to memory. **memorial** *n* **1** something serving to commemorate a person or thing. ♦ *adj* **2** serving as a memorial.

memsahib *n* (formerly, in India) term of respect used for a European married woman.

men *n* plural of MAN.

menace *n* **1** threat. **2** *Informal* nuisance. ♦ *v* **3** threaten, endanger. **menacing** *adj* **menacingly** *adv*

ménage [may-**nahzh**] *n* household.

menagerie [min-**naj**-er-ee] *n* collection of wild animals for exhibition.

mend *v* **1** repair or patch. **2** recover or heal. **3** make or become better. ♦ *n* **4** mended area. **on the mend** regaining health.

mendacity *n* (tendency to) untruthfulness. **mendacious** *adj*

mendelevium *n Chem* artificially produced radioactive element.

mendicant *adj* **1** begging. ♦ *n* **2** beggar.

menfolk *pl n* men collectively, esp. the men of a particular family.

menhir [**men**-hear] *n* single upright prehistoric stone.

menial [**mean**-nee-al] *adj* **1** involving boring work of low status. ♦ *n* **2** domestic servant.

meningitis [men-in-**jite**-iss] *n* inflammation of the membranes of the brain.

meniscus *n* **1** curved surface of a liquid. **2** crescent-shaped lens.

menopause *n* time when a woman's menstrual cycle ceases. **menopausal** *adj*

menstruation *n* approximately monthly discharge of blood and cellular debris from the womb of a nonpregnant woman. **menstruate** *v* **menstrual** *adj*

mensuration *n* measuring, esp. in geometry.

mental *adj* **1** of, in, or done by the mind. **2** of or for mental illness. **3** *Informal* insane. **mentally** *adv* **mentality** *n, pl* **-ties** way of thinking.

menthol *n* organic compound found in peppermint, used medicinally.

mention *v* **1** refer to briefly. **2** acknowledge. ♦ *n* **3** brief reference to a person or thing. **4** acknowledgment.

mentor *n* adviser or guide.

menu *n* **1** list of dishes to be served, or from which to order. **2** *Computers* list of options displayed on a screen.

MEP Member of the European Parliament.

mercantile *adj* of trade or traders.

Mercator projection [mer-**kate**-er] *n* method of map-making in which latitude and longitude form a rectangular grid.

mercenary *adj* **1** influenced by greed. **2** working merely for reward. ♦ *n, pl* **-aries 3** hired soldier.

mercerized *adj* (of cotton) given lustre by treating with chemicals.

merchandise *n* commodities.

merchant *n* person engaged in trade, wholesale trader. **merchant bank** bank dealing mainly with businesses and investment. **merchantman** *n* trading ship. **merchant navy** ships or crew engaged in a nation's commercial shipping.

mercury *n* **1** *Chem* silvery liquid metal. **2** (**M-**) *Roman myth* messenger of the gods. **3** (**M-**) planet nearest the sun. **mercurial** [mer-**cure**-ee-al] *adj* lively, changeable.

mercy *n, pl* **-cies 1** compassionate treatment of an offender or enemy who is in one's power. **2** merciful act. **merciful** *adj* **1** compassionate. **2** giving relief. **mercifully** *adv* **merciless** *adj* **mercilessly** *adv*

mere[1] *adj* nothing more than, e.g. *mere chance.* **merely** *adv*

mere[2] *n Obs* lake.

meretricious *adj* superficially or garishly attractive but of no real value.

merganser [mer-**gan**-ser] *n* large crested diving duck.

merge *v* combine or blend. **merger** *n* combination of business firms into one.

meridian *n* imaginary circle of the earth passing through both poles.

meringue [mer-**rang**] *n* **1** baked mixture of egg whites and sugar. **2** small cake of this.

merino *n, pl* **-nos 1** breed of sheep with fine soft wool. **2** this wool.

merit *n* **1** excellence or worth. ♦ *pl* **2** admirable qualities. ♦ *v* **-iting, -ited 3** deserve. **meritorious** *adj* deserving praise. **meritocracy** [mer-it-**tok**-rass-ee] *n* rule by people of superior talent or intellect.

merlin *n* small falcon.

mermaid *n* imaginary sea creature with the upper part of a woman and the lower part of a fish.

merry *adj* **-rier, -riest 1** cheerful or jolly. **2** *Informal* slightly drunk. **merrily** *adv* **merriment** *n* **merry-go-round** *n* roundabout. **merrymaking** *n* noisy, cheerful celebrations or fun.

mescaline *n* hallucinogenic drug obtained from the tops of mescals. **mescal** [mess-**kal**] *n* spineless globe-shaped cactus of Mexico and the SW of the USA.

mesdames *n* plural of MADAME.

mesdemoiselles *n* plural of MADEMOISELLE.

mesembryanthemum *n* low-growing plant with bright daisy-like flowers.

mesh *n* **1** network or net. **2** (open space between) strands forming a network. ♦ *v* **3** (of gear teeth) engage.

mesmerize *v* **1** hold spellbound. **2** *Obs* hypnotize. **mesmerizing** *adj*

meso- *combining form* middle or intermediate, e.g. *mesosphere.*

meson [**mee**-zon] *n* elementary atomic particle.

mess *n* **1** untidy or dirty confusion. **2** trouble or difficulty. **3** place where servicemen eat. **4** group of servicemen who regularly eat together. ♦ *v* **5** muddle or dirty. **6** (foll. by *about*) potter about. **7** (foll. by *with*) interfere with. **8** (of servicemen) eat in a group.

message *n* **1** communication sent. **2** meaning or moral. **messenger** *n* bearer of a message. **get the message** *Informal* understand.

Messiah *n* **1** Jews' promised deliverer. **2** Christ. **Messianic** *adj*

messieurs *n* plural of MONSIEUR.

Messrs [**mess**-erz] *n* plural of MR.

messy *adj* **messier, messiest** dirty, confused, or untidy. **messily** *adv*

met *v* past of MEET[1].

Met *adj, n Informal* Meteorological (Office).

metabolism [met-**tab**-oh-liz-zum] *n* chemical processes of a living body. **metabolic** *adj* **metabolize** *v* produce or be produced by metabolism.

metal *n* **1** chemical element, such as iron or copper, that is malleable and capable of conducting heat and electricity. **2** short for ROAD METAL. **3** *Informal* short for HEAVY METAL. ♦ *adj* **4** made of metal. **metallic** *adj* **metallurgy** *n* scientific study of the structure, properties, extraction, and refining of metals. **metallurgical** *adj* **metallurgist** *n* **metalwork** *n* **1** craft of making objects from metal. **2** metal part of something.

metamorphosis [met-a-**more**-foss-is] *n, pl* **-phoses** [-foss-eez] change of form or character. **metamorphic** *adj* (of rocks) changed in texture or structure by heat and pressure. **metamorphose** *v* transform.

metaphor *n* figure of speech in which a term is applied to something it does not literally denote in order to imply a resemblance, e.g. *he is a lion in battle.*

metaphorical *adj* **metaphorically** *adv*

metaphysics *n* branch of philosophy concerned with being and knowing. **metaphysical** *adj*

mete *v* (usu. with *out*) deal out as punishment.

meteor *n* small fast-moving heavenly body, visible as a streak of incandescence if it enters the earth's atmosphere. **meteoric** [meet-ee-**or**-rik] *adj* **1** of a meteor. **2** brilliant and very rapid, e.g. *his meteoric rise to power.* **meteorite** *n* meteor that has fallen to earth.

meteorology *n* study of the earth's atmosphere, esp. for weather forecasting. **meteorological** *adj* **meteorologist** *n*

meter *n* **1** instrument for measuring and recording something, such as the consumption of gas or electricity. ♦ *v* **2** measure by meter.

methane *n* colourless inflammable gas.

methanol *n* colourless poisonous liquid used as a solvent and fuel (also **methyl alcohol**).

methinks *v, past tense* **methought** *Obs* it seems to me.

method *n* **1** way or manner. **2** technique. **3** orderliness. **methodical** *adj* orderly. **methodically** *adv* **methodology** *n, pl* **-gies** particular method or procedure.

Methodist *n* **1** member of any of the Protestant churches originated by John Wesley and his followers. ♦ *adj* **2** of Methodists or their Church. **Methodism** *n*

meths *n Informal* methylated spirits.

methyl *n* (compound containing) a saturated hydrocarbon group of atoms. **methylated spirits** alcohol with methanol added, used as a solvent and for heating.

meticulous *adj* very careful about details. **meticulously** *adv*

métier [**met**-ee-ay] *n* **1** profession or trade. **2** one's strong point.

metonymy [mit-**on**-im-ee] *n* figure of speech in which one thing is replaced by another associated with it, such as 'the Crown' for 'the queen'.

metre *n* **1** basic unit of length equal to about 1.094 yards (100 centimetres). **2** rhythm of poetry. **metric** *adj* of the decimal system of weights and measures based on the metre. **metric ton** same as TONNE. **metrical** *adj* **1** of measurement. **2** of poetic metre. **metrication** *n* conversion to the metric system.

metro *n, pl* **metros** underground railway system, esp. in Paris.

metronome *n* instrument which marks musical time by means of a ticking pendulum.

metropolis [mit-**trop**-oh-liss] *n* chief city of a country or region. **metropolitan** *adj* of a metropolis.

mettle *n* courage or spirit. **on one's mettle** roused to making one's best efforts.

mew *n* **1** cry of a cat. ♦ *v* **2** utter this cry.

mews *n* yard or street orig. of stables, now often converted into houses.

Mexican *adj* **1** of Mexico. ♦ *n* **2** person from Mexico.

mezzanine [**mez**-zan-een] *n* intermediate storey, esp. between the ground and first floor.

mezzo-soprano [**met**-so-] *n* voice or singer between a soprano and contralto (also **mezzo**).

mezzotint [**met**-so-tint] *n* **1** method of engraving by scraping the roughened surface of a metal plate. **2** print so made.

mg milligram(s).

Mg *Chem* magnesium.

Mgr **1** manager. **2** Monseigneur. **3** Monsignor.

MHz megahertz.

mi *n Music* same as ME[2].

MI **1** Military Intelligence. **2** Michigan.

MI5 Military Intelligence, section five: British Government counterintelligence agency.

MI6 Military Intelligence, section six: British Government intelligence and espionage agency.

miaow [mee-**ow**] *n, v* same as MEW.

miasma [mee-**azz**-ma] *n* unwholesome

or foreboding atmosphere.

mica [**my**-ka] *n* glasslike mineral used as an electrical insulator.

mice *n* plural of MOUSE.

Michaelmas [**mik**-kl-mass] *n* Sept. 29th, feast of St Michael the archangel. **Michaelmas daisy** garden plant with small daisy-shaped flowers.

mickey *n* **take the mickey (out of)** *Informal* tease.

micro *n, pl* **-cros** short for MICROCOMPUTER or MICROPROCESSOR.

micro- *combining form* **1** small or minute, e.g. *microcopy.* **2** denoting a millionth part, e.g. *microsecond.*

microbe *n* minute organism, esp. one causing disease. **microbial** *adj*

microbiology *n* branch of biology involving the study of microorganisms. **microbiological** *adj* **microbiologist** *n*

microchip *n* small wafer of silicon containing electronic circuits.

microcircuit *n* miniature electronic circuit, esp. an integrated circuit.

microcomputer *n* computer with a central processing unit contained in one or more silicon chips.

microcosm *n* **1** miniature representation of something. **2** man regarded as epitomizing the universe.

microdot *n* photographic copy of a document reduced to pinhead size.

microelectronics *n* branch of electronics concerned with microcircuits. **microelectronic** *adj*

microfiche [**my**-kroh-feesh] *n* microfilm in sheet form.

microfilm *n* miniaturized recording of books or documents on a roll of film.

microlight, microlite *n* very small light private aircraft with large wings.

micrometer [my-**krom**-it-er] *n* instrument for measuring very small distances or angles.

micron [**my**-kron] *n* one millionth of a metre.

microorganism *n* organism of microscopic size.

microphone *n* instrument for amplifying or transmitting sounds.

microprocessor *n* integrated circuit acting as the central processing unit in a small computer.

microscope *n* instrument with lens(es) which produces a magnified image of a very small object. **microscopic** *adj* **1** too small to be seen except with a microscope. **2** very small. **3** of a microscope. **microscopically** *adv* **microscopy** *n* use of a microscope.

microstructure *n* structure on a microscopic scale, esp. of a metal or a cell.

microsurgery *n* intricate surgery using a special microscope and miniature precision instruments.

microwave *n* **1** electromagnetic wave with a wavelength of a few centimetres, used in radar and cooking. **2** microwave oven. ♦ *v* **3** cook in a microwave oven. **microwave oven** oven using microwaves to cook food quickly.

micturate *v* urinate. **micturition** *n*

mid *adj* intermediate, middle. **mid-off** *n Cricket* fielding position on the off side closest to the bowler. **mid-on** *n Cricket* fielding position on the on side closest to the bowler.

midair *n* some point above ground level, in the air.

midday *n* noon.

midden *n* dunghill or rubbish heap.

middle *adj* **1** equidistant from two extremes. **2** medium, intermediate. ♦ *n* **3** middle point or part. **middle age** period of life between youth and old age. **middle-aged** *adj* **Middle Ages** period from about 1000 AD to the 15th century. **middle class** social class of business and professional people. **middle-class** *adj* **middle ear** sound-conducting part of the ear immediately inside the eardrum. **Middle East** area around the eastern Mediterranean up to and including Iran. **middleman** *n* trader who buys from the producer and sells to the consumer. **middle-of-the-road** *adj* **1** politically moderate. **2** (of music) generally popular. **middleweight** *n* boxer weighing up to 160lb (professional) or

75kg (amateur).

middling *adj* **1** mediocre. **2** moderate. ♦ *adv* **3** moderately.

midfield *n Soccer* area between the two opposing defences.

midge *n* small mosquito-like insect.

midget *n* very small person or thing.

midland *n* **1** middle part of a country. ♦ *pl* **2** (**M-**) central England.

midnight *n* twelve o'clock at night.

midriff *n* middle part of the body.

midshipman *n* naval officer of the lowest commissioned rank.

midst *n* **in the midst of 1** surrounded by. **2** at a point during.

midsummer *n* **1** middle of summer. **2** summer solstice. **Midsummer's Day, Midsummer Day** June 24th.

midway *adj, adv* halfway.

midwife *n* trained person who assists at childbirth. **midwifery** [mid-**wiff**-fer-ree] *n*

midwinter *n* **1** middle or depth of winter. **2** winter solstice.

mien [**mean**] *n Lit* person's bearing, demeanour, or appearance.

miffed *adj Informal* offended or upset.

might[1] *v* past tense of MAY.

> Both *might* and *may* can be used to express a tentative request: *Might/may I ask a favour?*

might[2] *n* power or strength. **with might and main** energetically or forcefully. **mighty** *adj* **mightier, mightiest 1** powerful. **2** important. ♦ *adv* **3** *US & Aust informal* very. **mightily** *adv*

mignonette [min-yon-**net**] *n* grey-green plant with sweet-smelling flowers.

migraine [**mee**-grain] *n* severe headache, often with nausea and visual disturbances.

migrate *v* **1** move from one place to settle in another. **2** (of animals) journey between different habitats at specific seasons. **migration** *n* **migrant** *n* **1** person or animal that moves from one place to another. ♦ *adj* **2** moving from one place to another, e.g. *migrant workers.* **migratory** *adj* (of an animal) migrating every year.

mikado *n, pl* **-dos** *Old-fashioned* Japanese emperor.

mike *n Informal* microphone.

milch [**miltch**] *adj* (of a cow) giving milk.

mild *adj* **1** not strongly flavoured. **2** gentle. **3** calm or temperate. **mildly** *adv* **mildness** *n*

mildew *n* destructive fungus on plants or things exposed to damp. **mildewed** *adj*

mile *n* unit of length equal to 1760 yards or 1.609 kilometres. **mileage** *n* **1** distance travelled in miles. **2** miles travelled by a motor vehicle per gallon of petrol. **3** *Informal* usefulness of something. **mileometer** [mile-**om**-it-er] *n* device that records the number of miles a vehicle has travelled. **milestone** *n* **1** significant event. **2** stone marker showing the distance to a certain place.

milieu [meal-**yer**] *n, pl* **milieux, milieus** [meal-**yerz**] environment or surroundings.

militant *adj* aggressive or vigorous in support of a cause. **militancy** *n* **militantly** *adv*

military *adj* **1** of or for soldiers, armies, or war. ♦ *n* **2** armed services. **militarily** *adv* **militarism** *n* belief in the use of military force and methods. **militarist** *n* **militaristic** *adj* **militarized** *adj*

militate *v* (usu. with *against* or *for*) have a strong influence or effect.

> Do not confuse *militate* with *mitigate* 'make less severe'.

militia [mill-**ish**-a] *n* military force of trained citizens for use in emergency only. **militiaman** *n*

milk *n* **1** white fluid produced by female mammals to feed their young. **2** milk of cows, goats, etc., used by humans as food. **3** fluid in some plants. ♦ *v* **4** draw milk from. **5** exploit (a person or situation). **milking** *n* **milky** *adj* **milkier, milkiest Milky Way** luminous band of stars stretching across the night sky. **milk float** small electrically powered vehicle used to deliver milk to houses. **milkmaid** *n* (esp. in former times) woman who milks cows. **milkman** *n* man who delivers milk to people's houses. **milk round** **1** route along which a milkman regularly delivers milk. **2** regular series of visits to colleges made by recruitment officers from industry. **milkshake** *n* frothy flavoured cold milk drink. **milksop** *n* feeble man. **milk teeth** first set of teeth in young children.

mill *n* **1** factory. **2** machine for grinding, processing, or rolling. ♦ *v* **3** grind, press, or process in or as if in a mill. **4** cut fine grooves across the edges of (coins). **5** move in a confused manner. **miller** *n* person who works in a mill.

millennium [mill-**en**-nee-um] *n, pl* **-nia** [-nee-a], **-niums** **1** period of a thousand years. **2** future period of peace and happiness. **millennium bug** computer problem caused by the date change at the beginning of the 21st century.

millet *n* a cereal grass.

milli- *combining form* denoting a thousandth part, e.g. *millisecond.*

milliard *n Brit* one thousand millions.

millibar *n* unit of atmospheric pressure.

milligram, milligramme *n* thousandth part of a gram.

millilitre *n* thousandth part of a litre.

millimetre *n* thousandth part of a metre.

milliner *n* maker or seller of women's hats. **millinery** *n*

million *n* one thousand thousands. **millionth** *adj, n* **millionaire** *n* person who owns at least a million pounds, dollars, etc.

millipede *n* small animal with a jointed body and many pairs of legs.

millstone *n* flat circular stone for grinding corn. **millstone round one's neck** heavy burden of responsibility or obligation.

millwheel *n* waterwheel that drives a mill.

milometer [mile-**om**-it-er] *n* same as MILEOMETER.

milt *n* sperm of fish.

mime *n* **1** acting without the use of words. **2** performer who does this. ♦ *v* **3** act in mime. **4** perform as if singing or playing music that is prerecorded.

mimic *v* **-icking, -icked** **1** imitate (a person or manner), esp. for satirical effect. ♦ *n* **2** person or animal that is good at mimicking. **mimicry** *n*

mimosa *n* shrub with fluffy yellow flowers and sensitive leaves.

min. **1** minimum. **2** minute(s).

Min. **1** Minister. **2** Ministry.

minaret *n* tall slender tower of a mosque.

minatory *adj* threatening or menacing.

mince *v* **1** cut or grind into very small pieces. **2** walk or speak in an affected manner. **3** soften or moderate (one's words). ♦ *n* **4** minced meat. **mincer** *n* machine for mincing meat. **mincing** *adj* affected in manner. **mincemeat** *n* sweet mixture of dried fruit and spices. **mince pie** pie containing mincemeat.

mind *n* **1** thinking faculties. **2** memory or attention. **3** intention. **4** sanity. ♦ *v* **5** take offence at. **6** pay attention to. **7** take care of. **8** be cautious or careful about (something). **change one's mind** alter one's decision or opinion. **in one's mind's eye** in one's imagination. **make up one's mind** reach a decision. **minded** *adj* having an inclination as specified, e.g. *politically minded.* **minder** *n Informal* aide or bodyguard. **mindful** *adj* **1** heedful. **2** keeping aware. **mindless** *adj* **1** stupid. **2** requiring no thought. **3** careless.

mine[1] *pron* belonging to me.

mine[2] *n* **1** deep hole for digging out coal, ores, etc. **2** bomb placed under the ground or in water. **3** profitable source, e.g. *a mine of information.* ♦ *v* **4** dig for minerals. **5** dig (minerals) from a mine. **6** place explosive mines in or on. **miner** *n* person who works in a mine. **mining** *n* **minefield** *n* area of land or water containing mines. **minesweeper** *n* ship for clearing away mines.

mineral *n* **1** naturally occurring inorganic substance, such as metal. ♦ *adj* **2** of, containing, or like minerals. **mineralogy** [min-er-**al**-a-jee] *n* study of minerals. **mineralogist** *n* **mineral water** water containing dissolved mineral salts or gases.

minestrone [min-ness-**strone**-ee] *n* soup containing vegetables and pasta.

mingle *v* **1** mix or blend. **2** come into association (with).

mingy *adj* **-gier, -giest** *Informal* miserly.

mini *n, adj* **1** (something) small or miniature. **2** short (skirt).

mini- *combining form* smaller or shorter than usual, e.g. *mini-budget; minidress.*

miniature *n* **1** small portrait, model, or copy. ♦ *adj* **2** small-scale. **miniaturist** *n* **miniaturize** *v* make to a very small scale. **miniaturization** *n*

minibar *n* selection of drinks and confectionery provided in a hotel room.

minibus *n* small bus.

minicab *n* ordinary car used as a taxi.

minicomputer *n* computer smaller than a mainframe but more powerful than a microcomputer.

minim *n Music* note half the length of a semibreve.

minimum *adj, n, pl* **-mums, -ma** least possible (amount or number). **minimal** *adj* minimum. **minimally** *adv* **minimize** *v* **1** reduce to a minimum. **2** belittle. **minimization** *n*

minion *n* servile assistant.

miniseries *n* TV programme shown in several parts, often on consecutive days.

miniskirt *n* very short skirt.

minister *n* **1** head of a government department. **2** diplomatic representative. **3** clergyman. ♦ *v* **4** (foll. by *to*) attend to the needs of. **ministerial** *adj* **ministration** *n* giving of help. **ministry** *n, pl* **-tries 1** profession or duties of a clergyman. **2** ministers collectively. **3** government department.

mink *n* **1** stoatlike animal. **2** its highly valued fur.

minnow *n* small freshwater fish.

minor *adj* **1** lesser. **2** *Music* (of a scale) having a semitone between the second and third notes. ♦ *n* **3** person regarded legally as a child. **4** *Music* minor scale. **minority** *n, pl* **-ties 1** lesser number. **2** smaller party voting together. **3** group in a minority in any state.

minster *n* cathedral or large church.

minstrel *n* medieval singer or musician.

mint[1] *n* **1** plant with aromatic leaves used for seasoning and flavouring. **2** sweet flavoured with this.

mint[2] *n* **1** place where money is coined. ♦ *v* **2** make (coins).

minuet [min-new-**wet**] *n* **1** stately dance. **2** music for this.

minus *prep, adj* **1** indicating subtraction. ♦ *adj* **2** less than zero. ♦ *n* **3** sign (-) denoting subtraction or a number less than zero.

minuscule [**min**-niss-skyool] *adj* very small.

minute[1] [**min**-it] *n* **1** 60th part of an hour or degree. **2** moment. ♦ *pl* **3** record of the proceedings of a meeting. ♦ *v* **4** record in the minutes.

minute[2] [my-**newt**] *adj* **1** very small. **2** precise. **minutely** *adv* **minutiae** [my-**new**-shee-eye] *pl n* trifling or precise details.

minx *n* bold or flirtatious girl.

miracle *n* **1** wonderful supernatural event. **2** marvel. **miraculous** *adj* **miraculously** *adv* **miracle play** medieval play based on a sacred subject.

mirage [mir-**rahzh**] *n* optical illusion, esp. one caused by hot air.

mire *n* **1** swampy ground. **2** mud.

mirror *n* **1** coated glass surface for reflecting images. ♦ *v* **2** reflect in or as if in a mirror. **mirror image** image or object that has left and right reversed as if seen in a mirror.

mirth *n* laughter, merriment, or gaiety. **mirthful** *adj* **mirthless** *adj* **mirthlessly** *adv*

mis- *prefix* wrong(ly), bad(ly).

misadventure *n* unlucky chance.

misanthrope [**miz**-zan-thrope] *n* person who dislikes people in general. **misanthropic** [miz-zan-**throp**-ik] *adj* **misan-**

thropy [miz-**zan**-throp-ee] *n*

misapplication *n* use of something for the wrong purpose.

misapprehend *v* misunderstand. **misapprehension** *n*

misappropriate *v* take and use (money) dishonestly. **misappropriation** *n*

misbehave *v* behave badly. **misbehaviour** *n*

miscalculate *v* calculate or judge wrongly. **miscalculation** *n*

miscarriage *n* **1** spontaneous premature expulsion of a fetus from the womb. **2** failure, e.g. *a miscarriage of justice.* **miscarry** *v* **1** have a miscarriage. **2** fail.

miscast *v* **-casting, -cast** cast (a role or actor) in (a play or film) inappropriately.

miscegenation [miss-ij-in-**nay**-shun] *n* interbreeding of races.

miscellaneous [miss-sell-**lane**-ee-uss] *adj* mixed or assorted. **miscellany** [miss-**sell**-a-nee] *n* mixed assortment.

mischance *n* unlucky event.

mischief *n* **1** annoying but not malicious behaviour. **2** inclination to tease. **3** harm. **mischievous** [**miss**-chiv-uss] *adj* **1** full of mischief. **2** intended to cause harm. **mischievously** *adv*

miscible [**miss**-sib-bl] *adj* able to be mixed.

misconception *n* wrong idea or belief. **misconceived** *adj*

misconduct *n* immoral or unethical behaviour.

misconstrue *v* interpret wrongly. **misconstruction** *n*

miscreant [**miss**-kree-ant] *n* wrongdoer.

misdeed *n* wrongful act.

misdemeanour *n* minor wrongdoing.

misdirect *v* give (someone) wrong directions or instructions. **misdirection** *n*

miser *n* person who hoards money and hates spending it. **miserly** *adj*

miserable *adj* **1** very unhappy, wretched. **2** causing misery. **3** squalid. **4** mean. **miserably** *adv* **misery** *n, pl* **-eries 1** great unhappiness. **2** *Informal* complaining person.

misfire *v* **1** (of a firearm or engine) fail to fire correctly. **2** (of a plan) fail to turn out as intended.

misfit *n* person not suited to his or her social environment.

misfortune *n* (piece of) bad luck.

misgiving *n* feeling of fear or doubt.

misguided *adj* mistaken or unwise.

mishandle *v* handle badly or inefficiently.

mishap *n* minor accident.

mishear *v* hear (what someone says) wrongly.

mishmash *n* confused collection or mixture.

misinform *v* give incorrect information to. **misinformation** *n*

misinterpret *v* understand or represent (something) wrongly. **misinterpretation** *n*

misjudge *v* judge wrongly or unfairly. **misjudgment, misjudgement** *n*

mislay *v* lose (something) temporarily.

mislead *v* give false or confusing information to. **misleading** *adj* **misleadingly** *adv*

mismanage *v* organize or run (something) badly. **mismanagement** *n*

misnomer [miss-**no**-mer] *n* **1** incorrect or unsuitable name. **2** use of this.

misogyny [miss-**oj**-in-ee] *n* hatred of women. **misogynist** *n*

misplace *v* **1** mislay. **2** put in the wrong place. **3** give (trust or affection) inappropriately.

misprint *n* printing error.

mispronounce *v* pronounce (a word) wrongly. **mispronunciation** *n*

misquote *v* quote inaccurately. **misquotation** *n*

misread *v* **1** misinterpret (a situation etc.). **2** read incorrectly.

misrepresent *v* represent wrongly or inaccurately. **misrepresentation** *n*

misrule *v* **1** govern inefficiently or unjustly. ♦ *n* **2** inefficient or unjust government.

miss *v* **1** fail to notice, hear, hit, reach, find, or catch. **2** not be in time for. **3** notice or regret the absence of. **4** avoid.

5 (of an engine) misfire. ♦ *n* **6** fact or instance of missing. **missing** *adj* lost or absent. **miss out** *v* **1** leave out or overlook. **2** (foll. by *on*) fail to take part in (something enjoyable or beneficial).

Miss *n* title of a girl or unmarried woman.

missal *n* book containing the prayers and rites of the Mass.

misshapen *adj* badly shaped, deformed.

missile *n* **1** rocket with an exploding warhead, used as a weapon. **2** object or weapon thrown, shot, or launched at a target.

mission *n* **1** specific task or duty. **2** task or duty that a person believes he or she must achieve. **3** group of people sent on a mission. **4** building in which missionaries work. **missionary** *n, pl* **-aries** person sent abroad to do religious and social work.

missive *n* letter.

misspell *v* spell (a word) wrongly.

misspent *adj* wasted or misused.

missus, missis *n Informal* one's wife or the wife of the person addressed or referred to.

mist *n* **1** thin fog. **2** fine spray of liquid. **misty** *adj* **mistier, mistiest 1** full of mist. **2** dim or obscure. **mist over** *v* **1** (also **mist up**) (of glass) become covered with small drops of moisture causing a misty effect. **2** (of eyes) fill up with tears.

mistake *n* **1** error or blunder. ♦ *v* **-taking, -took, -taken 2** misunderstand. **3** confuse (a person or thing) with another. **mistaken** *adj* wrong in judgment or opinion. **mistakenly** *adv*

Mister *n* polite form of address to a man.

mistime *v* do (something) at the wrong time.

mistletoe *n* evergreen plant with white berries growing as a parasite on trees.

mistral *n* strong dry northerly wind of S France.

mistreat *v* treat (a person or animal) badly.

mistress *n* **1** woman who has a continuing sexual relationship with a married man. **2** woman in control of people or animals. **3** female teacher.

mistrial *n Law* trial made void because of some error.

mistrust *v* **1** have doubts or suspicions about. ♦ *n* **2** lack of trust. **mistrustful** *adj*

misunderstand *v* fail to understand properly. **misunderstanding** *n*

misuse *n* **1** incorrect, improper, or careless use. ♦ *v* **2** use wrongly. **3** treat badly.

mite *n* **1** very small spider-like animal. **2** very small thing or amount. **a mite** somewhat.

mitigate *v* make less severe. **mitigating** *adj* **mitigation** *n*

> *Mitigate* is often confused with *militate* 'have an influence on'.

mitosis *n* type of cell division in which the nucleus divides into two nuclei which each contain the same number of chromosomes as the original nucleus.

mitre [**my**-ter] *n* **1** bishop's pointed headdress. **2** joint between two pieces of wood bevelled to meet at right angles. ♦ *v* **3** join with a mitre joint.

mitt *n* **1** short for MITTEN. **2** *Slang* hand. **3** baseball catcher's glove.

mitten *n* glove with one section for the thumb and one for the four fingers together.

mix *v* **1** combine or blend into one mass. **2** form (something) by mixing. **3** be sociable. ♦ *n* **4** mixture. **mixed** *adj* **mixed blessing** something that has advantages as well as disadvantages. **mixed grill** dish of several kinds of grilled meat, tomatoes, and mushrooms. **mix up** *v* **1** confuse. **2** make into a mixture. **mixed up** *adj* **mix-up** *n* **mixer** *n* **1** kitchen appliance used for mixing foods. **2** *Informal* person considered in relation to his or her ability to mix socially, e.g. *a good mixer.* **3** nonalcoholic drink, e.g. tonic water, that is mixed with an alcoholic drink. **mixture** *n* **1** something mixed. **2** combination.

mizzenmast *n* (on a vessel with three

or more masts) third mast from the bow.

mks units *pl n* metric system of units based on the metre, kilogram, and second.

ml millilitre(s).

Mlle *pl* **Mlles** Mademoiselle.

mm millimetre(s).

MM plural of M (sense 1).

Mme *pl* **Mmes** Madame.

Mn *Chem* manganese.

MN Minnesota.

mnemonic [nim-**on**-ik] *n, adj* (something, such as a rhyme) intended to help the memory.

mo *n, pl* **mos** *Informal* short for MOMENT.

Mo *Chem* molybdenum.

MO **1** Medical Officer. **2** Missouri.

moan *n* **1** low cry of pain. **2** *Informal* grumble. ♦ *v* **3** make or utter with a moan. **4** *Informal* grumble. **moaner** *n*

moat *n* deep wide ditch, esp. round a castle.

mob *n* **1** disorderly crowd. **2** *Slang* gang. ♦ *v* **mobbing, mobbed** **3** surround in a mob to acclaim or attack.

mobile *adj* **1** able to move. ♦ *n* **2** same as MOBILE PHONE. **3** hanging structure designed to move in air currents. **mobile phone** cordless phone powered by batteries. **mobility** *n*

mobilize *v* **1** (of the armed services) prepare for active service. **2** organize for a purpose. **mobilization** *n*

moccasin *n* soft leather shoe.

mocha [**mock**-a] *n* **1** kind of strong dark coffee. **2** flavouring made from coffee and chocolate.

mock *v* **1** make fun of. **2** mimic. ♦ *adj* **3** sham or imitation. **mocks** *pl n Informal* (in England and Wales) practice exams taken before public exams. **put the mockers on** *Informal* ruin the chances of success of. **mockery** *n* **1** derision. **2** inadequate or worthless attempt. **mocking** *adj* **mockingbird** *n* N American bird which imitates other birds' songs. **mockingly** *adv* **mock orange** shrub with white fragrant flowers. **mock-up** *n* full-scale model for test or study.

mod[1] *n* member of a group of young people, orig. in the mid-1960s, who were very clothes-conscious and rode motor scooters.

mod[2] *n* annual Highland Gaelic meeting with musical and literary competitions.

MOD Ministry of Defence.

mod. **1** moderate. **2** modern.

mod cons *pl n Informal* modern conveniences, such as heating and hot water.

mode *n* **1** method or manner. **2** current fashion.

model *n* **1** (miniature) representation. **2** pattern. **3** person or thing worthy of imitation. **4** person who poses for an artist or photographer. **5** person who wears clothes to display them to prospective buyers. ♦ *adj* **6** excellent or perfect, e.g. *a model husband.* ♦ *v* **-elling, -elled** **7** make a model of. **8** mould. **9** plan or create according to a model or models. **10** display (clothing) as a model. **modelling** *n*

modem [**mode**-em] *n* device for connecting two computers by a telephone line.

moderate *adj* **1** not extreme. **2** self-restrained. **3** average. ♦ *n* **4** person of moderate views. ♦ *v* **5** make or become less violent or extreme. **moderately** *adv* **moderation** *n* **moderator** *n* **1** (Presbyterian Church) minister appointed to preside over a Church court, general assembly, etc. **2** person who presides over a public or legislative assembly.

modern *adj* **1** of present or recent times. **2** up-to-date. **modern languages** languages spoken in present-day Europe, with the exception of English. **modern pentathlon** athletic contest consisting of five different events. **modernity** *n* **modernism** *n* (support of) modern tendencies, thoughts, or styles. **modernist** *adj, n* **modernize** *v* bring up to date. **modernization** *n*

modest *adj* **1** not vain or boastful. **2** not excessive. **3** not showy. **4** shy. **modest-**

ly *adv* **modesty** *n*

modicum *n* small quantity.

modify *v* **fying, -fied 1** change slightly. **2** tone down. **3** (of a word) qualify (another word). **modifier** *n* word that qualifies the sense of another. **modification** *n*

modish [**mode**-ish] *adj* in fashion.

modulate *v* **1** vary in tone. **2** adjust. **3** change the key of (music). **modulation** *n* **modulator** *n*

module *n* **1** self-contained unit, section, or component with a specific function. **2** short study course that together with other such courses counts towards a qualification. **modular** *adj*

modus operandi [**mode**-uss op-er-**an**-die] *n Latin* method of operating.

modus vivendi [**mode**-uss viv-**venn**-die] *n Latin* working arrangement between conflicting interests.

moggy, moggie *n, pl* **-gies** *Slang* cat.

mogul [**moh**-gl] *n* important or powerful person.

MOH Medical Officer of Health.

mohair *n* **1** fine hair of the Angora goat. **2** yarn or fabric made from this.

mohican *n* punk hairstyle with shaved sides and a stiff central strip of hair, often brightly coloured.

moiety [**moy**-it-ee] *n, pl* **-ties** half.

moiré [**mwahr**-ray] *adj* **1** having a watered or wavelike pattern. ♦ *n* **2** any fabric that has such a pattern.

moist *adj* slightly wet. **moisten** *v* make or become moist. **moisture** *n* liquid diffused as vapour or condensed in drops. **moisturize** *v* add moisture to (the skin etc.). **moisturizer** *n*

moke *n Slang* donkey.

molar *n* large back tooth used for grinding.

molasses *n* dark syrup, a by-product of sugar refining.

mole[1] *n* small dark raised spot on the skin.

mole[2] *n* **1** small burrowing mammal. **2** *Informal* spy who has infiltrated and become a trusted member of an organization. **molehill** *n* small mound of earth thrown up by a burrowing mole. **make a mountain out of a molehill** exaggerate an unimportant matter out of all proportion.

mole[3] *n* unit of amount of substance.

mole[4] *n* **1** breakwater. **2** harbour protected by this.

molecule [**mol**-lik-kyool] *n* **1** simplest freely existing chemical unit, composed of two or more atoms. **2** very small particle. **molecular** [mol-**lek**-yew-lar] *adj*

molest *v* **1** interfere with sexually. **2** annoy or injure. **molester** *n* **molestation** *n*

moll *n Slang* gangster's female accomplice.

mollify *v* **-fying, -fied** pacify or soothe. **mollification** *n*

mollusc *n* soft-bodied, usu. hard-shelled, animal, such as a snail or oyster.

mollycoddle *v* pamper.

Molotov cocktail *n* petrol bomb.

molten *adj* liquefied or melted.

molybdenum [mol-**lib**-din-um] *n Chem* hard silvery-white metallic element.

moment *n* **1** short space of time. **2** (present) point in time. **momentary** *adj* lasting only a moment. **momentarily** *adv*

> Note that some American speakers use *momentarily* to mean 'soon' rather than 'for a moment'.

momentous [moh-**men**-tuss] *adj* of great significance.

momentum [moh-**men**-tum] *n* **1** impetus to go forward, develop, or get stronger. **2** impetus of a moving body. **3** product of a body's mass and velocity.

Mon. Monday.

monarch *n* sovereign ruler of a state. **monarchical** *adj* **monarchist** *n* supporter of monarchy. **monarchy** *n, pl* **-chies** government by or a state ruled by a sovereign.

monastery *n, pl* **-teries** residence of a community of monks. **monastic** *adj* **1** of monks, nuns, or monasteries. **2** simple and austere. **monasticism** *n*

monatomic *adj* consisting of single atoms.

Monday *n* second day of the week.

monetary *adj* of money or currency. **monetarism** *n* **1** theory that inflation is caused by an increase in the money supply. **2** economic policy based on this theory. **monetarist** *n, adj*

money *n* medium of exchange, coins or banknotes. **moneyed, monied** *adj* rich. **moneylender** *n* person who lends money at a high rate of interest as a living.

Mongolian *n* **1** person from Mongolia. **2** language of Mongolia. ♦ *adj* **3** of Mongolia or its language.

mongolism *n Offens* Down's syndrome. **mongol** *n, adj Offens* (person) affected by this.

mongoose *n, pl* **-gooses** stoatlike mammal of Asia and Africa that kills snakes.

mongrel *n* **1** animal, esp. a dog, of mixed breed. **2** something arising from a variety of sources. ♦ *adj* **3** of mixed breed or origin.

monitor *n* **1** person or device that checks, controls, warns, or keeps a record of something. **2** pupil assisting a teacher with duties. **3** television set used in a studio to check what is being transmitted. **4** type of large lizard. ♦ *v* **5** watch and check on.

monk *n* member of an all-male religious community bound by vows. **monkish** *adj* **monkshood** *n* poisonous plant with hooded flowers.

monkey *n* **1** long-tailed primate. **2** mischievous child. ♦ *v* **3** (usu. foll. by *about* or *around*) meddle or fool. **monkey nut** peanut. **monkey puzzle** coniferous tree with sharp stiff leaves. **monkey wrench** wrench with adjustable jaws.

mono *adj* **1** short for MONOPHONIC. ♦ *n* **2** monophonic sound.

mono- *combining form* single, e.g. *monosyllable.*

monochrome *adj* **1** *Photog* black-and-white. **2** in only one colour.

monocle [**mon**-a-kl] *n* eyeglass for one eye only.

monocotyledon [mon-no-kot-ill-**leed**-on] *n* flowering plant with a single embryonic seed leaf.

monocular *adj* having or for one eye only.

monogamy *n* custom of being married to one person at a time. **monogamous** *adj*

monogram *n* design of combined letters, esp. a person's initials. **monogrammed** *adj* marked with such a design.

monograph *n* book or paper on a single subject.

monolith *n* large upright block of stone. **monolithic** *adj*

monologue *n* **1** long speech by one person. **2** dramatic piece for one performer.

monomania *n* obsession with one thing. **monomaniac** *n, adj*

monophonic *adj* (of a system of broadcasting, recording, or reproducing sound) using only one channel between source and loudspeaker.

monoplane *n* aeroplane with one pair of wings.

monopoly *n* **1** (*pl* **-lies**) exclusive possession of or right to do something. **2** (**M-**) ® board game for four to six players who deal in 'property' as they move around the board. **monopolist** *n* **monopolistic** *adj* **monopolize** *v* have or take exclusive possession of.

monorail *n* single-rail railway.

monosodium glutamate *n* white crystalline substance used as a food additive to enhance protein flavours.

monosyllable *n* word of one syllable. **monosyllabic** *adj*

monotheism *n* belief in only one God. **monotheistic** *adj*

monotone *n* unvaried pitch in speech or sound. **monotonous** *adj* tedious due to lack of variety. **monotonously** *adv* **monotony** *n* wearisome routine, dullness.

monoxide *n* oxide that contains one oxygen atom per molecule.

Monseigneur [mon-sen-**nyur**] *n, pl* **Messeigneurs** [may-sen-**nyur**] title of

French prelates.

monsieur [muss-**syur**] *n, pl* **messieurs** [may-**syur**] French title of address equivalent to *sir* or *Mr.*

Monsignor *n RC Church* title attached to certain offices.

monsoon *n* **1** seasonal wind of SE Asia. **2** rainy season accompanying this.

monster *n* **1** imaginary, usu. frightening, beast. **2** huge person, animal, or thing. **3** very wicked person. ♦ *adj* **4** huge. **monstrosity** *n, pl* **-ities** large ugly thing. **monstrous** *adj* **1** unnatural or ugly. **2** outrageous or shocking. **3** huge. **monstrously** *adv*

monstrance *n RC Church* container in which the consecrated Host is exposed for adoration.

montage [**mon**-tahzh] *n* **1** (making of) a picture composed from pieces of others. **2** method of film editing incorporating several shots to form a single image.

month *n* **1** one of the twelve divisions of the calendar year. **2** period of four weeks. **monthly** *adj* **1** happening or payable once a month. ♦ *adv* **2** once a month. ♦ *n, pl* **-lies** **3** monthly magazine.

monument *n* something, esp. a building or statue, that commemorates something. **monumental** *adj* **1** large, impressive, or lasting. **2** of or being a monument. **3** *Informal* extreme. **monumentally** *adv Informal* extremely.

moo *n* **1** long deep cry of a cow. ♦ *v* **2** make this noise.

mooch *v Slang* loiter about aimlessly.

mood[1] *n* temporary (gloomy) state of mind. **moody** *adj* **moodier, moodiest** **1** sullen or gloomy. **2** changeable in mood. **moodily** *adv* **moodiness** *n*

mood[2] *n Grammar* form of a verb indicating whether it expresses a fact, wish, supposition, or command.

moon *n* **1** natural satellite of the earth. **2** natural satellite of any planet. ♦ *v* **3** (foll. by *about* or *around*) be idle in a listless or dreamy way. **moonless** *adj* **moony** *adj Informal* dreamy or listless. **moonbeam** *n* ray of moonlight. **moonlight** *n* **1** light from the moon. ♦ *adj* **2** illuminated by the moon, e.g. *a moonlight drive.* ♦ *v* **3** *Informal* work at a secondary job, esp. illegally. **moonlit** *adj* **moonshine** *n* **1** illicitly distilled whisky. **2** nonsense. **moonstone** *n* translucent semiprecious stone. **moonstruck** *adj* slightly mad or odd.

moor[1] *n* tract of open uncultivated ground covered with grass and heather. **moorhen** *n* small black water bird. **moorland** *n*

moor[2] *v* secure (a ship) with ropes etc. **mooring** *n* **1** place for mooring a ship. ♦ *pl* **2** ropes etc. used in mooring a ship.

Moor *n* member of a Muslim people of NW Africa who ruled Spain between the 8th and 15th centuries. **Moorish** *adj*

moose *n* large N American deer.

moot *adj* **1** debatable, e.g. *a moot point.* ♦ *v* **2** bring up for discussion.

mop *n* **1** long stick with twists of cotton or a sponge on the end, used for cleaning. **2** thick mass of hair. ♦ *v* **mopping, mopped** **3** clean or soak up with or as if with a mop.

mope *v* be gloomy and apathetic.

moped *n* light motorized cycle.

moraine *n* accumulated mass of debris deposited by a glacier.

moral *adj* **1** concerned with right and wrong conduct. **2** based on a sense of right and wrong. **3** (of support or a victory) psychological rather than practical. ♦ *n* **4** lesson to be obtained from a story or event. ♦ *pl* **5** principles of behaviour with respect to right and wrong. **morally** *adv* **moralist** *n* person with a strong sense of right and wrong. **moralistic** *adj* **morality** *n* **1** good moral conduct. **2** moral goodness or badness. **morality play** medieval play with a moral lesson. **moralize** *v* make moral pronouncements.

morale [mor-**rahl**] *n* degree of confidence or hope of a person or group.

morass *n* **1** marsh. **2** mess.

moratorium *n, pl* **-ria, -riums** legally authorized ban or delay.

moray *n* large voracious eel.

morbid *adj* **1** unduly interested in death or unpleasant events. **2** gruesome. **morbidly** *adv*

mordant *adj* **1** sarcastic or scathing. ♦ *n* **2** substance used to fix dyes.

more *adj* **1** greater in amount or degree. **2** comparative of MUCH *or* MANY. **3** additional or further. ♦ *adv* **4** to a greater extent. **5** in addition. ♦ *pron* **6** greater or additional amount or number. **moreover** *adv* in addition to what has already been said.

morel *n* edible mushroom with a pitted cap.

mores [**more**-rayz] *pl n* customs and conventions embodying the fundamental values of a community.

morganatic marriage *n* marriage of a person of high rank to a lower-ranking person whose status remains unchanged.

morgue *n* mortuary.

moribund *adj* without force or vitality.

Mormon *n* member of a religious sect founded in the USA.

morn *n Poetic* morning.

mornay *adj* served with a cheese sauce, e.g. *sole mornay*.

morning *n* part of the day before noon. **the morning after** *Informal* the aftereffects of overindulgence, hangover. **morning coat** frock coat. **morning dress** formal day dress for men, comprising a morning coat, grey trousers, and a top hat. **morning-glory** *n* plant with trumpet-shaped flowers which close in the late afternoon. **morning sickness** nausea shortly after rising, often experienced in early pregnancy.

Moroccan *adj* **1** of Morocco. ♦ *n* **2** person from Morocco.

morocco *n* goatskin leather.

moron *n* **1** *Informal* foolish or stupid person. **2** (formerly) person with a low intelligence quotient. **moronic** *adj*

morose [mor-**rohss**] *adj* sullen or moody. **morosely** *adv*

morphine, morphia *n* drug extracted from opium, used as an anaesthetic and sedative.

morphology *n* science of forms and structures of organisms or words. **morphological** *adj*

morris dance *n* traditional English folk dance performed by men.

morrow *n Poetic* next day.

Morse *n* system of signalling in which letters of the alphabet are represented by combinations of short and long signals.

morsel *n* small piece, esp. of food.

mortal *adj* **1** subject to death. **2** causing death. ♦ *n* **3** human being. **mortally** *adv* **mortality** *n* **1** state of being mortal. **2** great loss of life. **3** death rate. **mortal sin** *RC Church* sin meriting damnation.

mortar *n* **1** small cannon with a short range. **2** mixture of lime, sand, and water for holding bricks and stones together. **3** bowl in which substances are pounded. **mortarboard** *n* square academic cap.

mortgage *n* **1** conditional pledging of property, esp. a house, as security for the repayment of a loan. **2** the loan itself. ♦ *v* **3** pledge (property) as security thus. **mortgagee** *n* creditor in a mortgage. **mortgagor, mortgager** *n* debtor in a mortgage.

mortice, mortise [**more**-tiss] *n* hole in a piece of wood or stone shaped to receive a matching projection on another piece. **mortice lock** lock set into a door.

mortify *v* **-fying, -fied 1** humiliate. **2** subdue by self-denial. **3** (of flesh) become gangrenous. **mortification** *n*

mortuary *n, pl* **-aries** building where corpses are kept before burial or cremation.

mosaic [mow-**zay**-ik] *n* design or decoration using small pieces of coloured stone or glass.

Mosaic *adj* of Moses.

Moselle *n* light white German wine.

Moslem *n, adj* same as MUSLIM.

mosque *n* Muslim temple.

mosquito *n, pl* **-toes, -tos** bloodsucking flying insect.

moss *n* small flowerless plant growing in masses on moist surfaces. **mossy** *adj* **mossier, mossiest**

most *n* **1** greatest number or degree. ♦ *adj* **2** greatest in number or degree. **3** superlative of MUCH *or* MANY. ♦ *adv* **4** in the greatest degree. **mostly** *adv* for the most part, generally.

MOT, MOT test *n* compulsory annual test of the roadworthiness of vehicles over a certain age.

mote *n* tiny speck.

motel *n* roadside hotel for motorists.

motet [moh-**tet**] *n* short sacred choral song.

moth *n* nocturnal insect like a butterfly. **mothball** *n* **1** small ball of camphor or naphthalene used to repel moths from stored clothes. ♦ *v* **2** store (something operational) for future use. **3** postpone (a project etc.). **moth-eaten** *adj* **1** decayed or scruffy. **2** eaten or damaged by moth larvae.

mother *n* **1** female parent. **2** head of a female religious community. ♦ *adj* **3** native or inborn, e.g. *mother wit.* ♦ *v* **4** look after as a mother. **motherhood** *n* **motherly** *adj* **motherless** *adj* **mother country, motherland** country where one was born. **mother-in-law** *n, pl* **mothers-in-law** mother of one's husband or wife. **mother of pearl** iridescent lining of certain shells. **mother tongue** one's native language.

motif [moh-**teef**] *n* (recurring) theme or design.

motion *n* **1** process, action, or way of moving. **2** proposal in a meeting. **3** evacuation of the bowels. ♦ *v* **4** direct (someone) by gesture. **motionless** *adj* not moving. **motion picture** cinema film.

motive *n* **1** reason for a course of action. ♦ *adj* **2** causing motion. **motivate** *v* give incentive to. **motivation** *n*

motley *adj* **1** miscellaneous. **2** multicoloured.

motocross *n* motorcycle race over a rough course.

motor *n* **1** engine, esp. of a vehicle. **2** machine that converts electrical energy into mechanical energy. **3** car. ♦ *v* **4** travel by car. **motorist** *n* driver of a car. **motorized** *adj* equipped with a motor or motor transport. **motorbike** *n* **motorboat** *n* **motorcade** *n* procession of cars carrying important people. **motorcar** *n* **motorcycle** *n* **motorcyclist** *n* **motor scooter** light motorcycle with small wheels and an enclosed engine. **motorway** *n* main road for fast-moving traffic.

mottled *adj* marked with blotches.

motto *n, pl* **-toes, -tos** **1** saying expressing an ideal or rule of conduct. **2** verse or maxim in a paper cracker.

mould[1] *n* **1** hollow container in which metal etc. is cast. **2** shape, form, or pattern. **3** nature or character. ♦ *v* **4** shape. **5** influence or direct. **moulding** *n* moulded ornamental edging.

mould[2] *n* fungal growth caused by dampness. **mouldy** *adj* **mouldier, mouldiest** **1** stale or musty. **2** dull or boring.

mould[3] *n* loose soil. **moulder** *v* decay into dust.

moult *v* **1** shed feathers, hair, or skin to make way for new growth. ♦ *n* **2** process of moulting.

mound *n* **1** heap, esp. of earth or stones. **2** small hill.

mount *v* **1** climb or ascend. **2** get up on (a horse etc.). **3** increase or accumulate. **4** fix on a support or backing. **5** organize, e.g. *mount a campaign.* ♦ *n* **6** backing or support on which something is fixed. **7** horse for riding. **8** hill.

mountain *n* **1** hill of great size. **2** large heap. **mountainous** *adj* **1** full of mountains. **2** huge. **mountaineer** *n* person who climbs mountains. **mountaineering** *n* **mountain bike** bicycle with straight handlebars and heavy-duty tyres, for cycling over rough terrain. **mountain lion** same as PUMA.

mountebank *n* charlatan or fake.

Mountie *n Informal* member of the Royal Canadian Mounted Police.

mourn *v* feel or express sorrow for (a

dead person or lost thing). **mourner** *n* **mournful** *adj* sad or dismal. **mournfully** *adv* **mourning** *n* **1** grieving. **2** conventional symbols of grief for death, such as the wearing of black.

mouse *n, pl* **mice 1** small long-tailed rodent. **2** timid person. **3** *Computers* hand-held device for moving the cursor without keying. **mouser** *n* cat used to catch mice. **mousy** *adj* **mousier, mousiest 1** like a mouse, esp. in hair colour. **2** meek and shy.

moussaka *n* dish made with meat, aubergines, and tomatoes, topped with cheese sauce.

mousse *n* **1** dish of flavoured cream whipped and set. **2** foamy substance applied to the hair before styling to hold the style.

moustache *n* hair on the upper lip.

mouth *n* **1** opening in the head for eating and issuing sounds. **2** lips. **3** entrance. **4** point where a river enters the sea. **5** opening. ♦ *v* **6** form (words) with the lips without speaking. **7** speak or utter insincerely, esp. in public. **mouthful** *n* **1** amount of food or drink put into the mouth at any one time when eating or drinking. **2** word, phrase, or name that is difficult to say. **mouth organ** same as HARMONICA. **mouthpiece** *n* **1** part of a telephone into which a person speaks. **2** part of a wind instrument into which the player blows. **3** spokesperson. **mouthwash** *n* medicated liquid for gargling and cleansing the mouth.

move *v* **1** change in place or position. **2** change (one's house etc.). **3** take action. **4** stir the emotions of. **5** incite. **6** suggest (a proposal) formally. ♦ *n* **7** moving. **8** action towards some goal. **movable, moveable** *adj* **movement** *n* **1** action or process of moving. **2** group with a common aim. **3** division of a piece of music. **4** moving parts of a machine. **moving** *adj* arousing or touching the emotions. **movingly** *adv*

movie *n Informal* cinema film.

mow *v* **mowing, mowed, mowed** *or* **mown** cut (grass or crops). **mower** *n* **mow down** *v* kill in large numbers.

mozzarella [mot-sa-**rel**-la] *n* moist white cheese originally made in Italy from buffalo milk.

MP 1 Member of Parliament. **2** Military Police(man).

mpg miles per gallon.

mph miles per hour.

Mr Mister.

Mrs *n* title of a married woman.

Ms [**mizz**] *n* title used instead of Miss or Mrs.

MS 1 manuscript. **2** multiple sclerosis. **3** Mississippi.

MSc Master of Science.

MSS manuscripts.

Mt Mount.

MT Montana.

much *adj* **more, most 1** large amount or degree of. ♦ *n* **2** large amount or degree. ♦ *adv* **more, most 3** to a great degree. **4** nearly. **much of a muchness** very similar.

mucilage [**mew**-sill-ij] *n* gum or glue.

muck *n* **1** dirt, filth. **2** manure. **3** *Slang* something of poor quality, rubbish. **mucky** *adj* **muckier, muckiest muck about** *v Slang* waste time or misbehave. **muck in** *v Slang* share a task with other people. **muck out** *v* clean (a byre, stable, etc.). **muckraking** *n* seeking out and exposing scandal relating to well-known people. **muckraker** *n* **muck up** *v Slang* ruin or spoil.

mucus [**mew**-kuss] *n* slimy secretion of the mucous membranes. **mucous** *adj* **mucous membrane** tissue lining body cavities or passages.

mud *n* wet soft earth. **muddy** *adj* **-dier, -diest 1** covered or filled with mud. **2** not clear or bright, e.g. *muddy brown.* ♦ *v* **-dying, -dies 3** make muddy. **4** make (a situation or issue) less clear. **mud flat** area of low muddy land that is covered by the sea only at high tide. **mudguard** *n* cover over a wheel to prevent mud or water being thrown up by it. **mudpack** *n* cosmetic paste to improve the complexion.

muddle *v* **1** (often foll. by *up*) confuse. **2** mix up. ♦ *n* **3** state of confusion.

muesli [**mewz**-lee] *n* mixture of grain, nuts, and dried fruit, eaten with milk.

muezzin [moo-**ezz**-in] *n* official who summons Muslims to prayer.

muff[1] *n* tube-shaped covering to keep the hands warm.

muff[2] *v* bungle (an action).

muffin *n* **1** light round flat yeast cake. **2** small cup-shaped sweet bread roll.

muffle *v* wrap up for warmth or to deaden sound. **muffler** *n* scarf.

mufti *n* civilian clothes worn by a person who usually wears a uniform.

mug[1] *n* large drinking cup.

mug[2] *n* **1** *Slang* face. **2** *Slang* gullible person. ♦ *v* **mugging, mugged 3** *Informal* attack in order to rob. **mugger** *n* **mugging** *n* **mug shot** *Informal* photograph of the face of a suspect or criminal, held in a police file.

mug[3] *v* **mugging, mugged** (foll. by *up*) *Informal* study hard.

muggins *n Informal* stupid or gullible person.

muggy *adj* **-gier, -giest** (of weather) damp and stifling.

mujaheddin, mujahedeen [moo-ja-hed-**deen**] *pl n* fundamentalist Muslim guerrillas.

mulatto [mew-**lat**-toe] *n, pl* **-tos, -toes** child of one Black and one White parent.

mulberry *n* **1** tree whose leaves are used to feed silkworms. **2** purple fruit of this tree.

mulch *n* **1** mixture of wet straw, leaves, etc., used to protect the roots of plants. ♦ *v* **2** cover (land) with mulch.

mule[1] *n* offspring of a horse and a donkey. **mulish** *adj* obstinate. **muleteer** *n* mule driver.

mule[2] *n* backless shoe or slipper.

mull *v* think (over) or ponder. **mulled** *adj* (of wine or ale) flavoured with sugar and spices and served hot.

mullah *n* Muslim scholar, teacher, or religious leader.

mullet *n* edible sea fish.

mulligatawny *n* soup made with curry powder.

mullion *n* vertical dividing bar in a window. **mullioned** *adj* having mullions.

multi- *combining form* many, e.g. *multicultural; multistorey.*

multicoloured *adj* having many different colours.

multifarious [mull-tee-**fare**-ee-uss] *adj* having many various parts.

multilateral *adj* of or involving more than two nations or parties.

multilingual *adj* speaking or written in more than two languages.

multimillionaire *n* person who owns several million pounds, dollars, etc.

multinational *adj* **1** operating in several countries. **2** involving people from several countries. ♦ *n* **3** large company operating in several countries.

multiple *adj* **1** having many parts. ♦ *n* **2** quantity which contains another an exact number of times. **multiple-choice** *adj* having a number of possible given answers out of which the correct one must be chosen. **multiple sclerosis** chronic progressive disease of the nervous system, resulting in speech and visual disorders, tremor, and partial paralysis.

multiplex *n* **1** purpose-built complex containing several cinemas and usu. restaurants and bars. ♦ *adj* **2** having many elements, complex.

multiplicity *n, pl* **-ties** large number or great variety.

multiply *v* **-plying, -plied 1** (cause to) increase in number, quantity, or degree. **2** add (a number or quantity) to itself a given number of times. **3** increase in number by reproduction. **multiplication** *n* **multiplicand** *n Maths* number to be multiplied. **multiplier** *n Maths* number by which another number is multiplied.

multipurpose *adj* having many uses, e.g. *a multipurpose vehicle.*

multiracial *adj* made up of people from many races, e.g. *a multiracial society.*

multitude *n* **1** great number. **2** great

crowd. **multitudinous** *adj* very numerous.

mum[1] *n Informal* mother.

mum[2] *adj* **keep mum** remain silent.

mumble *v* **1** speak indistinctly, mutter. ♦ *n* **2** indistinct utterance.

mumbo jumbo *n* **1** meaningless language. **2** foolish religious ritual or incantation.

mummer *n* actor in a folk play or mime.

mummy[1] *n, pl* **-mies** body embalmed and wrapped for burial in ancient Egypt. **mummified** *adj* (of a body) preserved as a mummy.

mummy[2] *n, pl* **-mies** child's word for MOTHER.

mumps *n* infectious disease with swelling in the glands of the neck.

munch *v* chew noisily and steadily.

mundane *adj* **1** everyday. **2** earthly.

municipal *adj* relating to a city or town. **municipality** *n, pl* **-ities** **1** city or town with local self-government. **2** governing body of this.

munificent [mew-**niff**-fiss-sent] *adj* very generous. **munificence** *n*

muniments [**mew**-nim-ments] *pl n* title deeds or similar documents.

munitions [mew-**nish**-unz] *pl n* military stores.

mural [**myoor**-al] *n* painting on a wall.

murder *n* **1** unlawful intentional killing of a human being. ♦ *v* **2** kill in this way. **murderer, murderess** *n* **murderous** *adj*

murk *n* thick darkness. **murky** *adj* **murkier, murkiest** **1** dark or gloomy. **2** suspicious or shady.

murmur *v* **-muring, -mured** **1** speak or say in a quiet indistinct way. **2** complain. ♦ *n* **3** continuous low indistinct sound. **4** complaint, e.g. *she went without a murmur.* **5** abnormal soft blowing sound heard made by the heart.

murrain [**murr**-rin] *n* cattle plague.

muscle *n* **1** tissue in the body which produces movement by contracting. **2** strength or power. **muscular** *adj* **1** with well-developed muscles. **2** of muscles. **muscular dystrophy** disease with wasting of the muscles. **muscle in** *v Informal* force one's way in.

muse *v* ponder quietly.

Muse *n* **1** *Greek myth* one of nine goddesses, each of whom inspired an art or science. **2** (**m-**) force that inspires a creative artist.

museum *n* building where natural, artistic, historical, or scientific objects are exhibited and preserved. **museum piece** *Informal* very old object or building.

mush *n* **1** soft pulpy mass. **2** *Informal* cloying sentimentality. **mushy** *adj* **mushier, mushiest**

mushroom *n* **1** edible fungus with a stem and cap. ♦ *v* **2** grow rapidly. **mushroom cloud** large mushroom-shaped cloud produced by a nuclear explosion.

music *n* **1** art form using a melodious and harmonious combination of notes. **2** written or printed form of this. **musical** *adj* **1** of or like music. **2** talented in or fond of music. **3** pleasant-sounding. ♦ *n* **4** play or film with songs and dancing. **musically** *adv* **musician** *n* **musicianship** *n* **musicology** *n* scientific study of music. **musicologist** *n* **music centre** combined record or CD player, radio, and cassette player. **music hall** variety theatre.

musk *n* scent obtained from a gland of the musk deer or produced synthetically. **musky** *adj* **muskier, muskiest** **muskrat** *n* **1** N American beaver-like rodent. **2** its fur.

musket *n Hist* long-barrelled gun. **musketeer** *n* **musketry** *n* (use of) muskets.

Muslim *n* **1** follower of the religion of Islam. ♦ *adj* **2** of or relating to Islam.

muslin *n* fine cotton fabric.

musquash *n* muskrat fur.

mussel *n* edible shellfish with a dark hinged shell.

must[1] *v* **1** used as an auxiliary to express obligation, certainty, or resolution. ♦ *n* **2** essential or necessary thing.

must[2] *n* newly pressed grape juice.

mustang *n* wild horse of SW USA.

mustard *n* **1** paste made from the powdered seeds of a plant, used as a condiment. **2** the plant. **mustard gas** poisonous gas causing blistering burns and blindness.

muster *v* **1** summon up (strength, energy, or support). **2** assemble. ♦ *n* **3** assembly of military personnel. **pass muster** be acceptable.

musty *adj* **mustier, mustiest** smelling mouldy and stale. **mustiness** *n*

mutable [**mew**-tab-bl] *adj* liable to change. **mutability** *n*

mutation [mew-**tay**-shun] *n* (genetic) change. **mutate** [mew-**tate**] *v* (cause to) undergo mutation. **mutant** [**mew**-tant] *n* mutated animal, plant, etc.

mute *adj* **1** silent. **2** unable to speak. ♦ *n* **3** person who is unable to speak. **4** *Music* device to soften the tone of an instrument. **muted** *adj* **1** (of sound or colour) softened. **2** (of a reaction) subdued. **mutely** *adv*

mutilate [**mew**-till-ate] *v* **1** deprive of a limb or other part. **2** damage (a book or text). **mutilated** *adj* **mutilation** *n*

mutiny [**mew**-tin-ee] *n, pl* **-nies** **1** rebellion against authority, esp. by soldiers or sailors. ♦ *v* **-nying, -nied** **2** commit mutiny. **mutineer** *n* **mutinous** *adj*

mutt *n Slang* **1** stupid person. **2** mongrel dog.

mutter *v* **1** utter or speak indistinctly. **2** grumble. ♦ *n* **3** muttered sound or grumble. **muttering** *n*

mutton *n* flesh of sheep, used as food.

mutual [**mew**-chew-al] *adj* **1** felt or expressed by each of two people about the other. **2** common to both or all. **mutually** *adv*

> The objection that something *mutual* has to do with two people only is outdated; nowadays *mutual* is equivalent to 'shared, in common'.

Muzak *n* ® recorded light music played in shops etc.

muzzle *n* **1** animal's mouth and nose. **2** cover for these to prevent biting. **3** open end of a gun. ♦ *v* **4** prevent from being heard or noticed. **5** put a muzzle on.

muzzy *adj* **-zier, -ziest** **1** confused or muddled. **2** blurred or hazy.

mW milliwatt(s).

MW **1** megawatt(s). **2** medium wave.

my *adj* belonging to me.

mycology *n* study of fungi.

mynah *n* Asian bird which can mimic human speech.

myopia [my-**oh**-pee-a] *n* short-sightedness. **myopic** [my-**op**-ik] *adj* **myopically** *adv*

myriad [**mir**-ree-ad] *adj* **1** innumerable. ♦ *n* **2** large indefinite number.

myrrh [**mur**] *n* aromatic gum used in perfume, incense, and medicine.

myrtle [**mur**-tl] *n* flowering evergreen shrub.

myself *pron* emphatic or reflexive form of I[1] *or* ME[1].

mystery *n, pl* **-teries** **1** strange or inexplicable event or phenomenon. **2** obscure or secret thing. **3** story or film that arouses suspense. **mysterious** *adj* **mysteriously** *adv*

mystic *n* **1** person who seeks spiritual knowledge. ♦ *adj* **2** mystical. **mystical** *adj* having a spiritual or religious significance beyond human understanding. **mysticism** *n*

mystify *v* **-fying, -fied** bewilder or puzzle. **mystification** *n*

mystique [miss-**steek**] *n* aura of mystery or power.

myth *n* **1** tale with supernatural characters, usu. of how the world and mankind began. **2** untrue idea or explanation. **3** imaginary person or object. **mythical, mythic** *adj* **mythology** *n* **1** myths collectively. **2** study of myths. **mythological** *adj*

myxomatosis [mix-a-mat-**oh**-siss] *n* contagious fatal viral disease of rabbits.

N n

n *adj* **1** indefinite number (of), e.g. *there are n ways of doing this.* ♦ *n* **2** *Maths* number whose value is not stated, e.g. *two to the power n.* **nth** *adj*

N **1** *Chem* nitrogen. **2** *Physics* newton(s). **3** North(ern). **4** nuclear, e.g. *N test.*

n. **1** neuter. **2** noun. **3** number.

Na *Chem* sodium.

n/a, N.A. not applicable: used to indicate that a question on a form is not relevant to the person filling it in.

Naafi *n* canteen or shop for military personnel.

naan *n* same as NAN BREAD.

nab *v* **nabbing, nabbed** *Informal* **1** arrest (someone). **2** catch (someone) in wrongdoing.

nabob [**nay**-bob] *n Informal* rich or important person.

nacelle [nah-**sell**] *n* streamlined enclosure on an aircraft, esp. one housing an engine.

nacre [**nay**-ker] *n* mother of pearl. **nacreous** *adj*

nadir *n* **1** point in the sky opposite the zenith. **2** lowest point.

naevus [**nee**-vuss] *n, pl* **-vi** birthmark or mole.

naff *adj Slang* lacking quality or taste, e.g. *one of the naffest songs ever.*

nag[1] *v* **nagging, nagged** **1** scold or find fault constantly. **2** be a constant source of discomfort or worry to. ♦ *n* **3** person who nags. **nagging** *adj, n*

nag[2] *n Informal* old horse.

naiad [**nye**-ad] *n, pl* **naiads, naiades** [**nye**-ad-deez] *Greek myth* water nymph.

nail *n* **1** pointed piece of metal with a head, hit with a hammer to join two objects together. **2** hard covering of the upper tips of the fingers and toes. ♦ *v* **3** attach (something) with nails. **4** *Informal* catch or arrest. **hit the nail on the head** say something exactly correct. **on the nail** at once, esp. in *pay on the nail.* **nailfile** *n* small metal file used to smooth or shape the finger or toe nails. **nail varnish, polish** cosmetic lacquer applied to the finger or toe nails.

naive [nye-**eev**] *adj* **1** innocent and gullible. **2** simple and lacking sophistication. **naively** *adv* **naivety, naïveté** [nye-**eev**-tee] *n*

naked *adj* **1** without clothes. **2** not concealed, e.g. *naked hostility.* **3** without any covering, e.g. *naked flame.* **the naked eye** the eye unassisted by any optical instrument. **nakedly** *adv* **nakedness** *n*

namby-pamby *adj* sentimental or insipid.

name *n* **1** word by which a person or thing is known. **2** reputation, esp. a good one. **3** famous person, e.g. *a big name in the music business.* ♦ *v* **4** give a name to. **5** refer to by name. **6** fix or specify. **call someone names, a name** insult someone by using rude words to describe him or her. **in name only** not possessing the powers implied by his, her, or its title, e.g. *ruler in name only.* **nameless** *adj* **1** without a name. **2** unspecified. **3** too horrible to be mentioned. **namely** *adv* that is to say. **name day** *RC Church* feast day of a saint whose name one bears. **name-dropping** *n* referring to famous people as if they were friends, in order to impress others. **name-dropper** *n* **nameplate** *n* small sign on or by a door giving the occupant's name and, sometimes, profession. **namesake** *n* person with the same name as another.

nan bread *n* slightly leavened Indian bread in a large flat leaf shape.

nancy, nancy boy *n* effeminate or homosexual boy or man.

nanny *n, pl* **-nies** **1** woman whose job is looking after young children. ♦ *v* **2** be too protective towards. **nanny goat** female goat.

nano- *combining form* denoting one thousand millionth, e.g. *nanosecond.*

nap[1] *n* **1** short sleep. ♦ *v* **napping, napped 2** have a short sleep.

nap[2] *n* raised fibres of velvet or similar cloth.

nap[3] *n* **1** card game similar to whist. **2** *Horse racing* tipster's choice for a certain winner. ♦ *v* **napping, napped 3** name (a horse) as a certain winner.

napalm *n* **1** highly inflammable jellied petrol, used in bombs. ♦ *v* **2** attack (people or places) with napalm.

nape *n* back of the neck.

naphtha *n* liquid mixture distilled from coal tar or petroleum, used as a solvent and in petrol. **naphthalene** *n* white crystalline product distilled from coal tar or petroleum, used in disinfectants, mothballs, and explosives.

napkin *n* piece of cloth or paper for wiping the mouth or protecting the clothes while eating.

nappy *n, pl* **-pies** piece of absorbent material fastened round a baby's lower torso to absorb urine and faeces.

narcissism *n* exceptional interest in or admiration for oneself. **narcissistic** *adj*

narcissus *n, pl* **-cissi** yellow, orange, or white flower related to the daffodil.

narcotic *n, adj* (of) a drug, such as morphine or opium, which produces numbness and drowsiness, used medicinally but addictive. **narcosis** *n* effect of a narcotic.

nark *Slang* ♦ *v* **1** annoy. ♦ *n* **2** informer or spy. **3** someone who complains in an irritating manner. **narky** *adj* **narkier, narkiest** *Slang* irritable or complaining.

narrate *v* **1** tell (a story). **2** speak the words accompanying and telling what is happening in a film or TV programme. **narration** *n* **narrator** *n* **narrative** *n* **1** account, story. ♦ *adj* **2** telling a story, e.g. *a narrative poem.*

narrow *adj* **1** small in breadth in comparison to length. **2** limited in range, extent, or outlook. **3** with little margin, e.g. *a narrow escape.* ♦ *v* **4** make or become narrow. **5** (often foll. by *down*) limit or restrict. **narrows** *pl n* narrow part of a strait, river, or current. **narrowly** *adv* **narrowness** *n* **narrow boat** long bargelike canal boat. **narrow-gauge** *adj* (of a railway) having less than the standard distance of 56½ inches between the rails. **narrow-minded** *adj* intolerant or bigoted. **narrow-mindedness** *n*

narwhal *n* arctic whale with a long spiral tusk.

NASA *US* National Aeronautics and Space Administration.

nasal *adj* **1** of the nose. **2** (of a sound) pronounced with air passing through the nose. **3** (of a voice) characterized by nasal sounds. **nasally** *adv*

nascent *adj* starting to grow or develop.

nasturtium *n* plant with yellow, red, or orange trumpet-shaped flowers.

nasty *adj* **-tier, -tiest 1** unpleasant. **2** (of an injury) dangerous or painful. **3** spiteful or unkind. ♦ *n, pl* **-ties 4** something unpleasant. **nastily** *adv* **nastiness** *n*

nat. 1 national. **2** nationalist.

natal [**nay**-tal] *adj* of or relating to birth.

nation *n* people of one or more cultures or races organized as a single state. **nationwide** *adj* covering all of a nation.

national *adj* **1** of or serving a nation as a whole. **2** characteristic of a particular nation. ♦ *n* **3** citizen of a nation. **nationally** *adv* **national anthem** official patriotic song of a nation. **National Curriculum** curriculum of subjects taught in state schools in England and Wales since 1989. **national debt** total outstanding debt of a country's government. **national grid** network of high-voltage power lines linking power stations. **National Health Service** system of national medical services financed mainly by taxation. **national insurance** state insurance scheme providing payments to the unemployed, sick, and retired. **national park** area of countryside protected by a government for its natural or environmental importance. **national service** compulsory military service.

nationalism *n* **1** policy of national independence. **2** patriotism, sometimes to an excessive degree. **nationalist** *n, adj* **nationalistic** *adj* fiercely or excessively patriotic.

nationality *n, pl* **-ities** **1** fact of being a citizen of a particular nation. **2** group of people of the same race, e.g. *young men of all nationalities.*

nationalize *v* put (an industry or a company) under state control. **nationalization** *n*

native *adj* **1** relating to a place where a person was born. **2** born in a specified place. **3** (foll. by *to*) originating (in). **4** inborn. ♦ *n* **5** person born in a specified place. **6** indigenous animal or plant. **7** member of the original race of a country. **Native American** (person) descended from the original inhabitants of the American continent.

Nativity *n Christianity* birth of Jesus Christ.

NATO North Atlantic Treaty Organization.

natter *Informal* ♦ *v* **1** talk idly or chatter. ♦ *n* **2** long idle chat.

natty *adj* **-tier, -tiest** *Informal* smart and spruce.

natural *adj* **1** normal or to be expected. **2** genuine or spontaneous. **3** of, according to, existing in, or produced by nature. **4** not created by human beings. **5** not synthetic. **6** (of a parent) not adoptive. **7** (of a child) illegitimate. **8** *Music* not sharp or flat, e.g. *B natural.* ♦ *n* **9** person with an inborn talent or skill. **10** *Music* symbol cancelling the effect of a previous sharp or flat. **naturally** *adv* **1** of course. **2** in a natural or normal way. **3** instinctively. **naturalness** *n* **natural gas** gas found below the ground, used mainly as a fuel. **natural history** study of animals and plants in the wild. **natural number** positive integer, such as 1, 2, 3, etc. **natural philosophy** *Old-fashioned* physics. **natural science** science dealing with the physical world, such as physics, biology or geology. **natural selection** process by which only creatures and plants well adapted to their environment survive.

naturalism *n* movement in art and literature advocating detailed realism. **naturalistic** *adj*

naturalist *n* student of natural history.

naturalize *v* give citizenship to (a person born in another country). **naturalization** *n*

nature *n* **1** whole system of the existence, forces, and events of the physical world that are not controlled by human beings. **2** fundamental or essential qualities. **3** kind or sort.

naturism *n* nudism. **naturist** *n*

naught *n Lit* nothing.

naughty *adj* **-tier, -tiest** **1** disobedient or mischievous. **2** mildly indecent. **naughtily** *adv* **naughtiness** *n*

nausea [**naw**-zee-a] *n* feeling of being about to vomit. **nauseate** *v* **1** make (someone) feel sick. **2** disgust. **nauseous** *adj* **1** as if about to vomit. **2** sickening.

nautical *adj* of the sea or ships. **nautical mile** 1852 metres (6076.12 feet).

nautilus *n, pl* **-luses, -li** shellfish with many tentacles.

naval *adj* see NAVY.

nave *n* long central part of a church.

navel *n* hollow in the middle of the abdomen where the umbilical cord was attached. **navel orange** sweet orange with a navel-like hollow at the top.

navigate *v* **1** direct or plot the path or position of a ship, aircraft, or car. **2** travel over or through. **navigation** *n* **navigational** *adj* **navigator** *n* **navigable** *adj* **1** wide, deep, or safe enough to be sailed through. **2** able to be steered.

navvy *n, pl* **-vies** labourer employed on a road or a building site.

navy *n, pl* **-vies** **1** branch of a country's armed services comprising warships with their crews and organization. **2** warships of a nation. ♦ *adj* **3** navy-blue. **naval** *adj* of or relating to a navy or ships. **navy-blue** *adj* very dark blue.

nay *interj Obs* no.

Nazi *n* **1** member of the fascist National

Socialist Party, which came to power in Germany in 1933 under Adolf Hitler. ♦ *adj* **2** of or relating to the Nazis. **Nazism** *n*

Nb *Chem* niobium.

NB **1** New Brunswick. **2** note well.

NC North Carolina.

NCO noncommissioned officer.

Nd *Chem* neodymium.

ND North Dakota.

Ne *Chem* neon.

NE **1** Nebraska. **2** northeast(ern).

Neanderthal [nee-**ann**-der-tahl] *adj* of a type of primitive man that lived in Europe before 12 000 BC.

Neapolitan *n* **1** person from Naples. ♦ *adj* **2** of Naples.

neap tide *n* tide at the first and last quarters of the moon when there is the smallest rise and fall in tidal level.

near *prep, adv, adj* **1** indicating a place or time not far away. ♦ *adj* **2** almost being the thing specified, e.g. *a near disaster.* ♦ *v* **3** draw close (to). **nearly** *adv* almost. **nearness** *n* **nearby** *adj* not far away. **Near East** same as MIDDLE EAST. **nearside** *n* side of a vehicle that is nearer the kerb. **near-sighted** *adj* (of a person) short-sighted.

neat *adj* **1** tidy and clean. **2** smoothly or competently done. **3** undiluted. **neatly** *adv* **neatness** *n* **neaten** *v* make neat.

nebula [**neb**-yew-la] *n, pl* **-lae** [-lee] *Astronomy* hazy cloud of particles and gases. **nebular** *adj* **nebulous** *adj* vague, indistinct.

NEC National Executive Committee.

necessary *adj* **1** needed to obtain the desired result, e.g. *the necessary skills.* **2** certain or unavoidable, e.g. *the necessary consequences.* **necessaries** *pl n* essential items, e.g. *the necessaries of life.* **necessarily** *adv* **necessitate** *v* compel or require. **necessitous** *adj* very needy. **necessity** *n, pl* **-ties** **1** circumstances that inevitably require a certain result. **2** something needed. **3** great poverty.

neck *n* **1** part of the body joining the head to the shoulders. **2** part of a garment round the neck. **3** long narrow part of a bottle or violin. ♦ *v* **4** *Slang* kiss and cuddle. **neck and neck** absolutely level in a race or competition. **stick one's neck out** *Informal* risk criticism or ridicule by speaking one's mind. **neckerchief** *n* piece of cloth worn tied round the neck. **necklace** *n* decorative piece of jewellery worn around the neck. **neckline** *n* shape or position of the upper edge of a dress or top. **necktie** *n US* same as TIE (sense 5).

necromancy [**neck**-rome-man-see] *n* **1** communication with the dead. **2** sorcery. **necromancer** *n*

necrophilia *n* sexual attraction for or intercourse with dead bodies.

necropolis [neck-**rop**-pol-liss] *n* cemetery.

necrosis *n Biol, Med* death of cells in the body.

nectar *n* **1** sweet liquid collected from flowers by bees. **2** drink of the gods.

nectarine *n* smooth-skinned peach.

née [**nay**] *prep* indicating the maiden name of a married woman.

need *v* **1** require or be in want of. **2** be obliged (to do something). ♦ *n* **3** condition of lacking something. **4** requirement or necessity. **5** poverty. **needs** *adv* (preceded or foll. by *must*) necessarily. **needy** *adj* **needier, neediest** poor, in need of financial support. **needful** *adj* necessary or required. **needless** *adj* unnecessary. **needlessly** *adv*

needle *n* **1** thin pointed piece of metal with an eye through which thread is passed for sewing. **2** long pointed rod used in knitting. **3** pointed part of a hypodermic syringe. **4** small pointed part in a record player that touches the record and picks up the sound signals, stylus. **5** pointer on a measuring instrument or compass. **6** long narrow stiff leaf. **7** *Informal* intense rivalry or ill-feeling, esp. in a sports match. ♦ *v* **8** *Informal* goad or provoke. **needlecord** *n* finely-ribbed corduroy. **needlepoint** *n* embroidery done on canvas. **needlework** *n* sewing and embroidery.

ne'er *adv Lit* never. **ne'er-do-well** *n* useless or lazy person.

nefarious [nif-**fair**-ee-uss] *adj* wicked.

negate *v* **1** invalidate. **2** deny the existence of. **negation** *n*

negative *adj* **1** expressing a denial or refusal. **2** lacking positive qualities. **3** (of an electrical charge) having the same electrical charge as an electron. **4** *Med* indicating the absence of a condition for which a test was made. ♦ *n* **5** negative word or statement. **6** *Photog* image with a reversal of tones or colours from which positive prints are made.

neglect *v* **1** take no care of. **2** fail (to do something) through carelessness. **3** disregard. ♦ *n* **4** neglecting or being neglected. **neglectful** *adj*

negligee, négligée [**neg**-lee-zhay] *n* woman's lightweight usu. lace-trimmed dressing gown.

negligence *n* neglect or carelessness. **negligent** *adj* **negligently** *adv*

negligible *adj* so small or unimportant as to be not worth considering.

negotiate *v* **1** discuss in order to reach (an agreement). **2** succeed in passing round or over (a place or problem). **negotiation** *n* **negotiator** *n* **negotiable** *adj*

Negro *n, pl* **-groes** *Old-fashioned* member of any of the Black peoples originating in Africa. **Negroid** *adj* of or relating to the Negro race.

neigh *n* **1** loud high-pitched sound made by a horse. ♦ *v* **2** make this sound.

neighbour *n* person who lives or is situated near another. **neighbouring** *adj* situated nearby. **neighbourhood** *n* **1** district. **2** surroundings. **3** people of a district. **neighbourhood watch** scheme in which the residents of an area keep an eye on each other's property as a means of preventing crime. **neighbourly** *adj* kind, friendly, and helpful.

neither *adj, pron* **1** not one nor the other. ♦ *conj* **2** not.

> When *neither* is followed by a plural noun it is acceptable to make the verb plural too: *Neither of these books are useful.*

nelson *n* wrestling hold in which a wrestler places his arm(s) under his opponent's arm(s) from behind and exerts pressure with his palms on the back of his opponent's neck.

nematode, nematode worm *n* slender cylindrical unsegmented worm.

nemesis [**nem**-miss-iss] *n, pl* **-ses** retribution or vengeance.

neo- *combining form* new, recent, or a modern form of, e.g. *neoclassicism.*

neoclassicism *n* late 18th- and early 19th-century style of art and architecture, based on ancient Roman and Greek models. **neoclassical** *adj*

neocolonialism *n* political control yielded by one country over another through control of its economy. **neocolonial** *adj*

neodymium *n Chem* silvery-white metallic element of lanthanide series.

Neolithic *adj* of the later Stone Age.

neologism [nee-**ol**-a-jiz-zum] *n* newly-coined word or an established word used in a new sense.

neon *n Chem* colourless odourless gaseous element used in illuminated signs and lights.

neonatal *adj* relating to the first few weeks of a baby's life.

neophyte *n* **1** beginner or novice. **2** new convert.

nephew *n* son of one's sister or brother.

nephritis [nif-**frite**-tiss] *n* inflammation of a kidney.

nepotism [**nep**-a-tiz-zum] *n* favouritism in business shown to relatives and friends.

Neptune *n* **1** Roman god of the sea. **2** eighth planet from the sun.

neptunium *n Chem* synthetic radioactive metallic element.

nerd, nurd *n Slang* **1** boring person obsessed with a particular subject. **2** stupid and feeble person.

nerve *n* **1** cordlike bundle of fibres that conducts impulses between the brain and other parts of the body. **2** bravery and determination. **3** impudence. ♦ *pl* **4** anxiety or tension. **5** ability or inability to remain calm in a difficult situation. **get on someone's nerves** irritate someone. **nerve oneself** prepare oneself (to do something difficult or unpleasant). **nerveless** *adj* **1** numb, without feeling. **2** fearless. **nervy** *adj* **nervier, nerviest** excitable or nervous. **nerve centre** place from which a system or organization is controlled. **nerve gas** poisonous gas which affects the nervous system. **nerve-racking** *adj* very distressing or harrowing.

nervous *adj* **1** apprehensive or worried. **2** of or relating to the nerves. **nervously** *adv* **nervousness** *n* **nervous breakdown** mental illness in which the sufferer ceases to function properly. **nervous system** brain, spinal column and nerves, which together control thought, feeling and movement.

ness *n* headland, cape.

nest *n* **1** place or structure in which birds or certain animals lay eggs or give birth to young. **2** secluded place. **3** set of things of graduated sizes designed to fit together. ♦ *v* **4** make or inhabit a nest. **5** (of a set of objects) fit one inside another. **nest egg** fund of money kept in reserve.

nestle *v* **1** snuggle. **2** be in a sheltered position.

nestling *n* bird too young to leave the nest.

net[1] *n* **1** fabric of meshes of string, thread, or wire with many openings. **2** piece of net used to protect or hold things or to trap animals. **3** (in certain sports) piece of net over which the ball or shuttlecock must be hit. **4** goal in soccer or hockey. **5** strategy intended to trap people, e.g. *he had slipped through a police net.* ♦ *v* **netting, netted 6** catch (a fish or animal) in a net. **the Net** short for INTERNET. **netting** *n* material made of net. **netball** *n* team game in which a ball has to be thrown through a net hanging from a ring at the top of a pole.

net[2]**, nett** *adj* **1** left after all deductions. **2** (of weight) excluding the wrapping or container. **3** final or conclusive, e.g. *the net result.* ♦ *v* **netting, netted 4** yield or earn as a clear profit.

nether *adj* lower. **nethermost** *adj* lowest.

nettle *n* plant with stinging hairs on the leaves. **nettled** *adj* irritated or annoyed. **nettle rash** skin condition in which itchy red or white raised patches appear.

network *n* **1** system of intersecting lines, roads, etc. **2** interconnecting group or system. **3** (in broadcasting) group of stations that all transmit the same programmes simultaneously. **4** *Computers* system of interconnected circuits. ♦ *v* **5** broadcast (a programme) over a network.

neural *adj* of a nerve or the nervous system.

neuralgia *n* severe pain along a nerve.

neuritis [nyoor-**rite**-tiss] *n* inflammation of a nerve or nerves.

neurology *n* scientific study of the nervous system. **neurological** *adj* **neurologist** *n*

neuron, neurone *n* cell specialized to conduct nerve impulses.

neurosis *n, pl* **-ses** mental disorder producing hysteria, anxiety, depression, or obsessive behaviour. **neurotic** *adj* **1** emotionally unstable. **2** suffering from neurosis. ♦ *n* **3** neurotic person.

neurosurgery *n* branch of surgery concerned with the nervous system. **neurosurgical** *adj* **neurosurgeon** *n*

neuter *adj* **1** belonging to a particular class of grammatical inflections in some languages. **2** (of an animal) sexually underdeveloped. ♦ *v* **3** castrate (an animal).

neutral *adj* **1** taking neither side in a war or dispute. **2** of or belonging to a neutral party or country. **3** not displaying emotions or opinions. **4** (of a colour) not definite or striking. ♦ *n* **5** neutral person or nation. **6** neutral gear. **neutrality** *n* **neutralize** *v* make ineffective or neutral. **neutral gear** position of the controls of a gearbox that leaves the gears unconnected to the engine.

neutrino [new-**tree**-no] *n, pl* **-nos** elementary particle with no mass or electrical charge.

neutron *n* electrically neutral elementary particle of about the same mass as a proton. **neutron bomb** nuclear bomb designed to kill people and animals while leaving buildings virtually undamaged.

never *adv* at no time. **never-ending** *adj* long and boring. **nevermore** *adv Lit* never again. **nevertheless** *adv* in spite of that.

> Avoid the use of *never* with the past tense to mean *not: I didn't see her* (not *I never saw her*).

never-never *n Informal* hire-purchase. **never-never land** imaginary idyllic place.

new *adj* **1** not existing before. **2** recently acquired. **3** having lately come into some state. **4** additional. **5** (foll. by *to*) unfamiliar. ♦ *adv* **6** recently. **newness** *n* **New Age** late 1980s philosophy characterized by a belief in alternative medicine and spiritualism. **newborn** *adj* recently or just born. **newcomer** *n* recent arrival or participant. **newfangled** *adj* objectionably or unnecessarily modern. **new-found** *adj* newly or recently discovered. **newly** *adv* **newlyweds** *pl n* recently married couple. **new moon** moon when it appears as a narrow crescent at the beginning of its cycle. **New Testament** part of the Christian Bible dealing with life and teachings of Christ and his followers. **new town** town planned and built as a complete unit. **New World** the Americas; the western hemisphere. **New Year** (holiday marking) the first day or days of the year.

newel *n* post at the top or bottom of a flight of stairs that supports the handrail.

news *n* **1** important or interesting new happenings. **2** information about such events reported in the mass media. **3** television or radio programme presenting such information. **newsy** *adj* full of news. **newsagent** *n* shopkeeper who sells newspapers and magazines. **newsflash** *n* brief important news item, which interrupts a radio or television programme. **newsletter** *n* bulletin issued periodically to members of a group. **newspaper** *n* weekly or daily publication containing news. **newsprint** *n* inexpensive paper used for newspapers. **newsreader, newscaster** *n* person who reads the news on the television or radio. **newsreel** *n* short film giving news. **newsroom** *n* room where news is received and prepared for publication or broadcasting. **newsworthy** *adj* sufficiently interesting to be reported as news.

newt *n* small amphibious creature with a long slender body and tail.

newton *n* unit of force.

next *adj, adv* **1** immediately following. **2** nearest. **next door** *adj, adv* (often hyphenated) in, at, or to the adjacent house or flat. **next-of-kin** *n* closest relative.

nexus *n, pl* **nexus** connection or link.

NF Newfoundland.

NH New Hampshire.

NHS National Health Service.

Ni *Chem* nickel.

NI **1** *Brit* National Insurance. **2** Northern Ireland.

nib *n* writing point of a pen.

nibble *v* **1** take little bites (of). ♦ *n* **2** little bite. **3** light meal.

nibs *n* **his, her nibs** *Slang* mock title of respect.

nice *adj* **1** pleasant. **2** kind, e.g. *a nice gesture.* **3** good or satisfactory, e.g. *they made a nice job of it.* **4** subtle, e.g. *a nice distinction.* **nicely** *adv* **niceness** *n*

> It is mistaken to suggest that the adjective *nice* should never be used,

> but, since it has been overused, it should be used sparingly.

nicety *n, pl* **-ties** **1** subtle point. **2** refinement or delicacy.

niche [**neesh**] *n* **1** hollow area in a wall. **2** suitable position for a particular person.

nick *v* **1** make a small cut in. **2** *Slang* steal. **3** *Slang* arrest. ♦ *n* **4** small cut. **5** *Slang* prison or police station. **in good nick** *Informal* in good condition. **in the nick of time** just in time.

nickel *n* **1** *Chem* silvery-white metal often used in alloys. **2** US coin worth five cents.

nickelodeon *n US* early type of jukebox.

nicker *n, pl* **nicker** *Brit slang* pound sterling.

nickname *n* **1** familiar name given to a person or place. ♦ *v* **2** call by a nickname.

nicotine *n* poisonous substance found in tobacco.

nictitate *v* blink. **nictitating membrane** (in reptiles, birds, and some mammals) thin fold of skin that can be drawn across the eye beneath the eyelid.

niece *n* daughter of one's sister or brother.

nifty *adj* **-tier, -tiest** *Informal* neat or smart.

niggard *n* stingy person. **niggardly** *adj*

nigger *n Offens* Black person.

niggle *v* **1** worry slightly. **2** continually find fault (with). ♦ *n* **3** small worry or doubt.

nigh *adv, prep Lit* near.

night *n* **1** time of darkness between sunset and sunrise. **2** evening. **3** period between going to bed and morning. **4** nightfall or dusk. **5** an evening designated for a specified activity, e.g. *parents' night.* ♦ *adj* **6** of, occurring, or working at night, e.g. *the night shift.* **nightly** *adj, adv* (happening) each night. **nightcap** *n* **1** drink taken just before bedtime. **2** soft cap formerly worn in bed. **nightclub** *n* establishment for dancing, music, etc., open late at night. **nightdress** *n* woman's loose dress worn in bed. **nightfall** *n* approach of darkness. **nightgown** *n* loose garment worn in bed; nightdress or nightshirt. **nightie** *n Informal* nightdress. **nightingale** *n* small bird with a musical song usu. heard at night. **nightjar** *n* nocturnal bird with a harsh cry. **nightlife** *n* entertainment and social activities available at night in a town or city. **night-light** *n* dim light left on overnight. **nightmare** *n* **1** very bad dream. **2** very unpleasant experience. **nightmarish** *adj* **night safe** safe built into the outside wall of a bank, which customers can deposit money in when the bank is closed. **night school** place where adults can attend educational courses in the evenings. **nightshade** *n* plant with bell-shaped flowers which are often poisonous. **nightshirt** *n* long loose shirt worn in bed. **nighttime** *n* time from sunset to sunrise.

nihilism [**nye**-ill-liz-zum] *n* rejection of all established authority and institutions. **nihilist** *n* **nihilistic** *adj*

nil *n* nothing, zero.

nimble *adj* **1** agile and quick. **2** mentally alert or acute. **nimbly** *adv*

nimbus *n, pl* **-bi, -buses** **1** dark grey rain cloud. **2** halo.

nincompoop *n Informal* stupid person.

nine *adj, n* one more than eight. **ninth** *adj, n* (of) number nine in a series. **ninepins** *n* game of skittles.

nineteen *adj, n* ten and nine. **talk nineteen to the dozen** talk very fast. **nineteenth** *adj, n* **nineteenth hole** *Slang* bar in a golf clubhouse.

ninety *adj, n* ten times nine. **ninetieth** *adj, n*

niobium *n Chem* white superconductive metallic element.

nip[1] *v* **nipping, nipped** **1** *Informal* hurry. **2** pinch or squeeze. **3** bite lightly. **4** (of the cold) cause pain. ♦ *n* **5** pinch or light bite. **6** sharp coldness, e.g. *a nip in the air.* **nippy** *adj* **-pier, -piest** **1** frosty or chilly. **2** *Informal* quick or nimble. **nipper** *n Informal* small child.

nip[2] *n* small alcoholic drink.

nipple *n* **1** projection in the centre of a breast. **2** small projection through which oil or grease can be put into a machine or component.

nirvana [near-**vah**-na] *n Buddhism, Hinduism* absolute spiritual enlightenment and bliss.

nisi [**nye**-sigh] *adj* see DECREE NISI.

Nissen hut *n* tunnel-shaped military hut made of corrugated steel.

nit *n* **1** egg or larva of a louse. **2** *Informal* short for NITWIT. **nit-picking** *adj Informal* overconcerned with insignificant detail, esp. to find fault. **nitwit** *n Informal* stupid person.

nitrogen [**nite**-roj-jen] *n Chem* colourless odourless gas that forms four fifths of the air. **nitric, nitrous, nitrogenous** *adj* of or containing nitrogen. **nitrate** *n* compound of nitric acid, used as a fertilizer. **nitroglycerin, nitroglycerine** *n* explosive liquid. **nitric acid** corrosive liquid widely used in industry. **nitrous oxide** anaesthetic gas.

nitty-gritty *n Informal* basic facts.

NJ New Jersey.

NM New Mexico.

NNE north-northeast.

NNW north-northwest.

no *interj* **1** expresses denial, disagreement, or refusal. ♦ *adj* **2** not any, not a. ♦ *adv* **3** not at all. ♦ *n, pl* **noes, nos** **4** answer or vote of 'no'. **5** person who answers or votes 'no'. **no-ball** *n* (in cricket or rounders) improperly bowled ball. **no-claims bonus, no-claim bonus** reduction in the cost of an insurance policy made if no claims have been made in a specified period. **no-go area** district barricaded off so that the police or army can enter only by force. **no-man's-land** *n* land between boundaries, esp. contested land between two opposing forces. **no-one, no one** *pron* nobody.

> When *no-one* refers to 'people in general' it may be followed by a plural: *No-one finished their drink.*

no. number.

No[1]**, Noh** *n, pl* **No, Noh** Japanese classical drama, using music and dancing.

No[2] *Chem* nobelium.

n.o. *Cricket* not out.

nob *n Slang* person of wealth or social distinction.

nobble *v Slang* **1** attract the attention of (someone) in order to talk to him or her. **2** bribe or threaten.

nobelium *n Chem* artificially-produced radioactive element.

Nobel Prize [no-**bell**] *n* prize awarded annually for outstanding achievement in various fields.

noble *adj* **1** showing or having high moral qualities. **2** of the nobility. **3** impressive and magnificent. ♦ *n* **4** member of the nobility. **nobility** *n* **1** quality of being noble. **2** class of people holding titles and high social rank. **nobly** *adv* **nobleman, noblewoman** *n* **noble gas** *Chem* any of a group of very unreactive gases, including helium and neon.

noblesse oblige [no-**bless** oh-**bleezh**] *n Often ironic* supposed obligation of the nobility to be honourable and generous.

nobody *pron* **1** no person. ♦ *n, pl* **-bodies** **2** person of no importance.

> *Nobody* is equivalent in its uses to *no-one*.

nock *n* notch on an arrow or a bow for the bowstring.

nocturnal *adj* **1** of the night. **2** active at night.

nocturne *n* short dreamy piece of music.

nod *v* **nodding, nodded** **1** lower and raise (one's head) briefly in agreement or greeting. **2** let one's head fall forward with sleep. ♦ *n* **3** act of nodding. **nod off** *v Informal* fall asleep.

noddle *n Informal* the head.

node *n* **1** point on a plant stem from which leaves grow. **2** point at which a curve crosses itself. **nodal** *adj*

nodule *n* **1** small knot or lump. **2** rounded mineral growth on the root of a plant. **nodular** *adj*

Noel, Noël *n* Christmas.

nog *n* alcoholic drink containing beaten egg.

noggin *n* **1** *Informal* head. **2** small quantity of an alcoholic drink.

noise *n* sound, usu. a loud or disturbing one. **be noised abroad** be rumoured. **noisy** *adj* **noisier, noisiest 1** making a lot of noise. **2** full of noise. **noisily** *adv* **noiseless** *adj* **noiselessly** *adv*

noisome *adj* **1** (of smells) offensive. **2** harmful or poisonous.

nomad *n* member of a tribe with no fixed dwelling place, wanderer. **nomadic** *adj*

nom de plume *n, pl* **noms de plume** pen name.

nomenclature [no-**men**-klatch-er] *n* system of names used in a particular subject.

nominal *adj* **1** in name only. **2** very small in comparison with real worth. **nominally** *adv*

nominate *v* **1** suggest as a candidate. **2** appoint to an office or position. **nomination** *n* **nominee** *n* candidate. **nominative** *n* form of a noun indicating the subject of a verb.

non- *prefix* indicating: **1** negation, e.g. *nonexistent.* **2** refusal or failure, e.g. *noncooperation.* **3** exclusion from a specified class, e.g. *nonfiction.* **4** lack or absence, e.g. *nonevent.*

nonage *n* **1** *Law* state of being under full legal age for various actions. **2** any period of immaturity.

nonagenarian *n* person aged between ninety and ninety-nine.

nonaggression *n* policy of not attacking other countries.

nonagon *n* geometric figure with nine sides.

nonalcoholic *adj* containing no alcohol.

nonaligned *adj* (of a country) not part of a major alliance or power bloc. **nonalignment** *n*

nonbelligerent *adj* (of a country) not taking part in a war.

nonce *n* **for the nonce** for the present. **nonce word** word coined for a single occasion.

nonchalant [**non**-shall-ant] *adj* casually unconcerned or indifferent. **nonchalantly** *adv* **nonchalance** *n*

noncombatant *n* member of the armed forces whose duties do not include fighting.

noncommissioned officer *n* (in the armed forces) a subordinate officer, risen from the ranks.

noncommittal *adj* not committing oneself to any particular opinion.

non compos mentis *adj* of unsound mind.

nonconductor *n* substance that is a poor conductor of heat, electricity, or sound.

nonconformist *n* **1** person who does not conform to generally accepted patterns of behaviour or thought. **2** (**N-**) member of a Protestant group separated from the Church of England. ♦ *adj* **3** (of behaviour or ideas) not conforming to accepted patterns. **nonconformity** *n*

noncontributory *adj* denoting a pension scheme for employees, the premiums of which are paid entirely by the employer.

non-cooperation *n* refusal to do more than is legally or contractually required of one.

nondescript *adj* lacking outstanding features.

none *pron* **1** not any. **2** no-one. **nonetheless** *adv* despite that, however.

> Although *none* means 'not one', and can take a singular verb, it more often takes a plural: *None of them are mine.*

nonentity [non-**enn**-tit-tee] *n, pl* **-ties** insignificant person or thing.

nonessential *adj* not absolutely necessary.

nonevent *n* disappointing or insignificant occurrence.

nonexistent *adj* not existing, imaginary. **nonexistence** *n*

nonferrous *adj* **1** denoting metal other than iron. **2** not containing iron.

nonflammable *adj* not easily set on fire.

nonintervention *n* refusal to intervene in the affairs of others.

noniron *adj* not requiring ironing.

non-nuclear *adj* not involving or using nuclear power or weapons.

nonpareil [non-par-**rail**] *n* person or thing that is unsurpassed.

nonpartisan *adj* not supporting any single political party.

nonpayment *n* failure to pay money owed.

nonplussed *adj* perplexed.

non-profit-making *adj* not run with the intention of making a profit.

nonproliferation *n* limitation of the production or spread of something, such as nuclear weapons.

nonrepresentational *adj Art* abstract.

nonresident *n* person who does not live in a particular country or place.

nonsectarian *adj* not confined to any specific religion.

nonsense *n* **1** something that has or makes no sense. **2** absurd language. **3** foolish behaviour. **nonsensical** *adj*

non sequitur [**sek**-wit-tur] *n* statement with little or no relation to what preceded it.

nonsmoker *n* **1** person who does not smoke. **2** train carriage or compartment in which smoking is forbidden. **nonsmoking, no-smoking** *adj* denoting an area in which smoking is forbidden.

nonstandard *adj* denoting language that is not regarded as correct by educated native speakers.

nonstarter *n* person or idea that has little chance of success.

nonstick *adj* coated with a substance that food will not stick to when cooked.

nonstop *adj, adv* without a stop.

nontoxic *adj* not poisonous.

nonunion *adj* **1** (of a company) not employing trade union members. **2** (of a person) not belonging to a trade union.

nonviolent *adj* using peaceful methods to bring about change. **nonviolence** *n*

nonvoting *adj* (of shares in a company) not entitling the owner to vote at company meetings.

noodles *pl n* long thin strips of pasta.

nook *n* **1** corner or recess. **2** sheltered place.

noon *n* twelve o'clock midday. **noonday** *adj* happening at noon.

noose *n* loop in the end of a rope, tied with a slipknot.

nor *conj* and not.

Nordic *adj* of Scandinavia or its typically tall blond and blue-eyed people.

norm *n* standard that is regarded as normal.

normal *adj* **1** usual, regular, or typical. **2** free from mental or physical disorder. ♦ *n* **3** usual or regular state, degree or form. **normally** *adv* **normality** *n* **normalize** *v* **1** make or become normal. **2** make comply with a standard. **normalization** *n* **normative** *adj* of or setting a norm or standard.

Norman *n* **1** person from Normandy in N France, esp. one of the people who conquered England in 1066. **2** (also **Norman French**) medieval Norman and English dialect of French. ♦ *adj* **3** of the Normans or their dialect of French. **4** of Normandy. **5** of a style of architecture used in Britain from the Norman Conquest until the 12th century, with massive masonry walls and rounded arches.

Norse *n, adj* (language) of ancient and medieval Norway. **Norseman** *n* Viking.

north *n* **1** direction towards the North Pole, opposite south. **2** area lying in or towards the north. ♦ *adj* **3** to or in the north. **4** (of a wind) from the north. ♦ *adv* **5** in, to, or towards the north. **northerly** *adj* **northern** *adj* **northerner** *n* person from the north of a country or area. **northward** *adj, adv* **northwards** *adv* **northeast** *n, adj, adv* (in or to) direction between north and east. **northwest** *n, adj, adv* (in or to) direction between north and west. **North Pole** northernmost point on the earth's axis.

Norwegian *adj* **1** of Norway, its language, or its people. ♦ *n* **2** language of Norway. **3** person from Norway.

nos. numbers.

nose *n* **1** organ of smell, used also in breathing. **2** sense of smell. **3** front part of a vehicle. **4** distinctive smell of a wine, perfume, etc. **5** instinctive skill in finding something, e.g. *a nose for a bargain.* ♦ *v* **6** move forward slowly and carefully. **7** pry or snoop. **nosebag** *n* bag containing feed fastened round a horse's head. **nosebleed** *n* bleeding from the nose. **nose dive** sudden drop. **nosegay** *n* small bunch of flowers. **nose out** *v* discover by searching or prying. **nosey, nosy** *adj* **nosier, nosiest** *Informal* prying or inquisitive. **nosiness** *n*

nosh *Slang* ♦ *n* **1** food. ♦ *v* **2** eat. **nosh-up** *n Slang* large meal.

nostalgia *n* sentimental longing for the past. **nostalgic** *adj*

nostril *n* one of the two openings at the end of the nose.

nostrum *n* **1** quack medicine. **2** favourite remedy.

not *adv* expressing negation, refusal, or denial.

nota bene [**note**-a **ben**-nay] note well, take note.

notable [**note**-a-bl] *adj* **1** worthy of being noted, remarkable. ♦ *n* **2** person of distinction. **notably** *adv* **notability** [note-a-**bill**-lit-tee] *n*

notary, notary public [**note**-a-ree] *n, pl* **-ries** person authorized to witness the signing of legal documents.

notation [no-**tay**-shun] *n* **1** representation of numbers or quantities in a system by a series of symbols. **2** set of such symbols.

notch *n* **1** V-shaped cut. **2** *Informal* step or level. ♦ *v* **3** make a notch in. **4** (foll. by *up*) score or achieve.

note *n* **1** short letter. **2** brief comment or record. **3** banknote. **4** (symbol for) a musical sound. **5** hint or mood. ♦ *v* **6** notice, pay attention to. **7** record in writing. **8** remark upon. **noted** *adj* well-known. **notebook** *n* book for writing in. **notelet** *n* small folded card with a design on the front, used for writing informal letters. **notepaper** *n* paper used for writing letters. **noteworthy** *adj* worth noting, remarkable.

nothing *pron* **1** not anything. **2** matter of no importance. **3** figure 0. ♦ *adv* **4** not at all. **nothingness** *n* **1** nonexistence. **2** insignificance.

> *Nothing* is usually followed by a singular verb but, if it comes before a plural noun, this can sound odd: *Nothing but books was/were on the shelf.* A solution is to rephrase the sentence: *Only books were....*

notice *n* **1** observation or attention. **2** sign giving warning or an announcement. **3** advance notification of intention to end a contract of employment. **4** review in a newspaper of a book or play. ♦ *v* **5** observe, become aware of. **6** point out or remark upon. **noticeable** *adj* easily seen or detected, appreciable. **noticeably** *adv* **notice board** board on which notices are displayed.

notify *v* **-fying, -fied** inform. **notification** *n* **notifiable** *adj* having to be reported to the authorities.

notion *n* **1** idea or opinion. **2** whim. **notional** *adj* speculative, imaginary, or unreal.

notorious *adj* well known for something bad. **notoriously** *adv* **notoriety** *n*

notwithstanding *prep* **1** in spite of. ♦ *adv* **2** nevertheless.

nougat *n* chewy sweet containing nuts and fruit.

nought *n* **1** figure 0. **2** nothing.

noun *n* word that refers to a person, place, or thing.

nourish *v* **1** feed. **2** encourage or foster (an idea or feeling). **nourishment** *n* **nourishing** *adj* providing the food necessary for life and growth.

nous *n Old-fashioned slang* common

sense.

nouveau riche [**noo**-voh **reesh**] *n, pl* **nouveaux riches** [**noo**-voh **reesh**] person who has recently become rich and is regarded as vulgar.

nouvelle cuisine [**noo**-vell kwee-**zeen**] *n* style of preparing and presenting food with light sauces and unusual combinations of flavours.

Nov. November.

nova *n, pl* **-vae, -vas** star that suddenly becomes brighter and then gradually decreases to its original brightness.

novel[1] *n* long fictitious story in book form. **novelist** *n* writer of novels. **novelette** *n* short novel, esp. one regarded as trivial or sentimental. **novella** *n, pl* **-las, -lae** short novel.

novel[2] *adj* fresh, new, or original. **novelty** *n* **1** newness. **2** something new or unusual. **3** cheap toy or trinket.

November *n* eleventh month of the year.

novena [no-**vee**-na] *n, pl* **-nas** *RC Church* set of prayers or services on nine consecutive days.

novice [**nov**-viss] *n* **1** beginner. **2** person who has entered a religious order but has not yet taken vows.

novitiate, noviciate *n* **1** period of being a novice. **2** part of a monastery or convent where the novices live.

now *adv* **1** at or for the present time. **2** immediately. ♦ *conj* **3** seeing that, since. **just now** very recently. **now and again, then** occasionally. **nowadays** *adv* in these times.

Nowell *n* same as Noel.

nowhere *adv* not anywhere.

noxious *adj* **1** poisonous or harmful. **2** extremely unpleasant.

nozzle *n* projecting spout through which fluid is discharged.

Np *Chem* neptunium.

nr near.

NS Nova Scotia.

NSPCC National Society for the Prevention of Cruelty to Children.

NSW New South Wales.

NT **1** National Trust. **2** New Testament. **3** Northern Territory.

nuance [**new**-ahnss] *n* subtle difference in colour, meaning, or tone.

nub *n* point or gist (of a story etc.).

nubile [**new**-bile] *adj* (of a young woman) **1** sexually attractive. **2** old enough to get married.

nuclear *adj* **1** of nuclear weapons or energy. **2** of a nucleus, esp. the nucleus of an atom. **nuclear energy** energy released as a result of nuclear fission or fusion. **nuclear family** family consisting only of parents and their offspring. **nuclear fission** splitting of an atomic nucleus. **nuclear fusion** combination of two nuclei to form a heavier nucleus with the release of energy. **nuclear power** power produced by a nuclear reactor. **nuclear reaction** change in structure and energy content of an atomic nucleus by interaction with another nucleus or particle. **nuclear reactor** device in which a nuclear reaction is maintained and controlled to produce nuclear energy. **nuclear weapon** weapon whose force is due to uncontrolled nuclear fusion or fission. **nuclear winter** theoretical period of low temperatures and little light after a nuclear war.

nucleic acid *n* complex compound, such as DNA or RNA, found in all living cells.

nucleonics *n* branch of physics dealing with the applications of nuclear energy.

nucleus *n, pl* **-clei** **1** centre, esp. of an atom or cell. **2** central thing around which others are grouped.

nude *adj* **1** naked. ♦ *n* **2** naked figure in painting, sculpture, or photography. **nudity** *n* **nudism** *n* practice of not wearing clothes. **nudist** *n*

nudge *v* **1** push gently, esp. with the elbow. ♦ *n* **2** gentle push or touch.

nugatory [**new**-gat-tree] *adj* **1** of little value. **2** not valid.

nugget *n* **1** small lump of gold in its natural state. **2** something small but valuable.

nuisance *n* something or someone that

causes annoyance or bother.

nuke *Slang* ♦ *v* **1** attack with nuclear weapons. ♦ *n* **2** nuclear weapon.

null *adj* **null and void** not legally valid. **nullity** *n* **nullify** *v* **-fying, -fied 1** make ineffective. **2** cancel.

numb *adj* **1** without feeling, as through cold, shock, or fear. ♦ *v* **2** make numb. **numbly** *adv* **numbness** *n* **numbskull** *n* stupid person.

number *n* **1** sum or quantity. **2** word or symbol used to express a sum or quantity, numeral. **3** numeral or string of numerals used to identify a person or thing. **4** one of a series, such as a copy of a magazine. **5** song or piece of music. **6** group of people. **7** *Grammar* classification of words depending on how many persons or things are referred to. ♦ *v* **8** count. **9** give a number to. **10** amount to. **11** include in a group. **numberless** *adj* too many to be counted. **number crunching** *Computers* large-scale processing of numerical data. **number one** *n Informal* **1** oneself. **2** bestselling pop record in any one week. ♦ *adj* **3** first in importance or quality. **numberplate** *n* plate on a car showing the registration number.

numeral *n* word or symbol used to express a sum or quantity.

numerate *adj* able to do basic arithmetic. **numeracy** *n*

numeration *n* act or process of numbering or counting.

numerator *n Maths* number above the line in a fraction.

numerical *adj* measured or expressed in numbers. **numerically** *adv*

numerology *n* study of numbers and their supposed influence on human affairs.

numerous *adj* existing or happening in large numbers.

numinous *adj* **1** arousing religious or spiritual emotions. **2** mysterious or awe-inspiring.

numismatist *n* coin collector. **numismatics** *n* study or collection of coins. **numismatic** *adj*

numskull *n* same as NUMBSKULL.

nun *n* female member of a religious order. **nunnery** *n, pl* **-neries** convent.

nuncio *n, pl* **-cios** *RC Church* pope's ambassador.

nuptial *adj* relating to marriage. **nuptials** *pl n* wedding.

nurse *n* **1** person employed to look after sick people, usu. in a hospital. **2** (also **nursemaid, nursery nurse**) woman employed to look after children. ♦ *v* **3** look after (a sick person). **4** breast-feed (a baby). **5** try to cure (an ailment). **6** harbour or foster (a feeling). **nursing home** private hospital or home for old people. **nursing officer** administrative head of the nursing staff of a hospital.

nursery *n, pl* **-ries 1** room where children sleep or play. **2** place where children are taken care of while their parents are at work. **3** place where plants are grown for sale. **nurseryman** *n* person who raises plants for sale. **nursery rhyme** short traditional verse or song for children. **nursery school** school for children from 3 to 5 years old. **nursery slopes** gentle ski slopes for beginners.

nurture *n* **1** act or process of promoting the development of a child or young plant. ♦ *v* **2** promote or encourage the development of.

nut *n* **1** fruit consisting of a hard shell and a kernel. **2** small piece of metal that screws onto a bolt. **3** (also **nutcase**) *Slang* insane or eccentric person. **4** *Slang* head. **nuts** *adj Slang* insane or eccentric. **nuts and bolts** *Informal* essential or practical details. **nutshell** *n* **in a nutshell** in essence, briefly. **nutty** *adj* **-tier, -tiest 1** containing or resembling nuts. **2** *Slang* insane or eccentric. **nutter** *n Slang* insane person. **nutcracker** *n* device for cracking the shells of nuts. **nuthatch** *n* small songbird. **nutmeg** *n* spice made from the seed of a tropical tree.

nutria [**new**-tree-a] *n* fur of the coypu.

nutrient [**new**-tree-ent] *n* substance that provides nourishment.

nutriment [**new**-tree-ment] *n* food or

nourishment required by all living things to grow and stay healthy.

nutrition [new-**trish**-shun] *n* **1** process of taking in and absorbing nutrients. **2** process of being nourished. **3** study of nutrition. **nutritional** *adj* **nutritious, nutritive** *adj* nourishing.

nuzzle *v* push or rub gently with the nose or snout.

NV Nevada.

NW northwest(ern).

NWT Northwest Territories.

NY New York.

nylon *n* **1** synthetic material used for clothing etc. ♦ *pl* **2** stockings made of nylon.

nymph *n* **1** mythical spirit of nature, represented as a beautiful young woman. **2** larva of certain insects, resembling the adult form.

nymphet *n* sexually precocious young girl.

nymphomaniac *n* woman with an abnormally intense sexual desire. **nymphomania** *n* abnormally intense sexual desire in women.

NZ New Zealand.

O o

O[1] **1** *Chem* oxygen. **2** Old. **3** same as NOUGHT (sense 1).

O[2] *interj* same as OH.

o' *prep Informal* of, e.g. *a cup o' tea.*

oaf *n* stupid or clumsy person. **oafish** *adj*

oak *n* **1** deciduous forest tree. **2** its wood, used for furniture. **oaken** *adj* **oak apple** brownish lump found on oak trees.

oakum *n* fibre obtained by unravelling old rope.

OAP old-age pensioner.

oar *n* pole with a broad blade, used for rowing a boat. **oarsman, oarswoman** *n*

oasis *n, pl* **-ses** fertile area in a desert.

oast *n* oven for drying hops. **oast house** building containing oasts.

oat *n* **1** hard cereal grown as food. ♦ *pl* **2** grain of this cereal. **sow one's wild oats** have many sexual relationships when young. **oaten** *adj* **oatcake** *n* thin flat biscuit of oatmeal. **oatmeal** *n* **1** coarse flour made from oats. ♦ *adj* **2** pale brownish-cream.

oath *n* **1** solemn promise, esp. to be truthful in court. **2** swearword.

obbligato [ob-lig-**gah**-toe] *n, pl* **-tos** *Music* essential part or accompaniment.

obdurate *adj* hardhearted or stubborn. **obduracy** *n*

OBE Officer of the Order of the British Empire.

obedient *adj* obeying or willing to obey. **obedience** *n* **obediently** *adv*

obeisance [oh-**bay**-sanss] *n* **1** attitude of respect. **2** bow or curtsy.

obelisk [**ob**-bill-isk] *n* four-sided stone column tapering to a pyramid at the top.

obese [oh-**beess**] *adj* very fat. **obesity** *n*

obey *v* carry out instructions or orders.

obfuscate *v* make (something) confusing. **obfuscation** *n*

obituary *n, pl* **-aries** announcement of someone's death, esp. in a newspaper. **obituarist** *n*

object[1] *n* **1** physical thing. **2** focus of thoughts or action. **3** aim or purpose. **4** *Grammar* word that a verb or preposition affects. **no object** not a hindrance.

object[2] *v* express disapproval. **objection** *n* **objectionable** *adj* unpleasant. **objector** *n*

objective *n* **1** aim or purpose. ♦ *adj* **2** not biased. **3** existing in the real world outside the human mind. **objectively** *adv* **objectivity** *n*

objet d'art [**ob**-zhay **dahr**] *n, pl* **objets d'art** small object of artistic value.

oblation *n* religious offering.

oblige *v* **1** compel (someone) morally or by law to do something. **2** do a favour for (someone). **obliging** *adj* ready to help other people. **obligingly** *adv* **obligated** *adj* obliged to do something. **obligation** *n* **1** duty. **2** indebtedness for a favour. **obligatory** *adj* required by a rule or law.

oblique [oh-**bleak**] *adj* **1** slanting. **2** indirect. ♦ *n* **3** the symbol (/). **obliquely** *adv* **oblique angle** angle that is not a right angle.

obliterate *v* wipe out, destroy. **obliteration** *n*

oblivious *adj* unaware. **oblivion** *n* **1** state of being forgotten. **2** state of being unaware or unconscious.

oblong *adj* **1** having two long sides, two short sides, and four right angles. ♦ *n* **2** oblong figure.

obloquy [**ob**-lock-wee] *n, pl* **-quies** **1** verbal abuse. **2** discredit.

obnoxious *adj* offensive. **obnoxiousness** *n*

oboe *n* double-reeded woodwind instrument. **oboist** *n*

obscene *adj* **1** portraying sex offensively. **2** disgusting. **obscenity** *n*

obscure *adj* **1** not well known. **2** hard to understand. **3** indistinct. ♦ *v* **4** make (something) obscure. **obscurity** *n*

obsequies [**ob**-sick-weez] *pl n* funeral rites.

obsequious [ob-**seek**-wee-uss] *adj* over-attentive in order to gain favour. **obsequiousness** *n*

observe *v* **1** see or notice. **2** watch (someone or something) carefully. **3** remark. **4** act according to (a law or custom). **observation** *n* **1** action or habit of observing. **2** remark. **observer** *n* **observable** *adj* **observance** *n* **1** observing of a custom. **2** ritual or ceremony. **observant** *adj* quick to notice things. **observatory** *n* building equipped for studying the weather and the stars.

obsess *v* preoccupy (someone) compulsively. **obsessed** *adj* **obsessive** *adj* **obsession** *n* **obsessional** *adj*

obsidian *n* dark glassy volcanic rock.

obsolete *adj* no longer in use. **obsolescent** *adj* becoming obsolete. **obsolescence** *n*

obstacle *n* something that makes progress difficult.

obstetrics *n* branch of medicine concerned with pregnancy and childbirth. **obstetric** *adj* **obstetrician** *n*

obstinate *adj* **1** stubborn. **2** difficult to remove or change. **obstinately** *adv* **obstinacy** *n*

obstreperous *adj* unruly, noisy.

obstruct *v* **1** block with an obstacle. **2** make (progress) difficult. **obstruction** *n* **obstructive** *adj*

obtain *v* **1** acquire intentionally. **2** be customary. **obtainable** *adj*

obtrude *v* **1** push oneself or one's ideas on others. **2** stick out noticeably. **obtrusion** *n* **obtrusive** *adj* unpleasantly noticeable. **obtrusively** *adv*

obtuse *adj* **1** mentally slow. **2** *Maths* (of an angle) between 90° and 180°. **3** not pointed. **obtuseness** *n*

obverse *n* **1** opposite way of looking at an idea. **2** main side of a coin or medal.

obviate *v* make unnecessary.

obvious *adj* easy to see or understand, evident. **obviously** *adv*

ocarina *n* small oval wind instrument.

occasion *n* **1** time at which a particular thing happens. **2** reason, e.g. *no occasion for complaint.* **3** opportunity. **4** special event. ♦ *v* **5** cause. **occasional** *adj* happening sometimes. **occasionally** *adv*

Occident *n Lit* the West. **Occidental** *adj*

occiput [**ox**-sip-put] *n* back of the head.

occlude *v* **1** obstruct. **2** close off. **occlusion** *n* **occluded front** *Meteorol* front formed when a cold front overtakes a warm front and warm air rises.

occult *adj* relating to the supernatural. **the occult** knowledge or study of the supernatural.

occupant *n* person occupying a specified place. **occupancy** *n* (length of) a person's stay in a specified place.

occupation *n* **1** profession. **2** activity that occupies one's time. **3** control of a country by a foreign military power. **4** being occupied. **occupational** *adj* **occupational hazard** unpleasant thing that occurs due to one's job. **occupational therapy** purposeful activities, designed to aid recovery from illness etc.

occupy *v* **-pying, -pied 1** live or work in (a building). **2** take up the attention of (someone). **3** take up (space or time). **4** take possession of (a place) by force. **5** hold (an office or position). **occupier** *n*

occur *v* **-curring, -curred 1** happen. **2** exist. **occur to** come to the mind of. **occurrence** *n* **1** something that occurs. **2** fact of occurring.

> Avoid the use of *occur* (or *happen*) for events that are planned. Compare *An accident occurred* with *A wedding took place.*

ocean *n* **1** vast area of sea between continents. **2** large quantity or expanse. **oceanic** *adj* **oceanography** *n* scientific study of the oceans. **oceanographer** *n* **ocean-going** *adj* able to sail on the open sea.

ocelot [**oss**-ill-lot] *n* American wild cat with a spotted coat.

oche [**ok**-kee] *n Darts* mark on the floor

behind which a player must stand.

ochre [**oak**-er] *adj, n* brownish-yellow (earth).

o'clock *adv* used after a number to specify an hour.

Oct. October.

octagon *n* geometric figure with eight sides. **octagonal** *adj*

octahedron [ok-ta-**heed**-ron] *n, pl* **-drons, -dra** three-dimensional geometric figure with eight faces.

octane *n* hydrocarbon found in petrol. **octane rating** measure of petrol quality.

octave *n Music* (interval between the first and) eighth note of a scale.

octavo *n, pl* **-vos** book size in which the sheets are folded into eight leaves.

octet *n* **1** group of eight performers. **2** music for such a group.

October *n* tenth month of the year.

octogenarian *n* person aged between eighty and eighty-nine.

octopus *n, pl* **-puses** sea creature with a soft body and eight tentacles.

ocular *adj* relating to the eyes or sight.

OD *Informal* ♦ *n* **1** overdose. ♦ *v* **OD'ing, OD'd** **2** take an overdose.

odd *adj* **1** unusual. **2** occasional. **3** left-over or additional. **4** not divisible by two. **5** not part of a set. **odds** *pl n* **1** (ratio showing) the probability of something happening. **2** likelihood. **at odds** in conflict. **odds and ends** small miscellaneous items. **oddity** *n* odd person or thing. **oddly** *adv* **oddness** *n* quality of being odd. **oddball** *n Informal* eccentric person. **oddments** *pl n* things left over.

ode *n* lyric poem, usu. addressed to a particular subject.

odium [**oh**-dee-um] *n* widespread dislike. **odious** *adj* offensive.

odour *n* particular smell. **odorous** *adj* **odourless** *adj*

odyssey [**odd**-iss-ee] *n* long eventful journey.

OECD Organization for Economic Cooperation and Development.

oedema [id-**deem**-a] *n, pl* **-mata** *Med* abnormal swelling.

o'er *prep, adv Poetic* over.

oesophagus [ee-**soff**-a-guss] *n, pl* **-gi** passage between the mouth and stomach.

oestrogen [**ee**-stra-jen] *n* female hormone that controls the reproductive cycle.

of *prep* **1** belonging to. **2** consisting of. **3** connected with. **4** characteristic of.

> When *of* means 'belonging to' an apostrophe can be used: *Bill's dog* (*the dog of Bill*).

off *prep* **1** away from. ♦ *adv* **2** away. **3** so as to stop or disengage. ♦ *adj* **4** not operating. **5** cancelled. **6** not up to the usual standard. **7** (of food) gone bad. ♦ *n* **8** *Cricket* side of the field to which the batsman's feet point. **offbeat** *adj* unusual or eccentric. **off chance** slight possibility. **off colour** slightly ill. **off-line** *adj* (of a computer) not directly controlled by a central processor. **off-putting** *adj* rather unpleasant or disturbing.

> Avoid using *of* after *off*: *He got off the bus* (not *off of*). The use of *off* to mean *from* is very informal: *They brought milk from* (rather than *off*) *a farmer.*

offal *n* edible organs of an animal, such as liver or kidneys.

offcut *n* piece remaining after the required parts have been cut out.

offend *v* **1** hurt the feelings of, insult. **2** disgust. **3** commit a crime. **offender** *n* **offence** *n* **1** (cause of) hurt feelings or annoyance. **2** illegal act. **offensive** *adj* **1** disagreeable. **2** insulting. **3** aggressive. ♦ *n* **4** position or action of attack.

offer *v* **1** present (something) for acceptance or rejection. **2** provide. **3** be willing (to do something). **4** present for sale. **5** propose as payment. ♦ *n* **6** something offered. **7** instance of offering something. **offering** *n* thing offered.

offertory *n Christianity* **1** offering of the bread and wine for Communion. **2** collection of money at Communion.

offhand *adj* **1** (also **offhanded**) casual, curt. ♦ *adv* **2** without preparation.

office *n* **1** room or building where people work at desks. **2** department of a commercial organization. **3** formal position of responsibility. **4** place where tickets or information can be obtained. **5** religious ceremony. **officer** *n* **1** person in authority in the armed services. **2** member of the police force. **3** person with special responsibility in an organization.

official *adj* **1** of a position of authority. **2** approved or arranged by someone in authority. **3** formal. ♦ *n* **4** person who holds a position of authority. **officially** *adv* **officialdom** *n* officials collectively. **Official Receiver** person who deals with the affairs of a bankrupt company.

officiate *v* act in an official role.

officious *adj* interfering unnecessarily.

offing *n* area of the sea visible from the shore. **in the offing** likely to happen soon.

off-licence *n* shop licensed to sell alcohol for drinking elsewhere.

off-load *v* get rid of (something).

offset *v* cancel out, compensate for.

offshoot *n* **1** something developed from something else. **2** shoot growing on the main stem of a plant.

offside *adj, adv Sport* (positioned) illegally ahead of the ball.

offspring *n, pl* **offspring** child.

often *adv* frequently, much of the time. **oft** *adv Poetic* often.

ogle *v* stare at (someone) lustfully.

ogre *n* **1** giant that eats human flesh. **2** monstrous or cruel person.

oh *interj* exclamation of surprise, pain, etc.

OH Ohio.

ohm *n* unit of electrical resistance.

OHMS On Her *or* His Majesty's Service.

oil *n* **1** viscous liquid, insoluble in water and usu. flammable. **2** same as PETROLEUM. **3** petroleum derivative, used as a fuel or lubricant. ♦ *pl* **4** oil-based paints used in art. ♦ *v* **5** lubricate (a machine) with oil. **oily** *adj* **oilcloth** *n* waterproof material. **oilfield** *n* area containing oil reserves. **oil rig** platform constructed for drilling oil wells. **oilskin** *n* (garment made from) waterproof material. **oil well** well bored into the earth or sea bed to a supply of oil.

ointment *n* greasy substance used for healing skin or as a cosmetic.

OK Oklahoma.

O.K., okay *Informal* ♦ *interj* **1** expression of approval. ♦ *adj, adv* **2** in satisfactory condition. ♦ *v* **3** approve (something). ♦ *n* **4** approval.

okapi [ok-**kah**-pee] *n* African animal related to the giraffe but with a shorter neck.

okra *n* tropical plant with edible green pods.

old *adj* **1** having lived or existed for a long time. **2** of a specified age, e.g. *two years old.* **3** former. **olden** *adj* old, e.g. *in the olden days.* **oldie** *n Informal* old but popular song or film. **old age pensioner** retired person receiving an allowance from the government. **old boy, girl** former pupil of a school. **old-fashioned** *adj* no longer commonly used or valued. **old guard** group of people in an organization who have traditional values. **old hand** skilled and experienced person. **old hat** boring because so familiar. **old maid** elderly unmarried woman. **old master** European painter or painting from the period 1500–1800. **Old Nick** *Informal* the Devil. **old school tie** system of mutual help between former pupils of public schools. **Old Testament** part of the Bible recording Hebrew history. **Old World** world as it was known before the discovery of the Americas.

oleaginous [ol-lee-**aj**-in-uss] *adj* oily, producing oil.

oleander [ol-lee-**ann**-der] *n* Mediterranean flowering evergreen shrub.

O level *n* former basic level of the General Certificate of Education.

olfactory *adj* relating to the sense of

smell.

oligarchy [**ol**-lee-gark-ee] *n, pl* **-chies** **1** government by a small group of people. **2** state governed this way. **oligarchic, oligarchical** *adj*

olive *n* **1** small green or black fruit used as food or pressed for its oil. **2** tree on which this fruit grows. ♦ *adj* **3** greyish-green. **olive branch** peace offering.

Olympiad *n* staging of the Olympic Games.

Olympian *adj* **1** of Mount Olympus or the classical Greek gods. **2** majestic or godlike.

Olympic Games *pl n* four-yearly international sports competition. **Olympic** *adj*

OM Order of Merit.

ombudsman *n* official who investigates complaints against government organizations.

omega *n* last letter in the Greek alphabet.

omelette *n* dish of eggs beaten and fried.

omen *n* happening or object thought to foretell success or misfortune. **ominous** *adj* worrying, seeming to foretell misfortune.

omit *v* **omitting, omitted** **1** leave out. **2** neglect (to do something). **omission** *n*

omnibus *n* **1** several books or TV or radio programmes made into one. **2** *Old-fashioned* bus.

omnipotent [om-**nip**-a-tent] *adj* having unlimited power. **omnipotence** *n*

omnipresent *adj* present everywhere. **omnipresence** *n*

omniscient [om-**niss**-ee-ent] *adj* knowing everything. **omniscience** *n*

omnivorous [om-**niv**-vor-uss] *adj* **1** eating food obtained from both animals and plants. **2** taking in everything indiscriminately. **omnivore** *n* omnivorous animal.

on *prep* **1** indicating position above, attachment, closeness, etc., e.g. *lying on the ground; a puppet on a string; on the coast.* ♦ *adv* **2** in operation. **3** attached to or in contact with. **4** continuing. **5** forwards. ♦ *adj* **6** operating. **7** taking place. ♦ *n* **8** *Cricket* side of the field on which the batsman stands. **on-line** *adj* (of a computer) directly controlled by a central processor.

ON Ontario.

ONC Ordinary National Certificate.

once *adv* **1** on one occasion. **2** formerly. ♦ *conj* **3** as soon as. ♦ *n* **4** one occasion. **at once** **1** immediately. **2** simultaneously. **once-over** *n Informal* quick examination.

oncogene [**on**-koh-jean] *n* gene that can cause cancer when abnormally activated.

oncoming *adj* approaching from the front.

OND Ordinary National Diploma.

one *adj* **1** single, lone. **2** only. ♦ *n* **3** number or figure 1. **4** single unit. ♦ *pron* **5** any person. **at one** in harmony. **one by one** individually. **oneness** *n* unity. **oneself** *pron* reflexive form of ONE. **one-armed bandit** fruit machine operated by a lever on one side. **one-liner** *n* witty remark. **one-night stand** sexual encounter lasting one night. **one-off** *n* thing made or happening only once. **one-sided** *adj* considering only one point of view. **one-way** *adj* allowing movement in one direction only.

> Avoid overuse of the pronoun *one* as a substitute for *I*. Many listeners find it affected. The pronouns *I* and *one* should not be mixed within the same group of sentences. Choose one of them and continue with it.

onerous [**own**-er-uss] *adj* (of a task) difficult to carry out.

ongoing *adj* in progress, continuing.

onion *n* strongly flavoured edible bulb.

onlooker *n* person who watches without taking part.

only *adj* **1** alone of its kind. ♦ *adv* **2** exclusively. **3** merely. **4** no more than. ♦ *conj* **5** but.

> The use of *only* to connect sentences is rather informal: *I would come only*

I'm busy. In formal use *only* is placed directly before the words it modifies: *The club opens only on Thursdays* but in everyday use this becomes: *The club only opens on Thursdays.*

o.n.o. or near(est) offer.

onomatopoeia [on-a-mat-a-**pee**-a] *n* use of a word which imitates the sound it represents, such as *hiss.* **onomatopoeic** *adj*

onset *n* beginning.

onslaught *n* violent attack.

onto *prep* **1** to a position on. **2** aware of, e.g. *she's onto us.*

ontology *n* branch of philosophy concerned with existence. **ontological** *adj*

onus [**own**-uss] *n, pl* **onuses** responsibility or burden.

onward *adj* **1** directed or moving forward. ♦ *adv* **2** (also **onwards**) ahead, forward.

onyx *n* type of quartz with coloured layers.

oodles *pl n Informal* great quantities.

oops *interj* exclamation of surprise or apology.

ooze[1] *v* **1** flow slowly. **2** overflow with (a quality). ♦ *n* **3** sluggish flow. **oozy** *adj*

ooze[2] *n* soft mud at the bottom of a lake or river.

op *n Informal* operation.

op. opus.

opal *n* iridescent precious stone. **opalescent** *adj* iridescent like an opal.

opaque *adj* **1** not able to be seen through, not transparent. **2** hard to understand. **opacity** *n*

op. cit. [**op sit**] in the work cited.

OPEC Organization of Petroleum-Exporting Countries.

open *adj* **1** not closed. **2** not covered. **3** unfolded. **4** ready for business. **5** free from obstruction, accessible. **6** unrestricted. **7** not finalized. **8** frank. ♦ *v* **9** (cause to) become open. **10** begin. ♦ *n* **11** *Sport* competition which all may enter. **in the open** outdoors. **opener** *n* tool for opening cans and bottles. **openly** *adv* without concealment. **opening** *n* **1** beginning. **2** opportunity. **3** hole. ♦ *adj* **4** first. **open air** outdoors. **open-and-shut case** problem that is easily solved. **opencast mining** mining at the surface and not underground. **open day** day on which a school or college is open to the public. **open-ended** *adj* without definite limits. **open-handed** *adj* generous. **open-hearted** *adj* **1** generous. **2** frank. **open-heart surgery** surgery on the heart during which the blood circulation is maintained by machine. **open house** hospitality to visitors at any time. **open letter** letter to an individual that the writer makes public in a newspaper or magazine. **open-minded** *adj* receptive to new ideas. **open-plan** *adj* (of a house or office) having few interior walls. **open prison** prison with minimal security. **open verdict** coroner's verdict not stating the cause of death.

opera[1] *n* drama in which the text is sung to an orchestral accompaniment. **operatic** *adj* **operetta** *n* light-hearted comic opera. **opera glasses** small binoculars used by theatre audiences.

opera[2] *n* a plural of OPUS.

operate *v* **1** (cause to) work. **2** direct. **3** perform an operation. **operator** *n* **operation** *n* **1** method or procedure of working. **2** action or series of actions. **3** medical procedure in which the body is worked on to repair a damaged part. **4** military campaign. **operational** *adj* **1** in working order. **2** relating to an operation. **operative** [**op**-rat-tiv] *adj* **1** working. **2** having particular significance. ♦ *n* **3** worker with a special skill.

ophthalmic *adj* relating to the eye. **ophthalmia** *n* inflammation of the eye. **ophthalmology** *n* study of the eye and its diseases. **ophthalmologist** *n* **ophthalmoscope** *n* instrument for examining the interior of the eye. **ophthalmic optician** see OPTICIAN.

opiate [**oh**-pee-ate] *n* **1** narcotic drug containing opium. **2** thing producing a stupefying effect.

opinion *n* **1** personal belief or judgment. **2** judgment given by an expert. **opinionated** *adj* having strong opinions. **opine** *v Old-fashioned* express an opinion. **opinion poll** see POLL (sense 1).

opium [**oh**-pee-um] *n* addictive narcotic drug made from poppy seeds.

opossum *n* small marsupial of America or Australia.

opponent *n* person one is working against in a contest, battle, or argument.

opportunity *n, pl* **-ties** **1** favourable time or condition. **2** good chance. **opportune** *adj* happening at a suitable time. **opportunist** *n, adj* (person) doing whatever is advantageous without regard for principles. **opportunism** *n*

oppose *v* **1** work against. **2** contrast. **be opposed to** disagree with or disapprove of. **opposition** *n* **1** obstruction or hostility. **2** group opposing another. **3** political party not in power.

opposite *adj* **1** situated on the other side. **2** facing. **3** completely different. ♦ *n* **4** person or thing that is opposite. ♦ *prep* **5** facing. ♦ *adv* **6** on the other side.

oppress *v* **1** control by cruelty or force. **2** depress. **oppression** *n* **oppressor** *n* **oppressive** *adj* **1** tyrannical. **2** depressing. **3** (of weather) hot and humid. **oppressively** *adv*

opprobrium [op-**probe**-ree-um] *n* state of being criticized severely for wrong one has done. **opprobrious** *adj*

opt *v* show a preference, choose. **opt out** *v* choose not to be part (of).

optic *adj* relating to the eyes or sight. **optics** *n* science of sight and light. **optical** *adj* **optical character reader** device that electronically reads and stores text. **optical fibre** fine glass-fibre tube used to transmit information.

optician *n* **1** (also **ophthalmic optician**) person qualified to prescribe glasses. **2** (also **dispensing optician**) person who supplies and fits glasses.

optimism *n* tendency to take the most hopeful view. **optimist** *n* **optimistic** *adj* **optimistically** *adv*

optimum *n, pl* **-ma, -mums** **1** best possible conditions. ♦ *adj* **2** most favourable. **optimal** *adj* **optimize** *v* make the most of.

option *n* **1** choice. **2** thing chosen. **3** right to buy or sell something at a specified price within a given time. **optional** *adj* possible but not compulsory.

optometrist [op-**tom**-met-trist] *n* person qualified to prescribe glasses. **optometry** *n*

opulent [**op**-pew-lent] *adj* **1** having or indicating wealth. **2** abundant. **opulence** *n*

opus [**oh**-puss] *n, pl* **opuses, opera** artistic creation, esp. a musical work.

or *conj* used to join alternatives, e.g. *tea or coffee.*

OR Oregon.

oracle *n* **1** shrine of an ancient god. **2** prophecy, often obscure, revealed at a shrine. **3** person believed to make infallible predictions. **4** (**O-**) ® ITV teletext service. **oracular** *adj*

oral *adj* **1** spoken. **2** of or for the mouth. **3** (of a drug) to be taken by mouth. ♦ *n* **4** spoken examination. **orally** *adv*

orange *n* **1** reddish yellow citrus fruit. ♦ *adj* **2** reddish-yellow. **orangeade** *n* orange-flavoured, usu. fizzy drink. **orangery** *n* greenhouse for growing orange trees.

Orangeman *n* member of a society in Ireland for the upholding of Protestantism.

orang-utan, orang-utang *n* large reddish-brown ape with long arms.

orator [**or**-rat-tor] *n* skilful public speaker. **oration** *n* formal speech.

oratorio [or-rat-**tor**-ee-oh] *n, pl* **-rios** musical composition for choir and orchestra, usu. with a religious theme.

oratory[1] [**or**-rat-tree] *n* art of making speeches. **oratorical** *adj*

oratory[2] *n, pl* **-ries** small private chapel.

orb *n* **1** ceremonial decorated sphere with a cross on top, carried by a monarch. **2** globe.

orbit *n* **1** curved path of a planet, satellite, or spacecraft around another body.

2 sphere of influence. ♦ *v* **orbiting, orbited** 3 move in an orbit around. 4 put (a satellite or spacecraft) into orbit. **orbital** *adj*

Orcadian *n* 1 person from the Orkneys. ♦ *adj* 2 of the Orkneys.

orchard *n* area where fruit trees are grown.

orchestra *n* 1 large group of musicians, esp. playing a variety of instruments. 2 (also **orchestra pit**) area of a theatre in front of the stage, reserved for the musicians. **orchestral** *adj* **orchestrate** *v* 1 arrange (music) for orchestra. 2 organize (something) to produce a particular result. **orchestration** *n*

orchid *n* plant with flowers that have unusual lip-shaped petals.

ordain *v* 1 make (someone) a member of the clergy. 2 order or establish with authority.

ordeal *n* painful or difficult experience.

order *n* 1 instruction to be carried out. 2 methodical arrangement or sequence. 3 established social system. 4 condition of a law-abiding society. 5 request for goods to be supplied. 6 goods so supplied. 7 written instruction to pay money. 8 social class. 9 group of similar plants or animals. 10 kind, sort. 11 religious society of monks or nuns. 12 group of people who have been awarded an honour. ♦ *v* 13 give an instruction to. 14 request (something) to be supplied. 15 arrange methodically. **in order** 1 appropriate or fitting. 2 so that it is possible. **orderly** *adj* 1 well-organized. 2 well-behaved. ♦ *n, pl* **-lies** 3 male hospital attendant. 4 soldier attending an officer. **orderliness** *n*

ordinal number *n* number showing a position in a series, e.g. *first; second.*

ordinance *n* official rule or order.

ordinary *adj* 1 usual or normal. 2 dull or commonplace. **ordinarily** *adv* **ordinary seaman** navy rank equivalent to an army private.

ordination *n* act of making someone a member of the clergy.

ordnance *n* weapons and military supplies. **Ordnance Survey** official organization making maps of Britain.

ordure *n* excrement.

ore *n* (rock containing) a mineral which yields metal.

oregano [or-rig-**gah**-no] *n* sweet-smelling herb used in cooking.

organ *n* 1 part of an animal or plant that has a particular function, such as the heart or lungs. 2 musical keyboard instrument in which notes are produced by forcing air through pipes. 3 means of conveying information, esp. a newspaper. **organist** *n* organ player. **organ-grinder** *n* formerly, a person who played a barrel organ in the streets.

organdie *n* fine cotton fabric.

organic *adj* 1 of or produced from animals or plants. 2 grown without artificial fertilizers or pesticides. 3 *Chem* relating to compounds of carbon. 4 (of change or development) gradual and natural. 5 organized systematically. **organically** *adv* **organism** *n* 1 any living animal or plant. 2 organized body or system.

organize *v* 1 make arrangements for. 2 arrange systematically. **organization** *n* 1 group of people working together. 2 act of organizing. 3 method of arrangement. **organizational** *adj* **organized** *adj* **organizer** *n*

orgasm *n* most intense point of sexual pleasure. **orgasmic** *adj*

orgy *n, pl* **-gies** 1 party involving promiscuous sexual activity. 2 unrestrained indulgence, e.g. *an orgy of destruction.* **orgiastic** *adj*

oriel window *n* upper window built out from a wall.

orient, orientate *v* 1 position (oneself) according to one's surroundings. 2 position (a map) in relation to the points of the compass. **orientation** *n* **orienteering** *n* sport in which competitors hike over a course using a compass and map.

Orient *n* **the Orient** *Lit* East Asia. **Oriental** *adj* 1 of the Orient. 2 (**o-**) eastern. ♦ *n* 3 person from the Orient. **Orientalist** *n* specialist in the languages and history of the Far East.

orifice [**or**-rif-fiss] *n* opening or hole.

origami [or-rig-**gah**-mee] *n* Japanese decorative art of paper folding.

origin *n* **1** point from which something develops. **2** ancestry. **original** *adj* **1** first or earliest. **2** new, not copied or based on something else. **3** able to think up new ideas. ♦ *n* **4** first version, from which others are copied. **original sin** human imperfection and mortality as a result of Adam's disobedience. **originality** *n* **originally** *adv* **originate** *v* come or bring into existence. **origination** *n* **originator** *n*

oriole *n* tropical or American songbird.

ormolu *n* gold-coloured alloy used for decoration.

ornament *n* **1** decorative object. **2** decorations collectively. **3** person regarded as an asset to a group. ♦ *v* **4** decorate. **ornamental** *adj* **ornamentation** *n*

ornate *adj* highly decorated, elaborate.

ornithology *n* study of birds. **ornithological** *adj* **ornithologist** *n*

orphan *n* **1** child whose parents are dead. ♦ *v* **2** deprive of parents. **orphanage** *n* children's home for orphans. **orphaned** *adj* having no living parents.

orrery *n, pl* **-ries** mechanical model of the solar system.

orris *n* **1** kind of iris. **2** (also **orris root**) fragrant root used for perfume.

orthodontics *n* branch of dentistry concerned with correcting irregular teeth. **orthodontist** *n*

orthodox *adj* conforming to established views. **orthodoxy** *n* **Orthodox Church** dominant Christian Church in Eastern Europe.

orthography *n* correct spelling. **orthographic** *adj*

orthopaedics *n* branch of medicine concerned with disorders of the bones or joints. **orthopaedic** *adj*

oryx *n* large African antelope.

Os *Chem* osmium.

OS **1** Ordnance Survey. **2** outsize(d).

Oscar *n* award in the form of a statuette given for achievements in films.

oscillate [**oss**-ill-late] *v* **1** swing back and forth. **2** waver. **3** (of an electric current) vary between values. **oscillation** *n* **oscillator** *n* **oscilloscope** [oss-**sill**-oh-scope] *n* instrument that shows the shape of a wave on a cathode-ray tube.

osier [**oh**-zee-er] *n* **1** willow tree. **2** willow branch used in basketwork.

osmium *n Chem* heaviest known metallic element.

osmosis *n* **1** movement of a liquid through a membrane from a lower to a higher concentration. **2** process of subtle influence. **osmotic** *adj*

osprey *n* large fish-eating bird of prey.

ossify *v* **-fying, -fied** **1** (cause to) become bone, harden. **2** become inflexible. **ossification** *n*

ostensible *adj* apparent, seeming. **ostensibly** *adv*

ostentation *n* pretentious display. **ostentatious** *adj* **ostentatiously** *adv*

osteopathy *n* medical treatment involving manipulation of the joints. **osteopath** *n*

osteoporosis *n* brittleness of the bones, caused by lack of calcium.

ostler *n Hist* stableman at an inn.

ostracize *v* exclude (a person) from a group. **ostracism** *n*

ostrich *n* large African bird that runs fast but cannot fly.

OT Old Testament.

OTC Officers' Training Corps.

other *adj* **1** remaining in a group of which one or some have been specified. **2** different from the ones specified or understood. **3** additional. ♦ *n* **4** other person or thing. **otherwise** *conj* **1** or else, if not. ♦ *adv* **2** differently, in another way. **3** in other respects. **otherworldly** *adj* concerned with spiritual rather than practical matters.

otiose [**oh**-tee-oze] *adj* not useful, e.g. *otiose language.*

otter *n* small brown freshwater mammal that eats fish.

ottoman *n, pl* **-mans** storage chest with

a padded lid for use as a seat. **Ottoman** *n, adj Hist* (member) of the former Turkish empire.

oubliette [oo-blee-**ett**] *n* dungeon entered only by a trapdoor.

ouch *interj* exclamation of sudden pain.

ought *v* used to express: **1** obligation, e.g. *you ought to pay.* **2** advisability, e.g. *you ought to diet.* **3** probability, e.g. *you ought to know by then.*

> In standard English *did* and *had* are not used with *ought*: *ought not to* (not *didn't/hadn't ought to*).

Ouija board *n* ® lettered board on which supposed messages from the dead are spelt out.

ounce *n* **1** unit of weight equal to one sixteenth of a pound (28.4 grams). **2** a small amount.

our *adj* belonging to us. **ours** *pron* thing(s) belonging to us. **ourselves** *pron* emphatic and reflexive form of WE or US.

ousel *n* see DIPPER.

oust *v* force (someone) out, expel.

out *adv, adj* **1** denoting movement or distance away from, a state of being used up or extinguished, public availability, etc., e.g. *oil was pouring out; turn the light out; her new book is out.* ♦ *v* **2** *Informal* name (a public figure) as being homosexual. **out of** at or to a point outside. **out-of-date** *adj* old-fashioned. **out-of-the-way** *adj* remote. **outer** *adj* **1** on the outside. **2** further from the middle. **outermost** *adj* furthest out. **outer space** space beyond the earth's atmosphere. **outing** *n* leisure trip. **outward** *adj* **1** apparent. **2** of the outside. **3** away from a place. ♦ *adv* **4** (also **outwards**) away from somewhere. **outwardly** *adv*

out- *prefix* **1** surpassing, e.g. *outlive; outdistance.* **2** outside, away, e.g. *outpatient; outgrowth.*

outback *n* remote bush country of Australia.

outbid *v* offer a higher price than.

outboard motor *n* engine externally attached to the stern of a boat.

outbreak *n* sudden occurrence (of something unpleasant).

outbuilding *n* outhouse.

outburst *n* **1** sudden expression of emotion. **2** sudden period of violent activity.

outcast *n* person rejected by a particular group.

outclass *v* surpass in quality.

outcome *n* result.

outcrop *n* part of a rock formation that sticks out of the earth.

outcry *n, pl* **-cries** vehement or widespread protest.

outdated *adj* old-fashioned.

outdo *v* surpass in performance.

outdoors *adv* **1** in(to) the open air. ♦ *n* **2** the open air. **outdoor** *adj*

outface *v* subdue or disconcert (someone) by staring.

outfall *n* mouth of a river or drain.

outfield *n Cricket* area far from the pitch.

outfit *n* **1** matching set of clothes. **2** *Informal* group of people working together. **3** kit for a job. **outfitter** *n Old-fashioned* supplier of men's clothes.

outflank *v* **1** get round the side of (an enemy army). **2** outdo (someone).

outgoing *adj* **1** leaving. **2** sociable. **outgoings** *pl n* expenses.

outgrow *v* become too large or too old for. **outgrowth** *n* **1** natural development. **2** thing growing out from a main body.

outhouse *n* building near a main building.

outlandish *adj* extremely unconventional.

outlast *v* last longer than.

outlaw *n* **1** *Hist* criminal deprived of legal protection, bandit. ♦ *v* **2** make illegal. **3** *Hist* make (someone) an outlaw. **outlawed** *adj*

outlay *n* expenditure.

outlet *n* **1** means of expressing emotion. **2** market for a product. **3** place where a product is sold. **4** opening or way out.

outline *n* **1** short general explanation. **2**

line defining the shape of something. ♦ *v* **3** summarize. **4** show the general shape of.

outlive *v* **1** live longer than. **2** live through (an unpleasant experience).

outlook *n* **1** attitude. **2** probable outcome. **3** view.

outlying *adj* distant from the main area.

outmanoeuvre *v* get an advantage over.

outmoded *adj* no longer fashionable or accepted.

outnumber *v* exceed in number.

outpatient *n* patient who does not stay in hospital overnight.

outpost *n* outlying settlement.

outpouring *n* **1** great amount produced very rapidly. **2** passionate outburst.

output *n* **1** amount produced. **2** power, voltage, or current delivered by an electrical circuit. **3** *Computers* data produced. ♦ *v* **4** *Computers* produce (data) at the end of a process.

outrage *n* **1** great moral indignation. **2** gross violation of morality. ♦ *v* **3** offend morally. **outrageous** *adj* **1** shocking. **2** offensive. **outrageously** *adv*

outré [**oo**-tray] *adj* shockingly eccentric.

outrider *n* motorcyclist acting as an escort.

outrigger *n* stabilizing frame projecting from a boat.

outright *adj, adv* **1** absolute(ly). **2** open(ly) and direct(ly).

outrun *v* **1** run faster than. **2** exceed.

outsell *v* be sold in greater quantities than.

outset *n* beginning.

outshine *v* surpass (someone) in excellence.

outside *prep, adj, adv* **1** indicating movement to or position on the exterior. ♦ *adj* **2** unlikely, e.g. *an outside chance.* **3** coming from outside. ♦ *n* **4** external area or surface. **outsider** *n* **1** person outside a specific group. **2** contestant thought unlikely to win.

> *Outside* is not followed by *of* in standard English.

outsize, outsized *adj* larger than normal.

outskirts *pl n* outer areas, esp. of a town.

outsmart *v Informal* outwit.

outspoken *adj* **1** tending to say what one thinks. **2** said openly.

outstanding *adj* **1** excellent. **2** still to be dealt with or paid.

outstay *v* overstay.

outstretched *adj* stretched out as far as possible.

outstrip *v* **1** surpass. **2** go faster than.

outtake *n* unreleased take from a recording session, film, or TV programme.

outvote *v* defeat by getting more votes than.

outweigh *v* **1** be more important, significant, or influential than. **2** be heavier than.

outwit *v* **-witting, -witted** get the better of (someone) by cunning.

outworn *adj* no longer in use.

ouzel [**ooze**-el] *n* see DIPPER.

ouzo [**ooze**-oh] *n* strong aniseed-flavoured spirit from Greece.

ova *n* plural of OVUM.

oval *adj* **1** egg-shaped. ♦ *n* **2** anything that is oval in shape.

ovary *n, pl* **-ries** **1** female egg-producing organ. **2** part of a plant containing the ovules. **ovarian** *adj*

ovation *n* enthusiastic round of applause.

oven *n* heated compartment or container for cooking or for drying or firing ceramics.

over *prep, adv* **1** indicating position on the top of, movement to the other side of, amount greater than, etc., e.g. *a room over the garage; climbing over the fence; over fifty pounds.* ♦ *adj* **2** finished. ♦ *n* **3** *Cricket* series of six balls bowled from one end. **overly** *adv* excessively.

over- *prefix* **1** too much, e.g. *overeat.* **2** above, e.g. *overlord.* **3** on top, e.g. *overshoe.*

overact *v* act in an exaggerated way.

overall *adj, adv* **1** in total. ♦ *n* **2** coat-shaped protective garment. ♦ *pl* **3** protective garment consisting of trousers with a jacket or bib and braces attached.

overarm *adj, adv* (thrown) with the arm above the shoulder.

overawe *v* affect (someone) with an overpowering sense of awe.

overbalance *v* lose balance.

overbearing *adj* unpleasantly forceful.

overblown *adj* excessive.

overboard *adv* from a boat into the water. **go overboard** go to extremes, esp. in enthusiasm.

overcast *adj* (of the sky) covered by clouds.

overcharge *v* charge too much.

overcoat *n* heavy coat.

overcome *v* **1** gain control over after an effort. **2** (of an emotion) affect strongly. **3** defeat (someone) in a conflict.

overcrowded *adj* containing more people or things than is desirable. **overcrowding** *n*

overdo *v* **1** do to excess. **2** exaggerate (something). **3** cook too long. **overdo it** do something to a greater degree than is advisable.

overdose *n* **1** excessive dose of a drug. ♦ *v* **2** take an overdose.

overdraft *n* **1** overdrawing. **2** amount overdrawn.

overdraw *v* withdraw more money than is in (one's bank account). **overdrawn** *adj* **1** having overdrawn one's account. **2** (of an account) in debit.

overdressed *adj* dressed too elaborately or formally.

overdrive *n* **1** very high gear in a motor vehicle. **2** state of great activity or excitement.

overdue *adj* still due after the time allowed.

overestimate *v* estimate too highly.

overflow *v* **1** flow over. **2** be filled beyond capacity. ♦ *n* **3** something that overflows. **4** outlet for excess liquid. **5** excess amount.

overgrown *adj* thickly covered with plants and weeds.

overhang *v* **1** project beyond something. ♦ *n* **2** overhanging part.

overhaul *v* **1** examine and repair. **2** overtake. ♦ *n* **3** examination and repair.

overhead *adv, adj* above one's head. **overheads** *pl n* general cost of maintaining a business.

overhear *v* hear (a speaker or remark) unintentionally or without the speaker's knowledge.

overjoyed *adj* extremely pleased.

overkill *n* treatment that is greater than required.

overland *adj, adv* by land.

overlap *v* **1** share part of the same space or period of time (as). ♦ *n* **2** area overlapping.

overlay *v* cover with a thin layer.

overleaf *adv* on the back of the current page.

overload *v* **1** put too large a load on or in. ♦ *n* **2** excessive load.

overlook *v* **1** fail to notice. **2** ignore. **3** look at from above.

overman *v* provide with too many staff.

overmuch *adv, adj* too much.

overnight *adj, adv* **1** (taking place) during one night. **2** (happening) very quickly.

overpower *v* **1** subdue or overcome (someone). **2** make helpless or ineffective. **overpowering** *adj*

overrate *v* have too high an opinion of.

overreach *v* **overreach oneself** fail by trying to be too clever.

overreact *v* react more strongly than is necessary.

override *v* **1** overrule. **2** replace.

overrule *v* **1** reverse the decision of (a person with less power). **2** reverse (someone else's decision).

overrun *v* **1** conquer rapidly. **2** spread over (a place) rapidly. **3** extend beyond a set limit.

overseas *adv, adj* to, of, or from a distant country.

oversee *v* watch over from a position of authority. **overseer** *n*

overshadow *v* **1** reduce the significance

of (a person or thing) by comparison. **2** sadden the atmosphere of.

overshoe *n* protective shoe worn over an ordinary shoe.

overshoot *v* go beyond (a mark or target).

oversight *n* mistake caused by not noticing something.

oversleep *v* sleep beyond the intended time.

overspill *n* rehousing of people from crowded cities in smaller towns.

overstate *v* state too strongly. **overstatement** *n*

overstay *v* **overstay one's welcome** stay longer than one's host or hostess would like.

overstep *v* go beyond (a certain limit).

overt *adj* open, not hidden. **overtly** *adv*

overtake *v* **1** move past (a vehicle or person) travelling in the same direction. **2** come upon suddenly or unexpectedly.

overtax *v* **1** put too great a strain on. **2** tax too heavily.

overthrow *v* **1** defeat and replace. ♦ *n* **2** downfall, destruction.

overtime *n, adv* (paid work done) in addition to one's normal working hours.

overtone *n* additional meaning.

overture *n* **1** *Music* orchestral introduction. ♦ *pl* **2** opening moves in a new relationship.

overturn *v* **1** turn upside down. **2** overrule (a legal decision). **3** overthrow (a government).

overview *n* general survey.

overweening *adj* excessive or immoderate.

overweight *adj* weighing more than is healthy.

overwhelm *v* **1** overpower, esp. emotionally. **2** defeat by force. **overwhelming** *adj* **overwhelmingly** *adv*

overwork *v* **1** work too much. **2** use too much. ♦ *n* **3** excessive work.

overwrought *adj* nervous and agitated.

oviduct *n* tube through which eggs are conveyed from the ovary.

ovine *adj* of or like a sheep.

ovoid [**oh**-void] *adj* egg-shaped.

ovulate [**ov**-yew-late] *v* release an egg cell from an ovary. **ovulation** *n*

ovule *n* plant part that contains the egg cell and becomes the seed after fertilization.

ovum [**oh**-vum] *n, pl* **ova** unfertilized egg cell.

owe *v* **1** be obliged to pay (a sum of money) to (a person). **2** feel an obligation to do. **owe to** have as a result of. **owing to** as a result of.

owl *n* night bird of prey. **owlish** *adj*

own *adj* **1** used to emphasize possession, e.g. *my own idea.* ♦ *pron* **2** thing(s) belonging to a particular person. ♦ *v* **3** possess. **4** acknowledge. **hold one's own** be able to deal successfully with a situation. **on one's own 1** without help. **2** alone. **owner** *n* **ownership** *n* **own up** *v* confess.

ox *n, pl* **oxen** castrated bull.

oxalic acid *n* poisonous acid found in many plants.

Oxbridge *n* universities of Oxford and Cambridge.

Oxfam Oxford Committee for Famine Relief.

oxide *n* compound of oxygen and one other element. **oxidize** *v* combine chemically with oxygen, as in burning or rusting. **oxidation** *n* oxidizing.

oxygen *n* *Chem* gaseous element essential to life and combustion. **oxygenate** *v* add oxygen to.

oxymoron [ox-see-**more**-on] *n* figure of speech that combines two apparently contradictory ideas, e.g. *cruel kindness.*

oyez *interj* *Hist* shouted three times by a public crier, listen.

oyster *n* edible shellfish. **oystercatcher** *n* wading bird with black-and-white feathers.

oz. ounce.

ozone *n* **1** strong-smelling form of oxygen. **2** bracing seaside air. **ozone layer** layer of ozone in the upper atmosphere that filters out ultraviolet radiation.

P p

p penny *or* pence.
P **1** *Chem* phosphorus. **2** parking.
p. *pl* **pp.** page.
Pa *Chem* protactinium.
PA **1** Pennsylvania. **2** personal assistant. **3** public-address system.
p.a. each year.
pace[1] *n* **1** single step in walking. **2** length of a step. **3** rate of progress. ♦ *v* **4** walk up and down, esp. in anxiety. **5** (foll. by *out*) cross or measure with steps. **keep pace with** advance at the same rate as. **pace oneself** do something at a steady rate. **pacemaker** *n* **1** electronic device surgically implanted in a person with heart disease to regulate the heartbeat. **2** person who, by taking the lead early in a race, sets the pace for the rest of the competitors.
pace[2] *prep* with due respect to: used to express polite disagreement.
pachyderm [**pak**-ee-durm] *n* thick-skinned animal such as an elephant.
pacifist *n* person who refuses on principle to take part in war. **pacifism** *n*
pacify *v* **-fying, -fied** soothe, calm. **pacification** *n*
pack *v* **1** put (clothes etc.) together in a suitcase or bag. **2** put (goods) into containers or parcels. **3** fill with people or things. ♦ *n* **4** bag carried on a person's or animal's back. **5** *Chiefly US* same as PACKET. **6** set of playing cards. **7** group of dogs or wolves that hunt together. **8** group of people who do things together. **packing** *n* material, such as paper or plastic, used to protect packed goods. **pack ice** mass of floating ice in the sea. **pack in** *v Informal* stop doing, e.g. *I packed in the job.* **pack off** *v* send away. **pack up** *v* **1** put (one's belongings) in a case, bag, etc. **2** *Informal* stop (doing something), e.g. *I'd packed up smoking.* **3** *Informal* (of a machine) break down.
package *n* **1** small parcel. **2** (also **package deal**) deal in which separate items are presented together as a unit. ♦ *v* **3** put into a package. **packaging** *n* **package holiday** holiday in which everything is arranged by one company for a fixed price.
packet *n* **1** small container (and contents). **2** small parcel. **3** *Slang* large sum of money. **packet boat** (formerly) boat carrying mail, goods, or passengers on a fixed short route.
packhorse *n* horse used for carrying goods.
pact *n* formal agreement.
pad *n* **1** piece of soft material used for protection, support, absorption of liquid, etc. **2** number of sheets of paper fastened at the edge. **3** fleshy underpart of an animal's paw. **4** place for launching rockets. **5** *Slang* home. ♦ *v* **padding, padded** **6** protect or fill with soft material. **7** walk with soft steps. **padding** *n* **1** soft material used to pad something. **2** unnecessary words put into a speech or written work to make it longer. **pad out** *v* add unnecessary words to (a speech or written work) to make it longer.
paddle[1] *n* **1** short oar with a broad blade at one or each end. ♦ *v* **2** move (a canoe etc.) with a paddle. **paddle steamer** ship propelled by paddle wheels. **paddle wheel** wheel with crosswise blades that strike the water successively to propel a ship.
paddle[2] *v* walk barefoot in shallow water.
paddock *n* small field or enclosure for horses.
paddy *n Informal* fit of temper.
paddy field *n* field where rice is grown (also **paddy**).
padlock *n* **1** detachable lock with a hinged hoop fastened over a ring on the object to be secured. ♦ *v* **2** fasten (something) with a padlock.
padre [**pah**-dray] *n* chaplain to the

armed forces.

paean [**pee**-an] *n* song of triumph or thanksgiving.

paediatrics *n* branch of medicine concerned with diseases of children. **paediatrician** *n*

paedophilia *n* condition of being sexually attracted to children. **paedophile** *n* person who is sexually attracted to children.

paella [pie-**ell**-a] *n* Spanish dish of rice, chicken, shellfish, and vegetables.

pagan *n, adj* (person) not belonging to one of the world's main religions. **paganism** *n*

page[1] *n* **1** (one side of) a sheet of paper forming a book etc. **2** screenful of information from a website or teletext service.

page[2] *n* **1** (also **pageboy**) small boy who attends a bride at her wedding. **2** *Hist* boy in training for knighthood. ♦ *v* **3** summon (someone) by bleeper or loudspeaker, in order to pass on a message.

pageant *n* parade or display of people in costume, usu. illustrating a scene from history. **pageantry** *n*

paginate *v* number the pages of (a book etc.). **pagination** *n*

pagoda *n* pyramid-shaped Asian temple or tower.

paid *v* past of PAY. **put paid to** *Informal* end or destroy, e.g. *the recession put paid to most of our long-term plans.*

pail *n* (contents of) a bucket.

pain *n* **1** physical or mental suffering. ♦ *pl* **2** trouble, effort, e.g. *Taylor was at pains to reassure Wright.* ♦ *v* **3** cause (someone) mental or physical suffering. **on pain of** subject to the penalty of. **painful** *adj* **painfully** *adv* **painless** *adj* **painlessly** *adv* **painkiller** *n* drug that relieves pain.

painstaking *adj* extremely thorough and careful.

paint *n* **1** coloured substance, spread on a surface with a brush or roller. ♦ *v* **2** colour or coat with paint. **3** use paint to make a picture of. **painter** *n* **painting** *n*

painter *n* rope at the front of a boat, for tying it up.

pair *n* **1** set of two things matched for use together. **2** two people, animals, or things used or grouped together. ♦ *v* **3** group or be grouped in twos.

> *Pair* is followed by a singular verb if it refers to a unit: *A pair of shoes was on the floor,* and by a plural verb if it refers to two individuals: *That pair are good friends.*

paisley pattern *n* pattern of small curving shapes, used in fabric.

pajamas *pl n US* pyjamas.

Pakistani *n, adj* (person) from Pakistan.

pal *n Informal* friend.

palace *n* **1** residence of a king, bishop, etc. **2** large grand building.

paladin *n Hist* knight who did battle for a monarch.

palaeography [pal-ee-**og**-ra-fee] *n* study of ancient manuscripts.

Palaeolithic [pal-ee-oh-**lith**-ik] *adj* of the Old Stone Age.

palaeontology [pal-ee-on-**tol**-a-jee] *n* study of past geological periods and fossils. **palaeontologist** *n*

palatable *adj* **1** pleasant to taste. **2** acceptable or satisfactory, e.g. *that option is not very palatable.*

palate *n* **1** roof of the mouth. **2** sense of taste.

palatial *adj* like a palace, magnificent.

palaver [pal-**lah**-ver] *n* time-wasting fuss.

pale[1] *adj* **1** light, whitish. **2** whitish in the face, esp. through illness or shock. ♦ *v* **3** become pale. **pale in, by comparison with** appear inferior when compared with.

pale[2] *n* wooden or metal post used in fences. **beyond the pale** outside the limits of social convention.

palette *n* artist's flat board for mixing colours on. **palette knife** spatula with a broad flat flexible blade, used in painting or cookery.

palindrome *n* word or phrase that reads the same backwards as forwards.

paling *n* wooden or metal post used in fences.

palisade *n* fence made of wooden posts driven into the ground.

pall[1] *n* **1** cloth spread over a coffin. **2** dark cloud (of smoke). **3** depressing oppressive atmosphere. **pallbearer** *n* person who helps to carry the coffin at a funeral.

pall[2] *v* become boring.

palladium *n Chem* silvery-white element of the platinum metal group.

pallet[1] *n* portable platform for storing and moving goods.

pallet[2] *n* straw-filled mattress or bed.

palliasse *n* straw-filled mattress.

palliate *v* lessen the severity of (something) without curing it. **palliative** *adj* **1** giving temporary or partial relief. ♦ *n* **2** something, for example a drug, that palliates.

pallid *adj* pale, esp. because ill or weak. **pallor** *n*

pally *adj* **-lier, -liest** *Informal* on friendly terms.

palm[1] *n* inner surface of the hand. **palm off** *v* get rid of (an unwanted thing or person), esp. by deceit.

palm[2] *n* tropical tree with long pointed leaves growing out of the top of a straight trunk. **Palm Sunday** Sunday before Easter.

palmistry *n* fortune-telling from lines on the palm of the hand. **palmist** *n*

palomino *n, pl* **-nos** gold-coloured horse with a white mane and tail.

palpable *adj* **1** obvious, e.g. *a palpable hit.* **2** so intense as to seem capable of being touched, e.g. *the tension is almost palpable.* **palpably** *adv*

palpate *v Med* examine (an area of the body) by touching.

palpitate *v* **1** (of the heart) beat rapidly. **2** flutter or tremble. **palpitation** *n*

palsy [**pawl**-zee] *n* paralysis. **palsied** *adj* affected with palsy.

paltry *adj* **-trier, -triest** insignificant.

pampas *pl n* vast grassy plains in S America. **pampas grass** tall grass with feathery ornamental flower branches.

pamper *v* treat (someone) with great indulgence, spoil.

pamphlet *n* thin paper-covered booklet. **pamphleteer** *n* writer of pamphlets.

pan[1] *n* **1** wide long-handled metal container used in cooking. **2** bowl of a toilet. ♦ *v* **panning, panned 3** sift gravel from (a river) in a pan to search for gold. **4** *Informal* criticize harshly. **pan out** *v* result.

pan[2] *v* **panning, panned** (of a film camera) be moved slowly so as to cover a whole scene or follow a moving object.

pan- *combining form* all, e.g. *pan-American.*

panacea [pan-a-**see**-a] *n* remedy for all diseases or problems.

panache [pan-**ash**] *n* confident elegant style.

panama hat, panama *n* man's straw hat.

panatella *n* long slender cigar.

pancake *n* thin flat circle of fried batter. **Pancake Day** Shrove Tuesday, when people traditionally eat pancakes. **pancake landing** landing in which an aircraft comes down to a height of a few feet and then drops flat onto the ground. **pancake roll** small pancake filled with Chinese-style vegetables and rolled up.

panchromatic *adj Photog* sensitive to light of all colours.

pancreas [**pang**-kree-ass] *n* large gland behind the stomach that produces insulin and helps digestion. **pancreatic** *adj*

panda *n* large black-and-white bearlike mammal from China. **panda car** police patrol car.

pandemic *adj* (of a disease) occurring over a wide area.

pandemonium *n* wild confusion, uproar.

pander *n* person who procures a sexual partner for someone. **pander to** *v* indulge (a person or his or her desires).

p & p postage and packing.

pane *n* sheet of glass in a window or

door.

panegyric [pan-ee-**jire**-ik] *n* formal speech or piece of writing in praise of someone or something.

panel *n* **1** flat distinct section of a larger surface, for example in a door. **2** group of people as a team in a quiz etc. **3** list of jurors, doctors, etc. **4** board or surface containing switches and controls to operate equipment. ♦ *v* **-elling, -elled 5** cover or decorate with panels. **panelling** *n* panels collectively, esp. on a wall. **panellist** *n* member of a panel. **panel beater** person who repairs damage to car bodies.

pang *n* sudden sharp feeling of pain or sadness.

pangolin *n* animal of tropical countries with a scaly body and a long snout for eating ants and termites (also **scaly anteater**).

panic *n* **1** sudden overwhelming fear, often affecting a whole group of people. ♦ *v* **-icking, -icked 2** feel or cause to feel panic. **panicky** *adj* **panic-stricken** *adj*

panicle *n* loose, irregularly branched cluster of flowers.

pannier *n* **1** bag fixed on the back of a cycle. **2** basket carried by a beast of burden.

panoply [**pan**-a-plee] *n* magnificent array.

panorama *n* **1** wide unbroken view of a scene. **2** picture of a scene unrolled so as to appear continuous. **panoramic** *adj*

pansy *n, pl* **-sies 1** small garden flower with velvety purple, yellow, or white petals. **2** *Offens* effeminate or homosexual man.

pant *v* breathe quickly and noisily after exertion.

pantaloons *pl n* baggy trousers gathered at the ankles.

pantechnicon *n* large van for furniture removals.

pantheism *n* **1** belief that God is present in everything. **2** willingness to worship all gods. **pantheist** *n* **pantheistic** *adj*

pantheon *n* (in ancient Greece and Rome) temple built to honour all the gods.

panther *n* leopard, esp. a black one.

panties *pl n* women's underpants.

pantile *n* roofing tile with an S-shaped cross section.

pantomime *n* **1** play based on a fairy tale, performed at Christmas time. **2** same as MIME (sense 1). **3** confused or farcical situation.

pantry *n, pl* **-tries** small room or cupboard for storing food.

pants *pl n* **1** undergarment for the lower part of the body. **2** *US, Canadian, Aust & NZ* trousers.

pap *n* **1** soft food for babies or invalids. **2** worthless entertainment or information.

papacy [**pay**-pa-see] *n, pl* **-cies** position or term of office of a pope. **papal** *adj* of the pope.

paparazzo [pap-a-**rat**-so] *n, pl* **-razzi** photographer specializing in candid photographs of famous people.

papaya [pa-**pie**-ya] *n* large sweet West Indian fruit.

paper *n* **1** material made in sheets from wood pulp or other fibres. **2** printed sheet of this. **3** newspaper. **4** set of examination questions. **5** article or essay. ♦ *pl* **6** personal documents. ♦ *v* **7** cover (walls) with wallpaper. **on paper** in theory, as opposed to fact, e.g. *this system looks good on paper but it is expensive.* **paperback** *n* book with covers made of flexible card. **paper money** banknotes, rather than coins. **paperweight** *n* heavy decorative object placed on top of loose papers. **paperwork** *n* clerical work, such as writing reports and letters.

papier-mâché [**pap**-yay **mash**-ay] *n* material made from paper mixed with paste and moulded when moist.

papist *n, adj Offens* Roman Catholic.

papoose *n* Native American child.

paprika *n* mild powdered seasoning made from red peppers.

Pap smear, test *n* same as SMEAR TEST.

papyrus [pap-**ire**-uss] *n, pl* **-ri, -ruses 1** tall water plant. **2** (manuscript written on) a kind of paper made from this plant.

par *n* **1** usual or average condition, e.g. *feeling under par.* **2** *Golf* expected standard score. **3** face value of stocks and shares. **on a par with** equal to.

para- *combining form* beside, beyond, e.g. *parameter; parapsychology.*

parable *n* story that illustrates a religious teaching.

parabola [par-**ab**-bol-a] *n* regular curve resembling the course of an object thrown forward and up. **parabolic** *adj*

paracetamol *n* mild pain-relieving drug.

parachute *n* **1** large fabric canopy that slows the descent of a person or object from an aircraft. ♦ *v* **2** land or drop by parachute. **parachutist** *n*

parade *n* **1** procession or march. **2** street or promenade. ♦ *v* **3** display or flaunt. **4** march in procession. **parade ground** place where soldiers assemble regularly for inspection or display.

paradigm [**par**-a-dime] *n* example or model.

paradise *n* **1** heaven. **2** place or situation that is near-perfect.

paradox *n* **1** person or thing made up of contradictory elements. **2** statement that seems self-contradictory but may be true. **paradoxical** *adj* **paradoxically** *adv*

paraffin *n* liquid mixture distilled from petroleum and used as a fuel or solvent.

paragliding *n* cross-country gliding wearing a parachute shaped like wings.

paragon *n* model of perfection.

paragraph *n* section of a piece of writing starting on a new line.

parakeet *n* small long-tailed parrot.

parallax *n* apparent change in an object's position due to a change in the observer's position.

parallel *adj* **1** separated by an equal distance at every point. **2** exactly corresponding. ♦ *n* **3** line separated from another by an equal distance at every point. **4** thing with similar features to another. **5** line of latitude. ♦ *v* **6** correspond to.

parallelogram *n* four-sided geometric figure with opposite sides parallel.

paralysis *n* inability to move or feel, because of damage to the nervous system. **paralyse** *v* **1** affect with paralysis. **2** make temporarily unable to move or take action. **paralytic** *n, adj* **1** (person) affected with paralysis. ♦ *adj* **2** *Informal* very drunk.

paramedic *n* person working in support of the medical profession. **paramedical** *adj*

parameter [par-**am**-it-er] *n* limiting factor, boundary.

paramilitary *adj* organized on military lines.

paramount *adj* of the greatest importance.

paramour *n Old-fashioned* lover, esp. of a person married to someone else.

paranoia *n* **1** mental illness causing delusions of grandeur or persecution. **2** *Informal* intense fear or suspicion. **paranoid, paranoiac** *adj, n*

paranormal *adj* beyond scientific explanation. **the paranormal** paranormal events or matters.

parapet *n* low wall or railing along the edge of a balcony or roof.

paraphernalia *n* personal belongings or bits of equipment.

paraphrase *v* **1** put (a statement or text) into other words. ♦ *n* **2** expression of a statement or text in other words.

paraplegia [par-a-**pleej**-ya] *n* paralysis of the lower half of the body. **paraplegic** *adj, n*

parapsychology *n* study of mental phenomena such as telepathy.

Paraquat *n* ® extremely poisonous weedkiller.

parasite *n* **1** animal or plant living in or on another. **2** person who lives at the expense of others. **parasitic** *adj*

parasol *n* umbrella-like sunshade.

paratroops *pl n* troops trained to be dropped by parachute into a battle area. **paratrooper** *n* member of the paratroops.

parboil *v* boil until partly cooked.

parcel *n* **1** something wrapped up, package. ♦ *v* **-celling, -celled 2** (often foll. by *up*) wrap up. **parcel out** *v* divide into parts.

parch *v* **1** make very hot and dry. **2** make thirsty.

parchment *n* thick smooth writing material made from animal skin.

pardon *v* **1** forgive, excuse. ♦ *n* **2** forgiveness. **3** official release from punishment for a crime. **pardonable** *adj*

pare *v* **1** cut off the skin or top layer of. **2** (often foll. by *down*) reduce in size or amount. **paring** *n* piece pared off.

parent *n* father or mother. **parental** *adj* **parenthood** *n* **parentage** *n* ancestry or family. **parenting** *n* activity of bringing up children

parenthesis [par-**on**-thiss-iss] *n, pl* **-ses 1** word or sentence inserted into a passage, marked off by brackets or dashes. ♦ *pl* **2** round brackets, ( ). **parenthetical** *adj*

par excellence *adv* beyond comparison, e.g. *he is a travel writer par excellence.*

pariah [par-**rye**-a] *n* social outcast.

parietal [par-**rye**-it-al] *adj* of the walls of a body cavity such as the skull.

parish *n* area that has its own church and clergyman. **parishioner** *n* inhabitant of a parish.

parity *n* equality or equivalence.

park *n* **1** area of open land for recreational use by the public. **2** area containing a number of related enterprises, e.g. *a business park.* **3** area of private land around a large country house. ♦ *v* **4** stop and leave (a vehicle) temporarily. **parking meter** coin-operated device beside a parking space that indicates how long a vehicle may be parked there. **parking ticket** notice of a fine served on a motorist for a parking offence.

parka *n* long jacket with a quilted lining and a fur-trimmed hood.

Parkinson's disease *n* progressive disorder of the central nervous system which causes impaired muscular coordination and tremor (also **Parkinsonism**).

parky *adj* **parkier, parkiest** *Informal* (of the weather) chilly.

parlance *n* particular way of speaking, idiom.

parley *n* **1** meeting between leaders or representatives of opposing forces to discuss terms. ♦ *v* **2** have a parley.

parliament *n* law-making assembly of a country. **parliamentary** *adj* **parliamentarian** *n* expert in parliamentary procedures.

parlour *n* *Old-fashioned* living room for receiving visitors.

parlous *adj* *Old-fashioned* dangerous.

Parmesan *n* hard strong-flavoured Italian cheese, used grated on pasta dishes and soups.

parochial *adj* **1** narrow in outlook. **2** of a parish. **parochialism** *n*

parody *n, pl* **-dies 1** exaggerated and amusing imitation of someone else's style. ♦ *v* **-dying, -died 2** make a parody of.

parole *n* **1** early freeing of a prisoner on condition that he or she behaves well. ♦ *v* **2** put on parole. **on parole** (of a prisoner) released on condition that he or she behaves well.

paroxysm *n* **1** uncontrollable outburst of rage, delight, etc. **2** spasm or convulsion of coughing, pain, etc.

parquet [**par**-kay] *n* **1** floor covering made of wooden blocks arranged in a geometric pattern. ♦ *v* **2** cover with parquet. **parquetry** *n*

parricide *n* **1** crime of killing either of one's parents. **2** person who does this.

parrot *n* **1** tropical bird with a short hooked beak and an ability to imitate human speech. ♦ *v* **-roting, -roted 2** repeat (someone else's words) without thinking.

parry *v* **-rying, -ried 1** ward off (an attack). **2** cleverly avoid (an awkward question). ♦ *n* **3** parrying.

parse [**parz**] *v* analyse (a sentence) in terms of grammar.

parsimony *n* extreme caution in spending money. **parsimonious** *adj*

parsley *n* herb used for seasoning and decorating food.

parsnip *n* long tapering cream-coloured root vegetable.

parson *n* parish priest in the Church of England. **parsonage** *n* parson's house. **parson's nose** rump of a cooked fowl.

part *n* **1** one of the pieces that make up a whole. **2** one of several equal divisions. **3** actor's role. **4** (often pl) region, area. **5** component of a vehicle or machine. ♦ *v* **6** divide or separate. **7** (of people) leave each other. **part and parcel of** necessary part of. **take someone's part** support someone in an argument etc. **take (something) in good part** respond to (teasing or criticism) with good humour. **parting** *n* **1** occasion when one person leaves another. **2** line of scalp between sections of hair combed in opposite directions. **3** dividing or separating. **partly** *adv* not completely. **part of speech** particular grammatical class of words, such as noun or verb. **part time** for less than the full working week. **part-time** *adj* occupying or working less than the full working week. **part with** *v* give away, hand over.

partake *v* **-taking, -took, -taken 1** (foll. by *of*) take (food or drink). **2** (foll. by *in*) take part in.

partial *adj* **1** not complete. **2** prejudiced. **partial to** having a liking for. **partiality** *n* **partially** *adv*

participate *v* become actively involved. **participant** *n* **participation** *n*

participle *n* form of a verb used in compound tenses or as an adjective, e.g. *worried; worrying.*

particle *n* **1** extremely small piece or amount. **2** *Physics* minute piece of matter, such as a proton or electron.

particular *adj* **1** relating to one person or thing, not general. **2** exceptional or special. **3** very exact. **4** difficult to please, fastidious. ♦ *n* **5** item of information, detail. **6** separate distinct item as opposed to a generalization, e.g. *to go from the general to the particular.* **particularly** *adv* **particularize** *v* give details about.

partisan *n* **1** strong supporter of a party or group. **2** guerrilla, member of a resistance movement. ♦ *adj* **3** prejudiced or one-sided.

partition *n* **1** screen or thin wall that divides a room. **2** division of a country into independent parts. ♦ *v* **3** divide with a partition.

partner *n* **1** either member of a couple in a relationship or activity. **2** member of a business partnership. ♦ *v* **3** be the partner of. **partnership** *n* joint business venture between two or more people.

partridge *n* game bird of the grouse family.

parturition *n* act of giving birth.

party *n, pl* **-ties 1** social gathering for pleasure. **2** group of people travelling or working together. **3** group of people with a common political aim. **4** person or people forming one side in a lawsuit or dispute. ♦ *v* **5** celebrate, have fun. **party line 1** official view of a political party. **2** telephone line shared by two or more subscribers. **party wall** common wall separating adjoining buildings.

parvenu [**par**-ven-new] *n* person newly risen to a position of power or wealth.

pascal *n* unit of pressure.

paschal [**pass**-kal] *adj* of the Passover or Easter.

pass *v* **1** go by, past, or through. **2** move or extend in a particular direction. **3** be successful in (a test or examination). **4** spend (time) or (of time) go by. **5** give, hand. **6** be inherited by. **7** *Sport* hit, kick, or throw (the ball) to another player. **8** (of a law-making body) agree to (a law). **9** announce (a sentence or verdict) officially. **10** exceed. **11** choose not to answer a question or not to take one's turn in a game. **12** discharge (urine etc.) from the body. **13** come to an end. ♦ *n* **14** successful result in a test or examination. **15** *Sport* transfer of a ball. **16** narrow gap through mountains. **17** permit or licence. **make a pass at** *Informal* make sexual advances to. **pass**

for be accepted as. **passable** *adj* **1** (just) acceptable. **2** (of a road) capable of being travelled along. **passing** *adj* **1** brief or transitory. **2** cursory or casual. **pass away** *v* die. **pass out** *v Informal* faint. **pass over** *v* take no notice of, disregard. **pass up** *v Informal* fail to take advantage of (something).

passage *n* **1** channel or opening providing a way through. **2** hall or corridor. **3** section of a book etc. **4** journey by sea. **5** act of passing from one place or condition to another. **6** right or freedom to pass. **passageway** *n* passage or corridor.

passbook *n* book issued by a bank or building society for keeping a record of deposits and withdrawals.

passé [**pas**-say] *adj* out-of-date.

passenger *n* **1** person travelling in a vehicle driven by someone else. **2** member of a team who does not pull his or her weight.

passer-by *n, pl* **passers-by** person who is walking past something or someone.

passerine *adj* belonging to the order of perching birds.

passim *adv Latin* everywhere, throughout.

passion *n* **1** intense sexual love. **2** any strong emotion. **3** great enthusiasm. **4** (**P-**) *Christianity* the suffering of Christ. **passionate** *adj* **passionately** *adv* **passionflower** *n* tropical American plant. **passion fruit** edible fruit of the passionflower. **Passion play** play about Christ's suffering.

passive *adj* **1** not playing an active part. **2** submissive and receptive to outside forces. **3** *Grammar* (of a verb) in a form indicating that the subject receives the action, e.g. *was jeered* in *he was jeered by the crowd*. **passively** *adv* **passivity** *n* **passive resistance** resistance to a government, law, etc. by nonviolent acts. **passive smoking** inhalation of smoke from others' cigarettes by a nonsmoker.

Passover *n* Jewish festival commemorating the sparing of the Jews in Egypt.

passport *n* official document granting permission to travel abroad.

password *n* secret word or phrase that ensures admission.

past *adj* **1** of the time before the present. **2** ended, gone by. **3** *Grammar* (of a verb tense) indicating that the action specified took place earlier. ♦ *n* **4** period of time before the present. **5** person's earlier life, esp. a disreputable period. **6** *Grammar* past tense. ♦ *adv* **7** ago. **8** by, along. ♦ *prep* **9** beyond. **past it** *Informal* unable to do the things one could do when younger. **past master** person with great talent or experience in a particular subject.

pasta *n* type of food, such as spaghetti, that is made in different shapes from flour and water.

paste *n* **1** moist soft mixture, such as toothpaste. **2** adhesive, esp. for paper. **3** smooth preparation of fish etc. for spreading on bread. **4** pastry dough. **5** shiny glass used to make imitation jewellery. ♦ *v* **6** fasten with paste. **pasting** *n Informal* **1** heavy defeat. **2** strong criticism. **pasteboard** *n* stiff thick paper.

pastel *n* **1** coloured chalk crayon for drawing. **2** picture drawn in pastels. **3** pale delicate colour. ♦ *adj* **4** pale and delicate in colour.

pasteurize *v* sterilize by heating. **pasteurization** *n*

pastiche [pass-**teesh**] *n* work of art that mixes styles or copies the style of another artist.

pastille *n* small fruit-flavoured and sometimes medicated sweet.

pastime *n* activity that makes time pass pleasantly.

pastor *n* clergyman in charge of a congregation. **pastoral** *adj* **1** of or depicting country life. **2** of a clergyman or his duties. ♦ *n* **3** poem or picture portraying country life.

pastrami *n* highly seasoned smoked beef.

pastry *n, pl* **-ries** **1** baking dough made of flour, fat, and water. **2** cake or pie.

pasture *n* grassy land for farm animals

to graze on.

pasty[1] [**pay**-stee] *adj* **pastier, pastiest** (of a complexion) pale and unhealthy.

pasty[2] [**pass**-tee] *n, pl* **pasties** round of pastry folded over a savoury filling.

pat[1] *v* **patting, patted** **1** tap lightly. ♦ *n* **2** gentle tap or stroke. **3** small shaped mass of butter etc.

pat[2] *adj* quick, ready, or glib. **off pat** learned thoroughly.

patch *n* **1** piece of material sewn on a garment. **2** small contrasting section. **3** plot of ground. **4** protective pad for the eye. ♦ *v* **5** mend with a patch. **patchy** *adj* **patchier, patchiest** of uneven quality or intensity. **patch up** *v* **1** repair clumsily. **2** make up (a quarrel). **patchwork** *n* needlework made of pieces of different materials sewn together.

pate *n Old-fashioned* head.

pâté [**pat**-ay] *n* spread of finely minced liver etc.

patella *n, pl* **-lae** kneecap.

patent *n* **1** document giving the exclusive right to make or sell an invention. ♦ *adj* **2** open to public inspection, e.g. *letters patent.* **3** obvious. **4** protected by a patent. ♦ *v* **5** obtain a patent for. **patently** *adv* obviously. **patent leather** leather processed to give a hard glossy surface.

paternal *adj* **1** fatherly. **2** related through one's father. **paternity** *n* fact or state of being a father. **paternalism** *n* authority exercised in a way that limits individual responsibility. **paternalistic** *adj*

path *n* **1** surfaced walk or track. **2** course or direction. **3** course of action.

pathetic *adj* **1** causing feelings of pity or sadness. **2** distressingly inadequate. **pathetically** *adv*

pathogen *n* thing that causes disease. **pathogenic** *adj*

pathology *n* scientific study of diseases. **pathological** *adj* **1** of pathology. **2** *Informal* compulsively motivated. **pathologist** *n*

pathos *n* power of arousing pity or sadness.

patient *adj* **1** enduring difficulties or delays calmly. ♦ *n* **2** person receiving medical treatment. **patience** *n* **1** quality of being patient. **2** card game for one.

patina *n* **1** fine layer on a surface. **2** sheen of age on woodwork.

patio *n, pl* **-tios** paved area adjoining a house.

patois [**pat**-wah] *n, pl* **patois** [**pat**-wahz] regional dialect.

patriarch *n* **1** male head of a family or tribe. **2** highest-ranking bishop in Orthodox Churches. **patriarchal** *adj* **patriarchy** *n, pl* **-chies** society in which men have most of the power.

patrician *n* **1** member of the nobility. ♦ *adj* **2** of noble birth.

patricide *n* **1** crime of killing one's father. **2** person who does this.

patrimony *n, pl* **-nies** property inherited from ancestors.

patriot *n* person who loves his or her country and supports its interests. **patriotic** *adj* **patriotism** *n*

patrol *n* **1** regular circuit by a guard. **2** person or small group patrolling. **3** unit of Scouts or Guides. ♦ *v* **-trolling, -trolled** **4** go round on guard, or reconnoitring. **patrol car** police car used for patrolling streets.

patron *n* **1** person who gives financial support to charities, artists, etc. **2** regular customer of a shop, pub, etc. **patronage** *n* support given by a patron. **patronize** *v* **1** treat in a condescending way. **2** be a patron of. **patronizing** *adj* **patron saint** saint regarded as the guardian of a country or group.

patronymic *n* name derived from one's father or a male ancestor.

patter[1] *v* **1** make repeated soft tapping sounds. ♦ *n* **2** quick succession of taps.

patter[2] *n* glib rapid speech.

pattern *n* **1** arrangement of repeated parts or decorative designs. **2** regular way that something is done. **3** diagram or shape used as a guide to make something. **patterned** *adj* decorated with a pattern.

patty *n, pl* **-ties** small round meat pie.

paucity *n* **1** scarcity. **2** smallness of amount or number.

paunch *n* protruding belly.

pauper *n* very poor person.

pause *v* **1** stop for a time. **2** hesitate. ♦ *n* **3** stop or rest in speech or action. **4** *Music* continuation of a note or rest beyond its normal length.

pave *v* form (a surface) with stone or brick. **pavement** *n* paved path for pedestrians.

pavilion *n* **1** building on a playing field etc. **2** building for housing an exhibition etc.

pavlova *n* meringue cake topped with whipped cream and fruit.

paw *n* **1** animal's foot with claws and pads. ♦ *v* **2** scrape with the paw or hoof. **3** *Informal* touch in a rough or overfamiliar way.

pawl *n* pivoted lever shaped to engage with a ratchet to prevent motion in a particular direction.

pawn[1] *v* deposit (an article) as security for money borrowed. **in pawn** deposited as security with a pawnbroker. **pawnbroker** *n* lender of money on goods deposited.

pawn[2] *n* **1** chessman of the lowest value. **2** person manipulated by someone else.

pawpaw *n* same as PAPAYA.

pay *v* **paying, paid 1** give money etc. in return for goods or services. **2** settle a debt or obligation. **3** compensate (for). **4** give. **5** be profitable to. ♦ *n* **6** wages or salary. **payment** *n* **1** act of paying. **2** money paid. **payable** *adj* due to be paid. **payee** *n* person to whom money is paid or due. **paying guest** lodger. **pay off** *v* **1** pay (debt) in full. **2** turn out successfully. **pay out** *v* **1** spend. **2** release (a rope) bit by bit.

PAYE pay as you earn: system by which income tax is paid by an employer straight to the government.

payload *n* **1** passengers or cargo of an aircraft. **2** explosive power of a missile etc.

payola *n* *Informal* bribe to get special treatment, esp. to promote a commercial product.

payroll *n* list of employees who receive regular pay.

Pb *Chem* lead.

pc per cent.

PC **1** personal computer. **2** Police Constable. **3** politically correct. **4** Privy Councillor.

Pd *Chem* palladium.

PE **1** physical education. **2** Prince Edward Island.

pea *n* **1** climbing plant with seeds growing in pods. **2** its seed, eaten as a vegetable. **peasouper** *n* *Informal* thick fog.

peace *n* **1** calm, quietness. **2** absence of anxiety. **3** freedom from war. **4** harmony between people. **peaceable** *adj* inclined towards peace. **peaceably** *adv* **peaceful** *adj* **peacefully** *adv* **peacemaker** *n* person who brings about peace, esp. between others.

peach *n* **1** soft juicy fruit with a stone and a downy skin. **2** *Informal* very pleasing person or thing. ♦ *adj* **3** pinkish-orange.

peacock *n* large male bird with a brilliantly coloured fanlike tail. **peahen** *n fem* **peafowl** *n* peacock or peahen.

peak *n* **1** pointed top, esp. of a mountain. **2** point of greatest development etc. **3** projecting piece on the front of a cap. ♦ *v* **4** form or reach a peak. ♦ *adj* **5** of or at the point of greatest demand. **peaked** *adj* **peaky** *adj* **peakier, peakiest** pale and sickly.

peal *n* **1** long loud echoing sound, esp. of bells or thunder. ♦ *v* **2** sound with a peal or peals.

peanut *n* **1** pea-shaped nut that ripens underground. ♦ *pl* **2** *Informal* trifling amount of money.

pear *n* sweet juicy fruit with a narrow top and rounded base.

pearl *n* hard round shiny object found inside some oyster shells and used as a jewel. **pearly** *adj* **pearlier, pearliest** **pearl barley** barley ground into small round grains.

peasant *n* farmer or farmworker of a low social class. **peasantry** *n* peasants collectively.

pease pudding *n* dish of boiled split peas.

peat *n* decayed vegetable material found in bogs, used as fertilizer or fuel.

pebble *n* small roundish stone. **pebbly** *adj* **pebblier, pebbliest** **pebble dash** coating for exterior walls consisting of small stones set in plaster.

pecan [**pee**-kan] *n* edible nut of a N American tree.

peccadillo *n, pl* **-loes, -los** trivial misdeed.

peck[1] *v* **1** strike or pick up with the beak. **2** *Informal* kiss quickly. ♦ *n* **3** pecking movement. **peckish** *adj Informal* slightly hungry. **peck at** *v* nibble, eat reluctantly. **pecking order** order of seniority or power in a group.

peck[2] *n* fourth part of a bushel, 2 gallons.

pectin *n* substance in fruit that makes jam set.

pectoral *adj* **1** of the chest or thorax. ♦ *n* **2** pectoral muscle or fin.

peculiar *adj* **1** strange. **2** distinct, special. **3** belonging exclusively to. **peculiarity** *n, pl* **-ties** **1** oddity, eccentricity. **2** distinguishing trait.

pecuniary *adj* relating to, or consisting of, money.

pedagogue *n* schoolteacher, esp. a pedantic one.

pedal *n* **1** foot-operated lever used to control a vehicle or machine, or to modify the tone of a musical instrument. ♦ *v* **-alling, -alled** **2** propel (a bicycle) by using its pedals.

pedant *n* person who is excessively concerned with details and rules, esp. in academic work. **pedantic** *adj* **pedantry** *n*

peddle *v* sell (goods) from door to door. **peddler** *n* person who sells illegal drugs.

pederast *n* man who has homosexual relations with boys. **pederasty** *n*

pedestal *n* base supporting a column, statue, etc.

pedestrian *n* **1** person who walks. ♦ *adj* **2** dull, uninspiring. **pedestrian crossing** place marked where pedestrians may cross a road. **pedestrian precinct** (shopping) area for pedestrians only.

pedicure *n* medical or cosmetic treatment of the feet.

pedigree *n* register of ancestors, esp. of a purebred animal.

pediment *n* triangular part over a door etc.

pedlar *n* person who sells goods from door to door.

pedometer [pid-**dom**-it-er] *n* instrument which measures the distance walked.

pee *Informal* ♦ *v* **peeing, peed** **1** urinate. ♦ *n* **2** urine. **3** act of urinating.

peek *v, n* peep or glance.

peel *v* **1** remove the skin or rind of (a vegetable or fruit). **2** (of skin or a surface) come off in flakes. ♦ *n* **3** rind or skin. **peelings** *pl n*

peep[1] *v* **1** look slyly or quickly. ♦ *n* **2** peeping look. **Peeping Tom** man who furtively watches women undressing.

peep[2] *v* **1** make a small shrill noise. ♦ *n* **2** small shrill noise.

peer[1] *n* **1** (*fem* **peeress**) member of the nobility. **2** person of the same status, age, etc. **peerage** *n* **1** whole body of peers. **2** rank of a peer. **peerless** *adj* unequalled, unsurpassed. **peer group** group of people of similar age, status, etc.

peer[2] *v* look closely and intently.

peeved *adj Informal* annoyed.

peevish *adj* fretful or irritable. **peevishly** *adv*

peewit *n* same as LAPWING.

peg *n* **1** pin or clip for joining, fastening, marking, etc. **2** hook or knob for hanging things on. ♦ *v* **pegging, pegged** **3** fasten with pegs. **4** stabilize (prices). **off the peg** (of clothes) ready-to-wear, not tailor-made.

peignoir [**pay**-nwahr] *n* woman's light dressing gown.

pejorative [pij-**jor**-a-tiv] *adj* (of words etc.) with an insulting or critical meaning.

Pekingese, Pekinese *n, pl* **-ese** small dog with a short wrinkled muzzle.

pelargonium *n* plant with red, white, or pink flowers.

pelican *n* large water bird with a pouch beneath its bill for storing fish. **pelican crossing** road crossing with pedestrian-operated traffic lights.

pellagra *n* disease caused by lack of vitamin B.

pellet *n* small ball of something.

pell-mell *adv* in utter confusion, headlong.

pellucid *adj* very clear.

pelmet *n* ornamental drapery or board, concealing a curtain rail.

pelt[1] *v* **1** throw missiles at. **2** run fast, rush. **3** rain heavily. **at full pelt** at top speed.

pelt[2] *n* skin of a fur-bearing animal.

pelvis *n* framework of bones at the base of the spine, to which the hips are attached. **pelvic** *adj*

pen[1] *n* **1** instrument for writing in ink. ♦ *v* **penning, penned 2** write or compose. **pen friend** friend with whom a person corresponds without meeting. **penknife** *n* small knife with blade(s) that fold into the handle. **pen name** name used by a writer instead of his or her real name.

pen[2] *n* **1** small enclosure for domestic animals. ♦ *v* **penning, penned 2** put or keep in a pen. **penned in** trapped or confined.

pen[3] *n* female swan.

penal [**pee**-nal] *adj* of or used in punishment. **penalize** *v* **1** impose a penalty on. **2** handicap, hinder. **penalty** *n, pl* **-ties 1** punishment for a crime or offence. **2** *Sport* handicap or disadvantage imposed for breaking a rule.

penance *n* voluntary self-punishment to make amends for wrongdoing.

pence *n* a plural of PENNY.

penchant [**pon**-shon] *n* inclination or liking.

pencil *n* **1** thin cylindrical instrument containing graphite, for writing or drawing. ♦ *v* **-cilling, -cilled 2** draw, write, or mark with a pencil.

pendant *n* ornament worn on a chain round the neck.

pendent *adj* hanging.

pending *prep* **1** while waiting for. ♦ *adj* **2** not yet decided or settled.

pendulous *adj* hanging, swinging.

pendulum *n* suspended weight swinging to and fro, esp. as a regulator for a clock.

penetrate *v* **1** find or force a way into or through. **2** arrive at the meaning of. **penetrable** *adj* capable of being penetrated. **penetrating** *adj* **1** (of a sound) loud and unpleasant. **2** quick to understand. **penetration** *n*

penguin *n* flightless black-and-white Antarctic sea bird.

penicillin *n* antibiotic drug effective against a wide range of diseases and infections.

peninsula *n* strip of land nearly surrounded by water. **peninsular** *adj*

penis *n* organ of copulation and urination in male mammals.

penitent *adj* **1** feeling sorry for having done wrong. ♦ *n* **2** someone who is penitent. **penitence** *n* **penitentiary** *n, pl* **-ries 1** *US* prison. ♦ *adj* **2** (also **penitential**) relating to penance.

pennant *n* long narrow flag.

pennon *n* triangular or tapering flag.

penny *n, pl* **pence, pennies 1** British bronze coin worth one hundredth of a pound. **2** former British coin worth one twelfth of a shilling. **penniless** *adj* very poor. **penny-pinching** *adj* excessively careful with money.

penology [pee-**nol**-a-jee] *n* study of punishment and prison management.

pension[1] *n* regular payment to people above a certain age, retired employees, widows, etc. **pensionable** *adj* **pensioner** *n* person receiving a pension. **pension off** *v* force (someone) to retire from a job and pay him or her a pension.

pension[2] [**pon**-syon] *n* boarding house in Europe.

pensive *adj* deeply thoughtful, often with a tinge of sadness.

pentagon *n* **1** geometric figure with five sides. **2** (**P-**) headquarters of the US military. **pentagonal** *adj*

pentagram, pentacle *n* five-pointed star.

pentameter [pen-**tam**-it-er] *n* line of poetry with five metrical feet.

Pentateuch [**pent**-a-tyuke] *n* first five books of the Old Testament.

Pentecost *n* Christian festival celebrating the descent of the Holy Spirit to the apostles, Whitsuntide. **Pentecostal** *adj* of a Christian group that has a charismatic and fundamentalist approach to Christianity.

penthouse *n* flat built on the roof or top floor of a building.

pent-up *adj* (of an emotion) not released, repressed.

penultimate *adj* second last.

penumbra *n, pl* **-brae, -bras 1** (in an eclipse) the partially shadowed region which surrounds the full shadow. **2** partial shadow. **penumbral** *adj*

penury *n* extreme poverty. **penurious** *adj*

peony *n, pl* **-nies** garden plant with showy red, pink, or white flowers.

people *pl n* **1** persons generally. **2** the community. **3** one's family. ♦ *n* **4** race or nation. ♦ *v* **5** provide with inhabitants.

pep *n Informal* high spirits, energy, or enthusiasm. **pep pill** *Informal* tablet containing a stimulant drug. **pep talk** *Informal* talk designed to increase confidence and enthusiasm. **pep up** *v* **pepping, pepped** stimulate, invigorate.

pepper *n* **1** sharp hot condiment made from the fruit of an East Indian climbing plant. **2** colourful tropical fruit used as a vegetable, capsicum. ♦ *v* **3** season with pepper. **4** sprinkle, dot. **5** pelt with missiles. **peppery** *adj* **1** tasting of pepper. **2** irritable. **peppercorn** *n* dried berry of the pepper plant. **peppercorn rent** low or nominal rent. **pepper mill** small hand mill used to grind peppercorns.

peppermint *n* **1** plant that yields an oil with a strong sharp flavour. **2** sweet flavoured with this.

peptic *adj* relating to digestion or the digestive juices. **peptic ulcer** ulcer in the stomach or duodenum.

per *prep* for each. **as per** in accordance with.

perambulate *v* walk through or about (a place). **perambulation** *n* **perambulator** *n* pram.

per annum *adv Latin* in each year.

per capita *adj, adv Latin* of or for each person.

perceive *v* **1** become aware of (something) through the senses. **2** understand.

percentage *n* proportion or rate per hundred. **per cent** in each hundred.

perceptible *adj* discernible, recognizable. **perceptibly** *adv*

perception *n* **1** act of perceiving. **2** intuitive judgment. **perceptive** *adj*

perch[1] *n* **1** resting place for a bird. ♦ *v* **2** alight, rest, or place on or as if on a perch.

perch[2] *n* edible freshwater fish.

perchance *adv Old-fashioned* perhaps.

percipient *adj* quick to notice things, observant.

percolate *v* **1** pass or filter through small holes. **2** spread gradually. **3** make (coffee) or (of coffee) be made in a percolator. **percolation** *n* **percolator** *n* coffeepot in which boiling water is forced through a tube and filters down through coffee.

percussion *n* **1** striking of one thing against another. **2** *Music* percussion instruments collectively. **percussionist** *n* **percussion instrument** musical instrument played by being struck, such as drums or cymbals.

perdition *n* spiritual ruin.

peregrination *n* travels, roaming.

peregrine falcon *n* falcon with dark upper parts and a light underside.

peremptory *adj* authoritative, imperious.

perennial *adj* **1** lasting through many years. ♦ *n* **2** plant lasting more than two years. **perennially** *adv*

perestroika *n* (formerly, in the USSR) policy of restructuring the economy and political system.

perfect *adj* **1** having all the essential elements. **2** faultless. **3** correct, precise. **4** utter or absolute. **5** excellent. **6** *Grammar* denoting a tense of verbs describing completed actions. ♦ *n* **7** *Grammar* perfect tense. ♦ *v* **8** improve. **9** make fully correct. **perfectly** *adv* **perfection** *n* state of being perfect. **perfectionist** *n* person who demands the highest standards of excellence. **perfectionism** *n*

perfidious *adj* treacherous, disloyal. **perfidy** *n*

perforate *v* make holes in. **perforation** *n*

perforce *adv* of necessity.

perform *v* **1** carry out (an action). **2** act, sing, or present a play before an audience. **3** fulfil (a request etc.). **performance** *n* **performer** *n*

perfume *n* **1** liquid cosmetic worn for its pleasant smell. **2** fragrance. ♦ *v* **3** give a pleasant smell to. **perfumed** *adj* **perfumer** *n* person who makes or sells perfume. **perfumery** *n* perfumes in general.

perfunctory *adj* done only as a matter of routine, superficial. **perfunctorily** *adv*

pergola *n* arch or framework of trellis supporting climbing plants.

perhaps *adv* **1** possibly, maybe. **2** approximately.

pericardium *n, pl* **-dia** membrane enclosing the heart.

perigee *n* point in the orbit of the moon or a satellite that is nearest the earth.

perihelion *n, pl* **-lia** point in the orbit of a planet or comet that is nearest to the sun.

peril *n* great danger. **perilous** *adj* **perilously** *adv*

perimeter [per-**rim**-it-er] *n* (length of) the outer edge of an area.

perinatal *adj* of or in the weeks shortly before or after birth.

period *n* **1** particular portion of time. **2** single occurrence of menstruation. **3** division of time at school etc. when a particular subject is taught. **4** *US* full stop. ♦ *adj* **5** (of furniture, dress, a play, etc.) dating from or in the style of an earlier time. **periodic** *adj* recurring at intervals. **periodic table** *Chem* chart of the elements, arranged to show their relationship to each other. **periodical** *n* **1** magazine issued at regular intervals. ♦ *adj* **2** periodic.

peripatetic [per-rip-a-**tet**-ik] *adj* travelling about from place to place.

periphery [per-**if**-er-ee] *n, pl* **-eries** **1** boundary or edge. **2** fringes of a field of activity. **peripheral** [per-**if**-er-al] *adj* **1** unimportant, not central. **2** of or on the periphery. ♦ *n* **3** any extra device that can be attached to or put in a computer.

periscope *n* instrument used, esp. in submarines, to give a view of objects on a different level.

perish *v* **1** be destroyed or die. **2** decay, rot. **perishable** *adj* liable to rot quickly. **perishing** *adj Informal* very cold.

peritoneum [per-rit-toe-**nee**-um] *n, pl* **-nea, -neums** membrane lining the internal surface of the abdomen. **peritonitis** [per-rit-tone-**ite**-iss] *n* inflammation of the peritoneum.

periwinkle[1] *n* small edible shellfish, the winkle.

periwinkle[2] *n* plant with trailing stems and blue flowers.

perjury [**per**-jer-ee] *n, pl* **-juries** act or crime of lying while under oath in a court. **perjure oneself** commit perjury.

perk *n Informal* incidental benefit gained from a job, such as a company car.

perk up *v* cheer up. **perky** *adj* **perkier, perkiest** lively or cheerful.

perm *n* **1** long-lasting curly hairstyle produced by treating the hair with chemicals. ♦ *v* **2** give (hair) a perm.

permafrost *n* permanently frozen ground.

permanent *adj* lasting forever. **permanence** *n* **permanently** *adv*

permanganate *n* a salt of an acid of manganese.

permeate *v* pervade or pass through the

whole of (something). **permeable** *adj* able to be permeated, esp. by liquid.

permit *v* **-mitting, -mitted** **1** give permission, allow. ♦ *n* **2** document giving permission to do something. **permission** *n* authorization to do something. **permissible** *adj* **permissive** *adj* (excessively) tolerant, esp. in sexual matters. **permissiveness** *n*

permutation *n* **1** any of the ways a number of things can be arranged or combined. **2** *Maths* arrangement of a number of quantities in every possible order. **3** fixed combination for selections of results on football pools.

pernicious *adj* **1** wicked. **2** extremely harmful, deadly.

pernickety *adj Informal* (excessively) fussy about details.

peroration *n* concluding part of a speech, usu. summing up the main points.

peroxide *n* **1** hydrogen peroxide used as a hair bleach. **2** oxide containing a high proportion of oxygen.

perpendicular *adj* **1** at right angles to a line or surface. **2** upright or vertical. ♦ *n* **3** line or plane at right angles to another.

perpetrate *v* commit or be responsible for (a wrongdoing). **perpetration** *n* **perpetrator** *n*

perpetual *adj* **1** lasting forever. **2** continually repeated. **perpetually** *adv* **perpetuate** *v* cause to continue or be remembered. **perpetuation** *n* **perpetuity** *n* eternity. **in perpetuity** forever.

perplex *v* puzzle, bewilder. **perplexity** *n, pl* **-ties**

perquisite *n Formal* same as PERK.

perry *n, pl* **-ries** alcoholic drink made from fermented pears.

per se [per **say**] *adv Latin* in itself.

persecute *v* **1** treat cruelly because of race, religion, etc. **2** subject to persistent harassment. **persecution** *n* **persecutor** *n*

persevere *v* keep making an effort despite difficulties. **perseverance** *n*

Persian *adj* **1** of ancient Persia or modern Iran, their people, or their languages. ♦ *n* **2** person from modern Iran, Iranian. **Persian carpet, rug** handmade carpet *or* rug with flowing or geometric designs in rich colours. **Persian cat** long-haired domestic cat.

persiflage [**per**-sif-flahzh] *n* light frivolous talk or writing.

persimmon *n* sweet red tropical fruit.

persist *v* **1** continue to be or happen, last. **2** continue in spite of obstacles or objections. **persistent** *adj* **persistently** *adv* **persistence** *n*

person *n* **1** human being. **2** body of a human being. **3** *Grammar* form of pronouns and verbs that shows if a person is speaking, spoken to, or spoken of. **in person** actually present.

> *Person* is generally used in the singular and *people* is used to indicate more than one. The plural *persons* is restricted to formal notices.

persona [per-**soh**-na] *n, pl* **-nae** [-nee] someone's personality as presented to others.

personable *adj* pleasant in appearance and personality.

personage *n* important person.

personal *adj* **1** individual or private. **2** of the body, e.g. *personal hygiene.* **3** (of a remark etc.) offensive. **personalize** *v* **personalized** *adj* **personally** *adv* **1** directly, not by delegation to others. **2** in one's own opinion. **personal assistant** person employed to help someone, esp. with secretarial and administrative work. **personal column** newspaper column containing personal messages and advertisements. **personal computer** small computer used for word processing or computer games. **personal pronoun** pronoun like *I* or *she* that stands for a definite person. **personal stereo** very small portable cassette player with headphones.

personality *n, pl* **-ties** **1** person's distinctive characteristics. **2** celebrity. ♦ *pl* **3** personal remarks, e.g. *the discussion de-*

generated into personalities.

personify *v* **-fying, -fied 1** give human characteristics to. **2** be an example of, typify. **personification** *n*

personnel *n* people employed in an organization.

perspective *n* **1** view of the relative importance of situations or facts. **2** method of drawing that gives the effect of solidity and relative distances and sizes. **3** appearance of objects or buildings relative to each other.

Perspex *n* ® transparent acrylic substitute for glass.

perspicacious *adj* having quick mental insight. **perspicacity** *n*

perspire *v* sweat. **perspiration** *n*

persuade *v* **1** make (someone) do something by argument, charm, etc. **2** convince. **persuasion** *n* **1** act of persuading. **2** way of thinking or belief. **persuasive** *adj*

pert *adj* saucy and cheeky.

pertain *v* belong or be relevant (to).

pertinacious *adj* very persistent and determined. **pertinacity** *n*

pertinent *adj* relevant. **pertinence** *n*

perturb *v* disturb greatly. **perturbation** *n*

peruse *v* read in a careful or leisurely manner. **perusal** *n*

pervade *v* spread right through (something). **pervasive** *adj*

perverse *adj* deliberately doing something different from what is thought normal or proper. **perversely** *adv* **perversity** *n*

pervert *v* **1** use or alter for a wrong purpose. **2** lead into abnormal (sexual) behaviour. ♦ *n* **3** person who practises sexual perversion. **perversion** *n* **1** sexual act or desire considered abnormal. **2** act of perverting.

pervious *adj* able to be penetrated, permeable.

peseta [pa-**say**-ta] *n* monetary unit of Spain.

peso [**pay**-so] *n, pl* **pesos** monetary unit of Argentina, Mexico, etc.

pessary *n, pl* **-ries 1** appliance worn in the vagina, either to prevent conception or to support the womb. **2** vaginal suppository.

pessimism *n* tendency to expect the worst in all things. **pessimist** *n* **pessimistic** *adj* **pessimistically** *adv*

pest *n* **1** annoying person. **2** insect or animal that damages crops. **pesticide** *n* chemical for killing insect pests.

pester *v* annoy or nag continually.

pestilence *n* deadly epidemic disease. **pestilent** *adj* **1** annoying, troublesome. **2** deadly. **pestilential** *adj*

pestle *n* club-shaped implement for grinding things to powder in a mortar.

pet *n* **1** animal kept for pleasure and companionship. **2** person favoured or indulged. ♦ *adj* **3** kept as a pet. **4** particularly cherished. ♦ *v* **petting, petted 5** treat as a pet. **6** pat or stroke affectionately. **7** *Informal* kiss and caress erotically.

petal *n* one of the brightly coloured outer parts of a flower. **petalled** *adj*

petard *n* **hoist with one's own petard** being the victim of one's own schemes.

peter out *v* gradually come to an end.

petite *adj* (of a woman) small and dainty.

petition *n* **1** formal request, esp. one signed by many people and presented to parliament. ♦ *v* **2** present a petition to. **petitioner** *n*

petrel *n* sea bird with a hooked bill and tubular nostrils.

petrify *v* **-fying, -fied 1** frighten severely. **2** turn to stone. **petrification** *n*

petrochemical *n* substance, such as acetone, obtained from petroleum.

petrodollar *n* money earned by a country by exporting petroleum.

petrol *n* flammable liquid obtained from petroleum, used as fuel in internal-combustion engines. **petrol bomb** home-made incendiary device consisting of a bottle filled with petrol. **petrol station** place selling petrol, oil, etc.

petroleum *n* thick dark oil found underground.

petticoat *n* woman's skirt-shaped undergarment.

pettifogging *adj* excessively concerned with unimportant detail.

petty *adj* **-tier, -tiest 1** unimportant, trivial. **2** small-minded. **3** on a small scale, e.g. *petty crime.* **pettiness** *n* **petty cash** cash kept by a firm to pay minor expenses. **petty officer** noncommissioned officer in the navy.

petulant *adj* childishly irritable or peevish. **petulance** *n* **petulantly** *adv*

petunia *n* garden plant with funnel-shaped flowers.

pew *n* **1** fixed benchlike seat in a church. **2** *Informal* chair, seat.

pewter *n* greyish metal made of tin and lead.

pH *Chem* measure of the acidity of a solution.

phalanger *n* long-tailed Australian tree-dwelling marsupial.

phalanx *n, pl* **phalanxes, phalanges** closely grouped mass of people.

phallus *n, pl* **-luses, -li** penis, esp. as a symbol of reproductive power in primitive rites. **phallic** *adj*

phantasm *n* unreal vision, illusion. **phantasmal** *adj*

phantasmagoria *n* shifting medley of dreamlike figures.

phantasy *n, pl* **-sies** same as FANTASY.

phantom *n* **1** ghost. **2** unreal vision.

Pharaoh [**fare**-oh] *n* title of the ancient Egyptian kings.

Pharisee *n* **1** member of an ancient Jewish sect teaching strict observance of Jewish traditions. **2** self-righteous hypocrite.

pharmaceutical *adj* of pharmacy.

pharmacology *n* study of drugs. **pharmacological** *adj* **pharmacologist** *n*

pharmacopoeia [far-ma-koh-**pee**-a] *n* book with a list of and directions for the use of drugs.

pharmacy *n, pl* **-cies 1** preparation and dispensing of drugs and medicines. **2** pharmacist's shop. **pharmacist** *n* person qualified to prepare and sell drugs and medicines.

pharynx [**far**-rinks] *n, pl* **pharynges, pharynxes** cavity forming the back part of the mouth. **pharyngeal** *adj* **pharyngitis** [far-rin-**jite**-iss] *n* inflammation of the pharynx.

phase *n* **1** any distinct or characteristic stage in a development or chain of events. ♦ *v* **2** arrange or carry out in stages or to coincide with something else. **phase in, out** *v* introduce *or* discontinue gradually.

PhD Doctor of Philosophy.

pheasant *n* game bird with bright plumage.

phenobarbitone *n* drug inducing sleep or relaxation.

phenol *n* chemical used in disinfectants and antiseptics.

phenomenon *n, pl* **-ena 1** anything appearing or observed. **2** remarkable person or thing. **phenomenal** *adj* extraordinary, outstanding. **phenomenally** *adv*

> Avoid using *phenomena* as a singular.

phew *interj* exclamation of relief, surprise, etc.

phial *n* small bottle for medicine etc.

philadelphus *n* shrub with sweet-scented flowers.

philanderer *n* man who flirts or has many casual love affairs. **philandering** *adj, n*

philanthropy *n* practice of helping people less well-off than oneself. **philanthropic** *adj* **philanthropist** *n*

philately [fill-**lat**-a-lee] *n* stamp collecting. **philatelist** *n*

philharmonic *adj* (in names of orchestras etc.) music-loving.

philippic *n* bitter or impassioned speech of denunciation, invective.

philistine *adj, n* boorishly uncultivated (person). **philistinism** *n*

philology *n* science of the structure and development of languages. **philological** *adj* **philologist** *n*

philosophy *n, pl* **-phies** **1** study of the meaning of life, knowledge, thought, etc. **2** theory or set of ideas held by a particular philosopher. **3** person's outlook on life. **philosopher** *n* person who studies philosophy. **philosophical, philosophic** *adj* **1** of philosophy. **2** calm in the face of difficulties or disappointments. **philosophically** *adv* **philosophize** *v* discuss in a philosophical manner.

philtre *n* magic drink supposed to arouse love in the person who drinks it.

phlebitis [fleb-**bite**-iss] *n* inflammation of a vein.

phlegm [**flem**] *n* thick yellowish substance formed in the nose and throat during a cold.

phlegmatic [fleg-**mat**-ik] *adj* not easily excited, unemotional. **phlegmatically** *adv*

phlox *n, pl* **phlox, phloxes** flowering garden plant.

phobia *n* intense and unreasoning fear or dislike. **phobic** *adj*

phoenix *n* legendary bird said to set fire to itself and rise anew from its ashes.

phone *n, v Informal* telephone. **phonecard** *n* card used to operate certain public telephones. **phone-in** *n* broadcast in which telephone comments or questions from the public are transmitted live.

phonetic *adj* **1** of speech sounds. **2** (of spelling) written as it is sounded. **phonetics** *n* science of speech sounds. **phonetically** *adv*

phoney, phony *Informal* ♦ *adj* **phonier, phoniest** **1** not genuine. **2** insincere. ♦ *n, pl* **phoneys, phonies** **3** phoney person or thing.

phonograph *n US old-fashioned* record player.

phonology *n* study of the speech sounds in a language.

phosgene [**foz**-jean] *n* poisonous gas used in warfare.

phosphorescence *n* faint glow in the dark. **phosphorescent** *adj*

phosphorus *n Chem* toxic flammable nonmetallic element which appears luminous in the dark. **phosphate** *n* **1** compound of phosphorus. **2** fertilizer containing phosphorus.

photo *n, pl* **photos** short for PHOTOGRAPH. **photo finish** finish of a race in which the contestants are so close that a photograph is needed to decide the result.

photo- *combining form* light, e.g. *photometer.*

photocell *n* cell which produces a current or voltage when exposed to light or other electromagnetic radiation.

photocopy *n, pl* **-copies** **1** photographic reproduction. ♦ *v* **-copying, -copied** **2** make a photocopy of. **photocopier** *n*

photoelectric *adj* using or worked by electricity produced by the action of light.

Photofit *n* ® picture made by combining photographs of different facial features

photogenic *adj* always looking attractive in photographs.

photograph *n* **1** picture made by the chemical action of light on sensitive film. ♦ *v* **2** take a photograph of. **photographer** *n* **photographic** *adj* **photography** *n* art of taking photographs.

photogravure *n* process in which an etched metal plate for printing is produced by photography.

photometer [foe-**tom**-it-er] *n* instrument for measuring the intensity of light.

photon *n* quantum of electromagnetic radiation energy, such as light, having both particle and wave behaviour.

photostat *n* copy made by photocopying machine.

photosynthesis *n* process by which a green plant uses sunlight to build up carbohydrate reserves. **photosynthesize** *v*

phrase *n* **1** group of words forming a unit of meaning, esp. within a sentence. **2** short effective expression. ♦ *v* **3** express in words. **phrasal verb** phrase consisting of a verb and an adverb or preposition, with a meaning different from the parts, such as *take in* meaning *deceive*. **phrase book** book containing frequently used expressions and their equivalent in a foreign language.

phraseology *n, pl* **-gies** way in which words are used.

phrenology *n* formerly, the study of the shape and size of the skull as a means of finding out a person's character and mental ability. **phrenologist** *n*

phut *adv* **go phut** *Informal* (of a machine) break down.

phylactery *n, pl* **-teries** leather case containing religious texts, worn by Jewish men.

phylum *n, pl* **-la** major taxonomic division of animals and plants that contains one or more classes.

physical *adj* **1** of the body, as contrasted with the mind or spirit. **2** of material things or nature. **3** of physics. **physically** *adv* **physical education** training and practice in sports and gymnastics. **physical geography** branch of geography dealing with the features of the earth's surface.

physician *n* doctor of medicine.

physics *n* science of the properties of matter and energy. **physicist** *n* person skilled in or studying physics.

physio *n* **1** short for PHYSIOTHERAPY. **2** (*pl* **physios**) short for PHYSIOTHERAPIST.

physiognomy [fiz-ee-**on**-om-ee] *n* face.

physiology *n* science of the normal function of living things. **physiological** *adj* **physiologist** *n*

physiotherapy *n* treatment of disease or injury by physical means such as massage, rather than by drugs. **physiotherapist** *n*

physique *n* person's bodily build and muscular development.

pi *n* **1** sixteenth letter in the Greek alphabet. **2** *Maths* ratio of the circumference of a circle to its diameter.

pianissimo *adv Music* very quietly.

piano[1] *n, pl* **pianos** musical instrument with strings which are struck by hammers worked by a keyboard (also **pianoforte**). **pianist** *n* **Pianola** *n* ® mechanically played piano.

piano[2] *adv Music* quietly.

piazza *n* square or marketplace, esp. in Italy.

pibroch [**pee**-brok] *n* form of bagpipe music.

pic *n, pl* **pics, pix** *Informal* photograph or illustration.

picador *n* mounted bullfighter with a lance.

picaresque *adj* denoting a type of fiction in which the hero, a rogue, has a series of adventures.

piccalilli *n* pickle of vegetables in mustard sauce.

piccolo *n, pl* **-los** small flute.

pick[1] *v* **1** choose. **2** remove (flowers or fruit) from a plant. **3** take hold of and move with the fingers. **4** provoke (a fight etc.) deliberately. **5** steal from (someone's pocket). **6** open (a lock) by means other than a key. ♦ *n* **7** choice, e.g. *take your pick*. **8** best part. **pick-me-up** *n Informal* stimulating drink, tonic. **pick on** *v* continually treat unfairly. **pick out** *v* recognize, distinguish. **pick up** *v* **1** raise, lift. **2** collect. **3** improve, get better. **4** learn as one goes along. **5** become acquainted with for a sexual purpose. **pick-up** *n* **1** small truck. **2** casual acquaintance made for a sexual purpose. **3** device for conversion of vibrations into electrical signals, as in a record player.

pick[2] *n* tool with a curved iron crossbar and wooden shaft, for breaking up hard ground or rocks.

pickaxe *n* large pick.

picket *n* **1** person or group standing outside a workplace to deter would-be workers during a strike. **2** sentry or sentries posted to give warning of an attack. **3** pointed stick used as part of a fence. ♦ *v* **4** form a picket outside (a workplace). **picket line** line of people acting as pickets.

pickings *pl n* money easily acquired.

pickle *n* **1** food preserved in vinegar or salt water. **2** *Informal* awkward situation. ♦ *v* **3** preserve in vinegar or salt water. **pickled** *adj* **1** preserved in vinegar or salt water. **2** *Informal* drunk.

pickpocket *n* thief who steals from someone's pocket.

picnic *n* **1** informal meal out of doors. **2** *Informal* easy task. ♦ *v* **-nicking, -nicked** **3** have a picnic.

picot [**peek**-oh] *n* any of pattern of small loops, as on lace.

Pict *n* member of an ancient race of N Britain. **Pictish** *adj*

pictograph *n* picture or symbol standing for word or group of words, as in written Chinese.

pictorial *adj* **1** of or in painting or pictures. ♦ *n* **2** newspaper etc. with many pictures.

picture *n* **1** drawing or painting. **2** photograph. **3** mental image. **4** description or account of a situation. **5** beautiful or picturesque object. **6** image on a TV screen. ♦ *pl* **7** cinema. ♦ *v* **8** visualize, imagine. **9** represent in a picture. **picturesque** *adj* **1** (of a place or view) pleasant to look at. **2** (of language) forceful, vivid. **picture rail** narrow piece of wood near the top of a wall from which pictures are hung. **picture window** large window made of a single sheet of glass.

piddle *v Informal* urinate.

piddling *adj Informal* small or unimportant.

pidgin *n* language, not a mother tongue, made up of elements of two or more other languages.

pie *n* dish of meat, fruit, etc. baked in pastry. **pie chart** circular diagram with sectors representing quantities.

piebald *n, adj* (horse) with irregular black-and-white markings.

piece *n* **1** separate bit or part. **2** instance, e.g. *a piece of luck.* **3** example, specimen. **4** literary or musical composition. **5** coin. **6** small object used in draughts, chess, etc. **piece together** *v* make or assemble bit by bit.

pièce de résistance [**pyess** de ray-**ziss**-tonss] *n French* most impressive item.

piecemeal *adv* a bit at a time.

piecework *n* work paid for according to the quantity produced.

pied *adj* having markings of two or more colours.

pied-à-terre [**pyay** da **tair**] *n, pl* **pieds-à-terre** [**pyay** da **tair**] small flat or house for occasional use.

pie-eyed *adj Slang* drunk.

pier *n* **1** platform on stilts sticking out into the sea. **2** pillar, esp. one supporting a bridge.

pierce *v* **1** make a hole in or through with a sharp instrument. **2** make a way through. **piercing** *adj* **1** (of a sound) shrill and high-pitched. **2** (of wind or cold) fierce, penetrating.

Pierrot [**pier**-roe] *n* pantomime clown with a whitened face.

piety *n, pl* **-ties** deep devotion to God and religion.

piffle *n Informal* nonsense.

pig *n* **1** animal kept and killed for pork, ham, and bacon. **2** *Informal* greedy, dirty, or rude person. **piglet** *n* young pig. **piggish, piggy** *adj* **1** *Informal* dirty. **2** greedy. **3** stubborn. **piggery** *n, pl* **-geries** place for keeping and breeding pigs. **piggy bank** child's bank shaped like a pig with a slot for coins. **pig-headed** *adj* obstinate. **pig iron** crude iron produced in a blast furnace.

pigeon[1] *n* bird with a heavy body and short legs, sometimes trained to carry messages. **pigeonhole** *n* **1** compartment for papers in a desk etc. ♦ *v* **2** classify. **3** put aside and do nothing about. **pigeon-toed** *adj* with the feet or toes turned inwards.

pigeon[2] *n Informal* concern or responsibility.

piggyback *n* **1** ride on someone's shoulders. ♦ *adv* **2** carried on someone's shoulders.

pigment *n* colouring matter, paint or dye. **pigmentation** *n*

Pigmy *n, pl* **-mies** same as PYGMY.

pigsty *n, pl* **-sties** **1** pen for pigs. **2** untidy place.

pigtail *n* plait of hair hanging from the back or either side of the head.

pike[1] *n* large predatory freshwater fish.

pike[2] *n Hist* long-handled spear.

pilaster *n* square column, usu. set in a wall.

pilau, pilaf, pilaff *n* Middle Eastern dish of meat, fish, or poultry boiled with rice, spices, etc.

pilchard *n* small edible sea fish of the herring family.

pile[1] *n* **1** number of things lying on top of each other. **2** *Informal* large amount. **3** large building. ♦ *v* **4** collect into a pile. **5** (foll. by *in* or *out*) move in a group. **pile-up** *n Informal* traffic accident involving several vehicles.

pile[2] *n* beam driven into the ground, esp. as a foundation for building.

pile[3] *n* fibres of a carpet or a fabric, esp. velvet, that stand up from the weave.

piles *pl n* swollen veins in the rectum, haemorrhoids.

pilfer *v* steal in small quantities.

pilgrim *n* person who journeys to a holy place. **pilgrimage** *n*

pill *n* small ball of medicine swallowed whole. **the pill** pill taken by a woman to prevent pregnancy. **pillbox** *n* **1** small box for pills. **2** small concrete fort.

pillage *v* **1** steal property by violence in war. ♦ *n* **2** violent seizure of goods, esp. in war.

pillar *n* **1** upright post, usu. supporting a roof. **2** strong supporter. **pillar box** red pillar-shaped letter box in the street.

pillion *n* seat for a passenger behind the rider of a motorcycle.

pillory *n, pl* **-ries** **1** *Hist* frame with holes for the head and hands in which an offender was locked and exposed to public abuse. ♦ *v* **-rying, -ried** **2** ridicule publicly.

pillow *n* **1** stuffed cloth bag for supporting the head in bed. ♦ *v* **2** rest as if on a pillow. **pillowcase, pillowslip** *n* removable cover for a pillow.

pilot *n* **1** person qualified to fly an aircraft or spacecraft. **2** person employed to steer a ship entering or leaving a harbour. ♦ *adj* **3** experimental and preliminary. ♦ *v* **4** act as the pilot of. **5** guide, steer. **pilot light** small flame lighting the main one in a gas appliance. **pilot officer** most junior commissioned rank in certain air forces.

pimento *n, pl* **-tos** mild-tasting red pepper.

pimp *n* **1** man who gets customers for a prostitute in return for a share of his or her earnings. ♦ *v* **2** act as a pimp.

pimpernel *n* wild plant with small star-shaped flowers.

pimple *n* small pus-filled spot on the skin. **pimply** *adj*

pin *n* **1** short thin piece of stiff wire with a point and head, for fastening things. **2** wooden or metal peg or stake. ♦ *v* **pinning, pinned** **3** fasten with a pin. **4** seize and hold fast. **pin down** *v* **1** force (someone) to make a decision, take action, etc. **2** define clearly. **pin money** small amount earned to buy small luxuries. **pins and needles** *Informal* tingling sensation in a part of the body. **pin tuck** narrow ornamental fold in shirt etc. **pin-up** *n* picture of a sexually attractive person, esp. (partly) naked.

pinafore *n* **1** apron. **2** dress with a bib top.

pinball *n* electrically operated table game in which a small ball is shot through various hazards.

pince-nez [panss-**nay**] *n, pl* **pince-nez** glasses kept in place only by a clip on the bridge of the nose.

pincers *pl n* **1** tool consisting of two hinged arms, for gripping. **2** claws of a lobster etc.

pinch *v* **1** squeeze between finger and thumb. **2** cause pain by being too tight. **3** *Informal* steal. **4** *Informal* arrest. ♦ *n* **5** act of pinching. **6** as much as can be taken up between the finger and thumb. **at a pinch** if absolutely necessary. **feel the pinch** have to economize.

pinchbeck *n* alloy of zinc and copper, used as imitation gold.

pincushion *n* small cushion in which

pins are stuck ready for use.

pine[1] *n* **1** evergreen coniferous tree. **2** its wood. **pine cone** woody seed case of the pine tree. **pine marten** wild mammal of the coniferous forests of Europe and Asia.

pine[2] *v* **1** (foll. by *for*) feel great longing (for). **2** become thin and ill through grief etc.

pineal gland [**pin**-ee-al] *n* small cone-shaped gland at the base of the brain.

pineapple *n* large tropical fruit with juicy yellow flesh and a hard skin.

ping *v, n* (make) a short high-pitched sound. **pinger** *n* device, esp. a timer, that makes a pinging sound.

Ping-Pong *n* ® table tennis.

pinion[1] *n* **1** bird's wing. ♦ *v* **2** immobilize (someone) by tying or holding his or her arms.

pinion[2] *n* small cogwheel.

pink *n* **1** pale reddish colour. **2** fragrant garden plant. ♦ *adj* **3** of the colour pink. ♦ *v* **4** (of an engine) make a metallic noise because not working properly, knock. **in the pink** in good health.

pinking shears *pl n* scissors with a serrated edge that give a wavy edge to material to prevent fraying.

pinnace *n* ship's boat.

pinnacle *n* **1** highest point of success etc. **2** mountain peak. **3** small slender spire.

pinnate *adj* (of compound leaves) having leaflets growing opposite each other in pairs.

pinpoint *v* **1** locate or identify exactly. ♦ *adj* **2** exact.

pinprick *n* small irritation or annoyance.

pinstripe *n* **1** very narrow stripe in fabric. **2** the fabric itself.

pint *n* liquid measure, ⅛ gallon (.568 litre).

pintail *n* greyish-brown duck with a pointed tail.

Pinyin *n* system for representing Chinese in Roman letters.

pioneer *n* **1** explorer or early settler of a new country. **2** originator or developer of something new. ♦ *v* **3** be the pioneer or leader of.

pious *adj* deeply religious, devout.

pip[1] *n* small seed in a fruit.

pip[2] *n* **1** high-pitched sound used as a time signal on radio. **2** spot on a playing card, dice, etc. **3** *Informal* star on a junior army officer's shoulder showing rank.

pipe *n* **1** tube for conveying liquid or gas. **2** tube with a small bowl at the end for smoking tobacco. **3** tubular musical instrument. ♦ *pl* **4** bagpipes. ♦ *v* **5** play on a pipe. **6** utter in a shrill tone. **7** convey by pipe. **8** decorate with piping. **piper** *n* player on a pipe or bagpipes. **piping** *n* **1** system of pipes. **2** decoration of icing on a cake etc. **3** fancy edging on clothes etc. **piping hot** extremely hot. **pipe cleaner** piece of wire coated with tiny tufts of yarn for cleaning the stem of a tobacco pipe. **piped music** recorded music played as background music in public places. **pipe down** *v Informal* stop talking. **pipe dream** fanciful impossible plan. **pipeline** *n* **1** long pipe for transporting oil, water, etc. **2** means of communication. **in the pipeline** in preparation. **pipe up** *v* speak suddenly or shrilly.

pipette *n* slender glass tube used to transfer or measure fluids.

pipit *n* small brownish songbird.

pippin *n* type of eating apple.

piquant [**pee**-kant] *adj* **1** having a pleasant spicy taste. **2** mentally stimulating. **piquancy** *n*

pique [**peek**] *n* **1** feeling of hurt pride, baffled curiosity, or resentment. ♦ *v* **2** hurt the pride of. **3** arouse (curiosity).

piqué [**pee**-kay] *n* stiff ribbed cotton fabric.

piquet [pik-**ket**] *n* card game for two.

piranha *n* small fierce freshwater fish of tropical America.

pirate *n* **1** sea robber. **2** person who illegally publishes or sells work owned by someone else. **3** person or company that broadcasts illegally. ♦ *v* **4** sell or reproduce (artistic work etc.) illegally.

piracy *n* **piratical** *adj*

pirouette *v, n* (make) a spinning turn balanced on the toes of one foot.

piscatorial *adj* of fishing or fishes.

Pisces *pl n* (the fishes) twelfth sign of the zodiac.

piss *Taboo* ♦ *v* **1** urinate. ♦ *n* **2** act of urinating. **3** urine.

pistachio *n, pl* **-chios** edible nut of a Mediterranean tree.

piste [**peest**] *n* ski slope.

pistil *n* seed-bearing part of a flower.

pistol *n* short-barrelled handgun.

piston *n* cylindrical part in an engine that slides to and fro in a cylinder.

pit *n* **1** deep hole in the ground. **2** coal mine. **3** dent or depression. **4** servicing and refuelling area on a motor-racing track. **5** same as ORCHESTRA PIT. ♦ *v* **pitting, pitted 6** mark with small dents or scars. **pit one's wits against** compete against in a test or contest. **pit bull terrier** strong muscular terrier with a short coat.

pitapat *adv* **1** with quick light taps. ♦ *n* **2** such taps.

pitch[1] *v* **1** throw, hurl. **2** set up (a tent). **3** fall headlong. **4** (of a ship or plane) move with the front and back going up and down alternately. **5** set the level or tone of. ♦ *n* **6** area marked out for playing sport. **7** degree or angle of slope. **8** degree of highness or lowness of a (musical) sound. **9** act or manner of throwing a ball. **10** place where a street or market trader regularly sells. **11** *Informal* persuasive sales talk. **pitched battle** fierce fight. **pitch in** *v* join in enthusiastically. **pitch into** *v Informal* attack.

pitch[2] *n* dark sticky substance obtained from tar. **pitch-black, pitch-dark** *adj* very dark.

pitchblende *n* mineral composed largely of uranium oxide, yielding radium.

pitcher *n* large jug with a narrow neck.

pitchfork *n* **1** large long-handled fork for lifting hay. ♦ *v* **2** thrust abruptly or violently.

pitfall *n* hidden difficulty or danger.

pith *n* **1** soft white lining of the rind of oranges etc. **2** essential part. **3** soft tissue in the stems of certain plants. **pithy** *adj* **pithier, pithiest** short and full of meaning.

pithead *n* top of a mine shaft and the buildings and hoisting gear around it.

piton [**peet**-on] *n* metal spike used in climbing to secure a rope.

pitta bread, pitta *n* flat slightly leavened bread, orig. from the Middle East.

pittance *n* very small amount of money.

pitter-patter *n* **1** sound of light rapid taps or pats, as of raindrops. ♦ *v* **2** make a such sound.

pituitary *n, pl* **-taries** gland at the base of the brain, that helps to control growth (also **pituitary gland**).

pity *n, pl* **pities 1** sympathy or sorrow for others' suffering. **2** regrettable fact. ♦ *v* **pitying, pitied 3** feel pity for. **piteous, pitiable** *adj* arousing pity. **pitiful** *adj* **1** arousing pity. **2** woeful, contemptible. **pitifully** *adv* **pitiless** *adj* feeling no pity or mercy.

pivot *n* **1** central shaft on which something turns. ♦ *v* **2** provide with or turn on a pivot. **pivotal** *adj* of crucial importance.

pix *n Informal* a plural of PIC.

pixie *n* (in folklore) fairy.

pizza *n* flat disc of dough covered with a wide variety of savoury toppings and baked.

pizzazz *n Informal* attractive combination of energy and style.

pizzicato [pit-see-**kah**-toe] *adj Music* played by plucking the string of a violin etc. with the finger.

pl. 1 place. **2** plural.

placard *n* notice that is carried or displayed in public.

placate *v* make (someone) stop feeling angry or upset. **placatory** *adj*

place *n* **1** particular part of an area or space. **2** particular town, building, etc. **3** position or point reached. **4** open square lined with houses. **5** seat or space. **6** duty or right. **7** position of employment. **8** usual position. ♦ *v* **9** put in a particular place. **10** identify, put in context. **11** make (an order, bet, etc.). **be placed** (of a competitor in a race) be among the first three. **take place** happen, occur. **placement** *n* **1** arrangement. **2** temporary employment. **3** process of finding someone a job or a home. **place setting** cutlery, crockery, and glassware laid for one person at a meal.

placebo [plas-**see**-bo] *n, pl* **-bos, -boes** sugar pill etc. given to an unsuspecting patient instead of an active drug.

placenta [plass-**ent**-a] *n, pl* **-tas, -tae** organ formed in the womb during pregnancy, providing nutrients for the fetus. **placental** *adj*

placid *adj* not easily excited or upset, calm. **placidity** *n*

plagiarize [**play**-jer-ize] *v* steal ideas, passages, etc. from (someone else's work) and present them as one's own. **plagiarism** *n* **plagiarist** *n*

plague *n* **1** fast-spreading fatal disease. **2** *Hist* bubonic plague. **3** widespread infestation. ♦ *v* **plaguing, plagued 4** trouble or annoy continually.

plaice *n* edible European flatfish.

plaid *n* **1** long piece of tartan cloth worn as part of Highland dress. **2** tartan cloth or pattern.

plain *adj* **1** easy to see or understand. **2** expressed honestly and clearly. **3** without decoration or pattern. **4** not beautiful. **5** simple, ordinary. ♦ *n* **6** large stretch of level country. **plainly** *adv* **plainness** *n* **plain clothes** ordinary clothes, as opposed to uniform. **plain sailing** easy progress. **plain speaking** saying exactly what one thinks.

plainsong *n* unaccompanied singing, esp. in a medieval church.

plaintiff *n* person who sues in a court of law.

plaintive *adj* sad, mournful. **plaintively** *adv*

plait [**platt**] *n* **1** intertwined length of hair. ♦ *v* **2** intertwine separate strands in a pattern.

plan *n* **1** way thought out to do or achieve something. **2** diagram showing the layout or design of something. ♦ *v* **planning, planned 3** arrange beforehand. **4** make a diagram of. **planner** *n*

plane[1] *n* **1** an aircraft. **2** *Maths* flat surface. **3** level of attainment etc. ♦ *adj* **4** perfectly flat or level. ♦ *v* **5** glide or skim.

plane[2] *n* **1** tool for smoothing wood. ♦ *v* **2** smooth (wood) with a plane.

plane[3] *n* tree with broad leaves.

planet *n* large body in space that revolves round the sun or another star. **planetary** *adj*

planetarium *n, pl* **-iums, -ia** building where the movements of the stars, planets, etc. are shown by projecting lights on the inside of a dome.

plangent [**plan**-jent] *adj* (of sounds) mournful and resounding.

plank *n* long flat piece of sawn timber.

plankton *n* minute animals and plants floating in the surface water of a sea or lake.

plant *n* **1** living organism that grows in the ground and has no power to move. **2** equipment or machinery used in industrial processes. **3** factory or other industrial premises. ♦ *v* **4** put in the ground to grow. **5** place firmly in position. **6** *Informal* put (a person) secretly in an organization to spy. **7** *Informal* hide (stolen goods etc.) on a person to make him or her seem guilty. **planter** *n* **1** owner of a plantation. **2** ornamental pot for house plants.

plantain[1] *n* low-growing wild plant with broad leaves.

plantain[2] *n* tropical fruit like a green banana.

plantation *n* **1** estate for the cultivation of tea, tobacco, etc. **2** wood of cultivated trees.

plaque *n* **1** inscribed commemorative stone or metal plate. **2** filmy deposit on teeth that causes decay.

plasma *n* **1** clear liquid part of blood. **2** *Physics* hot ionized gas containing positive ions and free electrons.

plaster *n* **1** mixture of lime, sand, etc. for coating walls. **2** adhesive strip of material for dressing cuts etc. ♦ *v* **3** cover with plaster. **4** coat thickly. **plastered** *adj Slang* drunk. **plasterboard** *n* thin rectangular sheets of cardboard held together with plaster, used to cover interior walls etc. **plaster of Paris** white powder which dries to form a hard solid when mixed with water, used for sculptures and casts for broken limbs.

plastic *n* **1** synthetic material that can be moulded when soft but sets in a hard long-lasting shape. **2** credit cards etc. as opposed to cash. ♦ *adj* **3** made of plastic. **4** easily moulded, pliant. **plasticity** *n* ability to be moulded. **plastic bullet** solid PVC cylinder fired by police in riot control. **plastic explosive** jelly-like explosive substance. **plastic surgery** repair or reconstruction of missing or malformed parts of the body.

Plasticine *n* ® soft coloured modelling material used esp. by children.

plate *n* **1** shallow dish for holding food. **2** flat thin sheet of metal, glass, etc. **3** thin coating of metal on another metal. **4** dishes or cutlery made of gold or silver. **5** illustration, usu. on fine quality paper, in a book. **6** *Informal* set of false teeth. ♦ *v* **7** cover with a thin coating of gold, silver, or other metal. **plateful** *n* **plate glass** glass in thin sheets, used for mirrors and windows. **plate tectonics** study of the structure of the earth's crust, esp. the movement of layers of rocks.

plateau *n, pl* **-teaus, -teaux** **1** area of level high land. **2** stage when there is no change or development.

platelet *n* minute particle occurring in blood of vertebrates and involved in clotting of blood.

platen *n* **1** roller of a typewriter, against which the paper is held. **2** plate in a printing press by which the paper is pressed against the type.

platform *n* **1** raised floor. **2** raised area in a station from which passengers board trains. **3** structure in the sea which holds machinery, stores, etc. for drilling an oil well. **4** programme of a political party.

platinum *n Chem* valuable silvery-white metal. **platinum blonde** woman with silvery-blonde hair.

platitude *n* remark that is true but not interesting or original. **platitudinous** *adj*

platonic *adj* friendly or affectionate but not sexual.

platoon *n* smaller unit within a company of soldiers.

platteland *n S Afr* rural district.

platter *n* large dish.

platypus *n* Australian egg-laying amphibious mammal, with dense fur, webbed feet, and a ducklike bill (also **duck-billed platypus**).

plaudits *pl n* expressions of approval.

plausible *adj* **1** apparently true or reasonable. **2** persuasive but insincere. **plausibly** *adv* **plausibility** *n*

play *v* **1** occupy oneself in (a game or recreation). **2** compete against in a game or sport. **3** behave carelessly. **4** act (a part) on the stage. **5** perform on (a musical instrument). **6** cause (a radio, record player, etc.) to give out sound. **7** move lightly or irregularly, flicker. ♦ *n* **8** story performed on stage or broadcast. **9** activities children take part in for amusement. **10** playing of a game. **11** conduct, e.g. *fair play.* **12** (scope for) freedom of movement. **player** *n* **playful** *adj* lively. **play back** *v* listen to or watch (something recorded). **play down** *v* minimize the importance of. **playground** *n* outdoor area for children to play on, esp. one with swings etc. or adjoining a school. **playgroup** *n* regular meeting of very young children for supervised play. **playhouse** *n* theatre. **playing card** one of a set of 52 cards used in card games. **playing field** extensive piece of ground for sport. **play off** *v* set (two people) against each other for one's own ends. **play on** *v* exploit or encourage (someone's sympathy or weakness). **playpen** *n* small portable enclosure in which a young child can safely be left to play. **playschool** *n* nursery group for young children. **plaything** *n* **1** toy. **2** person regarded or treated as a toy. **play up** *v* **1** give prominence to. **2** cause trouble. **playwright** *n* author of plays.

playboy *n* rich man who lives only for pleasure.

plaza *n* **1** open space or square. **2** modern shopping complex.

PLC, plc Public Limited Company.

plea *n* **1** serious or urgent request, entreaty. **2** statement of a prisoner or defendant. **3** excuse.

plead *v* **1** ask urgently or with deep feeling. **2** give as an excuse. **3** *Law* declare oneself to be guilty or innocent of a charge made against one.

pleasant *adj* pleasing, enjoyable. **pleasantly** *adv* **pleasantry** *n, pl* **-tries** polite or joking remark.

please *v* **1** give pleasure or satisfaction to. ♦ *adv* **2** polite word of request. **please oneself** do as one likes. **pleased** *adj* **pleasing** *adj* giving pleasure or satisfaction.

pleasure *n* **1** feeling of happiness and satisfaction. **2** something that causes this. **pleasurable** *adj* giving pleasure. **pleasurably** *adv*

pleat *n* **1** fold made by doubling material back on itself. ♦ *v* **2** arrange (material) in pleats.

plebeian [pleb-**ee**-an] *adj* **1** of the lower social classes. **2** vulgar or rough. ♦ *n* **3** (also **pleb**) member of the lower social classes.

plebiscite [**pleb**-iss-ite] *n* decision by direct voting of the people of a country.

plectrum *n, pl* **-trums, -tra** small implement for plucking the strings of a guitar etc.

pledge *n* **1** solemn promise. **2** something valuable given as a guarantee that a promise will be kept or a debt paid. ♦ *v* **3** promise solemnly. **4** bind by or as if by a pledge, e.g. *pledge to secrecy*.

plenary *adj* (of a meeting) attended by all members.

plenipotentiary *adj* **1** having full powers. ♦ *n, pl* **-aries** **2** diplomat or representative having full powers.

plenitude *n* completeness, abundance.

plenteous *adj* plentiful.

plenty *n* **1** large amount or number. **2** quite enough. **plentiful** *adj* existing in large amounts or numbers. **plentifully** *adv*

pleonasm *n* use of more words than necessary.

plethora *n* excess.

pleurisy *n* inflammation of the membrane covering the lungs.

pliable *adj* **1** easily bent. **2** easily influenced. **pliability** *n*

pliant *adj* pliable. **pliancy** *n*

pliers *pl n* tool with hinged arms and jaws for gripping.

plight[1] *n* difficult or dangerous situation.

plight[2] *v* **plight one's troth** *Old-fashioned* promise to marry.

Plimsoll line *n* mark on a ship showing the level water should reach when the ship is fully loaded.

plimsolls *pl n* rubber-soled canvas shoes.

plinth *n* slab forming the base of a statue, column, etc.

PLO Palestine Liberation Organization.

plod *v* **plodding, plodded** **1** walk with slow heavy steps. **2** work slowly but determinedly. **plodder** *n*

plonk[1] *v* put (something) down heavily and carelessly.

plonk[2] *n Informal* cheap inferior wine.

plop *n* **1** sound of an object falling into water without a splash. ♦ *v* **plopping, plopped** **2** make this sound.

plot[1] *n* **1** secret plan to do something illegal or wrong. **2** story of a film, novel, etc. ♦ *v* **plotting, plotted** **3** plan secretly, conspire. **4** mark the position or course of (a ship or aircraft) on a map. **5** mark and join up (points on a graph).

plot[2] *n* small piece of land.

plough *n* **1** agricultural tool for turning over soil. ♦ *v* **2** turn over (earth) with a plough. **3** move or work through slowly and laboriously. **ploughman** *n* **ploughman's lunch** snack lunch of bread and cheese with pickle. **ploughshare** *n* blade of a plough.

plover *n* shore bird with a straight bill and long pointed wings.

ploy *n* manoeuvre designed to gain an advantage.

pluck *v* **1** pull or pick off. **2** pull out the feathers of (a bird for cooking). **3** sound the strings of (a guitar etc.) with the fingers or a plectrum. ♦ *n* **4** courage. **plucky** *adj* **pluckier, pluckiest** brave. **pluckily** *adv* **pluck up** *v* summon up (courage).

plug *n* **1** thing fitting into and filling a hole. **2** device connecting an appliance to an electricity supply. **3** *Informal* favourable mention of a product etc., to encourage people to buy it. ♦ *v* **plugging, plugged 4** block or seal (a hole or gap) with a plug. **5** *Informal* advertise (a product etc.) by constant repetition. **plug away** *v* *Informal* work steadily. **plug in** *v* connect (an electrical appliance) to a power source by pushing a plug into a socket.

plum *n* **1** oval usu. dark red fruit with a stone in the middle. ♦ *adj* **2** dark purplish-red. **3** very desirable.

plumage *n* bird's feathers.

plumb *v* **1** understand (something obscure). **2** test with a plumb line. ♦ *adv* **3** exactly. **plumb the depths of** experience the worst extremes of (an unpleasant quality or emotion). **plumber** *n* person who fits and repairs pipes and fixtures for water and drainage systems. **plumbing** *n* pipes and fixtures used in water and drainage systems. **plumb in** *v* connect (an appliance such as a washing machine) to a water supply. **plumb line** string with a weight at the end, used to test the depth of water or to test whether something is vertical.

plume *n* feather, esp. one worn as an ornament.

plummet *v* **-meting, -meted** plunge downward.

plump[1] *adj* moderately or attractively fat. **plumpness** *n* **plump up** *v* make (a pillow) fuller or rounded.

plump[2] *v* sit or fall heavily and suddenly. **plump for** *v* choose, vote for.

plunder *v* **1** take by force, esp. in time of war. ♦ *n* **2** things plundered, spoils.

plunge *v* **1** put or throw forcibly or suddenly (into). **2** descend steeply. ♦ *n* **3** plunging, dive. **take the plunge** *Informal* embark on a risky enterprise. **plunger** *n* rubber suction cup used to clear blocked pipes. **plunge into** *v* become deeply involved in.

plunk *v* pluck the strings of (a banjo etc.) to produce a twanging sound.

pluperfect *n, adj* *Grammar* (tense) expressing an action completed before a past time, e.g. *had gone* in *his wife had gone already*.

plural *adj* **1** of or consisting of more than one. ♦ *n* **2** word indicating more than one.

pluralism *n* existence and toleration of a variety of peoples, opinions, etc. in a society. **pluralist** *n* **pluralistic** *adj*

plus *prep, adj* **1** indicating addition. ♦ *adj* **2** more than zero. **3** positive. **4** advantageous. ♦ *n* **5** sign (+) denoting addition. **6** advantage.

> Avoid using *plus* to mean 'additionally' except in very informal contexts.

plus fours *pl n* trousers gathered in at the knee.

plush *n* **1** fabric with long velvety pile. ♦ *adj* **2** (also **plushy**) luxurious.

Pluto *n* **1** Greek god of the underworld. **2** farthest planet from the sun.

plutocrat *n* person who is powerful because of being very rich. **plutocracy** *n* **plutocratic** *adj*

plutonium *n* *Chem* radioactive metallic element used esp. in nuclear reactors and weapons.

pluvial *adj* of or caused by the action of rain.

ply[1] *v* **plying, plied 1** work at (a job or trade). **2** use (a tool). **3** (of a ship) travel regularly along or between. **ply with** *v* supply with or subject to persistently.

ply[2] *n* thickness of wool, fabric, etc.

plywood *n* board made of thin layers of wood glued together.

Pm *Chem* promethium.

PM prime minister.

p.m. **1** after noon. **2** postmortem.

PMS premenstrual syndrome.

PMT premenstrual tension.

pneumatic *adj* worked by or inflated with wind or air.

pneumonia *n* inflammation of the lungs.

Po *Chem* polonium.

PO **1** postal order. **2** Post Office.

poach[1] *v* **1** catch (animals) illegally on someone else's land. **2** encroach on or steal something belonging to someone else. **poacher** *n*

poach[2] *v* simmer (food) gently in liquid.

pocket *n* **1** small bag sewn into clothing for carrying things. **2** pouchlike container, esp. for catching balls at the edge of a snooker table. **3** isolated or distinct group or area. ♦ *v* **pocketing, pocketed** **4** put into one's pocket. **5** take secretly or dishonestly. ♦ *adj* **6** small. **out of pocket** having made a loss. **pocket money** **1** small regular allowance given to children by parents. **2** money for small personal expenses.

pockmarked *adj* (of the skin) marked with hollow scars where diseased spots have been.

pod *n* long narrow seed case of peas, beans, etc.

podgy *adj* **podgier, podgiest** short and fat.

podium *n, pl* **-diums, -dia** small raised platform for a conductor or speaker.

poem *n* imaginative piece of writing in rhythmic lines.

poesy *n Obs* poetry.

poet *n* writer of poems. **poetry** *n* **1** poems. **2** art of writing poems. **3** beautiful or pleasing quality. **poetic, poetical** *adj* of or like poetry. **poetically** *adv* **poetic justice** suitable reward or punishment for someone's past actions. **poetic licence** freedom from the normal rules of language and truth, as in poetry. **poet laureate** poet appointed by the British sovereign to write poems on important occasions.

po-faced *adj* wearing a disapproving stern expression.

pogo stick *n* pole with steps for the feet and a spring at the bottom, so that the user can bounce up, down, and along on it.

pogrom *n* organized persecution and massacre.

poignant *adj* sharply painful to the feelings. **poignancy** *n*

poinsettia *n* Central American shrub widely grown for its clusters of scarlet leaves, which resemble petals.

point *n* **1** main idea in a discussion, argument, etc. **2** aim or purpose. **3** detail or item. **4** characteristic. **5** particular position, stage, or time. **6** dot indicating decimals. **7** full stop. **8** sharp end. **9** headland. **10** unit for recording a value or score. **11** one of the direction marks of a compass. **12** movable rail used to change a train to other rails. **13** electrical socket. ♦ *pl* **14** electrical contacts in the distributor of an engine. ♦ *v* **15** show the direction or position of something or draw attention to it by extending a finger or other pointed object towards it. **16** direct or face towards. **17** finish or repair the joints in brickwork with mortar. **18** (of a gun dog) show where game is by standing rigidly with the muzzle towards it. **on the point of** very shortly going to. **pointed** *adj* **1** having a sharp end. **2** (of a remark) obviously directed at a particular person. **pointedly** *adv* **pointer** *n* **1** helpful hint. **2** indicator on a measuring instrument. **3** breed of gun dog. **pointless** *adj* meaningless, irrelevant. **point-blank** *adj* **1** fired at a very close target. **2** (of a remark or question) direct, blunt. ♦ *adv* **3** directly or bluntly. **point duty** control of traffic by a policeman at a road junction. **point of view** way of considering something. **point-to-point** *n* horse race across open country.

poise *n* calm dignified manner. **poised** *adj* **1** absolutely ready. **2** behaving with or showing poise.

poison *n* **1** substance that kills or injures when swallowed or absorbed. ♦ *v* **2** give poison to. **3** have a harmful or evil effect on, spoil. **poisoner** *n* **poisonous** *adj* **poison-pen letter** malicious anonymous letter.

poke *v* **1** jab or prod with one's finger, a stick, etc. **2** thrust forward or out. ♦ *n* **3** poking. **poky** *adj* **pokier, pokiest** small and cramped.

poker[1] *n* metal rod for stirring a fire.

poker[2] *n* card game in which players bet on the hands dealt. **poker-faced** *adj* expressionless.

polar *adj* of or near either of the earth's poles. **polar bear** white bear that lives in the regions around the North Pole.

polarize *v* **1** form or cause to form into groups with directly opposite views. **2** *Physics* restrict (light waves) to certain directions of vibration. **polarization** *n*

Polaroid *n* ® **1** plastic which polarizes light and so reduces glare. **2** camera that develops a print very quickly inside itself.

polder *n* land reclaimed from the sea.

pole[1] *n* long rounded piece of wood etc. **pole vault** event in which competitors try to clear a high bar with the aid of a flexible long pole.

pole[2] *n* **1** point furthest north or south on the earth's axis of rotation. **2** either of the opposite ends of a magnet or electric cell. **pole position** advantageous starting position. **Pole Star** star nearest to the North Pole in the northern hemisphere.

poleaxe *v* hit or stun with a heavy blow.

polecat *n* small animal of the weasel family.

polemic [pol-**em**-ik] *n* fierce attack on or defence of a particular opinion, belief, etc. **polemical** *adj*

police *n* **1** organized force in a state which keeps law and order. ♦ *v* **2** control or watch over with police or a similar body. **policeman, policewoman** *n* member of a police force. **police dog** dog trained to help the police. **police state** state or country in which the government controls people's freedom by means of esp. secret police. **police station** office of the police force of a district.

policy[1] *n, pl* **-cies** plan of action adopted by a person, group, or state.

policy[2] *n, pl* **-cies** document containing an insurance contract.

polio *n* disease affecting the spinal cord, which often causes paralysis (also **poliomyelitis**).

polish *v* **1** make smooth and shiny by rubbing. **2** make more nearly perfect. ♦ *n* **3** substance used for polishing. **4** shine or gloss. **5** pleasing elegant style. **polished** *adj* **1** accomplished. **2** done or performed well or professionally. **polish off** *v* finish completely, dispose of.

Polish *adj* **1** of Poland, its people, or their language. ♦ *n* **2** official language of Poland.

polite *adj* **1** showing consideration for others in one's manners, speech, etc. **2** socially correct or refined. **politely** *adv* **politeness** *n*

politic *adj* wise and likely to prove advantageous.

politics *n* **1** winning and using of power to govern society. **2** (study of) the art of government. **3** person's beliefs about how a country should be governed. **political** *adj* of the state, government, or public administration. **politically** *adv* **politically correct** (of language) intended to avoid any implied prejudice. **political prisoner** person imprisoned because of his or her political beliefs. **politician** *n* person actively engaged in politics, esp. a member of parliament.

polka *n* **1** lively 19th-century dance. **2** music for this. **polka dots** pattern of bold spots on fabric.

poll *n* **1** (also **opinion poll**) questioning of a random sample of people to find out general opinion. **2** voting. **3** number of votes recorded. ♦ *v* **4** receive (votes). **5** question in an opinion poll. **pollster** *n* person who conducts opinion polls. **polling booth** compartment in which a voter can mark his or her ballot paper in private. **polling station** building where people vote in an election. **poll tax** tax levied on every adult person.

pollarded *adj* (of a tree) growing very bushy because its top branches have been cut short.

pollen *n* fine dust produced by flowers to fertilize other flowers. **pollinate** *v* fertilize with pollen. **pollen count** measure of the amount of pollen in the air, esp. as a warning to people with hay fever.

pollute *v* contaminate with something poisonous or harmful. **pollution** *n* **pollutant** *n* something that pollutes.

polo *n* game like hockey played by teams of players on horseback. **polo neck** sweater with tight turned-over collar. **polo shirt** cotton short-sleeved shirt with a collar and three-button opening at the neck.

polonaise *n* **1** old stately dance. **2** music for this.

polonium *n Chem* radioactive element that occurs in trace amounts in uranium ores.

poltergeist *n* spirit believed to move furniture and throw objects around.

poltroon *n Obs* utter coward.

poly- *combining form* many, much.

polyandry *n* practice of having more than one husband at the same time.

polyanthus *n* garden primrose.

polychromatic *adj* many-coloured.

polyester *n* synthetic material used to make plastics and textile fibres.

polygamy [pol-**ig**-a-mee] *n* practice of having more than one husband or wife at the same time. **polygamous** *adj* **polygamist** *n*

polyglot *n, adj* (person) able to speak or write several languages.

polygon *n* geometrical figure with three or more angles and sides. **polygonal** *adj*

polygraph *n* instrument for recording pulse rate and perspiration, used esp. as a lie detector.

polyhedron *n, pl* **-drons, -dra** solid figure with four or more sides.

polymath *n* person of great and varied learning.

polymer *n* chemical compound with large molecules made of simple molecules of the same kind. **polymerize** *v* form into polymers. **polymerization** *n*

polynomial *adj* **1** of two or more names or terms. ♦ *n* **2** mathematical expression consisting of the sum of a number of terms.

polyp *n* **1** small simple sea creature with a hollow cylindrical body. **2** small growth on a mucous membrane.

polyphonic *adj Music* consisting of several melodies played simultaneously.

polystyrene *n* synthetic material used esp. as white rigid foam for packing and insulation.

polytechnic *n* formerly, college offering courses in many subjects at and below degree level.

polytheism *n* belief in many gods. **polytheist** *n* **polytheistic** *adj*

polythene *n* light plastic used for bags etc.

polyunsaturated *adj* of a group of fats that do not form cholesterol in the blood.

polyurethane *n* synthetic material used esp. in paints.

pomade *n* perfumed oil put on the hair to make it smooth and shiny.

pomander *n* (container for) a mixture of sweet-smelling petals, herbs, etc.

pomegranate *n* round tropical fruit with a thick rind containing many seeds in a red pulp.

Pomeranian *n* small dog with long straight hair.

pommel *n* **1** raised part on the front of a saddle. **2** knob at the top of a sword hilt.

pommy *n, pl* **-mies** *Aust & NZ slang* person from Britain (also **pom**).

pomp *n* stately display or ceremony.

pompom *n* decorative ball of tufted wool, silk, etc.

pompous *adj* foolishly serious and

grand, self-important. **pompously** *adv* **pompósity** *n*

ponce *n Offens* **1** effeminate man. **2** pimp. **ponce around** *v* act stupidly, waste time.

poncho *n, pl* **-chos** loose circular cloak with a hole for the head.

pond *n* small area of still water. **pondweed** *n* plant that grows in ponds.

ponder *v* think thoroughly or deeply (about).

ponderous *adj* **1** serious and dull. **2** heavy and unwieldy. **3** (of movement) slow and clumsy. **ponderously** *adv*

pong *v, n Informal* (give off) a strong unpleasant smell.

pontiff *n* the Pope. **pontificate** *v* **1** state one's opinions as if they were the only possible correct ones. ♦ *n* **2** period of office of a Pope.

pontoon[1] *n* floating platform supporting a temporary bridge.

pontoon[2] *n* gambling card game.

pony *n, pl* **ponies** small horse. **ponytail** *n* long hair tied in one bunch at the back of the head. **pony trekking** pastime of riding ponies cross-country.

poodle *n* dog with curly hair often clipped fancifully.

poof *n Offens* homosexual man.

pooh *interj* exclamation of disdain, contempt, or disgust. **pooh-pooh** *v* express disdain or scorn for.

pool[1] *n* **1** small body of still water. **2** puddle of spilt liquid. **3** swimming pool.

pool[2] *n* **1** shared fund or group of workers or resources. **2** game like snooker. ♦ *pl* **3** short for FOOTBALL POOLS. ♦ *v* **4** put in a common fund.

poop *n* raised part at the back of a sailing ship.

poor *adj* **1** having little money and few possessions. **2** less, smaller, or weaker than is needed or expected. **3** inferior. **4** unlucky, pitiable. **poorly** *adv* **1** in a poor manner. ♦ *adj* **2** not in good health.

pop[1] *v* **popping, popped 1** make or cause to make a small explosive sound. **2** *Informal* go, put, or come unexpectedly or suddenly. ♦ *n* **3** small explosive sound. **4** nonalcoholic fizzy drink. **popcorn** *n* grains of maize heated until they puff up and burst.

pop[2] *n* **1** music of general appeal, esp. to young people. ♦ *adj* **2** popular. **pop art** movement in modern art that uses the methods, styles, and themes of popular culture and mass media.

pop[3] *n Informal* father.

Pope *n* head of the Roman Catholic Church. **popish** *adj Offens* Roman Catholic.

popeyed *adj* staring in astonishment.

popinjay *n* conceited or talkative person.

poplar *n* tall slender tree.

poplin *n* ribbed cotton material.

poppadom *n* thin round crisp Indian bread.

poppet *n* term of affection for a small child or sweetheart.

poppy *n, pl* **-pies 1** plant with a large red flower. **2** artificial red poppy worn to mark Remembrance Sunday.

poppycock *n Informal* nonsense.

populace *n* the ordinary people.

popular *adj* **1** widely liked and admired. **2** of or for the public in general. **popularly** *adv* **popularity** *n* **popularize** *v* **1** make popular. **2** make (something technical or specialist) easily understood.

populate *v* **1** live in, inhabit. **2** fill with inhabitants. **population** *n* **1** all the people who live in a particular place. **2** the number of people living in a particular place. **populous** *adj* densely populated.

populist *n, adj* (person) appealing to the interests or prejudices of ordinary people. **populism** *n*

porbeagle *n* kind of shark.

porcelain *n* **1** fine china. **2** objects made of it.

porch *n* covered approach to the entrance of a building.

porcine *adj* of or like a pig.

porcupine *n* animal covered with long pointed quills.

pore *n* tiny opening in the skin or in the

surface of a plant.

pore over *v* make a careful study or examination of (a book, map, etc.).

pork *n* pig meat. **porker** *n* pig raised for food.

porn, porno *n, adj Informal* short for PORNOGRAPHY *or* PORNOGRAPHIC.

pornography *n* writing, films, or pictures designed to be sexually exciting. **pornographer** *n* producer of pornography. **pornographic** *adj*

porous *adj* allowing liquid to pass through gradually. **porosity** *n*

porphyry [**por**-fir-ee] *n* reddish rock with large crystals in it.

porpoise *n* fishlike sea mammal.

porridge *n* **1** breakfast food made of oatmeal cooked in water or milk. **2** *Slang* term in prison.

port[1] *n* (town with) a harbour.

port[2] *n* left side of a ship or aircraft when facing the front of it.

port[3] *n* strong sweet wine, usu. red.

port[4] *n* **1** opening in the side of a ship. **2** porthole.

portable *adj* easily carried. **portability** *n*

portage *n* (route for) transporting boats and supplies overland between navigable waterways.

portal *n* large imposing doorway or gate.

portcullis *n* grating suspended above a castle gateway, that can be lowered to block the entrance.

portend *v* be a sign of.

portent *n* sign of a future event. **portentous** *adj* **1** of great or ominous significance. **2** pompous, self-important.

porter[1] *n* **1** man who carries luggage. **2** hospital worker who transfers patients between rooms etc.

porter[2] *n* doorman or gatekeeper of a building.

portfolio *n, pl* **-os** **1** (flat case for carrying) examples of an artist's work. **2** area of responsibility of a government minister. **3** list of investments held by an investor.

porthole *n* small round window in a ship or aircraft.

portico *n, pl* **-coes, -cos** porch or covered walkway with columns supporting the roof.

portion *n* **1** part or share. **2** helping of food for one person. **3** destiny or fate. **portion out** *v* divide into shares.

portly *adj* **-lier, -liest** rather fat.

portmanteau *n, pl* **-teaus, -teaux** **1** *Old-fashioned* large suitcase that opens into two compartments. ♦ *adj* **2** combining aspects of different things.

portrait *n* **1** picture of a person. **2** lifelike description.

portray *v* describe or represent by artistic means, as in writing or film. **portrayal** *n*

Portuguese *adj* **1** of Portugal, its people, or their language. ♦ *n* **2** person from Portugal. **3** language of Portugal and Brazil. **Portuguese man-of-war** sea creature resembling a jellyfish, with stinging tentacles.

pose *v* **1** place in or take up a particular position to be photographed or drawn. **2** behave in an affected way. **3** raise (a problem). **4** ask (a question). ♦ *n* **5** position while posing. **6** behaviour adopted for effect. **pose as** pretend to be. **poser** *n* **1** puzzling question. **2** *Informal* person who likes to be seen in trendy clothes in fashionable places. **3** poseur. **poseur** *n* person who behaves in an affected way to impress others.

posh *adj Informal* **1** smart, luxurious. **2** affectedly upper-class.

posit [**pozz**-it] *v* lay down as a basis for argument.

position *n* **1** place. **2** usual or expected place. **3** way in which something is placed or arranged. **4** attitude, point of view. **5** social standing. **6** job. ♦ *v* **7** place. **positional** *adj*

positive *adj* **1** feeling no doubts, certain. **2** confident, hopeful. **3** helpful, providing encouragement. **4** absolute, downright. **5** *Maths* greater than zero. **6** (of an electrical charge) having a deficiency of electrons. **7** *Med* indicating the presence of a condition for which a test was made. **positively** *adv* **positive dis-**

crimination provision of special opportunities for a disadvantaged group.

positivism *n* philosophical system which accepts only things that can be seen or proved. **positivist** *n, adj*

positron *n Physics* particle with same mass as electron but positive charge.

posse [**poss**-ee] *n* **1** *US* group of men organized to maintain law and order. **2** *Informal* group or gang.

possess *v* **1** have as one's property. **2** (of a feeling, belief, etc.) have complete control of, dominate. **possessed** *adj* **possessor** *n* **possession** *n* **1** state of possessing, ownership. ♦ *pl* **2** things a person possesses. **possessive** *adj* **1** wanting all the attention or love of another person. **2** (of a word) indicating the person or thing that something belongs to. **possessiveness** *n*

possible *adj* **1** able to exist, happen, or be done. **2** worthy of consideration. ♦ *n* **3** person or thing that might be suitable or chosen. **possibility** *n, pl* **-ties** **possibly** *adv* perhaps, not necessarily.

possum *n* same as OPOSSUM. **play possum** pretend to be dead or asleep to deceive an opponent.

post[1] *n* **1** official system of delivering letters and parcels. **2** (single collection or delivery of) letters and parcels sent by this system. ♦ *v* **3** send by post. **keep someone posted** supply someone regularly with the latest information. **postage** *n* charge for sending a letter or parcel by post. **postal** *adj* **postal order** written money order sent by post and cashed at a post office by the person who receives it. **postbag** *n* **1** postman's bag. **2** post received by a magazine, famous person, etc. **postbox** *n* same as LETTER BOX (sense 2). **postcode** *n* system of letters and numbers used to aid the sorting of mail. **postman, postwoman** *n* person who collects and delivers post. **postmark** *n* official mark stamped on letters showing place and date of posting. **postmaster, postmistress** *n* official in charge of a post office. **post office** place where postal business is conducted.

post[2] *n* **1** length of wood, concrete, etc. fixed upright to support or mark something. ♦ *v* **2** put up (a notice) in a public place.

post[3] *n* **1** job. **2** position to which someone, esp. a soldier, is assigned for duty. **3** military establishment. ♦ *v* **4** send (a person) to a new place to work. **5** put (a guard etc.) on duty.

post- *prefix* after, later than, e.g. *postwar.*

postcard *n* card for sending a message by post without an envelope.

postdate *v* write a date on (a cheque) that is later than the actual date.

poster *n* large picture or notice stuck on a wall.

poste restante *n French* post-office department where a traveller's letters are kept until called for.

posterior *n* **1** buttocks. ♦ *adj* **2** behind, at the back of.

posterity *n* future generations, descendants.

postern *n* small back door or gate.

postgraduate *n* person with a degree who is studying for a more advanced qualification.

posthaste *adv* with great speed.

posthumous [**poss**-tume-uss] *adj* **1** occurring after one's death. **2** published after the author's death. **posthumously** *adv*

postilion, postillion *n Hist* person riding one of a pair of horses drawing a carriage.

postmortem *n* medical examination of a body to establish the cause of death.

postnatal *adj* occurring after childbirth.

postpone *v* put off to a later time. **postponement** *n*

postscript *n* passage added at the end of a letter.

postulant *n* candidate for admission to a religious order.

postulate *v* assume to be true as the basis of an argument or theory. **postulation** *n*

posture *n* **1** position or way in which

someone stands, walks, etc. ♦ *v* **2** behave in an exaggerated way to get attention.

posy *n, pl* **-sies** small bunch of flowers.

pot[1] *n* **1** round deep container. **2** teapot. ♦ *pl* **3** *Informal* a lot. ♦ *v* **potting, potted 4** plant in a pot. **5** *Snooker* hit (a ball) into a pocket. **potted** *adj* **1** grown in a pot. **2** (of meat or fish) cooked or preserved in a pot. **3** *Informal* abridged. **potbelly** *n* bulging belly. **potsherd** *n* broken fragment of pottery. **pot shot** shot taken without aiming carefully. **potting shed** shed where plants are potted.

pot[2] *n Slang* cannabis.

potable [**pote**-a-bl] *adj* drinkable.

potash *n* white powdery substance obtained from ashes and used as fertilizer.

potassium *n Chem* silvery metallic element.

potato *n, pl* **-toes** roundish starchy vegetable that grows underground.

poteen *n* (in Ireland) illegally made alcoholic drink.

potent *adj* **1** having great power or influence. **2** (of a male) capable of having sexual intercourse. **potency** *n*

potentate *n* ruler or monarch.

potential *adj* **1** possible but not yet actual. ♦ *n* **2** ability or talent not yet fully used. **3** *Electricity* level of electric pressure. **potentially** *adv* **potentiality** *n, pl* **-ties**

pothole *n* **1** hole in the surface of a road. **2** deep hole in a limestone area. **potholing** *n* sport of exploring underground caves. **potholer** *n*

potion *n* dose of medicine or poison.

potluck *n* **take potluck** accept whatever happens to be available.

potpourri [po-**poor**-ee] *n* **1** fragrant mixture of dried flower petals. **2** assortment or medley.

pottage *n* thick soup or stew.

potter[1] *n* person who makes pottery.

potter[2] *v* be busy in a pleasant but aimless way.

pottery *n, pl* **-ries 1** articles made from baked clay. **2** place where they are made. **3** craft of making such articles.

potty[1] *adj* **-tier, -tiest** *Informal* crazy or silly.

potty[2] *n, pl* **-ties** bowl used by a small child as a toilet.

pouch *n* **1** small bag. **2** baglike pocket of skin on an animal.

pouf, pouffe [**poof**] *n* large solid cushion used as a seat.

poulterer *n* person who sells poultry.

poultice [**pole**-tiss] *n* moist dressing, often heated, applied to inflamed skin.

poultry *n* domestic fowls.

pounce *v* **1** spring upon suddenly to attack or capture. ♦ *n* **2** pouncing.

pound[1] *n* **1** monetary unit of Britain and some other countries. **2** unit of weight equal to 0.454 kg.

pound[2] *v* **1** hit heavily and repeatedly. **2** crush to pieces or powder. **3** (of the heart) throb heavily. **4** run heavily.

pound[3] *n* enclosure for stray animals or officially removed vehicles.

poundage *n* charge of so much per pound of weight or sterling.

pour *v* **1** flow or cause to flow out in a stream. **2** rain heavily. **3** come or go in large numbers.

pout *v* **1** thrust out one's lips, look sulky. ♦ *n* **2** pouting look.

pouter *n* pigeon that can puff out its crop.

poverty *n* **1** state of being without enough food or money. **2** lack of, scarcity. **poverty-stricken** *adj* very poor. **poverty trap** situation of being unable to raise one's living standard because any extra income would result in state benefits being reduced.

POW prisoner of war.

powder *n* **1** substance in the form of tiny loose particles. **2** medicine or cosmetic in this form. ♦ *v* **3** apply powder to. **powdered** *adj* in the form of a powder, e.g. *powdered milk.* **powdery** *adj* **powder puff** soft pad used to apply cosmetic powder to the skin. **powder room** ladies' toilet.

power *n* **1** ability to do or act. **2** strength. **3** position of authority or control. **4** person or thing having authority. **5** *Maths* product from continuous multiplication of a number by itself. **6** *Physics* rate at which work is done. **7** electricity supply. **8** particular form of energy, e.g. *nuclear power.* **powered** *adj* having or operated by mechanical or electrical power. **powerful** *adj* **powerless** *adj* **power cut** temporary interruption in the supply of electricity. **power point** socket on a wall for plugging in electrical appliances. **power station** installation for generating and distributing electric power. **power steering** type of steering on vehicles in which the turning of the steering wheel is assisted by power from the engine.

powwow *n* talk, conference.

pox *n* **1** disease in which skin pustules form. **2** *Informal* syphilis.

pp **1** past participle. **2** (in signing a document) for and on behalf of. **3** *Music* pianissimo.

> The original meaning of *pp* (Latin *per procurationem*) is 'by delegation to', so traditionally *pp* is written before the name of the typist to show that she or he has signed the letter on behalf of someone else. Nowadays the meaning has been overtaken by the sense of 'on behalf of' and *pp* is often written before the name of the person who composed the letter.

pp. pages.

PQ Quebec.

Pr *Chem* praseodymium.

PR **1** proportional representation. **2** public relations.

practicable *adj* capable of being done successfully. **practicability** *n*

practical *adj* **1** involving experience or actual use rather than theory. **2** concerned with everyday matters. **3** sensible, useful, and effective. **4** good at making or doing things. **5** in effect though not in name. ♦ *n* **6** examination in which something has to be done or made. **practically** *adv* **practicality** *n, pl* **-ties** **practical joke** trick intended to make someone look foolish.

practice *n* **1** something done regularly or habitually. **2** repetition of something so as to gain skill. **3** doctor's or lawyer's place of work. **in practice** what actually happens as distinct from what is supposed to happen. **put into practice** carry out, do.

> Note the *-ice* ending for the noun, with *-ise* for the verb (*practise*).

practise *v* **1** do repeatedly so as to gain skill. **2** take part in, follow (a religion etc.). **3** work at, e.g. *practise medicine.* **4** do habitually.

> Note the *-ise* ending for the verb, with *-ice* for the noun (*practice*).

practitioner *n* person who practises a profession.

pragmatic *adj* concerned with practical consequences rather than theory. **pragmatism** *n* **pragmatist** *n*

prairie *n* large treeless area of grassland, esp. in N America and Canada. **prairie dog** rodent that lives in burrows in the N American prairies.

praise *v* **1** express approval or admiration of (someone or something). **2** express honour and thanks to (one's God). ♦ *n* **3** something said or written to show approval or admiration. **sing someone's praises** praise someone highly. **praiseworthy** *adj*

praline [**prah**-leen] *n* sweet made of nuts and caramelized sugar.

pram *n* four-wheeled carriage for a baby, pushed by hand.

prance *v* walk with exaggerated bouncing steps.

prang *v, n Old-fashioned slang* (have) a crash in a car or aircraft.

prank *n* mischievous trick.

praseodymium [pray-zee-oh-**dim**-ee-um] *n Chem* silvery-white metallic element of the lanthanide series.

prat *n Offens* stupid person.

prattle *v* **1** chatter in a childish or foolish way. ♦ *n* **2** childish or foolish talk.

prawn *n* edible shellfish like a large shrimp.

praxis *n* practice as opposed to theory.

pray *v* **1** say prayers. **2** ask earnestly, entreat. **prayer** *n* **1** thanks or appeal addressed to one's God. **2** set form of words used in praying. **3** earnest request.

pre- *prefix* before, beforehand, e.g. *prenatal; prerecorded; preshrunk.*

preach *v* **1** give a talk on a religious theme as part of a church service. **2** speak in support of (an idea, principle, etc.). **preacher** *n*

preamble *n* introductory part to something said or written.

prearranged *adj* arranged beforehand.

prebendary *n, pl* **-daries** clergyman who is a member of the chapter of a cathedral.

precarious *adj* insecure, unsafe, likely to fall or collapse. **precariously** *adv*

precaution *n* action taken in advance to prevent something bad happening. **precautionary** *adj*

precede *v* go or be before. **precedence** [**press**-ee-denss] *n* formal order of rank or position. **take precedence over** be more important than. **precedent** *n* previous case or occurrence regarded as an example to be followed.

precentor *n* person who leads the singing in a church.

precept *n* rule of behaviour.

precinct *n* **1** area in a town closed to traffic. **2** enclosed area round a building, e.g. *cathedral precinct.* **3** *US* administrative area of a city. ♦ *pl* **4** surrounding region.

precious *adj* **1** of great value and importance. **2** loved and treasured. **3** (of behaviour) affected, unnatural. **precious metal** gold, silver, or platinum. **precious stone** rare mineral, such as a ruby, valued as a gem.

precipice *n* very steep cliff or rockface. **precipitous** *adj* sheer.

precipitate *v* **1** cause to happen suddenly. **2** condense and fall as snow or rain. **3** *Chem* cause to be deposited in solid form from a solution. **4** throw headlong. ♦ *adj* **5** done rashly or hastily. ♦ *n* **6** *Chem* substance precipitated from a solution. **precipitately** *adv* **precipitation** *n* **1** precipitating. **2** rain, snow, etc.

précis [**pray**-see] *n, pl* **précis** **1** short written summary of a longer piece. ♦ *v* **2** make a précis of.

precise *adj* **1** exact, accurate in every detail. **2** strict in observing rules or standards. **precisely** *adv* **precision** *n*

preclude *v* make impossible to happen.

precocious *adj* having developed or matured early or too soon. **precocity** *n*

precognition *n* alleged ability to foretell the future.

preconceived *adj* (of an idea) formed without real experience or reliable information. **preconception** *n*

precondition *n* something that must happen or exist before something else can.

precursor *n* something that precedes and is a signal of something else, forerunner.

predate *v* **1** occur at an earlier date than. **2** write a date on (a document) that is earlier than the actual date.

predatory [**pred**-a-tree] *adj* habitually hunting and killing other animals for food. **predator** *n* predatory animal.

predecease *v* die before (someone else).

predecessor *n* **1** person who precedes another in an office or position. **2** ancestor.

predestination *n* belief that future events have already been decided by God or fate. **predestined** *adj*

predetermined *adj* decided in advance.

predicament *n* embarrassing or difficult situation.

predicate *n* **1** *Grammar* part of a sentence in which something is said about the subject, e.g. *went home* in *I went home.* ♦ *v* **2** declare or assert. **predicat-**

ed on based on. **predicative** *adj* of or in the predicate of a sentence.

predict *v* tell about in advance, prophesy. **predictable** *adj* **prediction** *n*

predilection *n* preference or liking.

predispose *v* **1** influence (someone) in favour of something. **2** make (someone) susceptible to something. **predisposition** *n*

predominate *v* be the main or controlling element. **predominance** *n* **predominant** *adj* **predominantly** *adv*

pre-eminent *adj* excelling all others, outstanding. **pre-eminence** *n*

pre-empt *v* prevent an action by doing something which makes it pointless or impossible. **pre-emption** *n* **pre-emptive** *adj*

preen *v* (of a bird) clean or trim (feathers) with the beak. **preen oneself 1** smarten oneself. **2** show self-satisfaction.

prefab *n* prefabricated house.

prefabricated *adj* (of a building) manufactured in shaped sections for rapid assembly on site.

preface [**pref**-iss] *n* **1** introduction to a book. ♦ *v* **2** serve as an introduction to (a book, speech, etc.). **prefatory** *adj*

prefect *n* **1** senior pupil in a school, with limited power over others. **2** senior administrative officer in some countries. **prefecture** *n* office or area of authority of a prefect.

prefer *v* **-ferring, -ferred 1** like better. **2** *Law* bring (charges) before a court. **preferable** *adj* more desirable. **preferably** *adv* **preference** *n* **preferential** *adj* showing preference. **preferment** *n* promotion or advancement.

prefigure *v* represent or suggest in advance.

prefix *n* **1** letter or group of letters put at the beginning of a word to make a new word, such as *un-* in *unhappy*. ♦ *v* **2** put as an introduction or prefix (to).

pregnant *adj* **1** carrying a fetus in the womb. **2** full of meaning or significance, e.g. *a pregnant pause.* **pregnancy** *n, pl* **-cies**

prehensile *adj* capable of grasping.

prehistoric *adj* of the period before written history begins. **prehistory** *n*

prejudge *v* judge beforehand without sufficient evidence.

prejudice *n* **1** unreasonable or unfair dislike or preference. ♦ *v* **2** cause (someone) to have a prejudice. **3** harm, cause disadvantage to. **prejudicial** *adj* harmful, disadvantageous.

prelate [**prel**-it] *n* bishop or other churchman of high rank.

preliminary *adj* **1** happening before and in preparation, introductory. ♦ *n, pl* **-naries 2** preliminary remark, contest, etc.

prelude [**prel**-yewd] *n* **1** introductory movement in music. **2** event preceding and introducing something else.

premarital *adj* occurring before marriage.

premature *adj* **1** happening or done before the normal or expected time. **2** (of a baby) born before the end of the normal period of pregnancy. **prematurely** *adv*

premedication *n* drugs given to prepare a patient for a general anaesthetic.

premeditated *adj* planned in advance. **premeditation** *n*

premenstrual *adj* occurring or experienced before a menstrual period, e.g. *premenstrual tension.*

premier *n* **1** prime minister. ♦ *adj* **2** chief, leading. **premiership** *n*

première *n* first performance of a play, film, etc.

premise, premiss *n* statement assumed to be true and used as the basis of reasoning.

premises *pl n* house or other building and its land.

premium *n* **1** additional sum of money, as on a wage or charge. **2** (regular) sum paid for insurance. **at a premium** in great demand because scarce. **premium bonds** savings certificates issued by the government, on which no interest is paid but cash prizes can be won.

premonition *n* feeling that something unpleasant is going to happen; foreboding. **premonitory** *adj*

prenatal *adj* before birth, during pregnancy.

preoccupy *v* **-pying, -pied** fill the thoughts or attention of (someone) to the exclusion of other things. **preoccupation** *n*

preordained *adj* decreed or determined in advance.

prep *n Old-fashioned* (period reserved for) homework.

prep. **1** preparatory. **2** preposition.

prepacked *adj* sold already wrapped.

prepaid *adj* paid for in advance.

prepare *v* make or get ready. **prepared** *adj* **1** willing. **2** ready. **preparation** *n* **1** preparing. **2** something done in readiness for something else. **3** mixture prepared for use as a cosmetic, medicine, etc. **preparatory** [prip-**par**-a-tree] *adj* preparing for. **preparatory school** private school for children going on to public school.

preponderance *n* greater force, amount, or influence. **preponderant** *adj*

preposition *n* word used before a noun or pronoun to show its relationship with other words, such as *by* in *go by bus*. **prepositional** *adj*

> The practice of ending a sentence with a preposition, as in: *Venice is a place I should like to go to,* was formerly regarded as incorrect, but is now acceptable and is the preferred form in many contexts.

prepossessing *adj* making a favourable impression, attractive.

preposterous *adj* utterly absurd.

prep school *n* short for PREPARATORY SCHOOL.

prepuce [**pree**-pyewss] *n* retractable fold of skin covering the tip of the penis, foreskin.

prerecorded *adj* recorded in advance to be played or broadcast later.

prerequisite *n, adj* (something) required before something else is possible.

prerogative *n* special power or privilege.

presage [**press**-ij] *v* be a sign or warning of.

Presbyterian *n, adj* (member) of a Protestant church governed by lay elders. **Presbyterianism** *n*

presbytery *n, pl* **-teries** **1** *Presbyterian Church* local church court. **2** *RC Church* priest's house.

prescience [**press**-ee-enss] *n* knowledge of events before they happen. **prescient** *adj*

prescribe *v* **1** recommend the use of (a medicine). **2** lay down as a rule. **prescription** *n* written instructions from a doctor for the making up and use of a medicine. **prescriptive** *adj* laying down rules.

presence *n* **1** fact of being in a specified place. **2** impressive dignified appearance. **presence of mind** ability to act sensibly in a crisis.

present[1] *adj* **1** being in a specified place. **2** existing or happening now. **3** *Grammar* (of a verb tense) indicating that the action specified is taking place now. ♦ *n* **4** present time or tense. **presently** *adv* **1** soon. **2** *US & Scot* now.

present[2] *n* **1** something given to bring pleasure to another person. ♦ *v* **2** introduce formally or publicly. **3** introduce and compère (a TV or radio show). **4** cause, e.g. *present a difficulty.* **5** give, award. **presentation** *n* **presentable** *adj* attractive, neat, fit for people to see. **presenter** *n* person introducing a TV or radio show.

presentiment [priz-**zen**-tim-ent] *n* sense of something unpleasant about to happen.

preserve *v* **1** keep from being damaged, changed, or ended. **2** treat (food) to prevent it decaying. ♦ *n* **3** area of interest restricted to a particular person or group. **4** fruit preserved by cooking in sugar. **5** area where game is kept for private hunting or fishing. **preservation** *n* **preservative** *n* chemical that prevents decay.

preshrunk *adj* (of fabric or a garment)

having been shrunk during manufacture so that further shrinkage will not occur when washed.

preside *v* be in charge, esp. of a meeting.

president *n* **1** head of state in countries without a king or queen. **2** head of a society, institution, etc. **presidential** *adj* **presidency** *n, pl* **-cies**

press[1] *v* **1** apply force or weight to. **2** squeeze. **3** smooth by applying pressure or heat. **4** urge insistently. **5** crowd, push. ♦ *n* **6** printing machine. **pressed for** short of, e.g. *pressed for time.* **the press 1** news media collectively, esp. newspapers. **2** reporters, journalists. **pressing** *adj* urgent. **press box** room at a sports ground reserved for reporters. **press conference** interview for reporters given by a celebrity. **press release** official announcement or account of a news item supplied to the press. **press stud** fastener in which one part with a projecting knob snaps into a hole on another part.

press[2] *v* **press into service** force to be involved or used. **press gang** *Hist* group of men used to capture men and boys and force them to join the navy.

press-up *n* exercise in which the body is raised from and lowered to the floor by straightening and bending the arms.

pressure *n* **1** force produced by pressing. **2** urgent claims or demands, e.g. *working under pressure.* **3** *Physics* force applied to a surface per unit of area. ♦ *v* **4** persuade forcefully. **bring pressure to bear on** use influence or authority to persuade. **pressurize** *v* **pressure cooker** airtight pot which cooks food quickly by steam under pressure. **pressure group** group that tries to influence policies, public opinion, etc.

prestidigitation *n* skilful quickness with the hands, conjuring.

prestige *n* high status or respect resulting from success or achievements. **prestigious** *adj*

presto *adv Music* very quickly.

prestressed *adj* (of concrete) containing stretched steel wires to strengthen it.

presume *v* **1** suppose to be the case. **2** dare (to). **presumably** *adv* one supposes (that). **presumption** *n* **1** basis on which an assumption is made. **2** bold insolent behaviour. **3** strong probability. **presumptuous** *adj* doing things one has no right or authority to do. **presumptive** *adj* assumed to be true or valid until the contrary is proved.

presuppose *v* need as a previous condition in order to be true. **presupposition** *n*

pretend *v* claim or give the appearance of (something untrue) to deceive or in play. **pretender** *n* person who makes a false or disputed claim to a position of power. **pretence** *n* behaviour intended to deceive, pretending. **pretentious** *adj* making (unjustified) claims to special merit or importance. **pretension** *n*

preternatural *adj* beyond what is natural, supernatural.

pretext *n* false reason given to hide the real one.

pretty *adj* **-tier, -tiest 1** pleasing to look at. ♦ *adv* **2** fairly, moderately, e.g. *I'm pretty certain.* **prettily** *adv* **prettiness** *n* **sitting pretty** in a favourable state.

pretzel *n* brittle salted biscuit.

prevail *v* **1** gain mastery. **2** be generally established. **prevailing** *adj* **1** widespread. **2** predominant. **prevalence** *n* **prevalent** *adj* widespread, common.

prevaricate *v* avoid giving a direct or truthful answer. **prevarication** *n*

prevent *v* keep from happening or doing. **preventable** *adj* **prevention** *n* **preventive** *adj, n*

preview *n* **1** advance showing of a film or exhibition before it is shown to the public. ♦ *v* **2** view in advance.

previous *adj* coming or happening before. **previously** *adv*

prey *n* **1** animal hunted and killed for food by another animal. **2** victim. **bird of prey** bird that kills and eats other birds or animals. **prey on** *v* **1** hunt and kill for food. **2** worry, obsess.

price *n* **1** amount of money for which a

thing is bought or sold. **2** unpleasant thing that must be endured to get something desirable. ♦ *v* **3** fix or ask the price of. **priceless** *adj* **1** very valuable. **2** *Informal* very funny. **pricey** *adj* **pricier, priciest** *Informal* expensive.

prick *v* **1** pierce lightly with a sharp point. **2** cause to feel mental pain. **3** (of an animal) make (the ears) stand erect. ♦ *n* **4** sudden sharp pain caused by pricking. **5** mark made by pricking. **6** remorse. **7** *Taboo slang* penis. **prick up one's ears** listen intently.

prickle *n* **1** thorn or spike on a plant. ♦ *v* **2** have a tingling or pricking sensation. **prickly** *adj* **prickly heat** itchy rash occurring in hot moist weather.

pride *n* **1** feeling of pleasure and satisfaction when one has done well. **2** too high an opinion of oneself. **3** sense of dignity and self-respect. **4** something that causes one to feel pride. **5** group of lions. **pride of place** most important position. **pride oneself on** feel pride about.

priest *n* **1** (in the Christian church) a person who can administer the sacraments and preach. **2** (in some other religions) an official who performs religious ceremonies. **priestess** *n fem* **priesthood** *n* **priestly** *adj*

prig *n* self-righteous person who acts as if superior to others. **priggish** *adj* **priggishness** *n*

prim *adj* **primmer, primmest** formal, proper, and rather prudish. **primly** *adv*

prima ballerina *n* leading female ballet dancer.

primacy *n, pl* **-cies** **1** state of being first in rank, grade, etc. **2** office of an archbishop.

prima donna *n* **1** leading female opera singer. **2** *Informal* temperamental person.

primaeval *adj* same as PRIMEVAL.

prima facie [**prime**-a **fay**-shee] *adv Latin* as it seems at first.

primal *adj* of basic causes or origins.

primary *adj* **1** chief, most important. **2** being the first stage, elementary. **primarily** *adv* **primary colours** (in physics) red, green, and blue or (in art) red, yellow, and blue, from which all other colours can be produced by mixing. **primary school** school for children from five to eleven years.

primate[1] *n* member of an order of mammals including monkeys and humans.

primate[2] *n* archbishop.

prime *adj* **1** main, most important. **2** of the highest quality. ♦ *n* **3** time when someone is at his or her best or most vigorous. ♦ *v* **4** give (someone) information in advance to prepare them for something. **5** prepare (a surface) for painting. **6** prepare (a gun, pump, etc.) for use. **primer** *n* special paint applied to bare wood etc. before the main paint. **Prime Minister** leader of a government. **prime number** number that can be divided exactly only by itself and one. **prime time** peak viewing time on television.

primer *n* beginners' school book or manual.

primeval [prime-**ee**-val] *adj* of the earliest age of the world.

primitive *adj* **1** of an early simple stage of development. **2** basic, crude, e.g. *a primitive hut.*

primogeniture *n* system under which the eldest son inherits all his parents' property.

primordial *adj* existing at or from the beginning.

primrose *n* pale yellow spring flower.

primula *n* type of primrose with brightly coloured flowers.

Primus *n* ® portable cooking stove used esp. by campers.

prince *n* **1** male member of a royal family, esp. the son of the king or queen. **2** male ruler of a small country. **princely** *adj* **1** of or like a prince. **2** generous, lavish, or magnificent. **prince consort** husband of a reigning queen. **Prince of Wales** eldest son of the British sovereign. **princess** *n* female member of a royal family, esp. the daughter of the king or queen. **Princess Royal** title sometimes given to the eldest daughter of the British sovereign.

principal *adj* **1** main, most important. ♦ *n* **2** head of a school or college. **3** person taking a leading part in something. **4** sum of money lent on which interest is paid. **principally** *adv* **principal boy** leading male role in pantomime, played by a woman.

> Distinguish the spellings of *principal* and *principle*. These are different words but often confused.

principality *n, pl* **-ties** territory ruled by a prince.

principle *n* **1** moral rule guiding behaviour. **2** general or basic truth, e.g. *the principle of equality.* **3** scientific law concerning the working of something. **in principle** in theory but not always in practice. **on principle** because of one's beliefs.

> Distinguish the spellings of *principle* and *principal*. These are different words but often confused.

print *v* **1** reproduce (a newspaper, book, etc.) in large quantities by mechanical or electronic means. **2** reproduce (text or pictures) by pressing ink onto paper etc. **3** write in letters that are not joined up. **4** stamp (fabric) with a design. **5** *Photog* produce (pictures) from negatives. ♦ *n* **6** printed words etc. **7** printed copy of a painting. **8** printed lettering. **9** photograph. **10** printed fabric. **11** mark left on a surface by something that has pressed against it. **out of print** no longer available from a publisher. **printer** *n* **1** person or company engaged in printing. **2** machine that prints. **3** machine connected to a computer that prints out results on paper. **printing** *n* **printed circuit** electronic circuit with wiring printed on an insulating base. **print-out** *n* printed information from a computer.

prior[1] *adj* earlier. **prior to** before.

prior[2] *n* head monk in a priory. **prioress** *n* deputy head nun in a convent. **priory** *n, pl* **-ries** place where certain orders of monks or nuns live.

priority *n, pl* **-ties 1** most important thing that must be dealt with first. **2** right to be or go before others.

prise *v* force open by levering.

prism *n* transparent block usu. with triangular ends and rectangular sides, used to disperse light into a spectrum or refract it in optical instruments. **prismatic** *adj* **1** of or shaped like a prism. **2** (of colour) as if produced by refraction through a prism, rainbow-like.

prison *n* building where criminals and accused people are held. **prisoner** *n* person held captive. **prisoner of war** serviceman captured by an enemy in wartime.

prissy *adj* **-sier, -siest** prim, correct, and easily shocked. **prissily** *adv*

pristine *adj* clean, new, and unused.

private *adj* **1** for the use of one person or group only. **2** secret. **3** personal, unconnected with one's work. **4** owned or paid for by individuals rather than by the government. **5** quiet, not likely to be disturbed. ♦ *n* **6** soldier of the lowest rank. **privately** *adv* **privacy** *n* **private company** limited company that does not issue shares for public subscription. **private detective** person hired by a client to do detective work. **private member's bill** law proposed by a Member of Parliament who is not a government minister. **private parts** *Euphemistic* genitals. **private school** school controlled by a private body, accepting mostly fee-paying pupils. **private sector** part of a country's economy not controlled or financially supported by the government.

privateer *n* **1** *Hist* privately owned armed vessel authorized by the government to take part in a war. **2** captain of such a ship.

privation *n* loss or lack of the necessities of life.

privatize *v* sell (a publicly owned company) to individuals or a private company. **privatization** *n*

privet *n* bushy evergreen shrub used for hedges.

privilege *n* **1** advantage or favour that only some people have. **2** rare opportunity to do something which gives great satisfaction. **privileged** *adj* enjoying a special right or immunity.

privy *adj* **1** sharing knowledge of something secret. ♦ *n, pl* **privies 2** *Obs* toilet, esp. an outside one. **Privy Council** private council of the British monarch.

prize[1] *n* **1** reward given for success in a competition etc. ♦ *adj* **2** winning or likely to win a prize. **prizefighter** *n* boxer who fights for money. **prizefight** *n*

prize[2] *v* value highly.

prize[3] *v* same as PRISE.

pro[1] *adv, prep* in favour of. **pros and cons** arguments for and against.

pro[2] *n, pl* **pros** *Informal* **1** professional. **2** prostitute.

pro- *prefix* **1** in favour of, e.g. *pro-Russian.* **2** instead of, e.g. *pronoun.*

probable *adj* likely to happen or be true. **probably** *adv* **probability** *n, pl* **-ties**

probate *n* **1** process of proving the validity of a will. **2** certificate stating that a will is genuine.

probation *n* **1** system of dealing with law-breakers, esp. juvenile ones, by placing them under supervision. **2** period when someone is assessed for suitability for a job etc. **probationer** *n* person on probation. **probationary** *adj* **probation officer** person who supervises offenders placed on probation.

probe *v* **1** search into or examine closely. ♦ *n* **2** surgical instrument used to examine a wound, cavity, etc. **3** thorough inquiry.

probity *n* honesty, integrity.

problem *n* **1** something difficult to deal with or solve. **2** question or puzzle set for solution. **problematic, problematical** *adj*

proboscis [pro-**boss**-iss] *n* **1** long trunk or snout. **2** elongated mouth of some insects.

procedure *n* way of doing something, esp. the correct or usual one. **procedural** *adj*

proceed *v* **1** start or continue doing. **2** *Formal* walk, go. **3** start a legal action. **4** arise from. **proceeds** *pl n* money obtained from an event or activity. **proceedings** *pl n* **1** organized or related series of events. **2** minutes of a meeting. **3** legal action.

process *n* **1** series of actions or changes. **2** method of doing or producing something. ♦ *v* **3** handle or prepare by a special method of manufacture. **processed** *adj* (of food) treated to prevent it decaying. **processor** *n* *Computers* same as CENTRAL PROCESSING UNIT.

procession *n* line of people or vehicles moving forward together in order.

proclaim *v* declare publicly. **proclamation** *n*

proclivity *n, pl* **-ties** inclination, tendency.

procrastinate *v* put off taking action, delay. **procrastination** *n* **procrastinator** *n*

procreate *v* *Formal* produce offspring. **procreation** *n*

procurator fiscal *n* (in Scotland) law officer who acts as public prosecutor and coroner.

procure *v* **1** get, provide. **2** obtain (people) to act as prostitutes. **procurement** *n* **procurer, procuress** *n* person who obtains people to act as prostitutes.

prod *v* **prodding, prodded 1** poke with something pointed. **2** goad (someone) to take action. ♦ *n* **3** prodding.

prodigal *adj* recklessly extravagant, wasteful. **prodigality** *n*

prodigy *n, pl* **-gies 1** person with some marvellous talent. **2** wonderful thing. **prodigious** *adj* **1** very large, immense. **2** wonderful. **prodigiously** *adv*

produce *v* **1** bring into existence. **2** present to view, show. **3** make, manufacture. **4** present on stage, film, or television. ♦ *n* **5** food grown for sale. **producer** *n* **1** person with control over the making of a film, record, etc. **2** person or company that produces something.

product *n* **1** something produced. **2** number resulting from multiplication. **production** *n* **1** producing. **2** things produced. **3** presentation of a play, opera, etc. **productive** *adj* **1** producing large quantities. **2** useful, profitable. **productivity** *n*

profane *adj* **1** showing disrespect for religion or holy things. **2** (of language) coarse, blasphemous. ♦ *v* **3** treat (something sacred) irreverently, desecrate. **profanation** *n* act of profaning. **profanity** *n, pl* **-ties** profane talk or behaviour, blasphemy.

profess *v* **1** state or claim (something as true), sometimes falsely. **2** have as one's belief or religion. **professed** *adj* supposed.

profession *n* **1** type of work, such as being a doctor, that needs special training. **2** all the people employed in a profession, e.g. *the legal profession.* **3** declaration of a belief or feeling. **professional** *adj* **1** working in a profession. **2** taking part in an activity, such as sport or music, for money. **3** very competent. ♦ *n* **4** person who works in a profession. **5** person paid to take part in sport, music, etc. **professionally** *adv* **professionalism** *n*

professor *n* teacher of the highest rank in a university. **professorial** *adj* **professorship** *n*

proffer *v* offer.

proficient *adj* skilled, expert. **proficiency** *n*

profile *n* **1** outline, esp. of the face, as seen from the side. **2** brief biographical sketch.

profit *n* **1** money gained. **2** benefit obtained. ♦ *v* **3** gain or benefit. **profitable** *adj* making profit. **profitably** *adv* **profitability** *n* **profiteer** *n* person who makes excessive profits at the expense of the public. **profiteering** *n*

profligate *adj* **1** recklessly extravagant. **2** shamelessly immoral. ♦ *n* **3** profligate person. **profligacy** *n*

pro forma *adj Latin* prescribing a set form.

profound *adj* **1** showing or needing great knowledge. **2** strongly felt, intense. **profoundly** *adv* **profundity** *n, pl* **-ties**

profuse *adj* plentiful. **profusion** *n*

progeny [**proj**-in-ee] *n, pl* **-nies** children. **progenitor** [pro-**jen**-it-er] *n* ancestor.

progesterone *n* hormone which prepares the womb for pregnancy and prevents further ovulation.

prognosis *n, pl* **-noses** **1** doctor's forecast about the progress of an illness. **2** any forecast.

prognostication *n* forecast or prediction.

program *n* **1** sequence of coded instructions for a computer. ♦ *v* **-gramming, -grammed** **2** arrange (data) so that it can be processed by a computer. **3** feed a program into (a computer). **programmer** *n* **programmable** *adj*

programme *n* **1** planned series of events. **2** broadcast on radio or television. **3** list of items or performers in an entertainment.

progress *n* **1** improvement, development. **2** movement forward. ♦ *v* **3** become more advanced or skilful. **4** move forward. **in progress** taking place. **progression** *n* **1** act of progressing, advance. **2** sequence of numbers in which each differs from the next by a fixed ratio. **progressive** *adj* **1** favouring political or social reform. **2** happening gradually. **progressively** *adv*

prohibit *v* forbid or prevent from happening. **prohibition** *n* **1** act of forbidding. **2** ban on the sale or drinking of alcohol. **prohibitive** *adj* (of prices) too high to be affordable. **prohibitively** *adv*

> The idiom is *prohibit* someone *from* doing something.

project *n* **1** planned scheme to do or examine something over a period. ♦ *v* **2** make a forecast based on known data. **3** make (a film or slide) appear on a screen. **4** communicate (an impression). **5** stick out beyond a surface or edge. **projector** *n* apparatus for projecting photographic images, films, or slides on a screen. **projection** *n* **projectionist** *n* person who operates a projector.

projectile *n* object thrown as a weapon or fired from a gun.

prolapse *n* slipping down of an internal organ of the body from its normal position. **prolapsed** *adj*

prole *adj, n Offens* proletarian.

proletariat [pro-lit-**air**-ee-at] *n* working class. **proletarian** *adj, n*

proliferate *v* grow or reproduce rapidly. **proliferation** *n*

prolific *adj* very productive. **prolifically** *adv*

prolix *adj* (of speech or a piece of writing) overlong and boring. **prolixity** *n*

prologue *n* introduction to a play or book.

prolong *v* make (something) last longer. **prolongation** *n*

prom *n* short for PROMENADE *or* PROMENADE CONCERT.

promenade *n* **1** paved walkway along the seafront at a holiday resort. ♦ *v, n* **2** *Old-fashioned* (take) a leisurely walk. **promenade concert** concert at which part of the audience stands rather than sits.

promethium [pro-**meeth**-ee-um] *n Chem* artificial radioactive element of the lanthanide series.

prominent *adj* **1** very noticeable. **2** famous, widely known. **prominently** *adv* **prominence** *n*

promiscuous *adj* having many casual sexual relationships. **promiscuity** *n*

promise *v* **1** say that one will definitely do or not do something. **2** show signs of, seem likely. ♦ *n* **3** undertaking to do or not to do something. **4** indication of future success. **show promise** seem likely to succeed. **promising** *adj* likely to succeed or turn out well. **promissory note** written promise to pay a sum of money to a particular person on a certain date or on demand.

promo *n, pl* **-mos** *Informal* short video film made to promote a pop record.

promontory *n, pl* **-ries** point of high land jutting out into the sea.

promote *v* **1** help to make (something) happen or increase. **2** raise to a higher rank or position. **3** encourage the sale of by advertising. **promoter** *n* person who organizes or finances an event etc. **promotion** *n* **promotional** *adj*

prompt *v* **1** cause (an action). **2** remind (an actor or speaker) of words that he or she has forgotten. ♦ *adj* **3** done without delay. ♦ *adv* **4** exactly, e.g. *six o'clock prompt.* **promptly** *adv* immediately, without delay. **promptness** *n* **prompter** *n* person offstage who prompts actors.

promulgate *v* **1** put (a law etc.) into effect by announcing it officially. **2** make widely known. **promulgation** *n* **promulgator** *n*

prone *adj* **1** (foll. by *to*) likely to do or be affected by (something). **2** lying face downwards.

prong *n* one spike of a fork or similar instrument. **pronged** *adj*

pronoun *n* word, such as *she* or *it*, used to replace a noun. **pronominal** *adj*

pronounce *v* **1** form the sounds of (words or letters), esp. clearly or in a particular way. **2** declare formally or officially. **pronounceable** *adj* **pronounced** *adj* very noticeable. **pronouncement** *n* formal announcement. **pronunciation** *n* way in which a word or language is pronounced.

> Note the difference in spelling between *pronounce* and *pronunciation.* The pronunciation also changes from 'nown' to 'nun'.

pronto *adv Informal* at once.

proof *n* **1** evidence that shows that something is true or has happened. **2** copy of something printed, such as the pages of a book, for checking before final production. **3** *Photog* trial print from a negative. ♦ *adj* **4** able to withstand, e.g.

proof against criticism. **5** denoting the strength of an alcoholic drink, e.g. *seventy proof.* **proofread** *v* read and correct (printer's proofs). **proofreader** *n*

prop[1] *v* **propping, propped** **1** support (something) so that it stays upright or in place. ♦ *n* **2** pole, beam, etc. used as a support.

prop[2] *n* movable object used on the set of a film or play.

prop[3] *n Informal* propeller.

propaganda *n* (organized promotion of) information to assist or damage the cause of a government or movement. **propagandist** *n*

propagate *v* **1** spread (information and ideas). **2** reproduce, breed, or grow. **propagation** *n*

propane *n* flammable gas found in petroleum and used as a fuel.

propel *v* **-pelling, -pelled** cause to move forward. **propellant** *n* **1** something that provides or causes propulsion. **2** gas used in an aerosol spray. **propeller** *n* revolving shaft with blades for driving a ship or aircraft. **propulsion** *n* **1** method by which something is propelled. **2** act of propelling or state of being propelled.

propensity *n, pl* **-ties** natural tendency.

proper *adj* **1** real or genuine. **2** appropriate. **3** suited to a particular purpose. **4** correct in behaviour. **5** excessively moral. **6** *Informal* complete. **properly** *adv* **proper noun** name of a person or place, as in *David* or *Iceland.*

property *n, pl* **-ties** **1** something owned. **2** possessions collectively. **3** land or buildings owned by somebody. **4** quality or attribute.

prophet *n* **1** person supposedly chosen by God to spread His word. **2** person who predicts the future. **prophetic** *adj* **prophetically** *adv* **prophecy** *n, pl* **-cies** **1** prediction. **2** message revealing God's will. **prophesy** *v* **-sying, -sied** foretell.

> Note the difference in spelling between the noun (*prophecy*) and the verb (*prophesy*).

prophylactic *n, adj* (drug) used to prevent disease.

propitiate *v* appease, win the favour of. **propitiation** *n* **propitious** *adj* favourable or auspicious.

proponent *n* person who argues in favour of something.

proportion *n* **1** relative size or extent. **2** correct relation between connected parts. **3** part considered with respect to the whole. ♦ *pl* **4** dimensions or size. ♦ *v* **5** adjust in relative amount or size. **in proportion** **1** comparable in size, rate of increase, etc. **2** without exaggerating. **proportional, proportionate** *adj* being in proportion. **proportionally, proportionately** *adv* **proportional representation** representation of political parties in parliament in proportion to the votes they win.

propose *v* **1** put forward for consideration. **2** nominate. **3** intend or plan (to do). **4** make an offer of marriage. **proposal** *n* **proposition** *n* **1** offer. **2** statement or assertion. **3** *Maths* theorem. **4** *Informal* thing to be dealt with. ♦ *v* **5** *Informal* ask (someone) to have sexual intercourse.

propound *v* put forward for consideration.

proprietor *n* owner of a business establishment. **proprietress** *n fem* **proprietary** *adj* **1** made and distributed under a trade name. **2** denoting or suggesting ownership.

propriety *n, pl* **-ties** **1** quality of being appropriate or fitting. **2** correct conduct.

propulsion *n* see PROPEL.

pro rata *adv, adj Latin* in proportion.

prorogue *v* suspend (parliament) without dissolving it. **prorogation** *n*

prosaic [pro-**zay**-ik] *adj* lacking imagination, dull. **prosaically** *adv*

proscenium *n, pl* **-nia, -niums** arch in a theatre separating the stage from the auditorium.

proscribe *v* prohibit, outlaw. **proscription** *n* **proscriptive** *adj*

prose *n* ordinary speech or writing in contrast to poetry.

prosecute *v* **1** bring a criminal charge against. **2** continue to do. **prosecution** *n* **prosecutor** *n*

proselyte [**pross**-ill-ite] *n* recent convert. **proselytize** [**pross**-ill-it-ize] *v* attempt to convert.

prosody [**pross**-a-dee] *n* study of poetic metre and techniques.

prospect *n* **1** something anticipated, e.g. *the prospect of defeat.* **2** *Old-fashioned* view from a place. ♦ *pl* **3** probability of future success. ♦ *v* **4** explore, esp. for gold. **prospective** *adj* **1** future. **2** expected. **prospector** *n* **prospectus** *n* booklet giving details of a university, company, etc.

prosper *v* be successful. **prosperity** *n* success and wealth. **prosperous** *adj*

prostate *n* gland in male mammals that surrounds the neck of the bladder.

prosthesis [pross-**theess**-iss] *n, pl* **-ses** [-seez] artificial body part, such as a limb or breast. **prosthetic** *adj*

prostitute *n* **1** person who offers sexual intercourse in return for payment. ♦ *v* **2** make a prostitute of. **3** offer (oneself or one's talents) for unworthy purposes. **prostitution** *n*

prostrate *adj* **1** lying face downwards. **2** physically or emotionally exhausted. ♦ *v* **3** lie face downwards. **4** exhaust physically or emotionally. **prostration** *n*

protactinium *n Chem* toxic radioactive metallic element.

protagonist *n* **1** supporter of a cause. **2** leading character in a play or a story.

protea [**pro**-tee-a] *n* African shrub with showy flowers.

protean [pro-**tee**-an] *adj* constantly changing.

protect *v* defend from trouble, harm, or loss. **protection** *n* **protectionism** *n* policy of protecting industries by taxing competing imports. **protectionist** *n, adj* **protective** *adj* **1** giving protection, e.g. *protective clothing.* **2** tending or wishing to protect someone. **protector** *n* **1** person or thing that protects. **2** regent. **protectorate** *n* **1** territory largely controlled by a stronger state. **2** (period of) rule of a regent.

protégé, (*fem*) **protégée** [**pro**-ti-zhay] *n* person who is protected and helped by another.

protein *n* any of a group of complex organic compounds that are essential for life.

pro tempore *adv, adj* for the time being (also **pro tem**).

protest *n* **1** declaration or demonstration of objection. ♦ *v* **2** object, disagree. **3** assert formally. **protester** *n* **protestation** *n* strong declaration.

Protestant *n* **1** follower of any of the Christian churches that split from the Roman Catholic Church in the sixteenth century. ♦ *adj* **2** of or relating to such a church. **Protestantism** *n*

protium *n* most common isotope of hydrogen.

proto- *combining form* first, e.g. *protohuman.*

protocol *n* rules of behaviour for formal occasions.

proton *n* positively charged particle in the nucleus of an atom.

protoplasm *n* substance forming the living contents of a cell.

prototype *n* original or model to be copied or developed.

protozoan [pro-toe-**zoe**-an] *n, pl* **-zoa** microscopic one-celled creature.

protract *v* lengthen or extend. **protracted** *adj* **protractor** *n* instrument for measuring angles.

protrude *v* stick out, project. **protrusion** *n*

protuberant *adj* swelling out, bulging. **protuberance** *n*

proud *adj* **1** feeling pleasure and satisfaction. **2** feeling honoured. **3** thinking oneself superior to other people. **4** dignified. **proudly** *adv*

prove *v* **proving, proved, proved** *or* **proven** **1** establish the validity of. **2** demonstrate, test. **3** be found to be. **proven** *adj* known from experience to work.

provenance [**prov**-in-anss] *n* place of

origin.

provender *n Old-fashioned* fodder.

proverb *n* short saying that expresses a truth or gives a warning. **proverbial** *adj*

provide *v* make available. **provider** *n* **provided that, providing** on condition that. **provide for** *v* **1** take precautions (against). **2** support financially.

> The usage is either *providing* on its own or *provided that* (not *providing that*).

providence *n* God or nature seen as a protective force that arranges people's lives. **provident** *adj* **1** thrifty. **2** showing foresight. **providential** *adj* lucky.

province *n* **1** area governed as a unit of a country or empire. **2** area of learning, activity, etc. ♦ *pl* **3** parts of a country outside the capital. **provincial** *adj* **1** of a province or the provinces. **2** unsophisticated and narrow-minded. ♦ *n* **3** unsophisticated person. **4** person from a province or the provinces. **provincialism** *n* narrow-mindedness and lack of sophistication.

provision *n* **1** act of supplying something. **2** something supplied. **3** *Law* condition incorporated in a document. ♦ *pl* **4** food. ♦ *v* **5** supply with food. **provisional** *adj* temporary or conditional. **provisionally** *adv*

proviso [pro-**vize**-oh] *n, pl* **-sos, -soes** condition, stipulation.

provoke *v* **1** deliberately anger. **2** cause (an adverse reaction). **provocation** *n* **provocative** *adj*

provost *n* **1** head of certain university colleges. **2** chief councillor of a Scottish town. **provost marshal** head of military police.

prow *n* bow of a vessel.

prowess *n* **1** superior skill or ability. **2** bravery, fearlessness.

prowl *v* **1** move stealthily around a place as if in search of prey or plunder. ♦ *n* **2** prowling. **prowler** *n*

proximity *n* **1** nearness in space or time. **2** nearness or closeness in a series. **proximate** *adj*

proxy *n, pl* **proxies 1** person authorized to act on behalf of someone else. **2** authority to act on behalf of someone else.

prude *n* person who is excessively modest, prim, or proper. **prudish** *adj* **prudery** *n*

prudent *adj* cautious, discreet, and sensible. **prudence** *n* **prudential** *adj Old-fashioned* prudent.

prune[1] *n* dried plum.

prune[2] *v* **1** cut off dead parts or excessive branches from (a tree or plant). **2** shorten, reduce.

prurient *adj* excessively interested in sexual matters. **prurience** *n*

pry *v* **prying, pried** make an impertinent or uninvited inquiry into a private matter.

PS postscript.

psalm *n* sacred song. **psalmist** *n* writer of psalms.

Psalter *n* book containing (a version of) psalms from the Bible. **psaltery** *n, pl* **-ries** ancient instrument played by plucking strings.

PSBR public sector borrowing requirement.

psephology [sef-**fol**-a-jee] *n* statistical study of elections.

pseud *n Informal* pretentious person.

pseudo- *combining form* false, pretending, or unauthentic, e.g. *pseudoclassical.*

pseudonym *n* fictitious name adopted esp. by an author. **pseudonymous** *adj*

psittacosis *n* disease of parrots that can be transmitted to humans.

psoriasis [so-**rye**-a-siss] *n* skin disease with reddish spots and patches covered with silvery scales.

psyche [**sye**-kee] *n* human mind or soul.

psychedelic *adj* **1** denoting a drug that causes hallucinations. **2** having vivid colours and complex patterns similar to those experienced during hallucinations.

psychiatry *n* branch of medicine concerned with mental disorders. **psychiatric** *adj* **psychiatrist** *n*

psychic *adj* (also **psychical**) **1** having mental powers which cannot be explained by natural laws. **2** relating to the mind. ♦ *n* **3** person with psychic powers.

psycho *n, pl* **-chos** *Informal* psychopath.

psycho- *combining form* mind, mental processes, e.g. *psychology; psychosomatic.*

psychoanalysis *n* method of treating mental and emotional disorders by discussion and analysis of one's thoughts and feelings. **psychoanalyse** *v* **psychoanalyst** *n*

psychology *n, pl* **-gies** **1** study of human and animal behaviour. **2** *Informal* person's mental make-up. **psychologist** *n* **psychological** *adj* **1** of or affecting the mind. **2** of psychology. **psychological moment** most appropriate time for producing a desired effect. **psychological warfare** military application of psychology, esp. to influence morale in time of war. **psychologically** *adv*

psychopath *n* person afflicted with a personality disorder causing him or her to commit antisocial or violent acts. **psychopathic** *adj*

psychosis *n, pl* **-ses** severe mental disorder in which the sufferer's contact with reality becomes distorted. **psychotic** *adj*

psychosomatic *adj* (of a physical disorder) thought to have psychological causes.

psychotherapy *n* treatment of nervous disorders by psychological methods. **psychotherapeutic** *adj* **psychotherapist** *n*

psych up *v* prepare (oneself) mentally for a contest or task.

pt **1** part. **2** point.

Pt *Chem* platinum.

PT *Old-fashioned* physical training.

pt. pint.

PTA Parent-Teacher Association.

ptarmigan [**tar**-mig-an] *n* bird of the grouse family which turns white in winter.

pterodactyl [terr-roe-**dak**-til] *n* extinct flying reptile with batlike wings.

PTO please turn over.

ptomaine [**toe**-main] *n* any of a group of poisonous alkaloids found in decaying matter.

Pu *Chem* plutonium.

pub *n* building with a bar licensed to sell alcoholic drinks.

puberty [**pew**-ber-tee] *n* beginning of sexual maturity. **pubertal** *adj*

pubescent *adj* **1** reaching or having reached puberty. **2** covered with fine short hairs or down, as some plants and animals. **pubescence** *n*

pubic [**pew**-bik] *adj* of the lower abdomen, e.g. *pubic hair.*

pubis *n, pl* **-bes** one of the three sections of the hipbone that forms part of the pelvis.

public *adj* **1** of or concerning the people as a whole. **2** for use by everyone. **3** well-known. **4** performed or made openly. ♦ *n* **5** the community, people in general. **publicly** *adv* **public company** limited company whose shares may be purchased by the public. **public house** pub. **public relations** promotion of a favourable opinion towards an organization among the public. **public school** private fee-paying school in Britain. **public sector** part of a country's economy controlled and financially supported by the government. **public-spirited** *adj* having or showing an active interest in the good of the community.

publican *n* person who owns or runs a pub.

publicity *n* **1** process or information used to arouse public attention. **2** public interest so aroused. **publicize** *v* advertise. **publicist** *n* person, esp. a press agent or journalist, who publicizes something.

publish *v* **1** produce and issue (printed matter) for sale. **2** announce formally or in public. **publication** *n* **publisher** *n*

puce *adj* purplish-brown.

puck[1] *n* small rubber disc used in ice hockey.

puck[2] *n* mischievous or evil spirit. **puckish** *adj*

pucker *v* **1** gather into wrinkles. ♦ *n* **2** wrinkle or crease.

pudding *n* **1** dessert, esp. a cooked one served hot. **2** savoury dish with pastry or batter, e.g. *steak-and-kidney pudding.* **3** sausage-like mass of meat, e.g. *black pudding.*

puddle *n* small pool of water, esp. of rain.

pudenda *pl n* human external genital organs, esp. of a female.

puerile *adj* silly and childish.

puerperal [pew-**er**-per-al] *adj* concerning the period following childbirth.

puff *n* **1** (sound of) a short blast of breath, wind, etc. **2** act of inhaling cigarette smoke. ♦ *v* **3** blow or breathe in short quick draughts. **4** take draws at (a cigarette). **5** send out in small clouds. **6** swell. **out of puff** out of breath. **puffy** *adj* **puff adder** large venomous African viper. **puffball** *n* ball-shaped fungus. **puff pastry** light flaky pastry.

puffin *n* black-and-white sea bird with a brightly-coloured beak.

pug *n* small snub-nosed dog. **pug nose** short stubby upturned nose.

pugilist [**pew**-jil-ist] *n* boxer. **pugilism** *n* **pugilistic** *adj*

pugnacious *adj* ready and eager to fight. **pugnacity** *n*

puissance *n* showjumping competition that tests a horse's ability to jump large obstacles.

puke *Slang* ♦ *v* **1** vomit. ♦ *n* **2** act of vomiting. **3** vomited matter.

pukka *adj Anglo-Indian* **1** properly done, constructed, etc. **2** genuine, real.

pulchritude *n Lit* beauty.

pull *v* **1** exert force on (an object) to move it towards the source of the force. **2** strain or stretch. **3** remove or extract. **4** attract. ♦ *n* **5** act of pulling. **6** force used in pulling. **7** act of taking in drink or smoke. **8** *Informal* power, influence. **pull oneself together** *Informal* regain one's self-control. **pull in** *v* **1** (of a vehicle or driver) draw in to the side of the road or stop. **2** reach a destination. **3** attract in large numbers. **4** *Slang* arrest. **pull off** *v Informal* succeed in performing. **pull out** *v* **1** (of a vehicle or driver) move away from the side of the road or move out to overtake. **2** (of a train) depart. **3** withdraw. **4** remove by pulling. **pull through** *v* survive or recover, esp. after a serious illness. **pull up** *v* **1** (of a vehicle or driver) stop. **2** remove by the roots. **3** reprimand.

pullet *n* young hen.

pulley *n* wheel with a grooved rim in which a belt, chain, or piece of rope runs in order to lift weights by a downward pull.

Pullman *n, pl* **-mans** luxurious railway coach.

pullover *n* sweater that is pulled on over the head.

pulmonary *adj* of the lungs.

pulp *n* **1** soft wet substance made from crushed or beaten matter. **2** flesh of a fruit. **3** poor-quality books and magazines. ♦ *v* **4** reduce to pulp.

pulpit *n* raised platform for a preacher.

pulsar *n* small dense star which emits regular bursts of radio waves.

pulse[1] *n* **1** regular beating of blood through the arteries at each heartbeat. **2** any regular beat or vibration. **pulsate** *v* throb, quiver. **pulsation** *n*

pulse[2] *n* edible seed of a pod-bearing plant such as a bean or pea.

pulverize *v* **1** reduce to fine pieces. **2** destroy completely. **pulverization** *n*

puma *n* large American wild cat with a greyish-brown coat.

pumice [**pumm**-iss] *n* light porous stone used for scouring.

pummel *v* **-melling, -melled** strike repeatedly with or as if with the fists.

pump[1] *n* **1** machine used to force a liquid or gas to move in a particular direction. ♦ *v* **2** raise or drive with a pump. **3** supply in large amounts. **4** operate or work in the manner of a pump. **5** extract information from.

pump[2] *n* light flat-soled shoe.

pumpernickel *n* sour black bread made of coarse rye flour.

pumpkin *n* large round fruit with an orange rind, soft flesh, and many seeds.

pun *n* **1** use of words to exploit double meanings for humorous effect. ♦ *v* **punning, punned 2** make puns.

punch[1] *v* **1** strike at with a clenched fist. ♦ *n* **2** blow with a clenched fist. **3** *Informal* effectiveness or vigour. **punchy** *adj* **punchier, punchiest** forceful. **punch-drunk** *adj* dazed by or as if by repeated blows to the head. **punch line** line of a joke or funny story that gives it its point. **punch-up** *n Informal* fight or brawl.

punch[2] *n* **1** tool or machine for shaping, piercing, or engraving. ♦ *v* **2** pierce, cut, stamp, shape, or drive with a punch.

punch[3] *n* drink made from a mixture of wine, spirits, fruit, sugar, and spices.

punctilious *adj* **1** paying great attention to correctness in etiquette. **2** careful about small details.

punctual *adj* arriving or taking place at the correct time. **punctuality** *n* **punctually** *adv*

punctuate *v* **1** put punctuation marks in. **2** interrupt at frequent intervals. **punctuation** *n* (use of) marks such as commas, colons, etc. in writing, to assist in making the sense clear. **punctuation mark** any of the signs used in punctuation, such as a comma.

puncture *n* **1** small hole made by a sharp object, esp. in a tyre. ♦ *v* **2** pierce a hole in.

pundit *n* expert who speaks publicly on a subject.

pungent *adj* having a strong sharp bitter flavour. **pungency** *n*

punish *v* cause (someone) to suffer or undergo a penalty for some wrongdoing. **punishing** *adj* harsh or difficult. **punishment** *n* **punitive** [**pew**-nit-tiv] *adj* relating to punishment.

punk *n* **1** anti-Establishment youth movement and style of rock music of the late 1970s. **2** follower of this music. **3** worthless person.

punkah *n* fan made of palm leaves.

punnet *n* small basket for fruit.

punt[1] *n* **1** open flat-bottomed boat propelled by a pole. ♦ *v* **2** travel in a punt.

punt[2] *Sport* ♦ *n* **1** kick of a ball before it touches the ground when dropped from the hands. ♦ *v* **2** kick (a ball) in this way.

punt[3] *n* monetary unit of the Irish Republic.

punter *n* **1** person who bets. **2** any member of the public.

puny *adj* **-nier, -niest** small and feeble.

pup *n* young of certain animals, such as dogs and seals.

pupa [**pew**-pa] *n, pl* **-pae, -pas** insect at the stage of development between a larva and an adult. **pupal** *adj*

pupil[1] *n* person who is taught by a teacher.

pupil[2] *n* round dark opening in the centre of the eye.

puppet *n* **1** small doll or figure moved by strings or by the operator's hand. **2** person or country controlled by another. **puppeteer** *n*

puppy *n, pl* **-pies** young dog. **puppy fat** fatty tissue in a child or adolescent, usu. disappearing with maturity.

purchase *v* **1** obtain by payment. ♦ *n* **2** thing that is bought. **3** act of buying. **4** leverage, grip. **purchaser** *n*

purdah *n* Muslim and Hindu custom of keeping women in seclusion, with clothing that conceals them completely when they go out.

pure *adj* **1** unmixed, untainted. **2** innocent. **3** complete, e.g. *pure delight.* **4** concerned with theory only, e.g. *pure mathematics.* **purely** *adv* **purity** *n* **purify** *v* **-fying, -fied** make or become pure. **purification** *n* **purist** *n* person obsessed with strict obedience to the traditions of a subject.

purée [**pure**-ray] *n* **1** pulp of cooked food. ♦ *v* **-réeing, -réed 2** make into a purée.

purgatory *n* **1** place or state of temporary suffering. **2** (**P-**) *RC Church* place where souls of the dead undergo punishment for their sins before being admitted to Heaven. **purgatorial** *adj*

purge *v* **1** rid (a thing or place) of (unwanted things or people). ♦ *n* **2** purging. **purgative** *n, adj* (medicine) designed to cause defecation.

Puritan *n* **1** *Hist* member of the English Protestant group who wanted simpler church ceremonies. **2** (**p-**) person with strict moral and religious principles. **puritanical** *adj* **puritanism** *n*

purl *n* **1** stitch made by knitting a plain stitch backwards. ♦ *v* **2** knit in purl.

purlieus [**per**-lyooz] *pl n Lit* outskirts.

purloin *v* steal.

purple *adj, n* (of) a colour between red and blue.

purport *v* **1** claim (to be or do something). ♦ *n* **2** apparent meaning, significance.

purpose *n* **1** reason for which something is done or exists. **2** determination. **3** practical advantage or use, e.g. *use the time to good purpose.* **purposeful** *adj* with a definite purpose, determined. **purposely** *adv* intentionally (also **on purpose**).

purr *v* **1** (of cats) make low vibrant sound, usu. when pleased. ♦ *n* **2** this sound.

purse *n* **1** small bag for money. **2** *Chiefly US* handbag. **3** financial resources. **4** prize money. ♦ *v* **5** draw (one's lips) together into a small round shape. **purser** *n* ship's officer who keeps the accounts.

pursue *v* **1** chase. **2** follow (a goal). **3** engage in. **4** continue to discuss or ask about (something). **pursuer** *n* **pursuit** *n* **1** pursuing. **2** occupation or pastime.

purulent [**pure**-yoo-lent] *adj* of or containing pus.

purvey *v* supply (provisions). **purveyor** *n*

purview *n* scope or range of activity or outlook.

pus *n* yellowish matter produced by infected tissue.

push *v* **1** move or try to move by steady force. **2** drive or spur (oneself or another person) to do something. **3** *Informal* sell (drugs) illegally. ♦ *n* **4** act of pushing. **5** drive or determination. **6** special effort. **the push** *Slang* dismissal from a job or relationship. **pusher** *n* person who sells illegal drugs. **pushy** *adj* **pushier, pushiest** too assertive or ambitious. **push-bike** *n Informal* bicycle. **pushchair** *n* folding chair on wheels for a baby. **pushover** *n Informal* **1** something easily achieved. **2** person or team easily taken advantage of or defeated.

pusillanimous *adj* timid and cowardly. **pusillanimity** *n*

puss, pussy *n, pl* **pusses, pussies** *Informal* cat.

pussyfoot *v Informal* **1** move about stealthily. **2** behave too cautiously.

pustule *n* pimple containing pus.

put *v* **putting, put 1** cause to be (in a position, state, or place). **2** estimate or judge. **3** express. **4** throw (the shot) in the shot put. ♦ *n* **5** throw in putting the shot. **put about** *v* make widely known. **put across** *v* express successfully. **put down** *v* **1** make a written record of. **2** repress (a rebellion). **3** put (an animal) to death. **4** *Slang* belittle or humiliate. **put-down** *n* cruelly crushing remark. **put off** *v* **1** postpone. **2** evade (a person) by delay. **3** disconcert. **4** repel. **put out** *v* annoy or anger. **put over** *v Informal* communicate (facts or information). **put up** *v* **1** erect. **2** accommodate. **3** offer. **4** nominate. **put up with** *v* tolerate. **put-upon** *adj* taken advantage of.

putative [**pew**-tat-iv] *adj* reputed, supposed.

putrid *adj* rotten and foul-smelling. **putrefy** *v* **-fying, -fied** rot and produce an offensive smell. **putrefaction** *n* **putrescent** *adj* rotting.

putsch *n* sudden violent attempt to remove a government from power.

putt *Golf* ♦ *n* **1** stroke on the putting green to roll the ball into or near the hole. ♦ *v* **2** strike (the ball) in this way. **putter** *n* golf club for putting. **putting green** *Golf* area of closely mown grass around the hole.

putty *n* paste used to fix glass into frames and fill cracks in woodwork.

puzzle *v* **1** perplex and confuse or be perplexed or confused. ♦ *n* **2** problem that cannot be easily solved. **3** toy, game, or question that requires skill or ingenuity to solve. **puzzlement** *n* **puzzled** *adj* **puzzling** *adj*

PVC polyvinyl chloride: plastic material used in clothes etc.

Pygmy *n, pl* **-mies** **1** member of one of the very short peoples of Equatorial Africa. **2** (**p-**) very small person or thing. ♦ *adj* **3** (**p-**) very small.

pyjamas *pl n* loose-fitting trousers and top worn in bed.

pylon *n* steel tower-like structure supporting electrical cables.

pyorrhoea [pire-**ree**-a] *n* disease of the gums and tooth sockets which causes bleeding of the gums and the formation of pus.

pyramid *n* **1** solid figure with a flat base and triangular sides sloping upwards to a point. **2** building of this shape, esp. an ancient Egyptian one. **pyramidal** *adj*

pyre *n* pile of wood for burning a corpse on.

Pyrex *n* ® heat-resistant glassware.

pyromania *n* uncontrollable urge to set things on fire. **pyromaniac** *n*

pyrotechnics *n* **1** art of making fireworks. **2** firework display. **pyrotechnic** *adj*

Pyrrhic victory [**pir**-ik] *n* victory in which the victor's losses are as great as those of the defeated.

python *n* large nonpoisonous snake that crushes its prey.

Q q

QC Queen's Counsel.

QED which was to be shown or proved.

QLD Queensland.

QM Quartermaster.

qr. **1** quarter. **2** quire.

qt. quart.

q.t. *n* **on the q.t.** *Informal* secretly.

qua [**kwah**] *prep* in the capacity of.

quack[1] *v* **1** (of a duck) utter a harsh guttural sound. **2** make a noise like a duck. ♦ *n* **3** sound made by a duck.

quack[2] *n* **1** unqualified person who claims medical knowledge. **2** *Informal* doctor.

quad *n* **1** see QUADRANGLE (sense 1). **2** *Informal* quadruplet. ♦ *adj* **3** short for QUADRAPHONIC.

quadrangle *n* **1** (also **quad**) rectangular courtyard with buildings on all four sides. **2** geometric figure consisting of four points connected by four lines. **quadrangular** *adj*

quadrant *n* **1** quarter of a circle. **2** quarter of a circle's circumference. **3** instrument for measuring the altitude of the stars.

quadraphonic *adj* using four independent channels to reproduce or record sound.

quadratic *Maths* ♦ *n* **1** equation in which the variable is raised to the power of two, but nowhere raised to a higher power. ♦ *adj* **2** of the second power.

quadrennial *adj* **1** occurring every four years. **2** lasting four years.

quadri- *combining form* four, e.g. *quadrilateral.*

quadrilateral *adj* **1** having four sides. ♦ *n* **2** polygon with four sides.

quadrille *n* square dance for four couples.

quadriplegia *n* paralysis of all four limbs. **quadriplegic** *adj*

quadruped [**kwod**-roo-ped] *n* any animal with four legs.

quadruple *v* **1** multiply by four. ♦ *adj* **2** four times as much or as many. **3** consisting of four parts.

quadruplet *n* one of four offspring born at one birth.

quaff [**kwoff**] *v* drink heartily or in one draught.

quagga *n, pl* **-ga, -gas** recently extinct zebra, striped only on the head and shoulders.

quagmire [**kwog**-mire] *n* soft wet area of land.

quail[1] *n, pl* **quail, quails** small game bird of the partridge family.

quail[2] *v* shrink back with fear.

quaint *adj* attractively unusual, esp. in an old-fashioned style. **quaintly** *adv*

quake *v* **1** shake or tremble with or as if with fear. ♦ *n* **2** *Informal* earthquake.

Quaker *n* member of a Christian sect, the Society of Friends. **Quakerism** *n*

qualify *v* **-fying, -fied** **1** provide or be provided with the abilities necessary for a task, office, or duty. **2** moderate or restrict (a statement). **3** be classified as, e.g. *their romance hardly qualifies as news.* **4** reach the later stages of a competition, as by being successful in earlier rounds. **5** *Grammar* modify the sense of a word. **qualified** *adj* **qualifier** *n* **qualification** *n* **1** official record of achievement in a course or examination. **2** quality or skill needed for a particular activity. **3** condition that modifies or limits. **4** act of qualifying.

quality *n, pl* **-ties** **1** degree or standard of excellence. **2** distinguishing characteristic or attribute. **3** basic character or nature of something. ♦ *adj* **4** excellent or superior. **5** (of a newspaper) concentrating on detailed and serious accounts of the news, business affairs and the arts. **qualitative** *adj* of or relating to quality. **quality control** checking of the relative quality of products, usu. by testing samples.

qualm [**kwahm**] *n* **1** pang of conscience. **2** sudden sensation of misgiving.

quandary *n, pl* **-ries** difficult situation or dilemma.

quango *n, pl* **-gos** quasi-autonomous nongovernmental organization: any partly independent official body set up by a government.

quanta *n* plural of QUANTUM.

quantify *v* **-fying, -fied** discover or express the quantity of. **quantifiable** *adj* **quantification** *n*

quantity *n, pl* **-ties** **1** specified or definite amount or number. **2** aspect of anything that can be measured, weighed, or counted. **3** large amount. **quantitative** *adj* of or relating to quantity. **quantity surveyor** person who estimates the cost of the materials and labour necessary for a construction job.

quantum *n, pl* **-ta** **1** desired or required amount, esp. a very small one. **2** *Physics* smallest amount of some physical property, such as energy, that a system can possess. **quantum leap, jump** *Informal* sudden large change, increase, or advance. **quantum theory** physics theory based on the idea that energy of electrons is discharged in discrete quanta.

quarantine *n* **1** period of isolation of people or animals to prevent the spread of disease. ♦ *v* **2** isolate in or as if in quarantine.

quark *n Physics* subatomic particle thought to be the fundamental unit of matter.

quarrel *n* **1** angry disagreement. **2** cause of dispute. ♦ *v* **-relling, -relled** **3** have a disagreement or dispute. **quarrelsome** *adj*

quarry[1] *n, pl* **-ries** **1** place where stone is dug from the surface of the earth. ♦ *v* **-rying, -ried** **2** extract (stone) from a quarry.

quarry[2] *n, pl* **-ries** person or animal that is being hunted.

quart *n* unit of liquid measure equal to two pints.

quarter *n* **1** one of four equal parts of something. **2** fourth part of a year. **3** *Informal* unit of weight equal to 4 ounces. **4** region or district of a town or city. **5** *US* 25-cent piece. **6** mercy or pity, as shown towards a defeated opponent. **7** either of two phases of the moon when it appears as a semicircle. **8** (sometimes pl) unspecified people or group of people, e.g. *the highest quarters.* ♦ *pl* **9** lodgings. ♦ *v* **10** divide into four equal parts. **11** billet or be billeted in lodgings. **quarterly** *adj* **1** occurring, due, or issued at intervals of three months. ♦ *n, pl* **-lies** **2** magazine issued every three months. ♦ *adv* **3** once every three months. **quarterback** *n* player in American football who directs attacking play. **quarter day** any of the four days in the year when certain payments become due. **quarterdeck** *n Naut* rear part of the upper deck of a ship. **quarterfinal** *n* round before the semifinal in a competition. **quarterlight** *n* small triangular window in the door of a car. **quartermaster** *n* military officer responsible for accommodation, food, and equipment.

quartet *n* **1** group of four performers. **2** music for such a group. **3** any group of four people or things.

quarto *n, pl* **-tos** book size in which the sheets are folded into four leaves.

quartz *n* hard glossy mineral. **quartz clock, watch** very accurate clock *or* watch operated by a vibrating crystal of quartz.

quasar [**kway**-zar] *n* extremely distant starlike object that emits powerful radio waves.

quash *v* **1** annul or make void. **2** subdue forcefully and completely.

quasi- [**kway**-zie] *combining form* almost but not really, e.g. *quasi-religious; a quasi-scholar.*

quassia [**kwosh**-a] *n* tropical American tree, the wood of which yields a substance used in insecticides.

quaternary *adj* having four parts.

quatrain *n* stanza or poem of four lines.

quatrefoil *n* **1** leaf composed of four leaflets. **2** *Archit* carved ornament having four arcs arranged about a common centre.

quaver *v* **1** (of a voice) quiver or tremble. ♦ *n* **2** *Music* note half the length of a crotchet. **3** tremulous sound or note.

quay [**kee**] *n* wharf built parallel to the shore.

queasy *adj* **-sier, -siest 1** having the feeling that one is about to vomit. **2** feeling or causing uneasiness. **queasily** *adv* **queasiness** *n*

queen *n* **1** female sovereign who is the official ruler or head of state. **2** wife of a king. **3** woman, place, or thing considered to be the best of her or its kind. **4** *Slang* effeminate male homosexual. **5** only fertile female in a colony of bees, wasps, or ants. **6** the most powerful piece in chess. **queen it** *Informal* behave in an overbearing manner. **queenly** *adj* **Queen Mother** widow of a former king who is also the mother of the current monarch. **Queen's Counsel** barrister or advocate appointed Counsel to the Crown.

Queensberry rules *pl n* **1** code of rules followed in modern boxing. **2** *Informal* gentlemanly conduct, esp. in a dispute.

queer *adj* **1** not normal or usual. **2** dubious or suspicious. **3** faint, giddy, or queasy. **4** *Offens* homosexual. ♦ *n* **5** *Offens* homosexual. **queer someone's pitch** *Informal* spoil someone's chances of something. **in queer street** *Informal* in debt or facing bankruptcy.

> Although the term *queer* meaning homosexual is still considered derogatory when used by non-homosexuals, it is now being used by homosexuals of themselves as a positive term: *queer politics, queer cinema.*

quell *v* **1** suppress. **2** overcome.

quench *v* **1** satisfy (one's thirst). **2** put out or extinguish.

quern *n* stone hand mill for grinding corn.

querulous [**kwer**-yoo-luss] *adj* complaining or whining. **querulously** *adv*

query *n, pl* **-ries 1** question, esp. one raising doubt. **2** question mark. ♦ *v* **-rying, -ried 3** express uncertainty, doubt, or an objection concerning (something).

quest *n* **1** long and difficult search. ♦ *v* **2** (foll. by *for* or *after*) go in search of.

question *n* **1** form of words addressed to a person in order to obtain an answer. **2** point at issue. **3** difficulty or uncertainty. ♦ *v* **4** put a question or questions to (a person). **5** express uncertainty about. **in question** under discussion. **out of the question** impossible. **questionable** *adj* of disputable value or authority. **questionably** *adv* **questionnaire** *n* set of questions on a form, used to collect information from people. **question mark 1** punctuation mark (?) written at the end of questions. **2** a doubt or uncertainty, e.g. *a question mark still hangs over their success.* **question master** chairman of a radio or television quiz or panel game. **question time** (in a parliament) period when MPs can question government ministers.

queue *n* **1** line of people or vehicles waiting for something. ♦ *v* **queuing** *or* **queueing, queued 2** (often foll. by *up*) form or remain in a line while waiting.

quibble *v* **1** make trivial objections. ♦ *n* **2** trivial objection.

quiche [**keesh**] *n* savoury flan with an egg custard filling to which vegetables etc. are added.

quick *adj* **1** speedy, fast. **2** lasting or taking a short time. **3** alert and responsive. **4** easily excited or aroused. ♦ *n* **5** area of sensitive flesh under a nail. ♦ *adv* **6** *Informal* in a rapid manner. **cut someone to the quick** hurt someone's feelings deeply. **quickly** *adv* **quicken** *v* **1** make or become faster. **2** make or become more lively. **3** (of a fetus) reach the stage of development where its movements can be felt. **quickie** *n Informal* anything done or made hurriedly. **quicklime** *n* white solid used in the manufacture of glass and steel. **quicksand** *n* deep mass of loose wet sand that sucks anything on top of it into it. **quicksilver** *n* mercury. **quickstep** *n* fast modern ballroom dance.

quid[1] *n, pl* **quid** *Brit slang* pound (sterling).

quid[2] *n* piece of tobacco for chewing.

quid pro quo *n, pl* **quid pro quos** one thing, esp. an advantage or object, given in exchange for another.

quiescent [kwee-**ess**-ent] *adj* quiet, inactive, or dormant. **quiescence** *n*

quiet *adj* **1** with little noise. **2** calm or tranquil. **3** untroubled. **4** private or low-key. ♦ *n* **5** quietness. ♦ *v* **6** make or become quiet. **on the quiet** without other people knowing, secretly. **quietly** *adv* **quietness** *n* **quieten** *v* (often foll. by *down*) make or become quiet. **quietude** *n* quietness, peace, or tranquillity.

quietism *n* passivity and calmness of mind towards external events. **quietist** *n, adj*

quietus *n* **1** release from life; death. **2** discharge or settlement of debts or duties.

quiff *n* tuft of hair brushed up above the forehead.

quill *n* **1** pen made from the feather of a bird's wing or tail. **2** stiff hollow spine of a hedgehog or porcupine. **3** large stiff feather in a bird's wing or tail.

quilt *n* padded covering for a bed. **quilted** *adj* consisting of two layers of fabric with a layer of soft material between them.

quin *n* short for QUINTUPLET.

quince *n* acid-tasting pear-shaped fruit.

quinine *n* bitter drug used as a tonic and formerly to treat malaria.

quinquennial *adj* **1** occurring every five years. **2** lasting five years.

quinquereme *n* ancient Roman galley with five banks of oars.

quinsy *n* inflammation of the throat or tonsils.

quintessence *n* most perfect representation of a quality or state. **quintessential** *adj*

quintet *n* **1** group of five performers. **2** music for such a group.

quintuple *v* **1** multiply by five. ♦ *adj* **2** five times as much or as many. **3** consisting of five parts. ♦ *n* **4** quantity or number five times as great as another.

quintuplet *n* one of five offspring born at one birth.

quip *n* **1** witty saying. ♦ *v* **quipping, quipped** **2** make a quip.

quire *n* set of 24 or 25 sheets of paper.

quirk *n* **1** peculiarity of character. **2** unexpected twist or turn, e.g. *a quirk of fate.* **quirky** *adj* **quirkier, quirkiest**

quisling *n* traitor who aids an occupying enemy force.

quit *v* **quitting, quit** **1** stop (doing something). **2** give up (a job). **3** depart from. **quitter** *n* person who lacks perseverance. **quits** *adj Informal* on an equal footing.

quite *adv* **1** somewhat, e.g. *she's quite pretty.* **2** absolutely, e.g. *you're quite right.* **3** in actuality, truly. ♦ *interj* **4** expression of agreement.

> Note that because *quite* can mean 'extremely': *quite amazing;* or can express a reservation: *quite friendly,* it should be used carefully.

quiver[1] *v* **1** shake with a tremulous movement. ♦ *n* **2** shaking or trembling.

quiver[2] *n* case for arrows.

quixotic [kwik-**sot**-ik] *adj* romantic and unrealistic. **quixotically** *adv*

quiz *n, pl* **quizzes** **1** entertainment in which the knowledge of the players is tested by a series of questions. ♦ *v* **quizzing, quizzed** **2** investigate by close questioning. **quizzical** *adj* questioning and mocking, e.g. *a quizzical look.* **quizzically** *adv*

quod *n Brit slang* jail.

quoin *n* **1** external corner of a building. **2** small wedge.

quoit *n* **1** large ring used in the game of quoits. ♦ *pl* **2** game in which quoits are tossed at a stake in the ground in attempts to encircle it.

quondam *adj Formal* of an earlier time;

former.

quorum *n* minimum number of people required to be present at a meeting before any transactions can take place. **quorate** *adj* having or being a quorum.

quota *n* **1** share that is due from, due to, or allocated to a group or person. **2** prescribed number or quantity allowed, required, or admitted.

quote *v* **1** repeat (words) exactly from (an earlier work, speech, or conversation). **2** state (a price) for goods or a job of work. ♦ *n* **3** *Informal* quotation. **quotable** *adj* **quotation** *n* **1** written or spoken passage repeated exactly in a later work, speech, or conversation. **2** act of quoting. **3** estimate of costs submitted by a contractor to a prospective client. **quotation marks** raised commas used in writing to mark the beginning and end of a quotation or passage of speech.

quoth *v Obs* said.

quotidian *adj* **1** daily. **2** commonplace.

quotient *n* result of the division of one number or quantity by another.

Quran *n* same as KORAN.

q.v. which see: used to refer a reader to another item in the same book.

qwerty, QWERTY keyboard *n* standard English language typewriter or computer keyboard.

R r

r **1** radius. **2** ratio. **3** right.

R **1** Queen. **2** King. **3** River.

Ra *Chem* radium.

RA **1** Royal Academy. **2** Royal Artillery.

rabbi [**rab**-bye] *n, pl* **-bis** Jewish spiritual leader. **rabbinical** *adj*

rabbit *n* small burrowing mammal with long ears. **rabbit on** *v* **rabbiting, rabbited** *Informal* talk too much.

rabble *n* disorderly crowd of noisy people. **rabble-rouser** *n* person who stirs up the feelings of the mob.

Rabelaisian *adj* characterized by broad, often bawdy humour and sharp satire.

rabid *adj* **1** fanatical. **2** having rabies. **rabidly** *adv*

rabies [**ray**-beez] *n* usu. fatal viral disease transmitted by dogs and certain other animals.

RAC Royal Automobile Club.

raccoon *n* small N American mammal with a long striped tail.

race[1] *n* **1** contest of speed. **2** any competition or rivalry, e.g. *the arms race.* **3** rapid current or channel. ♦ *pl* **4** meeting for horse racing. ♦ *v* **5** compete with in a race. **6** run swiftly. **7** (of an engine) run faster than normal. **racer** *n* **racecourse** *n* **racehorse** *n* **racetrack** *n*

race[2] *n* group of people of common ancestry with distinguishing physical features, such as skin colour. **racial** *adj* **racism, racialism** *n* hostile attitude or behaviour to members of other races, based on a belief in the innate superiority of one's own race. **racist, racialist** *adj, n*

raceme [rass-**eem**] *n* cluster of flowers along a central stem, as in the foxglove.

rack[1] *n* **1** framework for holding particular articles, such as coats or luggage. **2** straight bar with teeth on its edge, to work with a cogwheel. **3** *Hist* instrument of torture that stretched the victim's body. ♦ *v* **4** cause great suffering to. **rack one's brains** try very hard to remember.

rack[2] *n* **go to rack and ruin** be destroyed.

racket[1] *n* **1** noisy disturbance. **2** occupation by which money is made illegally. **3** *Slang* business or occupation. ♦ *v* **-eting, -eted** **4** (often foll. by *about* or *around*) make a commotion.

racket[2], **racquet** *n* bat with strings stretched in an oval frame, used in tennis etc. **rackets** *n* ball game played in a paved walled court.

racketeer *n* person making illegal profits. **racketeering** *n*

raconteur [rak-on-**tur**] *n* skilled storyteller.

racoon *n* same as RACCOON.

racy *adj* **racier, raciest** **1** slightly shocking. **2** spirited or lively. **racily** *adv*

radar *n* device for tracking distant objects by bouncing high-frequency radio pulses off them.

raddled *adj* (of a person) unkempt or run-down in appearance.

radial *adj* **1** spreading out from a common central point. **2** of a radius. **3** (also **radial-ply**) (of a tyre) having flexible sides strengthened with radial cords.

radian *n* unit for measuring angles, equal to 57.296°.

radiant *adj* **1** looking happy. **2** shining. **3** emitted as radiation, e.g. *radiant heat.* **4** emitting radiation. **radiantly** *adv* **radiance** *n*

radiate *v* **1** spread out from a centre. **2** show (an emotion or quality) to a great degree. **3** emit or be emitted as radiation. **radiator** *n* **1** arrangement of pipes containing hot water or steam to heat a room. **2** tubes containing water as cooling apparatus for a car engine.

radiation *n* **1** transmission of energy from one body to another. **2** particles or waves emitted in nuclear decay. **3** process of radiating. **radiation sickness** illness caused by overexposure to radioactive material or x-rays.

radical *adj* **1** fundamental. **2** thorough. **3** advocating fundamental change. ♦ *n* **4** person advocating fundamental (political) change. **5** number expressed as the root of another. **6** group of atoms which acts as a unit during chemical reactions. **radically** *adv* **radicalism** *n*

radicle *n* small or developing root.

radii *n* a plural of RADIUS.

radio *n, pl* **-dios 1** use of electromagnetic waves for broadcasting, communication, etc. **2** device for receiving and amplifying radio signals. **3** communications device for sending and receiving messages using radio waves. **4** sound broadcasting. ♦ *v* **5** transmit (a message) by radio. ♦ *adj* **6** of, relating to, or using radio, e.g. *radio drama.* **radio-controlled** *adj* controlled by signals sent by radio. **radio telephone** telephone which sends and receives messages using radio waves rather than wires. **radio telescope** instrument which picks up and analyses radio signals from space.

radio- *combining form* of radio, radiation, or radioactivity.

radioactive *adj* emitting radiation as a result of nuclear decay. **radioactivity** *n*

radiocarbon *n* radioactive form of carbon used in calculating the age of very old objects.

radiography [ray-dee-**og**-ra-fee] *n* production of an image on a film or plate by radiation. **radiographer** *n*

radioisotope *n* radioactive isotope.

radiology [ray-dee-**ol**-a-jee] *n* science of using x-rays in medicine. **radiologist** *n*

radiotherapy *n* treatment of disease, esp. cancer, by radiation. **radiotherapist** *n*

radish *n* small hot-flavoured root vegetable eaten raw in salads.

radium *n Chem* radioactive metallic element.

radius *n, pl* **radii, radiuses 1** (length of) a straight line from the centre to the circumference of a circle. **2** outer of two bones in the forearm. **3** circular area of a specified size round a central point, e.g. *everyone within a two-mile radius.*

radon [**ray**-don] *n Chem* radioactive gaseous element.

RAF Royal Air Force.

raffia *n* prepared palm fibre for weaving mats etc.

raffish *adj* slightly disreputable.

raffle *n* **1** lottery with goods as prizes. ♦ *v* **2** offer as a prize in a raffle.

raft *n* floating platform of logs, planks, etc.

rafter *n* one of the main beams of a roof.

rag[1] *n* **1** fragment of cloth. **2** *Informal* newspaper. ♦ *pl* **3** tattered clothing. **from rags to riches** from being extremely poor to being extremely wealthy. **ragged** [**rag**-gid] *adj* **1** dressed in shabby or torn clothes. **2** torn. **3** lacking smoothness. **ragbag** *n* confused assortment, jumble.

rag[2] *v* **ragging, ragged 1** tease. **2** play practical jokes on. ♦ *adj, n* **3** (of) events organized by students to raise money for charities.

ragamuffin *n* ragged dirty child.

rage *n* **1** violent anger or passion. ♦ *v* **2** speak or act with fury. **3** proceed violently and without check, e.g. *a storm was raging.* **all the rage** very popular.

raglan *adj* (of a sleeve) joined to a garment by diagonal seams from the neck to the underarm.

ragout [rag-**goo**] *n* richly seasoned stew of meat and vegetables.

ragtime *n* style of jazz piano music.

raid *n* **1** sudden surprise attack or search. ♦ *v* **2** make a raid on. **3** sneak into (a place) in order to steal. **raider** *n*

rail[1] *n* **1** horizontal bar, esp. as part of a fence or track. **2** railway. **go off the rails** start behaving eccentrically or improperly. **railing** *n* fence made of rails supported by posts. **railcard** *n* card which pensioners, young people, etc. can buy, entitling them to cheaper rail travel. **railroad** *n* **1** *US* railway. ♦ *v* **2** *Informal* force (a person) into an action with haste or by unfair means. **railway** *n* **1** track of iron rails on which trains run. **2** company operating a railway.

rail[2] *v* (foll. by *at* or *against*) complain bitterly or loudly. **raillery** *n* teasing or joking.

rail[3] *n* small marsh bird.

raiment *n Obs* clothing.

rain *n* **1** water falling in drops from the clouds. **2** large quantity of anything falling rapidly. ♦ *v* **3** fall or pour down as rain. **4** fall rapidly and in large quantities. **the rains** season in the tropics when there is a lot of rain. **rainy** *adj* **rainy day** future time of need, esp. financial need. **rainbow** *n* arch of colours in the sky. **rainbow trout** freshwater trout with black spots and two red stripes. **raincoat** *n* water-resistant overcoat. **rainfall** *n* amount of rain. **rainforest** *n* dense forest in the tropics.

raise *v* **1** lift up. **2** set upright. **3** increase in amount or intensity. **4** collect or levy. **5** bring up (a family). **6** grow (a crop). **7** put forward for consideration. **8** build. **9** end, e.g. *raise a siege.* ♦ *n* **10** *US* increase in pay. **raised** *adj* higher than the surrounding area.

raisin *n* dried grape.

raison d'être [**ray**-zon **det**-ra] *n, pl* **raisons d'être** [**ray**-zon **det**-ra] *French* reason or justification for existence.

raita [**rye**-ta] *n* Indian dish of chopped cucumber, mint, etc., in yogurt, served with curries.

Raj *n* **the Raj** former British rule in India.

raja, rajah *n Hist* Indian prince or ruler.

rake[1] *n* **1** tool with a long handle and a crosspiece with teeth, used for smoothing earth or gathering leaves, hay, etc. ♦ *v* **2** gather or smooth with a rake. **3** search (through). **4** sweep (with gunfire). **rake it in** *Informal* make a large amount of money. **rake-off** *n Slang* share of profits, esp. illegal. **rake up** *v* revive memories of (a forgotten unpleasant event).

rake[2] *n* dissolute or immoral man. **rakish** *adj*

rake[3] *n* **1** slope, esp. backwards, of an object. ♦ *v* **2** slope from the vertical. **raked** *adj* (of a surface) sloping so that it is higher at the back than the front.

rakish [**ray**-kish] *adj* dashing or jaunty.

rally *n, pl* **-lies** **1** large gathering of people for a meeting. **2** marked recovery of strength. **3** *Tennis etc.* lively exchange of strokes. **4** car-driving competition on public roads. ♦ *v* **-lying, -lied** **5** bring or come together after dispersal or for a common cause. **6** regain health or strength, revive. **rally round** *v* group together to help someone.

ram *n* **1** male sheep. **2** hydraulic machine. ♦ *v* **ramming, rammed** **3** strike against with force. **4** force or drive. **5** cram or stuff. **ram (something) down someone's throat** put forward or emphasize (an idea or argument) with excessive force. **ram raid** *Informal* raid on a shop in which a stolen car is driven into the window. **ram raider**

RAM *Computers* random access memory.

Ramadan *n* **1** 9th Muslim month. **2** strict fasting from dawn to dusk observed during this time.

ramble *v* **1** walk without a definite route. **2** talk incoherently. ♦ *n* **3** walk, esp. in the country. **rambler** *n* **1** person who rambles. **2** climbing rose. **rambling** *adj* **1** large and irregularly shaped. **2** (of speech or writing) confused and long-winded. ♦ *n* **3** activity of going for long walks in the country.

ramekin [**ram**-ik-in] *n* small ovenproof dish for a single serving of food.

ramifications *pl n* consequences resulting from an action.

ramp *n* **1** slope joining two level surfaces. **2** place where the level of a road surface changes because of road works. **3** mobile stairs by which passengers enter or leave an aircraft.

rampage *v* dash about violently. **on the rampage** behaving violently or destructively.

rampant *adj* **1** growing or spreading uncontrollably. **2** (of a heraldic beast) on its hind legs.

rampart *n* mound or wall for defence.

ramrod *n* **1** long thin rod used for cleaning the barrel of a gun or forcing gunpowder into an old-fashioned gun. ♦ *adj* **2** (of someone's posture) very straight and upright.

ramshackle *adj* tumbledown, rickety, or makeshift.

ran *v* past tense of RUN.

ranch *n* large cattle farm in the American West. **rancher** *n*

rancid *adj* (of butter, bacon, etc.) stale and having an offensive smell. **rancidity** *n*

rancour *n* deep bitter hate. **rancorous** *adj*

rand *n* monetary unit of S Africa.

R & B rhythm and blues.

R & D research and development.

random *adj* made or done by chance or without plan. **at random** haphazard(ly). **randomly** *adv*

randy *adj* **randier, randiest** *Informal* sexually aroused. **randiness** *n*

ranee *n* same as RANI.

rang *v* past tense of RING[1].

range *n* **1** limits of effectiveness or variation. **2** distance that a missile or plane can travel. **3** distance of a mark shot at. **4** difference in pitch between the highest and lowest note a voice or instrument can make. **5** whole set of related things. **6** chain of mountains. **7** place for shooting practice or rocket testing. **8** kitchen stove. ♦ *v* **9** vary between one point and another. **10** cover or extend over. **11** roam. **ranger** *n* **1** official in charge of a nature reserve etc. **2** (**R-**) member of the senior branch of Guides. **rangefinder** *n* instrument for finding how far away an object is.

rangy [**rain**-jee] *adj* **rangier, rangiest** having long slender limbs.

rani *n* wife or widow of a rajah.

rank[1] *n* **1** relative place or position. **2** status. **3** social class. **4** row or line. **5** *Brit* place where taxis wait to be hired. ♦ *v* **6** have a specific rank or position. **7** arrange in rows or lines. **rank and file** ordinary people or members. **the ranks** common soldiers.

rank[2] *adj* **1** complete or absolute, e.g. *rank favouritism.* **2** smelling offensively strong. **3** growing too thickly.

rankle *v* continue to cause resentment or bitterness.

ransack *v* **1** search thoroughly. **2** pillage, plunder.

ransom *n* **1** money demanded in return for the release of someone who has been kidnapped. ♦ *v* **2** pay money to obtain the release of a captive. **3** release a captive in return for money.

rant *v* talk in a loud and excited way. **ranter** *n* **ranting** *n, adj*

ranunculus *n, pl* **-luses, -li** genus of plants including the buttercup.

rap *v* **rapping, rapped 1** hit with a sharp quick blow. **2** utter (a command) abruptly. **3** perform a rhythmic monologue with musical backing. ♦ *n* **4** quick sharp blow. **5** rhythmic monologue performed to music. **take the rap** *Slang* suffer punishment for something whether guilty or not. **rapper** *n*

rapacious *adj* greedy or grasping. **rapacity** *n*

rape[1] *v* **1** force to submit to sexual intercourse. ♦ *n* **2** act of raping. **3** any violation or abuse. **rapist** *n*

rape[2] *n* plant with oil-yielding seeds, also used as fodder.

rapid *adj* quick, swift. **rapids** *pl n* part of a river with a fast turbulent current. **rapidly** *adv* **rapidity** *n*

rapier [**ray**-pyer] *n* fine-bladed sword.

rapine [**rap**-pine] *n* pillage or plundering.

rapport [rap-**pore**] *n* harmony or agreement.

rapprochement [rap-**prosh**-mong] *n* re-establishment of friendly relations, esp. between nations.

rapscallion *n* *Old-fashioned* rascal or rogue.

rapt *adj* engrossed or spellbound. **rapture** *n* ecstasy. **rapturous** *adj*

raptor *n* any bird of prey. **raptorial** *adj*

rare[1] *adj* **1** uncommon. **2** infrequent. **3** of uncommonly high quality. **4** (of air at high altitudes) having low density, thin. **rarely** *adv* seldom. **rarity** *n, pl* **-ities**

rare[2] *adj* (of meat) lightly cooked.

rarebit *n* see WELSH RAREBIT.

rarefied [**rare**-if-ide] *adj* **1** highly specialized, exalted. **2** (of air) thin.

raring *adj* **raring to** enthusiastic, willing, or ready to.

rascal *n* **1** rogue. **2** naughty (young) person. **rascally** *adj*

rase *v* same as RAZE.

rash[1] *adj* hasty, reckless, or incautious. **rashly** *adv*

rash[2] *n* **1** eruption of spots or patches on the skin. **2** outbreak of (unpleasant) occurrences.

rasher *n* thin slice of bacon.

rasp *n* **1** harsh grating noise. **2** coarse file. ♦ *v* **3** speak in a grating voice. **4** make a scraping noise.

raspberry *n* **1** red juicy edible berry. **2** *Informal* spluttering noise made with the tongue and lips, to show contempt.

Rastafarian *n, adj* (member) of a religion originating in Jamaica and regarding Haile Selassie as God (also **Rasta**).

rat *n* **1** small rodent. **2** *Informal* contemptible person, esp. a deserter or informer. ♦ *v* **ratting, ratted 3** *Informal* inform (on). **4** hunt rats. **smell a rat** detect something suspicious. **ratty** *adj* **-tier, -tiest** *Informal* bad-tempered, irritable. **rat race** continual hectic competitive activity.

ratafia [rat-a-**fee**-a] *n* **1** liqueur made from fruit. **2** almond-flavoured biscuit.

ratatouille [rat-a-**twee**] *n* vegetable casserole of tomatoes, aubergines, etc.

ratchet *n* set of teeth on a bar or wheel allowing motion in one direction only.

rate[1] *n* **1** degree of speed or progress. **2** proportion between two things. **3** charge. ♦ *pl* **4** local tax on business. **5** (in Australia and formerly in Britain) local tax on domestic property. ♦ *v* **6** consider or value. **7** estimate the value of. **8** be worthy of, deserve. **at any rate** in any case. **rateable** *adj* **1** able to be rated. **2** (of property) liable to payment of rates. **ratepayer** *n*

rate[2] *v* scold or criticize severely.

rather *adv* **1** to some extent. **2** more truly or appropriately. **3** more willingly.

ratify *v* **-fying, -fied** give formal approval to. **ratification** *n*

rating *n* **1** valuation or assessment. **2** classification. **3** noncommissioned sailor. ♦ *pl* **4** size of the audience for a TV programme.

ratio *n, pl* **-tios** relationship between two numbers or amounts expressed as a proportion.

ration *n* **1** fixed allowance of food etc. ♦ *v* **2** limit to a certain amount per person. **3** (often foll. by *out*) distribute a fixed amount of food etc. to each person in a group.

rational *adj* **1** reasonable, sensible. **2** capable of reasoning. **3** *Maths* (of a number) able to be expressed as a ratio of two integers. **rationally** *adv* **rationality** *n* **rationale** [rash-a-**nahl**] *n* reason for an action or decision. **rationalism** *n* philosophy that regards reason as the only basis for beliefs or actions. **rationalist** *n, adj* **rationalistic** *adj* **rationalize** *v* **1** justify by plausible reasoning. **2** reorganize to improve efficiency or profitability. **rationalization** *n*

rattan *n* climbing palm with jointed stems used for canes.

rattle *v* **1** give out a succession of short sharp sounds. **2** send, move or drive with such a sound. **3** shake briskly causing sharp sounds. **4** *Informal* confuse or fluster. **5** (often foll. by *off* or *out*) recite perfunctorily or rapidly. **6** (often foll. by *on* or *away*) talk quickly and at length about something unimportant. ♦ *n* **7** short sharp sound. **8** instrument for making such a sound. **rattling** *adv* **1** *Informal, old-fashioned* exceptionally, very. ♦ *n* **2** succession of short sharp sounds. **rattlesnake** *n* poisonous snake with loose horny segments on the tail that make a rattling sound. **rattle through** *v* do very quickly.

raucous *adj* hoarse or harsh.

raunchy *adj* **-chier, -chiest** *Slang* earthy, sexy.

ravage *v* cause extensive damage to. **ravages** *pl n* damaging effects.

rave *v* **1** talk wildly or with enthusiasm. ♦ *n* **2** *Informal* enthusiastically good review. **3** *Slang* large-scale party with electronic dance music. **raving** *adj* **1** delirious. **2** *Informal* exceptional, e.g. *a raving beauty.*

ravel *v* **-elling, -elled** tangle or become entangled.

raven *n* **1** black bird like a large crow. ♦ *adj* **2** (of hair) shiny black.

ravening *adj* (of animals) hungrily searching for prey.

ravenous *adj* very hungry.

ravine [rav-**veen**] *n* narrow steep-sided valley worn by a stream.

ravioli *pl n* small squares of pasta with a savoury filling.

ravish *v* **1** enrapture. **2** *Lit* rape. **ravishing** *adj* lovely or entrancing.

raw *adj* **1** uncooked. **2** not manufactured or refined. **3** (of the skin or a wound) painful, with the surface scraped away. **4** inexperienced, e.g. *raw recruits.* **5** chilly. **raw deal** unfair or dishonest treatment. **rawhide** *n* untanned hide.

ray[1] *n* **1** single line or narrow beam of light. **2** any of a set of radiating lines. **3** slight indication of something desirable, e.g. *a ray of hope.*

ray[2] *n* large sea fish with a flat body and a whiplike tail.

ray[3] *n Music* (in tonic sol-fa) second note of any major scale.

rayon *n* (fabric made of) a synthetic fibre.

raze *v* destroy (buildings or a town) completely.

razor *n* sharp instrument for shaving. **razorbill** *n* sea bird with a stout sideways flattened bill. **razor shell** (burrowing shellfish with) a long narrow shell. **razor wire** strong wire with pieces of sharp metal set across it at intervals.

razzle-dazzle, razzmatazz *n Slang* showy activity.

Rb *Chem* rubidium.

RC **1** Roman Catholic. **2** Red Cross.

Rd Road.

re[1] *prep* with reference to, concerning.

> In commercial correspondence the use of *re* is becoming less frequent in favour of *with reference to* or *about*.

re[2] *n* same as RAY[3].

Re *Chem* rhenium.

RE religious education.

re- *prefix* again, e.g. *re-enter; retrial.*

reach *v* **1** arrive at. **2** make a movement in order to grasp or touch. **3** succeed in touching. **4** make contact or communication with. **5** extend as far as. ♦ *n* **6** distance that one can reach. **7** range of influence. ♦ *pl* **8** stretch of a river. **reachable** *adj*

react *v* **1** act in response (to). **2** (foll. by *against*) act in an opposing or contrary manner. **3** undergo a chemical reaction. **reaction** *n* **1** physical or emotional response to a stimulus. **2** any action resisting another. **3** opposition to change. **4** chemical or nuclear change, combination, or decomposition. **reactionary** *n, pl* **-aries,** *adj* (person) opposed to change, esp. in politics. **reactance** *n Electricity* resistance to the flow of an alternating current caused by the inductance or capacitance of the circuit. **reactive** *adj* chemically active. **reactor** *n* apparatus in which a nuclear reaction is maintained and controlled to produce nuclear energy.

read *v* **reading, read** **1** look at and understand or take in (written or printed matter). **2** look at and say aloud. **3** have a certain wording, e.g. *the statement reads as follows.* **4** interpret the significance or meaning of. **5** (of an instrument) register. **6** make out the true mood of. **7** study. ♦ *n* **8** matter suitable for reading, e.g. *a good read.* **9** spell of reading. **readable** *adj* **1** enjoyable to read. **2** legible. **reader** *n* **1** person who reads. **2** textbook. **3** senior university lecturer. **readership** *n* readers of a publication collectively. **reading** *n*

readjust *v* adapt to a new situation. **readjustment** *n*

readmit *v* **-mitting, -mitted** let (a person, country, etc.) back in to a place or organization.

ready *adj* **readier, readiest** **1** prepared

for use or action. **2** willing, prompt. **readily** *adv* **readiness** *n* **ready-made** *adj* for immediate use by any customer. **ready money, the ready, the readies** *Informal* cash for immediate use.

reaffirm *v* state again, confirm. **reaffirmation** *n*

reafforest *v* plant new trees in (an area that was formerly forested). **reafforestation** *n*

reagent [ree-**age**-ent] *n* chemical substance that reacts with another, used to detect the presence of the other.

real *adj* **1** existing in fact. **2** actual. **3** genuine. **really** *adv* **1** very. **2** truly. ♦ *interj* **3** exclamation of dismay, doubt, or surprise. **reality** *n* state of things as they are. **real ale** beer allowed to ferment in the barrel. **real estate** property consisting of land and houses. **real number** any rational or irrational number. **real tennis** old form of tennis played in a four-walled indoor court. **real-time** *adj* (of a computer system) processing data as it is received.

> To intensify an adjective, use the adverb form *really*, not *real: He's really strong.*

realistic *adj* seeing and accepting things as they really are, practical. **realistically** *adv* **realism** *n* **1** awareness or acceptance of things as they are. **2** style in art or literature that attempts to portray the world as it really is. **realist** *n*

realize *v* **1** become aware or grasp the significance of. **2** achieve (a plan, hopes, etc.). **3** convert into money. **realization** *n*

realm *n* **1** kingdom. **2** sphere of interest.

ream *n* **1** twenty quires of paper, generally 500 sheets. ♦ *pl* **2** *Informal* large quantity (of written matter).

reap *v* **1** cut and gather (a harvest). **2** receive as the result of a previous activity. **reaper** *n*

reappear *v* appear again. **reappearance** *n*

reappraise *v* consider or review to see if changes are needed. **reappraisal** *n*

rear[1] *n* **1** back part. **2** part of an army, procession, etc. behind the others. **bring up the rear** come last. **rearmost** *adj* **rearward** *adj, adv* **rear admiral** high-ranking naval officer. **rearguard** *n* troops protecting the rear of an army. **rear-view mirror** mirror inside a vehicle which allows the driver to see out of the rear window.

rear[2] *v* **1** care for and educate (children). **2** breed (animals). **3** (of a horse) rise on its hind feet.

rearm *v* **1** arm again. **2** equip with better weapons. **rearmament** *n*

rearrange *v* organize differently, alter. **rearrangement** *n*

reason *n* **1** cause or motive. **2** faculty of rational thought. **3** sanity. ♦ *v* **4** think logically in forming conclusions. **reason with** persuade by logical argument into doing something. **reasonable** *adj* **1** sensible. **2** not excessive. **3** logical. **reasonably** *adv*

reassess *v* reconsider the value or importance of.

reassure *v* restore confidence to. **reassurance** *n* **reassuring** *adj*

rebate *n* discount or refund.

rebel *v* **-belling, -belled** **1** revolt against the ruling power. **2** reject accepted conventions. ♦ *n* **3** person who rebels. **rebellion** *n* **1** organized open resistance to authority. **2** rejection of conventions. **rebellious** *adj*

rebirth *n* revival or renaissance. **reborn** *adj* active again after a period of inactivity.

rebore, reboring *n* boring of a cylinder to restore its true shape.

rebound *v* **1** spring back. **2** misfire so as to hurt the perpetrator of a plan or deed. ♦ *n* **3** act of rebounding. **on the rebound** *Informal* while recovering from rejection.

rebuff *v* **1** reject or snub. ♦ *n* **2** blunt refusal, snub.

rebuke *v* **1** scold sternly. ♦ *n* **2** stern scolding.

rebus [**ree**-buss] *n, pl* **-buses** puzzle consisting of pictures and symbols representing words or syllables.

rebut *v* **-butting, -butted** prove that (a claim) is untrue. **rebuttal** *n*

recalcitrant *adj* wilfully disobedient. **recalcitrance** *n*

recall *v* **1** recollect or remember. **2** order to return. **3** annul or cancel. ♦ *n* **4** ability to remember. **5** order to return.

recant *v* withdraw (a statement or belief) publicly. **recantation** *n*

recap *Informal* ♦ *v* **-capping, -capped 1** recapitulate. ♦ *n* **2** recapitulation.

recapitulate *v* state again briefly, repeat. **recapitulation** *n*

recapture *v* **1** experience again. **2** capture again.

recast *v* **-casting, -cast 1** organize or set out in a different way. **2** assign a part in a play or film to an actor other than the one originally intended.

recce *Slang* ♦ *v* **-ceing, -ced** *or* **-ceed 1** reconnoitre. ♦ *n* **2** reconnaissance.

recede *v* **1** move to a more distant place. **2** (of the hair) stop growing at the front.

receipt *n* **1** written acknowledgment of money or goods received. **2** receiving or being received.

receive *v* **1** take, accept, or get. **2** experience. **3** greet (guests). **4** have (an honour) bestowed. **5** admit (a person) to a society or condition. **6** convert radio or television signals into sound or vision. **7** support or sustain (the weight of something). **received** *adj* generally accepted. **receiver** *n* **1** part of telephone that is held to the ear. **2** equipment in a telephone, radio, or television that converts electrical signals into sound. **3** person appointed by a court to manage the property of a bankrupt. **4** person who handles stolen goods knowing they have been stolen. **receivership** *n* state of being administered by a receiver.

recent *adj* **1** having happened lately. **2** new. **recently** *adv*

receptacle *n* object used to contain something.

reception *n* **1** area for receiving guests, clients, etc. **2** formal party. **3** manner of receiving. **4** welcome. **5** (in broadcasting) quality of signals received. **receptionist** *n* person who receives guests, clients, etc. **reception room** room in a house suitable for entertaining guests.

receptive *adj* willing to accept new ideas, suggestions, etc. **receptivity, receptiveness** *n*

recess *n* **1** niche or alcove. **2** holiday between sessions of work. **3** secret hidden place. **recessed** *adj* hidden or placed in a recess.

recession *n* **1** period of economic difficulty when little is being bought or sold. **2** act of receding. **recessive** *adj* receding.

recharge *v* cause (a battery etc.) to take in and store electricity again. **rechargeable** *adj*

recherché [rish-**air**-shay] *adj* **1** refined or elegant. **2** known only to experts.

recidivism *n* habitual relapse into crime. **recidivist** *n*

recipe *n* **1** directions for cooking a dish. **2** method for achieving something.

recipient *n* person who receives something.

reciprocal [ris-**sip**-pro-kl] *adj* **1** mutual. **2** given or done in return. ♦ *n* **3** *Maths* number or quantity that gives a product of one when multiplied by a given number or quantity, e.g. *0.25 is the reciprocal of 4.* **reciprocally** *adv* **reciprocate** *v* **1** give or feel in return. **2** (of a machine part) move backwards and forwards. **reciprocation** *n* **reciprocity** *n*

recite *v* **1** repeat (a poem etc.) aloud to an audience. **2** give a detailed account of. **recital** [ris-**site**-al] *n* **1** musical performance by a soloist or soloists. **2** act of reciting. **recitation** *n* recital, usu. from memory, of poetry or prose. **recitative** [ress-it-a-**teev**] *n* speechlike style of singing, used esp. for narrative passages in opera.

reckless *adj* heedless of danger. **recklessly** *adv* **recklessness** *n*

reckon *v* **1** consider or think. **2** make calculations, count. **3** expect. **4** (foll. by *with* or *without*) take into account *or* fail to take into account. **5** (foll. by *on* or *upon*) rely on. **reckoning** *n*

reclaim *v* **1** regain possession of. **2** make fit for cultivation. **3** recover (useful substances) from waste. **reclamation** *n*

recline *v* rest in a leaning position. **reclining** *adj*

recluse *n* person who avoids other people. **reclusive** *adj*

recognize *v* **1** identify as (a person or thing) already known. **2** accept as true or existing. **3** treat as valid. **4** notice, show appreciation of. **recognition** *n* **recognizable** *adj* **recognizance** [rik-**og**-nizz-anss] *n* undertaking before a court to observe some condition.

recoil *v* **1** jerk or spring back. **2** draw back in horror. **3** (of an action) go wrong so as to hurt the doer. ♦ *n* **4** backward jerk. **5** recoiling.

recollect *v* call back to mind, remember. **recollection** *n*

recommend *v* **1** advise or counsel. **2** praise or commend. **3** make acceptable. **recommendation** *n*

recompense *v* **1** pay or reward. **2** compensate or make up for. ♦ *n* **3** compensation. **4** reward or remuneration.

reconcile *v* **1** harmonize (conflicting beliefs etc.). **2** bring back into friendship. **3** accept or cause to accept (an unpleasant situation). **reconciliation** *n*

recondite *adj* difficult to understand.

recondition *v* restore to good condition or working order.

reconnaissance [rik-**kon**-iss-anss] *n* survey for military or engineering purposes.

reconnoitre [rek-a-**noy**-ter] *v* make a reconnaissance of.

reconsider *v* think about again, consider changing.

reconstitute *v* **1** reorganize. **2** restore (dried food) to its former state by adding water. **reconstitution** *n*

reconstruct *v* **1** rebuild. **2** use evidence to re-create. **reconstruction** *n*

record *n* [**rek**-ord] **1** document or other thing that preserves information. **2** disc with indentations which a record player transforms into sound. **3** best recorded achievement. **4** known facts about a person's past. ♦ *v* [rik-**kord**] **5** put in writing. **6** preserve (sound, TV programmes, etc.) on plastic disc, magnetic tape, etc., for reproduction on a playback device. **7** show or register. **off the record** not for publication. **recorder** *n* **1** person or machine that records, esp. a video, cassette, or tape recorder. **2** type of flute, held vertically. **3** judge in certain courts. **recording** *n* **recorded delivery** postal service by which an official receipt is obtained for the posting and delivery of a letter or parcel. **record player** instrument for reproducing sound on records.

recount *v* tell in detail.

re-count *v* **1** count again. ♦ *n* **2** second or further count, esp. of votes.

recoup [rik-**koop**] *v* **1** regain or make good (a loss). **2** recompense or compensate.

recourse *n* source of help. **have recourse to** turn to a source of help or course of action.

recover *v* **1** become healthy again. **2** regain a former condition. **3** find again. **4** get back (a loss or expense). **5** obtain (useful substances) from waste. **recovery** *n* **recoverable** *adj*

re-create *v* make happen or exist again. **re-creation** *n*

recreation *n* agreeable or refreshing occupation, relaxation, or amusement. **recreational** *adj*

recrimination *n* mutual blame. **recriminatory** *adj*

recrudescence *n* outbreak of trouble or a disease after a period of quiet.

recruit *v* **1** enlist (new soldiers, members, etc.). ♦ *n* **2** newly enlisted soldier. **3** new member or supporter. **recruitment** *n*

rectal *adj* see RECTUM.

rectangle *n* oblong four-sided figure with four right angles. **rectangular** *adj*

rectify *v* **-fying, -fied 1** put right, correct. **2** *Chem* purify by distillation. **3** *Electricity* convert (alternating current) into direct current. **rectification** *n*

rectifier *n*

rectilinear [rek-tee-**lin**-ee-er] *adj* **1** in a straight line. **2** characterized by straight lines.

rectitude *n* moral correctness.

recto *n, pl* **-tos** **1** right-hand page of a book. **2** front of a sheet of paper.

rector *n* **1** clergyman in charge of a parish. **2** head of certain academic institutions. **rectory** *n, pl* **-ories** rector's house.

rectum *n, pl* **-tums, -ta** final section of the large intestine. **rectal** *adj*

recumbent *adj* lying down.

recuperate *v* recover from illness. **recuperation** *n* **recuperative** *adj*

recur *v* **-curring, -curred** happen again. **recurrence** *n* repetition. **recurrent** *adj* **recurring decimal** number in which a pattern of digits is repeated indefinitely after the decimal point.

recycle *v* reprocess (used materials) for further use. **recyclable** *adj*

red *adj* **redder, reddest** **1** of a colour varying from crimson to orange and seen in blood, fire, etc. **2** flushed in the face from anger, shame, etc. ♦ *n* **3** red colour. **4** (**R-**) *Informal* communist. **in the red** *Informal* in debt. **see red** *Informal* be angry. **redness** *n* **redden** *v* make or become red. **reddish** *adj* **red blood cell** same as ERYTHROCYTE. **red-blooded** *adj Informal* vigorous or virile. **redbrick** *adj* (of a university) founded in the late 19th or early 20th century. **red card** *Soccer* piece of red pasteboard shown by a referee to indicate that a player has been sent off. **red carpet** very special welcome for an important guest. **redcoat** *n* **1** *Hist* British soldier. **2** *Canadian informal* Mountie. **Red Crescent** name and symbol used by the Red Cross in Muslim countries. **Red Cross** international organization providing help for victims of war or natural disasters. **redcurrant** *n* small round edible red berry. **red flag** **1** symbol of revolution. **2** danger signal. **red-handed** *adj Informal* (caught) in the act of doing something wrong or illegal. **redhead** *n* person with reddish hair. **redheaded** *adj* **red herring** something which diverts attention from the main issue. **red-hot** *adj* **1** glowing red. **2** extremely hot. **3** very keen. **Red Indian** *Offens* Native American. **red-letter day** memorably happy or important occasion. **red light** **1** traffic signal to stop. **2** danger signal. **red-light district** area where prostitutes work. **red meat** dark meat, esp. beef or lamb. **red rag** something that infuriates or provokes. **redshank** *n* large sandpiper with red legs. **red shift** appearance of lines in the spectra of distant stars nearer the red end of the spectrum than on earth: used to calculate the velocity of objects in relation to the earth. **redskin** *n Informal, offens* Native American. **redstart** *n* European bird of the thrush family, the male of which has an orange-brown tail and breast. **red tape** excessive adherence to official rules. **redwood** *n* giant Californian conifer with reddish bark.

redeem *v* **1** make up for. **2** reinstate (oneself) in someone's good opinion. **3** free from sin. **4** buy back. **5** pay off (a loan or debt). **the Redeemer** Jesus Christ. **redeeming** *adj* **redeemable** *adj* **redemption** *n* **redemptive** *adj*

redeploy *v* assign to a new position or task. **redeployment** *n*

redevelop *v* rebuild or renovate (an area or building). **redevelopment** *n*

redirect *v* **1** send in a new direction or course. **2** send (mail) to a different address.

redolent *adj* **1** reminiscent (of). **2** smelling strongly (of). **redolence** *n*

redouble *v* increase, multiply, or intensify.

redoubt *n* small fort defending a hilltop or pass.

redoubtable *adj* formidable.

redound *v* cause advantage or disadvantage (to).

redox *n* chemical reaction in which one substance is reduced and the other is oxidized.

redress *v* **1** make amends for. ♦ *n* **2** compensation or amends.

reduce *v* **1** bring down, lower. **2** lessen, weaken. **3** bring by force or necessity to some state or action. **4** slim. **5** simplify. **6** make (a sauce) more concentrated. **7** lose oxygen atoms in a chemical reaction. **reducible** *adj* **reduction** *n*

redundant *adj* **1** (of a worker) no longer needed. **2** superfluous. **redundancy** *n, pl* **-cies**

reduplicate *v* make double, repeat.

re-echo *v* **-echoing, -echoed** echo over and over again, resound.

reed *n* **1** tall grass that grows in swamps and shallow water. **2** tall straight stem of this plant. **3** *Music* vibrating cane or metal strip in certain wind instruments. **reedy** *adj* **reedier, reediest 1** harsh and thin in tone. **2** full of reeds.

reef[1] *n* **1** ridge of rock or coral near the surface of the sea. **2** vein of ore.

reef[2] *n* **1** part of a sail which can be rolled up to reduce its area. ♦ *v* **2** take in a reef of. **reefer** *n* **1** short thick jacket worn esp. by sailors. **2** *Old-fashioned slang* hand-rolled cigarette containing cannabis. **reef knot** two simple knots turned opposite ways.

reek *v* **1** smell strongly. ♦ *n* **2** strong unpleasant smell. **reek of** give a strong suggestion of.

reel[1] *n* **1** cylindrical object on which film, tape, thread, or wire is wound. **2** winding apparatus, as of a fishing rod. **3** roll of film. **reel in** *v* draw in by means of a reel. **reel off** *v* recite or write fluently or quickly.

reel[2] *v* stagger, sway, or whirl.

reel[3] *n* lively Scottish dance.

re-enter *v* **1** come back into a place, esp. a country. **2** (of a spacecraft) return into the earth's atmosphere. **re-entry** *n*

ref *n Informal* referee in sport.

refectory *n, pl* **-tories** room for meals in a college etc. **refectory table** long narrow dining table supported by two trestles.

refer *v* **-ferring, -ferred** (foll. by *to*) **1** allude (to). **2** be relevant (to). **3** send (to) for information. **4** direct (a patient) to another doctor. **5** submit (to) for decision. **referable, referrable** *adj* **referral** *n* **reference** *n* **1** act of referring. **2** citation or direction in a book. **3** written testimonial regarding character or capabilities. **with reference to** concerning. **reference book** book, such as an encyclopedia or dictionary, containing information or facts. **reference library** library in which books may be consulted but not borrowed.

> *Refer* includes the sense 'back' in its meaning. Avoid using *refer back* unless the context involves sending papers back to a committee for further consideration.

referee *n* **1** umpire in sports, esp. football or boxing. **2** person willing to testify to someone's character etc. **3** arbitrator. ♦ *v* **-eeing, -eed 4** act as referee of.

referendum *n, pl* **-dums, -da** direct vote of the electorate on an important question.

refill *v* **1** fill again. ♦ *n* **2** second or subsequent filling. **3** replacement supply of something in a permanent container.

refine *v* **1** purify. **2** improve. **3** separate (a mixture) into its components. **refined** *adj* **1** cultured or polite. **2** purified. **refinement** *n* **1** improvement or elaboration. **2** fineness of taste or manners. **3** subtlety. **refinery** *n, pl* **-eries** place where sugar, oil, etc. is refined.

refit *v* **1** make ready for use again by repairing or re-equipping. ♦ *n* **2** repair or re-equipping for further use.

reflation *n* increase in the supply of money and credit designed to encourage economic activity. **reflate** *v* **reflationary** *adj*

reflect *v* **1** throw back, esp. rays of light, heat, etc. **2** form an image of. **3** show. **4** consider at length. **5** bring credit or discredit upon. **reflecting telescope** telescope in which the initial image is formed by a concave mirror. **reflection** *n* **1** act of reflecting. **2** return of rays of heat, light, etc. from a surface. **3** image of an object given back by a mirror etc. **4** conscious thought or meditation. **5** attribution of discredit or blame. **reflective** *adj* **1** quiet, contemplative. **2** capable of reflecting images. **reflector** *n* **1** polished surface for reflecting light etc. **2** reflecting telescope.

reflex *n* **1** involuntary response to a stimulus or situation. ♦ *adj* **2** (of a muscular action) involuntary. **3** reflected. **4** (of an angle) more than 180°. **reflexive** *adj Grammar* **1** denoting a pronoun that refers back to the subject of a sentence or clause. **2** denoting a verb whose subject is the same as its object, e.g. *dress oneself.* **reflex camera** camera which uses a mirror to channel light from a lens to the viewfinder, so that the image seen is the same as the image photographed.

reflexology *n* foot massage as a therapy in alternative medicine.

reform *n* **1** improvement. ♦ *v* **2** improve. **3** abandon evil practices. **reformer** *n* **reformation** [ref-fer-**may**-shun] *n* **1** a reforming. **2** (**R-**) religious movement in 16th-century Europe that resulted in the establishment of the Protestant Churches. **reformatory** *n, pl* **-ries** (formerly) institution for reforming young offenders. **reformist** *n, adj* (person) seeking the reform of something rather than its abolition or overthrow.

refract *v* change the course of (light etc.) passing from one medium to another. **refraction** *n* **refractive** *adj* **refractor** *n* **refracting telescope** telescope in which the image is formed by a series of lenses (also **refractor**).

refractory *adj* **1** unmanageable or rebellious. **2** *Med* resistant to treatment. **3** resistant to heat.

refrain[1] *v* **refrain from** keep oneself from doing.

refrain[2] *n* frequently repeated part of a song.

refresh *v* **1** revive or reinvigorate, as through food, drink, or rest. **2** stimulate (the memory). **refresher** *n* **refreshing** *adj* **1** having a reviving effect. **2** pleasantly different or new. **refreshment** *n* something that refreshes, esp. food or drink.

refrigerate *v* cool or freeze in order to preserve. **refrigeration** *n* **refrigerator** *n* full name for FRIDGE. **refrigerant** *n* **1** fluid capable of vaporizing at low temperatures, used in refrigerators. ♦ *adj* **2** refrigerating.

refuel *v* **-elling, -elled** supply or be supplied with fresh fuel.

refuge *n* (source of) shelter or protection. **refugee** *n* person who seeks refuge, esp. in a foreign country.

refulgent *adj* shining, radiant.

refund *v* **1** pay back. ♦ *n* **2** return of money. **3** amount returned.

refurbish *v* renovate and brighten up. **refurbishment** *n*

refuse[1] *v* **1** decline, deny, or reject. **2** (of a horse) be unwilling to jump a fence. **refusal** *n* denial of anything demanded or offered. **refusenik** *n* person who refuses to obey a law or cooperate with the government because of strong beliefs.

refuse[2] *n* rubbish or useless matter.

refute *v* disprove. **refutation** *n*

> *Refute* is not the same as *deny*. It means 'show evidence to disprove something', while *deny* means only 'say something is not true'.

regain *v* **1** get back or recover. **2** reach again.

regal *adj* of or like a king or queen. **regally** *adv* **regalia** *pl n* ceremonial emblems of royalty or high office.

regale *v* entertain (someone) with stories etc.

regard *v* **1** consider. **2** look at. **3** heed. ♦ *n* **4** respect or esteem. **5** attention. **6** look. ♦ *pl* **7** expression of goodwill. **as regards, regarding** in respect of, concerning. **regardless** *adj* **1** heedless. ♦ *adv* **2** in spite of everything.

regatta *n* meeting for yacht or boat races.

regenerate *v* [ri-**jen**-er-ate] **1** (cause to)

undergo spiritual, moral, or physical renewal. **2** reproduce or re-create. ♦ *adj* [ri-**jen**-er-it] **3** spiritually, morally, or physically renewed. **regeneration** *n* **regenerative** *adj*

regent *n* **1** ruler of a kingdom during the absence, childhood, or illness of its monarch. ♦ *adj* **2** ruling as a regent, e.g. *prince regent.* **regency** *n, pl* **-cies** status or period of office of a regent.

reggae *n* style of Jamaican popular music with a strong beat.

regicide *n* **1** killing of a king. **2** person who kills a king.

regime [ray-**zheem**] *n* **1** system of government. **2** particular administration. **3** *Med* regimen.

regimen *n* prescribed system of diet etc.

regiment *n* **1** organized body of troops as a unit of the army. **2** large number or group. **regimental** *adj* **regimentals** *pl n* military uniform. **regimentation** *n* **regimented** *adj* very strictly controlled.

region *n* **1** administrative division of a country. **2** area considered as a unit but with no definite boundaries. **3** part of the body. **in the region of** approximately **regional** *adj* **regionalism** *n* **1** division of a country or organization into geographical regions each having some autonomy. **2** loyalty to one's home region.

register *n* **1** (book containing) an official list or record of things. **2** range of a voice or instrument. ♦ *v* **3** enter in a register or set down in writing. **4** show or be shown on a meter or the face. **5** *Informal* have an effect or make an impression. **registered** *adj* (of mail) insured against loss by the Post Office, e.g. *a registered letter.* **registration** *n* **registration document** document giving identification details of a vehicle, including its owner's name. **registration number** numbers and letters displayed on a vehicle to identify it. **registrar** *n* **1** keeper of official records. **2** senior hospital doctor, junior to a consultant. **registry** *n, pl* **-tries 1** place where official records are kept. **2** registration of a ship's place of origin, e.g. *a tanker of Liberian registry.* **register office, registry office** place where births, marriages, and deaths are recorded.

Regius professor [**reej**-yuss] *n* professor appointed by the Crown to a university chair founded by a royal patron.

regress *v* revert to a former worse condition. **regression** *n* **1** act of regressing. **2** *Psychol* use of an earlier (inappropriate) mode of behaviour. **regressive** *adj*

regret *v* **-gretting, -gretted 1** feel sorry about. **2** express apology or distress. ♦ *n* **3** feeling of repentance, guilt, or sorrow. **regretful** *adj* **regrettable** *adj* **regrettably** *adv*

regular *adj* **1** normal, customary, or usual. **2** symmetrical or even. **3** done or occurring according to a rule. **4** periodical. **5** employed continuously in the armed forces. ♦ *n* **6** regular soldier. **7** *Informal* frequent customer. **regularity** *n* **regularize** *v* **regularly** *adv*

regulate *v* **1** control, esp. by rules. **2** adjust slightly. **regulation** *n* **1** rule. **2** regulating. ♦ *adj* **3** in accordance with rules or conventions. **regulator** *n* device that automatically controls pressure, temperature, etc. **regulatory** *adj*

regurgitate *v* **1** vomit. **2** (of some birds and animals) bring back (partly digested food) into the mouth. **3** reproduce (ideas, facts, etc.) without understanding them. **regurgitation** *n*

rehabilitate *v* **1** help (a person) to readjust to society after illness, imprisonment, etc. **2** restore to a former position or rank. **3** restore the good reputation of. **rehabilitation** *n*

rehash *v* **1** rework or reuse. ♦ *n* **2** old ideas presented in a new form.

rehearse *v* **1** practise (a play, concert, etc.). **2** repeat aloud. **rehearsal** *n*

rehouse *v* provide with a new (and better) home.

Reich [**rike**] *n German* kingdom or regime. **Third Reich** Nazi dictatorship in Germany from 1933–45.

reign *n* **1** period of a sovereign's rule. **2** period when a person or thing is dominant, e.g. *reign of terror.* ♦ *v* **3** rule (a country). **4** be supreme.

reimburse *v* refund, pay back. **reimbursement** *n*

rein *v* **1** check or manage with reins. **2** control or limit. **reins** *pl n* **1** narrow straps attached to a bit to guide a horse. **2** narrow straps attached to a harness to control a young child. **3** means of control. **give (a) free rein** allow a considerable amount of freedom.

reincarnation *n* **1** rebirth of a soul in successive bodies. **2** one of a series of such transmigrations. **reincarnate** *v*

reindeer *n, pl* **-deer, -deers** deer of arctic regions with large branched antlers.

reinforce *v* **1** give added emphasis to. **2** strengthen with new support, material, or force. **3** strengthen with additional troops, ships, etc. **reinforcement** *n* **reinforced concrete** concrete strengthened by having steel mesh or bars embedded in it.

reinstate *v* restore to a former position. **reinstatement** *n*

reiterate *v* repeat again and again. **reiteration** *n*

reject *v* **1** refuse to accept or believe. **2** rebuff (a person). **3** discard as useless. **4** fail to accept (a tissue graft or organ transplant). ♦ *n* **5** person or thing rejected as not up to standard. **rejection** *n*

rejig *v* **-jigging, -jigged 1** re-equip (a factory or plant). **2** rearrange.

rejoice *v* feel or express great happiness. **rejoicing** *n*

rejoin[1] *v* join again.

rejoin[2] *v* reply. **rejoinder** *n* answer, retort.

rejuvenate *v* restore youth or vitality to. **rejuvenation** *n*

rekindle *v* arouse former emotions or interests.

relapse *v* **1** fall back into bad habits, illness, etc. ♦ *n* **2** return of bad habits, illness, etc.

relate *v* **1** establish a relation between. **2** have reference or relation to. **3** have an understanding (of people or ideas). **4** tell (a story) or describe (an event). **related** *adj*

relation *n* **1** connection between things. **2** relative. **3** connection by blood or marriage. **4** act of relating (a story). ♦ *pl* **5** social or political dealings. **6** family. **7** *Euphemistic* sexual intercourse. **relationship** *n* **1** dealings and feelings between people or countries. **2** emotional or sexual affair. **3** connection between two things. **4** association by blood or marriage, kinship.

relative *adj* **1** true to a certain degree or extent. **2** dependent on relation to something else, not absolute. **3** having reference or relation (to). **4** *Grammar* referring to a word or clause earlier in the sentence. ♦ *n* **5** person connected by blood or marriage. **relatively** *adv* **relativity** *n* **1** subject of two theories of Albert Einstein, dealing with relationships of space, time, and motion, and acceleration and gravity. **2** state of being relative.

relax *v* **1** make or become looser, less tense, or less rigid. **2** ease up from effort or attention, rest. **3** be less strict about. **4** become more friendly. **relaxed** *adj* **relaxing** *adj* **relaxation** *n*

relay *n* **1** fresh set of people or animals relieving others. **2** *Electricity* device for making or breaking a local circuit. **3** broadcasting station receiving and retransmitting programmes. ♦ *v* **-laying, -layed 4** pass on (a message). **relay race** race between teams in which each runner races part of the distance.

release *v* **1** set free. **2** let go or fall. **3** issue (a record, film, etc.) for sale or public showing. **4** emit heat, energy, etc. ♦ *n* **5** setting free. **6** statement to the press. **7** act of issuing for sale or publication. **8** newly issued film, record, etc.

relegate *v* **1** put in a less important position. **2** demote (a sports team) to a lower league. **relegation** *n*

relent *v* give up a harsh intention, become less severe. **relentless** *adj* **1** unremitting. **2** merciless.

relevant *adj* to do with the matter in hand. **relevance** *n*

reliable *adj* able to be trusted, dependable. **reliably** *adv* **reliability** *n*

reliance *n* dependence, confidence, or trust. **reliant** *adj*

relic *n* **1** something that has survived from the past. **2** body or possession of a saint, regarded as holy. ♦ *pl* **3** remains or traces. **relict** *n Obs* **1** relic. **2** widow.

relief *n* **1** gladness at the end or removal of pain, distress, etc. **2** release from monotony or duty. **3** money or food given to victims of disaster, poverty, etc. **4** freeing of a besieged city etc. **5** person who replaces another. **6** projection of a carved design from the surface. **7** any vivid effect resulting from contrast, e.g. *comic relief.* **relieve** *v* bring relief to. **relieve oneself** urinate or defecate. **relief map** map showing the shape and height of land by shading.

religion *n* system of belief in and worship of a supernatural power or god. **religious** *adj* **1** of religion. **2** pious or devout. **3** scrupulous or conscientious. **religiously** *adv*

relinquish *v* give up or abandon. **relinquishment** *n*

reliquary [**rel**-lik-wer-ee] *n, pl* **-quaries** case or shrine for holy relics.

relish *v* **1** enjoy, like very much. **2** anticipate eagerly. ♦ *n* **3** liking or enjoyment. **4** pleasurable anticipation. **5** appetizing savoury food, such as pickle. **6** zestful quality or flavour.

relive *v* experience (a sensation etc.) again, esp. in the imagination.

relocate *v* move to a new place to live or work. **relocation** *n*

reluctant *adj* unwilling or disinclined. **reluctantly** *adv* **reluctance** *n*

rely *v* **-lying, -lied 1** depend (on). **2** trust.

remain *v* **1** continue. **2** stay, be left behind. **3** be left (over). **4** be left to be done, said, etc. **remains** *pl n* **1** relics, esp. of ancient buildings. **2** dead body. **remainder** *n* **1** part which is left. **2** amount left over after subtraction or division. **3** copy of a book sold cheaply because it has been impossible to sell at full price. ♦ *v* **4** offer (copies of a poorly selling book) at reduced prices.

remand *v* send back into custody or put on bail before trial. **on remand** in custody or on bail before trial. **remand centre** place where accused people are detained awaiting trial.

remark *v* **1** make a casual comment (on). **2** say. **3** observe or notice. ♦ *n* **4** observation or comment. **remarkable** *adj* **1** worthy of note or attention. **2** striking or unusual. **remarkably** *adv*

remarry *v* **-rying, -ried** marry again following a divorce or the death of one's previous husband or wife.

rematch *n Sport* second or return game or contest between two players.

remedy *n, pl* **-edies 1** means of curing pain or disease. **2** means of solving a problem. ♦ *v* **-edying, -edied 3** put right. **remediable** *adj* able to be put right. **remedial** *adj* intended to correct a specific disability, handicap, etc.

remember *v* **1** retain in or recall to one's memory. **2** keep in mind. **3** give money to, as in a tip or through a will. **remember to** pass on someone's greeting to, e.g. *remember me to your mother.* **remembrance** *n* **1** memory. **2** token or souvenir. **3** honouring of the memory of a person or event. **Remembrance Day, Remembrance Sunday** Sunday closest to November 11th, on which the dead of both World Wars are commemorated.

remind *v* **1** cause to remember. **2** put in mind (of). **reminder** *n* **1** something that recalls the past. **2** note to remind a person of something not done.

reminisce *v* talk or write of past times, experiences, etc. **reminiscence** *n* **1** remembering. **2** thing recollected. ♦ *pl* **3** memoirs. **reminiscent** *adj* reminding or suggestive (of).

remiss *adj* negligent or careless.

remission *n* **1** reduction in the length of a prison term. **2** pardon or forgiveness. **3** easing of intensity, as of an illness.

remit *v* [rim-**mitt**] **-mitting, -mitted 1** send (money) for goods, services, etc., esp. by post. **2** cancel (a punishment or debt). **3** refer (a decision) to a higher authority or later date. ♦ *n* [**ree**-mitt] **4** area of competence or authority. **remittance** *n* money sent as payment.

remix *v* **1** change the relative prominence of each performer's part of (a recording). ♦ *n* **2** remixed version of a recording.

remnant *n* **1** small piece, esp. of fabric, left over. **2** surviving trace.

remonstrate *v* argue in protest. **remonstrance, remonstration** *n*

remorse *n* feeling of sorrow and regret for something one did. **remorseful** *adj* **remorseless** *adj* **1** pitiless. **2** persistent. **remorselessly** *adv*

remote *adj* **1** far away, distant. **2** aloof. **3** slight or faint. **remotely** *adv* **remote control** control of an apparatus from a distance by an electrical device.

remould *v* **1** change completely. **2** renovate (a worn tyre). ♦ *n* **3** renovated tyre.

remove *v* **1** take away or off. **2** get rid of. **3** dismiss from office. ♦ *n* **4** degree of difference. **removable** *adj* **removal** *n* removing, esp. changing residence.

remunerate *v* reward or pay. **remuneration** *n* **remunerative** *adj*

renaissance *n* **1** revival or rebirth. **2** (**R-**) revival of learning in the 14th–16th centuries. ♦ *adj* **3** (**R-**) of the Renaissance.

renal [**ree**-nal] *adj* of the kidneys.

renascent *adj* becoming active or vigorous again.

rend *v* **rending, rent 1** tear or wrench apart. **2** (of a sound) break (the silence) violently.

render *v* **1** cause to become. **2** give or provide (aid, a service, etc.). **3** submit or present (a bill). **4** portray or represent. **5** cover with plaster. **6** melt down (fat).

rendezvous [**ron**-day-voo] *n, pl* **-vous 1** appointment. **2** meeting place. ♦ *v* **3** meet as arranged.

rendition *n* **1** performance. **2** translation.

renegade *n* person who deserts a cause.

renege [rin-**nayg**] *v* go back (on a promise etc.).

renew *v* **1** begin again. **2** make valid again. **3** grow again. **4** restore to a former state. **5** replace (a worn part). **6** restate or reaffirm. **renewable** *adj* **renewal** *n*

rennet *n* substance for curdling milk to make cheese.

renounce *v* **1** give up (a belief, habit, etc.) voluntarily. **2** give up (a title or claim) formally. **renunciation** *n*

renovate *v* restore to good condition. **renovation** *n*

renown *n* widespread good reputation. **renowned** *adj* famous.

rent[1] *v* **1** give or have use of in return for regular payments. ♦ *n* **2** regular payment for use of land, a building, machine, etc. **rental** *n* **1** sum payable as rent. ♦ *adj* **2** of or relating to rent.

rent[2] *n* **1** tear or fissure. ♦ *v* **2** past of REND.

rentier [**ron**-tee-ay] *n French* person who lives off unearned income such as rents or interest.

renunciation *n* see RENOUNCE.

reorganize *v* organize in a new and more efficient way. **reorganization** *n*

rep[1] *n* short for REPERTORY COMPANY.

rep[2] *n* short for REPRESENTATIVE.

repaid *v* past of REPAY.

repair[1] *v* **1** restore to good condition, mend. ♦ *n* **2** act of repairing. **3** repaired part. **4** state or condition, e.g. *in good repair.* **repairable** *adj* **reparation** *n* something done or given as compensation.

repair[2] *v* go (to).

repartee *n* **1** interchange of witty retorts. **2** witty retort.

repast *n* meal.

repatriate *v* send (someone) back to his or her own country. **repatriation** *n*

repay *v* **repaying, repaid 1** pay back, refund. **2** do something in return for, e.g. *repay hospitality.* **repayable** *adj* **repayment** *n*

repeal *v* **1** cancel (a law) officially. ♦ *n* **2** act of repealing.

repeat *v* **1** say or do again. **2** happen again, recur. ♦ *n* **3** act or instance of repeating. **4** programme broadcast again. **5** *Music* passage that is identical to the one before it. **repeated** *adj* **repeatedly** *adv* **repeater** *n* firearm that may be discharged many times without reloading.

repel *v* **-pelling, -pelled 1** be disgusting to. **2** drive back, ward off. **3** resist. **repellent** *adj* **1** distasteful. **2** resisting water etc. ♦ *n* **3** something that repels, esp. a chemical to repel insects.

repent *v* feel regret for (a deed or omission). **repentance** *n* **repentant** *adj*

repercussions *pl n* indirect effects, often unpleasant.

repertoire *n* **1** stock of plays, songs, etc. that a player or company can give. **2** range of things someone or something is capable of doing.

repertory *n, pl* **-ries** repertoire. **repertory company** permanent theatre company producing a succession of plays.

repetition *n* **1** act of repeating. **2** thing repeated. **repetitive, repetitious** *adj* full of repetition.

rephrase *v* express in different words.

repine *v* fret or complain.

replace *v* **1** substitute for. **2** put back. **replacement** *n*

replay *n* **1** (also **action replay**) immediate reshowing on TV of an incident in sport, esp. in slow motion. **2** second sports match, esp. one following an earlier draw. ♦ *v* **3** play (a match, recording, etc.) again.

replenish *v* fill up again, resupply. **replenishment** *n*

replete *adj* filled or gorged. **repletion** *n*

replica *n* exact copy. **replicate** *v* make or be a copy of. **replication** *n*

reply *v* **-plying, -plied 1** answer or respond. ♦ *n, pl* **-plies 2** answer or response.

report *v* **1** give an account of. **2** make a report (on). **3** make a formal complaint about. **4** present oneself (to). **5** be responsible (to). ♦ *n* **6** account or statement. **7** rumour. **8** written statement of a child's progress at school. **9** bang. **reportedly** *adv* according to rumour. **reporter** *n* person who gathers news for a newspaper, TV, etc. **reported speech** report that gives the content of what someone said but not the actual words.

repose[1] *n* **1** peace. **2** composure. **3** sleep. ♦ *v* **4** lie or lay at rest. **5** lie when dead.

repose[2] *v* place one's trust (in).

repository *n, pl* **-ries** place where valuables are deposited for safekeeping, store.

repossess *v* (of a lender) take back property from a customer who is behind with payments. **repossession** *n*

reprehend *v* find fault with. **reprehensible** *adj* open to criticism, unworthy.

represent *v* **1** act as a delegate or substitute for. **2** stand for. **3** symbolize. **4** make out to be. **5** portray, as in art. **representation** *n* **representational** *adj* (of art) portraying people or things, not abstract. **representative** *n* **1** person chosen to stand for a group. **2** (travelling) salesperson. ♦ *adj* **3** typical.

repress *v* **1** keep (feelings) in check. **2** restrict the freedom of. **repression** *n* **repressive** *adj*

reprieve *v* **1** postpone the execution of (a condemned person). **2** give temporary relief to. ♦ *n* **3** (document granting) postponement or cancellation of a punishment. **4** temporary relief.

reprimand *v* **1** blame (someone) officially for a fault. ♦ *n* **2** official blame.

reprint *v* **1** print further copies of (a book). ♦ *n* **2** reprinted copy.

reprisal *n* retaliation.

reproach *n, v* blame, rebuke. **reproachful** *adj* **reproachfully** *adv*

reprobate [**rep**-roh-bate] *adj, n* depraved or disreputable (person). **reprobation** *n* disapproval or blame.

reproduce *v* **1** produce a copy of. **2** bring new individuals into existence. **3** re-create. **reproducible** *adj* **reproduction** *n* **1** process of reproducing. **2** facsimile, as of a painting etc. **3** quality of sound from an audio system. ♦ *adj* **4** made in imitation of an earlier style, e.g. *reproduction furniture.*

reproductive *adj*

reprove *v* speak severely to (someone) about a fault. **reproof** *n* severe blaming of someone for a fault.

reptile *n* cold-blooded egg-laying vertebrate with horny scales or plates, such as a snake or tortoise. **reptilian** *adj*

republic *n* **1** form of government in which the people or their elected representatives possess the supreme power. **2** country in which a president is the head of state. **republican** *adj* **1** of or supporting a republic. ♦ *n* **2** person who supports or advocates a republic. **republicanism** *n* **Republican** *n, adj* **1** (member or supporter) of the Republican Party, the more conservative of the two main political parties in the US. **2** (member or supporter) of the Irish Republican Army. **Republicanism** *n*

repudiate [rip-**pew**-dee-ate] *v* **1** reject the authority or validity of. **2** disown. **repudiation** *n*

repugnant *adj* offensive or distasteful. **repugnance** *n*

repulse *v* **1** be disgusting to. **2** drive (an army) back. **3** rebuff or reject. ♦ *n* **4** driving back. **5** rejection or rebuff. **repulsion** *n* **1** distaste or aversion. **2** *Physics* force separating two objects. **repulsive** *adj* loathsome, disgusting.

reputation *n* estimation in which a person is held. **reputable** [**rep**-pew-tab-bl] *adj* of good reputation, respectable. **repute** *n* reputation. **reputed** *adj* supposed. **reputedly** *adv*

request *v* **1** ask. ♦ *n* **2** asking. **3** thing asked for.

Requiem [**rek**-wee-em] *n* **1** Mass for the dead. **2** music for this.

require *v* **1** want or need. **2** demand. **requirement** *n* **1** essential condition. **2** specific need or want.

> *Require* suggests a demand imposed by some regulation. *Need* is usually something that comes from a person.

requisite [**rek**-wizz-it] *adj* **1** necessary, essential. ♦ *n* **2** essential thing.

requisition *v* **1** demand (supplies). ♦ *n* **2** formal demand, such as for materials or supplies.

requite *v* return to someone (the same treatment or feeling as received). **requital** *n*

reredos [**rear**-doss] *n* ornamental screen behind an altar.

rerun *n* **1** film or programme that is broadcast again, repeat. **2** race that is run again. ♦ *v* **3** put on (a film or programme) again. **4** run (a race) again.

resale *n* selling of something purchased earlier.

rescind *v* annul or repeal.

rescue *v* **-cuing, -cued 1** deliver from danger or trouble, save. ♦ *n* **2** rescuing. **rescuer** *n*

research *n* **1** systematic investigation to discover facts or collect information. ♦ *v* **2** carry out investigations. **researcher** *n*

resemble *v* be or look like. **resemblance** *n*

resent *v* feel indignant or bitter about. **resentful** *adj* **resentment** *n*

reservation *n* **1** doubt. **2** exception or limitation. **3** seat, room, etc. that has been reserved. **4** area of land reserved for use by a particular group. **5** (also **central reservation**) strip of ground separating the two carriageways of a dual carriageway or motorway.

reserve *v* **1** set aside, keep for future use. **2** obtain by arranging beforehand, book. **3** retain. ♦ *n* **4** something, esp. money or troops, kept for emergencies. **5** area of land reserved for a particular purpose. **6** *Sport* substitute. **7** concealment of feelings or friendliness. **reserved** *adj* **1** not showing one's feelings, lacking friendliness. **2** set aside for use by a particular person. **reservist** *n* member of a military reserve. **reserve price** minimum price acceptable to the owner of property being auctioned.

reservoir *n* **1** natural or artificial lake storing water for community supplies. **2** store or supply of something.

reshuffle *n* **1** reorganization. ♦ *v* **2** reorganize.

reside *v* dwell permanently. **residence** *n* **1** home or house. **2** (period of) living in a place. **in residence** (of an artist) working for a set period at a college, gallery, etc., e.g. *writer in residence.* **resident** *n* **1** person who lives in a place. **2** bird or animal that does not migrate. ♦ *adj* **3** living in a place. **4** (of a bird or animal) not migrating. **residential** *adj* **1** (of part of a town) consisting mainly of houses. **2** providing living accommodation.

residue *n* **1** what is left, remainder. **2** *Law* what is left of an estate after debts have been paid and specific gifts made. **residual** *adj* **residuum** *n, pl* **-ua** residue.

resign *v* **1** give up office, a job, etc. **2** reconcile (oneself) to. **3** give up a right, claim, etc. **resigned** *adj* content to endure. **resignation** *n* **1** resigning. **2** passive endurance of difficulties.

resilient *adj* **1** (of a person) recovering quickly from a shock etc. **2** able to return to normal shape after stretching etc. **resilience** *n*

resin [**rezz**-in] *n* **1** sticky substance from plants, esp. pines. **2** similar synthetic substance. **resinous** *adj*

resist *v* **1** withstand or oppose. **2** refrain from despite temptation. **3** be proof against. **resistance** *n* **1** act of resisting. **2** capacity to withstand something. **3** *Electricity* opposition offered by a circuit to the passage of a current through it. **4** any force that slows or hampers movement, e.g. *wind resistance.* **5** (**R-**) illegal organization fighting for national liberty in a country under enemy occupation. **resistant** *adj* **resistible** *adj* **resistor** *n* component of an electrical circuit producing resistance.

resit *v* **-sitting, -sat 1** take (an exam) again. ♦ *n* **2** exam that has to be taken again.

resolute *adj* firm in purpose. **resolutely** *adv* **resolution** *n* **1** firmness of conduct or character. **2** thing resolved upon. **3** decision of a court or vote of an assembly. **4** act of resolving. **5** ability of a television, microscope, etc. to show fine detail.

resolve *v* **1** decide with an effort of will. **2** form (a resolution) by a vote. **3** separate the component parts of. **4** make clear, settle. ♦ *n* **5** absolute determination. **resolved** *adj* determined.

resonance *n* **1** echoing, esp. with a deep sound. **2** sound produced in one object by sound waves coming from another object. **resonant** *adj* **resonate** *v* **resonator** *n*

resort *v* **1** have recourse (to) for help etc. ♦ *n* **2** place for holidays. **3** recourse.

resound [riz-**zownd**] *v* **1** echo or ring with sound. **2** (of sounds) echo or ring. **3** be widely known, e.g. *his fame resounded through the land.* **resounding** *adj* **1** echoing. **2** clear and emphatic.

resource *n* **1** thing resorted to for support. **2** ingenuity. **3** means of achieving something. ♦ *pl* **4** sources of economic wealth. **5** stock that can be drawn on, funds. **resourceful** *adj* **resourcefulness** *n*

respect *n* **1** consideration. **2** deference or esteem. **3** point or aspect. **4** reference or relation, e.g. *with respect to.* ♦ *pl* **5** polite greetings. ♦ *v* **6** treat with esteem. **7** show consideration for. **respecter** *n* **respectful** *adj* **respectfully** *adv* **respecting** *prep* concerning.

respectable *adj* **1** worthy of respect. **2** having good social standing and reputation. **3** fairly good. **respectably** *adv* **respectability** *n*

respective *adj* relating separately to each of those in question. **respectively** *adv*

respiration [ress-per-**ray**-shun] *n* **1** breathing. **2** process in plants and animals of taking in oxygen and giving out carbon dioxide. **3** breakdown of complex organic substances by living cells to produce energy and carbon dioxide. **respirator** *n* apparatus worn over the mouth and breathed through as protection against dust, poison gas, etc., or to provide artificial respiration. **respiratory** *adj* **respire** *v* breathe.

respite *n* **1** pause, interval of rest. **2**

delay.

resplendent *adj* **1** brilliant or splendid. **2** shining. **resplendence** *n*

respond *v* **1** answer. **2** act in answer to any stimulus. **3** react favourably. **respondent** *n Law* defendant. **response** *n* **1** answer. **2** reaction to a stimulus. **3** (in some Christian churches) words sung or recited in reply to a priest during a service. **responsive** *adj* readily reacting to some influence. **responsiveness** *n*

responsible *adj* **1** having control and authority. **2** being the cause (of some action). **3** reporting or accountable (to). **4** sensible and dependable. **5** involving responsibility. **responsibly** *adv* **responsibility** *n, pl* **-ties** **1** state of being responsible. **2** person or thing for which one is responsible.

respray *n* new coat of paint applied to a car, van, etc.

rest[1] *n* **1** freedom from exertion etc. **2** repose. **3** pause, esp. in music. **4** object used for support. ♦ *v* **5** take a rest. **6** give a rest (to). **7** be supported. **8** place on a support. **9** depend or rely, e.g. *their hopes rested on an early end to the dispute.* **10** (of someone's gaze) direct at or settle on, e.g. *her eyes rested on the dog.* **restful** *adj* **restless** *adj*

rest[2] *n* **1** what is left. **2** others. ♦ *v* **3** remain, continue to be.

restaurant *n* commercial establishment serving meals. **restaurateur** [rest-er-a-**tur**] *n* person who owns or runs a restaurant. **restaurant car** railway coach where meals are served.

restitution *n* **1** giving back. **2** reparation or compensation.

restive *adj* restless or impatient.

restore *v* **1** return (a building, painting, etc.) to its original condition. **2** cause to recover health or spirits. **3** give back, return. **4** re-establish. **restoration** *n* **restorative** [rest-**or**-a-tiv] *adj* **1** restoring. ♦ *n* **2** food or medicine to strengthen etc. **restorer** *n*

restrain *v* **1** hold (someone) back from action. **2** control or restrict. **restraint** *n* **1** something that restrains. **2** control, esp. self-control. **3** restraining. **restrained** *adj* not displaying emotion.

restrict *v* confine to certain limits. **restriction** *n* **restrictive** *adj* **restrictive practice** trading or industrial agreement which is against the interests of the public or other business interests.

restructure *v* reorganize.

result *n* **1** outcome or consequence. **2** score. **3** number obtained from a calculation. **4** exam mark or grade. ♦ *v* **5** (foll. by *from*) be the outcome or consequence (of). **6** (foll. by *in*) end (in). **resultant** *adj* **1** arising as a result. ♦ *n* **2** *Maths, physics* sum of two or more vectors, such as the force resulting from two or more forces acting on a single point.

resume *v* **1** begin again. **2** occupy or take again. **resumption** *n*

résumé [**rezz**-yew-may] *n* summary.

resurgence *n* rising again to vigour. **resurgent** *adj*

resurrect *v* **1** restore to life. **2** use once more (something discarded etc.), revive. **resurrection** *n* **1** rising again (esp. from the dead). **2** revival.

resuscitate [ris-**suss**-it-tate] *v* restore to consciousness. **resuscitation** *n*

retail *n* **1** selling of goods individually or in small amounts to the public. ♦ *adj* **2** of or engaged in such selling. ♦ *adv* **3** by retail. ♦ *v* **4** sell or be sold retail. **5** recount in detail. **retailer** *n*

retain *v* **1** keep in one's possession. **2** be able to hold or contain. **3** engage the services of. **retainer** *n* **1** fee to retain someone's services. **2** payment to reserve a room or flat for future use. **3** old-established servant of a family.

retake *v* **-taking, -took, -taken** **1** recapture. **2** take something, such as an examination, again. ♦ *n* **3** *Films* act of rephotographing a scene.

retaliate *v* repay an injury or wrong in kind. **retaliation** *n* **retaliatory** *adj*

retard *v* delay or slow (progress or development). **retarded** *adj* underdeveloped, esp. mentally. **retardation** *n*

retch *v* try to vomit.

retention *n* **1** retaining. **2** ability to remember. **3** abnormal holding of something, esp. fluid, in the body. **retentive** *adj* capable of retaining or remembering.

rethink *v* consider again, esp. with a view to changing one's tactics.

reticent *adj* uncommunicative, reserved. **reticence** *n*

retina *n, pl* **-nas, -nae** light-sensitive membrane at the back of the eye.

retinue *n* band of attendants.

retire *v* **1** (cause to) give up office or work, esp. through age. **2** go away or withdraw. **3** go to bed. **retired** *adj* having retired from work etc. **retirement** *n* **retirement pension** weekly pension paid by the government to retired people over a specified age. **retiring** *adj* shy.

retort[1] *v* **1** reply quickly, wittily, or angrily. ♦ *n* **2** quick, witty, or angry reply.

retort[2] *n* glass container with a bent neck used for distilling.

retouch *v* restore or improve by new touches, esp. of paint.

retrace *v* go back over (a route etc.) again.

retract *v* **1** withdraw (a statement etc.). **2** draw in or back. **retractable, retractile** *adj* able to be retracted. **retraction** *n*

retread *v, n* same as REMOULD.

retreat *v* **1** move back from a position, withdraw. ♦ *n* **2** act of or military signal for retiring or withdrawal. **3** place to which anyone retires, refuge. **4** period of seclusion, esp. for religious contemplation.

retrench *v* reduce expenditure, cut back. **retrenchment** *n*

retrial *n* second trial of a case or defendant in a court of law.

retribution *n* punishment or vengeance for evil deeds. **retributive** *adj*

retrieve *v* **1** fetch back again. **2** restore to a better state. **3** rescue or save. **4** recover (information) from a computer. **retrievable** *adj* **retrieval** *n* **retriever** *n* dog trained to retrieve shot game.

retro *adj* associated with or revived from the past, e.g. *retro fashion.*

retro- *prefix* back or backwards, e.g. *retroactive.*

retroactive *adj* effective from a date in the past.

retrograde *adj* **1** tending towards an earlier worse condition. **2** moving or bending backwards.

retrogress *v* go back to an earlier worse condition. **retrogression** *n* **retrogressive** *adj*

retrorocket *n* small rocket engine used to slow a spacecraft.

retrospect *n* **in retrospect** when looking back on the past. **retrospective** *adj* **1** looking back in time. **2** applying from a date in the past. ♦ *n* **3** exhibition of an artist's life's work.

retroussé [rit-**troo**-say] *adj* (of a nose) turned upwards.

retsina *n* Greek wine flavoured with resin.

return *v* **1** go or come back. **2** give, put, or send back. **3** repay with something of equivalent value, e.g. *return the compliment.* **4** *Sport* hit, throw, or play (a ball) back. **5** reply. **6** elect. ♦ *n* **7** returning. **8** (thing) being returned. **9** profit. **10** official report, as of taxable income. **11** return ticket. ♦ *adj* **12** of or being a return, e.g. *a return visit.* **returnable** *adj* **returning officer** person in charge of an election. **return ticket** ticket allowing a passenger to travel to a place and back.

reunify *v* bring together again something previously divided. **reunification** *n*

reunion *n* meeting of people who have been apart. **reunite** *v* bring or come together again after a separation.

reuse *v* use again. **reusable** *adj*

rev *Informal* ♦ *n* **1** revolution (of an engine). ♦ *v* **revving, revved 2** (foll. by *up*) increase the speed of revolution of (an engine).

Rev., Revd. Reverend.

revalue *v* adjust the exchange value of

(a currency) upwards. **revaluation** *n*

revamp *v* renovate or restore.

reveal *v* **1** make known. **2** expose or show. **revealing** *adj* **revelation** *n*

reveille [riv-**val**-ee] *n* morning bugle call to waken soldiers.

revel *v* **-elling, -elled 1** take pleasure (in). **2** make merry. **revels** *pl n* merry-making. **reveller** *n* **revelry** *n* festivity.

revenge *n* **1** retaliation for wrong done. ♦ *v* **2** make retaliation for. **3** avenge (oneself or another). **revengeful** *adj*

revenue *n* income, esp. of a state. **Inland Revenue** see INLAND.

reverberate *v* echo or resound. **reverberation** *n*

revere *v* be in awe of and respect greatly. **reverence** *n* awe mingled with respect and esteem. **Reverend** *adj* title of respect for a clergyman. **reverent** *adj* showing reverence. **reverently** *adv* **reverential** *adj* marked by reverence.

reverie *n* absent-minded daydream.

revers [riv-**veer**] *n* turned back part of a garment, such as the lapel.

reverse *v* **1** turn upside down or the other way round. **2** change completely. **3** move (a vehicle) backwards. ♦ *n* **4** opposite. **5** back side. **6** change for the worse. **7** reverse gear. ♦ *adj* **8** opposite or contrary. **reverse the charges** make a telephone call at the recipient's expense. **reversal** *n* **reversible** *adj* **reverse gear** mechanism enabling a vehicle to move backwards. **reversing lights** lights on the back of a motor vehicle that go on when the vehicle is moving backwards.

revert *v* **1** return to a former state. **2** come back to a subject. **3** (of property) return to its former owner. **reversion** *n* **1** return to a former state, practice, or belief. **2** (of property) rightful passing to the owner, designated heir, etc.

review *n* **1** critical assessment of a book, concert, etc. **2** publication with critical articles. **3** general survey. **4** formal inspection. ♦ *v* **5** hold or write a review of. **6** examine, reconsider, or look back on. **7** inspect formally. **reviewer** *n* writer of reviews.

revile *v* be abusively scornful of.

revise *v* **1** change or alter. **2** prepare a new edition of (a book etc.). **3** restudy (work) in preparation for an examination. **revision** *n*

revive *v* bring or come back to life, vigour, use, etc. **revival** *n* **1** reviving or renewal. **2** movement seeking to restore religious faith. **3** new production of a play that has not been recently performed. **revivalism** *n* **revivalist** *n*

revoke *v* cancel (a will, agreement, etc.). **revocation** *n*

revolt *n* **1** uprising against authority. ♦ *v* **2** rise in rebellion. **3** cause to feel disgust. **revolting** *adj* disgusting, horrible.

revolution *n* **1** overthrow of a government by the governed. **2** great change. **3** spinning round. **4** complete rotation. **revolutionary** *adj* **1** advocating or engaged in revolution. **2** radically new or different. ♦ *n, pl* **-aries 3** person advocating or engaged in revolution. **revolutionize** *v* change considerably.

revolve *v* turn round, rotate. **revolve around** be centred on. **revolver** *n* repeating pistol.

revue *n* theatrical entertainment with topical sketches and songs.

revulsion *n* strong disgust.

reward *n* **1** something given in return for a service. **2** sum of money offered for finding a criminal or missing property. ♦ *v* **3** pay or give something to (someone) for a service, information, etc. **rewarding** *adj* giving personal satisfaction, worthwhile.

rewind *v* run (a tape or film) back to an earlier point in order to replay.

rewire *v* provide (a house, engine, etc.) with new wiring.

rewrite *v* **1** write again in a different way. ♦ *n* **2** something rewritten.

Rh 1 *Chem* rhodium. **2** rhesus.

rhapsody *n, pl* **-dies 1** freely structured emotional piece of music. **2** expression of ecstatic enthusiasm. **rhapsodic** *adj* **rhapsodize** *v* speak or write with extravagant enthusiasm.

rhea [**ree**-a] *n* S American three-toed ostrich.

rhenium *n Chem* silvery-white metallic element with a high melting point.

rheostat *n* instrument for varying the resistance of an electrical circuit.

rhesus [**ree**-suss] *n* small long-tailed monkey of S Asia. **rhesus factor, Rh factor** antigen commonly found in human blood.

rhetoric [**ret**-a-rik] *n* **1** art of effective speaking or writing. **2** artificial or exaggerated language. **rhetorical** [rit-**tor**-ik-kal] *adj* **1** (of a question) not requiring an answer. **2** of, like, or using rhetoric. **rhetorically** *adv*

rheum [**room**] *n* watery discharge from the eyes or nose. **rheumy** *adj*

rheumatism *n* painful inflammation of joints or muscles. **rheumatic** *n, adj* (person) affected by rheumatism. **rheumatoid** *adj* of or like rheumatism. **rheumatoid arthritis** chronic disease characterized by inflammation and swelling of the joints.

Rh factor *n* see RHESUS.

rhinestone *n* imitation diamond.

rhino *n, pl* **rhinos** short for RHINOCEROS.

rhinoceros *n, pl* **-oses, -os** large thick-skinned animal with one or two horns on its nose.

rhizome *n* thick underground stem producing new plants.

rhodium *n Chem* hard metallic element.

rhododendron *n* evergreen flowering shrub.

rhombus *n, pl* **-buses, -bi** parallelogram with sides of equal length but no right angles, diamond-shaped figure. **rhomboid** *n* parallelogram with adjacent sides of unequal length.

rhubarb *n* garden plant of which the fleshy stalks are cooked as fruit.

rhyme *n* **1** sameness of the final sounds at the ends of lines of verse, or in words. **2** word identical in sound to another in its final sounds. **3** verse marked by rhyme. ♦ *v* **4** make a rhyme. **rhyming slang** slang in which a word is replaced by a word or phrase which rhymes with it.

rhythm *n* **1** any regular movement or beat. **2** arrangement of the durations of and stress on the notes of a piece of music, usu. grouped into a regular pattern. **3** (in poetry) arrangement of words to form a regular pattern of stresses. **rhythmic, rhythmical** *adj* **rhythmically** *adv* **rhythm and blues** popular music, orig. Black American, influenced by the blues. **rhythm method** method of contraception in which intercourse is avoided at times when conception is most likely.

RI Rhode Island.

rib[1] *n* **1** one of the curved bones forming the framework of the upper part of the body. **2** cut of meat including the rib(s). **3** curved supporting part, as in the hull of a boat. **4** raised series of rows in knitting. ♦ *v* **ribbing, ribbed 5** provide or mark with ribs. **6** knit to form a rib pattern. **ribbed** *adj* **ribbing** *n* **ribcage** *n* bony structure of ribs enclosing the lungs.

rib[2] *v* **ribbing, ribbed** *Informal* tease or ridicule. **ribbing** *n*

ribald *adj* humorously or mockingly rude or obscene. **ribaldry** *n*

ribbon *n* **1** narrow band of fabric used for trimming, tying, etc. **2** any long strip, for example of inked tape in a typewriter. **3** (also **riband, ribband**) small strip of coloured cloth worn as a badge or as the symbol of an award. ♦ *pl* **4** ragged strips or shreds.

riboflavin [rye-boe-**flay**-vin] *n* form of vitamin B.

ribonucleic acid *n* see RNA.

rice *n* **1** cereal plant grown on wet ground in warm countries. **2** its seeds as food. **rice paper** thin edible paper.

rich *adj* **1** owning a lot of money or property, wealthy. **2** abounding. **3** fertile. **4** (of food) containing much fat or sugar. **5** mellow. **6** intense or vivid. **7** amusing. **riches** *pl n* wealth. **richly** *adv* **1** elaborately. **2** fully. **richness** *n*

Richter scale *n* scale for measuring the intensity of earthquakes.

rick[1] *n* stack of hay etc.
rick[2] *v, n* sprain or wrench.
rickets *n* disease of children marked by softening of the bones, bow legs, etc., caused by vitamin D deficiency.
rickety *adj* shaky or unstable.
rickshaw *n* light two-wheeled man-drawn Asian vehicle.
ricochet [**rik**-osh-ay] *v* **1** (of a bullet) rebound from a solid surface. ♦ *n* **2** such a rebound.
rid *v* **ridding, rid** clear or relieve (of). **get rid of** free oneself of (something undesirable). **good riddance** relief at getting rid of something or someone.
ridden *v* **1** past participle of RIDE. ♦ *adj* **2** afflicted or affected by the thing specified, e.g. *disease-ridden.*
riddle[1] *n* **1** question made puzzling to test one's ingenuity. **2** puzzling person or thing. ♦ *v* **3** speak in riddles.
riddle[2] *v* **1** pierce with many holes. ♦ *n* **2** coarse sieve for gravel etc. **riddled with** full of.
ride *v* **riding, rode, ridden 1** sit on and control or propel (a horse, bicycle, etc.). **2** go on horseback or in a vehicle. **3** travel over. **4** be carried on or across. **5** lie at anchor. ♦ *n* **6** journey on a horse etc., or in a vehicle. **7** type of movement experienced in a vehicle. **rider** *n* **1** person who rides. **2** supplementary clause added to a document. **riding** *n* art or practice of horsemanship. **ride out** *v* survive (a period of difficulty or danger) successfully. **ride up** *v* (of a garment) move up from the proper position.
ridge *n* **1** long narrow hill. **2** long narrow raised part on a surface. **3** line where two sloping surfaces meet. **4** *Meteorol* elongated area of high pressure. **ridged** *adj*
ridiculous *adj* deserving to be laughed at, absurd. **ridicule** *n* **1** treatment of a person or thing as ridiculous. ♦ *v* **2** laugh at, make fun of.
Riding *n* former administrative district of Yorkshire.
riesling *n* type of white wine.
rife *adj* widespread or common. **rife with** full of.
riff *n Jazz, rock* short repeated melodic figure.
riffle *v* flick through (pages etc.) quickly.
riffraff *n* rabble, disreputable people.
rifle[1] *n* **1** firearm with a long barrel. ♦ *v* **2** cut spiral grooves inside the barrel of a gun.
rifle[2] *v* **1** search and rob. **2** steal.
rift *n* **1** break in friendly relations. **2** crack, split, or cleft. **rift valley** long narrow valley resulting from subsidence between faults.
rig *v* **rigging, rigged 1** arrange in a dishonest way. **2** equip, esp. a ship. ♦ *n* **3** apparatus for drilling for oil and gas. **4** way a ship's masts and sails are arranged. **5** (also **rigout**) *Informal* outfit of clothes. **rigging** *n* ship's spars and ropes. **rig up** *v* set up or build temporarily.
right *adj* **1** just. **2** true or correct. **3** proper. **4** most favourable or convenient. **5** in a satisfactory condition. **6** of the side that faces east when the front is turned to the north. **7** of the outer side of a fabric. ♦ *adv* **8** correctly. **9** properly. **10** straight or directly. **11** on or to the right side. **12** all the way. **13** exactly or precisely. ♦ *n* **14** claim, title, etc. allowed or due. **15** what is just or due. **16** (**R-**) conservative political party or group. ♦ *v* **17** bring or come back to a normal or correct state. **18** bring or come back to a vertical position. **19** compensate for. **in the right** morally or legally correct. **right away** immediately. **rightly** *adv* **rightful** *adj* **rightfully** *adv* **rightist** *n, adj* (person) on the political right. **right angle** angle of 90°. **right-handed** *adj* using or for the right hand. **right-hand man** person's most valuable assistant. **right-minded, right-thinking** *adj* having opinions or principles deemed acceptable by the speaker. **right of way 1** right of one vehicle to go before another. **2** legal right to pass over someone's land. **right-wing** *adj* **1** conservative or reactionary. **2** belonging to the more conservative part of a political par-

ty. **right-winger** *n*

righteous [**rye**-chuss] *adj* **1** upright, godly, or virtuous. **2** morally justified. **righteousness** *n*

rigid *adj* **1** inflexible or strict. **2** unyielding or stiff. **rigidly** *adv* **rigidity** *n*

rigmarole *n* **1** long complicated procedure. **2** meaningless string of words.

rigor mortis *n* stiffening of the body after death.

rigour *n* **1** harshness, severity, or strictness. **2** hardship. **rigorous** *adj* harsh, severe, or stern.

rile *v* anger or annoy.

rill *n* small stream.

rim *n* **1** edge or border. **2** outer ring of a wheel. **rimmed** *adj*

rime *n Lit* hoarfrost.

rind *n* tough outer coating of fruits, cheese, or bacon.

ring[1] *v* **ringing, rang, rung 1** give out a clear resonant sound, as a bell. **2** cause (a bell) to sound. **3** telephone. **4** resound. ♦ *n* **5** ringing. **6** telephone call. **7** inherent quality, e.g. *the ring of truth.* **ring off** *v* end a telephone call. **ring up** *v* **1** telephone. **2** record on a cash register.

> The simple past is *rang: He rang the bell.* Avoid the use of the past participle *rung* for the simple past.

ring[2] *n* **1** circle of gold etc., esp. for a finger. **2** any circular band, coil, or rim. **3** circle of people. **4** circular course. **5** enclosed area, esp. a circle for a circus or a roped-in square for boxing. **6** group operating (illegal) control of a market. ♦ *v* **7** put a ring round. **8** mark (a bird) with a ring. **9** kill (a tree) by cutting the bark round the trunk. **ringer** *n Slang* person or thing apparently identical to another (also **dead ringer**). **ringlet** *n* curly lock of hair. **ring binder** binder with metal rings that can be opened to insert perforated paper. **ringdove** *n* large pigeon with white patches on the wings and neck. **ring finger** third finger, esp. of the left hand, on which the wedding ring is worn. **ringleader** *n* instigator of a mutiny, riot, etc. **ringmaster** *n* master of ceremonies in a circus. **ring road** main road that bypasses a town (centre). **ringside** *n* row of seats nearest a boxing or circus ring. **ringworm** *n* fungal skin disease in circular patches.

rink *n* **1** sheet of ice for skating or curling. **2** floor for roller-skating. **3** building for ice-skating or roller-skating.

rinkhals *n* S African cobra that can spit venom.

rinse *v* **1** remove soap from (washed clothes, hair, etc.) by applying clean water. **2** wash lightly. ♦ *n* **3** rinsing. **4** liquid to tint hair.

riot *n* **1** disorderly unruly disturbance. **2** loud revelry. **3** profusion. **4** *Slang* very amusing person or thing. ♦ *v* **5** take part in a riot. **read the riot act** reprimand severely. **run riot 1** behave without restraint. **2** grow profusely. **rioter** *n* **riotous** *adj* **1** unrestrained. **2** unruly or rebellious.

rip *v* **ripping, ripped 1** tear violently. **2** tear away. **3** *Informal* rush. ♦ *n* **4** split or tear. **let rip** act or speak without restraint. **ripcord** *n* cord pulled to open a parachute. **rip off** *v Slang* cheat by overcharging. **rip-off** *n Slang* **1** overpriced article. **2** cheat or swindle. **rip-roaring** *adj Informal* boisterous and exciting.

RIP rest in peace.

riparian [rip-**pair**-ee-an] *adj* of or on the banks of a river.

ripe *adj* **1** ready to be reaped, eaten, etc. **2** matured. **3** ready or suitable. **ripen** *v* **1** grow ripe. **2** mature.

riposte [rip-**posst**] *n* **1** verbal retort. **2** counterattack, esp. in fencing. ♦ *v* **3** make a riposte.

ripple *n* **1** slight wave or ruffling of a surface. **2** sound like ripples of water. ♦ *v* **3** flow or form into little waves (on). **4** (of sounds) rise and fall gently.

rise *v* **rising, rose, risen 1** get up from a lying, sitting, or kneeling position. **2** get out of bed. **3** move upwards. **4** (of the sun or moon) appear above the horizon. **5** reach a higher level. **6** (of an amount or price) increase. **7** rebel. **8** (of a court) adjourn. **9** have its source. ♦ *n* **10** rising. **11** upward slope. **12** increase, esp. of wages. **take a rise out of** *Slang* provoke an angry reaction from. **give rise to** cause. **riser** *n* **1** person who rises, esp. from bed. **2** vertical part of a step. **rising** *n* **1** revolt. ♦ *adj* **2** increasing in rank or maturity.

risible [**riz**-zib-bl] *adj* causing laughter, ridiculous.

risk *n* **1** chance of disaster or loss. **2** person or thing considered as a potential hazard. ♦ *v* **3** act in spite of the possibility of (injury or loss). **4** expose to danger or loss. **risky** *adj* **riskier, riskiest** full of risk, dangerous.

risotto *n, pl* **-tos** dish of rice cooked in stock with vegetables, meat, etc.

risqué [**risk**-ay] *adj* bordering on indecency.

rissole *n* cake of minced meat, coated with breadcrumbs and fried.

rite *n* formal practice or custom, esp. religious. **rite of passage** event that marks an important change in a person's life.

ritual *n* **1** prescribed order of rites. **2** regular repeated action or behaviour. ♦ *adj* **3** concerning rites. **ritually** *adv* **ritualistic** *adj* like a ritual.

ritzy *adj* **ritzier, ritziest** *Slang* luxurious or elegant.

rival *n* **1** person or thing that competes with or equals another for favour, success, etc. ♦ *adj* **2** in the position of a rival. ♦ *v* **-valling, -valled 3** (try to) equal. **rivalry** *n* keen competition.

riven *adj* **1** split apart. **2** torn to shreds.

river *n* **1** large natural stream of water. **2** plentiful flow.

rivet [**riv**-vit] *n* **1** bolt for fastening metal plates, the end being put through holes and then beaten flat. ♦ *v* **riveting, riveted 2** fasten with rivets. **3** cause to be fixed, as in fascination. **riveting** *adj* very interesting and exciting.

rivulet *n* small stream.

Rn *Chem* radon.

RN Royal Navy.

RNA ribonucleic acid: substance in living cells essential for the synthesis of protein.

roach[1] *n* freshwater fish.

roach[2] *n US* same as COCKROACH.

road *n* **1** way prepared for passengers, vehicles, etc. **2** route in a town or city with houses along it. **3** way or course, e.g. *the road to fame.* **4** roadstead. **on the road** travelling. **roadie** *n Informal* person who transports and sets up equipment for a band. **roadblock** *n* barricade across a road to stop traffic for inspection etc. **road hog** *Informal* selfish aggressive driver. **roadholding** *n* extent to which a vehicle does not skid on bends or wet surfaces. **roadhouse** *n* pub or restaurant on a country road. **road metal** broken stones used in building roads. **road rage** aggressive behaviour by a motorist in response to another motorist's driving. **road show** *Radio* live broadcast from a radio van taking a particular programme on a tour of the country. **roadside** *n, adj* **roadstead** *n Naut* partly sheltered anchorage. **road test** test of a vehicle etc. in actual use. **road-test** *v* test (a vehicle etc.) in actual use. **roadway** *n* the part of a road used by vehicles. **roadworks** *pl n* repairs to a road, esp. blocking part of the road. **roadworthy** *adj* (of a vehicle) mechanically sound.

roam *v* wander about.

roan *adj* **1** (of a horse) having a brown or black coat sprinkled with white hairs. ♦ *n* **2** roan horse.

roar *v* **1** make or utter a loud deep hoarse sound like that of a lion. **2** shout (something) as in anger. **3** laugh loudly. ♦ *n* **4** such a sound. **a roaring trade** *Informal* brisk and profitable business. **roaring drunk** noisily drunk.

roast *v* **1** cook by dry heat, as in an oven. **2** make or be very hot. ♦ *n* **3** roasted joint of meat. ♦ *adj* **4** roasted. **roasting** *Informal* ♦ *adj* **1** extremely hot. ♦ *n* **2** severe criticism or scolding.

rob *v* **robbing, robbed 1** steal from. **2** deprive. **robber** *n* **robbery** *n, pl* **-beries**

robe *n* **1** long loose outer garment. ♦ *v* **2** put a robe on.

robin *n* small brown bird with a red breast.

robot *n* **1** automated machine, esp. one performing functions in a human manner. **2** person of machine-like efficiency. **robotic** *adj* **robotics** *n* science of designing and using robots.

robust *adj* **1** very strong and healthy. **2** sturdily built. **3** requiring physical strength. **robustly** *adv* **robustness** *n*

roc *n* monstrous bird of Arabian mythology.

rock[1] *n* **1** hard mineral substance that makes up part of the earth's crust, stone. **2** large rugged mass of stone. **3** *US & Aust* a stone. **4** hard sweet in sticks. **on the rocks 1** (of a marriage) about to end. **2** (of an alcoholic drink) served with ice. **rocky** *adj* **rockier, rockiest** having many rocks. **rockery** *n, pl* **-eries** mound of stones in a garden for rock plants. **rock bottom** lowest possible level. **rock cake** small fruit cake with a rough surface. **rock plant** any plant which grows on rocky ground. **rock salt** common salt as a naturally occurring mineral.

rock[2] *v* **1** (cause to) sway to and fro. **2** (cause to) feel shock, e.g. *the scandal rocked the government.* ♦ *n* **3** (also **rock music**) style of pop music with a heavy beat. ♦ *adj* **4** of or relating to rock music. **rocky** *adj* **rockier, rockiest** shaky or unstable. **rock and roll, rock'n'roll** style of pop music blending rhythm and blues and country music. **rocking chair** chair allowing the sitter to rock backwards and forwards. **rocking horse** toy horse on which a child can rock to and fro.

rocker *n* **1** rocking chair. **2** curved piece of wood etc. on which something may rock. **3** rock music performer, fan, or song. **off one's rocker** *Informal* insane.

rocket *n* **1** self-propelling device powered by the burning of explosive contents (used as a firework, weapon, etc.). **2** vehicle propelled by a rocket engine, as a weapon or carrying a spacecraft. **3** *Informal* severe reprimand. ♦ *v* **-eting, -eted 4** move fast, esp. upwards, like a rocket.

rococo [rok-**koe**-koe] *adj* (of furniture, architecture, etc.) having much elaborate decoration in an early 18th-century style.

rod *n* **1** slender straight bar, stick. **2** cane.

rode *v* past tense of RIDE.

rodent *n* animal with teeth specialized for gnawing, such as a rat, mouse, or squirrel.

rodeo *n, pl* **-deos** display of skill by cowboys, such as bareback riding.

roe[1] *n* mass of eggs in a fish, sometimes eaten as food.

roe[2] *n* small species of deer.

roentgen [**ront**-gan] *n* unit measuring a radiation dose.

roger *interj* (used in signalling) message received and understood.

rogue *n* **1** dishonest or unprincipled person. **2** mischief-loving person. **3** inferior or defective specimen, esp. of a plant. ♦ *adj* **4** (of a wild beast) having a savage temper and living apart from the herd. **roguery** *n* **roguish** *adj*

roister *v* make merry noisily or boisterously.

role, rôle *n* **1** task or function. **2** actor's part. **role model** person regarded by others, esp. younger people, as a good example to follow.

roll *v* **1** move by turning over and over. **2** move or sweep along. **3** wind round. **4** undulate. **5** smooth out with a roller. **6** (of a ship or aircraft) turn from side to side about a line from nose to tail. **7** (of machinery) (begin to) operate. **8** (of a drum, thunder, etc.) make a continuous deep loud noise. **9** walk with a swaying gait. ♦ *n* **10** act of rolling over or from side to side. **11** piece of paper etc. rolled up. **12** small round individually baked piece of bread. **13** list or register. **14** complete rotation of an aircraft about a line from nose to tail. **15** continuous sound, as of drums, thunder, etc. **16** swaying unsteady movement or gait. **rolling** *adj* **1** (of hills) gently sloping, undulating. **2** (of a gait) slow and swaying. **roll call** calling out of a list of names, as in a school or the army, to check who is present. **rolled gold** metal coated with a thin layer of gold. **rolling pin** cylindrical roller for flattening pastry. **rolling stock** locomotives and coaches of a railway. **rolling stone** restless wandering person. **rollmop** *n* herring fillet rolled round onion slices and pickled. **roll-on/roll-off** *adj* denoting a ship allowing vehicles to be driven straight on and off. **roll-top** *adj* (of a desk) having a flexible lid sliding in grooves. **roll up** *v Informal* appear or arrive. **roll-up** *n Informal* cigarette made by the smoker from loose tobacco and cigarette paper.

roller *n* **1** rotating cylinder used for smoothing or supporting a thing to be moved, spreading paint, etc. **2** small tube around which hair is wound to make it curly. **3** long wave of the sea. **Rollerblade** *n* ® roller skate with the wheels set in one straight line. **roller coaster** (at a funfair) narrow railway with steep slopes. **roller skate** skate with wheels.

rollicking *adj* boisterously carefree.

roly-poly *adj* round or plump.

ROM *Computers* read only memory.

Roman *adj* of Rome or the Roman Catholic Church. **Roman alphabet** alphabet used for writing W European languages, including English. **Roman candle** firework that emits a steady stream of coloured sparks. **Roman Catholic** (member) of that section of the Christian Church that acknowledges the supremacy of the Pope. **Roman nose** nose with a high prominent bridge. **Roman numerals** the letters I, V, X, L, C, D, M, used to represent numbers. **roman type** plain upright letters in printing.

romance *n* **1** love affair. **2** love idealized for its purity or beauty. **3** mysterious or exciting quality. **4** novel or film dealing with love, esp. sentimentally. **5** story with scenes remote from ordinary life. ♦ *v* **6** exaggerate or fantasize.

Romance *adj* (of a language) developed from Latin, such as French or Spanish.

Romanesque *adj, n* (in) a style of architecture of the 9th–12th centuries, characterized by round arches.

romantic *adj* **1** of or dealing with love. **2** idealistic but impractical. **3** (of literature, music, etc.) displaying passion and imagination rather than order and form. ♦ *n* **4** romantic person or artist. **romantically** *adv* **romanticism** *n* **romanticize** *v* describe or regard in an idealized and unrealistic way.

Romany *n, pl* **-nies,** *adj* Gypsy.

Romeo *n, pl* **Romeos** ardent male lover.

romp *v* **1** play wildly and joyfully. ♦ *n* **2** boisterous activity. **romp home** win easily. **rompers** *pl n* child's overalls.

rondavel *n S Afr* circular building, often thatched.

rondo *n, pl* **-dos** piece of music with a leading theme continually returned to.

roo *n Aust informal* kangaroo.

rood *n* **1** *Christianity* the Cross. **2** crucifix. **rood screen** (in a church) screen separating the nave from the choir.

roof *n, pl* **roofs 1** outside upper covering of a building, car, etc. ♦ *v* **2** put a roof on. **roof rack** rack for carrying luggage attached to the roof of a car.

rook[1] *n* **1** bird of the crow family. ♦ *v* **2** *Old-fashioned slang* swindle. **rookery** *n, pl* **-eries** colony of rooks, penguins, or seals.

rook[2] *n* chess piece shaped like a castle.

rookie *n Informal* new recruit.

room *n* **1** enclosed area in a building. **2** unoccupied space. **3** scope or opportunity. ♦ *pl* **4** lodgings. ♦ *v* **5** *US* occupy or share a room. **roomy** *adj* **roomier, roomiest** spacious.

roost *n* **1** perch for fowls. ♦ *v* **2** perch. **rooster** *n* domestic cock.

root[1] *n* **1** part of a plant that grows down into the earth obtaining nourishment. **2** plant with an edible root, such as a carrot. **3** part of a tooth, hair, etc.

below the skin. **4** source or origin. **5** form of a word from which other words and forms are derived. **6** *Maths* factor of a quantity which, when multiplied by itself the number of times indicated, gives the quantity. ♦ *pl* **7** person's sense of belonging. ♦ *v* **8** establish a root and start to grow. **rootless** *adj* having no sense of belonging. **root for** *v Informal* cheer on. **root out** *v* get rid of completely. **rootstock** *n* rhizome.

root[2], **rootle** *v* **1** dig or burrow. **2** *Informal* search vigorously but unsystematically.

rope *n* thick cord. **know the ropes** be thoroughly familiar with an activity. **rope in** *v* persuade to join in. **rope off** *v* enclose or divide with a rope.

ropey, ropy *adj* **ropier, ropiest** *Informal* **1** inferior or inadequate. **2** not well.

Roquefort *n* strong blue-veined cheese made from ewes' or goats' milk.

rorqual *n* toothless whale with a dorsal fin.

rosary *n, pl* **-saries** **1** series of prayers. **2** string of beads for counting these prayers.

rose[1] *n* **1** shrub or climbing plant with prickly stems and fragrant flowers. **2** flower of this plant. **3** perforated flat nozzle for a hose. **4** pink colour. ♦ *adj* **5** pink. **roseate** [**roe**-zee-ate] *adj* rose-coloured. **rose window** circular window with spokes branching from the centre. **rosewood** *n* fragrant wood used to make furniture.

rose[2] *v* past tense of RISE.

rosé [**roe**-zay] *n* pink wine.

rosehip *n* berry-like fruit of a rose plant.

rosemary *n* **1** fragrant flowering shrub. **2** its leaves as a herb.

rosette *n* rose-shaped ornament, esp. a circular bunch of ribbons.

Rosh Hashanah, Rosh Hashana *n Hebrew* Jewish New Year festival.

rosin [**rozz**-in] *n* **1** resin used for treating the bows of violins etc. ♦ *v* **2** apply rosin to.

roster *n* list of people and their turns of duty.

rostrum *n, pl* **-trums, -tra** platform or stage.

rosy *adj* **rosier, rosiest** **1** pink-coloured. **2** hopeful or promising.

rot *v* **rotting, rotted** **1** decompose or decay. **2** slowly deteriorate physically or mentally. ♦ *n* **3** decay. **4** *Informal* nonsense.

rota *n* list of people who take it in turn to do a particular task.

rotary *adj* **1** revolving. **2** operated by rotation.

rotate *v* **1** (cause to) move round a centre or on a pivot. **2** (cause to) follow a set sequence. **3** plant different crops from one year to the next to maintain the fertility of the soil. **rotation** *n*

rote *n* mechanical repetition. **by rote** by memory.

rotisserie *n* rotating spit for cooking meat.

rotor *n* **1** revolving portion of a dynamo, motor, or turbine. **2** rotating device with long blades that provides thrust to lift a helicopter.

rotten *adj* **1** decaying. **2** *Informal* very bad. **3** corrupt. **rottenness** *n*

rotter *n Slang* despicable person.

Rottweiler [**rot**-vile-er] *n* large sturdy dog with a smooth black and tan coat and usu. a docked tail.

rotund [roe-**tund**] *adj* **1** round and plump. **2** sonorous. **rotundity** *n*

rotunda *n* circular building or room, esp. with a dome.

rouble [**roo**-bl] *n* monetary unit of Russia, Belarus, and Tajikistan.

roué [**roo**-ay] *n* man given to immoral living.

rouge *n* **1** red cosmetic used to colour the cheeks. ♦ *v* **2** apply rouge to.

rough *adj* **1** uneven or irregular. **2** not careful or gentle. **3** difficult or unpleasant. **4** approximate. **5** violent, stormy, or boisterous. **6** in preliminary form. **7** lacking refinement. ♦ *v* **8** make rough. ♦ *n* **9** rough state or area. **10** sketch. **rough it** live without the usual comforts etc. **roughen** *v* **roughly** *adv* **roughness** *n* **roughage** *n* indigestible constituents of food which aid digestion. **rough-and-ready** *adj* hastily prepared but adequate. **rough-and-tumble** *n* playful fight. **rough-hewn** *adj* roughly shaped. **roughhouse** *n Slang* fight. **roughneck** *n Slang* **1** violent person. **2** worker on an oil rig. **rough out** *v* prepare (a sketch or report) in preliminary form.

roughcast *n* **1** mixture of plaster and small stones for outside walls. ♦ *v* **2** coat with this.

roughshod *adv* **ride roughshod over** act with total disregard for.

roulette *n* gambling game played with a revolving wheel and a ball.

round *adj* **1** spherical, cylindrical, circular, or curved. **2** complete or whole, e.g. *round numbers.* ♦ *adv, prep* **3** indicating an encircling movement, presence on all sides, etc., e.g. *tied round the waist; books scattered round the room.* ♦ *v* **4** move round. ♦ *n* **5** round shape. **6** recurrent duties. **7** customary course, as of a milkman. **8** game (of golf). **9** stage in a competition. **10** one of several periods in a boxing match etc. **11** number of drinks bought at one time. **12** bullet or shell for a gun. **13** part song in which singers join at equal intervals. **14** circular movement. **15** set of sandwiches. **roundly** *adv* thoroughly. **rounders** *n* bat-and-ball team game. **round on** *v* attack angrily. **round robin** petition signed with names in a circle to conceal the order. **round table** meeting of people on equal terms for discussion. **round-the-clock** *adj* throughout the day and night. **round trip** journey out and back again. **round up** *v* gather (people or animals) together. **roundup** *n*

roundabout *n* **1** road junction at which traffic passes round a central island. **2** revolving circular platform on which people ride for amusement. ♦ *adj* **3** not straightforward.

roundel *n* small disc. **roundelay** *n* simple song with a refrain.

Roundhead *n Hist* supporter of Parliament against Charles I in the English Civil War.

rouse *v* **1** wake up. **2** provoke or excite. **rousing** *adj* lively, vigorous.

roustabout *n* labourer on an oil rig.

rout *n* **1** overwhelming defeat. **2** disorderly retreat. ♦ *v* **3** defeat and put to flight.

route *n* **1** roads taken to reach a destination. **2** chosen way. ♦ *v* **3** send by a particular route. **routemarch** *n* long military training march.

routine *n* **1** usual or regular method of procedure. **2** set sequence. ♦ *adj* **3** ordinary or regular.

roux [**roo**] *n* fat and flour cooked together as a basis for sauces.

rove *v* wander. **rover** *n*

row[1] [rhymes with **go**] *n* straight line of people or things. **in a row** in succession.

row[2] [rhymes with **go**] *v* **1** propel (a boat) by oars. ♦ *n* **2** spell of rowing. **rowing boat** boat propelled by oars.

row[3] [rhymes with **now**] *Informal* ♦ *n* **1** dispute. **2** disturbance. **3** reprimand. ♦ *v* **4** quarrel noisily.

rowan *n* tree producing bright red berries, mountain ash.

rowdy *adj* **-dier, -diest 1** disorderly, noisy, and rough. ♦ *n, pl* **-dies 2** person like this.

rowel [rhymes with **towel**] *n* small spiked wheel on a spur.

rowlock [**rol**-luk] *n* device on a boat that holds an oar in place.

royal *adj* **1** of, befitting, or supported by a king or queen. **2** splendid. ♦ *n* **3** *Informal* member of a royal family. **royally** *adv* **royalist** *n* supporter of monarchy. **royalty** *n* **1** royal people. **2** rank or power of a monarch. **3** (*pl* **-ties**) payment to an author, musician, inventor, etc. **royal blue** deep blue.

RPI retail price index: measure of change in the average level of prices.

rpm revolutions per minute.

RR Right Reverend.

RSI repetitive strain injury.

RSPCA Royal Society for the Prevention

of Cruelty to Animals.

RSVP please reply.

Rt Hon. Right Honourable.

Ru *Chem* ruthenium.

rub *v* **rubbing, rubbed 1** apply pressure and friction to (something) with a circular or backwards-and-forwards movement. **2** clean, polish, or dry by rubbing. **3** chafe or fray through rubbing. ♦ *n* **4** act of rubbing. **5** difficulty. **rub it in** emphasize an unpleasant fact. **rub along** *v* have a friendly relationship. **rub off** *v* affect through close association. **rub out** *v* remove with a rubber.

rubato *adv, n Music* (with) expressive flexibility of tempo.

rubber[1] *n* **1** strong waterproof elastic material, orig. made from the dried sap of a tropical tree, now usu. synthetic. **2** piece of rubber used for erasing writing. ♦ *adj* **3** made of or producing rubber. **rubberize** *v* coat or treat with rubber. **rubbery** *adj* **rubberneck** *v US* stare with unthinking curiosity. **rubber plant** house plant with glossy leaves. **rubber stamp 1** device for imprinting the date, a name, etc. **2** automatic authorization.

rubber[2] *n* **1** match consisting of three games of bridge, whist, etc. **2** series of matches.

rubbish *n* **1** waste matter. **2** anything worthless. **3** nonsense. ♦ *v* **4** *Informal* criticize. **rubbishy** *adj*

rubble *n* fragments of broken stone, brick, etc.

rubella [roo-**bell**-a] *n* same as GERMAN MEASLES.

rubicund [**roo**-bik-kund] *adj* ruddy.

rubidium [roo-**bid**-ee-um] *n Chem* soft highly reactive radioactive element.

rubric [**roo**-brik] *n* **1** set of rules for behaviour. **2** heading or explanation inserted in a text.

ruby *n, pl* **-bies 1** red precious gemstone. ♦ *adj* **2** deep red. **ruby wedding** fortieth wedding anniversary.

ruche *n* pleat or frill of lace etc. as a decoration.

ruck[1] *n* **1** rough crowd of common people. **2** *Rugby* loose scrummage.

ruck[2] *n, v* wrinkle or crease.

rucksack *n* large pack carried on the back.

ructions *pl n Informal* noisy uproar.

rudder *n* vertical hinged piece at the stern of a boat or at the rear of an aircraft, for steering.

ruddy *adj* **-dier, -diest 1** of a fresh healthy red colour. ♦ *adv, adj* **2** *Slang* bloody.

rude *adj* **1** impolite or insulting. **2** coarse, vulgar, or obscene. **3** unexpected and unpleasant. **4** roughly made. **5** robust. **rudely** *adv* **rudeness** *n*

rudiments *pl n* simplest and most basic stages of a subject. **rudimentary** *adj* basic, elementary.

rue[1] *v* **ruing, rued** feel regret for. **rueful** *adj* regretful or sorry. **ruefully** *adv*

rue[2] *n* plant with evergreen bitter leaves.

ruff[1] *n* **1** starched and frilled collar. **2** natural collar of feathers, fur, etc. on certain birds and animals. **3** kind of sandpiper.

ruff[2] *n, v Cards* same as TRUMP[1].

ruffian *n* violent lawless person.

ruffle *v* **1** disturb the calm of. **2** annoy, irritate. ♦ *n* **3** frill or pleat.

rufous *adj* reddish-brown.

rug *n* **1** small carpet. **2** thick woollen blanket.

rugby *n* form of football played with an oval ball which may be handled by the players.

rugged [**rug**-gid] *adj* **1** rocky or steep. **2** uneven and jagged. **3** strong-featured. **4** tough and sturdy.

rugger *n Informal* rugby.

ruin *v* **1** destroy or spoil completely. **2** impoverish. ♦ *n* **3** destruction or decay. **4** loss of wealth, position, etc. **5** broken-down unused building. **ruination** *n* **1** act of ruining. **2** state of being ruined. **3** cause of ruin. **ruinous** *adj* **1** causing ruin. **2** more expensive than can be afforded. **ruinously** *adv*

rule *n* **1** statement of what is allowed, for example in a game or procedure. **2** what is usual. **3** government, authority, or control. **4** measuring device with a straight edge. ♦ *v* **5** govern. **6** be pre-eminent. **7** give a formal decision. **8** mark with straight line(s). **9** restrain. **as a rule** usually. **ruler** *n* **1** person who governs. **2** measuring device with a straight edge. **ruling** *n* formal decision. **rule of thumb** practical but imprecise approach. **rule out** *v* exclude.

rum[1] *n* alcoholic drink distilled from sugar cane.

rum[2] *adj Informal* odd, strange.

rumba *n* lively ballroom dance of Cuban origin.

rumble *v* **1** make a low continuous noise. **2** *Informal* discover the (disreputable) truth about. ♦ *n* **3** deep resonant sound.

rumbustious *adj* boisterous or unruly.

ruminate *v* **1** chew the cud. **2** ponder or meditate. **ruminant** *adj, n* cud-chewing (animal, such as a cow, sheep, or deer). **rumination** *n* quiet meditation and reflection. **ruminative** *adj*

rummage *v* **1** search untidily and at length. ♦ *n* **2** untidy search through a collection of things.

rummy *n* card game in which players try to collect sets or sequences.

rumour *n* **1** unproved statement. **2** gossip or common talk. **rumoured** *adj* suggested by rumour.

rump *n* **1** buttocks. **2** rear of an animal.

rumple *v* make untidy, crumpled, or dishevelled.

rumpus *n, pl* **-puses** noisy commotion.

run *v* **running, ran, run** **1** move with a more rapid gait than walking. **2** go quickly (across). **3** compete in a race, election, etc. **4** operate a vehicle. **5** travel according to schedule. **6** function. **7** manage. **8** continue in a particular direction or for a specified period. **9** expose oneself to (a risk). **10** flow. **11** spread. **12** (of stitches) unravel. **13** (of a newspaper) publish (a story). **14** smuggle (goods, esp. arms). ♦ *n* **15** act or spell of running. **16** ride in a car. **17** unrestricted access. **18** continuous period. **19** sequence. **20** heavy demand. **21** series of unravelled stitches, ladder. **22** steep snow-covered course for skiing. **23** enclosure for domestic fowls. **24** migration of fish upstream to spawn. **25** score of one at cricket. **run across** *v* meet by chance. **run away** *v* make one's escape, flee. **runaway** *n* person or animal that runs away. **run down** *v* **1** be rude about. **2** reduce in number or size. **3** stop working. **rundown** *n* **run-down** *adj* **1** exhausted. **2** dilapidated. **run in** *v* **1** run (an engine) gently. **2** *Informal* arrest. **run-in** *n Informal* argument. **run into** *v* meet. **run-of-the-mill** *adj* ordinary. **run out** *v* be completely used up. **run over** *v* knock down (a person) with a moving vehicle. **run up** *v* incur (a debt). **run-up** *n* time just before an event.

rune *n* **1** any character of the earliest Germanic alphabet. **2** obscure piece of writing using mysterious symbols. **runic** *adj*

rung[1] *n* crossbar on a ladder.

rung[2] *v* past participle of RING[1].

runnel *n* small brook.

runner *n* **1** competitor in a race. **2** messenger. **3** smuggler. **4** part underneath an ice skate etc., on which it slides. **5** slender horizontal stem of a plant, such as a strawberry, running along the ground and forming new roots at intervals. **6** long strip of carpet or decorative cloth. **runner bean** seeds and pod of a climbing bean plant. **runner-up** *n* person who comes second in a competition.

running *adj* **1** continuous. **2** consecutive. **3** (of water) flowing. ♦ *n* **4** act of moving or flowing quickly. **5** management of a business etc. **in, out of the running** having *or* not having a good chance in a competition.

runny *adj* **-nier, -niest** **1** tending to flow. **2** exuding moisture.

runt *n* **1** smallest animal in a litter. **2** undersized person.

runway *n* hard level roadway where aircraft take off and land.

rupee *n* monetary unit of India and Pakistan.

rupture *n* **1** breaking, breach. **2** hernia. ♦ *v* **3** break, burst, or sever.

rural *adj* in or of the countryside.

ruse [**rooz**] *n* stratagem or trick.

rush[1] *v* **1** move or do very quickly. **2** force (someone) to act hastily. **3** make a sudden attack upon (a person or place). ♦ *n* **4** sudden quick or violent movement. **5** sudden demand. ♦ *pl* **6** first unedited prints of a scene for a film. ♦ *adj* **7** done with speed, hasty. **rush hour** period at the beginning and end of the working day, when many people are travelling to or from work.

rush[2] *n* marsh plant with a slender pithy stem. **rushy** *adj* full of rushes.

rusk *n* hard brown crisp biscuit, used esp. for feeding babies.

russet *adj* **1** reddish-brown. ♦ *n* **2** apple with rough reddish-brown skin.

Russian *adj* **1** of Russia. ♦ *n* **2** person from Russia. **3** official language of Russia and, formerly, of the Soviet Union. **Russian roulette** act of bravado in which a person spins the cylinder of a revolver loaded with only one cartridge and presses the trigger with the barrel against his or her own head.

rust *n* **1** reddish-brown coating formed on iron etc. that has been exposed to moisture. **2** disease of plants which produces rust-coloured spots. ♦ *adj* **3** reddish-brown. ♦ *v* **4** become coated with rust. **5** deteriorate through lack of use. **rusty** *adj* **rustier, rustiest 1** coated with rust. **2** of a rust colour. **3** out of practice.

rustic *adj* **1** of or resembling country people. **2** rural. **3** crude, awkward, or uncouth. **4** (of furniture) made of untrimmed branches. ♦ *n* **5** person from the country. **rusticity** *n*

rusticate *v* **1** banish temporarily from university as a punishment. **2** retire to the country.

rustle[1] *v, n* (make) a low whispering sound.

rustle[2] *v US* steal (cattle). **rustler** *n US* cattle thief. **rustle up** *v* prepare at short notice.

rut[1] *n* **1** furrow made by wheels. **2** dull settled habits or way of living.

rut[2] *n* **1** recurrent period of sexual excitability in male deer. ♦ *v* **rutting, rutted 2** be in a period of sexual excitability.

ruthenium *n Chem* rare hard brittle white element.

ruthless *adj* pitiless, merciless. **ruthlessly** *adv* **ruthlessness** *n*

rye *n* **1** kind of grain used for fodder and bread. **2** *US* whiskey made from rye.

rye-grass *n* any of several grasses cultivated for fodder.

S s

s second(s).

S **1** South(ern). **2** *Chem* sulphur.

SA **1** Salvation Army. **2** South Africa. **3** South Australia.

Sabbath *n* day of worship and rest: Saturday for Jews, Sunday for Christians. **sabbatical** *adj, n* (denoting) leave for study.

sable *n* **1** dark fur from a small weasel-like Arctic animal. ♦ *adj* **2** black.

sabot [**sab**-oh] *n* wooden shoe, clog.

sabotage *n* **1** intentional damage done to machinery, systems, etc. ♦ *v* **2** damage intentionally. **saboteur** *n* person who commits sabotage.

sabre *n* **1** curved cavalry sword. **2** light fencing sword.

sac *n* pouchlike structure in an animal or plant.

saccharin *n* artificial sweetener. **saccharine** *adj* **1** excessively sweet. **2** of or like sugar.

sacerdotal *adj* of priests.

sachet *n* **1** small envelope or bag containing a single portion. **2** small bag of perfumed powder for scenting clothing.

sack[1] *n* **1** large bag made of coarse material. **2** *Informal* dismissal. **3** *Slang* bed. ♦ *v* **4** *Informal* dismiss. **sacking** *n* rough woven material used for sacks. **sackcloth** *n* coarse fabric used for sacks, formerly worn as a penance.

sack[2] *n* **1** plundering of a captured town. ♦ *v* **2** plunder (a captured town).

sacrament *n* ceremony of the Christian Church, esp. Communion. **sacramental** *adj*

sacred *adj* **1** holy. **2** connected with religion. **3** set apart, reserved. **sacred cow** person, custom, etc. regarded as being beyond criticism.

sacrifice *n* **1** giving something up. **2** thing given up. **3** making of an offering to a god. **4** thing offered. ♦ *v* **5** offer as a sacrifice. **6** give (something) up. **sacrificial** *adj*

sacrilege *n* misuse or desecration of something sacred. **sacrilegious** *adj*

sacristan *n* person in charge of the contents of a church. **sacristy** *n, pl* **-ties** room in a church where sacred objects are kept.

sacrosanct *adj* regarded as sacred, inviolable.

sacrum [**say**-krum] *n, pl* **-cra** wedge-shaped bone at the base of the spine.

sad *adj* **sadder, saddest** **1** sorrowful, unhappy. **2** causing or expressing sorrow. **3** deplorably bad. **sadden** *v* make sad. **sadly** *adv* **sadness** *n*

saddle *n* **1** rider's seat on a horse or bicycle. **2** joint of meat. ♦ *v* **3** put a saddle on (a horse). **4** burden (with a responsibility). **saddler** *n* maker or seller of saddles. **saddlery** *n*

sadism [**say**-dizz-um] *n* gaining of (sexual) pleasure from inflicting pain. **sadist** *n* **sadistic** *adj* **sadistically** *adv*

sadomasochism *n* combination of sadism and masochism. **sadomasochist** *n*

s.a.e. stamped addressed envelope.

safari *n, pl* **-ris** expedition to hunt or observe wild animals, esp. in Africa. **safari park** park where lions, elephants, etc. are kept uncaged so that people can see them from cars.

safe *adj* **1** secure, protected. **2** uninjured, out of danger. **3** not involving risk. **4** not dangerous, e.g. *the beef is safe to eat.* ♦ *n* **5** strong lockable container. **safely** *adv* **safe-conduct** *n* permit allowing travel through a dangerous area. **safe deposit** place where valuables can be stored safely. **safekeeping** *n* protection.

safeguard *v* **1** protect. ♦ *n* **2** protection.

safety *n, pl* **-ties** state of being safe. **safety belt** same as SEAT BELT. **safety lamp** miner's lamp designed to prevent it from igniting gas. **safety net** net to catch performers on a trapeze or high wire if they fall. **safety pin** pin with a spring fastening and a guard over the point when closed. **safety valve** 1 valve that allows steam etc. to escape if pressure becomes excessive. 2 harmless outlet for emotion.

safflower *n* thistle-like plant with flowers used for dye and oil.

saffron *n* **1** orange-coloured flavouring obtained from a crocus. ♦ *adj* **2** orange.

sag *v* **sagging, sagged 1** sink in the middle. **2** tire. **3** (of clothes) hang loosely. ♦ *n* **4** droop.

saga [**sah**-ga] *n* **1** legend of Norse heroes. **2** any long story.

sagacious *adj* wise. **sagacity** *n*

sage[1] *n* **1** very wise man. ♦ *adj* **2** *Lit* wise. **sagely** *adv*

sage[2] *n* aromatic herb with grey-green leaves.

sagebrush *n* aromatic plant of West N America.

Sagittarius *n* (the archer) ninth sign of the zodiac.

sago *n* starchy cereal from the powdered pith of the sago palm tree.

sahib *n* Indian term of address placed after a man's name as a mark of respect.

said *v* past of SAY.

sail *n* **1** sheet of fabric stretched to catch the wind for propelling a sailing boat. **2** journey by boat. **3** arm of a windmill. ♦ *v* **4** travel by water. **5** begin a voyage. **6** navigate a vessel. **7** move smoothly. **sailor** *n* **1** member of a ship's crew. **2** person considered as liable or not liable to seasickness, e.g. *a bad sailor; a good sailor.* **sailboard** *n* board with a mast and single sail, used for windsurfing. **sailcloth** *n* **1** fabric for making sails. **2** light canvas for making clothes.

saint *n* **1** *Christianity* person venerated after death as specially holy. **2** exceptionally good person. **saintly** *adj* **saintliness** *n* **sainthood** *n*

saithe *n* dark-coloured edible sea fish.

sake[1] *n* **1** benefit. **2** purpose. **for the sake of 1** for the purpose of. **2** to please or benefit (someone).

sake[2], **saki** [**sah**-kee] *n* Japanese alcoholic drink made from fermented rice.

salaam [sal-**ahm**] *n* **1** low bow of greeting among Muslims. ♦ *v* **2** make a salaam.

salacious *adj* excessively concerned with sex.

salad *n* dish of raw vegetables, eaten as a meal or part of a meal. **salad days** period of youth and inexperience. **salad dressing** sauce of oil and vinegar or mayonnaise.

salamander *n* amphibian which looks like a lizard.

salami *n* highly spiced sausage.

salary *n, pl* **-ries** fixed regular payment, usu. monthly, to an employee. **salaried** *adj*

sale *n* **1** exchange of goods for money. **2** amount sold. **3** selling of goods at unusually low prices. **4** auction. ♦ *pl* **5** department that sells its company's products. **saleable** *adj* fit or likely to be sold. **saleroom** *n* place where goods are sold by auction. **salesman, saleswoman, salesperson** *n* person who sells goods. **salesmanship** *n* skill in selling.

salient [**say**-lee-ent] *adj* **1** prominent, noticeable. ♦ *n* **2** *Mil* projecting part of a front line.

saline [**say**-line] *adj* containing salt. **salinity** *n*

saliva [sal-**lie**-va] *n* liquid that forms in the mouth, spittle. **salivary** *adj* **salivate** *v* produce saliva.

sallow *adj* of an unhealthy pale or yellowish colour.

sally *n, pl* **-lies 1** witty remark. **2** sudden brief attack by troops. ♦ *v* **-lying, -lied** (foll. by *forth*) **3** rush out. **4** go out.

salmon *n* **1** large fish with orange-pink flesh valued as food. ♦ *adj* **2** orange-pink.

salmonella *n, pl* **-lae** bacterium causing food poisoning.

salon *n* **1** commercial premises of a hairdresser, beautician, etc. **2** elegant reception room for guests. **3** informal gathering of important people.

saloon *n* **1** car with a fixed roof. **2** large public room, as on a ship. **3** *US* bar serving alcoholic drinks. **saloon bar** more expensive bar in a pub.

salt *n* **1** white crystalline substance used to season food. **2** chemical compound of acid and metal. **3** liveliness, wit. ♦ *pl* **4** mineral salts used as a medicine. ♦ *v* **5** season or preserve with salt. **6** scatter salt over (an icy road) to melt the ice. **old salt** experienced sailor. **with a pinch of salt** allowing for exaggeration. **worth one's salt** efficient. **salty** *adj* **salt away** *v* hoard or save. **saltcellar** *n* small container for salt at table. **saltwater** *adj* living in the sea.

saltpetre *n* compound used in gunpowder and as a preservative.

salubrious *adj* favourable to health.

Saluki *n* tall hound with a silky coat.

salutary *adj* producing a beneficial result.

salute *n* **1** motion of the arm as a formal military sign of respect. **2** firing of guns as a military greeting of honour. ♦ *v* **3** greet with a salute. **4** make a salute. **5** acknowledge with praise. **salutation** *n* greeting by words or actions.

salvage *n* **1** saving of a ship or other property from destruction. **2** property so saved. ♦ *v* **3** save from destruction or waste. **4** gain (something beneficial) from a failure.

salvation *n* **1** fact or state of being saved from harm or the consequences of sin. **2** person or thing that preserves from harm.

salve *n* **1** healing or soothing ointment. ♦ *v* **2** soothe or appease, e.g. *salve one's conscience.*

salver *n* (silver) tray on which something is presented.

salvia *n* plant with blue or red flowers.

salvo *n, pl* **-vos, -voes 1** simultaneous discharge of guns etc. **2** burst of applause or questions.

sal volatile [sal vol-**at**-ill-ee] *n* preparation of ammonia, used to revive a person who feels faint.

SAM surface-to-air missile.

Samaritan *n* person who helps people in distress.

samarium *n Chem* silvery metallic element.

samba *n* lively Brazilian dance.

same *adj* **1** identical, not different, unchanged. **2** just mentioned. **all the same, just the same** nevertheless. **sameness** *n*

samovar *n* Russian tea urn.

Samoyed *n* dog with a thick white coat and tightly curled tail.

sampan *n* small boat with oars used in China.

samphire *n* plant found on rocks by the seashore.

sample *n* **1** part taken as representative of a whole. ♦ *v* **2** take and test a sample of. **sampler** *n* piece of embroidery showing the embroiderer's skill. **sampling** *n*

samurai *n, pl* **-rai** member of an ancient Japanese warrior caste.

sanatorium *n, pl* **-riums, -ria 1** institution for invalids or convalescents. **2** room for sick pupils at a boarding school.

sanctify *v* **-fying, -fied 1** make holy. **2** approve as religiously binding.

sanctimonious *adj* pretending to be religious and virtuous.

sanction *n* **1** permission, authorization. **2** coercive measure or penalty. ♦ *v* **3** allow, authorize.

sanctity *n* sacredness, inviolability.

sanctuary *n, pl* **-aries 1** holy place. **2** part of a church nearest the altar. **3** place of safety for a fugitive. **4** place where animals or birds can live undisturbed.

sanctum *n, pl* **-tums, -ta 1** sacred place. **2** person's private room.

sand *n* **1** substance consisting of small grains of rock, esp. on a beach or in a desert. ♦ *pl* **2** stretches of sand forming a beach or desert. ♦ *v* **3** smooth with sandpaper. **4** fill with sand. **sander** *n* power tool for smoothing surfaces. **sandy** *adj* **1** covered with sand. **2** (of hair) reddish-fair. **sandbag** *n* **1** bag filled with sand, used as protection against gunfire or flood water. ♦ *v* **2** protect with sandbags. **sandbank** *n* bank of sand below the surface of a river or sea. **sandblast** *v, n* (clean with) a jet of sand blown from a nozzle under pressure. **sand castle** model of a castle made from sand. **sandpaper** *n* **1** paper coated with sand for smoothing a surface. ♦ *v* **2** smooth with sandpaper. **sandpiper** *n* shore bird with a long bill and slender legs. **sandstone** *n* rock composed of sand. **sandstorm** *n* desert wind that whips up clouds of sand.

sandal *n* light shoe consisting of a sole attached by straps.

sandalwood *n* sweet-scented wood.

sandwich *n* **1** two slices of bread with a layer of food between. ♦ *v* **2** insert between two other things. **sandwich board** pair of boards hung over a person's shoulders to display advertisements in front and behind. **sandwich course** course consisting of alternate periods of study and work.

sane *adj* **1** of sound mind. **2** sensible, rational. **sanity** *n*

sang *v* past tense of SING.

sang-froid [sahng-**frwah**] *n* composure and calmness.

sangria *n* Spanish drink of wine and fruit juice.

sanguinary *adj* **1** accompanied by bloodshed. **2** bloodthirsty.

sanguine *adj* **1** cheerful, optimistic. **2** ruddy.

Sanhedrin [**san**-id-rin] *n Judaism* highest court of the ancient Jewish nation.

sanitary *adj* **1** promoting health by getting rid of dirt and germs. **2** hygienic. **sanitation** *n* sanitary measures, esp. drainage or sewerage. **sanitary towel** absorbent pad worn externally during menstruation.

sank *v* past tense of SINK.

Sanskrit *n* ancient language of India.

Santa Claus *n* legendary patron saint of children, who brings presents at Christmas.

sap[1] *n* **1** moisture that circulates in plants. **2** *Informal* gullible person. **sappy** *adj*

sap[2] *v* **sapping, sapped 1** undermine. **2** weaken. ♦ *n* **3** trench dug to undermine an enemy position. **sapper** *n* soldier in an engineering unit.

sapient [**say** pee-ent] *adj Lit* wise, shrewd. **sapience** *n*

sapling *n* young tree.

sapphire *n* **1** blue precious stone. ♦ *adj* **2** deep blue.

saprophyte *n* plant that lives on dead organic matter.

sarabande, saraband *n* slow stately Spanish dance.

Saracen *n Hist* Arab or Muslim who opposed the Crusades.

sarcasm *n* (use of) bitter or wounding ironic language. **sarcastic** *adj* **sarcastically** *adv*

sarcoma *n, pl* **-mata, -mas** malignant tumour beginning in connective tissue.

sarcophagus *n, pl* **-gi, -guses** stone coffin.

sardine *n* small fish of the herring family, usu. preserved in tightly packed tins.

sardonic *adj* mocking or scornful. **sardonically** *adv*

sardonyx *n* brown-and-white gemstone.

sargassum, sargasso *n* type of floating seaweed.

sari, saree *n* long piece of cloth draped around the body and over one shoulder, worn by Hindu women.

sarong *n* long piece of cloth tucked around the waist or under the armpits, worn esp. in Malaysia.

sarsaparilla *n* soft drink, orig. made from the root of a tropical American plant.

sartorial *adj* of men's clothes or tailoring.

SAS Special Air Service.

sash[1] *n* decorative strip of cloth worn round the waist or over one shoulder.

sash[2] *n* wooden frame containing the panes of a window. **sash window** window consisting of two sashes that can be opened by sliding one over the other.

sassafras *n* American tree with aromatic bark used medicinally.

Sassenach *n Scot* English person.
sat *v* past of SIT.
Sat. Saturday.
Satan *n* the Devil. **satanic** *adj* **1** of Satan. **2** supremely evil. **Satanism** *n* worship of Satan.
satchel *n* bag, usu. with a shoulder strap, for carrying school books.
sate *v* satisfy (a desire or appetite) fully.
satellite *n* **1** man-made device orbiting in space. **2** heavenly body that orbits another. **3** country that is dependent on a more powerful one. ♦ *adj* **4** of or used in the transmission of television signals from a satellite to the home.
satiate [**say**-she-ate] *v* provide with more than enough, so as to disgust. **satiable** *adj* **satiety** [sat-**tie**-a-tee] *n* feeling of having had too much.
satin *n* silky fabric with a glossy surface on one side. **satiny** *adj* of or like satin. **satinwood** *n* tropical tree yielding hard wood.
satire *n* **1** use of ridicule to expose vice or folly. **2** poem or other work that does this. **satirical** *adj* **satirist** *n* **satirize** *v* ridicule by means of satire.
satisfy *v* **-fying, -fied 1** please, content. **2** provide amply for (a need or desire). **3** convince, persuade. **4** fulfil the requirements of. **satisfaction** *n* **satisfactory** *adj*
satsuma *n* kind of small orange.
saturate *v* **1** soak thoroughly. **2** cause to absorb the maximum amount of something. **saturation** *n* **saturation point** point at which some capacity is at its fullest.
Saturday *n* seventh day of the week.
Saturn *n* **1** Roman god of agriculture. **2** sixth planet from the sun. **saturnine** *adj* gloomy in temperament or appearance. **saturnalia** *n* wild party or orgy.
satyr *n* **1** woodland god, part man, part goat. **2** lustful man.
sauce *n* **1** liquid added to food to enhance flavour. **2** *Informal* impudence. **saucy** *adj* **1** impudent. **2** pert, jaunty. **saucily** *adv* **saucepan** *n* cooking pot with a long handle.
saucer *n* small round dish put under a cup.
sauerkraut *n* shredded cabbage fermented in brine.
sauna *n* Finnish-style steam bath.
saunter *v* **1** walk in a leisurely manner, stroll. ♦ *n* **2** leisurely walk.
saurian *adj* of or like a lizard.
sausage *n* minced meat in an edible tube-shaped skin. **sausage roll** skinless sausage covered in pastry.
sauté [**so**-tay] *v* **-téing** *or* **-téeing, -téed** fry quickly in a little fat.
savage *adj* **1** wild, untamed. **2** cruel and violent. **3** uncivilized, primitive. ♦ *n* **4** uncivilized person. ♦ *v* **5** attack ferociously. **6** criticize violently. **savagely** *adv* **savagery** *n*
savannah, savanna *n* extensive open grassy plain in Africa.
savant *n* learned person.
save *v* **1** rescue or preserve from harm, protect. **2** avoid the waste or loss of. **3** keep for the future. **4** set aside (money). **5** prevent the necessity for. **6** *Sport* prevent the scoring of (a goal). ♦ *n* **7** *Sport* act of preventing a goal. ♦ *prep* **8** *Old-fashioned* except. **saver** *n* **saving** *n* **1** economy. ♦ *pl* **2** money put by for future use. ♦ *prep* **3** except. **saving grace** good quality that prevents a person from being worthless.
saveloy *n* spicy smoked sausage.
saviour *n* **1** person who rescues another. **2** (**S-**) Christ.
savoir-faire [sav-wahr-**fair**] *n French* ability to do and say the right thing in any situation.
savory *n* aromatic herb used in cooking.
savour *v* **1** enjoy, relish. **2** (foll. by *of*) have a flavour or suggestion of. ♦ *n* **3** characteristic taste or odour. **4** slight but distinctive quality. **savoury** *adj* **1** salty or spicy. **2** pleasant or acceptable. ♦ *n, pl* **-vouries 3** savoury dish served before or after a meal.
savoy *n* variety of cabbage.
savvy *Slang* ♦ *v* **-vying, -vied 1** understand. ♦ *n* **2** understanding, intelligence.

saw[1] *n* **1** cutting tool with a toothed metal blade. ♦ *v* **sawing, sawed, sawed** *or* **sawn 2** cut with a saw. **3** move (something) back and forth. **sawyer** *n* person who saws timber for a living. **sawdust** *n* fine wood fragments made in sawing. **sawfish** *n* fish with a long toothed snout. **sawmill** *n* mill where timber is sawn into planks.

saw[2] *v* past tense of SEE[1].

saw[3] *n* wise saying, proverb.

sax *n Informal* short for SAXOPHONE.

saxifrage *n* alpine rock plant with small flowers.

Saxon *n* **1** member of the W Germanic people who settled widely in Europe in the early Middle Ages. ♦ *adj* **2** of the Saxons.

saxophone *n* brass wind instrument with keys and a curved body. **saxophonist** *n*

say *v* **saying, said 1** speak or utter. **2** express (an idea) in words. **3** give as one's opinion. **4** indicate or show. **5** suppose as an example or possibility. ♦ *n* **6** right or chance to speak. **7** share in a decision. **saying** *n* maxim, proverb. **say-so** *n Informal* permission.

SAYE save as you earn: system by which regular payments are made into a savings account from a salary.

Sb *Chem* antimony.

Sc *Chem* scandium.

SC South Carolina.

scab *n* **1** crust formed over a wound. **2** *Offens* blackleg. **3** disease of plants and animals. **scabby** *adj* **1** covered with scabs. **2** *Informal* despicable.

scabbard *n* sheath for a sword or dagger.

scabies [**skay**-beez] *n* itchy skin disease.

scabrous [**skay**-bruss] *adj* **1** rough and scaly. **2** indecent.

scaffold *n* **1** temporary platform for workmen. **2** gallows. **scaffolding** *n* (materials for building) scaffolds.

scalar *n, adj* (variable quantity) having magnitude but no direction.

scald *v* **1** burn with hot liquid or steam. **2** sterilize with boiling water. **3** heat (liquid) almost to boiling point. ♦ *n* **4** injury by scalding.

scale[1] *n* **1** one of the thin overlapping plates covering fishes and reptiles. **2** thin flake. **3** coating which forms in kettles etc. due to hard water. **4** tartar formed on the teeth. ♦ *v* **5** remove scales from. **6** come off in scales. **scaly** *adj*

scale[2] *n* (often pl) weighing instrument.

scale[3] *n* **1** graduated table or sequence of marks at regular intervals, used as a reference in making measurements. **2** ratio of size between a thing and a representation of it. **3** graded system, e.g. *a wage scale.* **4** relative degree or extent. **5** fixed series of notes in music. **6** notation of a number system. ♦ *v* **7** climb. **scale up, down** *v* increase *or* decrease proportionately in size.

scalene *adj* (of a triangle) with three unequal sides.

scallion *n* spring onion.

scallop *n* **1** edible shellfish with two fan-shaped shells. **2** one of a series of small curves along an edge. **scalloped** *adj* decorated with small curves along the edge.

scallywag *n Informal* scamp, rascal.

scalp *n* **1** skin and hair on top of the head. **2** part of this taken as a trophy from a slain person by a Native American. ♦ *v* **3** cut off the scalp of.

scalpel *n* small surgical knife.

scamp *n* mischievous child.

scamper *v* **1** run about hurriedly or in play. ♦ *n* **2** scampering.

scampi *pl n* large prawns.

scan *v* **scanning, scanned 1** scrutinize carefully. **2** glance over quickly. **3** examine or search (an area) by passing a radar or sonar beam over it. **4** (of verse) conform to metrical rules. ♦ *n* **5** scanning. **scanner** *n* electronic device used for scanning. **scansion** *n* metrical scanning of verse.

scandal *n* **1** disgraceful action or event. **2** shame or outrage. **3** malicious gossip. **scandalize** *v* shock by scandal.

scandalmonger *n* person who spreads gossip. **scandalous** *adj*

Scandinavian *n, adj* (inhabitant or language) of Scandinavia (Norway, Denmark, Sweden, Finland, and Iceland).

scandium *n Chem* rare silvery-white metallic element.

scant *adj* barely sufficient, meagre.

scanty *adj* **scantier, scantiest** barely sufficient or not sufficient. **scantily** *adv* **scantiness** *n*

scapegoat *n* person made to bear the blame for others.

scapula *n, pl* **-lae, -las** shoulder blade. **scapular** *adj* of the scapula.

scar[1] *n* **1** mark left by a healed wound. **2** permanent emotional damage left by an unpleasant experience. ♦ *v* **scarring, scarred 3** mark or become marked with a scar.

scar[2] *n* bare craggy rock formation.

scarab *n* sacred beetle of ancient Egypt.

scarce *adj* **1** insufficient to meet demand. **2** not common, rarely found. **make oneself scarce** *Informal* go away. **scarcely** *adv* **1** hardly at all. **2** definitely or probably not. **scarcity** *n*

> As *scarcely* has a negative sense it is followed by *ever* or *any* (not *never* or *no*).

scare *v* **1** frighten or be frightened. **2** (foll. by *away* or *off*) drive away by frightening. ♦ *n* **3** fright, sudden panic. **4** period of general alarm. **scary** *adj Informal* frightening. **scarecrow** *n* **1** figure dressed in old clothes, set up to scare birds away from crops. **2** raggedly dressed person. **scaremonger** *n* person who spreads alarming rumours.

scarf[1] *n, pl* **scarves, scarfs** piece of material worn round the neck, head, or shoulders.

scarf[2] *n* **1** joint between two pieces of timber made by notching the ends and fastening them together. ♦ *v* **2** join in this way.

scarify *v* **-fying, -fied 1** scratch or cut slightly all over. **2** break up and loosen (topsoil). **3** criticize mercilessly. **scarification** *n*

scarlatina *n* scarlet fever.

scarlet *adj, n* brilliant red. **scarlet fever** infectious fever with a scarlet rash.

scarp *n* steep slope.

scarper *v Slang* run away.

scat[1] *v* **scatting, scatted** *Informal* go away.

scat[2] *n* jazz singing using improvised vocal sounds instead of words.

scathing *adj* harshly critical.

scatological *adj* preoccupied with obscenity, esp. with references to excrement. **scatology** *n*

scatter *v* **1** throw about in various directions. **2** disperse. ♦ *n* **3** scattering. **scatterbrain** *n* empty-headed person.

scatty *adj* **-tier, -tiest** *Informal* empty-headed.

scavenge *v* search for (anything usable) among discarded material. **scavenger** *n* **1** person who scavenges. **2** animal that feeds on decaying matter.

SCE Scottish Certificate of Education.

scenario *n, pl* **-rios 1** summary of the plot of a play or film. **2** imagined sequence of future events.

scene *n* **1** place of action of a real or imaginary event. **2** subdivision of a play or film in which the action is continuous. **3** scenery. **4** view of a place. **5** display of emotion. **6** *Informal* specific activity or interest, e.g. *the fashion scene*. **behind the scenes 1** backstage. **2** in secret. **scenery** *n* **1** natural features of a landscape. **2** painted backcloths or screens used on stage to represent the scene of action. **scenic** *adj* **1** picturesque. **2** of stage scenery.

scent *n* **1** pleasant smell. **2** smell left in passing, by which an animal can be traced. **3** series of clues. **4** perfume. ♦ *v* **5** detect by smell. **6** suspect. **7** fill with fragrance.

sceptic [**skep**-tik] *n* person who habitually doubts generally accepted beliefs. **sceptical** *adj* **sceptically** *adv* **scepticism** *n*

sceptre *n* ornamental rod symbolizing

royal power.
schedule *n* **1** plan of procedure for a project. **2** list. **3** timetable. ♦ *v* **4** plan to occur at a certain time. **5** make or place in a schedule.
schema *n, pl* **-mata** overall plan or diagram. **schematic** *adj* presented as a plan or diagram. **schematize** *v* arrange in a scheme.
scheme *n* **1** systematic plan. **2** systematic arrangement. **3** secret plot. ♦ *v* **4** plan in an underhand manner. **schemer** *n* **scheming** *adj, n*
scherzo [**skairt**-so] *n, pl* **-zos, -zi** brisk lively piece of music.
schilling *n* standard monetary unit of Austria.
schism [**skizz**-um] *n* (group resulting from) division in an organization. **schismatic** *adj, n*
schist [**skist**] *n* crystalline rock which splits into layers.
schizo [**skit**-so] *adj, n, pl* **-os** *Offens* schizophrenic (person).
schizoid *adj* **1** abnormally introverted. **2** *Informal* contradictory. ♦ *n* **3** schizoid person.
schizophrenia *n* **1** mental disorder involving deterioration of or confusion about the personality. **2** *Informal* contradictory behaviour or attitudes. **schizophrenic** *adj, n*
schmaltz *n* excessive sentimentality. **schmaltzy** *adj*
schnapps *n* strong alcoholic spirit.
schnitzel *n* thin slice of meat, esp. veal.
scholar *n* **1** learned person. **2** student receiving a scholarship. **3** pupil. **scholarly** *adj* learned. **scholarship** *n* **1** learning. **2** financial aid given to a student because of academic merit. **scholastic** *adj* of schools or scholars.
school[1] *n* **1** place where children are taught or instruction is given in a subject. **2** staff and pupils of a school. **3** department specializing in a subject. **4** group of artists, thinkers, etc. with shared principles or methods. ♦ *v* **5** educate or train. **schooling** *n* education. **schoolboy, schoolgirl** *n* child attending school. **schoolteacher, schoolmaster, schoolmistress** *n* person who teaches in a school.
school[2] *n* shoal of fish, whales, etc.
schooner *n* **1** sailing ship rigged fore-and-aft. **2** large glass.
schottische *n* type of slow polka.
sciatica *n* severe pain in the large nerve in the back of the leg. **sciatic** *adj* **1** of the hip. **2** of or afflicted with sciatica.
science *n* **1** systematic study and knowledge of natural or physical phenomena. **2** branch of this knowledge. **3** skill or technique. **scientific** *adj* **1** of science. **2** systematic. **scientifically** *adv* **scientist** *n* person who studies or practises a science. **science fiction** stories making imaginative use of scientific knowledge. **science park** area where scientific research and commercial development are carried on in cooperation.
sci-fi *n* short for SCIENCE FICTION.
scimitar *n* curved oriental sword.
scintillate *v* give off sparks. **scintillating** *adj* very lively and amusing. **scintillation** *n*
scion [**sy**-on] *n* **1** descendant or heir. **2** shoot of a plant for grafting.
scissors *pl n* cutting instrument with two crossed pivoted blades.
sclerosis *n, pl* **-ses** abnormal hardening of body tissues.
scoff[1] *v* **1** express derision. ♦ *n* **2** mocking expression.
scoff[2] *v Informal* eat rapidly.
scold *v* **1** find fault with, reprimand. ♦ *n* **2** person who scolds. **scolding** *n*
scollop *n* same as SCALLOP.
sconce *n* bracket on a wall for holding candles or lights.
scone *n* small plain cake baked in an oven or on a griddle.
scoop *n* **1** shovel-like tool for ladling or hollowing out. **2** news story reported in one newspaper before all its rivals. ♦ *v* **3** take up or hollow out with or as if with a scoop. **4** beat (rival newspapers) in reporting a news item.
scoot *v Slang* leave or move quickly.

scooter *n* **1** child's vehicle propelled by pushing on the ground with one foot. **2** light motorcycle.

scope *n* **1** opportunity for using abilities. **2** range of activity.

scorch *v* **1** burn on the surface. **2** parch or shrivel from heat. ♦ *n* **3** slight burn. **scorcher** *n Informal* very hot day.

score *n* **1** points gained in a game or competition. **2** twenty. **3** written version of a piece of music showing parts for each musician. **4** mark or cut. **5** record of amounts due. **6** reason. **7** grievance, e.g. *settle old scores.* ♦ *pl* **8** lots. ♦ *v* **9** gain (points) in a game. **10** keep a record of points. **11** mark or cut. **12** (foll. by *out*) cross out. **13** arrange music (for). **14** achieve a success. **score off** *v* gain an advantage at someone else's expense.

scorn *n* **1** open contempt. ♦ *v* **2** despise. **3** reject with contempt. **scornful** *adj* **scornfully** *adv*

Scorpio *n* (the scorpion) eighth sign of the zodiac.

scorpion *n* small lobster-shaped animal with a sting at the end of a jointed tail.

Scot *n* person from Scotland. **Scottish** *adj* of Scotland, its people, or their languages. **Scotch** *n* whisky distilled in Scotland. **Scotch broth** thick soup of beef or lamb and vegetables. **Scotch egg** hard-boiled egg encased in sausage meat and breadcrumbs. **Scots** *adj* **1** Scottish. ♦ *n* **2** English dialect spoken in Scotland. **Scotsman, Scotswoman** *n*

> *Scotch* is used only in certain fixed expressions like *Scotch egg*. The use of *Scotch* for *Scots* or *Scottish* is otherwise felt to be incorrect, esp. when applied to people.

scotch *v* **1** put an end to. **2** wound.

scot-free *adj* without harm or punishment.

Scotland Yard *n* headquarters of the police force of metropolitan London.

scoundrel *n Old-fashioned* cheat or deceiver.

scour[1] *v* **1** clean or polish by rubbing with something rough. **2** clear or flush out. ♦ *n* **3** scouring. **scourer** *n* small rough nylon pad used for cleaning pots and pans.

scour[2] *v* **1** search thoroughly and energetically. **2** move swiftly over.

scourge *n* **1** person or thing causing severe suffering. **2** whip. ♦ *v* **3** cause severe suffering to. **4** whip.

Scouse *Informal* ♦ *n* **1** (also **Scouser**) person from Liverpool. **2** dialect of Liverpool. ♦ *adj* **3** of Liverpool, its people, or their dialect.

scout *n* **1** person sent out to reconnoitre. **2** (**S-**) member of the Scout Association, an organization for boys which aims to develop character and promotes outdoor activities. ♦ *v* **3** act as a scout. **4** reconnoitre. **Scouter** *n* leader of a troop of Scouts.

scow *n* unpowered barge.

scowl *v, n* (have) an angry or sullen expression.

scrabble *v* **1** scrape at with the hands, feet, or claws. ♦ *n* **2** (**S-**) ® board game in which words are formed by letter tiles.

scrag *n* **1** thin end of a neck of mutton. **2** scrawny person or animal. **scraggy** *adj* thin, bony.

scram[1] *v* **scramming, scrammed** *Informal* go away quickly.

scram[2] *n* **1** emergency shutdown of a nuclear reactor. ♦ *v* **scramming, scrammed 2** (of a nuclear reactor) shut or be shut down in an emergency.

scramble *v* **1** climb or crawl hastily or awkwardly. **2** struggle with others (for). **3** mix up. **4** cook (eggs beaten up with milk). **5** (of an aircraft or aircrew) take off hurriedly in an emergency. **6** make (transmitted speech) unintelligible by the use of an electronic device. ♦ *n* **7** scrambling. **8** rough climb. **9** disorderly struggle. **10** motorcycle race over rough ground. **scrambler** *n* electronic device that makes transmitted speech unintelligible.

scrap[1] *n* **1** small piece. **2** waste metal collected for reprocessing. ♦ *pl* **3** leftover food. ♦ *v* **scrapping, scrapped 4** discard as useless. **scrappy** *adj* fragmentary, disjointed. **scrapbook** *n* book with blank pages in which newspaper cuttings or pictures are stuck.

scrap[2] *n, v* **scrapping, scrapped** *Informal* fight or quarrel.

scrape *v* **1** rub with something rough or sharp. **2** clean or smooth thus. **3** rub with a harsh noise. **4** economize. ♦ *n* **5** act or sound of scraping. **6** mark or wound caused by scraping. **7** *Informal* awkward situation. **scraper** *n* **scrape through** *v* succeed in or obtain with difficulty.

scratch *v* **1** mark or cut with claws, nails, or anything rough or sharp. **2** scrape (skin) with nails or claws to relieve itching. **3** cross out. **4** withdraw from a race or competition. ♦ *n* **5** wound, mark, or sound made by scratching. ♦ *adj* **6** put together at short notice. **7** *Sport* with no handicap allowed. **from scratch** from the very beginning. **up to scratch** up to standard. **scratchy** *adj* **scratchcard** *n* ticket that reveals whether or not the holder has won a prize when the surface is removed by scratching.

scrawl *v* **1** write carelessly or hastily. ♦ *n* **2** scribbled writing.

scrawny *adj* **scrawnier, scrawniest** thin and bony.

scream *v* **1** utter a piercing cry, esp. of fear or pain. **2** utter with a scream. ♦ *n* **3** shrill piercing cry. **4** *Informal* very funny person or thing.

scree *n* slope of loose shifting stones.

screech *v, n* (utter) a shrill cry. **screech owl** barn owl.

screed *n* long tedious piece of writing.

screen *n* **1** surface of a television set, VDU, etc., on which an image is formed. **2** white surface on which films or slides are projected. **3** movable structure used to shelter, divide, or conceal something. ♦ *v* **4** shelter or conceal with or as if with a screen. **5** examine (a person or group) to determine suitability for a task or to detect the presence of disease or weapons. **6** show (a film). **the screen** cinema generally. **screenplay** *n* script for a film

screw *n* **1** metal pin with a spiral ridge along its length, twisted into materials to fasten them together. **2** *Slang* prison guard. ♦ *v* **3** turn (a screw). **4** twist. **5** fasten with screw(s). **6** *Informal* extort. **screwy** *adj Informal* crazy or eccentric. **screwdriver** *n* tool for turning screws. **screw up** *v* **1** *Informal* bungle. **2** distort. **3** summon up (courage).

scribble *v* **1** write hastily or illegibly. **2** make meaningless or illegible marks. ♦ *n* **3** something scribbled.

scribe *n* **1** person who copied manuscripts before the invention of printing. **2** *Bible* scholar of the Jewish Law.

scrimmage *n* **1** rough or disorderly struggle. ♦ *v* **2** engage in a scrimmage.

scrimp *v* be very economical.

scrip *n* certificate representing a claim to stocks or shares.

script *n* **1** text of a film, play, or TV programme. **2** particular system of writing, e.g. *Arabic script.* **3** candidate's answer paper in an exam. **4** handwriting. ♦ *v* **5** write a script for.

scripture *n* **1** sacred writings of a religion. **2** (**S-**) Old and New Testaments. **scriptural** *adj*

scrofula *n* tuberculosis of the lymphatic glands. **scrofulous** *adj*

scroll *n* **1** roll of parchment or paper. **2** ancient book in scroll form. **3** ornamental carving shaped like a scroll. ♦ *v* **4** move (text) up or down on a VDU screen.

Scrooge *n* miserly person.

scrotum *n, pl* **-ta, -tums** pouch of skin containing the testicles.

scrounge *v Informal* get by cadging or begging. **scrounger** *n*

scrub[1] *v* **scrubbing, scrubbed 1** clean by rubbing, often with a hard brush and water. **2** *Informal* delete or cancel. ♦ *n* **3** scrubbing.

scrub[2] *n* **1** stunted trees. **2** area of land

covered with scrub. **scrubby** *adj* **1** covered with scrub. **2** stunted. **3** *Informal* shabby.

scruff[1] *n* nape (of the neck).

scruff[2] *n Informal* untidy person. **scruffy** *adj* unkempt or shabby.

scrum, scrummage *n* **1** *Rugby* restarting of play in which opposing packs of forwards push against each other to gain possession of the ball. **2** disorderly struggle.

scrump *v Brit dialect* steal (apples) from an orchard or garden.

scrumptious *adj Informal* delicious.

scrumpy *n* rough dry cider.

scrunch *v* **1** crumple or crunch or be crumpled or crunched. ♦ *n* **2** act or sound of scrunching.

scrunchie *n* loop of elastic covered loosely with fabric, used to hold the hair in a ponytail.

scruple *n* **1** doubt produced by one's conscience or morals. ♦ *v* **2** have doubts on moral grounds. **scrupulous** *adj* **1** very conscientious. **2** very careful or precise. **scrupulously** *adv*

scrutiny *n, pl* **-nies** **1** close examination. **2** searching look. **scrutinize** *v* examine closely.

scuba diving *n* sport of swimming under water using cylinders containing compressed air attached to breathing apparatus.

scud *v* **scudding, scudded** **1** move along swiftly. **2** run before a gale.

scuff *v* **1** drag (the feet) while walking. **2** scrape (one's shoes) by doing so. ♦ *n* **3** mark caused by scuffing.

scuffle *v* **1** fight in a disorderly manner. ♦ *n* **2** disorderly struggle. **3** scuffling sound.

scull *n* **1** small oar. ♦ *v* **2** row (a boat) using sculls.

scullery *n, pl* **-leries** small room where washing-up and other kitchen work is done.

sculpture *n* **1** art of making figures or designs in wood, stone, etc. **2** product of this art. ♦ *v* **3** (also **sculpt**) represent in sculpture. **sculptor, sculptress** *n* **sculptural** *adj*

scum *n* **1** impure or waste matter on the surface of a liquid. **2** worthless people. **scummy** *adj*

scupper[1] *v Informal* defeat or ruin.

scupper[2] *n* drain in the side of a ship.

scurf *n* flaky skin on the scalp. **scurfy** *adj*

scurrilous *adj* untrue and defamatory.

scurry *v* **-rying, -ried** **1** move hastily. ♦ *n* **2** act or sound of scurrying.

scurvy *n* **1** disease caused by lack of vitamin C. ♦ *adj* **2** mean and despicable.

scut *n* short tail of the hare, rabbit, or deer.

scuttle[1] *n* fireside container for coal.

scuttle[2] *v* **1** run with short quick steps. ♦ *n* **2** hurried run.

scuttle[3] *v* make a hole in (a ship) to sink it.

scythe *n* **1** long-handled tool with a curved blade for cutting grass. ♦ *v* **2** cut with a scythe.

SD South Dakota.

Se *Chem* selenium.

SE southeast(ern).

sea *n* **1** mass of salt water covering three quarters of the earth's surface. **2** particular area of this. **3** vast expanse. **at sea** **1** in a ship on the ocean. **2** confused or bewildered. **sea anemone** sea animal with suckers like petals. **seaboard** *n* coast. **sea dog** experienced sailor. **seafaring** *adj* working or travelling by sea. **seafood** *n* edible saltwater fish or shellfish. **seagoing** *adj* built for travelling on the sea. **seagull** *n* gull. **sea horse** small sea fish with a plated body and horselike head. **sea legs** ability to keep one's balance at sea and resist seasickness. **sea level** average level of the sea's surface in relation to the land. **sea lion** kind of large seal. **seaman** *n* sailor. **seaplane** *n* aircraft designed to take off from and land on water. **seascape** *n* picture of a scene at sea. **seashell** *n* empty shell of a mollusc. **seasick** *adj* suffering from nausea caused by the motion of a ship. **seasickness** *n* **seaside** *n* area, esp. a holiday resort, on the coast. **sea urchin** sea animal with a round spiky shell. **seaweed** *n* plant growing in the sea. **seaworthy** *adj* (of a ship) in fit condition for a sea voyage.

seal[1] *n* **1** piece of wax, lead, etc. with a special design impressed upon it, attached to a letter or document as a mark of authentication. **2** device for making such an impression. **3** device or material used to close an opening tightly. ♦ *v* **4** close with or as if with a seal. **5** make airtight or watertight. **6** affix a seal to or stamp with a seal. **7** decide (one's fate) irrevocably. **sealant** *n* any substance used for sealing. **sealing wax** hard material which softens when heated, used to make a seal. **seal off** *v* enclose or isolate (a place) completely.

seal[2] *n* **1** amphibious mammal with flippers as limbs. ♦ *v* **2** hunt seals. **sealskin** *n*

seam *n* **1** line where two edges are joined, as by stitching. **2** thin layer of coal or ore. ♦ *v* **3** mark with furrows or wrinkles. **seamless** *adj* **seamy** *adj* sordid.

seamstress *n* woman who sews.

seance [**say**-anss] *n* meeting at which spiritualists attempt to communicate with the dead.

sear *v* scorch, burn the surface of. **searing** *adj* **1** (of pain) very sharp. **2** highly critical.

search *v* **1** examine closely in order to find something. **2** make a search. ♦ *n* **3** searching. **searching** *adj* keen or thorough, e.g. *a searching look.* **searchlight** *n* powerful light with a beam that can be shone in any direction. **search warrant** document permitting the entry and search of premises.

season *n* **1** one of four divisions of the year, each of which has characteristic weather conditions. **2** period during which a thing happens or is plentiful. **3** any definite or indefinite period, e.g. *the busy season.* **4** fitting or proper time. ♦ *v* **5** flavour with salt, herbs, etc. **6** dry (timber) till ready for use. **seasonable** *adj* **1** appropriate for the season. **2** timely or opportune. **seasonal** *adj* depending on or varying with the seasons. **seasoned** *adj* experienced. **seasoning** *n* salt, herbs, etc. added to food to enhance flavour. **season ticket** ticket for a series of journeys or events within a specified period.

seat *n* **1** thing designed or used for sitting on. **2** part of a chair on which one sits. **3** place to sit in a theatre, esp. one that requires a ticket. **4** buttocks. **5** part of a garment covering the buttocks. **6** place in which something is based. **7** country house. **8** membership of a legislative or administrative body. ♦ *v* **9** cause to sit. **10** provide seating for. **seating** *n* supply or arrangement of seats. **seat belt** belt worn in a car or aircraft to prevent a person being thrown forward in a crash.

sebaceous *adj* of, like, or secreting fat or oil.

sec[1] *adj* (of wines) dry.

sec[2] *n Informal* second (of time).

sec. **1** second (of time). **2** secondary. **3** secretary.

secateurs *pl n* small pruning shears.

secede *v* withdraw formally from a political alliance or federation. **secession** *n* **secessionist** *n*

seclude *v* keep (a person) from contact with others. **secluded** *adj* private, sheltered. **seclusion** *n*

second[1] *adj* **1** coming directly after the first. **2** alternate, additional. **3** inferior. ♦ *n* **4** person or thing coming second. **5** attendant in a duel or boxing match. ♦ *pl* **6** inferior goods. ♦ *v* **7** express formal support for (a motion proposed in a meeting). **secondly** *adv* **second-best** *adj* next to the best. **second-class** *adj* **1** inferior. **2** cheaper, slower, or less comfortable than first-class. **second-hand** *adj* **1** bought after use by another. **2** not from an original source. **second nature** something so habitual that it seems part of one's character. **second-rate** *adj* not of the highest quality. **second sight** supposed ability to predict events. **second thoughts** revised opinion on a matter already considered.

second wind renewed ability to continue effort.

second[2] *n* **1** sixtieth part of a minute of an angle or time. **2** moment.

second[3] [si-**kawnd**] *v* transfer (a person) temporarily to another job. **secondment** *n*

secondary *adj* **1** of less importance. **2** coming after or derived from what is primary or first. **3** relating to the education of people between the ages of 11 and 18.

secret *adj* **1** kept from the knowledge of others. **2** secretive. ♦ *n* **3** something kept secret. **4** mystery. **5** underlying explanation, e.g. *the secret of my success.* **in secret** without other people knowing. **secretly** *adv* **secrecy** *n* **secretive** *adj* inclined to keep things secret. **secretiveness** *n* **secret agent** spy. **secret service** government department concerned with spying.

secretariat *n* administrative office or staff of a legislative body.

secretary *n, pl* **-ries** **1** person who deals with correspondence and general clerical work. **2** (**S-**) head of a state department, e.g. *Home Secretary.* **3** person who keeps records for a company. **secretarial** *adj* **Secretary of State** head of a major government department.

secrete[1] *v* (of an organ, gland, etc.) produce and release (a substance). **secretion** *n* **secretory** [sek-**reet**-or-ee] *adj*

secrete[2] *v* hide or conceal.

sect *n* subdivision of a religious or political group, esp. one with extreme beliefs. **sectarian** *adj* **1** of a sect. **2** narrow-minded. **sectarianism** *n*

section *n* **1** part cut off. **2** part or subdivision of something. **3** distinct part of a country or community. **4** cutting. **5** drawing of something as if cut through. ♦ *v* **6** cut or divide into sections. **sectional** *adj*

sector *n* **1** part or subdivision. **2** part of a circle enclosed by two radii and the arc which they cut off. **3** portion of an area for military operations.

secular *adj* **1** worldly, as opposed to sacred. **2** not connected with religion or the church. **secularism** *n* belief that religion should have no place in education. **secularize** *v* remove from the influence of the Church.

secure *adj* **1** free from danger. **2** free from anxiety. **3** firmly fixed. **4** reliable. ♦ *v* **5** obtain. **6** make safe. **7** make firm. **8** guarantee payment of (a loan) by giving something as security. **securely** *adv* **security** *n, pl* **-ties** **1** precautions against theft, espionage, or other danger. **2** state of being secure. **3** certificate of ownership of a share, stock, or bond. **4** something given or pledged to guarantee payment of a loan.

sedan *n US & Aust* saloon car. **sedan chair** *Hist* enclosed chair for one person, carried on poles by two bearers.

sedate[1] *adj* **1** calm and dignified. **2** slow or unhurried. **sedately** *adv*

sedate[2] *v* give a sedative drug to. **sedation** *n* **sedative** *adj* **1** having a soothing or calming effect. ♦ *n* **2** sedative drug.

sedentary [**sed**-en-tree] *adj* done sitting down, involving little exercise.

sedge *n* coarse grasslike plant growing on wet ground. **sedgy** *adj*

sediment *n* **1** matter which settles to the bottom of a liquid. **2** material deposited by water, ice, or wind. **sedimentary** *adj*

sedition *n* speech or action encouraging rebellion against the government. **seditious** *adj*

seduce *v* **1** persuade into sexual intercourse. **2** tempt into wrongdoing. **seducer, seductress** *n* **seduction** *n* **seductive** *adj*

sedulous *adj* diligent or persevering. **sedulously** *adv*

sedum *n* rock plant.

see[1] *v* **seeing, saw, seen** **1** perceive with the eyes or mind. **2** understand. **3** watch. **4** find out. **5** make sure (of something). **6** consider or decide. **7** have experience of. **8** meet or visit. **9** interview. **10** frequent the company of. **11** accompany. **seeing** *n* **1** use of the eyes.

♦ *conj* 2 in view of the fact that. **see about** *v* attend to. **see off** *v* be present at the departure of. **see through** *v* 1 perceive the true nature of. 2 remain with until the end. **see-through** *adj* transparent.

see[2] *n* diocese of a bishop.

seed *n* 1 mature fertilized grain of a plant. 2 such grains used for sowing. 3 origin. 4 *Obs* offspring. 5 *Sport* player ranked according to his or her ability. ♦ *v* 6 sow with seed. 7 produce seeds. 8 remove seeds from. 9 arrange (the draw of a sports tournament) so that the outstanding competitors will not meet in the early rounds. **go, run to seed** 1 (of plants) produce or shed seeds after flowering. 2 lose vigour or usefulness. **seedling** *n* young plant raised from a seed. **seedy** *adj* 1 shabby. 2 *Informal* unwell. 3 full of seeds.

seek *v* **seeking, sought** 1 try to find or obtain. 2 try (to do something).

seem *v* 1 appear to be. 2 have the impression. **seeming** *adj* apparent but not real. **seemingly** *adv*

seemly *adj* **-lier, -liest** proper or fitting.

seen *v* past participle of SEE[1].

seep *v* trickle through slowly, ooze. **seepage** *n*

seer *n* prophet.

seersucker *n* light cotton fabric with a slightly crinkled surface.

seesaw *n* 1 plank balanced in the middle so that two people seated on either end ride up and down alternately. ♦ *v* 2 move up and down.

seethe *v* **seething, seethed** 1 be very agitated. 2 (of a liquid) boil or foam.

segment *n* 1 one of several sections into which something may be divided. 2 part of a circle cut off by an intersecting line. ♦ *v* 3 divide into segments. **segmentation** *n*

segregate *v* 1 set apart. 2 keep (a racial or minority group) apart from the rest of the community. **segregation** *n*

seigneur *n* feudal lord.

seine [**sane**] *n* large fishing net that hangs vertically from floats.

seismic *adj* relating to earthquakes. **seismology** *n* study of earthquakes. **seismological** *adj* **seismologist** *n* **seismograph, seismometer** *n* instrument that records the strength of earthquakes.

seize *v* 1 take hold of forcibly or quickly. 2 take immediate advantage of. 3 take legal possession of. 4 understand quickly. 5 (usu. foll. by *up*) (of mechanical parts) stick tightly through overheating. **seizure** *n* 1 sudden violent attack of an illness. 2 seizing or being seized.

seldom *adv* not often, rarely.

select *v* 1 pick out or choose. ♦ *adj* 2 chosen in preference to others. 3 restricted to a particular group, exclusive. **selection** *n* 1 selecting. 2 things that have been selected. 3 range from which something may be selected. **selective** *adj* chosen or choosing carefully. **selectively** *adv* **selectivity** *n* **selector** *n*

selenium *n Chem* nonmetallic element with photoelectric properties.

self *n, pl* **selves** 1 distinct individuality or identity of a person or thing. 2 one's basic nature. 3 one's own welfare or interests. **selfish** *adj* caring too much about oneself and not enough about others. **selfishly** *adv* **selfishness** *n* **selfless** *adj* unselfish.

self- *prefix* used with many main words to mean: 1 of oneself or itself. 2 by, to, in, due to, for, or from the self. 3 automatic(ally). **self-addressed** *adj* addressed to the sender. **self-assertion** *n* putting forward one's opinions, esp. aggressively. **self-assertive** *adj* **self-assured** *adj* confident. **self-catering** *adj* (of accommodation) for people who provide their own food. **self-centred** *adj* totally preoccupied with one's own concerns. **self-coloured** *adj* having only a single colour. **self-confessed** *adj* according to one's own admission. **self-confidence** *n* belief in one's own abilities. **self-confident** *adj* **self-conscious** *adj* embarrassed at being the object of others' attention. **self-contained** *adj* 1 containing everything needed, complete. **2** (of a flat) having its own facilities. **self-control** *n* ability to control one's feelings and reactions. **self-defence** *n* defending of oneself or one's property. **self-determination** *n* the right of a nation to decide its own form of government. **self-effacing** *adj* unwilling to draw attention to oneself. **self-employed** *adj* earning a living from one's own business. **self-esteem** *n* favourable opinion of oneself. **self-evident** *adj* obvious without proof. **self-government** *n* government of a nation or community by its own people. **self-help** *n* **1** use of one's own abilities to solve problems. **2** practice of solving one's problems within a group of people with similar problems. **self-important** *adj* having an unduly high opinion of one's importance. **self-importance** *n* **self-indulgent** *adj* tending to indulge one's desires. **self-interest** *n* one's own advantage. **self-made** *adj* having achieved wealth or status by one's own efforts. **self-opinionated** *adj* clinging stubbornly to one's own opinions. **self-possessed** *adj* having control of one's emotions, calm. **self-raising** *adj* (of flour) containing a raising agent. **self-respect** *n* sense of one's dignity and integrity. **self-righteous** *adj* thinking oneself more virtuous than others. **selfsame** *adj* the very same. **self-satisfied** *adj* conceited. **self-seeking** *adj, n* seeking to promote only one's own interests. **self-service** *adj* denoting a shop, café, or garage where customers serve themselves and then pay a cashier. **self-styled** *adj* using a title or name that one has taken without right. **self-sufficient** *adj* able to provide for oneself without help. **self-willed** *adj* stubbornly determined to get one's own way.

sell *v* **selling, sold 1** exchange (something) for money. **2** stock, deal in. **3** (of goods) be sold. **4** (foll. by *for*) have a specified price. **5** promote. **6** be in demand. **7** *Informal* persuade (someone) to accept (something). **8** give up for a price or reward. ♦ *n* **9** manner of selling. **seller** *n* **sell-by date** date printed on packaged food specifying the date after which the food should not be sold. **past one's sell-by date** *Informal* beyond one's prime. **sell out** *v* **1** dispose of (something) completely by selling. **2** *Informal* betray. **sellout** *n* **1** performance of a show etc. for which all the tickets are sold. **2** *Informal* betrayal. **sell up** *v* sell all one's goods.

Sellotape *n* **1** ® type of adhesive tape. ♦ *v* **2** stick with Sellotape.

selvage, selvedge *n* edge of cloth, woven so as to prevent unravelling.

selves *n* plural of SELF.

semantic *adj* relating to the meaning of words. **semantics** *n* study of linguistic meaning.

semaphore *n* system of signalling by holding two flags in different positions to represent letters of the alphabet.

semblance *n* outward or superficial appearance.

semen *n* sperm-carrying fluid produced by male animals.

semester *n* either of two divisions of the academic year.

semi *n Informal* semidetached house.

semi- *prefix* used with many main words to mean: **1** half, e.g. *semicircle.* **2** partly or almost, e.g. *semiprofessional.* **3** occurring twice in a specified period, e.g. *semiweekly.*

semibreve *n* musical note four beats long.

semicircle *n* half of a circle. **semicircular** *adj*

semicolon *n* the punctuation mark (;).

semiconductor *n* substance with an electrical conductivity that increases with temperature.

semidetached *adj* (of a house) joined to another on one side.

semifinal *n* match or round before the final. **semifinalist** *n*

seminal *adj* **1** original and influential. **2** capable of developing. **3** of semen or seed.

seminar *n* meeting of a group of students for discussion.

seminary *n, pl* **-ries** college for priests.

semiotics *n* study of human communications, esp. signs and symbols.

semiprecious *adj* (of gemstones) having less value than precious stones.

semiquaver *n* musical note half the length of a quaver.

semiskilled *adj* partly trained but not for specialized work.

Semite *n* member of the group of peoples including Jews and Arabs. **Semitic** *adj*

semitone *n* smallest interval between two notes in Western music.

semolina *n* hard grains of wheat left after the milling of flour, used to make puddings and pasta.

Senate *n* **1** upper house of some parliaments. **2** governing body of some universities. **senator** *n* member of a Senate. **senatorial** *adj*

send *v* **sending, sent 1** cause (a person or thing) to go to or be taken or transmitted to a place. **2** (foll. by *for*) issue a request for. **3** bring into a specified state or condition. **sender** *n* **send down** *v* **1** expel from university. **2** *Informal* send to jail. **sendoff** *n* demonstration of good wishes at a person's departure. **send up** *v Informal* make fun of by imitating. **send-up** *n Informal* imitation.

senescent *adj* growing old. **senescence** *n*

senile *adj* mentally or physically weak because of old age. **senility** *n*

senior *adj* **1** superior in rank or standing. **2** older. **3** of or for older pupils. ♦ *n* **4** senior person. **seniority** *n* **senior citizen** old person, esp. a pensioner.

senna *n* **1** tropical plant. **2** its dried leaves or pods used as a laxative.

señor [sen-**nyor**] *n, pl* **-ores** Spanish term of address equivalent to *sir* or *Mr.* **señora** [sen-**nyor**-a] *n* Spanish term of address equivalent to *madam* or *Mrs.* **señorita** [sen-nyor-**ee**-ta] *n* Spanish term of address equivalent to *madam* or *Miss.*

sensation *n* **1** ability to feel things physically. **2** physical feeling. **3** general feeling or awareness. **4** state of excitement. **5** exciting person or thing. **sensational** *adj* **1** causing intense shock, anger, or excitement. **2** *Informal* very good. **sensationalism** *n* deliberate use of sensational language or subject matter. **sensationalist** *adj, n*

sense *n* **1** any of the faculties of perception or feeling (sight, hearing, touch, taste, or smell). **2** ability to perceive. **3** feeling perceived through one of the senses. **4** awareness. **5** moral discernment. **6** (sometimes pl) sound practical judgment or intelligence. **7** reason or purpose. **8** specific meaning. ♦ *v* **9** perceive. **senseless** *adj* **1** foolish. **2** unconscious.

sensible *adj* **1** having or showing good sense. **2** practical, e.g. *sensible shoes.* **3** capable of being perceived by the senses. **4** (foll. by *of*) aware. **sensibly** *adv* **sensibility** *n* **1** ability to experience deep feelings. **2** (usu. pl) tendency to be influenced or offended.

sensitive *adj* **1** easily hurt or offended. **2** responsive to external stimuli. **3** (of a subject) liable to arouse controversy or strong feelings. **4** (of an instrument) responsive to slight changes. **sensitively** *adv* **sensitivity** *n* **sensitize** *v* make sensitive.

sensor *n* device that detects or measures the presence of something, such as radiation.

sensory *adj* of the senses or sensation.

sensual *adj* **1** giving pleasure to the body and senses rather than the mind. **2** having a strong liking for physical pleasures. **sensually** *adv* **sensuality** *n* **sensualist** *n*

sensuous *adj* pleasing to the senses. **sensuously** *adv*

sent *v* past of SEND.

sentence *n* **1** sequence of words capable of standing alone as a statement, question, or command. **2** punishment passed on a criminal. ♦ *v* **3** pass sentence on (a convicted person).

sententious *adj* **1** trying to sound wise. **2** pompously moralizing. **sententiously** *adv*

sentient [**sen**-tee-ent] *adj* capable of feeling. **sentience** *n*

sentiment *n* **1** thought, opinion, or attitude. **2** feeling expressed in words. **3** exaggerated or mawkish emotion. **sentimental** *adj* excessively romantic or nostalgic. **sentimentalism** *n* **sentimentality** *n* **sentimentalize** *v* make sentimental.

sentinel *n* sentry.

sentry *n, pl* **-tries** soldier on watch.

sepal *n* leaflike division of the calyx of a flower.

separate *v* **1** act as a barrier between. **2** distinguish between. **3** divide up into parts. **4** sever or be severed. **5** (of a couple) stop living together. ♦ *adj* **6** not the same, different. **7** set apart. **8** not shared, individual. ♦ *pl n* **9** clothes that only cover half the body, such as skirts and blouses. **separately** *adv* **separation** *n* **1** separating or being separated. **2** *Law* living apart of a married couple without divorce. **separable** *adj* **separatist** *n* person who advocates the separation of a group from an organization or country. **separatism** *n*

sepia *adj, n* reddish-brown (pigment).

sepoy *n* (formerly) Indian soldier in the service of the British.

sepsis *n* poisoning caused by pus-forming bacteria.

Sept. September.

September *n* ninth month of the year.

septet *n* **1** group of seven performers. **2** music for such a group.

septic *adj* **1** (of a wound) infected. **2** of or caused by harmful bacteria. **septic tank** tank in which sewage is decomposed by the action of bacteria.

septicaemia [sep-tis-**see**-mee-a] *n* infection of the blood.

septuagenarian *n* person aged between seventy and seventy-nine.

septum *n, pl* **-ta** dividing partition between two cavities in the body.

sepulchre [**sep**-pull-ker] *n* tomb or burial vault. **sepulchral** [sip-**pulk**-ral] *adj* gloomy.

sequel *n* **1** novel, play, or film that continues the story of an earlier one. **2** thing that follows something else. **3** consequence.

sequence *n* **1** arrangement of two or more things in successive order. **2** the successive order of two or more things. **3** section of a film showing a single uninterrupted episode. **sequential** *adj*

sequester *v* **1** seclude. **2** sequestrate.

sequestrate *v* confiscate (property) until its owner's debts are paid or a court order is complied with. **sequestration** *n*

sequin *n* small ornamental metal disc on a garment. **sequined** *adj*

sequoia *n* giant Californian coniferous tree.

seraglio [sir-**ah**-lee-oh] *n, pl* **-raglios** **1** harem of a Muslim palace. **2** Turkish sultan's palace.

seraph *n, pl* **-aphs, -aphim** member of the highest order of angels. **seraphic** *adj*

Serbian, Serb *adj* **1** of Serbia. ♦ *n* **2** person from Serbia. **3** dialect of Serbo-Croat spoken in Serbia. **Serbo-Croat, Serbo-Croatian** *adj, n* (of) the chief official language of Serbia and Croatia.

serenade *n* **1** music played or sung to a woman by a lover. **2** piece of music for a small orchestra. ♦ *v* **3** sing or play a serenade to (someone).

serendipity *n* gift of making fortunate discoveries by accident.

serene *adj* **1** calm, peaceful. **2** (of the sky) clear. **serenely** *adv* **serenity** *n*

serf *n* medieval farm labourer who could not leave the land he worked on. **serfdom** *n*

serge *n* strong woollen fabric.

sergeant *n* **1** noncommissioned officer in the army. **2** police officer ranking between constable and inspector. **sergeant at arms** parliamentary or court officer with ceremonial duties. **sergeant major** highest rank of noncommissioned officer in the army.

serial *n* **1** story or play produced in successive instalments. ♦ *adj* **2** of or forming a series. **3** published or presented as a serial. **serialize** *v* publish or present as a serial. **serial killer** person who commits a series of murders.

series *n, pl* **-ries** **1** group or succession of related things, usu. arranged in order. **2** set of radio or TV programmes about the same subject or characters.

serious *adj* **1** giving cause for concern. **2** concerned with important matters. **3** not cheerful, grave. **4** sincere, not joking. **5** *Informal* impressive, e.g. *serious money.* **seriously** *adv* **seriousness** *n*

sermon *n* **1** speech on a religious or moral subject by a clergyman in a church service. **2** long moralizing speech. **sermonize** *v* make a long moralizing speech.

serpent *n* snake. **serpentine** *adj* twisting like a snake.

serrated *adj* having a notched or sawlike edge. **serration** *n*

serried *adj* in close formation.

serum [**seer**-um] *n* **1** watery fluid left after blood has clotted. **2** this fluid from the blood of immunized animals used for inoculation or vaccination.

serval *n* feline African mammal.

servant *n* person employed to do household work for another.

serve *v* **1** work for (a person, community, or cause). **2** perform official duties. **3** attend to (customers). **4** provide with food or drink. **5** present (food or drink). **6** provide with a service. **7** be a member of the armed forces. **8** spend (time) in prison. **9** be useful or suitable. **10** *Tennis etc.* put (the ball) into play. **11** deliver (a legal document) to (a person). ♦ *n* **12** *Tennis etc.* act of serving the ball. **serve someone right** *Informal* be what someone deserves for doing something wrong. **serving** *n* portion of food.

service *n* **1** serving. **2** system that provides something needed by the public. **3** department of public employment and its employees. **4** maintenance of goods provided by a dealer after sale. **5** availability for use. **6** overhaul of a machine or vehicle. **7** set of dishes etc. for serving a meal. **8** formal religious ceremony. **9** *Tennis etc.* act, manner, or right of serving the ball. ♦ *pl* **10** armed forces. ♦ *adj* **11** serving the public rather than producing goods, e.g. *service industry.* ♦ *v* **12** provide a service or services to. **13** overhaul (a machine or vehicle). **serviceable** *adj* **1** useful or helpful. **2** able or ready to be used. **service area** area beside a motorway with garage, restaurant, and toilet facilities. **service charge** additional cost on a restaurant bill to pay for service. **service flat** flat where domestic services are provided. **serviceman, servicewoman** *n* member of the armed forces. **service road** narrow road giving access to houses and shops. **service station** garage selling fuel for motor vehicles.

serviette *n* table napkin.

servile *adj* **1** too eager to obey people, fawning. **2** suitable for a slave. **servility** *n*

servitude *n* bondage or slavery.

sesame [**sess**-am-ee] *n* plant cultivated for its seeds and oil, which are used in cooking.

session *n* **1** period spent in an activity. **2** meeting of a court, parliament, or council. **3** series or period of such meetings. **4** academic term or year.

set[1] *v* **setting, set** **1** put in a specified position or state. **2** make ready. **3** make or become firm or rigid. **4** put (a broken bone) or (of a broken bone) be put into a normal position for healing. **5** adjust (a clock) to a particular position. **6** establish, arrange. **7** prescribe, assign. **8** arrange (hair) while wet, so that it dries in position. **9** place (a jewel) in a setting. **10** put to music. **11** arrange (type) for printing. **12** (of the sun) go down. **13** (of plants) produce (fruit or seeds). **14** (of a gun dog) face game. ♦ *n* **15** setting or being set. **16** bearing or posture. **17** scenery used in a play or film. ♦ *adj* **18** fixed or established beforehand. **19**

rigid or inflexible. **20** conventional or stereotyped. **21** determined (to do something). **22** ready. **set back** *v* **1** hinder. **2** cost. **setback** *n* anything that delays progress. **set off** *v* **1** embark on a journey. **2** cause to begin. **3** cause to explode. **4** act as a contrast to. **set square** flat right-angled triangular instrument used for drawing angles. **set to** *v* begin working. **set-to** *n* brief fight. **set up** *v* arrange or establish. **setup** *n* way in which anything is organized or arranged.

set[2] *n* **1** number of things or people grouped or belonging together. **2** *Maths* group of numbers or objects that satisfy a given condition or share a property. **3** television or radio receiver. **4** *Sport* group of games in a match. **5** series of songs performed by a musician or group. **set theory** branch of mathematics concerned with the properties of sets.

sett, set *n* **1** badger's burrow. **2** small paving stone.

settee *n* couch.

setter *n* long-haired gun dog.

setting *n* **1** background or surroundings. **2** time and place where a film, book, etc. is supposed to have taken place. **3** music written for the words of a text. **4** decorative metalwork in which a gem is set. **5** plates and cutlery for a single place at table. **6** position or level to which the controls of a machine can be adjusted.

settle[1] *v* **1** arrange or put in order. **2** come to rest. **3** establish or become established as a resident. **4** colonize. **5** make quiet, calm, or stable. **6** pay (a bill). **7** dispose of, conclude. **8** bestow (property) legally. **9** end (a dispute). **settlement** *n* **1** act of settling. **2** place newly colonized. **3** subsidence (of a building). **4** property bestowed legally. **settler** *n* colonist. **settle down** *v* **1** make or become calm. **2** (foll. by *to*) concentrate on. **3** adopt a routine way of life. **settle for** *v* accept in spite of dissatisfaction.

settle[2] *n* long wooden bench with high back and arms.

seven *adj, n* one more than six. **seventh** *adj, n* (of) number seven in a series. **seventeen** *adj, n* ten and seven. **seventeenth** *adj, n* **seventy** *adj, n* ten times seven. **seventieth** *adj, n*

sever *v* **1** cut through or off. **2** break off (a relationship). **severance** *n* **severance pay** compensation paid by a firm to an employee who leaves because the job he or she was appointed to do no longer exists.

several *adj* **1** some, a few. **2** various, separate. **3** distinct or different. **severally** *adv* separately.

severe *adj* **1** strict or harsh. **2** very intense or unpleasant. **3** strictly restrained in appearance. **severely** *adv* **severity** *n*

sew *v* **sewing, sewed, sewn** *or* **sewed** **1** join with thread repeatedly passed through with a needle. **2** make or fasten by sewing.

sewage *n* waste matter or excrement carried away in sewers. **sewer** *n* drain to remove waste water and sewage. **sewerage** *n* system of sewers.

sewn *v* a past participle of SEW.

sex *n* **1** state of being male or female. **2** male or female category. **3** sexual intercourse. **4** sexual feelings or behaviour. ♦ *v* **5** find out the sex of. **sexy** *adj* **1** sexually exciting or attractive. **2** *Informal* exciting or trendy. **sexism** *n* discrimination on the basis of a person's sex. **sexist** *adj, n* **sexual** *adj* **sexually** *adv* **sexuality** *n* **sexual intercourse** sexual act in which the male's penis is inserted into the female's vagina.

sexagenarian *n* person aged between sixty and sixty-nine.

sextant *n* navigator's instrument for measuring angles, as between the sun and horizon, to calculate one's position.

sextet *n* **1** group of six performers. **2** music for such a group.

sexton *n* official in charge of a church and churchyard.

sextuplet *n* one of six children born at one birth.

SF science fiction.

SFA Scottish Football Association.

Sgt. Sergeant.

sh *interj* be quiet!

shabby *adj* **-bier, -biest 1** worn or dilapidated in appearance. **2** mean or unworthy, e.g. *shabby treatment.* **shabbily** *adv* **shabbiness** *n*

shack *n* rough hut. **shack up with** *v* *Slang* live with (one's lover).

shackle *n* **1** one of a pair of metal rings joined by a chain, for securing a person's wrists or ankles. **2** anything that restricts freedom. ♦ *v* **3** fasten with shackles. **4** hinder.

shad *n* herring-like fish.

shade *n* **1** relative darkness. **2** place sheltered from sun. **3** screen or cover used to protect from a direct source of light. **4** depth of colour. **5** slight amount. **6** *Lit* ghost. ♦ *pl* **7** *Slang* sunglasses. ♦ *v* **8** screen from light. **9** darken. **10** represent (darker areas) in drawing. **11** change slightly or by degrees. **shady** *adj* **1** situated in or giving shade. **2** of doubtful honesty or legality. **in the shade** in a position of relative obscurity.

shadow *n* **1** dark shape cast on a surface when something stands between a light and the surface. **2** patch of shade. **3** slight trace. **4** threatening influence. **5** inseparable companion. **6** person who secretly trails another. ♦ *v* **7** cast a shadow over. **8** follow secretly. **shadowy** *adj* **shadow-boxing** *n* boxing against an imaginary opponent for practice. **Shadow Cabinet** members of the main opposition party in Parliament who would be ministers if their party were in power.

shaft *n* **1** long narrow straight handle of a tool or weapon. **2** ray of light. **3** revolving rod that transmits power in a machine. **4** vertical passageway, as for a lift or a mine. **5** one of the bars between which an animal is harnessed to a vehicle. **6** something directed like a missile, e.g. *shafts of wit.* **7** middle part of a column.

shag[1] *n* **1** coarse shredded tobacco. **2** tangled hair or wool. ♦ *adj* **3** (of a carpet) having a long pile. **shaggy** *adj* **1** covered with rough hair or wool. **2** tousled, unkempt. **shaggy-dog story** long anecdote with a humorous twist at the end.

shag[2] *n* kind of cormorant.

shag[3] *Brit taboo slang* ♦ *v* **1** to have sexual intercourse with (a person). ♦ *n* **2** an act of sexual intercourse.

shagreen *n* **1** sharkskin. **2** rough grainy untanned leather.

shah *n* formerly, ruler of Iran.

shake *v* **shaking, shook, shaken 1** move quickly up and down or back and forth. **2** make unsteady. **3** tremble. **4** grasp (someone's hand) in greeting or agreement. **5** shock or upset. **6** undermine or weaken. ♦ *n* **7** shaking. **8** vibration. **9** *Informal* short period of time. **shaker** *n* container in which drinks are mixed or from which powder is shaken. **shaky** *adj* **1** unsteady. **2** uncertain or questionable. **shakily** *adv* **shake off** *v* **1** remove. **2** escape from. **shake up** *v* **1** mix by shaking. **2** reorganize drastically. **3** shock.

shale *n* flaky sedimentary rock.

shall *v, past tense* **should** used as an auxiliary to make the future tense or to indicate intention, obligation, or inevitability.

> The use of *shall* with *I* and *we* is a matter of preference, not rule. *Shall* is commonly used for questions in southern England but less often in the north and Scotland.

shallot [shal-**lot**] *n* kind of small onion.

shallow *adj* **1** not deep. **2** lacking depth of character or intellect. **shallows** *pl n* area of shallow water. **shallowness** *n*

sham *n* **1** thing or person that is not genuine. ♦ *adj* **2** not genuine. ♦ *v* **shamming, shammed 3** fake, feign.

shamble *v* walk in a shuffling awkward way.

shambles *n* **1** disorderly event or place. **2** slaughterhouse. **shambolic** *adj* *Infor-*

mal completely disorganized.

shame *n* **1** painful emotion caused by awareness of having done something dishonourable or foolish. **2** capacity to feel shame. **3** disgrace. **4** cause of shame. **5** cause for regret. ♦ *v* **6** cause to feel shame. **7** disgrace. **8** compel by shame, e.g. *she was shamed into helping.* **shameful** *adj* causing or deserving shame. **shamefully** *adv* **shameless** *adj* with no sense of shame. **shamefaced** *adj* looking ashamed.

shammy *n, pl* **-mies** *Informal* piece of chamois leather.

shampoo *n* **1** liquid soap for washing hair, carpets, or upholstery. **2** process of shampooing. ♦ *v* **3** wash with shampoo.

shamrock *n* clover leaf, esp. as the Irish emblem.

shandy *n, pl* **-dies** drink made of beer and lemonade.

shanghai *v* **-haiing, -haied** force or trick (someone) into doing something.

shank *n* **1** lower leg. **2** shaft or stem.

shan't shall not.

shantung *n* soft Chinese silk with a knobbly surface.

shanty[1] *n, pl* **-ties** shack or crude dwelling. **shantytown** *n* slum consisting of shanties.

shanty[2] *n, pl* **-ties** sailor's traditional song.

shape *n* **1** outward form of an object. **2** way in which something is organized. **3** pattern or mould. **4** condition or state. ♦ *v* **5** form or mould. **6** devise or develop. **shapeless** *adj* **shapely** *adj* having an attractive shape. **shape up** *v Informal* develop satisfactorily.

shard *n* broken piece of pottery or glass.

share[1] *n* **1** part of something that belongs to or is contributed by a person. **2** one of the equal parts into which the capital stock of a public company is divided. ♦ *v* **3** give or take a share of (something). **4** join with others in doing or using (something). **5** divide and distribute. **shareholder** *n*

share[2] *n* blade of a plough.

shark *n* **1** large usu. predatory sea fish. **2** person who cheats others.

sharkskin *n* stiff glossy fabric.

sharp *adj* **1** having a keen cutting edge or fine point. **2** not gradual. **3** clearly defined. **4** mentally acute. **5** clever but underhand. **6** shrill. **7** bitter or sour in taste. **8** *Music* above the true pitch. ♦ *adv* **9** promptly. **10** *Music* too high in pitch. ♦ *n* **11** *Music* symbol raising a note one semitone above natural pitch. **sharply** *adv* **sharpness** *n* **sharpen** *v* make or become sharp or sharper. **sharpener** *n* **sharper** *n* person who cheats. **sharpshooter** *n* marksman.

shatter *v* **1** break into pieces. **2** destroy completely. **shattered** *adj Informal* **1** completely exhausted. **2** badly upset.

shave *v* **shaving, shaved, shaved** *or* **shaven 1** remove (hair) from (the face, head, or body) with a razor or shaver. **2** pare away. **3** touch lightly in passing. ♦ *n* **4** shaving. **close shave** *Informal* narrow escape. **shaver** *n* electric razor. **shavings** *pl n* parings.

shawl *n* piece of cloth worn over a woman's head or shoulders or wrapped around a baby.

she *pron* refers to: **1** female person or animal previously mentioned. **2** something regarded as female, such as a car, ship, or nation.

sheaf *n, pl* **sheaves 1** bundle of papers. **2** tied bundle of reaped corn. ♦ *v* **3** tie into a sheaf.

shear *v* **shearing, sheared, sheared** *or* **shorn 1** clip hair or wool from. **2** cut through. **3** cause (a part) to break or (of a part) break through strain or twisting. **shears** *pl n* large scissors or a cutting tool shaped like these. **shearer** *n*

sheath *n* **1** close-fitting cover, esp. for a knife or sword. **2** condom. **sheathe** *v* **1** put into a sheath. **2** cover with a sheath.

sheaves *n* plural of SHEAF.

shed[1] *n* building used for storage or shelter or as a workshop.

shed[2] *v* **shedding, shed 1** get rid off. **2** pour forth (tears). **3** cast off (skin, hair, or leaves).

sheen *n* glistening brightness on the surface of something.

sheep *n, pl* **sheep** **1** ruminant animal bred for wool and meat. **2** timid person. **sheep-dip** *n* liquid disinfectant in which sheep are immersed. **sheepdog** *n* dog used for herding sheep. **sheepskin** *n* skin of a sheep with the fleece still on, used for clothing or rugs.

sheepish *adj* embarrassed because of feeling foolish. **sheepishly** *adv*

sheer[1] *adj* **1** absolute, complete, e.g. *sheer folly.* **2** perpendicular, steep. **3** (of material) so fine as to be transparent. ♦ *adv* **4** steeply.

sheer[2] *v* **1** change course suddenly. **2** avoid an unpleasant person or thing.

sheet[1] *n* **1** large piece of cloth used as an inner bed cover. **2** broad thin piece of any material. **3** large expanse. **sheeting** *n* material from which sheets are made. **sheet lightning** lightning that appears to flash across a large part of the sky at once.

sheet[2] *n* rope for controlling the position of a sail. **sheet anchor** **1** strong anchor for use in an emergency. **2** person or thing relied on.

sheikh, sheik [**shake**] *n* Arab chief. **sheikhdom, sheikdom** *n*

sheila *n Aust slang* girl or woman.

shekel *n* **1** monetary unit of Israel. ♦ *pl* **2** *Informal* money.

shelf *n, pl* **shelves** **1** board fixed horizontally for holding things. **2** ledge. **on the shelf** past the age where marriage is likely. **shelf life** time a packaged product will remain fresh.

shell *n* **1** hard outer covering of an egg, nut, or certain animals. **2** external frame of something. **3** explosive projectile fired from a large gun. **4** light rowing boat. ♦ *v* **5** take the shell from. **6** fire at with artillery shells. **shellfish** *n* sea-living animal, esp. one that can be eaten, with a shell. **shell out** *v Informal* pay out or hand over (money). **shell shock** nervous disorder caused by exposure to battle conditions. **shell suit** lightweight tracksuit made of a waterproof nylon layer over a cotton layer.

shellac *n* **1** resin used in varnishes. ♦ *v* **-lacking, -lacked** **2** coat with shellac.

shelter *n* **1** structure providing protection from danger or the weather. **2** protection. ♦ *v* **3** give shelter to. **4** take shelter.

shelve[1] *v* **1** put aside or postpone. **2** provide with shelves. **shelving** *n* (material for) shelves.

shelve[2] *v* slope.

shelves *n* plural of SHELF.

shenanigans *pl n Informal* **1** mischief or nonsense. **2** trickery.

shepherd *n* **1** person who tends sheep. ♦ *v* **2** guide or watch over (people). **shepherdess** *n fem* **shepherd's pie** baked dish of mince covered with mashed potato.

sherbet *n* fruit-flavoured fizzy powder.

sheriff *n* **1** (in the US) chief law enforcement officer of a county. **2** (in England and Wales) chief executive officer of the Crown in a county. **3** (in Scotland) chief judge of a district.

Sherpa *n* member of a people of Tibet and Nepal.

sherry *n, pl* **-ries** pale or dark brown fortified wine.

Shetland pony *n* very small sturdy breed of pony.

shibboleth *n* slogan or principle, usu. considered outworn, characteristic of a particular group.

shied *v* past of SHY.

shield *n* **1** piece of armour carried on the arm to protect the body from blows or missiles. **2** anything that protects. **3** sports trophy in the shape of a shield. ♦ *v* **4** protect.

shift *v* **1** move. **2** transfer (blame or responsibility). **3** remove or be removed. ♦ *n* **4** shifting. **5** group of workers who work during a specified period. **6** period of time during which they work. **7** loose-fitting straight underskirt or dress. **shiftless** *adj* lacking in ambition or initiative. **shifty** *adj* evasive or untrustworthy. **shiftiness** *n*

shillelagh [shil-**lay**-lee] *n* (in Ireland) a cudgel.

shilling *n* **1** former British coin, replaced by the 5p piece. **2** monetary unit in some E African countries.

shillyshally *v* **-lying, -lied** *Informal* be indecisive.

shimmer *v, n* (shine with) a faint unsteady light.

shin *n* **1** front of the lower leg. ♦ *v* **shinning, shinned 2** climb by using the hands or arms and legs. **shinbone** *n* tibia.

shindig *n Informal* **1** noisy party. **2** brawl.

shine *v* **shining, shone 1** give out or reflect light. **2** aim (a light). **3** polish. **4** excel. ♦ *n* **5** brightness or lustre. **take a shine to** *Informal* take a liking to (someone). **shiny** *adj* **shiner** *n Informal* black eye.

shingle[1] *n* **1** wooden roof tile. ♦ *v* **2** cover (a roof) with shingles.

shingle[2] *n* coarse gravel found on beaches.

shingles *n* disease causing a rash of small blisters along a nerve.

Shinto *n* Japanese religion in which ancestors and nature spirits are worshipped. **Shintoism** *n*

shinty *n* game like hockey.

ship *n* **1** large seagoing vessel. **2** airship or spaceship. ♦ *v* **shipping, shipped 3** send or transport by carrier, esp. a ship. **4** bring or go aboard a ship. **5** *Informal* send away. **6** be hired to work on a ship. **shipment** *n* **1** act of shipping cargo. **2** consignment of goods shipped. **shipping** *n* **1** freight transport business. **2** ships collectively. **shipmate** *n* sailor serving on the same ship as another. **shipshape** *adj* orderly or neat. **shipwreck** *n* **1** destruction of a ship through storm or collision. **2** ruin or destruction. ♦ *v* **3** cause to undergo shipwreck. **shipyard** *n* place where ships are built.

shire *n* county.

shire horse *n* large powerful breed of horse.

shirk *v* avoid (duty or work). **shirker** *n*

shirt *n* garment for the upper part of the body. **shirtsleeves** *pl n* **in one's shirtsleeves** not wearing a jacket.

shirty *adj* **-tier, -tiest** *Slang* bad-tempered or annoyed.

shish kebab *n* meat and vegetable dish cooked on a skewer.

shit *Taboo* ♦ *v* **shitting, shitted, shit** *or* **shat 1** defecate. ♦ *n* **2** excrement. **3** *Slang* nonsense. **4** *Slang* worthless person. ♦ *interj* **5** *Slang* exclamation of anger or disgust. **shitty** *adj*

shiver[1] *v* **1** tremble, as from cold or fear. ♦ *n* **2** shivering. **shivery** *adj*

shiver[2] *v* **1** splinter into pieces. ♦ *n* **2** splintered piece.

shoal[1] *n* **1** large number of fish swimming together. **2** large group of people.

shoal[2] *n* **1** stretch of shallow water. **2** sandbank.

shock[1] *v* **1** horrify, disgust, or astonish. ♦ *n* **2** sudden violent emotional disturbance. **3** sudden violent blow or impact. **4** something causing this. **5** state of bodily collapse caused by physical or mental shock. **6** pain and muscular spasm caused by an electric current passing through the body. **shocker** *n* **shocking** *adj* **1** causing horror, disgust, or astonishment. **2** *Informal* very bad. **shock absorber** device on a car for reducing the effects of travelling over bumps. **shock therapy** electroconvulsive therapy.

shock[2] *n* bushy mass (of hair).

shod *v* past of SHOE.

shoddy *adj* **-dier, -diest** made or done badly.

shoe *n* **1** outer covering for the foot, ending below the ankle. **2** horseshoe. ♦ *v* **shoeing, shod 3** fit with a shoe or shoes. **shoehorn** *n* smooth curved implement inserted at the heel of a shoe to ease the foot into it. **shoelace** *n* cord for fastening shoes. **shoestring** *n* **on a shoestring** using a very small amount of money. **shoetree** *n* piece of metal, wood, or plastic inserted in a shoe to keep its shape.

shone *v* past of SHINE.

shoo *interj* **1** go away! ♦ *v* **2** drive away as by saying 'shoo'.

shook *v* past tense of SHAKE.

shoot *v* **shooting, shot 1** hit, wound, or kill with a missile fired from a weapon. **2** fire (a missile from) a weapon. **3** hunt. **4** send out or move rapidly. **5** (of a plant) sprout. **6** photograph or film. **7** *Sport* take a shot at goal. ♦ *n* **8** new branch or sprout of a plant. **9** hunting expedition. **10** *Informal* photographic assignment. **shooting star** meteor. **shooting stick** stick with a spike at one end and a folding seat at the other.

shop *n* **1** place for sale of goods and services. **2** workshop. ♦ *v* **shopping, shopped 3** visit a shop or shops to buy goods. **4** *Slang* inform against (someone). **talk shop** discuss one's work, esp. on a social occasion. **shopper** *n* **shopping** *n* **1** act of going to shops and buying things. **2** things bought. **shopping centre** area or building with many shops. **shop around** *v* visit various shops to compare goods and prices. **shop assistant** person serving in a shop. **shop floor 1** production area of a factory. **2** workers in a factory. **shoplifter** *n* person who steals from a shop. **shopsoiled** *adj* soiled or faded from being displayed in a shop. **shop steward** trade-union official elected to represent his or her fellow workers.

shore[1] *n* **1** edge of a sea or lake. **2** land.

shore[2] *v* **1** (foll. by *up*) prop or support. ♦ *n* **2** prop set under or against something as a support.

shorn *v* a past participle of SHEAR.

short *adj* **1** not long. **2** not tall. **3** not lasting long, brief. **4** deficient, e.g. *short of cash.* **5** abrupt, rude. **6** (of a drink) consisting chiefly of a spirit. **7** (of pastry) crumbly. ♦ *adv* **8** abruptly. ♦ *n* **9** drink of spirits. **10** short film. **11** *Informal* short circuit. ♦ *pl* **12** short trousers. ♦ *v* **13** short-circuit. **shortage** *n* deficiency. **shorten** *v* make or become shorter. **shortly** *adv* **1** soon. **2** rudely. **shortbread, shortcake** *n* crumbly biscuit made with butter. **short-change** *v* **1** give (someone) less than the correct amount of change. **2** *Slang* swindle. **short circuit** faulty or accidental connection in a circuit, which deflects current through a path of low resistance. **short-circuit** *v* **1** develop a short circuit. **2** bypass. **shortcoming** *n* failing or defect. **short cut** quicker route or method. **shortfall** *n* deficit. **shorthand** *n* system of rapid writing using symbols to represent words. **short-handed** *adj* not having enough workers. **short list** selected list of candidates for a job or prize, from which the final choice will be made. **short-list** *v* put on a short list. **short-lived** *adj* lasting a short time. **short shrift** brief and unsympathetic treatment. **short-sighted** *adj* **1** unable to see distant things clearly. **2** lacking in foresight. **short-tempered** *adj* easily angered. **short-term** *adj* of or lasting a short time. **short wave** radio wave with a wavelength of less than 60 metres.

shot[1] *n* **1** shooting. **2** small lead pellets used in a shotgun. **3** person with specified skill in shooting. **4** *Slang* attempt. **5** *Sport* act or instance of hitting, kicking, or throwing the ball. **6** photograph. **7** uninterrupted film sequence. **8** *Informal* injection. **9** *Informal* drink of spirits. **shotgun** *n* gun for firing a charge of shot at short range. **shotgun wedding** wedding enforced because the bride is pregnant.

shot[2] *v* **1** past of SHOOT. ♦ *adj* **2** woven to show changing colours, e.g. *shot silk.* **3** streaked with colour.

shot put *n* athletic event in which contestants hurl a heavy metal ball as far as possible. **shot-putter** *n*

should *v* past tense of SHALL: used as an auxiliary to make the subjunctive mood or to indicate obligation or possibility.

shoulder *n* **1** part of the body to which an arm, foreleg, or wing is attached. **2** cut of meat including the upper foreleg. **3** part of a garment which covers the shoulder. **4** side of a road. ♦ *v* **5** bear (a burden or responsibility). **6** push with one's shoulder. **7** put on one's shoulder. **shoulder blade** large flat triangular bone at the shoulder.

shouldn't should not.

shout *n* **1** loud cry. ♦ *v* **2** cry out loudly. **shout down** *v* silence (someone) by shouting.

shove *v* **1** push roughly. **2** *Informal* put. ♦ *n* **3** rough push. **shove off** *v Informal* go away.

shovel *n* **1** tool for lifting or moving loose material. ♦ *v* **-elling, -elled** **2** lift or move as with a shovel.

show *v* **showing, showed, shown** *or* **showed** **1** make, be, or become noticeable or visible. **2** exhibit or display. **3** indicate. **4** instruct by demonstration. **5** prove. **6** guide. **7** reveal or display (an emotion). ♦ *n* **8** public exhibition. **9** theatrical or other entertainment. **10** mere display or pretence. **11** *Slang* thing or affair. **showy** *adj* **1** gaudy. **2** ostentatious. **showily** *adv* **showing** *n* **1** exhibition. **2** manner of presentation. **show business** the entertainment industry. **showcase** *n* **1** situation in which something is displayed to best advantage. **2** glass case used to display objects. **showdown** *n* confrontation that settles a dispute. **showjumping** *n* competitive sport of riding horses to demonstrate skill in jumping. **showman** *n* man skilled at presenting anything spectacularly. **showmanship** *n* **show off** *v* **1** exhibit to invite admiration. **2** *Informal* behave flamboyantly in order to attract attention. **show-off** *n Informal* person who shows off. **showpiece** *n* excellent specimen shown for display or as an example. **showroom** *n* room in which goods for sale are on display. **show up** *v* **1** reveal or be revealed clearly. **2** expose the faults or defects of. **3** *Informal* embarrass. **4** *Informal* arrive.

shower *n* **1** kind of bath in which a person stands while being sprayed with water. **2** wash in this. **3** short period of rain, hail, or snow. **4** sudden abundant fall of objects, e.g. *shower of sparks.* ♦ *v* **5** wash in a shower. **6** sprinkle with or as if with a shower. **7** bestow (things) or present (someone) with things liberally. **showery** *adj*

shown *v* a past participle of SHOW.

shrank *v* a past tense of SHRINK.

shrapnel *n* **1** artillery shell filled with pellets which scatter on explosion. **2** fragments from this.

shred *n* **1** long narrow strip torn from something. **2** small amount. ♦ *v* **shredding, shredded** *or* **shred** **3** tear to shreds.

shrew *n* **1** small mouselike animal. **2** bad-tempered nagging woman. **shrewish** *adj*

shrewd *adj* clever and perceptive. **shrewdly** *adv* **shrewdness** *n*

shriek *n* **1** shrill cry. ♦ *v* **2** utter (with) a shriek.

shrike *n* songbird with a heavy hooked bill.

shrill *adj* **1** (of a sound) sharp and high-pitched. ♦ *v* **2** utter shrilly. **shrillness** *n* **shrilly** *adv*

shrimp *n* **1** small edible shellfish. **2** *Informal* small person. **shrimping** *n* fishing for shrimps.

shrine *n* **1** place of worship associated with a sacred person or object. **2** container for holy relics.

shrink *v* **shrinking, shrank** *or* **shrunk, shrunk** *or* **shrunken** **1** become or make smaller. **2** recoil or withdraw. ♦ *n* **3** *Slang* psychiatrist. **shrinkage** *n* decrease in size, value, or weight.

shrivel *v* **-elling, -elled** shrink and wither.

shroud *n* **1** piece of cloth used to wrap a dead body. **2** anything which conceals. ♦ *v* **3** conceal.

Shrove Tuesday *n* day before Ash Wednesday.

shrub *n* woody plant smaller than a tree. **shrubbery** *n, pl* **-beries** area planted with shrubs.

shrug *v* **shrugging, shrugged** **1** raise and then drop (the shoulders) as a sign of indifference, ignorance, or doubt. ♦ *n* **2** shrugging. **shrug off** *v* dismiss as unimportant.

shrunk *v* a past of SHRINK.

shrunken *v* a past participle of SHRINK.

shudder *v* **1** shake or tremble violently,

esp. with horror. ♦ *n* **2** shaking or trembling.

shuffle *v* **1** walk without lifting the feet. **2** jumble together. **3** rearrange. ♦ *n* **4** shuffling. **5** rearrangement.

shun *v* **shunning, shunned** avoid.

shunt *v* **1** move (objects or people) to a different position. **2** move (a train) from one track to another. ♦ *n* **3** shunting. **4** railway point.

shush *interj* **1** be quiet! ♦ *v* **2** quiet by saying 'shush'.

shut *v* **shutting, shut** **1** bring together or fold, close. **2** prevent access to. **3** (of a shop etc.) stop operating for the day. **shutter** *n* **1** hinged doorlike cover for closing off a window. **2** device in a camera letting in the light required to expose a film. ♦ *v* **3** close or equip with a shutter. **shut down** *v* close or stop (a factory, machine, or business). **shutdown** *n* **shuteye** *n Slang* sleep. **shut up** *v* **1** *Informal* stop talking. **2** confine.

shuttle *n* **1** vehicle going to and fro over a short distance. **2** instrument which passes the weft thread between the warp threads in weaving. **3** small thread-holding device in a sewing machine. ♦ *v* **4** travel by or as if by shuttle.

shuttlecock *n* small light cone with feathers stuck in one end, struck to and fro in badminton.

shy[1] *adj* **1** not at ease in company. **2** timid. **3** (foll. by *of*) cautious or wary. **4** reluctant, e.g. *workshy.* ♦ *v* **shying, shied** **5** start back in fear. **6** (foll. by *away from*) avoid (doing something) through fear or lack of confidence. **shyly** *adv* **shyness** *n*

shy[2] *v* **shying, shied** **1** throw. ♦ *n, pl* **shies** **2** throw.

Si *Chem* silicon.

SI *French* Système International (d'Unités), international metric system of units of measurement.

Siamese *adj* of Siam, former name of Thailand. **Siamese cat** breed of cat with cream fur, dark ears and face, and blue eyes. **Siamese twins** twins born joined to each other at some part of the body.

sibilant *adj* **1** hissing. ♦ *n* **2** consonant pronounced with a hissing sound.

sibling *n* brother or sister.

sibyl *n* (in ancient Greece and Rome) prophetess.

sic *Latin* thus: used to indicate that an odd spelling or reading is in fact accurate.

sick *adj* **1** vomiting or likely to vomit. **2** physically or mentally unwell. **3** *Informal* amused by something sadistic or morbid. **4** (foll. by *of*) *Informal* disgusted (by) or weary (of). ♦ *n* **5** *Informal* vomit. **sickness** *n* **sicken** *v* **1** make nauseated or disgusted. **2** become ill. **sickly** *adj* **1** unhealthy, weak. **2** looking pale and ill. **3** causing revulsion or nausea. **sickbay** *n* place for sick people, such as that on a ship.

sickle *n* tool with a curved blade for cutting grass or grain.

side *n* **1** line or surface that borders anything. **2** either of two halves into which something can be divided. **3** either surface of a flat object. **4** slope of a hill. **5** right or left part of the body. **6** area immediately next to a person or thing. **7** region. **8** aspect or part. **9** one of two opposing groups or teams. **10** line of descent through one parent. **11** *Slang* conceit. ♦ *adj* **12** at or on the side. **13** subordinate. **on the side** **1** as an extra. **2** unofficially. **siding** *n* short stretch of railway track on which trains or wagons are shunted from the main line. **sideboard** *n* piece of furniture for holding plates, cutlery, etc. in a dining room. **sideburns, sideboards** *pl n* man's side whiskers. **sidecar** *n* small passenger car on the side of a motorcycle. **side effect** additional undesirable effect. **sidekick** *n Informal* close friend or associate. **sidelight** *n* either of two small lights on the front of a vehicle. **sideline** *n* **1** subsidiary interest or source of income. **2** *Sport* line marking the boundary of a playing area. **sidelong** *adj* **1** sideways. ♦ *adv* **2** obliquely. **side-saddle** *n* saddle designed to allow a woman rider to sit with both legs on the same side of the horse. **sideshow** *n* entertainment offered along with the main show. **sidestep** *v* **1** dodge (an issue). **2** avoid by stepping sideways. **sidetrack** *v* divert from the main topic. **sidewalk** *n US* pavement. **sideways** *adv* **1** to or from the side. **2** obliquely. **side with** *v* support (one side in a dispute).

sidereal [side-**eer**-ee-al] *adj* of or determined with reference to the stars.

sidle *v* move in a furtive manner.

SIDS sudden infant death syndrome, cot death.

siege *n* surrounding and blockading of a place.

siemens *n* SI unit of electrical conductance.

sienna *n* reddish- or yellowish-brown pigment made from natural earth.

sierra *n* range of mountains in Spain or America with jagged peaks.

siesta *n* afternoon nap, taken in hot countries.

sieve [**siv**] *n* **1** utensil with mesh through which a substance is sifted or strained. ♦ *v* **2** sift or strain through a sieve.

sift *v* **1** remove the coarser particles from a substance with a sieve. **2** examine (information or evidence) to select what is important.

sigh *n* **1** long audible breath expressing sadness, tiredness, relief, or longing. ♦ *v* **2** utter a sigh. **sigh for** *v* long for.

sight *n* **1** ability to see. **2** instance of seeing. **3** range of vision. **4** thing seen. **5** *Informal* unsightly thing. **6** device for guiding the eye while using a gun or optical instrument. **7** thing worth seeing. **8** *Informal* a lot. ♦ *v* **9** catch sight of. **10** aim (a weapon) using a sight. **sightless** *adj* blind. **sight-read** *v* play or sing printed music without previous preparation. **sightseeing** *n* visiting places of interest. **sightseer** *n*

sign *n* **1** indication of something not immediately or outwardly observable. **2** gesture, mark, or symbol conveying a meaning. **3** notice displayed to advertise, inform, or warn. **4** visible indication. **5** omen. ♦ *v* **6** write (one's name) on (a document or letter) to show its authenticity or one's agreement. **7** communicate using sign language. **8** make a sign or gesture. **9** engage by signing a contract. **sign language** system of communication by gestures, as used by deaf people (also **signing**). **sign on** *v* **1** register as unemployed. **2** sign a document committing oneself to a job, course, etc. **signpost** *n* **1** post bearing a sign that shows the way. ♦ *v* **2** mark with signposts.

signal *n* **1** sign or gesture to convey information. **2** sequence of electrical impulses or radio waves transmitted or received. ♦ *adj* **3** *Formal* very important. ♦ *v* **-nalling, -nalled 4** convey (information) by signal. **signally** *adv* **signal box** building from which railway signals are operated. **signalman** *n* railwayman in charge of signals and points.

signatory [**sig**-na-tree] *n, pl* **-ries** one of the parties who sign a document.

signature *n* **1** person's name written by himself or herself in signing something. **2** identifying characteristic. **3** sign at the start of a piece of music to show the key or tempo. **signature tune** tune used to introduce a particular television or radio programme.

signet *n* small seal used to authenticate documents. **signet ring** finger ring bearing a signet.

significant *adj* **1** important. **2** having or expressing a meaning. **significantly** *adv* **significance** *n*

signify *v* **-fying, -fied 1** indicate or suggest. **2** be a symbol or sign for. **3** be important. **signification** *n* meaning.

signor [see-**nyor**] *n* Italian term of address equivalent to *sir* or *Mr*. **signora** [see-**nyor**-a] *n* Italian term of address equivalent to *madam* or *Mrs*. **signorina** [see-nyor-**ee**-na] *n* Italian term of address equivalent to *madam* or *Miss*.

Sikh [**seek**] *n* member of an Indian religion having only one God. **Sikhism** *n*

silage [**sile**-ij] *n* fodder crop harvested while green and partially fermented in a silo.

silence *n* **1** absence of noise or speech. **2** refusal or failure to speak or communicate. ♦ *v* **3** make silent. **4** put a stop to. **silent** *adj* **silently** *adv* **silencer** *n* device to reduce the noise of an engine exhaust or gun.

silhouette *n* **1** outline of a dark shape seen against a light background. **2** outline drawing of a profile. ♦ *v* **3** show in silhouette.

silica *n* hard glossy mineral found as quartz and in sandstone. **silicosis** *n* lung disease caused by inhaling silica dust.

silicate *n* compound of silicon, oxygen, and a metal.

silicon *n Chem* brittle nonmetallic element widely used in chemistry and industry. **silicone** *n* tough synthetic substance made from silicon and used in lubricants, paints, and resins. **silicon chip** tiny wafer of silicon processed to form an integrated circuit.

silk *n* **1** fibre made by the larva (**silkworm**) of a certain moth. **2** thread or fabric made from this. **take silk** become a Queen's (or King's) Counsel. **silky, silken** *adj* of or like silk.

sill *n* ledge at the bottom of a window or door.

silly *adj* **-lier, -liest** foolish. **silliness** *n*

silo *n, pl* **-los** **1** pit or airtight tower for storing silage. **2** underground structure in which nuclear missiles are kept ready for launching.

silt *n* **1** mud deposited by moving water. ♦ *v* **2** (foll. by *up*) fill or be choked with silt.

silvan *adj* same as SYLVAN.

silver *n* **1** white precious metal. **2** coins or articles made of silver. ♦ *adj* **3** made of or of the colour of silver. ♦ *v* **4** coat with silver. **silvery** *adj* **1** like silver. **2** having a clear ringing sound. **silver birch** tree with silvery-white bark. **silverfish** *n* small wingless silver-coloured insect. **silver medal** medal given to the runner-up in a competition or race. **silver-plated** *adj* covered with a thin layer of silver. **silverside** *n* cut of beef from below the rump and above the leg. **silversmith** *n* person who makes articles of silver. **silver wedding** twenty-fifth wedding anniversary

silviculture *n* cultivation of forest trees.

simian *adj, n* (of or like) a monkey or ape.

similar *adj* alike but not identical. **similarity** *n* **similarly** *adv*

> Do not confuse *similar* and *same*. *Similar* is 'alike but not identical'; *same* means 'identical'.

simile [**sim**-ill-ee] *n* figure of speech comparing one thing to another, using 'as' or 'like', e.g. *as blind as a bat.*

similitude *n* similarity, likeness.

simmer *v* **1** cook gently at just below boiling point. **2** be in a state of suppressed rage. **simmer down** *v Informal* calm down.

simnel cake *n* fruit cake covered with marzipan.

simper *v* **1** smile in a silly or affected way. **2** utter (something) with a simper. ♦ *n* **3** simpering smile.

simple *adj* **1** easy to understand or do. **2** plain or unpretentious. **3** not combined or complex. **4** sincere or frank. **5** feeble-minded. **simply** *adv* **1** in a simple manner. **2** merely. **3** absolutely. **simplicity** *n* **simplify** *v* **-fying, -fied** make less complicated. **simplification** *n* **simplistic** *adj* too simple or naive. **simple fraction** fraction in which the numerator and denominator are whole numbers. **simple-minded** *adj* unsophisticated. **simpleton** *n* foolish or half-witted person.

simulate *v* **1** make a pretence of. **2** imitate the conditions of (a particular situation). **3** have the appearance of. **simulation** *n* **simulator** *n*

simultaneous *adj* occurring at the same time. **simultaneity** *n* **simultaneously** *adv*

sin[1] *n* **1** breaking of a religious or moral law. **2** offence against a principle or standard. ♦ *v* **sinning, sinned** **3** commit a sin. **sinful** *adj* **1** guilty of sin. **2** being a sin. **sinfully** *adv* **sinner** *n*

sin[2] *Maths* sine.

since *prep* **1** during the period of time after. ♦ *conj* **2** from the time when. **3** for the reason that. ♦ *adv* **4** from that time.

> Avoid the use of *ago* with *since*. It is redundant: *It is ten years since he wrote his book* (not *ten years ago since*).

sincere *adj* without pretence or deceit. **sincerely** *adv* **sincerity** *n*

sine *n* (in trigonometry) ratio of the length of the opposite side to that of the hypotenuse in a right-angled triangle.

sinecure [**sin**-ee-cure] *n* paid job with minimal duties.

sine die [**sin**-ay **dee**-ay] *adv Latin* with no date fixed for future action.

sine qua non [**sin**-ay kwah **non**] *n Latin* essential requirement.

sinew *n* **1** tough fibrous tissue joining muscle to bone. **2** muscles or strength. **sinewy** *adj*

sing *v* **singing, sang, sung** **1** make musical sounds with the voice. **2** perform (a song). **3** make a humming or whistling sound. **singer** *n* **singing telegram** service in which a messenger presents greetings to a person by singing. **singsong** *n* **1** informal singing session. ♦ *adj* **2** (of the voice) repeatedly rising and falling in pitch.

> The simple past of *sing* is *sang*: *He sang the chorus*. Avoid the use of the past participle *sung* for the simple past.

singe *v* **singeing, singed** **1** burn the surface of. ♦ *n* **2** superficial burn.

single *adj* **1** one only. **2** distinct from others of the same kind. **3** unmarried. **4** designed for one user. **5** formed of only one part. **6** (of a ticket) valid for an outward journey only. ♦ *n* **7** single thing. **8** thing intended for one person. **9** record with one short song or tune on each side. **10** single ticket. ♦ *pl* **11** game between two players. ♦ *v* **12** (foll. by *out*) pick out from others. **singly** *adv* **single-breasted** *adj* (of a garment) having only slightly overlapping fronts and one row of buttons. **single file** (of people or things) arranged in one line. **single-handed** *adj* without assistance. **single-minded** *adj* having one aim only.

singlet *n* sleeveless vest.

singular *adj* **1** (of a word or form) denoting one person or thing. **2** remarkable, unusual. ♦ *n* **3** singular form of a word. **singularity** *n* **singularly** *adv*

Sinhalese, Singhalese *n, adj* (member or language) of a people living mainly in Sri Lanka.

sinister *adj* threatening or suggesting evil or harm.

sink *v* **sinking, sank, sunk** *or* **sunken** **1** submerge (in liquid). **2** descend or cause to descend. **3** decline in value or amount. **4** become weaker in health. **5** seep or penetrate. **6** dig or drill (a hole or shaft). **7** invest (money). **8** *Golf, snooker* hit (a ball) into a hole or pocket. ♦ *n* **9** fixed basin with a water supply and drainage pipe. **sinker** *n* weight for a fishing line. **sink in** *v* penetrate the mind. **sinking fund** money set aside regularly to repay a long-term debt.

Sino- *combining form* Chinese.

sinuous *adj* **1** curving. **2** lithe. **sinuously** *adv*

sinus [**sine**-uss] *n* hollow space in a bone, esp. an air passage opening into the nose. **sinusitis** *n* inflammation of a sinus membrane.

sip *v* **sipping, sipped** **1** drink in small mouthfuls. ♦ *n* **2** amount sipped.

siphon *n* **1** bent tube which uses air pressure to draw liquid from a container. ♦ *v* **2** draw off thus. **3** redirect (resources).

sir *n* **1** polite term of address for a man. **2** (**S-**) title of a knight or baronet.

sire *n* **1** male parent of a horse or other domestic animal. **2** respectful term of address to a king. ♦ *v* **3** father.

siren *n* **1** device making a loud wailing noise as a warning. **2** dangerously alluring woman.

sirloin *n* prime cut of loin of beef.

sirocco *n, pl* **-cos** hot wind blowing from N Africa into S Europe.

sisal [**size**-al] *n* (fibre of) plant used in making ropes.

siskin *n* yellow-and-black finch.

sissy *adj, n, pl* **-sies** weak or cowardly (person).

sister *n* **1** girl or woman with the same parents as another person. **2** female fellow-member of a group. **3** senior nurse. **4** nun. ♦ *adj* **5** closely related, similar. **sisterhood** *n* **1** state of being a sister. **2** group of women united by common aims or beliefs. **sisterly** *adj* **sister-in-law** *n, pl* **sisters-in-law** **1** sister of one's husband or wife. **2** one's brother's wife.

sit *v* **sitting, sat** **1** rest one's body upright on the buttocks. **2** cause to sit. **3** perch. **4** (of a bird) incubate (eggs) by sitting on them. **5** be situated. **6** pose for a portrait. **7** occupy an official position. **8** (of an official body) hold a session. **9** fit or hang as specified. **10** take (an examination). **sit tight** *Informal* wait patiently without taking action. **sitter** *n* **1** baby-sitter. **2** person posing for a picture. **sitting** *n* **1** time when a meal is served. **2** meeting of an official body. ♦ *adj* **3** current. **4** seated. **sitting room** room in a house where people sit and relax. **sit down** *v* (cause to) adopt a sitting posture. **sit-in** *n* protest in which demonstrators occupy a place and refuse to move. **sit on** *v Informal* delay action on. **sit out** *v* endure to the end.

sitar *n* Indian stringed musical instrument.

sitcom *n Informal* situation comedy.

site *n* **1** place where something is, was, or is intended to be located. ♦ *v* **2** provide with a site.

situate *v* place. **situation** *n* **1** state of affairs. **2** location and surroundings. **3** position of employment. **situation comedy** radio or television series involving the same characters in various situations.

six *adj, n* one more than five. **sixth** *adj, n* (of) number six in a series. **sixteen** *adj, n* six and ten. **sixteenth** *adj, n* **sixty** *adj, n* six times ten. **sixtieth** *adj, n* **sixpence** *n* former British coin worth six pennies. **sixth sense** perception beyond the five senses.

size[1] *n* **1** dimensions, bigness. **2** one of a series of standard measurements of goods. ♦ *v* **3** arrange according to size. **sizeable, sizable** *adj* quite large. **size up** *v Informal* assess.

size[2] *n* **1** gluey substance used as a protective coating. ♦ *v* **2** treat with size.

sizzle *v* **1** make a hissing sound like frying fat. ♦ *n* **2** hissing sound.

SK Saskatchewan.

skate[1] *n* **1** boot with a steel blade or sets of wheels attached to the sole for gliding over ice or a hard surface. ♦ *v* **2** glide on or as if on skates. **skateboard** *n* board mounted on small wheels for riding on while standing up. **skate over, round** *v* avoid discussing or dealing with (a matter) fully.

skate[2] *n* large marine flatfish.

skean-dhu *n* dagger worn in the stocking as part of the Highland dress.

skedaddle *v Informal* run off.

skein *n* **1** yarn wound in a loose coil. **2** flock of geese in flight.

skeleton *n* **1** framework of bones inside a person's or animal's body. **2** essential framework of a structure. **3** skinny person or animal. **4** outline of bare essentials. ♦ *adj* **5** reduced to a minimum. **skeletal** *adj* **skeleton key** key which can open many different locks.

skerry *n, pl* **-ries** rocky island or reef.

sketch *n* **1** rough drawing. **2** brief description. **3** short humorous play. ♦ *v* **4** make a sketch (of). **sketchy** *adj* incomplete or inadequate. **sketch out** *v* make a brief description of.

skew *v* **1** make slanting or crooked. ♦ *adj* **2** slanting or crooked. **skewed** *adj* distorted or biased because of lack of information. **skewwhiff** *adj Informal* slanting or crooked.

skewbald *n, adj* (horse) marked with patches of white and another colour.

skewer *n* **1** pin to hold meat together during cooking. ♦ *v* **2** fasten with a skewer.

ski *n* **1** one of a pair of long runners fastened to boots for gliding over snow or water. ♦ *v* **skiing, skied** *or* **ski'd** **2** travel on skis. **skier** *n*

skid *v* **skidding, skidded** **1** (of a moving vehicle) slide sideways uncontrollably. ♦ *n* **2** skidding. **skid row** *US slang* dilapidated part of a city frequented by down-and-outs.

skiff *n* small boat.

skill *n* **1** special ability or expertise. **2** something requiring special training or expertise. **skilful** *adj* having or showing skill. **skilfully** *adv* **skilled** *adj*

skillet *n* small frying pan or shallow cooking pot.

skim *v* **skimming, skimmed** **1** remove floating matter from the surface of (a liquid). **2** glide smoothly over. **3** throw across a surface. **4** read quickly. **skimmed, skim milk** milk from which the cream has been removed.

skimp *v* not invest enough time, money, material, etc. **skimpy** *adj* scanty or insufficient.

skin *n* **1** outer covering of the body. **2** complexion. **3** outer layer or covering. **4** film on a liquid. **5** animal skin used as a material or container. ♦ *v* **skinning, skinned** **6** remove the skin of. **7** graze. **8** *Slang* swindle. **skinless** *adj* **skinny** *adj* thin. **skin-deep** *adj* superficial. **skin diving** underwater swimming using flippers and light breathing apparatus. **skin-diver** *n* **skinflint** *n* miser. **skinhead** *n* youth with very short hair. **skintight** *adj* fitting tightly over the body.

skint *adj Slang* having no money.

skip[1] *v* **skipping, skipped** **1** leap lightly from one foot to the other. **2** jump over a rope as it is swung under one. **3** *Informal* pass over, omit. **4** change quickly from one subject to another. ♦ *n* **5** skipping.

skip[2] *n* **1** large open container for builders' rubbish. **2** cage used as a lift in mines.

skipper *n, v* captain.

skirl *n* sound of bagpipes.

skirmish *n* **1** brief or minor fight or argument. ♦ *v* **2** take part in a skirmish.

skirt *n* **1** woman's garment hanging from the waist. **2** part of a dress or coat below the waist. **3** circular hanging part. **4** cut of beef from the flank. ♦ *v* **5** border. **6** go round. **7** avoid dealing with (an issue). **skirting board** narrow board round the bottom of an interior wall.

skit *n* brief satirical sketch.

skittish *adj* **1** playful or lively. **2** (of a horse) easily frightened.

skittle *n* **1** bottle-shaped object used as a target in some games. ♦ *pl* **2** game in which players try to knock over skittles by rolling a ball at them.

skive *v Informal* evade work or responsibility.

skivvy *n, pl* **-vies** female servant who does menial work.

skua *n* large predatory gull.

skulduggery *n Informal* trickery.

skulk *v* **1** move stealthily. **2** lurk.

skull *n* **1** bony framework of the head. **2** *Informal* brain or mind. **skullcap** *n* close-fitting brimless cap.

skunk *n* **1** small black-and-white N American mammal which emits a foul-smelling fluid when attacked. **2** *Slang* despicable person.

sky *n, pl* **skies** **1** upper atmosphere as seen from the earth. ♦ *v* **skying, skied** **2** *Informal* hit high in the air. **skydiving** *n* sport of jumping from an aircraft and performing manoeuvres before opening one's parachute. **skylark** *n* lark that sings while soaring at a great height. **skylight** *n* window in a roof or ceiling. **skyline** *n* outline of buildings, trees, etc. against the sky. **skyscraper** *n* very tall building.

slab *n* broad flat piece.

slack[1] *adj* **1** not tight. **2** negligent. **3** (of water) moving slowly. **4** not busy. ♦ *n* **5** slack part. **6** slack period. ♦ *pl* **7** informal trousers. ♦ *v* **8** neglect one's work or duty. **9** loosen or slacken. **slackness** *n* **slacken** *v* make or become slack. **slacker** *n*

slack[2] *n* coal dust or small pieces of coal.

slag *n* **1** waste left after metal is smelted. **2** *Brit slang* a sexually immoral woman. ♦ *v* **slagging, slagged 3** (foll. by *off*) *Slang* criticize. **slag heap** pile of waste from smelting or mining.

slain *v* past participle of SLAY.

slake *v* **1** satisfy (thirst or desire). **2** combine (quicklime) with water.

slalom *n* skiing or canoeing race over a winding course.

slam *v* **slamming, slammed 1** shut, put down, or hit violently and noisily. **2** *Informal* criticize harshly. ♦ *n* **3** act or sound of slamming. **grand slam** see GRAND.

slander *n* **1** false and malicious statement about a person. **2** crime of making such a statement. ♦ *v* **3** utter slander about. **slanderous** *adj*

slang *n* very informal language. **slangy** *adj* **slanging match** abusive argument.

slant *v* **1** lean at an angle, slope. **2** present (information) in a biased way. ♦ *n* **3** slope. **4** point of view, esp. a biased one. **slanting** *adj*

slap *n* **1** blow with the open hand or a flat object. ♦ *v* **slapping, slapped 2** strike with the open hand or a flat object. **3** *Informal* place forcefully or carelessly. **slapdash** *adj* careless and hasty. **slaphappy** *adj Informal* cheerfully careless. **slapstick** *n* boisterous knockabout comedy. **slap-up** *adj* (of a meal) large and luxurious.

slash *v* **1** cut with a sweeping stroke. **2** gash. **3** reduce drastically. **4** criticize harshly. ♦ *n* **5** sweeping stroke. **6** gash.

slat *n* narrow strip of wood or metal.

slate[1] *n* **1** rock which splits easily into thin layers. **2** piece of this for covering a roof or, formerly, for writing on. ♦ *v* **3** cover with slates. **4** *US* plan or arrange. ♦ *adj* **5** dark grey.

slate[2] *v Informal* criticize harshly. **slating** *n*

slattern *n Old-fashioned* slovenly woman. **slatternly** *adj*

slaughter *v* **1** kill (animals) for food. **2** kill (people) savagely or indiscriminately. ♦ *n* **3** slaughtering. **slaughterhouse** *n* place where animals are killed for food.

Slav *n* member of any of the peoples of E Europe or the former Soviet Union who speak a Slavonic language. **Slavonic** *n* **1** language group including Russian, Polish, and Czech. ♦ *adj* **2** of this language group.

slave *n* **1** person owned by another for whom he or she has to work. **2** person dominated by another or by a habit. **3** drudge. ♦ *v* **4** work like a slave. **slaver** *n* person or ship engaged in the slave trade. **slavery** *n* **1** state or condition of being a slave. **2** practice of owning slaves. **slavish** *adj* **1** of or like a slave. **2** imitative. **slave-driver** *n* person who makes others work very hard.

slaver [**slav**-ver] *v* **1** dribble saliva from the mouth. ♦ *n* **2** saliva dribbling from the mouth.

slay *v* **slaying, slew, slain** kill.

sleazy *adj* **-zier, -ziest** run-down or sordid. **sleaze** *n*

sledge[1], **sled** *n* **1** carriage on runners for sliding on snow. **2** light wooden frame for sliding over snow. ♦ *v* **3** travel by sledge.

sledge[2], **sledgehammer** *n* heavy hammer with a long handle.

sleek *adj* **1** glossy, smooth, and shiny. **2** elegantly dressed.

sleep *n* **1** state of rest characterized by unconsciousness. **2** period of this. ♦ *v* **sleeping, slept 3** be in or as if in a state of sleep. **4** have sleeping accommodation for (a specified number). **sleeper** *n* **1** railway car fitted for sleeping in. **2** beam supporting the rails of a railway. **3** ring worn in a pierced ear to stop the hole from closing up. **4** person who sleeps. **sleepy** *adj* **1** needing sleep. **2**

without activity or bustle. **sleepily** *adv* **sleepiness** *n* **sleepless** *adj* **sleep in** *v* sleep longer than usual. **sleeping bag** padded bag for sleeping in. **sleeping partner** business partner who does not play an active role. **sleeping sickness** African disease spread by the tsetse fly. **sleepwalk** *v* walk while asleep. **sleepwalker** *n* **sleep with, together** *v* have sexual intercourse (with).

sleet *n* **1** rain and snow or hail falling together. ♦ *v* **2** fall as sleet.

sleeve *n* **1** part of a garment which covers the arm. **2** tubelike cover. **3** gramophone record cover. **up one's sleeve** secretly ready. **sleeveless** *adj*

sleigh *n, v* sledge.

sleight of hand [**slite**] *n* skilful use of the hands when performing conjuring tricks.

slender *adj* **1** slim. **2** small in amount.

slept *v* past of SLEEP.

sleuth [**slooth**] *n* detective.

slew[1] *v* past tense of SLAY.

slew[2] *v* twist or swing round.

slice *n* **1** thin flat piece cut from something. **2** share. **3** kitchen tool with a broad flat blade. **4** *Sport* hitting of a ball so that it travels obliquely. ♦ *v* **5** cut into slices. **6** cut (through). **7** *Sport* hit (a ball) with a slice.

slick *adj* **1** persuasive and glib. **2** skilfully devised or carried out. **3** well-made and attractive, but superficial. ♦ *n* **4** patch of oil on water. ♦ *v* **5** make smooth or sleek.

slide *v* **sliding, slid 1** slip smoothly along (a surface). **2** pass unobtrusively. **3** go into or become (something) by degrees, e.g. *the states slid into barbarism.* ♦ *n* **4** sliding. **5** piece of glass holding an object to be viewed under a microscope. **6** photographic transparency. **7** surface or structure for sliding on or down. **8** ornamental hair clip. **9** sliding curved part of a trombone. **slide rule** mathematical instrument formerly used for rapid calculations. **sliding scale** variable scale according to which things such as wages alter in response to changes in other factors.

slight *adj* **1** small in quantity or extent. **2** not important. **3** slim and delicate. ♦ *v, n* **4** snub. **slightly** *adv*

slim *adj* **slimmer, slimmest 1** not heavy or stout, thin. **2** slight. ♦ *v* **slimming, slimmed 3** make or become slim by diet and exercise. **slimmer** *n*

slime *n* unpleasant thick slippery substance. **slimy** *adj* **slimier, slimiest 1** of, like, or covered with slime. **2** ingratiating.

sling[1] *n* **1** bandage hung from the neck to support an injured hand or arm. **2** rope or strap for lifting something. **3** strap with a string at each end for throwing a stone. ♦ *v* **slinging, slung 4** throw. **5** carry, hang, or throw with or as if with a sling. **slingback** *n* shoe with a strap that goes around the back of the heel.

sling[2] *n* sweetened drink with a spirit base, e.g. *gin sling.*

slink *v* **slinking, slunk** move furtively or guiltily. **slinky** *adj* **slinkier, slinkiest** (of clothes) figure-hugging.

slip[1] *v* **slipping, slipped 1** lose balance by sliding. **2** move smoothly, easily, or quietly. **3** place quickly or stealthily. **4** (foll. by *on* or *off*) put on or take off easily or quickly. **5** pass out of (the mind). **6** become worse. **7** dislocate (a bone). ♦ *n* **8** slipping. **9** mistake. **10** petticoat. **11** *Cricket* fielding position behind and to the offside of the wicketkeeper. **give someone the slip** escape from someone. **slippy** *adj Informal* slippery. **slipknot** *n* knot tied so that it will slip along the rope round which it is made. **slip-on** *adj* (of a garment or shoe) made to be put on easily. **slipped disc** painful condition in which one of the discs connecting the bones of the spine becomes displaced. **slip road** narrow road giving access to a motorway. **slipshod** *adj* (of an action) careless. **slipstream** *n* stream of air forced backwards by a fast-moving object. **slip up** *v* make a mistake. **slipway** *n* launching slope on which ships are built or repaired.

slip[2] *n* **1** small piece (of paper). **2** cutting from a plant. **3** slender person.

slip[3] *n* clay mixed with water used for decorating pottery.

slipper *n* light shoe for indoor wear.

slippery *adj* **1** so smooth or wet as to cause slipping or be difficult to hold. **2** (of a person) untrustworthy.

slit *n* **1** long narrow cut or opening. ♦ *v* **slitting, slit 2** make a long straight cut in.

slither *v* **1** slide unsteadily. **2** move in a twisting way.

sliver [**sliv**-ver] *n* **1** small thin piece. ♦ *v* **2** cut into slivers.

slob *n Informal* lazy and untidy person. **slobbish** *adj*

slobber *v* **1** dribble or drool. **2** behave in a gushy way. **slobbery** *adj*

sloe *n* sour blue-black fruit.

slog *v* **slogging, slogged 1** work hard and steadily. **2** make one's way with difficulty. **3** hit hard. ♦ *n* **4** long and exhausting work or walk.

slogan *n* catchword or phrase used in politics or advertising.

sloop *n* small single-masted ship.

slop *v* **slopping, slopped 1** splash or spill. ♦ *n* **2** spilt liquid. **3** liquid food. ♦ *pl* **4** liquid refuse and waste food used to feed animals. **sloppy** *adj* **-pier, -piest 1** careless or untidy. **2** gushingly sentimental.

slope *v* **1** slant. ♦ *n* **2** sloping surface. **3** degree of inclination. ♦ *pl* **4** hills. **slope off** *v Informal* go furtively.

slosh *v* **1** pour carelessly. **2** splash carelessly. **3** *Slang* hit hard. ♦ *n* **4** splashing sound. **sloshed** *adj Slang* drunk.

slot *n* **1** narrow opening for inserting something. **2** *Informal* place in a series or scheme. ♦ *v* **slotting, slotted 3** make a slot or slots in. **4** fit into a slot. **slot machine** automatic machine worked by placing a coin in a slot.

sloth [rhymes with **both**] *n* **1** slow-moving animal of tropical America. **2** laziness. **slothful** *adj* lazy or idle.

slouch *v* **1** sit, stand, or move with a drooping posture. ♦ *n* **2** drooping posture. **be no slouch** *Informal* be very good or talented.

slough[1] [rhymes with **now**] *n* bog.

slough[2] [**sluff**] *v* **1** (of a snake) shed (its skin) or (of a skin) be shed. ♦ *n* **2** outer covering that has been shed. **slough off** *v* get rid of (something unwanted or unnecessary).

Slovak *adj, n* **1** (person) from Slovakia. ♦ *n* **2** language of Slovakia.

sloven *n* habitually dirty or untidy person. **slovenly** *adj* **1** dirty or untidy. **2** careless.

Slovene *adj, n* **1** (also **Slovenian**) (person) from Slovenia. ♦ *n* **2** language of Slovenia.

slow *adj* **1** taking a longer time than is usual or expected. **2** not fast. **3** (of a clock or watch) showing a time earlier than the correct one. **4** stupid. **5** dull or uninteresting. ♦ *adv* **6** slowly. ♦ *v* **7** reduce the speed (of). **slowly** *adv* **slowness** *n* **slowcoach** *n Informal* person who moves or works slowly. **slow motion** movement on film made to appear much slower than it actually is.

slowworm *n* small legless lizard.

sludge *n* **1** thick mud. **2** sewage.

slug[1] *n* land snail with no shell. **sluggish** *adj* slow-moving, lacking energy. **sluggishly** *adv* **sluggishness** *n* **sluggard** *n* lazy person.

slug[2] *n* **1** bullet. **2** *Informal* mouthful of an alcoholic drink.

slug[3] *v* **slugging, slugged 1** hit hard. ♦ *n* **2** heavy blow.

sluice *n* **1** channel carrying off water. **2** sliding gate used to control the flow of water in this. **3** water controlled by a sluice. ♦ *v* **4** pour a stream of water over or through.

slum *n* **1** squalid overcrowded house or area. ♦ *v* **slumming, slummed 2** temporarily and deliberately experience poorer places or conditions than usual. **slummy** *adj*

slumber *v, n Lit* sleep.

slump *v* **1** (of prices or demand) decline suddenly. **2** sink or fall heavily. ♦ *n* **3**

sudden decline in prices or demand. **4** time of substantial unemployment.

slung *v* past of SLING[1].

slunk *v* past of SLINK.

slur *v* **slurring, slurred 1** pronounce or utter (words) indistinctly. **2** disparage. **3** *Music* sing or play (notes) smoothly without a break. **4** treat carelessly. ♦ *n* **5** slurring of words. **6** remark intended to discredit someone. **7** *Music* slurring of notes. **8** curved line indicating notes to be slurred.

slurp *Informal* ♦ *v* **1** eat or drink noisily. ♦ *n* **2** slurping sound.

slurry *n, pl* **-ries** muddy liquid mixture.

slush *n* **1** watery muddy substance. **2** sloppy sentimental talk or writing. **slushy** *adj* **slush fund** fund for financing bribery or corruption.

slut *n Offens* dirty or immoral woman. **sluttish** *adj*

sly *adj* **slyer, slyest** *or* **slier, sliest 1** crafty. **2** secretive and cunning. **3** roguish. **on the sly** secretly. **slyly** *adv* **slyness** *n*

Sm *Chem* samarium.

smack[1] *v* **1** slap sharply. **2** open and close (the lips) loudly in enjoyment or anticipation. ♦ *n* **3** sharp slap. **4** loud kiss. **5** slapping sound. ♦ *adv* **6** *Informal* squarely or directly, e.g. *smack in the middle.* **smacker** *n Slang* **1** loud kiss. **2** pound note or dollar bill.

smack[2] *n* **1** slight flavour or trace. **2** *Slang* heroin. ♦ *v* **3** have a slight flavour or trace (of).

smack[3] *n* small single-masted fishing boat.

small *adj* **1** not large in size, number, or amount. **2** unimportant. **3** mean or petty. ♦ *n* **4** narrow part of the lower back. ♦ *pl* **5** *Informal* underwear. ♦ *adv* **6** into small pieces. **smallness** *n* **small change** coins of low value. **smallholding** *n* small area of farming land. **small hours** hours just after midnight. **small-minded** *adj* intolerant, petty. **smallpox** *n* contagious disease with blisters that leave scars. **small talk** light social conversation. **small-time** *adj* insignificant or minor.

smarmy *adj* **smarmier, smarmiest** *Informal* unpleasantly suave or flattering.

smart *adj* **1** well-kept and neat. **2** astute. **3** witty. **4** fashionable. **5** brisk. **6** causing a stinging pain. ♦ *v* **7** feel or cause stinging pain. ♦ *n* **8** stinging pain. **smartly** *adv* **smartness** *n* **smart aleck** *Informal* irritatingly clever person. **smart card** plastic card used for storing and processing computer data. **smarten** *v* make or become smart.

smash *v* **1** break violently and noisily. **2** throw (against) violently. **3** collide forcefully. **4** destroy. ♦ *n* **5** act or sound of smashing. **6** violent collision of vehicles. **7** *Informal* popular success. **8** *Sport* powerful overhead shot. ♦ *adv* **9** with a smash. **smasher** *n Informal* attractive person or thing. **smashing** *adj Informal* excellent.

smattering *n* slight knowledge.

smear *v* **1** spread with a greasy or sticky substance. **2** rub so as to produce a dirty mark or smudge. **3** slander. ♦ *n* **4** dirty mark or smudge. **5** slander. **6** *Med* sample of a secretion smeared on to a slide for examination under a microscope. **smear test** *Med* examination of stained cells in a specimen taken from the neck or lining of the womb for detection of cancer.

smell *v* **smelling, smelt** *or* **smelled 1** perceive (a scent or odour) by means of the nose. **2** have or give off a smell. **3** have an unpleasant smell. **4** detect by instinct. **5** (foll. by *of*) indicate, suggest. ♦ *n* **6** ability to perceive odours by the nose. **7** odour or scent. **8** smelling. **smelly** *adj* having a nasty smell. **smelling salts** preparation of ammonia used to revive a person who feels faint.

smelt[1] *v* extract (a metal) from (an ore) by heating. **smelter** *n*

smelt[2] *n* small fish of the salmon family.

smelt[3] *v* a past of SMELL.

smile *n* **1** turning up of the corners of the mouth to show pleasure, amusement, or friendliness. ♦ *v* **2** give a smile. **3** express by a smile. **smile on, upon** *v* regard favourably.

smirch *v, n* disgrace.

smirk *n* **1** smug smile. ♦ *v* **2** give a smirk.

smite *v* **smiting, smote, smitten** **1** *Old-fashioned* strike hard. **2** affect severely.

smith *n* worker in metal. **smithy** *n* blacksmith's workshop.

smithereens *pl n* shattered fragments.

smitten *v* **1** past participle of SMITE. ♦ *adj* **2** affected by love.

smock *n* **1** loose overall. **2** woman's loose blouselike garment. ♦ *v* **3** gather (material) by sewing in a honeycomb pattern. **smocking** *n*

smog *n* mixture of smoke and fog.

smoke *n* **1** cloudy mass that rises from something burning. **2** act of smoking tobacco. **3** *Informal* cigarette or cigar. ♦ *v* **4** give off smoke. **5** inhale and expel smoke of (a cigar, cigarette, or pipe). **6** do this habitually. **7** cure (meat, fish, or cheese) by treating with smoke. **smokeless** *adj* **smoker** *n* **smoky** *adj* **smoke out** *v* drive out of hiding, esp. by using smoke. **smoke screen** something said or done to hide the truth. **smokestack** *n* tall chimney of a factory.

smolt *n* young salmon at the stage when it migrates to the sea.

smooch *Informal* ♦ *v* **1** kiss and cuddle. ♦ *n* **2** smooching.

smooth *adj* **1** even in surface, texture, or consistency. **2** without obstructions or difficulties. **3** charming and polite but possibly insincere. **4** free from jolts. **5** not harsh in taste. ♦ *v* **6** make smooth. **7** calm. **smoothly** *adv*

smorgasbord *n* buffet meal of assorted dishes.

smote *v* past tense of SMITE.

smother *v* **1** suffocate or stifle. **2** surround or overwhelm (with). **3** suppress. **4** cover thickly.

smoulder *v* **1** burn slowly with smoke but no flame. **2** (of feelings) exist in a suppressed state.

smudge *v* **1** make or become smeared or soiled. ♦ *n* **2** dirty mark. **3** blurred form. **smudgy** *adj*

smug *adj* **smugger, smuggest** self-satisfied. **smugly** *adv* **smugness** *n*

smuggle *v* **1** import or export (goods) secretly and illegally. **2** take somewhere secretly. **smuggler** *n*

smut *n* **1** obscene jokes, pictures, etc. **2** speck of soot or dark mark left by soot. **3** fungal disease of cereals. **smutty** *adj*

Sn *Chem* tin.

snack *n* light quick meal. **snack bar** place where snacks are sold.

snaffle *n* **1** jointed bit for a horse. ♦ *v* **2** *Slang* steal.

snag *n* **1** difficulty or disadvantage. **2** sharp projecting point. **3** hole in fabric caused by a sharp object. ♦ *v* **snagging, snagged** **4** catch or tear on a point.

snail *n* slow-moving mollusc with a spiral shell. **snail's pace** very slow speed.

snake *n* **1** long thin scaly limbless reptile. ♦ *v* **2** move in a winding course like a snake. **snake in the grass** treacherous person. **snaky** *adj* twisted or winding.

snap *v* **snapping, snapped** **1** break suddenly. **2** (cause to) make a sharp cracking sound. **3** move suddenly. **4** bite (at) suddenly. **5** speak sharply and angrily. **6** take a snapshot of. ♦ *n* **7** act or sound of snapping. **8** fastener that closes with a snapping sound. **9** *Informal* snapshot. **10** thin crisp biscuit. **11** sudden brief spell of cold weather. **12** card game in which the word 'snap' is called when two similar cards are put down. ♦ *adj* **13** made on the spur of the moment. ♦ *adv* **14** with a snap. **snappy** *adj* **1** (also **snappish**) irritable. **2** *Slang* quick. **3** *Slang* smart and fashionable. **snapdragon** *n* plant with flowers that can open and shut like a mouth. **snapshot** *n* informal photograph. **snap up** *v* take eagerly and quickly.

snare[1] *n* **1** trap with a noose. ♦ *v* **2** catch in or as if in a snare.

snare[2] *n* *Music* set of gut strings wound with wire fitted across the bottom of a drum to increase vibration. **snare drum** cylindrical double-headed drum with snares.

snarl[1] *v* **1** (of an animal) growl with

bared teeth. **2** speak or utter fiercely. ♦ *n* **3** act or sound of snarling.

snarl[2] *n* **1** tangled mess. ♦ *v* **2** make tangled. **snarl-up** *n Informal* confused situation such as a traffic jam.

snatch *v* **1** seize or try to seize suddenly. **2** take (food, rest, etc.) hurriedly. **3** remove suddenly. ♦ *n* **4** snatching. **5** fragment.

snazzy *adj* **-zier, -ziest** *Informal* stylish and flashy.

sneak *v* **1** move furtively. **2** bring, take, or put furtively. **3** *Informal* tell tales. ♦ *n* **4** cowardly or underhand person. **sneaking** *adj* **1** slight but persistent. **2** secret. **sneaky** *adj*

sneakers *pl n Chiefly US* canvas shoes with rubber soles.

sneer *n* **1** contemptuous expression or remark. ♦ *v* **2** show contempt by a sneer.

sneeze *v* **1** expel air from the nose suddenly, involuntarily, and noisily. ♦ *n* **2** act or sound of sneezing. **sneeze at** *v Informal* dismiss lightly.

snib *n Scot* catch of a door or window.

snick *v, n* (make) a small cut or notch.

snicker *n, v* same as SNIGGER.

snide *adj* critical in an unfair and nasty way.

sniff *v* **1** inhale through the nose in short audible breaths. **2** smell by sniffing. ♦ *n* **3** act or sound of sniffing. **sniffle** *v* **1** sniff repeatedly, as when suffering from a cold. ♦ *n* **2** slight cold. **sniff at** *v* express contempt for. **sniffer dog** police dog trained to detect drugs or explosives by smell.

snifter *n Informal* small quantity of alcoholic drink.

snigger *n* **1** sly disrespectful laugh, esp. one partly stifled. ♦ *v* **2** utter a snigger.

snip *v* **snipping, snipped** **1** cut in small quick strokes with scissors or shears. ♦ *n* **2** *Informal* bargain. **3** act or sound of snipping. **4** piece snipped off. **snippet** *n* small piece.

snipe *n* **1** wading bird with a long straight bill. ♦ *v* **2** (foll. by *at*) shoot at (a person) from cover. **3** make critical remarks about. **sniper** *n*

snitch *Informal* ♦ *v* **1** act as an informer. **2** steal. ♦ *n* **3** informer.

snivel *v* **-elling, -elled** **1** cry in a whining way. **2** have a runny nose.

snob *n* **1** person who judges others by social rank. **2** person who feels smugly superior in his or her tastes or interests. **snobbery** *n* **snobbish** *adj*

snog *v* **snogging, snogged** *Informal* kiss and cuddle.

snood *n* pouch, often of net, loosely holding a woman's hair at the back.

snook *n* **cock a snook at** show contempt for.

snooker *n* **1** game played on a billiard table. ♦ *v* **2** leave (a snooker opponent) in a position such that another ball blocks the target ball. **3** *Informal* put (someone) in a position where he or she can do nothing.

snoop *Informal* ♦ *v* **1** pry. ♦ *n* **2** snooping. **snooper** *n*

snooty *adj* **snootier, snootiest** *Informal* haughty.

snooze *Informal* ♦ *v* **1** take a brief light sleep. ♦ *n* **2** brief light sleep.

snore *v* **1** make snorting sounds while sleeping. ♦ *n* **2** sound of snoring.

snorkel *n* **1** tube allowing a swimmer to breathe while face down on the surface of the water. **2** device supplying air to a submarine when under water. ♦ *v* **-kelling, -kelled** **3** swim using a snorkel.

snort *v* **1** exhale noisily through the nostrils. **2** express contempt or anger by snorting. **3** say with a snort. ♦ *n* **4** act or sound of snorting. **5** *Informal* small drink of alcohol.

snot *n Slang* mucus from the nose. **snotty** *adj Slang* **1** covered with mucus from the nose. **2** haughty.

snout *n* animal's projecting nose and jaws.

snow *n* **1** frozen vapour falling from the sky in flakes. **2** *Slang* cocaine. ♦ *v* **3** fall as or like snow. **be snowed under** be overwhelmed, esp. with paperwork. **snowy** *adj* **snowball** *n* **1** snow pressed into a ball for throwing. ♦ *v* **2** increase rapidly. **snow-blind** *adj* temporarily blinded by the brightness of the sun on snow. **snowbound** *adj* shut in by snow. **snowdrift** *n* bank of deep snow. **snowdrop** *n* small white bell-shaped spring flower. **snowflake** *n* single crystal of snow. **snow line** (on a mountain) height above which there is permanent snow. **snowman** *n* figure shaped out of snow. **snowplough** *n* vehicle for clearing away snow. **snowshoes** *pl n* racket-shaped shoes for travelling on snow.

SNP Scottish National Party.

snub *v* **snubbing, snubbed 1** insult deliberately. ♦ *n* **2** deliberate insult. ♦ *adj* **3** (of a nose) short and blunt. **snub-nosed** *adj*

snuff[1] *n* powdered tobacco for sniffing up the nostrils.

snuff[2] *v* extinguish (a candle). **snuff it** *Informal* die. **snuff out** *v Informal* put an end to.

snuff[3] *v* take in air through the nose.

snuffle *v* **1** breathe noisily or with difficulty. **2** speak through the nose.

snug *adj* **snugger, snuggest 1** warm and comfortable. **2** comfortably close-fitting. ♦ *n* **3** small room in a pub. **snugly** *adv*

snuggle *v* nestle into a person or thing for warmth or from affection.

so[1] *adv* **1** to such an extent. **2** in such a manner. **3** very. **4** also. **5** thereupon. ♦ *conj* **6** in order that. **7** with the result that. **8** therefore. ♦ *interj* **9** exclamation of surprise, triumph, or realization. **or so** approximately. **so-and-so** *n* **1** *Informal* person whose name is not specified. **2** unpleasant person or thing. **so-called** *adj* called (in the speaker's opinion, wrongly) by that name. **so long** goodbye. **so that** in order that.

so[2] *n Music* same as SOH.

soak *v* **1** make wet. **2** put or lie in liquid so as to become thoroughly wet. **3** (of liquid) penetrate. ♦ *n* **4** soaking. **5** *Slang* drunkard. **soaking** *n, adj* **soak up** *v* absorb.

soap *n* **1** compound of alkali and fat, used with water as a cleaning agent. **2** *Informal* soap opera. ♦ *v* **3** apply soap to. **soapy** *adj* **soapbox** *n* crate used as a platform for speech-making. **soap opera** radio or television serial dealing with domestic themes.

soapstone *n* soft mineral used for making table tops and ornaments.

soar *v* **1** rise or fly upwards. **2** increase suddenly.

sob *v* **sobbing, sobbed 1** weep with convulsive gasps. **2** utter with sobs. ♦ *n* **3** act or sound of sobbing. **sob story** tale of personal distress told to arouse sympathy.

sober *adj* **1** not drunk. **2** temperate. **3** serious. **4** (of colours) plain and dull. ♦ *v* **5** make or become sober. **soberly** *adv* **sobriety** *n* state of being sober.

sobriquet [**so**-brik-ay] *n* nickname.

Soc. Society.

soccer *n* football played by two teams of eleven kicking a spherical ball.

sociable *adj* **1** friendly or companionable. **2** (of an occasion) providing companionship. **sociability** *n* **sociably** *adv*

social *adj* **1** living in a community. **2** of society or its organization. **3** of the behaviour of people living in groups. **4** sociable. ♦ *n* **5** informal gathering. **socially** *adv* **socialize** *v* **1** meet others socially. **2** prepare for life in society. **socialite** *n* member of fashionable society. **social democrat** socialist who believes in the gradual transformation of capitalism into democratic socialism. **social science** scientific study of society and its relationships. **social security** state provision for the unemployed, aged, or sick. **social services** welfare services provided by the local authorities. **social work** work which involves helping people with serious financial or family problems.

socialism *n* political system which advocates public ownership of industries, resources, and transport. **socialist** *n, adj*

society *n, pl* **-ties 1** human beings considered as a group. **2** organized community. **3** structure and institutions of such a community. **4** organized group with common aims and interests. **5** upper-class or fashionable people collectively. **6** companionship.

sociology *n* study of human societies. **sociological** *adj* **sociologist** *n*

sock[1] *n* cloth covering for the foot.

sock[2] *Slang* ♦ *v* **1** hit hard. ♦ *n* **2** hard blow.

socket *n* hole or recess into which something fits.

sod[1] *n* (piece of) turf.

sod[2] *n Slang* obnoxious person.

soda *n* **1** compound of sodium. **2** soda water. **soda water** fizzy drink made from water charged with carbon dioxide.

sodden *adj* **1** soaked. **2** dulled, esp. by drink.

sodium *n Chem* silvery-white metallic element. **sodium bicarbonate** white soluble compound used in baking powder. **sodium hydroxide** white alkaline substance used in making paper and soap.

sodomy *n* anal intercourse. **sodomite** *n* person who practises sodomy.

sofa *n* couch.

soft *adj* **1** easy to shape or cut. **2** not hard, rough, or harsh. **3** (of a breeze or climate) mild. **4** (too) lenient. **5** easily influenced or imposed upon. **6** feeble or silly. **7** not robust. **8** (of drugs) not liable to cause addiction. **9** *Informal* easy. **10** (of water) containing few mineral salts. ♦ *adv* **11** softly. **softly** *adv* **soften** *v* **1** make or become soft or softer. **2** make or become more gentle. **softie, softy** *n Informal* person who is easily upset. **soft drink** nonalcoholic drink. **soft furnishings** curtains, rugs, lampshades, and furniture covers. **soft option** easiest alternative. **soft-pedal** *v* deliberately avoid emphasizing something. **soft-soap** *v Informal* flatter. **soft touch** *Informal* person easily persuaded, esp. to lend money. **software** *n* computer programs. **softwood** *n* wood of a coniferous tree.

soggy *adj* **-gier, -giest 1** soaked. **2** moist and heavy. **sogginess** *n*

soh *n Music* (in tonic sol-fa) fifth degree of any major scale.

soigné, (*fem*) **soignée** [**swah**-nyay] *adj* well-groomed, elegant.

soil[1] *n* **1** top layer of earth. **2** country or territory.

soil[2] *v* **1** make or become dirty. **2** disgrace. ♦ *n* **3** soiled spot. **4** refuse.

soiree [**swah**-ray] *n* evening party or gathering.

sojourn [**soj**-urn] *n* **1** temporary stay. ♦ *v* **2** stay temporarily.

sol *n Music* same as SOH.

solace [**sol**-iss] *n, v* comfort in distress.

solar *adj* **1** of the sun. **2** using the energy of the sun. **solar plexus 1** network of nerves at the pit of the stomach. **2** this part of the stomach. **solar system** the sun and the heavenly bodies that go round it.

solarium *n, pl* **-lariums, -laria** place with beds and ultraviolet lights used for acquiring an artificial suntan.

sold *v* past of SELL.

solder *n* **1** soft alloy used to join two metal surfaces. ♦ *v* **2** join with solder. **soldering iron** tool for melting and applying solder.

soldier *n* **1** member of an army. ♦ *v* **2** serve in an army. **soldierly** *adj* **soldier on** *v* persist doggedly.

sole[1] *adj* **1** one and only. **2** not shared, exclusive. **solely** *adv* **1** only, completely. **2** alone.

sole[2] *n* **1** underside of the foot. **2** underside of a shoe. **3** lower surface of something. ♦ *v* **4** provide (a shoe) with a sole.

sole[3] *n* small edible flatfish.

solecism [**sol**-iss-izz-um] *n* **1** minor grammatical mistake. **2** breach of etiquette.

solemn *adj* **1** serious, deeply sincere. **2** formal. **3** glum. **solemnly** *adv* **solemnity** *n* **solemnize** *v* **1** celebrate or perform (a ceremony). **2** make solemn.

solenoid [**sole**-in-oid] *n* coil of wire magnetized by passing a current through it.

sol-fa *n* system of syllables used as names for the notes of a scale.

solicit *v* **-iting, -ited 1** request. **2** (of a

prostitute) offer (a person) sex for money. **solicitation** *n*

solicitor *n* lawyer who advises clients and prepares documents and cases.

solicitous *adj* **1** anxious about someone's welfare. **2** eager. **solicitude** *n*

solid *adj* **1** (of a substance) keeping its shape. **2** not liquid or gas. **3** not hollow. **4** of the same substance throughout. **5** strong or substantial. **6** sound or reliable. **7** having three dimensions. ♦ *n* **8** three-dimensional shape. **9** solid substance. **solidly** *adv* **solidify** *v* make or become solid or firm. **solidity** *n*

solidarity *n* agreement in aims or interests, total unity.

solidus *n, pl* **-di** short oblique stroke (/) used to separate items in text.

soliloquy *n, pl* **-quies** speech made by a person while alone, esp. in a play. **soliloquize** *v* utter a soliloquy.

solipsism *n* doctrine that the self is the only thing known to exist. **solipsist** *n*

solitaire *n* **1** game for one person played with pegs set in a board. **2** gem set by itself. **3** *US* card game for one person.

solitary *adj* **1** alone, single. **2** (of a place) lonely. ♦ *n, pl* **-aries 3** hermit. **solitude** *n* state of being alone. **solitary confinement** isolation of a prisoner in a special cell.

solo *n, pl* **-los 1** music for one performer. **2** any act done without assistance. ♦ *adj* **3** done alone. ♦ *adv* **4** by oneself, alone. **soloist** *n*

solstice *n* either the shortest (in winter) or longest (in summer) day of the year.

soluble *adj* **1** able to be dissolved. **2** able to be solved. **solubility** *n*

solution *n* **1** answer to a problem. **2** act of solving a problem. **3** liquid with something dissolved in it. **4** process of dissolving.

solve *v* find the answer to (a problem). **solvable** *adj*

solvent *adj* **1** having enough money to pay one's debts. ♦ *n* **2** liquid capable of dissolving other substances. **solvency** *n* **solvent abuse** deliberate inhaling of intoxicating fumes from certain solvents.

somatic *adj* of the body, as distinct from the mind.

sombre *adj* dark, gloomy.

sombrero *n, pl* **-ros** wide-brimmed Mexican hat.

some *adj* **1** unknown or unspecified. **2** unknown or unspecified quantity or number of. **3** considerable number or amount of. **4** a little. **5** *Informal* remarkable. ♦ *pron* **6** certain unknown or unspecified people or things. **7** unknown or unspecified number or quantity. ♦ *adv* **8** approximately. **somebody** *pron* **1** some person. ♦ *n* **2** important person. **somehow** *adv* in some unspecified way. **someone** *pron* somebody. **something** *pron* **1** unknown or unspecified thing or amount. **2** impressive or important thing. **sometime** *adv* **1** at some unspecified time. ♦ *adj* **2** former. **sometimes** *adv* from time to time, now and then. **somewhat** *adv* to some extent, rather. **somewhere** *adv* in, to, or at some unspecified or unknown place.

> *Somebody* and *someone* are singular and in formal usage are followed by a singular verb or pronoun. Informal usage favours the use of the plural *they* to avoid the use of the clumsy *he or she*: *If I annoy somebody, they* (rather than *he or she*) *will take it out on me.*

somersault *n* **1** leap or roll in which the trunk and legs are turned over the head. ♦ *v* **2** perform a somersault.

somnambulist *n* person who walks in his or her sleep. **somnambulism** *n*

somnolent *adj* drowsy. **somnolence** *n*

son *n* **1** male offspring. **2** man who comes from a certain place or is connected with a certain thing. **son-in-law** *n, pl* **sons-in-law** daughter's husband.

sonar *n* device for detecting underwater objects by the reflection of sound waves.

sonata *n* piece of music in several movements for one instrument with or without piano. **sonatina** *n* short sonata.

son et lumière [**sawn** eh **loo**-mee-er] *n French* night-time entertainment with lighting and sound effects, telling the story of the place where it is staged.

song *n* **1** music for the voice. **2** tuneful sound made by certain birds. **3** singing. **for a song** very cheaply. **songster, songstress** *n* singer. **songbird** *n* any bird with a musical call.

sonic *adj* of or producing sound. **sonic boom** loud bang caused by an aircraft flying faster than sound.

sonnet *n* fourteen-line poem with a fixed rhyme scheme.

sonny *n Informal* term of address to a boy.

sonorous *adj* **1** (of sound) deep or resonant. **2** (of speech) pompous. **sonorously** *adv* **sonority** *n*

soon *adv* in a short time. **as soon as** at the very moment that. **sooner** *adv* rather, e.g. *I'd sooner go alone.* **sooner or later** eventually.

soot *n* black powder formed by the incomplete burning of an organic substance. **sooty** *adj*

soothe *v* **1** make calm. **2** relieve (pain etc.).

soothsayer *n* seer or prophet.

sop *n* **1** concession to pacify someone. ♦ *pl* **2** food soaked in liquid. ♦ *v* **sopping, sopped 3** mop up or absorb (liquid). **sopping** *adj* completely soaked. **soppy** *adj Informal* oversentimental.

sophist *n* person who uses clever but invalid arguments. **sophistry, sophism** *n* clever but invalid argument.

sophisticate *v* **1** make less natural or innocent. **2** make more complex or refined. ♦ *n* **3** sophisticated person. **sophisticated** *adj* **1** having or appealing to refined or cultured tastes and habits. **2** complex and refined. **sophistication** *n*

sophomore *n US* student in second year at college.

soporific *adj* **1** causing sleep. ♦ *n* **2** drug that causes sleep.

soprano *n, pl* **-pranos 1** (singer with) the highest female or boy's voice. **2** highest pitched of a family of instruments.

sorbet *n* flavoured water ice.

sorcerer *n* magician. **sorceress** *n fem* **sorcery** *n* witchcraft or magic.

sordid *adj* **1** dirty, squalid. **2** base, vile. **3** selfish and grasping. **sordidly** *adv* **sordidness** *n*

sore *adj* **1** painful. **2** causing annoyance. **3** resentful. **4** (of need) urgent. ♦ *n* **5** painful area on the body. ♦ *adv* **6** *Obs* greatly. **sorely** *adv* greatly. **soreness** *n*

sorghum *n* kind of grass cultivated for grain.

sorority *n, pl* **-ties** *US* society for female students.

sorrel *n* bitter-tasting plant.

sorrow *n* **1** grief or sadness. **2** cause of sorrow. ♦ *v* **3** grieve. **sorrowful** *adj* **sorrowfully** *adv*

sorry *adj* **-rier, -riest 1** feeling pity or regret. **2** pitiful or wretched. **3** of poor quality.

sort *n* **1** group all sharing certain qualities or characteristics. **2** *Informal* type of character. ♦ *v* **3** arrange according to kind. **4** mend or fix. **out of sorts** slightly unwell or bad-tempered. **sort out** *v* **1** find a solution. **2** put in order. **3** *Informal* scold or punish.

> Note the singular/plural usage: *this* (or *that*) *sort of thing; these* (or *those*) *sorts of thing*. In the second, plural example you can also say *these sorts of things*.

sortie *n* **1** relatively short return trip. **2** raid into enemy territory. **3** operational flight made by military aircraft.

SOS *n* **1** international code signal of distress. **2** call for help.

so-so *adj* **1** *Informal* mediocre. ♦ *adv* **2** in an average way.

sot *n* habitual drunkard.

sotto voce [**sot**-toe **voe**-chay] *adv* in an undertone.

sou *n* **1** former French coin. **2** small amount of money.

soubriquet [**so**-brik-ay] *n* same as SOBRIQUET.

soufflé [**soo**-flay] *n* light fluffy dish made with beaten egg whites and other ingredients.

sough [rhymes with **now**] *v* (of the wind) make a sighing sound.

sought [**sawt**] *v* past of SEEK.

souk [**sook**] *n* marketplace in Muslim countries, often open-air.

soul *n* **1** spiritual and immortal part of a human being. **2** essential part or fundamental nature. **3** deep and sincere feelings. **4** person regarded as typifying some quality. **5** person. **6** (also **soul music**) type of Black music combining blues, pop, and gospel. **soulful** *adj* full of emotion. **soulless** *adj* **1** lacking human qualities, mechanical. **2** (of a person) lacking sensitivity. **soul-destroying** *adj* extremely monotonous. **soul-searching** *n* deep examination of one's actions and feelings.

sound[1] *n* **1** something heard, noise. **2** vibrations travelling in waves through air, water, etc. ♦ *v* **3** make or cause to make a sound. **4** seem to be as specified. **5** announce by a sound. **6** pronounce. **sound barrier** *Informal* sudden increase in air resistance against an object as it approaches the speed of sound. **soundproof** *adj* **1** not penetrable by sound. ♦ *v* **2** make soundproof. **soundtrack** *n* recorded sound accompaniment to a film.

sound[2] *adj* **1** in good condition. **2** firm, substantial. **3** financially reliable. **4** showing good judgment. **5** ethically correct. **6** (of sleep) deep. **7** thorough. **soundly** *adv*

sound[3] *v* **1** find the depth of (water etc.). **2** examine (the body) by tapping or with a stethoscope. **3** ascertain the views of. **soundings** *pl n* measurements of depth taken by sounding. **sounding board** person or group used to test a new idea.

sound[4] *n* channel or strait.

soup *n* liquid food made from meat, vegetables, etc. **soupy** *adj* **soup kitchen** place where food and drink is served to needy people. **souped-up** *adj* (of an engine) adjusted so as to be more powerful than normal.

soupçon [**soop**-sonn] *n* small amount.

sour *adj* **1** sharp-tasting. **2** (of milk) gone bad. **3** (of a person's temperament) sullen. ♦ *v* **4** make or become sour. **sourly** *adv* **sourness** *n* **sour cream** cream soured by bacteria for use in cooking. **sour grapes** attitude of claiming to despise something when one cannot have it oneself.

source *n* **1** origin or starting point. **2** person, book, etc. providing information. **3** spring where a river or stream begins.

souse *v* **1** plunge (something) into liquid. **2** drench. **3** pickle. **soused** *adj* *Slang* drunk.

soutane [soo-**tan**] *n* Roman Catholic priest's cassock.

south *n* **1** direction towards the South Pole, opposite north. **2** area lying in or towards the south. ♦ *adj* **3** to or in the south. **4** (of a wind) from the south. ♦ *adv* **5** in, to, or towards the south. **southerly** *adj* **southern** *adj* **southerner** *n* person from the south of a country or area. **southward** *adj, adv* **southwards** *adv* **southeast** *n, adj, adv* (in or to) direction between south and east. **southwest** *n, adj, adv* (in or to) direction between south and west. **southpaw** *n Informal* left-handed person, esp. a boxer. **South Pole** southernmost point on the earth's axis.

souvenir *n* keepsake, memento.

sou'wester *n* seaman's waterproof hat covering the head and back of the neck.

sovereign *n* **1** king or queen. **2** former British gold coin worth one pound. ♦ *adj* **3** (of a state) independent. **4** supreme in rank or authority. **5** excellent. **sovereignty** *n*

soviet *n* **1** formerly, elected council at various levels of government in the USSR. ♦ *adj* **2** (**S-**) of the former USSR.

sow[1] [rhymes with **know**] *v* **sowing, sowed, sown** *or* **sowed** **1** scatter or plant (seed) in or on (the ground). **2** implant or introduce.

sow[2] [rhymes with **cow**] *n* female adult pig.

soya *n* plant whose edible bean (**soya bean**) is used for food and as a source of oil. **soy sauce** sauce made from fermented soya beans, used in Chinese and Japanese cookery.

sozzled *adj Slang* drunk.

spa *n* resort with a mineral-water spring.

space *n* **1** unlimited expanse in which all objects exist and move. **2** interval. **3** blank portion. **4** unoccupied area. **5** the universe beyond the earth's atmosphere. ♦ *v* **6** place at intervals. **spacious** *adj* having a large capacity or area. **spacecraft, spaceship** *n* vehicle for travel beyond the earth's atmosphere. **space shuttle** manned reusable vehicle for repeated space flights. **space station** artificial satellite used as a base for people travelling and researching in space. **spacesuit** *n* sealed pressurized suit worn by an astronaut.

spade[1] *n* tool for digging. **spadework** *n* hard preparatory work.

spade[2] *n* playing card of the suit marked with black leaf-shaped symbols.

spaghetti *n* pasta in the form of long strings.

span *n* **1** space between two points. **2** complete extent. **3** distance from thumb to little finger of the expanded hand. ♦ *v* **spanning, spanned 4** stretch or extend across.

spangle *n* **1** small shiny metallic ornament. ♦ *v* **2** decorate with spangles.

Spaniard *n* person from Spain.

spaniel *n* dog with long ears and silky hair.

Spanish *n* **1** official language of Spain and most countries of S and Central America. ♦ *adj* **2** of Spain or its language or people.

spank *v* **1** slap with the open hand, on the buttocks or legs. ♦ *n* **2** such a slap. **spanking** *n*

spanking *adj* **1** *Informal* outstandingly fine or smart. **2** quick.

spanner *n* tool for gripping and turning a nut or bolt.

spar[1] *n* pole used as a ship's mast, boom, or yard.

spar[2] *v* **sparring, sparred 1** box or fight using light blows for practice. **2** argue (with someone). ♦ *n* **3** argument.

spare *adj* **1** extra. **2** in reserve. **3** (of a person) thin. **4** very plain or simple. **5** *Slang* upset or angry. ♦ *n* **6** duplicate kept in case of damage or loss. ♦ *v* **7** refrain from punishing or harming. **8** protect (someone) from (something unpleasant). **9** afford to give. **to spare** in addition to what is needed. **sparing** *adj* economical. **spare ribs** pork ribs with most of the meat trimmed off. **spare tyre** *Informal* roll of fat at the waist.

spark *n* **1** fiery particle thrown out from a fire or caused by friction. **2** flash of light produced by an electrical discharge. **3** trace or hint (of a particular quality). **4** liveliness or humour. ♦ *v* **5** give off sparks. **6** initiate. **spark plug** device in an engine that ignites the fuel by producing an electric spark.

sparkle *v* **1** glitter with many points of light. **2** be vivacious or witty. ♦ *n* **3** sparkling points of light. **4** vivacity or wit. **sparkler** *n* hand-held firework that emits sparks. **sparkling** *adj* (of wine or mineral water) slightly fizzy.

sparrow *n* small brownish bird. **sparrowhawk** *n* small hawk.

sparse *adj* thinly scattered. **sparsely** *adv* **sparseness** *n*

spartan *adj* strict and austere.

spasm *n* **1** involuntary muscular contraction. **2** sudden burst of activity or feeling. **spasmodic** *adj* occurring in spasms. **spasmodically** *adv*

spastic *n* **1** person with cerebral palsy. ♦ *adj* **2** suffering from cerebral palsy. **3** affected by spasms.

spat[1] *n* slight quarrel.

spat[2] *v* past of SPIT[1].

spate *n* **1** large number of things happening within a period of time. **2** sudden outpouring or flood.

spathe *n* large sheathlike leaf enclosing a

flower cluster.

spatial *adj* of or in space.

spats *pl n* coverings formerly worn over the ankle and instep.

spatter *v* **1** scatter or be scattered in drops over (something). ♦ *n* **2** spattering sound. **3** something spattered.

spatula *n* utensil with a broad flat blade for spreading or stirring.

spawn *n* **1** jelly-like mass of eggs of fish, frogs, or molluscs. ♦ *v* **2** (of fish, frogs, or molluscs) lay eggs. **3** generate.

spay *v* remove the ovaries from (a female animal).

speak *v* **speaking, spoke, spoken 1** say words, talk. **2** communicate or express in words. **3** give a speech or lecture. **4** know how to talk in (a specified language). **speaker** *n* **1** person who speaks, esp. at a formal occasion. **2** loudspeaker. **3** (**S-**) official chairman of a body. **speak out, speak up** *v* **1** state one's beliefs firmly. **2** speak more loudly.

spear[1] *n* **1** weapon consisting of a long shaft with a sharp point. ♦ *v* **2** pierce with or as if with a spear. **spearhead** *v* **1** lead (an attack or campaign). ♦ *n* **2** leading force in an attack or campaign.

spear[2] *n* slender shoot.

spearmint *n* type of mint.

spec *n* **on spec** *Informal* as a risk or gamble.

special *adj* **1** distinguished from others of its kind. **2** for a specific purpose. **3** exceptional. **4** particular. ♦ *n* **5** product, programme, etc. which is only available at a certain time. **specially** *adv* **specialist** *n* expert in a particular activity or subject. **speciality** *n* **1** special interest or skill. **2** product specialized in. **specialize** *v* be a specialist. **specialization** *n* **Special Branch** British police department concerned with political security.

specie *n* coins as distinct from paper money.

species *n, pl* **-cies** group of plants or animals that are related closely enough to interbreed naturally.

specific *adj* **1** particular, definite. **2** relating to a particular thing. ♦ *n* **3** drug used to treat a particular disease. ♦ *pl* **4** particular details. **specifically** *adv* **specification** *n* detailed description of something to be made or done. **specify** *v* **1** refer to or state specifically. **2** state as a condition. **specific gravity** ratio of the density of a substance to that of water.

specimen *n* **1** individual or part typifying a whole. **2** sample of blood etc. taken for analysis. **3** *Informal* person.

specious [**spee**-shuss] *adj* apparently true, but actually false.

speck *n* small spot or particle. **speckle** *n* **1** small spot. ♦ *v* **2** mark with speckles.

specs *pl n Informal* short for SPECTACLES.

spectacle *n* **1** strange, interesting, or ridiculous sight. **2** impressive public show. ♦ *pl* **3** pair of glasses for correcting faulty vision. **spectacular** *adj* **1** impressive. ♦ *n* **2** spectacular public show. **spectacularly** *adv*

spectate *v* watch. **spectator** *n* person viewing anything, onlooker.

spectre *n* **1** ghost. **2** menacing mental image. **spectral** *adj*

spectrum *n, pl* **-tra 1** range of different colours, radio waves, etc. in order of their wavelengths. **2** entire range of anything. **spectroscope** *n* instrument for producing or examining spectra.

speculate *v* **1** guess, conjecture. **2** buy property, shares, etc. in the hope of selling them at a profit. **speculation** *n* **speculative** *adj* **speculator** *n*

speculum *n, pl* **-la, -lums** medical instrument for examining body cavities.

sped *v* a past of SPEED.

speech *n* **1** act, power, or manner of speaking. **2** utterance. **3** talk given to an audience. **4** language or dialect. **speechify** *v* make speeches, esp. boringly. **speechless** *adj* unable to speak because of great emotion. **speech therapy** treatment of people with speech problems.

speed *n* **1** swiftness. **2** rate at which something moves or acts. **3** measure of the light sensitivity of photographic film. **4** *Slang* amphetamine. ♦ *v* **speed-**

ing, sped *or* **speeded 5** go quickly. **6** drive faster than the legal limit. **speedy** *adj* **1** prompt. **2** rapid. **speedily** *adv* **speedboat** *n* light fast motorboat. **speed limit** maximum legal speed for travelling on a particular road. **speedometer** *n* instrument to show the speed of a vehicle. **speed up** *v* accelerate. **speedway** *n* track for motorcycle racing. **speedwell** *n* plant with small blue flowers.

speleology *n* study and exploration of caves. **speleologist** *n*

spell[1] *v* **spelling, spelt** *or* **spelled 1** give in correct order the letters that form (a word). **2** (of letters) make up (a word). **3** indicate. **spelling** *n* **1** way a word is spelt. **2** person's ability to spell. **spell out** *v* make explicit.

spell[2] *n* **1** formula of words supposed to have magic power. **2** effect of a spell. **3** fascination. **spellbound** *adj* entranced.

spell[3] *n* period of time of weather or activity.

spelt *v* a past of SPELL[1].

spend *v* **spending, spent 1** pay out (money). **2** use or pass (time). **3** use up completely. **spendthrift** *n* person who spends money wastefully.

sperm *n* **sperms** *or* **sperm 1** male reproductive cell. **2** semen. **spermicide** *n* substance that kills sperm. **sperm whale** large toothed whale.

spermaceti [sper-ma-**set**-ee] *n* waxy solid obtained from the sperm whale.

spermatozoon [sper-ma-toe-**zoe**-on] *n, pl* **-zoa** sperm.

spew *v* **1** vomit. **2** send out in a stream.

sphagnum *n* moss found in bogs.

sphere *n* **1** perfectly round solid object. **2** field of activity. **3** social class. **spherical** *adj*

sphincter *n* ring of muscle which controls the opening and closing of a hollow organ.

Sphinx *n* **1** statue in Egypt with a lion's body and human head. **2** (**s-**) enigmatic person.

spice *n* **1** aromatic substance used as flavouring. **2** something that adds zest or interest. ♦ *v* **3** flavour with spices. **4** add zest or interest to. **spicy** *adj* **1** flavoured with spices. **2** *Informal* slightly scandalous.

spick-and-span *adj* neat and clean.

spider *n* small eight-legged creature which spins a web to catch insects for food. **spidery** *adj*

spiel *n* speech made to persuade someone to do something.

spigot *n* stopper for, or tap fitted to, a cask.

spike[1] *n* **1** sharp point. **2** sharp pointed metal object. ♦ *pl* **3** sports shoes with spikes for greater grip. ♦ *v* **4** put spikes on. **5** pierce or fasten with a spike. **6** add alcohol to (a drink). **spike someone's guns** thwart someone. **spiky** *adj*

spike[2] *n* **1** long pointed flower cluster. **2** ear of corn.

spill[1] *v* **spilling, spilt** *or* **spilled 1** pour from or as if from a container. **2** come out of a place. **3** shed (blood). ♦ *n* **4** fall. **5** amount spilt. **spill the beans** *Informal* give away a secret. **spillage** *n*

spill[2] *n* thin strip of wood or paper for lighting pipes or fires.

spin *v* **spinning, spun 1** revolve or cause to revolve rapidly. **2** draw out and twist (fibres) into thread. **3** (of a spider) form (a web) from a silky fibre from the body. **4** grow dizzy. ♦ *n* **5** revolving motion. **6** continuous spiral descent of an aircraft. **7** spinning motion given to a ball in sport. **8** *Informal* short drive for pleasure. **spin a yarn** tell an improbable story. **spinner** *n* **spin-dry** *v* dry (clothes) in a spin-dryer. **spin-dryer** *n* machine in which washed clothes are spun in a perforated drum to remove excess water. **spinning wheel** wheel-like machine for spinning, worked by hand or foot. **spin-off** *n* incidental benefit. **spin out** *v* prolong.

spina bifida *n* condition in which part of the spinal cord protrudes through a gap in the backbone, often causing paralysis.

spinach *n* dark green leafy vegetable.

spindle *n* **1** rotating rod that acts as an

axle. **2** weighted rod rotated for spinning thread by hand. **spindly** *adj* long, slender, and frail.

spindrift *n* spray blown up from the sea.

spine *n* **1** backbone. **2** edge of a book on which the title is printed. **3** sharp point on an animal or plant. **spinal** *adj* of the spine. **spinal cord** cord of nerves inside the spine, which connects the brain to the nerves in the body. **spineless** *adj* lacking courage. **spiny** *adj* covered with spines. **spine-chiller** *n* terrifying film or story.

spinet *n* small harpsichord.

spinnaker *n* large sail on a racing yacht.

spinneret *n* organ through which silk threads come out of a spider.

spinney *n* small wood.

spinster *n* unmarried woman.

spiral *n* **1** continuous curve formed by a point winding about a central axis at an ever-increasing distance from it. **2** steadily accelerating increase or decrease. ♦ *v* **-ralling, -ralled 3** move in a spiral. **4** increase or decrease with steady acceleration. ♦ *adj* **5** having the form of a spiral.

spire *n* pointed part of a steeple.

spirit[1] *n* **1** nonphysical aspect of a person concerned with profound thoughts. **2** nonphysical part of a person believed to live on after death. **3** prevailing feeling. **4** mood or attitude. **5** temperament or disposition. **6** liveliness. **7** courage. **8** essential meaning as opposed to literal interpretation. **9** ghost. ♦ *pl* **10** emotional state. ♦ *v* **-iting, -ited 11** carry away mysteriously. **spirited** *adj* **1** lively. **2** characterized by the mood specified, e.g. *low-spirited.*

spirit[2] *n* liquid obtained by distillation. **spirit level** glass tube containing a bubble in liquid, used to check whether a surface is level.

spiritual *adj* **1** relating to the spirit. **2** relating to sacred things. ♦ *n* **3** type of religious folk song originating among Black slaves in America. **spiritually** *adv* **spirituality** *n* **spiritualism** *n* belief that the spirits of the dead can communicate with the living. **spiritualist** *n*

spit[1] *v* **spitting, spat 1** eject (saliva or food) from the mouth. **2** throw out particles explosively. **3** rain slightly. **4** utter (words) in a violent manner. ♦ *n* **5** saliva. **spitting image** *Informal* person who looks very like another. **spittle** *n* fluid produced in the mouth, saliva. **spittoon** *n* bowl to spit into.

spit[2] *n* **1** sharp rod on which meat is skewered for roasting. **2** long strip of land projecting into the sea.

spite *n* **1** deliberate nastiness. ♦ *v* **2** annoy or hurt from spite. **in spite of** in defiance of. **spiteful** *adj* **spitefully** *adv*

spitfire *n* person with a fiery temper.

spiv *n Slang* smartly dressed man who makes a living by shady dealings.

splash *v* **1** scatter liquid on (something). **2** scatter (liquid) or (of liquid) be scattered in drops. **3** print (a story or photograph) prominently in a newspaper. ♦ *n* **4** splashing sound. **5** amount splashed. **6** patch (of colour or light). **7** extravagant display. **8** small amount of liquid added to a drink. **splashdown** *n* landing of a spacecraft on water. **splash out** *v Informal* spend extravagantly.

splatter *v, n* splash.

splay *v* spread out, with ends spreading in different directions.

spleen *n* **1** abdominal organ which filters bacteria from the blood. **2** bad temper. **splenetic** *adj* spiteful or irritable.

splendid *adj* **1** excellent. **2** brilliant in appearance. **splendidly** *adv* **splendour** *n*

splice *v* join by interweaving or overlapping ends. **get spliced** *Slang* get married.

splint *n* rigid support for a broken bone.

splinter *n* **1** thin sharp piece broken off, esp. from wood. ♦ *v* **2** break into fragments. **splinter group** group that has broken away from an organization.

split *v* **splitting, split 1** break into separate pieces. **2** separate. **3** separate because of disagreement. **4** share. **5** (foll. by *on*) *Slang* inform. ♦ *n* **6** splitting. **7** crack or division caused by splitting. **8** dessert of sliced fruit, ice cream, and cream. ♦ *pl* **9** act of sitting with the legs outstretched in opposite directions. **splitting** *adj* (of a headache) very painful. **split-level** *adj* (of a house or room) having the ground floor on different levels. **split personality 1** tendency to change mood rapidly. **2** *Informal* schizophrenia. **split second** very short period of time.

splotch, splodge *n, v* splash, daub.

splurge *v* **1** spend money extravagantly. ♦ *n* **2** bout of extravagance.

splutter *v* **1** utter with spitting or choking sounds. **2** make hissing spitting sounds. ♦ *n* **3** spluttering.

spoil *v* **spoiling, spoilt** *or* **spoiled 1** damage. **2** harm the character of (a child) by giving it all it wants. **3** rot, go bad. **spoils** *pl n* **1** booty. **2** benefits of public office. **spoiling for** eager for. **spoiler** *n* device on an aircraft or car to increase drag. **spoilsport** *n* person who spoils the enjoyment of others.

spoke[1] *v* past tense of SPEAK.

spoke[2] *n* bar joining the hub of a wheel to the rim.

spoken *v* past participle of SPEAK.

spokesman, spokeswoman, spokesperson *n* person chosen to speak on behalf of a group.

spoliation *n* plundering.

sponge *n* **1** sea animal with a porous absorbent skeleton. **2** skeleton of a sponge, or a substance like it, used for cleaning. **3** type of light cake. **4** rub with a wet sponge. ♦ *v* **5** wipe with a sponge. **6** live at the expense of others. **sponger** *n Slang* person who sponges on others. **spongy** *adj* **sponge bag** small bag for holding toiletries.

sponsor *n* **1** person who promotes something. **2** person who agrees to give money to a charity on completion of a specified activity by another. **3** godparent. **4** person who pays the costs of a programme in return for advertising. ♦ *v* **5** act as a sponsor for. **sponsorship** *n*

spontaneous *adj* **1** not planned or arranged. **2** occurring through natural processes without outside influence. **spontaneously** *adv* **spontaneity** *n*

spoof *n* **1** mildly satirical parody. **2** trick.

spook *n Informal* ghost. **spooky** *adj*

spool *n* cylinder round which something can be wound.

spoon *n* **1** shallow bowl attached to a handle for eating, stirring, or serving food. ♦ *v* **2** lift with a spoon. **spoonful** *n* **spoon-feed** *v* **1** feed with a spoon. **2** give (someone) too much help.

spoonerism *n* accidental changing over of the initial sounds of a pair of words, such as *half-warmed fish* for *half-formed wish*.

spoor *n* trail of an animal.

sporadic *adj* intermittent, scattered. **sporadically** *adv*

spore *n* minute reproductive body of some plants.

sporran *n* pouch worn in front of a kilt.

sport *n* **1** activity for pleasure, competition, or exercise. **2** such activities collectively. **3** enjoyment. **4** playful joking. **5** person who reacts cheerfully. ♦ *v* **6** wear proudly. **sporting** *adj* **1** of sport. **2** behaving in a fair and decent way. **sporting chance** reasonable chance of success. **sporty** *adj* **sportive** *adj* playful. **sports car** fast low-built car, usu. open-topped. **sports jacket** man's casual jacket. **sportsman, sportswoman** *n* **1** person who plays sports. **2** person who plays fair and is good-humoured when losing. **sportsmanlike** *adj* **sportsmanship** *n*

spot *n* **1** small mark on a surface. **2** pimple. **3** location. **4** *Informal* small quantity. **5** *Informal* awkward situation. **6** part of a show assigned to a performer. ♦ *v* **spotting, spotted 7** notice. **8** mark with spots. **9** watch for and take note of. **10** rain lightly. **on the spot 1** at the place in question. **2** immediately. **3** in an awkward predicament. **spotless** *adj* absolutely clean. **spotlessly** *adv* **spotted** *adj* **spotty** *adj* **1** with spots. **2** inconsistent. **spot check** random examination. **spotlight** *n* **1** powerful light illuminating a small area. **2** centre of attention. ♦ *v* 3 draw attention to. **spot-on** *adj Informal* absolutely accurate.

spouse *n* husband or wife.

spout *v* 1 pour out in a stream or jet. 2 *Slang* utter (a stream of words) lengthily. ♦ *n* 3 projecting tube or lip for pouring liquids. 4 stream or jet of liquid. **up the spout** *Slang* ruined or lost.

sprain *v* 1 injure (a joint) by a sudden twist. ♦ *n* 2 such an injury.

sprang *v* a past tense of SPRING.

sprat *n* small sea fish.

sprawl *v* 1 lie or sit with the limbs spread out. 2 spread out in a straggling manner. ♦ *n* 3 part of a city that has spread untidily over a large area.

spray[1] *n* 1 (device for producing) fine drops of liquid. 2 number of small objects flying through the air. ♦ *v* 3 scatter in fine drops. 4 cover with a spray. **spray gun** device for spraying paint etc.

spray[2] *n* 1 branch with buds, leaves, flowers, or berries. 2 ornament like this.

spread *v* **spreading, spread** 1 open out or be displayed to the fullest extent. 2 extend over a larger expanse. 3 apply as a coating. 4 send or be sent in all directions. ♦ *n* 5 spreading. 6 extent. 7 *Informal* large meal. 8 soft food which can be spread. 9 two facing pages in a magazine or book. **spread-eagled** *adj* with arms and legs outstretched.

spreadsheet *n* computer program used for entering and arranging figures, used mainly for financial planning.

spree *n* session of overindulgence, usu. in drinking or spending money.

sprig *n* 1 twig or shoot. 2 design like this. **sprigged** *adj*

sprightly *adj* **-lier, -liest** lively and brisk. **sprightliness** *n*

spring *v* **springing, sprang** *or* **sprung, sprung** 1 move suddenly upwards or forwards in a single motion, jump. 2 cause to happen unexpectedly. 3 develop unexpectedly. 4 originate (from). 5 provide with springs. 6 *Informal* arrange the escape of (someone) from prison. ♦ *n* 7 season between winter and summer. 8 jump. 9 coil which can be compressed, stretched, or bent and returns to its original shape when released. 10 natural pool forming the source of a stream. 11 elasticity. **springy** *adj* elastic. **springboard** *n* 1 flexible board used to gain height or momentum in diving or gymnastics. 2 thing acting as an impetus. **spring-clean** *v* clean (a house) thoroughly. **spring onion** onion with a tiny bulb and long green leaves. **spring tide** high tide at new or full moon. **springtime** *n* season of spring.

springbok *n* S African antelope.

springer *n* small spaniel.

sprinkle *v* 1 scatter (liquid or powder) in tiny drops or particles over (something). 2 distribute over. **sprinkler** *n* **sprinkling** *n* small quantity or number.

sprint *n* 1 short race run at top speed. 2 fast run. ♦ *v* 3 run a short distance at top speed. **sprinter** *n*

sprit *n* small spar set diagonally across a sail to extend it. **spritsail** *n* sail extended by a sprit.

sprite *n* elf.

sprocket *n* wheel with teeth on the rim, that drives or is driven by a chain.

sprout *v* 1 put forth shoots. 2 begin to grow or develop. ♦ *n* 3 shoot. 4 short for BRUSSELS SPROUT.

spruce[1] *n* kind of fir.

spruce[2] *adj* neat and smart. **spruce up** *v* make neat and smart.

sprung *v* a past of SPRING.

spry *adj* **spryer, spryest** *or* **sprier, spriest** active or nimble.

spud *n Informal* potato.

spume *n, v* froth.

spun *v* past of SPIN.

spunk *n Informal* courage, spirit. **spunky** *adj*

spur *n* 1 stimulus or incentive. 2 spiked wheel on the heel of a rider's boot used to urge on a horse. 3 projection. ♦ *v* **spurring, spurred** 4 urge on, incite (someone). **on the spur of the moment** on impulse.

spurge *n* plant with milky sap.

spurious *adj* not genuine.

spurn *v* reject with scorn.
spurt *v* **1** gush or cause to gush out in a jet. ♦ *n* **2** short sudden burst of activity or speed. **3** sudden gush.
sputnik *n* early Soviet artificial satellite.
sputter *v, n* splutter.
sputum *n, pl* **-ta** spittle, usu. mixed with mucus.
spy *n, pl* **spies 1** person employed to obtain secret information. **2** person who secretly watches others. ♦ *v* **spying, spied 3** act as a spy. **4** catch sight of. **spyglass** *n* small telescope.
Sq. Square.
squab *n* young bird yet to leave the nest.
squabble *v, n* (engage in) a petty or noisy quarrel.
squad *n* small group of people working or training together.
squadron *n* division of an air force, fleet, or cavalry regiment.
squalid *adj* **1** dirty and unpleasant. **2** morally sordid. **squalor** *n* disgusting dirt and filth.
squall[1] *n* sudden strong wind.
squall[2] *v* **1** cry noisily, yell. ♦ *n* **2** harsh cry.
squander *v* waste (money or resources).
square *n* **1** geometric figure with four equal sides and four right angles. **2** open area in a town in this shape. **3** product of a number multiplied by itself. ♦ *adj* **4** square in shape. **5** denoting a measure of area. **6** straight or level. **7** fair and honest. **8** with all accounts or debts settled. **9** *Informal* old-fashioned. ♦ *v* **10** multiply (a number) by itself. **11** make square. **12** settle (a debt). **13** level the score. **14** be or cause to be consistent. ♦ *adv* **15** squarely, directly. **squarely** *adv* **1** in a direct way. **2** in an honest and frank manner. **square dance** formation dance in which the couples form squares. **square meal** substantial meal. **square root** number of which a given number is the square. **square up to** *v* prepare to confront (a person or problem).
squash[1] *v* **1** crush flat. **2** suppress. **3** push into a confined space. **4** humiliate with a crushing retort. ♦ *n* **5** sweet fruit drink diluted with water. **6** crowd of people in a confined space. **7** (also **squash rackets**) game played in an enclosed court with a rubber ball and long-handled rackets. **squashy** *adj*
squash[2] *n* marrow-like vegetable.
squat *v* **squatting, squatted 1** crouch with the knees bent and the weight on the feet. **2** occupy unused premises to which one has no legal right. ♦ *n* **3** place where squatters live. ♦ *adj* **4** short and broad. **squatter** *n* illegal occupier of unused premises.
squaw *n Offens* Native American woman.
squawk *n* **1** loud harsh cry. **2** loud complaint. ♦ *v* **3** utter a squawk.
squeak *n* **1** short shrill cry or sound. ♦ *v* **2** make or utter a squeak. **narrow squeak** *Informal* narrow escape. **squeaky** *adj*
squeal *n* **1** long shrill cry or sound. ♦ *v* **2** make or utter a squeal. **3** *Slang* inform on someone to the police.
squeamish *adj* easily sickened or shocked.
squeegee *n* tool with a rubber blade for clearing water from a surface.
squeeze *v* **1** grip or press firmly. **2** crush or press to extract liquid. **3** push into a confined space. **4** hug. **5** obtain (something) by force or great effort. ♦ *n* **6** squeezing. **7** amount extracted by squeezing. **8** hug. **9** crush of people in a confined space. **10** restriction on borrowing.
squelch *v* **1** make a wet sucking sound, as by walking through mud. ♦ *n* **2** squelching sound.
squib *n* small firework that hisses before exploding.
squid *n* sea creature with a long soft body and ten tentacles.
squiffy *adj Informal* slightly drunk.
squiggle *n* wavy line. **squiggly** *adj*
squint *v* **1** have eyes which face in different directions. **2** glance sideways. ♦ *n* **3** squinting condition of the eye. **4** *Informal* glance. ♦ *adj* **5** crooked.
squire *n* **1** country gentleman, usu. the

main landowner in a community. **2** *Hist* knight's apprentice. ♦ *v* **3** (of a man) escort (a woman).

squirm *v* **1** wriggle, writhe. **2** feel embarrassed. ♦ *n* **3** wriggling movement.

squirrel *n* small bushy-tailed tree-living animal.

squirt *v* **1** force (a liquid) or (of a liquid) be forced out of a narrow opening. **2** squirt liquid at. ♦ *n* **3** jet of liquid. **4** *Informal* small or insignificant person.

squish *v, n* (make) a soft squelching sound. **squishy** *adj*

Sr **1** Senior. **2** Señor. **3** *Chem* strontium.

SRN State Registered Nurse.

SS **1** Schutzstaffel: Nazi paramilitary security force. **2** steamship.

SSE south-southeast.

SSW south-southwest.

St **1** Saint. **2** Street.

st. stone (weight).

stab *v* **stabbing, stabbed** **1** pierce with something pointed. **2** jab (at). ♦ *n* **3** stabbing. **4** sudden unpleasant sensation. **5** *Informal* attempt.

stabilize *v* make or become stable. **stabilization** *n* **stabilizer** *n* device for stabilizing a child's bicycle, an aircraft, or a ship.

stable[1] *n* **1** building in which horses are kept. **2** establishment that breeds and trains racehorses. **3** establishment that manages or trains several entertainers or athletes. ♦ *v* **4** put or keep (a horse) in a stable.

stable[2] *adj* **1** firmly fixed or established. **2** firm in character. **3** *Science* not subject to decay or decomposition. **stability** *n*

staccato [stak-**ah**-toe] *adj, adv* **1** *Music* with the notes sharply separated. ♦ *adj* **2** consisting of short abrupt sounds.

stack *n* **1** ordered pile. **2** large amount. **3** chimney. ♦ *v* **4** pile in a stack. **5** control (aircraft waiting to land) so that they fly at different altitudes.

stadium *n, pl* **-diums, -dia** sports arena with tiered seats for spectators.

staff[1] *n* **1** people employed in an organization. **2** stick used as a weapon, support, etc. ♦ *v* **3** supply with personnel. **staff nurse** qualified nurse of the rank below a sister.

staff[2] *n, pl* **staves** set of five horizontal lines on which music is written.

stag *n* adult male deer. **stag beetle** beetle with large branched jaws. **stag night, party** party for men only.

stage *n* **1** step or period of development. **2** platform in a theatre where actors perform. **3** scene of action. **4** portion of a journey. ♦ *v* **5** put (a play) on stage. **6** organize and carry out (an event). **the stage** theatre as a profession. **stagey** *adj* overtheatrical. **stagecoach** *n* large horse-drawn vehicle formerly used to carry passengers and mail. **stage door** theatre door leading backstage. **stage fright** nervousness felt by a person about to face an audience. **stagehand** *n* person who moves props and scenery on a stage. **stage-manage** *v* arrange from behind the scenes. **stage-manager** *n* **stage whisper** loud whisper intended to be heard by an audience.

stagger *v* **1** walk unsteadily. **2** astound. **3** set apart to avoid congestion. ♦ *n* **4** staggering. **staggering** *adj*

stagnant *adj* **1** (of water or air) stale from not moving. **2** not growing or developing. **stagnate** *v* be stagnant. **stagnation** *n*

staid *adj* sedate, serious, and rather dull.

stain *v* **1** discolour, mark. **2** colour with a penetrating pigment. ♦ *n* **3** discoloration or mark. **4** moral blemish or slur. **5** penetrating liquid used to colour things. **stainless** *adj* **stainless steel** steel alloy that does not rust.

stairs *pl n* flight of steps between floors, usu. indoors. **stair** *n* one step in a flight of stairs. **staircase, stairway** *n* flight of stairs with a handrail or banisters.

stake[1] *n* **1** pointed stick or post driven into the ground as a support or marker. ♦ *v* **2** support or mark out with stakes. **stake a claim to** claim a right to. **stake out** *v Slang* (of police) keep (a place) under surveillance.

stake[2] *n* **1** money wagered. **2** interest, usu. financial, held in something. ♦ *pl* **3** prize in a race or contest. ♦ *v* **4** wager, risk. **5** support financially. **at stake** being risked.

stalactite *n* lime deposit hanging from the roof of a cave.

stalagmite *n* lime deposit sticking up from the floor of a cave.

stale *adj* **1** not fresh. **2** lacking energy or ideas through overwork or monotony. **3** uninteresting from overuse. **staleness** *n*

stalemate *n* **1** *Chess* position in which any of a player's moves would put his king in check, resulting in a draw. **2** deadlock, impasse.

stalk[1] *n* plant's stem.

stalk[2] *v* **1** follow or approach stealthily. **2** pursue persistently and, sometimes, attack (a person with whom one is obsessed). **3** walk in a stiff or haughty manner. **stalking-horse** *n* pretext.

stall[1] *n* **1** small stand for the display and sale of goods. **2** compartment in a stable. **3** small room or compartment. ♦ *pl* **4** ground-floor seats in a theatre or cinema. **5** row of seats in a church for the choir or clergy. ♦ *v* **6** stop (a motor vehicle or engine) or (of a motor vehicle or engine) stop accidentally.

stall[2] *v* employ delaying tactics.

stallion *n* uncastrated male horse.

stalwart [**stawl**-wart] *adj* **1** strong and sturdy. **2** dependable. ♦ *n* **3** stalwart person.

stamen *n* pollen-producing part of a flower.

stamina *n* enduring energy and strength.

stammer *v* **1** speak or say with involuntary pauses or repetition of syllables. ♦ *n* **2** tendency to stammer.

stamp *n* **1** (also **postage stamp**) piece of gummed paper stuck to an envelope or parcel to show that the postage has been paid. **2** act of stamping. **3** instrument for stamping a pattern or mark. **4** pattern or mark stamped. **5** characteristic feature. ♦ *v* **6** bring (one's foot) down forcefully. **7** walk with heavy footsteps. **8** characterize. **9** impress (a pattern or mark) on. **10** stick a postage stamp on. **stamping ground** favourite meeting place. **stamp out** *v* suppress by force.

stampede *n* **1** sudden rush of frightened animals or of a crowd. ♦ *v* **2** (cause to) take part in a stampede.

stance *n* **1** attitude. **2** manner of standing.

stanch [**stahnch**] *v* same as STAUNCH[2].

stanchion *n* upright bar used as a support.

stand *v* **standing, stood 1** be in, rise to, or place in an upright position. **2** be situated. **3** be in a specified state or position. **4** remain unchanged or valid. **5** tolerate. **6** survive. **7** offer oneself as a candidate. **8** *Informal* treat to. ♦ *n* **9** stall for the sale of goods. **10** structure for spectators at a sports ground. **11** firmly held opinion. **12** *US & Aust* witness box. **13** rack or piece of furniture on which things may be placed. **14** act of standing. **15** halt to counter-attack. **standing** *adj* **1** permanent, lasting. **2** used to stand in. ♦ *n* **3** reputation or status. **4** duration. **stand by** *v* **1** be available and ready. **2** watch without taking any action. **3** be faithful to. **stand-by** *n* person or thing ready to be used in an emergency. **stand down** *v* resign or withdraw. **stand for** *v* **1** represent or mean. **2** *Informal* tolerate. **stand in** *v* act as a substitute. **stand-in** *n* substitute. **standing order** instruction to a bank to pay a stated sum at regular intervals. **standoffish** *adj* reserved or haughty. **stand out** *v* be distinctive. **stand up** *v* **1** rise to one's feet. **2** *Informal* fail to keep an appointment. **3** withstand examination. **stand up for** *v* support or defend. **stand up to** *v* **1** confront and resist. **2** withstand and endure.

standard *n* **1** level of quality. **2** example against which others are judged or measured. **3** moral principle. **4** distinctive flag. **5** upright pole. ♦ *adj* **6** usual, regular, or average. **7** of recognized authority. **8** accepted as correct. **stand-**

ardize *v* cause to conform to a standard. **standardization** *n* **standard-bearer** *n* leader of a movement. **standard lamp** lamp attached to an upright pole on a base.

standpipe *n* tap attached to a water main to provide a public water supply.

standpoint *n* point of view.

standstill *n* complete halt.

stank *v* a past tense of STINK.

stanza *n* verse of a poem.

staple[1] *n* **1** U-shaped piece of metal used to fasten papers or secure things. ♦ *v* **2** fasten with staples. **stapler** *n* small device for fastening papers together.

staple[2] *adj* **1** of prime importance, principal. ♦ *n* **2** main constituent of anything.

star *n* **1** hot gaseous mass in space, visible in the night sky as a point of light. **2** star-shaped mark used to indicate excellence. **3** asterisk. **4** celebrity in the entertainment or sports world. ♦ *pl* **5** astrological forecast, horoscope. ♦ *v* **starring, starred 6** feature or be featured as a star. **7** mark with a star or stars. ♦ *adj* **8** leading, famous. **stardom** *n* status of a star in the entertainment or sports world. **starlet** *n* young actress presented as a future star. **starry** *adj* full of or like stars. **starry-eyed** *adj* full of naive optimism. **starfish** *n* star-shaped sea creature. **Stars and Stripes** national flag of America. **star sign** sign of the zodiac under which a person was born.

starboard *n* **1** right-hand side of a ship, when facing forward. ♦ *adj* **2** of or on this side.

starch *n* **1** carbohydrate forming the main food element in bread, potatoes, etc., and used mixed with water for stiffening fabric. ♦ *v* **2** stiffen (fabric) with starch. **starchy** *adj* **1** containing starch. **2** stiff and formal.

stare *v* **1** look or gaze fixedly (at). ♦ *n* **2** fixed gaze.

stark *adj* **1** harsh, unpleasant, and plain. **2** desolate, bare. **3** absolute. ♦ *adv* **4** completely. **stark-naked** *adj* completely naked.

starling *n* songbird with glossy black speckled feathers.

start *v* **1** take the first step, begin. **2** set or be set in motion. **3** make a sudden involuntary movement from fright. **4** establish or set up. ♦ *n* **5** first part of something. **6** place or time of starting. **7** advantage or lead in a competitive activity. **8** sudden movement made from fright. **starter** *n* **1** first course of a meal. **2** device for starting a car's engine. **3** person who signals the start of a race.

startle *v* slightly surprise or frighten.

starve *v* **1** die or suffer or cause to die or suffer from hunger. **2** deprive of something needed. **starvation** *n*

stash *Informal* ♦ *v* **1** store in a secret place. ♦ *n* **2** secret store.

state *n* **1** condition of a person or thing. **2** sovereign political power or its territory. **3** (**S-**) the government. **4** *Informal* excited or agitated condition. **5** pomp. ♦ *adj* **6** of or concerning the State. **7** involving ceremony. ♦ *v* **8** express in words. **the States** United States of America. **stately** *adj* dignified or grand. **statement** *n* **1** something stated. **2** printed financial account. **stateroom** *n* **1** private cabin on a ship. **2** large room in a palace, used for ceremonial occasions. **statesman, stateswoman** *n* experienced and respected political leader. **statesmanship** *n*

static *adj* **1** stationary or inactive. **2** (of a force) acting but producing no movement. ♦ *n* **3** crackling sound or speckled picture caused by interference in radio or television reception. **4** (also **static electricity**) electric sparks produced by friction. **statics** *n* branch of mechanics dealing with the forces producing a state of equilibrium.

station *n* **1** place where trains stop for passengers. **2** headquarters or local offices of the police or a fire brigade. **3** building with special equipment for a particular purpose, e.g. *power station*. **4** television or radio channel. **5** place or position assigned to a person. **6** position in society. **7** large Australian sheep or cattle ranch. ♦ *v* **8** assign (someone) to a particular place. **stationmaster** *n* official in charge of a railway station. **station wagon** *US & Aust* estate car.

stationary *adj* not moving.

stationery *n* writing materials such as paper and pens. **stationer** *n* dealer in stationery.

statistic *n* numerical fact collected and classified systematically. **statistics** *n* science of classifying and interpreting numerical information. **statistical** *adj* **statistically** *adv* **statistician** *n* person who compiles and studies statistics.

statue *n* large sculpture of a human or animal figure. **statuary** *n* statues collectively. **statuesque** [stat-yoo-**esk**] *adj* (of a woman) tall and well-proportioned. **statuette** *n* small statue.

stature *n* **1** person's height. **2** reputation of a person or their achievements.

status *n* **1** social position. **2** prestige. **3** person's legal standing. **status quo** existing state of affairs. **status symbol** possession regarded as a sign of position or wealth.

statute *n* written law. **statutory** *adj* required or authorized by law.

staunch[1] *adj* loyal, firm.

staunch[2], **stanch** *v* stop (a flow of blood).

stave *n* **1** one of the strips of wood forming a barrel. **2** *Music* same as STAFF[2] **3** thick stick. **4** stanza. **stave in** *v* **staving, stove** burst a hole in. **stave off** *v* **staving, staved** ward off.

staves *n* plural of STAFF[2] *or* STAVE.

stay[1] *v* **1** remain in a place or condition. **2** reside temporarily. **3** endure. ♦ *n* **4** period of staying in a place. **5** postponement. **staying power** stamina.

stay[2] *n* **1** prop or buttress. ♦ *pl* **2** corset.

stay[3] *n* rope or wire supporting a ship's mast.

STD 1 sexually transmitted disease. **2** subscriber trunk dialling.

stead *n* **in someone's stead** in someone's place. **stand someone in good stead** be useful to someone.

steadfast *adj* firm, determined. **steadfastly** *adv*

steady *adj* **steadier, steadiest 1** not shaky or wavering. **2** regular or continuous. **3** sensible and dependable. ♦ *v* **steadying, steadied 4** make steady. ♦ *adv* **5** in a steady manner. **steadily** *adv* **steadiness** *n*

steak *n* **1** thick slice of meat, esp. beef. **2** slice of fish.

steal *v* **stealing, stole, stolen 1** take unlawfully or without permission. **2** move stealthily.

stealth *n* **1** moving carefully and quietly. **2** secret or underhand behaviour. **stealthy** *adj* **stealthily** *adv*

steam *n* **1** vapour into which water changes when boiled. **2** power, energy, or speed. ♦ *v* **3** give off steam. **4** (of a vehicle) move by steam power. **5** cook or treat with steam. **steamer** *n* **1** steam-propelled ship. **2** container used to cook food in steam. **steamy** *adj* **steamier, steamiest 1** full of steam. **2** *Informal* erotic. **steam engine** engine worked by steam. **steamroller** *n* **1** steam-powered vehicle with heavy rollers, used to level road surfaces. ♦ *v* **2** use overpowering force to make (someone) do what one wants.

steatite [**stee**-a-tite] *n* same as SOAPSTONE.

steed *n Lit* horse.

steel *n* **1** hard malleable alloy of iron and carbon. **2** steel rod used for sharpening knives. **3** hardness of character or attitude. ♦ *v* **4** prepare (oneself) for something unpleasant. **steely** *adj* **steel band** band of people playing on metal drums, popular in the West Indies.

steep[1] *adj* **1** sloping sharply. **2** *Informal* (of a price) unreasonably high. **steeply** *adv* **steepness** *n*

steep[2] *v* soak or be soaked in liquid. **steeped in** filled with, e.g. *steeped in history.*

steeple *n* church tower with a spire. **steeplejack** *n* person who repairs steeples and chimneys.

steeplechase *n* **1** horse race with obstacles to jump. **2** track race with hurdles and a water jump.

steer[1] *v* **1** direct the course of (a vehicle or ship). **2** direct (one's course). **steerage** *n* cheapest accommodation on a passenger ship. **steering wheel** wheel turned by the driver of a vehicle in order to steer it.

steer[2] *n* castrated male ox.

stein [**stine**] *n* earthenware beer mug.

stellar *adj* of stars.

stem[1] *n* **1** long thin central part of a plant. **2** long slender part, as of a wineglass. **3** part of a word to which inflections are added. ♦ *v* **stemming, stemmed 4 stem from** originate from.

stem[2] *v* **stemming, stemmed** stop (the flow of something).

stench *n* foul smell.

stencil *n* **1** thin sheet with cut-out pattern through which ink or paint passes to form the pattern on the surface below. **2** pattern made thus. ♦ *v* **-cilling, -cilled 3** make (a pattern) with a stencil.

stenographer *n* shorthand typist.

stentorian *adj* (of a voice) very loud.

step *v* **stepping, stepped 1** move and set down the foot, as when walking. **2** walk a short distance. ♦ *n* **3** stepping. **4** distance covered by a step. **5** sound made by stepping. **6** foot movement in a dance. **7** one of a sequence of actions taken in order to achieve a goal. **8** degree in a series or scale. **9** flat surface for placing the foot on when going up or down. ♦ *pl* **10** stepladder. **11** flight of stairs. **step in** *v* intervene. **stepladder** *n* folding portable ladder with supporting frame. **stepping stone 1** one of a series of stones for stepping on in crossing a stream. **2** means of progress towards a goal. **step up** *v* increase (something) by stages.

step- *prefix* denoting a relationship created by the remarriage of a parent, e.g. *stepmother.*

steppes *pl n* wide grassy treeless plains.

stereo *adj* **1** short for STEREOPHONIC. ♦ *n* **2** stereophonic record player. **3** stereophonic sound.

stereophonic *adj* using two separate loudspeakers to give the effect of naturally distributed sound.

stereoscopic *adj* having a three-dimensional effect.

stereotype *n* **1** standardized idea of a type of person or thing. **2** monotonously familiar idea. ♦ *v* **3** form a stereotype of.

sterile *adj* **1** free from germs. **2** unable to produce offspring or seeds. **3** lacking inspiration or vitality. **sterility** *n* **sterilize** *v* make sterile. **sterilization** *n*

sterling *n* **1** British money system. ♦ *adj* **2** genuine and reliable. **sterling silver** alloy with 92.5 per cent silver.

stern[1] *adj* severe, strict. **sternly** *adv* **sternness** *n*

stern[2] *n* rear part of a ship.

sternum *n, pl* **-na, -nums** same as BREASTBONE.

steroid *n* organic compound containing a carbon ring system, such as many hormones.

stertorous *adj* (of breathing) laboured and noisy.

stet *interj* instruction to ignore an alteration previously made by a proofreader.

stethoscope *n* medical instrument for listening to sounds made inside the body.

Stetson *n* ® tall broad-brimmed hat, worn mainly by cowboys.

stevedore *n* person who loads and unloads ships.

stew *n* **1** food cooked slowly in a closed pot. **2** *Informal* troubled or worried state. ♦ *v* **3** cook slowly in a closed pot.

steward *n* **1** person who looks after passengers on a ship or aircraft. **2** official who helps at a public event such as a race. **3** person who administers another's property. **stewardess** *n fem*

stick[1] *n* **1** long thin piece of wood. **2** such a piece of wood shaped for a special purpose, e.g. *hockey stick.* **3** something like a stick, e.g. *stick of celery.* **4** *Slang* verbal abuse, criticism. **the sticks** *Informal* remote country area. **stick insect** tropical insect resembling a twig.

stick[2] *v* **sticking, stuck 1** push (a pointed object) into (something). **2** fasten or be fastened by or as if by pins or glue. **3** (foll. by *out*) extend beyond something else, protrude. **4** *Informal* put. **5** jam. **6** come to a standstill. **7** remain for a long time. **8** *Slang* tolerate, abide. **sticker** *n* adhesive label or sign. **sticky** *adj* **1** covered with an adhesive substance. **2** *Informal* difficult, unpleasant. **3** (of weather) warm and humid. **stick around** *v Informal* remain in a place. **stick-in-the-mud** *n* person who does not like anything new. **stick-up** *n Slang* robbery at gunpoint. **stick up for** *v Informal* support or defend.

stickleback *n* small fish with sharp spines on its back.

stickler *n* person who insists on something, e.g. *stickler for detail.*

stiff *adj* **1** not easily bent or moved. **2** moving with pain. **3** difficult. **4** severe, e.g. *stiff punishment.* **5** unrelaxed or awkward. **6** firm in consistency. **7** strong, e.g. *a stiff drink.* ♦ *n* **8** *Slang* corpse. **stiffly** *adv* **stiffness** *n* **stiffen** *v* make or become stiff. **stiff-necked** *adj* haughtily stubborn.

stifle *v* **1** suppress. **2** feel difficulty in breathing. **3** suffocate. **stifling** *adj* uncomfortably hot and stuffy.

stigma *n, pl* **-mas, -mata** **1** mark of social disgrace. **2** part of a plant that receives pollen. **stigmata** *pl n* marks resembling the wounds of the crucified Christ. **stigmatize** *v* mark as being shameful.

stile *n* set of steps allowing people to climb a fence.

stiletto *n, pl* **-tos** **1** (also **stiletto heel**) high narrow heel on a woman's shoe. **2** small slender dagger.

still[1] *adv* **1** now or in the future as before. **2** up to this or that time. **3** even or yet, e.g. *still more insults.* **4** nevertheless. **5** quietly or without movement. ♦ *adj* **6** motionless. **7** silent and calm, undisturbed. **8** (of a drink) not fizzy. ♦ *n* **9** calmness. **10** photograph from a film scene. ♦ *v* **11** make still. **12** relieve or end. **stillness** *n* **stillborn** *adj* born dead. **still life** painting of inanimate objects.

still[2] *n* apparatus for distilling alcoholic drinks.

stilted *adj* stiff and formal in manner.

Stilton *n* ® strong-flavoured cheese.

stilts *pl n* **1** pair of poles with footrests for walking raised from the ground. **2** long posts supporting a building above ground level.

stimulus *n, pl* **-li** something that rouses a person or thing to activity. **stimulant** *n* something, such as a drug, that acts as a stimulus. **stimulate** *v* act as a stimulus (on). **stimulation** *n*

sting *v* **stinging, stung** **1** (of certain animals or plants) wound by injecting with poison. **2** feel or cause to feel sharp physical or mental pain. **3** incite. **4** *Slang* cheat (someone) by overcharging. ♦ *n* **5** wound or pain caused by or as if by stinging. **6** mental pain. **7** sharp pointed organ of certain animals or plants by which poison can be injected. **stingray** *n* flatfish capable of inflicting painful wounds.

stingy *adj* **-gier, -giest** mean or miserly. **stinginess** *n*

stink *n* **1** strong unpleasant smell. **2** *Slang* unpleasant fuss. ♦ *v* **stinking, stank** *or* **stunk, stunk** **3** give off a strong unpleasant smell. **4** *Slang* be very unpleasant. **stinker** *n Informal* difficult or unpleasant person or thing. **stinking** *Informal* ♦ *adj* **1** unpleasant. ♦ *adv* **2** extremely.

stint *v* **1** (foll. by *on*) be miserly with (something). ♦ *n* **2** allotted amount of work.

stipend [**sty**-pend] *n* regular allowance or salary, esp. that paid to a clergyman. **stipendiary** *adj* receiving a stipend.

stipple *v* paint, draw, or engrave using dots.

stipulate *v* specify as a condition of an agreement. **stipulation** *n*

stir *v* **stirring, stirred** **1** mix up (a liquid) by moving a spoon etc. around in it. **2** move. **3** excite or stimulate (a person) emotionally. ♦ *n* **4** a stirring. **5** strong reaction, usu. of excitement.

stir up *v* instigate.

stirrup *n* metal loop attached to a saddle for supporting a rider's foot.

stitch *n* **1** link made by drawing thread through material with a needle. **2** loop of yarn formed round a needle or hook in knitting or crochet. **3** sharp pain in the side. ♦ *v* **4** sew. **in stitches** *Informal* laughing uncontrollably. **not a stitch** *Informal* no clothes at all.

stoat *n* small mammal of the weasel family, with brown fur that turns white in winter.

stock *n* **1** total amount of goods available for sale in a shop. **2** supply stored for future use. **3** financial shares in, or capital of, a company. **4** livestock. **5** lineage. **6** handle of a rifle. **7** liquid produced by boiling meat, fish, bones, or vegetables. **8** fragrant flowering plant. **9** standing or status. ♦ *pl* **10** *Hist* instrument of punishment consisting of a wooden frame with holes into which the hands and feet of the victim were locked. ♦ *adj* **11** kept in stock, standard. **12** hackneyed. ♦ *v* **13** keep for sale or future use. **14** supply (a farm) with livestock or (a lake etc.) with fish. **stockist** *n* dealer who stocks a particular product. **stocky** *adj* (of a person) broad and sturdy. **stockbroker** *n* person who buys and sells stocks and shares for customers. **stock car** car modified for a form of racing in which the cars often collide. **stock exchange, market** institution for the buying and selling of shares. **stock in trade** thing constantly used as part of a profession. **stockpile** *v* **1** store a large quantity of (something) for future use. ♦ *n* **2** accumulated store. **stock-still** *adj* motionless. **stocktaking** *n* counting and valuing of the goods in a shop. **stockyard** *n* yard where farm animals are sold.

stockade *n* enclosure or barrier made of stakes.

stockinette *n* machine-knitted elastic fabric.

stocking *n* close-fitting covering for the foot and leg. **stocking stitch** alternate rows of plain and purl in knitting.

stodgy *adj* **stodgier, stodgiest** **1** (of food) heavy and starchy. **2** (of a person) serious and boring. **stodge** *n* heavy starchy food.

stoic [**stow**-ik] *n* **1** person who suffers hardship without showing his or her feelings. ♦ *adj* **2** (also **stoical**) suffering hardship without showing one's feelings. **stoically** *adv* **stoicism** [**stow**-iss-izz-um] *n*

stoke *v* feed and tend (a fire or furnace). **stoker** *n*

stole[1] *v* past tense of STEAL.

stole[2] *n* long scarf or shawl.

stolen *v* past participle of STEAL.

stolid *adj* showing little emotion or interest. **stolidity** *n* **stolidly** *adv*

stomach *n* **1** organ in the body which digests food. **2** front of the body around the waist. **3** desire or inclination. ♦ *v* **4** put up with.

stomp *v Informal* tread heavily.

stone *n* **1** material of which rocks are made. **2** piece of this. **3** gem. **4** piece of rock for a specific purpose. **5** hard central part of a fruit. **6** unit of weight equal to 14 pounds or 6.350 kilograms. **7** hard deposit formed in the kidney or bladder. ♦ *v* **8** throw stones at. **9** remove stones from (a fruit). **stoned** *adj Slang* under the influence of alcohol or drugs. **stony** *adj* **1** of or like stone. **2** unfeeling or hard. **stony-broke** *adj Slang* completely penniless. **stonily** *adv* **Stone Age** prehistoric period when tools were made of stone. **stone-cold** *adj* completely cold. **stone-deaf** *adj* completely deaf. **stonewall** *v* obstruct or hinder discussion. **stoneware** *n* hard kind of pottery fired at a very high temperature. **stonework** *n* part of a building made of stone.

stood *v* past of STAND.

stooge *n* **1** actor who feeds lines to a comedian or acts as the butt of his jokes. **2** *Slang* person taken advantage of by a superior.

stool *n* **1** chair without arms or back. **2** piece of excrement.

stool pigeon *n* informer for the police.

stoop *v* **1** bend (the body) forward and downward. **2** carry oneself habitually in this way. **3** degrade oneself. ♦ *n* **4** stooping posture.

stop *v* **stopping, stopped 1** cease or cause to cease from doing (something). **2** bring to or come to a halt. **3** prevent or restrain. **4** withhold. **5** block or plug. **6** stay or rest. **7** instruct a bank not to honour (a cheque). ♦ *n* **8** stopping or being stopped. **9** place where something stops. **10** device that prevents, limits, or ends the motion of a mechanism. **11** full stop. **12** knob on an organ that is pulled out to allow a set of pipes to sound. **stoppage** *n* **stoppage time** same as INJURY TIME. **stopper** *n* plug for closing a bottle etc. **stopcock** *n* valve to control or stop the flow of fluid in a pipe. **stopgap** *n* temporary substitute. **stopover** *n* short break in a journey. **stop press** news item put into a newspaper after printing has been started. **stopwatch** *n* watch which can be stopped instantly for exact timing of a sporting event.

store *v* **1** collect and keep (things) for future use. **2** put (furniture etc.) in a warehouse for safekeeping. **3** stock (goods). **4** *Computers* enter or retain (data). ♦ *n* **5** shop. **6** supply kept for future use. **7** storage place, such as a warehouse. ♦ *pl* **8** stock of provisions. **in store** about to happen. **set great store by** value greatly. **storage** *n* **1** storing. **2** space for storing. **storage heater** electric device that can accumulate and radiate heat generated by off-peak electricity.

storey *n* floor or level of a building.

stork *n* large wading bird.

storm *n* **1** violent weather with wind, rain, or snow. **2** strongly expressed reaction. **3** heavy shower of missiles. ♦ *v* **4** attack or capture (a place) suddenly. **5** shout angrily. **6** rush violently or angrily. **stormy** *adj* **1** characterized by storms. **2** involving violent emotions. **storm trooper** member of the Nazi militia.

story *n, pl* **-ries 1** description of a series of events told or written for entertainment. **2** plot of a book or film. **3** news report. **4** *Informal* lie.

stoup [**stoop**] *n* small basin for holy water.

stout *adj* **1** fat. **2** thick and strong. **3** brave and resolute. ♦ *n* **4** strong dark beer. **stoutly** *adv*

stove[1] *n* apparatus for cooking or heating.

stove[2] *v* a past of STAVE.

stow *v* pack or store. **stowage** *n* space or charge for stowing goods. **stowaway** *n* person who hides on a ship or aircraft in order to travel free. **stow away** *v* hide as a stowaway.

straddle *v* have one leg or part on each side of (something).

strafe *v* attack (an enemy) with machine guns from the air.

straggle *v* **1** go or spread in a rambling or irregular way. **2** linger behind. **straggler** *n* **straggly** *adj*

straight *adj* **1** not curved or crooked. **2** level or upright. **3** orderly. **4** honest or frank. **5** in continuous succession. **6** (of spirits) undiluted. **7** *Theatre* serious. **8** *Slang* heterosexual. **9** *Slang* conventional. ♦ *adv* **10** in a straight line. **11** immediately. **12** in a level or upright position. **13** uninterruptedly. ♦ *n* **14** straight part, esp. of a racetrack. **go straight** *Informal* reform after being a criminal. **straighten** *v* **straightaway** *adv* immediately. **straight face** serious facial expression concealing a desire to laugh. **straightforward** *adj* **1** honest, frank. **2** (of a task) easy.

strain[1] *v* **1** subject to mental tension. **2** cause (something) to be used or tested beyond its limits. **3** make an intense effort. **4** injure by overexertion. **5** sieve. **6** draw or be drawn taut. ♦ *n* **7** tension or tiredness. **8** force exerted by straining. **9** injury from overexertion. **10** great demand on strength or resources. **11** melody or theme. **strained** *adj* **1** not natural, forced. **2** not relaxed, tense. **strainer** *n* sieve.

strain[2] *n* **1** breed or race. **2** trace or streak

strait *n* **1** narrow channel connecting two areas of sea. ♦ *pl* **2** position of acute difficulty. **straitjacket** *n* strong jacket with long sleeves used to bind the arms of a violent person. **strait-laced, straight-laced** *adj* prudish or puritanical.

straitened *adj* **in straitened circumstances** not having much money.

strand[1] *v* **1** run aground. **2** leave in difficulties. ♦ *n* **3** *Poetic* shore.

strand[2] *n* **1** single thread of string, wire, etc. **2** element of something.

strange *adj* **1** odd or unusual. **2** not familiar. **3** inexperienced (in) or unaccustomed (to). **strangely** *adv* **strangeness** *n* **stranger** *n* person who is not known or is new to a place or experience.

strangle *v* **1** kill by squeezing the throat. **2** prevent the development of. **strangler** *n* **strangulation** *n* strangling. **stranglehold** *n* **1** strangling grip in wrestling. **2** powerful control

strap *n* **1** strip of flexible material for lifting, fastening, or holding in place ♦ *v* **strapping, strapped 2** fasten with a strap or straps. **strapping** *adj* tall and sturdy.

strata *n* plural of STRATUM.

stratagem *n* clever plan, trick.

strategy *n, pl* **-gies 1** overall plan. **2** art of planning in war. **strategic** [strat-**ee**-jik] *adj* **1** advantageous. **2** (of weapons) aimed at an enemy's homeland. **strategically** *adv* **strategist** *n*

strathspey *n* Scottish dance with gliding steps.

stratosphere *n* atmospheric layer between about 15 and 50 kilometres above the earth.

stratum [**strah**-tum] *n, pl* **strata 1** layer, esp. of rock. **2** social class. **stratified** *adj* divided into strata. **stratification** *n*

straw *n* **1** dried stalks of grain. **2** single stalk of straw. **3** long thin tube used to suck up liquid into the mouth. **straw-coloured** *adj* pale yellow. **straw poll** unofficial poll taken to determine general opinion.

strawberry *n* sweet fleshy red fruit with small seeds on the outside. **strawberry mark** red birthmark.

stray *v* **1** wander. **2** digress. **3** deviate from certain moral standards. ♦ *adj* **4** having strayed. **5** scattered, random. ♦ *n* **6** stray animal.

streak *n* **1** long band of contrasting colour or substance. **2** sudden flash. **3** quality or characteristic. **4** short stretch (of good or bad luck). ♦ *v* **5** mark with streaks. **6** move rapidly. **7** *Informal* run naked in public. **streaker** *n* **streaky** *adj*

stream *n* **1** small river. **2** steady flow, as of liquid, speech, or people. **3** schoolchildren grouped together because of similar ability. ♦ *v* **4** flow steadily. **5** move in unbroken succession. **6** float in the air. **7** group (pupils) in streams. **streamer** *n* **1** strip of coloured paper that unrolls when tossed. **2** long narrow flag.

streamline *v* **1** make more efficient by simplifying. **2** give (a car, plane, etc.) a smooth even shape to offer least resistance to the flow of air or water.

street *n* public road, usu. lined with buildings. **streetcar** *n US* tram. **streetwalker** *n* prostitute. **streetwise** *adj* knowing how to survive in big cities.

strength *n* **1** quality of being strong. **2** quality or ability considered an advantage. **3** degree of intensity. **4** total number of people in a group. **on the strength of** on the basis of. **strengthen** *v*

strenuous *adj* requiring great energy or effort. **strenuously** *adv*

streptococcus [strep-toe-**kok**-uss] *n, pl* **-cocci** bacterium occurring in chains, many species of which cause disease.

streptomycin *n* antibiotic drug.

stress *n* **1** tension or strain. **2** emphasis. **3** stronger sound in saying a word or syllable. **4** *Physics* force producing strain. ♦ *v* **5** emphasize. **6** put stress on (a word or syllable). **stressed-out** *adj Informal* suffering from tension. **stressful** *adj*

stretch *v* **1** extend or be extended. **2** be able to be stretched. **3** extend the limbs or body. **4** pull tight. **5** strain (resources or abilities) to the utmost. ♦ *n* **6** stretching. **7** continuous expanse. **8** period. **9** *Informal* term of imprisonment. **stretchy** *adj* **stretcher** *n* frame covered with canvas, on which an injured person is carried.

strew *v* **strewing, strewed, strewed** *or* **strewn** scatter (things) over a surface.

striation *n* **1** scratch or groove. **2** pattern of scratches or grooves. **striated** *adj*

stricken *adj* seriously affected by disease, grief, pain, etc.

strict *adj* **1** stern or severe. **2** adhering closely to specified rules. **3** complete, absolute. **strictly** *adv* **strictness** *n*

stricture *n* severe criticism.

stride *v* **striding, strode, stridden 1** walk with long steps. ♦ *n* **2** long step. **3** regular pace. ♦ *pl* **4** progress.

strident *adj* loud and harsh. **stridently** *adv* **stridency** *n*

strife *n* conflict, quarrelling.

strike *v* **striking, struck 1** cease work as a protest. **2** hit. **3** attack suddenly. **4** ignite (a match) by friction. **5** sound (a note) on a musical instrument. **6** (of a clock) indicate (a time) by sounding a bell. **7** affect in a particular way. **8** enter the mind of. **9** render. **10** afflict. **11** discover (gold, oil, etc.). **12** agree (a bargain). **13** take up (a posture). **14** make (a coin) by stamping it. ♦ *n* **15** stoppage of work as a protest. **16** striking. **17** military attack. **18** discovery of gold, oil, etc. **strike camp** dismantle and pack up tents. **strike home** have the desired effect. **striker** *n* **1** striking worker. **2** attacking footballer. **striking** *adj* **1** impressive. **2** noteworthy. **strikebreaker** *n* person who works while others are on strike. **strike off, out** *v* cross out. **strike up** *v* **1** begin (a conversation or friendship). **2** begin to play music.

string *n* **1** thin cord used for tying. **2** set of objects threaded on a string. **3** series of things or events. **4** stretched wire or cord on a musical instrument that produces sound when vibrated. ♦ *pl* **5** restrictions or conditions. **6** section of an orchestra consisting of stringed instruments. ♦ *v* **stringing, strung 7** provide with a string or strings. **8** thread on a string. **9** extend in a line. **pull strings** use one's influence. **stringed** *adj* (of a musical instrument) having strings that are plucked or played with a bow. **stringy** *adj* **1** like string. **2** (of meat) fibrous. **string along** *v* **1** *Informal* accompany. **2** deceive over a period of time. **string up** *v Informal* kill by hanging.

stringent [**strin**-jent] *adj* strictly controlled or enforced. **stringently** *adv* **stringency** *n*

strip[1] *v* **stripping, stripped 1** take (the covering or clothes) off. **2** take a title or possession away from (someone). **3** remove (paint) from (a surface). **4** dismantle (an engine). ♦ *n* **5** act of stripping. **stripper** *n* person who performs a striptease. **striptease** *n* entertainment in which a performer undresses to music.

strip[2] *n* **1** long narrow piece. **2** clothes a football team plays in. **strip cartoon** sequence of drawings telling a story.

stripe *n* **1** long narrow band of contrasting colour or substance. **2** chevron on a uniform to indicate rank. **striped, stripy, stripey** *adj*

stripling *n* youth.

strive *v* **striving, strove, striven** make a great effort.

strobe *n* short for STROBOSCOPE.

stroboscope *n* instrument producing a very bright flashing light.

strode *v* past tense of STRIDE.

stroke *v* **1** touch or caress lightly with the hand. ♦ *n* **2** light touch or caress with the hand. **3** rupture of a blood vessel in the brain. **4** blow. **5** action or occurrence of the kind specified, e.g. *a stroke of luck.* **6** chime of a clock. **7** mark made by a pen or paintbrush. **8** hitting of the ball in some sports. **9** style or method of swimming. **10** single pull on the oars in rowing.

stroll *v* **1** walk in a leisurely manner. ♦ *n* **2** leisurely walk.

strong *adj* **1** having physical power. **2** not easily broken. **3** great in degree or intensity. **4** having moral force. **5** having a powerful taste or smell. **6** having a specified number, e.g. *twenty strong.* **going strong** *Informal* thriving. **strongly** *adv* **strong-arm** *adj* involving violence. **stronghold** *n* **1** area of predominance of a particular belief. **2** fortress. **strong point** thing at which one excels. **strongroom** *n* room designed for the safekeeping of valuables.

strontium *n Chem* silvery-white metallic element. **strontium-90** *n* radioactive isotope present in the fallout of nuclear explosions.

strop *n* leather strap for sharpening razors.

stroppy *adj* **-pier, -piest** *Slang* angry or awkward.

strove *v* past tense of STRIVE.

struck *v* past of STRIKE.

structure *n* **1** complex construction. **2** manner or basis of construction or organization. ♦ *v* **3** give a structure to. **structural** *adj* **structuralism** *n* approach to literature, social sciences, etc., which sees changes in the subject as caused and organized by a hidden set of universal rules. **structuralist** *n, adj*

strudel *n* thin sheet of filled dough rolled up and baked, usu. with an apple filling.

struggle *v* **1** work, strive, or make one's way with difficulty. **2** move about violently in an attempt to get free. **3** fight (with someone). ♦ *n* **4** striving. **5** fight.

strum *v* **strumming, strummed** play (a guitar or banjo) by sweeping the thumb or a plectrum across the strings.

strumpet *n Old-fashioned* prostitute.

strung *v* past of STRING.

strut *v* **strutting, strutted 1** walk pompously, swagger. ♦ *n* **2** bar supporting a structure.

strychnine [**strik**-neen] *n* very poisonous drug used in small quantities as a stimulant.

stub *n* **1** short piece left after use. **2** counterfoil of a cheque or ticket. ♦ *v* **stubbing, stubbed 3** strike (the toe) painfully against an object. **4** put out (a cigarette) by pressing the end against a surface. **stubby** *adj* short and broad.

stubble *n* **1** short stalks of grain left in a field after reaping. **2** short growth of hair on the chin of a man who has not shaved recently. **stubbly** *adj*

stubborn *adj* **1** refusing to agree or give in. **2** difficult to deal with. **stubbornly** *adv* **stubbornness** *n*

stucco *n* plaster used for coating or decorating walls. **stuccoed** *adj*

stuck *v* past of STICK[2]. **stuck-up** *adj Informal* conceited or snobbish.

stud[1] *n* **1** small piece of metal attached to a surface for decoration. **2** disc-like removable fastener for clothes. **3** one of several small round objects fixed to the sole of a football boot to give better grip. ♦ *v* **studding, studded 4** set with studs.

stud[2] *n* **1** male animal, esp. a stallion, kept for breeding. **2** (also **stud farm**) place where horses are bred. **3** *Slang* virile or sexually active man.

student *n* person who studies a subject, esp. at university.

studio *n, pl* **-dios 1** workroom of an artist or photographer. **2** room or building in which television or radio programmes, records, or films are made. **studio flat** one-room flat with a small kitchen and bathroom.

study *v* **studying, studied 1** be engaged in learning (a subject). **2** investigate by observation and research. **3** scrutinize. ♦ *n, pl* **studies 4** act or process of studying. **5** room for studying in. **6** book or paper produced as a result of study. **7** sketch done as practice or preparation. **8** musical composition designed to improve playing technique. **studied** *adj* carefully practised or planned. **studious** [**styoo**-dee-uss] *adj* **1** fond of study. **2** careful and deliberate. **studiously** *adv*

stuff *n* **1** substance or material. **2** collection of unnamed things. **3** raw material of something. **4** subject matter. **5** woollen fabric. ♦ *v* **6** pack, cram, or fill completely. **7** fill (food) with a seasoned mixture. **8** fill (an animal's skin) with material to restore the shape of the live animal. **stuff oneself** *Informal* eat large quantities. **stuffing** *n* **1** seasoned mixture with which food is stuffed. **2** padding.

stuffy *adj* **stuffier, stuffiest 1** lacking fresh air. **2** *Informal* dull or conventional.

stultifying *adj* very boring and repetitive.

stumble *v* **1** trip and nearly fall. **2** walk in an unsure way. **3** make frequent mistakes in speech. ♦ *n* **4** stumbling. **stumble across** *v* discover accidentally. **stumbling block** obstacle or difficulty.

stump *n* **1** base of a tree left when the main trunk has been cut away. **2** part of a thing left after a larger part has been removed. **3** *Cricket* one of the three upright sticks forming the wicket. ♦ *v* **4** baffle. **5** *Cricket* dismiss (a batsman) by breaking his wicket with the ball. **6** walk with heavy steps. **stumpy** *adj* short and thick. **stump up** *v Informal* give (the money required).

stun *v* **stunning, stunned 1** shock or overwhelm. **2** knock senseless. **stunner** *n Informal* beautiful person or thing. **stunning** *adj* very attractive or impressive.

stung *v* past of STING.

stunk *v* a past of STINK.

stunt[1] *v* prevent or impede the growth of. **stunted** *adj*

stunt[2] *n* **1** acrobatic or dangerous action. **2** anything spectacular done to gain publicity.

stupefy *v* **-fying, -fied 1** make insensitive or lethargic. **2** astound. **stupefaction** *n*

stupendous *adj* very large or impressive. **stupendously** *adv*

stupid *adj* **1** lacking intelligence. **2** silly. **3** in a stupor. **stupidity** *n* **stupidly** *adv*

stupor *n* dazed or unconscious state.

sturdy *adj* **-dier, -diest 1** healthy and robust. **2** strongly built. **sturdily** *adv*

sturgeon *n* fish from which caviar is obtained.

stutter *v* **1** speak with repetition of initial consonants. ♦ *n* **2** tendency to stutter.

sty *n, pl* **sties** pen for pigs.

stye, sty *n, pl* **styes, sties** inflammation at the base of an eyelash.

Stygian [**stij**-jee-an] *adj Lit* gloomy.

style *n* **1** shape or design. **2** manner of writing, speaking, or doing something. **3** elegance, refinement. **4** prevailing fashion. **5** part of a flower that bears the stigma. ♦ *v* **6** shape or design. **7** name or call. **stylish** *adj* smart, elegant, and fashionable. **stylishly** *adv* **stylist** *n* **1** hairdresser. **2** person who writes or performs with great attention to style. **stylistic** *adj* of literary or artistic style. **stylize** *v* cause to conform to an established stylistic form.

stylus *n* needle-like device on a record player that rests in the groove of the record and picks up the sound signals.

stymie *v* **-mieing, -mied** hinder or thwart.

styptic *n, adj* (drug) used to stop bleeding.

suave [**swahv**] *adj* smooth and sophisticated in manner. **suavely** *adv*

sub *n* **1** subeditor. **2** submarine. **3** subscription. **4** substitute. **5** *Informal* advance payment of wages or salary. ♦ *v* **subbing, subbed 6** act as a substitute. **7** grant advance payment to.

sub- *prefix* used with many main words to mean: **1** under or beneath, e.g. *submarine.* **2** subordinate, e.g. *sublieutenant.* **3** falling short of, e.g. *subnormal.* **4** forming a subdivision, e.g. *subheading.*

subaltern *n* army officer below the rank of captain.

subatomic *adj* of or being one of the particles which make up an atom.

subcommittee *n* small committee formed from some members of a larger committee.

subconscious *adj* **1** happening or existing without one's awareness. ♦ *n* **2** *Psychoanalysis* that part of the mind of which one is not aware but which can influence one's behaviour. **subconsciously** *adv*

subcontinent *n* large land mass that is a distinct part of a continent.

subcontract *n* **1** secondary contract by which the main contractor for a job puts work out to others. ♦ *v* **2** put out (work) on a subcontract. **subcontractor** *n*

subcutaneous [sub-cute-**ayn**-ee-uss] *adj* under the skin.

subdivide *v* divide (a part of something) into smaller parts. **subdivision** *n*

subdue *v* **-duing, -dued 1** overcome. **2** make less intense.

subeditor *n* person who checks and edits text for a newspaper or magazine.

subhuman *adj* less than human.

subject *n* **1** person or thing being dealt with or studied. **2** figure, scene, etc. portrayed by an artist or photographer. **3** *Grammar* word or phrase that represents the person or thing performing the action of the verb in a sentence. **4** person under the rule of a monarch or government. ♦ *adj* **5** being under the rule of a monarch or government. ♦ *v* (foll. by *to*) **6** cause to undergo. **7** bring under the control (of). **subject to 1** liable to. **2** conditional upon. **subjection** *n* **subjective** *adj* based on personal feelings or prejudices. **subjectively** *adv*

sub judice [sub **joo**-diss-ee] *adj Latin* before a court of law.

subjugate *v* bring (a group of people) under one's control. **subjugation** *n*

subjunctive *Grammar* ♦ *n* **1** mood of verbs used when the content of the clause is doubted, supposed, or wished. ♦ *adj* **2** in or of that mood.

sublet *v* **-letting, -let** rent out (property rented from someone else).

sublieutenant *n* naval officer of the lowest rank.

sublimate *v Psychol* direct the energy of (a strong desire, esp. a sexual one) into socially acceptable activities. **sublimation** *n*

sublime *adj* **1** of high moral, intellectual, or spiritual value. **2** unparalleled, supreme. ♦ *v* **3** *Chem* change from a solid to a vapour without first melting. **sublimely** *adv*

subliminal *adj* relating to mental processes of which the individual is not aware.

sub-machine-gun *n* portable machine gun with a short barrel.

submarine *n* **1** vessel which can operate below the surface of the sea. ♦ *adj* **2** below the surface of the sea.

submerge *v* **1** put or go below the surface of water or other liquid. **2** involve totally. **submersion** *n* **submersible** *n, adj* (vehicle) able to work under water.

submit *v* **-mitting, -mitted 1** surrender. **2** put forward for consideration. **3** be (voluntarily) subjected to a process or treatment. **submission** *n* **1** submitting. **2** something submitted for consideration. **3** state of being submissive. **submissive** *adj* meek and obedient.

subnormal *adj* less than normal, esp. in intelligence.

subordinate *adj* **1** of lesser rank or importance. ♦ *n* **2** subordinate person or thing. ♦ *v* **3** make or treat as subordinate. **subordination** *n*

suborn *v Formal* bribe or incite (a person) to commit a wrongful act.

subpoena [sub-**pee**-na] *n* **1** writ requiring a person to appear before a lawcourt. ♦ *v* **2** summon (someone) with a subpoena.

sub rosa [sub **rose**-a] *adv Latin* in secret.

subscribe *v* **1** pay (a subscription). **2** give support or approval (to). **subscriber** *n* **subscription** *n* **1** payment for issues of a publication over a period. **2** money contributed to a charity etc. **3** membership fees paid to a society.

subscript *n, adj* (character) printed below the line.

subsection *n* division of a section.

subsequent *adj* occurring after, succeeding. **subsequently** *adv*

subservient *adj* submissive, servile. **subservience** *n*

subside *v* **1** become less intense. **2** sink

to a lower level. **subsidence** *n* act or process of subsiding.

subsidiary *adj* **1** of lesser importance. ♦ *n, pl* **-aries** **2** subsidiary person or thing.

subsidize *v* help financially. **subsidy** *n, pl* **-dies** financial aid.

subsist *v* manage to live. **subsistence** *n*

subsoil *n* earth just below the surface soil.

subsonic *adj* moving at a speed less than that of sound.

substance *n* **1** physical composition of something. **2** solid, powder, liquid, or paste. **3** essential meaning of something. **4** solid or meaningful quality. **5** wealth. **substantial** *adj* **1** of considerable size or value. **2** (of food or a meal) sufficient and nourishing. **3** solid or strong. **4** real. **substantially** *adv* **substantiate** *v* support (a story) with evidence. **substantiation** *n* **substantive** *n* **1** noun. ♦ *adj* **2** of or being the essential element of a thing.

substitute *v* **1** take the place of or put in place of another. ♦ *n* **2** person or thing taking the place of (another). **substitution** *n*

subsume *v* include (an idea, case, etc.) under a larger classification or group.

subterfuge *n* trick used to achieve an objective.

subterranean *adj* underground.

subtitle *n* **1** secondary title of a book. ♦ *pl* **2** printed translation at the bottom of the picture in a film with foreign dialogue. ♦ *v* **3** provide with a subtitle or subtitles.

subtle *adj* **1** not immediately obvious. **2** delicate. **3** having or requiring ingenuity. **subtly** *adv* **subtlety** *n*

subtract *v* take (one number or quantity) from another. **subtraction** *n*

subtropical *adj* of the regions bordering on the tropics.

suburb *n* residential area on the outskirts of a city. **suburban** *adj* **1** of or inhabiting a suburb. **2** narrow or unadventurous in outlook. **suburbanite** *n* **suburbia** *n* suburbs and their inhabitants.

subvention *n Formal* subsidy.

subvert *v* overthrow the authority of. **subversion** *n* **subversive** *adj, n*

subway *n* **1** passage under a road or railway. **2** underground railway.

succeed *v* **1** accomplish an aim. **2** turn out satisfactorily. **3** come next in order after (something). **4** take over a position from (someone). **success** *n* **1** achievement of something attempted. **2** attainment of wealth, fame, or position. **3** successful person or thing. **successful** *adj* having success. **successfully** *adv* **succession** *n* **1** series of people or things following one another in order. **2** act or right by which one person succeeds another in a position. **successive** *adj* consecutive. **successively** *adv* **successor** *n* person who succeeds someone in a position.

succinct *adj* brief and clear. **succinctly** *adv*

succour *v, n* help in distress.

succubus *n, pl* **-bi** female demon believed to have sex with sleeping men.

succulent *adj* **1** juicy and delicious. **2** (of a plant) having thick fleshy leaves. ♦ *n* **3** succulent plant. **succulence** *n*

succumb *v* **1** (foll. by *to*) give way (to something overpowering). **2** die of (an illness).

such *adj* **1** of the kind specified. **2** so great, so much. ♦ *pron* **3** such things. **such-and-such** *adj* specific, but not known or named. **suchlike** *pron* such or similar things.

suck *v* **1** draw (liquid or air) into the mouth. **2** take (something) into the mouth and moisten, dissolve, or roll it around with the tongue. **3** (foll. by *in*) draw in by irresistible force. ♦ *n* **4** sucking. **sucker** *n* **1** *Slang* person who is easily deceived or swindled. **2** organ or device which adheres by suction. **3** shoot coming from a plant's root or the base of its main stem. **suck up to** *v Informal* flatter (someone) for one's own profit.

suckle *v* feed at the breast. **suckling** *n* unweaned baby or young animal.

sucrose [**soo**-kroze] *n* chemical name for sugar.

suction *n* **1** sucking. **2** force produced by drawing air out of a space to make a vacuum that will suck in a substance from another space.

sudden *adj* done or occurring quickly and unexpectedly. **all of a sudden** quickly and unexpectedly. **suddenly** *adv* **suddenness** *n* **sudden death** *Sport* period of extra time in which the first competitor to score wins.

sudorific [syoo-dor-**if**-ik] *n, adj* (drug) causing sweating.

suds *pl n* froth of soap and water, lather.

sue *v* **suing, sued** start legal proceedings against.

suede *n* leather with a velvety finish on one side.

suet *n* hard fat obtained from sheep and cattle, used in cooking.

suffer *v* **1** undergo or be subjected to. **2** tolerate. **sufferer** *n* **suffering** *n* **sufferance** *n* **on sufferance** tolerated with reluctance.

suffice [suf-**fice**] *v* be enough for a purpose. **sufficiency** *n* adequate amount **sufficient** *adj* enough, adequate. **sufficiently** *adv*

suffix *n* letter or letters added to the end of a word to form another word.

suffocate *v* **1** kill or be killed by deprivation of oxygen. **2** feel uncomfortable from heat and lack of air. **suffocation** *n*

suffragan *n* bishop appointed to assist an archbishop.

suffrage *n* right to vote in public elections. **suffragette** *n* (in Britain in the early 20th century) a woman who campaigned militantly for the right to vote.

suffuse *v* spread through or over (something). **suffusion** *n*

sugar *n* **1** sweet crystalline carbohydrate found in many plants and used to sweeten food and drinks. ♦ *v* **2** sweeten or cover with sugar. **sugary** *adj* **sugar beet** beet grown for the sugar obtained from its roots. **sugar cane** tropical grass grown for the sugar obtained from its canes. **sugar daddy** *Slang* elderly man who gives a young woman money and gifts in return for sexual favours.

suggest *v* **1** put forward (an idea) for consideration. **2** bring to mind by the association of ideas. **3** give a hint of. **suggestible** *adj* easily influenced. **suggestion** *n* **1** thing suggested. **2** hint or indication. **suggestive** *adj* **1** suggesting something indecent. **2** conveying a hint (of). **suggestively** *adv*

suicide *n* **1** killing oneself intentionally. **2** person who kills himself intentionally. **3** self-inflicted ruin of one's own prospects or interests. **suicidal** *adj* liable to commit suicide. **suicidally** *adv*

suit *n* **1** set of clothes designed to be worn together. **2** outfit worn for a specific purpose. **3** one of the four sets into which a pack of cards is divided. **4** lawsuit. ♦ *v* **5** be appropriate for. **6** be acceptable to. **suitable** *adj* appropriate or proper. **suitably** *adv* **suitability** *n* **suitcase** *n* portable travelling case for clothing.

suite *n* **1** set of connected rooms in a hotel. **2** matching set of furniture. **3** set of musical pieces in the same key.

suitor *n Old-fashioned* man who is courting a woman.

sulk *v* **1** be silent and sullen because of resentment or bad temper. ♦ *n* **2** resentful or sullen mood. **sulky** *adj* **sulkily** *adv* **sulkiness** *n*

sullen *adj* unwilling to talk or be sociable. **sullenly** *adv* **sullenness** *n*

sully *v* **-lying, -lied** **1** ruin (someone's reputation). **2** make dirty.

sulphate *n* salt or ester of sulphuric acid.

sulphide *n* compound of sulphur with another element.

sulphite *n* salt or ester of sulphurous acid.

sulphonamide [sulf-**on**-a-mide] *n* any of a class of drugs that prevent the growth of bacteria.

sulphur *n Chem* pale yellow nonmetallic element. **sulphuric, sulphurous** *adj* of or containing sulphur. **sulphuric acid** colourless corrosive liquid used for making explosives. **sulphurous acid** acid used for bleaching and as a preservative.

sultan *n* sovereign of a Muslim country. **sultana** *n* **1** kind of raisin. **2** sultan's wife, mother, or daughter. **sultanate** *n* territory of a sultan.

sultry *adj* **-trier, -triest 1** (of weather or climate) hot and humid. **2** passionate, sensual.

sum *n* **1** result of addition, total. **2** problem in arithmetic. **3** quantity of money. **4** gist of a matter. **sum total** complete or final total. **sum up** *v* **summing, summed 1** summarize. **2** form a quick opinion of.

summary *n, pl* **-ries 1** brief account giving the main points of something. ♦ *adj* **2** done quickly, without formalities. **summarily** *adv* **summarize** *v* make or be a summary of (something). **summation** *n* **1** summary. **2** adding up.

summer *n* warmest season of the year, between spring and autumn. **summery** *adj* **summerhouse** *n* small building in a garden. **summer school** academic course held during the summer. **summertime** *n* period or season of summer.

summit *n* **1** top of a mountain or hill. **2** highest point. **3** conference between heads of state.

summon *v* **1** order (someone) to come. **2** send for (someone) to appear in court. **3** call upon (someone) to do something. **4** gather (one's courage, strength, etc.). **summons** *n* **1** command summoning someone. **2** order requiring someone to appear in court. ♦ *v* **3** order (someone) to appear in court.

sumo *n* Japanese style of wrestling.

sump *n* **1** container in an internal-combustion engine into which oil can drain. **2** hollow into which liquid drains.

sumptuous *adj* lavish, magnificent. **sumptuously** *adv*

sun *n* **1** star around which the earth and other planets revolve. **2** any star around which planets revolve. **3** heat and light from the sun. ♦ *v* **sunning, sunned 4** expose (oneself) to the sun's rays. **sunless** *adj* **sunny** *adj* **1** full of or exposed to sunlight. **2** cheerful. **sunbathe** *v* lie in the sunshine in order to get a suntan. **sunbeam** *n* ray of sun. **sunburn** *n* painful reddening of the skin caused by overexposure to the sun. **sunburnt, sunburned** *adj* **sundial** *n* device showing the time by means of a pointer that casts a shadow on a marked dial. **sundown** *n* sunset. **sunflower** *n* tall plant with large golden flowers. **sunglasses** *pl n* dark glasses to protect the eyes from the sun. **sun lamp** lamp that gives off ultraviolet rays. **sunrise** *n* **1** daily appearance of the sun above the horizon. **2** time of this. **sunroof** *n* panel in the roof of a car that opens to let in air. **sunset** *n* **1** daily disappearance of the sun below the horizon. **2** time of this. **sunshine** *n* light and warmth from the sun. **sunspot** *n* dark patch appearing temporarily on the sun's surface. **sunstroke** *n* illness caused by prolonged exposure to intensely hot sunlight. **suntan** *n* browning of the skin caused by exposure to the sun. **sun-up** *n US* sunrise.

Sun. Sunday.

sundae *n* ice cream topped with fruit etc.

Sunday *n* first day of the week and the Christian day of worship. **Sunday school** school for teaching children about Christianity.

sundry *adj* several, various. **sundries** *pl n* several things of various sorts. **all and sundry** everybody.

sung *v* past participle of SING.

sunk *v* a past participle of SINK.

sunken *v* **1** a past participle of SINK. ♦ *adj* **2** unhealthily hollow. **3** situated at a low level. **4** underwater.

sup *v* **supping, supped 1** take (liquid) by sips. ♦ *n* **2** sip.

super *adj Informal* excellent.

super- *prefix* used with many main words to mean: **1** above or over, e.g. *superimpose.* **2** outstanding, e.g. *superstar.* **3** of greater size or extent, e.g. *supermarket.*

superannuation *n* **1** regular payment

by an employee into a pension fund. **2** pension paid from this. **superannuated** *adj* discharged with a pension, owing to old age or illness.

superb *adj* excellent, impressive, or splendid. **superbly** *adv*

superbug *n Informal* bacterium resistant to antibiotics.

supercharged *adj* (of an engine) having a supercharger. **supercharger** *n* device that increases the power of an internal-combustion engine by forcing extra air into it.

supercilious *adj* showing arrogant pride or scorn.

superconductor *n* substance which has almost no electrical resistance at very low temperatures. **superconductivity** *n*

superficial *adj* **1** not careful or thorough. **2** (of a person) without depth of character, shallow. **3** of or on the surface. **superficially** *adv* **superficiality** *n*

superfluous [soo-**per**-flew-uss] *adj* more than is needed. **superfluity** *n*

supergrass *n* person who acts as a police informer on a large scale.

superhuman *adj* beyond normal human ability or experience.

superimpose *v* place (something) on or over something else.

superintend *v* supervise (a person or activity). **superintendent** *n* **1** senior police officer. **2** supervisor.

superior *adj* **1** greater in quality, quantity, or merit. **2** higher in position or rank. **3** believing oneself to be better than others. ♦ *n* **4** person of greater rank or status. **superiority** *n*

superlative [soo-**per**-lat-iv] *adj* **1** of outstanding quality. **2** *Grammar* denoting the form of an adjective or adverb indicating *most*. ♦ *n* **3** *Grammar* superlative form of a word.

superman *n* man with great physical or mental powers.

supermarket *n* large self-service store selling food and household goods.

supermodel *n* famous and highly-paid fashion model.

supernatural *adj* of or relating to things beyond the laws of nature. **the supernatural** supernatural forces, occurrences, and beings collectively.

supernova *n, pl* **-vae, -vas** star that explodes and briefly becomes exceptionally bright.

supernumerary *adj* **1** exceeding the required or regular number. ♦ *n, pl* **-ries 2** supernumerary person or thing.

superphosphate *n* chemical fertilizer containing phosphates.

superpower *n* extremely powerful nation.

superscript *n, adj* (character) printed above the line.

supersede *v* replace, supplant.

supersonic *adj* of or travelling at a speed greater than the speed of sound.

superstar *n* very famous entertainer or sportsperson.

superstition *n* **1** belief in omens, ghosts, etc. **2** idea or practice based on this. **superstitious** *adj*

superstore *n* large supermarket.

superstructure *n* **1** structure erected on something else. **2** part of a ship above the main deck.

supertanker *n* large fast tanker.

supertax *n* extra tax on incomes above a certain level.

supervene *v* occur as an unexpected development. **supervention** *n*

supervise *v* watch over to direct or check. **supervision** *n* **supervisor** *n* **supervisory** *adj*

supine [**soo**-pine] *adj* lying flat on one's back.

supper *n* light evening meal.

supplant *v* take the place of, oust.

supple *adj* **1** (of a person) moving and bending easily and gracefully. **2** bending easily without damage. **suppleness** *n*

supplement *n* **1** thing added to complete something or make up for a lack. **2** magazine inserted into a newspaper. **3** section added to a publication to supply further information. ♦ *v* **4** provide or be a supplement to (something).

supplementary *adj*

supplication *n* humble request. **supplicant** *n* person who makes a humble request.

supply *v* **-plying, -plied 1** provide with something required. ♦ *n, pl* **-plies 2** supplying. **3** amount available. **4** *Economics* willingness and ability to provide goods and services. ♦ *pl* **5** food or equipment. ♦ *adj* **6** acting as a temporary substitute. **supplier** *n*

support *v* **1** bear the weight of. **2** provide the necessities of life for. **3** give practical or emotional help to. **4** take an active interest in (a sports team, political principle, etc.). **5** help to prove (a theory etc.). **6** speak in favour of. **7** play a subordinate part. ♦ *n* **8** supporting. **9** means of support. **supporter** *n* person who supports a team, principle, etc. **supportive** *adj*

suppose *v* **1** presume to be true. **2** consider as a proposal for the sake of discussion. **3** presuppose. **supposed** *adj* presumed to be true without proof, doubtful. **supposed to 1** expected or required to, e.g. *you were supposed to phone me.* **2** permitted to, e.g. *we're not supposed to swim here.* **supposedly** *adv* **supposition** *n* **1** supposing. **2** something supposed.

suppository *n, pl* **-ries** solid medication inserted into the rectum or vagina and left to melt.

suppress *v* **1** put an end to. **2** prevent publication of (information). **3** restrain (an emotion or response). **suppression** *n*

suppurate *v* (of a wound etc.) produce pus.

supreme *adj* highest in authority, rank, or degree. **supremely** *adv* extremely. **supremacy** *n* **1** supreme power. **2** state of being supreme. **supremo** *n Informal* person in overall authority.

surcharge *n* additional charge.

surd *n Maths* number that cannot be expressed in whole numbers.

sure *adj* **1** free from uncertainty or doubt. **2** reliable. **3** inevitable. **4** physically secure. ♦ *adv, interj* **5** *Informal* certainly. **for sure** without a doubt. **surely** *adv* it must be true that. **sure-fire** *adj Informal* certain to succeed. **surefooted** *adj* unlikely to slip or stumble.

surety *n, pl* **-ties** person who takes responsibility, or thing given as a guarantee, for the fulfilment of another's obligation.

surf *n* **1** foam caused by waves breaking on the shore. ♦ *v* **2** take part in surfing. **3** move quickly through a medium such as the Internet. **surfing** *n* sport of riding towards the shore on a surfboard on the crest of a wave. **surfer** *n* **surfboard** *n* long smooth board used in surfing.

surface *n* **1** outside or top of an object. **2** material covering the surface of an object. **3** superficial appearance. **4** top level of the land or sea. ♦ *v* **5** become apparent. **6** rise to the surface. **7** put a surface on.

surfeit *n* excessive amount.

surge *n* **1** sudden powerful increase. **2** strong rolling movement, esp. of the sea. ♦ *v* **3** increase suddenly. **4** move forward strongly.

surgeon *n* doctor who specializes in surgery. **surgery** *n* **1** treatment in which the patient's body is cut open in order to treat the affected part. **2** (*pl* **-geries**) place where, or time when, a doctor, dentist, MP, etc. can be consulted. **surgical** *adj* **surgically** *adv* **surgical spirit** spirit used for sterilizing and cleaning.

surly *adj* **-lier, -liest** ill-tempered and rude. **surliness** *n*

surmise *v, n* guess, conjecture.

surmount *v* **1** overcome (a problem). **2** be on top of (something). **surmountable** *adj*

surname *n* family name.

surpass *v* be greater than or superior to.

surplice *n* loose white robe worn by clergymen and choristers.

surplus *n* **1** amount left over in excess of what is required. ♦ *adj* **2** extra.

surprise *n* **1** unexpected event. **2** amazement and wonder. **3** act of taking someone unawares. ♦ *v* **4** cause to feel amazement or wonder. **5** come upon, attack, or catch suddenly and unexpectedly. **take someone by surprise** catch someone unprepared.

surrealism *n* movement in art and literature involving the combination of incongruous images, as in a dream. **surreal** *adj* bizarre. **surrealist** *n, adj* **surrealistic** *adj*

surrender *v* **1** give oneself up. **2** give (something) up to another. **3** yield (to a temptation or influence). ♦ *n* **4** surrendering.

surreptitious *adj* done secretly or stealthily. **surreptitiously** *adv*

surrogate *n* substitute. **surrogate mother** woman who gives birth to a child on behalf of a couple who cannot have children.

surround *v* **1** be, come, or place all around (a person or thing). ♦ *n* **2** border or edging. **surroundings** *pl n* area or environment around a person, place, or thing.

surtax *n* extra tax on incomes above a certain level.

surveillance *n* close observation.

survey *v* **1** view or consider in a general way. **2** make a map of (an area). **3** inspect (a building) to assess its condition and value. **4** find out the incomes, opinions, etc. of (a group of people). ♦ *n* **5** surveying. **6** report produced by a survey. **surveyor** *n*

survive *v* **1** continue to live or exist after (a difficult experience). **2** live after the death of (another). **survival** *n* **1** condition of having survived. **2** thing that has survived from an earlier time. **survivor** *n*

susceptible *adj* liable to be influenced or affected by. **susceptibility** *n*

suspect *v* **1** believe (someone) to be guilty without having any proof. **2** think (something) to be false or questionable. **3** believe (something) to be the case. ♦ *adj* **4** not to be trusted. ♦ *n* **5** person who is suspected.

suspend *v* **1** hang from a high place. **2** cause to remain floating or hanging. **3** cause to cease temporarily. **4** remove (someone) temporarily from a job or team. **suspenders** *pl n* **1** straps for holding up stockings. **2** *US* braces. **suspended sentence** prison sentence that is not served unless the offender commits another crime during a specified period.

suspense *n* state of uncertainty while awaiting news, an event, etc.

suspension *n* **1** suspending or being suspended. **2** system of springs and shock absorbers supporting the body of a vehicle. **3** mixture of fine particles of a solid in a fluid. **suspension bridge** bridge hanging from cables attached to towers at each end.

suspicion *n* **1** feeling of not trusting a person or thing. **2** belief that something is true without definite proof. **3** slight trace. **suspicious** *adj* feeling or causing suspicion. **suspiciously** *adv*

suss out *v Slang* work out using one's intuition.

sustain *v* **1** maintain or prolong. **2** keep up the vitality or strength of. **3** suffer (an injury or loss). **4** support. **5** confirm. **sustenance** *n* food.

suture [**soo**-cher] *n* stitch joining the edges of a wound.

suzerain *n* **1** state or sovereign with limited authority over another self-governing state. **2** feudal lord. **suzerainty** *n*

svelte *adj* attractively or gracefully slim.

SW southwest(ern).

swab *n* **1** small piece of cotton wool used to apply medication, clean a wound, etc. ♦ *v* **swabbing, swabbed 2** clean (a wound) with a swab. **3** clean (the deck of a ship) with a mop.

swaddle *v* wrap (a baby) in swaddling clothes. **swaddling clothes** long strips of cloth formerly wrapped round a newborn baby.

swag *n Slang* stolen property. **swagman** *n Aust* tramp who carries his belongings in a bundle on his back.

swagger *v* **1** walk or behave arrogantly.

♦ *n* **2** arrogant walk or manner.

swain *n Poetic* **1** suitor. **2** country youth.

swallow[1] *v* **1** cause to pass down one's throat. **2** make a gulping movement in the throat, as when nervous. **3** *Informal* believe (something) gullibly. **4** refrain from showing (a feeling). **5** engulf or absorb. ♦ *n* **6** swallowing. **7** amount swallowed.

swallow[2] *n* small migratory bird with long pointed wings and a forked tail.

swam *v* past tense of SWIM.

swamp *n* **1** watery area of land, bog. ♦ *v* **2** cause (a boat) to fill with water and sink. **3** overwhelm. **swampy** *adj*

swan *n* **1** large usu. white water bird with a long graceful neck. ♦ *v* **swanning, swanned 2** *Informal* wander about idly. **swan song** person's last performance before retirement or death.

swank *Slang* ♦ *v* **1** show off or boast. ♦ *n* **2** showing off or boasting. **swanky** *adj Slang* expensive and showy, stylish.

swap *v* **swapping, swapped 1** exchange (something) for something else. ♦ *n* **2** exchange.

sward *n* stretch of short grass.

swarm[1] *n* **1** large group of bees or other insects. **2** large crowd. ♦ *v* **3** move in a swarm. **4** (of a place) be crowded or overrun.

swarm[2] *v* (foll. by *up*) climb (a ladder or rope) by gripping with the hands and feet.

swarthy *adj* **-thier, -thiest** dark-complexioned.

swashbuckling *adj* having the exciting behaviour of pirates, esp. those depicted in films. **swashbuckler** *n*

swastika *n* symbol in the shape of a cross with the arms bent at right angles, used as the emblem of Nazi Germany.

swat *v* **swatting, swatted 1** hit sharply. ♦ *n* **2** sharp blow.

swatch *n* sample of cloth.

swath [**swawth**] *n* see SWATHE.

swathe *v* **1** wrap in bandages or layers of cloth. ♦ *n* **2** long strip of cloth wrapped around something. **3** (also **swath**) the width of one sweep of a scythe or mower. **4** strip cut in one sweep.

sway *v* **1** swing to and fro or from side to side. **2** waver or cause to waver in opinion. ♦ *n* **3** power or influence. **4** swaying motion.

swear *v* **swearing, swore, sworn 1** use obscene or blasphemous language. **2** state or promise on oath. **3** state earnestly. **swear by** *v* have complete confidence in. **swear in** *v* cause to take an oath. **swearword** *n* word considered obscene or blasphemous.

sweat *n* **1** salty liquid given off through the pores of the skin. **2** *Slang* drudgery or hard labour. **3** *Informal* state of anxiety. ♦ *v* **4** have sweat coming through the pores. **5** be anxious. **sweaty** *adj* **sweatband** *n* strip of cloth tied around the forehead or wrist to absorb sweat. **sweatshirt** *n* long-sleeved cotton jersey. **sweatshop** *n* place where employees work long hours in poor conditions for low pay.

sweater *n* (woollen) garment for the upper part of the body.

swede *n* **1** kind of turnip. **2** (**S-**) person from Sweden. **Swedish** *n, adj* (language) of Sweden.

sweep *v* **sweeping, swept 1** remove dirt from (a floor) with a broom. **2** move smoothly and quickly. **3** spread rapidly. **4** move majestically. **5** carry away suddenly or forcefully. **6** stretch in a long wide curve. ♦ *n* **7** sweeping. **8** sweeping motion. **9** wide expanse. **10** curving line. **11** sweepstake. **12** chimney sweep. **sweeping** *adj* **1** wide-ranging. **2** indiscriminate. **sweepstake** *n* lottery in which the stakes of the participants make up the prize.

sweet *adj* **1** tasting of or like sugar. **2** kind and charming. **3** agreeable to the senses or mind. **4** (of wine) with a high sugar content. ♦ *n* **5** shaped piece of food consisting mainly of sugar. **6** dessert. **sweetly** *adv* **sweetness** *n* **sweeten** *v* **sweetener** *n* **1** sweetening agent that does not contain sugar. **2** *Slang* bribe. **sweetie** *n Informal* **1** lovable person. **2** sweet. **sweetbread** *n* animal's pancreas used as food. **sweet corn** type of maize with sweet yellow kernels, eaten as a vegetable. **sweetheart** *n* lover. **sweetmeat** *n Old-fashioned* sweet delicacy such as a small cake. **sweet pea** climbing plant with bright fragrant flowers. **sweet potato** tropical root vegetable with yellow flesh. **sweet-talk** *v Informal* coax or flatter. **sweet tooth** strong liking for sweet foods. **sweet william** garden plant with clusters of scented flowers.

swell *v* **swelling, swelled, swollen** *or* **swelled 1** expand or increase. **2** (of an emotion) become more intense. **3** (of a sound) become gradually louder. ♦ *n* **4** swelling or being swollen. **5** movement of waves in the sea. **6** *Old-fashioned slang* fashionable person. ♦ *adj* **7** *US slang* excellent or fine. **swelling** *n* enlargement of part of the body, caused by injury or infection

sweltering *adj* uncomfortably hot. **swelter** *v*

swept *v* past of SWEEP.

swerve *v* **1** turn aside from a course sharply or suddenly. ♦ *n* **2** swerving.

swift *adj* **1** moving or able to move quickly. **2** performed or happening quickly. ♦ *n* **3** fast-flying bird with pointed wings. **swiftly** *adv* **swiftness** *n*

swig *n* **1** large mouthful of drink. ♦ *v* **swigging, swigged 2** drink in large mouthfuls.

swill *v* **1** drink greedily. **2** rinse (something) in large amounts of water. ♦ *n* **3** sloppy mixture containing waste food, fed to pigs. **4** deep drink.

swim *v* **swimming, swam, swum 1** move along in water by movements of the limbs. **2** be covered or flooded with liquid. **3** float on a liquid. **4** reel, e.g. *her head was swimming.* ♦ *n* **5** act or period of swimming. **swimmer** *n* **swimmingly** *adv* successfully and effortlessly. **swimming costume, swimsuit** *n* swimming garment that leaves the arms and legs bare. **swimming pool** (building containing) an artificial pond for swimming in.

swindle *v* **1** cheat (someone) out of money. ♦ *n* **2** instance of swindling. **swindler** *n*

swine *n* **1** contemptible person. **2** pig.

swing *v* **swinging, swung 1** move to and fro, sway. **2** turn, as on a hinge. **3** move in a curve. **4** (of an opinion or mood) change sharply. **5** hit out with a sweeping motion. **6** *Slang* be hanged. **7** *Informal* manipulate or influence. ♦ *n* **8** swinging. **9** suspended seat on which a child can swing to and fro. **10** style of popular dance music played by big bands in the 1930s. **11** sudden or extreme change.

swingeing [**swin**-jing] *adj* punishing, severe.

swipe *v* **1** strike (at) with a sweeping blow. **2** *Slang* steal. **3** pass (a credit card) through a machine which electronically reads information stored in the card. ♦ *n* **4** hard blow.

swirl *v* **1** turn with a whirling motion. ♦ *n* **2** whirling motion. **3** twisting shape.

swish *v* **1** move with a whistling or hissing sound. ♦ *n* **2** whistling or hissing sound. ♦ *adj* **3** *Informal* fashionable, smart.

Swiss *adj* **1** of Switzerland or its people. ♦ *n, pl* **Swiss 2** person from Switzerland. **swiss roll** sponge cake spread with jam or cream and rolled up.

switch *n* **1** device for opening and closing an electric circuit. **2** abrupt change. **3** exchange or swap. **4** flexible rod or twig. ♦ *v* **5** change abruptly. **6** exchange or swap. **switchback** *n* road or railway with many sharp hills or bends. **switchboard** *n* installation in a telephone exchange or office where telephone calls are connected. **switch on, off** *v* turn (a device) on *or* off by means of a switch.

swivel *v* **-elling, -elled 1** turn on a central point. ♦ *n* **2** coupling device that allows an attached object to turn freely.

swizz, swiz *n Brit informal* swindle or

disappointment.

swizzle stick *n* small stick used to stir cocktails.

swollen *v* a past participle of SWELL.

swoon *v, n* faint.

swoop *v* **1** sweep down or pounce on suddenly. ♦ *n* **2** swooping.

swop *v* **swopping, swopped,** *n* same as SWAP.

sword *n* weapon with a long sharp blade. **sword dance** Highland dance performed over swords on the ground. **swordfish** *n* large fish with a very long upper jaw. **swordsman** *n* person skilled in the use of a sword.

swore *v* past tense of SWEAR.

sworn *v* **1** past participle of SWEAR. ♦ *adj* **2** bound by or as if by an oath, e.g. *sworn enemies.*

swot *Informal* ♦ *v* **swotting, swotted 1** study hard. ♦ *n* **2** person who studies hard.

swum *v* past participle of SWIM.

swung *v* past of SWING.

sybarite [**sib**-bar-ite] *n* lover of luxury. **sybaritic** *adj*

sycamore *n* tree with five-pointed leaves and two-winged fruits.

sycophant *n* person who uses flattery to win favour from people with power or influence. **sycophantic** *adj* **sycophancy** *n*

syllable *n* part of a word pronounced as a unit. **syllabic** *adj*

syllabub *n* dessert of beaten cream, sugar, and wine.

syllabus *n, pl* **-buses, -bi** list of subjects for a course of study.

> The usual plural is *syllabuses.*

syllogism *n* form of logical reasoning consisting of two premises and a conclusion. **syllogistic** *adj*

sylph *n* **1** slender graceful girl or woman. **2** imaginary being supposed to inhabit the air. **sylphlike** *adj*

sylvan *adj Lit* relating to woods and trees.

symbiosis *n* close association of two species living together to their mutual benefit. **symbiotic** *adj*

symbol *n* sign or thing that stands for something else. **symbolic** *adj* **symbolically** *adv* **symbolism** *n* **1** representation of something by symbols. **2** movement in art and literature using symbols to express abstract and mystical ideas. **symbolist** *n, adj* **symbolize** *v* **1** be a symbol of. **2** represent with a symbol.

symmetry *n* **1** state of having two halves that are mirror images of each other. **2** beauty resulting from a balanced arrangement of parts. **symmetrical** *adj* **symmetrically** *adv*

sympathy *n, pl* **-thies 1** compassion for someone's pain or distress. **2** agreement with someone's feelings or interests. **3** feelings of loyalty and support for an idea. **sympathetic** *adj* **1** feeling or showing sympathy. **2** likeable or appealing. **sympathetically** *adv* **sympathize** *v* **1** feel or express sympathy. **2** agree with. **sympathizer** *n*

symphony *n, pl* **-nies 1** composition for orchestra, with several movements. **2** visually pleasing arrangement. **symphonic** *adj*

symposium *n, pl* **-siums, -sia 1** conference for discussion of a particular topic. **2** collection of essays on a topic.

symptom *n* **1** sign indicating the presence of an illness. **2** sign that something is wrong. **symptomatic** *adj*

synagogue *n* Jewish place of worship and religious instruction.

sync, synch *Informal* ♦ *n* **1** synchronization. ♦ *v* **2** synchronize.

synchromesh *adj* (of a gearbox) having a device that synchronizes the speeds of gears before they engage.

synchronize *v* **1** (of two or more people) perform (an action) at the same time. **2** set (watches) to show the same time. **3** match (the soundtrack and action of a film) precisely. **synchronization** *n* **synchronous** *adj* happening or existing at the same time.

syncopate *v Music* stress the weak beats

in (a rhythm) instead of the strong ones. **syncopation** *n*

syncope [**sing**-kop-ee] *n Med* a faint.

syndicate *n* **1** group of people or firms undertaking a joint business project. **2** agency that sells material to several newspapers. ♦ *v* **3** publish (material) in several newspapers. **4** form a syndicate. **syndication** *n*

syndrome *n* **1** combination of symptoms indicating a particular disease. **2** set of characteristics indicating a particular problem.

synergy *n* potential ability for people or groups to be more successful working together than on their own.

synod *n* church council.

synonym *n* word with the same meaning as another. **synonymous** *adj*

synopsis *n, pl* **-ses** summary or outline.

syntax *n Grammar* way in which words are arranged to form phrases and sentences. **syntactic** *adj*

synthesis *n, pl* **-ses** **1** combination of objects or ideas into a whole. **2** artificial production of a substance. **synthesize** *v* produce by synthesis. **synthesizer** *n* electronic musical instrument producing a range of sounds. **synthetic** *adj* **1** (of a substance) made artificially. **2** not genuine, insincere. **synthetically** *adv*

syphilis *n* serious sexually transmitted disease. **syphilitic** *adj*

syphon *n, v* same as SIPHON.

Syrian *adj* **1** of Syria, its people, or their dialect of Arabic. ♦ *n* **2** person from Syria.

syringe *n* **1** device for withdrawing or injecting fluids, consisting of a hollow cylinder, a piston, and a hollow needle. ♦ *v* **2** wash out or inject with a syringe.

syrup *n* **1** solution of sugar in water. **2** thick sweet liquid. **3** sugar solution containing medicine. **syrupy** *adj* **1** thick and sweet. **2** excessively sentimental.

system *n* **1** method or set of methods. **2** orderliness. **3** scheme of classification or arrangement. **4** network or assembly of parts that form a whole. **5** body considered as a whole. **the system** society or government regarded as oppressive and exploitative. **systematic** *adj* **systematically** *adv* **systematize** *v* organize using a system. **systematization** *n* **systemic** *adj* affecting the entire animal or body. **systemically** *adv*

systole [**siss**-tol-ee] *n* regular contraction of the heart as it pumps blood. **systolic** *adj*

T t

t tonne.

T *n* **to a T 1** in every detail. **2** perfectly.

t. ton.

ta *interj Informal* thank you.

Ta *Chem* tantalum.

TA Territorial Army.

tab *n* small flap or projecting label. **keep tabs on** *Informal* watch closely.

tabard *n* short sleeveless tunic decorated with a coat of arms, worn in medieval times.

Tabasco *n* ® very hot red pepper sauce.

tabby *n, pl* **-bies,** *adj* (cat) with dark stripes on a lighter background.

tabernacle *n* **1** portable shrine of the Israelites. **2** Christian place of worship not called a church. **3** *RC Church* receptacle for the consecrated Host.

tabla *n, pl* **-bla, -blas** one of a pair of Indian drums played with the hands.

table *n* **1** piece of furniture with a flat top supported by legs. **2** arrangement of information in columns. ♦ *v* **3** submit (a motion) for discussion by a meeting. **4** *US* suspend discussion of (a proposal). **tablecloth** *n* cloth for covering the top of a table, esp. during meals. **tableland** *n* high plateau. **tablespoon** *n* large spoon for serving food. **table tennis** game like tennis played on a table with small bats and a light ball.

tableau [**tab**-loh] *n, pl* **-leaux** silent motionless group arranged to represent some scene.

table d'hôte [**tah**-bla **dote**] *n, pl* **tables d'hôte,** *adj* (meal) having a set number of dishes at a fixed price.

tablet *n* **1** pill of compressed medicinal substance. **2** flattish cake of soap etc. **3** inscribed slab of stone etc.

tabloid *n* small-sized newspaper with many photographs and a concise, usu. sensational style.

taboo *n, pl* **-boos 1** prohibition resulting from religious or social conventions. ♦ *adj* **2** forbidden by a taboo.

tabor *n* small drum, used esp. in the Middle Ages.

tabular *adj* arranged in a table. **tabulate** *v* arrange (information) in a table. **tabulation** *n*

tachograph *n* device for recording the speed and distance travelled by a motor vehicle.

tachometer *n* device for measuring speed, esp. that of a revolving shaft.

tacit [**tass**-it] *adj* implied but not spoken. **tacitly** *adv*

taciturn [**tass**-it-turn] *adj* habitually uncommunicative. **taciturnity** *n*

tack[1] *n* **1** short nail with a large head. **2** long loose stitch. ♦ *v* **3** fasten with tacks. **4** stitch with tacks. **tack on** *v* append.

tack[2] *n* **1** course of a ship sailing obliquely into the wind. **2** course of action. ♦ *v* **3** sail into the wind on a zigzag course.

tack[3] *n* riding harness for horses.

tackle *v* **1** deal with (a task). **2** confront (an opponent). **3** *Sport* attempt to get the ball from (an opposing player). ♦ *n* **4** *Sport* act of tackling an opposing player. **5** equipment for a particular activity. **6** set of ropes and pulleys for lifting heavy weights.

tacky[1] *adj* **tackier, tackiest** slightly sticky. **tackiness** *n*

tacky[2] *adj* **tackier, tackiest 1** *Informal* vulgar and tasteless. **2** shabby. **tackiness** *n*

tact *n* skill in avoiding giving offence. **tactful** *adj* **tactfully** *adv* **tactless** *adj* **tactlessly** *adv* **tactlessness** *n*

tactics *n* art of directing military forces in battle. **tactic** *n* method or plan to achieve an end. **tactical** *adj* **tactically** *adv* **tactician** *n*

tactile *adj* of or having the sense of touch.

tadpole *n* limbless tailed larva of a frog or toad.

taffeta *n* shiny silk or rayon fabric.

tag[1] *n* **1** label bearing information. **2** pointed end of a cord or lace. **3** trite quotation. ♦ *v* **tagging, tagged 4** attach a tag to. **tag along** *v* accompany someone, esp. if uninvited.

tag[2] *n* **1** children's game where the person being chased becomes the chaser upon being touched. ♦ *v* **tagging, tagged 2** touch and catch in this game.

tagliatelle *n* pasta in long narrow strips.

tail *n* **1** rear part of an animal's body, usu. forming a flexible appendage. **2** rear or last part or parts of something. **3** *Informal* person employed to follow and spy on another. ♦ *pl* **4** *Informal* tail coat. ♦ *adj* **5** at the rear. ♦ *v* **6** *Informal* follow (someone) secretly. **turn tail** run away. **tailless** *adj* **tails** *adv* with the side of a coin uppermost that does not have a portrait of a head on it. **tailback** *n* queue of traffic stretching back from an obstruction. **tailboard** *n* removable or hinged rear board on a lorry etc. **tail coat** man's coat with a long back split into two below the waist. **tail off, away** *v* diminish gradually. **tailplane** *n* small stabilizing wing at the rear of an aircraft. **tailspin** *n* uncontrolled spinning dive of an aircraft. **tailwind** *n* wind coming from the rear.

tailor *n* **1** person who makes men's clothes. ♦ *v* **2** cut or style (a garment) to specific requirements. **3** adapt to suit a purpose. **tailored** *adj* made to fit close to a particular person's body. **tailor-made** *adj* **1** made by a tailor. **2** perfect for a purpose.

taint *v* **1** spoil with a small amount of decay, contamination, or other bad quality. ♦ *n* **2** something that taints.

take *v* **taking, took, taken 1** remove from a place. **2** carry or accompany. **3** use. **4** get possession of, esp. dishonestly. **5** capture. **6** select. **7** require (time, resources, or ability). **8** assume. **9** accept. **10** perform, do, or make. **11** write down. **12** subtract or deduct. ♦ *n* **13** one of a series of recordings from which the best will be used. **take place** happen. **taking** *adj* charming. **takings** *pl n* money received by a shop. **take after** *v* look or behave like (a parent etc.). **take against** *v* start to dislike. **take away** *v* remove or subtract. **takeaway** *adj* **1** (of food) sold for consumption away from the premises. ♦ *n* **2** shop or restaurant selling meals for eating elsewhere. **3** meal bought at a takeaway. **take in** *v* **1** understand. **2** deceive or swindle. **3** make (clothing) smaller. **take off** *v* **1** (of an aircraft) leave the ground. **2** *Informal* depart. **3** *Informal* become successful. **4** *Informal* parody. **takeoff** *n* **takeover** *n* act of taking control of a company by buying a large number of its shares. **take up** *v* **1** occupy or fill (space or time). **2** adopt the study or activity of. **3** shorten (a garment). **4** accept (an offer).

talc *n* **1** talcum powder. **2** soft mineral of magnesium silicate. **talcum powder** powder, usu. scented, used to dry or perfume the body.

tale *n* **1** story. **2** malicious piece of gossip.

talent *n* **1** natural ability. **2** *Informal* attractive members of the opposite sex. **3** ancient unit of weight or money. **talented** *adj*

talisman *n, pl* **-mans** object believed to have magic power. **talismanic** *adj*

talk *v* **1** express ideas or feelings by means of speech. **2** utter. **3** discuss, e.g. *let's talk business.* **4** reveal information. **5** (be able to) speak in a specified language. ♦ *n* **6** speech or lecture. **7** conversation. **talker** *n* **talkative** *adj* fond of talking. **talk back** *v* answer impudently. **talking-to** *n Informal* telling-off. **talk into** *v* persuade (someone) to do something by talking. **talk out of** *v* dissuade (someone) from doing something by talking.

tall *adj* **1** higher than average. **2** of a specified height. **tall order** difficult task. **tall story** unlikely and probably untrue tale.

tallboy *n* high chest of drawers.

tallow *n* hard animal fat used to make candles.

tally *v* **-lying, -lied 1** (of two things) correspond. ♦ *n, pl* **-lies** 2 record of a debt or score.

tally-ho *interj* huntsman's cry when the quarry is sighted.

Talmud *n* body of Jewish law. **Talmudic** *adj*

talon *n* bird's hooked claw.

tamarind *n* **1** tropical tree. **2** its acid fruit.

tamarisk *n* evergreen shrub with slender branches and feathery flower clusters.

tambourine *n* percussion instrument like a small drum with jingling metal discs attached.

tame *adj* **1** (of animals) brought under human control. **2** (of animals) not afraid of people. **3** meek or submissive. **4** uninteresting. ♦ *v* **5** make tame. **tamely** *adv* **tamer** *n*

Tamil *n* **1** member of a people of Sri Lanka and S India. **2** their language.

tam-o'-shanter *n* brimless wool cap with a bobble in the centre.

tamp *v* pack down by repeated taps.

tamper *v* (foll. by *with*) interfere.

tampon *n* absorbent plug of cotton wool inserted into the vagina during menstruation.

tan *n* **1** brown coloration of the skin from exposure to sunlight. ♦ *v* **tanning, tanned 2** (of skin) go brown from exposure to sunlight. **3** convert (a hide) into leather. ♦ *adj* **4** yellowish-brown. **tannery** *n, pl* **-eries** place where hides are tanned.

tandem *n* bicycle for two riders, one behind the other. **in tandem** together.

tandoori *adj* (of food) cooked in an Indian clay oven.

tang *n* **1** strong taste or smell. **2** trace or hint. **tangy** *adj* **tangier, tangiest**

tangent *n* **1** line that touches a curve without intersecting it. **2** (in trigonometry) ratio of the length of the opposite side to that of the adjacent side of a right-angled triangle. **go off at a tangent** suddenly take a completely different line of thought or action. **tangential** *adj* **1** of superficial relevance only. **2** of a tangent. **tangentially** *adv*

tangerine *n* small orange-like fruit of an Asian citrus tree.

tangible *adj* **1** able to be touched. **2** clear and definite. **tangibly** *adv* **tangibility** *n*

tangle *n* **1** confused mass or situation. ♦ *v* **2** twist together in a tangle. **3** (often foll. by *with*) come into conflict.

tango *n, pl* **-gos 1** S American dance. ♦ *v* **2** dance a tango.

tank *n* **1** container for liquids or gases. **2** armoured fighting vehicle moving on tracks. **tanker** *n* ship or lorry for carrying liquid in bulk.

tankard *n* large beer-mug, often with a hinged lid.

tannin, tannic acid *n* vegetable substance used in tanning.

Tannoy *n* ® type of public-address system.

tansy *n, pl* **-sies** yellow-flowered plant.

tantalize *v* torment by showing but withholding something desired. **tantalizing** *adj* **tantalizingly** *adv*

tantalum *n Chem* hard greyish-white metallic element.

tantamount *adj* **tantamount to** equivalent in effect to.

tantrum *n* childish outburst of temper.

Taoism [**tow**-iz-zum] *n* system of religion and philosophy advocating a simple, honest life and noninterference with the course of natural events. **Taoist** *n, adj*

tap[1] *v* **tapping, tapped 1** knock lightly and usu. repeatedly. ♦ *n* **2** light knock. **tap dancing** style of dancing in which the feet beat out an elaborate rhythm.

tap[2] *n* **1** valve to control the flow of liquid from a pipe or cask. ♦ *v* **tapping, tapped 2** listen in on (a telephone call) secretly by making an illegal connection. **3** obtain something useful or desirable from (something). **4** draw off with or as if with a tap. **on tap 1** *Informal* readily available. **2** (of beer etc.) drawn from a cask.

tape *n* **1** narrow long strip of material. **2** (recording made on) a cassette containing magnetic tape. **3** string stretched across a race track to mark the finish. ♦ *v* **4** record on magnetic tape. **5** bind or fasten with tape. **have a person, situation taped** *Informal* have full understanding and control of a person or situation. **tape measure** tape marked off in centimetres or inches for measuring. **tape recorder** device for recording and reproducing sound on magnetic tape. **tapeworm** *n* long flat parasitic worm living in the intestines of vertebrates.

taper *v* **1** become narrower towards one end. ♦ *n* **2** long thin candle. **3** narrowing. **taper off** *v* become gradually less.

tapestry *n, pl* **-tries** fabric decorated with coloured woven designs.

tapioca *n* beadlike starch made from cassava root, used in puddings.

tapir [**tape**-er] *n* piglike mammal of tropical America and SE Asia, with a long snout.

tappet *n* short steel rod in an engine, transferring motion from one part to another.

taproot *n* main root of a plant, growing straight down.

tar *n* **1** thick black liquid distilled from coal etc. ♦ *v* **tarring, tarred 2** coat with tar.

taramasalata *n* creamy pink pâté made from fish roe.

tarantella *n* **1** lively Italian dance. **2** music for this.

tarantula *n* large hairy spider with a poisonous bite.

tardy *adj* **tardier, tardiest** slow or late. **tardily** *adv* **tardiness** *n*

tare[1] *n* **1** weight of the wrapping or container of goods. **2** unladen weight of a vehicle.

tare[2] *n* **1** type of vetch plant. **2** *Bible* weed.

target *n* **1** object or person a missile is aimed at. **2** goal or objective. **3** object of criticism. ♦ *v* **-geting, -geted 4** aim or direct.

tariff *n* **1** tax levied on imports. **2** list of fixed prices.

Tarmac *n* **1** ® mixture of tar, bitumen, and crushed stones used for roads etc. **2** (**t-**) airport runway.

tarn *n* small mountain lake.

tarnish *v* **1** make or become stained or less bright. **2** damage or taint. ♦ *n* **3** discoloration or blemish.

tarot [**tarr**-oh] *n* special pack of cards used mainly in fortune-telling. **tarot card** card in a tarot pack.

tarpaulin *n* (sheet of) heavy waterproof fabric.

tarragon *n* aromatic herb.

tarry *v* **-rying, -ried** *Old-fashioned* **1** linger or delay. **2** stay briefly.

tarsus *n, pl* **-si** bones of the heel and ankle collectively.

tart[1] *n* pie or flan with a sweet filling.

tart[2] *adj* sharp or bitter. **tartly** *adv* **tartness** *n*

tart[3] *n Informal* sexually provocative or promiscuous woman. **tart up** *v Informal* dress or decorate in a smart or flashy way.

tartan *n* **1** design of straight lines crossing at right angles, esp. one associated with a Scottish clan. **2** cloth with such a pattern.

tartar[1] *n* **1** hard deposit on the teeth. **2** deposit formed during the fermentation of wine.

tartar[2] *n* fearsome or formidable person.

Tartar, Tatar *n* **1** member of a Mongoloid people who established a powerful state in central Asia in the 13th century. **2** descendant of this people. ♦ *adj* **3** of the Tartars.

tartare sauce *n* mayonnaise sauce mixed with chopped herbs and capers, served with seafood.

tartrazine [**tar**-traz-zeen] *n* artificial yellow dye used in food etc.

TAS Tasmania.

task *n* (difficult or unpleasant) piece of work to be done. **take to task** criticize or scold. **task force** (military) group formed to carry out a specific task. **taskmaster** *n* person who enforces hard work.

Tasmanian devil *n* small carnivorous

marsupial found in Tasmania.

tassel *n* decorative fringed knot of threads.

taste *n* **1** sense by which the flavour of a substance is distinguished in the mouth. **2** distinctive flavour. **3** small amount tasted. **4** brief experience of something. **5** liking. **6** ability to appreciate what is beautiful or excellent. ♦ *v* **7** distinguish the taste of (a substance). **8** take a small amount of (something) into the mouth. **9** have a specific taste. **10** experience briefly. **tasteful** *adj* having or showing good taste. **tastefully** *adv* **tasteless** *adj* **1** bland or insipid. **2** showing bad taste. **tastelessly** *adv* **tasty** *adj* pleasantly flavoured. **taste bud** small organ on the tongue which perceives flavours.

tat *n* tatty or tasteless article(s).

Tatar *n, adj* same as TARTAR.

tattered *adj* ragged or torn. **in tatters** in ragged pieces.

tattle *v, n* gossip or chatter.

tattoo[1] *n* **1** pattern made on the body by pricking the skin and staining it with indelible inks. ♦ *v* **-tooing, -tooed 2** make such a pattern on the skin. **tattooist** *n*

tattoo[2] *n* **1** military display or pageant. **2** drumming or tapping.

tatty *adj* **-tier, -tiest** shabby or worn out.

taught *v* past of TEACH.

taunt *v* **1** tease with jeers. ♦ *n* **2** jeering remark.

taupe *adj* brownish-grey.

Taurus *n* (the bull) second sign of the zodiac.

taut *adj* **1** drawn tight. **2** showing nervous strain. **tauten** *v* make or become taut.

tautology *n, pl* **-gies** use of words which merely repeat something already stated. **tautological** *adj*

tavern *n Old-fashioned* pub.

tawdry *adj* **-drier, -driest** cheap, showy, and of poor quality.

tawny *adj* **-nier, -niest** yellowish-brown.

tax *n* **1** compulsory payment levied by a government on income, property, etc. to raise revenue. ♦ *v* **2** levy a tax on. **3** make heavy demands on. **taxable** *adj* **taxation** *n* levying of taxes. **taxing** *adj* demanding, onerous. **tax-free** *adj* (of goods and services) not taxed. **taxpayer** *n* **tax relief** reduction in the amount of tax a person or company has to pay. **tax return** statement of personal income for tax purposes.

taxi *n* **1** (also **taxicab**) car with a driver that may be hired to take people to any specified destination. ♦ *v* **taxiing, taxied 2** (of an aircraft) run along the ground before taking off or after landing. **taximeter** *n* meter in a taxi that registers the fare. **taxi rank** place where taxis wait to be hired.

taxidermy *n* art of stuffing and mounting animal skins to give them a lifelike appearance. **taxidermist** *n*

taxonomy *n* classification of plants and animals into groups. **taxonomic** *adj* **taxonomist** *n*

Tb *Chem* terbium.

TB tuberculosis.

T-bone steak *n* steak cut from the sirloin of beef, containing a T-shaped bone.

tbs., tbsp. tablespoon(ful).

Tc *Chem* technetium.

te *n Music* (in tonic sol-fa) seventh degree of any major scale.

Te *Chem* tellurium.

tea *n* **1** drink made from infusing the dried leaves of an Asian bush in boiling water. **2** leaves used to make this drink. **3** main evening meal. **4** light afternoon meal of tea, cakes, etc. **5** drink like tea, made from other plants. **tea bag** small porous bag of tea leaves. **tea cosy** covering for a teapot to keep the tea warm. **teapot** *n* container with a lid, spout, and handle for making and serving tea. **teaspoon** *n* small spoon for stirring tea. **tea towel, tea cloth** towel for drying dishes.

teach *v* **teaching, taught 1** tell or show (someone) how to do something. **2** give lessons in (a subject). **3** cause to learn or understand. **teacher** *n* **teaching** *n*

teak *n* very hard wood of an E Indian tree.

teal *n* kind of small duck.

team *n* **1** group of people forming one side in a game. **2** group of people or animals working together. **teamster** *n US* lorry driver. **team spirit** willingness to cooperate as part of a team. **team up** *v* make or join a team. **teamwork** *n* cooperative work by a team.

tear[1], **teardrop** *n* drop of fluid appearing in and falling from the eye. **in tears** weeping. **tearful** *adj* weeping or about to weep. **tear gas** gas that stings the eyes and causes temporary blindness. **tear-jerker** *n Informal* excessively sentimental film or book.

tear[2] *v* **tearing, tore, torn 1** rip a hole in. **2** rip apart. **3** rush. **4** remove by force. ♦ *n* **5** hole or split. **tearaway** *n* wild or unruly person.

tease *v* **1** make fun of (someone) in a provoking or playful way. ♦ *n* **2** person who teases. **teaser** *n* annoying or difficult problem. **teasing** *adj, n* **tease out** *v* remove tangles from (hair etc.) by combing.

teasel, teazel, teazle *n* plant with prickly leaves and flowers.

teat *n* **1** nipple of a breast or udder. **2** rubber nipple of a feeding bottle.

tech *n Informal* technical college.

technetium [tek-**neesh**-ee-um] *n Chem* artificially produced silvery-grey metallic element.

technical *adj* **1** of or specializing in industrial, practical, or mechanical arts and applied sciences. **2** skilled in technical subjects. **3** relating to a particular field. **4** according to the letter of the law. **5** showing technique, e.g. *technical brilliance.* **technically** *adv* **technicality** *n, pl* **-ties** petty point based on a strict application of rules. **technician** *n* person skilled in a particular technical field. **technical college** higher educational institution with courses in art and technical subjects.

Technicolor *n* ® system of colour photography used for the cinema.

technique *n* **1** method or skill used for a particular task. **2** technical proficiency.

techno *n* type of electronic dance music with a very fast beat.

technocracy *n, pl* **-cies** government by technical experts. **technocrat** *n*

technology *n* **1** application of practical or mechanical sciences to industry or commerce. **2** scientific methods used in a particular field. **technological** *adj* **technologist** *n*

tectonics *n* study of the earth's crust and the forces affecting it.

teddy *n, pl* **-dies 1** teddy bear. **2** combined camisole and knickers. **teddy bear** soft toy bear.

teddy boy *n* youth who wore mock Edwardian fashions in Britain esp. in the mid-1950s.

Te Deum [tee **dee**-um] *n* ancient Latin hymn of praise.

tedious *adj* causing fatigue or boredom. **tediously** *adv* **tedium** *n* monotony.

tee *n* **1** small peg from which a golf ball can be played at the start of each hole. **2** area of a golf course from which the first stroke of a hole is made. **tee off** *v* make the first stroke of a hole in golf.

teem[1] *v* be full of.

teem[2] *v* rain heavily.

teenage *adj* of the period of life between the ages of 13 and 19. **teenager** *n* person aged between 13 and 19.

teens *pl n* period of being a teenager.

teeny *adj* **-nier, -niest** *Informal* extremely small.

teepee *n* same as TEPEE.

tee-shirt *n* same as T-SHIRT.

teeter *v* wobble or move unsteadily.

teeth *n* plural of TOOTH.

teethe *v* (of a baby) grow his or her first teeth. **teething troubles** problems during the early stages of something.

teetotal *adj* drinking no alcohol. **teetotaller** *n*

TEFL Teaching of English as a Foreign Language.

Teflon *n* ® substance used for nonstick coatings on saucepans etc.

telecommunications *n* communications using telephone, radio, television, etc.

telegram *n* formerly, a message sent by telegraph.

telegraph *n* **1** formerly, a system for sending messages over a distance along a cable. ♦ *v* **2** communicate by telegraph. **telegraphic** *adj* **telegraphist** *n* **telegraphy** *n* science or use of a telegraph.

telekinesis *n* movement of objects by thought or willpower.

Telemessage *n* ® message sent by telephone or telex and delivered in printed form.

telemetry *n* use of electronic devices to record or measure a distant event and transmit the data to a receiver.

teleology *n* belief that all things have a predetermined purpose. **teleological** *adj*

telepathy *n* direct communication between minds. **telepathic** *adj* **telepathically** *adv*

telephone *n* **1** device for transmitting sound over a distance along wires. ♦ *v* **2** call or talk to (a person) by telephone. **telephony** *n* **telephonic** *adj* **telephonist** *n* person operating a telephone switchboard.

telephoto lens *n* camera lens producing a magnified image of a distant object.

teleprinter *n* apparatus like a typewriter for sending and receiving typed messages by wire.

Teleprompter *n* ® device under a television camera enabling a speaker to read the script while appearing to look at the camera.

telesales *n* selling of a product or service by telephone.

telescope *n* **1** optical instrument for magnifying distant objects. ♦ *v* **2** shorten. **telescopic** *adj*

Teletext *n* ® system which shows information and news on television screens.

television *n* **1** system of producing a moving image and accompanying sound on a distant screen. **2** device for receiving broadcast signals and converting them into sound and pictures. **3** content of television programmes. **televise** *v* broadcast on television. **televisual** *adj*

telex *n* **1** international communication service using teleprinters. **2** machine used in such a service. **3** message sent by telex. ♦ *v* **4** transmit by telex.

tell *v* **telling, told 1** make known in words. **2** order or instruct. **3** give an account of. **4** discern or distinguish. **5** have an effect. **6** *Informal* reveal secrets. **teller** *n* **1** narrator. **2** bank cashier. **3** person who counts votes. **telling** *adj* having a marked effect. **tell off** *v* reprimand. **telling-off** *n* **telltale** *n* **1** person who reveals secrets. ♦ *adj* **2** revealing.

tellurium *n Chem* brittle silvery-white nonmetallic element.

telly *n, pl* **-lies** *Informal* television.

temerity [tim-**merr**-it-tee] *n* boldness or audacity.

temp *Informal* ♦ *n* **1** temporary employee, esp. a secretary. ♦ *v* **2** work as a temp.

temp. **1** temperature. **2** temporary.

temper *n* **1** outburst of anger. **2** tendency to become angry. **3** calm mental condition, e.g. *I lost my temper.* **4** frame of mind. ♦ *v* **5** make less extreme. **6** strengthen or toughen (metal).

tempera *n* painting medium for powdered pigments.

temperament *n* person's character or disposition. **temperamental** *adj* **1** having changeable moods. **2** *Informal* erratic and unreliable. **temperamentally** *adv*

temperate *adj* **1** (of climate) not extreme. **2** self-restrained or moderate. **temperance** *n* **1** moderation. **2** abstinence from alcohol.

temperature *n* **1** degree of heat or cold. **2** *Informal* abnormally high body temperature.

tempest *n* violent storm. **tempestuous** *adj* **1** violent or stormy. **2** extremely emotional or passionate. **tempestuously** *adv*

template *n* pattern used to cut out shapes accurately.

temple[1] *n* building for worship.

temple[2] *n* region on either side of the forehead. **temporal** *adj*

tempo *n, pl* **-pi, -pos 1** rate or pace. **2** speed of a piece of music.

temporal *adj* **1** of time. **2** worldly rather than spiritual.

temporary *adj* lasting only for a short time. **temporarily** *adv*

temporize *v* **1** gain time by negotiation or evasiveness. **2** adapt to circumstances.

tempt *v* entice (a person) to do something wrong. **tempt fate** take foolish or unnecessary risks. **tempter, temptress** *n* **temptation** *n* **1** tempting. **2** tempting thing. **tempting** *adj* attractive or inviting.

ten *adj, n* one more than nine. **tenth** *adj, n* (of) number ten in a series.

tenable *adj* able to be upheld or maintained.

tenacious *adj* **1** holding fast. **2** stubborn. **tenaciously** *adv* **tenacity** *n*

tenant *n* person who rents land or a building. **tenancy** *n*

tench *n, pl* **tench** freshwater game fish of the carp family.

tend[1] *v* **1** be inclined. **2** go in the direction of. **tendency** *n* inclination to act in a certain way. **tendentious** *adj* biased, not impartial.

tend[2] *v* take care of.

tender[1] *adj* **1** not tough. **2** gentle and affectionate. **3** vulnerable or sensitive. **tenderly** *adv* **tenderness** *n* **tenderize** *v* soften (meat) by pounding or treatment with a special substance. **tenderizer** *n* **tenderloin** *n* tender cut of pork from between the sirloin and the ribs.

tender[2] *v* **1** offer. **2** make a formal offer to supply goods or services at a stated cost. ♦ *n* **3** such an offer. **legal tender** currency that must, by law, be accepted as payment.

tender[3] *n* **1** small boat that brings supplies to a larger ship in a port. **2** carriage for fuel and water attached to a steam locomotive.

tendon *n* strong tissue attaching a muscle to a bone.

tendril *n* slender stem by which a climbing plant clings.

tenement *n* building divided into several flats.

tenet [**ten**-nit] *n* doctrine or belief.

tenner *n Informal* ten-pound note.

tennis *n* game in which players use rackets to hit a ball back and forth over a net.

tenon *n* projecting end on a piece of wood fitting into a slot in another.

tenor *n* **1** (singer with) the second highest male voice. **2** general meaning. ♦ *adj* **3** (of a voice or instrument) between alto and baritone.

tenpin bowling *n* game in which players try to knock over ten skittles by rolling a ball at them.

tense[1] *adj* **1** emotionally strained. **2** stretched tight. ♦ *v* **3** make or become tense.

tense[2] *n Grammar* form of a verb showing the time of action.

tensile *adj* of tension. **tensile strength** measure of the ability of a material to withstand lengthways stress.

tension *n* **1** hostility or suspense. **2** emotional strain. **3** degree of stretching.

tent *n* portable canvas shelter.

tentacle *n* flexible organ of many invertebrates, used for grasping, feeding, etc.

tentative *adj* **1** provisional or experimental. **2** cautious or hesitant. **tentatively** *adv*

tenterhooks *pl n* **on tenterhooks** in anxious suspense.

tenuous *adj* slight or flimsy. **tenuously** *adv*

tenure *n* **1** (period of) the holding of an office or position. **2** legal right to live in a building or use land for a period of time.

tenuto *adj, adv Music* (of a note) to be

held for or beyond its full time value.

tepee [**tee**-pee] *n* cone-shaped tent, formerly used by Native Americans.

tepid *adj* **1** slightly warm. **2** half-hearted.

tequila *n* Mexican alcoholic drink.

terbium *n Chem* rare metallic element.

tercentenary *adj, n, pl* **-naries** (of) a three hundredth anniversary.

term *n* **1** word or expression. **2** fixed period. **3** period of the year when a school etc. is open or a lawcourt holds sessions. ♦ *pl* **4** conditions. **5** mutual relationship. ♦ *v* **6** name or designate.

termagant *n* unpleasant and bad-tempered woman.

terminal *adj* **1** (of an illness) ending in death. **2** at or being an end. ♦ *n* **3** place where people or vehicles begin or end a journey. **4** point where current enters or leaves an electrical device. **5** keyboard and VDU having input and output links with a computer. **terminally** *adv* **terminal velocity** *Physics* maximum velocity reached by a body falling under gravity.

terminate *v* bring or come to an end. **termination** *n* **terminable** *adj* capable of being terminated.

terminology *n* technical terms relating to a subject. **terminological** *adj*

terminus *n, pl* **-ni, -nuses** railway or bus station at the end of a line.

termite *n* white antlike insect that destroys timber.

tern *n* gull-like sea bird with a forked tail and pointed wings.

ternary *adj* **1** consisting of three parts. **2** *Maths* (of a number system) to the base three.

Terpsichorean *adj* of dancing.

terrace *n* **1** row of houses built as one block. **2** paved area next to a building. **3** level tier cut out of a hill. ♦ *pl* **4** (also **terracing**) tiered area in a stadium where spectators stand. ♦ *v* **5** form into or provide with a terrace.

terracotta *adj, n* **1** (made of) brownish-red unglazed pottery. ♦ *adj* **2** brownish-red.

terra firma *n Latin* dry land or solid ground.

terrain *n* area of ground, esp. with reference to its physical character.

terrapin *n* small turtle-like reptile.

terrarium *n, pl* **-raria, -rariums** enclosed container for small plants or animals.

terrazzo *n, pl* **-zos** floor of marble chips set in mortar and polished.

terrestrial *adj* **1** of the earth. **2** of or living on land.

terrible *adj* **1** very serious. **2** *Informal* very bad. **3** causing fear. **terribly** *adv*

terrier *n* any of various breeds of small active dog.

terrific *adj* **1** great or intense. **2** *Informal* excellent.

terrify *v* **-fying, -fied** fill with fear. **terrified** *adj* **terrifying** *adj* **terrifyingly** *adv*

terrine [terr-**reen**] *n* **1** earthenware dish with a lid. **2** pâté or similar food.

territory *n, pl* **-ries** **1** district. **2** area under the control of a particular government. **3** area inhabited and defended by an animal. **4** area of knowledge. **5** (**T-**) region of a country, esp. of a federal state, that does not enjoy full rights. **territorial** *adj* **Territorial Army** reserve army. **territorial waters** parts of the sea over which a country exercises control, esp. with regard to fishing rights.

terror *n* **1** great fear. **2** terrifying person or thing. **3** *Informal* troublesome person or thing. **terrorism** *n* use of violence and intimidation to achieve political ends. **terrorist** *n, adj* **terrorize** *v* force or oppress by fear or violence.

terry *n* fabric with small loops covering both sides, used esp. for making towels.

terse *adj* **1** neat and concise. **2** curt. **tersely** *adv*

tertiary [**tur**-shar-ee] *adj* third in degree, order, etc.

Terylene *n* ® synthetic polyester yarn or fabric.

TESSA Tax Exempt Special Savings Account.

tessellated *adj* paved or inlaid with a mosaic of small tiles. **tessera** *n, pl*

-serae small square tile used in mosaics.

test *v* **1** try out to ascertain the worth, capability, or endurance of. **2** carry out an examination on. ♦ *n* **3** critical examination. **4** Test match. **testing** *adj* **test case** lawsuit that establishes a precedent. **Test match** one of a series of international cricket or rugby matches. **test pilot** pilot who tests the performance of new aircraft. **test tube** narrow round-bottomed glass tube used in scientific experiments. **test-tube baby** baby conceived outside the mother's body.

testament *n* **1** proof or tribute. **2** *Law* will. **3** (**T-**) one of the two main divisions of the Bible.

testate *adj* having left a valid will. **testacy** *n* **testator** [test-**tay**-tor], (*fem*) **testatrix** [test-**tay**-triks] *n* maker of a will.

testicle *n* either of the two male reproductive glands.

testify *v* **-fying, -fied** give evidence under oath. **testify to** be evidence of.

testimony *n, pl* **-nies** **1** declaration of truth or fact. **2** evidence given under oath. **testimonial** *n* **1** recommendation of the worth of a person or thing. **2** tribute for services or achievement.

> A *testimonial* is an open letter of recommendation about someone. A *reference* is a confidential report that is not read by the person who is the subject.

testis *n, pl* **-tes** testicle.

testosterone *n* male sex hormone secreted by the testes.

testy *adj* **-tier, -tiest** irritable or touchy. **testily** *adv* **testiness** *n*

tetanus *n* acute infectious disease producing muscular spasms and convulsions.

tetchy *adj* **tetchier, tetchiest** cross and irritable.

tête-à-tête *n, pl* **-têtes, -tête** private conversation.

tether *n* **1** rope or chain for tying an animal to a spot. ♦ *v* **2** tie up with rope. **at the end of one's tether** at the limit of one's endurance.

tetragon *n* figure with four angles and four sides. **tetragonal** *adj*

tetrahedron [tet-ra-**heed**-ron] *n, pl* **-drons, -dra** solid figure with four faces.

tetralogy *n, pl* **-gies** series of four related works.

tetrameter [tet-**tram**-it-er] *n* **1** line of poetry with four metrical feet. **2** verse composed of such lines.

Teutonic [tew-**tonn**-ik] *adj* of or like the (ancient) Germans.

text *n* **1** main body of a book as distinct from illustrations etc. **2** any written material. **3** passage of the Bible as the subject of a sermon. **4** novel or play studied for a course. **textual** *adj* **textbook** *n* **1** standard book on a particular subject. ♦ *adj* **2** perfect, e.g. *a textbook landing.*

textile *n* **1** fabric or cloth, esp. woven. ♦ *adj* **2** of (the making of) fabrics.

texture *n* structure, feel, or consistency. **textured** *adj* **textural** *adj*

Th *Chem* thorium.

Thai *adj* **1** of Thailand. ♦ *n* **2** (*pl* **Thais, Thai**) person from Thailand. **3** language of Thailand.

thalidomide [thal-**lid**-oh-mide] *n* drug formerly used as a sedative, but found to cause abnormalities in developing fetuses.

thallium *n Chem* highly toxic metallic element.

than *conj, prep* used to introduce the second element of a comparison.

thane *n Hist* Anglo-Saxon or medieval Scottish nobleman.

thank *v* **1** express gratitude to. **2** hold responsible. **thanks** *pl n* **1** words of gratitude. ♦ *interj* **2** (also **thank you**) polite expression of gratitude. **thanks to** because of. **thankful** *adj* grateful. **thankless** *adj* unrewarding or unappreciated. **Thanksgiving Day** autumn public holiday in Canada and the US.

> When *thank you* is used to express gratitude it should be written as two words: *Thank you for the gift.* When it

is used as an adjective, use a hyphen: *a thank-you note.*

that *adj, pron* **1** used to refer to something already mentioned or familiar, or further away. ♦ *conj* **2** used to introduce a clause. ♦ *pron* **3** used to introduce a relative clause.

The relative pronoun *that* may often be used interchangeably with *which* in defining clauses: *the coat that/which you bought.* Some people, however, prefer to reserve *which* for the type of clause (called nondefining) that contains explanations and amplifications and is divided by a comma from the rest of the sentence; *he found the book, which was a start.*

thatch *n* **1** roofing material of reeds or straw. ♦ *v* **2** roof (a house) with reeds or straw. **thatched** *adj*

thaw *v* **1** make or become unfrozen. **2** become more relaxed or friendly. ♦ *n* **3** thawing. **4** weather causing snow or ice to melt.

the *adj* the definite article, used before a noun.

theatre *n* **1** place where plays etc. are performed. **2** hospital operating room. **3** drama and acting in general. **4** region in which a war takes place. **theatrical** *adj* **1** of the theatre. **2** exaggerated or affected. **theatricals** *pl n* (amateur) dramatic performances. **theatrically** *adv* **theatricality** *n*

thee *pron Obs* objective form of THOU.

theft *n* act or an instance of stealing.

their *adj* of or associated with them. **theirs** *pron* (thing or person) belonging to them.

Be careful not to confuse *their* with *there. Their* is used for possession: *their new baby. There* indicates place and has a similar '-ere' spelling pattern to *here* and *where.*

theism [**thee**-iz-zum] *n* belief in a God or gods. **theist** *n, adj* **theistic** *adj*

them *pron* refers to people or things other than the speaker or those addressed. **themselves** *pron* emphatic and reflexive form of THEY *or* THEM.

Them may be used after a singular to avoid the clumsy *him or her: If you see a person looking lost, help them.*

theme *n* **1** main idea or subject being discussed. **2** recurring idea in literature, art, etc. **3** recurring melodic figure in music. **thematic** *adj* **thematically** *adv* **theme park** leisure area in which all the activities and displays are based on a single theme. **theme tune, song** tune *or* song used to introduce a television or radio programme.

then *adv* **1** at that time. **2** after that. **3** that being so.

thence *adv* **1** from that place or time. **2** therefore.

theocracy *n, pl* **-cies** government by a god or priests. **theocratic** *adj*

theodolite [thee-**odd**-oh-lite] *n* surveying instrument for measuring angles.

theology *n, pl* **-gies** study of religions and religious beliefs. **theologian** *n* **theological** *adj* **theologically** *adv*

theorem *n* proposition that can be proved by reasoning.

theory *n, pl* **-ries** **1** set of ideas to explain something. **2** abstract knowledge or reasoning. **3** idea or opinion. **in theory** in an ideal or hypothetical situation. **theoretical** *adj* based on theory rather than practice or fact. **theoretically** *adv* **theorist** *n* **theorize** *v* form theories, speculate.

theosophy *n* religious or philosophical system claiming to be based on intuitive insight into the divine nature. **theosophical** *adj*

therapy *n, pl* **-pies** curing treatment. **therapist** *n* **therapeutic** [ther-rap-**pew**-tik] *adj* curing. **therapeutics** *n* art of curing.

there *adv* **1** in or to that place. **2** in that respect. **thereabouts** *adv* near that place, time, amount, etc. **thereafter** *adv Formal* from that time onwards. **thereby** *adv* by that means. **therefore** *adv* consequently, that being so. **thereupon** *adv* immediately after that.

> Be careful not to confuse *there* with *their*. *There* indicates place and has a similar '-ere' spelling pattern to *here* and *where*. *Their* indicates possession: *their new baby*.

therm *n* unit of measurement of heat. **thermal** *adj* **1** of heat. **2** hot or warm. **3** (of clothing) retaining heat. ♦ *n* **4** rising current of warm air.

thermionic valve *n* electronic valve in which electrons are emitted from a heated rather than a cold cathode.

thermodynamics *n* scientific study of the relationship between heat and other forms of energy.

thermometer *n* instrument for measuring temperature.

thermonuclear *adj* **1** involving nuclear fusion. **2** involving atomic weapons.

thermoplastic *adj* (of a plastic) softening when heated and resetting on cooling.

Thermos *n* ® vacuum flask.

thermosetting *adj* (of a plastic) remaining hard when heated.

thermostat *n* device for automatically regulating temperature. **thermostatic** *adj* **thermostatically** *adv*

thesaurus [thiss-**sore**-uss] *n, pl* **-ruses** book containing lists of synonyms and related words.

these *adj, pron* plural of THIS.

thesis *n, pl* **theses** **1** written work submitted for a degree. **2** opinion supported by reasoned argument.

Thespian *n* **1** actor or actress. ♦ *adj* **2** of the theatre.

they *pron* refers to: **1** people or things other than the speaker or people addressed. **2** people in general. **3** *Informal* he or she.

> *They* may be used after a singular to avoid the clumsy *he or she: If a person is born gloomy, they cannot help it.*

thiamine *n* vitamin found in the outer coat of rice and other grains.

thick *adj* **1** of great or specified extent from one side to the other. **2** having a dense consistency. **3** *Informal* stupid or insensitive. **4** (of an accent) very noticeable. **5** *Informal* friendly. **a bit thick** *Informal* unfair or unreasonable. **the thick** busiest or most intense part. **thick with** full of. **thicken** *v* make or become thick or thicker. **thickener** *n* substance used to thicken liquids. **thickly** *adv* **thickness** *n* **1** state of being thick. **2** dimension through an object. **3** layer. **thickset** *adj* **1** stocky in build. **2** set closely together. **thick-skinned** *adj* insensitive to criticism or hints.

thicket *n* dense growth of small trees.

thief *n, pl* **thieves** person who steals. **thieve** *v* steal. **thieving** *adj*

thigh *n* upper part of the human leg.

thimble *n* cap protecting the end of the finger when sewing.

thin *adj* **thinner, thinnest** **1** not thick. **2** slim or lean. **3** sparse or meagre. **4** of low density. **5** poor or unconvincing. ♦ *v* **thinning, thinned** **6** make or become thin. **thinly** *adv* **thinness** *n* **thin-skinned** *adj* sensitive to criticism or hints.

thine *pron, adj Obs* (something) of or associated with you (thou).

thing *n* **1** material object. **2** object, fact, or idea considered as a separate entity. **3** *Informal* obsession. ♦ *pl* **4** possessions, clothes, etc.

think *v* **thinking, thought** **1** consider, judge, or believe. **2** make use of the mind. **3** be considerate enough or remember to do something. **thinker** *n* **thinking** *adj, n* **think-tank** *n* group of experts studying specific problems. **think up** *v* invent or devise.

third *adj* **1** of number three in a series. **2** rated or graded below the second level. ♦ *n* **3** one of three equal parts. **third degree** violent interrogation. **third party**

(applying to) a person involved by chance or only incidentally in legal proceedings, an accident, etc. **Third World** developing countries of Africa, Asia, and Latin America.

thirst *n* **1** desire to drink. **2** craving or yearning. ♦ *v* **3** feel thirst. **thirsty** *adj* **thirstier, thirstiest** **thirstily** *adv*

thirteen *adj, n* three plus ten. **thirteenth** *adj, n*

thirty *adj, n* three times ten. **thirtieth** *adj, n*

this *adj, pron* **1** used to refer to a thing or person nearby, just mentioned, or about to be mentioned. ♦ *adj* **2** used to refer to the present time, e.g. *this morning*.

thistle *n* prickly plant with dense flower heads. **thistledown** *n* mass of feathery plumed seeds produced by thistles.

thither *adv Obs* to or towards that place.

tho', tho *conj, adv* short for THOUGH.

thole, tholepin *n* wooden pin set in the side of a rowing boat to serve as a fulcrum for rowing.

thong *n* thin strip of leather etc.

thorax *n, pl* **thoraxes, thoraces** part of the body between the neck and the abdomen. **thoracic** *adj*

thorium *n Chem* radioactive metallic element.

thorn *n* **1** prickle on a plant. **2** bush with thorns. **thorn in one's side, flesh** source of irritation. **thorny** *adj* **1** covered with thorns. **2** (of a problem, subject) difficult or unpleasant.

thorough *adj* **1** complete. **2** careful or methodical. **thoroughly** *adv* **thoroughness** *n* **thoroughbred** *n, adj* (animal) of pure breed. **thoroughfare** *n* way through from one place to another. **thoroughgoing** *adj* extremely thorough.

those *adj, pron* plural of THAT.

thou *pron Obs* singular form of YOU.

though *conj* **1** despite the fact that. ♦ *adv* **2** nevertheless.

thought *v* **1** past of THINK. ♦ *n* **2** thinking. **3** concept or idea. **4** ideas typical of a time or place. **5** consideration. **6** intention or expectation. **thoughtful** *adj* **1** considerate. **2** showing careful thought. **3** pensive or reflective. **thoughtfully** *adv* **thoughtless** *adj* inconsiderate. **thoughtlessly** *adv*

thousand *adj, n* **1** ten hundred. **2** large but unspecified number. **thousandth** *adj, n* (of) number one thousand in a series.

thrall *n* state of being in the power of another person.

thrash *v* **1** beat, esp. with a stick or whip. **2** defeat soundly. **3** move about wildly. **4** thresh. **thrashing** *n* severe beating. **thrash out** *v* solve by thorough argument.

thread *n* **1** fine strand or yarn. **2** unifying theme. **3** spiral ridge on a screw, nut, or bolt. ♦ *v* **4** pass thread through. **5** pick (one's way etc.). **threadbare** *adj* **1** (of fabric) with the nap worn off. **2** hackneyed. **3** shabby.

threat *n* **1** declaration of intent to harm. **2** strong possibility of something dangerous happening. **3** dangerous person or thing. **threaten** *v* **1** make or be a threat to. **2** be a menacing indication of. **threatening** *adj* **threateningly** *adv*

three *adj, n* one more than two. **threefold** *adj, adv* (having) three times as many or as much. **threesome** *n* group of three. **three-dimensional, 3-D** *adj* having three dimensions. **three-ply** *adj* having three layers or strands. **three-point turn** complete turn of a motor vehicle using forward and reverse gears. **three-quarter** *adj* being three quarters of something.

threnody *n, pl* **-dies** lament for the dead.

thresh *v* beat (wheat etc.) to separate the grain from the husks and straw. **thresh about** move about wildly.

threshold *n* **1** bar forming the bottom of a doorway. **2** entrance. **3** starting point. **4** point at which something begins to take effect.

threw *v* past tense of THROW.

thrice *adv Lit* three times.

thrift *n* **1** wisdom and caution with money. **2** low-growing plant with pink flowers. **thrifty** *adj* **thriftier, thriftiest**

thrill *n* **1** sudden feeling of excitement. ♦ *v* **2** (cause to) feel a thrill. **thrilling** *adj*

thriller *n* book, film, etc. with an atmosphere of mystery or suspense.

thrive *v* **thriving, thrived** *or* **throve, thrived** *or* **thriven 1** flourish or prosper. **2** grow well.

throat *n* **1** passage from the mouth and nose to the stomach and lungs. **2** front of the neck. **throaty** *adj* (of the voice) hoarse.

throb *v* **throbbing, throbbed 1** pulsate repeatedly. **2** vibrate rhythmically. ♦ *n* **3** throbbing.

throes *pl n* violent pangs or pains. **in the throes of** struggling to cope with.

thrombosis *n, pl* **-ses** forming of a clot in a blood vessel or the heart.

throne *n* **1** ceremonial seat of a monarch or bishop. **2** sovereign power.

throng *n, v* crowd.

throstle *n* song thrush.

throttle *n* **1** device controlling the amount of fuel entering an engine. ♦ *v* **2** strangle.

through *prep* **1** from end to end or side to side of. **2** because of. **3** during. ♦ *adj* **4** finished. **5** (of transport) going directly to a place. **through and through** completely. **throughout** *prep, adv* in every part (of). **throughput** *n* amount of material processed.

throve *v* a past tense of THRIVE.

throw *v* **throwing, threw, thrown 1** hurl through the air. **2** move or put suddenly or carelessly. **3** bring into a specified state, esp. suddenly. **4** move (a switch, lever, etc.). **5** shape (pottery) on a wheel. **6** give (a party). **7** *Informal* baffle or disconcert. **8** direct (a look, light, etc.). **9** project (the voice) so that it seems to come from elsewhere. ♦ *n* **10** throwing. **11** distance thrown. **throwaway** *adj* **1** done or said casually. **2** designed to be discarded after use. **throwback** *n* person or thing that reverts to an earlier type. **throw up** *v* vomit.

thrum *v* **thrumming, thrummed 1** strum rhythmically but without expression on (a musical instrument). **2** make a low beating or humming sound.

thrush[1] *n* brown songbird.

thrush[2] *n* fungal disease of the mouth or vagina.

thrust *v* **thrusting, thrust 1** push forcefully. ♦ *n* **2** forceful stab. **3** force or power. **4** essential part. **5** intellectual or emotional drive.

thud *n* **1** dull heavy sound. ♦ *v* **thudding, thudded 2** make such a sound.

thug *n* violent man, esp. a criminal. **thuggery** *n* **thuggish** *adj*

thulium *n Chem* malleable ductile silvery-grey element.

thumb *n* **1** short thick finger set apart from the others. ♦ *v* **2** touch or handle with the thumb. **3** signal with the thumb for a lift in a vehicle. **thumb through** flick through (a book or magazine). **thumb index** series of notches cut into the edge of a book to allow quick reference.

thump *n* **1** (sound of) a dull heavy blow. ♦ *v* **2** strike heavily. **thumping** *adj Informal* huge or excessive.

thunder *n* **1** loud noise accompanying lightning. **2** any loud sound. ♦ *v* **3** rumble with thunder. **4** shout. **5** move fast, heavily, and noisily. **thunderous** *adj* **thundery** *adj* **thunderbolt** *n* **1** lightning flash. **2** something sudden and unexpected. **thunderclap** *n* peal of thunder. **thunderstorm** *n* storm with lightning and thunder. **thunderstruck** *adj* amazed.

Thurs. Thursday.

Thursday *n* fifth day of the week.

thus *adv* **1** therefore. **2** in this way.

thwack *v, n* whack.

thwart *v* **1** foil or frustrate. ♦ *n* **2** seat across a boat.

thy *adj Obs* of or associated with you (thou). **thyself** *pron Obs* emphatic form of THOU.

thyme [**time**] *n* aromatic herb.

thymol *n* substance obtained from thyme, used as an antiseptic.

thymus *n, pl* **-muses, -mi** small gland at the base of the neck.

thyroid *adj, n* (of) a gland in the neck controlling body growth.

ti *n Music* same as TE.

Ti *Chem* titanium.

tiara *n* semicircular jewelled headdress.

tibia *n, pl* **tibiae, tibias** inner bone of the lower leg. **tibial** *adj*

tic *n* spasmodic muscular twitch.

tick[1] *n* **1** mark (✓) used to check off or indicate the correctness of something. **2** recurrent tapping sound, as of a clock. **3** *Informal* moment. ♦ *v* **4** mark with a tick. **5** make a ticking sound. **tick off** *v* **1** mark with a tick. **2** reprimand. **tick over** *v* **1** (of an engine) idle. **2** function smoothly. **ticktack** *n* bookmakers' sign language.

tick[2] *n* tiny bloodsucking parasitic animal.

tick[3] *n Informal* credit or account.

ticket *n* **1** card or paper entitling the holder to admission, travel, etc. **2** label, esp. showing price. **3** official notification of a parking or traffic offence. **4** declared policy of a political party. ♦ *v* **-eting, -eted 5** attach or issue a ticket to.

ticking *n* strong material for mattress covers.

tickle *v* **1** touch or stroke (a person) to produce laughter. **2** itch or tingle. **3** please or amuse. ♦ *n* **4** tickling. **ticklish** *adj* **1** sensitive to tickling. **2** requiring care or tact.

tiddly[1] *adj* **-dlier, -dliest** tiny. **tiddler** *n Informal* very small fish.

tiddly[2] *adj* **-dlier, -dliest** *Informal* slightly drunk.

tiddlywinks *n* game in which players try to flip small plastic discs into a cup.

tide *n* **1** rise and fall of the sea caused by the gravitational pull of the sun and moon. **2** current caused by this. **3** widespread feeling or tendency. **tidal** *adj* **tidal wave** large destructive wave. **tideline** *n* mark left by the highest or lowest point of the tide. **tide over** *v* help (someone) temporarily.

tidings *pl n* news.

tidy *adj* **-dier, -diest 1** neat and orderly. **2** *Informal* considerable. ♦ *v* **-dying, -died 3** put in order. **tidily** *adv* **tidiness** *n*

tie *v* **tying, tied 1** fasten or be fastened with string, rope, etc. **2** make (a knot or bow) in (something). **3** restrict or limit. **4** score the same as another competitor. ♦ *n* **5** long narrow piece of material worn knotted round the neck. **6** bond or fastening. **7** match in an eliminating competition. **8** drawn game or contest. **tie-break, tie-breaker** *n* extra game or question that decides the result of a contest ending in a draw. **tied** *adj* **1** (of a pub) allowed to sell only the beer of a particular brewery. **2** (of a cottage etc.) rented to the tenant only as long as he or she is employed by the owner.

tier *n* one of a set of rows placed one above and behind the other.

tiff *n* petty quarrel.

tiger *n* large yellow-and-black striped Asian cat. **tigress** *n* **1** female tiger. **2** *Informal* fierce woman.

tight *adj* **1** stretched or drawn taut. **2** closely fitting. **3** secure or firm. **4** cramped. **5** (of a situation) difficult or dangerous. **6** *Informal* not generous. **7** (of a match or game) very close. **8** *Informal* drunk. **tights** *pl n* one-piece clinging garment covering the body from the waist to the feet. **tightly** *adv* **tighten** *v* make or become tight or tighter. **tight-fisted** *adj* very mean. **tight-lipped** *adj* **1** secretive. **2** with lips pressed tightly together, as through anger. **tightrope** *n* rope stretched taut on which acrobats perform.

tikka *adj Indian cookery* marinated in spices and dry-roasted, e.g. *chicken tikka.*

tilde *n* mark (˜) used in Spanish to indicate that the letter 'n' is to be pronounced in a particular way.

tile *n* **1** flat piece of ceramic, plastic, etc. used to cover a roof, floor, or wall. ♦ *v* **2** cover with tiles. **tiled** *adj* **tiling** *n* tiles collectively.

till[1] *conj, prep* until.

till[2] *v* cultivate (land). **tillage** *n*

till[3] *n* drawer for money, usu. in a cash register.

tiller *n* lever to move a rudder of a boat.

tilt *v* **1** slant at an angle. **2** *Hist* compete against in a jousting contest. ♦ *n* **3** slope. **4** *Hist* jousting contest. **5** attempt. **at full tilt** at full speed or force.

tilth *n* (condition of) land that has been tilled.

timber *n* **1** wood as a building material. **2** trees collectively. **3** wooden beam in the frame of a house, boat, etc. **timbered** *adj* **timber line** limit beyond which trees will not grow.

timbre [**tam**-bra] *n* distinctive quality of sound of a voice or instrument.

time *n* **1** past, present, and future as a continuous whole. **2** specific point in time. **3** unspecified interval. **4** instance or occasion. **5** period with specific features. **6** musical tempo. **7** *Slang* imprisonment. ♦ *v* **8** note the time taken by. **9** choose a time for. **timeless** *adj* **1** unaffected by time. **2** eternal. **timely** *adj* at the appropriate time. **times** *prep* multiplied by. **timing** *n* ability to judge when to do or say something so as to make the best effect. **time-honoured** *adj* sanctioned by custom. **time-lag** *n* period between cause and effect. **timepiece** *n* watch or clock. **timeserver** *n* person who changes his or her views to gain support or favour. **time sharing** **1** system of part ownership of a holiday property for a specified period each year. **2** system enabling users at different terminals of a computer to use it at the same time. **time signature** *Music* sign that indicates the number and length of beats in the bar. **timetable** *n* plan showing the times when something takes place, the departure and arrival times of trains or buses, etc. **time zone** region throughout which the same standard time is used.

timid *adj* **1** easily frightened. **2** shy, not bold. **timidly** *adv* **timidity** *n* **timorous** [**tim**-mor-uss] *adj* timid.

timpani [**tim**-pan-ee] *pl n* set of kettle-drums. **timpanist** *n*

tin *n* **1** soft metallic element. **2** (airtight) metal container. **tinned** *adj* (of food) preserved by being sealed in a tin. **tinny** *adj* (of sound) thin and metallic. **tinpot** *adj Informal* worthless or unimportant.

tincture *n* medicinal extract in a solution of alcohol.

tinder *n* dry easily-burning material used to start a fire. **tinderbox** *n* formerly, small box for tinder, esp. one fitted with a flint and steel.

tine *n* prong of a fork or antler.

ting *n* high metallic sound, as of a small bell.

tinge *n* **1** slight tint. **2** trace. ♦ *v* **tingeing, tinged** **3** give a slight tint or trace to.

tingle *v, n* (feel) a prickling or stinging sensation.

tinker *n* **1** travelling mender of pots and pans. **2** *Scot & Irish* Gypsy. ♦ *v* **3** fiddle with (an engine etc.) in an attempt to repair it.

tinkle *v* **1** ring with a high tinny sound like a small bell. ♦ *n* **2** this sound or action.

tinsel *n* **1** decorative metallic strips or threads. **2** anything cheap and gaudy.

tint *n* **1** (pale) shade of a colour. **2** dye for the hair. ♦ *v* **3** give a tint to.

tintinnabulation *n* ringing or pealing of bells.

tiny *adj* **tinier, tiniest** very small.

tip[1] *n* **1** narrow or pointed end of anything. **2** small piece forming an end. ♦ *v* **tipping, tipped** **3** put a tip on.

tip[2] *n* **1** money given in return for service. **2** helpful hint or warning. **3** piece of inside information. ♦ *v* **tipping, tipped** **4** give a tip to. **tipster** *n* person who sells tips about races.

tip[3] *v* **tipping, tipped** **1** tilt or overturn. **2** dump (rubbish). ♦ *n* **3** rubbish dump.

tipple *v* **1** drink alcohol habitually, esp. in small quantities. ♦ *n* **2** alcoholic drink. **tippler** *n*

tipsy *adj* **-sier, -siest** slightly drunk.

tiptoe *v* **-toeing, -toed** walk quietly with the heels off the ground.

tiptop *adj* of the highest quality or condition.

tirade *n* long angry speech.

tire *v* **1** reduce the energy of, as by exertion. **2** weary or bore. **tired** *adj* **1** exhausted. **2** bored. **3** hackneyed or stale. **tiring** *adj* **tireless** *adj* energetic and determined. **tirelessly** *adv* **tiresome** *adj* boring and irritating.

tissue *n* **1** substance of an animal body or plant. **2** piece of thin soft paper used as a handkerchief etc. **3** interwoven series, e.g. *a tissue of lies.*

tit[1] *n* any of various small songbirds.

tit[2] *n Slang* female breast.

titanic *adj* huge or very important. **titan** *n* person who is huge, strong, or very important.

titanium *n Chem* strong light metallic element used to make alloys.

titbit *n* **1** tasty piece of food. **2** pleasing scrap of scandal.

tit-for-tat *adj* done in retaliation.

tithe *n* **1** esp. formerly, one tenth of one's income or produce paid to the church as a tax. ♦ *v* **2** charge or pay a tithe.

Titian [**tish**-an] *adj* (of hair) reddish-gold.

titillate *v* excite or stimulate pleasurably. **titillating** *adj* **titillation** *n*

titivate *v* smarten up. **titivation** *n*

title *n* **1** name of a book, film, etc. **2** book or periodical. **3** name signifying rank or position. **4** formal designation, such as *Mrs.* **5** *Sport* championship. **6** *Law* legal right of possession. **titled** *adj* aristocratic. **title deed** legal document of ownership. **titleholder** *n* person who holds a title, esp. a sporting championship. **title role** role of the character after whom a film or play is named.

titration *n Chem* operation in which a measured amount of one solution is added to a known quantity of another solution until the reaction between the two is complete.

titter *v* **1** laugh in a suppressed way. ♦ *n* **2** suppressed laugh.

tittle-tattle *n, v* gossip.

titular *adj* **1** in name only. **2** of a title.

tizzy *n, pl* **-zies** *Informal* confused or agitated state.

Tl *Chem* thallium.

Tm *Chem* thulium.

TN Tennessee.

TNT *n* trinitrotoluene, a powerful explosive.

to *prep* **1** indicating movement towards, equality or comparison, etc., e.g. *walking to school; forty miles to the gallon.* **2** used to mark the indirect object or infinitive of a verb. ♦ *adv* **3** to a closed position, e.g. *pull the door to.* **to and fro** back and forth.

toad *n* animal like a large frog.

toad-in-the-hole *n* sausages baked in batter.

toadstool *n* poisonous fungus like a mushroom.

toady *n, pl* **toadies** **1** ingratiating person. ♦ *v* **toadying, toadied** **2** be ingratiating.

toast[1] *n* **1** sliced bread browned by heat. ♦ *v* **2** brown (bread) by heat. **3** warm or be warmed. **toaster** *n* electrical device for toasting bread.

toast[2] *n* **1** tribute or proposal of health or success marked by people raising glasses and drinking together. **2** person or thing so honoured. ♦ *v* **3** drink a toast to.

tobacco *n, pl* **-cos, -coes** plant with large leaves dried for smoking. **tobacconist** *n* person or shop selling tobacco, cigarettes, etc.

toboggan *n* **1** narrow sledge for sliding over snow. ♦ *v* **-ganing, -ganed** **2** ride a toboggan.

toby jug *n* mug in the form of a stout seated man.

toccata [tok-**kah**-ta] *n* rapid piece of music for a keyboard instrument.

today *n* **1** this day. **2** the present age. ♦ *adv* **3** on this day. **4** nowadays.

toddle *v* walk with short unsteady steps. **toddler** *n* child beginning to walk.

toddy *n, pl* **-dies** sweetened drink of spirits and hot water.

to-do *n, pl* **-dos** fuss or commotion.

toe *n* **1** digit of the foot. **2** part of a shoe or sock covering the toes. ♦ *v* **toeing, toed 3** touch or kick with the toe. **toe-cap** *n* strengthened covering for the toe of a shoe. **toehold** *n* **1** small space on a mountain for supporting the toe of the foot in climbing. **2** means of gaining access or advantage. **toerag** *n Slang* contemptible person. **toe the line** conform.

toff *n Slang* well-dressed or upper-class person.

toffee *n* chewy sweet made of boiled sugar. **toffee-apple** *n* apple fixed on a stick and coated with toffee. **toffee-nosed** *adj Informal* snobbish.

tofu *n* soft food made from soya-bean curd.

tog *n* **1** unit for measuring the insulating power of duvets. ♦ *pl* **2** *Informal* clothes.

toga [**toe**-ga] *n* garment worn by citizens of ancient Rome.

together *adv* **1** in company. **2** simultaneously. ♦ *adj* **3** *Informal* organized.

> Two nouns linked by *together with* do not make a plural subject so the following verb must be singular: *Jones, together with his partner, has had great success.*

toggle *n* **1** small bar-shaped button inserted through a loop for fastening. **2** switch used to turn a machine or computer function on or off.

toil *n* **1** hard work. ♦ *v* **2** work hard. **3** progress with difficulty.

toilet *n* **1** (room with) a bowl connected to a drain for receiving and disposing of urine and faeces. **2** washing and dressing. **toiletry** *n, pl* **-ries** object or cosmetic used to clean or groom oneself. **toilet paper** thin absorbent paper used for cleaning oneself after defecation. **toilet water** light perfume.

token *n* **1** sign or symbol. **2** voucher exchangeable for goods of a specified value. **3** disc used as money in a slot machine. ♦ *adj* **4** nominal or slight. **tokenism** *n* policy of making only a token effort, esp. to comply with a law.

told *v* past of TELL.

tolerate *v* **1** allow to exist or happen. **2** endure patiently. **tolerable** *adj* **1** bearable. **2** *Informal* quite good. **tolerably** *adv* **tolerance** *n* **1** acceptance of other people's rights to their own opinions or actions. **2** ability to endure something. **tolerant** *adj* **tolerantly** *adv* **toleration** *n*

toll[1] *v* **1** ring (a bell) slowly and regularly, esp. to announce a death. ♦ *n* **2** tolling.

toll[2] *n* **1** charge for the use of a bridge or road. **2** total loss or damage from a disaster.

toluene *n* colourless volatile flammable liquid obtained from petroleum and coal tar.

tom *n* male cat.

tomahawk *n* fighting axe of the Native Americans.

tomato *n, pl* **-toes** red fruit used in salads and as a vegetable.

tomb *n* **1** grave. **2** monument over a grave. **tombstone** *n* gravestone.

tombola *n* lottery with tickets drawn from a revolving drum.

tomboy *n* girl who acts or dresses like a boy.

tome *n* large heavy book.

tomfoolery *n* foolish behaviour.

Tommy *n, pl* **-mies** *Brit informal* private soldier in the British army.

Tommy gun *n* light sub-machine-gun.

tomorrow *adv, n* **1** (on) the day after today. **2** (in) the future.

tom-tom *n* drum beaten with the hands.

ton *n* unit of weight equal to 2240 pounds or 1016 kilograms (**long ton**) or, in the US, 2000 pounds or 907 kilograms (**short ton**). **tonnage** *n* weight capacity of a ship.

tone *n* **1** sound with reference to its pitch, volume, etc. **2** *US* musical note. **3** *Music* (also **whole tone**) interval of two semitones. **4** quality of a sound or colour. **5** general character. **6** healthy bodily condition. ♦ *v* **7** harmonize (with). **8**

give tone to. **tonal** *adj Music* written in a key. **tonality** *n* **toneless** *adj* **tone-deaf** *adj* unable to perceive subtle differences in pitch. **tone down** *v* make or become more moderate. **tone up** *v* make or become more healthy.

tongs *pl n* large pincers for grasping and lifting.

tongue *n* **1** muscular organ in the mouth, used in speaking and tasting. **2** language. **3** animal tongue as food. **4** thin projecting strip. **5** flap of leather on a shoe. **tonguing** *n* technique of playing a wind instrument by obstructing and uncovering the air passage through the lips with the tongue. **tongue-tied** *adj* speechless, esp. with shyness or embarrassment. **tongue twister** sentence or phrase that is difficult to say quickly.

tonic *n* **1** medicine to improve body tone. **2** anything that is strengthening or cheering. **3** tonic water. **4** *Music* first note of a scale. ♦ *adj* **5** invigorating. **tonic water** mineral water containing quinine.

tonight *adv, n* (in or during) the night or evening of this day.

toning table *n* exercise table with mechanically moving parts, which is programmed to repeat certain movements for a set time, in order to exercise specific parts of the body of the person lying on it.

tonne [**tunn**] *n* unit of weight equal to 1000 kilograms.

tonsil *n* small gland in the throat. **tonsillectomy** *n* surgical removal of the tonsils. **tonsillitis** *n* inflammation of the tonsils.

tonsure *n* **1** shaving of all or the top of the head as a religious or monastic practice. **2** shaved part of the head. **tonsured** *adj*

too *adv* **1** also, as well. **2** to excess. **3** extremely.

took *v* past tense of TAKE.

tool *n* **1** implement used by hand. **2** person used by another to perform unpleasant or dishonourable tasks. ♦ *v* **3** work on with a tool.

toot *n* **1** short hooting sound. ♦ *v* **2** (cause to) make such a sound.

tooth *n, pl* **teeth** **1** bonelike projection in the jaws of most vertebrates for biting and chewing. **2** toothlike prong or point. **sweet tooth** strong liking for sweet food. **toothless** *adj* **1** lacking teeth. **2** (of an official body) lacking power or influence. **toothpaste** *n* paste used to clean the teeth. **toothpick** *n* small stick for removing scraps of food from between the teeth.

top[1] *n* **1** highest point or part. **2** lid or cap. **3** highest rank. **4** garment for the upper part of the body. ♦ *adj* **5** at or of the top. ♦ *v* **topping, topped** **6** form a top on. **7** be at the top of. **8** exceed or surpass. **topping** *n* sauce or garnish for food. **topless** *adj* (of a costume or woman) with no covering for the breasts. **topmost** *adj* highest or best. **top brass** most important officers or leaders. **top-dress** *v* spread fertilizer on the surface of the land. **top dressing** layer of fertilizer spread on the surface of land. **top hat** man's tall cylindrical hat. **top-heavy** *adj* unstable through being overloaded at the top. **top-notch** *adj* excellent, first-class. **top-secret** *adj* (of military or government information) classified as needing the highest level of secrecy and security. **topsoil** *n* surface layer of soil.

top[2] *n* toy which spins on a pointed base.

topaz [**toe**-pazz] *n* semiprecious stone in various colours.

tope[1] *v* drink alcohol regularly.

tope[2] *n* small European shark.

topee, topi [**toe**-pee] *n* lightweight hat worn in tropical countries.

topiary [**tope**-yar-ee] *n* art of trimming trees and bushes into decorative shapes. **topiarist** *n*

topic *n* subject of a conversation, book, etc. **topical** *adj* relating to current events. **topicality** *n*

topography *n, pl* **-phies** (science of describing) the surface features of a place. **topographer** *n* **topographical** *adj*

topology *n* geometry of the properties

of a shape which are unaffected by continuous distortion. **topological** *adj*

topple *v* **1** (cause to) fall over. **2** overthrow (a government etc.).

topsy-turvy *adj* **1** upside down. **2** in confusion.

toque [**toke**] *n* small round hat.

tor *n* high rocky hill.

Torah *n* body of traditional Jewish teaching.

torch *n* **1** small portable battery-powered lamp. **2** wooden shaft dipped in wax and set alight. ♦ *v* **3** *Informal* deliberately set (a building) on fire. **carry a torch for** be in love with (someone).

tore *v* past tense of TEAR[2].

toreador [**torr**-ee-a-dor] *n* bullfighter.

torment *v* **1** cause (someone) great suffering. **2** tease cruelly. ♦ *n* **3** great suffering. **4** source of suffering. **tormentor** *n*

torn *v* past participle of TEAR[2].

tornado *n, pl* **-dos, -does** violent whirlwind.

torpedo *n, pl* **-does** **1** self-propelled underwater missile. ♦ *v* **-doing, -doed** **2** attack or destroy with or as if with torpedoes.

torpid *adj* sluggish and inactive. **torpor** *n* torpid state.

torque [**tork**] *n* **1** force causing rotation. **2** Celtic necklace or armband of twisted metal.

torrent *n* **1** rushing stream. **2** rapid flow of questions, abuse, etc. **torrential** *adj* (of rain) very heavy.

torrid *adj* **1** very hot and dry. **2** highly emotional.

torsion *n* twisting of a part by equal forces being applied at both ends but in opposite directions.

torso *n, pl* **-sos** **1** trunk of the human body. **2** statue of a nude human trunk.

tort *n Law* civil wrong or injury for which damages may be claimed.

tortilla *n* thin Mexican pancake.

tortoise *n* slow-moving land reptile with a dome-shaped shell. **tortoiseshell** *n* **1** mottled brown shell of a turtle, used for making ornaments. ♦ *adj* **2** having brown, orange, and black markings.

tortuous *adj* **1** winding or twisting. **2** not straightforward.

torture *v* **1** cause (someone) severe pain or mental anguish. ♦ *n* **2** severe physical or mental pain. **3** torturing. **torturer** *n*

Tory *n, pl* **Tories** **1** member of the Conservative Party in Great Britain or Canada. ♦ *adj* **2** of Tories. **Toryism** *n*

toss *v* **1** throw lightly. **2** fling or be flung about. **3** coat (food) by gentle stirring or mixing. **4** (of a horse) throw (its rider). **5** move (one's head) suddenly backwards. **6** throw up (a coin) to decide between alternatives by guessing which side will land uppermost. ♦ *n* **7** tossing. **toss up** *v* toss a coin. **toss-up** *n* even chance or risk.

tot[1] *n* **1** small child. **2** small drink of spirits.

tot[2] *v* **totting, totted. tot up** add (numbers) together.

total *n* **1** whole, esp. a sum of parts. ♦ *adj* **2** complete. **3** of or being a total. ♦ *v* **-talling, -talled** **4** amount to. **5** add up. **totally** *adv* **totality** *n* **totalizator** *n* machine operating a betting system in which money is paid out to the winners in proportion to their stakes.

totalitarian *adj* of a dictatorial one-party government. **totalitarianism** *n*

tote[1] *v* carry (a gun etc.).

tote[2] *n* short for TOTALIZATOR.

totem *n* tribal badge or emblem. **totem pole** post carved or painted with totems by Native Americans.

totter *v* **1** move unsteadily. **2** be about to fall.

toucan *n* tropical American bird with a large bill.

touch *v* **1** come into contact with. **2** tap, feel, or stroke. **3** affect. **4** move emotionally. **5** eat or drink. **6** equal or match. **7** *Slang* ask for money. ♦ *n* **8** sense by which an object's qualities are perceived when they come into contact with part of the body. **9** contact with the body. **10** gentle tap, push, or caress. **11** small amount. **12** characteristic style. **13** detail. **touch and go** risky or critical. **touched** *adj* **1** emotionally moved. **2** slightly mad. **touching** *adj* emotionally moving. **touchy** *adj* easily offended. **touch down** *v* (of an aircraft) land. **touchline** *n* side line of the pitch in some games. **touch on** *v* refer to in passing. **touch-type** *v* type without looking at the keyboard. **touchy-feely** *adj Informal, sometimes offens.* sensitive and caring.

touché [**too**-shay] *interj* acknowledgment of the striking home of a remark or witty reply.

touchstone *n* standard by which a judgment is made.

tough *adj* **1** strong or resilient. **2** difficult to chew or cut. **3** firm and determined. **4** rough and violent. **5** difficult. **6** *Informal* unlucky or unfair. ♦ *n* **7** *Informal* rough violent person. **toughness** *n* **toughen** *v* make or become tough or tougher.

toupee [**too**-pay] *n* small wig.

tour *n* **1** journey visiting places of interest along the way. **2** trip to perform or play in different places. ♦ *v* **3** make a tour (of). **tourism** *n* tourist travel as an industry. **tourist** *n* person travelling for pleasure. **touristy** *adj Informal, often derogatory* full of tourists or tourist attractions.

tour de force *n, pl* **tours de force** *French* brilliant stroke or achievement.

tourmaline *n* crystalline mineral used for optical instruments and as a gem.

tournament *n* **1** sporting competition with several stages to decide the overall winner. **2** *Hist* contest between knights on horseback.

tourniquet [**tour**-nick-kay] *n* something twisted round a limb to stop bleeding.

tousled *adj* ruffled and untidy.

tout [rhymes with **shout**] *v* **1** seek business in a persistent manner. **2** recommend (a person or thing). ♦ *n* **3** person who sells tickets for a popular event at inflated prices.

tow[1] *v* **1** drag, esp. by means of a rope. ♦ *n* **2** towing. **in tow** following closely behind. **on tow** being towed. **towbar** *n* metal bar on a car for towing vehicles. **towpath** *n* path beside a canal or river, originally for horses towing boats. **towrope** *n* rope or cable used for towing a vehicle or vessel.

tow[2] *n* fibre of hemp or flax.

towards, toward *prep* **1** in the direction of. **2** with regard to. **3** as a contribution to.

> *Towards* is usual. The form *toward* is chiefly American.

towel *n* **1** cloth for drying things. ♦ *v* **-elling, -elled 2** dry or wipe with a towel. **throw in the towel** give up completely. **towelling** *n* material used for making towels.

tower *n* tall structure, often forming part of a larger building. **towering** *adj* very tall or impressive. **tower block** tall building divided into flats or offices. **tower of strength** person who supports or comforts. **tower over** *v* be much taller than.

town *n* **1** group of buildings larger than a village. **2** central part of this. **3** people of a town. **township** *n* **1** small town. **2** (in S Africa) urban settlement of Black or Coloured people. **town hall** large building used for council meetings, concerts, etc. **town planning** comprehensive planning of the physical and social development of a town.

toxaemia [tox-**seem**-ya] *n* **1** blood poisoning. **2** high blood pressure in pregnancy.

toxic *adj* **1** poisonous. **2** caused by poison. **toxicity** *n* **toxicology** *n* study of poisons. **toxin** *n* poison of bacterial origin.

toy *n* **1** something designed to be played with. ♦ *adj* **2** designed to be played with. **3** (of a dog) of a variety much smaller than is normal for that breed. **toy with** *v* play or fiddle with.

trace *v* **1** locate or work out (the cause of something). **2** track down and find. **3** follow the course of. **4** copy exactly by drawing on a thin sheet of transparent paper set on top of the original. ♦ *n* **5** track left by something. **6** minute quantity. **7** indication. **traceable** *adj* **tracer** *n* projectile which leaves a visible trail. **tracery** *n* pattern of interlacing lines. **tracing** *n* traced copy. **trace element** chemical element occurring in very small amounts in soil etc.

traces *pl n* strap by which a horse pulls a vehicle. **kick over the traces** escape or defy control.

trachea [track-**kee**-a] *n, pl* **tracheae** windpipe. **tracheotomy** [track-ee-**ot**-a-mee] *n* surgical incision into the trachea.

track *n* **1** rough road or path. **2** mark or trail left by the passage of anything. **3** railway line. **4** course for racing. **5** separate section on a record, tape, or CD. **6** course of action or thought. **7** endless band round the wheels of a tank, bulldozer, etc. ♦ *v* **8** follow the trail or path of. **track down** *v* hunt for and find. **track event** athletic sport held on a running track. **track record** past accomplishments of a person or organization. **track shoe** light running shoe fitted with spikes for better grip. **tracksuit** *n* warm loose-fitting suit worn by athletes etc., esp. during training.

tract[1] *n* **1** wide area. **2** *Anat* system of organs with a particular function.

tract[2] *n* pamphlet, esp. a religious one.

tractable *adj* easy to manage or control.

traction *n* **1** pulling, esp. by engine power. **2** *Med* application of a steady pull on an injured limb by weights and pulleys. **3** grip of the wheels of a vehicle on the ground. **traction engine** old-fashioned steam-powered vehicle for pulling heavy loads.

tractor *n* motor vehicle with large rear wheels for pulling farm machinery.

trade *n* **1** buying, selling, or exchange of goods. **2** person's job or craft. **3** (people engaged in) a particular industry or business. ♦ *v* **4** buy and sell. **5** exchange. **6** engage in trade. **trader** *n* **trading** *n* **trade-in** *n* used article given in part payment for a new one. **trademark** *n* (legally registered) name or symbol used by a firm to distinguish its goods. **trade-off** *n* exchange made as a compromise. **trade secret** secret formula, technique, or process known and used to advantage by only one manufacturer. **tradesman** *n* **1** skilled worker **2** shopkeeper. **trade union** society of workers formed to protect their interests. **trade wind** wind blowing steadily towards the equator.

tradescantia [trad-dess-**kan**-shee-a] *n* widely cultivated plant with striped variegated leaves.

tradition *n* **1** handing down from generation to generation of customs and beliefs. **2** body of beliefs, customs, etc. handed down from generation to generation. **3** custom or practice of long standing. **traditional** *adj* **traditionally** *adv* **traditionalist** *n* person who supports established customs or beliefs. **traditionalism** *n*

traduce *v* slander.

traffic *n* **1** vehicles coming and going on a road. **2** (illicit) trade. ♦ *v* **-ficking, -ficked 3** trade, usu. illicitly. **trafficker** *n* **traffic lights** set of coloured lights at a junction to control the traffic flow. **traffic warden** person employed to control the movement and parking of traffic.

tragedy *n, pl* **-dies 1** shocking or sad event. **2** serious play, film, etc. in which the hero is destroyed by a personal failing in adverse circumstances. **tragedian** [traj-**jee**-dee-an], **tragedienne** [traj-jee-dee-**enn**] *n* person who acts in or writes tragedies. **tragic** *adj* of or like a tragedy. **tragically** *adv* **tragicomedy** *n* play with both tragic and comic elements.

trail *n* **1** path, track, or road. **2** tracks left by a person, animal, or object. ♦ *v* **3** drag along the ground. **4** lag behind. **5** follow the tracks of. **trailer** *n* **1** vehicle designed to be towed by another vehicle. **2** extract from a film or programme used to advertise it.

train *v* **1** instruct in a skill. **2** learn the skills needed to do a particular job or activity. **3** prepare for a sports event etc. **4** aim (a gun etc.). **5** cause (an animal) to perform or (a plant) to grow in a particular way. ♦ *n* **6** line of railway coaches or wagons drawn by an engine. **7** sequence or series. **8** long trailing back section of a dress. **trainer** *n* **1** person who trains an athlete or sportsman. **2** person who trains racehorses. **3** piece of equipment employed in training, such as a simulated aircraft cockpit. **4** sports shoe. **trainee** *n* person being trained. **train spotter** person who collects the numbers of railway trains.

traipse *v Informal* walk wearily.

trait *n* characteristic feature.

traitor *n* person guilty of treason or treachery. **traitorous** *adj*

trajectory *n, pl* **-ries** line of flight, esp. of a projectile.

tram *n* public transport vehicle powered by an overhead wire and running on rails laid in the road. **tramlines** *pl n* track for trams.

tramp *v* **1** travel on foot, hike. **2** walk heavily. ♦ *n* **3** homeless person who travels on foot. **4** hike. **5** sound of tramping. **6** cargo ship available for hire. **7** *US & Aust slang* promiscuous woman.

trample *v* tread on and crush.

trampoline *n* **1** tough canvas sheet attached to a frame by springs, used by acrobats etc. ♦ *v* **2** bounce on a trampoline.

trance *n* unconscious or dazed state.

tranche *n* portion of something large, esp. a sum of money.

tranquil *adj* calm and quiet. **tranquilly** *adv* **tranquillity** *n* **tranquillize** *v* make calm. **tranquillizer** *n* drug which reduces anxiety or tension.

trans- *prefix* across, through, or beyond.

transact *v* conduct or negotiate (a business deal). **transaction** *n* business deal transacted.

transatlantic *adj* on, from, or to the other side of the Atlantic.

transceiver *n* transmitter and receiver of radio or electronic signals.

transcend *v* **1** rise above. **2** be superior to. **transcendence** *n* **transcendent** *adj* **transcendental** *adj* **1** based on intuition rather than experience. **2** supernatural or mystical. **transcendentalism** *n*

transcribe *v* **1** write down (something said). **2** record for a later broadcast. **3** arrange (music) for a different instrument. **transcript** *n* copy.

transducer *n* device that converts one form of energy to another.

transept *n* either of the two shorter wings of a cross-shaped church.

transfer *v* **-ferring, -ferred 1** move or send from one person or place to another. ♦ *n* **2** transferring. **3** design which can be transferred from one surface to another. **transferable** *adj* **transference** *n* transferring.

transfigure *v* change in appearance. **transfiguration** *n*

transfix *v* **1** astound or stun. **2** pierce through.

transform *v* change the shape or character of. **transformation** *n* **transformer** *n* device for changing the voltage of an alternating current.

transfusion *n* injection of blood into the blood vessels of a patient. **transfuse** *v* **1** give a transfusion to. **2** permeate or infuse.

transgress *v* break (a moral law). **transgression** *n* **transgressor** *n*

transient *adj* lasting only for a short time. **transience** *n*

transistor *n* **1** semiconducting device used to amplify electric currents. **2** portable radio using transistors. **transistorized** *adj*

transit *n* movement from one place to another. **transition** *n* change from one state to another. **transitional** *adj* **transitive** *adj Grammar* (of a verb) requiring a direct object. **transitory** *adj* not lasting long.

translate *v* turn from one language into another. **translatable** *adj* **translation** *n* **1** piece of writing or speech translated into another language. **2** *Maths* transformation in which the origin of a coordinate system is moved to another position so that each axis retains the same direction. **translator** *n*

transliterate *v* convert to the letters of a different alphabet. **transliteration** *n*

translucent *adj* letting light pass through, but not transparent. **translucency, translucence** *n*

transmigrate *v* (of a soul) pass into another body. **transmigration** *n*

transmit *v* **-mitting, -mitted 1** pass (something) from one person or place to another. **2** send out (signals) by radio waves. **3** broadcast (a radio or television programme). **transmission** *n* **1** transmitting. **2** shafts and gears through which power passes from a vehicle's engine to its wheels. **transmittable** *adj* **transmitter** *n* **1** piece of equipment used for broadcasting radio or television programmes. **2** person or thing that transmits.

transmogrify *v* **-fying, -fied** *Informal* change completely.

transmute *v* change the form or nature of. **transmutation** *n*

transom *n* **1** horizontal bar across a window. **2** bar separating a door from the window over it.

transparent *adj* **1** able to be seen through, clear. **2** easily understood or recognized. **transparently** *adv* **transparency** *n* **1** transparent quality. **2** (*pl* **-cies**) colour photograph on transparent film that can be viewed by means of a projector.

transpire *v* **1** become known. **2** *Informal* happen. **3** give off water vapour through pores. **transpiration** *n*

> *Transpire* is so often used for 'happen' or 'occur' that the objection that it should be used only for 'become known' is no longer valid.

transplant *v* **1** transfer (an organ or tissue) surgically from one part or body to another. **2** remove and transfer (a plant) to another place. ♦ *n* **3** surgical transplanting. **4** thing transplanted. **transplantation** *n*

transport *v* **1** convey from one place to another. **2** *Hist* exile (a criminal) to a penal colony. **3** enrapture. ♦ *n* **4** business or system of transporting. **5** vehicle used in transport. **6** ecstasy or rapture. **transportation** *n* **transporter** *n* large goods vehicle.

transpose *v* **1** interchange two things. **2** put (music) into a different key. **3** *Maths* move (a term) from one side of an equation to the other with a corresponding reversal in sign. **transposition** *n*

transsexual, transexual *n* **1** person of one sex who believes his or her true identity is of the opposite sex. **2** person who has had a sex-change operation.

transubstantiation *n Christianity* doctrine that the bread and wine consecrated in Communion changes into the substance of Christ's body and blood.

transuranic [tranz-yoor-**ran**-ik] *adj* (of an element) having an atomic number greater than that of uranium.

transverse *adj* crossing from side to side.

transvestite *n* person who seeks sexual pleasure by wearing the clothes of the opposite sex. **transvestism** *n*

trap *n* **1** device for catching animals. **2** plan for tricking or catching a person. **3** situation from which it is difficult to escape. **4** bend in a pipe containing liquid to prevent the escape of gas. **5** stall in which greyhounds are enclosed before a race. **6** two-wheeled carriage. **7** *Slang* mouth. ♦ *v* **trapping, trapped 8** catch. **9** trick. **trapper** *n* person who traps animals for their fur. **trapdoor** *n* door in floor or roof.

trapeze *n* horizontal bar suspended from two ropes, used by circus acrobats.

trapezium *n, pl* **-ziums, -zia** quadrilateral with two parallel sides of unequal length. **trapezoid** [**trap**-piz-zoid] *n* **1** quadrilateral with no sides parallel. **2** *Chiefly US* trapezium.

trappings *pl n* accessories that symbolize an office or position.

Trappist *n* member of an order of Christian monks who observe strict silence.

trash *n* **1** anything worthless. **2** *US* rubbish. **trashy** *adj*

trauma [**traw**-ma] *n* **1** emotional shock. **2** injury or wound. **traumatic** *adj* **traumatically** *adv* **traumatize** *v*

travail *n Lit* labour or toil.

travel *v* **-elling, -elled 1** go from one place to another, through an area, or for a specified distance. ♦ *n* **2** travelling, esp. as a tourist. ♦ *pl* **3** (account of) travelling. **traveller** *n* person who makes a journey or travels a lot. **travelogue** *n* film or talk about someone's travels. **travel agency** agency that arranges holidays. **traveller's cheque** cheque sold by a bank to the bearer, who signs it on purchase and cashes it abroad by signing it again.

traverse *v* move over or back and forth over.

travesty *n, pl* **-ties 1** grotesque imitation or mockery. ♦ *v* **-tying, -tied 2** make or be a travesty of.

trawl *n* **1** net dragged at deep levels behind a fishing boat. ♦ *v* **2** fish with such a net. **trawler** *n* trawling boat.

tray *n* **1** flat board, usu. with a rim, for carrying things. **2** open receptacle for office correspondence.

treachery *n, pl* **-eries** wilful betrayal. **treacherous** *adj* **1** disloyal. **2** unreliable or dangerous. **treacherously** *adv*

treacle *n* thick dark syrup produced when sugar is refined. **treacly** *adj*

tread *v* **treading, trod, trodden** *or* **trod 1** set one's foot on. **2** crush by walking on. ♦ *n* **3** way of walking or dancing. **4** upper surface of a step. **5** part of a tyre or shoe that touches the ground. **tread water** stay afloat in an upright position by moving the legs in a walking motion. **treadmill** *n* **1** *Hist* cylinder turned by treading on steps projecting from it. **2** dreary routine.

treadle [**tred**-dl] *n* lever worked by the foot to turn a wheel.

treason *n* **1** betrayal of one's sovereign or country. **2** treachery or disloyalty. **treasonable, treasonous** *adj*

treasure *n* **1** collection of wealth, esp. gold or jewels. **2** valued person or thing. ♦ *v* **3** prize or cherish. **treasurer** *n* official in charge of funds. **treasury** *n* **1** storage place for treasure. **2** (**T-**) government department in charge of finance. **treasure-trove** *n* treasure found with no evidence of ownership.

treat *v* **1** deal with or regard in a certain manner. **2** give medical treatment to. **3** subject to a chemical or industrial process. **4** provide (someone) with (something) as a treat. ♦ *n* **5** pleasure, entertainment, etc. given or paid for by someone else. **treatment** *n* **1** medical care. **2** way of treating a person or thing.

treatise [**treat**-izz] *n* formal piece of writing on a particular subject.

treaty *n, pl* **-ties** signed contract between states.

treble *adj* **1** triple. **2** *Music* high-pitched. ♦ *n* **3** (singer with or part for) a soprano voice. ♦ *v* **4** increase three times. **trebly** *adv*

tree *n* large perennial plant with a woody trunk. **treeless** *adj* **tree surgery** repair of damaged trees. **tree surgeon**

trefoil [**tref**-foil] *n* **1** plant, such as clover, with a three-lobed leaf. **2** carved ornament like this.

trek *n* **1** long difficult journey, esp. on foot. **2** *S Afr* migration by ox wagon. ♦ *v* **trekking, trekked 3** make such a journey.

trellis *n* framework of horizontal and vertical strips of wood.

tremble *v* **1** shake or quiver. **2** feel fear or anxiety. ♦ *n* **3** trembling. **trembling** *adj*

tremendous *adj* **1** huge. **2** *Informal* great in quality or amount. **tremendously** *adv*

tremolo *n, pl* **-los** *Music* quivering effect in singing or playing.

tremor *n* **1** involuntary shaking. **2** minor earthquake.

tremulous *adj* trembling, as from fear or excitement. **tremulously** *adv*

trench *n* long narrow ditch, esp. one used as a shelter in war. **trench coat** double›breasted waterproof coat.

trenchant *adj* **1** incisive. **2** effective.

trencher *n Hist* wooden plate for serving food. **trencherman** *n* hearty eater.

trend *n* **1** general tendency or direction. **2** fashion. **trendy** *adj, n Informal* con›sciously fashionable (person). **trendi-ness** *n* **trendsetter** *n* person or thing that creates, or may create, a new fash›ion. **trendsetting** *adj*

trepidation *n* fear or anxiety.

trespass *v* **1** go onto another's property without permission. ♦ *n* **2** trespassing. **3** *Old-fashioned* sin or wrongdoing. **tres-passer** *n* **trespass on** *v* take unfair ad›vantage of (someone's friendship, pa›tience, etc.).

tresses *pl n* long flowing hair.

trestle *n* board fixed on pairs of spread›ing legs, used as a support.

trews *pl n* close›fitting tartan trousers.

tri- *combining form* three.

triad *n* **1** group of three. **2** (**T-**) Chinese criminal secret society

trial *n* **1** *Law* investigation of a case be›fore a judge. **2** trying or testing. **3** thing or person straining endurance or pa›tience. ♦ *pl* **4** sporting competition for individuals. **trial and error** method of discovery based on practical experience and experiment rather than theory.

triangle *n* **1** geometric figure with three sides. **2** triangular percussion instru›ment. **3** situation involving three peo›ple. **triangular** *adj*

tribe *n* group of clans or families be›lieved to have a common ancestor. **trib-al** *adj* **tribalism** *n* loyalty to a tribe.

tribulation *n* great distress.

tribunal *n* **1** board appointed to inquire into a specific matter. **2** lawcourt.

tribune *n* people's representative, esp. in ancient Rome.

tributary *n, pl* **-taries** **1** stream or river flowing into a larger one. ♦ *adj* **2** (of a stream or river) flowing into a larger one.

tribute *n* **1** sign of respect or admiration. **2** tax paid by one state to another.

trice *n* **in a trice** instantly.

triceps *n* muscle at the back of the up›per arm.

trichology [trick›**ol**›a›jee] *n* study and treatment of hair and its diseases. **tri-chologist** *n*

trick *n* **1** deceitful or cunning action or plan. **2** joke or prank. **3** feat of skill or cunning. **4** deceptive illusion. **5** manner›ism. **6** cards played in one round. ♦ *v* **7** cheat or deceive. **trickery** *n* **trickster** *n* **tricky** *adj* **1** difficult, needing careful handling. **2** crafty.

trickle *v* **1** (cause to) flow in a thin stream or drops. **2** move gradually. ♦ *n* **3** gradual flow.

tricolour [**trick**›kol›lor] *n* three›coloured striped flag.

tricycle *n* three›wheeled cycle.

trident *n* three›pronged spear.

triennial *adj* happening every three years.

trifle *n* **1** insignificant thing or amount. **2** dessert of sponge cake, fruit, custard, and cream. **trifling** *adj* insignificant. **trifle with** *v* toy with.

trigger *n* **1** small lever releasing a catch on a gun or machine. **2** action that sets off a course of events. ♦ *v* **3** (usu. foll. by *off*) set (an action or process) in mo›tion. **trigger-happy** *adj* too quick to use guns.

trigonometry *n* branch of mathematics dealing with relations of the sides and angles of triangles.

trike *n Informal* tricycle.

trilateral *adj* having three sides.

trilby *n, pl* **-bies** man's soft felt hat.

trill *n* **1** *Music* rapid alternation between two notes. **2** shrill warbling sound made by some birds. ♦ *v* **3** play or sing a trill.

trillion *n* **1** one million million, 10^{12}. **2** *Brit* (formerly) one million million mil›lion, 10^{18}.

> A *trillion* is what British speakers used to call 'a billion'.

trilobite [**trile**-oh-bite] *n* small prehistoric sea animal.

trilogy [**trill**-a-jee] *n, pl* **-gies** series of three related books, plays, etc.

trim *adj* **trimmer, trimmest** **1** neat and smart. **2** slender. ♦ *v* **trimming, trimmed** **3** cut or prune into good shape. **4** decorate with lace, ribbons, etc. **5** adjust the balance of (a ship or aircraft) by shifting the cargo etc. **6** adjust the sails of a ship to take advantage of the wind. ♦ *n* **7** decoration. **8** upholstery and decorative facings in a car. **9** trim state. **10** haircut that neatens the existing style. **trimming** *n* **1** decoration. ♦ *pl* **2** usual accompaniments, e.g. *turkey with all the trimmings.*

trimaran [**trime**-a-ran] *n* three-hulled boat.

trinitrotoluene *n* full name for TNT.

trinity *n, pl* **-ties** **1** group of three. **2** (**T-**) *Christianity* union of three persons, Father, Son, and Holy Spirit, in one God.

trinket *n* small or worthless ornament or piece of jewellery.

trio *n, pl* **trios** **1** group of three. **2** piece of music for three performers.

trip *n* **1** journey to a place and back, esp. for pleasure. **2** stumble. **3** act of causing someone to stumble. **4** *Informal* hallucinogenic drug experience. **5** switch on a mechanism. ♦ *v* **tripping, tripped** **6** (cause to) stumble. **7** (often foll. by *up*) catch (someone) in a mistake. **8** move or tread lightly. **9** *Informal* experience the hallucinogenic effects of a drug. **tripper** *n* tourist.

tripartite *adj* involving or composed of three people or parts.

tripe *n* **1** stomach of a cow used as food. **2** *Informal* nonsense.

triple *adj* **1** having three parts. **2** (of musical time or rhythm) having three beats in each bar. **3** three times as great or as many. ♦ *v* **4** increase three times. **triplet** *n* one of three babies born at one birth. **triple jump** athletic event in which competitors make a hop, a step, and a jump as a continuous movement.

triplicate *adj* triple. **in triplicate** in three copies.

tripod [**tripe**-pod] *n* three-legged stand, stool, etc.

tripos [**tripe**-poss] *n* final examinations for an honours degree at Cambridge University.

triptych [**trip**-tick] *n* painting or carving on three hinged panels, often forming an altarpiece.

trite *adj* (of a remark or idea) commonplace and unoriginal.

tritium *n* radioactive isotope of hydrogen.

triumph *n* **1** (happiness caused by) victory or success. ♦ *v* **2** be victorious or successful. **3** rejoice over a victory. **triumphal** *adj* celebrating a triumph. **triumphant** *adj* feeling or showing triumph. **triumphantly** *adv*

triumvirate [try-**umm**-vir-rit] *n* group of three people in joint control.

trivalent *adj Chem* **1** having a valency of three. **2** having three valencies. **trivalency** *n*

trivet [**triv**-vit] *n* metal stand for a pot or kettle.

trivial *adj* of little importance. **trivially** *adv* **trivia** *pl n* trivial things or details. **triviality** *n* . **trivialize** *v* make (something) seem less important or complex than it is.

trod *v* past tense and a past participle of TREAD.

trodden *v* a past participle of TREAD.

troglodyte *n* cave dweller.

troika *n* **1** Russian vehicle drawn by three horses abreast. **2** group of three people in authority.

Trojan *adj* **1** of Ancient Troy. ♦ *n* **2** person from ancient Troy. **3** hard-working person. **Trojan Horse** trap intended to undermine an enemy.

troll[1] *n* giant or dwarf in Scandinavian folklore.

troll[2] *v* fish by dragging a baited hook through the water.

trolley *n* **1** small wheeled table for food and drink. **2** wheeled cart for moving goods. **trolley bus** bus powered by electricity from an overhead wire but not running on rails.

trollop *n* promiscuous or slovenly woman.

trombone *n* brass musical instrument with a sliding tube. **trombonist** *n*

troop *n* **1** large group. **2** artillery or cavalry unit. **3** Scout company. ♦ *pl* **4** soldiers. ♦ *v* **5** move in a crowd. **6** *Brit mil* parade (the colour or flag of a regiment) ceremonially. **trooper** *n* cavalry soldier.

trope *n* figure of speech.

trophy *n, pl* **-phies 1** cup, shield, etc. given as a prize. **2** memento of success.

tropic *n* **1** either of two lines of latitude at 23½°N (**tropic of Cancer**) or 23½°S (**tropic of Capricorn**). ♦ *pl* **2** part of the earth's surface between these lines. **tropical** *adj* **1** of or in the tropics. **2** (of climate) very hot.

tropism *n* tendency of a plant or animal to turn or curve in response to an external stimulus.

troposphere *n* lowest layer of the earth's atmosphere.

trot *v* **trotting, trotted 1** (of a horse) move at a medium pace, lifting the feet in diagonal pairs. **2** (of a person) move at a steady brisk pace. ♦ *n* **3** trotting. **trotter** *n* pig's foot. **trot out** *v* repeat (old ideas etc.) without fresh thought.

troth [rhymes with **growth**] *n Obs* pledge of devotion, esp. a betrothal.

Trotskyist, Trotskyite *n, adj* (supporter) of the theories of Leon Trotsky, Russian communist writer.

troubadour [**troo**-bad-oor] *n* medieval travelling poet and singer.

trouble *n* **1** (cause of) distress or anxiety. **2** disease or malfunctioning. **3** state of disorder or unrest. **4** care or effort. ♦ *v* **5** (cause to) worry. **6** exert oneself. **7** cause inconvenience to. **troubled** *adj* **troublesome** *adj* **troublemaker** *n* person who causes trouble, esp. between people. **troubleshooter** *n* person employed to locate and deal with faults or problems. **trouble spot** place where there is frequent fighting or violence.

trough [**troff**] *n* **1** long open container, esp. for animals' food or water. **2** narrow channel between two waves or ridges. **3** low point in a cycle. **4** *Meteorol* area of low pressure.

trounce *v* defeat utterly.

troupe [**troop**] *n* company of performers. **trouper** *n*

trousers *pl n* two-legged outer garment with legs reaching usu. to the ankles. **trouser** *adj* of trousers.

trousseau [**troo**-so] *n, pl* **-seaux, -seaus** bride's collection of clothing etc. for her marriage.

trout *n* game fish related to the salmon.

trowel *n* hand tool with a wide blade for spreading mortar, lifting plants, etc.

troy weight, troy *n* system of weights used for gold, silver, and jewels.

truant *n* pupil who stays away from school without permission. **play truant** stay away from school without permission. **truancy** *n*

truce *n* temporary agreement to stop fighting.

truck¹ *n* **1** railway goods wagon. **2** lorry. **trucker** *n Chiefly US* lorry driver.

truck² *n* **have no truck with** refuse to be involved with.

truckle bed *n* low bed on wheels, stored under a larger bed.

truculent [**truck**-yew-lent] *adj* aggressively defiant. **truculence** *n*

trudge *v* **1** walk heavily or wearily. ♦ *n* **2** long tiring walk.

true *adj* **truer, truest 1** in accordance with facts. **2** genuine. **3** faithful. **4** exact. **truly** *adv* **1** in a true manner. **2** really. **truism** *n* self-evident truth. **truth** *n* **1** state of being true. **2** something true. **truthful** *adj* **1** honest. **2** exact. **truthfully** *adv* **true-blue** *adj* fiercely loyal. **true blue** *Brit* staunch Royalist or Conservative.

truffle *n* **1** edible underground fungus. **2** sweet flavoured with chocolate.

trug *n* long shallow basket used by gardeners.

trump¹ *n, adj* **1** (card) of the suit outranking the others. ♦ *v* **2** play a trump card on (another card). ♦ *pl n* **3** suit outranking the others. **turn up trumps** achieve an unexpected success. **trumped up** invented or concocted.

trump[2] *n Lit* (sound of) a trumpet.

trumpery *n, pl* **-eries 1** something useless or worthless. ♦ *adj* **2** useless or worthless.

trumpet *n* **1** valved brass instrument with a flared tube. ♦ *v* **-peting, -peted 2** proclaim loudly. **3** (of an elephant) cry loudly. **trumpeter** *n*

truncate *v* cut short.

truncheon *n* small club carried by a policeman.

trundle *v* move heavily on wheels.

trunk *n* **1** main stem of a tree. **2** large case or box for clothes etc. **3** person's body excluding the head and limbs. **4** elephant's long nose. **5** *US* car boot. ♦ *pl* **6** man's swimming shorts. **trunk call** long-distance telephone call. **trunk road** main road.

truss *v* **1** tie or bind up. ♦ *n* **2** device for holding a hernia in place. **3** framework supporting a roof, bridge, etc.

trust *v* **1** believe in and rely on. **2** consign to someone's care. **3** expect or hope. ♦ *n* **4** confidence in the truth, reliability, etc. of a person or thing. **5** obligation arising from responsibility. **6** arrangement in which one person administers property, money, etc. on another's behalf. **7** property held for another. **8** *Brit* self-governing hospital or group of hospitals within the National Health Service. **9** group of companies joined to control a market. **trustee** *n* person holding property on another's behalf. **trustful, trusting** *adj* inclined to trust others. **trustworthy** *adj* reliable or honest. **trusty** *adj* faithful or reliable. **trust fund** money or securities held in trust.

truth *n* see TRUE.

try *v* **trying, tried 1** make an effort or attempt. **2** test or sample. **3** put strain on, e.g. *he tries my patience.* **4** investigate (a case). **5** examine (a person) in a lawcourt. ♦ *n, pl* **tries 6** attempt or effort. **7** *Rugby* score gained by touching the ball down over the opponent's goal line. **try it on** *Informal* try to deceive or fool someone. **trying** *adj Informal* difficult or annoying.

> The idiom *try to* can be used at any time. The alternative *try and* is less formal and often signals a 'dare': *Just try and stop me!*.

tryst *n* arrangement to meet.

tsar, czar [**zahr**] *n Hist* Russian emperor.

tsetse fly [**tset**-see] *n* bloodsucking African fly whose bite transmits disease, esp. sleeping sickness.

T-shirt *n* short-sleeved casual shirt or top.

tsp. teaspoon.

T-square *n* T-shaped ruler.

tsunami *n, pl* **-mis, -mi** tidal wave, usu. caused by an earthquake under the sea.

TT teetotal.

tub *n* **1** open, usu. round container. **2** bath. **tubby** *adj* (of a person) short and fat.

tuba [**tube**-a] *n* valved low-pitched brass instrument.

tube *n* **1** hollow cylinder. **2** flexible cylinder with a cap to hold pastes. **the tube** underground railway, esp. the one in London. **tubing** *n* **1** length of tube. **2** system of tubes. **tubular** [**tube**-yew-lar] *adj* of or shaped like a tube.

tuber [**tube**-er] *n* fleshy underground root of a plant such as a potato. **tuberous** *adj*

tubercle [**tube**-er-kl] *n* small rounded swelling.

tuberculosis [tube-berk-yew-**lohss**-iss] *n* infectious disease causing tubercles, esp. in the lungs. **tubercular** *adj* **tuberculin** *n* extract from a bacillus used to test for tuberculosis.

TUC Trades Union Congress.

tuck *v* **1** push or fold into a small space. **2** thrust the loose ends or sides of (a shirt etc.) into a space. **3** stitch in folds. ♦ *n* **4** stitched fold. **5** *Informal* food. **tuck away** *v* **1** eat (a large amount of food). **2** store in a safe place.

Tudor *adj* **1** of the English royal house ruling from 1485–1603. **2** in an architectural style characterized by half-timbered buildings.

Tues. Tuesday.

Tuesday *n* third day of the week.

tufa [**tew**-fa] *n* porous rock formed as a deposit from springs.

tuffet *n* small mound or seat.

tuft *n* bunch of feathers, grass, hair, etc. held or growing together at the base. **tufted** *adj*

tug *v* **tugging, tugged 1** pull hard. ♦ *n* **2** hard pull. **3** (also **tugboat**) small ship used to tow other vessels. **tug of war** contest in which two teams pull against one another on a rope.

tuition *n* instruction, esp. received individually or in a small group.

tulip *n* plant with bright cup-shaped flowers.

tulle [**tewl**] *n* fine net fabric of silk etc.

tumble *v* **1** (cause to) fall, esp. awkwardly or violently. **2** roll or twist, esp. in play. **3** rumple. ♦ *n* **4** fall. **5** somersault. **tumbler** *n* **1** stemless drinking glass. **2** acrobat. **3** spring catch in a lock. **tumbledown** *adj* dilapidated. **tumble dryer, drier** machine that dries laundry by rotating it in warm air. **tumble to** *v* *Informal* realize, understand.

tumbril, tumbrel *n* farm cart used during the French Revolution to take prisoners to the guillotine.

tumescent [tew-**mess**-ent] *adj* swollen or becoming swollen.

tummy *n, pl* **-mies** *Informal* stomach.

tumour [**tew**-mer] *n* abnormal growth in or on the body.

tumult [**tew**-mult] *n* uproar or commotion. **tumultuous** [tew-**mull**-tew-uss] *adj*

tumulus [**tew**-mew-luss] *n, pl* **-li** [-lie] burial mound.

tun *n* large beer cask.

tuna [**tune**-a] *n* large marine food fish.

tundra *n* vast treeless Arctic region with permanently frozen subsoil.

tune *n* **1** (pleasing) sequence of musical notes. **2** correct musical pitch, e.g. *she sang out of tune.* ♦ *v* **3** adjust (a musical instrument) so that it is in tune. **4** adjust (a machine) to obtain the desired performance. **tuneful** *adj* **tunefully** *adv* **tuneless** *adj* **tuner** *n* part of a radio or television receiver for selecting channels. **tune in** *v* adjust (a radio or television) to receive (a station or programme). **tuning fork** small steel instrument which produces a note of a fixed musical pitch when struck.

tungsten *n Chem* greyish-white metal.

tunic *n* **1** close-fitting jacket forming part of some uniforms. **2** loose knee-length garment.

tunnel *n* **1** underground passage. ♦ *v* **-nelling, -nelled 2** make a tunnel (through). **tunnel vision 1** condition in which a person is unable to see things that are not straight in front of him or her. **2** narrowness of viewpoint caused by concentration on a single idea or opinion.

tunny *n, pl* **-nies, -ny** same as TUNA.

tup *n* male sheep.

turban *n* Muslim, Hindu, or Sikh man's head covering, made by winding cloth round the head.

turbid *adj* muddy, not clear.

turbine *n* machine or generator driven by gas, water, etc. turning blades.

turbocharger *n* device that increases the power of an internal-combustion engine by using the exhaust gases to drive a turbine.

turbofan *n* engine in which a large fan driven by a turbine forces air rearwards to increase the thrust.

turboprop *n* gas turbine for driving an aircraft propeller.

turbot *n* large European edible flatfish.

turbulence *n* **1** confusion, movement, or agitation. **2** atmospheric instability causing gusty air currents. **turbulent** *adj*

tureen *n* serving dish for soup.

turf *n, pl* **turfs, turves 1** short thick even grass. **2** square of this with roots and soil attached. ♦ *v* **3** cover with turf. **the**

turf **1** racecourse. **2** horse racing. **turf accountant** bookmaker. **turf out** *v Informal* throw out.

turgid [**tur**-jid] *adj* **1** (of language) pompous. **2** swollen and thick. **turgidity** *n*

turkey *n* large bird bred for food.

Turkish *adj* **1** of Turkey, its people, or their language. ♦ *n* **2** Turkish language. **Turkish bath** steam bath. **Turkish delight** jelly-like sweet coated with icing sugar.

turmeric *n* yellow spice obtained from the root of an Asian plant.

turmoil *n* agitation or confusion.

turn *v* **1** change the position or direction (of). **2** move around an axis, rotate. **3** (usu. foll. by *into*) change in nature or character. **4** reach or pass in age, time, etc., e.g. *she has just turned twenty.* **5** shape on a lathe. **6** become sour. ♦ *n* **7** turning. **8** opportunity to do something as part of an agreed succession. **9** direction or drift. **10** period or spell. **11** short excursion. **12** slight attack of an illness. **13** short theatrical performance. **good, bad turn** helpful *or* unhelpful act. **turner** *n* **turning** *n* road or path leading off a main route. **turncoat** *n* person who deserts one party or cause to join another. **turn down** *v* **1** reduce the volume or brightness (of). **2** refuse or reject. **turn in** *v* **1** go to bed. **2** hand in. **turning circle** smallest circle in which a vehicle can turn. **turning point** moment when a decisive change occurs. **turn off** *v* stop (something) working by using a knob etc. **turn on** *v* **1** start (something) working by using a knob etc. **2** become aggressive towards. **3** *Informal* excite, esp. sexually. **turnout** *n* number of people appearing at a gathering. **turn out** *v* **1** produce or create. **2** be discovered. **3** end up or result. **turnover** *n* **1** total sales made by a business over a certain period. **2** small pastry. **3** rate at which staff leave and are replaced. **turnpike** *n* road where a toll is collected at barriers. **turnstile** *n* revolving gate for admitting one person at a time. **turntable** *n* revolving platform. **turn up** *v* **1** arrive or appear. **2** find or be found. **3** increase the volume or brightness (of). **turn-up** *n* **1** turned-up fold at the bottom of a trouser leg. **2** *Informal* unexpected event.

turnip *n* root vegetable with orange or white flesh.

turpentine *n* (oil made from) the resin of certain trees. **turps** *n* turpentine oil.

turpitude *n* wickedness.

turquoise *adj* **1** blue-green. ♦ *n* **2** blue-green precious stone.

turret *n* **1** small tower. **2** revolving gun tower on a warship or tank. **turreted** *adj*

turtle *n* sea tortoise. **turn turtle** capsize. **turtledove** *n* small wild dove. **turtleneck** *n* (sweater with) a round high close-fitting neck.

tusk *n* long pointed tooth of an elephant, walrus, etc.

tussle *n, v* fight or scuffle.

tussock *n* tuft of grass.

tutelage [**tew**-till-lij] *n* **1** instruction or guidance, esp. by a tutor. **2** state of being supervised by a guardian or tutor. **tutelary** [**tew**-till-lar-ee] *adj*

tutor *n* **1** person teaching individuals or small groups. ♦ *v* **2** act as a tutor to. **tutorial** *n* period of instruction with a tutor.

tutti *adj, adv Music* to be performed by the whole orchestra or choir.

tutti-frutti *n* ice cream or other sweet food containing small pieces of candied or fresh fruits.

tutu *n* short stiff skirt worn by ballerinas.

tuxedo *n, pl* **-dos** *US & Aust* dinner jacket.

TV television.

twaddle *n* silly or pretentious talk or writing.

twain *n Obs* two.

twang *n* **1** sharp ringing sound. **2** nasal speech. ♦ *v* **3** (cause to) make a twang. **twangy** *adj*

tweak *v* **1** pinch or twist sharply. ♦ *n* **2** tweaking.

twee *adj Informal* too sentimental,

sweet, or pretty.

tweed *n* **1** thick woollen cloth. ♦ *pl* **2** suit of tweed. **tweedy** *adj* **1** of or made of tweed. **2** showing a fondness for country life, often associated with wearers of tweed.

tweet *n, v* chirp. **tweeter** *n* loudspeaker reproducing high-frequency sounds.

tweezers *pl n* small pincer-like tool.

twelve *adj, n* two more than ten. **twelfth** *adj, n* (of) number twelve in a series.

twenty *adj, n* two times ten. **twentieth** *adj, n*

twerp *n Informal* silly person.

twice *adv* two times.

twiddle *v* fiddle or twirl in an idle way. **twiddle one's thumbs** be bored, have nothing to do.

twig[1] *n* small branch or shoot.

twig[2] *v* **twigging, twigged** *Informal* realize or understand.

twilight *n* **1** soft dim light just after sunset. **2** period in which strength or importance is gradually declining. **twilit** *adj*

twill *n* fabric woven to produce parallel ridges.

twin *n* **1** one of a pair, esp. of two children born at one birth. ♦ *v* **twinning, twinned** **2** pair or be paired. **twin town** *Brit* town that has cultural and social links with a foreign town.

twine *n* **1** string or cord. ♦ *v* **2** twist or coil round.

twinge *n* sudden sharp pain or emotional pang.

twinkle *v* **1** shine brightly but intermittently. ♦ *n* **2** flickering brightness. **in the twinkling of an eye** in a very short time.

twirl *v* **1** turn or spin around quickly. **2** twist or wind, esp. idly.

twist *v* **1** turn out of the natural position. **2** distort or pervert. **3** wind or twine. ♦ *n* **4** twisting. **5** twisted thing. **6** unexpected development in the plot of a film, book, etc. **7** bend or curve. **8** distortion. **twisted** *adj* (of a person) cruel or perverted. **twister** *n Informal* swindler.

twit[1] *v* **twitting, twitted** poke fun at (someone).

twit[2] *n Informal* foolish person.

twitch *v* **1** move spasmodically. **2** pull sharply. ♦ *n* **3** nervous muscular spasm. **4** sharp pull.

twitter *v* **1** (of birds) utter chirping sounds. **2** talk nervously. ♦ *n* **3** act or sound of twittering.

two *adj, n* one more than one. **two-edged** *adj* (of a remark) having both a favourable and an unfavourable interpretation. **two-faced** *adj* deceitful, hypocritical. **two-ply** *adj* having two layers or strands. **two-stroke** *adj* (of an internal-combustion engine) making one explosion to every two strokes of the piston. **two-time** *v Informal* deceive (a lover) by having an affair with someone else. **two-way** *adj* **1** moving in, or allowing movement in, two opposite directions. **2** involving mutual involvement or cooperation. **3** (of a radio or transmitter) capable of both transmission and reception of messages.

TX Texas.

tycoon *n* powerful wealthy businessman.

tyke *n Informal* small cheeky child.

tympanum *n, pl* **-nums, -na** **1** cavity of the middle ear. **2** tympanic membrane. **3** *Archit* space between the arch and the lintel above a door. **tympanic** *adj* **tympanic membrane** thin membrane separating the external ear from the middle ear.

type *n* **1** class or category. **2** *Informal* person, esp. of a specified kind. **3** block with a raised character used for printing. **4** printed text. ♦ *v* **5** print with a typewriter or word processor. **6** typify. **7** classify. **typist** *n* person who types with a typewriter or word processor. **typecast** *v* continually cast (an actor or actress) in similar roles. **typeface** *n Printing* style of the type. **typescript** *n* typewritten document. **typewriter** *n* machine which prints a character when the appropriate key is pressed.

typhoid fever *n* acute infectious feverish disease.

typhoon *n* violent tropical storm.

typhus *n* infectious feverish disease.

typical *adj* true to type, characteristic. **typically** *adv* **typify** *v* **-fying, -fied** be typical of.

typography *n* art or style of printing. **typographical** *adj* **typographer** *n*

tyrannosaurus [tirr-ran-oh-**sore**-uss] *n* large two-footed flesh-eating dinosaur.

tyrant *n* **1** oppressive or cruel ruler. **2** person who exercises authority oppressively. **tyrannical** *adj* like a tyrant, oppressive. **tyrannize** *v* exert power (over) oppressively or cruelly. **tyrannous** *adj* **tyranny** *n* tyrannical rule.

tyre *n* rubber ring, usu. inflated, over the rim of a vehicle's wheel to grip the road.

tyro *n, pl* **-ros** novice or beginner.

tzar *n* same as TSAR.

tzetze fly *n* same as TSETSE FLY.

U u

U *Chem* uranium.

UB40 *n Brit* registration card issued to an unemployed person.

ubiquitous [yew-**bik**-wit-uss] *adj* being or seeming to be everywhere at once. **ubiquity** *n*

U-boat *n* German submarine.

udder *n* large baglike milk-producing gland of cows, sheep, or goats.

UDI Unilateral Declaration of Independence.

UEFA Union of European Football Associations.

UFO unidentified flying object.

ugh [**uhh**] *interj* exclamation of disgust.

ugly *adj* **uglier, ugliest 1** of unpleasant appearance. **2** ominous or menacing. **ugliness** *n*

UHF ultrahigh frequency.

UHT (of milk or cream) ultra-heat-treated.

UK United Kingdom.

ukulele, ukelele [yew-kal-**lay**-lee] *n* small guitar with four strings.

ulcer *n* open sore on the surface of the skin or mucous membrane. **ulcerated** *adj* made or becoming ulcerous. **ulceration** *n* **ulcerous** *adj* of, like, or characterized by ulcers.

ulna *n, pl* **-nae, -nas** inner and longer of the two bones of the human forearm.

ulster *n* man's heavy double-breasted overcoat.

ulterior [ult-**ear**-ee-or] *adj* (of an aim, reason, etc.) concealed or hidden, e.g. *ulterior motives.*

ultimate *adj* **1** final in a series or process. **2** highest or supreme. **3** most extreme. **ultimately** *adv*

ultimatum [ult-im-**may**-tum] *n* final warning stating that action will be taken unless certain conditions are met.

ultra- *prefix* **1** beyond a specified extent, range, or limit, e.g. *ultrasonic.* **2** extremely, e.g. *ultramodern.*

ultrahigh frequency *n* radio frequency between 3000 and 300 megahertz.

ultramarine *adj* vivid blue.

ultrasonic *adj* of or producing sound waves with a higher frequency than the human ear can hear.

ultrasound *n* ultrasonic waves, used in medical diagnosis and therapy and in echo sounding.

ultraviolet *adj, n* (of) light beyond the limit of visibility at the violet end of the spectrum.

ululate [**yewl**-yew-late] *v* howl or wail. **ululation** *n*

umbel *n* umbrella-like flower cluster with the stalks springing from the central point. **umbelliferous** *adj* denoting a plant with flowers in umbels.

umber *adj* dark brown to reddish-brown.

umbilical [um-**bill**-ik-al] *adj* of the navel. **umbilical cord** long flexible tube of blood vessels that connects a fetus with the placenta.

umbra *n, pl* **-brae, -bras** shadow, esp. the shadow cast by the moon onto the earth during a solar eclipse.

umbrage *n* **take umbrage** feel offended or upset.

umbrella *n* **1** portable device used for protection against rain, consisting of a folding frame covered in material attached to a central rod. **2** single organization, idea, etc. that contains or covers many different organizations, ideas, etc.

umiak [**oo**-mee-ak] *n* Inuit boat made of skins.

umlaut [**oom**-lowt] *n* mark (¨) placed over a vowel, esp. in German, to indicate a change in its sound.

umpire *n* **1** official who rules on the playing of a game. ♦ *v* **2** act as umpire in (a game).

umpteen *adj Informal* very many. **umpteenth** *n, adj*

UN United Nations.

un- *prefix* **1** not, e.g. *unidentified.* **2** denoting reversal of an action, e.g. *untie.* **3** denoting removal from, e.g. *unthrone.*

unabated *adv* without any reduction in force, e.g. *the storm continued unabated.*

unable *adj* **unable to** lacking the necessary power, ability, or authority to (do something).

unaccountable *adj* **1** unable to be explained. **2** (foll. by *to*) not answerable to. **unaccountably** *adv*

unadulterated *adj* with nothing added, pure.

unaffected *adj* **1** unpretentious, natural, sincere. **2** not influenced or moved by something.

unanimous [yew-**nan**-im-uss] *adj* **1** in complete agreement. **2** agreed by all. **unanimously** *adv* **unanimity** *n*

unannounced *adv* without warning, e.g. *he turned up unannounced.*

unapproachable *adj* discouraging friendliness, aloof.

unarmed *adj* without weapons.

unassailable *adj* unable to be attacked or disputed.

unassuming *adj* modest or unpretentious.

unattached *adj* **1** not connected with any specific group or organization. **2** not married or involved in a steady relationship.

unavailing *adj* useless or futile.

unavoidable *adj* unable to be avoided or prevented. **unavoidably** *adv*

unaware *adj* not aware or conscious, e.g. *unaware of the danger.* **unawares** *adv* **1** by surprise, e.g. *caught unawares.* **2** without knowing.

> Note the difference between the adjective *unaware,* usually followed by *of* or *that,* and the adverb *unawares.*

unbalanced *adj* **1** biased or one-sided. **2** mentally deranged.

unbearable *adj* not able to be endured. **unbearably** *adv*

unbecoming *adj* unattractive or unsuitable.

unbeknown *adv* **unbeknown to** without the knowledge of (a person).

unbelievable *adj* **1** too unlikely to be believed. **2** *Informal* marvellous, amazing. **3** *Informal* terrible, shocking. **unbelievably** *adv*

unbend *v Informal* become less strict or more informal in one's attitudes or behaviour. **unbending** *adj* rigid or inflexible.

unbidden *adj* not ordered or asked.

unborn *adj* not yet born.

unbosom *v* relieve (oneself) of (secrets or feelings) by telling someone.

unbridled *adj* (of feelings or behaviour) not controlled in any way.

unburden *v* relieve (one's mind or oneself) of a worry by confiding in someone.

uncalled-for *adj* not fair or justified.

uncanny *adj* weird or mysterious. **uncannily** *adv*

unceremonious *adj* **1** relaxed and informal. **2** abrupt or rude. **unceremoniously** *adv*

uncertain *adj* **1** not able to be accurately known or predicted. **2** not able to be depended upon. **3** changeable. **uncertainty** *n*

uncharacteristic *adj* not typical. **uncharacteristically** *adv*

uncharitable *adj* unkind or harsh. **uncharitably** *adv*

un-Christian *adj* not in accordance with Christian principles.

uncivilized *adj* **1** (of a tribe or people) not yet civilized. **2** lacking culture or sophistication.

uncle *n* **1** brother of one's father or mother. **2** husband of one's aunt.

unclean *adj* lacking moral, spiritual, or physical cleanliness.

uncomfortable *adj* **1** not physically relaxed. **2** anxious or uneasy. **uncomfortably** *adv*

uncommon *adj* **1** not happening or encountered often. **2** in excess of what is normal. **uncommonly** *adv*

uncompromising *adj* not prepared to compromise. **uncompromisingly** *adv*

unconcerned *adj* lacking in concern or involvement. **unconcernedly** [un-kon-**sern**-id-lee] *adv*

unconditional *adj* without conditions or limitations. **unconditionally** *adv*

unconscionable *adj* **1** having no principles, unscrupulous. **2** excessive in amount or degree.

unconscious *adj* **1** lacking normal awareness through the senses. **2** not aware of one's actions or behaviour. ♦ *n* **3** part of the mind containing instincts and ideas that exist without one's awareness. **unconsciously** *adv* **unconsciousness** *n*

unconventional *adj* not conforming to accepted rules or standards.

uncooperative *adj* not willing to help other people with what they are doing.

uncouth *adj* lacking in good manners, refinement, or grace.

uncover *v* **1** reveal or disclose. **2** remove the cover, top, etc., from.

unction *n* act of anointing with oil in sacramental ceremonies.

unctuous *adj* pretending to be kind and concerned.

undecided *adj* **1** not having made up one's mind. **2** (of an issue or problem) not agreed or decided upon.

undeniable *adj* unquestionably true. **undeniably** *adv*

under *prep, adv* **1** indicating movement to or position beneath the underside or base. ♦ *prep* **2** less than. **3** subject to.

under- *prefix* **1** below, e.g. *underground.* **2** insufficient or insufficiently, e.g. *underrate.*

underachieve *v* fail to achieve a performance appropriate to one's age or talents. **underachiever** *n*

underage *adj* below the required or standard age.

underarm *adj* **1** *Sport* denoting a style of throwing, bowling, or serving in which the hand is swung below shoulder level. **2** of or denoting the armpit. ♦ *adv* **3** *Sport* in an underarm style.

undercarriage *n* **1** landing gear of an aircraft. **2** framework supporting the body of a vehicle.

underclass *n* class consisting of the most disadvantaged people, such as the long-term unemployed.

undercoat *n* coat of paint applied before the final coat.

undercover *adj* done or acting in secret.

undercurrent *n* **1** current that is not apparent at the surface. **2** underlying opinion or emotion.

undercut *v* charge less than (a competitor) to obtain trade.

underdeveloped *adj* **1** immature or undersized. **2** (of a country) lacking the finance, industries, and organization necessary to advance.

underdog *n* person or team in a weak or underprivileged position.

underdone *adj* not cooked enough.

underestimate *v* **1** make too low an estimate of. **2** not realize the full potential of.

underfelt *n* thick felt laid under a carpet to increase insulation.

underfoot *adv* under the feet.

undergarment *n* any piece of underwear.

undergo *v* experience, endure, or sustain.

undergraduate *n* person studying in a university for a first degree.

underground *adj* **1** occurring, situated, used, or going below ground level. **2** secret. ♦ *n* **3** electric passenger railway operated in underground tunnels. **4** movement dedicated to overthrowing a government or occupation forces.

undergrowth *n* small trees and bushes growing beneath taller trees in a wood or forest.

underhand *adj* sly, deceitful, and secretive.

underlay *n* felt or rubber laid beneath a carpet to increase insulation and resilience.

underlie *v* **1** lie or be placed under. **2** be the foundation, cause, or basis of. **underlying** *adj* fundamental or basic.

underline *v* **1** draw a line under. **2** state

forcibly, emphasize.

underling *n* subordinate.

undermine *v* **1** weaken gradually. **2** (of the sea or wind) wear away the base of (cliffs).

underneath *prep, adv* **1** under or beneath. ♦ *adj, n* **2** lower (part or surface).

underpants *pl n* man's undergarment for the lower part of the body.

underpass *n* section of a road that passes under another road or a railway line.

underpin *v* give strength or support to.

underprivileged *adj* lacking the rights and advantages of other members of society.

underrate *v* not realize the full potential of. **underrated** *adj*

underseal *n* coating of tar etc. applied to the underside of a motor vehicle to prevent corrosion.

undersecretary *n* senior civil servant or junior minister in a government department.

underside *n* bottom or lower surface.

undersized *adj* smaller than normal.

underskirt *n* skirtlike garment worn under a skirt or dress, petticoat.

understand *v* **1** know and comprehend the nature or meaning of. **2** realize or grasp (something). **3** assume, infer, or believe. **understandable** *adj* **understandably** *adv* **understanding** *n* **1** ability to learn, judge, or make decisions. **2** personal interpretation of a subject. **3** mutual agreement, usu. an informal or private one. ♦ *adj* **4** kind and sympathetic.

understate *v* **1** describe or represent (something) in restrained terms. **2** state that (something, such as a number) is less than it is. **understatement** *n*

understudy *n* **1** actor who studies a part in order to be able to replace the usual actor if necessary. ♦ *v* **2** act as an understudy for.

undertake *v* **1** agree or commit oneself to (something) or to do (something). **2** promise. **undertaking** *n* **1** task or enterprise. **2** agreement to do something.

undertaker *n* person whose job is to prepare corpses for burial or cremation and organize funerals.

undertone *n* **1** quiet tone of voice. **2** underlying quality or feeling.

undertow *n* strong undercurrent flowing in a different direction from the surface current.

underwater *adj, adv* (situated, occurring, or for use) below the surface of the sea, a lake, or a river.

underwear *n* clothing worn under the outer garments and next to the skin.

underworld *n* **1** criminals and their associates. **2** *Greek & Roman myth* regions below the earth's surface regarded as the abode of the dead.

underwrite *v* **1** accept financial responsibility for (a commercial project). **2** sign and issue (an insurance policy), thus accepting liability. **underwriter** *n*

undesirable *adj* **1** not desirable or pleasant, objectionable. ♦ *n* **2** objectionable person.

undies *pl n Informal* underwear, esp. women's.

undistinguished *adj* not particularly good or bad, mediocre.

undo *v* **1** open, unwrap. **2** reverse the effects of. **3** cause the downfall of. **undone** *adj* **undoing** *n* cause of someone's downfall.

undoubted *adj* certain or indisputable. **undoubtedly** *adv*

undress *v* **1** take off the clothes of (oneself or another person). ♦ *n* **2** **in a state of undress** naked or nearly naked.

undue *adj* greater than is reasonable, excessive. **unduly** *adv*

undulate *v* move in waves. **undulation** *n*

undying *adj* never ending, eternal.

unearned income *n* income from property or investments rather than work.

unearth *v* **1** reveal or discover by searching. **2** dig up out of the earth.

unearthly *adj* **1** ghostly or eerie. **2** ridiculous or unreasonable, e.g. *an unearthly hour.*

uneasy *adj* **1** (of a person) anxious or apprehensive. **2** (of a condition) precarious or uncomfortable. **uneasily** *adv* **uneasiness** *n* **unease** *n* **1** feeling of anxiety. **2** state of dissatisfaction.

unemployed *adj* **1** out of work. ♦ *pl n* **2 the unemployed** people who are out of work. **unemployment** *n*

unequivocal *adj* completely clear in meaning. **unequivocally** *adv*

unerring *adj* never mistaken, consistently accurate.

UNESCO United Nations Educational, Scientific, and Cultural Organization.

uneven *adj* **1** not level or flat. **2** not consistent in quality, e.g. *an uneven performance.* **3** not fairly matched, e.g. *an uneven race.*

unexceptionable *adj* beyond criticism or objection.

unexceptional *adj* ordinary or normal.

unexpected *adj* surprising or unforeseen. **unexpectedly** *adv*

unfailing *adj* continuous or reliable. **unfailingly** *adv*

unfair *adj* not right, fair, or just. **unfairly** *adv* **unfairness** *n*

unfaithful *adj* **1** having sex with someone other than one's regular partner. **2** not true to a promise or vow. **unfaithfulness** *n*

unfathomable *adj* too strange or too complicated to be understood.

unfavourable *adj* **1** unlikely to produce the desired outcome, inauspicious, e.g. *unfavourable weather conditions.* **2** disapproving, e.g. *an unfavourable opinion.* **unfavourably** *adv*

unfeeling *adj* without sympathy.

unfit *adj* **1** unqualified or unsuitable. **2** in poor physical condition.

unflappable *adj Informal* not easily upset. **unflappability** *n*

unfold *v* **1** open or spread out from a folded state. **2** reveal or be revealed.

unforeseen *adj* surprising because not expected.

unforgettable *adj* impossible to forget, memorable. **unforgettably** *adv*

unfortunate *adj* **1** unlucky, unsuccessful, or unhappy. **2** regrettable or unsuitable. ♦ *n* **3** unlucky person. **unfortunately** *adv*

unfounded *adj* not based on facts or evidence.

unfrock *v* deprive (a priest in holy orders) of his priesthood.

unfurl *v* unroll or unfold.

ungainly *adj* **-lier, -liest** lacking grace when moving. **ungainliness** *n*

ungodly *adj* **1** *Informal* unreasonable or outrageous, e.g. *an ungodly hour.* **2** wicked or sinful. **ungodliness** *n*

ungovernable *adj* not able to be disciplined or restrained.

ungrateful *adj* not grateful or thankful.

unguarded *adj* **1** not protected. **2** incautious or careless.

unguent [**ung**-gwent] *n Lit* ointment.

unhand *v Old-fashioned or lit* release from one's grasp.

unhappy *adj* **1** sad or depressed. **2** unfortunate or wretched. **unhappily** *adv* **unhappiness** *n*

unhealthy *adj* **1** likely to cause poor health. **2** not fit or well. **3** morbid, unnatural.

unheard-of *adj* **1** without precedent. **2** highly offensive or shocking.

unhinge *v* derange or unbalance (a person or his or her mind).

unholy *adj* **1** immoral or wicked. **2** *Informal* unnatural or outrageous, e.g. *an unholy mess.*

uni- *combining form* of, consisting of, or having only one, e.g. *unicellular.*

UNICEF *n* agency of United Nations that funds education and children's health.

unicorn *n* imaginary horselike creature with one horn growing from its forehead.

uniform *n* **1** special identifying set of clothes for the members of an organization, such as soldiers. ♦ *adj* **2** regular and even throughout, unvarying. **3** alike or like. **uniformly** *adv* **uniformity** *n*

unify *v* **-fying, -fied** make or become one. **unification** *n*

unilateral *adj* made or done by only one person or group. **unilaterally** *adv*

unimpeachable *adj* completely honest and reliable.

uninterested *adj* having or showing no interest in someone or something.

union *n* **1** uniting or being united. **2** short for TRADE UNION. **3** association or confederation of individuals or groups for a common purpose. **unionist** *n* member or supporter of a trade union. **unionism** *n* **unionize** *v* organize (workers) into a trade union. **unionization** *n* **Union Jack, Flag** national flag of the United Kingdom.

unique [yoo-**neek**] *adj* **1** being the only one of a particular type. **2** without equal or like. **unique to** concerning or belonging to a particular person, thing, or group. **uniquely** *adv*

> Because of its meaning, avoid using *unique* with modifiers like *very* and *rather.*

unisex *adj* designed for use by both sexes.

unison *n* **1** complete agreement. **2** *Music* singing or playing of the same notes together at the same time. **in unison** at the same time as another person or other people.

UNISON *n* British trade union consisting mainly of council and hospital workers.

unit *n* **1** single undivided entity or whole. **2** group or individual regarded as a basic element of a larger whole. **3** fixed quantity etc., used as a standard of measurement. **4** piece of furniture designed to be fitted with other similar pieces, e.g. *kitchen units.* **unit trust** investment trust that issues units for public sale and invests the money in many different businesses.

Unitarian *n* person who believes that God is one being and rejects the Trinity. **Unitarianism** *n*

unitary *adj* **1** consisting of a single undivided whole. **2** of a unit or units.

unite *v* **1** make or become an integrated whole. **2** (cause to) enter into an association or alliance.

unity *n* **1** state of being one. **2** mutual agreement.

universe *n* **1** whole of all existing matter, energy, and space. **2** the world. **universal** *adj* **1** of or typical of the whole of mankind or of nature. **2** existing everywhere. **universally** *adv* **universality** *n*

university *n, pl* **-ties** institution of higher education with the authority to award degrees.

unkempt *adj* **1** (of the hair) not combed. **2** slovenly or untidy.

unkind *adj* unsympathetic or cruel. **unkindly** *adv* **unkindness** *n*

unknown *adj* **1** not known. **2** not famous. ♦ *n* **3** unknown person, quantity, or thing.

unleaded *adj* (of petrol) containing less tetraethyl lead, in order to reduce environmental pollution.

unleash *v* set loose or cause (something bad).

unleavened [un-**lev**-vend] *adj* (of bread) made without yeast.

unless *conj* except under the circumstances that.

unlike *adj* **1** dissimilar or different. ♦ *prep* **2** not like or typical of.

unlikely *adj* improbable.

unload *v* **1** remove (cargo) from (a ship, lorry, or plane). **2** tell someone your problems or worries. **3** remove the ammunition from (a firearm).

unlooked-for *adj* unexpected or unforeseen.

unlucky *adj* **1** having bad luck, unfortunate. **2** ill-omened or inauspicious.

unman *v* cause to lose courage or nerve.

unmanned *adj* having no personnel or crew.

unmask *v* **1** remove the mask or disguise from. **2** (cause to) appear in true character.

unmentionable *adj* unsuitable as a topic of conversation.

unmistakable, unmistakeable *adj*

not ambiguous, clear. **unmistakably, unmistakeably** *adv*

unmitigated *adj* **1** not reduced or lessened in severity etc. **2** total and complete.

unmoved *adj* not affected by emotion, indifferent.

unnatural *adj* **1** strange and frightening because not usual. **2** not in accordance with accepted standards of behaviour. **unnaturally** *adv* **not unnaturally** as one would expect.

unnecessary *adj* not essential, or more than is essential. **unnecessarily** *adv*

unnerve *v* cause to lose courage, confidence, or self-control. **unnerving** *adj*

unnumbered *adj* **1** countless. **2** not counted or given a number.

UNO United Nations Organization.

unobtrusive *adj* not drawing attention to oneself or itself, inconspicuous. **unobtrusively** *adv*

unorthodox *adj* **1** (of ideas, methods, etc.) unconventional and not generally accepted. **2** (of a person) having unusual opinions or methods.

unpack *v* **1** remove the contents of (a suitcase, trunk, etc.). **2** take (something) out of a packed container.

unpalatable *adj* **1** (of food) unpleasant to taste. **2** (of a fact, idea, etc.) unpleasant and hard to accept.

unparalleled *adj* not equalled, supreme.

unpick *v* undo (the stitches) of (a piece of sewing).

unpleasant *adj* not pleasant or agreeable. **unpleasantly** *adv* **unpleasantness** *n*

unpopular *adj* generally disliked or disapproved of. **unpopularity** *n*

unprecedented *adj* never having happened before, unparalleled.

unprepossessing *adj* unattractive in appearance.

unpretentious *adj* modest, unassuming, and down-to-earth.

unprincipled *adj* lacking moral principles, unscrupulous.

unprintable *adj* unsuitable for printing for reasons of obscenity or libel.

unprofessional *adj* contrary to the accepted code of a profession. **unprofessionally** *adv*

unprofitable *adj* **1** not making a profit. **2** not helpful or beneficial.

unqualified *adj* **1** lacking the necessary qualifications. **2** total or complete.

unquestionable *adj* not to be doubted, indisputable. **unquestionably** *adv*

unquote *interj* expression used to indicate the end of a quotation that was introduced with the word 'quote'.

unravel *v* **-elling, -elled 1** reduce (something knitted or woven) to separate strands. **2** become unravelled. **3** explain or solve.

unreadable *adj* **1** unable to be read or deciphered. **2** too difficult or dull to read.

unreal *adj* **1** (as if) existing only in the imagination. **2** insincere or artificial. **unreality** *n*

unreasonable *adj* **1** immoderate or excessive. **2** refusing to listen to reason. **unreasonably** *adv*

unremitting *adj* never slackening or stopping. **unremittingly** *adv*

unrequited *adj* not returned, e.g. *unrequited love.*

unreserved *adj* completely, without reservation. **unreservedly** [un-re-**zerv**-id-lee] *adv*

unrest *n* rebellious state of discontent.

unrivalled *adj* having no equal.

unroll *v* open out or unwind (something rolled or coiled) or (of something rolled or coiled) become opened out or unwound.

unruffled *adj* **1** calm and unperturbed. **2** smooth and still.

unruly *adj* **-lier, -liest** difficult to control or organize.

unsaturated *adj* **1** (of an organic compound) containing a double or triple bond and therefore capable of combining with other substances. **2** (of a fat, esp. a vegetable fat) containing a high proportion of fatty acids with double bonds.

unsavoury *adj* distasteful or objectionable.

unscathed *adj* not harmed or injured.

unscrupulous *adj* prepared to act dishonestly, unprincipled.

unseasonable *adj* inappropriate or unusual for the time of year. **unseasonably** *adv*

unseat *v* **1** throw or displace from a seat or saddle. **2** depose from an office or position.

unseemly *adj* not according to expected standards of behaviour.

unsettled *adj* **1** lacking order or stability. **2** disturbed and restless. **3** constantly changing or moving from place to place.

unshakable, unshakeable *adj* (of beliefs) completely firm, not wavering. **unshakably, unshakeably** *adv*

unsightly *adj* unpleasant to look at.

unsocial *adj* **1** (also **unsociable**) avoiding the company of other people. **2** falling outside the normal working day, e.g. *unsocial hours.*

unsound *adj* **1** unhealthy or unstable. **2** not based on truth or fact.

unspeakable *adj* indescribably bad or evil. **unspeakably** *adv*

unstable *adj* **1** lacking stability or firmness. **2** having abrupt changes of mood or behaviour.

unsteady *adj* **1** not securely fixed. **2** shaky or staggering. **unsteadily** *adv*

unstinting *adj* generous, gladly given, e.g. *unstinting praise.*

unstructured *adj* without formal or systematic organization.

unstuck *adj* **come unstuck** *Informal* fail badly.

unstudied *adj* natural or spontaneous.

unsuccessful *adj* not achieving success. **unsuccessfully** *adv*

unsuitable *adj* not right or appropriate for a particular purpose. **unsuitably** *adv*

unsuited *adj* **1** not appropriate for a particular task or situation. **2** (of a couple) having different personalities or tastes and unlikely to form a lasting relationship.

unsung *adj* not acclaimed or honoured, e.g. *unsung heroes.*

unswerving *adj* firm, constant, not changing.

unsympathetic *adj* **1** not feeling or showing sympathy. **2** unpleasant, not likeable. **3** (foll. by *to*) opposed to.

untapped *adj* not yet used, e.g. *untapped resources.*

untenable *adj* (of a theory, idea, etc.) incapable of being defended.

unthinkable *adj* out of the question, inconceivable.

untidy *adj* messy and disordered. **untidily** *adv* **untidiness** *n*

untie *v* **1** open or free (something that is tied). **2** free from constraint.

until *conj* **1** up to the time that. ♦ *prep* **2** in or throughout the period before. **not until** not before (a time or event).

untimely *adj* **1** occurring before the expected or normal time. **2** inappropriate to the occasion or time. **untimeliness** *n*

unto *prep Old-fashioned* to.

untold *adj* **1** incapable of description. **2** incalculably great in number or quantity.

untouchable *adj* **1** above reproach or suspicion. **2** unable to be touched. ♦ *n* **3** member of the lowest Hindu caste in India.

untoward *adj* causing misfortune or annoyance.

untrue *adj* **1** incorrect or false. **2** disloyal or unfaithful. **untruth** *n* statement that is not true, lie. **untruthful** *adj* **untruthfully** *adv*

unusual *adj* uncommon or extraordinary. **unusually** *adv*

unutterable *adj* incapable of being expressed in words. **unutterably** *adv*

unvarnished *adj* not elaborated upon, e.g. *the unvarnished truth.*

unveil *v* **1** ceremonially remove the cover from (a new picture, plaque, etc.). **2** make public (a secret). **unveiling** *n*

unwarranted *adj* not justified, not necessary.

unwell *adj* not healthy, ill.
unwieldy *adj* too heavy, large, or awkward to be easily handled.
unwind *v* **1** relax after a busy or tense time. **2** slacken, undo, or unravel.
unwitting *adj* **1** not intentional. **2** not knowing or conscious. **unwittingly** *adv*
unwonted *adj* out of the ordinary.
unworthy *adj* **1** not deserving or worthy. **2** lacking merit or value. **unworthy of** beneath the level considered befitting (to).
unwrap *v* remove the wrapping from (something).
unwritten *adj* **1** not printed or in writing. **2** operating only through custom, e.g. *an unwritten rule.*
up *prep, adv* **1** indicating movement to or position at a higher place. ♦ *adv* **2** indicating readiness, intensity or completeness, etc., e.g. *warm up; drink up.* ♦ *adj* **3** of a high or higher position. **4** out of bed. ♦ *v* **upping, upped 5** increase or raise. **up against** having to cope with. **up and** *Informal* do something suddenly, e.g. *he upped and left.* **ups and downs** alternating periods of good and bad luck. **up to 1** engaged in (usu. something shady, secretive, or mischievous). **2** the responsibility of, e.g. *it's up to you to lock the doors.* **3** equal to or capable of (doing something). **what's up?** *Informal* what is wrong? **upward** *adj* **1** directed or moving towards a higher place or level. ♦ *adv* **2** (also **upwards**) from a lower to a higher place, level, or condition.
up-and-coming *adj* likely to be successful in the future.
upbeat *adj* **1** *Informal* cheerful and optimistic. ♦ *n* **2** *Music* unaccented beat.
upbraid *v* scold or reproach.
upbringing *n* education of a person during the formative years.
update *v* bring up to date.
upend *v* turn or set (something) on its end.
upfront *adj* **1** open and frank. ♦ *adv, adj* **2** (of money) paid out at the beginning of a business arrangement.
upgrade *v* promote (a person or job) to a higher rank. **upgrading** *n*
upheaval *n* strong, sudden, or violent disturbance.
uphill *adj* **1** sloping or leading upwards. **2** requiring a great deal of effort. ♦ *adv* **3** up a slope.
uphold *v* **1** maintain or defend against opposition. **2** give moral support to. **upholder** *n*
upholster *v* fit (a chair or sofa) with padding, springs, and covering. **upholstered** *adj* **upholsterer** *n* **upholstery** *n* soft covering on a chair or sofa.
upkeep *n* act, process, or cost of keeping something in good repair.
upland *adj* of or in an area of high or relatively high ground. **uplands** *pl n* area of high or relatively high ground.
uplift *v* **1** raise or lift up. **2** raise morally or spiritually. ♦ *n* **3** act or process of improving moral, social, or cultural conditions. **uplifting** *adj*
up-market *adj* expensive and of superior quality.
upon *prep* **1** on. **2** up and on.
upper *adj* **1** higher or highest in physical position, wealth, rank, or status. ♦ *n* **2** part of a shoe above the sole. **on one's uppers** destitute. **uppermost** *adj* **1** highest in position, power, or importance. ♦ *adv* **2** in or into the highest place or position. **upper case** capital letters. **upper class** highest social class. **upper-class** *adj* **upper crust** *Informal* upper class. **uppercut** *n* short swinging upward punch delivered to the chin. **upper hand** position of control.
uppish, uppity *adj Informal* snobbish, arrogant, or presumptuous.
upright *adj* **1** vertical or erect. **2** honest or just. ♦ *adv* **3** vertically or in an erect position. ♦ *n* **4** vertical support, such as a post. **uprightness** *n*
uprising *n* rebellion or revolt.
uproar *n* disturbance characterized by loud noise and confusion. **uproarious** *adj* **1** very funny. **2** (of laughter) loud and boisterous. **uproariously** *adv*
uproot *v* **1** pull up by or as if by the

roots. **2** displace (a person or people) from their native or usual surroundings.

upset *adj* **1** emotionally or physically disturbed or distressed. ♦ *v* **2** tip over. **3** disturb the normal state or stability of. **4** disturb mentally or emotionally. **5** make physically ill. ♦ *n* **6** unexpected defeat or reversal. **7** disturbance or disorder of the emotions, mind, or body. **upsetting** *adj*

upshot *n* final result or conclusion.

upside down *adj* **1** turned over completely. **2** *Informal* confused or jumbled. ♦ *adv* **3** in an inverted fashion. **4** in a chaotic manner.

upstage *adj* **1** at the back half of the stage. ♦ *v* **2** *Informal* draw attention to oneself from (someone else).

upstairs *adv* **1** to or on an upper floor of a building. ♦ *n* **2** upper floor. ♦ *adj* **3** situated on an upper floor.

upstanding *adj* of good character.

upstart *n* person who has risen suddenly to a position of power and behaves arrogantly.

upstream *adv, adj* in or towards the higher part of a stream.

upsurge *n* rapid rise or swell.

uptake *n* **quick, slow on the uptake** *Informal* quick *or* slow to understand or learn.

uptight *adj Informal* nervously tense, irritable, or angry.

up-to-date *adj* modern or fashionable.

upturn *n* upward trend or improvement. **upturned** *adj* facing upwards.

uranium [yew-**rain**-ee-um] *n Chem* radioactive silvery-white metallic element, used chiefly as a source of nuclear energy.

Uranus *n* **1** *Greek myth* god of the sky. **2** seventh planet from the sun.

urban *adj* of or living in a city or town. **urbanize** *v* make (a rural area) more industrialized and urban. **urbanization** *n*

urbane *adj* characterized by courtesy, elegance, and sophistication. **urbanity** *n*

urchin *n* mischievous child.

Urdu [**oor**-doo] *n* language of Pakistan.

ureter [yew-**reet**-er] *n* tube that conveys urine from the kidney to the bladder.

urethra [yew-**reeth**-ra] *n* canal that carries urine from the bladder out of the body.

urge *n* **1** strong impulse, inner drive, or yearning. ♦ *v* **2** plead with or press (a person to do something). **3** advocate earnestly. **4** force or drive onwards.

urgent *adj* requiring speedy action or attention. **urgency** *n* **urgently** *adv*

uric acid *n* white odourless crystalline acid present in the blood and urine.

urine *n* pale yellow fluid excreted by the kidneys to the bladder and passed as waste from the body. **urinary** *adj* **urinate** *v* discharge urine. **urination** *n* **urinal** *n* sanitary fitting used by men for urination.

urn *n* **1** vase used as a container for the ashes of the dead. **2** large metal container with a tap, used for making and holding tea or coffee.

ursine *adj* of or like a bear.

us *pron* objective case of WE.

US, USA United States (of America).

use *v* **1** put into service or action. **2** take advantage of, exploit. **3** consume or expend. ♦ *n* **4** using or being used. **5** ability or permission to use. **6** usefulness or advantage. **7** purpose for which something is used. **user** *n* **user-friendly** *adj* easy to familiarize oneself with, understand, and use. **usable** *adj* able to be used. **usage** *n* **1** regular or constant use. **2** way in which a word is used in a language. **used** *adj* second-hand. **used to** *adj* **1** accustomed to. ♦ *v* **2** used as an auxiliary to express past habitual or accustomed actions, e.g. *I used to live there.* **useful** *adj* **1** able to be used advantageously or for several different purposes. **2** *Informal* commendable or capable, e.g. *a useful day's work.* **usefully** *adv* **usefulness** *n* **useless** *adj* **1** having no practical use. **2** *Informal* ineffectual, weak, or stupid, e.g. *useless at maths.* **uselessly** *adv* **uselessness** *n*

In the negative there are two common combinations: *didn't use to* and *used not to*. The abbreviated form is *usedn't to*.

usher *n* **1** official who shows people to their seats, as in a church. ♦ *v* **2** conduct or escort. **usherette** *n* female assistant in a cinema who shows people to their seats.

USSR (formerly) Union of Soviet Socialist Republics.

usual *adj* of the most normal, frequent, or regular type. **as usual** as happens normally. **usually** *adv* most often, in most cases.

usurp [yewz-**zurp**] *v* seize (a position or power) without authority. **usurpation** *n* **usurper** *n*

usury *n* practice of lending money at an extremely high rate of interest. **usurer** [**yewz**-yoor-er] *n*

UT Utah.

utensil *n* tool or container for practical use.

uterus [**yew**-ter-russ] *n* womb. **uterine** *adj*

utilitarian *adj* **1** useful rather than beautiful. **2** of utilitarianism. **utilitarianism** *n* doctrine that the right action is the one that brings about the greatest good for the greatest number of people.

utility *n* **1** usefulness. (**2** *pl* **-ties**) public service, such as electricity. ♦ *adj* **3** designed for use rather than beauty. **utility room** room used for large domestic appliances and equipment.

utilize *v* make practical use of. **utilization** *n*

utmost *adj, n* (of) the greatest possible degree or amount.

Utopia [yew-**tope**-ee-a] *n* any real or imaginary society, place, or state considered to be perfect or ideal. **Utopian** *adj*

utter[1] *v* express (something) in sounds or words. **utterance** *n* **1** something uttered. **2** act or power of uttering.

utter[2] *adj* total or absolute. **utterly** *adv*

uttermost *adj, n* same as UTMOST.

U-turn *n* **1** turn, made by a vehicle, in the shape of a U, resulting in a reversal of direction. **2** complete change in policy.

UV ultraviolet.

uvula [**yew**-view-la] *n* small fleshy part of the soft palate that hangs in the back of the throat.

uxorious [ux-**or**-ee-uss] *adj* excessively fond of or dependent on one's wife.

V v

V **1** *Chem* vanadium. **2** volt. **3** the Roman numeral for five.

v. **1** verb. **2** versus. **3** very.

VA Virginia.

vacant *adj* **1** (of a toilet, room, etc.) unoccupied. **2** without interest or understanding. **vacantly** *adv* **vacancy** *n, pl* **-cies** **1** unfilled job. **2** unoccupied room in a guesthouse. **3** state of being unoccupied.

vacate *v* **1** cause (something) to be empty by leaving. **2** give up (a job or position). **vacation** *n* **1** time when universities and law courts are closed. **2** *Chiefly US* holiday.

vaccinate *v* inject with a vaccine. **vaccination** *n* **vaccine** *n* substance designed to cause a mild form of a disease to make a person immune to the disease itself.

vacillate [**vass**-ill-late] *v* keep changing one's mind or opinions. **vacillation** *n*

vacuous *adj* not expressing intelligent thought. **vacuity** *n*

vacuum *n, pl* **vacuums, vacua** **1** empty space from which all or most air or gas has been removed. **2** same as VACUUM CLEANER. ♦ *v* **3** clean with a vacuum cleaner. **vacuum cleaner** electrical appliance which sucks up dust and dirt from carpets and upholstery. **vacuum flask** double-walled flask with a vacuum between the walls that keeps drinks hot or cold. **vacuum-packed** *adj* contained in packaging from which the air has been removed.

vagabond *n* person with no fixed home, esp. a beggar.

vagary [**vaig**-a-ree] *n, pl* **-garies** **1** unpredictable change. **2** whim.

vagina [vaj-**jine**-a] *n, pl* **-nas, -nae** (in female mammals) passage from the womb to the external genitals. **vaginal** *adj*

vagrant [**vaig**-rant] *n* **1** person with no settled home. ♦ *adj* **2** wandering. **vagrancy** *n*

vague *adj* **1** not clearly explained. **2** deliberately withholding information. **3** unable to be seen or heard clearly. **4** absent-minded. **vaguely** *adv*

vain *adj* **1** excessively proud, esp. of one's appearance. **2** bound to fail, futile. **in vain** unsuccessfully.

vainglorious *adj Lit* boastful.

valance [**val**-lenss] *n* piece of drapery round the edge of a bed.

vale *n Lit* valley.

valedictory [val-lid-**dik**-tree] *adj* (of a speech, performance, etc.) intended as a farewell. **valediction** *n* farewell speech.

valence [**vale**-ence] *n* molecular bonding between atoms.

valency *n, pl* **-cies** power of an atom to make molecular bonds.

valentine *n* (person to whom one sends) a romantic card on Saint Valentine's Day, 14th February.

valerian *n* herb used as a sedative.

valet *n* man's personal male servant.

valetudinarian [val-lit-yew-din-**air**-ee-an] *n* **1** person with a long-term illness. **2** person overconcerned about his or her health.

valiant *adj* brave or courageous. **valiantly** *adv*

valid *adj* **1** soundly reasoned. **2** having legal force. **validate** *v* make valid. **validation** *n* **validity** *n*

valise [val-**leez**] *n Old-fashioned* small suitcase.

Valium *n* fi drug used as a tranquillizer.

valley *n* low area between hills, often with a river running through it.

valour *n Lit* bravery.

value *n* **1** importance, usefulness. **2** monetary worth. **3** satisfaction, e.g. *value for money.* **4** *Maths* particular number represented by a figure or symbol. ♦ *pl* **5** moral principles. ♦ *v* **valuing, valued** **6**

assess the worth or desirability of. **7** have a high regard for. **valuable** *adj* having great worth. **valuables** *pl n* valuable personal property. **valuation** *n* assessment of worth. **valueless** *adj* **valuer** *n* **value-added tax** *Brit* see VAT. **value judgment** opinion based on personal belief.

valve *n* **1** device to control the movement of fluid through a pipe. **2** *Anat* flap in a part of the body allowing blood to flow in one direction only. **3** *Physics* tube containing a vacuum, allowing current to flow from a cathode to an anode. **4** *Zool* one of the hinged shells of an oyster or clam. **5** *Music* device on brass instruments to lengthen the tube. **valvular** *adj* **1** of or having valves. **2** like valves.

vamp[1] *n Informal* sexually attractive woman who seduces men.

vamp[2] *v* **vamp up** make (a story, piece of music, etc.) seem new by inventing additional parts.

vampire *n* (in folklore) corpse that rises at night to drink the blood of the living. **vampire bat** tropical bat that feeds on blood.

van[1] *n* **1** motor vehicle for transporting goods. **2** *Brit & Aust* railway carriage for goods, luggage, or mail.

van[2] *n* short for VANGUARD.

vanadium *n Chem* metallic element, used in steel.

vandal *n* person who deliberately damages property. **vandalism** *n* **vandalize** *v*

vane *n* flat blade on a rotary device such as a weathercock or propeller.

vanguard *n* **1** unit of soldiers leading an army. **2** most advanced group or position in a movement or activity.

vanilla *n* seed pod of a tropical climbing orchid, used for flavouring.

vanish *v* **1** disappear suddenly or mysteriously. **2** cease to exist.

vanity *n, pl* **-ties** (display of) excessive pride. **vanity case** small bag for carrying cosmetics.

vanquish *v Lit* defeat (someone) utterly.

vantage *n* **vantage point** position that gives one an overall view.

vapid *adj* lacking character, dull. **vapidity** *n*

vapour *n* **1** moisture suspended in air as steam or mist. **2** gaseous form of something that is liquid or solid at room temperature. **vaporize** *v* change into a vapour. **vaporizer** *n* **vaporous** *adj*

variable *adj* **1** not always the same, changeable. ♦ *n* **2** something that is subject to variation. **3** *Maths* expression with a range of values. **variability** *n*

variant *adj* **1** differing from a standard or type. ♦ *n* **2** something that differs from a standard or type. **at variance** in disagreement.

variation *n* **1** something presented in a slightly different form. **2** difference in level, amount, or quantity. **3** *Music* repetition in different forms of a basic theme.

varicose veins *pl n* knotted and swollen veins, esp. in the legs.

variegated *adj* having patches or streaks of different colours. **variegation** *n*

variety *n, pl* **-ties** **1** state of being diverse or various. **2** different things of the same kind. **3** particular sort or kind. **4** light entertainment composed of unrelated acts.

various *adj* of several kinds. **variously** *adv*

varnish *n* **1** solution of oil and resin, put on a surface to make it hard and glossy. ♦ *v* **2** apply varnish to.

varsity *n Brit informal* university.

vary *v* **varying, varied** **1** change. **2** cause differences in. **varied** *adj*

vascular *adj Biol* relating to vessels.

vas deferens *n, pl* **vasa deferentia** *Anat* sperm-carrying duct in each testicle.

vase *n* ornamental jar, esp. for flowers.

vasectomy *n, pl* **-mies** surgical removal of part of the vas deferens, as a contraceptive method.

Vaseline *n* ® thick oily cream made from petroleum, used in skin care.

vassal *n* **1** *Hist* man given land by a lord

in return for military service. **2** subordinate person or nation. **vassalage** *n*

vast *adj* extremely large. **vastly** *adv* **vastness** *n*

vat *n* large container for liquids.

VAT *Brit* value-added tax: tax on the difference between the cost of materials and the selling price.

Vatican *n* **1** the Pope's palace. **2** authority of the Pope.

vaudeville *n* variety entertainment of songs and comic turns.

vault[1] *n* **1** secure room for storing valuables. **2** underground burial chamber. **vaulted** *adj* having an arched roof.

vault[2] *v* **1** jump over (something) by resting one's hand(s) on it. ♦ *n* **2** such a jump.

vaunt *v* describe or display (success or possessions) boastfully. **vaunted** *adj*

VC **1** Vice Chancellor. **2** Victoria Cross.

VCR video cassette recorder.

VD venereal disease.

VDU visual display unit.

veal *n* calf meat.

vector *n* **1** *Maths* quantity that has size and direction, such as force. **2** animal, usu. an insect, that carries disease.

veer *v* change direction suddenly.

vegan [**vee**-gan] *n* **1** person who eats no meat, fish, eggs, or dairy products. ♦ *adj* **2** suitable for a vegan. **veganism** *n*

vegetable *n* **1** edible plant. **2** *Informal* severely brain-damaged person. ♦ *adj* **3** of or like plants or vegetables.

vegetarian *n* **1** person who eats no meat or fish. ♦ *adj* **2** suitable for a vegetarian. **vegetarianism** *n*

vegetate *v* live a dull boring life with no mental stimulation.

vegetation *n* plant life of a given place. **vegetative** *adj* of plant life or growth.

vehement *adj* expressing strong feelings. **vehemence** *n* **vehemently** *adv*

vehicle *n* **1** machine, esp. with an engine and wheels, for carrying people or objects. **2** something used to achieve a particular purpose or as a means of expression. **vehicular** *adj*

veil *n* **1** piece of thin cloth covering the head or face. **2** something that masks the truth, e.g. *a veil of secrecy.* ♦ *v* **3** cover with or as if with a veil. **take the veil** become a nun. **veiled** *adj* disguised.

vein *n* **1** tube that takes blood to the heart. **2** line in a leaf or an insect's wing. **3** layer of ore or mineral in rock. **4** streak in marble, wood, or cheese. **5** feature of someone's writing or speech, e.g. *a vein of humour.* **6** mood or style, e.g. *in a lighter vein.* **veined** *adj*

Velcro *n* ® fastening consisting of one piece of fabric with tiny hooked threads and another with a coarse surface that sticks to it.

veld, veldt *n* high grassland in southern Africa.

vellum *n* **1** fine calfskin parchment. **2** type of strong good-quality paper.

velocity [vel-**loss**-it-ee] *n, pl* **-ties** speed of movement in a given direction.

velour, velours [vel-**loor**] *n* fabric similar to velvet.

velvet *n* fabric with a thick soft pile. **velvety** *adj* soft and smooth. **velveteen** *n* cotton velvet.

venal [**vee**-nal] *adj* **1** easily bribed. **2** characterized by bribery. **venally** *adv*

vend *v* sell. **vendor** *n* **vending machine** machine that dispenses goods when coins are inserted.

vendetta *n* **1** long-lasting quarrel between people or organizations in which they attempt to harm each other. **2** prolonged quarrel between families, esp. one involving revenge killings.

veneer *n* **1** thin layer of wood etc. covering a cheaper material. **2** superficial appearance, e.g. *a veneer of sophistication.*

venerable *adj* worthy of deep respect. **venerate** *v* hold (a person) in deep respect. **veneration** *n*

venereal disease [ven-**ear**-ee-al] *n* disease transmitted sexually.

Venetian *adj* **1** of Venice, port in NE Italy. ♦ *n* **2** native or inhabitant of Venice. **Venetian blind** window blind made of thin horizontal slats that turn to let in more or less light.

vengeance *n* revenge. **with a vengeance** to an excessive degree. **vengeful** *adj* wanting revenge.

venial [**veen**-ee-al] *adj* (of a sin or fault) easily forgiven.

venison *n* deer meat.

venom *n* **1** malice or spite. **2** poison produced by snakes etc. **venomous** *adj* **venomously** *adv*

venous [**vee**-nuss] *adj Anat* of veins.

vent[1] *n* **1** outlet releasing fumes or fluid. ♦ *v* **2** express (an emotion) freely. **give vent to** release (an emotion) in an outburst.

vent[2] *n* vertical slit in a jacket.

ventilate *v* **1** let fresh air into. **2** discuss (ideas or feelings) openly. **ventilation** *n* **ventilator** *n* device to let fresh air into a room or building.

ventral *adj* relating to the front of the body.

ventricle *n Anat* one of the four cavities of the heart or brain.

ventriloquist *n* entertainer who can speak without moving his or her lips, so that a voice seems to come from elsewhere. **ventriloquism** *n*

venture *n* **1** risky undertaking, esp. in business. ♦ *v* **2** do something risky. **3** dare to express (an opinion). **4** go to an unknown place. **venturesome** *adj* daring.

venue *n* place where an organized gathering is held.

Venus *n* **1** planet second nearest to the sun. **2** Roman goddess of love. **Venus flytrap, Venus's flytrap** plant that traps and digests insects between hinged leaves.

veracious *adj* habitually truthful. **veracity** *n*

verandah, veranda *n* open porch attached to a house.

verb *n* word that expresses the idea of action, happening, or being. **verbal** *adj* **1** spoken. **2** of a verb. **verbally** *adv* **verbalize** *v* express (something) in words.

verbatim [verb-**bait**-im] *adv, adj* word for word.

verbena *n* plant with sweet-smelling flowers.

verbiage *n* excessive use of words.

verbose [verb-**bohss**] *adj* speaking at tedious length. **verbosity** *n*

verdant *adj Lit* covered in green vegetation.

verdict *n* **1** decision of a jury. **2** opinion formed after examining the facts.

verdigris [**ver**-dig-riss] *n* green film on copper, brass, or bronze.

verdure *n Lit* flourishing green vegetation.

verge *n* grass border along a road. **on the verge of** having almost reached (a point or condition). **verge on** *v* be near to (a condition).

verger *n C of E* church caretaker.

verify *v* **-ifying, -ified** check the truth or accuracy of. **verifiable** *adj* **verification** *n*

verily *adv Obs* in truth.

verisimilitude *n* appearance of being real or true.

veritable *adj* rightly called, without exaggeration, e.g. *a veritable feast.* **veritably** *adv*

verity *n, pl* **-ties** true statement or principle.

vermicelli [ver-me-**chell**-ee] *n* **1** fine strands of pasta. **2** tiny strands of chocolate.

vermiform *adj* shaped like a worm. **vermiform appendix** *Anat* same as APPENDIX.

vermilion *adj* orange-red.

vermin *pl n* **1** animals, esp. insects and rodents, that spread disease or cause damage. **2** people who are considered dangerous or harmful to others. **verminous** *adj*

vermouth [**ver**-muth] *n* wine flavoured with herbs.

vernacular [ver-**nak**-yew-lar] *n* **1** most widely spoken language of a particular people or place. ♦ *adj* **2** in or using the vernacular.

vernal *adj* occurring in spring.

vernier [**ver**-nee-er] *n* movable scale on

a graduated measuring instrument for taking readings in fractions.

veronica *n* plant with small blue, pink, or white flowers.

verruca [ver-**roo**-ka] *n* wart, usu. on the foot.

versatile *adj* having many skills or uses. **versatility** *n*

verse *n* **1** group of lines forming part of a song or poem. **2** poetry as distinct from prose. **3** subdivision of a chapter of the Bible. **versed in** knowledgeable about. **versify** *v* **-fying, -fied** write in verse. **versification** *n*

version *n* **1** form of something, such as a piece of writing, with some differences from other forms. **2** account of an incident from a particular point of view.

verso *n, pl* **-sos 1** left-hand page of a book. **2** back of a sheet of printed paper.

versus *prep* **1** in opposition to or in contrast with. **2** *Sport, Law* against.

vertebra [**ver**-tib-ra] *n, pl* **vertebrae** [**ver**-tib-ree] one of the bones that form the spine. **vertebral** *adj* **vertebrate** *n, adj* (animal) having a spine.

vertex *n, pl* **-texes, -tices 1** *Maths* point on a geometric figure where the sides form an angle. **2** highest point of a triangle.

vertical *adj* **1** straight up and down. ♦ *n* **2** vertical direction. **vertically** *adv*

vertigo *n* dizziness, usu. when looking down from a high place. **vertiginous** *adj*

vervain *n* plant with spikes of blue, purple, or white flowers.

verve *n* enthusiasm or liveliness.

very *adv* **1** more than usually, extremely. ♦ *adj* **2** absolute, exact, e.g. *the very top; the very man.*

vesicle *n Biol* sac or small cavity, esp. one containing fluid.

vespers *pl n RC Church* (service of) evening prayer.

vessel *n* **1** ship. **2** *Lit* container, esp. for liquids. **3** *Biol* tubular structure in animals and plants that carries body fluids, such as blood or sap.

vest *n* **1** undergarment worn on the top half of the body. **2** *US & Aust* waistcoat. ♦ *v* **3** (foll. by *in* or *with*) give (authority) to (someone). **vested interest** interest someone has in a matter because he or she might benefit from it.

vestal *adj* pure, chaste. **vestal virgin** (in ancient Rome) one of the virgin priestesses dedicated to the goddess Vesta and to maintaining the sacred fire in her temple.

vestibule *n* small entrance hall.

vestige [**vest**-ij] *n* small amount or trace. **vestigial** [vest-**ij**-ee-al] *adj*

vestments *pl n* priest's robes.

vestry *n, pl* **-tries** room in a church used as an office by the priest or minister.

vet[1] *n* **1** short for VETERINARY SURGEON. ♦ *v* **vetting, vetted 2** check the suitability of.

vet[2] *n US & Aust* military veteran.

vetch *n* climbing plant with a beanlike fruit used as fodder.

veteran *n* **1** person with long experience in a particular activity, esp. military service. ♦ *adj* **2** long-serving. **veteran car** car built before 1919, esp. before 1905.

veterinarian *n US* veterinary surgeon.

veterinary *adj* concerning animal health. **veterinary surgeon** medical specialist who treats sick animals.

veto [**vee**-toe] *n, pl* **-toes 1** official power to cancel a proposal. ♦ *v* **-toing, -toed 2** enforce a veto against.

vex *v* frustrate, annoy. **vexation** *n* **1** something annoying. **2** being annoyed. **vexatious** *adj* **vexed question** much debated subject.

VHF very high frequency: radio frequency band between 30 and 300 MHz.

VHS ® Video Home System: format for recording on video.

VI Vancouver Island.

via *prep* by way of.

viable *adj* **1** able to be put into practice. **2** *Biol* able to live and grow independently. **viability** *n*

viaduct *n* bridge over a valley.

Viagra *n* ® drug used to treat impotence

in men.

vial *n* same as PHIAL.

viands *pl n Obs* food.

viaticum *n, pl* **-ca, -cums** Holy Communion given to a person who is dying or in danger of death.

vibes *pl n Informal* **1** emotional reactions between people. **2** atmosphere of a place. **3** short for VIBRAPHONE.

vibrant [**vibe**-rant] *adj* **1** vigorous in appearance, energetic. **2** (of a voice) resonant. **3** (of a colour) strong and bright. **vibrancy** *n*

vibraphone *n* musical instrument with metal bars that resonate electronically when hit.

vibrate *v* **1** move back and forth rapidly. **2** (cause to) resonate. **vibration** *n* **vibrator** *n* device that produces vibratory motion, used for massage or as a sex aid. **vibratory** *adj*

vibrato *n, pl* **-tos** *Music* rapid fluctuation in the pitch of a note.

viburnum [vie-**burn**-um] *n* subtropical shrub with white flowers and berry-like fruits.

VIC Victoria (Australian state).

vicar *n C of E* clergyman in charge of a parish. **vicarage** *n* vicar's house.

vicarious [vick-**air**-ee-uss] *adj* **1** felt indirectly by imagining what another person experiences. **2** delegated. **vicariously** *adv*

vice[1] *n* **1** immoral or evil habit or action. **2** habit regarded as a weakness in someone's character. **3** criminal immorality, esp. involving sex.

vice[2] *n* tool with a pair of jaws for holding an object while working on it.

vice[3] *adj* serving in place of.

vice chancellor *n* chief executive of a university.

vice president *n* officer ranking immediately below the president and serving as his or her deputy. **vice-presidency** *n*

viceroy *n* governor of a colony who represents the monarch. **viceregal** *adj*

vice versa [**vie**-see **ver**-sa] *adv Latin* conversely, the other way round.

Vichy water [**vee**-shee **waw**-ter] *n* mineral water from Vichy in France, reputed to be good for the health.

vicinity [viss-**in**-it-ee] *n* surrounding area.

vicious *adj* cruel and violent. **viciously** *adv* **vicious circle, cycle** situation in which an attempt to resolve one problem creates new problems that recreate the original one.

vicissitudes [viss-**iss**-it-yewds] *pl n* changes in fortune.

victim *n* **1** person or thing harmed or killed. **2** person who has suffered because of misfortune or other people's actions. **victimize** *v* **1** punish unfairly. **2** discriminate against. **victimization** *n*

victor *n* person who has defeated an opponent, esp. in war or in sport. **victorious** *adj* **victory** *n, pl* **-tories** winning of a battle or contest.

victoria *n* large sweet plum, red and yellow in colour.

Victoria Cross *n Brit* highest award for bravery.

Victorian *adj* **1** of or in the reign of Queen Victoria (1837–1901). **2** characterized by prudery or hypocrisy. ♦ *n* **3** person who lived during Victoria's reign.

victuals [**vit**-tals] *pl n Old-fashioned* food and drink. **victual** *v* **victualling, victualled** *Old-fashioned* supply with or obtain victuals. **victualler** *n*

vicuña [vik-**koo**-nya] *n* **1** S American animal like the llama. **2** fine cloth made from its wool.

vide [**vie**-dee] *Latin* see.

videlicet [vid-**deal**-ee-set] *Latin* namely.

video *n, pl* **-os** **1** short for VIDEO CASSETTE (RECORDER). ♦ *v* **videoing, videoed** **2** record (a TV programme or event) on video. ♦ *adj* **3** relating to or used in producing television images. **video nasty** horrific or pornographic film, usu. made for video. **videotext** *n* means of representing on a TV screen information that is held in a computer.

video cassette *n* cassette containing video tape. **video cassette recorder** tape recorder for recording and playing back TV programmes and films.

video tape *n* **1** magnetic tape used to record video-frequency signals in TV production. **2** magnetic tape used to record programmes when they are broadcast. **videotape** *v* record (a TV programme) on video tape. **video tape recorder** tape recorder for vision signals, used in TV production.

Videotex *n* ® same as VIEWDATA.

vie *v* **vying, vied** compete (with someone).

Vietnamese *adj* **1** of Vietnam, in SE Asia. ♦ *n* **2** (*pl* **-ese**) native of Vietnam. **3** language of Vietnam.

view *n* **1** opinion or belief. **2** understanding of or outlook on something. **3** everything that can be seen from a given place. **4** picture of this. ♦ *v* **5** think of (something) in a particular way. **6** see or watch. **in view of** taking into consideration. **on view** exhibited to the public. **viewer** *n* **1** person who watches television. **2** hand-held device for looking at photographic slides. **viewfinder** *n* window on a camera showing what will appear in a photograph.

Viewdata *n* ® videotext service linking users to a computer by telephone.

vigil [**vij**-ill] *n* night-time period of staying awake to look after a sick person, pray, etc. **vigilant** *adj* watchful in case of danger. **vigilance** *n*

vigilante [vij-ill-**ant**-ee] *n* person, esp. as one of a group, who takes it upon himself or herself to enforce the law.

vignette [vin-**yet**] *n* **1** concise description of the typical features of something. **2** small decorative illustration in a book.

vigour *n* physical or mental energy. **vigorous** *adj* **vigorously** *adv*

Viking *n Hist* seafaring raider and settler from Scandinavia.

vile *adj* **1** very wicked. **2** disgusting. **vilely** *adv* **vileness** *n*

vilify [**vill**-if-fie] *v* **-ifying, -ified** attack the character of. **vilification** *n*

villa *n* **1** large house with gardens. **2** holiday home, usu. in the Mediterranean.

village *n* **1** small group of houses in a country area. **2** rural community. **villager** *n*

villain *n* **1** wicked person. **2** main wicked character in a play. **villainous** *adj* **villainy** *n*

villein [**vill**-an] *n Hist* peasant bound in service to his lord.

vim *n Informal* force, energy.

vinaigrette *n* salad dressing of oil and vinegar.

vindicate *v* **1** clear (someone) of guilt. **2** provide justification for. **vindication** *n*

vindictive *adj* maliciously seeking revenge. **vindictiveness** *n* **vindictively** *adv*

vine *n* climbing plant, esp. one producing grapes. **vineyard** [**vinn**-yard] *n* plantation of grape vines, esp. for making wine.

vinegar *n* acid liquid made from wine, beer, or cider. **vinegary** *adj*

viniculture *n* process or business of growing grapes and making wine.

vino [**vee**-noh] *n Informal* wine.

vintage *n* **1** wine from a particular harvest of grapes. ♦ *adj* **2** best and most typical. **vintage car** car built between 1919 and 1930.

vintner *n* dealer in wine.

vinyl [**vine**-ill] *n* type of plastic, used in mock leather and records.

viol [**vie**-oll] *n* early stringed instrument preceding the violin.

viola[1] [vee-**oh**-la] *n* stringed instrument lower in pitch than a violin.

viola[2] [**vie**-ol-la] *n* variety of pansy.

violate *v* **1** break (a law or agreement). **2** disturb (someone's privacy). **3** treat (a sacred place) disrespectfully. **4** rape. **violation** *n* **violator** *n*

violence *n* **1** use of physical force, usu. intended to cause injury or destruction. **2** great force or strength in action, feeling, or expression. **violent** *adj* **violently** *adv*

violet *n* **1** plant with bluish-purple flowers. ♦ *adj* **2** bluish-purple.

violin *n* small four-stringed musical instrument played with a bow. **violinist** *n*

violoncello [vie-oll-on-**chell**-oh] *n, pl* **-los** same as CELLO.
VIP very important person.
viper *n* poisonous snake.
virago [vir-**rah**-go] *n, pl* **-goes, -gos** aggressive woman.
viral [**vie**-ral] *adj* of or caused by a virus.
virgin *n* **1** person, esp. a woman, who has not had sexual intercourse. ♦ *adj* **2** not having had sexual intercourse. **3** not yet exploited or explored. **virginal** *adj* **1** like a virgin. **2** extremely pure or fresh. ♦ *n* **3** early keyboard instrument like a small harpsichord. **virginity** *n* **the Virgin, the Virgin Mary** *Christianity* Mary, the mother of Christ.
Virginia creeper *n* climbing plant that turns red in autumn.
Virgo *n* (the virgin) sixth sign of the zodiac.
virile *adj* having the traditional male characteristics of physical strength and a high sex drive. **virility** *n*
virology *n* study of viruses.
virtual *adj* **1** having the effect but not the form of. **2** of or relating to virtual reality. **virtual reality** computer-generated environment that seems real to the user. **virtually** *adv* practically, almost.
virtue *n* **1** moral goodness. **2** positive moral quality. **3** merit. **by virtue of** by reason of. **virtuous** *adj* morally good. **virtuously** *adv*
virtuoso *n, pl* **-sos, -si** person with impressive esp. musical skill. **virtuosity** *n*
virulent [**vir**-yew-lent] *adj* **1** extremely bitter or hostile. **2** very infectious. **3** violently harmful. **virulently** *adv* **virulence** *n*
virus *n* **1** microorganism that causes disease in humans, animals, and plants. **2** *Computers* program that propagates itself, via disks and electronic networks, to cause disruption.
visa *n* permission to enter a country, granted by its government and shown by a stamp on one's passport.
visage [**viz**-zij] *n Lit* face.
vis-à-vis [veez-ah-**vee**] *prep* in relation to, regarding.
viscera [**viss**-er-a] *pl n* large abdominal organs. **visceral** *adj* **1** instinctive. **2** of or relating to the viscera.
viscid [**viss**-id] *adj* sticky.
viscose *n* synthetic fabric made from cellulose.
viscount [**vie**-count] *n* British nobleman ranking between an earl and a baron. **viscountcy** *n, pl* **-cies**
viscountess [**vie**-count-iss] *n* **1** woman holding the rank of viscount in her own right. **2** wife or widow of a viscount.
viscous *adj* thick and sticky. **viscosity** *n*
visible *adj* **1** able to be seen. **2** able to be perceived by the mind. **visibly** *adv* **visibility** *n* range or clarity of vision.
vision *n* **1** ability to see. **2** mental image of something. **3** foresight. **4** hallucination. **visionary** *adj* **1** showing foresight. **2** idealistic but impractical. ♦ *n, pl* **-aries** **3** visionary person.
visit *v* **-iting, -ited** **1** go or come to see. **2** stay temporarily with. **3** (foll. by *upon*) *Lit* afflict. ♦ *n* **4** instance of visiting. **5** official call. **visitor** *n* **visitation** *n* **1** formal visit or inspection. **2** catastrophe seen as divine punishment.
visor [**vize**-or] *n* **1** transparent part of a helmet that pulls down over the face. **2** eyeshade, esp. in a car. **3** peak on a cap.
vista *n* (beautiful) extensive view.
visual *adj* **1** done by or used in seeing. **2** designed to be looked at. **visualize** *v* form a mental image of. **visualization** *n* **visual display unit** device with a screen for displaying data held in a computer.
vital *adj* **1** essential or highly important. **2** lively. **3** necessary to maintain life. **vitals** *pl n* bodily organs necessary to maintain life. **vitally** *adv* **vitality** *n* physical or mental energy. **vital statistics** **1** statistics of births, deaths, and marriages. **2** *Informal* woman's bust, waist, and hip measurements.
vitamin *n* one of a group of substances that are essential in the diet for specific body processes.
vitiate [**vish**-ee-ate] *v* spoil the effective-

ness of. **vitiation** *n*

viticulture *n* cultivation of grapevines.

vitreous *adj* like or made from glass. **vitreous humour** gelatinous substance that fills the eyeball.

vitrify *v* **-ifying, -ified** change or be changed into glass or a glassy substance. **vitrification** *n*

vitriol *n* **1** language expressing bitterness and hatred. **2** sulphuric acid. **vitriolic** *adj*

vituperative [vite-**tyew**-pra-tiv] *adj* bitterly abusive. **vituperation** *n*

viva[1] *interj* long live (a person or thing).

viva[2] *n* examination in the form of an interview.

vivace [viv-**vah**-chee] *adv Music* in a lively manner.

vivacious *adj* full of energy and enthusiasm. **vivacity** *n*

vivarium *n, pl* **-iums, -ia** place where animals are kept in natural conditions.

viva voce [**vive**-a **voh**-chee] *adv* **1** by word of mouth. ♦ *n* **2** same as VIVA[2].

vivid *adj* **1** very bright. **2** conveying images that are true to life. **vividly** *adv* **vividness** *n*

vivify *v* **-ifying, -ified** animate, inspire.

viviparous [viv-**vip**-a-russ] *adj* producing live offspring.

vivisection *n* performing surgical experiments on living animals. **vivisectionist** *n*

vixen *n* **1** female fox. **2** *Informal* spiteful woman.

viz. (introducing specified items) namely.

vizier [viz-**zeer**] *n* high official in certain Muslim countries.

vizor *n* same as VISOR.

VLF, vlf *Radio* very low frequency.

V neck *n* neck on a garment shaped like the letter 'V'. **V-neck, V-necked** *adj*

vocabulary *n, pl* **-aries** **1** all the words that a person knows. **2** all the words in a language. **3** specialist terms used in a given subject. **4** list of words in another language with their translation.

vocal *adj* **1** relating to the voice. **2** outspoken. **vocals** *pl n* singing part of a piece of pop music. **vocally** *adv* **vocalist** *n* singer. **vocalize** *v* express with or use the voice. **vocalization** *n* **vocal cords** membranes in the larynx that vibrate to produce sound.

vocation *n* **1** profession or trade. **2** occupation that someone feels called to. **vocational** *adj* directed towards a particular profession or trade.

vocative *n* (in some languages) case of nouns used when addressing a person.

vociferate *v* exclaim, cry out. **vociferation** *n*

vociferous *adj* shouting, noisy. **vociferously** *adv*

vodka *n* (Russian) spirit distilled from potatoes or grain.

vogue *n* **1** popular style. **2** period of popularity. **in vogue** fashionable.

voice *n* **1** (quality of) sound made when speaking or singing. **2** expression of opinion by a person or group. **3** property of verbs that makes them active or passive. ♦ *v* **4** express verbally. **voiceless** *adj* **voice-over** *n* film commentary spoken by someone off-camera.

void *adj* **1** not legally binding. **2** empty. ♦ *n* **3** feeling of deprivation. **4** empty space. ♦ *v* **5** make invalid. **6** empty.

voile [**voyl**] *n* light semitransparent fabric.

vol. volume.

volatile [**voll**-a-tile] *adj* **1** liable to sudden change, esp. in behaviour. **2** evaporating quickly. **volatility** *n*

vol-au-vent [**voll**-oh-von] *n* small puff-pastry case with a savoury filling.

volcano *n, pl* **-noes, -nos** mountain with a vent through which lava is ejected. **volcanic** *adj*

vole *n* small rodent.

volition *n* ability to decide things for oneself. **of one's own volition** through one's own choice.

volley *n* **1** simultaneous discharge of ammunition. **2** burst of questions or critical comments. **3** *Sport* stroke or kick at a moving ball before it hits the ground. ♦ *v* **4** discharge (ammunition) in a volley. **5** hit or kick (a ball) in a volley.

volleyball *n* team game where a ball is hit with the hands over a high net.

volt *n* unit of electric potential. **voltaic** *adj* same as GALVANIC (sense 1). **voltage** *n* electric potential difference expressed in volts. **voltmeter** *n* instrument for measuring voltage.

volte-face [volt-**fass**] *n* reversal of opinion.

voluble *adj* talking easily and at length. **volubility** *n* **volubly** *adv*

volume *n* **1** size of the space occupied by something. **2** amount. **3** loudness of sound. **4** control on a radio or TV for adjusting this. **5** book, esp. one of a series. **voluminous** *adj* **1** (of clothes) large and roomy. **2** (of writings) extensive. **volumetric** *adj* relating to measurement by volume.

voluntary *adj* **1** done by choice. **2** done or maintained without payment. **3** (of muscles) controlled by the will. ♦ *n, pl* **-taries 4** organ solo in a church service. **voluntarily** *adv*

volunteer *n* **1** person who offers voluntarily to do something. **2** person who voluntarily undertakes military service. ♦ *v* **3** offer one's services. **4** give (information) willingly. **5** offer the services of (another person).

voluptuous *adj* **1** (of a woman) sexually alluring through fullness of figure. **2** sensually pleasurable. **voluptuary** *n, pl* **-aries** person devoted to sensual pleasures.

volute *n* spiral or twisting turn, form, or object.

vomit *v* **-iting, -ited 1** eject (the contents of the stomach) through the mouth. ♦ *n* **2** matter vomited.

voodoo *n* religion involving ancestor worship and witchcraft, practised by Black people in the West Indies, esp. in Haiti.

voracious *adj* **1** craving great quantities of food. **2** insatiably eager. **voraciously** *adv* **voracity** *n*

vortex *n, pl* **-texes, -tices 1** whirlpool. **2** situation which people are drawn into against their will.

votary *n, pl* **-ries** person dedicated to religion or to a cause.

vote *n* **1** choice made by a participant in a shared decision, esp. in electing a candidate. **2** right to this choice. **3** total number of votes cast. **4** collective voting power of a given group, e.g. *the Black vote.* ♦ *v* **5** make a choice by a vote. **6** authorize (something) by vote. **voter** *n*

votive *adj* done or given to fulfil a vow.

vouch *v* **vouch for 1** give one's personal assurance about. **2** provide evidence for.

voucher *n* **1** ticket used instead of money to buy specified goods. **2** record of a financial transaction, receipt.

vouchsafe *v* **1** *Old-fashioned* give, entrust. **2** offer assurances about.

vow *n* **1** solemn and binding promise. ♦ *pl* **2** formal promises made when marrying or entering a religious order. ♦ *v* **3** promise solemnly.

vowel *n* **1** speech sound made without obstructing the flow of breath. **2** letter representing this.

vox pop *n* interviews with members of the public on TV or radio.

vox populi *n* public opinion.

voyage *n* **1** long journey by sea or in space. ♦ *v* **2** make a voyage. **voyager** *n*

voyeur *n* person who obtains pleasure from watching people undressing or having sex. **voyeurism** *n* **voyeuristic** *adj*

vs versus.

V-sign *n* **1** offensive gesture made by sticking up the index and middle fingers with the palm inwards. **2** similar gesture, with the palm outwards, meaning victory or peace.

VSO Voluntary Service Overseas.

VSOP (of brandy or port) very superior old pale.

VT Vermont.

VTOL vertical takeoff and landing.

VTR video tape recorder.

vulcanize *v* strengthen (rubber) by treating it with sulphur. **vulcanization** *n* **vulcanite** *n* vulcanized rubber.

vulgar *adj* showing lack of good taste, decency, or refinement. **vulgarly** *adv* **vulgarity** *n* **vulgarian** *n* vulgar (rich) person. **vulgarism** *n* coarse word or phrase. **vulgarize** *v* make vulgar or too common. **vulgarization** *n* **vulgar fraction** simple fraction.

Vulgate *n* fourth-century Latin version of the Bible.

vulnerable *adj* **1** liable to be physically or emotionally hurt. **2** exposed to attack. **3** financially weak and likely to fail. **vulnerability** *n*

vulpine *adj* of or like a fox.

vulture *n* large bird that feeds on the flesh of dead animals.

vulva *n* woman's external genitals.

vying *v* present participle of VIE.

W w

W 1 *Chem* tungsten. **2** watt. **3** West(ern).
WA **1** Washington. **2** Western Australia.
wacky *adj* **wackier, wackiest** *Informal* eccentric or funny. **wackiness** *n*
wad *n* **1** small mass of soft material. **2** roll or bundle, esp. of banknotes. **wadded** *adj* **wadding** *n* soft material used for padding or stuffing.
waddle *v* **1** walk with short swaying steps. ♦ *n* **2** swaying walk.
wade *v* **1** walk with difficulty through water or mud. **2** proceed with difficulty. **wader** *n* **1** long-legged water bird. ♦ *pl* **2** angler's long waterproof boots.
wadi [**wod**-dee] *n, pl* **-dies** (in N Africa and Arabia) river which is dry except in the wet season.
wafer *n* **1** thin crisp biscuit. **2** thin disc of unleavened bread used at Communion. **3** thin slice. **wafer-thin** *adj* extremely thin.
waffle[1] *Informal* ♦ *v* **1** speak or write in a vague wordy way. ♦ *n* **2** vague wordy talk or writing.
waffle[2] *n* square crisp pancake with a gridlike pattern.
waft *v* **1** drift or carry gently through the air. ♦ *n* **2** something wafted.
wag *v* **wagging, wagged** **1** move rapidly from side to side. ♦ *n* **2** wagging movement. **3** *Old-fashioned* humorous witty person. **waggish** *adj* **wagtail** *n* small long-tailed bird.
wage *n* **1** (often pl) payment for work done, esp. when paid weekly. ♦ *v* **2** engage in (an activity).
wager *n, v* bet on the outcome of something.
waggle *v* move with a rapid shaking or wobbling motion. **waggly** *adj*
wagon, waggon *n* **1** four-wheeled vehicle for heavy loads. **2** railway freight truck.
waif *n* young person who is, or seems, homeless or neglected.
wail *v* **1** cry out in pain or misery. ♦ *n* **2** mournful cry.
wain *n* *Poetic* farm wagon.
wainscot, wainscoting *n* wooden lining of the lower part of the walls of a room.
waist *n* **1** part of the body between the ribs and hips. **2** narrow middle part. **waistband** *n* band of material sewn on to the waist of a garment to strengthen it. **waistcoat** *n* sleeveless garment which buttons up the front, usu. worn over a shirt and under a jacket. **waistline** *n* (size of) the waist of a person or garment.
wait *v* **1** remain inactive in expectation (of something). **2** be ready (for something). **3** delay or be delayed. **4** serve in a restaurant etc. ♦ *n* **5** act or period of waiting. **waiter** *n* man who serves in a restaurant etc. **waitress** *n fem* **waiting list** list of people who have applied for something that is not immediately available. **waiting-room** *n* room for waiting in, as at a station or surgery.
waive *v* refrain from enforcing (a law, right, etc.). **waiver** *n* (written statement of) this act.
wake[1] *v* **waking, woke, woken** **1** rouse from sleep or inactivity. ♦ *n* **2** vigil beside a corpse the night before the funeral. **wake up to** become aware of. **waken** *v* wake. **wakeful** *adj* **wakefulness** *n*
wake[2] *n* track left by a moving ship. **in the wake of** following, often as a result.
walk *v* **1** move on foot with at least one foot always on the ground. **2** pass through or over on foot. **3** escort or accompany on foot. ♦ *n* **4** short journey on foot, usu. for pleasure. **5** act or instance of walking. **6** distance walked. **7** manner of walking. **8** place or route for walking. **walk of life** social position or profession. **walker** *n* **walkabout** *n* informal walk among the public by royalty etc. **walkie-talkie** *n* portable radio transmitter and receiver. **walking stick**

stick used as a support when walking. **walk into** *v* meet with unwittingly. **Walkman** *n* ® small portable cassette player with headphones. **walk-on** *adj* (of a part in a film or play) small and not involving speaking. **walkout** *n* **1** strike. **2** act of leaving as a protest. **walkover** *n* easy victory.

wall *n* **1** structure of brick, stone, etc. used to enclose, divide, or support. **2** something having the function or effect of a wall. ♦ *v* **3** enclose or seal with a wall or walls. **go to the wall** be ruined, esp. financially. **wall-to-wall** *adj* (of carpeting) completely covering a floor. **wallflower** *n* **1** fragrant garden plant. **2** (at a dance) woman who remains seated because she has no partner. **wallpaper** *n* decorative paper to cover interior walls.

wallaby *n, pl* **-bies** marsupial like a small kangaroo.

wallet *n* small folding case for paper money, documents, etc.

walleyed *adj* having eyes with an abnormal amount of white showing due to a squint.

wallop *Informal* ♦ *v* **-loping, -loped** **1** hit hard. ♦ *n* **2** hard blow. **walloping** *Informal* ♦ *n* **1** thrashing. ♦ *adj* **2** large or great.

wallow *v* **1** revel in an emotion. **2** roll in liquid or mud. ♦ *n* **3** act or instance of wallowing. **4** muddy place where animals wallow.

wally *n, pl* **-lies** *Slang* stupid person.

walnut *n* **1** edible nut with a wrinkled shell. **2** tree it grows on. **3** its wood, used for making furniture.

walrus *n, pl* **-ruses, -rus** large sea mammal with long tusks.

waltz *n* **1** ballroom dance. **2** music for this. ♦ *v* **3** dance a waltz. **4** *Informal* move in a relaxed confident way.

wampum [**wom**-pum] *n* shells woven together, formerly used by Native Americans for money and ornament.

wan [rhymes with **swan**] *adj* **wanner, wannest** pale and sickly looking.

wand *n* thin rod, esp. one used in performing magic tricks.

wander *v* **1** move about without a definite destination or aim. **2** go astray, deviate. **3** (of the mind) lose concentration. ♦ *n* **4** act or instance of wandering. **wanderer** *n* **wanderlust** *n* great desire to travel.

wane *v* **1** decrease gradually in size or strength. **2** (of the moon) decrease in size. **on the wane** decreasing in size, strength, or power.

wangle *v* *Informal* get by devious methods.

want *v* **1** need or long for. **2** desire or wish. ♦ *n* **3** act or instance of wanting. **4** thing wanted. **5** lack or absence, e.g. *a want of foresight.* **6** state of being in need, poverty. **wanted** *adj* sought by the police. **wanting** *adj* **1** lacking. **2** not good enough.

wanton *adj* **1** without motive, provocation, or justification. **2** maliciously and unnecessarily cruel. **3** *Old-fashioned* (of a woman) sexually unrestrained or immodest. **wantonly** *adv*

wapiti [**wop**-pit-tee] *n, pl* **-tis** large N American and NZ deer.

war *n* **1** fighting between nations. **2** conflict or contest. ♦ *adj* **3** of, like, or caused by war. ♦ *v* **warring, warred** **4** conduct a war. **warring** *adj* **warlike** *adj* **1** of or relating to war. **2** hostile and eager to have a war. **on the warpath** *Informal* angry and prepared for conflict. **war crime** crime, such as killing, committed during a war in violation of accepted conventions. **war criminal** person who has committed war crimes. **war cry** **1** shout used in battle. **2** slogan for rallying support for a cause. **warfare** *n* fighting or hostilities. **warhead** *n* explosive front part of a missile. **warmonger** *n* person who encourages war. **warmongering** *n, adj* **warship** *n* ship designed and equipped for naval combat.

warble *v* sing in a trilling voice. **warbler** *n* any of various small songbirds.

ward *n* **1** room in a hospital for patients needing a similar kind of care. **2** electoral division of a town. **3** child under the care of a guardian or court. **warder** *n* prison officer. **wardress** *n fem* **wardship** *n* state of being a ward. **ward off** *v* avert or repel. **wardroom** *n* officers' quarters on a warship.

warden *n* **1** person in charge of a building and its occupants. **2** official responsible for the enforcement of regulations.

wardrobe *n* **1** cupboard for hanging clothes in. **2** person's collection of clothes. **3** costumes of a theatrical company.

ware *n* **1** articles of a specified type or material, e.g. *silverware.* ♦ *pl* **2** goods for sale. **warehouse** *n* building for storing goods prior to sale or distribution.

warlock *n* man who practises black magic.

warm *adj* **1** moderately hot. **2** providing warmth. **3** (of a colour) predominantly yellow or red. **4** affectionate. **5** enthusiastic. ♦ *v* **6** make or become warm. **warmly** *adv* **warmth** *n* **1** mild heat. **2** cordiality. **3** intensity of emotion. **warm-blooded** *adj* **1** *Zool* (of mammals and birds) having a constant body temperature, usu. higher than the surroundings. **2** passionate. **warm up** *v* **1** make or become warmer. **2** do preliminary exercises before a race or more strenuous exercise. **3** make or become more lively. **warm-up** *n*

warn *v* **1** make aware of possible danger or harm. **2** caution or scold. **3** inform (someone) in advance. **warning** *n* **1** something that warns. **2** scolding or caution. **warn off** *v* advise (someone) not to become involved with.

warp *v* **1** twist out of shape. **2** pervert. ♦ *n* **3** state of being warped. **4** lengthwise threads on a loom.

warrant *n* **1** (document giving) official authorization. ♦ *v* **2** make necessary. **3** guarantee. **warranty** *n, pl* **-ties** (document giving) a guarantee. **warrant officer** officer in certain armed services with a rank between a commissioned and noncommissioned officer.

warren *n* **1** series of burrows in which rabbits live. **2** overcrowded building or part of a town.

warrior *n* person who fights in a war.

wart *n* small hard growth on the skin. **warty** *adj* **wart hog** kind of African wild pig.

wary [**ware**-ree] *adj* **warier, wariest** watchful or cautious. **warily** *adv* **wariness** *n*

was *v* first and third person singular past tense of BE.

wash *v* **1** clean (oneself, clothes, etc.) with water and usu. soap. **2** be washable. **3** flow or sweep over or against. **4** *Informal* be believable or acceptable, e.g. *that excuse won't wash.* ♦ *n* **5** act or process of washing. **6** clothes washed at one time. **7** thin coat of paint. **8** disturbance in the water after a ship has passed by. **washable** *adj* **washer** *n* ring put under a nut or bolt or in a tap as a seal. **washing** *n* clothes to be washed. **washing machine** electric machine for washing clothes and linen. **washing-up** *n* (washing of) dishes and cutlery needing to be cleaned after a meal. **wash away** *v* carry or be carried off by moving water. **washbasin** *n* basin for washing the face and hands. **washout** *n Informal* complete failure. **washed-out** *adj* **1** exhausted. **2** faded. **wash up** *v* wash dishes and cutlery after a meal.

wasp *n* stinging insect with a slender black-and-yellow striped body. **waspish** *adj* bad-tempered.

Wasp, WASP *n US derogatory* White Anglo-Saxon Protestant.

wassail *n* **1** formerly, festivity when much drinking took place. ♦ *v* **2** drink health of (a person) at a wassail.

waste *v* **1** use pointlessly or thoughtlessly. **2** fail to take advantage of. ♦ *n* **3** act of wasting or state of being wasted. **4** anything wasted. **5** rubbish. ♦ *pl* **6** desert. ♦ *adj* **7** rejected as worthless or surplus to requirements. **8** not cultivated or inhabited. **waste away** (cause to) decline in health or strength. **wastage** *n* **1** loss by wear or waste. **2** reduction in size of a workforce by not filling vacancies. **wasted** *adj* **1** unnecessary or unfruitful. **2** pale, thin, and unhealthy. **wasteful** *adj* extravagant. **wastefully** *adv* **waster, wastrel** *n* layabout. **wasteland** *n* barren or desolate area of land. **wastepaper basket** container for discarded paper.

watch *v* **1** look at closely. **2** look after. **3** maintain a careful interest in. **4** guard or supervise. ♦ *n* **5** portable timepiece for the wrist or pocket. **6** (period of) watching. **7** sailor's spell of duty. **watchable** *adj* **watcher** *n* **watchful** *adj* vigilant or alert. **watchfully** *adv* **watchfulness** *n* **watchdog** *n* **1** dog kept to guard property. **2** person or group guarding against inefficiency or illegality. **watch for** *v* be keenly alert to or cautious about. **watchman** *n* man employed to guard a building or property. **watchword** *n* word or phrase that sums up the attitude of a particular group.

water *n* **1** clear colourless tasteless liquid that falls as rain and forms rivers etc. **2** body of water, such as a sea or lake. **3** level of the tide. **4** urine. ♦ *v* **5** put water on or into. **6** (of the eyes) fill with tears. **7** (of the mouth) salivate. **watery** *adj* **water buffalo** oxlike Asian animal. **water closet** *Old-fashioned* (room containing) a toilet flushed by water. **watercolour** *n* **1** paint thinned with water. **2** painting done in this. **watercourse** *n* bed of a stream or river. **watercress** *n* edible plant growing in clear ponds and streams. **water down** *v* dilute, make less strong. **waterfall** *n* place where the waters of a river drop vertically. **waterfront** *n* part of a town alongside a body of water. **waterhole** *n* pond or pool in a dry area where animals drink. **water ice** ice cream made from frozen fruit-flavoured syrup. **watering place** **1** place where drinking water may be obtained for people or animals. **2** resort or spa. **water lily** water plant with large floating leaves. **waterline** *n* level to which a ship's hull will be immersed when afloat. **waterlogged** *adj* saturated with water. **watermark** *n* faint translucent design in a sheet of paper. **watermelon** *n* melon with green skin and red flesh. **water polo** team game played by swimmers with a ball. **waterproof** *adj* **1** not letting water through. ♦ *n* **2** waterproof garment. ♦ *v* **3** make waterproof. **watershed** *n* **1** important period or factor serving as a dividing line. **2** line separating two river systems. **water-skiing** *n* sport of riding over water on skis towed by a speedboat. **watertight** *adj* **1** not letting water through. **2** with no loopholes or weak points. **water wheel** large wheel which is turned by flowing water to drive machinery.

watt [**wott**] *n* unit of power. **wattage** *n* electrical power expressed in watts.

wattle [**wott**-tl] *n* **1** branches woven over sticks to make a fence. **2** fold of skin hanging from the neck of certain birds.

wave *v* **1** move the hand to and fro as a greeting or signal. **2** direct (someone) to move in a particular direction by waving. **3** move or flap to and fro. ♦ *n* **4** moving ridge on water. **5** curve(s) in the hair. **6** prolonged spell of something, e.g. *the recent wave of violence.* **7** gesture of waving. **8** vibration carrying energy through a medium. **wavy** *adj* **wavier, waviest** **wavelength** *n* distance between the same points of two successive waves.

waver *v* **1** hesitate or be irresolute. **2** be or become unsteady. **waverer** *n* **wavering** *adj*

wax[1] *n* **1** solid shiny fatty or oily substance used for sealing, making candles, etc. **2** similar substance made by bees. **3** waxy secretion of the ear. ♦ *v* **4** coat or polish with wax. **waxed** *adj* **waxen** *adj* made of or like wax. **waxy** *adj* **waxier, waxiest** **waxwork** *n* **1** lifelike wax model of a (famous) person. ♦ *pl* **2** place exhibiting these.

wax[2] *v* **1** increase in size or strength. **2** (of the moon) get gradually larger.

way *n* **1** manner or method. **2** characteristic manner. **3** route or direction. **4** track or path. **5** distance. **6** room for movement or activity, e.g. *you're in the way.* **7** passage or journey. **8** *Informal* state or condition, e.g *In a bad way.* ♦ *pl* **9** habits or customs. **wayfarer** *n* traveller. **waylay** *v* lie in wait for and accost or attack. **way-out** *adj Informal* extremely unconventional. **wayside** *adj, n* (situated by) the side of a road.

wayward *adj* erratic, selfish, or stubborn. **waywardness** *n*

Wb *Physics* weber.

WC water closet.

we *pron* (used as the subject of a verb) **1** the speaker or writer and one or more others. **2** people in general. **3** formal word for 'I' used by editors and monarchs.

weak *adj* **1** lacking strength. **2** liable to give way. **3** unconvincing. **4** lacking flavour. **weaken** *v* make or become weak. **weakling** *n* feeble person or animal. **weakly** *adv* **1** feebly. ♦ *adj* **2** weak or sickly. **weakness** *n* **1** being weak. **2** failing. **3** self-indulgent liking. **weak-kneed** *adj Informal* lacking determination.

weal[1] *n* raised mark left on the skin by a blow.

weal[2] *n Obs* prosperity or wellbeing, esp. in *the common weal.*

wealth *n* **1** state of being rich. **2** large amount of money and valuables. **3** great amount or number. **wealthy** *adj* **wealthier, wealthiest**

wean *v* **1** accustom (a baby or young mammal) to food other than mother's milk. **2** coax (someone) away from former habits.

weapon *n* **1** object used in fighting. **2** anything used to get the better of an opponent. **weaponry** *n* weapons collectively.

wear *v* **wearing, wore, worn 1** have on the body as clothing or ornament. **2** show as one's expression. **3** have (the hair) in a particular style. **4** (cause to) deteriorate by constant use or action. **5** *Informal* tolerate. **6** endure constant use. ♦ *n* **7** clothes suitable for a particular time or purpose, e.g. *beach wear.* **8** damage caused by use. **9** ability to endure constant use. **wearable** *adj* **wearer** *n* **wearing** *adj* tiring and sometimes trying. **wear and tear** damage or loss from ordinary use. **wear off** *v* gradually decrease in intensity. **wear on** *v* (of time) pass slowly. **wear out** *v* **1** make or become useless through wear. **2** exhaust or tire.

weary *adj* **-rier, -riest 1** tired or exhausted. **2** tiring. ♦ *v* **-rying, -ried 3** make or become weary. **wearily** *adv* **weariness** *n* **wearisome** *adj* tedious. **wearying** *adj*

weasel *n* small carnivorous mammal with a long body and short legs.

weather *n* **1** day-to-day atmospheric conditions of a place. ♦ *v* **2** (cause to) be affected by the weather. **3** come safely through. **under the weather** *Informal* slightly ill. **weather-beaten** *adj* worn, damaged, or (of skin) tanned by exposure to the weather. **weathercock, weathervane** *n* device that revolves to show the direction of the wind. **weatherman** *n Informal* person who forecasts the weather on television or radio.

weave *v* **weaving, wove** *or* **weaved, woven** *or* **weaved 1** make (fabric) by interlacing (yarn) on a loom. **2** compose (a story). **3** move from side to side while going forwards. **weaver** *n* **weaving** *n*

web *n* **1** net spun by a spider. **2** anything intricate or complex, e.g. *web of deceit.* **3** skin between the toes of a duck, frog, etc. **the Web** short for WORLD WIDE WEB. **webbed** *adj* **webbing** *n* strong fabric woven in strips. **website** *n* group of connected pages on the World Wide Web.

weber [**vay**-ber] *n* SI unit of magnetic flux.

wed *v* **wedding, wedded** *or* **wed 1** marry. **2** unite closely. **wedded** *adj* **1** of marriage. **2** firmly in support of an idea or institution. **wedding** *n* act or ceremony of marriage. **wedlock** *n* marriage.

Wed. Wednesday.

wedge *n* **1** piece of material thick at one end and thin at the other. ♦ *v* **2** fasten or split with a wedge. **3** squeeze into a narrow space.

Wednesday *n* fourth day of the week.

wee *adj* small.

weed *n* **1** plant growing where undesired. **2** *Informal* thin ineffectual person. ♦ *v* **3** clear of weeds. **weedy** *adj* **weedier, weediest 1** *Informal* (of a person) thin and weak. **2** full of or like weeds. **weed out** *v* remove or eliminate (what is unwanted).

weeds *pl n Obs* widow's mourning clothes.

week *n* **1** period of seven days, esp. one beginning on a Sunday. **2** hours or days of work in a week. **weekly** *adj, adv* **1** happening, done, etc. once a week. ♦ *n, pl* **-lies 2** newspaper or magazine published once a week. **weekday** *n* any day of the week except Saturday or Sunday. **weekend** *n* Saturday and Sunday.

weep *v* **weeping, wept 1** shed tears. **2** ooze liquid. ♦ *n* **3** spell of weeping. **weepy** *adj* **weepier, weepiest** liable to cry. **weeping willow** willow with drooping branches.

weevil *n* small beetle which eats grain etc.

weft *n* cross threads in weaving.

weigh *v* **1** have a specified weight. **2** measure the weight of. **3** consider carefully. **4** be influential. **5** be burdensome. **weigh anchor** raise a ship's anchor or (of a ship) have its anchor raised. **weighbridge** *n* machine for weighing vehicles by means of a metal plate set into the road.

weight *n* **1** heaviness of an object. **2** unit of measurement of weight. **3** object of known mass used for weighing. **4** heavy object. **5** importance or influence. ♦ *v* **6** add weight to. **7** slant (a system) so that it favours one side rather than another. **weightless** *adj* **weightlessness** *n* **weightlifting** *n* sport of lifting heavy weights. **weightlifter** *n* **weight training** physical exercise using weights to improve muscles.

weighting *n* extra allowance paid in special circumstances.

weighty *adj* **weightier, weightiest 1** important or serious. **2** very heavy. **weightily** *adv*

weir *n* river dam.

weird *adj* **1** strange or bizarre. **2** unearthly or eerie. **weirdly** *adv*

weirdo *n, pl* **-dos** *Informal* peculiar person.

welch *v* same as WELSH.

welcome *v* **-coming, -comed 1** greet with pleasure. **2** receive gladly. ♦ *n* **3** kindly greeting. ♦ *adj* **4** received gladly. **5** freely permitted.

weld *v* **1** join (pieces of metal or plastic) by softening with heat. **2** unite closely. ♦ *n* **3** welded joint. **welder** *n*

welfare *n* **1** wellbeing. **2** help given to people in need. **welfare state** system in which the government takes responsibility for the wellbeing of its citizens.

well[1] *adv* **better, best 1** satisfactorily. **2** skilfully. **3** completely. **4** prosperously. **5** suitably. **6** intimately. **7** favourably. **8** considerably. **9** very likely. ♦ *adj* **10** in good health. **11** satisfactory. ♦ *interj* **12** exclamation of surprise, interrogation, etc.

well[2] *n* **1** hole sunk into the earth to reach water, oil, or gas. **2** deep open shaft. ♦ *v* **3** flow upwards or outwards.

wellbeing *n* state of being well, happy, or prosperous.

well-built *adj* strong and muscular.

well-disposed *adj* inclined to be friendly or sympathetic.

well-done *adj* **1** accomplished satisfactorily. **2** (of food, esp. meat) thoroughly cooked.

well-heeled *adj Informal* wealthy.

wellies *pl n Informal* wellingtons.

wellingtons *pl n* high waterproof rubber boots.

well-known *adj* famous.

well-meaning *adj* having good intentions.

well-nigh *adv* almost.

well-off *adj* **1** moderately wealthy. **2** in a fortunate position.

well-spoken *adj* speaking in a polite or articulate way.

well-to-do *adj* moderately wealthy.

well-worn *adj* **1** (of a word or phrase) stale from overuse. **2** so much used as to be affected by wear.

welsh *v* fail to pay a debt or fulfil an obligation.

Welsh *adj* **1** of Wales. ♦ *n* **2** language or people of Wales. **Welsh rarebit, rabbit** dish of melted cheese on toast.

welt *n* **1** raised mark on the skin produced by a blow. **2** raised or strengthened seam.

welter *n* jumbled mass.

welterweight *n* boxer weighing up to 147lb (professional) or 67kg (amateur).

wen *n* cyst on the scalp.

wench *n Facetious* young woman.

wend *v* go or travel.

wensleydale *n* type of white cheese of flaky texture.

went *v* past tense of GO.

wept *v* past of WEEP.

were *v* **1** form of the past tense of BE: used after *we, you, they,* or a plural noun. **2** subjunctive of BE.

we're we are.

weren't were not.

werewolf *n* (in folklore) person who can turn into a wolf.

west *n* **1** (direction towards) the part of the horizon where the sun sets. **2** region lying in this direction. **3** (**W-**) western Europe and the US. ♦ *adj* **4** to or in the west. **5** (of a wind) from the west. ♦ *adv* **6** in, to, or towards the west. **westerly** *adj* **western** *adj* **1** of or in the west. ♦ *n* **2** film or story about cowboys in the western US. **westerner** *n* person from the west of a country or area. **westernize** *v* adapt to the customs and culture of the West. **westward** *adj, adv* **westwards** *adv*

wet *adj* **wetter, wettest 1** covered or soaked with water or another liquid. **2** not yet dry, e.g. *wet paint.* **3** rainy. **4** *Informal* (of a person) feeble or foolish. ♦ *n* **5** moisture or rain. **6** *Informal* feeble or foolish person. **7** *Brit* moderate Conservative politician. ♦ *v* **wetting, wet** *or* **wetted 8** make wet. **wetly** *adv* **wetness** *n* **wet blanket** *Informal* person who has a depressing effect on others. **wetland** *n* area of marshy land. **wet nurse** woman employed to breast-feed another's child. **wet suit** close-fitting rubber suit worn by divers etc.

whack *v* **1** strike with a resounding blow. ♦ *n* **2** such a blow. **3** *Informal* share. **4** *Informal* attempt. **whacked** *adj* exhausted. **whacking** *adj Informal* huge.

whale *n* large fish-shaped sea mammal. **a whale of a time** *Informal* a very enjoyable time. **whaling** *n* hunting of whales. **whaler** *n* ship or person involved in whaling. **whalebone** *n* horny substance hanging from the upper jaw of toothless whales.

wham *interj* expression indicating suddenness or forcefulness.

wharf *n, pl* **wharves, wharfs** platform at a harbour for loading and unloading ships.

what *pron* **1** which thing. **2** that which. **3** request for a statement to be repeated. ♦ *interj* **4** exclamation of anger, surprise, etc. ♦ *adv* **5** in which way, how much, e.g. *what do you care?* **what for?** why? **whatever** *pron* **1** everything or anything that. **2** no matter what. **whatnot** *n Informal* similar unspecified things. **whatsoever** *adj* at all.

wheat *n* **1** grain used in making flour, bread, and pasta. **2** plant producing this. **wheaten** *adj* made of the grain or flour of wheat. **wheatear** *n* small so[illegible] bird. **wheatgerm** *n* vitamin-ric[illegible] bryo of the wheat kernel. **wh**[illegible] *adj, n* (made with) brow[illegible] wholemeal, flour.

wheedle *v* coax or cajole.

wheel *n* **1** disc that revolves

2 something repeated in cycles, e.g *wheel of life.* **3** pivoting movement. ♦ *v* **4** push or pull (something with wheels). **5** turn as if on an axis. **6** turn round suddenly. **wheeling and dealing** use of shrewd and sometimes unscrupulous methods to achieve success. **wheeler-dealer** *n* **wheelie** *n* manoeuvre on a bike in which the front wheel is raised off the ground. **wheelie bin** large container for household rubbish, mounted on wheels for easy movement. **wheelbarrow** *n* shallow box for carrying loads, with a wheel at the front and two handles. **wheelbase** *n* distance between a vehicle's front and back axles. **wheelchair** *n* chair mounted on wheels for use by people who cannot walk. **wheel clamp** immobilizing device fixed to one wheel of an illegally parked car. **wheelwright** *n* person who makes or mends wheels as a trade.

wheeze *v* **1** breathe with a hoarse whistling noise. ♦ *n* **2** wheezing sound. **3** *Informal* trick or plan. **wheezy** *adj* **wheezier, wheeziest**

whelk *n* edible snail-like shellfish.

whelp *n* **1** pup or cub. **2** *Offens* youth. ♦ *v* **3** (of an animal) give birth.

when *adv* **1** at what time? ♦ *conj* **2** at the time that. **3** although. **4** considering the fact that. ♦ *pron* **5** at which time. **whenever** *adv, conj* at whatever time.

> Some people dislike the use of *when* in definitions: *famine is when food runs low,* but it is very common in informal usage. More formally, write *...a situation/condition in which....*

whence *adv, conj Obs* from what place or source.

where *adv* **1** in, at, or to what place? ♦ *pron* **2** in, at, or to which place. ♦ *conj* **3** in the place at which. **whereabouts** *n* **1** present position. ♦ *adv* **2** at what place. **whereas** *conj* but on the other hand. **whereby** *pron* by which. **wherefore** *Obs* ♦ *adv* **1** why. ♦ *conj* **2** consequently. **whereupon** *conj* at which point. **wherever** *conj, adv* at whatever place. **wherewithal** *n* necessary funds, resources, etc.

> *Where* includes the ideas *to* and *at* so avoid the use of these prepositions: *where was it?* (not *where was it at?*).

whet *v* **whetting, whetted** sharpen (a tool). **whet someone's appetite** increase someone's desire. **whetstone** *n* stone for sharpening tools.

whether *conj* used to introduce an indirect question or a clause expressing doubt or choice.

whew *interj* exclamation expressing relief, delight, etc.

whey [**way**] *n* watery liquid that separates from the curd when milk is clotted.

which *adj, pron* **1** used to request or refer to a choice from different possibilities. ♦ *pron* **2** used to refer to a thing already mentioned. **whichever** *adj, pron* **1** any out of several. **2** no matter which.

whiff *n* **1** puff of air or odour. **2** trace or hint.

Whig *n* member of a British political party of the 18th–19th centuries that sought limited reform.

while *conj* **1** at the same time that. **2** during the time that. **3** whereas. ♦ *n* **4** period of time. **whilst** *conj* while. **while away** *v* pass (time) idly but pleasantly.

whim *n* sudden fancy. **whimsy** *n, pl* **-sies 1** capricious idea. **2** light or fanciful humour. **whimsical** *adj* unusual, playful, and fanciful.

whimper *v* **1** cry in a soft whining way. ♦ *n* **2** soft plaintive whine.

whin *n* gorse.

whine *n* **1** high-pitched plaintive cry. **2** peevish complaint. ♦ *v* **3** make such a sound. **whining** *n, adj*

whinge *Informal* ♦ *v* **1** complain. ♦ *n* **2** complaint.

whinny *v* **-nying, -nied 1** neigh softly. ♦ *n, pl* **-nies 2** soft neigh.

whip *n* **1** cord attached to a handle, used for beating animals or people. **2**

politician responsible for organizing and disciplining fellow party members. **3** call made on members of Parliament to attend for important votes. **4** dessert made from beaten cream or egg whites. ♦ *v* **whipping, whipped 5** strike with a whip, strap, or cane. **6** *Informal* pull, remove, or move quickly. **7** beat (esp. eggs or cream) to a froth. **8** rouse into a particular condition. **9** *Informal* steal. **whip hand** advantage. **whiplash injury** neck injury caused by a sudden jerk to the head, as in a car crash. **whipping boy** scapegoat. **whip-round** *n Informal* collection of money.

whippet *n* racing dog like a small greyhound.

whirl *v* **1** spin or revolve. **2** be dizzy or confused. ♦ *n* **3** whirling movement. **4** bustling activity. **5** confusion or giddiness. **whirlpool** *n* strong circular current of water. **whirlwind** *n* **1** column of air whirling violently upwards in a spiral. ♦ *adj* **2** much quicker than normal.

whirr, whir *n* **1** prolonged soft buzz. ♦ *v* **whirring, whirred 2** (cause to) make a whirr.

whisk *v* **1** move or remove quickly. **2** beat (esp. eggs or cream) to a froth. ♦ *n* **3** quick movement. **4** egg-beating utensil.

whisker *n* **1** any of the long stiff hairs on the face of a cat or other mammal. ♦ *pl* **2** hair growing on a man's face. **by a whisker** *Informal* only just. **whiskered, whiskery** *adj*

whisky *n, pl* **-kies** spirit distilled from fermented cereals. **whiskey** *n, pl* **-keys** Irish or American whisky.

whisper *v* **1** speak softly, without vibration of the vocal cords. **2** rustle. ♦ *n* **3** soft voice. **4** *Informal* rumour. **5** rustling sound.

whist *n* card game in which one pair of players tries to win more tricks than another pair. **whist drive** social event at which whist is played.

whistle *v* **1** produce a shrill sound, esp. by forcing the breath through pursed lips. **2** signal by a whistle. ♦ *n* **3** whistling sound. **4** instrument blown to make a whistling sound. **blow the whistle on** *Informal* inform on or put a stop to. **whistling** *n, adj*

whit *n* **not a whit** not the slightest amount.

white *adj* **1** of the colour of snow. **2** pale. **3** light in colour. **4** (of coffee) served with milk. ♦ *n* **5** colour of snow. **6** clear fluid round the yolk of an egg. **7** white part, esp. of the eyeball. **8** (**W-**) member of the race of people with light-coloured skin. **whiten** *v* make or become white or whiter. **whiteness** *n* **whitish** *adj* **white blood cell** same as LEUCOCYTE. **white-collar** *adj* denoting professional and clerical workers. **white elephant** useless or unwanted possession. **white fish** any sea fish with white flesh used as food. **white flag** signal of surrender or truce. **white goods** large household appliances such as cookers and fridges. **white-hot** *adj* very hot. **White House 1** official residence of the US president. **2** US presidency. **white lie** minor unimportant lie. **white paper** report by the government, outlining its policy on a matter. **white sauce** thick sauce made from butter, flour, and milk or stock.

whitebait *n* small edible fish.

whitewash *n* **1** substance for whitening walls. **2** attempt to conceal unpleasant facts. ♦ *v* **3** cover with whitewash. **4** conceal or gloss over unpleasant facts.

whither *adv Obs* to what place.

whiting [**white**-ing] *n* edible sea fish.

whitlow *n* inflamed sore on a finger or toe, esp. round a nail.

Whitsun, Whitsuntide *n* Christian festival celebrating the descent of the Holy Spirit to the apostles.

whittle *v* cut or carve (wood) with a knife. **whittle down, away** *v* reduce or wear away gradually.

whizz, whiz *v* **whizzing, whizzed 1** make a loud buzzing sound. **2** *Informal* move quickly. ♦ *n, pl* **whizzes 3** loud buzzing sound. **4** *Informal* person skilful at something. **whizz kid, whiz kid** *In-*

formal person who is outstandingly able for his or her age.

who *pron* **1** which person. **2** used to refer to a person or people already mentioned. **whoever** *pron* **1** any person who. **2** no matter who.

WHO World Health Organization.

whoa *interj* command used, esp. to horses, to stop or slow down.

whodunnit, whodunit [hoo-**dun**-nit] *n Informal* detective story, play, or film.

whole *adj* **1** containing all the elements or parts. **2** uninjured or undamaged. ♦ *n* **3** complete thing or system. **on the whole** taking everything into consideration. **wholly** *adv* **wholefood** *n* food that has been processed as little as possible. **wholehearted** *adj* sincere or enthusiastic. **wholemeal** *adj* **1** (of flour) made from the whole wheat grain. **2** made from wholemeal flour. **whole number** number that does not contain a fraction.

wholesale *adj, adv* **1** dealing by selling goods in large quantities to retailers. **2** on a large scale. **wholesaler** *n*

wholesome *adj* physically or morally beneficial.

whom *pron* objective form of WHO.

whoop *v, n* shout or cry to express excitement.

whoopee *interj Informal* cry of joy.

whooping cough *n* infectious disease marked by convulsive coughing and noisy breathing.

whoops *interj* exclamation of surprise or of apology.

whopper *n Informal* **1** anything unusually large. **2** huge lie. **whopping** *adj*

whore [**hore**] *n* prostitute.

whorl *n* **1** ring of leaves or petals. **2** one turn of a spiral. **3** something coiled.

whose *pron* of whom or of which.

why *adv* **1** for what reason. ♦ *pron* **2** because of which.

WI **1** Wisconsin. **2** *Brit* Women's Institute.

wick *n* cord through a lamp or candle which carries fuel to the flame.

wicked *adj* **1** morally bad. **2** mischievous. **3** dangerous. **4** *Slang* very good. **wickedly** *adv* **wickedness** *n*

wicker *adj* made of woven cane. **wickerwork** *n*

wicket *n* **1** set of three cricket stumps and two bails. **2** ground between the two wickets on a cricket pitch. **wicketkeeper** *n* fielder positioned directly behind the wicket.

wide *adj* **1** large from side to side. **2** having a specified width. **3** spacious or extensive. **4** far from the target. **5** opened fully. ♦ *adv* **6** to the full extent. **7** over an extensive area. **8** far from the target. **widely** *adv* **widen** *v* make or become wider. **wide-awake** *adj* fully awake. **wide-eyed** *adj* **1** naive or innocent. **2** surprised or frightened. **widespread** *adj* affecting a wide area or a large number of people.

widgeon *n* same as WIGEON.

widow *n* woman whose husband is dead and who has not remarried. **widowed** *adj* **widowhood** *n* **widower** *n* man whose wife is dead and who has not remarried.

width *n* **1** distance from side to side. **2** quality of being wide.

wield *v* **1** hold and use (a weapon). **2** have and use (power).

wife *n, pl* **wives** woman to whom a man is married. **wifely** *adj*

wig *n* artificial head of hair.

wigeon *n* duck found in marshland.

wigging *n Brit slang* reprimand.

wiggle *v* **1** move jerkily from side to side. ♦ *n* **2** wiggling movement. **wiggly** *adj* **wigglier, wiggliest**

wigwam *n* Native American's tent.

wilco *interj* expression in telecommunications etc., indicating that the message just received will be complied with.

wild *adj* **1** (of animals) not tamed or domesticated. **2** (of plants) not cultivated. **3** not civilized. **4** lacking restraint or control. **5** violent or stormy. **6** *Informal* excited. **7** *Informal* furious. **8** random. **wilds** *pl n* desolate or uninhabited place. **wildly** *adv* **wildness** *n* **wild-goose chase** search that has little chance of success. **Wild West** western US, which was lawless during settlement.

wildcat *n* European wild animal like a large domestic cat. **wildcat strike** sudden unofficial strike.

wildebeest *n* gnu.

wilderness *n* **1** uninhabited uncultivated region. **2** state of no longer being in a prominent position.

wildfire *n* **spread like wildfire** spread quickly and uncontrollably.

wildlife *n* wild animals and plants collectively.

wiles *pl n* tricks or ploys. **wily** *adj* **wilier, wiliest** crafty or sly.

wilful *adj* **1** headstrong or obstinate. **2** intentional. **wilfully** *adv* **wilfulness** *n*

will[1] *v, past* **would** used as an auxiliary to form the future tense or to indicate intention, ability, or expectation.

> *Will* is normal for discussing the future. The use of *shall* with *I* and *we* is a matter of preference, not of rule. *Shall* is commonly used for questions in Southern England but less often in the North and Scotland.

will[2] *n* **1** strong determination. **2** desire or wish. **3** directions written for disposal of one's property after death. ♦ *v* **4** use one's will in an attempt to do (something). **5** wish or desire. **6** leave (property) by a will. **willing** *adj* **1** ready or inclined (to do something). **2** keen and obliging. **willingly** *adv* **willingness** *n* **willpower** *n* ability to control oneself and one's actions.

willies *pl n* **give someone the willies** *Slang* cause nervousness or fright.

will-o'-the-wisp *n* **1** elusive person or thing. **2** pale light sometimes seen over marshes at night.

willow *n* **1** tree with thin flexible branches. **2** its wood, used for making cricket bats. **willowy** *adj* slender and graceful.

willy-nilly *adv* whether desired or not.

wilt *v* (cause to) become limp or lose strength.

wimp *n Informal* feeble ineffectual person.

wimple *n* garment framing the face, worn by medieval women and now by nuns.

win *v* **winning, won** **1** come first in (a competition, fight, etc.). **2** gain (a prize) in a competition. **3** get by effort. ♦ *n* **4** victory, esp. in a game. **winner** *n* **winning** *adj* **1** gaining victory. **2** charming. **winnings** *pl n* sum won, esp. in gambling. **win over** *v* gain the support or consent of (someone).

wince *v* **1** draw back, as if in pain. ♦ *n* **2** wincing.

winch *n* **1** machine for lifting or hauling using a cable wound round a drum. ♦ *v* **2** lift or haul using a winch.

wind[1] *n* **1** current of air. **2** hint or suggestion. **3** breath. **4** flatulence. **5** idle talk. ♦ *v* **6** render short of breath. **windy** *adj* **windier, windiest** **windward** *adj, n* (of or in) the direction from which the wind is blowing. **windbag** *n Slang* person who talks much but uninterestingly. **windbreak** *n* fence or line of trees providing shelter from the wind. **windfall** *n* **1** unexpected good luck. **2** fallen fruit. **wind instrument** musical instrument played by blowing. **windmill** *n* machine for grinding or pumping driven by sails turned by the wind. **windpipe** *n* tube linking the throat and the lungs. **windscreen** *n* front window of a motor vehicle. **windscreen wiper** device that wipes rain etc. from a windscreen. **windsock** *n* cloth cone on a mast at an airfield to indicate wind direction. **windsurfing** *n* sport of riding on water using a surfboard propelled and steered by a sail. **windswept** *adj* exposed to the wind.

wind[2] *v* **winding, wound** **1** coil or wrap around. **2** tighten the spring of (a clock or watch). **3** move in a twisting course. **wind up** *v* **1** bring to or reach an end. **2** tighten the spring of (a clock or watch). **3** *Informal* make tense or agitated. **4** *Slang* tease.

windlass *n* winch worked by a crank.

window *n* **1** opening in a wall to let in light or air. **2** glass pane or panes fitted in such an opening. **3** display area behind the window of a shop. **4** area on a computer screen that can be manipulated separately from the rest of the display area. **5** period of unbooked time in a diary or schedule. **window-dressing** *n* **1** arrangement of goods in a shop window. **2** attempt to make something more attractive than it really is. **window-shopping** *n* looking at goods in shop windows without intending to buy. **windowsill** *n* ledge below a window.

wine *n* **1** alcoholic drink made from fermented grapes. **2** similar drink made from other fruits. ♦ *adj* **3** of a dark purplish-red colour. **wine and dine** entertain or be entertained with fine food and drink.

wing *n* **1** one of the limbs or organs of a bird, insect, or bat that are used for flying. **2** one of the winglike supporting parts of an aircraft. **3** projecting side part of a building. **4** faction of a political party. **5** part of a car body surrounding the wheels. **6** *Sport* (player on) either side of the pitch. ♦ *pl* **7** sides of a stage. ♦ *v* **8** fly. **9** wound slightly in the wing or arm. **winged** *adj* **winger** *n Sport* player positioned on a wing. **wing commander** middle-ranking commissioned air-force officer. **wingspan** *n* distance between the wing tips of an aircraft, bird, or insect.

wink *v* **1** close and open (an eye) quickly as a signal. **2** twinkle. ♦ *n* **3** winking. **4** smallest amount of sleep.

winkle *n* shellfish with a spiral shell. **winkle out** *v Informal* extract or prise out.

winnow *v* **1** separate (chaff) from (grain). **2** examine to select desirable elements.

winsome *adj* charming or winning.

winter *n* **1** coldest season. ♦ *v* **2** spend the winter. **wintry** *adj* **wintrier, wintriest 1** of or like winter. **2** cold or unfriendly. **winter sports** open-air sports held on snow or ice.

wipe *v* **1** clean or dry by rubbing. **2** erase (a tape). ♦ *n* **3** wiping. **wipe out** *v* destroy completely.

wire *n* **1** thin flexible strand of metal. **2** length of this used to carry electric current. **3** wire or cable connecting points in a telephone or telegraph system. **4** *Obs* telegram. ♦ *v* **5** fasten with wire. **6** equip with wires. **wiring** *n* system of wires. **wiry** *adj* **wirier, wiriest 1** lean and tough. **2** like wire. **wire-haired** *adj* (of a dog) having a stiff wiry coat. **wire netting** net made of wire, used for fences.

wireless *n Old-fashioned* same as RADIO.

wisdom *n* **1** good sense and judgment. **2** accumulated knowledge. **wisdom tooth** any of the four large molar teeth that come through usu. after the age of twenty.

wise[1] *adj* having wisdom. **wisely** *adv* **wiseacre** *n* person who wishes to seem wise.

wise[2] *n Obs* manner.

-wise *adv suffix* **1** indicating direction or manner, e.g. *clockwise; likewise.* **2** with reference to, e.g. *businesswise.*

> The ending *-wise* can frequently be replaced by *-ways: sidewise/sideways; lengthwise/lengthways.* Adding *-wise* to a noun to create the meaning 'in respect of', as in: *Defencewise, the team is strong,* is generally unacceptable except in very informal usage.

wisecrack *Informal* ♦ *n* **1** clever, sometimes unkind, remark. ♦ *v* **2** make a wisecrack.

wish *v* **1** want or desire. **2** feel or express a hope about someone's wellbeing, success, etc. ♦ *n* **3** expression of a desire. **4** thing desired. **wishful** *adj* too optimistic. **wishful thinking** interpretation of the facts as one would like them to be, rather than as they are. **wishbone** *n* V-shaped bone above the breastbone of a fowl.

wishy-washy *adj Informal* insipid or

bland.

wisp *n* **1** light delicate streak. **2** twisted bundle or tuft. **wispy** *adj* **wispier, wispiest**

wisteria *n* climbing shrub with blue or purple flowers.

wistful *adj* sadly longing. **wistfully** *adv* **wistfulness** *n*

wit[1] *n* **1** ability to use words or ideas in a clever and amusing way. **2** person with this ability. **3** (sometimes pl) practical intelligence. **witless** *adj* foolish.

wit[2] *v* **to wit** that is to say; namely.

witch *n* **1** person, usu. female, who practises (black) magic. **2** ugly or wicked woman. **witchcraft** *n* use of magic. **witch doctor** (in certain societies) a man appearing to cure or cause injury or disease by magic. **witch-hunt** *n* campaign against people with unpopular views.

with *prep* indicating presence alongside, possession, means of performance, characteristic manner, etc., e.g. *walking with his dog; a man with two cars; hit with a hammer; playing with skill.* **within** *prep, adv* in or inside. **without** *prep* not accompanied by, using, or having.

withdraw *v* **-drawing, -drew, -drawn** take or move out or away. **withdrawal** *n* **withdrawn** *adj* unsociable.

wither *v* **1** wilt or dry up. **2** fade or waste. **withering** *adj* (of a look or remark) scornful.

withers *pl n* ridge between a horse's shoulder blades.

withhold *v* **-holding, -held** refrain from giving.

withstand *v* **-standing, -stood** oppose or resist successfully.

witness *n* **1** person who has seen something happen. **2** person giving evidence in court. **3** person who confirms that a document is genuine by signing it. **4** evidence or testimony. ♦ *v* **5** see at first hand. **6** be the scene of. **7** sign (a document) to certify that it is genuine. **witness box** place in a court where a witness stands to give evidence.

witter *v* chatter pointlessly or at unnecessary length.

wittingly *adv* intentionally.

witty *adj* **wittier, wittiest** clever and amusing. **wittily** *adv* **witticism** *n* witty remark.

wives *n* plural of WIFE.

wizard *n* **1** magician. **2** person with outstanding skill in a particular field. **wizardry** *n*

wizened [**wiz**-zend] *adj* shrivelled or wrinkled.

woad *n* blue dye obtained from a plant.

wobble *v* **1** move unsteadily. **2** shake. ♦ *n* **3** wobbling movement or sound. **wobbly** *adj* **wobblier, wobbliest**

wodge *n Informal* thick lump or chunk.

woe *n* grief. **woeful** *adj* **1** extremely sad. **2** pitiful. **woefully** *adv* **woebegone** *adj* looking miserable.

wok *n* bowl-shaped Chinese cooking pan, used for stir-frying.

woke *v* past tense of WAKE[1]. **woken** *v* past participle of WAKE[1].

wold *n* high open country.

wolf *n, pl* **wolves** **1** wild predatory canine mammal. ♦ *v* **2** eat ravenously. **cry wolf** raise a false alarm. **wolfhound** *n* very large breed of dog. **wolf whistle** whistle by a man indicating that he thinks a woman is attractive.

wolverine *n* carnivorous mammal of Arctic regions.

woman *n, pl* **women** **1** adult human female. **2** women collectively. **womanhood** *n* **womanish** *adj* effeminate. **womanly** *adj* having qualities traditionally associated with a woman. **womanizing** *n* practice of indulging in casual affairs with women. **womanizer** *n* **Women's Liberation** movement for the removal of inequalities between women and men (also **women's lib**).

womb *n* hollow organ in female mammals where babies are conceived and develop.

wombat *n* small heavily-built burrowing Australian marsupial.

won *v* past of WIN.

wonder *v* **1** be curious about. **2** be

amazed. ♦ *n* **3** wonderful thing. **4** emotion caused by an amazing or unusual thing. ♦ *adj* **5** spectacularly successful, e.g. *a wonder drug*. **wonderful** *adj* **1** very fine. **2** remarkable. **wonderfully** *adv* **wonderment** *n* **wondrous** *adj Old-fashioned* wonderful. **wonderland** *n* real or imaginary place full of wonders.

wonky *adj* **-kier, -kiest** *Informal* **1** shaky or unsteady. **2** insecure or unreliable.

wont [rhymes with **don't**] *adj* **1** accustomed. ♦ *n* **2** custom.

won't will not.

woo *v* **1** try to persuade. **2** *Old-fashioned* try to gain the love of.

wood *n* **1** substance trees are made of, used in carpentry and as fuel. **2** area where trees grow. **3** long-shafted golf club, usu. with wooden head. ♦ *adj* **4** made of or using wood. **wooded** *adj* covered with trees. **wooden** *adj* **1** made of wood. **2** without expression. **woody** *adj* **woodier, woodiest** **woodbine** *n* honeysuckle. **woodcock** *n* game bird. **woodcut** *n* (print made from) an engraved block of wood. **woodland** *n* forest. **woodlouse** *n* small insect-like creature with many legs. **woodpecker** *n* bird which searches tree trunks for insects. **woodwind** *adj, n* (of) a type of wind instrument made of wood. **woodwork** *n* **1** parts of a room or building made of wood. **2** skill of making things in wood. **woodworm** *n* insect larva that bores into wood.

woof[1] *n* cross threads in weaving.

woof[2] *n* barking noise made by a dog. **woofer** *n* loudspeaker reproducing low-frequency sounds.

wool *n* **1** soft hair of sheep, goats, etc. **2** yarn spun from this. **woollen** *adj* **woolly** *adj* **woollier, woolliest** **1** of or like wool. **2** vague or muddled. ♦ *n, pl* **-lies** **3** knitted woollen garment. **woolgathering** *n* daydreaming.

woozy *adj* **woozier, wooziest** *Informal* weak, dizzy, and confused.

word *n* **1** smallest single meaningful unit of speech or writing. **2** chat or discussion. **3** brief remark. **4** message. **5** promise. **6** command. ♦ *v* **7** express in words. **wordless** *adj* **wordy** *adj* **wordier, wordiest** using too many words. **wording** *n* choice and arrangement of words. **word-perfect** *adj* (of a speaker or actor) knowing one's speech or role perfectly. **word processor** keyboard, microprocessor, and VDU for electronic organization and storage of text. **word processing**

wore *v* past tense of WEAR.

work *n* **1** physical or mental effort directed to making or doing something. **2** paid employment. **3** duty or task. **4** something made or done. ♦ *pl* **5** factory. **6** total of a writer's or artist's achievements. **7** *Informal* full treatment. **8** mechanism of a machine. ♦ *adj* **9** of or for work. ♦ *v* **10** (cause to) do work. **11** be employed. **12** (cause to) operate. **13** (of a plan etc.) be successful. **14** cultivate (land). **15** manipulate, shape, or process. **16** (cause to) reach a specified condition. **work-to-rule** *n* protest in which workers keep strictly to all regulations to reduce the rate of work. **workable** *adj* **worker** *n* **workaday** *adj* ordinary. **workaholic** *n* person obsessed with work. **workforce** *n* total number of workers. **workhorse** *n* person or thing that does a lot of dull or routine work. **workhouse** *n Hist* institution where the poor were given food and lodgings in return for work. **working class** social class consisting of wage earners, esp. manual workers. **working-class** *adj* **working party** committee investigating a specific problem. **workman** *n* manual worker. **workmanship** *n* skill with which an object is made. **work out** *v* **1** solve by reasoning or calculation. **2** happen in a particular way. **3** take part in physical exercise. **workout** *n* session of physical exercise for training or fitness. **workshop** *n* **1** room or building for a manufacturing process. **2** session of group study or practice of a subject. **work station** area in an office where one person works. **worktop** *n* surface in a kitchen, used for food preparation. **work up** *v* **1** make angry or excited. **2** build up.

world *n* **1** the planet earth. **2** mankind. **3** society of a particular area or period. **4** sphere of existence. ♦ *adj* **5** of the whole world. **worldly** *adj* **1** not spiritual. **2** concerned with material things. **3** wise in the ways of the world. **world-weary** *adj* no longer finding pleasure in life. **worldwide** *adj* applying or extending throughout the world. **World Wide Web** global network of linked computer files.

worm *n* **1** small limbless invertebrate animal. **2** *Informal* wretched or spineless person. **3** shaft with a spiral thread forming part of a gear system. ♦ *pl* **4** illness caused by parasitic worms in the intestines. ♦ *v* **5** rid of worms. **worm one's way 1** crawl. **2** insinuate (oneself). **wormy** *adj* **wormier, wormiest** **wormcast** *n* coil of earth excreted by a burrowing worm. **worm-eaten** *adj* eaten into by worms. **worm out** *v* extract (information) craftily.

wormwood *n* bitter plant.

worn *v* past participle of WEAR. **worn-out** *adj* **1** threadbare, valueless, or useless. **2** completely exhausted.

worry *v* **-rying, -ried** **1** (cause to) be anxious or uneasy. **2** annoy or bother. **3** (of a dog) chase and try to bite (sheep etc.). ♦ *n, pl* **-ries** **4** (cause of) anxiety or concern. **worried** *adj* **worrying** *adj, n*

worse *adj, adv* comparative of BAD *or* BADLY. **worst** *adj, adv* **1** superlative of BAD *or* BADLY. ♦ *n* **2** worst thing. **worsen** *v* make or grow worse.

worship *v* **-shipping, -shipped** **1** show religious devotion to. **2** love and admire. ♦ *n* **3** act or instance of worshipping. **4** (**W-**) title for a mayor or magistrate. **worshipper** *n* **worshipful** *adj* worshipping.

worsted [**wooss**-tid] *n* type of woollen yarn or fabric.

worth *prep* **1** having a value of. **2** meriting or justifying. ♦ *n* **3** value or price. **4** excellence. **5** amount to be had for a given sum. **worthless** *adj* **worthy** *adj* **-thier, -thiest** **1** deserving admiration or respect. ♦ *n, pl* **-thies** **2** *Informal* notable person. **worthy of** deserving of. **worthily** *adv* **worthiness** *n* **worthwhile** *adj* worth the time or effort involved.

would *v* used as an auxiliary to express a request, describe a habitual past action, or form the past tense or subjunctive mood of WILL[1]. **would-be** *adj* wishing or pretending to be.

wouldn't would not.

wound[1] *n* **1** injury caused by violence. **2** injury to the feelings. ♦ *v* **3** inflict a wound on.

wound[2] *v* past of WIND[2].

wove *v* a past tense of WEAVE. **woven** *v* a past participle of WEAVE.

wow *interj* **1** exclamation of astonishment. ♦ *n* **2** *Informal* astonishing person or thing. ♦ *v* **3** *Informal* be a great success with.

wpm words per minute.

WRAC Women's Royal Army Corps.

wrack *n* seaweed.

WRAF Women's Royal Air Force.

wraith *n* ghost.

wrangle *v* **1** argue noisily. ♦ *n* **2** noisy argument.

wrap *v* **wrapping, wrapped** **1** fold (something) round (a person or thing) so as to cover. ♦ *n* **2** garment wrapped round the shoulders. **wrapper** *n* cover for a product. **wrapping** *n* material used to wrap. **wrap up** *v* **1** fold paper round. **2** put warm clothes on. **3** *Informal* finish or settle (a matter).

wrasse *n* colourful sea fish.

wrath [**roth**] *n* intense anger. **wrathful** *adj*

wreak *v* **wreak havoc** cause chaos. **wreak vengeance on** take revenge on.

wreath *n* twisted ring or band of flowers or leaves used as a memorial or tribute. **wreathed** *adj* surrounded or encircled.

wreck *v* **1** destroy. ♦ *n* **2** remains of something that has been destroyed or badly damaged, esp. a ship. **3** person in very poor condition. **wrecker** *n* formerly, person who lured ships onto the rocks in order to plunder them. **wreckage** *n* wrecked remains.

wren *n* small brown songbird.

Wren *n Informal* member of the Women's Royal Naval Service.

wrench *v* **1** twist or pull violently. **2** sprain (a joint). ♦ *n* **3** violent twist or pull. **4** sprain. **5** difficult or painful parting. **6** adjustable spanner.

wrest *v* **1** twist violently. **2** take by force.

wrestle *v* **1** fight, esp. as a sport, by grappling with and trying to throw down an opponent. **2** struggle hard with. **wrestler** *n* **wrestling** *n*

wretch *n* **1** despicable person. **2** pitiful person. **wretched** [**retch**-id] *adj* **1** miserable or unhappy. **2** worthless. **wretchedly** *adv* **wretchedness** *n*

wrier *adj* a comparative of WRY. **wriest** *adj* a superlative of WRY.

wriggle *v* **1** move with a twisting action. **2** manoeuvre oneself by devious means. ♦ *n* **3** wriggling movement.

wright *n* maker, e.g. *wheelwright.*

wring *v* **wringing, wrung 1** twist, esp. to squeeze liquid out of. **2** clasp and twist (the hands). **3** obtain by forceful means.

wrinkle *n* **1** slight crease, esp. one in the skin due to age. ♦ *v* **2** make or become slightly creased. **wrinkled** *adj* **wrinkly** *adj*

wrist *n* joint between the hand and the arm. **wristwatch** *n* watch worn on the wrist.

writ *n* written legal command.

write *v* **writing, wrote, written 1** mark paper etc. with symbols or words. **2** set down in words. **3** communicate by letter. **4** be the author or composer of. **writing** *n* **writer** *n* **1** author. **2** person who has written something specified. **write-off** *n Informal* something damaged beyond repair. **write-up** *n* published account of something.

writhe *v* twist or squirm in or as if in pain.

WRNS Women's Royal Naval Service.

wrong *adj* **1** incorrect or mistaken. **2** immoral or bad. **3** not intended or suitable. **4** not working properly. ♦ *adv* **5** in a wrong manner. ♦ *n* **6** something immoral or unjust. ♦ *v* **7** treat unjustly. **8** malign. **wrongly** *adv* **wrongful** *adj* **wrongfully** *adv* **wrongdoing** *n* immoral or illegal behaviour. **wrongdoer** *n*

wrote *v* past tense of WRITE.

wrought [**rawt**] *v* **1** *Lit* past of WORK. ♦ *adj* **2** (of metals) shaped by hammering or beating. **wrought iron** pure form of iron used for decorative work.

wrung *v* past of WRING.

WRVS Women's Royal Voluntary Service.

wry *adj* **wrier, wriest** *or* **wryer, wryest 1** dryly humorous. **2** (of a facial expression) contorted. **wryly** *adv*

wt. weight.

WV West Virginia.

WWI World War One.

WWII World War Two.

WY Wyoming.

wych-elm *n* elm with large rough leaves.

X x Y y Z z

X **1** indicating an error, a choice, or a kiss. **2** indicating an unknown, unspecified, or variable factor, number, person, or thing. **3** the Roman numeral for ten.

X-chromosome *n* sex chromosome that occurs in pairs in the females of many animals, and as one of a pair with the Y-chromosome in males.

Xe *Chem* xenon.

xenon *n Chem* colourless odourless gas found in very small quantities in the air.

xenophobia [zen-oh-**fobe**-ee-a] *n* fear or hatred of people from other countries. **xenophobic** *adj*

Xerox [**zeer**-ox] *n* **1** ® machine for copying printed material. **2** ® copy made by a Xerox machine. ♦ *v* **3** copy (a document) using such a machine.

Xmas [**eks**-mass] *n Informal* Christmas.

X-ray, x-ray *n* **1** stream of radiation that can pass through some solid materials. **2** picture made by sending X-rays through someone's body to examine internal organs. ♦ *v* **3** photograph, treat, or examine using X-rays.

xylem [**zy**-lem] *n* plant tissue that conducts water and minerals from the roots to all other parts.

xylophone [**zile**-oh-fone] *n* musical instrument made of a row of wooden bars played with hammers.

Y *Chem* yttrium.

Y2K *n Informal* name for the year 2000 AD (esp. referring to the millennium bug).

yacht [**yott**] *n* **1** large boat with sails or an engine, used for racing or pleasure cruising. ♦ *v* **2** sail in a yacht. **yachting** *n* **yachtsman, yachtswoman** *n*

yahoo *n* crude coarse person.

yak[1] *n* Tibetan ox with long shaggy hair.

yak[2] *v* **yakking, yakked** *Slang* talk continuously about unimportant matters.

Yale lock *n* ® cylinder lock using a flat serrated key.

yam *n* tropical root vegetable.

yank *v* **1** pull or jerk suddenly. ♦ *n* **2** sudden pull or jerk.

Yankee, Yank *n Slang* **1** person from the United States. **2** *US* person from the Northern United States.

yap *v* **yapping, yapped** **1** bark with a high-pitched sound. **2** *Informal* talk continuously. ♦ *n* **3** high-pitched bark.

yard[1] *n* **1** unit of length equal to 36 inches or about 91.4 centimetres. **2** spar slung across a ship's mast to extend the sail. **yardarm** *n* outer end of a ship's yard. **yardstick** *n* standard against which to judge other people or things.

yard[2] *n* **1** enclosed area, usu. next to a building and often used for a particular purpose, e.g. *builder's yard.* **2** *US* garden of a house.

yarmulke [**yar**-mull-ka] *n* skullcap worn by Jewish men.

yarn *n* **1** thread used for knitting or making cloth. **2** *Informal* long involved story.

yashmak *n* veil worn by a Muslim woman to cover her face in public.

yaw *v* (of an aircraft or ship) turn to one side or from side to side while moving.

yawl *n* two-masted sailing boat.

yawn *v* **1** open the mouth wide and take in air deeply, often when sleepy or bored. **2** (of an opening) be large and wide. ♦ *n* **3** act of yawning. **yawning** *adj*

yaws *n* infectious tropical skin disease.

Yb *Chem* ytterbium.

Y-chromosome *n* sex chromosome that occurs as one of a pair with the X-chromosome in the males of many animals.

yd yard.

ye [**yee**] *pron Obs* you.

yea *interj Old-fashioned* yes.

yeah *interj Informal* yes.

year *n* **1** time taken for the earth to make one revolution around the sun, about

365 days. **2** twelve months from January 1 to December 31. **3** any period of twelve months. **4** group of people who have started a course at the same time. ♦ *pl* **5** a long time. **6** age. **yearly** *adj, adv* (happening) every year or once a year. **yearling** *n* animal between one and two years old. **yearbook** *n* reference book published annually containing details of the previous year's events.

yearn *v* **1** want (something) very much. **2** feel tenderness. **yearning** *n, adj*

yeast *n* fungus used to make bread rise and to ferment alcoholic drinks. **yeasty** *adj*

yell *v* **1** shout or scream in a loud or piercing way. ♦ *n* **2** loud cry of pain, anger, or fear.

yellow *n* **1** the colour of gold, a lemon, etc. ♦ *adj* **2** of this colour. **3** *Informal* cowardly. ♦ *v* **4** make or become yellow. **yellow card** *Soccer* piece of yellow pasteboard shown by a referee to indicate that a player has been booked. **yellow fever** serious infectious tropical disease. **yellowhammer** *n* European songbird with a yellow head and body. **Yellow Pages** fi telephone directory which lists businesses under the headings of the type of service they provide.

yelp *v, n* (give) a short sudden cry.

yen[1] *n, pl* **yen** main unit of currency in Japan.

yen[2] *n Informal* longing or desire.

yeoman [**yo**-man] *n, pl* **-men** *Hist* farmer owning and farming his own land. **yeomanry** *n* **1** yeomen. **2** (in Britain) former volunteer cavalry force. **yeoman of the guard** member of the ceremonial bodyguard of the British monarchy.

yes *interj* **1** expresses consent, agreement, or approval. **2** used to answer when one is addressed. ♦ *n* **3** answer or vote of yes. **yes man** person who always agrees with their superior.

yesterday *adv, n* **1** (on) the day before today. **2** (in) the recent past.

yet *conj* **1** nevertheless, still. ♦ *adv* **2** up until then or now. **3** still. **4** now. **5** eventually.

yeti *n* same as ABOMINABLE SNOWMAN.

yew *n* evergreen tree with needle-like leaves and red berries.

YHA Youth Hostels Association.

Yiddish *adj, n* (of or in) a language of German origin spoken by many Jews in Europe and elsewhere.

yield *v* **1** produce or bear. **2** give up control of, surrender. **3** give in. **4** agree (to). **5** grant or allow. ♦ *n* **6** amount produced. **yielding** *adj* **1** submissive. **2** soft or flexible.

yippee *interj* exclamation of joy or pleasure.

YMCA Young Men's Christian Association.

yob, yobbo *n Slang* bad-mannered aggressive youth.

yodel *v* **-delling, -delled** sing with abrupt changes between a normal and a falsetto voice. **yodelling** *n*

yoga *n* Hindu method of exercise and discipline aiming at spiritual, mental, and physical wellbeing. **yogi** *n* person who practises yoga.

yogurt, yoghurt *n* slightly sour custard-like food made from milk that has had bacteria added to it, often sweetened and flavoured with fruit.

yoke *n* **1** wooden bar put across the necks of two animals to hold them together. **2** frame fitting over a person's shoulders for carrying buckets. **3** *Lit* oppressive force, e.g. *the yoke of the tyrant.* **4** fitted part of a garment to which a fuller part is attached. ♦ *v* **5** put a yoke on. **6** unite or link.

yokel *n Offens* person who lives in the country and is usu. simple and old-fashioned.

yolk *n* yellow part of an egg that provides food for the developing embryo.

Yom Kippur *n* annual Jewish religious holiday.

yon *adj Old-fashioned or dialect* that or those over there.

yonder *adj, adv* (situated) over there.

yonks *pl n Informal* very long time.

yoo-hoo *interj* call to attract attention.

yore *n Lit* **of yore** a long time ago.
yorker *n Cricket* ball that pitches just under the bat.
Yorkshire pudding *n* baked batter made from flour, milk, and eggs.
you *pron* refers to: **1** the person or people addressed. **2** an unspecified person or people in general.
young *adj* **1** in an early stage of life or growth. ♦ *pl n* **2** young people in general. **3** offspring, esp. young animals. **youngish** *adj* **youngster** *n* young person.
your *adj* **1** of, belonging to, or associated with you. **2** of, belonging to, or associated with an unspecified person or people in general. **yours** *pron* something belonging to you. **yourself** *pron*
youth *n* **1** time of being young. **2** state of being young. **3** boy or young man. **4** young people as a group. **youthful** *adj* **youthfulness** *n* **youth club** club that provides leisure activities for young people. **youth hostel** inexpensive lodging place for young people travelling cheaply.
yowl *v, n* (produce) a loud mournful cry.
yo-yo *n, pl* **-yos** toy consisting of a spool attached to a string, by which it is repeatedly spun out and reeled in.
YT Yukon Territory.
ytterbium [it›**terb**›ee›um] *n Chem* soft silvery element.
yttrium [**it**›ree›um] *n Chem* silvery metallic element used in various alloys.
yucca *n* tropical plant with spikes of white leaves.
yucky *adj* **yuckier, yuckiest** *Slang* disgusting, nasty.
Yugoslav *n* **1** person from the former Yugoslavia. ♦ *adj* **2** of the former Yugoslavia.
Yule *n Lit* Christmas (season).
yummy *adj* **-mier, -miest** *Informal* delicious.
yuppie *n* **1** young highly-paid professional person, esp. one who has a fashionable way of life. ♦ *adj* **2** typical of or reflecting the values of yuppies.
YWCA Young Women's Christian Association.
Z *Chem* atomic number.
zany [**zane**›ee] *adj* **zanier, zaniest** comical in an endearing way.
zap *v* **zapping, zapped 1** *Slang* kill (by shooting). **2** change TV channels rapidly by remote control. **3** move quickly.
zeal *n* great enthusiasm or eagerness. **zealot** [**zel**›lot] *n* fanatic or extreme enthusiast. **zealous** [**zel**›luss] *adj* extremely eager or enthusiastic. **zealously** *adv*
zebra *n* black-and-white striped African animal of the horse family. **zebra crossing** pedestrian crossing marked by black and white stripes on the road.
zebu [**zee**›boo] *n* Asian ox with a humped back and long horns.
Zen *n* Japanese form of Buddhism that concentrates on learning through meditation and intuition.
zenith *n* **1** highest point of success or power. **2** point in the sky directly above an observer.
zephyr [**zef**›fer] *n* soft gentle breeze.
zeppelin *n Hist* large cylindrical airship.
zero *n, pl* **-ros, -roes 1** (symbol representing) the number 0. **2** point on a scale of measurement from which the graduations commence. **3** lowest point. **4** nothing, nil. ♦ *adj* **5** having no measurable quantity or size. **zero hour** time at which something is set to happen. **zero in on** *v* **1** aim at. **2** *Informal* concentrate on.
zest *n* **1** enjoyment or excitement. **2** interest, flavour, or charm. **3** peel of an orange or lemon.
zigzag *n* **1** line or course having sharp turns in alternating directions. ♦ *v* **-zagging, -zagged 2** move in a zigzag. ♦ *adj* **3** formed in or proceeding in a zigzag. ♦ *adv* **4** in a zigzag manner.
zilch *n Slang* nothing.
zinc *n Chem* bluish-white metallic element used in alloys and to coat metal.
zing *n Informal* quality in something that makes it lively or interesting.
Zionism *n* movement to found and sup-

port a Jewish homeland in Israel. **Zionist** *n, adj*

zip *n* **1** fastener with two rows of teeth that are closed or opened by a small clip pulled between them. **2** *Informal* energy, vigour. **3** short whizzing sound. ♦ *v* **zipping, zipped 4** fasten with a zip. **5** move with a sharp whizzing sound. **6** rush.

zircon *n* mineral used as a gemstone and in industry.

zirconium *n Chem* greyish-white metallic element that is resistant to corrosion.

zither *n* musical instrument consisting of strings stretched over a flat box and plucked to produce musical notes.

zloty *n, pl* **-tys, -ty** monetary unit of Poland.

Zn *Chem* zinc.

zodiac *n* imaginary belt in the sky within which the sun, moon, and planets appear to move, divided into twelve equal areas, called signs of the zodiac, each named after a constellation.

zombie, zombi *n* **1** person who appears to be lifeless, apathetic, or totally lacking in independent judgment. **2** corpse brought back to life by witchcraft.

zone *n* **1** area with particular features or properties. **2** one of the divisions of the earth's surface according to temperature. ♦ *v* **3** divide into zones. **zonal** *adj*

zoo *n, pl* **zoos** place where live animals are kept for show.

zoology *n* study of animals. **zoologist** *n* **zoological** *adj* **zoological garden** zoo.

zoom *v* **1** move or rise very rapidly. **2** make or move with a buzzing or humming sound. **zoom lens** lens that can make the details of a picture larger or smaller while keeping the picture in focus.

Zr *Chem* zirconium.

zucchini [zoo-**keen**-ee] *n, pl* **-ni, -nis** *US & Aust* courgette.

Zulu *n* **1** member of a tall Black people of southern Africa. **2** language of this people.

zygote *n* fertilized egg cell.